The
BIBLE
COMPANION

The BIBLE COMPANION

Abingdon Press

Nashville

The Bible Companion

Copyright © 1985 by Abingdon Press

This book is printed on acid-free paper.

Library of Congress Cataloging in Publication Data

Main entry under title:
The Bible companion.
 Bibliography: p.
 1. Bible—Handbooks, manuals, etc.
BS417.B44 1985   220.6'1   85-1215

ISBN 0-687-03148-6

Excerpts from *Introducing the Bible* by William Barclay copyright Bible Reading Fellowship and International Bible Reading Association, England.

Selections from *The Abingdon Bible Handbook* by Edward P. Blair. Copyright © 1975 by Abingdon Press. Used by permission.

Text from *Animals, Birds, and Plants of the Bible*, copyright 1971 by Church Art, Inc. Used by permission of the estate of Carroll E. Whittemore.

Abridged Concordance to *Holy Bible: New International Version* (NIV Mini Concordance) © 1982, 1984 by the Zondervan Corporation. Used by permission of Zondervan Corporation and the International Bible Society.

Chronology of Biblical Events and Measures and Money in the Bible excerpted from *The Interpreter's One-Volume Commentary on the Bible.* Copyright © 1971 by Abingdon Press. Primary resource material for this volume is *The Interpreter's Dictionary of the Bible*, copyright © 1962 by Abingdon Press.

Definitions from *Young Readers Dictionary of the Bible.* Copyright © 1969 by Abingdon Press.

Endsheet maps used by permission of Oxford University Press.

Selections from *The Interpreter's Dictionary of the Bible*, copyright © 1962 by Abingdon Press.

MANUFACTURED BY THE PARTHENON PRESS AT
NASHVILLE, TENNESSEE, UNITED STATES OF AMERICA

CONTENTS

PREFACE

T*he Bible Companion* is designed for the general reader of Scripture. William Barclay gives a readable introduction to the value of the Bible, how both the Old and New Testaments came to be, and how to study the Bible. The cross-referenced Bible dictionary gives concise definitions, explanations, and identifications of more than 1300 different people, places, and events in the Bible, together with descriptions of numerous birds, plants, and animals of the biblical world. The concordance section will point to the location of more than 4600 different topics in the Bible. The section of study helps is made up of four parts. A chronology of biblical events presents events from the time of Abraham to the death of the apostles. An explanation of measures and money in the Bible describes the modern equivalents of biblical measurements and money. The Hebrew calendar describes how the people of the Old Testament measured their year. The program for reading the Bible gives two sequences for reading through the Bible. The longer plan will lead through the entire Bible, the shorter plan through the major books and portions of books. Finally, the four maps visually depict the world of the Bible.

All of these features together provide a helpful aid to the study of the Bible. *The Bible Companion* offers information about how the Bible came to us and how to study it, answers questions about unfamiliar subjects in the Bible, and includes more than 35,000 Scripture citations that will lead to the correct verse of Scripture in the study of the Bible.

INTRODUCING THE BIBLE

PRAYERS FOR BIBLE STUDY

It was the prayer of the psalmist:
> Open my eyes, that I may behold
> wondrous things out of thy law (Psalm 119: 18).

O God, our Father,
> Open our eyes and enlighten our minds,
> as we study your word.

So grant that
> our minds may know your truth,
> and our hearts may feel your love;

And then confirm and strengthen our wills,
> that we may go out to live what we have learned:
> through Jesus Christ our Lord. Amen.

O God,
> Help us to study your word,
> > not only to know about our blessed Lord,
> > > but also to know him;
> > not only to learn about him,
> > > but also to encounter him;
> > not only to grow in knowledge,
> > > but also to increase in love;
> > not only to love him with our hearts,
> > > but also to obey him with our lives;
> So that knowing him, loving him, and obeying him,
> we too may say: For me to live is Christ.
> > This we ask for your love's sake. Amen.

O God,
   as we study your word,
   grant us persistence,
      that we may not cease from study,
         until we find its meaning.
   Take from us the prejudice,
      which would shut our eyes to the truth.
   Never let us love systems
      more than we love you.
And then give us the humility which will accept and obey
what you say to us and what you tell us to do:
         through Jesus Christ our Lord. Amen.

O God, our Father,
   as we read your word,
      humble us at the sight of your holiness,
         and then comfort us with the memory of your mercy.
      Humiliate us with the realization of our sinfulness,
         and then uplift us at the sight of your love.
            Help us in your word
            to know our sin
            and to find our Savior:
         through Jesus Christ our Lord. Amen.

O God, our Father,
   help us in the study of your word to find
      guidance for our problems,
      strength for our temptations;
      power for our tasks;
      comfort for our sorrows;
      your fellowship for our loneliness.
   When we are lazy and lethargic,
      let your word stimulate us to thought and to action.
   When we are restless and distracted,
      let your word calm our troubled hearts
      with the peace that passes understanding.
In the study of your word, open your hand
and satisfy our every need:
         through Jesus Christ our Lord. Amen.

THE ANCIENT BOOK

The first chapter of the Westminster Confession of Faith is entitled "Of the Holy Scripture." Right at the beginning of that document basic to the Church of Scotland it is laid down that the books of the Bible "are given by inspiration of God, to be the rule of faith and life." The Confession goes on to say that the authority of Scripture "depends wholly upon God," and that therefore it is "the word of God." We are then told that "the whole counsel of God, concerning all things necessary for his own glory, man's salvation, faith and life, is either expressly set down in Scripture, or by good and necessary consequence may be deduced from Scripture; unto which nothing at any time is to be added, whether by new revelations of the Spirit, or traditions of men." And in all the controversies of religion the Scriptures are to be the final court of appeal.

Such then is the position that is given to the Bible. At first sight it is an extraordinary position. The earliest parts of the Bible were written almost three thousand years ago; there is no part of the Bible which is less than eighteen hundred years old; and yet the church accepts this ancient book as having final and binding authority.

In one sense the position is unique. True, there are many ancient textbooks still extant, but they are not accepted as final and binding. The doctors do not dictate their treatment by Galen and Hippocrates; the architects do not use the work of Vitruvius as their authority; the farmers do not follow the advice of Varro in their agricultural practice; the astronomers do not follow the astronomy of Ptolemy. To this day these books are read, but they are read as stages on the way, not the end; they are read for their interest, not for their authority. But the Bible, in its earlier parts older than any of them, is still for the Christian the supreme rule of faith and life.

13

In another sense we do have parallels to this. So long as people read poetry, they will read Homer; so long as people study philosophy, they will read Plato and Aristotle; so long as people are interested in the ethics of the good life, they will read Epictetus and Marcus Aurelius; so long as people love beauty, they will study the statues of Praxiteles. That a thing is old does not necessarily make it irrelevant; many of the oldest things are among the most precious possessions of mankind. But even in these cases there is no claim to the absolute authority to which the Bible lays claim; there is no claim, as the Westminster Confession claims for the Bible, that to this there is nothing left to add. What then is so special about this book?

1. The Bible has in it a sheer beauty which makes it, apart from anything else, an immortal work of literature. We have only to listen to it even in short passages to be moved to the heart with the magic of its words; and this is especially so in the Authorized Version.

> Many waters cannot quench love, neither can the floods drown it: if a man would give all the substance of his house for love, it would be utterly contemned. (Song of Solomon 8:7)

> Saul and Jonathan were lovely and pleasant in their lives, and in their death they were not divided. (II Samuel 1:23)

> O my son Absalom, my son, my son Absalom! would God I had died for thee, O Absalom, my son, my son! (II Samuel 18:33)

> Comfort ye, comfort ye my people, saith your God. Speak ye comfortably to Jerusalem, and cry unto her, that her warfare is accomplished, that her iniquity is pardoned. (Isaiah 40: 1, 2)

> They shall hunger no more, neither thirst any more; neither shall the sun light on them, nor any heat. For the Lamb which is in the midst of the throne shall feed them, and shall lead them unto living fountains of waters: and God shall wipe away all tears from their eyes. (Revelation 7:16, 17)

It would be easy to fill half this book with such passages. Everyone will have the passages and the verses which are fixed immovably and forever in his memory, with their inescapable beauty.

If on no other grounds than beauty, the Bible has unanswerable rights to greatness. Coleridge said that constant study of the Bible will keep anyone from being vulgar in point of style. Whatever a person's religious beliefs may be, and even if he has none, no one can claim to be fully educated unless he has read this monument of English prose.

The Greek Longinus wrote one of the great books on literary criticism and called it *On the Sublime*. For him sublimity was the supreme quality in any writer. When a coin is dropped it gives out a ring, and from that ring you can tell at once whether it is true or base metal, and Longinus said, in a

great phrase, that sublimity is the ring of a great soul. And there is no book in the world which has this quality of sublimity as the Bible has.

Undoubtedly, the Bible has the title to greatness for its sheer beauty. But at least to some extent this would mean that the Bible belongs to the luxuries rather than to the basic necessities of life. We must look for more than beauty to explain its claim to its unique place.

2. The Bible is an indispensable history book. The Bible is written against the background of the world movements of the great empires of the Middle East—Egypt, Assyria, Babylonia, Persia, Greece, Rome. Our knowledge of the history of the Middle East would be very considerably lessened without the Bible.

It is quite true that the Jewish idea of history was not that of the professional historian. The one test of any figure in biblical history was his obedience or his disobedience to God. So it is said of Asa that he did that which was right in the eyes of the Lord (I Kings 15:11), and it is said of Jehoram that he did what was evil in the sight of the Lord (II Kings 3:2). Omri of Samaria is dismissed in a few lines; he did what was evil in the sight of the Lord (I Kings 16:25-28); and yet we know from nonbiblical sources that politically Omri was one of the most important of all the kings. The biblical historian will spend more time on the stories of Elijah and Elisha than on the background of world-shaking events. Ahab's conduct in regard to Naboth's vineyard gets a whole chapter to itself (I Kings 21). All this is true, but without the historians and the prophets of the Old Testament our knowledge of Middle East history would be seriously curtailed. As a history book the Bible occupies a very important place.

But again this is not enough. It is not only time with which the Bible is concerned; it is also eternity. We must look further for the reason of its uniqueness.

3. From the point of view of language the Bible is a very important book. It is the great monument of classical Hebrew; the whole of a nation's early literature, the whole of Hebrew literature, is there. And what is linguistically even more important, the New Testament is the only written example of the colloquial Greek which people spoke to each other every day in the first century. To this we shall return, but for the moment briefly, the case is this. When Alexander the Great conquered the world, he took the Greek language with him; but it obviously could not be the classical Greek of the great days of Greece. It was a much simplified form of Greek, called *Koinê* Greek, which means the Greek of *common* speech. That kind of Greek did not normally get into literature, and the New Testament is the only written example of it. In fact, Greek linguists will assert that, if the New Testament were ever to lose all its religious value, it would still remain one of the most important linguistic books in the world.

Once again this is not enough. Even if a book is a linguist's paradise, that is no guarantee that it will open the way to a far higher paradise.

4. The Bible is indispensable as a treasury of ethical wisdom. In the ancient world there was a kind of literature called Wisdom Literature. The wisdom in question is practical wisdom; it is the wisdom which enables people to live honestly and successfully. The great example of it is the book of Proverbs; open it anywhere and you will find good advice for life, and advice written in the most vivid and memorable way.

> My son, do not despise the Lord's discipline
> or be weary of his reproof.
> The Lord reproves him whom he loves,
> as a father the son in whom he delights.
> Happy is the man who finds wisdom,
> and the man who gets understanding,
> for the gain from it is better than the gain from silver,
> and its profit better than gold.
> She is more precious than jewels,
> and nothing you desire can compare with her.
> Long life is in her right hand;
> in her left hand are riches and honour.
> Her ways are ways of pleasantness,
> and all her paths are peace. (Proverbs 3:11-17)

> Go to the ant. O sluggard;
> consider her ways and be wise.
> Without having any chief,
> officer or ruler,
> she prepares her food in summer,
> and gathers her sustenance in harvest.
> How long will you lie there, O sluggard?
> When will you arise from your sleep?
> A little sleep, a little slumber,
> A little folding of the hands to rest,
> And poverty will come upon you like a vagabond,
> and want like an armed man. (Proverbs 6:6-11)

With proverbs as a guide for practical living, no one need go wrong.

As for the New Testament, always Paul finishes his letters with the most practical of practical advice, and even the non-Christian will often say that we could build heaven on earth, if only people would accept and live the teaching of the Sermon on the Mount.

There is no doubt at all that as a guide to the good life the Bible is supreme; and as a mine of good advice it is inexhaustible. But it is also true that the unfortunate lesson of life is that good advice by itself never made anyone good. If it did, we would have arrived at perfection long ago. To find the unique character of the Bible we must go deeper than the claim that the Bible is an unsurpassable source-book for the conditions of the good life.

5. We come nearer to the heart of the matter when we make the claim that the Bible is a uniquely effective book. In his book *The Bible in Modern Evangelism* A. M. Chirgwin has a chapter entitled "Achievements" from which the following incidents are selected from among many others.

In Brazil there lived a man called Signor Antonio of Minas. For some time a friend had been pressing him to buy a Bible. He bought one, and thereupon vowed to take it home and burn it. When he reached home he found the fire out, but he was so eager to burn the book that he rekindled it. Before he threw the book on to the fire, he naturally opened it, so that it would burn the more easily. It opened at the Sermon on the Mount. He paused for a moment to do no more than glance at it. "The words had in them something that held him. He read on, forgetful of time, through the hours of the night, and just as the dawn was breaking he stood up and declared, 'I believe.' "

A New York gangster had been very recently released from prison. He was on his way to join his old gang with a view to another burglary when he stopped to pick a man's pocket on Fifth Avenue. He slipped into Central Park to see what he had acquired. He found himself in possession of a New Testament—no doubt to his deep disappointment. He had time before his appointment, so idly he began to read it, and soon he was deep in the book. A few hours later he went to meet his comrades. He told them what he had been reading, and then once and for all he broke with them and with crime.

Once in a Sicilian forest, in the middle of the night, a colporteur was stopped by a brigand at the point of the revolver. He was ordered by the brigand to light a fire and to burn the books he was carrying. He lit the fire and asked if he might read a little from the books before he burned them. From the first he read the Twenty-third Psalm; from another the story of the Good Samaritan; from another the Sermon on the Mount; from another the hymn of love. In each case the brigand intervened. "That's a good book," he said. "We won't burn that one. Give it to me." In the end not a book was burned and the brigand went off with the lot. Years later the brigand and the colporteur met again. This time the one-time brigand was an ordained minister of the Christian church. "It was your books that did it," he said to the colporteur.

This is only a brief selection of stories of what the Bible has done. Here, then, there is a book of power, a book operative, effective, dynamic. Here we are coming much nearer to the secret. If a book can do things like that, then it may justly be called unique.

6. We now come to the point of the whole matter, the reason why the ancient book is still relevant and still powerful. The Bible is about the one thing which does not change. Laws and customs change. To some extent even morality changes. For example, the very early parts of the Old Testament have no objection to polygamy, in patriarchal times. To some extent even religion changes. For example, the Jewish religion was a religion of sacrifice, but animal sacrifice is no longer a part of religion for

us. The one thing that does not change is personal relationships. So long as people are people, personal relationships will remain the same. Love and hate, loyalty and treachery, fellowship and enmity remain.

This is what the Bible is about. It is about the personal relationship between man and man, between man and woman, and above all between people and God, and God and people; here is why the Bible is ancient and modern at the same time. Take a simple and a lovely example. Jacob had to serve seven years before Laban would give him his daughter to marry. "So Jacob served seven years for Rachel; and they seemed to him but a few days because of the love he had for her" (Genesis 29:20). That is the kind of story, and that is the kind of situation, which will never go out of date, so long as men are men and women are women.

So then the Bible remains forever new because its whole concentration is essentially not upon laws and rules and regulations, but upon men and women and their relationship with each other and their relationship with God. The Bible is the book of love for each other, and love for God—and this is timeless and forever.

7. So this brings us to the last and the supreme reason why the Bible is unique and forever indispensable—a reason to which we shall have cause to return again and again. The Bible is the one place where we find Jesus Christ. The Bible is literally the only source-book for the life and the words and the teaching of Jesus. Take the Bible away, and we would be left with fugitive memories and subjective opinions.

And this is inextricably linked with the last point we made. It is only in and through Jesus Christ that our relationship with our fellowmen is the relationship of love, and that our relationship with God is possible at all.

Ancient in years the Bible is, but it is always relevant because it deals with the unchanging personal relationships between man and man, man and woman, and people and God, and it is always essential, for in it alone we are confronted with the portrait of the one person in heaven and earth in whom these relationships become what they ought to be.

8. There remains one other thing to be said—and it is said in the Westminster Confession, from which we began. The Confession lays it down that the Bible contains all that is necessary for salvation, and then it goes on to say: "Yet notwithstanding, our full persuasion and assurance of the infallible truth and divine authority thereof, is from the inward work of the Holy Spirit, bearing witness by and with the word in our hearts." And then it goes on to say: "We acknowledge the inward illumination of the Spirit of God to be necessary for the saving understanding of such things as are revealed in the word."

The Jewish doctrine of the Spirit was very simple and very comprehensive. As the Jews saw it, the Spirit did two things. The Spirit revealed God's truth to people, and the Spirit enabled people to recognize that truth, when the truth was revealed. So then, people need the Spirit in their hearts if they are fully to understand and to appropriate the meaning of the word of God.

And that is simply to say that reading and prayer must go hand in hand. We do well to approach the Bible with George Adam Smith's great prayer on our lips:

> Almighty and most merciful God, who hast given the Bible to be the revelation of thy great love to man, and of thy power and will to save him; grant that our study of it may not be made vain by any callousness or carelessness of our hearts, but that by it we may be confirmed in penitence, lifted to hope, made strong for service, and filled with the true knowledge of thee and of thy Son Jesus Christ: this we ask for thy love's sake. Amen.

THE MAKING OF THE OLD TESTAMENT

We are going to begin by studying how the Bible was built up and came into being. To put it in technical language, we are going to study the formation of the *canon* of Scripture. The canon of Scripture is that list of books which have been accepted as the Christian Church's written rule of faith; it is the list of the "official" books of the church; it is the list of books which the church regards as authoritative and determinative for the story of its own history and for the formation of its life and doctrine.

The word *canon* is itself an interesting word. It comes from a semitic word *kaneh* which means a reed. A straight reed can be used as a rule to draw straight lines. Then the word *canon* goes on to mean a rule, not in the sense of a rule for drawing straight lines, but a rule in the sense of a rule for living a straight life. A canon becomes a rule which decides what is right in any sphere.

But the word *canon* develops another meaning, probably from the fact that the rule which draws straight lines is often marked off in graduations of length. The word *canon* comes to mean a list. For instance, the canon of the Mass is the list of people commemorated in the Mass.

So the canon of Scripture comes to mean the list of the church's authoritative books. But a list in this sense and usage contains books *which have had something done to them*; they have been put on the list; but these same books *do something to everything else*; they become the standard by which all other things are judged. So the canon of Scripture was formulated by the church; in this sense it was not the Bible which made the church, it was the church which made the Bible; for the church existed long before the Bible existed. The early church did not possess the New Testament; it was busy writing it. On the other hand these books are not merely books which

have had the passive experience of having had something done to them; they are books which have the active power of guiding and directing the life and work of the church.

So we go on to study how there came into being that list of books which the church accepted as authoritative and which became the basic documents of the Christian faith.

If we go into a shop nowadays and ask for a copy of the Bible we will be handed one single volume, one book. But if we open that book we will find lists of the books of the Old Testament and of the New Testament. We will find that by the usual reckoning there are thirty-nine books in the Old Testament and twenty-seven in the New Testament, a total of sixty-six books. This is to say that, when we buy a one-volume Bible, we are really buying a library between two covers. When we go on to investigate this portable library a little more closely, we will find that the writing of it was spread over at least one thousand years, and that its books were written all over the ancient world from distant Babylon to Rome.

If we had lived in biblical times, we would never have made the mistake of thinking of the Bible as one book, because we would never have seen it in the form of one book; it did not exist in that form. In the ancient world literary works were written on rolls. The book form, called the *codex*, did not emerge until round about the second century A.D. The Old Testament books were written on skins. The New Testament books were originally written on papyrus. Papyrus was made from the papyrus reed, which grew almost exclusively on the banks of the Nile. It is a bulrush. It can be taller than a man and thicker than a man's wrist. The pith was cut into long strips; it was then laid down vertically and another row of strips horizontally. It was then moistened; pressure was applied; and there emerged a substance rather like brown paper, after the papyrus had been smoothed off with pumice stone. *Biblos* or *bublos* is the Greek word from which our word *bible* comes. *Biblos* originally was the word for the papyrus bulrush itself; it then became the word for the papyrus writing material made from that bulrush; it then went on to mean a roll of papyrus; and finally it came to mean a book. Papyrus lasts almost forever, so long as it is kept dry, but it becomes increasingly brittle.

Papyrus was not a cheap material. It was made in sheets which measured about ten by eight inches. It cost anything from five cents a sheet for the cheapest quality to about twenty cents for the best quality, and these prices have to be evaluated in light of the fact that a working-man's wage was eight cents a day. The sheets were joined edge to edge to form a long strip of papyrus. A wooden roller was placed at each end. The roll was unrolled with the one hand, and rolled up again with the other as it was read. The writing was in narrow columns, two and a half to three inches wide.

There is an overlap period when the roll was vanishing and when the book or codex form was coming into use, during which the codex too was made of papyrus. But usually the codex is made of vellum or parchment.

Vellum was originally made of calves' skin. *Vitulina charta* it was called, and from that phrase the word *vellum* is derived. Its greatest center of manufacture was Pergamum, and it was also called *Pergamênê charta* from which the word *parchment* is derived.

Parchment and papyrus have one advantage—they are both extremely durable. But the whole situation in the ancient world had two disadvantages.

The roll was unwieldy to use. The result is that the maximum length of roll for all practical purposes was thirty feet, and it would take a roll of almost exactly that size to hold the Gospel of Luke or of Matthew, or the book of Acts. This is why no one in the ancient world would ever think of the Old Testament or the New Testament as one book. To such a person the Old and New Testaments would be quite extensive collections of rolls. Even when the codex came in, ancient binding was such that three or four volumes would be needed for even the New Testament. The fact that the Bible is a library would not be lost sight of in the ancient world.

The other disadvantage was expense, both of the papyrus material itself and of the cost of copying.

The unit of measurement for copying was the *stichos* (plural, *stichoi*). A *stichos* was not a line; to pay by the line would not be satisfactory, for different writers might well get a very different number of words into a line. A *stichos* was the average length of one of Homer's hexameter lines which is sixteen syllables. Books were reckoned in *stichoi*. There is a sixth-century New Testament manuscript, Codex Claromontanus, which gives the number of *stichoi* in each book. For example, there are 2,900 *stichoi* in Luke; 2,600 in Matthew; 1,040 in Romans; 251 in Colossians; 20 in II John; 2,600 in Acts; 1,200 in the Revelation. In the time of Diocletian a price-fixing edict was issued, and the cost of copying was twenty to twenty-five *denarii* per hundred *stichoi*. A *denarius* was about ten cents, so this means it cost about two dollars to copy one hundred lines, which means that Matthew itself, apart from the papyrus, would cost about $50. This costliness was something which remained until printing arrived. There were few who could own a Bible; and until the printed book emerged the Bible could not exist in one volume.

Let us now move on to see the process by which the divine library of the Old Testament came into being and grew up into completeness.

The Jews divided their sacred writings into three sections—the Law, the Prophets, and the Writings. This classification goes back to about 180 B.C. Jesus the son of Sirach had written a book of wisdom which we now commonly call *Ecclesiasticus*. It was originally written in Hebrew. In the year 132 B.C. his grandson, thinking it a valuable book and a book deserving to be widely known, while he was staying in Egypt translated it into Greek, and in the prologue he refers to the teachings of the Law, the Prophets, and the others who followed them. He speaks again of the Law, the Prophets, and "the other books of our fathers."

The Law consists of the first five books of the Old Testament—Genesis, Exodus, Leviticus, Numbers, Deuteronomy. This section of the Bible is commonly known as the *Pentateuch*, which is a Greek word, meaning the five rolls.

The Prophets came to be divided into two sections. First, there are the Former Prophets. These are the books of Joshua, Judges, Samuel, and Kings. These were reckoned as four books, I and II Samuel and I and II Kings each being reckoned as one book. We usually look on these books as historical books, but the Jews looked on them as prophetic, partly because they tell the story of the great prophets like Elijah and Elisha, and partly because the Jews thought of God as revealing himself in the events of history just as much as, and even more than, in the words of men. Second, there were the Latter Prophets. These were Isaiah, Jeremiah, Ezekiel, and the Twelve. We call the Twelve the Minor Prophets—Hosea, Joel, Amos, Obadiah, Jonah, Micah, Nahum, Habakkuk, Zephaniah, Haggai, Zechariah, Malachi. They are not *minor* in the sense that they are in any way lesser or inferior; they are *minor* only in the sense that they are *shorter* than the first three. The Latter Prophets are also reckoned as four books, because the Twelve are reckoned as one.

The Writings are a miscellaneous collection. They are variously classified. One classification is, first, three books of poetry—Psalms, Proverbs, Job; second, the five *megilloth* (*megillah* means a roll); each of them was connected specially with some great Jewish festival. The Song of Solomon, allegorized to make it speak of the deliverance from Egypt, was associated with the Passover and was read on the eighth day of the Passover celebrations. Ruth was connected with Pentecost, because it was a harvest idyll, and Pentecost was harvest feast; it was read on the second day of Pentecost. Lamentations was read on 9th Ab, which is the anniversary day of the destruction of Solomon's Temple. Ecclesiastes was read on the third day of the Feast of Tabernacles. Tabernacles commemorated the journey through the wilderness, and during it for a week the people left their houses and lived out of doors in booths made of branches. Ecclesiastes was read to remind people to remember God in the midst of material blessings. Esther was read at the Feast of Purim, for which it provides the reason and the warrant. The five *megilloth* were the only books of the Writings to be read in the synagogue, and they were read only on the occasions with which they were specially connected. Third, there was one book of prophecy—Daniel. Finally, there were two books of history—Ezra-Nehemiah, counting as one, and Chronicles.

The Jews often counted these books as twenty-four. This number was arrived at by reckoning

five books of the Law;

four books of the Former Prophets, I and II Samuel and I and II Kings each being reckoned as one book;

four books of the Latter Prophets, the Twelve being reckoned as one
book;

eleven books of the Writings, Ezra and Nehemiah, and I and II
Chronicles each being reckoned as one book.

So then let us see how and when each of these three parts of the Old
Testament acquired the character of Scripture.

For the Jew the Law was, and is, the most important thing in the world,
the center of the Synagogue service, and the essence of all true religion. The
word *law* is not quite an adequate title for it; the word *law* is in English too
legalistic to describe the Jewish Law. There is much more in it and to it than
rules and regulations, prohibitions and commands. The Hebrew word is
Torah, and it means instruction rather than law. The Torah is God's
instruction to people, by obeying which people find life in this world and
life in the world to come. They held that the Law had been created before
the creation of the world itself, and that God had looked into the Law and
then created the world. When the kingdom of God fully came, the Prophets
and the Writings would pass away, but the Law would last forever.

It was held to have been delivered to Moses verbatim and entire by the
very hand of God himself. It was even held that God began each day by
himself setting time apart to study the Law. The aim was that Jewish
children should have the Law "graven on their souls." From their infancy
they were instructed in the Law, and many a Jew died rather than be false
to the Law which to him was nothing less than the word of God. The center
of everything was the Law, and even the rest of Scripture, great as it was,
was no more than commentary on the Law. The center of the Synagogue
service was the reading of the Law. It was read one verse at a time in
Hebrew, and translated into whatever language the congregation
understood. How then did it reach its exalted position? In what follows we
try to reconstruct the situation. This is a reconstruction and not a certainty;
but it does fit the facts, and the majority of Old Testament scholars would
agree with it.

In regard to the Law we have one date from which we can start, and a
dramatic start it is. Religion in Judah had been in a sorry state. The good
king Hezekiah had been followed by Manasseh and Amon, who were little
better than heathen (II Kings 21). Their combined reigns lasted for more
than half a century, and religion was at its lowest ebb. Then in 621 B.C. the
young Josiah came to the throne. And Josiah "did that which was right in
the eyes of the Lord." One of the things he did was to initiate the repair and
the restoration of the neglected temple; and during that work the book of
the Law was found by Hilkiah in the house of the Lord. The reading of that
book of the Law moved the king and the people to repentance and
reformation, and that book of the Law became for them the very word of
God (II Kings 22 and 23). There is little doubt what that book was. It was the
book of Deuteronomy. Someone who was at once prophet and priest wrote

it in the dark days of Manasseh and Amon, when it was impossible to speak openly, and then hid it in the temple, to be found in due time.

Here is the beginning of the whole movement; here is the first time that a book is, so to speak, canonized, and becomes the word of God to God's people. There were other statements of the Law, and they too were recovered and collected and cherished. There was the oldest statement of all about the Law, commonly called the little book of the covenant, in Exodus 34. There was the book of the covenant itself, the conditions to which the people of God agreed, when God took them as his people and promised to be their God. This is found in Exodus 20:22–23:33, and in its present form dates back to 900 B.C. Then in the middle of the sixth century B.C. another great section was added. The very essence of Judaism is in the phrase: "You shall be holy, for I the Lord your God am holy" (Leviticus 19:2). So there arose what is called the Holiness Code. The word *holy* here really means *different*. God is the supremely different one, as he has been called, The Wholly Other. His people too are to be different; they are not to live like other nations; they are to accept the fact that they are a people destined to be different. And the life of difference they are to lead is summed up in the Holiness Code in Leviticus 17 to 26. So we have the great sections of the Law, the voice of God coming ever more fully and directly to his people—the ancient little book of the covenant, and book of the covenant itself, the book of Deuteronomy, and the Code of Holiness. Slowly the Law is building up. It is of the greatest importance to remember one fact that is emerging. People did not sit down and write a book with the intention of writing a book of Scripture. The books which became Scripture had for years and centuries been the help and the strength of the people. These books had already proved themselves over the centuries to be nothing less than the word of God. They were books which by their own proved value had established their right to be recognized as God's word to humankind. These books which became Scripture were not new books; they were books which time had already proved.

But there is more in the Pentateuch than laws and instruction. The law material in the Pentateuch stands in the context of a narrative which takes the story from the creation of the world to the entry into the Promised Land, and within this narrative there are certain very interesting phenomena. When we study this material, it becomes clear that it is composite and that it comes from more than one source.

Traditionally, it is the work of Moses, but it soon becomes clear that more than Moses had a hand in it. In Genesis there is a list of the kings of Edom, and then there is the sentence, "These are the kings who reigned in the land of Edom, before any king reigned over the Israelites" (Genesis 36:31). The first of the kings is Saul, and Saul is centuries after Moses, so Moses could hardly have spoken of kings reigning over the Israelites. Genesis 14:14 tells of Abraham's pursuit of his enemies *as far as Dan*. But Dan did not get its name until the time of the Judges (Judges 18:29) after the time of

Moses. In Genesis (21:34; 26:14-18) the Philistines are mentioned, but in fact the Philistines did not appear on the scene of history until about 1200 B.C., again after the time of Moses. And, above all in this connection, Deuteronomy 34:1-8 tells of the death of Moses, and it is hardly likely that Moses told the story of his own death!

Unquestionably, Moses was the great law-giver of Israel, but equally unquestionably more than his hand is to be seen in the first five books of the Old Testament. There is more than one narrative here, and there is more than one author here.

There are other signs that the narrative is composite. Often there are two accounts of the same event. There are two stories about how Beer-sheba got its name, one connected with Abraham and one connected with Isaac (Genesis 21:31; 26:31). There are two stories of how Bethel got its name, one telling how Jacob gave it its name on the way to Paddan-aram, the other telling how he gave it its name on the way back from Paddan-aram (Genesis 28:19; 35:15). There are two accounts of the banishment of Hagar and Ishmael, in one of which Hagar is banished *before* the child is born (Genesis 16:6-16), and in the other of which she is banished *after* the child is born (Genesis 21:9-21).

There are two versions of the Creation story. In the one, man is created at the end of the whole process of creation, after the sea and the land and the growing things and the beasts and the birds have been created, and in this version man and woman are created at the same time (Genesis 1). In the other man is created at the beginning of the process; then the garden is created; then the beasts and the birds are formed; then woman is made out of the rib taken from man (Genesis 2). Two stories of the ark in the days of the Flood are interwoven. In the one story the animals are to go into the ark seven pairs of each; in the other story they are to go in in single pairs (Genesis 7:2, 3; 7:8, 9). All over the narrative it can be seen that two versions, two sources, two accounts are being put together. The compiler of the final form is so honest, so full of respect for his sources, that when he has two sources he gives both of them.

Now in this compilation there are times when something else is seen. In Hebrew there are two words for God. There is the word *elôhim*, and there is the word *Jahweh* or *Yahweh*. This latter is very interesting and very important; it is the same word as the word *Jehovah*, which is its much commoner form. In Hebrew there are no vowels in the original script, only consonants, and it was only later that little signs for the vowels were put below the consonants to show what the right pronunciation was. The name of God is represented by the four consonants YHWH. The Jews would never pronounce these four letters as they really sounded; the name of God was too sacred even to be said. Now there was another word *Adonai* which means Lord; and what the Jews did was to take the vowels of the word *Adonai* and to attach them to the sacred letters YHWH, and from that they got the form Jehovah. Jehovah is really the letters YHWH spelled with the

vowels of the word for Lord, but the real form is Jahweh (Yahweh), which was too sacred and too holy to say.

In our English translation of the Old Testament, *elôhim* is translated simply God; but YHWH is translated LORD and is printed in special capital letters, as for instance in Genesis 2:4, 5. This way of printing LORD for Jahweh, or Jehovah, is used in the Authorized Version, the Revised Standard Version, and the New English Bible. Now when we examine these early books carefully we find that in some sections God is called *elôhim*, God, and in some sections he is called Jahweh, LORD. For instance, right at the beginning of the Bible, in the first Creation story God is called *elôhim*, God (Genesis 1:1–2:3), whereas in the second Creation story God is called Jahweh, LORD (Genesis 2:4-24). We saw that in the ark story of the Flood there is one version of the story in which the animals are taken in in seven pairs and another in which the animals are taken in in single pairs. In the version in which the animals are taken in in seven pairs the command is given by the LORD, Jahweh (Genesis 7:1, 2); in the version in which the animals go in in single pairs the command is given by God, *elôhim* (Genesis 7:9). So we find that in the very early parts of the Bible there are two interwoven sources, in one of which God is called *elôhim*, and in the other of which he is called Jahweh; that is to say in one source God is called God, and in the other he is called LORD. After a time both sources call God Jahweh, LORD, for in the source which began by calling God *elôhim*, God, we find the famous story of how Moses discovered that the name of God is Jahweh, the One Who Is (Exodus 3:13-16), for this was the lesson that Moses received in the mysterious incident of the burning bush (Exodus 3:1-6).

What becomes clear is that the Law, the Pentateuch, did not spring into being ready-made. It is the product of the centuries. It is the essence and the distillation of the voice of God to people both in words and in events over the years. Here is the concentrated voice of God over the centuries—first the little book of the covenant; then the larger book of the covenant; then Deuteronomy; then the Holiness Code; then the story of the ways of God to humankind compiled by the two different writers; then its molding and interweaving into one, with that complete honesty which would omit nothing and change nothing; until in the end there emerged that wonderful amalgam of law and history which to the Jew was and is the word of God as nothing else on earth.

But there remains one question still to ask. When did the Law stop being simply a wonderful book, and when did it become Scripture? When did it stop being only a book and become a Bible? This is to ask, when did the oldest part of the Bible begin to be regarded as definitely the word of God? There are three indications to help us to fix a date.

1. One of the great dates was the date when the Old Testament was translated into Greek. We shall tell the story of that translation later. At the

present moment we are concerned only with the date when the Septuagint, as the Greek translation of the Old Testament is called, came into being. It is obviously a great date. When the Old Testament remained in Hebrew its sphere was strictly limited to the Jews; when it was translated into Greek it became the possession of the world. The Old Testament was translated into Greek in the reign of Ptolemy the Second, called Philadelphus, in Egypt, and this Ptolemy reigned from 285 until 246 B.C. At first, it was only the Law which was translated, for it was the Law above all which was Scripture for the Jew by that time. We can therefore begin by saying that the Law was certainly Scripture by about 270 B.C. Can we trace it further back?

2. The Samaritans even to the present day accept only the Law, the Pentateuch, as Scripture; they do not so accept the rest of the Old Testament. This will mean that they split from the rest of the nation when the Law had become Scripture, but the rest of the Old Testament had not. The Samaritan split dates to about 400 B.C. Therefore away back in 400 B.C. the Law was already regarded as the word of God.

3. When we read Nehemiah 8–10 we find Ezra the scribe reading "the book of the Law" to the people, and the people taking it as the Law of God and the law of their lives. This happened after they had returned from exile. From then on the Jews were to be forever the people of the Book, and that book, the book of the Law. And that also happened about 400 B.C. Everything points to the fact that the Law became Scripture, the Law was established as the word of God to people, four hundred years before Jesus came into the world as a man. We may take it that people have regarded the Law, the Pentateuch, the first five books of the Old Testament, as Scripture since 400 B.C. For very nearly 2,400 years men have found the word of God in the books of the Law. And there is something unique about a book by which people have guided their lives not only for hundreds but for thousands of years.

It will be remembered that we began the story of the formation of the Old Testament by seeing that the Jews divided it into three sections—the Law, the Prophets, and the Writings. We have now seen how the Law was built up and how by 400 B.C. it had become Scripture, and now we turn our attention to the Prophets.

As we have seen, to the Jew the Law was incomparably the greatest part of Scripture; for most modern students of the Bible the Prophets would stand higher than the Law. They would indeed, with the exception of the Psalms, be the most precious part of the Old Testament for most of us. Let us see then how they too became part of the word of God.

We have already seen that the Prophets were divided into two sections—the Former Prophets and the Latter Prophets. The Former Prophets consist of the books of Joshua, Judges, Samuel, and Kings. The authors of these books are completely unknown. There are not even any traditional titles ascribed to them as the books of the Law are all ascribed to Moses. But Jewish tradition did say that Joshua wrote the book of Joshua,

that Samuel wrote the book of Judges and Samuel, and that Jeremiah wrote the books of Kings. These four books, as the Jews reckoned them, were completed in the sixth and the fifth centuries B.C.

It may seem strange to us to find what we regard as history books ranked among the prophetic books. There are two reasons for this. These books tell of the great prophets who functioned before the literary prophets emerged, the nonliterary prophets—Samuel and Nathan and Elijah and Elisha. They certainly had prophetic material in them. Second, the Jews took history very seriously. For them the events of history were God in action; history for them was the arena of the activity of God. God, for them, was speaking in events. The events of history were, for them, the demonstration of the truth of the prophetic message. History too was for them the voice of God. History for them was the voice of God proclaiming across the centuries that it is well with the good, and it is disaster for the wicked. It was perfectly natural to look on history as prophetic, for history was for them the manifestation of the rule of God.

When we come to the Latter Prophets, the great named prophets, it is well to have a time scheme in our minds as we read them, and to know the events of history which were the background of their writings.

First of them to come in the latter half of the eighth century were Amos and Micah. They were writing near the days when the Assyrians invaded Palestine and when the Kingdom of Samaria was wiped out forever in 722 B.C. These two prophets strike the note which is from beginning to end the center of the prophetic message. That message is summed up in a famous phrase—it was the proclamation of *ethical monotheism*. Let us take the second word first, the word *monotheism*. There are three forms of belief in God. First, there is *polytheism*. *Polloi* is the Greek for many; *theos* is the Greek for God or a god; and *polytheism* is the word which describes a religion which has many gods. This was the way of the early Greek and Roman religion with Zeus and Apollo and Athene and Aphrodite and all the rest of them. This is the stage of many gods. Second, there is *henotheism*. At this stage people still believed in many gods, but they had come to believe that only one of these gods was valid for them. Each country had its own god, and beyond that country the writ of that god did not run. So each country had its own god, but no one denied that the gods of the other countries were equally real and in their own sphere equally powerful. So Jephthah says to the Ammonites: "Will you not possess what Chemosh your god gives you to possess? And all that the Lord (Jahweh) our God has dispossessed before us we will possess" (Judges 11:24). At this stage Jahweh was the only God for the Hebrews, but that did not mean that Chemosh was not real enough for the Ammonites. At this stage a nation had its own god, and for them that god was the only god, but there was no denial of the rights of other gods in regard to other nations. Lastly, there is the belief in *monotheism*, which is the belief that there is only one God, who

is the God of all, the God of this universe and of any other universe that does exist or ever will exist.

This was the first message of the Prophets, the message that there is one God and one God only, and to him Israel must be true. Nor was this altogether easy. In the days when people believed that each country had its own god, then when a person came to stay in a strange country he brought, as it were, his own god with him, and built a shrine for him. This is what happened in the case of Solomon. In the days of Solomon, Israel was politically a great nation. This led to foreign alliances. Very often a foreign alliance was cemented by the king of the one country marrying the daughter of the king of the other. This is exactly what Solomon did, and these foreign princesses brought their own gods and goddesses with them and so infected the true religion with false faiths (I Kings 11:1-8). To us monotheism is the only natural belief; in the days of the prophets it was a great discovery, and the prophets were the guardians of it.

Not only did these great early prophets teach monotheism; they also taught *ethical* monotheism. Nowadays religion and morality go hand in hand. But strangely in the ancient days religion and immorality were apt to go hand in hand. Take three instances of this. In the ancient world, when a man founded a new city, it was the custom to lay the foundations of it, and to fix the gateposts of it, in the body of his slaughtered and sacrificed son (I Kings 16:34). In the worship of the god Molech little children were sacrificed in the fire (II Kings 23:10). The worship of Baal was the worship of the fertility cult. The baals were the powers who made the corn grow and the grape ripen. The greatest fertility force of all is sex. So to the temples of the baals there were attached many sacred priestesses who were nothing other than sacred prostitutes, and to have sexual intercourse with one of them was an act of worship. These so-called priestesses were the cult-prostitutes whom Hosea condemns (Hosea 4:14). The prophets had to teach that the most elaborate ritual in the world is no substitute for personal chastity, for social justice, and for love for people and love for God. The whole book of Amos has been called "a cry for social justice," and no text in the Bible is better known than Micah's saying that God does not want sacrifice. What he wants is that people should do justice, and love kindness, and walk humbly with him (Micah 6:6-8). For us these things are part of religion. For the great early prophets they were epoch-making discoveries. The prophets were the great ethical monotheists, insisting that there is one God, and that chastity, mercy, and fidelity are the true sacrifices.

Also from the eighth century B.C. come two more of the great early prophets, and they too have their dominant ideas. As we have seen, the great cry of Amos and Micah is the insistence on social justice. But Hosea is above all the prophet of undefeatable love. Hosea argued from himself to God. Hosea had taken on God's orders a wife from the streets. He treated her with love, but she went back to her old life; but every time she went

back, he took her back again with a love which would not own defeat. And, so Hosea argued, if I a man can love like that, how much more God?

So we have Amos and Micah with their stress on social justice; and we have Hosea with his stress on love. But there is still another of the great eighth-century prophets. The book of Isaiah falls into three parts, and the first part of it (chapters 1–39) belongs to this same period. Isaiah was an aristocrat and the friend of kings, and he too has his dominant note; and his note is holiness. "Holy, holy, holy is the Lord of hosts" (Isaiah 6:3). Always he confronts people with the holy God. And always he too is insistent that nothing can take the place of justice and of love. Sacrifices, new moons, sabbaths, prayers—by themselves they are without avail.

Seek justice,
    correct oppression;
defend the fatherless,
    plead for the widow. (Isaiah 1:10-17)

So each of the great eighth-century prophets has his note—Amos and Micah, social justice; Hosea, love; Isaiah, holiness; and it is while remembering their note that we should read them.

In the seventh and the sixth centuries B.C. there was another group of prophets, proclaiming the word of God in the light of their contemporary history, and always interpreting that history in the light of the purpose of God. In 627 B.C. Zephaniah saw the Scythian hordes arriving from the East, and saw in that invasion the beginning of the time of judgment for Assyria, and for Moab and for Philistia, and for Judah too. It was for him the warning of the coming of the Day of the Lord. At the same time Nahum was vividly portraying the fall of Nineveh. For a moment it looked as if God was going to strike in history, but the event was the rise of still another great power, the rise of Babylon, and Habakkuk writes wondering at the delay of God, as one tyranny succeeds another.

Then there came two of the greatest of the prophets who both made the discovery which saved Jewish religion from collapse. Jeremiah saw the fall of Jerusalem at the hands of the Babylonians in 586 B.C., and Ezekiel lived through the exile with the people in Babylon, where he dreamed of the new order of things which would someday be. But the great contribution of these two was the reminder that religion is not only a national thing; it is a personal thing too, and that even more.

It is hard for us to understand, but it took centuries for the individual fully to emerge. For centuries people did not think of themselves principally as individuals; they thought of themselves as members of the group or the tribe or the family or the nation to which they belonged. A very good Old Testament example of that is the story of the sin of Achan. In spite of the command of God to destroy all the spoils of Jericho, Achan kept some. The consequence was disastrous. Disaster fell on the nation. It was

discovered that it was Achan who was guilty, and, when that discovery had been made, Achan "and his sons and his daughters and his oxen and asses and sheep, and his tent and all that he had" were utterly destroyed (Joshua 7:1-26). The punishment fell not simply on the man but on the whole group.

A modern example of all this comes from Australia. The Australian aborigines are among the most primitive of people left in the world, and, until quite recently, if you asked an aborigine his name, it was not his name that he would tell you; it was his tribe: "I am a man of such and such a tribe," he would say.

Now, if you think always in terms of the group, then if the nation is in the midst of disaster, faith may well collapse; but if you make the discovery that a man is connected with God, not because he is the member of a nation or a tribe, but because he is a person, then the connection between the individual and God can survive any national trial or disaster. This is exactly what Jeremiah and Ezekiel discovered. They discovered that a man was connected with God, not because he was a Jew, but because he was a man. They discovered personal religion. Like all great discoveries it is a very simple discovery, but few could be more important.

But a new world power was emerging, the power of Persia, and the second section of Isaiah has something of quite extraordinary interest to say about this; the section is chapters 40 to 55. The leader of the Persians was Cyrus, who had no intention of liberating the Jews from the power of Babylon, and it is very unlikely that Cyrus had ever heard of Jahweh, or would have thought Jahweh of any importance if he had heard of him. But in spite of that Cyrus has his place in the plan and the purpose of God. God says of Cyrus: "He is my shepherd, and he shall fulfil all my purpose." Cyrus is the anointed whose right hand God has grasped (Isaiah 44:28; 45:1). Cyrus was to be the liberator of the Jews. He did not know it, but he was working out the purposes of God. Here indeed is a philosophy of history. All history is in the hand of God, and even the man who has never heard of God may be, all unknown to himself, the servant of God and the instrument in the hand of God. Truly, a man can face the world with a faith like that.

It is in this section of Isaiah that we find the picture of the Suffering Servant, that figure who was to have so great an influence on the thought of the New Testament, and almost certainly on the thought of Jesus himself. The picture of the Suffering Servant culminates in Isaiah 53 in the one who was wounded for our transgressions and bruised for our iniquities (Isaiah 53:5). The complete picture of the Suffering Servant is drawn in what are known as the four Servant Songs (Isaiah 42:1-4; 49:1-6; 50:4-9; 52:13–53:12). It is to be noted that in Isaiah 53 all the verbs up to verse 10 are in the past tense. On the face of it, they are a description of someone whom the prophet knew and who had suffered, rather than of someone who was to come. It is true that sometimes a prophet was so sure that what he was

saying was going to happen that he spoke of it as having already happened, but Isaiah 53 does not read like that.

Who was the sufferer in Isaiah 53? This is one of the questions which has always fascinated and eluded the minds of scholars. The best book on the subject is C. R. North's *The Suffering Servant in Deutero-Isaiah*, and in it North tells us that S. R. Driver, the great Old Testament scholar, planned to write a commentary on Isaiah, and abandoned the task because of the tangled maze of interpretations in regard to the Servant.

Is the Servant Isaiah himself, who according to Jewish tradition was martyred and buried in a felon's grave, as the Ethiopian thought it might be (Acts 8:34)? Is he Jeremiah who speaks of himself as "a gentle lamb led to the slaughter" (Jeremiah 11:19)? Is he Jehoiachin who according to Jewish tradition sacrificed himself to Nebuchadnezzar in order to save the city of Jerusalem from devastation (II Kings 24:8-20)? Is he Zerubbabel who after playing a foremost part in the return from exile strangely vanishes from history (Haggai 1:1, 12, 14; 2:21-23; Zechariah 4:6-10)? Or is the Servant the nation of Israel, redemptively suffering for its own sins and the sins of the world? We cannot tell, but we do know beyond a doubt that this figure of the Suffering Servant found its complete fulfilment in Jesus Christ. All over the New Testament Jesus is identified with the Suffering Servant (Acts 3:13; 3:26; 4:27, 30; 8:26-35; Matthew 8:14-17; 12:14-21; Luke 22:37; II Corinthians 5:21; I Peter 1:19; 2:22-25). No Old Testament figure is so built into the New Testament as the Suffering Servant of Second Isaiah.

So we have the rise of another world power. Assyria had left the scene and so had Babylon, and now it was the turn of Persia to dominate the stage of history. This was very important for the Jews, for the Persians allowed the Jews to return to Jerusalem, from which the Babylonians had removed them in exile, so in the late sixth century and in the fifth century we find Haggai and Zechariah urging them on to rebuild the shattered temple and to try to restore the lost glory.

We find Obadiah condemning Edom because she had stood aside and seen Judah reduced to slavery. We find Joel cheering the people when days were difficult, and Malachi rousing them to new devotion when devotion had grown cold. In the slackening of devotion the people had come to try to put God off with second-bests, and with the cheapest and the shoddiest things they could offer (Malachi 1:6-14). And in the day of despair and depression Malachi tried to rekindle the flame of devotion in their hearts.

There is one book included among the prophets which we have not yet mentioned—the book of Jonah. This little book is one of the greatest books in the Old Testament because it calls on the Jews to abandon their exclusiveness, to bring God's word to the Gentiles, to rejoice when the Gentiles accept the message, to believe that even Nineveh can be saved, if Nineveh repents. Jonah is the one supremely missionary book in the Old Testament. It is also one of the latest books, for it comes most probably from the fourth century B.C.

We have now to ask when the books of the prophets ceased to be merely precious works of devotional literature and became Scripture.

1. We have to note regarding the prophets that which we have noted about the other books of the Old Testament. Long before they became Scripture they were known and used and loved. It was because they had proved their power to illuminate the mind and to comfort and strengthen the heart that they did earn a place in Scripture.

It was in the days of the exile that the works of the prophets came to be known and loved. This was so because these books did two things. They foretold the fate of the sinner and of the disobedient and of those who forsook the way of God for their own way. And that part of them had been amply fulfilled. The nation knew only too well now what happened to a nation which disregarded the voice of God. What the prophets had said would happen had happened. But the prophets did not end their message there. Just as they had a message of doom for the disobedient, so they had a message of hope for the penitent. And the Jews had the conviction that just as the message of doom had come true, so the message of hope would also come true. F. C. Grant in his book *How to Read the Bible* (pp. 84, 85) points out that the prophetic message follows a pattern:

(a) Your sins are about to find you out, justice is certain to overtake you—soon; (b) if God's punishment is severe, he is still concerned with those whom he punishes, and his purpose is to save, not to annihilate; (c) in this final hour before the stroke of doom, repent!—for, if you repent, God may turn away the threatened punishment and restore you to his favour; (d) indeed, God, who foresees all things is aware that a "remnant" will survive, a penitent few, like the living stump of a fallen tree; out of this small handful he will be able to build up once more the nation or the family or the covenant-people of his choice.

In other words, the message of the prophets was compounded in equal parts of threat and promise, of doom and rescue, of the midnight and the dawn. And so the Jews read and studied and drew strength from the prophets in the certainty that, if the prophets had been right about the doom, they would also be right about the restoration. In the darkest days they drew their hope from the prophetic hope.

2. But these prophetic books drew their special place from another factor in the situation. They were regarded as the great examples of a voice that was now silenced forever. No longer was there anyone to say: "Thus saith the Lord." As the Psalmist said wistfully: "We do not see our signs; there is no longer any prophet, and there is none among us who knows how long" (Psalm 74:9). By the time of Zechariah it was true that anyone who claimed to be a prophet was to be regarded as a fraud: "And if anyone again appears as a prophet, his father and mother who bore him will say to him, 'You shall not live, for you speak lies in the name of the Lord'; and his father and

mother who bore him shall pierce him through when he prophesies" (Zechariah 13:3). So in I Maccabees it is said: "Thus there was great distress in Israel, such as had not been since the time that prophets ceased to appear among them" (I Maccabees 9:27). Simon is made leader and priest, "until a trustworthy prophet should arise" (I Maccabees 14:41). They will wait until a prophet comes and tells them what to do (I Maccabees 4:46). There came a time as early as the fourth century B.C. when the prophets belonged to the splendor of the past; they had spoken with a voice and an accent which was forever silent. Obviously this gives them a greatness which could never be repeated.

3. When then did they actually come to be regarded as Scripture? This is something which we can only deduce. In II Maccabees 2:13 it is said of Nehemiah that "he also founded a library and collected the books about the kings and prophets, and the writings of David and letters of kings about votive offerings." It was always part of Jewish tradition that Ezra had a great deal to do with the construction of the collection of Scripture. This is no more than tradition, but it may well be that at that time—about 400 B.C.—the writings of the prophets were collected and set in order.

But there is one fact which may well give us our clue. Daniel is clearly a prophetic book; it is a book which characteristically foretells the future. And yet the strange fact is that in Jewish practice Daniel was never ranked with the Prophets but always with the Writings. This can only mean that Daniel comes from a time when the list of the prophets was closed. If that list had been open, surely Daniel would have been on it. Now the date of Daniel is about 165 B.C., and this is an indication that the list of the prophets was probably closed by the time. So it is likely that the prophets came to be regarded as Scripture by round about 200 B.C.

Slowly the Old Testament is being built up; slowly book after book is gaining admittance, because it could not be denied, and because it bore its inspiration on its face. By about 400 B.C. the Law was Scripture; and probably by 200 B.C. the Prophets stood beside the Law. It only remains to see how the Writings won their place.

So then let us turn our attention to these Writings. There were, as we have already noted, eleven of them—Psalms, Proverbs, Job, Ecclesiastes, the Song of Solomon, Ruth, Lamentations, Esther, Ezra-Nehemiah, Chronicles, Daniel. The Writings do not form a unified and homogeneous group like the Law or the Prophets. They are very much a miscellaneous collection, a miscellany, as someone has called them, of independent books. They never quite attained to the place of the other two groups. Some of them had their place on special occasions in the synagogue worship, but they were not read regularly and systematically at the synagogue services as the Law and the Prophets were. When the Jews spoke about their Scriptures, they usually spoke about the Law and the Prophets. Jesus said that he came not to abolish the Law and the Prophets, but to fulfil them (Matthew 5:17). He said that the principle which commands us to do to

others as we would have them do to us is the Law and the Prophets (Matthew 7:12). It was the Law and the Prophets which preceded the coming of the Kingdom (Luke 16:16). It was Moses and all the Prophets which Jesus expounded and interpreted on the way to Emmaus (Luke 24:27). It is the Law and the Prophets which are read in the synagogue (Acts 13:15). If in the New Testament another section is added to Scripture, it is the Law, the Prophets, and the Psalms (Luke 24:44).

In the Writings there was something of everything. E. J. Goodspeed in *How Came the Bible?* (p. 39) divides them into philosophical discussion of religion—Job and Ecclesiastes; dirges—Lamentations; love songs—the Song of Solomon; stories—Ruth and Esther; history written from the priestly point of view—Chronicles. F. C. Grant in *How to Read the Bible* (p. 87) distinguishes poetry—Job, Psalms, Song of Solomon, Lamentations; Wisdom books—Ecclesiastes and Proverbs; stories—Esther and Ruth; a prophetic book—Daniel; history—Ezra-Nehemiah and Chronicles. In the Writings we really have the religious literature of a nation, and they won their place, not as a single whole, but piece-meal.

We have first to ask how they got into Scripture at all. We saw that from the fourth century onward it was the conviction of the Jews that the direct voice of God had ceased to speak. Now this would in effect mean that no book written after Ezra had any chance of becoming Scripture. It lay outside the period of direct inspiration. The rabbis arrived at an odd conclusion about this. If the author of a book was known, and if he was known to have written outside the period of inspiration, then the book did not get into the list of books which were Scripture. That is what kept out Ecclesiasticus, which is one of the very great books, and the omission of which many regret. It was known to be the writing of one Jesus the son of Sirach, and that he wrote it about 180 B.C. and that his grandson translated it into Greek about 132 B.C. Its date and author were known, and therefore it was out. On the other hand, the rabbis held that if the author of a book was unknown, and if it was a book of sufficient religious value to make it desirable as Scripture, then it was possible to attribute it to one of the great figures who did fall within the period of inspiration. Thus since no one really knew who wrote them, Ruth could be attributed to Samuel; Lamentations to Jeremiah; Proverbs and Ecclesiastes to Solomon; Job to Moses; the Song of Solomon to Solomon, or at least to the time of Hezekiah; all the Psalms to David, although in the middle of the book we find the verse, "The prayers of David, the son of Jesse, are ended" (Psalm 72:20); Ezra and Nehemiah to Ezra. The place that Ezra acquired in Jewish tradition was unique. The rabbis said: "The Torah was forgotten by Israel, until Ezra went up from Babylon and re-established it," and they also held that, if the Law had not already been given to Moses, Ezra was fit to have received it. To Ezra's place in tradition we will return. It is indeed fortunate that the Jewish rabbis found a way to preserve these books, for otherwise they might well have vanished.

We shall now look at the process by which these Writings were established as Scripture, and then after that we shall look at them individually. There are five pieces of evidence which will combine to give us our date.

1. We have already had cause to cite what II Maccabees 2:13 says about Nehemiah. It says of him that he founded a library and collected the books about the kings and the prophets and the writings of David. If this is to be taken as historical, then we could say that Nehemiah began the collection of the Psalms, and thereby laid the foundation of that section of Scripture which became the Writings.

2. We have also referred before to the prologue which the grandson of Jesus son of Sirach wrote to his Greek translation of his grandfather's book. In that prologue he refers to the great things handed down—the writings of the Law and the prophets and of others who have followed in their steps. He tells how his grandfather had studied the Law and the Prophets and the books of our fathers. He speaks of the Law and the Prophets and the rest of the books. He never uses the term the Writings, but it is clear that for him there was in addition to the Law and the Prophets a third section of Scripture.

3. As we have already noted, in Luke 24:44 Jesus is said to have expounded to his disciples after his resurrection the things about himself in the Law of Moses, the Prophets, and the Psalms.

4. In the apocryphal book IV Ezra, called in the printed Apocrypha II Esdras, there is a highly colored fictional account of the work of Ezra (chapter 14). In Ezra's time the Law had been lost, and it was Ezra's divinely appointed task to restore it. He was taken to a field with five men and given a cup of liquid like fire to drink. For forty days and forty nights he dictated non-stop to the five men. During that time ninety-four books were written. Then the Most High said to him: "Make public the twenty-four books that you wrote first and let the worthy and the unworthy read them; but keep the seventy that were written last, in order to give them to the wise among your people." This is obvious legend, but the point is that when this book of IV Ezra was written in the latter half of the first century A.D. the Jewish Scriptures were composed of twenty-four books, which is the number including the Writings. By that time the Writings were Scripture.

5. Round about A.D. 100 Josephus the Jewish historian laid it down that the Jewish books were fixed and settled, with none to be added and none to be subtracted.

This all fits in, for it is usually held that it was in A.D. 90 at the Council of Jamnia, near Jaffa, that the Jewish rabbis finally fixed the contents of Scripture. The Writings were now complete.

When we remember how varied a miscellany the Writings are, we will not be surprised to learn that they did not all become Scripture with the same speed and the same unanimity.

About some of them there never was any question. There was never any question about the Psalms. The Psalms were the hymnbook and the prayer book of the temple. They were intimately connected with the worship and the liturgy of the temple. Each day of the week had its special psalm with a rabbinic reason to explain its attachment.

Psalm 24 was the psalm for the first day of the week. "The earth is the Lord's and the fullness thereof"—this commemorated the first day of creation, "when God possessed the world and ruled in it." Psalm 48 was the psalm for the second day of the week. "Great is the Lord and greatly to be praised"—because on the second day of creation "God divided his works and reigned over them." Psalm 82 was the psalm for the third day of the week. "God has taken his place in the divine council"—"because on that day the earth appeared on which are the Judge and the judged." Psalm 94 was the psalm for the fourth day. "O Lord, thou God of vengeance"—"because on the fourth day God made the sun, moon and stars, and will be avenged on those that worship them." Psalm 81 was the psalm for the fifth day. "Sing aloud to God our strength"—"because of the variety of creatures created on that day to praise his name." Psalm 93 was the psalm for the sixth day. "The Lord reigns"—"because on that day God finished his works and made man, and the Lord ruled over all his works." For the seventh day, the sabbath, the psalm was Psalm 92. "It is good to give thanks to the Lord"—"because the sabbath is symbolic of the day, when after the six thousand years dispensation, God will reign over all, and his glory and service will fill the earth with thanksgiving."

Both for public worship and for private devotion the Psalms stood supreme, and never was their right to a place within Scripture challenged.

The five rolls, the *Megilloth*, which were connected with the great festivals and memorials had a secure place, although as we shall see some of them were challenged.

Chronicles, Job, Ezra-Nehemiah, and Daniel had a special place, because the high priest read publicly from them on the eve of the greatest of all Jewish religious occasions, the Day of Atonement.

Three books were particularly questioned. The Song of Solomon came under question because, unless it is read as an allegory, which it was originally never meant to be, it is a passionate love poem of very physical love, indeed one of the supreme love poems of the world. Ecclesiastes came under question because of its weary pessimism. Do your best here, and live your hardest here, is its message, because there is nothing on the other side of death but the land of shadows (Ecclesiastes 9:10). Esther came under question, because, extraordinary as it may seem, the name of God is never mentioned in it from beginning to end, and it is the warrant for the Festival of Purim, which commemorates the victory of Mordecai over Haman, but which is not one of the festivals laid down in the Law at all.

But after the Council of Jamnia the doubts were stilled and the questions were silenced.

So then, in the guidance and the providence of God the Old Testament reached its present form. And we may well note three things about it.

1. It is composed of books which, before they entered the sacred realm of Scripture, had stood the test of the years. It was not that a man wrote a book with the intention of writing a book which should be Scripture. The man wrote his book; he delivered it to people and to the years. Throughout the years and the centuries people came to love that book and to stay their hearts on it, and God used that book for his purposes. And then there came a day when people recognized that that book was nothing less than a message of God. If we liked to do so, we could say that books became Scripture by the principle of the survival of the fittest. A book became part of the Bible because it was so effective and so obviously used by God that none could stop it.

2. We must always remember that it took from the eighth century to the second century to write the Old Testament. Think of that in terms of modern history. The equivalent would be a book which men began to write in the fourteenth century and finished writing in the twentieth century. This is something to which we must return, but it is easy to see the difference in the world between 1300 and 1900. Six hundred years is a long time.

3. Further, the establishment of the Old Testament as Scripture began with the finding of Deuteronomy in 621 B.C. and ended with the Council of Jamnia in A.D. 90. This is to say that it took rather more than seven hundred years to build up the Old Testament to the point when there was a canon of Scripture. The roots of the Old Testament go very deep.

THE MAKING OF THE NEW TESTAMENT

The New Testament as we now possess it consists of twenty-seven books. There are four Gospels, one book of church history, twenty-one letters, and one apocalypse. The first time we meet the New Testament exactly in this shape is in A.D. 367. The great bishop Athanasius was accustomed at Easter time to send a pastoral letter to his people. In the year 367 he decided to deal with the books which it was right and proper for a Christian to read and which the church approved. He listed them, and for the first time the list contains all the books which make up our New Testament. This is to say that the making of the New Testament took more than three hundred years to complete.

From the beginning of its existence, the Christian faith was the faith of a book. Christianity was cradled in Judaism, and Judaism was centered in the synagogue. In its very earliest days the Christian church had no intention of breaking away from the ancestral worship of the Jews. We find Peter and John on their way up to pray in the temple (Acts 3:1). We find that both Stephen and Paul began their career as preachers by debating in the synagogue (Acts 6:8-10; 9:20, 21). The center of the synagogue service was the reading of the Scripture. That is what the service existed for. It began with a recital of the creed of Judaism and with the offering of a series of prayers. It ended with an address by a rabbi or a distinguished stranger. But right in the middle there came the reading of Scripture, and it was for this that the people had assembled.

When it was no longer possible for the Christians to worship in the synagogue, when the doors of the synagogue were closed against them, they took the form of the synagogue service with them. More than that—they took the book of the synagogue service with them too. In the

early days of the church the New Testament had not yet been written. It was not the New Testament which produced the church; it was the church which produced the New Testament. So, in the beginning, it was the Old Testament which was read every Sunday at the Christian services, and usually it was read in the form of its Greek translation, the Septuagint, which is usually denoted by the letters LXX. So in the first days of the church it was the Old Testament which was the book of the church; it was the Old Testament which was quoted and read.

For example in Peter's sermon at Pentecost (Acts 2:14-40) ten out of twenty-seven verses are Old Testament quotations—Acts 2:17-21 = Joel 2:28-32; Acts 2:25-28 = Psalm 16:8-11; Acts 2:34, 35 = Psalm 110:1. In Paul's sermon in Antioch (Acts 13:16-41) nine out of twenty-six verses go back to the Old Testament—Acts 13:16-22 is a straight summary out of Old Testament history up to David; Acts 13:33 = Psalm 2:7; Acts 13:34 = Isaiah 55:3; Acts 13:35 = Psalm 16:10; Acts 13:41 = Habakkuk 1:5; Acts 13:47 = Isaiah 49:6. In the early days it was the Old Testament which was the sacred book of the church.

How then did the New Testament arise at all? First of all, let us see in what order the New Testament was written. The most interesting fact to begin with is that the letters of Paul were almost certainly written before any of the rest of the New Testament. They were written between the years—approximately—A.D. 49 and A.D. 62.

Paul's letters were real letters. For the most part they were written to meet a local and a temporary situation. Something went wrong in Thessalonica or in Corinth, and Paul wrote to correct the situation. F. C. Grant has said truly, "Had telephones been invented, Paul certainly would have used them—and we should never have had any epistles from his pen!" (*How to Read the Bible*, p. 131). Paul wrote to correct some situation in Thessalonica or Galatia or Corinth. He wrote as a pastor, not as an author. And it must be remembered that Paul was writing long before the days of printing. His letters *were* letters, handwritten because there was no such thing as print, existing to begin with as one single copy, often written to correct some temporary, local situation in which things had gone wrong. Of course, Paul dealt with the local and temporary situation in the light of eternal truth, but nonetheless his letters were letters in the real sense of the term, and there is nothing so temporary and local and evanescent as a letter. It is always of the first importance to remember that there was no question of Paul's *publishing* his letters in a modern sense.

How then did they ever become Scripture? What follows is necessarily a reconstruction. It is not certainty, but it does seem to meet the facts. We begin by remembering that for the most part Paul's letters existed in the churches to which they were sent and nowhere else. They were not published as books; they were sent as letters. How were they ever rescued and recovered and published? It was probably about A.D. 90 when the book of Acts was published. Now it is a strange thing that if we had no more than

the book of Acts we would never have known that Paul ever wrote a letter. Acts has absolutely nothing to say about Paul as a letter-writer. What likely happened was that, when Acts was published, it was suddenly realized what an extraordinary figure Paul was. Suddenly Paul came to life, and in consequence of that every church which had a letter of Paul suddenly realized over again what a treasure it had; and so the letters were searched for and collected and shared and became the possession of the church at large rather than merely the correspondence of a congregation. We may well take it that it was the publication of Acts which showed the greatness of Paul, and which was the mainspring of the movement to collect his letters. At this stage, about A.D. 90, Paul's letters have not yet been ranked as Scripture, but they have become one of the most treasured possessions of the church.

So then Paul's letters were written between A.D. 49 and A.D. 62, and they were probably rediscovered in all their greatness as a consequence of the publication of Acts about A.D. 90. But what was happening to the rest of the New Testament, and in particular what was happening to the Gospels? Roughly speaking, the dates of the Gospels in the form in which we have them are A.D. 65–70 for Mark; A.D. 80–90 for Matthew and Luke; A.D. 100 for John. Why were they so long in being written, and why were they so long in becoming the books of the church? And what in the end did cause them finally to be written?

1. In the first place, Christianity was born into a nonliterary civilization, at least in its early stages. It came into the world long before the invention of printing, and there was no way of really mass-producing books as can be done in modern times. People did not think in terms of the mass production of books as they do nowadays. This was specially true of Judaism. The rabbis had the strongest possible objection to writing down their teaching. "Commit nothing to writing," they said. The memory of a good teacher or a good student was "like a well-plastered cistern which never loses a drop." There may well have also been a hesitation among the Jews to writing things down because, if a thing was written, it seemed in a way to challenge the authority of Scripture, and so Scripture tended to be the only thing that was written and so all other teaching was passed down by word of mouth. The *Mishnah* is what we might call the commentary on and the expansion of the laws of the Old Testament. It is the application of the written laws of the Old Testament to particular cases. It was never written down at all until the third century A.D., and when it was written down, even a summary account of it today in English translation makes a book of over eight hundred pages. All this was carried in the memory of the rabbis. The written word did not have in the ancient world the place that it has today. Papias, who was one of the great collectors of information in the early church, wrote: "I did not think that what was to be gotten from books would profit me as much as what came from the living and abiding voice"

(quoted, Eusebius, *The Ecclesiastical History* 3:39.4). The first age of the church was not a literary age in anything like the sense in which modern ages became literary after printing was invented. At least in the East, where Christianity originated, it was much more natural to transmit knowledge and teaching by word of mouth than on the printed page.

2. There was further the fact that Christianity made its first impact on the poorer and the more uncultured classes. "Consider your call, brethren," Paul writes to the Corinthians, "not many of you were wise according to worldly standards, not many were powerful, not many were of noble birth" (I Corinthians 1:26). It was indeed among the poor and the underprivileged and the slaves that the Christian message made its first main impact.

Early in the third century a pagan philosopher called Celsus made an attack on Christianity. He attacked it on the ground that it appealed only to the poor and the ignorant and the uncultured. He says that the attitude and the invitation of the Christians is: "Let no one cultured draw near, none wise, none sensible, for all that kind of thing we count evil; but, if any man is ignorant, if any man is wanting in sense and culture, if any man is a fool, let him come boldly. . . . It is only the simpletons, the ignoble, the senseless, slaves, and womenfolk and children whom they wish to persuade, or can persuade" (Origen, *Against Celsus* 3.44). In its early days the Christian community was neither a book-reading nor a book-producing community.

3. There were, as we shall see, methods of book production which foreshadowed mass production. But where was the market for Christian books?

Writing materials were not cheap. The writing substance which was made from the papyrus plant was produced in sheets measuring the equivalent of eight by ten inches. One sheet cost at the cheapest the equivalent of five cents per sheet, and in the best quality range it cost twenty cents per sheet. And this has to be evaluated in the light of the fact that the average wage of a working-man was about eight cents per day. In other words, it would cost more than a day's wage to buy a single sheet of the best papyrus. Very few people are going to be able to afford books made of papyrus which cost that kind of figure.

Nor was the process of expert copying cheap, as we have seen. Clearly the cost would be well beyond the reach of most Christians and even of most Christian churches. The very expense of book production tended to delay the formation of anything like a Christian literature.

4. So long as the original apostles continued to live, there was little demand for written books. The apostles and their immediate associates were the living books on which the Christian message was written. They were the eyewitnesses, and so long as they lived, books were not necessary.

5. It may well be that the factor which most of all discouraged the production of books was the belief in the imminence of the Second Coming. We have only to read a chapter like I Corinthians 7, where in the light of the short time before the end, as they then expected, Paul discourages marriage in a world which is hastening, as was thought, to its end. If the Second Coming was just round the corner, there was neither the time nor the reason to write books in a world in which the end was due to come at any moment.

These were the main factors which delayed the formation of a Christian literature; but inevitably there came a time when literature was a necessity.

1. The time when the story was passed down by word of mouth was bound to come to an end with the death of the apostles and of those who had been eyewitnesses. By A.D. 70 of the original apostles probably only John was left alive. The story had therefore to be set down. In the nature of things the written word had to take the place of "the living and abiding voice." Eusebius quotes Irenaeus' account of how the Gospels were written. Irenaeus says that after the death of Peter and Paul, "Mark, the disciple and interpreter of Peter, transmitted to us in writing those things which Peter had preached; and Luke, the attendant of Paul, recorded in a book the gospel which Paul had declared" (*Against Heresies* 3.1.1; quoted by Eusebius, *The Ecclesiastical History* 5.8.2, 3). The idea is that the written record was meant to take the place of the living voice. The age of the eyewitness had to come to an end; the time of the written record had come.

2. When Christianity went out of Palestine into the larger world, and particularly when Christianity made contact with Roman culture and civilization, it entered a society which was literate and literary, a society in which the book was part of life. Rome had its bookshops, with the pillars covered with advertisements for the latest books, and these bookshops were not only shops; they were the meeting places of cultured society. In Rome the publishers produced books by slave labor. What happened was that fifty or a hundred slaves would write to dictation. Of course, mistakes were made, but by this mass dictation books could be copied and produced quickly and cheaply. The first book of Martial has one hundred and nineteen epigrams in about seven hundred lines of verse, and copied thus it sold for five *denarii*, which was the equivalent of about fifty cents. Once Christianity left Palestine and went out into the world of culture and literature, it went out to a world which knew all about books, and where the Christian story would soon be written down.

3. From the beginning Christianity was a missionary religion. It was obvious that with a world to evangelize, the missionaries could not stay for any length of time in any one place. It was therefore necessary to leave a written record of the story they had told with the new converts in each place. To this day one of the first tasks of the missionary is to produce a written record of the Christian story, even if it involves the invention of an

alphabet to do so. A missionary religion is almost obliged to be a literary religion.

4. As the church grew and developed, there came into the church people with strange, and even dangerous, ideas. In other words, it was not long before heresies developed. And in that situation the church needed some "official" book, some standard account of the life and teaching of Jesus. It was precisely such that the New Testament supplied, especially in the Gospels.

5. We saw that one of the factors which delayed the production of a Christian literature was the supposed imminence of the Second Coming. But the Second Coming was delayed, and the church began to see that it was living in a more or less permanent situation, and in a situation like that a written literature was no longer an irrelevance but a necessity.

In the nature of things it became necessary for the church to produce a Christian literature.

When we have reached this stage in our thinking about the Gospels, a question arises. We have seen that there was considerable delay in the production of a written Gospel. If Jesus died round about A.D. 30 and if the first written Gospel did not emerge until some time between A.D. 65 and 70, what was happening in that thirty-five to forty years when there was no official written account of the life and teaching of Jesus? Is it possible that within this period the story of the life of Jesus and the account of his teaching grew less and less accurate, and more and more a matter of invention? From the point of view of the twentieth century that is a natural question to ask. But in the first century things were very different.

In the first place the ancient memory was much more retentive than the modern memory. It had to be. It may well be said that the printed book, especially when the book is cheap or readily available, has tended to kill the memory. In the ancient days, if a person wanted to retain some story, or some set of facts, he had to do it by memorizing, because books were scarce and expensive. Xenophon tells of Niceratus, "My father," said Niceratus, "was anxious to see me develop into a good man, and as a means to this end he compelled me to memorise all Homer: and so even now I can repeat the whole *Iliad and Odyssey* by heart" (*Symposium* 3.6). The *Iliad* and the *Odyssey* each contain twenty-four books, and a book will average about five hundred lines, and this feat of memorization was something that many a Greek boy achieved as part of the education of a cultured man. Nowadays, when we want to enjoy or to refer to a passage, we look it up in a printed book; in the ancient days, when there were few or no books to look up, people carried things in their memories. There was no real fear of the story getting lost or becoming distorted in a day when the memory was strong.

But there was another process operating. There is a necessary corollary to the retentive memory. When things have to be remembered, they tend to become stereotyped. A story comes to be told always in exactly the same way. This process can be seen in the way in which children regard stories.

When a child knows and loves a story, it must be told to him always in exactly the same way; he will not accept any deviation from the form of the story which he knows and loves.

So the gospel stories became stereotyped into certain *forms*, and in fairly recent years there has arisen a form of study of the Gospels called Form Criticism, which has made it its objective to find out the *forms* in which the gospel tradition circulated before it came to be set down in the shape of the written Gospels. Those who have studied these matters have identified a number of different kinds of forms in which the stories are stereotyped. Three of these follow:

1. There are what are called paradigms or apothegms or pronouncement stories. These are pieces of tradition whose one reason for existing is that they are intended to preserve a saying of Jesus. The story is not important; the details are few; the one important thing is the saying. To take two examples—the story in Mark 2:23-28 exists simply to enshrine the saying of Jesus: "The sabbath was made for man, not man for the sabbath; so the Son of man is lord even of the sabbath." The story in Matthew 9:10-13 exists to preserve the saying of Jesus: "I came not to call the righteous, but sinners." These stories exist, not for the sake of the story, but for the sake of the saying. The saying is the jewel of which the story is the casket.

2. There are stories which are called tales or novellen. These are stories which tell of some healing deed of Jesus. They all follow the same pattern. There is first a statement of the illness; second, an account of the cure; third, a statement of the consequence of the cure. To take a very simple example, there is the story of the cure of Peter's mother-in-law (Mark 1:29-31). There are:

   a. The statement of the illness—"Now Simon's mother-in-law lay sick with a fever."
   b. The account of the cure—"He came and took her by the hand and lifted her up, and the fever left her."
   c. The consequence or result—"And she served them." Nearly all of Jesus' miracles are told in this pattern. This is the stereotype which was fixed long before the story was written down.

3. There are sayings. Sayings are epigrammatic and memorable sayings of Jesus which have no context. The pronouncement stories with which we began all arise from an incident; the sayings are detached sayings of Jesus. The sermon on the Mount is almost entirely composed of such sayings.

It was in these forms that the gospel stories were quickly stereotyped in the time between the earthly life of Jesus and the writing down of the Gospels as we now have them. And there is another thing to note which is of the greatest importance. These stories were repeated over and over again for one purpose—for preaching and for the instruction of those entering the Christian community. The importance of this is that these stories were therefore never what we might call private property; they were always public possessions. If there was a change in the telling, the audience would

at once ask why. They were not stories told once; they were told again and again and again. The check on them was not simply the memory of the teller; the check on them was the memory of the Christian church. They were not simply the product of one man; they did not depend on any one man's memory. From the beginning they were the possession of the community; they were the material which preachers and teachers continually used, and to which groups of Christians continually listened. The possibility of distortion or falsification is very much reduced when the story is being continually repeated not only to individuals but also to groups. The guarantor of the truth of any story is not any individual; the guarantor is the united witness of the church.

This leads us to note one more very important fact about the Gospels. The Gospels are not primarily historical documents; they are not intended to be regarded as biographies of Jesus. They are in fact the preaching material of the early church. John tells us the aim of his Gospel: "These are written that you may believe that Jesus is the Christ, the Son of God, and that believing you may have life in his name" (John 20:30). The aim is not to write a life of Jesus. Many of the things that we would look for in a biography are not there. There is, for instance, no description of what Jesus looked like. It is impossible to construct a timetable of the life of Jesus from the Gospels.

It has been said that there are two ways of writing a story. You may follow the story from day to day and from hour to hour and from event to event in strict chronological order, trying to make the record as complete as possible and trying to leave nothing out. Or, you may take a series of significant incidents and episodes and use them as windows to see into the mind and the heart of the person you are seeking to know. It is the second method that the gospel writers use. They make no attempt to follow Jesus from place to place and day to day. They take a series of things he said and did to open a series of windows through which we catch glimpses of his mind and heart. It is the difference between a photograph and a portrait. A photograph shows us the subject reproduced in every detail; a portrait seizes on the special characteristics of the person being painted and brings them out. A photograph reproduces in every detail what the person looks like externally; a portrait tries to reveal his inner character and mind and heart. The Gospels are not biographies; they are not photographs. They are attempts to show the mind and the heart and the character of Jesus; and they make this attempt, not simply as matter of interest, and not simply as a contribution to history, but so that those who read may see the mind of God in Jesus. The Gospels are not simply descriptions of Jesus; they are invitations to believe in him as the Son of God.

We have looked at the Letters of Paul, and we have looked at the Gospels. There were other letters in the New Testament also—the Letters of James and Peter and Jude and John. And we have looked at the Gospels, and we have seen what they are meant to be.

Between the Gospels and the letters there comes the book of Acts. It could be argued that Acts is the most important single book in the New Testament, for without it we would know nothing about the history of the early church except what we could guess and deduce from the letters. Even if we lost three of the Gospels, we would still have one left, and we would still have some kind of portrait of Jesus; but, if Acts had been lost, the history of the early church would have been shrouded in entire darkness. It is misleading to call the book *The Acts of the Apostles*. The only apostles mentioned are James, whose death is given in one sentence (Acts 12:2), Peter, John, who is always with Peter and who never himself speaks, and Paul. It is better to call the book *Acts of Apostolic Men*. In the Greek title there is no *the* before either Acts or Apostles. The book does not attempt to give a comprehensive account. What it does do is to open a series of windows through which significant events in the history of the early church may be seen.

Acts does three things. First, it tells the story of the expansion of the church, of how, as Jesus gave his orders, the message went out from Jerusalem, to Judaea and to Samaria and to the ends of the earth (Acts 1:8). Second, it tells how this astonishing crusade began with no more than one hundred and twenty people (Acts 1:15), and how it was the work of the Spirit (Acts 1:8). The first great story is the story of Pentecost (Acts 2), when the Holy Spirit came. Thereafter it is the Holy Spirit who dictates every outgoing movement of the Christian church. It was the Holy Spirit who instructed Philip to approach the Ethiopian (Acts 8:29); who told Peter to welcome the deputation from Cornelius (Acts 10:19); who was responsible for the dispatch of Paul and Barnabas from Antioch on the first missionary journey (Acts 13:2); who guided the church into receiving the Gentiles in its membership (Acts 15:28); who guided Paul's steps from Asia Minor to Europe (Acts 16:7). Acts is in reality the book of the acts of the Holy Spirit.

Third, Acts tells us of the message of the early church. In it we have the summaries of speeches by Peter (2:14-36; 3:12-26; 4:8-12; 4:24-30); by Stephen (7:2-53); by Paul (13:16-41; 14:15-17; 17:22-31). There is no reason to doubt that, though these are not verbatim reports, they do give the substance of what early Christian sermons were about.

From them we learn the essence of the early Christian message.

1. The new age has dawned, and it has dawned through the life, death, and resurrection of Jesus Christ.

2. Jesus' life and all that happened to him, and especially his death and resurrection, are the fulfilment of prophecy.

3. He will come again to judge the living and the dead.

4. Therefore repent and receive forgiveness and the gift of the Holy Spirit.

5. He who will not repent will reap the consequences of his refusal.

One thing specially interests us about these speeches. The early Christian preachers never failed to mention the Resurrection. The

Resurrection, as it has been put, was "the star in the firmament of early Christianity." And—very surprisingly—these early sermons do not connect the death of Jesus with the forgiveness of sins. The early church was dominated by the resurrection faith, and by the experience of the Holy Spirit. It had not yet become what W. D. Davies has called, cross conscious. The cruciality of the cross, as P. T. Forsyth called it, and the interpretation of the cross had to wait for the great mind and heart of Paul.

There is one book in the New Testament which is neither a letter nor a gospel, and it is one of the most puzzling books in the New Testament. It is the book which we call the Revelation, or the Apocalypse. Although it is so strange a book to us, and although it is the only book of its kind in the New Testament, it is in fact a specimen of a kind of book which was very common in the days when the New Testament books were being written.

The Jews divided all time into two ages. There was this present age, and as they saw it, this present age is wholly bad; it is so bad that it cannot be reformed; it is fit only to be destroyed. Contrasted with this there is the age which is to come, and as they believed, the age which is to come is the golden age of God, when everything will be as God meant it to be, and when the good will enter into their joy and the evil into their destruction. The question is, how was the one age to turn into the other? How was the evil of this present age to become the glory of the age which is to come? By the time of the New Testament, the Jews were sure that this change could never come about by human means; it could not come about by any process of reformation. It could come about only by the total destruction of this present age, and the birth of a new age which would be the age of God. How then would the change take place? They believed that it would take place at the Day of the Lord. The Day of the Lord would be a time when the present world and all that is in it would disintegrate and be destroyed, when there would be a last and final judgment, and when there would arise out of the chaos a new world which would be the world of God recreated for the people of God.

So there came into being a whole series of books, each of them called an apocalypse. The word *apocalypse* literally means "an unveiling." And the aim of these books was to tell of the terrible events of the last days, of the terror of judgment, and of the golden age which was to come. In the nature of things these books were unintelligible except to those who understood the "code," for the books were seeking to tell of things which no eye had seen, which no ear had heard, and which had never entered into the minds of people. Many of these books survive, for the darker the history of the Jewish people, the harder their fate, the sorer their subjugation and slavery, the more eagerly they dreamed of the day when God would invade history, when the dramatic change would come, and when the new age would dawn. Mostly these are Jewish books, but our Apocalypse is a Christian specimen of this kind of literature, and this is why it is the most difficult book in the New Testament for us to understand. But it must be

remembered that, strange as it is, it is a specimen of one of the commonest kinds of religious literature in New Testament times.

So, then, as we have it now, the New Testament is composed of the Four Gospels, Acts, a series of letters written by Paul, James, Peter, John, Jude, and others, and one Apocalypse. Most people would agree that it took about seventy years to write. The Letter to the Galatians is probably the earliest book in it—about A.D. 49—and the Second Letter of Peter is probably the latest book in it—about A.D. 120; and having been written, as we have already seen, the New Testament took until A.D. 367 to assume the form in which we have it today.

There are certain milestones on the way to the completion of the New Testament at which we must now look. The great steps in the final definition of the contents of the New Testament were the result of the mistakes into which certain heretics tried to lead the church.

The first of these heretics was Marcion. He was a wealthy shipowner from Sinope on the Black Sea coast, and he came to Rome about A.D. 140. Marcion was a Gnostic. The Gnostics—from a word meaning "knowledge"—were among the most dangerous heretics who ever threatened the church. They set out to explain the existence of sin and evil. Their basic assumption was that from the beginning of time there have been two principles—matter and spirit, matter and God. Matter was not created; it, as the Gnostics believed, was a basic substance which was always there. It is the basic material out of which the world was made. The matter was essentially evil, just as spirit is essentially good. This is to say that from the beginning the world is made out of flawed material. That is the explanation of sorrow and sin and suffering and pain. The world is made out of bad stuff. But, if matter is evil, this means that the true God who is spirit and who is altogether good could not have touched it. And this means that the true and good God, who is spirit, cannot have been responsible for creation. What happened, as the Gnostics taught, was that the good God put out a series of emanations or aeons, each one more distant from himself. Each emanation was more ignorant of God, and at the end of the scale there was an emanation who was not only ignorant of God, but also hostile to God; and it was this distant, ignorant, hostile emanation who was the creator of the world. This meant that the Gnostics believed that all created things, including the body, are essentially evil. All matter is bad and only spirit is good.

And then the Gnostics took another step. They held that the creator, the distant, hostile, ignorant emanation is the God of the Old Testament, and the real God, the God of spirit, the true God, is the God of the New Testament. This had one obvious consequence. The Gnostic completely, totally and altogether abandoned and discarded the Old Testament. The

Old Testament was the book of the ignorant and hostile God. But it also meant that everything in the New Testament which had anything to do with the God of the Old Testament had to go. So of the Christian books Marcion kept only an expurgated version of Luke's Gospel. But Paul was Marcion's hero, for Marcion misunderstood Paul and thought that Paul's attack on the Law was an attack on the Old Testament, and so Marcion kept the Letters of Paul as his most sacred books. So just as the Old Testament consisted of the Law and the Prophets, Marcion's Christian book consisted of the Gospel—Luke—and the Apostle—Paul. Clearly, this was something to which the church had to offer an answer.

Marcion's attack left the church with two obligations. First, the church had to define its attitude to the Old Testament, which Marcion wished completely to discard, and it had also to make up its mind just what books composed the New Testament. The church affirmed its faith in the Old Testament; it had no intention of jettisoning it. And there are signs that the church did face up to the task of defining the New Testament.

There exists a list of New Testament books formulated about A.D. 170. It is called the Muratorian Canon, after the discoverer of it. It is slightly mutilated at the beginning, but it is easy to see just what it contained. Its contents were as follows: the Four Gospels, Matthew, Mark, Luke, John; the Acts of the Apostles; Paul's Letters, which it enumerates in the unusual order Corinthians, Ephesians, Philippians, Colossians, Galatians, Thessalonians, Romans; to these it adds the Pastoral Epistles, that is, the Letters to Timothy and to Titus, and the Letter to Philemon; it includes the Letter of Jude and the First and Second Letters of John; and the Revelation. It included the Wisdom of Solomon, and—with a doubt—a second Apocalypse, the Apocalypse of Peter. The one surprise is the omission of First Peter. The other books which are omitted—James, Second Peter, Third John, Hebrews—are the books which took longest to make their place in the Canon of the New Testament unquestioned and secure. So we can see that toward the end of the second century the New Testament is well on the way to being in the form which it finally took.

For the moment we must turn aside from the story of the final formation of the New Testament to another question. How did the process of writing the New Testament come to an end? Why and when did the Christian church come to the conclusion that no more New Testament books could be written, or, to put it more accurately, when did the church decide, and why, that the quota of sacred books was complete and not to be added to any more?

This too happened under the influence of a heretic. Some time toward the end of the second century a man called Montanus appeared on the scene. Montanus felt that the original standards of the church had been lowered. He remembered that Jesus had said that the Spirit would come to the church and bring the church fresh truth and fresh strength. As the Fourth Gospel put it, Jesus had said: "I have yet many things to say to you,

but you cannot bear them now. When the Spirit of truth comes, he will guide you into all the truth. . . . He will take what is mine and declare it to you" (John 16:12-14). Jesus had promised that the Holy Spirit, the Paraclete, would come, and would, as it were, develop and complete his message. What happened was that Montanus arrived on the scene and claimed that he in fact was the promised Paraclete and that he proposed to give to people the new revelation which Jesus had promised.

This indeed presented the church with a problem; and the church solved it by holding that the revelation of God had been given and completed, and that the days of revelation in the full sense of the term were ended. The church in effect declared that all the sacred books which should be written had been written, and that Scripture was closed. As Tertullian, who later became a Montanist, put it bitterly, the Holy Spirit had been chased into a book. In any event, the Canon of Scripture was regarded as closed. It would never have done, so the church felt, if every now and then someone were to come up with an entirely new revelation. There had to be a time of full revelation by which all other revelations were to be judged. It was decided that that time had come and that no more sacred books could be written. It was not that they had ceased to believe in the revealing power of the Holy Spirit. The difference was that in the first days the Holy Spirit had enabled men to write the sacred books of the Christian religion; in the later days the Holy Spirit enabled people to understand, to interpret and to apply what had been written.

What then was the qualification for a book to gain entry into the church's list of supremely sacred books? The one question asked was whether or not a book was apostolic—that is, whether or not it was written by an actual apostle, or at least by an apostolic man. Thus, as far as the Gospels go, Matthew and John were the work of apostles, and Mark and Luke qualified, because Mark was held to be the disciple and the interpreter of Peter, while Luke was held to have put down in a book the gospel preached by Paul (Irenaeus, *Against Heresies* 3.1.1, 2; Eusebius, *The Ecclesiastical History* 5.8.2). This was in the end why the Letter to the Hebrews was ascribed to Paul. It was known well enough that it was not actually the writing of Paul. As Origen said in the famous sentence: "Who wrote the Letter to the Hebrews only God really knows" (Eusebius, 6.25.11-14). Paul was the great letter-writer; the Letter to the Hebrews was so valuable that the church wanted to keep it as one of the sacred books; and so to give it the status it needed it was added to the Letters of Paul.

There was a good reason for making apostolic authorship the standard of acceptance of any book as one of the church's sacred and authoritative books. Christianity is a historical religion. Christianity took its origin and its power from a historical person, Jesus of Nazareth. Therefore the one necessity was an unbroken chain of evidence going right back to him. The world was full of the stories of dying and rising gods. The only way to make it certain that the Christian gospel was not simply another of these stories

was to trace it back to someone who could say: "I know that this is true, because with my own eyes I saw it."

This stressing of apostolic authorship had one interesting consequence. On general grounds it seems strange that the church kept four different Gospels. The fact that there were four Gospels could produce embarrassing situations. For instance, the Fourth Gospel has the incident of the cleansing of the temple at the beginning of the ministry of Jesus, and the other three have it at the end. The fact that there are four Gospels often produces problems of harmonization. There was an experiment in harmonizing the Gospels made by a man called Tatian about A.D. 180. Tatian produced the *Diatessaron*, which literally means "through four," and in it he made a harmony of the Gospels in which by a scissors-and-paste method he managed to include almost everything. A fragment of the Diatessaron read like this:

> And the day was Preparation; the Sabbath was dawning (Luke 23:54). And when it was evening, on the Preparation, that is the day before the Sabbath (Matthew 27:57; Mark 15:42), there came up a man, being a member of the council (Matthew 27:57; Luke 23:50), from Arimathaea, a city of Judah, by name Joseph (Matthew 27:57; Luke 23:50), good and righteous, being a disciple of Jesus, but secretly for fear of the Jews (Matthew 27:57; Luke 23:50; John 19:38). And he was looking for the kingdom of God (Luke 23:51). This man had not consented to their purpose (Luke 23:51).

It is true that Tatian's *Diatessaron* was not put together with any great artistry, but one would have expected the Four Gospels to be woven into one narrative. What stopped that was the overwhelming importance of apostolic testimony. The Gospels were all of them the work of apostolic men or of apostles; and it was therefore more important to keep them as they were than to harmonize them. So much so, that on there being four Gospels, Irenaeus could write; "As there are four quarters of the world in which we live, as there are four universal winds, and as the church is scattered all over the earth, and the gospel is the pillar and base of the church and the breath of life, it is likely that it should have four pillars breaching immortality on every side and kindling afresh the life of men. Whence it is evident that the Word, the architect of all things, who sits upon the cherubim and holds all things together, having been made manifest to men, gave us the gospel in a fourfold shape, but held together by one Spirit" (*Against Heresies* 3.11.8). So in the end it came to be argued that it was just as natural that there should be four Gospels as that there should be four points of the compass.

So then the Gospels and the Letters took their place as the books of the church; and that place became secure when they began to be read at the public worship of the church. When, as the years passed on, they became part of every service of the church, they were fully established.

We may complete this story by noting still one other thing. For a time there were certain books whose position was not secure. Two of the great early scholars of the church made investigations about the contents of the Christian Scriptures.

The first was Origen, who lived from A.D. 182 to 251. In his time the situation was that the place of the Four Gospels, of the Letters of Paul, including Hebrews, of I Peter, I John, and the Revelation was undisputed and secure. Origen goes on to say that Peter may have left another letter, but that this was doubtful. Second and Third John he knew but not everyone, he said, considered them genuine. And James and Jude he never mentions at all.

The second was Eusebius of Caesarea, the great church historian who lived from A.D. 270 to 330. He divided the books of the church into three classes—the universally accepted, the disputed, and the spurious. The universally accepted are the Four Gospels, Acts, the Letters of Paul, including Hebrews, I John, and I Peter. The Revelation hovered between the universally accepted and the disputed. The disputed books are James, Jude, II Peter, and II and III John. He says that II Peter is not generally accepted, but that because it has been found profitable by many it may well be Scripture. He says that many regard the Letter of James as spurious, and that very few of the early writers of the church have ever mentioned it. The list of Eusebius is to all intents and purposes the same as that of Origen.

So finally we come to the last stage. The first time, as we began by saying, that we find the books of the New Testament listed exactly as we have them today is in the Easter Letter of Athanasius to his people in A.D. 367, and it marks such an epoch that the relevant section must be quoted in full:

> There must be no hesitation to state again the books of the New Testament, for they are these: Four Gospels, according to Matthew, according to Mark, according to Luke and according to John. Further, after these, also the Acts of the Apostles, and the seven so-called Catholic Epistles of the Apostles, as follows: one of James, but two of Peter, then three of John, and after these one of Jude; in addition to these there are fourteen Epistles of the apostle Paul put down in the following order: the first to the Romans, then two to the Corinthians, and after these the Epistles to the Galatians, and then to the Ephesians: further, the Epistles to the Philippians and to the Colossians and two to the Thessalonians, and the Epistle to the Hebrews. And next two Letters to Timothy, but one to Titus, and the last one to Philemon. Moreover also, the Apocalypse of John.

Here for the first time is the complete New Testament as we know it.

So then by 367 the New Testament was completed and the canon was closed. There was never again to be any variation in it. It is, however, worthwhile to see what Luther has to say on the subject. To us nowadays the attitude of the Reformers seems quite astonishingly free and radical. They claimed a sovereign liberty in regard to the place they gave to certain

books. Luther had only one touchstone, and he expressed it with his usual vivid violence: "That which does not teach Christ is not apostolic," though Peter or Paul should have said it; on the contrary, that which does preach Christ is apostolic, even if it should come from Judas, Annas, Herod, or Pilate.

There were certain books to which Luther gave a supreme place, and certain books to which he gave a secondary place. There are twenty-seven books in the New Testament. On the title page of his own translation of the New Testament Luther printed and numbered twenty-three of them; then at the end in a little group of their own, indented and not numbered, he placed James, Hebrews, Jude, and the Revelation. James, he said, was "an epistle of straw; for it has nothing of the nature of the gospel about it." It teaches justification by works; it contradicts Paul; and it has nothing to say about the life and the death and the resurrection of Jesus, and about the Holy Spirit. Hebrews in three places, in chapters 6, 10, 12, says that there can be no repentance after baptism, and this, says Luther, is in flat contradiction to the teaching of the Gospels and of Paul. Jude is no more than an extract from II Peter; it is in fact included very largely in II Peter. As for the Revelation, Luther said of it: "I hold it to be neither apostolic nor prophetic. . . . My spirit cannot acquiesce in the book." He went on to say: "I abide by the books which present Christ pure and clear. . . . After all, in it Christ is neither taught nor acknowledged."

Luther's standards were completely clear. In his Preface to the New Testament he writes—and we must quote the passage in full:

John's Gospel and St. Paul's epistles, especially that to the Romans, and St. Peter's first Epistle are the true kernel and marrow of all the books. . . .

In them you find not many works and miracles of Christ described, but you do find it depicted, in masterly fashion, how faith in Christ overcomes sin, death and hell, and gives life, righteousness and salvation. This is the real nature of the Gospel. . . . If I had to do without one or the other—either the works or the preaching of Christ—I would rather do without his works than his preaching; for the works do not help me, but his words give life, as he himself says. . . . Now John writes very little about the works of Christ, but very much about his preaching; therefore John's Gospel is the one, tender, true, chief Gospel, far, far, to be preferred to the other three and placed high above them. So too the Epistles of St. Paul and St. Peter far surpass the other three Gospels—Matthew, Mark and Luke.

In a word, John's Gospel and his First Epistle, St. Paul's Epistles, especially Romans, Galatians, and Ephesians, and St. Peter's First Epistle are the books that show you Christ and teach you all that it is necessary and good for you to know, even though you were never to see or hear any other book or doctrine.

Luther has no hesitation in drawing distinctions between the books of the New Testament. He makes it clear that this preference is a personal thing. At the end of his Introduction to James he writes: "Therefore, I cannot put

him among the chief books, though I would not thereby prevent anyone from putting him where he pleases and estimating him as he pleases, for there are many good things in him."

For Luther all the New Testament books were holy, but within the New Testament there was a special Holy of Holies of books where above all Jesus Christ is to be encountered.

This then is the story of how the New Testament came to be what it is today, and although to Luther and others there have always been some books which are dearer and more precious than others, for the last sixteen hundred years no book has been added and no book has been taken away.

HOW TO STUDY THE BIBLE

All through this chapter I am going to assume that the person who wants to engage in the study of the Bible is a Christian, or at least wishes to be a Christian. We are to be thinking all the time of the person whose desire it is to widen his knowledge and to deepen and enrich his Christian life and experience by the study of the Bible. We begin with the assumption of Arminius that "the Church is that community which recognizes the word of God in the Scriptures."

The Bible, of course, must be studied as any other book is studied. To it we must bring all the rigor and the apparatus of scholarship. It must be approached with all the willingness to make an effort with which the student approaches the study of any of the world's great books.

But there is another side of this question which is no less important. If it is true that the Bible is to be studied with the *methods* with which any great book is studied, it is equally true that the Bible is not studied for the *purpose* for which any other book is studied. An ordinary book is studied for information, for instruction, for interest, for pleasure, as a textbook, as a task; but the Bible is written that in it the reader may find life and encounter God. In about A.D. 1000 Aelfric, one of the very early translators of the Bible, wrote a noble passage on what he felt the Bible to be.

Whoever would be one with God must often and often read the Holy Scriptures. For when we pray we speak to God; and, when we read the Bible, God speaks to us. The reading of the Scriptures produces a twofold advantage to the reader. It renders him wiser by informing his mind; and also leads him from the vanities of the world to the love of God. The reading of the Scriptures is truly an honorable employment, and greatly conduces to the purity of the soul. For as the body is nourished by natural food, so the

sublimer man, that is, the soul, is nourished by the divine saying, according to the words of the Psalmist: "How sweet are thy words unto my taste, yea, sweeter than honey to my mouth." Happy is he, then, who reads the Scriptures if he convert the words into actions. The whole of the Scriptures are written for our salvation, and by them we obtain the knowledge of the truth. The blind man stumbles oftener than he who sees; so he who is ignorant of the precepts of Scripture offends more frequently than he who knows them.

1. So then, in the very first place, the reader must bring reverence to the Bible. His duty will be to begin his reading with prayer. Luther said of the student of Scripture that his "first duty is to begin with a prayer of such a nature that God in his great mercy may grant you the true understanding of his words." The Psalmist prayed: "Open my eyes that I may behold wondrous things out of thy law" (Psalm 119:18), and we may well use the prayer that many of us know and love:

Blessed Lord, who hast caused all holy Scriptures to be written for our learning, grant that we may in such wise hear them, read, mark, learn, and inwardly digest them, that by patience and comfort of thy holy word, we may embrace and ever hold fast the blessed hope of everlasting life, which thou hast given us in our Savior Jesus Christ.

We will do well to take our thoughts back to the Jewish idea of the Spirit. As the Jew saw it, the Spirit of God does two things. First, the Spirit brings God's truth to people. Second, and just as important, the Spirit enables people to recognize God's truth when they see it. This is to say that the same Spirit who moved the writers of the Bible to write their books is the Spirit who now enables us to study and to interpret these books.

We may see how the Spirit came to open the Bible to one of the greatest Christians of all time. Writing in 1545 Luther tells us how in his younger days he hated the very word *righteousness*. To him it always brought the idea that God in his righteousness is out to punish the unrighteous and the sinner. It was to him a word of terror. He never could understand the connection of the two halves of Romans 1:17: "For therein is the righteousness of God revealed from faith to faith: as it is written, The just shall live by faith." For days and nights he thought and meditated upon this text; and then he began to see that the word *righteousness* means that God in his mercy justifies a person by faith. To put it very simply, he began to see that the righteousness of God is not the righteousness with which he threatens us, but *the righteousness which he offers us and gives us*. Then he writes:

At this point I felt completely reborn, and as if I had entered paradise with its open gate. In a moment the whole meaning of Scripture seemed to have changed. Thereafter I ran through the Scriptures as if I had them in my

memory, and collected analogical meanings in other words, such as the work of God, which means the work that God works in *us*, the virtue of God, which means the virtue through which he makes us powerful, the wisdom of God, which means the wisdom through which he makes *us* wise, the courage of God, the salvation of God, the glory of God. My love for that sweetest word *righteousness of God* was henceforth as great as my hatred for it had been hitherto. In this way this passage of Paul was truly the gate of Paradise.

In one blinding flash of illumination the meaning of the passage had blazed upon him, and the meaning was not the way to knowledge but the way to paradise, when he saw that anything that is *of* God is *for* the person who has faith. To study Scripture with reverence is the way to illumination by the continued action of the Spirit of God.

Let us take another example. Luther and Erasmus were two of the great figures of the Reformation, but they were very different. Erasmus was the grammarian, the philologist. He would identify the meaning of a word, disentangle the grammar of a passage—none could do so better—but there he left it. With theological definition he refused to become entangled. But Luther began where Erasmus left off. He asked, not only, What does this mean? but also, What does this mean *for me*? Erasmus had defined the meaning of *penitence*—it is "a change of mind and the understanding of one's own sin, after having suffered harm, and having recognized the mistake." There he left it, and there Luther took it up. Luther said—and said rightly—that such a change and such a recognition cannot take place "without a change of sentiment and love." A person's affections have to be set on different things before he sees the error of the old things. Then Luther went on to say further—and rightly—such a change of sentiment and love can only be effected by the grace of God. A person cannot change himself—grace has to do that. So then Luther took the third step and declared that penitence is "a transmutation of mind and sentiment effected by grace"—and that, he said, is the translation of *metanoia*, penitence.

Here we have the difference. Erasmus approached the word penitence in the spirit of the man who would make a definition of it to grace a dictionary; Luther approached it in the spirit of the man who wanted to find salvation for his own soul, and for the souls of persons. The grammarian and the theologian, the philologist and the evangelist—both are needed. But the really Christian study of Scripture approaches it in the attitude of that reverence which is seeking more than grammatical accuracy; it is seeking and finding the grace of God.

2. The second rule for the study of Scripture is that it is best done within the fellowship of the church. This does not mean ruling out Bible study on one's own. But the Second Letter of Peter lays it down: "First of all you must understand this, that no prophecy of Scripture is a matter of one's own interpretation" (II Peter 1:20). To study Scripture wisely we must study it within the tradition of the church.

To take the matter at its simplest this is the only sensible thing to do. If a person begins to study medicine, he does not start as if no one had ever studied medicine before. He enters into the discoveries and the works and the wisdom of all who went before. If a person embarks on the study of any branch of science, the first thing he does is to study the work that has been done on that part of the subject up until now. It would be a matter of folly—and arrogant folly at that—if when we came to the study of any passage of Scripture we completely neglected all that the scholarship and the devotion of the past had learned about it. It is an obvious fact that all learning begins in a fellowship of learning, and Christian learning should begin in the Christian church. Luther said that the study of Scripture is only possible for a Christian. He held, and he held rightly, that to study any work profitably the experience of the reader must at least to some extent correspond with the experience of the writer. He held that it was a condition of any understanding of Scripture that the person who studies it must have a knowledge of Christ, since he, "the sun and truth in Scripture," is spoken of everywhere in the Bible, in the Old Testament as in the New. "The deeper the understanding of Christ," as Schwartz puts it in *Biblical Translation*, "the deeper the understanding of Scripture." The Christian studies Scripture both because he knows Christ and wants to know Christ.

Luther always held that Jerome's Latin Bible, the Vulgate, was not a good translation, because Jerome had produced it alone, and had thereby lost the promise that, where two or three are gathered together in his name, Jesus Christ is with them (Matthew 18:20). The study of the Bible in a Christian fellowship is richer than the study of the Bible in isolation and alone.

We have here three principles. First, no one can find the truth alone. Second, no human endeavor is effective without the Spirit and the grace of God. Third, no conclusion is valid if it is arrived at having no regard for the fellowship of the church.

3. The student of the Bible must study the Bible honestly. This is to say, he must go to the Bible to find out and to seek the truth, and not to prove a case about which he has already made up his mind. It is common—it is almost usual—for people to use the Bible as an arsenal of proof texts to prove things about which they have already made up their minds. A person can use the Bible to find in it what he wants to find. He can use it to hear the echo of his own voice rather than the sound of the voice of God. Tyndale once said that the students who were taught by the priests and the monks came to the Bible "armed with false principles, with which they are clean shut out of the understanding of Scripture." Arminius once said: "Nothing is more obstructive to the investigation of the truth than prior commitments to partial truths." This is simply to say that not even God can teach a person who comes to the Bible with his mind made up.

F. C. Grant in *How to Read the Bible* tells how an ancient rabbi once satirized his rival by saying: "When Rabbi Eliezer expounds, he begins by

saying, 'Scripture, be silent, while I am interpreting.' " Hugh Pope in *English Versions of the Bible* quotes Gardiner as saying: "Scripture is a sweet, pure flower, whereof spiders gather poison and bees honey. . . . Go thither instructed with wholesome doctrine and thou shalt see it confirmed. Go thither infected with malicious opinions and then thou shalt writhe out matter wherewith to maintain them." When we study the Bible we should be very sure that we are listening for God and not for the echo of our own voice.

4. If we are going to make the honest approach to Scripture, it specially means one thing. It means that our approach must be to *the whole of Scripture*. It is possible by making a selective approach to Scripture to argue in precisely opposite directions. If we quote Ecclesiastes 9:10: "Whatever your hand finds to do, do it with your might; for there is no work or thought or knowledge or wisdom in Sheol, to which you are going," we can argue that there is no life after death. If we quote I Corinthians 15:19: "If for this life only we have hoped in Christ, we are of all men most to be pitied," we can argue that to remove the belief in a life after death is to cut the vital nerve of the Christian faith. If we quote the Old Testament law of an eye for an eye and a tooth for a tooth (Exodus 21:24; Leviticus 24:20; Deuteronomy 19:21) we can argue for the punishment of criminals by force, and, for instance, for the death penalty. If on the other hand we quote the command of Jesus to turn the other cheek and to love our enemies (Matthew 5:39, 44), then we can argue that purely retributory and vindictive punishment has no place in Christian society. If we quote Matthew 25:46: "And they will go away into eternal punishment, but the righteous into eternal life," we can argue that after death some go to eternal bliss and some to eternal hell by the judgment of God. If we quote John 12:32: "I, when I am lifted up from the earth, will draw all men to myself," we can argue for universal salvation.

There is nothing which so bedevils theological discussion as the one-sided and selective approach to Scripture, the approach in which a person quotes and cites that which suits his own point of view and agrees with his own case, and at the same time deliberately ignores all the material on the other side. That is why argument and discussion based on the quotation of texts can never get anywhere.

When we study Scripture we have to take the whole of Scripture to our problem and to our thought. We have to look at the matter, not in the light of any text or series of texts, but in the light of the whole mind and character of Jesus Christ as we know them, and in the light of the mind and heart of that God, who is the God and Father of our Lord Jesus Christ. An honest approach to the Bible is an approach to the whole Bible, and not a selection from the Bible to suit ourselves.

5. Still further, and equally important, we have to take the whole of ourselves to the study of Scripture. Jesus said that we must love God with

all our heart and soul and strength and mind (Luke 10:27), and that is the way in which we have to study the Bible.

There always have been some people who consciously or unconsciously left their minds behind them when they began to study Scripture. F. C. Grant in his book *How to Read the Bible* tells of an experience of a friend of his. His friend had been talking of how to study the Old Testament, and of how there are times when the Old Testament can be a difficult book. At the end of the talk a bright, attractive young woman rose and said: "You don't need someone to tell you how to read the Bible. Open it anywhere, read three verses, make your mind a blank, then the Holy Spirit will do the rest!" The one thing you did not need, as she saw it, was intelligence; the one thing you did not use was your mind.

So then there is with some this suspicion of human reason, "the devil's whore," as Luther called it. But Luther was like so many great preachers who are people of passion and enthusiasm and conviction. He was very apt to stress one side of a question at a time, and it is often quite unsafe to regard anything he says as his final view of any subject until you have checked up on the other side. Luther can argue—and argue rightly—that more than intellect is needed for the study of the Bible. He can and does argue that human and celestial wisdom are not the same thing. He can and does argue that it is not in human power, it is not in the scope of the human intellect, to understand the word of God. He can say, "Offer your empty heart to God, and the truth will be revealed.

Luther can certainly argue that the human intellect is quite inadequate to understand the word of God; he can certainly argue that a person's intellect may be his biggest handicap. "Reason is the devil's whore, and can do nothing but shame and disgrace everything that God does." "Faith strikes dead this reason, and kills this beast, which heaven and earth and all creatures cannot destroy." "Reason cannot rightly accord to God his deity nor attribute it to him as his own, though it rightly belongs to him alone. It knows that God exists. But who or what person it may be who is properly called God it does not know. . . . Thus reason plays blind man's bluff with God, and makes vain errors, and always misses the mark, calling God what is not God, and not calling God what is God." No one has ever spoken more contemptuously about human reason than Martin Luther.

But there is another side to this, and when it is stated by Luther, the matter is perfectly reasonable. True, Scripture is given by the Spirit and can be understood only by the Spirit. It is only the author of Scripture who can interpret Scripture. "But the message of the Spirit is transmitted through language." "Words are the vehicles of thought; they are like the shrine in which God's truth is found." And there is need of the hardest kind of thought, the most intense kind of study, the most strenuous bringing to bear of the reason on the subject, to find the meaning of the words. This is where reason comes in. Reason has to be brought to bear on the givenness of the message of the Spirit. Devotion will grasp the message of the Spirit

through grace; scholarship will toil at the meaning of the words in which the message is expressed.

So Melanchthon writes in the *Encomium Eloquentiae (In Praise of Eloquence)*: "I have not the mistaken view that the holy can be penetrated through the industry of human talent. There is something in the holy that no one can ever see, unless it is shown to him by God: and Christ cannot be known to use without the Holy Spirit teaching us. . . . But apart from prophecy, the meaning of words must be known, in which, as in a shrine, the divine mysteries are hidden. For what is the use of reciting in a magic way words that have not been understood? Is it not like telling a story to a deaf person?" The mind of a person has to toil to understand and to communicate the message of the Spirit. Luther himself said that the Scripture teaches eternal life, and for that very reason it cannot be understood without the Spirit. Therefore a person must pray to receive illumination, guidance, and understanding. "But God will grant understanding only to him who perseveres in the study of words themselves, and meditates upon the meaning with which they are informed by that Holy Spirit."

The interaction between the Spirit of God and the mind of the person is established. The Spirit helps the person who toils to help himself. God does not spoonfeed a man. The more a man brings to the Bible, the more he gets from it. When the grace and guidance of the Spirit meet the study, the toil, and the endeavor of a dedicated mind, then indeed Scripture opens its riches. A person has to bring the whole of himself—heart and mind—to the whole of Scripture.

6. One last general point concerning our attitude to Scripture must be noted before we turn to detail. The study of Scripture is meant to lead to action. We often hear of a *discussion* circle, but if the work of a circle ends in discussion there is something far wrong; it must end in action. J. A. Bengel had on his New Testament the famous two lines:

Te totum applica ad textum;
Rem totam applica ad te.

This we may paraphrase: "Apply the whole of yourself to the study of Scripture; and then apply the whole of the result of your study to yourself."

And as Luther noted, in the last analysis it is not the regulations of a book with which we are dealing; it is the commands of a person, Jesus Christ. As Luther wrote in a letter to John Staupitz: "For thus do the commands of God become sweet, when we understand that they are not to be read in books only, but in the wounds of the sweetest Savior."

When we study the word of God in a group, we should not do so for the sake of a pleasant argument and discussion; we should do so to find for ourselves the will of God, and having found it, we should not only know, we should also obey.

We have spoken about the attitude of study. Let us now come to the actual technique of our study. We begin with one thing which must be clear. Our aim from beginning to end must be to find out what the Bible means. That sounds comparatively easy, but it is just here that the task of study has so often been complicated and wrongly conceived.

The ancient Jewish scholars used to say that Scripture has four meanings. First, there is *Peshat*, the simple literal meaning. Second, there is *Remez*, the meaning by allusion, the meaning which the student can arrive at when he treats a passage not just as a straightforward narrative but as an allegory. Third, there is *Derash*, which means the homiletic application of the passage after it has been studied with all the aids to study available. And fourth there is *Sod*, which is the inner meaning, the meaning to which only the spiritual expert can penetrate. *Peshat, Remez, Derash, Sod*—note the initial letters of the words—P R D S. Hebrew has no vowels, only consonants; the vowels have to be specially inserted, and PRDS are the consonants of the Hebrew word for Paradise, and so the ancient scholars claimed that, if a student penetrated fully into these four meanings, he would be here and now in Paradise! But where they went wrong was that they neglected the simple, literal meaning, and went all out for the allegorical and the inner meanings, and once we start allegorizing Scripture we can make it mean anything.

Here is a comparatively simple example of how they allegorized. The passage is Ecclesiastes 9:14, 15:

> There was a little city with few men in it; and a great king came against it and besieged it, building great siegeworks against it. But there was found in it a poor wise man, and he by his wisdom delivered the city. Yet no one remembered that poor man.

That is a simple parable of the way in which people forget what has been done for them and are guilty of ingratitude. Now one of the basic beliefs of the Jews about human nature is that in everyone there are two natures, the good nature and the bad nature; the good nature urges the person to goodness, and the evil nature tries to seduce him into sin. So the rabbis allegorized this parable. "There was a little city"—that is, the body. "With few men in it"—the few men are the limbs of the body. "A great king came against it"—that is the evil nature, the evil impulse. "Building great siegeworks against it"—the great siegeworks are the sins. "But there was found in it a poor wise man"—that is, the good nature, the good impulse. "He by his wisdom delivered the city"—this means repentance and good works by which a person is saved. "Yet no one remembered that poor man"—because at the time the evil impulse holds sway the good impulse is altogether forgotten. Thus a simple story of ingratitude is turned into a complicated allegory of human nature.

Christian scholars for many centuries did exactly the same. The scholars of the Middle Ages had four Latin lines which spoke of the fourfold meaning of Scripture:

Litera gesta docet;
Quid credas, allegoria;
Moralis, quid agat;
Quid speres, anagogia.

The translation is:

The literal tells what happened;
The allegorical, what you are to believe;
The moral, what you are to do;
The anagogical, what you may hope for.

Schwartz (*Biblical Translation,* p. 47) fills it out: "The literal sense explains the historical contents, the allegorical elucidates matters of faith by revealing the allegory contained in the biblical text, the moral sense indicates rules of human conduct, the anagogical sense deals with the future you may hope for (in the life to come)."

The trouble in the Christian approach to the Bible has often tended to be the way in which inner meanings were always being looked for in Scripture, and in which simple stories were given mystical meanings. The Greeks did this with Homer long before the Jews began doing it with the Old Testament. Take a Greek example. The Greeks had a god named Hermes. They then went on to derive *Hermes* from the Greek verb *erein*, which means *to speak*. Next they went on to say that Hermes is not meant to be taken as a person at all; he is a symbol, an allegory of the power of speech. They then went on to explain on these lines the various ways in which Hermes is described. He is called the *conductor*, because speech *conducts* one person's thoughts into his neighbor's soul. He is represented with *winged* feet, which stand for *winged words*. He is called *the leader of souls* because words soothe the soul to rest. He is called *the awakener from sleep*, because words rouse people to action. He carries a staff with serpents twined round it, and the serpents stand for the savage natures which are calmed by words (Edwin Hatch, *The Influence of Greeks Ideas and Usages upon the Christian Church*, p. 63). So the god Hermes is allegorized into the power of speech.

The Jews did this regularly. Sarah and Hagar are the symbols of true wisdom and pagan philosophy. Lot's wife symbolizes the attachment of the soul to earthly things, an attachment which produces blindness to God and to his truth.

It is obvious that, if you treat Scripture like this, you can make it mean almost anything you choose. The most notorious example of this is

Augustine's interpretation of the Parable of the Good Samaritan, which C. H. Dodd quotes in his book on the *Parables of the Kingdom*.

A certain man went down from Jerusalem to Jericho—Adam is meant; *Jerusalem* is the heavenly city of peace from the blessedness of which Adam fell; *Jericho* means the moon, and signifies our mortality, because it is born, waxes, wanes and dies. *Thieves* are the devil and his angels. *Who stripped him*—that is, of his immortality; *and left him half dead*—because insofar as a man can understand and know God, he lives, but insofar as he is wasted and oppressed by sin, he is dead; he is therefore called *half-dead*. The *Priest* and the *Levite* who saw him and passed by signify the priesthood and ministry of the Old Testament, which could profit nothing for salvation, *Samaritan* came from a Hebrew derivation meaning *guardian*, and therefore the Lord himself is signified by this name. *The binding of the wounds* is the restraint of sin. *Oil* is the comfort of a good hope, *wine* is the exhortation to work with a fervent spirit. The *beast* is the flesh in which Jesus came to us. The being *set upon the beast* is belief in the incarnation of Christ. The *inn* is the Church, where travellers are refreshed on their return from pilgrimage to their heavenly country. The *morrow* is after the Resurrection of the Lord. The *two pence* are either the two precepts of love, or, possibly, the two sacraments. The *innkeeper* is the apostle Paul. *The promise he makes to pay any extra expense* incurred is either his counsel of celibacy, or the fact that he worked with his hands lest he be a burden to the brethren.

If this is what the parable really means, it is obvious that no ordinary person could ever be expected to discover its meaning for himself; and it is also obvious that there is no limit to the number of meanings that a person could find in any passage of Scripture.

There is another famous instance of what allegorization can do in the Letter of Barnabas 9:7-9. Barnabas starts out from Genesis 17:23, 27. We there learn of the beginning of circumcision and that Abraham circumcised all the males in his household. By adding Genesis 14:14 to this we find that the number of them can be reckoned as *three hundred and eighteen*. In the Greek of the Septuagint, from which Barnabas is working, the number comes in the order *eighteen men and three hundred*. Now Greek has no figures for the numerals; the numerals are represented by letters of the alphabet, as if in English A were to equal 1, B were to equal 2, and so on. Well then, the Greek for *eighteen* is the letter *iota*, I, which stands for 10, and *eta*, the long Greek E, which stands for 8. That is to say, 18 is IE, which as anyone can see is the first two letters of the name IESOUS, which is Jesus. The Greek for *three hundred* is the letter *tau*, T, and T is the shape of the Roman cross on which Jesus was crucified. So Barnabas says that *three hundred and eighteen* is IE, which stands for Jesus, and T which stands for the cross, and therefore when Abraham performed the first act of circumcision he did so "looking forward to the spirit of Jesus."

This is a fatal way of interpreting Scripture. It is a method which we should entirely avoid. The meaning for which we look is the meaning

which the writer originally meant, not the meaning which later ingenuity can read into the text. To this day preachers often use allegorizations, not, it is true, with the perverted ingenuity with which the ancient interpreters used it, but in a more restrained way. That very great preacher James S. Stewart in his book of sermons *The Gates of New Life* has a sermon on Acts 27:29: "Then fearing lest we should have fallen upon rocks, they cast four anchors out of the stern, and wished for the day." He calls the sermon "Anchors of the Soul." He goes on to say that every soul should have four anchors—the anchors of hope, duty, prayer, and the cross of Christ. A simple action of sailors in the middle of a storm has been turned into an allegorization of the supports of the soul in the storms of life. The use of this method by even so great a preacher cannot justify it for us. It is the original meaning of Scripture that we must set out to find.

If our primary task is to find out the meaning of Scripture, then the beginning of our study must be the study of words. We take only two illustrations of how illuminating the study of words can be.

Three times Paul speaks about the *earnest of the Spirit*. The word for earnest is *arrabôn*. *Arrabôn* is a word from business and commercial Greek. An *arrabôn* was the part of a purchase price or a contract price, paid in advance, as a guarantee that the full price would in due time be paid. So a woman sells a cow, and gets so much as *arrabôn* in guarantee that the full price will be paid. A man engages a mousecatcher. Mice did a great deal of harm in the vineyards at harvest time, and he pays him so much as *arrabôn*, so that he will begin on the extermination of the pests straight away. A group of castanet dancing-girls are engaged for a village festivity, and they are at once paid so much as *arrabôn*, as a guarantee that the full contract price will be paid after they have performed. An *arrabôn* was a first installment of the full purchase price, and a guarantee that the full purchase price would be paid. So Paul speaks of the Holy Spirit as God's *arrabôn*. This is to say that for the Christian the gift of the Spirit is the first installment of the life of heaven, and the guarantee that someday that heavenly life in all its fullness will come.

Very commonly the Holy Spirit is called the Comforter. In the Authorized Version in John's Gospel, Comforter is the title and description of the Holy Spirit (John 14:16, 26; 15:26; 16:7). There are few things which have so limited and truncated the real work of the Holy Spirit as the consistent use of this word *Comforter*. The word in Greek is *Paraklêtos*, which is sometimes transliterated into English in the form *Paraclete*, as in the hymn, "Come, thou holy Paraclete."

The Greek word *paraklêtos* literally means *someone who is called in to the side of someone else*. In Greek the meaning of the word is always decided by the purpose for which the person is called in. It may mean someone called in to give evidence for the defense, a witness in favor. It may mean someone called in to plead one's cause, an advocate for the defense. It could mean

someone summoned to render medical aid, a physician. It is used to describe someone speaking to the men of a depressed and dispirited army, who by his words and the impact of his personality puts fresh strength and courage into them.

It can be seen from these examples that a *paraklêtos* is someone who is called in to help one who is in difficulties to cope with the situation. So then the Holy Spirit is the person through whom there come to us the strength and grace of God to enable us to cope with life. Certainly, part of this work is to comfort, but only part. To call the Holy Spirit the Comforter, and to stop there, is to have a limited and rather sentimental view of the Spirit, whereas in the Greek the word is full of power and of the promise of the God-given ability to face and to master any situation in life.

How then did this word *Comforter* get into the English translation of the Bible? It came in with Wycliffe about 1386, and it has stayed ever since. But in the days of Wycliffe it was a perfect translation. The word *comfort* is derived from the Latin word *fortis*, which means brave, and originally the word meant someone who puts courage into you. Let us take two other examples of it in Wycliffe. Wycliffe translates Ephesians 6:10, "Be ye *comforted* in the Lord." And he translates I Timothy 1:12, "I do thankings to him who *comforted* me." In both cases the word in the Greek is *endunamoun*, whose root word is *dunamis*, power, from which the word *dynamite* comes. In Wycliffe's day to comfort a person was to fill that person with a power like spiritual dynamite. The Holy Spirit does not simply come and wipe our tears away; he gives us a dynamic power to cope with life.

So then the first step in the technique of the study of the Bible must be to ascertain the meaning of the passage which is being studied, and that study must start with the investigation into the meaning of words. This means that, ideally speaking, a Bible study group should be led by someone who knows the original languages Hebrew and Greek. This will be an obviously impossible demand. Failing that, the group should have access to someone who possesses such knowledge. But even that is an impossible demand. The assumption would be that the minister of the church would be such a person, but modern methods of ministerial training do not necessarily include training in the original languages. So the group will probably need to depend on the use of commentaries which have been made for English-speaking readers and which are in English, but which are founded on the original languages. Some such commentaries are listed at the end of this chapter.

Our search for meaning will bring us to another necessity. If we are to ascertain the meaning of any passage of Scripture, we shall need to use a modern translation. The Authorized Version is a version which will always be known and loved as one of the supreme achievements of the English language, but there are at least three reasons why, from the point of view of study, it is now an inadequate translation.

1. There are passages in it which have now ceased to be intelligible to modern ears, or in which the meaning of words has altered. The astonishing thing in a translation made in 1611 is not that such things exist in it, but that on the whole there are so few. Here are some examples of that.

They *fetched a compass* of seven days' journey. (II Kings 3:9)

From thence *we fetched a compass* and came to Rhegium. (Acts 28:13)

To fetch a compass means to make a circuit.

There is in the AV a now-abandoned and often-misleading use of the word *prevent*.

The sorrows of hell compassed me about; the snares of death *prevented* me. (Psalm 18:5)

Why did the knees *prevent* me? or why the breasts that I should suck? (Job 3:12)

In the morning shall my prayer *prevent* thee. (Psalm 88:13)

The inhabitants of the land of Tema brought water to him that was thirsty, they *prevented* with their bread him that fled. (Isaiah 21:14)

In modern English the word *prevent* means to hinder, to impede, to stop a person doing something; in the language of 1611 it meant to go before, to precede, and therefore to meet or to encounter, but with no thought of hindrance, or prevention in the modern sense of the term.

There is a still more misleading use of the word *conversation*.

Ye have heard of my *conversation* in time past in the Jews' religion. (Galatians 1:13)

Be thou an example of the believers, in word, in *conversation*, in charity, in spirit, in faith, in purity. (I Timothy 4:12)

Who is a wise man and endued with knowledge among you? let him show out of a good *conversation* his works with meekness of wisdom. (James 3:13)

Be ye holy in all manner of *conversation*. (I Peter 1:15)

Having your *conversation* honest among the Gentiles. (I Peter 2:12)

In modern language a person's *conversation* is the way in which he talks; it is his speech, his language, his thought. But the word *conversation* comes from the Latin *conversari*, which means to walk up and down, to go to and

fro, and it therefore means, not his talk, but his whole conduct and behavior. In all these instances we have quoted it is not a question of being careful of our talk, but of being careful of our whole behavior, of our whole life and conduct. The last instance is doubly deceiving. In it *honest* does not mean telling the truth. In 1611 the word *honest* far more commonly meant *honorable*. And so I Peter 2:12 really means: "In your contact with the Gentile world see that your conduct is always honorable."

It is quite clear that in our search for meaning we need a translation which speaks the language not of the seventeenth but of the twentieth century.

2. There is another characteristic of the Authorized Version which it is relevant to note. The great characteristic of the Authorized Version is the beauty of its English, and this beauty is accompanied by a certain archaism. The language is beautiful, but the language is not the language of the twentieth century, and it is precisely this combination of beauty and archaism which gives the Authorized Version the solemnity and the dignity which are dear to so many. Now a translation should reproduce not only the meaning of the original but also the atmosphere of the original.

In the case of the Old Testament the atmosphere of the Authorized Version is not at fault, for the Hebrew of the Old Testament is for the most part classical Hebrew, Hebrew at its best. But in the case of the New Testament the matter is very different. The Greek of the New Testament is colloquial Greek; it is the kind of Greek that people spoke on the street in the first century. It is not classical Greek. We have noted that, even if the New Testament were to lose all its religious importance, it would still have a unique importance in that it is the only written monument of that colloquial spoken Greek of the first century. Now here is the point—the more solemn and dignified and beautiful and archaic a translation of the New Testament is, the worse a translation it is. The New Testament in translation should not sound beautiful and dignified and solemn and old; it should sound modern, colloquial, the kind of language people speak in their homes and on the street, the kind of language they read in their newspapers. In the case of the New Testament a solemn, dignified, archaic translation could not be a worse translation, for that is all that the New Testament Greek is not.

Any translation of the New Testament ought to speak to a person in the vernacular in which he speaks; any other kind of translation is a bad translation.

So then in 1611 the Authorized Version was a good translation—but not now. When Luther spoke about his own translation of the Bible, he said that it was not to those who spoke Latin that the translator must go. "We must ask the mother in the home, the children on the street, the common man in the marketplace about this, and look them in the mouth to see how they speak, and afterward do our translating." The first essential of a New Testament for use in the study of its meaning is a New Testament in the language of our own generation.

3. The third fact about the Authorized Version is the most serious of all. It is obvious that no translation can be better than the manuscripts on which it is founded. Before printing was invented manuscripts were of course copied by hand. Even with the most careful copying by hand new errors crept in with each successive copying. Therefore, the older a manuscript is the more correct it is likely to be. The nearer it is to the original, the fewer removes there are between it and the author's original writing, the more accurate it will be. Further, the more manuscripts there are available, the more likely it is that in some of them the original readings will be preserved.

The Authorized Version was published in 1611. It was made from a Greek text, in the case of the New Testament, which was largely that of Erasmus, revised by Beza and Stephanus. This Greek text was based on not more than ten Greek manuscripts, of which the earliest was not earlier than the tenth century. This is to say that the Authorized Version is a translation of a Greek text of the New Testament which is quite inadequate. This was not the fault of the translators; nor was it the fault of those who constructed the text which was used. They used the best that was available in 1611. But since then all kinds of discoveries have been made, and many new manuscripts have come to light. We have now available manuscripts which go back to the third and fourth centuries, and the manuscripts which are now available can be numbered by the score, and even by the hundred. This is to say that in the twentieth century there are available manuscripts which are up to seven or eight hundred years older than the manuscripts which were the basis of the Greek text from which the Authorized Version was translated, and there are hundreds more of them.

Much as we love the Authorized Version as a monument of English prose, much as we rest our hearts in its music and in its cadences, we cannot do anything other than recognize that in the twentieth century it is no longer an adequate translation. This is not to say that we are to stop reading the Authorized Version for spiritual and devotional purposes; but it is to say that it can no longer be properly used as the basis of real Bible study. For the purposes of study we must use either the Revised Standard Version, or, better still, the New English Bible. To refuse to make the change is to shut our eyes deliberately to the new knowledge of his word which God in our day and generation has made available for us.

When we have established the meaning of the passage, so far as the actual wording goes, the next task is to put the passage into its context and into its background. It is impossible to understand a person without understanding something about his background. It is, for instance, impossible to understand why a person is what he is until we know something about his home and his parents and how he was brought up. So it is important to know *that* a thing happened; it is even more important to know *why* it happened; and to know this it is necessary to know the context and the background of the event. Let us take two examples of this, one from the area of geography and one from the area of life and customs.

One of the supreme differences between modern and ancient times is the annihilation of distance. A person may nowadays breakfast in London and lunch in New York over three thousand miles away. The world today is a small place, and the life people live today is a mobile life. Jesus, however, in his life in Palestine was never as far as we know more than a hundred miles from home. When we read the Samuel story in the first two chapters of I Samuel, it seems that Hannah and the boy Samuel are very far apart. Once a year she goes to see him and takes with her the little coat that she had made for him. The journey has all the atmosphere of an expedition, and yet in fact Ramah, where Hannah lived, and Shiloh, where the child Samuel served, were about seventeen miles apart! Take the case of the Flood in Genesis 6. There the Flood is told of in terms of a world event. But for the writer of that story the world is Mesopotamia and the Euphrates Valley. America, Africa, Australia, Britain—the ancient writer had no conception that these continents and countries even existed. To him the world was that small part of it he knew. And that there was a flood in that area is one of the facts of history about which there is no doubt whatever. The flood devastated the only world the ancient writer knew, but we must not think that the word *world* meant to him a world in which three thousand miles is a morning's journey.

Take a more detailed example—Jesus' cleansing of the Temple. The cleansing of the Temple is one of the most terrifying stories in the Gospel history. The idea of the white hot anger of Jesus, the picture of the Jesus with the whip, are frightening conceptions. Let us then see first of all where this incident happened. It happened in the Court of the Gentiles. The Temple in Jerusalem was composed of a series of courts, and the entry into each court was increasingly limited. Into the Court of the Gentiles, anyone, Jew or Gentile might come. Next came the Court of the Women beyond which no woman could go. Between it and the Court of the Gentiles there was a low wall, into which there were inset stone tablets warning any Gentile that for him to proceed beyond this wall was a crime for which the penalty was instant death. Beyond the Court of the Women was the Court of the Israelites beyond which no layman could go. Finally there was the Court of the Priests in which were the great altar, and the seven-branched candlestick, and the table of the showbread, and the altar of the incense, and into it only the priests could go. At the far end of the Court of the Priests stood the Temple proper, the Holy Place and the Holy of Holies, into which only the High Priest could go, and he on the occasion of the Day of Atonement only. So then the farther into the Temple the various courts went, the fewer people were allowed into them. And this incident of the cleansing of the Temple happened in the one area of the Temple into which a Gentile might come. If the Gentile was to worship and pray in the Temple at all, here alone he might do so.

Next, who are the characters involved? First, there are the money-changers. Every male Jew and proselyte—women and minors were

exempt—had to pay a Temple tax of one half-shekel per year. A half-shekel was the equivalent of about fifteen cents. But this must be evaluated in light of the fact that a working man's daily wage averaged about eight cents. The tax was near enough two days' pay—which is quite something. Further, this Temple tax had to be paid in either sanctuary shekels or Galilean shekels. This was so because these were the only coins which had no king's head on them, and a coin with a king's head was for a Jew a graven image, especially since so many kings were given divine honor. For all ordinary purposes in Palestine any coinage would do and was valid—Greek, Roman, Phoenician, Egyptian, Syrian, and so on. The tax was paid at Passover time, and people came from all over the world to keep the Passover and to pay their tax. With them they brought all kinds of money. They were bound to pay. Within Palestine, if a man did not pay, the Temple authorities could and did distrain upon his goods. So the pilgrims went to the money-changers to have their money changed into the right kind of shekels. For every coin changed the changers charged one *maah*, which was the equivalent of one penny, and, if the coin presented was larger than a half-shekel and change had to be given, another *maah* was charged for giving change—and remember a *maah* was the equivalent of a quarter of a day's pay. So the pilgrim had to pay his tax, which was the equivalent of nearly two days' pay, and, he might well have to pay another half day's pay to get his coin changed and to receive his change. It was one colossal ramp in which poor pilgrims were being mercilessly fleeced. It brought in between sixteen to eighteen thousand dollars a year, which in modern terms would be millions, and such was the wealth of the Temple treasury that when Crassus, the Roman general, plundered it in 54 B.C., he took away the equivalent of five million dollars, and that did not exhaust it. The modern purchasing power of such a sum would be in the category of hundreds of milions of dollars. The pilgrims were being victimized by the money-changers.

The others involved were the pigeon-sellers. Almost all the visitors to the Temple would make some offering or other, and for the poorer people the commonest victim was the pigeon or the dove. A sacrificial victim had to be without spot or blemish, and the Temple authorities had appointed inspectors to see that victims were perfect. It was possible for a pilgrim to buy his pigeons outside the Temple; there were shops where they were on sale. But all the likelihood was that the inspector would find a blemish. So it was safer to buy the victims at the Temple shops where they had already been inspected. Outside the Temple a pair of pigeons could cost as little as five cents, but inside the Temple they could cost as much as $1.50. Here was a still more lucrative racket, and the shops in the Court of the Gentiles, where the trading went on, were called the Bazaars of Annas.

So then we see why Jesus was enraged. Poor pilgrims were being fleeced. The one place where the Gentile could worship was turned into a shouting, arguing, bargaining oriental market. And we can see why Annas and

company hated Jesus; their vested interest had been attacked. Put into its background, the cleansing of the Temple becomes vividly meaningful.

Insofar as it is possible every Bible incident should be read against its background. This often means work and research in order to understand—but the result is worth it.

There is another fact which often has a large part to play in our interpretation of the Bible, especially in the case of the Old Testament. The Jew knew nothing of secondary causes. The Jew in Old Testament times attributed everything to the direct action of God. In modern times, if there is thunder, we explain the thunder by certain atmospheric conditions. The Jew says quite simply: "God thundered," or, "God sent the thunder." If the crops are destroyed by blasting and mildew, we explain it by soil conditions and by the action of pests. The Jew says: "God sent blasting and mildew." Modern man would explain plague and pestilence by telling of the conditions which caused them. The Jew would simply say: "God sent the plague or the pestilence."

There is one vivid example of this in II Kings 19:35, 36. The story comes from the invasion of Palestine by Sennacherib the King of Assyria. He had besieged Jerusalem, and all seemed lost. It seemed but a matter of time until there would be nothing for the city to do but surrender. And then there come the two verses:

> And that night the angel of the Lord went forth and slew a hundred and eighty-five thousand in the camp of the Assyrians; and when men arose early in the morning, behold, these were all dead bodies. Then Sennacherib king of Assyria departed, and went home and dwelt at Nineveh.

It so happens that this is a piece of history of which we have two other accounts. The first is in the Greek historian Herodotus, who tells us that the King of Assyria retreated because mice gnawed the strings of the bows and the thongs of the shields of his army. The angel of the Lord or mice? The third account is from a Chaldean historian called Berosus, who says that Sennacherib was compelled to retreat because pestilence decimated his army. The angel of the Lord—mice—pestilence—which was it? Which account is true? Surely the answer is—all of them. It was plague which caused the army to retreat—so Berosus is right. Plague, especially bubonic plague, is carried by rats and mice—so Herodotus is right. It was not the will of God that Sennacherib and his hosts should conquer Jerusalem— therefore the Hebrew historian is right. The pagan historians fixed on the secondary causes of Sennacherib's retreat; the Hebrew historian eliminated the secondary cause and went straight to God.

This is something which we have to remember especially when we read the Old Testament. The Old Testament moves in a world that is full of God. Events are always being attributed to the direct action of God instead of to the secondary cause. The result is that in the Old Testament many a thing is

regarded as miraculous of which we now know the secondary cause. It might well be said that the Jew knew *that* God did things; we know more of *how* he does them.

Still another important point for interpretation emerges. There are parts of the Old Testament which are poetry, and to treat them as prose is to misunderstand them and to do them injustice.

We take one outstanding example of that, Joshua 10:12, 13:

> Then spoke Joshua to the Lord in the day when the Lord gave the Amorites over to the men of Israel; and he said in the sight of Israel,
> "Sun, stand thou still at Gibeon,
> and thou Moon in the valley of Aijalon."
> And the sun stood still, and the moon stayed,
> until the nation took vengeance on their enemies.

This is clearly a passage at which we would have to look with some care, in order to arrive at a correct interpretation of it. The first thing that strikes us about it is that it cannot in any event be taken literally for the very simple and sufficient reason that the sun does not in fact move; the sun always stands still. It is the earth which moves, and if at any time the earth had ceased to move, then life as we know it would have come suddenly and catastrophically to an end. Further, if anything resembling this had somehow or other happened, if there had been an occasion when it could be said that the sun or the earth stood still, then this would be an event, not simply of Jewish history, but also of world history, and there would be some record or memory of it in the history of every nation in the world. It is not possible to approach this with a crude literalism.

But then we note something else about it. It is a quotation from the Book of Jashar (Joshua 10:13). This Book of Jashar is quoted again. It is quoted as the origin of David's great lament over the death of Saul (II Samuel 1:18). And so the fact becomes clear that the Book of Jashar is in fact a book of poetry, and the material that is in it is poetry. The Revised Standard Version prints the Joshua story as poetry and correctly so.

So then in this passage we have a poet speaking. The poet here speaks of the sun in the same kind of way as the poet of Psalm 19, who speaks of the sun daily leaving his chamber like a bridegroom and running his daily race from one end of the heavens to the other (Psalm 19:5, 6). This is the language of poetry; it is even the language we use in everyday life. We say of an occasion: "It was the longest half hour that I spent in all my life," but all half hours are thirty minutes, neither more nor less. We say of a golden day: "Never did the time pass more quickly," but the time always passes at the same rate.

So we need not worry trying to find explanations of the Joshua passage. It means that by the help of God that day was long enough for the victory to be won, that into it there were by the grace of God packed these events

which gave victory to God's people Israel. We do the Bible an ill service when we turn the beauty of its poetry into prose.

We come now to what may well be the most important single thing to remember when we are seeking to interpret the Bible. It took all of one thousand years to write the Bible, and the period of history covered in the Bible—apart from the parts of the Bible which deal with the things which happened before history can be said to have begun—amounts to something like three thousand years. Take one thousand years in modern terms. Go back a thousand years, and we arrive somewhere about the time of Alfred the Great. Clearly, life and thoughts and society and civilization were very different one thousand years ago. It is so with the Bible. If the Bible story stretches over scores of centuries, there cannot be in it one flat level of thought and religion and ethics. There is bound to be development. God could only tell people what people were able and willing to receive. God's message had to be adapted to the state of people's minds when that message was given. If we are going to teach a child algebra, we do not start with the binomial theorem; we lead slowly up to it. If we are going to teach a child to play the piano, we do not start with Bach's preludes and fugues; they are a summit, not a beginning. If we are going to teach a child Greek, we do not start with the odes of Pindar, or the choruses of Aeschylus; something much easier has to be the beginning. It is so with the Bible. God had to lead the minds of people from less to more, from lower to higher levels, from the glimmerings to the full blaze. This is obvious, for if people knew it all already why should the great prophets come, and above all why should Jesus come? Revelation is an ongoing process all the time.

Very commonly this is called the principle of *developing revelation*. God's revelation, so to say, developed with people's ability to receive it. It would be better to speak, not of a *developing revelation*, but rather of a *developing grasp of revelation*. It is not so much that God doled out his revelation in small doses; it is rather that he was offering the blaze of truth all the time, but the human mind was capable of and willing to receive only a limited amount of it.

When we find in the Bible things which are sub-Christian, there is no need to defend them, and there is no need to explain them away. They represent the stage to which people had reached at that particular time. This we know, because Jesus more than once said: "You have heard that it was said . . . But I say to you" (Matthew 5:21, 27, 31, 33, 38, 43). We accept this in practice, for there are few or no Christians who live out all the ceremonial laws of the Old Testament. We know that with Jesus Christ these have been left behind. It is not that they were wrong; it is not that they were in error. But that they were incomplete. Behind every one of them there is a great and unchanging truth, and these old laws are imperfect grasps of that truth. They represent what people made of that truth at that particular stage. We can see this in many things in the Bible, but we shall

illustrate it, first, by looking at certain religious practices, and second, at certain religious principles in which there has been development.

1. Let us look first at the answer to the question, *How do I show my religion?* as that question is answered in the legal parts of the Old Testament.

a. The Jew showed his religion by abstaining from certain kinds of food. As everyone knows the Jew would not, and will not, eat pigs' flesh. "And the swine . . . is unclean to you. Of their flesh you shall not eat, and their carcasses you shall not touch; they are unclean to you" (Leviticus 11:7, 8). That is laid down as a law in Leviticus, but it does not stop our eating bacon for breakfast, or a pork chop for dinner.

b. The Jew showed his religion by wearing the tasselled cloak, the phylacteries or prayer boxes, and by putting the *mezuzah*, the little cylindrical wooden fixture with words of Scripture in it, on his doorpost. The phylacteries were little leather boxes with certain texts written in parchment inside them, and were strapped to the wrist and the forehead at prayer.

> The Lord said to Moses: Speak to the people of Israel, and bid them to make tassels on the corners of their garments. . . . And it shall be to you a tassel to look upon and remember all the commandments of the Lord. (Numbers 15:37-39)

> And these words which I command you this day shall be upon your heart . . . and you shall bind them as a sign upon your hand, and they shall be as frontlets between your eyes [phylacteries], and you shall write them on the doorposts of your house, and on your gates [*mezuzah*]. (Deuteronomy 6:6-9)

The Jew still wears his tasselled prayer shawl and his phylacteries at prayer; he still fixes the *mezuzah* to the door of his house or flat. But the Christian does not consider these commandments in any way binding upon him.

c. Above all the Jew showed his religion by circumcision. This was the sign of the covenant. This was the sign that he was a member of the people of God. So important is it that it is said, "Any uncircumcised male, who is not circumcised in the flesh of his foreskin, shall be cut off from his people; he has broken my covenant" (Genesis 17:14). But no Christian accepts the obligation of circumcision.

The Jew shows his religion by abstention from certain foods, by the wearing of certain objects, by affixing certain things to his house, and by circumcision. Let no one belittle these things; they are a public demonstration of the faith of the Jew, and it would be a good thing if Christians showed their faith as openly. But this is the way in which a Christian shows his religion: "By this all men will know that you are my disciples, if you have love for one another" (John 13:35).

In the Old Testament there are ways of showing a man's religion—and they are honorable ways. They grasp the fact that a person must show his faith, but they have not reached the full revelation that a person must show his faith by his love. This had to wait for Jesus.

2. Next, let us look at the answer to the question, *How do I protect my religion?* How do I keep it safe from any infection which would make it less pure?

It is in the answer to this question that we find some of these things which fill us with horror as we read. In the event of war if a city surrenders, then its inhabitants are to be put to forced labor.

> But if it makes no peace with you, but makes war against you, then you shall besiege it; and when the Lord your God gives it into your hand, you shall put all its males to the sword, but the women and the little ones, the cattle and everything else in the city, all its spoil, you shall take as booty for yourselves. . . . But in the cities of these peoples that the Lord your God gives you for an inheritance, you shall save alive nothing that breathes, but you shall utterly destroy them. (Deuteronomy 20:12-17)

The instructions are followed at the siege of Jericho and the result is: "Then they utterly destroyed all in the city, both men and women, young and old, oxen, sheep and asses, with the edge of the sword" (Joshua 6:21).

In the war with Amalek Samuel's instructions from God to Saul are: "Now go and smite Amalek, and utterly destroy all that they have; do not spare them, but kill both man and woman, infant and suckling, ox and sheep, camel and ass" (I Samuel 15:3). It sounds, and it is, so bloodthirsty. But what must be remembered is this—in this there was no personal hatred, there was no blood lust, there was no murderous passion for slaughter. What was behind it was this—all foreign faiths were an infection; they were a threat to the purity of the worship of Jahweh; and everything to do with them had for safety's and for purity's sake to be wiped out. This is actually said, for the instructions in Deuteronomy conclude with the words which give the reason for all this, "that they may not teach you to do according to all their abominable practices which they have done in the service of their gods, and so to sin against the Lord your God" (Deuteronomy 20:18). The whole point is that these foreign nations were idolaters, and were therefore the enemies of God, and therefore had to be wiped out lest the infection of their heathen practices taint the purity of Hebrew religion.

But when Jesus comes, we get a new conception. We get the conception that we are not to wipe out God's enemies by killing them; we are to wipe them out by converting them. In the American civil war over slavery Abraham Lincoln was charged with being far too gracious and kindly to the southern states. "They are your enemies," people said to him, "and it is your task to destroy them." Lincoln answered: "Do I not destroy my

enemies when I make them my friends?" The Old Testament had got hold of half of a great truth, the truth that the enemies of God must be destroyed. But we have to wait for Jesus to discover that the way to destroy the enemies of God is to convert them so that they become the friends of God.

3. The third question which it is natural to ask is, *What is it that I ought to give to God*? What gift can I take to him to please him?

There is a great part of the Old Testament which is all about the sheep and lambs and calves and bulls and oxen and doves and pigeons and wine and flour and oil which form part of the ceremonial sacrifices to God. The theory behind this is quite clear. The worshiper says to himself: "I must give to God my most precious possession," and in an agricultural society his most precious possession was the animals and the crops over which he had toiled.

But even in the Old Testament itself the inadequacy of this is seen. Isaiah hears God say:

What to me is the multitude of your sacrifices?
  says the Lord
I have had enough of burnt offerings of rams
  and the fat of fed beasts;
I do not delight in the blood of bulls,
  or of lambs, or of he-goats.
When you come to appear before me
  who requires of you
  this trampling of my courts?
Bring no more vain offerings;
  incense is an abomination to me . . .
Wash yourselves; make yourselves clean;
  remove the evil of your doings
  from before my eyes;
cease to do evil;
  learn to do good;
seek justice;
  correct oppression;
defend the fatherless,
plead for the widow. (Isaiah 1:11-13, 16-17)

As Isaiah saw it, the whole paraphernalia of sacrifice was one vast irrelevance. Micah said the same.

With what shall I come before the Lord,
  and bow myself before God on high?
Shall I come before him with burnt-offerings,
  with calves a year old?
Will the Lord be pleased with thousands of rams,
  with ten thousands of rivers of oil?

> Shall I give my first-born for my transgression,
>> the fruit of my body for the sin of my soul?
> He hath showed you, O man, what is good,
>> and what does the Lord require of you
> but to do justice, and to love kindness,
>> and to walk humbly with your God? (Micah 6:6-8)

And it is in Hosea that we find what looks as if it was Jesus' favorite text. "For I desire steadfast love and not sacrifice" (Hosea 6:6; Matthew 9:13; 12:7).

It is clear God never wanted the sacrifice of animals. The Jews thought he did, because they saw in these animals their most precious possession, and to God they were willing to give them. But the prophets saw the irrelevance of animal sacrifice, and Jesus above all saw it. The most precious thing a man has is his heart, his self, a heart and a self filled with love for God and love for people—that is the only gift God wants.

So in the Old Testament we see time and time again that a great truth is grasped, but it is imperfectly grasped. For the full grasp we have to wait for Jesus. It is not that the Old Testament is wrong—far from that; it is an essential stage to that goal which is Jesus Christ.

Let us now take two of the very great conceptions of the Christian faith, and let us see how they develop throughout the Bible until they culminate in Jesus Christ.

First, let us take the conception *of the forgiveness of our enemies and of those who have injured us.*

1. In the beginning so far from any desire to forgive there was a cry for unlimited vengeance. Genesis 4:23, 24 is one of the oldest fragments in the Bible, and in it the cry is for vengeance:

> Lamech said to his wives:
> Adah and Zillah, hear my voice;
> you wives of Lamech, hearken to what I say:
> I have slain a man for wounding me,
>> a young man for striking me.
> If Cain is avenged sevenfold,
>> truly Lamech seventy-sevenfold.

It is Lamech's boast that he has exacted vengeance for injury. He has killed a man for injuring him, and his desire is for a vengeance which will exceed the injury seventy-sevenfold. Here in the most primitive of all passages there is no thought of forgiveness, only for vengeance.

2. The next stage is a stage at which the Old Testament has often been, and still is, much misunderstood. It is often said that the Old Testament believes in "an eye for an eye, and a tooth for a tooth," and this is claimed to be one of "the bloodthirsty laws of the Old Testament."

If any harm follows, then you shall give life for life, eye for eye, tooth for tooth, hand for hand, foot for foot, burn for burn, wound for wound, stripe for stripe. (Exodus 21:23-25)

When a man causes a disfigurement in his neighbour, as he has done, it shall be done to him, fracture for fracture, eye for eye, tooth for tooth; as he has disfigured a man, he shall be disfigured. He who kills a beast shall make it good, and he who kills a man shall be put to death. (Leviticus 24:19-21)

Your eye shall not pity; it shall be life for life, eye for eye, tooth for tooth, hand for hand, foot for foot. (Deuteronomy 19:21)

To call these bloodthirsty laws is totally to misunderstand them; they are the precise reverse of that.

In the early days the vendetta or blood feud was typical of tribal society. In the vendetta, if any man injured a member of another tribe, it was the duty of all the members of the injured man's tribe to take all possible vengeance on all the members of the tribe of the man who injured him. And thus a comparatively slight injury could lead to a war between two tribes in which many lives were lost. These laws which we have just quoted were the first attempt to *limit* vengeance. If vengeance was to be taken, it must be only to the precise extent to which injury had been inflicted, and no longer must injury issue in a bloodthirsty tribal war.

In later times this law of precise retribution became modified. Suppose a man's tooth is knocked out, and the tooth is a decayed tooth, it will be unjust to knock out in retribution a tooth which is a healthy tooth. Suppose the eye which was injured to be a very inefficient eye, it will be wrong to knock out in revenge a perfectly healthy eye. So each injury came to be assessed at a money penalty, and not as a physical exchange of injuries. But the main point is that here there is the first step toward the controlled limitation of vengeance, and it is therefore a very big step in the right direction.

3. At the third stage we arrive at a stage when forgiveness and nonretaliation are urged, but with certain limitations and for certain conditions.

a. Forgiveness is urged, with the limitation that it is to extend only to fellow Hebrews.

You shall not hate your brother in your heart, but you shall reason with your neighbour, lest you bear sin because of him. You shall not take vengeance nor bear any grudge against the sons of your own people, but you shall love your neighbour as yourself; I am the Lord. (Leviticus 19:17, 18)

This is definite enough but the forgiveness is limited to "your brother," and to "the sons of your own people." It does not necessarily extend to the Gentile.

b. Forgiveness is urged, because vengeance belongs to God, and if a man's cause is just, he can leave the vengeance to God:

Do not say, I will repay evil.
Wait for the Lord and he will help you. (Proverbs 20:22)

The same attitude is seen in the intertestamental book *The Testament of the Twelve Patriarchs*:

Love one another from the heart; and if a man sins against you, cast forth the poison of hate and speak peaceably to him, and retain no guile in your soul. And if he confesses and repents, forgive him. . . . And if he is shameless and persists in his wrong-doing, even so forgive him from the heart, and leave the avenging to God. (The Testament of Gad 6:3, 7)

True, forgiveness is urged, but God will exercise the vengeance for the good man.

c. Most commonly of all, forgiveness is urged in order to win the favor of God:

If your enemy is hungry, give him bread to eat,
    and if he is thirsty, give him water to drink;
for you will heap coals of fire on his head,
    and the Lord will reward you. (Proverbs 25:21)

Do not rejoice when your enemy falls,
    and let not your heart be glad when he stumbles;
lest the Lord see it, and be displeased,
    and turn away his anger from him. (Proverbs 24:17, 18)

Even a passage like Lamentations 3:30, "Let him give his cheek to the smiter, / and be filled with insults," derives from the fact that "the Lord is good to those who wait for him, to the soul that seeks him" (Lamentations 5:25).

It is the same with a passage from Ecclesiasticus 28:2:

Forgive your neighbour the wrong he has done,
and then your sins will be pardoned when you pray.

So again, "If anyone seeks to do evil to you, do good to him, and pray for him, and then you shall be redeemed by the Lord from all evil" (The Testamant of Joseph 18:2).

One of the few Old Testament passages on forgiveness in which there is no limitation and no condition is Proverbs 24:29:

Do not say, "I will do him as he had done to me:
    I will pay the man back for what he has done."

So then the Old Testament begins with unlimited vengeance; it moves on to a strictly controlled exchange of penalty; it moves still further on to the urging of forgiveness, but within certain limits and conditions.

4. And so finally we come to Jesus. The essence of the teaching of Jesus on forgiveness is in the Sermon on the Mount:

> You have heard that it was said, "An eye for an eye, and a tooth for a tooth." But I say to you, Do not resist one who is evil. But if anyone strikes you on the right cheek, turn to him the other also. . . . You have heard that it was said, You shall love your neighbour and hate your enemy. But I say to you, Love your enemies and pray for those who persecute you, so that you may be sons of your Father who is in heaven; for he makes his sun rise on the evil and on the good, and sends rain on the just and on the unjust. For if you love those who love you, what reward have you? Do not even the tax-collectors do the same? And if you salute only your brethren, what more are you doing than others? Do not even the Gentiles do the same? You, therefore, must be perfect, as your heavenly Father is perfect. (Matthew 5:38-48)

There are no limitations and no conditions. Forgiveness is absolute. There is a reward, but the reward is that he who forgives becomes like God. As Paul put it, "Be kind to one another, tenderhearted, forgiving one another, as God in Christ forgave you" (Ephesians 4:32). So the wheel has gone full circle; it began with unlimited vengeance, and it ends in Christ with unlimited forgiveness. (Contrast Christ's seventy times seven, Matthew 18:22, with Genesis 4:24.) On this matter we have to say unequivocally, "It is not by the Old Testament but by the New Testament, not by the Law but by the Gospel, not by anyone other than Jesus Christ, that I judge my duty to forgive." So when people quote the Old Testament to us, we have to say quite frankly, "This is the stage which at that time men had reached. This is the part of God's revelation which they had grasped. But the full revelation is in Jesus Christ, and we take our orders and our pattern from no one but him."

The second great idea at which we must look is *life after death*. We shall look at the development of that idea throughout the Bible.

1. In the earliest times the Hebrews had no real belief in any life after death. They believed that the souls of all who died went to Sheol or Hades. Sheol is not hell; Sheol was the place of all the dead. It was a gray, shadowy land, from which all the color and the strength and the meaning had been evacuated. It was separated from people and from God alike, and the souls who lived there lived a ghostly, specter-like existence. It was not extinction, but it was no more than the shadow of life. Again and again this hopelessness comes out in the Old Testament.

> For in death there is no remembrance of thee;
> in Sheol who can give thee praise? (Psalm 6:5)

What profit is there in my death,
   if I go down to the Pit?
Will the dust praise thee?
   Will it tell of my faithfulness? (Psalm 30:9)

Look away from me, that I may know gladness.
   before I depart and be no more! (Psalm 39:13)

For my soul is full of troubles
   and my life draws near to Sheol.
I am reckoned among those who go down to the Pit;
   I am a man who has no strength,
like one forsaken among the dead,
   like the slain that lie in the grave,
like those whom thou dost remember no more,
   for they are cut off from thy hand . . .
   Dost thou work wonders for the dead?
   Do the shades rise up to praise thee?
Is thy steadfast love declared in the grave?
   or thy faithfulness in Abaddon?
Are thy wonders known in the darkness,
   or thy saving help in the land of forgetfulness? (Psalm 88:3-12)

The dead do not praise the Lord,
   nor do any that go down into silence (Psalm 115:17)

For the fate of the sons of men and the fate of beasts is the same; as one dies, so dies the other. They all have the same breath, and man has no advantage over the beasts; for all is vanity. All go to one place; all are from the dust and all turn to dust again. (Ecclesiastes 3:19, 20)

He who is joined with all the living has hope, for a living dog is better than a dead lion. For the living know that they will die, but the dead know nothing, and they have no more reward; but the memory of them is lost... Whatever your hand finds to do, do it with your might; for there is no work or thought or knowledge of wisdom in Sheol to which you are going. (Ecclesiastes 9:4-10)

For Sheol cannot thank thee,
   death cannot praise thee;
those who go down to the pit cannot hope
   for thy faithfulness. (Isaiah 38:18)

For there is hope for a tree,
   if it be cut down, that it will sprout again,
   and that its shoots will not cease.
Though its root grow old in the earth,
   and its stump die in the ground,
yet at the scent of water it will bud
   and put forth branches like a young plant.

But man dies, and is laid low;
   man breathes his last, and where is he?
As waters fail from a lake,
   and a river wastes away and dries up,
so man lies down, and rises not again;
   till the heavens are no more he will not awake,
   or be roused out of his sleep. (Job 14:7-12)

It is clear that in the Old Testament there is little to hope for after death—a land of shadows, a land of the dark, a land of silence, a land of forgetfulness, a land which is cut off from God and from people. J. E. McFadyen wrote in *The Message of Israel* (p. 46); "There are few more wonderful things than this in the long story of religion, that for centuries men lived the noblest lives, doing their duties and bearing their sorrows, without hope of future reward; and they did this because in all their going out and coming in they were very sure of God." Then McFadyen went on to say: "An American scholar has said that 'it has never been possible for man, thinking man, on a basis of *this life only*, to make life anything but meaningless nonsense.' The Old Testament is the triumphant refutation of such an assertion." In the earliest form of Hebrew religion there was no belief in any real life beyond the grave and on the other side of death.

2. But this is not the end of the matter in the Old Testament. In the Old Testament there are many passages which are at least on the way to a belief in life after death. Isaiah can say:

Thy dead shall live, their bodies shall rise.
   O dwellers in the dust, awake and sing for joy!
For thy dew is a dew of light,
   and on the land of the shades thou wilt let it fall. (Isaiah 26:19)

In Daniel we find the belief:

And many of those who sleep in the dust of the earth shall awake, some to everlasting life, and some to shame and everlasting contempt. And those who are wise shall shine like the brightness of the firmament; and those who turn many to righteousness, like the stars for ever and ever. (Daniel 12:2, 3)

Let us trace the process and the reasons by which the real belief in life after death came into being.

a. The greater people's conception of God, the more they came to be certain that there was no part of the universe outside the being of God. When people thought of their God as only the god of their nation, and when they were willing to grant that each nation had its own god, then the area of God's power was strictly limited; but when they moved on to believe in only one God, the God of all people and all nations and all

possible worlds, then they could not avoid thinking of him also as the God of that world which came after death.

> Whither shall I go from thy Spirit?
>   Or whither shall I flee from thy presence?
> If I ascend to heaven, thou art there!
>   If I make my bed in Sheol, thou art there! (Psalm 139:7, 8)

Once people began to believe in one God of all the universe, then this life and any other life are in the presence of God, and the idea of Sheol was bound to change.

b. Sometimes people's glimpse of a life to come was like a leap in the dark. It was not a settled belief to begin with. It was something which a person grasped like a life-belt in a sea of trouble. It was that way with Job. We have already quoted Job's words of despair, and Job could despair:

> As the cloud fades and vanishes,
>   so he who goes down to Sheol does not come up. (7:9)

But Job felt that it would make all the difference in the world if he could only hope for something. As Galloway once said, "The enigmas of life become at least less baffling, when we come to rest in the thought that this is not the last act of the human drama." So Moffatt translates Job's hope:

> If only man might die and live again,
>   I could endure my weary post until relief arrived;
> thou wouldst call, and I would come,
>   when thou didst yearn for life that thou hadst made. (14:14, 15)

So in Job's heart there was the longing—if only there was something still to come! And then suddenly he makes the leap:

> I know that my Redeemer lives,
>   and at last he will stand upon the earth;
> and after my skin has been thus destroyed,
>   then from my flesh I shall see God,
> whom I shall see on my side,
>   and my eyes shall behold and not another. (19:25-27)

It is not a settled doctrine; it is not a reasoned faith; it is not part of a creed. It is the first leap in the dark to grasp at God, not just in this life, but forever.

c. Sometimes that belief in the life to come came not from any sudden leap, but from the growing conviction that a relationship, a connection, a friendship, a link established with God is in its essence unbreakable, just because God is God. So the person who had found God in this world believed that, since God is always God, you cannot lose him. To say that love is immortal would mean the same thing. So the psalmists write:

Nevertheless I am continually with thee;
   thou dost hold my right hand.
Thou dost guide me with thy counsel
   and afterward thou wilt receive me to glory.
Whom have I in heaven but thee?
   And there is nothing on earth that I desire besides thee.
My flesh and my heart may fail,
   but God is the strengh of my heart,
     and my portion for ever. (Psalm 73:23-26)

I keep the Lord always before me;
   because he is at my right hand,
     I shall not be moved.
Therefore my heart is glad, and my soul rejoices;
   my body also dwells secure.
For thou dost not give me up to Sheol,
   or let thy godly one see the Pit.
Thou dost show me the path of life;
   in thy presence there is fullness of joy,
     in thy right hand are pleasures for evermore. (Psalm 16:8-11)

In these two passages there is the confidence of a heart which has established a connection with God which it is convinced cannot be terminated by death.

d. But perhaps that which most of all brought to the Hebrews a real belief in a life to come was simply the fact that, unless they brought another world into the scheme of things, then neither God's promises to the nation nor to the individual would ever be fulfilled. There was a time when people looked for God's rewards and punishments within this present time scheme. The psalmist said:

I have been young, and now am old;
   yet I have not seen the righteous forsaken.
   or his children begging bread. (Psalm 37:25)

But it became less and less possible to say that. The good person might die in agony in the cruelty of the persecutor. The person of principle was so often—as he still is—the one the world hates. Israel was the chosen people, but Israel was a nation subjugated by the Assyrians, the Babylonians, the Persians, the Greeks, the Romans. The plain fact was that without a life to come it was impossible to believe in either the love or the justice of God. In the famous phrase, the new world was called in to redress the balance of the old. Thus between the Testaments this belief in a life to come became strong, so that those who had been true to God might find their reward and that the promises of God might yet be fulfilled.

They that fear the Lord shall arise to eternal life; their life shall be in light, and it will never cease. (Psalms of Solomon 3:12)

> After that, when the time of the Advent of the Messiah is completed, he shall return in glory into the heavens. And then shall all those arise who slept with their hope in him. (Apocalypse of Baruch 30:1)

Since God's man never received God's blessing in this distressful life, people were driven to believe in the life to come.

3. But at the best this was a hope, and not till the coming of Jesus does the hope turn to certainty. It is the word of Jesus.

> In my Father's house are many rooms; if it were not so, would I have told you that I go to prepare a place for you? And when I go and prepare a place for you, I will come again and will take you to myself, that where I am you may be also. . . . Because I live you will live also. (John 14:2, 3, 19)

As Paul sees it, the Christian certainty of the life to come comes from the fact that the Christian's Savior is one who was dead and is alive again. "As in Adam all die, so also in Christ shall all be made alive" (I Corinthians 15:22). In Jesus Christ what had been a hope became a certainty, and what had been a theory became a fact. And so within the Bible we see the belief in the life to come developing from the gray shadowy Sheol to life forever with the Lord. And once again, when people quote the grim parts of the Old Testament where belief in the life to come does not in any real way exist, then we do not need to defend these parts, and we do not need to explain them away. Once again we can say, "Yes, that is as far as men had reached at that time. But that is not the Christian belief. These are only steps on the way to the conviction of life in Christ here and hereafter."

There is one more big demand on us in our study of the Bible. To understand any book we have to try to enter into the mind and the heart and the life and the circumstances of the person who wrote it. We have to try to see how his mind works; we have to try to understand his general world view. This is just as true of the Bible as of any other book. We must try to enter into the mind of the people who wrote it. To go to the Bible with the eyes and the ideas and the preconceptions of twentieth-century western people is the surest way to misunderstand it. We have to try to think ourselves into the mind of a man of the date at which each book was written. And we have continually to remind ourselves what the object of the writers of the Bible was in writing at all. Their one object was to show the ways of God with humanity; their one aim was to show life in terms of the sovereignty of God. Their aim was exclusively religious. They were not writing history; they knew no more of scientific history than any of their contemporaries did. They were not writing science; their science was as primitive as that of their age. Their aim was to show God in action.

There is nothing at all unnatural in this. A person is always an expert within an area. My mother knew no Hebrew and no Greek and no

theology, but she was the greatest saint I ever knew. I would never have gone to her for the translation of a word or for the expounding of a doctrine; but I would have gone to her every time to learn how to live with God as a constant companion. So in the Bible I do not look in the first place for history; I do not look at all for science; but I do look for God—and I find him. Let us then see some of the things which we must remember if we are to enter into the minds of the biblical writers.

1. They have a quite different view of the world. For them the earth was the fixed center of things, and the sun emerged each day to run his daily race across the heavens (Psalm 19:4, 5). The earth is like a flat plate sitting on the waters with the solid dome of the firmament overarching it, across which the great lights of the sun and moon traveled and which opened for the waters above to make the rain (Genesis 1:1-19). But the important thing is not what they believed the earth to be like; the important thing is what they believed people to be like, and what they believed God to be like, and that they were quite certain that, whatever the earth is like, the creating power of God is behind it.

2. They have a quite different view of sickness. They attributed sickness to the demons or to the sin of the sick person. It was not only mental illness that they ascribed to the demons. Any part of the body might, as they thought, be occupied and rendered ill by a demon. All illness, so they believed, had some sin behind it.

We no longer attribute illness to the demons or necessarily to the sin of the sick person himself. But in one way these ancient thinkers were curiously modern. What we have been saying is that, in the modern term, they believed illness to be psychosomatic. *Psychê* is the Greek for *soul*, and *sôma* is the Greek for *body*. And to say that illness is psychosomatic means that it has more than a physical cause; it has its spiritual causes as well. It may indeed have no physical cause, only a physical effect. This means that it is never enough to concentrate on a person as a body, but that he has a spirit as well, and the body will never be healthy until the spirit also is whole. Healing—and in their own way the ancient writers saw this—is always more than a physical matter.

3. They have quite a different way of thinking, and this is the most important and the most difficult point of all. Among the Hebrews in biblical times there were few—perhaps none—who thought, or could think, in abstract terms and abstract arguments. *They thought in pictures.* Now, the pictures in which they thought were bound to be the pictures of their own time, the pictures which were part of the scene of day-to-day living in their own day, for the simple reason that these were the only pictures which the people of their day could understand. So, then, inevitably what happens to us is that we are confronted with a piece of timeless truth enclosed in a quite

local and temporary picture. Time and time again our task is to penetrate beyond the husk of the picture to the kernel of the truth.

This process has a name—and it is a name which very unfortunately and very unfairly has become to many people a bad word. It is called *demythologizing*. The trouble about this is that the word *myth* (*mythos*) means one thing in Greek and another in English. In English a myth is a piece of fiction, and to say that a thing is mythical is well nigh the same as to say that it is untrue. But in Greek a myth is a story designed to make clear some truth which it is difficult or impossible to put into plain language which an ordinary person can follow. A myth is truth in a picture.

There is, for instance, the famous myth in the sixth book of Plato's *Republic*. There is a cave, and in it there are men so fettered that they can look only inward. In front of them there is a wall, and they can look only at the wall. Behind them there is a raised path, and behind that there is a bright light of a burning fire. People and things are always passing along the path between the fire and the backs of the fettered men, and the shadows of the people and the things are continually thrown on the wall in front. Inevitably men bound in a position like that would come to think that the shadows were the realities, because they were so fettered that they could not see the real objects at all; and, if all their lives men had been so fettered, even if they were freed, it would be hard to convince them that the shadows were unreal and that the real people and things were the realities. This is a myth, and it is designed to show how people become so attached to the shadows of life that they become incapable of seeing the realities. That is the Greek idea of myth. A myth is a story constructed to demonstrate and illustrate and bring home a truth, which would have no impact upon people, if it was expressed in abstract language.

Time and time again our task in studying the Bible is to get at the timeless truth at the back of the temporary picture. The twentieth-century scholars were far from being the first to recognize this need. Origen, the great scholar, knew all about it and stated it clearly and forcibly half way through the third century (*De Principiis* 1:16):

> What man of sense will suppose that the first and the second and the third day, and the evening and the morning, existed without a sun and moon and stars? Who is so foolish as to believe that God like a farmer planted a garden in Eden, and placed in it a tree of life, that might be seen and touched, so that one who has tasted of the fruit by his bodily lips obtained life? Or again, that one was partaker of good and evil by eating that which was taken from a tree? And if God is said to have walked in a garden in the evening, and Adam to have hidden under a tree, I do not suppose that anyone doubts that these things figuratively indicate certain mysteries, the history being apparently but not literally true. . . . Nay, the Gospels themselves are filled with the same kind of narratives. Take, for example, the story of the Devil taking Jesus up into a high mountain to show him from thence the kingdoms of the world and the glory of them: what thoughtful reader would not condemn those who

teach that it was with the eye of the body—which needs a lofty height that even the near neighbourhood may be seen—that Jesus beheld the kingdoms of the Persians, and Scythians, and Indians, and Parthians, and the manner in which their rulers were glorified among men?

Origen begins by noting that in the creation story it is three times said that there was evening and morning *before* the sun and moon were created (Genesis 1:5, 8, 13, 14). What Origen is saying is that here we have truth, but truth in a picture. The picture is the husk; the truth is the kernel. Let us take briefly the three stories to which Origen refers.

a. There is the creation story, or rather there are two different creation stories. If you ask any intelligent schoolboy to put into one sentence what Genesis 1 and 2 are saying, he will at once answer: "They are saying that God made the world." That *is* the answer. The *method* by which he made it is not in question. The *fact* that God's creating power is behind this universe and is responsible for this universe is the kernel, however that creating power was exercised.

b. There is the story of the Fall in Genesis 3. This story is in fact the story of *the fall of every man*. It is worthwhile noting that the name Adam is not a proper name at all; it is in fact the Hebrew word for *man*. This is everyman's story. The man who wrote it would not even know that there was such a word as *psychology*, but there never was written a story more psychologically true than this one. Take it step by step.

(1) God gives a command.

(2) There comes the temptation to break it. Sin always implies that we know better than God; it is putting our wish above God's will.

(3) The wrong thing is attractive (verse 6). It looks good; it was good to eat; to take it would be to win something apparently well worthwhile. Sin is always attractive. If I can only have this, I will be happy. If the forbidden thing was ugly and repulsive, there would be no power in temptation. Temptation has power, because the forbidden things look attractive and desirable and profitable.

(4) Sin is committed and the first instinct is to hide (verse 8). No sooner has a person committed a sin than he wants to hide it from people, to hide it from God, and, if possible, to refuse to look at it himself. And there is no greater folly than thinking that anything can be hidden from God.

(5) When confronted with his sin, man's first instinct is to push the blame on to someone else. Adam said, "Don't blame me; blame Eve." Eve said, "Don't blame me; blame the serpent." The sinner blames everyone but himself.

Genesis 3 is a story which was never meant to tell of something which happened in a moment of time. It is the story of what happens to Adam—to man, to every man, to you and to me.

c. Finally, let us take the story of the temptations of Jesus (Matthew 4:1-11; Luke 4:1-13). Origen was right; there is one thing which should

make us stop and think—there is no mountain from which anyone can literally see all the kingdoms of the world. Jesus had gone out into the desert to decide how he was to do the task God had given him to do. Was he to use the way of force, of material things, of sensations, of compromise—or the way of the Cross? All that this story tells was not happening visibly and externally. It was going on in the mind of Jesus. He was fighting the battle with all that was trying to lure him from the way God wanted him to take. If you had seen him during it, you would have seen a man alone—or not alone—with God. Just as temptation comes to us, so it came to him, not physically, visibly, but with the attack in the mind and in the heart.

Always we have to remember as we read the Bible that we are reading the work of men who thought in pictures. We must never waste time in argument about whether this is literally and physically true or not. It is spiritually forever true, and beyond the husk of story we must find the kernel of truth—and live by it.

There are just three things more to say about reading and studying the Bible.

1. While we should study the Bible in detail, we should often, to get the best of it, read it in long sections. We should, for instance, read Mark's Gospel at a sitting, and see the four-act drama—preparation, conflict, tragedy, triumph—opening before us. It is possible sometimes to spend too much time on detail and too little on the panoramic and the dramatic pictures of the whole.

2. However long and however devotedly we study the Bible, there will still be passages which are too difficult and which we cannot understand. A man once came to Spurgeon complaining that there were parts of the Bible he did not understand, and saying that he had stopped reading it. Spurgeon said: "When I am eating a nice bit of fish and come upon a bone, I don't fling the whole fish away; I put the bone at the side of the plate and leave it there; and I go on enjoying the fish." When we come to something in the Bible that, even after study, we still do not understand, then we can leave it and pass on. The day will come when we may understand; and for the present there is wealth enough and more to be going on with.

3. One last thing—there is everything to be said for regular and systematic reading of the Bible. In his autobiographical study, . . . *And Another Thing*, Howard Spring tells how he got the habit. It was during the war in 1940, when things were at their worst. He went to his desk to work, and he found that he could not concentrate for thinking of the threat to our country. It so happened that very recently someone had given him a copy of Marcus Aurelius' *Meditations*. He picked it up and began to read, and somehow the gallant and astringent Stoic philosophy did something to him. "Thereafter," he said,

I made a practice of beginning the morning not by sitting down at my desk with a mind inflamed by all the surging incertitude of the times, but by standing up and reading erect for half-an-hour or so from Marcus Aurelius. I found it a salutary and strengthening custom. . . . In this way I read twice through the *Meditations*, and by then it seemed to me that no day should be begun with a plunge straight into "business," whatever that business might be. A few moments of quietness in the company of a supreme and tranquil mind seemed to pay dividends that would make a company promoter lick his chops. It is so easy to begin the day with a rush through the morning paper and a rush through the morning mail, and then to make a rush at the work in hand, but I now think so foolish and so unnecessary. It is like playing the fiddle before it has been keyed up; it will be off pitch all day.

But Howard Spring did not stop there. He goes on, "After the second reading of the *Meditations*, I began the morning with readings from the Bible, and it was during these readings of a book neglected for a quarter of a century that the central importance of a loving God and love of the brethren took possession of my mind."

Howard Spring found that that daily reading brought a serenity and a strength into life, and through it God took possession of his mind. We too ought to be regular in reading the Bible. Howard Spring, being an author, could do his work at home and was not the slave of the clock. It may be that for us with a train to catch and an office to get to and a family to live among the morning reading will not be possible, or will at least be very difficult. But the reading can just as well be the last thing at night, and we can go to rest thinking of God and of his ways with people.

If we adopt this method of regular reading, it will not be the best of plans to begin at the beginning of the Bible and to go on to the end. We will be far better to use a carefully prepared scheme of daily readings with comments such as the Bible Reading Fellowship or the International Bible Reading Association offers. In that way our reading will be guided and directed; the difficulties will be explained; the meanings will be brought out; and we will have the sense of being one of a great company reading with us all over the world. To read the Bible with system and with help is the way to get the best out of it, for thus we will get strength for the way, wisdom for our minds, and the love of God for our hearts.*

And if we read, what translation shall we use? There are some who are troubled with the large number of translations which exist; but of translations we cannot have too many. No translation can be perfect; words will never come completely out of one language into another. Every translation is another attempt to achieve the impossible, the perfect translation. Every translation has something to offer. Away back about

---

*Two programs for reading the Bible can be found in the "Helps for Bible Study" section—ED.

1560 the Geneva Bible was most popular, but the Bishops' Bible, an official translation, was being planned. John Bodley, the father of the founder of Oxford's famous library, had the patent to print the Geneva Bible, and he wondered if he would be allowed to continue to do so when the new official translation was being planned. Matthew Parker, the Archbishop of Canterbury, had no doubt. It was true, he wrote, that the official volume was being planned, "Yet should it nothing hinder but rather do much good to have diversity of translations and readings." The more the better so that each person might find that which spoke to him, and that the struggle for perfection might go on.

Translations can differ vastly. There is—or was—a series of schoolboy cribs called "Kelly's Keys to the Classics." They are absolutely literal and are not English at all. Here is a paragraph from Sophocles' *Oedipus Coloneus*: it is Oedipus who is speaking:

> O dearest son of Aegeus, exemption from old age and death comes to gods alone. But all-powerful Time brings everything else to confusion. The strength of the earth decays, the strength of the body decays, faith dies and faithlessness arises, and the same spirit no longer exists between friends or between city and city. With some at once and with others later on, what is a source of pleasure becomes bitter, and then again is pleasant.

No doubt with that the schoolboy would gain a passing mark—but the haunting beauty of Sophocles is gone. Here is the same passage in Gilbert Murray's translation:

> Fair Aegeus' son, only to gods on high
> Not to grow old is given, nor yet to die,
> All else is turmoiled by our master, Time.
> Decay is in earth's bloom and manhood's prime,
> Faith dies and unfaith blossoms like a flower,
> And who of men shall find from hour to hour,
> Or in loud cities or the marts thereof,
> Or silent chambers of his own heart's love,
> One wind blows true forever? Soon or late
> Hate shall be love and love veer back to hate.

Here the beauty of the Greek speaks again. It is easy to see how different translations can be.

But, suppose we find a good translation, why not stick to it? Why the many? There are many reasons. Nothing changes so quickly and so imperceptibly as language—and remember that the New Testament was in the colloquial language of the ordinary people. My way of speaking is not my son's, nor his mine. Again, there are continuous new discoveries. Fifty years ago there were more than six hundred words in the New Testament which were listed as "biblical Greek"; now there are fewer than fifty. There

have been continuous discoveries of the letters people wrote and the deeds they drew up and the documents they used. And the words that once were strange have been discovered to be common words, and their meaning has been far more closely fixed. New manuscripts of the New Testament are discovered. We have now at least seventy items of New Testament manuscripts which go back to A.D. 150, which is perhaps two centuries older than any manuscripts scholars could use seventy-five years ago. Language does not stand still, and scholarship does not stand still. And if the Bible is, as we believe it is, the word of God, then nothing but the most accurate translation will do. Translation is a never-ending task. Let a student of the Bible use all the translations he can find—and thank God for them.

Books for Further Study

The following series of commentaries will be found useful. In each of them there is a volume or part-volume on each Bible book.

Clarke's Commentary (Abingdon). This commentary covers the entire Bible. Although it is one of the older commentaries, it still remains helpful.

Interpreter's Bible (Abingdon). This is a complete and scholarly commentary on the whole Bible. It is consistently valuable.

Of the one-volume commentaries the best known of the older ones is A. S. Peake's. This *Commentary on the Bible* (Nelson) was fairly recently revised and rewritten. One of the newest of these commentaries is *The Interpreter's One-Volume Commentary on the Bible* (Abingdon). It should be remembered that one-volume commentaries are necessarily brief in their comments.

There are two older books on the Bible which are still of the greatest use. The first is *The Bible: Its Origin, Its Significance, and Its Abiding Worth* by A. S. Peake, and *A Guide to Understanding the Bible* by H. E. Fosdick (Harper). No better books on the Bible have ever been published. One of the most useful and significant of recent books is G. E. Ladd's *The New Testament and Criticism* (Eerdmans). Whatever else is read, these books should not be missed.

Of books on the background of the Bible, the *Cambridge History of the Bible*; the *Oxford Bible Atlas*, ed. Herbert G. May and G. H. Hunt; and the *Westminster Historical Atlas to the Bible*, ed. George G. Wright and F. V. Filson, are worth noting.

Two useful aids are *Eerdman's Handbook to the Bible* by David Alexander and Patricia Alexander, and the *Abingdon Bible Handbook* by Edward P. Blair.

Finally, a book to lead us back again to the Bible itself: A. E. Harvey, *The New English Bible, Companion to the New Testament* (Oxford). ◑

DICTIONARY

OF THE

BIBLE

AARON. The elder brother of Moses. Aaron served as spokesman for his brother when Moses asked the pharaoh to let the Israelites leave Egypt, and he assisted Moses in helping the Israelites escape from Egyptian slavery. During the Israelites' long stay in the wilderness Moses anointed Aaron priest of the tabernacle, the tent of meeting in which the ark with the Ten Commandments was kept. Descendants of Aaron also became priests. In the OT they are sometimes referred to as Levites—from Levi, the family or tribal name. (See *Ark of the Covenant, Levi, Priests and Levites, Tabernacle.*) *Exodus 6:20-29; 28:1-4; 29:4-7; 32:1-5.*

ABADDON. A poetic name used in the OT to indicate a place under the earth where the dead were supposed to dwell. It was also called Sheol. Other early peoples had similar ideas about the dwelling places of the dead. *Job 26:6; 28:22; 31:12; Psalm 88:11; Proverbs 15:11; 27:20.*

ABBA. An Aramaic word meaning "the father," "my father," or "our father." In the NT Jesus used this word as a familiar name for God, the Father. *Mark 14:36; Romans 8:15; Galatians 4:6.*

ABEDNEGO. See *Shadrach, Meshach, Abednego.*

ABEL. The second son of Adam and Eve. In the OT story Abel, said to have been a shepherd, was murdered by his brother Cain. The NT mentions Abel as the first person to die for his faith. *Genesis 4:1-9; Hebrews 11:4.*

ABIATHAR. A priest of David's time. After David's death Abiathar and the priest Zadok disagreed over which of David's sons should be made king. Zadok anointed Solomon king, and Abiathar was sent into exile in the city of Anathoth. It is possible that Abiathar, his son, and Zadok's son were responsible for some of the records preserved in the Books of Samuel. *I Samuel 22:20-23; 23:6-14;*

ABIGAIL

II Samuel 15: 24-29; I Kings 2:26-27; Mark 2:23-28. (Here Abiathar is mentioned as high priest when David ate the bread of the Presence in the house of God. In I Samuel 21:5-6 Ahimelech is named as the one who gave David the bread. See Ahimelech.)

ABIGAIL. Wife of Nabal the owner of large flocks of sheep and goats. When Nabal refused to invite David to his sheepshearing feast or to give him and his men any food, Abigail rode to meet David and apologize, asking him not to harm her husband. David respected her wishes. After Nabal's death David married Abigail. Also the name of one of David's sisters. *I Samuel 25:1-42; I Chronicles 2:16-17.*

ABIJAM. King of Judah from about 913 to 911 B.C. He was the son and successor of Rehoboam. His name also appears as Abijah. *I Kings 14:31–15:8; II Chronicles 13:1-22.*

ABIMELECH. One of the seventy sons of Gideon (or Jerubbaal). He persuaded the men of Shechem to help him become king after his father's death. He murdered all of his brothers except the youngest, Jotham, who told a fable warning the people that Abimelech would be a cruel king. The bramble in Jotham's fable represents Abimelech. *Judges 9:1-57.*

ABISHAI. A nephew of David. He is remembered as one of David's brave and loyal men who volunteered to go with David on a dangerous and daring venture. *I Samuel 26:6-9; II Samuel 23:18-19.*

ABLUTION. Ceremonial or symbolic washing of hands, cups, pots, or other utensils to make these objects fit for use in worship, or fit for a place in the religious life of the community. *Matthew 15:1-20; 23:25-26; Mark 7:1-23; Hebrews 6:2; 9:10.*

ABNER. Commander of the Israelite army under Saul, he fought in the battles against the Philistines. At the festival of the new moon he was seated in the place of honor beside King Saul. Abner introduced David to Saul. *I Samuel 14:50; 17:55-58; 20:25; 26:5; II Samuel 2:8-10; 3:17-39.*

ABOMINATION. In the Bible anything vile or detestable, especially something offensive to God. For the Hebrews the foods and objects used by pagans in the worship of idols, and the worship itself, were the worst abominations. Certain diseases, certain foods, and the breaking of certain moral laws were also abominations. *Leviticus 11:9-23; 19:5-8; Deuteronomy 12:31; 18:9-12; 25:14-16; Proverbs 12:22.*

ABRAHAM or **ABRAM.** OT patriarch known as the father, or ancestor, of the Hebrew people. He was noted for his obedience to God. Born near Ur in Mesopotamia, Abraham wandered with his family close to Haran. Abraham, in obedience to God, left Haran and led his family to Canaan, the Land of Promise. God made a covenant, or agreement, with Abraham promising that he would be the father of a great nation, and that through him God would bless all the families of the earth. A son, Isaac, was born to Abraham's wife, Sarah. The

faith of Abraham was tested when God asked him to offer Isaac as a sacrifice. Abraham consented, and God spared the son. In the NT, Abraham is often mentioned because of his great example of obedience and trust. *Genesis 11:27–25:11; John 8:39-40; Galatians 3:6-9.*

ABRAHAM'S BOSOM. In NT
times a way of speaking of the state in which the faithful who died awaited the resurrection. The picture it gives is one of faithful sons finding rest and close companionship with their father Abraham. (See *Abraham.*) *Luke 16:22-23.*

ABSALOM. The third son of King
David. Absalom was handsome and ambitious. He led a revolt against his father and tried to take the throne. *II Samuel 13:1–19:8.*

ABYSS. An unmeasured, deep,
bottomless pit. This word is used in the NT to refer to the place of the dead. (See *Sheol, Abaddon.*) *Luke 8:31; Romans 10:7.*

ACACIA. The acacia is native to
Egypt and so was known to the early Hebrews who called it the "shittah tree" (Isaiah 41:19). On their exodus from Egypt they carried with them wood of this tree and used it in building the ark of the covenant (Exodus 25:10.) Considered sacred, it was never used for other than religious purposes. Some scholars think its spiny growth might have been used to make Jesus' crown of thorns.

ACANTHUS. See *Nettle.*

ACHAIA. The Roman province
that made up most of ancient Greece. Achaia is mentioned frequently in the NT in connection with Paul and the early Christian churches. *Acts 18:12, 27; 19:21; Romans 15:26; I Corinthians 16:15; II Corinthians 1:1; 9:2; 11:10; I Thessalonians 1:7-8.*

ACORUS. Oil pressed from the
roots of the acorus was used for anointing. It is a rush-like plant, native to the eastern Mediterranean region. Leaves of the plant were sometimes strewn on the floors of places of worship in place of carpeting.

ACTS OF THE APOSTLES.
The fifth book in the NT. It was written as a sequel to the Gospel of Luke. Acts records many of the experiences of Jesus' followers after the Resurrection and describes how the Christian church began and spread.

ADAM. A Hebrew word meaning
"man." This is the name given the first man in the stories of creation. In the NT Adam is spoken of as representing all mankind. *Genesis 2:7–5:5; Romans 5:14; I Corinthians 15:22, 45.*

ADDAX. Several kinds of antelope
were known in ancient Israel. One of the most common was the addax. It is about the size of a donkey, off-white in color except for its brown head. A short mane on the underside of the neck gives it the appearance of a large goat. It has a donkey-like tail, flat hoofs to keep it from sinking into the desert sand and long, thin, double-

twisted horns, probably the most unusual of any animal.

Like other antelope, the addax was clean under the dietary laws and so was widely hunted. It is so fast that no dog can catch it. They are used, but falcons are usually a necessary part of the hunting team.

ADDER. See *Viper*.

ADONIJAH. The fourth son of David whose plot to take over the throne as the old king lay dying failed and led finally to his own destruction. Since his older brothers were dead, Adonijah claimed the right to reign after David. Solomon, aided by his mother, by Zadok the priest, and by the prophet Nathan, took the reign away from Adonijah. *II Samuel 3.4; I Kings 1:5–2:25.*

ADULLAM. An OT town which was in the territory of the tribe of Judah. Joshua defeated the king of Adullam during the Hebrew conquest of Canaan. In a cave near Adullam, David took refuge when Saul was trying to kill him. *Joshua 12:15; I Samuel 22:1-2.*

ADULTERY. Intimate and sinful physical relations between a married man and a woman who is not his wife, or between a married woman and a man who is not her husband. In both the OT and NT adultery is a most serious offense against God, and because it damaged the life of families, it was seen as an offense against the whole community. *Exodus 20:14; Leviticus 20:10; Matthew 5:27-28; Mark 10:2-12.*

AGAMID. A large lizard, often three feet in length, covered with scales and thornlike protrusions, the agamid presents a very frightening appearance. Actually it is harmless, living mainly on insects. Though not mentioned by name in the Bible, the word *tortoise* in Leviticus 11:29 is now generally thought to be some kind of lizard, quite possibly the agamid.

AGAPE. This Greek word does not appear in the Bible, but it was used by Christians to mean the love of God. When early Christians broke bread and ate together, the meal was sometimes called "the Agape." (See *Love*.)

AGRIPPA. Agrippa II was the king of Judea before whom Paul made his defense after the Jewish authorities accused him of crimes against the laws of the Jews and of Caesar. *Acts 25:13–26:32.*

AHAB. Seventh king of the northern kingdom of Israel. He reigned for twenty years from about 874 to 853 B.C. During most of his reign he was at war with the Assyrians. Probably influenced by his Baal-worshiping wife, Jezebel, Ahab built a temple to Baal, erected an altar, and worshiped this god. Ahab was condemned by the prophet Elijah. One of the stories about Ahab's reign tells of Elijah's triumph over the prophets of Baal in a contest to prove to the people that the Lord was God. Ahab was fatally wounded in a battle with the king of Syria (not the same as Assyria) even though he had disguised himself so no one would recognize him. He died

in his capital city, Samaria. (See *Elijah, Jezebel.*) *I Kings 16:29–22:40.*

AHASUERUS. A king of the Persian Empire, who made Esther, a Jewess, his wife. (See *Esther.*) *Ezra 4:6; Esther 1:1–10:3.*

AHAZ. King of the southern kingdom of Judah from about 732 to 716 B.C. His reign had important and long-lasting results for the religious and political life of Judah, and also for Israel. The kings of Israel and Syria joined forces and invaded Judah, besieging Jerusalem. It is reported that Ahaz burned his son as an offering, which was probably a desperate attempt to avoid defeat. When this failed, Ahaz appealed to Tiglath-pileser, king of Assyria, for help. The Assyrian king responded quickly and began the campaigns which finally ended in the destruction of the northern kingdom of Israel. Judah, however, was forced to pay heavy tribute to the Assyrians. Ahaz also introduced Assyrian worship into the temple. *II Kings 16:1-20; II Chronicles 28:1-6, 16-27; Isaiah 1:1; 7:1-17.*

AHAZIAH. 1. King of Israel from about 853 to 852 B.C. He was the son and successor of Ahab. *I Kings 22:49-53; II Kings 1:2-17.* 2. See *Jehoahaz* (1).

AHIJAH. A priest and prophet from the town of Shiloh. Meeting Jeroboam on the road outside Jerusalem, Ahijah foretold one of the most important events in the history of Israel, the division of Solomon's kingdom into two separate kingdoms. *I Kings 11:29-40; 12:12-15; II Chronicles 9:29.*

AHIMELECH. A priest of the sanctuary at Nob who helped David when he was fleeing from Saul by giving him the holy bread of the sanctuary and the sword of Goliath. When Saul heard of this, he was very angry and had Ahimelech and all the other priests put to death. (See *Abiathar.*) *I Samuel 21:1–22:23.*

ALABASTER. A soft calcite stone, light and creamy in color and often having a banded or striped appearance that adds to its beauty. In Bible times it was most frequently used for vases and for flasks or boxes to hold perfume and precious ointments. *Song of Solomon 5:15; Matthew 26:7; Mark 14:3; Luke 7:37.*

ALEXANDRIA. The capital city and great seaport of Egypt. This city was built by Alexander the Great in 331 B.C. Many Jews settled there at that time, and the OT was translated into Greek there. It had a great library and became a center of learning. Next to Rome it was the most important city in NT times. *Acts 18:24; 27:6; 28:11.*

ALLEGORY. A story with a double meaning. In the Bible there are some stories in which the characters and events tell one obvious story, but because these characters and events also have a hidden meaning, there is another story below the surface. (See *Fable, Myth, Parable.*) *Judges 9:7-15 and II Samuel 12:14 are examples of allegory.*

ALLOTMENT. In early OT times the portion of land distributed or assigned by lot to each of the tribes occupying Canaan. The Hebrews had a very special attitude toward their

land. They lived in Canaan, the Promised Land, promised by God to Abraham and his descendants. For this reason they thought of God as their landlord, that is, he was the owner of the land. As the years went by, the people lost sight of this idea. *Joshua 11:23; 16:1-3; Ezekiel 48:10-13.*

ALMIGHTY. Having absolute power. The word is often used as an adjective with "God" to show his greatness, power, and might. As a noun it is a synonym for God, and "the Almighty" is often used in hymns and psalms in place of the word *God. Genesis 17:1; Psalm 91:1; Revelation 4:8.*

ALMOND. Only the olive and the fig are more commonly cultivated in the Holy Land than the almond. The pink or white blossoms cover the branches before the leaves appear as early as January. They resemble our peach blossoms which is not strange since botanically the almond is a member of the peach family. While the nut is universally popular and delicious eating, it is also crushed to produce almond oil, widely used for flavoring and in cosmetics. Wild almonds grow in some sections of Palestine.

ALMS. Gifts given to the poor. OT laws directed the Hebrews to be generous to the poor (see Deuteronomy 15:7-11). The NT records the directions of Jesus and the apostles for remembering the needy. *Matthew 6:2-4; Luke 12:33; Acts 3:2-3.*

ALMUG. A special kind of sweet-scented wood used in musical instruments such as lyres and harps. It was also used in the construction of Solomon's Temple. Almug may have been sandlewood, but this is uncertain. *I Kings 10:11-12.*

ALOES (OT). There are two "aloes" referred to in the Bible, differing widely. The "lign aloes" of Numbers 24:6, also called "eaglewood, " is a large, spreading tree with leaves resembling those of the peach. The inner wood is soft and fragrant leading the psalmist to write. "All thy garments smell of myrrh and aloes" (Psalm 45:8). *Proverbs 7:17.*

Aloes

ALOES (NT). Entirely different from the aloes above is the aloes mixed with myrrh that Nicodemus and Joseph of Arimathea used in preparing the body of Jesus for burial (John 19:38-40). This aloes is a succulent plant with large spike-like leaves and bearing bell-shaped reddish yellow flowers. It is common in the warmer sections of this country. The crushed leaves yield a sap quite commonly used in medicinal lotions.

ALPHA AND OMEGA. The first and last letters of the Greek alphabet. In the NT the two letters are always used together as symbols for God and for Jesus Christ. They indicate that in God all things begin and end, but God himself is without beginning or end. *Revelation 1:8; 21:6; 22:13.*

ALTAR. In early OT times this was usually a mound of earth or a block of stone supported by a pile of smaller stones. Often these were built in a place where God had made himself known. Sacrificial offerings of animals were made to God on the altar, and often incense was burned. In later OT times altars were more elaborate and were often of great size. Other people than the Hebrews also built altars for their gods. *Genesis 8:20; 12:7; 26:23-25; 35:1; Exodus 17:15; Matthew 5:23-24; Acts 17:22-23.*

AMALEKITES. A nomadic desert tribe in the OT, descendants of Esau. The Amalekites continually raided and threatened the Israelites in the time of Moses. Later they were badly defeated by King Saul and were completely wiped out in Hezekiah's reign. *Numbers 13:29; 14:42-45; I Samuel 15:4-8; I Chronicles 4:43.*

AMAZIAH. 1. King of the southern kingdom of Judah from about 797 to 792 B.C., son of King Joash. *II Chronicles 25:1-28.*

2. Priest of the shrine at Bethel. It was this Amaziah who tried to keep the prophet Amos from coming to Bethel and denouncing the sins of the people. *Amos 7:10-15.*

AMBUSH. Lying in wait in a hiding place in order to attack an enemy by surprise. Also, the place where one lies in wait. *Judges 9:25, 34-35; Acts 25:2-3.*

AMEN. A Hebrew word meaning "truly" or "surely." In the Bible its use signified the listener's willingness to acknowledge and agree with the statement or the prayer of a previous speaker. Often it was used as a blessing at the end of a letter. "Amen" is usually used today at the end of a prayer or a hymn. It signifies that the one who uses the word sincerely means what he has said or sung. *Deuteronomy 27:15-26; I Kings 1:36; I Chronicles 16:36; Nehemiah 8:6; I Corinthians 14:16; II Corinthians 1:20; Ephesians 3:20-21.*

AMON. 1. Governor of the city of Samaria during the reign of Ahab. He was in charge of the prophet Micaiah who had been imprisoned after predicting the failure of Ahab's expedition against Ramothgilead. *I Kings 22:26-28; II Chronicles 18:25-27.*

2. King of Judah from about 643 to 641 B.C. He was the son of Manasseh and apparently continued in the ways of his father worshiping the Assyrian gods. He was murdered by his servants. *II Kings 21:19-26; II Chronicles 33:21-25.*

AMOS. A prophet who lived in Tekoa, a town in Judah. He made his prophecies sometime between 760 and 745 B.C. Amos was a shepherd and also "a dresser of sycamore trees." The sycamores mentioned in the Bible are a type of fig-mulberry tree common in Palestine. Just before the fruit

ripens it is necessary for the dresser to pinch or pierce the fruit to allow insects to escape. Otherwise the fruit will not be edible. When Amos took his produce to the marketplaces of the cities, he saw the dishonesty of the people and the way the rich mistreated the poor. In the marketplace at Bethel in the northern kingdom of Israel he warned the people that they could not please God by worship if they continued to be dishonest and unjust to the poor, for God was a holy and just God. "Hate the evil and love the good and establish justice and God will be with you," Amos declared. (See *Amos, Book of.*)

AMOS, BOOK OF. A prophetic book in the OT. The messages of Amos were the first prophetic messages to be gathered into a book. His brief book is included among the last twelve books in the OT, known as the Minor Prophets.

ANATHOTH. In the OT a priestly city near Jerusalem. Jeremiah the prophet was born there and in this city made his first prophecies. The citizens were so angry with the prophet that they threatened his life (see *Jeremiah*). *I Kings 2:26; Isaiah 10:30; Jeremiah 1:1; 11:21-23.*

ANDREW. A fisherman from Capernaum and a brother of Simon Peter. Andrew was one of Jesus' first disciples and was one of the twelve apostles. *Matthew 4:18-20; 10:2; Mark 1:16.*

ANEMONE. Sometimes called the "wildflower," the anemone is related to the buttercup. It grows profusely in Palestine. In early spring its vividly colored flowers carpet the plains with acres of color, ranging from white to purple, with the red anemone especially striking. It is believed by many scholars that these were the "lilies of the field" to which Jesus was referring when he told his listeners that "Soloman in all his glory was not arrayed like one of these" (Luke 12:27).

ANGEL. In Bible usage a spiritual being or messenger from God sometimes said to appear in human form. Angels are reported as announcing special events and giving help in time of crisis. In the OT angels are mentioned in the stories of Abraham. In the NT angels appear in the accounts of Jesus' birth and his temptation. *Genesis 22:11; 21:11; Exodus 3:2; 23:20-24; I Kings 19:5; Psalm 91:11; Matthew 4:6,11; Luke 1:26-38; 2:9-15.*

ANISE (Dill). When Jesus berated the scribes and Pharisees for confining

Anise

their holiness to the tithing of "mint and anise" (Matthew 23:23) the reference was most likely to the common dill since anise was rare in the Holy Land. But the tall feathery plants of dill with their clusters of small yellow flowers and abundant seed were found everywhere. Even as today, it was used as a spice and for flavoring.

ANNUNCIATION. In the NT the angel Gabriel's announcement to Mary that she would give birth to a son whose name was to be Jesus. *Luke 1:26-38.*

ANOINT. To smear ointment or pour oil on the head or body of a person or on an object. In biblical times anointing was often done as part of a religious ceremony to indicate that a person or object had been set apart for the service of the Lord. When a king was crowned he was also anointed by a priest or a prophet. There are many references in the Bible to the kings as "anointed ones." It was a title for the expected ultimate or great King. Jesus was called "the Anointed." Anointing was also done for the sake of good grooming, for medical treatment, and in preparing a body for burial. *Exodus 29:36; 30:30; Ruth 3:3; I Samuel 9:15-16; II Kings 9:1-3; Matthew 6:17; Mark 16:1; Luke 7:44-46.*

ANT. The ant is one of the most common insects on earth. Solomon recognized its industry and skill in one of his familiar proverbs: "Go to the ant, thou sluggard; consider her ways and be wise." And in Proverbs 30:24-25 the wisdom of the ant is

mentioned as one of the "four things which are little upon the earth, but they are exceeding wise: the ants are a people not strong, yet they prepare their meat in the summer." The ability and skill of the ant in building a community of galleries and corridors underground was well known to Hebrews.

ANTICHRIST. As used in the NT a demonic being in opposition to the Christ. The word is also used to refer to actual historical rulers who fight against the faithful. *I John 2:18, 22; 4:3; II John 1:7.*

ANTIOCH. 1. A city near the seacoast north of Israel (the modern city of Antakya, Turkey). It was the third largest city in the Roman Empire. It was in Antioch that the followers of Christ first came to be called Christians and from Antioch that Paul set out on his missionary journeys. *Acts 11:19-30.*

2. A Greek city in Pisidia also visited by Paul. *Acts 13:14.*

AOUDAD. Also known as the "Barbary sheep" the aoudad was quite common in Palestine, especially on and near Mt. Sinai. Today it is found only in the mountains of North Africa. It has large, smooth, widespread horns and a liberal display of "chin whiskers" which gives it a resemblance to a large billy goat. It is related to the Big Horn of the Rocky Mountains.

APE. The ape was not native to the Holy Land, but we read of the navy of Tharsish bringing King Solomon apes, along with "gold, silver, ivory

and peacocks" on the long voyage from India and Ethiopia (I Kings 10:22). Since the ape, along with other kinds of monkeys, was highly prized in Egypt, the Hebrews were familiar with it.

APOCRYPHA. The title given to fourteen or fifteen books written during the last two centuries B.C. and the first century A.D. but not included in the Hebrew Scriptures when these Scriptures were made official by the Council of Jamnia about A.D. 90. These books were, however, included in the Septuagint, or Greek translation of the OT. The word originally meant "hidden books." "Hidden" referred to the secret wisdom they contained. Gradually the word came to refer to books not in the canon, that is, not officially recognized as sacred Scripture. When any apocryphal books appear in Protestant Bibles, they are usually placed between the OT and NT.

APOLLOS. An important member and worker in the early Christian church. He was an evangelist and a scholarly and fluent preacher. *Acts 18:24–19:1; I Corinthians 1:12; 3:4-9; 4:6; 16:12.*

APOSTLE. A title meaning "messenger" or "someone who is sent." It was the title applied to the twelve disciples sent out by Jesus. It was also used to refer to Paul and to certain other first-generation leaders in the early church. *Matthew 10:1-5; Mark 6:30; Luke 6:13-16; 9:10; Acts 14:4, 14; Romans 16:7; I Corinthians 15:9; Ephesians 4:11.*

APRICOT. The apricot is one of the most abundant fruits in Palestine. It grows profusely on the highlands and in the lowlands around the Jordan. Since the apple is comparatively recent, the forbidden fruit growing in the Garden of Eden may well have been the apricot. The Hebrew word translated "apple" in the Song of Solomon 2:3 and the fruit mentioned in Joel 1:12 could have been the Golden Apricot.

AQUILA AND PRISCILLA. A husband and wife who were companions of Paul in Corinth and Ephesus and like Paul were tentmakers. They became partners with Paul in his missionary work, possibly as teachers. *Acts 18:2-3, 18, 26; Romans 16:3-4; I Corinthians 16:19.*

ARABAH. One of the main regions of Israel lying below sea level. It contains the Jordan Valley, Sea of Galilee, the Dead Sea, and the land south to the Gulf of Aqabah. In the Bible "the Arabah" meant any part of this long valley. The southern Arabah was one of the areas through which the Israelites traveled on their journey from Egypt to Canaan. *Deuteronomy 1:1; 2:8; 4:49; Joshua 8:14; Ezekiel 47:8.*

ARABIA. A large peninsula in southwest Asia. Its present-day boundaries are the Red Sea on the west, the Gulf of Aden and the Indian Ocean on the south, the Gulf of Oman and the Persian Gulf on the east, and by Jordan and Iraq on the north. The name probably means "desert." Arabia is often mentioned in the Bible as the source of gold, silver, precious

stones, perfumes, and spices. The northwest portion of Arabia was the scene of some important biblical events. *I Kings 10:14-15; II Chronicles 9:13-14; Isaiah 21:13; Jeremiah 25:24; Ezekiel 27:21; Galatians 1:17; 4:25.*

ARAM, ARAMEANS. See *Syria, Syrians.*

ARAMAIC. The name of a group of dialects closely related to the Hebrew language. In the time of Jesus it was the everyday language of the Jews and was spoken by Jesus and the disciples. It still survives in a few villages in the eastern mountain range running parallel to Lebanon and called the Anti-Lebanon. Some parts of the OT were originally written in Aramaic. *II Kings 18:26; Ezra 4:7; Isaiah 36:11.*

ARARAT. A country in the region of Armenia. It refers to the mountains located in this region that emerged first from the waters in the OT account of the Flood. The Assyrian name was Urartu. *Genesis 8:4; Jeremiah 51:27.*

ARCHAEOLOGY. Study of man's past made through the examination of things that he has left behind. These remains are found by digging in the places where ancient towns or burial grounds once were located. Bowls, baskets, tools, tablets of writing, jewelry, and many things of this kind give valuable clues to the history of the people. Archaeologists have made important discoveries that have helped in an understanding of biblical history.

ARCHANGEL. As used in the Bible, a chief angel. *I Thessalonians 4:16; Jude 1:9.*

ARCHIVES, HOUSE OF THE. Meaning "house of books." In the OT, the house of the archives was the place where historical documents, public records, and probably worn-out scrolls were stored. *Ezra 5:17–6:1.*

AREOPAGUS. A rocky hill in Athens, Greece. It is also the name for a council or court that met there in NT times. Paul was taken to the Areopagus for questioning about his teaching. *Acts 17:19.*

ARIMATHEA. A town where the Jewish official Joseph lived. After the crucifixion of Jesus, Joseph asked for the body, and he took it and buried it in his own tomb. The location of the town is uncertain. *Matthew 27:57-60; Mark 15:43-46; Luke 23:50-53; John 19:38.*

ARISTARCHUS. A Gentile Christian from Thessalonica who was closely associated with Paul from the time of Paul's missionary journey in Macedonia until Paul's death. Tradition says Aristarchus was martyred in Rome under the emperor Nero. *Acts 19:29; 20:4; Colossians 4:10; Philemon 1:24.*

ARK OF NOAH. In the OT account a floating vessel like a houseboat in which Noah, his family, and at least one pair each of all living creatures took refuge during the Great Flood. *Genesis 6:14–8:19.*

ARK OF THE COVENANT. A box or chest of acacia wood overlaid

ARMLET

with gold. It was too holy to be touched and so was carried by priests and Levites on poles. Inside the ark the stone tablets containing the Ten Commandments were kept. On the ark was the mercy seat, which represented the throne of God and signified his presence and guidance. For this reason the Israelites carried it with them during their wanderings in the wilderness and when they went into battle. Later when Solomon built the temple in Jerusalem, the ark was placed in it. *Exodus 25:10-22; Numbers 10:35-36; Deuteronomy 10:1-5; I Samuel 4:4–7:2; I Kings 8:6-21; II Chronicles 5:2-10.*

ARMLET. In the OT a metal ring or band worn on the upper arm as jewelry. Armlets were worn by kings and other persons in authority. *Exodus 35:22; Numbers 31:50; II Samuel 1:10; Isaiah 3:20.*

ARMOR OF GOD. A figurative, or pictorial, way of speaking of the protection God gives the faithful to stand against evil. Armor was actually part of the protective equipment of a soldier. It consisted of helmet, girdle, shield, breastplate, mail, and leg guards. These protected the soldier from the blows of his enemies. The armor of God refers to truth, righteousness, peace, faith, and prayer, which strengthen a person to stand against evil. *Ephesians 6:11, 13.*

ARTAXERXES. King of Persia who reigned in the fifth century B.C. It was this king who gave Ezra permission to go to Jerusalem. Later Artaxerxes stopped the reconstruction of Jerusalem for a while. But he later permitted Nehemiah, his cupbearer, to go to Jerusalem to direct the rebuilding. Artaxerxes decreed that exiles in Babylonia could freely return to Jerusalem. *Ezra 4:11-13, 23-24; 7:1, 7-8, 11-26; Nehemiah 2:1.*

ARTEMIS. A goddess worshiped more widely than any other goddess in the Greek world. She was called Diana by the Romans. The NT mentions "silver shrines of Artemis" made in the city of Ephesus by Demetrius, a worker in silver. These were probably small silver pieces made to resemble the shrine of the goddess. The temple to Artemis of the Ephesians was an elaborate building, one of the wonders of the ancient world. It contained a "sacred stone that fell from the sky," which was probably a meteorite. *Acts 19:23-40.*

ASA. King of Judah from about 911 to 870 B.C. He undertook to rid the land of idols and incense altars to foreign gods, and to restore the worship of the Lord to its rightful place among the Hebrews. *I Kings 15:9-24; II Chronicles 14:1–16:14.*

ASCENTS, SONG OF. Title of Psalms 120–34. Probably the songs the people chanted when going up to Jerusalem at festival times or in procession going up to the temple. The word *ascent* means "a going up."

ASHDOD. One of the five principal cities of the Philistines in OT times. At one time the ark of the covenant was captured by the Philistines and brought to Ashdod and placed beside the pagan god Dagon. *Joshua 13:3; I Samuel 5:1-8; II Chronicles 26:6.*

ASHERAH. Hebrew name for an Amorite or Canaanite goddess associated with the worship of Baal. The word also means an image of Asherah. *Judges 6:25-30; II Kings 23:4; II Chronicles 33:3.*

ASHKELON. One of the five principal cities of the Philistines in OT times. It was the only one located on the shores of the Mediterranean Sea. The Israelites captured and held Ashkelon for a brief time. *Joshua 13:3; Judges 1:18; I Samuel 6:17; II Samuel 1:20.*

ASPALATHUS. This is a thorny shrub, growing from four to five feet high with narrow leaves along the stem. The very fragrant white and pink blossoms are shaped somewhat like the morning glory. From it was derived ointment and perfume. The writer of Ecclesiasticus (24:15) refers to it: "I gave a sweet smell like cinnamon and aspalathus."

ASS. The ass, mentioned over 130 times in the Bible, was probably the most useful of all domestic animals to the Israelites. Because of its ability to thrive on a minimum of food, even a poor family might own an ass. It was used as a pack animal, for working in the fields, and for transportation. Yet it was also a measure of wealth. Pharoah's gift to Abraham was many asses (Genesis 12:16). Job counted "five hundred she-asses" among his possessions (Job 1:3) which later (Job 42:12) had multiplied to "one thousand."

The ass of biblical times was a larger and more stately animal than the ass, or donkey, of today. It was usually tawny in color, the occassional white

ass being greatly prized. Although once used in warfare, the horse superseded it in this capacity and the ass became a symbol of peace. Thus it was most fitting that the Prince of Peace should enter Jerusalem that first Palm Sunday riding on a lowly ass.

ASSYRIA. An ancient civilization in Mesopotamia east of the Tigris River. The territory now lies within the borders of Iraq. The Assyrians had many kings who were able military leaders. These people were noted for their cruelty to their captives, often skinning them alive. The Assyrian armies with their horses and chariots often invaded the lands of the Israelites. The Assyrians achieved a strong empire which dominated the world in the eighth century B.C. (See map on page 112.) At this time they destroyed the northern kingdom of Israel and deported the people into other countries. *II Kings 17:1-6; 18:13–19:36; Psalm 83:8.*

ASTRAGAL. This spiny dwarf shrub yields the "gum tragacanth" of commerce. It has pale yellow pealike flowers and long, needle-sharp thorns that point in all directions. There are many varieties, some found on the shores of the Dead Sea, others growing high up on the summit of Mount Hermon.

ATHALIAH. Wife of Jehoram (Joram) and daughter of Ahab and Jezebel. She reigned as queen over the northern kingdom of Israel from about 797 to 792 B.C. She was a worshiper of Baal and seems to have had much influence over the life of Israel

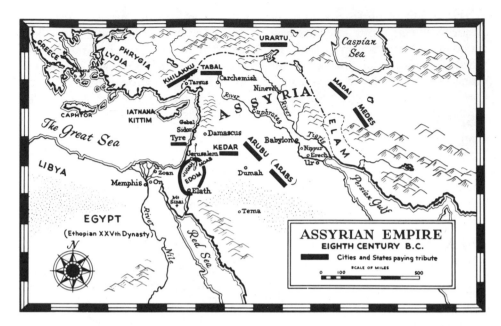

ASSYRIAN EMPIRE
EIGHTH CENTURY B.C.
Cities and States paying tribute
SCALE OF MILES
0   100   500

as the power behind the throne of her son Ahaziah. She seized the throne when he died. The OT account gives the picture of a cold-blooded and ruthless woman. There was a revolt against her led by the priest Jehoida. He and his wife had taken the infant son of Ahaziah and hidden him away. They raised him in secret and had him anointed king when he was seven years old. *II Kings 11:1-21; II Chronicles 22:10-15.*

ATHENS. Chief city of the ancient district of Attica, now the capital of modern Greece. In NT times Paul visited this old city and spoke in the marketplace and in the Areopagus (see *Areopagus*). *Acts 17:15-22; 18:1; I Thessalonians 3:1.*

ATONEMENT. The achievement of a state of harmony, or the overcoming of conflict or separation. In the biblical accounts, the Hebrews were deeply conscious of man's separation from God due to man's sin. The Hebrews made sacrifices and offerings to the Lord to achieve reconciliation. These sacrifices, usually animals, symbolized the unworthiness of the person who made the offering and also his desire to be united with God. (See *Reconcile, Reconciliation.*) *Exodus 29:33; Leviticus 4:20; 16:1-22; 23:27-28; Numbers 29:11; Nehemiah 10:32-33.*

ATONEMENT, DAY OF. For the Hebrews a day of fasting and repentance. In OT times this was the one day of the year when the most holy place of the temple was entered, and then only by the high priest. Here he sprinkled the blood of a sacrifice to atone for the sins of all the people. As a symbol that the people were

cleansed of their sins, a goat, called the scapegoat, was led through the wilderness and pushed over a precipice. Still a most solemn holy day for Jews everywhere, the Day of Atonement (Yom Kippur) comes in the autumn. *Leviticus 16:1-34; 25:9.*

AUGUSTUS CAESAR. Founder of the Roman Empire and ruler over it when Jesus Christ was born. *Luke 2:1.*

AUROCH (Urus). The huge auroch, or "urus," was also known as the "wild ox." Familiar to the Israelites, the animal was unknown to the translators of Hebrew Scripture some 1500 years later. To them the many references to the very large horns of the animal (Deuteronomy 33:17; Psalm 22:21; Isaiah 34:7) led these scholars to believe that the Hebrew writers referred to the unicorn. Hence "unicorn" in most references very likely should be "auroch."

Probably the auroch is the only "extinct" animal to be "re-created." The last known auroch died in Poland over three hundred years ago. Zoologists, knowing much about the animal, reconstructed it by what might be called reverse cross-breeding of cattle believed to be ancestors of the auroch. Thus this huge animal of the far distant past, or a very close copy, lives again.

AZARIAH. See *Uzziah.*

BAAL. A Canaanite word which meant "lord." The Canaanites called their chief god Baal, but there were many less important gods also known as Baals. These were connected with a particular place. The high places and the pagan ceremonies which the OT prophets cried out against were connected with Baal worship. The Israelites were often tempted by Baal worship. Jezebel, King Ahab's wife, tried to persuade Ahab to make the worship of Baal the official religion of Israel. The names of many places in Palestine were combined with Baal to indicate that the place belonged to the god. Some of the Hebrews even called their children by names ending in Baal, such as Eshbaal and Meribbaal (see *I Chronicles 8:33-34). Deuteronomy 4:1-3; Judges 2:11-13; 8:33; I Kings 16:31-32; Psalm 106:28; Hosea 2:17.*

BAASHA. King of the northern kingdom of Israel about 909 to 886 B.C. He became king following the reign of Nadab, whom he murdered during a military campaign against the Philistines. He reigned at Tirzah, which was the capital of the northern kingdom before Omri built up Samaria. *I Kings 15:27-30, 33; 16:1-7.*

BABEL. The Hebrew form of the name Babylon. Also, a play on a Hebrew word meaning "to mix." The OT account of the tower of Babel tells how the people of the world, after the Great Flood, gathered on a plain to build for themselves a city and unite. They decided to make a tower that would reach to heaven. This was the occasion for the mixing of their languages so that they no longer understood one another. It is interesting to note that the Babylonians

worshiped their god Marduk in a tower-like structure. *Genesis 11:1-9.*

BABOON. The baboon is not mentioned in the Bible, and like the ape and other monkeys, it never lived in Palestine. Since it is quite likely that baboons were included in the exotic cargo brought to King Solomon's court from India and Africa, they may well have been known to the Hebrew people. Certainly the generations that lived in Egypt knew them, for the Egyptians looked upon the baboon with near reverence, sufficient reason for the Israelites to ignore the creature in their Scriptures. However, some scholars believe that the word *peacock* in I Kings 10:22 should be translated "baboon."

BABYLON. A ancient city of Mesopotamia whose ruins are situated on the lower Euphrates River. It lies southwest of Baghdad in modern Iraq. Babylon was the capital city of the great Babylonian Empire under King Nebuchadnezzar. When Nebuchadnezzar captured Judah, the Hebrew people were taken as captives to Babylonia. *II Kings 24:1-25:30.*

BACKSLIDING. A term used by the prophets to describe the Hebrew people's rejection of and disobedience to God. The word means "sliding back from" or "turning away from" what the people knew to be right. *Isaiah 57:17; Jeremiah 8:5.*

BADGER. See *Hyrax.*

BALAAM. A prophet in early OT times. When Balak, king of Moab, feared an invasion of the Israelites, he summoned Balaam to pronounce a curse on them. Instead Balaam, even though he was not an Israelite, uttered a blessing as God commanded him. There is also a story about Balaam's talking donkey. NT references to Balaam are unfavorable. *Numbers 22:5–24:25; 31:8, 16; Deuteronomy 23:4-5; Joshua 13:22; 24:9-10; Nehemiah 13:2; Micah 6:5; II Peter 2:15; Jude 1:11; Revelation 2:14.*

BALANCES. A type of scale made by hanging two pans from each end of a beam which is balanced by being suspended on a cord or from a shaft. To weigh metal or grain, blocks or stones of a given size were put in one pan and the material to be weighed in the other. Material or weights were added until the pans hung evenly. Hebrew law required honest balances. The term is used as a figure of speech in Hebrew poetry to express the idea that man must be "weighed," or measured, against the standards of goodness. *Leviticus 19:35-36; Isaiah 40:12; Amos 8:5; Daniel 5:27.*

BALSAM. A low-growing tree, the balsam is native to southern Arabia. It is said that the Queen of Sheba brought seeds to King Solomon who had groves of balsam planted so that the fragrant and medicinal "balm" made from the sap of the tree might be available. The "balm of Gilead," mentioned several times in the Old Testament (Jeremiah 8:22; Ezekiel 27:17), is believed by many to be this product of the balsam.

BANKING. The business of making loans, receiving deposits of money,

and changing the money of one nation to the money of another. In NT times bankers carried on their business at tables in the marketplace. *Matthew 25:27; Luke 19:23.*

BANNER. A sign, symbol, or standard held high on a pole as the emblem of a tribe (see Numbers 2:10). Troops of soldiers used banners rather like flags to rally the men and trumpets were sounded when the banners were raised or paraded (see Isaiah 18:3). The Egyptians, Assyrians, Babylonians, Persians, and Romans all had banners which they carried. The eagle was used on the banners of imperial Rome; the god Asher drawing a bow was used on the banners of Assyria. *Exodus 17:15-16; Song of Solomon 6:4, 10; Jeremiah 50:2.*

BANQUET. A meal consisting of large quantities of rich foods. The prophet Amos described banquet customs in OT times when guests would eat lying on beds, or couches, of ivory (see Amos 6:4-6). Banquets were held on many occasions such as harvests, birthdays, weddings, and important national occasions like the crowning of a king or the signing of a treaty. *Esther 1:1-9; 2:18; Mark 6:21; Luke 14:12-24.*

BAPTISM. A ceremonial act using water to symbolize washing or making pure in the sight of God. In the NT John the Baptist used baptism as a sign of repentance. Later Jesus' disciples used baptism as an outward sign of belief in Jesus Christ and the new, clean life of faith. This ceremony

Assyrian standards

Roman standards

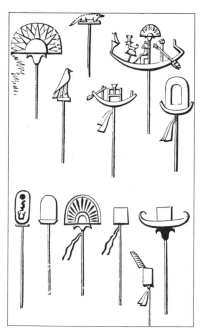

Standards used in ancient Egypt

marks a person's acceptance into the fellowship of the Christian community. Most Christian churches baptize either by sprinkling water on the head, by immersion where the whole body is lowered under the water, or by pouring water over the head or body. *Matthew 28:18-20; Mark 1:4-5, 9-11; Luke 3:3; Acts 2:37-38, 41; 8:12; 16:14-15.*

BARABBAS. A prisoner of the Roman authorities at the time of Jesus' trial. The Roman rulers made it a practice at times, especially on holidays, to please the people by freeing a prisoner. During the feast of the Passover, Jesus and Barabbas were among those from whom one was to be chosen. The people, urged on by the chief priests and other leaders, chose Barabbas to be set free. Jesus was crucified. *Matthew 27:15-21; Mark 15:6-15; Luke 23:18-19; John 18:39-40.*

BARAK. A Hebrew leader during the time of the judges, who with the prophetess Deborah led an Israelite army in a victorious campaign against the Canaanites. Barak is also mentioned in a NT list of ancient people whose faithfulness was commendable. *Judges 4:6–5:15; Hebrews 11:32.*

BARBARIAN. Originally someone who spoke a different language; in the NT the word means "foreigner"—someone neither Greek nor Jew. Paul used the term *barbarian* when he said that he was under obligation to preach the gospel to all mankind. *Romans 1:14; Colossians 3:11.*

BARBARY SHEEP. See *Aoudad.*

BARLEY. An important grain or cereal in Bible times that was cheaper than wheat and ripened earlier. It was used as food for animals and humans and was especially important to the poor. At the beginning of the barley harvest, the people brought a sheaf of the first fruits to the priest (see Leviticus 23:10-14) as a dedication of the entire harvest. *Exodus 9:31; Deuteronomy 8:7-10; Judges 7:13; Ruth 1:22; 2:17; II Samuel 17:27-29; I Kings 4:28; II Kings 7:1, 16, 18; II Chronicles 2:10, 15.*

BARNABAS. One of the first men in Jerusalem to accept Christianity. His first home was on the island of Cyprus. After the crucifixion of Jesus, Barnabas worked with the apostles and later became a leader of the Antioch church. He introduced Paul to the disciples in Jerusalem and was Paul's companion on several missionary journeys. His name meant "son of encouragement," and his work was important in his homeland of Cyprus. *Acts 4:36-37; 9:26-30; 11:22-30; 13:1-4; and other places in Acts; I Corinthians 9:6; Galatians 2:1, 9, 13.*

BARRACKS. Buildings for lodging soldiers. In the NT these were headquarters of Roman officers stationed in Jerusalem. Paul was taken to the barracks for protection when he was seized in Jerusalem. *Acts 21:30-37; 22:24; 23:10, 16, 32.*

BARTHOLOMEW. One of the twelve apostles. His name meant "son of Talmai." He may also have been known as Nathanael (see John 1:45-51). In the Armenian church there is a tradition that the gospel was

brought to Armenia by Thaddeus and Bartholomew. *Matthew 10:3; Mark 3:18; Luke 6:14; Acts 1:13.*

BARTIMAEUS. A blind beggar of Jericho. He was healed by Jesus. *Mark 10:46-52.*

BARUCH. Scribe or secretary to the prophet Jeremiah. It is likely that some of the scrolls which Jeremiah dictated to Baruch are part of the book of Jeremiah. Baruch may also have written some of the material himself. *Jeremiah 32:12-16; 36:4-32.*

BASHAN. A wide, fertile plain in the northern part of the land east of the Jordan River A seminomadic people called Amorites or Westerners settled here in 2000 B.C. The area was well suited for growing wheat and raising cattle, and reference to this often appears in the poetry of the Bible. Bashan was taken by the Israelites and divided among the tribes of Israel. *Deuteronomy 3:1-14; Joshua 9:9-10; I Kings 4:13 19; II Kings 10:32-33; I Chronicles 5:11; Psalms 22:12; 68:15, 22; Isaiah 2:13; Amos 4:1.*

BASILISK. This fabulous creature, half snake and half cock, a product of a superstitious imagination, was "looked upon" with terror by many of the ancients. According to legend, the glance of the basilisk was sufficient to cause death. It was the symbol of the devil, a natural interpretation of Psalm 91:13, which in the Douay version reads, "Thou shalt tread upon the adder and the basilisk."

BASIN. A bowl-like vessel of any size. The words *basin* and *bowl* are often used to indicate the same thing in the Bible. Basins of many sizes and types were used in making sacrifices. These vessels were also used for table service and for cleaning, much as they are used today. Small bowls were placed on tables for washing before meals. Water was poured from a pitcher over the hands and caught in the bowls. Basins were placed at the doors of houses for washing dusty feet before entering. *Exodus 12:22; 24:6; Numbers 4:14; 7:84; John 13:5.*

BAT. We know the bat to be a flying mammal, but it is not strange that the ancient writers thought of it as a bird and so included it with the stork, the heron, and the lapwing as unclean fowl (Leviticus 11:19). There are over a dozen species of bats in Palestine, living in caves and old buildings where they hang upside down through the day, flying out at night to frighten nervous humans, as is the case the world over. Isaiah, writing of "the day of the Lord," could think of nothing more degrading for the fate of the "idols of silver and gold" in "the last days" than that they be cast "to the moles and the bats" (Isaiah 2:20).

BATHSHEBA. The beautiful wife of Uriah, a soldier in the army of King David. The king desired to make Bathsheba his wife, and so he ordered that Uriah be put in a dangerous spot in battle so that he would be killed. When this happened, David took the woman as his own wife. The prophet Nathan condemned this sinful affair. Solomon, who later became king, was the son of Bathsheba and David. (See

117

The Bible Companion

Solomon.) II Samuel 11:1-17, 26-27; I Kings 1:11-40; 2:13-25.

BATTERING RAM. An antique engine of warfare. It was used by the Assyrians. The battering ram was a large pole with a heavy head supported in a framework set on wheels so that it could be rammed against the gates and walls of a city to break them down (see II Samuel 20:15). *Ezekiel 4:2; 21:22; 26:9.*

BAY TREE. David's reference to the "green bay tree" (Psalm 37:35) as a symbol of the spreading power of the wicked is an apt illustration. Actually the "spreading" is from the many shoots that sprout near the main stem. It is the "laurel" later used by Rome for the crown awarded the victors in sports and in war.

BDELLIUM. According to Genesis 2:12 bdellium was planted in the Garden of Eden. It is an ancient tree having small, inconspicuous blossoms and long thorns. From it comes a fragrant gum which, hardening on exposure to the air, forms almost transparent globules with a whitish tinge. Hence the reference in Numbers 11:7, "the manna was as coriander seed, and the color thereof as the color of bdellium."

BEAN. The bean is an ancient vegetable and has long been a staple article of diet in the Middle East. The bean referred to in II Samuel 17:28 was not unlike the bush bean known to present day gardeners; though more robust, sometimes growing to a height of two or three feet. The familiar pea-shaped blossoms are white with a black spot on some of the petals. The system of voting with white and black balls, still used in some places, originated in ancient times when beans were used. Then, as now, white showed approval, black signified a "no" vote.

BEAR. Though bears are now rare in Palestine, found only occasionally in the mountains of Lebanon, they were numerous in biblical times. The Syrian bear, indigenous to the area, may grow to six feet in length and weigh up to five hundred pounds. It has a prominent forehead, short paws, and long claws. As a cub it is dark brown, but as it matures it becomes a yellowish brown, and in its old age it is a dirty white.

Though they rarely attack a person without provocation, they are extremely dangerous when aroused. Evidently Hushai knew this when he reminded Absalom that his father David and his followers were, when enraged, like "a bear robbed of her whelps" (II Samuel 17:8).

BEARD. The hair growing on a man's face. Hebrew men wore full

Upper row: Egyptian beards; lower row: beards of other nations

beards and cut them only in times of mourning. The Egyptians and Romans shaved their faces, and the pharaohs sometimes wore artificial beards. *Leviticus 14:9; 19:27; II Samuel 19:24; Isaiah 7:20; 15:2.*

BEARDED VULTURE. See *Lammergier.*

BEATEN OIL. The high quality olive oil made by crushing ripe olives in a mortar. This oil was used in the lamp in the sanctuary and with the daily sacrifices. *Exodus 27:20; 29:40; I Kings 5:11.*

BEATITUDE. A form of writing which begins with the word *blessed.* There are beatitudes in the OT and NT, but the most familiar are those in the Sermon on the Mount. (See Psalms 1:1; 119:1-2; Isaiah 56:2; Matthew 5:3-12.)

BEE. The bee is the smallest "domestic animal" in the world. Beekeeping was common in Egypt as far back as 4000 B.C. Honey was used for embalming since it was the least expensive ingredient. And of course its food value was well known. The Hebrews evidently took their knowledge of beekeeping with them when they left Egypt since Ezekiel lists honey as one of the chief exports of Judah (Ezekiel 27:17). Some of this might well have been wild honey, for wild honeybees were, and are, common in Palestine. But it is quite certain that Palestinian farmers kept domestic honeybees, selling both honey and beeswax.

Evidence that the potency of an attack of angry bees was well known is found in Deuteronomy 1:44 and in Psalm 118:12. In both references the attack of enemies is likened to an attack by a swarm of bees.

BEE EATER. The bee eater, or bee catcher as it is sometimes called, is aptly named since its preferred diet is bees. It is a close relative of the kingfisher, though somewhat smaller. There are several species. The most common is gaily colored with feathers of green, blue, and brown. An unusual characteristic, and one which makes the bee eater easily identifiable, is the tail feathers, two of which project noticeably from the middle of the tail.

BEELZEBUL. A name for Satan, also spelled Beelzebub. *Matthew 10:25; 12:24, 27; Mark 3:22; Luke 11:15, 18-19.*

BEER. A word meaning "well" that is often used in combination with place names as in the name Beersheba. Also the place where the Israelites dug a well which offered such an adequate water supply that the people sang praises to it. *Numbers 21:16-18; Judges 9:21.*

BEER-SHEBA. The principal city of the Negeb in the southern part of Palestine. In the time of Abraham a religious sanctuary was located there. Beer-sheba was at the southern tip of the Israelite country while Dan was at the northern tip, so the expression "from Dan to Beer-sheba" meant the entire nation. There is an important modern city just west of the old site. (See *Beer.*) *Genesis 21:25-33; 26:32-33; 46:1, 5; Judges 20:1; I Samuel 3:20; 8:2; I Kings 4:25; 19:3; II Kings 12:1; Nehemiah 11:27,30.*

BEHEMOTH. Job's mention and description of "behemoth" (Job 40:15-24) has raised speculation among scholars as to just what animal he referred to. It was once thought that the elephant was meant. Now it is generally agreed that the description of its habitat, its great size and strength, its feeding and drinking habits best fit the hippopotamus. The behemoth is the subject of many legends in Hebrew folklore, a mythical creature along with the unicorn and the cockatrice.

BELIAL. Meaning worthless or ungodly. In the OT it is used in such Hebrew expressions as son, daughter, or man of Belial and is translated as "worthless one," or something similar. (See I Samuel 2:12; Job 34:18.) In the NT it refers to Satan or an enemy of Christ. *II Corinthians 6:15.*

BENEDICTION. A prayer for God's blessing. Several NT letters close with benedictions. *Numbers 6:24-26; Romans 15:13; II Corinthians 13:14; Hebrews 13:20-21.*

BENJAMIN. A son of Jacob for whom one of the twelve tribes of Israel was named. As a son of Rachel, the favored wife, he was especially loved by his father. The name also refers to the territory occupied by the Benjamites. *Genesis 35:16-18, 24; 42:4, 36; 43:14-16, 34; 44:12; 45:12, 14, 22; Joshua 18:11-20.*

BETHANY. A small village just under two miles from Jerusalem near the Mount of Olives. It was the home of Mary, Martha, and Lazarus, close friends of Jesus with whom he sometimes stayed. *Matthew 21:17; 26:6; Mark 11:1, 11-12; 14:3; Luke 24:50; John 11:1, 18.*

BETHEL. Meaning "house of God." A city of major importance mentioned in the OT. It was located on a major road running along the ridge where the territories of Ephraim and Benjamin met. When Abraham stopped near Bethel, he built an altar to God. There years later, Jacob's name was changed to Israel. *Genesis 12:8; 13:3; 28:10-22; 31:13; 35:1-15; Judges 1:22-26; 20:18-28; I Kings 12:28-33; II Kings 2:2-3; I Chronicles 7:28; II Chronicles 13:19; Amos 7:12-13.*

BETHLEHEM. A town in Judah about six miles south of Jerusalem. Most of the story in the book of Ruth took place in and near Bethlehem. It was also the home of David. It is best known as the birthplace of Jesus. *Genesis 35:19; Judges 17:7-9; Ruth 1:1-2, 19, 22; 2:4; 4:11; I Samuel 16:14, 18; 17:12, 15; 20:6, 28; II Samuel 23:14-16; I Chronicles 11:16-18; II Chronicles 11:6; Micah 5:2; Matthew 2:1-16; John 7:42.*

BETHLEHEM STAR. Though its half dozen elongated yellow petals forming a "star" appear fragile, the Bethlehem star is a hardy plant. It favors northern exposures and grows in damp, stony ground, blossoming in early winter. This plant is not to be confused with the Star of Bethlehem.

BETHPHAGE. A village near Jerusalem, probably east of Bethany. The name means "house of unripe figs," referring to a kind of figs which never looks ripe, even when ready to eat. Bethphage is mentioned in the report

of Palm Sunday, that is, Jesus' entry into Jerusalem the week before he was crucified. Bethphage was probably the village where the disciples found the colt on which Jesus rode into the city. *Matthew 21:1; Mark 11:1; Luke 19:29.*

BETH-SAIDA. Meaning "house of the fisher," it was a town in NT times, located on the shore of the Sea of Galilee. Beth-saida is mentioned several times in connection with the ministry of Jesus, and it was probably close to this town that the feeding of five thousand people with the loaves and fishes took place. *Matthew 11:21; Mark 6:45; 8:22; Luke 9:10-17; John 1:44.*

BEZALEL. A skilled and inspired craftsman from the tribe of Judah who was put in charge of making the tabernacle in the wilderness and the ark, altars, tables, and other equipment. He created artistic designs in metal, stone, and wood for decorating the ancient sanctuary. His name means "in the shadow or protection of God." (See *Tabernacle, Ark of the Covenant.*) *Exodus 31:1-5; 35:30–36:2; 37:1; 38:22; I Chronicles 2:20; II Chronicles 1:5.*

BIRTHRIGHT. The special rights and privileges of the firstborn or eldest son. In OT times the eldest son inherited more of his father's wealth than did his younger brothers and became head of the family after his father's death (see *Firstborn*). The OT reports that Jacob deceived his father to obtain the birthright that was rightly his brother's. In the NT Paul's Roman citizenship is mentioned as

his birthright (see Acts 22:28). *Genesis 25:29-34; 43:33; Hebrews 12:16.*

BITTER HERBS. Herbs eaten with lamb during the Passover as a reminder of the bitter experience of the Israelites during the Exodus. Horseradish is the herb commonly used with lamb when Jews eat the Passover meal today. *Exodus 12:8.*

BITTERN. A shy, solitary bird, and a night prowler, the bittern lives in swampy places where its mottled and striped back of a black and brown color pattern provides excellent camouflage. Unlike most birds of the heron family, of which it is a member, its neck is short. Nor has it the long, wading legs of the heron. The unusually powerful call of the male bittern can be heard a mile away.

References to the bittern in Isaiah (14:23) and in Zephaniah (2:14) imply that Babylon and Nineveh were to become as desolate as the swamps in which the bittern lives and sounds its eerie cry.

BITUMEN. Mineral tar asphalt found in wells. Bitumen was mentioned in the OT story of the Tower of Babel as being used for mortar in the building of a city on the Plain of Shinar. It was also used to seal and waterproof the basket of bulrushes in which the infant Moses was placed. *Genesis 11:3; 14:10; Exodus 2:3.*

BLACKBIRD. The blackbird of the Holy Land is a different bird than our well-known variety. It is nearer brown than black and belongs to the thrush family.

The Bible Companion

BLASPHEMY. Any dishonoring of the name of God by slandering, cursing, or an act of irreverence. For the Hebrews the name of God was so sacred that it could be spoken only with great reverence, and to use the name of God for a wrong or foolish purpose was a serious sin. In the NT some of the religious leaders of the Jews accused Jesus of blasphemy because he spoke of a familiar relationship with God. In the early church blasphemy included active interference with the preaching of the gospel of Jesus Christ. *Leviticus 24:11; I Samuel 3:13; Nehemiah 9:18-19; Matthew 12:31; 26:63-65; Mark 14:61-64; John 10:33-36; Romans 2:24; I Timothy 1:12-13; James 2:7.*

BLESSED. To be favored with spiritual happiness. In the OT the term usually included in its meaning long life and prosperity in harmony with God and his law. When "blessed" is applied to God, it is an exclamation of worship. In the NT "blessed" is used for faithful Christians, especially those who suffer for their faithfulness. (See *Beatitude.*) *Genesis 48:14-15; II Samuel 6:11; Psalms 1:1-2; 28:6; Matthew 13:16; 16:17; Luke 6:20-23; I Timothy 1:11; 6:15; James 1:12.*

BLIND. Without sight. The blind had a difficult life in Bible times. They could only beg for a living. Many times people considered that such afflictions were caused by sin, so the blind were often outcasts. *Leviticus 19:14; Deuteronomy 27:18; Luke 4:18-19; John 9:1-41.*

BLOODGUILT. The guilt of one who shed the blood of an innocent person, even if the killing was accidental. This guilt could not be atoned for or taken away by offering a sacrifice. By OT law the entire community shared in the bloodguilt, and for this reason everyone helped find the killer and saw that the punishment required by law was carried out. If the killing was intentional, the murderer must die. If accidental, the killer could serve a period of time in a city of refuge. (See *Cities of Refuge.*) *Exodus 22:2-3; Deuteronomy 19:8-10; I Samuel 25:26, 33; Psalm 51:14.*

BOAR, WILD. Though once common in Palestine the only mention of the wild boar in the Bible is in Psalm 80:13. It was a constant menace to farmers since a field of grain or a vineyard might be destroyed by wild boars in a single night. Since the boar is a wild pig, it was unclean by Mosaic law. Hence the farmer who killed the boars ravaging his crops did not have the compensation of using it for food.

It is interesting to note that in Albrecht Durer's painting *The Prodigal Son*, the swine with their tusks resemble the wild boar rather than the domesticated pig.

BOAT. A small open vessel, usually a sailboat and sometimes having oars, used for fishing on the Sea of Galilee. Also a smaller craft used for ferrying across the Jordan River. *Matthew 4:21-22; Mark 3:9; Luke 5:1-3; John 6:22-24.*

BOAZ. A wealthy landowner of Bethlehem. He married Ruth, the Moabitess, and became the great grandfather of David. *Ruth 2:1–4:22; Matthew 1:5.*

BODY. In the OT "body" refers to the whole physical makeup of a person. In the NT the word has added spiritual meanings. Jesus used bread as a symbol of his body. Paul talked about disciplining the body because physical desires often interfere with a person's good intentions. The church is called the body of Christ. *Job 14:)2; Psalm 109:24; Matthew 6:22; 26:26; Luke 12:22-23; I Corinthians 6:19; 10:16-17; 12:12-27; Ephesians 2:3; James 3:2-3.*

BOOK. In Bible times a strip of leather or papyrus upon which were written laws history, stories, prophecies and other literary compositions. These were rolled up and often sealed. Several books which are not part of the Bible are mentioned by name in the OT, for example the "Book of Jashar." *Exodus 24:7; Joshua 10:13; II Kings 22:8; II Chronicles 27:7.*

BOOTHS, FEAST OF. One of Israel's three great festivals. It was celebrated with joy and thanksgiving at the end of the harvest season. Each family built a booth of branches and vines as the harvest time approached. The father and older son slept in it to guard the ripening grain. At the time of the feast the family ate meals in the booth for seven days. The celebration also recalled the wilderness life of the Israelites during their long journey from Egypt to Canaan. The festival is also known as the Feast of Tabernacles, the Feast of Ingathering, and the Feast of the Lord. *Leviticus 23:34, 39-43; Deuteronomy 16:13-17; Ezra 3:4; Nehemiah 8:13-18; Zechariah 14:16-19.*

BOW AND ARROW. A weapon used by hunters and warriors. In Bible times the bow was made of wood or bone with a gut or hide string. The arrows were made of a shaft of reed or light wood to which a pointed head of flint, bone, or metal was fastened. Sometimes the arrows were given barbs or dipped in poison to make them more painful or deadly. *Genesis 21:20; Isaiah 7:24; Hosea 1:7.*

BRAMBLE. The Palestinian bramble (Judges 9:14) is similar to our common blackberry. It is just as strong a grower with equally numerous sharp thorns. The blossoms have a pinkish tinge. The delicious berries are a deep purple.

BREAD. An important item of food made from wheat or barley flour, mixed with water, kneaded, and baked. People who were wandering nomads did not have much bread since they did not raise the grain needed to make flour or meal. However, for settled people of all periods in history, bread has been a basic food. This was true in OT and NT times. Bread also had a religious use. In OT times the Hebrews made offerings of flour alone or of loaves. In NT times it was unleavened bread that Jesus used as a symbol of his body. *Genesis 14:18; 18:5-6; 41:54; Leviticus 23:17; Psalm 104:15; Mark 14:22; Luke 22:19.*

BREAD OF THE PRESENCE. Also called showbread. Twelve loaves of bread made of fine flour, arranged in two rows on a table in the temple or sanctuary as an offering to God. The

number twelve suggested the twelve tribes of Israel. Fresh loaves were brought each sabbath, and the old loaves were eaten by the priests (see Leviticus 24:5-9). This offering of holy bread was required to be in the sanctuary continually. *Exodus 25:30; I Samuel 21:6; I Kings 7:48; I Chronicles 9:32; II Chronicles 4:19; 13:11; Matthew 12:1-4.*

Table of the bread of the Presence of Herod's Temple, from the Arch of Titus

BREASTPIECE. An ornamental piece of folded material attached by golden rings to the ephod, a garment worn by the high priest in the sanctuary. It had four rows of three jewels each, set in gold. Each jewel represented one of the tribes of Israel. This pouchlike piece carried the Urim and Thummim (probably stones and sticks of uneven lengths) with which the priest, in the early days, determined by lot God's judgments on the people. (See *Ephod, Urim and Thummim.*) *Exodus 28:4, 15-30.*

BREASTPLATE. A piece of armor made of solid metal, attached to or worn over a tunic to protect the chest, shoulders, and back of a soldier.

Before the use of metal, leather or padded cloth was used. *I Kings 22:34; II Chronicles 18:33; Isaiah 59:17; Ephesians 6:14; I Thessalonians 5:8.*

BRETHREN. Meaning "brothers." Fellow members of a tribe in OT usage. The descendants of Abraham were considered one family, and therefore all Hebrews were brothers. In the NT Jesus looked upon all who had faith in him and who wanted to do God's will as his brothers. Paul addressed the people in the Christian churches as brethren. *Joshua 17:4; Judges 20:13; Matthew 12:46-50; I Corinthians 1:10-13; Galatians 6:1-5.*

BRICK. The most common building material of the Bible lands. Clay was shaped into blocks and dried in the sun or in an oven called a kiln. During their stay in Egypt the Hebrews were forced to make bricks of clay, bound with straw, for the pharaoh. *Exodus 1:14; 5:7-19.*

BROOM. A desert shrub or bush with pale pink flowers like pea blossoms. It frequently grows large enough to offer shade. Its roots and foilage burn with intense heat and make a fine charcoal. *I Kings 19:5, Job 30:4; Psalm 120:4.*

BUBAL. The bubal, or hartebeest, is one of several species of antelope found in parts of the Middle East. The Arabs call it a "wild cow." In ancient times it lived in the arid regions of Egypt and probably as far as northern Arabia and into southern Palestine.

Since the bubal seems to have been the only animal of the deer or the antelope family to survive in these

arid regions, this may have been the source of the venison that Esau brought to Isaac (Genesis 25:28). The bubal would have been an important source of meat for the wandering Children of Israel.

BUCKLER. A shield. The words *shield* and *buckler* were used to refer to the same thing. In OT times it was a small, movable guard made of leather or metal and carried in the hand or worn on one arm of a soldier while he carried his weapon in the other. With this movable shield the soldier protected parts of his body not covered with armor and warded off the blows and weapons of his enemies. The terms *shield* and *buckler* were sometimes used as figures of speech for God's protection and his truth. (See *Armor of God.*) I Kings 10:16-17; II Chronicles 14:8; Psalms 35:2; 91:4.

BULBUL. The Hebrews discovered that the bulbul was an easy bird to tame, and with a pleasing song. They kept them in cages outside the doors of their homes, much as we keep canaries and "love birds" today. The bulbul is rather a handsome bird with shiny black feathers. White around the eyes gives it the appearance of wearing spectacles.

BULL. Since cattle were an important factor in Hebrew living, the bull was a practical necessity. While the Israelites did not deify the bull as did the Egyptians with their bull-formed god Apis, and the Babylonians who worshiped the winged bull-god, some of this obeisance found its way into Hebrew religious literature. A literal translation of "the Mighty One" (Genesis 49:24; Isaiah 1:24) is "Bull of Jacob (Israel)." Horns of the bull adorned the top of the altar in King Solomon's Temple (I Kings 7:44), a practice condemned by the later prophets.

BULRUSH. A kind of reed that grows in swampy places and beside streams. Baskets were woven from bulrushes. It was also called papyrus plant (see Isaiah 18:2), and from it came the earliest known material for the making of paper. *Exodus 2:3.*

BULWARK. A wall or barrier built for defense purposes, sometimes called a rampart. In the OT "bulwark" is used in figures of speech to describe God's protection. The church is sometimes called a bulwark of truth. *Psalm 8:2; Jeremiah 50:15; 51:32; I Timothy 3:15.*

BUSH, THE BURNING. The flaming bush through which Moses became aware of God's presence and his plans for Israel. *Exodus 3:2–4:17.*

CAESAR. The family name of Julius Caesar. The name was taken by his adopted son, Octavius or Octavian, who was also Julius Caesar's grandnephew. Octavian became the first emperor of the Roman Empire, and the title Caesar Augustus was conferred on him by the Roman Senate. The term became the title of all succeeding Roman emperors. Caesar Augustus ruled from 27 B.C. to A.D. 14 and was the emperor when

Jesus was born. Several other Caesars are mentioned in the NT. Caesar Augustus—*Luke 2:1-7; Tiberius Caesar—Mark 12: 14-17; Luke 3:1; 23:2; John 19:12-15;* Claudius Caesar—*Acts 18:2;* Nero (probably)—*Acts 25:8-12; 28:17-19.*

CAESAREA. A city of NT times on the coast of Judea, twenty-three miles south of Mt. Carmel. The city was rebuilt in Greek style by Herod the Great and named in honor of Caesar Augustus. Caesarea was the headquarters of the Roman government in Judea. The city is mentioned in the stories of Paul. *Acts 8:40; 9:30; 10:1, 24; 11:11; 18:22; 21:8; 23:23; 25:13.*

CAESAREA PHILIPPI. A city located in NT times on the southwestern slope of Mt. Hermon in Judea. The city probably controlled a large area around it, for there are references in the NT to districts and villages of Caesarea Philippi. It was here that Jesus asked Peter and the other disciples the question, "But who do you say that I am?" *Matthew 16:13-20; Mark 8:27-30.*

CAIAPHAS. The high priest before whom Jesus was brought to trial (see Mark 14:53; Luke 22:54). He is also named among those who plotted the arrest and crucifixion of Jesus. *Matthew 26:3-4 57; John 11:47-50; 18:13-14.*

CAIN. Eldest son of Adam and Eve. Cain became jealous of his brother Abel and murdered him. He was punished by being exiled from his land. *Genesis 4:1-16.*

CALEB. One of the spies sent into Cannan by Moses to find out more about the land before the people of Israel tried to enter it. *Numbers 13:1-30.*

CALF. Besides reference to the calf as a young cow, it is mentioned many times in the Bible in other connections. Probably the best known is the incident of the golden calf which Aaron had made for the Children of Israel to worship (Exodus 32). Nor were the Hebrew people ever allowed to forget their idolatrous transgression which so aroused the wrath of Moses. The golden calf is cited by the psalmist (Psalm 106:19), by the prophet Hosea (Hosea 8:6), and in the New Testament by Stephen (Acts 6:39-41) in his eloquent speech just before his death. A young calf was deemed an appropriate sin offering.

CALF, GOLDEN. In the OT an image of a bull made of wood and overlaid with gold before which the people made sacrifices and offerings and indulged in heathen celebrations—especially the calf image made by Aaron while the people of Israel camped near Mt. Sinai. It was also called "molten calf." *Exodus 32:3-6; Deuteronomy 9:16,21; II Kings 10:29; 17:16; II Chronicles 11:15; 13:8; Nehemiah 9:18; Psalm 106:19.*

CALYCOTOME. The golden color of the calycotome, a gray, prickly shrub, welcomes spring in most regions of the Holy Land. The fragrant yellow blossoms resemble small orchids. The hairy seedpods, much like peapods, begin to ripen as soon as the petals fall, the ripening continuing

through the dry summer months. Though used extensively for fencing and for fuel the calycotome is always plentiful, spreading rapidly in dry soil where little other vegetation can survive.

CAMEL. The camel is one of the first animals mentioned in the Bible. The fact that it could go for days without water and with little food: its ability to scent water before an oasis was sighted: its stamina and, when necessary, its speed—a camel can outrun a horse—made it of great importance to the Israelites. The species used was the single-humped dromedary.

Not only was the camel important as a means of transportation, but it was also much used as a work animal. Its milk, along with butter and cheese, was an important item in the Hebrew diet. Cloth was made from its hair (Matthew 3:4), its hide was tanned for leather, and the dried dung was used as fuel and as an ingredient in roofing.

CAMPHIRE. When King Solomon writes, "My beloved is unto me as a cluster of camphire in the vineyards" (Song of Solomon 1:14), we can be sure that the camphire is a delightful plant. It is shrub-like plant, about ten feet high with very fragrant creamy-white blossoms that grow in clusters. The camphire is the "henna" from which comes the rusty-red commercial dye of that name.

CAMPION. Also called Egyptian pink or catchfly, the campion is one of the most common varieties of pinks found in Palestine. Only about six inches high, it grows abundantly around the Sea of Galilee, its blossoming in early February marking the beginning of spring.

CANA. A village of Galilee not far from Nazareth. It was the home of Nathanael, one of the disciples. It was the scene of Jesus' first miracle, when he turned water into wine. *John 2:1-11; 4:46; 21:2.*

CANAAN. In the OT the territory bounded on the west by the Mediterranean Sea, on the east by the Jordan River, on the south by Sinai, and on the north by Syria. It was sometimes called the Land of Promise because this was the land promised to Abraham. This was the territory invaded and finally conquered by the Israelites after they left Egypt and crossed the wilderness. The people of the land were called Canaanites, and they spoke a Semitic language. The whole area was divided into several local kingdoms which had strongly fortified cities. When conquered, some Canaanites remained in the land and others migrated to Phoenicia. Canaan came to be called Palestine. The area today includes the countries of Israel, Lebanon, and part of Jordan (see *Palestine*). *Genesis 12:5-7; Deuteronomy 32:48-49; Joshua 14:1; Psalm 105:8-11.*

CANANAEAN. A name given to a certain Simon, a disciple of Jesus, to distinguish him from Simon Peter. In Luke 6:15 and Acts 1:13 Simon is referred to as the Zealot. Cananaen means "zealot." This may indicate that he was a member of one of the Jewish political parties that grew up in

protest against the Roman domination of the Jewish nation. *Matthew 10:4; Mark 3:18.*

CAPER. This small, inconspicuous plant with flowers of white, having rose-magenta filaments with yellow tips, trails over the rocky cliffs so profusely as to cover the ground with its dark green leaves. Thorns grow along the stem. In the familiar passage of Ecclesiastes 12:5 we read, "the grasshopper shall be a burden, and *desire* shall fail." The original Hebrew reads, "the *caper* shall fail" (to grow?).

CAPERNAUM. One of the most important cities on the shore of the Sea of Galilee. Capernaum was the scene for much of Jesus' teaching and healing and is the only place where Jesus is said to be "at home." It was the home of Peter, Andrew, James, and John and probably the home of Matthew (Levi). *Matthew 4:13; 8:5-6; 11:23; 17:24; Mark 1:21; 2:1; 9:33; Luke 4:23, 31; 10:15; John 2:12; 4:46; 6:16, 24, 59.*

CAPTAIN. A person having authority over others. This word is applied in the Bible to many different kinds of people: heads of the camps in the wilderness, men in charge of armies, and priests in charge of the temple guard were all called captains. *I Samuel 22:2; II Kings 1:9-14; Luke 22:3; Acts 4:1; 5:24.*

CAPTIVITY. Being taken and kept captive by force, especially being taken from one's own country and made to live in another land. In the OT it usually refers to the Babylonian captivity when the people of Judah were conquered by Nebuchadnezzar and carried off to Babylon in the sixth century B.C. (See *Exile, The.*) *II Kings 24:15; Ezra 3:8; Nehemiah 8:17.*

CARAVAN. A group of people, especially merchants with pack animals, traveling together, often through dangerous territory. Caravan routes crisscrossed the ancient world. Asses and camels were used to transport goods, and it may be that there were escorts or guards mounted on horses. *Genesis 37:25; Judges 5:6; 8:11; Job 6:18-19.*

CARMEL, MOUNT. A prominent mountain at the head of a mountain range on the eastern coast of the Mediterranean Sea which divides the coastal plain of Palestine into two parts. It was the scene of the contest between the prophets of Baal and the prophet Elijah. *Joshua 19:26; I Kings 18:19-20; Jeremiah 46:18.*

CAROB TREE. While not mentioned by name in the Bible, the carob tree was familiar to the Hebrew people since it is native to the lands of the eastern Mediterranean area. An evergreen, it grows up to fifty feet in height. It bears large thick pods used for food for swine and cattle, and even for people. The "husks" which the swine and the prodigal son ate were very likely these pods which are called "locusts." In the East they are known as "John's bread" and accepted as the "locusts" eaten by John the Baptist (Matthew 3:4).

CARPENTER. In Bible times a craftsman who worked with wood, making yokes, plows, threshing

boards, benches, beds, chests, boats. The workshop was usually in the home. Carpenters also worked on the upper stories of stone houses and sometimes repaired gates. Jesus was closely connected with the trade and was probably trained in it since Joseph was a carpenter. *II Samuel 5:11; II Kings 12:11; I Chronicles 14:1; 22:15; II Chronicles 34:11; Isaiah 44:13; Matthew 13:55; Mark 6:3.*

CASSIA. An oriental tree with sweet-smelling bark, probably used in making anointing oil. Buds of the tree were used as we use cloves to season food, and the smaller leaves and pods were used in medicines. *Exodus 30:24; Psalm 45:8; Ezekiel 27:19.*

CAT. The cat is not mentioned in the Bible. The Israelites looked on it with contempt. This may have been due to the fact that the Egyptians, their masters for generations, worshiped the cat, and to kill one was a crime punishable by death. When a cat died the Egyptians often embalmed it and buried it in an ornate coffin. Such pagan animal worship must have galled the Hebrews and made the cat dispicable. This attitude was probably hardened long after when their later captors, the Babylonians, kept cats in the sacred places of the temple. Yet, in spite of this general feeling, it is quite probable that the cat was a household pet among the Israelites of a later date.

CATERPILLAR. Since moths, grasshoppers, and butterflies were common in Palestine, caterpillars were familiar. They are mentioned many times in the Bible, often when pestilence is the theme (I Kings 8:37; Psalm 78:46; Isaiah 33:4), giving the impression that the writers made no definite distinction between the worm-like larvae of insects found in refuse and the fuzzy, innocent caterpillars of butterflies. But no doubt the Hebrews were aware of the wonder of the metamorphosis of the egg-larvae-flying insect cycle.

CATTLE. In biblical usage a general term for domesticated animals including sheep, goats, cows, oxen, asses, and camels. Possession of many cattle was a sign of wealth as these animals were the source of meat, milk, hides, wool, and transportation. They also had an important place in sacrificial worship. *Numbers 31:9, 33; Psalms 50:10; 144:14; John 4:12.*

CEDAR. An evergreen tree with fragrant and beautiful wood which is long lasting. The trees usually grow to a height of twenty feet, but the cedars of Lebanon grew to as much as 120 to 140 feet. Cedar wood was used in burning sacrifices in the temple. A great deal of cedar was used in the building of the temple. The large logs needed for this were made into rafts in the Lebanon mountains and floated down the coast from Tyre to Joppa. Many poets mentioned cedar in their poetry and songs as a symbol of strength and glory. *Numbers 19:6; I Kings 7:2-3; Psalms 29:5; 92:12; Ezekiel 31:3-9.*

CENTAUR. Whether or not the people of the Bible knew of the

centaur we cannot be certain. It is quite likely they did believe in this mythical creature that has come down through the ages—in imagination. It was supposed to have the head and torso of a man and the body of a horse. Symbolically it represented man divided against himself, torn between good and evil.

CENTURION. The commanding officer of one hundred foot soldiers, part of a cohort or division in the Roman army. His duty included the punishment of prisoners and the supervision of the executions. In NT stories centurions are mentioned more often than any other army officer. *Matthew 8:5-13; Mark 15:39, 44-45; Luke 7:2-10; 23:44-47; Acts 10:1; 21:31-32; 27:1.*

CHAFF. The useless dry husks of grain which were blown away from the good seed in the process of winnowing. Many Bible references use the word *chaff* as a figure of speech to indicate someone or something worthless. (See *Winnow.*) *Job 13:25; 21:18; Psalms 1:4; 35:5; 83:13; Isaiah 17:13; 29:5; 41:15; Jeremiah 13:24; Hosea 13:3; Zephaniah 2:1-2; Matthew 3:12; Luke 3:17.*

CHALDEANS. The inhabitants of a region in south Babylonia between the Tigris and Euphrates rivers. The term came to mean "Babylonians." They conquered the Assyrian Empire, and their kings ruled from the city Babylon. Nebuchadnezzar was their greatest king (605–562 B.C.). Under him Judea was conquered, Jerusalem destroyed, and the Hebrews carried away into Babylonia (see II Kings 24:10-17). *Genesis 11:28; II Chronicles 36:17-21; Jeremiah 21:4; 32:4-5; and other places in Jeremiah; Ezekiel 23:23.*

CHAMELEON. The chameleon was as familiar to the ancients as it is to people today. Its unique ability to change its color, not so much to match the background as a means of camouflage, but because of the temperature and its emotions, is well known. A most peculiar characteristic of the chameleon is its eyes. Each eyeball can move independently, thus giving the weird effect of the animal looking two ways at once—which it actually does! The chameleon is harmless, its diet consisting mostly of insects which it traps with a quick jab of its long tongue.

CHAMOIS. The Hebrew word translated "chamois" in Deuteronomy 14:5 is the broad description of "antelope" and might refer to any one of several species. While there is a remote variety of chamois native to Asia Minor it is doubtful if the true chamois ever lived in the Holy Land. The Barbary sheep might be the animal intended in the Deuteronomy passage.

CHAMPION. In the OT a mighty warrior. This word referred to a man who went into the space between two warring armies and as a representative of his army challenged someone from the other army to come out and fight in single combat. Goliath was called a champion. (See *Goliath.*) *I Samuel 17:4-51.*

CHARIOT. A two-wheeled, horse-drawn vehicle used in war and for

travel, especially by kings and officials. The use of swift horses and chariots of wood, wicker, or metal with a built-in case for carrying weapons changed the nature of war. They gave armies that used them a great advantage over foot soldiers. Chariots played an important part in establishing large empires like those of Assyria and Babylonia. The hilly land of Judah kept the Judeans from making good use of chariots in war, but King Solomon had hundreds and built chariot cities like Megiddo. *Genesis 41:43; 46:29; Exodus 14:5-9; I Kings 10:26; Acts 8:27-29, 38.*

Assyrian relief of a royal chariot, with the king being shielded by an umbrella held by a servant.

CHERUB, CHERUBIM. In the

OT the reference is to winged angelic creatures. Cherubim are often mentioned in the myths and folklore of the Canaanites. Some of the Canaanite figures have the bodies of animals and the heads of men. There were images of two cherubim on the ark of the covenant. What they looked like we do not know, though they were made of wood and covered with gold. They were placed on either side of the mercy seat, which represented the throne of God, and their outstretched wings touched above it. There were also cherubim embroidered on tapestries hung in the tabernacle and carved on doors of the temple. *Genesis 3:24; Exodus 25:18-22; II Chronicles 3:7, 10-14; Psalms 80:1; 99:1; Isaiah 37:16; Ezekiel 10:l-20.*

CHICKEN. The chicken is a de-

scendant of the Red Jungle Fowl of southern and southwestern Asia. It was domesticated long before the time of the Jewish settlement in the Holy Land. Though the Talmud forbade them from keeping chickens, probably for sanitary reasons lest the flesh of sacrificial animals be contaminated by the insects and larvae that breed in chicken droppings, the regulation was not strictly observed. This is indicated by the familiar words of Jesus: "How often would I have gathered thy children together, even as a hen gathereth her chickens under her wings, and ye would not!" (Matthew 23:34: Luke 13:34).

CHILDREN OF GOD. The spir-

itual family of God. In the OT the Hebrews were often referred to as sons or children of God because of their special relation to God as his chosen people (see Jeremiah 3:14, 22). In the NT a special spiritual relationship with God is still indicated by the term which is used for the followers of Jesus Christ, who are the new people of God. *John 1:12; 11:52; Romans 8:15-16; 9:8; Philippians 2:14-15; I John 3:1.*

CHINNERETH, SEA OF. See

Galilee, Sea of.

The Bible Companion

CHORAZIN. In NT times a city of Galilee on the hills above Capernaum. One of the cities reproved by Jesus for its unbelief. *Matthew 11:21; Luke 10:13.*

CHRIST. Greek word meaning "the Anointed One," "the Messiah." A title given to the king expected by the Jews. In the NT it is the title most commonly applied to Jesus by his disciples. It soon became almost a name or surname for Jesus. *Mark 1:1; 8:29; Luke 2:26; John 1:41; 4:25; Acts 5:42; Romans 5:8; 6:3; and many other references.*

CHRISTIAN. A term referring to a follower of Jesus, meaning "Christ's man." It was probably used first by pagans or unbelievers when speaking of and belittling the followers of Jesus Christ. The word is used only three time in the Bible. *Acts 11:26; 26:28; I Peter 4:16.*

CHRONICLES, FIRST AND SECOND. Two books in the OT. The word means "history" or "events of the past." These books contain a history of Israel from Adam to Cyrus, king of Persia. The author, whose name is not known, is called the Chronicler. His purpose was to write about the Hebrews—their national achievements, their temple worship, and their kings. He records especially events in the reigns of David and Solomon.

CHRYSANTHEMUM. There is little resemblance between the cultivated chrysanthemum with which we are familiar and the garland chrysanthemum of Palestine. The yellow flower, blossoming along the top of the two-foot stem, looks more like a daisy with widespread petals, or a small sunflower. It blooms in March.

CHURCH. In the NT a fellowship of believers in Jesus Christ gathered together for the purpose of worship, prayer, instruction, and fellowship. The word was used by Paul for a group or congregation in a local community. The first organized church in the NT was made up of the followers of Jesus in Jerusalem. Today "church" also refers to the whole group of believers in Jesus Christ from every land and continent, which is the church universal. *Acts 8:1; 9:31; 11:22, 26; 12:5; I Corinthians 1:2; 11:18; 14:4-5, 19, 28; Ephesians 1:22-23; 5:23; Colossians 1:18; I Timothy 3:15; Philemon 1:2.*

CIRCUMCISION. The act of cutting off the foreskin of a baby boy. Among the Hebrews it was a religious ceremony performed on the eighth day after birth. This act dedicated the child and was a sign of the covenant between God and the Hebrews. In the early Christian church some of the leaders insisted that the non-Jews, who were known as Gentiles, be circumcised and obey all the laws of Moses. But Paul argued that this was unnecessary, and at the first church council in Jerusalem it was officially decided that Christians would not be required to obey the Jewish laws or to be circumcised. *Genesis 17:10-14; Exodus 12:48; Luke 2:21; Romans 2:25-29; I Corinthians 7:18-19; Galatians 5:2-3.*

CISTERN. A pit dug in the earth and lined with a lime plaster for the storage of water. *II Kings 18:31; Jeremiah 38:6-13.*

CISTUS. The large lavender-pink cistus is a spring flower. It has commercial value since ladanum, a fragrant gum, is derived from the plant. Some scholars believe that the "myrrh" referred to in Genesis 43:11 was from the cistus.

CITADEL. A fortified building or stronghold within a city, sometimes attached to a palace or temple for the purpose of defense. The last citadel of the Jews in Jerusalem was the Tower of Antonia in Herod's temple. The Romans overran it in A.D. 70. *I Kings 16:18; II Kings 15:25; Psalm 48:3, 13.*

CITIES OF REFUGE. Six cities given to the Levites or priests in OT times to provide refuge for persons who had bloodguilt by accidentally killing someone. In these cities the refugee was safe from anyone wanting to get revenge. The fugitive could remain protected until a congregation judged him to see whether the killing was accidental or intentional. (See *Bloodguilt.*) *Numbers 35:6-14, 25-33; Joshua 20:1-9.*

CITY. In OT times a walled town, in contrast to a village which lay open. The walls served as protection from enemy attack, and people living in the surrounding farmland came inside in times of danger. Cities provided a market and had cisterns to provide water in times of siege. Cities were built on hills as a safeguard against surprise attack. Except in royal cities the streets were narrow and unpaved. *Numbers 13:17-20; Deuteronomy 3:5; I Kings 16:24.*

CLAM. Since clams, along with other marine animals that have no fins or scales, were classed as unclean in the Mosaic dietary ruling, they were not used as food by the Israelites. But they must have been known to the inhabitants of the seacoast towns.

CLEMATIS. This is also known as buckthorn. Growing in dry, unfertile areas where only a few plants survive, the clematis seems to prepare for a grand exhibit when the rainy season comes. Then the hills are covered with its green tinted creamy-white blossoms. Though a shrub, a fully grown plant is almost tree-size. The flowers grow at the end of short branches, hanging downward. The bark of the clematis has a sweet taste of which ants are very fond.

CLOAK. A square of cloth worn as an outer garment over a coat. It was used also by a traveler and by the poor as a bed cover. If borrowed, a cloak had to be returned by nightfall. *Deuteronomy 24:10-13; Matthew 5:40.*

COAT. A long tunic-like shirt usually made of linen and worn by men and women as an undergarment. Coats were sometimes referred to as robes with long sleeves. A coat of mail was a protective garment made of leather and metal and worn into battle over a cloth coat. *Leviticus 8:5-7; I Samuel 17:5; II Chronicles 26:14; Jeremiah 46:4; Luke 3:11; Acts 9:39.*

COCK. When "cock" is mentioned there comes to mind the picture of the cringing Peter denying his Lord "before the cock crows thrice" (Matthew 26:34). Most often the cock is mentioned in reference to its habit of

crowing an hour or two before dawn. The "cockcrow" was the third watch. Jesus refers to this in Mark 13:35: "Watch ye therefore: for ye know not when the master of the house cometh, at even, or at midnight, or at the cockcrowing, or in the morning." No doubt the crowing of a rooster (cock) was the "alarm clock" of the Israelite farmer then, even as today.

COCKATRICE. It would do no good to look up the cockatrice in a nature book: there never has been such an animal. Mention of it in several Bible passages of early translations (Isaiah 11:8; 50:5; Jeremiah 8:17) was logical to the English translators to whom the cockatrice—a kind of serpent hatched from a chicken egg—was a generally accepted creature, even though never seen. Later translators have changed this mythical "animal" into the very real "adder," as do footnotes in the King James passages.

COCKLE. "Let cockle [grow] instead of barley" (Job 31:40) was Job's way of insisting on his integrity, inviting punishment if he were guilty of wrongdoing. Though a rather beautiful plant, some four feet high with veined pink flowers on its spreading stalks, it is a noxious weed. The seeds are poisonous if used as flour.

COHORT. In NT times a part of the Roman army. A cohort consisted of six hundred men. These were usually posted in small forts on the frontiers. In Jerusalem the cohort was stationed in the Tower of Antonia north of the temple. *Acts 10:1; 21:31; 27:1.*

COLOSSIANS, LETTER TO THE. A letter written by Paul to the Christians of Colossae, a city in southwestern Asia Minor. Paul was a prisoner in Rome when he had news of false teachings in Colossae. He wrote to remind the people there of the Christian way of life. This letter makes up the twelfth book in the NT.

COLT. A young horse or ass. In the OT it is also a young camel. A colt which had never been ridden was brought by the disciples for Jesus to ride into Jerusalem. *Zechariah 9:9; Matthew 21:2-7; Mark 11:1-7.*

COMMANDMENT. A law or order from someone in authority. In the Bible it is used most frequently for the laws of God found in the early OT books, especially the Ten Commandments, which form the core of the laws given to Moses. *Genesis 26:5; Exodus 24:12; Deuteronomy 11:22-23; Psalm 119:6; Matthew 5:19; 21:35-40: Mark 12:28-31.*

COMMONWEALTH. A body of people making up a community. Paul used the term to indicate that a Christian is first of all a citizen of heaven and that his conduct and welfare are determined by this citizenship. *Ephesians 2:12; Philippians 3:20-21.*

COMMUNION. A term meaning the act of sharing. It is important in the covenant relationship between God and his people and indicates close friendship (see Exodus 25:8). In the NT a deeper relationship between God and man was established through Jesus Christ. This relationship is remembered in the sacrament of the

Lord's Supper which is also called Communion. (See Matthew 26:26-29; Mark 14:22-25; Luke 22:14-20; I Corinthians 11:23-26.)

CONCUBINE. In OT times a slave girl or servant who belonged to a Hebrew family and bore children (see Exodus 21:7-10). Such a girl achieved certain honor if she had sons. *Genesis 22:24; 25:6; I Kings 11:3.*

CONDUIT. A water channel or tunnel. One of these ancient water-supply channels was built in Jerusalem by King Hezekiah to bring water into the city. *II Kings 18:17; 20:20; Isaiah 7:3; 36:2.*

CONEY. See *Hyrax.*

CONFESSION. An act in the worship of God in which a person humbly admits his sins and asks for God's forgiveness. *Leviticus 26:40-42; Numbers 5:7; Psalm 32:5; Mark 1:5; I John 1:9.*

CONGREGATION. A gathering or assembly. A term used for all the Israelites encamped in the wilderness. It is also used for the assembly of people before God for worship or for judgment. *Exodus 12:3-6; 16:1-2; Leviticus 4:13-14; Joshua 22:16-18; Psalm 1:5; Acts 15:30; Hebrews 2:12.*

CONIAH. See *Jehoiachin.*

CONSECRATE. To set apart or dedicate an offering, a building, or a person for some sacred purpose. *Exodus 13:2; I Kings 9:3, 7; II Chronicles 29:31, 33; John 17:19; I Timothy 4:4-5.*

CONVOCATION, HOLY. A solemn assembly to fulfill a sacred obligation. In the OT this term was used when the people of Israel were summoned together for worship and for rest on the sabbaths and on feast days, especially the Day of Atonement. *Leviticus 23:2-4, 7-8, 21, 24, 27, 35-37; Numbers 28:18.*

COR. In the OT a large measure for grain and oil. It contained about six bushels of dry material or sixty gallons of liquid. *I Kings 5:11; II Chronicles 2:10; Ezekiel 45:14.*

CORAL. Whether the Hebrews realized that coral, abundant in the sea waters of the Middle East, is the skeleton remains of tiny animals is questionable. But the wealthy used it in decorating their homes, particularly the red coral. Possibly this is what Job had in mind when he reminded Bildad the Shuhite that "no mention shall be made of coral or crystal" in setting a price on wisdom (Job 28:18). Ezekiel's inclusion of coral with "emeralds, fine linen and agate" (Ezekiel 27:16) indicates that it was considered a valuable commodity.

CORIANDER SEED. A small, gray seed used as a seasoning in food, much the way poppy and sesame seeds are used on breads and cakes today. It is mentioned in the OT in describing manna, the food of the Israelites during their long journey out of Egypt. It comes from a plant of the carrot family. *Exodus 16:31; Numbers 11:7-9.*

CORINTH. The chief commercial city on the Isthmus of Corinth in Greece and the capital of the Roman province of Achaia in NT times.

Because of its location on the isthmus, which was only three and a half miles across at its narrowest point, ships from east and west were unloaded and the goods hauled across on land. Some of the smaller vessels were themselves dragged over. Paul preached here to the Jews and Greeks. *Acts 18:1; 19:1; I Corinthians 1:2; II Corinthians 1:1, 23; II Timothy 4:20.*

CORINTHIANS, FIRST AND SECOND LETTER TO THE.

The letters written by Paul to the Christians at Corinth, now the seventh and eighth books in the NT. They are letters full of advice, admonition, and encouragement to the people in the church in that city.

CORMORANT.

Common to the Asian warm countries, the cormorant has two interesting characteristics: though it has webbed feet it often perches on tree branches, and it swims beneath the surface of the water in pursuit of fish. It is nearly three feet long, covered with shiny feathers. Its habit of diving in deep water where it fishes has given it the nickname of "plunger." Today the oriental fishermen train the cormorant to dive and retrieve fish. A ring is first placed around the bird's neck to prevent it from swallowing its catch.

CORN.

"Corn" in the Bible refers to almost all kinds of grain, as it does today in many countries. Our corn was unknown to the people of the Bible.

CORNELIUS.

A centurion of the Italian Cohort, stationed in Caesarea. Cornelius was a Gentile and not a Jew. However, he was a religious man, worshiping the God of the Hebrews and giving liberally to the poor. His dramatic vision and conversion to the Christian faith through the preaching of Peter is one of the great stories in the book of Acts. This even also taught Peter that all foods had been cleansed through the word of Jesus so that the old Jewish food laws were no longer needed. *Acts 10:1-48.*

CORNFLOWER.

The Palestinian cornflower is much the same as our familiar "bachelor button." It is a deep blue, growing profusely over the hills of much of the Middle East.

COTTON.

Cotton is not mentioned by name in the King James Version of the Bible, but the later versions describe the hangings in the king's palace as "white cotton curtains" (Esther 1:6). Cotton was grown in Egypt for centuries before the Christian era and was cultivated by the Jews after their settlement in the Holy Land. It was processed much as it was in this country before the advent of the cotton gin.

COUNCIL.

In the OT an assembly made up of men of authority. Their duty was to consider and direct the affairs of the community in government, law, and religion. The council was made up of the wise men and elders of Israel, who directed matters according to the laws of the Hebrews. There are several references in the OT to the council of God, made up of God himself and the heavenly beings. In NT times the term referred to local

councils and to the high council in Jerusalem, the Sanhedrin. This powerful body made judgments under Jewish law, including cases in which the punishment was death. However, the Roman government kept the power of carrying out the execution in the hands of its own officials. This can be seen in the judgment against Jesus by the council and the necessity of having the Roman governor, Pilate, accept their verdict (see Matthew 26:65-66; Mark 14:63-64; 15:1-15; John 19:7, 10-16). *II Kings 9:5; 25:19; Job 15:8; Psalm 82:1; Jeremiah 23:18, 22; 52:25; Mark 15:43; Luke 23:50; John 11:47.*

COVENANT. An agreement or solemn promise binding persons together in a firm relationship. It was of great importance in OT law and religion. *Covenant* was the word used for the special relationship which God had established between himself and Israel. He was to be their God, and they were to be his people. This was the meaning of the original covenant which God made with Abraham. The covenant was dramatically renewed through Moses at Mt. Sinai as the Israelites journeyed toward the Promised Land. Against this background the early Christians in the NT thought of their relationships to one another and to Jesus as a covenant binding them together. Jesus spoke of a new covenant. *Genesis 15:18; 17:1-11; 21:31-32; 26:28; Exodus 24:8; I Samuel 18:3; II Samuel 23:5; Job 41:4; Jeremiah 31:31-34; Ezekiel 17:13-14; Matthew 26:28; Mark 14:24; I Corinthians 11:25; II Corinthians 3:14; Hebrews 8:6-13; 10:29; 13:20-21.*

COVETOUSNESS. A desire to have something that belongs to someone else or to have more than one already possesses. Throughout the Bible covetousness is considered sinful. In the NT especially, covetousness is considered a hindrance to true worship and faith in God. *Exodus 20:17; Luke 12:15; Romans 1:29; Ephesians 5:3; Colossians 3:5.*

CRADLEWORT. This is also called "Our Lady's bedstraw," legend saying that cradlewort filled the manger in which Mary placed the Christ child. Some of the paintings of the old masters show cradlewort in pictures of the Nativity. It is a fragile plant, covered with puffs of small, sweet-scented yellow flowers.

CRANE. The crane referred to in Jeremiah 8:7 and again in Isaiah 38:14—"like a crane did I chatter"—was the European variety. Reference to its "chatter" was an understatement, perhaps in the translation, as all cranes have powerful voices. They live mostly in swampy areas, subsisting mainly on snakes, insects, and small rodents, a fact that makes them useful to the natives and probably fostered the belief that it is considered bad luck to kill a crane. All varieties have long legs and necks.

CREATION. God's act of bringing the world and all of life into being. Two stories of creation are found at the very beginning of the Bible, reminding us that creation is the starting point of history. *Genesis 1:1–2:25; Mark 13:19; Ephesians 3:9; Revelation 4:11; 10:6.*

The Bible Companion

CRICKET. Translation of the Hebrew word as "beetle" in the King James Version of the Bible (Leviticus 11:22) is changed to "cricket" in the Revised Version, leaving us uncertain as to just what member of the grasshopper family was meant. In any case we can be quite sure that the chirp of crickets, made by the cricket rubbing its hind legs together, was as familiar to the people of Bible times as it is today.

CRISPUS. A leader of the synagogue in Corinth. He and all his family became Christians after hearing Paul preach. They were among the few early believers whom Paul personally baptized. *Acts 18:8; I Corinthians 1:14-15.*

CROCODILE. Even though the crocodile is not mentioned in the Bible it must have been known to the Children of Israel because of their long sojourn in Egypt where it was, and still is, plentiful. Since the Egyptians worshiped the crocodile as one of their gods, we can be sure the animal was abhorrent to the Israelites. Some scholars believe that the crocodile once inhabited the Jordan River and the swamps of northern Israel.

CROCUS. This harbinger of spring, blossoming before the snow has gone, was familiar to the people of the Bible. One form is native to the Mediterranean area and no doubt was as eagerly looked for as a sign of spring as it is today.

CROSS. A large stake set upright in the ground as an instrument of execution. Often a horizontal piece was attached either at the top to form a "T" or just below the top to make the type of cross that is most familiar. Jesus was put to death on a cross, and this event is described in all four Gospels. The Jews were unable to believe that the long-expected Messiah, or king, would die in so painful and humiliating a way. For pagans too it made no sense that one who claimed to be God would die so. In spite of all this the cross has become the most important symbol of the Christian faith. Also the word was used by Jesus to mean the suffering and death that men must bear. (See *Crucifixion.*) *Matthew 10:38; 16:24; 27:32-50; Mark 8:34; 15:21-37; Luke 14:27; 23:26; I Corinthians 1:17-18; Galatians 6:12-14.*

CROSSBILL. The crossbill is a finch. It lives among evergreens, feeding mostly on conifer seed, its crossed bill being especially adapted for extracting the seed from the cone. It is only about four inches in length. The male is a brick red, the female greenish gray. They very much resemble small parrots as they hang from a twig and reach for food.

CROW. While the raucous crow we know is not found in the Holy Land, the carrion crow of Eurasia and the hooded crow no doubt were known. Since these were quite common it may seem strange that the crow is not referred to in the Bible. One logical explanation could be that crow belongs to the raven family and might have been intended in some places where "raven" is used.

CROWFOOT. The small, glossy, yellow blossom of the crowfoot (often called Jerusalem crowfoot) resembles the familiar buttercup. The finely divided foliage has a grayish tinge. It grows profusely in the rock soil of Palestine.

CROWN. A headdress for a priest or king often made of rich material and decorated with designs or jewels. There were also simple metal headbands which served as crowns. The wreath placed on the head of a winner in Greek games was called a crown. *Exodus 29:6; II Chronicles 23:11; Psalm 21:3; Revelation 6:2; 14:14.*

Royal crowns and headdresses: (1) red crown of Lower Egypt; (2) crown of Upper and Lower Egypt; (3) white crown of Upper Egypt; (4) Egyptian; (5) Assyrian; (6) Ptolemaic and Seleucid

CROWN OF THORNS. A circlet of thorny briers made by Roman soldiers and pushed down on Jesus' head as a part of their torture and mockery of him. They teased and taunted him with this make-believe crown. *Matthew 27:27-29; John 19:2-5.*

CRUCIFIXION. The act of putting a person to death by nailing or binding him to a cross or sometimes to a tree. It was a very slow death resulting from hunger, thirst and exposure. It was a form of execution practiced by the Romans at the time of Jesus' arrest and trial. Jesus' crucifixion is described in the four Gospels. (See *Cross*.) *Matthew 27:22-54; Mark 15:15-39; Luke 23:1-49; John 19:1-30.*

CRUSE. A small pottery jug four to six inches high used to hold olive oil. Also called a jar and bowl. *I Kings 17:12-16.*

CUBIT. A unit of measurement based on the length from the elbow to the tip of the middle finger—about eighteen inches. *Genesis 6:15; Exodus 25:10; I Samuel 17:4; Matthew 6:27.*

CUCKOO. The cuckoo, spelled "cookow" in all but the late translations of the Bible, was probably the European bird. Feeding mostly on insects, the fact that it does sometimes eat frogs, lizards, and small snakes made it unclean (Deuteronomy 14:15; Leviticus 11:16). It is a very clever imitator of other birds in calls and action. An unusual characteristic of the cuckoo is that some lay blue eggs, others lay buff eggs with black spots. Oftentimes it will lay its eggs in the nest of another bird with eggs of similar colorization, leaving them to be hatched by "foster parents."

CUMMIN. Cummin has been cultivated since ancient times. It is a

Cummin

small, rather fragile plant about twelve inches in height with umbels of dainty pink and white flowers. It is cultivated for the seeds which are crushed and used for flavoring and for medicinal purposes. It was valuable enough to be part of the required tithe, but not to be compared with the "weightier matters of the law" (Matthew 23:23).

CUPBEARER. In OT times an official who served wine to the king. He was obliged to test the wine by drinking it himself to make sure that it was not poisoned. He had to be a person whom the king trusted. *I Kings 10:5; II Chronicles 9:4; Nehemiah 1:11–2:1.*

CURDS. A thickened milk food made by churning fresh milk in a goatskin containing the leftover clots from the previous churning. In OT times curds were a part of the ordinary diet. *Genesis 18:8; Deuteronomy 32:14; Judges 5:25; II Samuel 17:27-29; Proverbs 30:33; Isaiah 7:14-15, 21-22.*

CURTAIN OF THE TEMPLE. The curtain that separated the Most Holy Place from the rest of the temple. Only the high priest could go through the curtain into the Most Holy Place. The curtain was torn in two at the death of Jesus, opening for all this place of meeting between God and man. In the OT the curtain was called the veil (see *Veil of the Temple*). *Matthew 27:51; Mark 15:38, Luke 23:45; Hebrews 10:19-20.*

CUSTODIAN. A slave who in Roman times had charge over a young boy, guarding him and taking him to school until he was sixteen. Paul used the term in a word picture to explain that the law had been the guardian or custodian of the Jews until Christ came. *Galatians 3:24-25.*

CYCLAMEN. Growing abundantly throughout much of the Middle East, the cyclamen is called "cock of the mountains" by the Arabs. It has been dedicated to Mary because the "red throat" at the heart of the flower looks like a drop of blood, symbolizing the sword of sorrow that pierced Mary's heart when her Son was crucified. It has been described as "a strange flower with bent back, curved petals, and crimson eye looking down as if expectant of the earth to yield treasure to it."

CYPRESS. This is the "gopher wood" referred to in Genesis 6:14, used to build the ark. It was once common on the mountains of Palestine. Because of its great durability it was extensively used for building ships. Gradually the supply was

depleted. Since "cypress" and "cedar" are both translations of the same Hebrew word, we cannot always be certain which was intended.

CYPRUS. An island in the Mediterranean Sea off the coast of Syria. Cyprus was the home of Barnabas, an early Christian who traveled with Paul on his missionary journeys. *Isaiah 23:1, 12; Jeremiah 2:10; Ezekiel 27:6; Acts 4:36; 11:19-20; 13:4; 15:39; 21:3; 27:4.*

CYRENE. A Greek city on the northern coast of Africa. A man from Cyrene named Simon carried Jesus' heavy cross to the place of the Crucifixion. *Matthew 27:32; Mark 15:21; Luke 23:26; Acts 2:10; 11:20; 13:1.*

CYRUS. A Persian king, founder of the Persian Empire, who reigned from 550 to 529 B.C. After he captured Babylon in 539 B.C., Cyrus proclaimed himself "king of the world." From this position of power Cyrus ruled with a tolerance, understanding, and wisdom that were unusual for those times. He allowed the many people who had been captured and deported by the Babylonians to return to their homes and to restore their old religions. This policy included the Jews who were in exile in Babylonia. They went home to Jerusalem and began to rebuild the temple. His empire, even before taking Babylon, extended from India across Asia to the Aegean Sea. Cyrus captured Babylon by digging a ditch around the city, and causing the Euphrates River to flow into the ditch. His army then marched up the dry river bed into the surprised city of Babylon. The city itself was not attacked. (See *Darius.*) *II Chronicles 36:22-23; Ezra 1:1-8; 6:3-5; Isaiah 44:28–45:4; Daniel 1:21.*

DAGON. A god worshiped by the Philistines in Gaza and in Ashdod, where there was a temple dedicated to Dagon. Very little is known about the nature of this god or the way in which he was worshiped. The name means "corn," and it seems likely that he was a god of vegetation. It is also known that Dagon was worshiped by other peoples of the Near East in ancient times. During a period of war between the Philistines and the Israelites, the Philistines captured the ark of the covenant. It was placed in the temple at Ashdod beside the god Dagon. While the ark was kept by the Philistines, they had so many misfortunes that they sent it back to the Israelites. *Judges 16:23-24, I Samuel 5:1-7; I Chronicles 10:10.*

DAISY. Although it does not grow as high as our daisy, nor is it as robust, the daisy of the Holy Land bears a close resemblance otherwise. Its petals are often edged with pink. It is especially abundant in moist areas of the hills, blooming in October and continuing to bloom until the following summer.

DAMASCUS. The capital city of Syria. Damascus is a very ancient city and was important in OT times. Its importance continues down to the present. It was located where

important military and commercial routes met. It was the capital of the Aramean kingdom at one time and a rival city of Jerusalem and Samaria. It was conquered by the Assyrians, the Babylonians, the Persians, and the Greeks. Damascus was also an important center for early Christians. It was on the road from Jerusalem to Damascus that Paul became a Christian. *Genesis 14:13-15; II Samuel 8:5-6; I Kings 11:24-25; 15:18-19; 19:15; 20:34; II Kings 8:7-9; 14:28; 16:10-13; Isaiah 7:8; 17:1-3; Acts 9:1-22; 26:19-20; Galatians 1:17.*

DAN. One of the twelve sons of Jacob and the ancestor of the tribe of Danites. The tribe settled in an area in the extreme northern part of Canaan at the foot of Mt. Hermon near the Jordan River and called the place Dan. In the OT the phrase "from Dan to Beer-sheba" (which was at the southern end of Canaan) meant the entire length of the land. The most famous Danite was Samson. *Exodus 1:1-4; Joshua 19:40-48; Judges 1:34; I Samuel 3:20; I Kings 4:25; 12:26-29; II Chronicles 16:4; 30:5.*

DANDELION. Lands bordering the Mediterranean were the original home of the dandelion. From there it spread around the world. In ancient times, as now, the leaves were used in salads. Quite likely it is one of the "bitter herbs" often mentioned in the Bible: the bitter taste of older dandelion leaves is familiar to us.

DANIEL. Meaning "God has judged." The name of a heroic Jewish youth in exile in Babylon. (See *Daniel, Book of.*)

DANIEL, BOOK OF. An OT book by an unknown author who probably wrote it when the Jews were ruled by the Greeks about 166 B.C. The book tells of Daniel, a very wise and upright young Jew, and three other persons who were loyal to their faith in God though far from their homeland and in exile in Babylon, where they were persecuted. The stories of Daniel's visions were probably meant to give a message of hope to the Jewish people that in spite of their troubles they would be triumphant. The stories were in a kind of secret language that represented persons and situations at that time. The writer knew his Jewish readers would understand what he was trying to say. This form of writing is similar to the book of Revelation. It is called apocalyptic.

DARIC. In the OT thick gold coin of Persia worth a little over five dollars. It was named for Darius, a Persian emperor, and is the first coin mentioned in the Bible. *I Chronicles 29:7; Ezra 2:69; 8:27; Nehemiah 7:70-72.*

DARIUS. 1. King of Persia from 522 to 486 B.C., known as Darius the Great. He decreed that all interference with the Jews' attempt to rebuild the temple in Jerusalem be stopped and that they be allowed to continue the restoration. *Ezra 5:6–6:13; Nehemiah 12:22; Haggai 1:1-2.*

2. The book of Daniel tells of another Darius called Darius the Mede. *Daniel 5:31–6:28.*

DATE PALM. It is thought that the date palm may be the oldest known species of tree cultivated by man.

After the exodus from Egypt the Hebrew people took the date palm as a sacred emblem, perhaps because of its importance as a source of food and because date palms growing in the desert were an indication of life-giving water in the area. It is the main food supply for man and beast in the desert regions today as it has been for countless centuries. The palm—there are several varieties—is referred to more than sixty times in the Bible, from Judges 4:5 when we read that "Deborah dwelt under the palm tree" to the waving of palm branches on the first Palm Sunday.

DAVID. The second and greatest king of Israel (from about 1000 to 965 B.C.). David was a shepherd boy living in Bethlehem when he was chosen to serve King Saul. His way of conducting himself soon made him a favorite at court. David is one of the most attractive personalities in the OT. He had many talents and used them with all his might. He was a gifted poet and musician and probably wrote some of the psalms. He was an excellent soldier, quick to realize what was needed in any military situation. He was also a man of inspiring courage. After Saul's death David became a great and powerful king, and proved to be as skilled in political affairs as he was in battle. David committed a great sin in taking Bathsheba while she was the wife of another man and having her husband killed. When the prophet Nathan accused King David to his face, the king repented with all his heart and asked God's forgiveness (see II Samuel 12:13). Under David's rule the kingdom of Israel reached its peak, and he was thought of ever after as their ideal king. The outstanding quality in David was his devotion to the Lord. *I Samuel 16:1–I Kings 2:11; I Chronicles 11:1–29:30; Jeremiah 33:15-17, 21; Ezekiel 37:24-25; Matthew 12:23; 22:42-45; Luke 1:32, 69; and other references (the name David appears nearly eight hundred times in the OT and around sixty in the NT).*

DAY. In OT times the period from sunrise to sunset with morning, noon, and night as the divisions of time. The sabbath was the only day with a name. Other days were counted by numbers. After the Babylonian exile the Hebrews divided the day into hours. *Psalm 55:10; Jeremiah 31:35.*

DAY OF THE LORD. The day when God will be fully revealed and will judge all the people. Many terms are used for this: Day of Judgment, Day of God, Day of the Lord, the Day, and others. There were many and varied ideas about this day. In the OT it was usually thought of as a day of vengeance on the enemies of Israel. Later the Hebrews came to understand that they also deserved judgment. Christians called Jesus "Lord," and in the NT "Day of the Lord" is understood to mean "Day of Christ." This refers to the expected Second Coming of Jesus Christ, who will exercise the judgment of God. *Joel 1:15; 2:31; Amos 5:18-20; Zephaniah 1:7; II Corinthians 1:14; Philippians 1:6, 10; 2:16; II Thessalonians 2:1-4; II Timothy 1:12.*

DAY'S JOURNEY. The distance traveled from sunrise to sunset, about eighteen to twenty-five miles. In Bible times the measurement of distances was not exact. A day's journey depended on the nature of the ground traveled and the person doing the traveling. *Genesis 30:36; Exodus 3:18; Numbers 11:31; Jonah 3:3-4; Luke 2:44.*

DEACON. Meaning "servant, attendant, minister." An officer in the early Christian church who probably had the responsibility for collecting and distributing the offerings of money or goods and of caring for the sick, the needy, and the elderly. *Philippians 1:1; I Timothy 3:8-13.*

DEACONESS. Women in the early Christian church who assisted in the baptism of women, visited and bathed the sick, and called in pagan homes where there were Christian women. *Romans 16:1.*

DEAD SEA. See *Salt Sea.*

DEBORAH. One of the early "judges" of ancient Israel. She was a remarkable woman with great qualities of leadership. She was endowed with wisdom, and the people called her a prophetess. Deborah aroused the tribes of Israel to fight the Canaanites, and a sense of unity and loyalty grew out of this common effort. Her achievements may be read in the poem called "The Song of Deborah." *Judges 4:1–5:31.*

DEBT. Something owed by one person to another. In the OT there are many rules and customs concerning debts. The older custom of the nomads was to lend to one another within a tribe without charging interest. However, there were violations of this rule, and the charge could become so high for a loan that the borrower's life was almost hopeless. Sometimes debtors had to sell themselves or their children into slavery to pay off their debts. OT laws stated that objects needed in daily living, such as a cloak or millstone, were not to be taken as a pledge for payment of debt unless they were returned to the owner as he needed them and that periodically people enslaved because of debts were to be freed (see Exodus 22: 25-27; Leviticus 25:35-37; Deuteronomy 23:19-20; 24:6, 10-13; II Kings 4:7). Jesus used these Jewish customs to illustrate his teachings. In the Lord's Prayer, "debts" is a figure of speech Jesus used for sins. Roman law permitted the imprisonment of debtors who could not pay. *I Samuel 22:2; Nehemiah 10:31; Matthew 6:12; 18:23-35.*

DECAPOLIS. The word means "ten cities." These Greek cities in Palestine, located along or near chief trade routes and military highways, were founded by the followers of Alexander the Great. When the Roman army entered Palestine, these cities banded together to protect themselves and the trade routes and to promote the interests of Rome. In Jesus' time "Decapolis" was the name for the federation of the ten cities in a specific region southeast of the Sea of Galilee in the Roman province of Syria. *Matthew 4:25; Mark 5:20; 7:31.*

DECREE. In biblical use a declaration or proclamation usually in writing

issued by a king and publicly read to the people to inform, instruct, or command them about what was to be done. *II Chronicles 30:5-6; Ezra 5:13; Isaiah 10:1; Daniel 3:10; Luke 2:1; Acts 17:6-7.*

DEDICATION, FEAST OF. A general term for a celebration in which something is set apart for a sacred purpose (see Numbers 7:10; I Kings 8:1-66; II Chronicles 7:9). In the Bible it referred specifically to the annual celebration commemorating the purification and rededication of the temple in 165 B.C. after the Greeks had defiled it by setting up an altar to pagan gods. This eight-day celebration is still kept by the Jews and is known as Hanukkah or the Feast of Lights. It falls in winter close to the Christmas season. *John 10:22-23.*

DEEP. A poetic term meaning ocean. This type of expression uses a quality of a thing, in this case, the deepness of the ocean, as a substitute word for the thing itself. *Genesis 7:11; Job 38:16; 41:31; Psalms 42:7; 104:6; 107:24-25.*

DEER, FALLOW. The fallow deer, a small animal only about three feet high, lived only in northern Palestine. Some scholars believe a species of antelope was referred to in Deuteronomy 14:5 where the fallow deer is mentioned with the hart. This is not a repetition as the hart is the male of the red deer.

DEER, RED. The red deer, a relative of the North American elk, was plentiful in the Holy Land. As mentioned above, the male red deer is called the hart: "As the hart panteth after the water brooks" (Psalm 42:1) is a graphic word picture of a tired, thirsty male deer. The psalmist continues, "so panteth my soul after thee, O God."

DEFILE. In OT usage to make persons, foods, places, or objects unclean in a religious sense so that they were unfit for a place in the community, especially in matters of worship. An important part of the duties of the OT priests was to judge between clean and unclean. It was also their duty to give instruction in the cleansing of whatever had been defiled. In the NT Jesus used the word in a deeper sense to mean that the words, thoughts, and actions of people may be ugly and unclean and that these defile them in the sight of God. *Leviticus 11:43; II Kings 23:13; Isaiah 59:3; Daniel 1:8; Matthew 15:10-20; Mark 7:15-23; Jude 1:8.*

DELILAH. In the OT story of Samson a woman who betrayed this hero of the Hebrew tribe of Dan to the Philistines. Pretending to have great affection for Samson, she persuaded him to tell her how he had such great strength. When she learned that his hair was the secret of his power, she cut it off while he was sleeping. He awoke to find the Philistines upon him. He was now no stronger than an ordinary man, and the Philistines captured him, put out his eyes, and imprisoned him. *Judges 16:4-22.*

DEMAS. One of Paul's co-workers in the early church. Later he gave up his work with Paul. *Colossians 4:14; II Timothy 4:10; Philemon 1:24.*

DEMETRIUS. A silversmith at Ephesus who made and sold silver pieces that resembled the temple of the goddess Artemis. He complained that Paul's preaching of Christ was interfering with the sale of his shrines. He aroused the people against Paul, causing a riot throughout the city. *Acts 19:24-41.*

DEMON. In the OT a nameless god or spirit which might be friendly or unfriendly. When this word appears in the NT it refers only to evil spirits who are the cause of all kinds of misfortune—disease, insanity, accidents. Demons were also thought of as the messengers of Satan. The word also refers at times to pagan gods. *Deuteronomy 32:17; Psalm 106:37; Matthew 8:16; 9:33; 15:22; Luke 8:26-39; 11:14-15; John 10:20-21.*

DEMONIAC. In the NT one possessed by a demon. Such a condition may be associated with insanity and diseases of the mind. Demoniacs were among those healed by Jesus. *Matthew 8:28-34; Mark 5:15.*

DENARIUS (plural, **DENARII**). A Roman silver coin. In the NT it was a day's pay for a laborer. *Matthew 18:28; 20:2, 9-10, 13; Mark 6:37; 14:5; Luke 10:35.*

DERBE. A city in the central part of southern Asia Minor in the Roman province of Galatia. It was twice visited by Paul, the first time with Barnabas. Here Paul and Barnabas made many disciples for Christ. *Acts 14:6, 20-21; 16:1; 20:4.*

DESTROYER, THE. A term used in the Bible for death or destruction or for the supernatural being that brings them. Sometimes Satan is referred to as the destroyer. *Exodus 12:23; Job 15:21; Isaiah 16:4; 21:2; Jeremiah 4:7; 48:8; I Corinthians 10:9-10; Hebrews 11:28.*

DEUTERONOMY. The fifth book in the OT. The name means "'second law" because it states again the Ten Commandments that are found in Exodus. It was probably put together from various sources written at different periods of time. It is written in the form of a farewell address by Moses to the people he had led out of Egypt. The sermons of Moses urge the people to remember always God's deliverance of them, to keep his commandments, and to be faithful in the covenant. Parts of Deuteronomy are probably the book that was found when King Josiah ordered the temple to be repaired in 622 B.C. (see II Kings 22:8-13).

DEVIL. A term used when speaking of evil as if it were a person. One who leads people to sin and disturbs their relation with God. In the NT it often refers to Satan. *Matthew 4:1-11; Luke 4:1-13; 8:12; John 13:2; Acts 10:38; Ephesians 4:26-27; 6:11; I Timothy 3:6-7.*

DEVOTED. Things forbidden for common use. In the OT persons or things set apart for God were said to be "devoted." In warfare all men, beasts, and objects that were captured were "devoted" to God and were usually destroyed. Sometimes, however, precious metals captured in battle were taken to the sanctuary or holy place. Captured sheep might be

used for burnt offerings to the Lord. *Leviticus 27:21, 28-29; Numbers 18:14; Deuteronomy 13:17; Joshua 6:18; I Samuel 15:21; I Kings 20:42; Ezekiel 44:29.*

DEVOUT. In the OT the word means "righteous," that is, being free from wrong or sin. In the NT it means "godly" and "reverent," that is, devoted to God. *Isaiah 57:1; Acts 10:2.*

DILL. A kind of seed similar to caraway used for seasoning and for medicine. One tenth of all the seed, stems, and leaves that were harvested was given to the temple. This was called a tithe. *Isaiah 28:25, 27; Matthew 23:23.*

DISCIPLE. A pupil or learner. One who accepts and follows a certain teaching or teacher. In the Bible we read of the disciples of Isaiah, of the Pharisees, and of John the Baptist, but the term is most familiar when used to indicate all those who followed Jesus and were called disciples. *Isaiah 8:16; Matthew 10:24-25; 11:1-3; 27:57; Mark 2:16, 18; 6:45; Luke 5:33; 6:13; John 1:35-37; 6:66-67; 9:27-28; Acts 6:1-2, 7; 9:10, 23-26, 36.*

DISCIPLINE. In the Bible this term refers to training and instruction. It also means "correction" and "punishment." This usually refers to the training of a child, but it is also used to indicate God's discipline of people through fortune and misfortune. *Deuteronomy 8:5; Proverbs 12:1; 13:24; Ephesians 6:4.*

DISPERSION. A word used for the settlement of the Jewish people away from their own land after the time of the Assyrian and Babylonian exiles. They had been scattered, or dispersed, until they came to live in many cities of the Greek and Roman empires and in parts of Asia and Africa. Wherever these people settled, they built their synagogues for prayer and study. The word *dispersion* is used sometimes today as a term for Jews who live outside Israel. *Nehemiah 1:9; Esther 3:8; Jeremiah 25:34; Ezekiel 36:19; Zephaniah 3:10; John 7:35; James 1:1; I Peter 1:1.*

DIVINATION. Any attempt to communicate with supernatural powers or to foretell the future by the aid of such natural events as dreams, the position of the stars, cloud formations, unexpected storms, and the like. In the OT divination was also practiced with objects or situations especially arranged for the purpose like the shooting of arrows, casting of lots, or examining of the insides of sacrificed animals. Divination was forbidden in Israel, and the prophets preached against it. *Genesis 30:27; Numbers 22:7; 23:23; Deuteronomy 18:10; I Samuel 15:23; Jeremiah 14:14; Ezekiel 12:24; 21:21; Acts 16:16-18.*

DOG. To the Hebrews of biblical times, as to most eastern people except the Egyptians, the dog was an outcast, a scavenger to be despised. It is referred to over forty times in the Bible and from Deuteronomy 23:18, where it is "an abomination," to Jesus' admonition, "Do not give that which is holy unto the dogs," this "abomination" is evident. The pariah dogs, belonging to no one, ran in packs, roaming and howling at night,

subsisting on refuge and even ravaging human corpses. However, the Jews learned that dogs could be trained to warn of wild animals and thieves. Job speaks of "the dogs of my flock" (Job 30:1). This could have been a type of shepherd dog somewhat similar to the ones we know today. But the dog was seldom a household pet. And even today the worst of insults in the Eastern countries is to call a person a dog.

DOLPHIN. The playful dolphin is one of the swiftest and strongest of fish. Some early writers believed the "big fish" in the story of Jonah's harrowing experience to be a dolphin. But the physical makeup of the dolphin readily dispenses this suggestion. In Christian art it has often been used to symbolize salvation and resurrection.

DOMINION. Meaning "rule," "to have power over," "authority," "kingship." In the Bible the word is used to mean the supreme rule of God, man's rule over nature, or power gained by conquest. It is often used in songs of praise for God. *Genesis 1:26; Numbers 24:19; Judges 14:4; I Kings 4:24; Nehemiah 9:28; Job 25:2; Psalms 8:6; 19:13; 22:28; 72:8; 119:133; I Timothy 6:14-16; I Peter 4:11; 5:11; Jude 1:25; Revelation 1:6.*

DONKEY. See *Ass*.

DOOR, DOORKEEPER. An entrance and one who watches or guards it. In the Bible "door" may refer to a swinging door set in sockets, to a gate, to an opening in a wall, a cavelike tomb, or a sheepfold. A doorkeeper guarded the entrance of the temple and collected money from the people. In the psalms the word *door* is used in a poetic sense as a "door of my lips." Jesus also used the term as a figure of speech when he said he was the "door" of the sheep, for at that time a shepherd slept at the opening in the wall of the sheepfold to protect his sheep from danger. *I Kings 14:27; Psalms 84:10; 141:3; Matthew 6:6; John 10:7-8.*

DORCAS. A woman disciple in Joppa. She was also called Tabitha. Dorcas was known for her good deeds especially among widows, for whom she made clothes. When Dorcas died, the apostle Peter was called, and he raised her from the dead. This the first report of an apostle raising a person from the dead. *Acts 9:36-42.*

DOTHAN. An ancient town located west of the Jordan River and southwest of the Sea of Galilee. In the OT story of Joseph he found his brothers keeping the sheep there. They put him into a well and later sold him to a caravan of Ishmaelites. The modern city of Tell Dotha stands where Dothan stood in Bible times. *Genesis 37:17; II Kings 6:13.*

DOVE. A small species of pigeon which was very plentiful in Palestine. The mournful cry of the dove, its way of flying, its habit of nesting in the rocks, and its gentleness and faithfulness to its mate made this bird a favorite. The Hebrew poets spoke of it often in their poetry. In the story of the Flood it was a dove which brought back an olive leaf to the ark. The dove

was also used as a sacrificial offering in the temple. At the baptism of Jesus the Holy Spirit is said to have descended "like a dove." For this reason the dove has become a symbol of the Holy Spirit for Christians. *Genesis 8:8-12; Psalm 74:19; Song of Solomon 2:12; 4:1; Isaiah 59:11; Jeremiah 48:28; Matthew 3:16; 10:16; John 1:32.*

DOXOLOGY. A short hymn or summary of praise to God. In the Jewish services blessings or doxologies were recited or chanted at the end of hymns (see I Chronicles 16:36; Psalms 41:13; 72: 18-19; 89:52; 106:48). Sometimes they are found at the beginning of a prayer (see Luke 1:68; II Corinthians 1:3; I Peter 1:3). Doxologies are a part of Christian worship.

DRAGON. In the OT a sea monster frightening to look at and very strong, sometimes called Leviathan or Rahab. In the book of Revelation the word is used to represent Satan as a dragon seeking to destroy. The dragon is defeated by the archangel Michael. *Psalm 74:13; Isaiah 27:1; 51:9; Revelation 12:3–13:4; 20:2-3.*

DUCK. Though not mentioned in the Bible, we can be sure that ducks were well known to the Israelites. Like the goose they doubtless were served at King Solomon's banquets and in the humblest Hebrew home. There is no record that they were domesticated. Wild ducks are still plentiful in Palestine.

DUGONG (Sea Cow). The dugong, a specie of sea cow, is found in the Indian Ocean and in the Red Sea. Hence it was known to the Hebrews.

It is one of nature's strangest creatures: a mammal, as the alternate name of "sea cow" implies, but living mostly in the water like a seal, which it somewhat resembles. Its hide makes excellent leather of a bluish tinge and no doubt was used by the Israelites.

EAGLE. Any of several large birds of prey of the falcon family. The eagle and the vulture are the largest birds mentioned in the Bible. The two types of eagles of Bible times were the golden eagle and the imperial eagle. Being birds of prey, they were considered unclean (see *Unclean, Uncleanness*). The OT writers were impressed by the sweep and speed of the eagle's flight. The eagle's long life, its majestic appearance, its lofty nesting places in the tallest trees or on craggy, hard-to-reach places in the mountains, its care for its young, and its awesome ways were used as figures of speech. *Psalm 103:5; Proverbs 23:4-5; 30:18-19; Jeremiah 4:13; 49:14-16.*

EARTH. Dry land, in biblical usage. In OT poetry the Hebrews often pictured the earth as a flat strip of land suspended over the ocean by pillars which mountains grounded into the seas. It was covered with a dome-like canopy, or covering of sky, called the firmament. The stars showed through openings in the firmament, and the rain and snow came through windows in the firmament. Heaven was up above the firmament. There are

many references to the four corners of the earth. *Exodus 20:4; Job 9:6-10; Psalms 24:1-2; 69:34; Isaiah 11:12.*

EARTHQUAKE. A shaking of the earth caused by volcanic activity or by movement of the earth's crust. The lands of the Bible are within an active earthquake zone. The Jordan Valley of upper Galilee, the Samaritan territory near biblical Shechem, and the edge of the Judean mountains near Lydda, Jericho, and Tiberias were centers of these disturbances. Fault lines, or cracks in the earth's crust along which some shifting can be observed, run into the Jordan Valley on an angle from east and west creating a condition that causes the earth's surface to move. *I Kings 19:9-14; Amos 1:1; Zechariah 14:5; Acts 16:25-26.*

EBAL, MOUNT. A mountain north of and opposite to Mt. Gerizim near Jerusalem. Mt. Ebal and Mt. Gerizim together form the sides of an important east-west pass. After the Israelites had entered Canaan, Joshua led them in a ceremony confirming the covenant which they had made with God, agreeing to obey his commandments. For this covenant ceremony six tribes were stationed in front of Mt. Ebal and six in front of Mt. Gerizim. The ark of the covenant was placed between them. Those tribes standing before Mt. Ebal pronounced curses on all who would fail to keep the commandments. Those tribes standing before Mt. Gerizim announced the blessings that would come to those who served the Lord. Joshua also built an altar on Mt. Ebal.

(See *Covenant; Gerizim, Mount.*) *Deuteronomy 11:29; 27:4-13; Joshua 8:30-33.*

EBED-MELECH. An Ethiopian servant in the court of King Zedekiah who rescued the prophet Jeremiah from a cistern. The title "ebed" means "slave" and was used to designate the class of court official. Here it is a proper name. *Jeremiah 36:7-13; 39:16.*

EBENEZER. Meaning "stone of help." A place near Aphek northeast of Joppa where the Israelites fought two battles with the Philistines and where the ark was captured by them. Also the name of a stone or monument which was set up near Mizpah, northwest of the Dead Sea, to commemorate a victory over the Philistines. The stone was a reminder that: "Hitherto the Lord has helped us." This shows plainly how the Hebrews understood that the hand of God was in all their victories and defeats, in fact, in all of their life as a nation. *I Samuel 4:1-11; 5:1; 7:12.*

ECCLESIASTES. Meaning "preacher," "speaker before an assembly." The pen name of the author and the name of his book, which is the twenty-first book of the OT. It was probably written during the time when the Jews were ruled by Greek kings about 250 B.C. Very little is known of the author, but he was a wise man and a philosopher. He explored and considered life and wrote down what he thought best for the person who wanted a good, satisfying life and one that was pleasing to God. His writings suggest that he wanted his readers to think of him as another Solomon.

EDICT. A public proclamation or ruling written, sealed with the king's ring, and read aloud before all the people. An edict was always written, and this is the way it differs from a decree, which did not have to be written down although it usually was. (See *Decree.*) *Esther 8:8-10; 9:1, 13; Hebrews 11:23.*

EDOM. In the OT a country located southeast of Judah. Edom received its name, which means "the red region," because of its red rocks and soil. Another name for this territory was Seir (see Joshua 12:7). Esau, the brother of Jacob, was called Edom possibly because of his ruddy complexion or from the redness of the lentil porridge which Jacob sold to Esau in exchange for his birthright. *Genesis 25:30; 36:1; Numbers 20:14-21; Deuteronomy 2:2-8; I Samuel 14:47; I Kings 11:14-17; 22:47; II Kings 8:20-22; Isaiah 11:14; Ezekiel 35:1-15; Amos 1:6, 9, 11; 2:1.*

EDOMITES. The people of Edom. The Israelites and Edomites were constantly at war, and in the time of the kings nearly all of the Judean prophets preached against the Edomites for their slavery and cruelty. Just as the Israelites were identified with Jacob, the Edomites were identified with his twin brother Esau. *Genesis 36:9; Deuteronomy 23:7-8; II Kings 8:21.*

EEL. Eels were found in the local lakes of Palestine, and the salt water variety in the Mediterranean. Since they have neither scales nor fins their use as food was forbidden under the prescribed dietary law. (Leviticus 11:10). It is quite possible that "eel" instead of "serpent" was used by Jesus when he asked, "If [his son] asks for a fish, will he give him a serpent?" (Matthew 7:10). An eel would be more familiar, and as worthless to a hungry Israelite as a stone.

EGYPT. A land on the southern coast of the Mediterranean Sea in northwestern Africa. Egypt lies along the valley of the great Nile River and because of this was probably the most fertile land of the ancient world. One of the names for Egypt was the "Black Land" because her rich, river-valley soil was such a contrast to the red, barren soil of her neighbors. There is very little rain in Egypt. The yearly flood brings a constant supply of fresh, rich soil and enough water to be stored for the rest of the season. The soil was so precious that not an inch of it was wasted. Instead of cutting into it with roads, the people used the river and its branches for transportation. Even the villages were crowded into the smallest possible space, while the fields for farming spread out all around them. For centuries Egypt was a rich and powerful nation. Egyptians had many contacts with the Hebrews, sometimes friendly and sometimes not. Abraham and later Jacob and all his family journeyed into Egypt to get food during times of famine, and this planted the Hebrews in Egypt. A hostile pharaoh later made them slaves. It was from Egypt that Moses led the Hebrew people into the land of Canaan. After the

establishment of the kingdom of Israel there were treaties and trade with the Egyptians. The famous stone pyramids and other tombs of the Egyptians are monuments to their former greatness. *Genesis 12:10–13:1; 39:1; 41:1-57; 47:1-31; II Kings 23:29, II Chronicles 12:2-3; Matthew 2:13-15.*

ELAH. King of the northern kingdom of Israel about 886 to 885 B.C. He was killed by Zimri in the revolt which brought the Omride family to the throne. *I Kings 16:6-14.*

ELAH, VALLEY OF. A fertile and strategic valley to the west of Bethlehem where Saul and the Israelites camped before the battle with the Philistines. It was here that David killed Goliath and won the battle for Israel. *I Samuel 17:2, 19; 21:9.*

ELAM. A mountainous country located east of the Tigris River at the north end of the Persian Gulf. The capital was Susa. The NT records the Elamites as among those present in Jerusalem on the day of Pentecost. Several men mentioned in the OT had the name Elam. *Ezra 4:9; Isaiah 21:2; Jeremiah 49:34-39; Acts 2:9.*

ELDER. In the OT a mature man, head of a family or tribe who had authority to judge in disputes or arguments and to give advice. The elders were the leaders in war. In NT times each synagogue and Jewish community had its council of elders. The most important council was the Sanhedrin in Jerusalem. Among the early Christians, elders presided over the churches and were associated with the apostles in governing the churches. *Genesis 25:23; Numbers 11:16-17; Ruth 4:2-12; I Samuel 15:30; Matthew 26:3; Acts 14:23; 15:2-4; I Timothy 5:17; I Peter 5:1-5.*

ELEAZAR. Son of Aaron and the successor to his father's priestly office as Moses' helper on the journey to the land of Canaan. Later Eleazar and Joshua divided the land by lots among the tribes of Israel. *Numbers 20:25-28; 34:17; Joshua 14:1.*

ELEPHANT. Though there is not direct reference to the elephant in the Bible, ivory is mentioned often. A symbol of great wealth, it was one of the wonders of King Solomon's Temple. Since the main source of ivory was the tusks of the elephant, the Hebrews must have known of this huge animal even though they never saw one. It it interesting to note that the Hebrew word for ivory is almost the same as that of southern India and Ceylon.

The Asiatic elephant once lived much closer to the Mediterranean than it does today. When Egypt conquered Syria about 1480 B.C., a herd of war elephants was part of the army.

ELI. The priest of the sanctuary, or shrine, at Shiloh and judge of Israel for forty years. Eli trained the boy Samuel to help him in the work in the sanctuary. *I Samuel 1:3–3:18; I Kings 2:27.*

ELIJAH. A prophet of the northern kingdom of Israel during the reign of Ahab in the ninth century B.C. Elijah opposed King Ahab and his wife Jezebel in their movement to establish

the worship of Baal in Israel. Elijah is reported to have performed many miracles. He foretold a severe drought, warning King Ahab that it was a punishment from the Lord. At the end of the drought Elijah challenged 450 prophets of Baal to a great contest. The Baal prophets prepared a sacrifice but got no response from their god. Elijah also prepared a sacrifice, and at his prayer to the Lord, fire came from heaven and burned it. At the end of his life Elijah gave the cloak of his office to Elisha, who was to be his successor. The younger prophet witnessed the translation of Elijah, that is, his being taken up into heaven in a chariot of fire by a whirlwind. The memory of Elijah was so cherished by the Hebrews that in NT times many people thought Jesus was Elijah. *I Kings 17:1–19:21; 21:17-29; II Kings 1:1–2:12; Malachi 4:5-6; Matthew 11:13-14; 16:13-14; 17:3-4, 10-13.*

ELISHA. A prophet of the northern kingdom of Israel in the ninth century B.C. He was the disciple and successor of Elijah. He continued the task of Elijah in fighting against the worship of Baal. Many miracles are credited to Elisha including the healing of Naaman, commander of the Syrian army, who had leprosy; the reviving of a dead boy; and the feeding of a hundred men with twenty loaves of bread. He advised and attempted to guide the kings of Israel for fifty years. *II Kings 2:1–13:21; Luke 4:27.*

ELIZABETH. Mother of John the Baptist and a relative of Mary the mother of Jesus. *Luke 1:5-60.*

EMMAUS. A Judean town about seven miles from Jerusalem. Cleopas and another disciple who were friends set out to walk from Jerusalem to Emmaus a short while after the crucifixion. They met the risen Jesus and though they did not recognize him, they walked along talking with him. They invited him to have supper with them, and when he blessed the bread and broke it, they realized that he was the risen Lord. *Luke 24:13-53.*

EN-ROGEL. A spring near Jerusalem in the Kidron Valley. It marked the limit between the tribes of Benjamin and Judah. When David had to flee from Jerusalem during a revolt, two of his spies remained near En-rogel to gather information concerning the revolt. Also Adonijah, a son of David who hoped to get the throne instead of Solomon, had himself secretly crowned near this spring as David lay dying. *Joshua 15:7; 18:16; II Samuel 17:17; I Kings 1:9.*

ENROLLMENT. A public census, or counting of people according to family position and tribe (see Numbers 1:2-3). In NT times Rome under Emperor Augustus Caesar required all families to return to their native cities to be enrolled for tax purposes. It was at the time of that enrollment that Jesus was born. *I Chronicles 9:1; Luke 2:1-7.*

EPAPHRAS. An early Christian who was a native of the city of Colossae. It was through Epaphras that the Colossians had come to know the Christian gospel. He preached in Colossae, Laodicea, and Hierapolis.

He was a co-worker and close friend of Paul. The two men were in prison together in Rome. *Colossians 1:3-8; 4:12-13; Philemon 1:23.*

EPAPHRODITUS. A friend and co-worker of Paul and a leader in the church at Philippi. He took a gift from that church to Paul in prison and stayed for a time to help him. *Philippians 2:25-30.*

EPHAH. A measure for dry ingredients nearly equal to a bushel. *Leviticus 19:36; Ezekiel 45:10-11; Zechariah 5:5-11.*

EPHESIANS, LETTER TO THE. The tenth book in the NT. A letter addressed to the Christians in Ephesus about the plan of God to bring all people together in Christ. It explains the place of the church and Christians in the world. It may have been sent to churches in many other cities. It is not certain who wrote this letter, but it may well have been Paul.

EPHESUS. In NT times a large seaport city in the Roman province of Asia which is now Turkey. It was a commercial and religious center for the worship of the goddess Artemis. Paul lived for a time at Ephesus, teaching in the synagogue and in the hall of Tyrannus. An outdoor theater may still be seen in the ruins of this old city. *Acts 18:19-21, 24; 19:1-10, 23-41; 20:16-21; I Corinthians 16:8-9; I Timothy 1:3-4; II Timothy 1:18; 4-12; Revelation 1:11; 2:1.*

EPHOD. An OT name for a ceremonial garment worn by a priest. Also, it may have been an object carried by the priest when he was seeking direction from God. *Exodus 28:4, 28-29; 35:27; 39:1-22; Judges 17:5; 18:14, 17-18, 20; I Samuel 2:18; 14:3.*

EPHRAIM. A son of Joseph and brother of Manasseh. Though Ephraim was the younger, his good fortune and his landholdings in Palestine overshadowed his brother's. Originally the name of a geographical area, "Ephraim" became the name of one of the twelve tribes of Israel. It also came to be a name for Israel after the territory of the northern kingdom had been reduced by war, first with Syria and then Assyria, until little more than the original Ephraimite territory remained. *Genesis 41:50-52; 46:20; 48:1-5, 13-22; 50:23; Numbers 1:32-33; Joshua 24:30; Judges 7:24; Hosea 4:17; 7:1; John 11:54.*

EPHRATHAH. A city in Judah, an ancient settlement that became a part of Bethlehem. Often the two names are combined—Bethlehem-Ephrathah. *Genesis 35:19; 48:7; Ruth 1:2; I Samuel 17:12; Micah 5:2.*

EPICUREANS. In NT times the followers of a Greek philosopher named Epicurus who taught in Athens in the fourth century B.C. His philosophy was that happiness was the chief aim of life. The happy state could be reached without any belief in God or gods. He taught that religion disturbed or destroyed the contentment of people. *Acts 17:18.*

ESAU. A son of Isaac and Rebekah and elder twin brother of Jacob. His name means "red" and "hairy," indicating that Esau was a hairy, red-complexioned man. He loved the

rugged outdoor life of a hunter. He sold his birthright to Jacob in exchange for some food once when he was very hungry. On another occasion Jacob deceived his father Isaac into bestowing upon him the blessing rightfully belonging to the older son. Esau was the ancestor of the Edomites as Jacob was of the Israelites. The unfriendly relations between the two nations through the years reflected this conflict between the brothers. (See *Edom.*) *Genesis 25:24-34; 27:1–28:9; 33:1-16; I Chronicles 1:34.*

ESTHER. A Jewish girl who was among the beautiful maidens chosen by the Persian king Ahasuerus to fill the place of the banished queen Vashti. She pleased the king so that he made her his queen. Haman, the prime minister, aroused the king against the Jews because of their religious beliefs and practices, which were different from any others in the kingdom. With great courage Esther approached the king and explained that his edict authorizing the destruction of the Jews would mean the end of her people. The king was persuaded, and Haman was executed on the gallows he had prepared for Esther's cousin Mordecai. (See *Esther, Book of.*)

ESTHER, BOOK OF. The OT book which tells the story of how Esther, the Jewish wife of a Persian king, saved the Jews from persecution. The book explains the festival of Purim, which is the annual Jewish observance of this deliverance.

ETERNAL LIFE. Life with God that is not destroyed by death and which can begin here and now. In the OT God was often spoken as the living God (see Deuteronomy 5:26; Joshua 3:10). This meant that God had the rule over death and could defeat it. The NT points to this victory over death in the crucifixion of Jesus Christ, in his rising again from the tomb, and in his offer of everlasting life to all those who believe in him. (See *Immortality; Resurrection, The.*) *Matthew 25:46; John 3:15-16; 6:39-40, 47-51, 54; Romans 6:22-23; I John 5:11-12.*

ETHIOPIA. The ancient name of the African territory south of Egypt corresponding roughly to the present Sudan. In the Bible it is also called Cush. *II Kings 19:9; Psalm 68:31; Isaiah 20:3-5; 45:14; Jeremiah 13:23; Acts 8:26-28.*

EUNUCH. In Bible times a man servant whose male organs had been removed. Such men served in the women's quarters of the royal household. They were sometimes called "officers" and "captains." *II Kings 9:30-33; 20:18; Esther 2:3; Isaiah 39:7; 56:3-5; Jeremiah 38:7; 41:16; Matthew 19:12; Acts 8:27.*

EUPHRATES. The largest river in western Asia, originating in Armenia and emptying into the Persian Gulf. According to biblical tradition it was one of the four rivers into which the river that flowed from the Garden of Eden divided. In Bible times the Euphrates formed the north boundary of the territories promised by God to Israel in his covenant with Abraham. Because of its importance it was often called simply "the River."

EVANGELIST

UNIVERSITY MUSEUM, UNIVERSITY OF PENNSYLVANIA

ORIENTAL INSTITUTE, UNIVERSITY OF CHICAGO

Left: Cylinder of Nebuchadrezzar (King of Babylon 605–562 B.C.) inscribed with three columns of text *ca.* 586 B.C. found buried in the foundation of a temple in Babylon. Above: City of Babylon, showing the Tower of Babel (from a painting by Maurice Bardin of the reconstruction by Unger).

Genesis 2:14; 15:18; Joshua 1:4; I Kings 4:24; I Chronicles 18:3.

EVANGELIST. Meaning "one who announces good news." A title of early Christian missionaries and preachers of the gospel. It is used in a more limited way to indicate the authors of the NT gospels. *Acts 21:8; Ephesians 4:11; II Timothy 4:5.*

EVE. In the Genesis stories of creation, the first woman, the wife given by God to Adam to be his companion and helper. She was the "woman" who listened to the serpent and ate the forbidden fruit. She persuaded Adam to eat, and they were banished from the Garden of Eden. *Genesis 3:1–4:2.*

EWE. The female sheep was often a household pet of the Hebrews as indicated in Nathan's story in II

Samuel 12:1-6. It was seldom used for food or for sacrificial purposes for the very practical reason that the ewe was the mother of the next generation.

EXILE, THE. The time in biblical history when the Babylonians conquered the country of Judah and the city of Jerusalem and carried many of the Jews away to live in Babylonia. The first of the exiles left their homes in 597 B.C. Other exiles went in 586 and 582 B.C. Many returned home in 538 B.C. when Cyrus, the Persian king, conquered Babylonia and permitted the exiles and prisoners of war to go home. The word *exile* is also used to refer to an individual's banishment from his home or country. Kings were sometimes banished to other lands because they were weak or poor rulers. *II Samuel 15:19; II Chronicles 36:19-20; Ezra 6:16.*

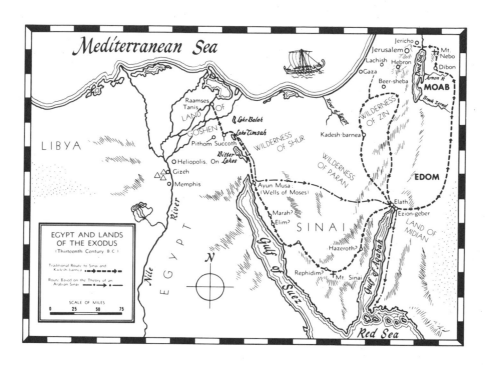

EGYPT AND LANDS
OF THE EXODUS
(Thirteenth Century B.C.)

Traditional Route to Sinai and
Kadesh-barnea

Route Based on the Theory of an
Arabian Sinai

SCALE OF MILES
0   25   50   75

EXODUS, BOOK OF. Meaning "a going out." The second book of the OT telling of the "going out" from Egypt by the Hebrew people under the leadership of Moses. It tells of the deliverance of the people from slavery and the long journey to the land of Canaan.

EXPIATION. An action of atonement that takes away a sin or "covers" it and thus restores a person to holiness and divine favor. (See *Atonement.*) *Numbers 35:33; Deuteronomy 32:43; Romans 3:23-25; Hebrews 2:17; I John 2:1-2; 4:10.*

EZEKIEL. A prophet of the Babylonian exile. Ezekiel was the son of a priest and had grown up close to the temple in Jerusalem. He was carried to Babylonia in 597 B.C. There among the exiles Ezekiel had a vision of God and received the call to be a prophet to Israel. He preached to the Jews in exile and prepared them for the time when God would restore them to their own land. (See *Ezekiel, Book of.*)

EZEKIEL, BOOK OF. An OT book containing the prophecies and sermons of Ezekiel. The prophecies are in poetic language with much symbolism. One of Ezekiel's most important messages to the Jews was that being separated from their land and from the temple in Jerusalem did not separate them from God.

EZRA. A priest and scribe who led a group of Jewish exiles from Babylonia back to Jerusalem around the middle of the fifth century or the beginning of the fourth century B.C. In a royal

EZRA, BOOK OF

decree King Artaxerxes gave Ezra great authority in supervising the rebuilding of Jerusalem. He made a great effort to restore the community life of the Jews according to the old Jewish law. (See *Ezra, Book of.*)

EZRA, BOOK OF. Originally the book of Ezra and the book of Nehemiah were a single book. The two books are a continuation of the books called Chronicles I and II and relate the history of the Jews from 536 to 432 B.C. The book of Ezra lists the exiles who returned to Jerusalem with Ezra and the temple vessels they brought with them. *Nehemiah 8:1–10:39.*

FABLE. A form of short story which teaches a lesson and in which plants and animals speak and act as persons do. A fable could not possibly happen, but it has some truth the reader or listener will find helpful. The Bible has two fables. Each tells some truth about a king. (See *Allegory, Myth, Parable.*) *Judges 9:8-15; II Kings 14:9.*

FACE. The front part of the head of people or animals. The face expresses most clearly the thoughts and feelings of a person. In the Bible such phrases as "to set one's face against" or "to hide one's face" express anger and displeasure. "Face" is used also as a figure of speech to suggest God's presence, as in "the Lord make his face to shine upon you." *Numbers 6:24-26; Psalm 27:8-9.*

FAIR HAVENS. A harbor at the south side of the island of Crete where the Alexandrian ship on which Paul was sailing to Rome stopped for a while. Paul suggested remaining there for the winter. Against his advice the ship continued on and was shipwrecked. *Acts 27:6-12.*

FAITH. As used in the Bible, faith is belief in, trust in, and loyalty to God. Faith is the confident response people make to the love, care, and seeking of God. With the NT, faith in God became also faith in Jesus. He gave a new understanding of God as the father, and in his decisive acts (especially the crucifixion and the resurrection) he charged mankind with responding in faith to the highest, the ultimate. *II Chronicles 19:9; Psalms 78:22; 116:10; Habakkuk 2:4; Matthew 21:22; Mark 2:5; 5:34; 11:22; Luke 7:9; 18:8; Acts 14:9; 20:21; 24:24; Romans 1:16-17; 4:13-22; I Corinthians 13:13; Galatians 2:16; Hebrews 11:1-31; I John 5:4.*

FALCON. Several varieties of the falcon, a branch of the hawk family, are found in the Holy Land. In most species the male is smaller than the female. Usually a pair remain mated for life. Both help build the nest, incubate the eggs and raise the young. The peregrine falcon has been used for hunting since ancient times. Falconry was a common sport in medieval England, but there is no record that the Hebrews used them in this way.

FAMILY. A group of persons related to each other by kinship or marriage. In early OT times families were very large because a man was permitted to have more than one wife and to have children by more than one

wife. The family group would consist of wives, children, grandparents, concubines, servants, and grown children with their own family circles. In later times it became the custom to have only one wife. Among the Hebrews the family was a religious community which had a solemn duty to pass on the traditions of their worship, history, and knowledge of God. So close were these ties that the entire nation was thought of as a family, the family of God. In the NT the community of Christian believers is also referred to as the family of God. *Genesis 37:1-2; Ruth 2:1-2; Psalm 22:27; Jeremiah 31:1; Acts 3:25.*

FAMINE. Scarcity of food caused by drought, insects, disease of the grain or cattle, war, and other disasters. *Genesis 12:10; 41:54-57; Job 5:20; Jeremiah 14:15-16; Acts 11:28.*

FAST. To go without food and water for a period of time as religious and moral discipline. In early OT times there was often public fasting to express personal grief or to express sorrow and alarm at a national disaster. Fasting was also an act of repentance for sin. After the Exile fast days were appointed at regular times of the year. In the NT Jesus emphasized that fasting should be done in sincerity and for the glory of God, not for the praise of people. The early church used it as a discipline. *Judges 20:26; II Chronicles 20:3; Ezra 8:21-23; 9:5-6; Nehemiah 9:1; Matthew 4:2; 6:16-18; 9:14-15; Acts 13:2-3; 14:23.*

FATHER. The male head of a household, family, or tribe. The name was sometimes used as a title of respect for an ancestor or a person in authority. Jesus used the name in speaking of God to help people understand his nature. *Genesis 28:13; Deuteronomy 5:16; I Samuel 24:8-11; Matthew 6:9, 14, 32; Luke 2:48-49; 6:36; Ephesians 5:19-20.*

FATHOM. In NT times a unit of measurement based on the length from the tip of one outstretched hand to the tip of the other, usually about six feet. It is a term used today in measuring the depth of water. *Acts 27:28.*

FATLING. A well-cared-for and well-fed animal, such as a cow or sheep, important for its use in Israel's sacrificial worship. *II Samuel 6:13; I Kings 1:9, 25; Psalm 66:15; Isaiah 11:6.*

FEAR. Alarm, dread. In the Bible the term appears with many different meanings. The expressions "fear of God" and "fear of the Lord" also have the meanings of awe, reverence, respect, love, trust, and faith. This sort of fear is a recognition of God's holiness. *Deuteronomy 6:13; Joshua 24:14; II Samuel 23:3-4; II Chronicles 19:7; 26:5; Psalms 23:4; 33:8; 130:4; Acts 9:31; I Peter 2:17.*

FELIX, ANTONIUS. Roman governor of Judea from A.D. 52 to 60. He was governor when Paul last visited Jerusalem and was arrested there. Paul was brought to Caesarea to be tried by Felix. The governor kept him in prison for two years, hoping that Paul would pay to secure his release. *Acts 23:24–24:27.*

FESTAL GARMENT. Fine clothing worn on special days or occasions. *Genesis 45:22; Judges 14:12-13, 19; II Kings 5:5, 22-23.*

FESTUS, PORCIUS. Roman governor of Judea probably from A.D. 60 to 62. Successor to Felix. Festus was forced to send Paul to Rome for trial when Paul as a Roman citizen appealed to Caesar. Paul had already been in prison in Caesarea for two years. *Acts 24:27–26:32.*

FETTER. Anything that restrains a person's movements; a shackle. In Bible times fetters were made of wood, bronze, or iron. A prisoner's feet might be placed in fetters or shackles. The fetters were joined together by a rope and allowed him to take only short steps. A captive's hands were often placed in a fetter suspended from his neck by a rope. *Judges 16.21; Psalms 105:18; 149:8; Mark 5:4; Acts 16:25-26.*

FIG. Ranking with the date palm as one of the most valuable trees of ancient time is the fig. Its pear-shaped fruit was important as food. To the Hebrews this beautiful spreading tree was a symbol of abundance and peace. It is mentioned in Genesis 3:7 as growing in the Garden of Eden and Jesus refers to the fig and the fig tree several times. To the Egyptians it represented the Tree of Life. Its importance to the life and commerce of peoples in the Middle East is still great.

FILLET. A metal band joining the tops of the pillars in the tabernacle. Hooks were probably fixed to the band by which the curtains were hung. *Exodus 27:10-11; 36:38; 38:10-12, 17, 19.*

FINCH. Of the many varieties of finch, several are found in Palestine. Both the trumpeter bullfinch with its distinctive piping note, and the brightly colored goldfinch were kept as caged pets in Jesus' time, as they are today in many parts of Asia. Because of its habit of eating thistles and thorns the goldfinch became the symbol of Christ's crown of thorns and so of the Passion of Christ.

FINGER OF GOD. A figure of speech used in the Bible to indicate the power of God. *Exodus 8:19; 31:18; Deuteronomy 9:10, Psalm 8:3; Luke 11:20.*

FIR. The fir of the Holy Land is a variety of pine, common in the area west of the Jordan. It is similar to our pines, having silver-gray bark and reddish-brown cones that take on a grayish tinge when fully opened. The needles grow in pairs.

Hiram, king of Tyre, "gave Solomon . . . fir trees" (I Kings 5:10) to be used in the building of the temple. Turpentine and resin were by-products of the fir in ancient times.

FIRMAMENT. An OT word meaning "a strip of beaten metal." The Hebrews sometimes pictured the sky as a metallic sheet that separated the upper waters from the lower waters. (See *Earth.*) *Genesis 1:6-7; Psalms 19:1; 150:1.*

FIRSTBORN. In the OT the term is used mainly to mean the eldest son.

The Hebrews gave a special place to the firstborn son. He became the next head of the family or tribe, responsible for its welfare. He claimed the family blessing and received a double portion of the family inheritance (see *Birthright*). The term refers also to the sacrifice of the firstlings of animals. In the NT the term is applied to Jesus and indicates his relationship to God. *Exodus 4:22-23; 13:11-15; Numbers 18:15-18; Deuteronomy 21:15-17; Luke 2:7; Romans 8:29; Colossians 1:15, 18; Hebrews 1:6.*

FIRST FRUITS. The sacrificial offering to God from the annual crop of vegetables, grain, and animals. The Hebrews were very conscious of the fact that their land was a gift of God; he was their landlord, so to speak. For this reason all the fruit of the earth belonged to God, but by offering the first and best back to him, the rest of the harvest was free for people to use as they needed. The first fruits were offered by the Hebrews at the Festival of Weeks, or Pentecost. In the later calendar this fell fifty days from the second day of Passover. This thanksgiving festival is still kept by the Jews. *Exodus 34:22; Leviticus 23:15-22; Numbers 28:26.*

FISH. Plentiful as fish were in Bible times, and as often as they are referred to in both the old and new testaments, no particular kind is named. But doubtless those caught by "the big fisherman," Simon, and his fellow fishermen were the same as those caught today in the Sea of Galilee and the freshwater streams of the Holy Land. Familiar with fish and the vocation of fisherman, Jesus used them many times as illustrations in his preaching. One of his most challenging pronouncements was that his disciples should be "fishers of men."

A fish (in Greek, ΙΧΘΥΣ)

$I = \text{'}I\eta\sigma o\hat{v}s = \text{Jesus}$
$X = X\rho\iota\sigma\tau\acute{o}s = \text{Christ}$
$\Theta = \Theta\epsilon o\hat{v} = \text{God's}$
$\Upsilon = \text{'}\Upsilon\iota\acute{o}s = \text{Son}$
$\Sigma = \Sigma\omega\tau\acute{\eta}\rho = \text{Savior}$

The Greek acrostic for "fish," which means: "Jesus Christ, God's Son, Savior." The inscribed fish, with such a hidden meaning, was frequently found in the catacombs of the early Christians.

FLAG. In Exodus 2:3, 5 the flag is mentioned in connection with the hiding of the baby Moses. It was one of the many rank growing plants that thrive in wet ground. It is natural that they be mentioned along with the bulrushes. As Job asks, "Can the flag grow without water?" (Job 8:11).

Entirely different from the swampland flag mentioned above is the corn flag indigenous to Palestine. It grows mostly in the grainfields, its deep pink blossoms changing to purple as they grow older, coloring the fields before the grain ripens in early April.

FLAGON. A large pitcher of pottery or metal usually having a cover. Oil, wine, and other liquids were kept in flagons. *Exodus 25:29; 37:16; Numbers 4:7; Isaiah 22:24.*

FLAMINGO. The long-legged, long-necked flamingo was one of the

many wading birds abundant in the Nile delta close to the site of the Israelites' sojourn in Egypt. They must have been familiar to the Hebrews then, and later in Palestine when flocks of water birds, including the flamingo, inhabited the swamps around the Sea of Galilee.

FLASK. A small, bottle-like container for oil, water, perfume, or ointment. In ancient times flasks were made of pottery or alabaster; later they were made of glass. *II Kings 9:1-3; Jeremiah 19:1, 10; Matthew 25:4; Luke 7:37.*

FLAX. The plant from which linen comes. In Bible times it was cultivated in Egypt and Canaan. The fibers of the plant are soaked, combed, and spun into linen thread, then woven into linen cloth and rope. *Exodus 9:31; Joshua 2:6, Judges 15:14; Proverbs 31:13; Isaiah 19:9; Ezekiel 40:3.*

FLEA. The pestiferous flea was doubtless as much of a nuisance to the ancients as it is today. Certainly the unsanitary conditions common in ancient times would have made it a common pest. The only direct reference to the flea in the Bible is by David, who chides Saul and sucessfully seeks to appease him be reminding the king that he is wasting his strength seeking "a flea as one doth hunt a partridge in the mountains" (I Samuel 26:20).

FLESH. The soft, muscular part of the body. However, the word was used in the OT to refer to the whole body of a person. In this sense it means the person's humanity. "Flesh" is often used to indicate weakness, especially in contrast to the spiritual part of a person which is thought of as the seat of what is best in him. *Genesis 2:23; II Chronicles 32:8; Psalm 78:39; Matthew 26:41; John 1:14; 8:15; Galatians 5:16-24; I Peter 1:24-25.*

FLY. Flies swarming over the land are listed as the fourth plague that ravished Egypt (Exodus 8:24). They are one of the most widely distributed of insects, as prevalent thousands of years ago as now, and of many varieties. The common housefly was a pest, but equally so were the "botfly," or "gadfly," which deposits its eggs in the fur of a cow or other animal (Jeremiah 46:20). The tsetse fly, carrier of the germ of "sleeping sickness," was familiar to the Hebrews in Egypt.

FOOTSTOOL. A footrest for a king's throne or steps leading to the throne. Solomon's throne had a footstool of gold. Some ancient kings had carvings on the steps or footstool, representing other peoples and nations. Thus, they felt they walked over their captives or enemies as they mounted the throne. In the Bible this word is often used as a symbol to represent the earth as God's footstool to show the dominion or authority of God as king and sovereign over all things. *I Chronicles 28:2; II Chronicles 9:18; Psalms 99:5; 110:1; 132:7; Isaiah 66:1; Lamentations 2:1; Matthew 5:34-35; Acts 7:49.*

FORD. A place where a river is shallow enough to cross by wading. Until recent times fording was the most common way to cross rivers

except in the prosperous and well-traveled places where bridges were built. *Genesis 32:22; Joshua 2:7; Judges 3:28; 12:5-6; I Samuel 13:7; II Samuel 15:28; 17:16; 19:18; Isaiah 16:2.*

FORGIVENESS. The plainest meanings of forgiveness are the pardoning of an offender, the giving up of a claim to a debt, or the release from an obligation. In the relationship of people to God, forgiveness is God's gracious taking away of the barriers which separate people from him. The central fact of the NT is that in the life and death of Jesus Christ the obstacles of man's sin and disobedience are removed for those who, believing in Christ, repent of their sins. Their guilt is wiped away, forgiven. In the relationship of persons, forgiveness is the pardoning of an offender. The person who has been wronged excuses the offender and counts the wrong as if it had not happened. *Genesis 50:17; Numbers 15:25-26; Psalm 130:4; Luke 3:3; 6:37; Acts 2:38; 10:43; Hebrews 9:22.*

FORUM OF APPIUS. A stopping place or station on the Appian Way between Puteoli, where ships unloaded passengers and cargo, and the city of Rome. It was about forty-three miles, slightly more than a day's journey, from Rome; though because the road was good, the trip could be made in a day. Paul passed through this place on his way to prison in Rome. *Acts 28:15.*

FOUNTAIN. A spring of water flowing from an opening in a hillside or valley. In the dry Bible lands a fountain was an important source of water. The presence of a fountain often determined the location of a village. This is shown by the fact that names of many villages began with *en*, meaning "fountain," for instance, En-gedi. Fountains were also mentioned in the OT in figures of speech for the power and wisdom of God as the source of life and refreshment. *Deuteronomy 33:28; Nehemiah 2:14; 3:15; Psalms 36: 9; 68:26; Proverbs 13:14; 14:27; Ecclesiastes 12:6; Jeremiah 17:13; Joel 3:18.*

FOWL. We think of a hen as a fowl, and this has come to be the common meaning of the word. But "fowl" in the Bible had little if any reference to adult chickens. Rather the word is used in a general sense to include all birds: God gave man "domination over the fowl of the air" (Genesis 1:26). When Jesus bids his listeners to "behold the fowls of the air" that "neither toil nor spin" (Matthew 6:26), he obviously was not thinking of barnyard fowl, that is, the hen.

FOX. The red fox was the most common in Bible lands, but the smaller Egyptian fox, rust-colored with a white-belly, was prevalent in southern Palestine. The shiny, golden-colored Syrian fox was common in the northern forests. The fox has always been noted for its craftiness and cunning: Jesus referred to Herod as "that fox" (Luke 13:32). And rather pensively he reminds his disciples that "foxes have holes . . . but the Son of Man hath not where to lay his head" (Matthew 8:20).

In the Song of Solomon (2:15) mention is made of "the little foxes

that spoil the vines" of the vineyard. Foxes like the sweet juice of the grapes, and also they burrow tunnels in the vineyards that destroy the roots of the vines. Samson's "three hundred foxes" (Judges 15:4) more likely were jackals.

FRANKINCENSE. A fragrant gum resin taken from the bark of a tree that grows in northern Arabia. The resin hardens into small white chunks and beads that are easily ground into a powder. This powder was an important ingredient in incense and has a balsam-like odor when burned. Frankincense was used in many ways in the sacrificial worship of Israel. It was set with the bread of the presence before the holy of holies and was mixed with oil in the offerings of grain, vegetables, or fruit. As a gift to the infant Jesus it symbolized worship. *Exodus 30:34-38; Leviticus 2:1-2; 24:7; Isaiah 43:23; 60:6; Matthew 2:10-11.*

FRINGE. A cord or thread which ended in a kind of tassel sewn on the corners of an outer garment (see Deuteronomy 22: 12). The fringe, or tassel, was to remind the Hebrews of the commandments of God. *Matthew 9:20; 14:36; 23:5; Mark 6:56; Luke 8:44.*

FROG. Not only were frogs abhorrent to the early Israelites, and unclean, but the fact that their Egyptian masters paid obeisance to the frog god Hequet made the creature even more despicable.

Frogs of many species were common in Egypt. The plague of frogs, second of the ten, is described in detail in Exodus 8:1-14. The psalmist reminds the Children of Israel of this event in Psalms 78:45 and 105:34. The only other time the frog is mentioned in the Bible is in Revelation 16:13, when John tells of seeing "three unclean spirits like frogs."

FRONTLET. A band worn on the forehead between the eyes at prayer times as a reminder of the commandments of God. It may occasionally have been thought of as being effective against certain kinds of evil. *Exodus 13-16; Deuteronomy 6:4-9; 11:18.*

FRUIT. A product of a plant or tree useful to man. The word is used as a figure of speech in the Bible to mean the result of any specific action, good or evil. *Genesis 30:2; Psalms 104:13; 127:3; Proverbs 1:31; 12:14; 31:31; Isaiah 3:10; 13:18; 57:18; Jeremiah 17:10; Hosea 10:12-13; Amos 6:12; Matthew 3:10; 7:15-20; 21:43; Mark 4:20; Luke 1:42; Ephesians 5:9; Hebrews 12:11; 13:15.*

FULLER'S FIELD. A place outside the city of Jerusalem near the canal of the Upper Pool. Probably the location where cloth had once been "fulled." This process involved thickening and shrinking newly shorn wool or newly woven cloth. The natural oils were removed and the material cleaned and bleached. The worker who did this was called a "fuller." *II Kings 18:17; Isaiah 7:3; 36:2.*

GABRIEL. In the Bible, a messenger angel. The name

means "man of God" or "God has shown himself mighty." Gabriel is specifically named in the NT as the messenger from God sent to announce the births of John the Baptist and of Jesus. *Daniel 8:16; 9:21; Luke 1:11-20, 26-38.*

GAD. The seventh son of Jacob and the ancestor of the tribe of Gad, called Gadites. The territory of the Gadites was east of the Jordan River. *Genesis 35:26; Numbers 1:24-25; I Samuel 13:6-7; I Chronicles 5:11; 12:8-15.*

GAIUS. 1. A Christian baptized by Paul in Corinth. Gaius made Paul welcome in his home there. At this time Paul wrote a letter to the Romans. *Romans 16:23; I Corinthians 1:14.*

2. Gaius of Macedonia was one of Paul's traveling companions who was arrested with Paul in Ephesus. *Acts 19:29.*

3. Gaius of Derbe is also mentioned as another traveling companion of Paul. Gaius of Macedonia and Gaius of Derbe may possibly have been the same person. *Acts 20:4.*

4. Another Gaius was a Christian leader to whom the third letter of John was addressed. *III John 1:1.*

GALATIA. In NT times a Roman province in central Asia Minor named for the Celtic (Gallic) tribe of the Galatians. It is now a part of Turkey. Important NT cities in Galatia were Derbe, Antioch of Pisidia, Iconium, and Lystra. *Acts 16:6; 18:23; I Corinthians 16:1; Galatians 1:2; II Timothy 4:10; I Peter 1:1.*

GALATIANS, LETTER TO THE. The ninth book in the NT. A letter written by Paul to "the churches of Galatia." In it Paul tells of his own conversion. He explains that Christians are not required to keep all the Jewish laws and regulations. Their faith in Christ makes them free to follow the law of love. He gives a description of the kind of goodness a Christian should practice.

GALBANUM. The galbanum plant resembles anise (dill). A perennial, it grows several feet in height. It has finely divided leaves and umbels of small greenish-white blossoms. As indicated in Exodus 30:34, it was one of the "sweet spices" to be used in the preparation of sacred ointment.

GALILEE. A small region in northern Palestine east of the Mediterranean Sea. In OT times its boundaries changed many times, and for centuries it was ruled by one nation after another. In 63 B.C. Galilee became a fixed area under Roman rule with Sepphoris and then Tiberias as the capital. It was bounded on the west by the Mediterranean Sea and on the east by the Sea of Galilee and the Jordan River. Oil, wine, fish, and grain were the common exports. Almost all Jesus' career lay within the borders of this tiny region. Galileans spoke with an accent different from that of Judeans. The modern state of Israel, established in 1948, includes all of Galilee. *Joshua 21:32; I Kings 9:11; II Kings 15:29; Isaiah 9:1; Matthew 2:22; 4:12-15; Mark 1:9, 28, 39; Luke 4:31; 17:11; John 4:43-47; 7:1, 41, 52; Acts 1:11; 9:31.*

GALILEE, SEA OF. A freshwater, heart-shaped, inland lake that empties

into the Jordan River. It is about thirteen miles long and seven miles wide with an abundance of fish and birds. Almost surrounded by mountains, the lake reaches to a depth of two hundred feet. The surface of the lake is about six hundred feet below sea level. It has been called by several names during the period of Hebrew history—"Chinnereth," "Gennesaret," and "Tiberias." It is best known as the Sea of Galilee. Many persons and places associated with Jesus came from this area. Here fishing was an important means of making a living. *Numbers 34:11; Joshua 12:3; 13:27; Matthew 4:18; Mark 1:16; 7:31; Luke 5:1; John 6:1; 21:1.*

GALL. The juice of a bitter herb. The term is also used to describe or symbolize a feeling of bitterness. The gall offered to Jesus on the cross was made from the juice of the poppy added to sour wine. It was supposed to have the effect of easing pain. Jesus refused to take it. *Job 20:14; Lamentations 3:19; Matthew 27:34; Acts 8:23.*

GALLIO. Proconsul of Achaea about A.D. 52 with headquarters at Corinth. Paul was brought before him on the charge that faith in Christ was contrary to Roman law, but Gallio was unwilling to be the judge and dismissed the case. *Acts 18:12-17.*

GAMALIEL. A Pharisee, a famous interpreter of the Jewish law, and an honored member of the Sanhedrin in Jerusalem. He is said to have been Paul's teacher. He was a man of generous spirit, and he cautioned his fellow council members to be careful

about how they opposed the apostles who preached and healed in the name of Jesus Christ. If their teaching were false, it would fade away, he pointed out. If it were true, the council would be working against God. *Acts 5:34-39; 22:3.*

GARRISON. A body of troops stationed for defense, usually at a frontier post. *I Samuel 10:5; 13:3-4; II Samuel 8:6, 14; 23:14; I Chronicles 11:16; 18:13; II Chronicles 17:2.*

GASH. In the OT to cut oneself as a sign of mourning or as a part of the worship of pagan gods. *Jeremiah 41:5; 47:5; 48:37; Hosea 7:14.*

GATE. In the OT an opening in the wall of a city built so that it could be well defended. There were usually an outer and an inner gate built at angles to the wall with a lookout tower. Gates were closed at night. The gate was the center of interest in the town, and most business was carried on there. News was best gathered there, and it was also the place of judgment. The elders sat between the outer and inner gates to judge cases brought to them. Just inside the gate was the busy marketplace. *Deuteronomy 21:19; Joshua 20:4; Ruth 4.1-2; II Samuel 18:24; II Kings 7:1, 18; Amos 5:10, 12, 15.*

GATH. In the OT one of the five principal cities of the Philistines. It was nearer Judah than the others; therefore, now and again it came under Judah's control. It was an old city once inhabited by the Anakim, a race of giants. Goliath and other giant Philistine warriors came from Gath. David's lament "Tell it not in Gath" is

often quoted in works of literature when mentioning some disastrous or regrettable event which might give one's enemies cause to rejoice. *Joshua 11:22; 13:3; I Samuel 5:8; 17:4, 52; 21:10-12; 27:2-4; II Samuel 1:20; I Chronicles 18:1; 20:6-8; II Chronicles 26:6; Micah 1:10.*

GAZA. An ancient city southeast of the Mediterranean Sea located three miles from the seacoast of Philistia on the road to Egypt. It was a place of importance because it was on a trade route. Gaza was one of the five principal cities of the Philistines and fought against the Israelites. The prophet Amos condemned Gaza for its slave trade. *Genesis 10:19; Deuteronomy 2:23; Joshua 10:41; 11:22; 13:3; 15:47; Judges 1:18; 6:4; 16:1-2; I Samuel 6:17, Amos 1:6-7; Acts 8:26.*

GAZELLE. The gazelle is common in Palestine today. It is a member of the antelope family, especially noted for its graceful body and movements. It is one of the fastest of animals, leaping as much as three feet in the air as it runs. Very shy, it travels in herds of forty or fifty. It is hunted for food, but its speed makes special techniques necessary for the hunter. The animals are sometimes driven into narrow valleys where they can more easily be shot. Sometimes they are captured in nets or driven into pitfalls. The Egyptians made pets of the gazelle.

GEBA. A city on the northern boundary of the kingdom of Judah about six miles northeast of Jerusalem. Here Saul, Jonathan, and David fought the Philistines. After the Exile,

Geba became the home of many Jews returning from Babylon. *Joshua 18:24; 21:17; Judges 20:33; I Samuel 13:3, 16; 14:5; II Samuel 5:25; II Kings 23:8, I Chronicles 6:60; 8:6, II Chronicles 16:6, Nehemiah 7:30; 11:31; 12:29.*

GECKO. The gecko has always been a common type of lizard in the Holy Land. The difficulty of the early translators is evident in the translation of the name in Leviticus 11:30, where listed among the unclean "creeping things" is the "ferret." But there have never been ferrets in Palestine. Later scholars concluded that the correct name was "gecko."

There is an old superstition that a gecko walking on one's body causes leprosy. Even today many Arabs believe that it poisons all it touches. Actually it is harmless, though rather repulsive in appearance.

GEHENNA. Meaning "fiery hell." A valley south of Jerusalem called the valley of Hinnom (see *Hinnom, Valley of the Son of*) where in OT times in the pagan worship of Molech, children were passed through fire as a sacrifice. This was forbidden by Jewish law. Later and in NT times rubbish was burned there. So all through its history ill-smelling and disagreeable smokes had risen from this valley (see II Kings 23:10; II Chronicles 28:3; 33:6; Jeremiah 7:31; 19:5; 32:35). By the first century B.C. the term *Gehenna* was being used to mean a place of fiery punishment after death—a hell of fire or lake of fire for those who did not repent (see Matthew 5:22, 29-30; 10:28; 18:9; 23:15; Mark 9:43, 45, 47; Luke 12:5; James 3:6).

GENEALOGY. An orderly list of names recording the ancestry of individuals or the relationships of families, clans, tribes, or nations. In Bible times the purpose of this listing was to establish legal rights to property and to show which of the sons of a king or a priest would inherit the father's kingdom or priestly office. Early genealogies often included traditions about the origin of the nations. In many cases the writers were interested in telling of the people who had maintained a strong relationship with God. Some of the lists are not accurate because names were forgotten. Lacking some names, biblical writers often made an orderly division of generations. Today a generation is estimated to be about thirty-three to forty years. *Genesis 10:32; I Chronicles 5:17; Ezra 2:62; 8:1; Nehemiah 7:5; Matthew 1:1-17; I Timothy 1:4; Titus 3:9.*

GENESIS. Meaning "beginning." This is the first book of the Bible, and it covers the time from the very first beginnings of history until the journey of the Israelites into Egypt. There are two divisions to the book of Genesis. The first eleven chapters contain some of the most noble and poetic images ever written. The stories of Adam and Eve in the Garden of Eden, the Great Flood, the attempt to build the Tower of Babel, suggest and symbolize the grandeur and mystery of creation in a way that has inspired and instructed readers for thousands of years. The rest of Genesis tells of God's dealing with a particular man, Abraham. There is the call of God to Abraham; the covenant between them; the birth of Isaac, Jacob, and the twelve sons of Jacob; the exile of Joseph into Egypt; and the reunion of the family with Joseph there. These stories trace the development of this family of Abraham into the people of Israel. The significance of the book of Genesis lies in the light it sheds on the relationship between God and his creation before man rebelled. It indicates how God entered into history after his creation had been damaged by the sinfulness of people. He did this through the Hebrew people, and the entire Bible focuses on them and the working out of God's purpose through them.

GENNESARET. The name for the Sea of Galilee in NT times; also, a fruitful valley northwest of the Sea of Galilee. (See *Galilee, Sea of.*) *Mark 6:53; Luke 5:1.*

GENTILE. NT word for a person who was not a Jew. In the plural it meant "nations" in general. *Matthew 5:47; 6:32; 10:5; Acts 11:1; Romans 3:29; 9:24.*

GERAH. A small Hebrew weight, one-twentieth of a shekel. *Exodus 30:13; Numbers 18:16; Ezekiel 45:12.*

GERANIUM. We think of the geranium as a cultivated bedding plant in our gardens, growing the year around where winters are warm. In the lands of the Bible it grows wild on the hillsides and in the valleys. It closely resembles our popular member of the family.

GERIZIM, MOUNT. A mountain in Canaan directly south of

Mt. Ebal. The sides of this mountain and of Mt. Ebal form a pass, now an important east-west highway about forty miles from Jerusalem. Ancient Shechem lies at the eastern entrance to the narrow valley between the mountains. In this pass and from the sides of the two mountains the ceremony of covenant renewal was held (see *Ebal, Mount*). The modern name of Mt. Gerizim is Jebel et-Tor. The Samaritan woman whom Jesus met at the well mentioned to him that her ancestors worshiped on "this mountain," and she indicated Mt. Gerizim (see John 4:20). The small groups of Samaritans that remain today still celebrate the Passover on its summit. *Deuteronomy 11:29; 27:12; Joshua 8:33; Judges 9:7.*

GERSHOM. The older son of Moses and Zipporah. He was born in Midian. Because Moses had escaped there from Egypt to save his life, he gave his son a name which meant, "I have been a sojourner in a foreign land." *Exodus 2:22; 18:3.*

GETHSEMANE. Meaning "oil press." The site on the Mount of Olives outside Jerusalem where Jesus went to pray after the Last Supper with his disciples. It was in this place that he was betrayed by Judas. *Matthew 26:36; Mark 14:32.*

GIANTS. Humans of huge proportions. When a group of men were sent by Moses into Canaan to spy out the land and see what sort of place it was, they brought back the report that there were giants, "the descendants of Anak," in this land. The Hebrews may have thought that in addition to their enormous size and strength these huge men had some supernatural power. In any case, they were afraid to enter Canaan (see Numbers 13:23-30). There were also some men among the Philistines who were unusually tall. Goliath is the most famous of these. *II Samuel 21:16-22.*

GIBEAH. A city in the hill country north of Jerusalem. Its name meant "hill" or "height." It was the home of Saul, and it became his provincial capital after he was acclaimed the first king of Israel. Gibeah played an important part in Saul's struggles with the Philistines. Part of a fortress dating from the time of Saul has been uncovered there. (There are other places mentioned in the OT with the same name.) *Judges 19:12-16; I Samuel 10:26; 14:16; 22:6; Hosea 10:9.*

GIBEON. An OT town six miles northwest of Jerusalem. Gibeon stood in the path of the victorious armies of Joshua as they invaded Canaan. The cities of Jericho and Ai had already been overcome, and the people of Gibeon were very frightened even though their city was strong and the men mighty. They hatched a clever plan by which they could prevent Joshua's attacking them. Many years later some of the battles between the forces of King Saul and the men loyal to David were fought near Gibeon. This was also the place in which Solomon had his famous dream in which he asked God for wisdom to be a good king. Still later, Nehemiah mentions that the men of Gibeon helped in rebuilding the wall of

Jerusalem after the Hebrews had returned from their exile in Babylon. *Joshua 9:3–10:10, I Kings 3:4-14; I Chronicles 14:16; 16:39; II Chronicles 1:3; Nehemiah 3:7; Jeremiah 28:1; 41:12.*

GIDEON. An OT hero, also known as Jerubbaal, who was a judge called by God to lead the Israelites. At the time of his call Gideon was a farmer. The whole land was gripped with fear of the fierce Midianites, who would ride into the country on their swift camels and ruin or steal whatever they wanted. For this reason the people hid their animals and their food as best they could. Gideon was told by the angel of the Lord that he was to defeat the Midianites. His confidence and enthusiasm aroused the whole tribe of Manasseh, and Gideon set out with ten thousand men. However, God told him that not nearly that many were needed. After testing them, he picked three hundred of the best soldiers and took them only. They completely defeated the enemy. The grateful Israelites wanted to make Gideon their king, but he refused. *Judges 6:11–9:5, 16; Hebrews 11:32-34.*

GILBOA, MOUNT. A ridge of limestone hills rising 1,737 feet above the Mediterranean Sea at the east end of the Valley of Jezreel. Because of its location it was often the scene of battles. King Saul chose this place to fight the Philistines. *I Samuel 31:1, 8; II Samuel 1:6, 21.*

GILEAD. Grandson of Manasseh and ancestor of the tribe of Gilead. It is also the name of a territory of hills and valleys located to the east of Jordan, where grapes and olives were grown. *Genesis 37:25; Numbers 26:29-30; 27:1; Judges 5:17; II Kings 10:32-33.*

GILEAD, BALM OF. A soothing medicine and antiseptic made from the bark of an evergreen tree. This substance did not come from Gilead as the name suggests. Jeremiah's cry "Is there no balm in Gilead?" is often quoted today when one wishes relief from suffering. *Jeremiah 8:22; 46:11.*

GILGAL. Meaning "circle of stones." Gilgal near Jericho was the site of the first encampment of the Israelites after crossing the Jordan River and entering Canaan. There they erected twelve memorial stones taken from the bed of the Jordan. Gilgal became the base city for the Israelites' military operations against the Canaanites. A great sanctuary was built there. At Gilgal Saul was made king of Israel, and here he was rejected from the kingship. Gilgal is mentioned frequently in OT history, and there are several towns with this name. *Joshua 4:19-20; I Samuel 7:15-16; 11:14-15; Hosea 9:15; 12:11; Amos 4:4-5; Micah 6:5.*

GIRDLE. A sashlike piece of the high priest's clothing of fine embroidered linen. The belts, or sashes, worn by ordinary men and women were also called girdles. These were used to fasten in the long, flowing robes. Money pouches or weapons were carried in the girdle. In the case of messengers and travelers who wished to free their legs for easier movement, the robe was brought between the legs toward the front and

tucked into the girdle. This was called "girding up the loins" (see I Kings 18:46; II Kings 4:29). *Exodus 39:29; II Kings 1:8; Proverbs 31:24; Isaiah 11:5; Matthew 3:4; Acts 21:11.*

GLADIOLI. Called "sword lily" in Palestine, the native gladiolus derives its name from the curved petals that resemble an eastern scimitar. The blossoms, smaller than our cultivated variety, are pink or purple and grow along one side of the short stem.

GLASSY SEA. See *Sea of Glass.*

GLEANING. The practice of gathering or picking up what had been left behind or overlooked in the fields or orchards after harvesting. The Hebrew law provided that the privilege of gleaning be granted to the needy. *Leviticus 19:9-10; 23:22; Deuteronomy 24:19-21; Ruth 2:2-19.*

GLORY. Honor, praise, importance, and splendor. The word was chiefly used to describe the presence of God. In the Bible glory is sometimes connected with riches, bravery, uprightness, beauty, and similar qualities in people and the works of people. *Leviticus 9:23; I Samuel 4:22; Psalms 8:5; 49:16; 148:13; Isaiah 60:13; Jeremiah 2:11; Matthew 6:28-29; Luke 2:14, 29-32; John 8:54; Acts 7:2; Ephesians 3:16; Hebrews 2:9; Revelation 4:11.*

GNAT. "Ye blind guides, which strain at a gnat and swallow a camel!" (Matthew 23:24). So Jesus, in strong hyperbole, indicates that he is familiar with the pestiferous gnat. It was a common practice to strain wine through cloth to remove insects and foreign matter. Hence Jesus' illustration was easily understood, effectively ridiculing the hypercritical legalism of the Pharisee's religious practices. While the King James Version lists lice as the third of the plagues to beset Egypt, all other translations list gnats.

GOAD. A pointed stick used for driving or guiding cattle, especially oxen when plowing. Sometimes it was tipped with iron. *Judges 3:31; I Samuel 13:21; Ecclesiastes 12:11; Acts 26:14.*

GOAT. The goat of the Hebrews was probably the species with long, floppy ears and covered with long, black silky hair. Both male and female had horns, but the male had an additional ornament of chin whiskers. It was an important domestic animal, providing meat, hair for weaving into cloth, hide for water bags, and even horns for trumpets. The skin was also used for the strings of the "nebal," a large harp, and for drum heads.

In addition to the above practical uses, the male goat was acceptable as a sin-offering. On the Day of Atonement one was chosen by chance. After the high priest had symbolically transferred the sins of the people to the goat it was turned loose in the wilderness (Leviticus 16:20-22). We still refer to a "scapegoat" as one who bares the blame for others.

Both goats and sheep grazed in the same pasture but since the male goat was often ill-tempered toward sheep, the flocks were kept separate. Hence Jesus' remarks in Matthew 25:32, "as a shepherd divideth his sheep from the goats."

GOD (NAMES OF). For the Hebrews every name represented the very selfhood of the person who bore it. It was the same for the holy name of God. His name expressed his power and holiness. The very fact that God had revealed his name to the Hebrews was a sign of his special care for them. They regarded the divine name with great reverence. It was not to be used carelessly. Advice and prophecies given in the name of God had his authority. Other ways of referring to God are: Lord (see *Holy One, Yahweh*), The Rock, Father, Savior, King, Judge, Shepherd, Creator, Redeemer, Maker, Almighty, and such descriptive expressions as the Living God, the Everlasting God, the First and the Last, the Ancient of Days, the God of our Fathers, the God of Abraham. *Genesis 17:1; 49:24-25; Exodus 3:13-15; 33:19; Isaiah 17:7; 33:22; 40:28; Jeremiah 3:19; Daniel 7:13; Matthew 6:6; Acts 4:24.*

GOD (NATURE OF). To the Hebrews of the OT, God was the living God who was the LORD, the ruler of their lives. The Hebrews did not ask, "Is there a God?" In the biblical accounts, the Hebrews never questioned the existence of God; they knew him because of what he had done for them. Their questions were: "What is he called? What is he like?" The OT reports the historical events in which the Hebrews were involved not as the acts of people so much as the acts of God. As the Hebrews lived out their special history as the people with whom God had made a covenant, or agreement, they found answers to their questions about God

(see *Covenant*). In the NT God revealed himself in Jesus Christ, and people's relation with God was made richer because it can be experienced in a very personal way as in the relationship with an earthly father or a beloved friend.

GOLDSMITH. A worker in gold, a maker of jewelry and idols frequently referred to in the OT. Gold was probably the first metal known to man. *Nehemiah 3:8, 31-32; Isaiah 40:19; 41:7; 46:6; Jeremiah 10:9, 14; 51:17.*

GOLGOTHA. Meaning "skull." A place of execution probably outside the city wall of Jerusalem where Jesus was crucified. The exact location is not certain. *Matthew 27:33-36; Mark 15:22; John 19:17-18.*

GOLIATH. The Philistine champion and giant who defied the Israelite army. In spite of Goliath's huge size and heavy armor the boy David accepted the challenge to fight him and went out to meet him with only a slingshot. He shot a small round stone that struck the forehead of the giant, and Goliath fell dead. *I Samuel 17:4-11, 23-49; 21:9; 22:10.*

GOMER. The wife of the prophet Hosea who was unfaithful to him. Hosea forgave her and took her back into his home. He used this sad experience in his prophecies about Israel. The Hebrews were behaving toward God like an unfaithful wife, Hosea pointed out, but God would forgive them if they would repent. *Hosea 1:3.*

GOMORRAH. An OT city usually mentioned together with Sodom. The two cities "in the Valley" were noted for their wickedness. Abraham pleaded with God not to destroy those cities if as many as ten good men could be found there. But according to the story there were not ten. It is thought that these cities may be buried under the waters at the southern end of the Dead Sea. *Genesis 18:20-33; 19:24-29; Isaiah 1:9; Jeremiah 49:18; Matthew 10:15.*

GOOSE. Though not mentioned by name in the Bible, carvings on the walls of ancient Egyptian tombs indicate that geese were known as early as 2500 B.C. The captive Children of Israel surely knew them. It is quite likely that the "fatted fowl," a part of Solomon's provisions for one day (I Kings 23:4) were geese, possibly the red-breasted goose, still seen in Egypt and in parts of the Holy Land.

GOPHER WOOD. A material, probably cypress, from which Noah was instructed to make the ark. *Genesis 6:14.*

GOSHEN. 1. An area of Egypt probably in the northeastern part of the Nile delta. It was occupied by the Israelites from the time of Joseph to the Exodus. *Genesis 46:28-47:6; Exodus 8:22.*

2. The same name refers to a hill country in Canaan and a town in Judah. *Joshua 10:41; 11:16; 15:51.*

GOSPEL. God's announcement of the good news that Jesus Christ is the Son of God. This new announcement was made in the same style as the message of the OT, through historical facts. The words and actions of Jesus—his birth, loving deeds, suffering, death, and rising from the dead—have fulfilled the plan of God. It is a plan in which all people can have a part. These deeds of Christ accomplished salvation. This means that those who believe in him and his works are saved from the worst results of their own sinfulness and weakness and may enjoy the benefit of Jesus' goodness and righteousness. "Gospel" is also the name given each of the first four books of the NT. In Matthew, Mark, Luke, and John we find accounts of the life of Jesus and the facts that make up the good news. *Matthew 4:23; 24:14; Mark 1:1; 8:35; 10:29-30; Acts 8:40; Romans 1:1-4; Philippians 1:12; I Thessalonians 2:9.*

GOVERNOR. In the OT a ruler appointed by a king to govern a specific territory or province. He governed by authority of the king, not in his own right. Joseph was a governor in Egypt. The king of Babylon left a governor named Gedaliah to rule Judah after the Babylonians had conquered it. In the NT these officials were appointed by the Roman emperor and had authority to give the sentence of death or to free a prisoner. Other Roman names for governor are proconsul, procurator, prefect, and legate. *Genesis 42:6; Ezra 2:63; 5:3, 14; Nehemiah 2:7; 5:14; Jeremiah 40:5; 51:23; Haggai 1:1; Matthew 10:18; Mark 13:9; Luke 2:2; 3:1; Acts 7:10.*

GRACE. God's great love for people which cannot be earned but which is offered by God as a free gift. In the OT a similar Hebrew word is translated

GRAPE

"steadfast love" (see Psalm 136:1-26). In the NT the grace of God is one of the most distinctive features of the Christian gospel. It is seen as divine power flowing through Jesus Christ into the lives of those who believe in him. This grace makes it possible for persons to think, act, and speak according to God's will. *Romans 5:15; I Corinthians 15:10; II Corinthians 6:1; 8:1; 9:14; Ephesians 3:7; II Thessalonians 1:12; I Peter 1:10, 13; 5:10.*

GRAPE. Grapes and vineyards are mentioned early and often in the Bible, from Genesis 9:20 to Revelation 14:18, sometimes literally (Deuteronomy 23:24), often as metaphor (Hosea 9:10). While the grapes themselves were of greatest importance as food and for making wine, the beauty of the vineyards in blossom could not have escaped attention. Except that the harvest began in June, vineculture was much the same in Bible times as now.

GRASSHOPPER. Many varieties of grasshopper are found in the Holy Land, probably the same ones that were common in ancient times. The locust, as the most destructive, is mentioned most often. But the name is also applied to crickets and katydids, especially when the reference is to something other than the havoc wrought by herds of locusts.

GRAVEN IMAGE. An image carved from stone, metal, or wood. These idols were used in ancient times to represent a deity, or god. The Ten Commandments forbade the Hebrews to make such things. *Exodus 20:4; Leviticus 26:1; Deuteronomy 4:23, 25; 5:8; 7:5; 12:3; 27:15; Judges 17:3-4; II Kings 21:7; II Chronicles 34:3-4; Isaiah 10:10-11; 30:22; Jeremiah 8:19.*

GREAT SEA. The name by which the Mediterranean Sea was known in Bible lands in ancient times. It was also referred to as the "western sea" and "the sea." The Mediterranean Sea is an inland ocean more than two thosuand miles long, stretching from Gibraltar to Lebanon between the continents of Europe and Africa. Its width varies from one hundred to six hundred miles. *Numbers 34:6; Joshua 1:4; Ezekiel 47:10.*

GREECE. In Bible times a land which occupied the southern end of the Balkan Peninsula and also included western Asia Minor and the islands of the Aegean Sea. There were also Greek settlements in southern Italy. The Greeks ruled their known world from the fourth to the first century B.C. Their arts, customs, literature, government, and religion had much to give to the Roman civilization that followed. While Greece was the domiant world power, its influence was spread very wide. The Greek language was the one most widely used. The OT was translated into Greek. At first the NT was written in common, everyday Greek known as Koine. The Greek language version of both testaments was the official Bible among early Christians. Some of the earliest Christian churches were started in Greece. The name "Hellenists" was given to Jews who adopted Greek manners and lived among the Greeks. *Mark 7:26; John 7:35; 19:20; Acts 11:20; 14:1; 16:1, 3; 17:4, 12;*

20:2; 21:37; Romans 1:14, 16; 10:12; I Corinthians 1:22-24; Galatians 2:3; 3:28; Colossians 3:11.

GRIFFIN. A species of vulture, the griffin glides gracefully high in the air, swooping down to earth with amazing speed and precision when its keen eyesight locates a meal, usually a dead animal, far below. Then it may gorge itself until it is unable to fly. It is light brown, its neck and head nearly bare, covered only with fine down. The Egyptians and the Persians used the griffin as an emblem of royal power.

GULL. An occasional seagull doubtless "wandered" inland as far as the Sea of Galilee, acquainting the natives with the bird. To those Israelites who lived near the coast of the Mediterranean Sea, and to Peter and the apostles who came to Joppa on the coast (Acts 9:36) soaring, screaming seagulls were a familiar sight.

HABAKKUK. A prophet of the southern kingdom of Judah during the reigns of Jehoiakim and Josiah. (See *Habakkuk, Book of.*)

HABAKKUK, BOOK OF. A small OT book and one of the Minor Prophets. It contains protests against the power and cruelty of the Babylonian Empire. It also contains prayers of faith and trust. The prayers have a form about them which suggests they may have been chanted by the worshipers on days of penitence.

HADES. The NT name for the place of the dead. The word *Hades* was adopted from the Greeks, who thought of the underground regions as a place of punishment for evildoers. (See *Gehenna.*) *Matthew 11:23; Luke 16:23; Acts 2:27, 31; Revelation 20:13-14.*

HAGAR. Servant of Sarah by whom Abraham had a son, Ishmael. *Genesis 16:1-16; Galatians 4:24-25.*

HAGGAI. A prophet in Babylon during the Exile. He returned to Jerusalem and was one of the leaders who encouraged the Jews to undertake the task of rebuilding the temple. (See *Haggai, Book of.*)

HAGGAI, BOOK OF. The tenth in the series of twelve short prophetic books that come at the end of the OT. It is a collection of prophecies by Haggai and gives an account of their effect in rallying the people to rebuild the ruined temple.

HALF-SHEKEL TAX. See *Moneychanger.*

HALLEL. A song of praise to the Lord. The Hebrew word means "praise." It was one of the duties of the Levites (the choirmasters of OT times, see II Chronicles 7:6; Ezra 3:11) to praise the Lord. Psalms 120–36 were called the Great Hallel. Psalms 113–18, called the Egyptian Hallel, were used at Passover in homes, the temple, and synagogues.

HALLELUJAH. A Hebrew word meaning "praise the Lord." It was a form of doxology used mainly in the psalms (see Psalms 104:35; 106:1). *Revelation 19:1, 3-4, 6.*

HALLOW. To make holy, to set apart, to treat with reverence. In ancient Israel a place in which God's presence had been experienced was often set apart for worship and as a memorial of the event. Anything that is separated from ordinary use and reserved for the service of God is said to be hallowed. Among things that were especially hallowed in Israel were God's name (see *God, Names of*), the sabbath, and the temple. *Exodus 20:11; Leviticus 16:19; 22:32; 25:10; Ezekiel 20:20; Matthew 6:9; Luke 11:2.*

HAM. Youngest of Noah's three sons. According to Genesis the nations of the world are descended from the sons of Noah. Ham was said to be the ancestor of the Egyptians and North Africans. The name is used in referring to Egypt in some of the poetry of Psalms. *Genesis 5:32; 6:10; 9:18; 10:1, 6, 20; I Chronicles 1:4, 8; Psalms 105:23, 27; 106:22.*

HAMAN. Prime minister of the Persian king Ahasuerus. He plotted to have all the Jews in Persia killed because Mordecai, a Jew and the cousin of Esther, would not bow down to him. *Esther 3:1–7:10.*

HAMATH. A town on the Orontes River north of Damascus in Syria. For long periods Hamath was the center of an independent kingdom to the north of the Israelite kingdom. The phrase "entrance of Hamath" might refer to Israel's northern border. *Numbers 13:21; 34:8; Joshua 13:5, II Kings 14:25, 28; 19:13; Jeremiah 52:27; Ezekiel 47:15; 48:1; Amos 6:14.*

HAMSTER. This small rodent is found in the Middle East but is most common in Syria where it is a source of food for the Arabs. The Syrian hamster is somewhat smaller than the common pet, with a longer tail and silky hair of a golden color. It has large cheek pouches into which it stuffs food to be taken to its nest, burrowed in the ground. Each animal occupies its own "quarters" consisting of a storage chamber and a "living room."

HANDBREADTH. A measure based on the width of the hand at the base of the fingers, about three inches. *Exodus 25:25; 37:12; I Kings 7:26; II Chronicles 4:5; Psalm 39:5; Ezekiel 40:5.*

HANNAH. Wife of Elkanah and mother of Samuel. Hannah and her husband waited many years for a child. Hannah prayed for a son and promised to dedicate him to the service of God. A son, Samuel, was born to her. As soon as he was old enough she took him to serve in the sanctuary in Shiloh. Samuel grew up to be one of the great judges and prophets of Israel. *I Samuel 1:1–2:11.*

HARAN. 1. Brother of Abraham and father of Lot. *Genesis 11:26-31.*

2. Also a city of northern Mesopotamia (now Turkey) where Abraham settled for a time after leaving Ur and before going on to Canaan. Rebekah, the wife of Isaac, came from Haran, and this was the place where Jacob went to be safe after he had tricked his brother out of his birthright and blessing. Jacob's wives also came from Haran. It was an important trade

city for caravans. Here archaeologists have found the ruins of a temple dedicated to a moon god, a library, a statue of a king with his name carved on his shoulder, and the king's palace. *Genesis 12:4-5; 27:43; 28:10; 29:4; II Kings 19:12; Ezekiel 27:23; Acts 7:2, 4.*

HARE. The hare and its close relative, the rabbit, are common to practically all of the temperature regions of the world. Two varieties of the hare are found in Palestine. One lives in the wooded inhabited areas; the other, somewhat smaller, species is found in the more barren regions.

Because of the ignorance of the times, the hare is classed as unclean "because he cheweth the cud" (Leviticus 11:6). However, neither the hare nor the rabbit is a ruminant. But the peculiar way they have of moving their lips does give the impression of cud chewing. On this presumption it was classed as unclean and not to be eaten.

HARLOT. A woman who offers her body to men for money. The OT often uses the word *harlot* as a figure of speech, such as "playing the harlot," to describe those in Israel who had forsaken God and turned to the worship of other gods. *Genesis 34:31; Exodus 34:15-16; Numbers 25:1-2; Joshua 2:1; Judges 2:17; Jeremiah 3:3, 6.*

HARP. A stringed musical instrument small enough to be carried. It was used alone; with other instruments; or with singing in processions, in the worship of the temple, and sometimes to go before the army as they marched to battle. (See *Musical Instruments.*) *I Samuel 10:5; II Chronicles 20:28; Psalms 71:22, 150:3; Isaiah 5:12; Amos 6:5; I Corinthians 14:7.*

HART. The adult male of the red deer. It was used as food. A leaping hart was used as a symbol of strength and nimbleness. *Deuteronomy 12:15, 22; 14:4-5; Psalm 42:1; Isaiah 35:6.*

HARVEST. The gathering of ripe crops. In Bible lands the barley harvest came in April or May; the wheat harvest, in May or June; summer fruits (figs, grapes, pomegranates) ripened in August and September; olives, September to November. *Leviticus 19:9-10; Deuteronomy 24:19-22; I Samuel 6:13; Isaiah 17: 5-6; Matthew 9:37-38.*

HAWK. Hawks of many kinds are common in the lands of the Bible. The most common in Palestine is the relatively small sparrow hawk. Job asks, "Doth the hawk fly by thy wisdom?" (Job 39:26). It builds its nest in the top of tall trees or in rock crannies from which its keen eyesight can detect a potential meal on the ground far below. Like all birds of prey, the hawk is unclean.

HAZAEL. A king of Damascus who had once been a servant of the king and had seized the throne by murdering his master. He was a mighty warrior, a builder, and a powerful king from about 841 to about 798 B.C. He frequently invaded the kingdoms of Israel and Judah. His attacks were seen by the prophet Elisha as the wrath of God turned against the Hebrews because of their sins. He

once approached Jerusalem but was bribed by King Joash to stay away. To get the treasure to pay the bribe to Hazael, Joash stripped his own palace and the temple. *I Kings 19:15; II Kings 8:13-15, 28-29; 10:32; 12:17-18; 13:3, 22, 24; Amos 1:3-4.*

HAZOR. A city in Galilee about ten miles north of the Sea of Galilee. Hazor has been destroyed and rebuilt many times throughout history. Because of this there is a huge mound containing the ruins of the many cities. These were uncovered by an Israeli archaeologist in 1955–56. At the bottom layer was found a Canaanite royal city. In the late thirteenth century B.C. Joshua conquered and destroyed Hazor. King Solomon rebuilt and fortified the city as did Ahab. In 732 B.C. the city was completely destroyed when Tiglath-pileser III of Assyria captured it and took the people into captivity. *Joshua 11:1-5, 10-13; 12:19; I Kings 9:15; II Kings 15:29.*

HEAP OF STONES. In OT times a pile of stones set up to help people remember an important event connected with a place, much as people set up monuments today (see *Gilgal*). A heap of stones was also made as a witness to an agreement. The phrase was sometimes used to indicate ruin or collapse as when some disaster destroyed an altar, a house, or a city, leaving it a "heap of stones." *Genesis 31:44-52; Joshua 7:26; 8:29; II Samuel 18:17.*

HEAVEN. This word is used in two ways in the Bible. The first and most important meaning is the place where God dwells. It is also used to refer to the sky. There were many figures of speech for this heaven. It was referred to as having "windows" to let the rain through and was called a "tent," a "curtain," a "mirror," and the "firmament." (See *Earth.*) *Genesis 1:6-8; 7:11; 8:2; I Kings 8:30; I Chronicles 27:23; Job 16:19; 22:12-14; 38:37; Psalms 19:1; 104:2; Isaiah 66:1; Jeremiah 10:2; 51:9; Daniel 2:28; 4:13, 15; Matthew 6:9, 20; Mark 1:10; 10:21; 12:25; John 6:32; Acts 1:11.*

HEBREW. 1. The ancient language of the Jews. Most of the books of the OT were written in the Hebrew language. A modern form of Hebrew is the common language of the country of Israel today.

2. "Hebrew" is also used to refer to the people descended from Abraham. The word is probably related to the name "Eber," one of Abraham's ancestors. "Hebrews" was used by the Israelites to refer to themselves, and it was also used by foreigners. *Genesis 14:13; 39:14; Exodus 1:15-16, 19; 2:11; Deuteronomy 15:12; John 20:16; Acts 22:2; Philippians 3:4-6.*

HEBREWS, LETTER TO THE. The nineteenth book of the NT, probably written at the end of the first century. Though called a letter, it is more like a sermon or lecture. The author is unknown. The title "To the Hebrews" indicates the first readers may have been Jewish (Hebrew) Christians. The author used the OT to prove that the religion of the covenant between God and the Hebrews is continued and fulfilled in Jesus Christ.

HEBRON. A Canaanite royal city in the hill country of Judah, about nineteen miles south of Jerusalem. It was founded about the middle of the fourteenth century B.C. It was conquered and destroyed by the Israelites but later rebuilt. It was David's capital during the first years of his reign. Today Hebron is still an important city in the Near East. *Genesis 13:18; Joshua 10:36; 20:7; I Kings 2:11; II Chronicles 11:5-10.*

HELL. The NT name for the place under the earth for the punishment of the dead. (See *Gehenna, Hades, Sheol.*) *Matthew 5:22; James 3:6.*

HELLENISTS. In the NT, Greek-speaking Jews and Jewish Christians, usually living in Greek-speaking countries. *Acts 6:1; 9:29.*

HEMLOCK. The hemlock that "springeth . . . in the furrows of the field" (Hosea 10:4) is a poisonous plant, some five feet in height with dark fern-like leaves. It has small white blossoms in umbels on branching stems. Both seed and plant when crushed yield a poisonous substance which can be fatal when taken internally. This was the hemlock which Socrates drank.

HERALD. An officer making public proclamations for the nation or the ruler, or one who bears ceremonial messages between countries or between royal persons. *Isaiah 40:9; 41:27; Daniel 3:4-6; II Peter 2:5.*

HERESY. A Greek term which meant a school or sect holding a special doctrine. In NT times as soon as the church was established the term came to be used for wrong beliefs held by some people within the Christian church. In the NT the word is only used once, but the presence of heresy is implied many times by such words as *divisions, dissensions,* and *factions. II Peter 2:1.*

HERITAGE. The accumulation of material possessions. For the Hebrews and for Christians the knowledge of God passed down from one generation to another is their special heritage. *II Kings 21:14; Job 20:29; Psalms 94:14; 119:111; Jeremiah 3:18-19; Revelation 21:7.*

HERMES. A Greek god. He was a master thief and clever player of tricks. He was also the god of eloquence, or good speech, and served as the herald of the gods. When Paul was preaching in Lystra, the people thought he must be Hermes because of his impresssive speech. There was a person with this name in the early church in Rome. *Acts 14:12; Romans 16:14.*

HERMON, MOUNT. A mountain in the southern end of the Lebanon mountain range. Rising over nine thousand feet, its snow-capped peak can be seen for many miles. Partly because of this majestic aspect it was always considered a sacred mountain. In ancient times a local Baal probably was worshiped there (see Judges 3:3). *Deuteronomy 3:8-9; 4:48; Joshua 11:16-17; I Chronicles 5:23; Psalm 42:6.*

HEROD. The name of a powerful family which ruled Jewish Palestine

The Bible Companion

under the Roman Empire from 37 B.C. to A.D. 70. They were Idumeans (Edomites) who had become Jews and were not liked by the people of Palestine. Several of the Herods figured prominently in the NT.

1. Herod the Great was king when Jesus was born but died very soon afterward. *Matthew 2:3, 13-16, 19-23; Luke 1:5.*

2. His son, Herod Antipas, had John the Baptist beheaded. It was to this Herod that Jesus was brought for trial after his arrest. *Matthew 14:1-2; Mark 6:14-26; Luke 3:1, 19-20; 9:7-9; 23:7-16.*

3. Herod Agrippa, a grandson of Herod the Great, persecuted the apostles and the Christians in Jerusalem. *Acts 4:27; 12:1-3; 13:1.*

HERODIANS. In the NT Jews who supported the dynasty of Herod. They are mentioned as opponents of Jesus. *Matthew 22:16; Mark 3:6; 12:13.*

HERODIAS. Wife of King Herod Antipas. She had first been the wife of Antipas' half-brother. John the Baptist criticized this marriage, and Salome, the daughter of Herodias, after pleasing the king with her dancing, demanded and got the head of John. *Mark 6:14-29.*

HERON. Herons are characterized by their long legs, long neck, and long, pointed beak. The blue-gray heron is common in the Holy Land where it winters. It builds its nest in swamps and along river banks, often in a tall tree, returning to the same nest year after year. Quite often many nests are close together forming a colony. Although some kinds of heron might be classed as unclean under the Mosaic dietary law, all are on the forbidden list.

The great white heron is found in the swamps of Syria. Common, too, is the black-crowned night heron with a thicker beak and shorter legs than most of the heron family.

HEWERS OF WOOD. In the OT one of the lowest classes of servants. They were the gatherers of firewood—an endless, dull task. The term has come to be used for persons of dull mind who can do nothing but the tiresome and menial jobs. (See *Gibeon.*) *Deuteronomy 29:11; Joshua 9:21, 23, 27.*

HEZEKIAH. King of Judah from about 716 to 687 B.C.; son and successor of Ahaz. Hezekiah was twenty-five when he became king at a critical time in Judah's history. The nation had been weakened by wars, and the annual payments of tribute to Assyria had become a burden. The people had rejected God and turned to idols. Hezekiah, influenced by Isaiah the prophet, realized the urgent need for reform. In his first year he removed the high places and destroyed the idols. He reopened and purified the temple and restored the true worship of God. He strengthened the defenses of Jerusalem and brought water from nearby into the city by means of a tunnel so that the city would have water during siege. In later generations he was remembered as an able, vigorous, and godly man. *II Kings 18:1–20:21; II Chronicles 29:1–32:33; Isaiah 36:1–39:8; Jeremiah 26:18-19; Matthew 1:9-10.*

HIGH PLACE. A religious place of sacrifice, worship, and festival. High places, usually on hilltops, were first used by the Canaanites as places to worship their gods. The Israelites were commanded by God to destroy the high places when they entered Canaan. However, they did not obey and frequently joined in the Canaanite worship associated with great trees and green groves. Sometimes the Israelites took over a Canaanite high place for the worship of God. These places often had buildings of various kinds: raised platforms, halls, altars, and stone pillars. An Israelite sanctuary was a place set apart for the worship of God, such as the tabernacle in the desert and later the temple at Jerusalem. But there were other, less-important sanctuaries built by people like Abraham, Jacob, and David in places where they had experienced a special sense of God's presence. Later in the NT the word *sanctuary* came to be used by Christians to mean the holy place set apart for the worship of God by the people. *Exodus 15:17; Numbers 33:50-52; Joshua 24:26; I Samuel 9:12; I Kings 3:2; 12:31; II Kings 17:32; 18:4; 23:8-9; II Chronicles 33:3, 17; Psalm 78:58; Hebrews 8:2, 5; 9:1, 24.*

HIGH PRIEST. Chief of the priests in the temple at Jerusalem. He acted as the representative of the people before God. (See *Priests and Levites.*) *Numbers 35:25, 28; II Kings 22:4, 8; Haggai 1:1, 12, 14; Matthew 26:57-66; Mark 14:53-54; John 11:49-52.*

HIGHWAY. The exact meaning is a road built up higher than the land on either side. But it is also used as a figure of speech for the route of returning exiles and to describe an upright way of living. *Numbers 20:17; Psalm 84:5; Proverbs 15:19; 16:17; Isaiah 35:8; 40:3; 49:11.*

HILKIAH. A high priest during the reign of King Josiah (about 641 to 609 B.C.). While the temple was being repaired, Hilkiah discovered the scrolls of the Book of the Law (which is Deuteronomy). These were taken and read to the king. Later, Hilkiah assisted the king in his religious reforms. Other persons in the OT have the same name. *II Kings 22:4-14; I Chronicles 6:13; II Chronicles 34:9-22; 35:8.*

HIN. A liquid measure about equal to an American gallon. *Exodus 29:40; 30:24; Ezekiel 4:11.*

HIND. The hind is the female of the red deer. Its use as food was forbidden. This was not for dietary reasons, but because the female was the bearer of the next generation.

HINNOM, VALLEY OF THE SON OF. A deep valley south of Jerusalem that marked the boundary between the tribes of Benjamin and Judah. It was the center of worship of foreign gods where children were sacrificed by fire in honor of Baal and Molech. (See *Gehenna.*) *Joshua 18:16; II Kings 23:10; II Chronicles 28:3; Jeremiah 2:23; 19:2, 5-6; 32:35.*

HIPPOPOTAMUS (Behemoth). This, one of the largest of animals, would have been known to the Israelites during their long sojourn in Egypt where it was found in and near the

Nile River. Job's reference to the behemoth (Job 40:15) was probably to the hippopotamus.

The young are born underwater and can swim before they can walk. They weigh up to a ton when full grown. Job saw this huge creature as a demonstration of the creative power of God. Eaten by the Egyptians, the flesh was unclean to the Israelites.

HIRAM (also HURAM). King of Tyre, 986 to 935 B.C. He enjoyed friendship and brisk trade relations with David and Solomon. These relations may have been based on a mutual need. Israel needed skilled workmen and raw materials for its building program, which included the temple, and Phoenicia needed agricultural products and olive oil. Hiram helped Solomon in his commercial enterprises by supplying ships and seamen for the merchant fleet. He probably received a share of the profits from these voyages. Later Solomon was so much in debt for these goods he was forced to sell twenty cities of Galilee to Hiram. *Hiram—II Samuel 5:11; I Kings 5:1-12; 9:10-14, 26-28; 10:11, 22; Huram—II Chronicles 2:1-16; 8:17-18; 9:10, 21.*

HIRELING. A servant or other worker paid wages. *Job 7:1-2; Malachi 3:5; John 10:12-13.*

HITTITES. A people of the ancient Near East who lived in the territory that is now Turkey. Probably some Hittites were living in Canaan before the coming of the Israelites. Several names of individuals with a Hittite background are mentioned in the OT.

It is almost certain that the Hittites first discovered the art of smelting and working iron. *Genesis 15:18-21; 23:3-20; 25:9-10; 26:34; 36:2; Exodus 3:8; Deuteronomy 7:1; Joshua 1:4; Judges 1:26; I Samuel 26:6; II Samuel 11:3, 6; 12:9-10; 23:39; I Kings 10:29; 11:1; 15:5; II Kings 7:6.*

HIVITES. People living in Canaan before the coming of the Israelites. The name is usually given in the OT list of nations conquered and sent out of the land by the Israelites. Hivite settlements were along the way between Sidon and Beer-sheba and Mt. Lebanon, and at the foot of Mt. Hermon. *Genesis 34:2; Exodus 3:8, 17; 23:23-33; Deuteronomy 7:1; 20:17; Joshua 3:10; Judges 3:3, 5; II Samuel 24:7; I Kings 9:20-21; Isaiah 17:9.*

HOBAB. One of the names for the father-in-law of Moses. He is also identified as Jethro and Reuel. *Numbers 10:29; Judges 4:11.*

HOLINESS. More than any other term *holiness* suggests the nature of God. It does not indicate some quality of God but his complete being. The idea of holiness includes some sense of a tremendous and mysterious energy that is beyond and above man. The Hebrews of the OT were very much aware of this power; they sensed the presence of God, his holy love, in the events of their history, in the lives of certain people, and also in the natural world. (It is interesting to note that in the religion of Israel nature worship had no place and there is no word for "nature" in the OT. See *Holy One.*) *Exodus 15:11; Psalm*

93:5; *Amos 4:2; Luke 1:75; II Corinthians 7:1; Ephesians 4:24; I Thessalonians 3:13; Hebrews 12:10.*

HOLY OF HOLIES. Sometimes called the most holy place (see Exodus 26:33-34). The innermost room of the temple, the place of the presence of God. The high priest entered the Holy of Holies only on the Day of Atonement. In Solomon's Temple it contained the ark and cherubim, but after the Jews returned from their exile in Babylon this room was left empty in later temples. *Hebrews 9:3-5.*

HOLY ONE. In the OT a name for God which emphasizes that God himself is absolute holiness and the source of holiness in all other things. In the NT "Holy One" referred to the Messiah, the one who would appear on earth among people and who would be holy as God is holy. (See *Holiness, Messiah.*) *II Kings 19:22; Psalms 71:22; 78:41; 89:18; Isaiah 5:19; 30:11-15; and many other places in Isaiah; Mark 1:24; Luke 4:34; Acts 3:14.*

HOLY PLACE. In the tent of meeting, the courts with the inner and outer rooms of the tabernacle; in the temple, the rooms and the surrounding courts. *Exodus 26:33; 28:29; 29:31; 39:1; 40:9; Leviticus 6:24-26.*

HOLY SPIRIT. The mysterious power of God. Sometimes called the Spirit or the Spirit of the Lord. In the OT this power, or spirit, was given to certain persons as a revelation which gave them strength, courage, wisdom, and the knowledge of God's will. In the NT the Holy Spirit is brought through Jesus Christ to be personally present to guide, comfort, and strengthen those who believe in him. *Spirit of the Lord—Judges 14:6; I Samuel 16:13; Isaiah 11:2; Holy Spirit—Matthew 3:11; Luke 2:25-32; 4:1; John 14:25-26; Acts 1:5; 2:1-4; 4:8, 31; 9:31; 10:38; II Corinthians 13:14; Ephesians 1:13-14.*

HOMER. An ancient Hebrew measure for dry materials. It was probably the load that a donkey could carry, ten bushels, more or less. *Numbers 11:32; Isaiah 5:10; Ezekiel 45:11*

HOOPOE. The hoopoe is an attractive bird, especially with its crest of reddish feathers erected and expanded when it is alarmed. It is a fairly large bird, about ten inches long, salmon-pink with zebra-like stripes on its back, wings and tail. The nesting and feeding habits of the hoopoe do not match the attractive appearance of the bird. It does nothing to keep its nest in repair once it is built. During the incubation period an oil gland at the base of the female's tail exudes an intensely unpleasant fluid to discourage would-be invaders. This, along with the fact that it has a habit of probing into filth for worms and insects, gave the Hebrews sufficient reason for classing it as unclean.

HOREB, MOUNT. Another name for Mt. Sinai, the place near the wilderness where the Israelites camped on their journey to Canaan. *Exodus 3:1; Deuteronomy 1:2; 5:2; II Chronicles 5:10; Psalm 106:19.*

HORNET. There are at least four species of hornets in the Holy Land. The most common is the large yellow

and reddish-brown variety armed with the familiar poisonous sting of all hornets. Whether the promise of God to use hornets as one means of combating the enemies of Israel (Exodus 23:28) was meant literally or figuratively, its meaning is plain (Joshua 24:12).

HORSE. Though mentioned often in the Bible—over 150 times—the horse never took the place of the lowly ass in the life of the Hebrews. Its use was mostly that of a war animal, vividly described as such by Job (Job 39:19-25). Used first to draw chariots—Solomon had 1400 (I Kings 10:26)—but later as cavalry (Ezekiel 38:15).

For a long time Mosaic law forbade the breeding of horses (Deuteronomy 17:16) and they were imported from Egypt. But when the superiority of the horse in warfare became apparent, this law was conveniently overlooked. We do not know the breed of horses common in Palestine, but it was probably the rather small, swift animal common in Egypt. The large Arabian horse was not known at that time.

HOSANNA. A term meaning "Save us, we beseech thee" (see Psalm 118:25). During the Feast of Tabernacles this verse was sung each day by the priests as they marched in procession around the altar while the congregation waved branches of myrtle, branches of willow, and a palm leaf. At Jesus' triumphal entry into Jerusalem the people greeted him by waving branches and singing "Hosanna." *Matthew 21:9; Mark 11:9-10; John 12:13.*

HOSEA. A prophet in Israel in the eighth century B.C. and the only one of the writing prophets who had his home in the northern kingdom. There were other prophets in Israel, but they were generally unreliable and had seen better days. Hosea criticized them and also the priests for their failure in leading the people, for giving them poor advice, and for their ignorance of the true nature of God. He accused them of guiding the people into pagan worship rather than into the true faith. (See *Hosea, Book of.*)

HOSEA, BOOK OF. The name of the first book of the Twelve Prophets in the OT. The book is partly biography and partly the prophecies of Hosea. Hosea compared his love for his unfaithful wife to God's love for unfaithful Israel. He pleaded with the people to return to God.

HOSHEA. The last king of the northern kingdom of Israel who reigned from about 732 to 722 B.C. The northern kingdom was under the domination of Assyria at this time, and with Assyrian approval Hoshea murdered King Pekah in order to gain the throne. Later Hoshea rebelled against the Assyrians with the result that King Shalmaneser V of Assyria took him prisoner and began a three-year siege of Samaria, the capital city of Israel. There are other Hosheas in the Bible. This was the original name of the prophet Hosea and of Joshua. It was also the name of one of David's officers. *II Kings 17:1-6.*

HOSPITALITY. Entertainment of a stranger or guest. Throughout the

ancient Mediterranean world it was a sacred duty to entertain strangers. The Hebrews also held this view (see Genesis 18:1-8; 19:1-11). Jesus depended upon hospitality for his food and lodging wherever he went (see Luke 9:58; 11:37). When the apostles were sent out, they were told to rely on hospitality (see Luke 10:7). This practice among the early Christians bound them together. *Romans 12:13; I Timothy 5:10; Hebrews 13:2; I Peter 4:9.*

HOSTS, HOST OF HEAVEN.

"Host" in military use means a body of men organized for war. The host of heaven includes the sun, moon, stars, and particularly angels. These forces are at God's command in carrying out his purpose for the world. In the OT the God of Israel is frequently called "God of hosts." *Exodus 7:4; 12:17; 14:17; Numbers 10:28; Deuteronomy 4:19; 17:3; I Samuel 17:46; I Kings 22:19; II Kings 21:3-5; Psalms 89:8; 103:21; Isaiah 1:9; and other places in Isaiah; Jeremiah 10:16; and other places in Jeremiah; Amos 5:27; Luke 2:13.*

HOUSEHOLD OF GOD. A

group of believers or the members of the church. *Ephesians 2:19; I Timothy 3:15; I Peter 4:17.*

HOUSEHOLDER. In the NT a

house steward or master of the house. *Matthew 13:27; 20:1; Mark 14:14.*

HULDAH. A prophetess, the wife

of Shallum. She was consulted by King Josiah after the Book of the Law had been found in the temple. It was very unusual for a woman to act as prophet. *II Kings 22:14; II Chronicles 34:22.*

HUMBUM. The Arabs named this

plant which decorates the rocky areas of Palestine and neighboring countries. The blossoms, ranging in color from white to blue, cover the tall stalks. The flowers resemble forget-me-nots. The plant has a practical use as the leaves are used as poultices and as food.

HURAM. See *Hiram.*

HYACINTH. The blue bell-shaped

flowers of the hyacinth bloom profusely throughout the Holy Land in February and March. They are especially abundant on Mt. Carmel and near Sidon. The smaller grape hyacinth is also found throughout Palestine.

HYENA. The hyena was probably

the most detested animal of the ancient world, due largely to its habit of digging up graves. Absalom was buried under a pile of stones to prevent this from happening to his corpse (II Samuel 18:17). It was also the subject of many superstitions: its scent was believed to corrupt the air; sandals and leggings made of its hide were said to be protection against hyena bites. Once plentiful in Palestine, the striped hyena is now rare. Strange as it seems, young hyenas are said to be easily tamed and the Egyptians kept them as pets and as a source of food.

HYMNS. Songs of praise. The

earliest Christians continued to use the psalms and religious songs of Judaism. The hymn sung at the conclusion of the Last Supper was probably the Hallel, or Psalms 113–

118, that was sung at the celebration of the chief Jewish festivals. In the NT there are many references to the use of songs in the churches' worship. *Matthew 26:30; Mark 14:26; Acts 16:25; I Corinthians 14:26; Ephesians 5:19; Colossians 3:16.*

HYPOCRISY, HYPOCRITE.
From a Greek word meaning the act of playing a part and one who plays a part. In the NT Jesus used the word to condemn those who were so firmly convinced of their own goodness that they were blind to their faults. *Matthew 6:2, 16; 23:13:15; Mark 7:6:7; Luke 6:42; 13:15.*

HYRAX (Coney). Probably the most familiar reference to the hyrax, or coney as it is more commonly known, is Psalm 104:8: "The high hills are a refuge for the wild goats and the rocks for the coneys." The translation "badger" in the Revised Version is misleading since the badger is unknown in Palestine. The hyrax resembles a large rodent and is sometimes called a "desert rat." It has a thick body covered with fine fur, short legs, a very short tail, and small, round ears. A marked peculiarity of the hyrax is the formation of its feet. There are skin folds between the toes. Glands on the bottom of the feet keep them moist and so provide a suction effect, most helpful to the animal as it climbs the sheer rocks among which it lives in colonies of up to fifty. It is a shy creature, its safety depending largely on its ability to scamper into rock crevices on a warning signal from stationed "lookouts."

Strange as it seems, zoologists believe that the hyrax is a survivor of an ancient type of hoofed animal, its nearest living relative being the elephant, or possibly the sea cow.

Hyssop

HYSSOP. There are two "hyssops" referred to in the Bible. In the Old Testament David prays, "Purge me with hyssop and I shall be clean" (Psalm 51:7). The reference here, as in other places in the Old Testament, is an herb-like plant belonging to the mint family. It has a pungent taste and a spicy odor. In some Jewish religious rites it was sprinkled over the sacrifice as a symbolic purifying agent.

The hyssop mentioned in the New Testament is a member of the sorghum family. It is sometimes called "Jerusalem corn." The large seed heads, ground into meal, constitute the main part of the diet for many people in the Near East. Some scholars believe that this was the "parched

corn" that Boaz gave to Ruth (Ruth 2:14).

The strong stems of the plant grow to a height of six feet or more, which indicates how this hyssop was used at Calvary when "they filled a sponge with vinegar, and put it upon hyssop, and put it to his mouth" (John 19:29).

IBEX. While the ibex is not mentioned by name in the Bible, most naturalists believe the "wild goat" refers to this animal. Traveling in herds of eight or ten, it lived high in the craggy mountains where sure-footedness and agility were essential. It is still found in Palestine.

When David and his followers were fleeing from the wrath of Saul, ibex may have been their main food supply "in the wilderness of En-gedi" (I Samuel 24:1). En-gedi was known as the "fountain of goats," quite possibly ibex.

IBIS. The ibis, sacred to Thoth, Egyptian god of learning, was common among the tall papyrus in which the baby Moses was hidden. Now it is seldom seen along the lower Nile. Over two feet from its slender arched bill to its tail feathers, with the long, thin legs of the wading birds, it was well known to the Children of Israel before the Exodus.

ICONIUM. In NT times a city in south central Asia Minor in the Roman province of Galatia. Iconium was visited by Paul and Barnabas on their first missionary journey. Today it is called Konya and is in the country of Turkey. *Acts 13:51–14:7, 19; 16:2; II Timothy 3:10-11.*

IDOL. Usually an image of a god made of wood, stone, or metal; but it may be any other symbol of the supernatural that is an object of worship. *Deuteronomy 29:16-17; I Chronicles 16:26; Psalm 96:5; Isaiah 44:9-17; Jeremiah 50:38; Acts 7:41; 17:16; I Corinthians 8:1-7; 10:7; I Thessalonians 1:9; I John 5:21.*

IDUMEA. In NT times the region south of Judea occupied by Edomites. In OT times it was known as Edom or Seir. *Mark 3:7-8.*

IMMORTALITY. This word, which means never-ending life, is not found in the OT and is found only five times in the NT. The belief that God is an eternal (ever living) God is assumed throughout the OT. There were varied ideas in Judaism about a person's life after death, but no one idea was accepted by all Jews. In the NT the death and resurrection of Jesus Christ signal a strong new hope of everlasting life for those who believe in him. For people death is a fact, but the NT mentions many times a life for a man after death, a life near God. The biblical writers imagined what it might be like, but there is no complete picture. (See *Eternal Life, Resurrection.*) *Romans 2:7; I Corinthians 15:53-54; I Timothy 6:15-16; II Timothy 1:8-10.*

INCENSE. A mixture of gums and spices made into a powder and burned so that the fragrance of the smoke would rise in the air as an offering to God or to the "gods." In

the OT the powder was burned on an incense altar. The offering of incense was a very sacred ceremony wherever mentioned in the OT. In both the OT and the NT the offering of incense was symbolic of the prayers offered by the people. *Exodus 30:1, 7-9, 34-38; I Kings 9:25; Psalm 141:2; Hosea 11:1-2; Luke 1:8-10.*

INGATHERING, FEAST OF. See *Booths, Feast of.*

INHERITANCE. A possession handed down from the past. In the Bible the word refers to material possessions, such as land, cattle, wealth, possessions given by God. In the NT the word more often refers to spiritual gifts from God, such as eternal life, or the kingdom of God. (See *Heritage.*) *Leviticus 27:24; Numbers 36:7; Deuteronomy 10:9; 19:14; Psalm 105:11; Proverbs 13:22; 17:2; Ezekiel 46:16-18; Luke 10:25; 12:13-21, Acts 20:32; Colossians 1:11-12; 3:23-24.*

INIQUITY. Another word for sin. It is any action that separates a person from God or destroys his relationship with another person as well as with God. (See *Sin, Transgression, Trespass.*) *Leviticus 26:39; II Samuel 24:10; Psalm 51:9-12; Isaiah 40:1-2; Ezekiel 18:19-22; Matthew 23:28.*

INK. In Bible times writing fluid made from soot or lampblack mixed with gum resin. Red ink was made by using red iron oxide as a substitute for the soot. The ink was probably dried into cakes and moistened when needed. Most of the scribes carried cakes of red and black ink with them. Writing was done on flat clay tablets and on pieces of broken pottery as well as on parchment, leather, and paper. *Jeremiah 36:18; II Corinthians 3:3; II John 1:12; III John 1:13.*

INN. A shelter for travelers and their animals. It was used like the hotels and motels of today. In most inns the guests brought their own bedding and food. Some inns were merely a village guest house where travelers could spend the night. Others had a square, walled-in place for the animals of a caravan and a place for the travelers to sleep and eat. *Luke 2:4-7; 10:33-35.*

INQUIRE OF GOD. To seek the will of God before acting or making a commitment. In early OT times God was consulted through seers, priests, and prophets. They asked for help on matters of personal and public welfare and before people went into battle. Many different methods were used. The priest tried to find God's will by using the sacred lots, Urim and Thummim (probably stones or sticks of uneven length), or by making a sacrifice. Prophets sometimes reported help through dreams. From the time of the establishment of synagogues during the Exile the people more and more prayed directly to God for guidance. By NT times prayer was the chief means of inquiring of God to find his will. *Exodus 18:15-23; I Samuel 9:9; II Chronicles 18:4-7; Psalm 27:4.*

IOTA. The ninth and the smallest letter of the Greek alphabet. The term is used to mean something very small. *Matthew 5:18.*

IRON, IRONSMITH. A silver-white metallic mineral substance found in ore. The one who works in iron, both smelting the ore and casting the finished pieces. Iron is the most abundant and cheapest of the hard metals. In ancient times, however, the use of iron spread slowly because it was difficult to work. The metal had to be heated, and that required great amounts of fuel. The Canaanites and Philistines were using iron when the Hebrews came to Canaan. They used chariots of iron in battle against the Hebrews and knew how to make weapons of steel. The invention of the bellows around 1500 B.C. made it easier to produce iron in quantities. Plowshares, kettles, and tools were then made of iron and steel. The Hebrews, however, did not possess a supply of iron or the skill to make use of iron until the time of David, about 1000 B.C. "Iron" is used in the Bible as a figure of speech for hardness, strength, and harshness. *Joshua 17:16; Judges 4:3; I Samuel 13:19-21; II Samuel 12:30-31; Job 19:24; Psalms 2:9; 107:10; Proverbs 27:17; Isaiah 44:12.*

ISAAC. Meaning "he laughs." The son which God promised Abraham and Sarah. He was born to them in their old age. The boy Isaac and his father shared a deep faith in each other and in God. In the story of the "sacrifice" of Isaac their faith and obedience were tested when Abraham was commanded to return Isaac to God by sacrificing him. Both the father and the son sadly consented to do this. At the moment when Abraham was about to kill his son, he was interrupted by the voice of God renewing the promise to Abraham on which the Hebrew covenant faith was based. Isaac married Rebekah when he was forty years old and became the father of Jacob and Esau. Abraham, Isaac, and Jacob are known as patriarchs, or fathers, of the Hebrew people. *Genesis 17:15-21; 21:1-12; 22:1-14; 24:62-67; 25:11, 20, 26; 26:6, 12-26: 27:1-40; 35:27-29; 49:31.*

ISAIAH. A prophet in the southern kingdom of Judah, born about 760 B.C. His name meant "God has saved." After Isaiah received his call from God to be a prophet, he became a man of action, fearless and frank. He came from an important family, and rulers listened to his advice even though it was unpleasant. Isaiah condemned the religious and social evils of his time and denounced injustice and greed. He opposed all alliances with foreign powers and urged the people to put their trust in God. He looked forward to the coming of an ideal king who would "reign in righteousness" and "rule with justice." He was the first of the major prophets. His ministry lasted about forty years (742–701 B.C.). (See *Isaiah, Book of.*)

ISAIAH, BOOK OF. The first book of a major prophet in the OT. The book contains the prophecies of Isaiah (chapters 1–39) and of his followers (chapters 40–66). These are set down in poetic form. One of the most important things emphasized in the book is the holiness of God. There is also some history in the book.

ISHBOSHETH. A son of King Saul, he ruled the northern tribes of Israel for about two years after his father's death (about 1000 B.C.). He struggled unsuccessfully with David for the leadership of all the tribes. Ishbosheth was murdered by two of his own men, a deed condemned by David even though it meant the last block to David's complete control of the land was removed. *II Samuel 2:1–4:12.*

ISHMAEL. Son of Abraham by the serving woman Hagar; older half-brother of Isaac. Jealous for her own son Isaac and annoyed by the behavior of her servant, Sarah forced Abraham to send Hagar and Ishmael into the wilderness of Paran. Later Ishmael married and had twelve sons. *Genesis 16:11, 15-16; 17:15-21; 25:9, 12-18.*

ISHMAELITES. In the OT the name of wandering caravan traders, tent dwellers, and camel herders who dwelt in settlements or camps in the desert of northern Arabia. The Ishmaelites traced their descent from their ancestor Ishmael, the son of Abraham and Hagar. Today a person who roams about and does not seem to settle down in any one place is sometimes called an Ishmaelite. *Genesis 37:25-28; 39:1; Judges 8:24; I Chronicles 2:17; 27:30; Psalm 83:6.*

ISLAND, ISLE. Land completely surrounded by water. When islands are referred to in the Bible, those in the Mediterranean Sea are meant. *Psalm 72:10; Isaiah 40:15; 42:15; Ezekiel 26:18; Acts 13:4, 6; 27:16; 28:11.*

ISRAEL. A name given to Jacob after his vision of God (see *Jacob*). It later came to refer to the descendants of Jacob. The history of Israel probably began with the time of Jacob. Abraham, Isaac, and Jacob were the earliest ancestors of the Israelites. They are known as the patriarchs. Jacob's twelve sons became the leaders of the twelve tribes of Israel. In the stories of their slavery in Egypt, the Exodus from there, their desert wanderings, and their entrance into Canaan, the name "Israel" is used for the people as a whole or for their land. It was also the name of the kingdom under Saul, David, and Solomon. With the death of Solomon the kingdom divided into two parts, the north and south. The northern kingdom continued to be called Israel. The southern kingdom became Judah. Israel, the northern kingdom, lasted about two centuries, until 722 B.C. It was overthrown by Assyria, and its people were taken into captivity. A century and a half later in 586 B.C. Judah, the southern kingdom, came to an end. There was no land called Israel for 2,670 years. The Israelites became a people instead of a nation. The idea that they were God's people always remained with them. On May 14, 1948, an independent Jewish state was formed at the eastern end of the Mediterranean Sea and once more took the ancient name Israel. *Genesis 32:22-28; 35:9-12; 46:29-30; Exodus 1:7-14; 12:40; Deuteronomy 6:3-4; Judges 6:2-3; II Samuel 2:9:10; I Kings 6:1; 11:42; 12:12-20; II Kings 17:1, 21-23; II Chronicles 7:3; Isaiah 1:3; 5:7; Luke 1:68-79; John 1:47, 49; Acts 2:22.*

ISRAELITES. The people descended from Israel and heirs of the spiritual gifts and historical purpose of God's chosen people.

ISSACHAR. A son of Jacob and Leah and the ancestor of one of the twelve tribes of Israel whose territory was between Mt. Tabor and the southern end of the Sea of Galilee. *Genesis 30:18; Numbers 1:28-29; Judges 5:15; I Chronicles 12:40; II Chronicles 30:18.*

IVORY. A hard, creamy-white, bone-like substance forming the tusks of elephants. It is mentioned in the Bible as a sign of wealth and luxury. Ivory was carved for inlaid decorations on thrones, beds, houses, and possibly decks of ships. The tribute, or tax, was often paid in ivory-inlaid pieces. *I Kings 10:18, 22; 22:39; II Chronicles 9:17; Psalm 45:8; Ezekiel 27:6, 15; Amos 3:15; 6:4.*

JABBOK. A stream about fifty miles long which empties into the Jordan River fifteen miles north of the Dead Sea. The waters of the Jabbok flow steadily downhill through an ever-deepening canyon so that its current is swift and strong. In Bible times it was the boundary between the Amorites and the Ammonites. Returning to be reconciled with his brother Esau, Jacob forded the Jabbok. It was near this stream that he had his encounter with God and received a blessing and a new name, Israel. *Genesis 32:22-30; Numbers 21:24; Deuteronomy 2:37; Joshua 12:2; Judges 11:13, 22.*

JACKAL. A bushy-tailed relative of the dog, the jackal is still common throughout the lands of the Bible. It was unknown to the English translators. "Fox" was the nearest they could come to identifying the animal from the Hebrew description. It is very likely that the three hundred "foxes" which Samson caught, tied tail to tail, and turned loose as living firebrands to destroy the crops of the Philistines were jackals (Judges 15:4). Foxes travel alone and capturing three hundred would be almost impossible. But jackals, traveling as they do in packs, would have made the capture of so large a number more plausible.

JACOB. Son of Isaac and Rebekah and younger twin brother of Esau. Jacob became head of the family by bargaining for his older brother's birthright. Through a trick he obtained his father's blessing that was meant for Esau. After this Jacob fled from his home and went to Haran. On the way there he had an unusual vision in which he saw God and received the covenant promise which had first been given to Abraham. He, Jacob, was to become the father of a nation (Israel) and to inherit the land of Canaan. The twelve sons born to him while he lived in exile with his uncle Laban became the ancestors of the twelve tribes of Israel. After a period of years Jacob returned to Palestine. He now had his large family and was very wealthy. On his way to meet Esau and make peace with him, Jacob received the name Israel. In all of his wrongdoing Jacob felt that God was with him, calling

him back to his true self. Jacob is linked with Abraham and Isaac as one of the great patriarchs. In the Bible the name Jacob, as well as Israel, is used to refer to the Hebrew nation. (See *Israel.*) *Genesis 25:21–49:33; Exodus 19:3; II Kings 13:23; Psalm 46:7; Isaiah 41:8-9; 44:1-2, 21; 48:20; Mark 12:26; Luke 1:33; Acts 3:13; 7:46, Hebrews 11:9.*

JACOB'S WELL. The well where Jesus met the Samaritan woman. It was near Sychar in Samaria. Today there is a Greek Orthodox church standing near the spot. *John 4:3-6.*

JAMES. 1. James, one of the twelve apostles, was the son of Zebedee and a brother of John. He was a fisherman by trade but left this prosperous business to become one of the first followers of Jesus. He was put to death by King Herod during the persecution of the Christians in Jerusalem about A.D. 43. *Matthew 4:21-22; 10:2; 17:1; Mark 1:19, 29; 3:17; 9:2; 10:35, 41; 13:3; Luke 5:10; 6:14; 8:51; 9:28; Acts 1:13; 12:1-2.*

2. James, the Son of Alphaeus, was also a disciple of Jesus. This may be the same James listed as "James the son of Mary." This woman was present at the crucifixion. *Matthew 27:56; Mark 3:18; 15:40; 16:1; Luke 6:15; 24:10; Acts 1:13.*

3. James, the brother of Jesus, was not at first a disciple, but after the resurrection he became a believer and an important leader in the church at Jerusalem. *Matthew 13:55; Mark 6:3; Acts 12:17; 15:13; 21:18; I Corinthians 15:7; Galatians 1:19, 2:9, 12.*

JAMES, LETTER OF. The twentieth book in the NT. It is really a sermon in the form of a letter addressed to Christians everywhere. It describes the way a Christian must make his faith and love work in his everyday living.

JAPHETH. A son of Noah. He was called the ancestor of the ancient people who lived to the north and west of the Hebrews. These people in Asia Minor in the region of the Aegean, Black, and Caspian seas are known as the Indo-European family of nations. *Genesis 5:32; 6:10; 7:13; 9:18-19; 10:1-5.*

JASHAR, BOOK OF. An ancient written document, containing songs and poetry, which is now lost. It must have been well known among the Hebrews, for it is mentioned several times in the OT. The short poem of Solomon (I Kings 8:12-13) is thought to be a quotation from this book. *Joshua 10:12-13; II Samuel 1:17-27.*

JEALOUSY. In the Bible this word has two very different meanings. It can mean the intense hatred and suspicion that grows out of envy and greed. It has another meaning that is something like "zeal." This type of jealousy is the single-minded devotion of people to God. God is also said to be jealous, and this means that he demands complete obedience and loyalty on the part of his people. *Genesis 37:11; Deuteronomy 4:24; 5:9; 6:15; I Kings 19:10, 14; Galatians 5:19-20; James 3:14-16.*

JEBUSITES. The name of a clan also called Jebus. The Jebusites occupied

Jerusalem before David captured the city. *Joshua 18:16, 28; Judges 19:10-11; I Chronicles 11:4-9.*

JECONIAH, JECHONIAH. See *Jehoiachin.*

JEHOAHAZ. Meaning "God has taken hold of." Name of three OT kings.

1. Jehoahaz, the son of Joram, was king of Judah about 841 B.C. He was greatly influenced by his mother Athaliah, who was a cruel and cold-blooded Baal worshiper. At her son's death she seized the throne. His name is sometimes written Ahaziah. *II Chronicles 21:17; 22:1-10.*

2. Jehoahaz, the son of Jehu, was king of Israel from about 814 to 798 B.C. During his reign Syria overcame Israel and forced the nation to pay tribute. *II Kings 13:1-9.*

3. Jehoahaz, the son of Josiah, was king of Judah about 609 B.C. He was also called Shallum. This Jehoahaz had reigned in Jerusalem three months when he was taken in captivity to Egypt by Pharaoh Neco. *II Kings 23:31-34; I Chronicles 3:15; II Chronicles 36:2-4; Jeremiah 22:10-12.*

JEHOASH. See *Joash* (1).

JEHOIACHIN. Also called Jeconiah, Coniah, and Jechoniah. He was the son and successor of Jehoiakim and king of Judah (598–597 B.C.) in the time of the prophet Jeremiah. After a reign of only three months he surrendered to Nebuchadnezzar, king of Babylon, and was taken into exile. *II Kings 24:8-17; 25:27-30; I Chronicles 3:16-17; Esther 2:6; Jeremiah 22:24-30; 24:1; 28:4; 52:31-34; Ezekiel 1:2; Matthew 1:11-12.*

JEHOIADA. High priest in Jerusalem in the ninth century B.C. He led the revolt that overthrew Queen Athaliah of Judah and the Baal worship that she supported. He helped to establish the seven-year-old King Joash (Jehoash) on the throne about 837 B.C. and apparently governed for him until Joash was old enough to govern the kingdom himself. Jehoiada inspired Joash to have the temple repaired. *II Kings 11:4–12:16; II Chronicles 22:10–24:27.*

JEHOIAKIM. Son of Josiah and brother of Jehoahaz. He was king of Judah from about 609 to 598 B.C. In the time of the prophet Jeremiah he succeeded to the throne when Jehoahaz was taken into Egypt. Jehoiakim was the throne name given the new king by Pharaoh Neco. His given name was Eliakim. Later Jehoiakim became subject to King Nebuchadnezzar of Babylon. After three years of paying tribute he ignored the advice of Jeremiah and rebelled against Nebuchadnezzar. This cost the king his life. *II Kings 23:34–24:6; I Chronicles 3:15-16; II Chronicles 36:4-8; Jeremiah 26:1-23, 46:2.*

JEHORAM. See *Joram.*

JEHOSHAPHAT. Several persons had this name.

1. A priest who blew a trumpet before the ark when the ark was brought to Jerusalem. *I Chronicles 15:24.*

2. A record keeper in the reigns of David and Solomon. *II Samuel 8:16; 20:24; I Kings 4:3; I Chronicles 18:15.*

3. An officer in Solomon's government. *I Kings 4:17.*

4. The son of Asa who reigned as king of Judah from about 870 to 848 B.C. He ended the warfare between the kingdoms of Israel and Judah. He was an able ruler who gained control of the trade routes from Arabia. He greatly improved the system of justice throughout his kingdom, and he led his people in a return to the worship of God and obedience to the law of Moses. *I Kings 22:41-45; II Chronicles 20:29–21:3, 12.*

JEHU. The son of Jehoshaphat, he was king of Israel from about 841 to 814 B.C., when Elisha was prophet in the land. After being secretly anointed as king, Jehu led a bloody revolt which was inspired by the prophet. His purpose was to rid the land of Baal worship and of the people who practiced it. Joram, king of Israel; Ahaziah, king of Judah; and Jezebel, the wife of Ahab, were assassinated. Finally Jehu summoned all the worshipers of Baal on the pretense of offering a great sacrifice in the temple which Ahab had built. Once these people were assembled, Jehu gave orders that they all be killed. *II Kings 9:1–10:36; II Chronicles 22:8-9.*

JELLYFISH. The jellyfish is found in the Mediterranean Sea and the Indian Ocean, so would have been known to the Israelites living near the seacoast, but it is not mentioned in the Bible.

JEPHTHAH. A Gileadite warrior who freed Israel from the constant raids by the Ammonites. His victories stopped invasions by the Ammonites until Saul became king. After his military victories he became a judge in Israel. Before defeating the Ammonites Jepthah vowed to offer as a sacrifice whatever came out of his house upon his return if God would give him success. His daughter and only child came dancing to meet him. When he sadly told her of his solemn promise, she insisted that he keep his word. *Judges 11:1–12:7; Hebrews 11:32.*

JERBOA. The jerboa is a rodent, somewhat larger than the rat, common to much of the Middle East. Its hind legs are five or six times longer than the front, giving it a kangaroo look and, in fact, enabling it to leap like a small kangaroo so effectively that it can "run" faster than a human. It has rabbit-like ears, large eyes, and is covered with a soft, sandy-colored fur except for its white belly and a black-and-white tassel at the end of its tail. It feeds on plants and insects. It lives in burrows made in the hard, sandy soil and, being very shy, is seldom seen.

JEREMIAH. One of the major OT prophets who lived in the last years before the Babylonians defeated Judah and destroyed Jerusalem. He lived from 626 to about 580 B.C. Jeremiah spoke to his own people throughout the reigns of five kings. There was a constant threat of disaster to the nation. He denounced the people of Judah for their neglect of the true service of God, for their injustices to one another, and for their worship of idols. He urged the people of Judah to repent and return to God. They would not listen, and the prophet was even punished for his efforts. As he

had foretold, Jerusalem was taken by the Babylonians in 586, and the people were sent into exile. Jeremiah was permitted to remain in Judah. Later he was taken to Egypt against his will and died there. (See *Jeremiah, Book of*.)

JEREMIAH, BOOK OF. The book contains the prophecies of Jeremiah, usually set down in poetic form. It also contains history of those critical times which Jeremiah dictated to his secretary Baruch. It is possible that Baruch added material based on his personal knowledge of Jeremiah.

JERICHO. A major city at the southern end of the Jordan Valley. It is the site of many ancient cities, the earliest of which dates back as far as 7000 B.C. At the time of the conquest Jericho, a strongly fortified city, stood in the path of the Hebrews as they entered Canaan under the leadership of Joshua. The OT tells how the armies of Israel marched around the city according to God's instruction, and the walls crumbled, and the city fell. Archaeologists have always been interested in the city. It was excavated long before science was as developed as it is today. For this reason much valuable evidence is lost. However, many scientists think one city of Jericho may have been destroyed by earthquake and fire a century before the time of Joshua and then rebuilt. The NT Jericho, founded by Herod the Great, was a mile south of the old city. Zacchaeus, the famous tax collector, lived here. There are many stories in the Gospels that tell of Jesus' ministry in Jericho. *Joshua 2:1-14;*

5:10–6:27; I Kings 16:34; II Kings 2:4-5, 15-18; Matthew 20:29; Mark 10:46; Luke 10:30; 18:35; 19:1-2; Hebrews 11:30.

JEROBOAM. 1. The first king of the northern kingdom Israel, who reigned from about 931 to 910 B.C. He was chosen by ten northern tribes when the kingdom was divided after the death of Solomon. He introduced pagan practices into the worship of God. Many later kings of Israel were described as following the ways of Jeroboam, "who made Israel to sin." *I Kings 11:26-40; 12:20–14:20; II Kings 14:24; II Chronicles 9:29; 10:2-5, 12-15; 13:3-20.*

2. A later king of Israel (782–753 B.C.), son and successor of Joash. Under him the kingdom prospered, but the prophet Amos declared everything in the land was crooked. *II Kings 14:23-29; Amos 1:1.*

JERUSALEM. In the Bible, Jerusalem is referred to by several other names, such as Salem, Zion, Moriah, City of David, and Jebus. David captured Jerusalem from the Jebusites and made it his capital city. When he brought the ark to Jerusalem, the city became the religious center of the Hebrew people. David's son Solomon built the temple, and Jerusalem became a holy city. After Solomon's death when the kingdom was divided, Jerusalem was the capital of the southern kingdom, Judah. Many nations threatened Jerusalem. Finally it was conquered and burned by Nebuchadnezzar and part of its population carried off to Babylon. When the refugees returned from exile, they rebuilt the temple, and later the city

and walls were restored. In NT times Jerusalem was under Roman rule, but the Jews were free to worship in the temple and to celebrate their feast days. Jesus spent his last days on earth in Jerusalem, and his trial and resurrection took place there. Jerusalem was very important in the early years of the Christian church. Today the city of Jerusalem is the capital of the state of Israel. It is sacred to Christians, Jews, and Muslims. *Joshua 15:8; II Samuel 5:6-10; 6:16-19; I Kings 3:1; 14:25-26; II Kings 12:17-18; 14:13; II Chronicles 3:1; 36:19; Ezra 1:5; 7:7-10; Nehemiah 2:17; Psalms 122:1-9; 137:5-7; Jeremiah 3:17; 39:1-3; Matthew 2:1; 16:21; Mark 11:11; Luke 2:22-25, 38, 41-45; 9:51; 13:33-35; Acts 1:8; 11:22.*

JESSE. The father of King David. He was of the tribe of Judah and lived in Bethlehem. *Ruth 4:17,22; I Samuel 16:1-23; 17:17-19; 20:27; I Chronicles 2:12-13; 10:14; Isaiah 11:1, 10; Matthew 1:5-6; Luke 3:32, Acts 13:22.*

JESUS CHRIST. The central figure in the NT. Both God and man, Jesus is the one in whom the whole of OT history takes on a new and deeper meaning. Jesus was the personal name of the one whose title is "the Christ," from which the Christian religion gets its name. The name Jesus in the original Hebrew is a form of the name Joshua, meaning "God saves." Jesus was born into an ordinary Jewish family from Nazareth—one which practiced deep devotion to God and which had ancestors in the line of David. After being baptized by John in the river Jordan, Jesus began his ministry. His words and teaching had such power that he was called a prophet (see Matthew 21:11). As he preached his message that the kingdom of God was coming, in fact had already begun (Mark 1:15), he healed the sick of every sort and did other works that indicated the power of God was working through him. Those who believed his message and understood his mission hailed him as the Son of David (see Matthew 21:15), the Son of God (see John 1:49), and the Messiah (see John 1:41). Jesus proclaimed the personal nearness of God and spoke of him as the Father. He declared of the mercy, the justice, and especially the love of God. Through his extraordinary life and mighty acts his disciples came to recognize him as the Christ or Anointed One. However, it was only after his death and resurrection that they began to understand his role as the Lord and Savior of mankind. *Matthew 1:1, 21; 16:13-20; 26:71; Mark 1:1, 24; 10:47; 14:67; Luke 4:22; 18:37-38; John 1:17; 20:31; Acts 2:36; Romans 8:39; Galatians 3:26; I Timothy 1:1.*

JETHRO. Priest of Midian and father-in-law of Moses. He is also called Hobab and Reuel. He advised Moses on giving counsel to the people in the wilderness. *Exodus 18:1-27.*

JEW. There are three ways in which this word is used in the Bible. In the OT it was used from the time of the Exile to refer to the members of the southern kingdom of Judah who were in Babylon. Later it was used to refer to any of the people who were not Gentiles and who lived in the province of Judah under the governance of Babylon or Persia. It also came to be

used for any person who worshiped God and followed Judaism even if that person were not a Jew by birth. *II Kings 25:25; Ezra 4:12; 5:5; Nehemiah 1:2; 4:1-2; Esther 3:6–9:31; Jeremiah 40:11-12; Daniel 3:8, Zechariah 8:23; Matthew 27:11; John 4:9; 11:33-36; Acts 2:10; 14:1; 21:39; Romans 2:28-29; Galatians 2:13; Colossians 3:11.*

JEZEBEL. A princess from Phoenicia who became the wife of King Ahab of Israel. Jezebel was a clever and strong-willed woman who influenced Ahab and the people of Israel to turn away from God and worship her god Baal. The prophet Elijah opposed the queen in her schemes. Jezebel succeeded in driving Elijah away, but not before he had won a victory over the prophets of Baal. *I Kings 16:31-33; 18:4, 19; 19:1-2; 21:5-15; II Kings 9:22, 30-37.*

JEZREEL. An OT town located at the foot of Mt. Gilboa southwest of the Sea of Galilee. Here King Ahab had a royal residence. It was also the name of the entire valley that separated Galilee from Samaria. Jezreel is mentioned frequently in biblical history after the division of the kingdom. The prophet Hosea named his first child Jezreel, recalling the bloodshed in the city of Jezreel by which King Jehu came to power. *Joshua 17:16; Judges 6:33; I Samuel 29:1, 11; II Samuel 2:9; 4:4; I Kings 4:12; 18:45-46; 21:1; II Kings 8:29; Hosea 1:4-5.*

JOAB. King David's nephew and commander of the army during many of David's important conquests. He was a fearless soldier and a loyal servant of the king in many private matters. In the dispute over who would be king after David's death—Adonijah or Solomon—Joab sided with Adonijah. Solomon, when he became king, had Joab put to death for this. *II Samuel 2:13-14, 18; 3:23-31; 8:16; 11:14-22; 18:10-16; 19:5-8; 20:7-11; 24: 1-4; I Kings 1:19, 41; 2:28-34.*

JOANNA. Wife of the steward of Herod Antipas. She was healed by Jesus, and provided for the needs of Jesus and the Twelve out of her own money. She was one of the women who visited the tomb of Jesus after his resurrection. *Luke 8:3; 24:10.*

JOASH. Sometimes written as Jehoash, it is the name of several people in the OT. The most important were two kings.

1. Joash, son of Ahaziah, who ruled the southern kingdom of Judah about 835 to 797 B.C. He came to the throne when he was seven years old with the priest Jehoiada acting as his teacher and regent until the boy king came of age. During his reign the temple was repaired. He is also called Jehoash. *II Kings 11:2-3, 21; 12:1-21.*

2. Joash, son of Jehoahaz, was king of the northern kingdom of Israel from about 798 to 782 B.C. He recovered for Israel the territory lost to Aram in the reign of his father. He was a friend of the prophet Elisha. *II Kings 13:10-13, 24-25; 14:8-16.*

JOB. A righteous and godly man who is the hero of the OT poem in the book of Job. For no reason that he could understand Job suffered terrible troubles. All his possessions, his

children, and finally his health were taken from him. Through all this his faith in God held steady (see James 5:11). He discussed his situation with his friends. They discussed the problem of why God allows good people to suffer, but they could not find the answer. At the end of the poem God himself speaks to Job and gives him the key to the answer. (See *Job, Book of.*)

JOB, BOOK OF. The eighteenth book in the OT which tells the story of Job. The author and the date are uncertain, but it may have been written sometime between 600 and 450 B.C.

JOEL. A common name in the OT, but the most famous Joel was a prophet. Little is known about him, but he probably lived in Jerusalem at a time when there was a plague of grasshopper-like locusts which destroyed crops and trees until there was a serious food shortage. (See *Joel, Book of.*)

JOEL, BOOK OF. The second of the twelve short books of prophecy that stand at the end of the OT. The prophet described a terrible locust plague which he understood to be a warning from God to the people of even worse disaster at the day of judgment. Joel urged the people to repent and predicted that they would be forgiven and the land restored. The book was probably written about 400 B.C.

JOHN. 1. One of the twelve apostles and a member of the inner circle of men—Peter, James, and John—who were closest to Jesus. He was the son of Zebedee and brother of James. He was a fisherman and followed his trade on the Sea of Galilee. He may have been the one called the beloved disciple. John became an outstanding leader in the church at Jerusalem and was concerned with preaching the gospel to his fellow Jews. *Matthew 4:21-22; 10:2; 17:1-2; Mark 1:19-20; Luke 5:10; 22:8; Acts 1:13; 3:1-4, 11; Galatians 2:9.*

2. A prophet whose father was a priest. His mother Elizabeth was related to Mary the mother of Jesus. He was called John the Baptist. John lived in Judea and began his ministry in the wilderness preaching repentance for the forgiveness of sins. Many came to hear him preach and to be baptized in the river Jordan, some of them thinking he was the Christ. Jesus came to be baptized by his cousin. John criticized King Herod for marrying his brother's wife. This made the woman so angry with the prophet that she had him beheaded (see *Herodias*). John the Baptist is often called the "forerunner" or the person who prepared the way for Jesus and the kingdom of God. *Matthew 3:1-15; 4:12; 11:2-19; 14:1-12; Mark 1:4-9; 6:14-29; Luke 7:18-27; John 1:6-8, 15-40; Acts 1:5; 13:24-25.*

JOHN, FIRST, SECOND, AND THIRD. Three letters in the NT written to Christians in the early church encouraging them to be faithful and loyal in a time of trouble and danger. The writer warned them against false teachers who claimed Jesus was not the Christ. He emphasized that love and concern for others

are important. The author of these letters does not identify himself by name. The letters were written toward the end of the first century.

JOHN, GOSPEL OF. The last of the four Gospels in the NT. It is different from the other three in that it does not tell a connected story of the life of Jesus but explains the importance of Jesus to all mankind. In small sermons John gives "signs" selected from Jesus' own acts that show Jesus to be the Christ, the Son of God. The book of John teaches that in Jesus people can better understand God. The book probably was written toward the end of the first century. It is not certain who the author was.

JOHN MARK. See *Mark, John.*

JONAH. The OT parable of a prophet who was commanded by God to go and preach to the people of Nineveh, a large and prosperous city. Jonah was unwilling to go to a non-Jewish city so he tried to run away by taking a ship. A storm so frightened the sailors that they threw Jonah overboard because they felt he was the cause of the storm. At this point a great fish swallowed him and took him the rest of his journey. He went into the city and urged the people to turn from their sins. When they listened and did repent, God spared the city. At first Jonah was angry at this. However, God showed Jonah that these people who were not Jews also had a place in God's purpose (See *Jonah, Book of.*)

JONAH, BOOK OF. The fifth of the twelve OT books known as the Minor Prophets. It is a story about a prophet rather than a book of prophetic sayings. It was written about 350 B.C. by an unknown writer who recognized that God's concern was not for Jews alone. It is a missionary book in which the chief character is a prophet called Jonah.

JONATHAN. Eldest son of King Saul. He was a warrior who assisted his father in many military campaigns. He was a dear friend of David and proved his love even when King Saul turned against David. Jonathan died with his father and brothers in a battle with the Philistines at Gilboa. David was deeply grieved at the loss of Jonathan. This personal name was used frequently in OT times. *I Samuel 13:2-3, 16; 14:1-45; 18:1-4; 19:1-7; 20:1-42; 23:16-18; II Samuel 1:4-5, 23-26; 21:12-14.*

JOPPA. A city thirty-five miles from Jerusalem on the Mediterranean coast. It is now called Jaffa and is a part of Tel Aviv. In OT times it was a major seaport serving Jerusalem. In NT times there was an early Christian community there with which Peter was closely connected. *II Chronicles 2:16; Ezra 3:7; Jonah 1:3; Acts 9:36-43; 10:5-6.*

JORAM. Sometimes spelled Jehoram.
1. King of the northern kingdom of Israel from 852 to 841 B.C. He was the brother and successor of Ahaziah and a son of Ahab. The prophet Elisha encouraged a revolt against the Omride family (the family of Ahab), and Jehu was secretly proclaimed king. When Jehu saw the wounded

king returning from battle he murdered Joram. *II Kings 1:17; 3:1; 8:28-29; 9:14-26.*

2. King of Judah from about 848 to 841 B.C. He was the son and successor of Jehoshaphat. His wife was Athaliah, daughter of Ahab. During his reign he encouraged Baal worship and was remembered as a wicked king. *II Kings 8:16-24; II Chronicles 21:16-17.*

JORDAN. The longest and most important river in Palestine. The name means "stream that descends rapidly." It rises 1,200 feet above sea level, flows south, and empties into the Dead Sea 1,200 feet below sea level. A straight line from its beginning to its end is about eighty miles, but its curves and twists make it a full two hundred miles long. It cannot be used for transportation, but there are many shallow places where it can be forded. In Bible times the Jordan was a great military barrier and armies fought for possession of the fords. Crossing the Jordan marked the Hebrews' entry into Canaan, and the stretch of river from the Sea of Galilee to the Dead Sea continued to play an important part in biblical history. *Genesis 13:10-11; 32:10; Numbers 13:29; Deuteronomy 3:8, 17, 23-27; Joshua 1:2; 3:1-17; 23:4; Judges 3:28; 7:24-25; Mark 1:5,9; Luke 3:3.*

JOSEPH. 1. The son of Rachel and the favorite of his father Jacob. His older brothers were envious and plotted to kill him. However, they changed their plan a bit and sold him to a caravan of traders. Joseph became a slave in Egypt. But his intelligence and attractive personality made it possible for him to rise to power and into favor with the pharaoh. He managed the grain supply in such a way that there was enough to feed the people during a great drought. Years later Joseph was reunited with his father and brothers, and his entire family came to live in Egypt. *Genesis 30:23-24; 37:2-35; 39:1–48:22; 50:1; Exodus 1:5-9; Joshua 16:1-4.*

2. The carpenter who was the husband of the mother of Jesus. He is mentioned only a few times in the NT. Matthew and Luke mention him in the birth and childhood stories of Jesus. Mark does not refer to him at all, and the Gospel of John twice refers to Jesus as the "son of Joseph." It is probable that Joseph died before Jesus' ministry began. Mary seems to have been a widow at the time of the crucifixion (see John 19:25-27). *Matthew 1:16, 19-25; 2:13-15, 19-23; 13:55; Luke 2:4-7, 16; 3:23; John 1:45; 6:42.*

3. Joseph of Arimathea was a wealthy member of the Jewish Sanhedrin who probably became a follower of Jesus. He begged the body of Jesus from the Roman governor and buried it in a newly hewn tomb on his own property. *Matthew 27:57-60; Mark 15:43-46; Luke 23:50-53; John 19:38-41.*

JOSHUA. The son of Nun and a major figure in the OT book of Joshua. He was Moses' assistant in the journey from Egypt to Canaan. Before Moses died, he appointed Joshua his successor. Joshua had great military skill and was a forceful leader. He brought the tribes together and led them in conquering the land of

Canaan. Before his death he challenged the people to be faithful in their worship and service of God and not to accept the gods of the Canaanites. (See *Joshua, Book of.*) *Exodus 24:13; Numbers 14:6-8, 38; 27:18-23; 34:17; Deuteronomy 1:38; 3:28; 31:7-8, 14, 23; 34:9; Judges 2:8; I Chronicles 7:27; Acts 7:45.*

JOSHUA, BOOK OF. The sixth book in the OT. It describes the invasion of Canaan after the exodus of the Israelites from Egypt and their wanderings in the wilderness. It tells of the division and allotment of the land of Canaan among the tribes of Israel. The central figure is Joshua, who was the leader at this time. The book probably was written by several authors drawing from various sources.

JOSIAH. King of Judah from about 641 to 609 B.C. He was the son and successor of Amon. Josiah was one of Judah's able and faithful kings. The discovery of the book of the law in the temple led him to make many major reforms in the life of the nation. He removed the idols and encouraged the worship of God. His death in the battle at Megiddo was a blow to the nation. In this battle Josiah tried to prevent reinforcements from Egypt from reaching the Assyrians, who had been enemies of Judah for so long and had overcome the northern kingdom of Israel. *II Kings 22:1–23:30; Jeremiah 1:1-2; 22:11.*

JOTHAM. 1. One of Gideon's sons who told the story of the fable of the trees. *Judges 9:7-15.*

2. A king of Judah from about 740 to 732 B.C. He was the son and successor of Uzziah (Azariah). During his reign there was great building activity in Jerusalem and all of Judah. It was a time of prosperity. *II Kings 15:32-36; II Chronicles 27:1-9.*

JUBILEE, YEAR OF. In OT times every fiftieth year was set by law as the time when all slaves of the preceding forty-nine years (seven, seven-year periods) were to be released and all property sold during that time was to be returned to its original owners. This year was also called the "year of liberty." The biblical records seem to show that this legislation never became effective. The probable use of the term *jubilee year* was to name a fifty-year period of time, like the present half-a-century. *Leviticus 25:8-14; Numbers 36:4.*

JUDAH. The fourth son of Jacob and leader of the tribe descended from him which took his name. In the OT, King David was the most famous descendant of the tribe. The NT genealogies of Jesus Christ list Judah as an ancestor. The territory of Judah was a narrow mountain ridge about twenty miles long between Jerusalem and Hebron. Judah and several other tribes gradually occupied the whole of the southern country of Palestine. There were none of the strong Canaanite cities to be dealt with, and the land was cleared of forest to make it suitable for farming. The tribe of Judah gradually expanded to the south and mingled with the other Judean hill clans. The tribes and

territory of Judah became the southern kingdom of Judah (see *Israel*) after the death of King Solomon. *Genesis 29:35; Judges 1:1-19; II Samuel 2:4; I Kings 12:17; 14:21; II Kings 18:1; 25:21-22; Psalm 78:68-70; Isaiah 40:9; Lamentations 1:3; Matthew 1:2-3; Luke 3:33; Revelation 5:5.*

JUDAISM. The belief and total way of life of the Jewish community. This community was unlike most in that it was bound together by its sense of election by God and bound to God himself by the covenant, their agreement to serve him. In Jesus' day the beliefs and practices differed in various Jewish sects, such as the Pharisees and Sadducees, but all Jews believed in the one God of Israel and acknowledged the Law. *Acts 13:43; Galatians 1:13-14.*

JUDAS. 1. Judas Iscariot, one of the twelve apostles and the betrayer of Jesus. There are many puzzling questions about this man: Why was he attracted to Jesus? Why did Jesus include him in the Twelve? Why did Judas turn against Jesus? For a sum of money he agreed to help the religious authorities in Jerusalem take Jesus in a quiet place where they would not arouse the people. Later Judas was sorry for his deed and killed himself. *Matthew 10:2-4; 26:14-16; 27:3-5; Mark 14:10-11; Luke 22:3-6; John 12:4-6; 13:2, 21-30; 18:2-5; Acts 1:16-26.*

2. Another apostle was called Judas and is referred to as a son of James. He is sometimes called Thaddaeus. Tradition tells that this apostle went to preach the gospel with Bartholomew

in Armenia. *Mark 3:18; Luke 6:13-16; John 14:22; Acts 1:13.*

3. A relative of Jesus was also called Judas. At the beginning of Jesus' ministry Judas doubted him and was not interested. This was also true of James, another "brother." After the resurrection they did believe and became leaders in the early church. *Matthew 13:55; Mark 6:3; Jude 1:1.*

JUDE, LETTER OF. A short letter in the NT written around the beginning of the second century. The writer appealed to all the churches to keep their faith strong and warned them against false teachings. It is not certain who was the author.

JUDEA. In NT times a division of the Roman province of Syria. It is a variation of the name Judah of OT times. During Judea's long history political changes at times enlarged the area, but Judea proper was a small area about forty-five miles square around Jerusalem, usually ruled by a tetrarch, or governor. In Judea the Herods rose to power with the support of Rome and were ruling when the Christian era began. Judea was important in the life of the Jewish people, chiefly because the holy city Jerusalem was located there. *Matthew 2:1; Mark 1:5; 10:1 Luke 3:1; John 3:22; Acts 8:1; 9:31; Galatians 1:22.*

JUDGE. An official with authority to settle disputes in a court of law; also the act of deciding disputes. In the OT between the time of Joshua and David the judges were military leaders who delivered the Israelites from their

enemies. After the establishment of the kingdom the king often acted as judge or appointed others to fill this office. "Judge" was also used as a title for God, who is the Judge of all the earth, and for Jesus, who set a new standard of judgment. *Genesis 18:25; 19:9; Exodus 2:14; 18:13-26; Leviticus 19:15; Deuteronomy 16:18; 17:8-12; I Samuel 7:15; II Samuel 15:1-6; I Chronicles 23:4; II Chronicles 19:5-7; Psalm 94:2; Isaiah 2:4; 33:22; Luke 6:37; John 7:24; 8:16; Acts 7:27; 10:42; II Timothy 4:1.*

JUDGES, BOOK OF. The seventh book in the OT. It records the history of the Israelites from the time of their entrance into Canaan to the beginning of the kingdom. The book emphasizes that the spirit of God was moving through the history of time. It tells the stories of the chief Israelite leaders who were called judges and contains stories, songs, poems, and some fragments of very ancient literature.

JUDGMENT SEAT. See *Tribunal*.

JULIUS. A Roman centurion, or officer, assigned to take Paul from Caesarea to Rome. He was kind to Paul and permitted him to go ashore at Sidon to visit friends. *Acts 27:1, 3, 9-11, 42-44; 28:16.*

JUNIPER. The "juniper" mentioned by Job (Job 30:4) and in Psalm 120:4 is an incorrect translation of the Hebrew name for one of the most common flowering shrubs in all Judea. It actually is the "flowering broom," a member of the pea family with pea-like clusters of delicate pale pink or white blossoms, followed by pods containing two rows of small, bitter pea-like seeds. It is used extensively as fuel. And although the leaves are small the plant furnishes a measure of welcome shade in the desert, as when Elijah "came down and sat under a juniper tree" (I Kings 19:4).

JUSTICE. See *Law, Righteousness*.

JUSTIFY. In biblical use a term for the action of God which forgives and restores people to goodness and righteousness. Several ideas are combined in this thought: (1) God is a holy and righteous God. (2) He demands holiness and righteousness of his people. (3) People are not holy, they are sinners. (4) This sinfulness deserves punishment. The NT solution for this problem was God's offer of forgiveness through Jesus Christ. When people respond to this offer they are justified. *Job 32:2; Psalm 51:4; Isaiah 43:9; Luke 10:29; Romans 3:20-26; 8:33; Galatians 2:15-21.*

KADESH, KADESH-BARNEA. An oasis in the Wilderness of Zin south of Canaan. Here the Israelites encamped for a lengthy time during their travels from Egypt to Canaan. It was from here that the Israelites sent men to spy out the land of Canaan. *Genesis 14:7; 16:14; Numbers 13:25-26; 20:14-16; 32:8, Deuteronomy 1:19; 2:14; Joshua 10:41; Psalm 29:8.*

KADMONITES. Meaning "easterners." The Kadmonites were a nomadic tribe living in the desert

between Canaan Syria and the river Euphrates. Their lands were included in those promised by God to Abraham and his descendants. *Genesis 15:18-19.*

KERMES. It is difficult to think of the kermes as an "animal" in any category. It is a node-like insect, about the size of a pea, found on the kermes oak. The dried body of the female is treated with vinegar to make a scarlet dye that will not bleach or fade. This is the "scarlet" referred to in the Bible. Its permanence is what Isaiah refers to when he promises that "though your sins be as scarlet they shall be white as snow" (Isaiah 1:18). This scarlet dye was very expensive and only the wealthy could afford garments of scarlet. Still, soldiers were often attired in scarlet. It was a scarlet robe that the soldiers placed on Jesus (Matthew 27:28).

KESTREL. The kestrel is one of the smaller falcons, and is still found in Palestine. Like all falcons, it is an excellent flyer, but a unique characteristic of the kestrel is its ability to hover in mid-air, its long, pointed wings extended. This has given it the name of "wind hover." It feeds mostly on small rodents and insects. Kestrels are often seen in flocks of twenty or more.

KIDRON, BROOK. A valley east of Jerusalem dividing the eastern parts of the city from the Mount of Olives. After heavy rainfalls a brook runs down the valley and waters the orchards and gardens near Jerusalem. Jesus crossed this valley on his way to Gethsemane. Part of the valley was used as a burial ground for the poor.

II Samuel 15:23; II Kings 23:6, 12; II Chronicles 15:16; 29:16; 30:14; John 18:1.

KING, KINGSHIP. A male ruler who had power over a city or a nation. He had the right to hand his royal power on to his descendants. A kingship refers to the office and dignity of a king, his power and authority, and the territory governed by him. In Israel the king was also the military leader who led the army into battle and the judge who settled disputes and corrected injustices. The king also had authority over the religious life of the people. The Israelites recognized the supreme kingship of God and looked on all earthly kings as his anointed representatives. By NT times "king" had become an honorary title for the governor appointed, as the Herods were, by Rome to rule a province. All four Gospels report that Pilate and others called Jesus King of the Jews when questioning him or when mocking him during the trial and crucifixion. *Joshua 12:9-24; I Samuel 8:4-22; II Samuel 5:1-3; 15:2; Psalms 10:16; 24:7-10; Matthew 27:11, 27, 37, 42; Mark 15:2, 9, 12, 18, 26; Luke 23:3, 37-38; John 19:14-15, 19-22; I Timothy 1:17; 6:14-16; Revelation 17:14.*

TABLE OF
OLD TESTAMENT KINGS

The United Kingdom

Saul..........................1020–1000 B.C.
David..........................1000–965 B.C.
Solomon...................... 965–931 B.C.

The Divided Kingdom

JUDAH

ISRAEL

KINGDOM OF GOD, OF HEAVEN. The rule or reign of God. This is one of the most important ideas in the Bible. It deals with a kingdom which is not only in the world that we know, but which includes all places and all times. It is a kingdom designed to carry out the purposes of God. There are three parts to the idea of the kingdom: First, the ruler is and always has been God. Second, the establishment of the kingdom on the earth becomes a reality whenever people pledge their allegiance to God and try to keep his law. Third, a fulfillment, or completing of, God's purpose is expected and hoped for by his people. The idea of the kingdom of God was important to the Hebrews of the OT, and when Jesus came the NT records that he began his ministry by announcing that the "kingdom of God is at hand." He taught that his life, work, and death were necessary for the coming of the kingdom. Jesus also spoke of a future completion. Therefore, the kingdom has come in the person and the acts of Jesus. Those individuals who believe that Jesus is lord become part of the community of the kingdom here and now. They may look forward to a place in the fulfilled kingdom of the future. *Matthew 4:17; 5:3, 10, 19-20; 6:10; 7:21; 10:7; 13:24-52; 18:1-4; Mark 1:14-15; 4:1-33; 12:28-34; Luke 9:2, 61-62; 10:9; 19:11-27; John 3:3, 5; Acts 14:21-22; Romans 14:17; Ephesians 5:5.*

KINGS, FIRST AND SECOND. The eleventh and twelfth books in the OT. They give the history of the Hebrews from the beginning of Solomon's reign, through the devision of the kingdom into two separate states, through the fall of Samaria to the Assyrians, through the fall of Jerusalem and the exile into Babylon. The materials in the books of Kings were collected from many sources such as old histories and court records. The writers, or authors, of the books show how the kings behaved toward God and tell of those who failed in their loyalty to God.

KING'S HIGHWAY. In Bible times a well-known road that ran from Damascus to the Gulf of Aqabah along the length of eastern Palestine. It passed through the territories of Bashan, Gilead, Ammon, Moab, and Edom and connected with other roads that led to Egypt. Fortresses lined the road. The Israelites on their way from Egypt to Canaan were prevented by the Edomites from using the highway through Edomite territory, and they had to go around it. There is a modern road which closely follows the course of the old road. *Numbers 20:17-21; 21:22.*

KISHON. A river draining the western part of the Valley of Jezreel. It winds for twenty-three miles to the Mediterranean Sea. During the rainy months of winter the river bed is boggy, but in summer it is usually dry. It is chiefly remembered as the scene of the defeat of Sisera by Barak and Deborah, recorded in the OT. *Judges 4:7, 13; 5:19-21; I Kings 18:40; Psalm 83:9.*

KITE. A migratory bird, the kite summers along the Dead Sea and in the mountains of southern Judea. Like the falcon, it is a member of the hawk family. It is the greatest scavanger of the family, feeding on carrion, which assures it a place among the unclean. But it is a magnificent bird with a long, forked tail and chestnut plumage. Like all hawks, its flight is graceful and buoyant.

KITTIM. OT name for the island of Cyprus. It was known to the Israelites as a land across the sea, and they associated Kittim with ships. People of Tyre and Sidon fled to Kittim to escape from the Assyrians. It was captured by the Assyrians under Sargon. Pine for the decks of Phoenician ships came from Cyprus. (See *Cyprus.*) *Numbers 24:24; Daniel 11:30.*

KNEAD. To pound or press dough with the hands until it forms a well-mixed mass. Flour and water were mixed along with a small piece of leavened dough left from the previous day in a shallow container made of wood, bronze, or pottery and called a kneading bowl or kneading trough. *Genesis 18:6; Exodus 8:3; 12:34; Deuteronomy 28:5, 17; I Samuel 28:24; II Samuel 13:8; Jeremiah 7:18; Hosea 7:4.*

KOHATH. A son of Levi and the grandfather of Aaron, Moses, and Miriam. *Exodus 6:16-20; Numbers 3:17-19; 4:1-15; 7:9.*

KOHATHITE. The Kohathites were one of three important Levitical

families who were responsible for the care and transportation of the tabernacle during the journey through the wilderness. *Numbers 3:27-31; 4:34-37; 10:21; 26:57; Joshua 21:4-5, 9-26; I Chronicles 9:32; II Chronicles 20:19.*

KORAH. 1. A son and a grandson of Esau. *Genesis 36:5, 14, 16, 18.*

2. An Israelite who quarreled with Moses because he felt Aaron and his family should not be the only ones who could be priests. Korah declared that all the families were holy and could be religious leaders. *Numbers 16:1-50.*

KORAHITES. In I Chronicles the Korahites are named with the Kohathites as gatekeepers and helpers in the temple service. The "Sons of Korah" appear in the headings of several psalms (Psalms 42; 44-49; 84-85; 87-88) indicating that there was a guild or group of temple singers called Sons of Korah. *I Chronicles 9:19, 26:1, 19; II Chronicles 24:19.*

LABAN. A relative of Abraham who lived in the area of Paddan-aram in northern Mesopotamia. He was the brother of Isaac's wife Rebekah and the father of Leah and Rachel, who became the wives of Isaac's son Jacob. *Genesis 25:20; 28:5; 29:1-30; 31:1-55.*

LACHISH. An ancient Canaanite city between Jerusalem and Gaza, captured and destroyed by the Israelites when Joshua led their invasion of the hill country. During Solomon's reign it was rebuilt, and it later became a city of the southern kingdom of Judah. Great fortifications were added. About 700 B.C. Lachish was captured and burned by the Assyrians. Wall carvings found in the ruins of Sennacherib's palace at Nineveh show the siege of Lachish. The city was rebuilt and stood until captured by Nebuchadnezzar in 588–586 B.C. Archaeologists have uncovered in the ruins of Lachish evidence of great fires and battles. They have also found bits of pottery with writing which appear to have been the letters of a military man, written just before Nebuchadnezzar's destruction of Jerusalem. *Joshua 10:3-5, 31-35; 12:11, II Kings 18:14-17; 19:8; II Chronicles 11:5-12; 25:25-28; 32:9-10; Nehemiah 11:30; Isaiah 36:1-2; 37:8; Jeremiah 34:6-7; Micah 1:13.*

LAMB. A young sheep. In OT times the lamb was used for food and in sacrifices in the temple. It was especially important at the Passover. For the Israelites, flocks of sheep and herds of goats were of great importance. Sheep were a source of meat, milk, cheese, wool, and hides. So the lamb offered as sacrifice was an object of great value. Unlike most animals, sheep quietly submit to such things as being sheared or clipped, and even to being sacrificed. It isn't surprising that for the Israelites the lamb symbolized innocence and gentleness. In the NT the term is used as a figure of speech in referring to Jesus. *Exodus 12:3-14; 29:38-42; I Samuel 7:9; II Chronicles 35:13; Isaiah 65:25; Luke 22:7; John 1:29, 35-36; Acts 8:32; I Corinthians 5:7.*

The Bible Companion

LAMENTATION. See *Mourning.*

LAMENTATIONS, BOOK OF. A OT book of five poems mourning the destruction of Jerusalem. The poems are sad, yet there is confession of sin and hope for the future in chapter 3. All the cruelty of the invading army of the Babylonians in 586 B.C., the sickness and hunger, the helplessness of the Jewish leaders, and the destruction of the temple are described. Yet the writer of chapter 3 had confidence in God and hope for the future (see Lamentations 3:21-27). Called the "Lamentations of Jeremiah," it was once thought that the prophet had written these pieces, but probably they were written by several authors.

LAMMERGIER. This is the "ossifrage" mentioned in Deuteronomy 14:12. It is a species of vulture and the largest of the species, with a wing spread of up to nine feet. It has been called the most magnificent of the birds of prey. Like most of the vulture family it nests on cliffs. It feeds largely on the marrow inside the bones that other vultures have picked clean. To get at the marrow it carries the bones high in the air, then lets them drop upon the rocks to shatter the bone. Because of the tassels of feathers that hang from its beak it is sometimes called the bearded vulture.

LAMP. In early Bible times a pottery saucer filled with olive oil, having a wick of twisted threads resting on the edge. Later the rim of the saucer was pinched in several places to hold the wick. Still later covered lamps with spouts for holding the wick became popular. Usually a lamp was kept burning in a house day and night. The word was also used in a figure of speech to represent the law, to symbolize life as opposed to death, or to symbolize the change from the darkness of evil into the light of goodness and truth. *Exodus 27:20; I Samuel 3:3; II Samuel 21:17; 22:29; II Chronicles 21:7; Psalm 119:105; Proverbs 31:18; Matthew 5:15; Mark 4:21; Luke 8:16-17; John 5:35; Revelation 21:23; 22:5.*

LAMPSTAND. A device for raising a lamp high so that its light will cover a large area. Lampstands were used in the tabernacle, the temple, and palaces. Originally the stand probably held a pottery lamp with seven spouts. This was developed into a seven-branched lamp which became and still is one of the best-known symbols of Judaism. *Exodus 25:31-40; 26:35; 37:17-24; I Kings 7:49; I Chronicles 28:15; Zechariah 4:2-14; Hebrews 9:2; Revelation 1:12-20; 2:5.*

LANDMARK. A mark showing the boundaries of an area of land. In Bible times stones were piled to mark the boundaries between the fields of one man and those of his neighbors. They also marked districts and nations. It was a serious offense to remove the landmarks. *Deuteronomy 19:14; 27:17; Job 24:2; Proverbs 22:28; 23:10; Hosea 5:10.*

LANGUAGES OF THE BIBLE. The OT in its final form was in Hebrew, and the NT in Greek. However, biblical writers sometimes used names, words, and phrases from languages of other nations with which

they had contact. In the story of Joseph in Egypt, Egyptian words are quoted (see Genesis 41:43, 45). Babylonian and Assyrian words and names found their way into the Bible (see II Kings 18:17; Daniel 1:7) as did Persian words (see Daniel 3:2-3). Whole chapters in Daniel and Ezra were written in Aramaic. Jesus spoke in Aramaic, and the NT contains many Aramaic expressions (see Matthew 27:46; Mark 5:41). The Gospels state that the inscriptions above the cross were in Latin, Greek, and Hebrew (see John 19:20). Many place names found in the Bible have come from a variety of languages, and there are some whose meaning and origin are unknown. *Nehemiah 13:23-24; Esther 3:12.*

LAODICEA. A city in southwestern Asia Minor. In NT times it was one of the main cities of Phrygia (now part of Turkey), located in the Lycus River Valley. Laodicea was a prosperous city, famous for its black sheep whose wool was woven into especially fine garments and carpets. In NT times the population included Greek-speaking Syrians, Romans, and also many wealthy Jews. *Colossians 2:1; 4:13-16; Revelation 1:11; 3:14-17.*

LAPWING. The lapwing of Eurasia is a colorful bird, its dark green irridescent feathers splashed with brown above and white below, and with a black chest band. A curving crest decorates the back of the neck. About a foot long, it has stubby wings and the long legs typical of the plover family to which it belongs. But unlike the plover it is not a shore bird and is usually found inland. Its eggs were once considered a delicacy.

LAST SUPPER, THE. The final meal which Jesus ate with his disciples on the evening before his death. Jesus spoke of his coming death and said it would be used by God to establish his kingdom. Christians recall the Last Supper in the sacrament, or sacred observance, called the Communion service. (See *Lord's Supper.*) The Last Supper is described in *Matthew 26:17-30; Mark 14:12-26; Luke 22:7-30; I Corinthians 11:23-26.*

LATIN. The language spoken by Romans in Bible times. In Italy in NT times every educated Roman spoke Greek as well as Latin, for Greek was the international language. In the Judean and Galilean provinces only those who were officers of the law, the government, and the army spoke Latin. *John 19:20.*

LAVER. A large metal basin or bowl for water in the tabernacle or temple. It was used by the priests for washing before they offered a sacrifice. *Exodus 30:17-19; I Kings 7:38.*

LAW. Rules or ordinances for living together in a community. The OT law was based on a covenant, or agreement, between God and the Hebrew people. The basis for Hebrew law was the Ten Commandments, but the first five books of the OT, called the Torah, contained most of the Hebrew laws and ordinances. The OT prophets constantly challenged the people to keep the laws in obedience to God. Jesus observed the customs and laws

of his people but criticized the way many religious leaders insisted upon exact performance of ceremonial laws and forgot that the most important law in all relationships is the law of love. *Exodus 13:9, 21:1; Leviticus 7:37; Deuteronomy 1:16-18; 4:8; 5:1-20; 6:1-9; Joshua 1:7; 24:25-26; Ezra 7:10, 14; Isaiah 5:24; Jeremiah 32:23; Daniel 6:5; Matthew 5:17; 22:34-40; John 7:19; Acts 13:15; Romans 2:17-23; Galatians 3:21-26.*

LAWYER. In NT times one who knew and interpreted the law, especially the law of Moses. The lawyers were among those who opposed Jesus for healing on the sabbath. In the NT a lawyer was also called a scribe. *Matthew 22:35; Luke 7:30; 10:25; 11:45-52; 14:3-5.*

LAZARUS. 1. The name of a beggar in Jesus' parable about a beggar and a rich man. His name means "God's help of a needy beggar." *Luke 16:19-31.*

2. A friend of Jesus whom Jesus raised from the dead. He lived in Bethany with his sisters Mary and Martha. *John 11:1-44.*

LEAH. The older daughter of Laban and Jacob's first wife. She was not as high in Jacob's favor as her younger and more beautiful sister Rachel. In fact, Jacob was tricked into marrying her. She was the mother of six sons. *Genesis 29:15-35; 30:17-21; 49:31.*

LEATHER. Animal skins tanned and prepared for use as garments, girdles, belts, footwear, coverings for tents, skin bottles for water or wine (see *I Samuel 1:24; Job 38:37*), and

writing materials. Some scrolls were made of strips of leather sewn together. *Exodus 26:14; II Kings 1:8; Ezekiel 16:10; Matthew 3:4; Mark 1:6.*

LEAVEN. Any substance such as yeast that was added to bread dough to make it rise. In biblical times leavening was done with a portion of active dough kept from a previous day's baking. During the Passover festival each year the Hebrews did not eat bread that had been made with leaven. They used unleavened bread as a reminder of the hardships their ancestors suffered during the exodus from Egypt. Only unleavened bread could be used in any sacrifices to God. In the NT "leaven" is often used as a figure of speech to show how the actions of a person, whether good or bad, can have a wide influence, affecting a group of people as yeast affects dough. *Exodus 12:19-20, 34, 39; 34:25; Leviticus 2:11; 27:13; Deuteronomy 16:3-4; Matthew 13:33; 16:6, 11-12; Mark 8:15; Luke 12:1; 13:21; I Corinthians 5:6-8; Galatians 5:9.*

LEBANON. The name of a country and of a mountain range that follows the eastern coastline of the Mediterranean Sea. In OT times it formed the northwestern boundary of the lands of the Hebrews and was famous for its great forests of cedars and cypresses. The snow-capped mountain peaks probably gave the mountains the name Lebanon, which means "white." *Deuteronomy 1:7; 3:25; 11:24; Judges 3:3; I Kings 5:6, 8-10, 14; 7:2; II Kings 19:23; Ezra 3:7; Psalms 37:35; 92:12; Isaiah 40:16; Jeremiah 18:14; Hosea 14:6-7.*

LEECH. The leech ("blood sucker") has not changed through the centuries. Its flat body is up to five inches long with the suction pads at either end. It has three knife-like projections of its mouth with which it pierces the skin to suck the blood of its host. No doubt it was as repulsively familiar in Jesus' time as it is today. It is the only true worm mentioned in the Bible where it is referred to as the "horse-leach" (Proverbs 30:15).

LEES. The dregs of wine which were allowed to settle at the bottom of a wineskin until the wine was strong and well flavored. In the Bible the word was used in a figure of speech to describe people who had never been unsettled by calamity. *Isaiah 25:6; Jeremiah 48:11; Zephaniah 1:12.*

LEGION. The main unit of the Roman army. In NT times a legion usually consisted of about six thousand men divided into ten cohorts or regiments. The legions were made up of the best and most-trusted Roman soldiers. In the NT the word is used to refer to a large number or group. *Matthew 26:53; Mark 5:9, 15; Luke 8:30.*

Lentil

LENTIL. The lentil, from which Jacob made the pottage for his weary brother Esau (Genesis 26:29ff) is a pea-like plant resembling vetch. The trailing vine grows in soil too poor for other plants. It is common in most of the Middle East and in Egypt.

LEOPARD. The derivation of the English name "leopard" is interesting. When first discovered by early European travelers, to whom such an animal was unknown, they thought it a cross between a lion and a panther. So they combined the Latin word for each: *leo* (lion) and *pard* (panther).

The leopard was well known in Bible times, especially in the forested regions of Lebanon where its swiftness and ferocity made it a constant menace to grazing flocks. It is one of the animals Isaiah mentions in his word picture of peace (Isaiah 11:6). Jeremiah indicates the familiarity of the people with the animal when he asks, "Can . . . the leopard change his spots?" (Jeremiah 13:23).

LEPROSY. A serious skin disease. In Bible times persons who had leprosy were forced to live apart from others. They were considered religiously unclean. The term *leprosy* in Bible times was probably used for many types of skin diseases. The priest had to observe the skin disease and determine whether or not it was leprosy. Today leprosy is often called Hansen's disease, and some forms are curable. *Leviticus 13:1–14:54; Numbers 5:2; II Kings 5:1-27; II Chronicles 26:19-21; Matthew 8:2-4; 10:8; Mark 1:40-44; Luke 5:12-15; 17:11-19.*

The Bible Companion

LETTER. A written message sent to a person or persons at a distance. The earliest letters were written on clay tablets or pieces of pottery. Later, writing was done on sheets of papyrus which were folded or rolled, then sealed and carried to their destination by runners. Many of the books in the NT were written in the form of letters. Paul is the most famous NT author of this type of book. *I Kings 21:8-12; II Chronicles 30:6; Ezra 4:7-24; Acts 15:22-31; Romans 16:22; Colossians 4:16.*

LEVI. 1. In the OT one of the twelve sons of Jacob whose descendants were called "sons of Levi," "tribe of Levi," or "Levites." *Genesis 29:34; 35:23; 49:5; Exodus 1:2; 6:16; 32:25-29; Deuteronomy 33:8-11; Joshua 13:14; I Chronicles 2:1.*

2. In the NT the name of a tax collector in Capernaum who became a follower of Jesus. He was sometimes called Matthew, but it is not certain that he was the same Matthew listed as one of the twelve apostles. *Mark 2:14; Luke, 5:27-32.*

LEVIATHAN. The ancient beliefs of the Hebrews in the field of nature coincided with those of other races in regard to strange and mythical creatures such as the unicorn, the cockatrice—and the leviathan. While Job might have been describing a crocodile in Job 41 where the word *leviathan* is used, his people believed it to be a large sea monster about which there were many fantastic legends. One such legend was that the leviathan was not capable of reproducing lest they crowd all other creatures out of the ocean! The psalmist pictures it as a playful animal (Psalm 104:26). In Isaiah 27:1 it is a serpent-like creature. Modern scholars are inclined to think that these and other references are to a mythical dragon.

LEVITES. See *Priests and Levites.*

LEVITICAL CITIES. Forty-eight cities in Canaan which were to be set apart as the dwelling places of the tribe of Levi, who were priests *Leviticus 25:32-34; Numbers 18:21-30; 35:1-34; Deuteronomy 14:28-29; Joshua 20:1–21:42.*

LEVITICUS. The third book of the Bible. It deals mainly with the duties of the priests and contains laws and regulations about worship, sacrifices, food, dress, and the conduct of everyday living. Jesus used Leviticus 19:18 as part of his summary of the law. Leviticus probably was compiled after the Exile.

LIBERTY. Freedom from bondage, slavery, or the control of another. In the OT it almost always refers to those who are free from slavery or forced labor. The NT uses "liberty" to mean freedom from the slavery of sin. This liberty is gained through Jesus Christ and makes one able to lead a new life ruled by God's love. *Isaiah 61:1; Luke 4:16-21; Romans 8:21.*

LICE. Human lice were as numerous among the ancients as among modern man where unsanitary conditions existed. Not only does the bite of the louse cause extreme itching, but the insect is the carrier of diseases, especially cholera and typhus. Human lice are of two kinds, head and body.

Plant lice of many species are older than civilization. The plague of lice was the third of the ten plagues to strike Egypt (Exodus 8:17).

LILY. The lily, in many varieties, has been growing in the Holy Land since time immemorial. As far back as 3000 B.C. it was a sacred emblem in Crete. Today it is a symbol of the Resurrection, and of the Virgin Mary. However, our "Easter lily" is a comparatively recent introduction.

One of the more common varieties in biblical times was the brilliant red Chalcedonecum lily, somewhat resembling the modern tulip. Though the lily is mentioned many times in the Song of Solomon and other places in the Bible, we have no way of knowing just what variety is meant. Or even if, as in Jesus' reference to "the lilies of the field" (Matthew 6:28), other flowers might have been meant, such as the field anemone.

LION. The lion, ensign of the tribe of Judah, is the most often mentioned wild animal in the Bible. It was probably the relatively small Persian lion, a species native to the Middle East. Though ferocious by nature and much feared, tamed lions were pets at the courts of the Pharaohs, and later of King Solomon. Untamed, they were also kept in pits ("dens"). Into one of these "dens" Darius, king of Persia, cast Daniel.

The lion is used in the Bible as a symbol of strong spiritual qualities: "the righteous are as bold as a lion" (Proverbs 28:1); as symbol for God (Isaiah 31:4); and, by contrast, the devil is likened to a "roaring lion . . .

seeking whom he may devour" (I Peter 5:8).

LIZARD. There are many kinds of lizards in the Holy Land. Unfortunately the early writers of the Scriptures, and later the translators, were very ambiguous in their references to them. The sand lizard very likely was the "snail" mentioned in Leviticus 11:30 amd Psalm 58:8, an example of the difficulty in establishing individual identity. Common in the area were the agamid, the chameleon, and the gecko.

Less common than the other varieties was the "land crocodile," some three feet in length, its body covered with green and yellow spots and with golden rings around its neck. The Nile monitor, common to Egypt as its name implies, grows up to six feet in length. It, too, must have been known to the Hebrew people.

LOBSTER. The lobster is a marine animal and was eaten by the Egyptians and other maritime neighbors of the Israelites. But to them it was unclean and apparently they considered it of no importance. It is not mentioned in the Bible.

LOCUST. The locust, plague of the Middle East since earliest times, is a species of grasshopper. It is about two inches long, reddish-brown and yellow, with a wing-spread of nearly five inches. In early or mid-summer hordes of them, borne on the prevailing winds, begin the destructive migration. The result is as devastating today as it was when the plague of locusts visited Egypt (Exodus 10:13-15).

The Mosaic dietary law permits the eating of locusts. While the locusts which John the Baptist subsisted on in the wilderness (flavored with honey) could have been the insect, it is also possible that the reference (Matthew 3:4) is to the fruit of the carob tree.

LOG. An OT liquid measure equal to about a pint in modern terms. Also a length of tree trunk. *Leviticus 14:10, 12, 15, 21, 24; II Kings 6:5; Matthew 7:3-5.*

LORD. A title for anyone who commands respect or has authority over others. The OT uses "Lord" as a title of honor and majesty for God. The NT uses the word as a title for God and also for Jesus. Early Christians used the expression "Jesus is Lord" to indicate that God had sent Jesus as the Christ. *Deuteronomy 14:1-2; Joshua 1:9; 13:33; I Samuel 2:1-10; Isaiah 42:5-8; Jeremiah 16:19-20; Amos 4:13; Matthew 1:20; Luke 2:22-23; 7:19; John 13:13-14; Acts 10:36; I Corinthians 1:3.*

LORD'S PRAYER. The title given to the prayer Jesus taught his disciples. *Matthew 6:9-13; Luke 11:2-4.*

LORD'S SUPPER. The title given by Paul to the holy meals of the church. These were a continuation of the fellowship of Jesus with his disciples begun at the Last Supper (see *Last Supper*). The celebration of the Lord's Supper or Holy Communion in Christian churches today is a continuing memorial to Jesus Christ. *I Corinthians 11:17-26.*

LOT. Nephew of Abraham who journeyed with him to the land of Canaan. Later when Abraham and Lot separated, Lot chose to live in the fertile and attractive region of the cities of Sodom and Gomorrah. *Genesis 11:27, 31; 12:4; 13:5-13; II Peter 2:7.*

LOTS. Marked stones, stones of different colors, or sticks of different lengths. Casting lots was rather like drawing straws or tossing a coin. It was solemnly done to make a decision or determine a course of action. The lots were thrown on the ground or drawn from a jar or shaken in a jar until one fell out. The land of Canaan was divided among the Hebrew tribes by the casting of lots. The first king of Israel was chosen by lot. The word also refers to the fortune or misfortune which may chance to happen to a person. *Leviticus 16:7-10; Joshua 14:2; I Samuel 10:20-21; Jonah 1:7; Matthew 27:35; I Thessalonians 3:3.*

LOTUS. When we think of the lotus we very likely think of Egypt. There it was dedicated to Horus, god of the sun. The Hebrew people must have known of its pagan religious connotation. Perhaps because of it, the lotus never found a place in the symbolism of Judaism or Christianity. It is a water lily, found in many tropical and sub-tropical countries of the world.

LOVE. The deep, personal attachment that includes loyalty, good will, devotion, knowledge, and responsibility. In the OT love is looked upon as God's activity in redeeming humankind and is seen most clearly in God's steadfast care for the Hebrews. Humankind is the object of God's love, while people's love for God is the response people make to God's

love. The love of person for person is based on God's love and requires love and justice in all relationships. In the NT Jesus showed clearly the meaning of God's love by his concern and care for others and by his life and his death. *Leviticus 19:18; Deuteronomy 6:5; 7:7; Psalms 17:7; 136:1-26; Matthew 22:37-39; Mark 12:30-31; Luke 6:27-36; John 14:23; 15:9-13, 17; Romans 5:8; 12:9-10; 13:8-10; I Corinthians 13:1-13; II Corinthians 5:14; Galatians 5:13-14; Ephesians 6:24; Hebrews 13:1; I John 3:1–4:21.*

LUKE, EVANGELIST. A Gentile Christian, probably the author of the Gospel of Luke and the book of Acts. Luke was a physician and a close friend and traveling companion of Paul. Luke's native country is uncertain. (See *Luke, Gospel of.*) *Colossians 4:14; II Timothy 4:11; Philemon 1:24.*

LUKE, GOSPEL OF. The third book of the NT, probably written by Luke, the beloved physician and companion of Paul. The book tells of the life, ministry, death, and resurrection of Jesus Christ. The author used information from reports and stories he had heard about Jesus and also from such written accounts as are found in the Gospel of Mark. He was writing to tell Gentile Christians that what they had been taught about Christ was true. He may have had in mind also recommending Christianity to members of the Roman court circle. The Gospel of Luke, probably written about A.D. 70–80, and the book of Acts make a two-volume account of the life of Jesus and the beginnings of the early church.

LUPINE. The lupine, which grows profusely in the Holy Land, is almost identical with the variety familiar to our flower gardens. The blue lupine is most common, its striking color covering whole fields in Galilee in the late spring. An unusual characteristic is the handshaped leaves.

LUTE. See *Musical Instruments.*

LYCAONIA. A region in south central Asia Minor bounded on the north by Galatia. Today the region lies in Turkey. Paul traveled and preached in the cities of Lycaonia, including Lystra, and made many disciples. *Acts 14:3-7.*

LYDIA. A woman from Thyatira in Asia Minor who sold purple-dyed cloth in Philippi. She heard Paul preach, and she and her family were baptized. Paul and his companions stayed in Lydia's house, and thus he did not have to earn his living while he was in Philippi. The church at Philippi supported Paul as he allowed no other church to do. Lydia's help may have been the chief reason Paul allowed the church to do this. *Acts 16:11-15, 40.*

LYRE. See *Musical Instruments.*

LYSTRA. A city in the highlands of the region of Lycaonia in southern Asia Minor in what is now Turkey. Paul and Barnabas preached in Lystra and made disciples there. *Acts 14:5-8, 21; 16:1-2; II Timothy 3:10-11.*

MACEDONIA. The region north of Achaia in

what is now the northern part of Greece. In NT times Macedonia was a Roman province. Its mountains and plains stretched from the Adriatic Sea to the Aegean Sea, with its most important cities situated on the Aegean coast. Macedonia was the first European territory in which the gospel was preached. Paul preached in many of the cities, among them Philippi and Thessalonica. Paul later wrote letters to the churches which he had started in these two cities. *Acts 16:9-12; 18:5; 19:21-22; 27:2; I Corinthians 16:5; II Corinthians 8:1; Philippians 4:15; I Thessalonians 1:7-8.*

MACHIR. 1. Son of Manasseh and grandson of Joseph. The name of a tribe that settled west of the Jordan. The Machirites probably helped to conquer part of Canaan. *Genesis 50:23; Numbers 26:29; 32:39-40; Deuteronomy 3:15; Joshua 13.-29-31; 17:1, 3; Judges 5:14; I Chronicles 7:14, 16.*

2. A follower of King Saul who gave shelter to Mephibosheth, the lame son of Jonathan, until David took the prince to his court. Machir was so moved by the king's kindness that he became a loyal supporter of King David. *II Samuel 9:3-5; 17:27-29.*

MACHPELAH. A field near Hebron where Abraham bought a cave to use as a family burying place. Sarah, Abraham, Isaac, Rebekah, Leah, and Jacob are buried there. *Genesis 23:19; 25:9; 49:29-32; 50:13.*

MAGADAN, MAGDALA, DALMANUTHA. A city on the western shore of the Sea of Galilee. In NT times the Greek name for Magadan,

or Magdala, was probably Tarichea. It was the center of a prosperous fishing industry and was the home of Mary Magdalene, one of the followers of Jesus. Today it is called Mejdel. *Matthew 15:39; Mark 8:10.*

MAGDALENE. Meaning "from Magadan" or "from Magdala." It is used in the Gospels to identify one of Jesus' followers, Mary Magdalene, a Galilean woman. (See *Magadan.*) *Matthew 27:55-56, 61; 28:1; Mark 15:40, 47; 16:1; Luke 8:2; 24:10; John 19:25; 20:1, 18.*

MAGGOT. The maggot, larval stage of the fly, is as well known as the fly itself. In most cases biblical writers have used the word "worm" in referring to maggots. "They shall lie down alike in the dust, and the worms shall cover them" (Job 21:28). Dead bodies are inferred here which earthworms would not molest but which would soon be covered with maggots. The loathsomeness of the maggot is manifested in the taunting challenge to the king of Babylon: "Thy pomp is brought down to the grave . . . the worm is spread under thee, and the worms cover thee" (Isaiah 14:11).

MAGIC, MAGICIAN. In ancient times power which did not belong to the gods or to men, but was believed to be supernatural. This power could be set into action, it was believed, by use of certain acts and words. Various kinds of magic and sorcery were practiced among ancient peoples. The laws of the Israelites forbade the practice of magic. The

prophets condemned its use. Still, some Hebrews were influenced by the Egyptian and Babylonian sorcery and did engage in magic practices. In the NT, Paul called magicians the enemies of all righteousness. Other terms used for a magician are *diviner*, *soothsayer*, *sorcerer*, *medium*, and *necromancer*. *Genesis 41:8; Deuteronomy 18:10-14; I Samuel 28:3, 7; II Chronicles 33:6; Isaiah 3:2-3; Jeremiah 27:9; Ezekiel 13:18-20; Acts 8:9-24; 13:6-8; 19:19.*

MAGISTRATE. In the NT the term was used for a judge or governing official in the Roman provinces. *Luke 12:58-59; Acts 16:20, 22, 35-36, 38.*

MALACHI. The last of the short books that make up the collection of the Twelve Prophets; the last book of the OT. It tells of the religious and social conditions after the Jews' return from exile, when the land was under Persian rule. The writer's chief concern was for the Jews to be faithful to their covenant with God. He urged them to practice proper worship in the temple. He warned against the danger of foreign religious practices which were introduced when Jews married non-Jews. The author probably wrote the book about 450 B.C.

MALLOW. The mallow found growing in swampy places in Palestine is very much like the thick, downy-leaved plant with which we are familiar. Its purple, pink, and white flowers cover marshy areas. Though the thick, fleshy leaves are not too palatable, the very poor sometimes use them for food.

MALTA. An island south of Sicily. In NT times Malta belonged to Rome. Paul was shipwrecked in a bay off the coast of Malta on his way to prison in Rome. Although Paul stayed for three months on the island, it is uncertain whether he organized a Christian group. But early art found on Malta shows Christian influence. Jewish and Christian catacombs have been found on the island. *Acts 28:1.*

MAMMON. A word meaning "wealth," "money," "property" or "profit." Jesus used the term to describe the love of material things which makes a person forget God and causes him to use his best energy to earn money instead of serving God. *Matthew 6:24; Luke 16:9, 11, 13.*

MAMRE. A place near ancient Hebron in Canaan in the general area in which Abraham lived. It is often associated with the oak trees near which Abraham built an altar. The burial place of Abraham's family was located nearby. *Genesis 13:18; 14:13, 24; 18:1; 23:17-19; 35:27.*

MANASSEH. 1. The firstborn son of Joseph and the ancestor of one of the twelve tribes of Israel. His mother was an Egyptian. The territory of Israel along the Jordan River was also called Manasseh. *Genesis 41:50-51; 48:1-20; Numbers 1:34-35; Joshua 4:12; 17:5-12; Judges 1:27; II Chronicles 30:10-11; Psalm 60:7; Isaiah 9:21.*

2. The name of a king of Judah who reigned about 687–643 B.C. He was the son and successor of Hezekiah. King Manasseh attempted to restore the places of pagan worship that his

father had destroyed. *II Kings 21:1-18; 23:26; 24:3-4; II Chronicles 33:10-20.*

MANDRAKE. A stemless herb with large leaves shooting out from the roots to form a flat circle on the earth. Creamy-yellow blossoms veined with purple come out on single stems. The small, bright yellow, pulpy fruit is sometimes eaten although it is slightly poisonous. The root of the plant is dark brown and is shaped so much like a person that many superstitious ideas about its magic powers were held in early Bible times. *Genesis 30:14; Song of Solomon 7:13.*

MANGER. In Bible times a trough or box made of stones or hollowed out of rock and used for feeding cattle. Sometimes it was located on the lower level of a Palestinian house where the poorer people kept their animals in bad weather or in a natural cave near the house. The first bed of the baby Jesus was a manger. *Luke 2:7, 12, 16; 13:15.*

MANNA. Meaning "What is it?" The substance that the Israelites gathered and ate for part of their food during the long journey through the wilderness. After the hungry people began to murmur for bread, God told Moses he would rain bread from heaven. From this time on the people found manna on the ground each morning. This may have been a natural substance secreted from certain insects. This sticky, sweet honeydew is still gathered and dried into wafers of sticky solids. Today Arabs eat it as a relish on bread. *Exodus 16:3-5, 13-17; Numbers 11:6-9; Deuteronomy 8:3, 16; Nehemiah 9:20; Psalm 78:23-24.*

MANTLE. A loose, sleeveless coat. A rough mantle made of hair was worn by the prophets as a sign of their office. Priests, kings, and other people in authority wore rich mantles suitable to their position. The word is used as a figure of speech in which praise, prosperity, or beauty is spoken of as a covering wrap, or adornment. *Exodus 12:34; Joshua 7:21, 24; I Kings 19:13, 19; II Kings 2:8, 13-14; Ezra 9:5; Isaiah 3:22; 59:17; 61:3; Zechariah 13:4; Mark 14:63; Luke 22:36.*

MARJORAM. This is one of the smallest flowering shrubs in the Holy Land. Its shrub-like stems are only a few inches in height, bearing clusters of white flowers among rocks and wall crevices. It belongs to the mint family.

MARK, JOHN. A member of the church in Jerusalem, who may have been the author of the Gospel of Mark. The home of his mother Mary was a gathering place for Christians. He was a close friend of Peter and became a companion of some of the early Christian missionaries. He traveled with Paul and Barnabas on their first missionary journey. (See *Mark, Gospel of.*) *Acts 12:12, 25; 15:37-39; Colossians 4:10; II Timothy 4:11; Philemon 1:23-24.*

MARK, GOSPEL OF. The second book in the NT. Most scholars believe it to be the first Gospel written down. This Gospel may have been written in Rome by John Mark between A.D. 65 and 70. It was based on

information Mark gathered from Peter and perhaps from some other eyewitnesses to the events in the life of Jesus. It is the story of Jesus' life, teachings, death, and resurrection; written to strengthen the church in Rome during persecution and for use in the church's mission to non-Christians. The writers of Matthew and Luke made use of the material in Mark.

MARTHA. Sister of Mary and Lazarus of Bethany and friend of Jesus. Martha was a homemaker and provided for Jesus' needs whenever he visited their home. It was to Martha that Jesus declared "I am the resurrection and the life." Her reply was, "I believe that you are the Christ, the Son of God." *Luke 10:38-42; John 11:1-6, 17-30; 12:1-2.*

MARY. 1. The mother of Jesus. Very little is said about Mary in the Gospels after the stories of Jesus' birth and childhood. The NT tells us that during Jesus' ministry Mary lived in Nazareth with his brothers and sisters, that she was present at the crucifixion, and afterwards with his brothers and disciples took part in a prayer meeting. *Matthew 1:18-25; 2:10-15, 21; Mark 3:31-35; 6:3; Luke 1:26-56; 2:1-19; John 2:1-12; 19:25-27; Acts 1:14.*

2. Mary Magdalene, a friend of Jesus who was present at the crucifixion and went to the tomb. (See *Magdalene.*) *Mark 16:9; Luke 8:1-2; John 20:1-2, 11-18.*

3. Mary of Bethany, the sister of Lazarus and Martha. This Mary felt a deep devotion to Jesus. The gospel stories show that she was a thoughtful person who spent much time considering the words of Jesus and their meaning. *Luke 10:38-42; John 11:1–12:8.*

4. There are several other Marys mentioned in the Gospels who were relatives of the disciples and so associated in the ministry of Jesus. *Matthew 27:55, 61; 28:1; Mark 15:40, 47; 16:1; Luke 24:9-11; John 19:25.*

MASTER. Meaning "manager" or "chief"; a person with authority over others. Used in the NT as a title for Jesus Christ. *Genesis 24:27; Judges 19:11-12; II Kings 6:23; Isaiah 37:4; Malachi 1:6; Matthew 24:45-51; 26:25; Mark 9:5; Luke 8:24; 9:49; Ephesians 6:9.*

MATTHEW. One of the twelve apostles of Jesus. A collector of taxes on the goods carried over the Damascus Road, and perhaps on the fishing industry and other industries in Capernaum. It is possible that Matthew and Levi are the same person. (See *Matthew, Gospel of.*) *Matthew 9:9; 10:3; Luke 6:15; Acts 1:13.*

MATTHEW, GOSPEL OF. First in the arrangement of books in the NT, this book probably was written sometime close to A.D. 100. Matthew based his writing on the material in Mark's Gospel and on a collection of Jesus' sayings which had been made at that time. Written especially for the Jewish Christians of the time, the book used many quotations from the OT to show how Jesus was the fulfillment of old prophecies and had given the old laws new meaning.

MATTHIAS. The apostle chosen by casting lots to fill the place left vacant by Judas Iscariot. He is credited with

helping to bring the gospel to Armenia, which is part of Russia today. *Acts 1:23-26.*

MEAL. A coarse type of flour ground from whole kernels of wheat or barley. Fine flour was prepared from the inner kernels only. In early Bible history meal was more commonly used than flour. Meal was ground by the women before dawn and only enough was ground for a day's use. *Genesis 18:6; Numbers 5:15; I Kings 17:12; I Chronicles 12:40; Nehemiah 10:37; Hosea 8:7; Luke 13:21.*

MEDIA. In OT times a province in the Persian Empire in what is now northwestern Iran. The Israelites were exiled to the "cities of the Medes" by the Assyrian king who conquered Samaria in 722 B.C. According to the report in Daniel, the laws of the Medes and Persians could not be changed. Today the phrase "of the Medes and Persians" is used to indicate any law that is firm. *II Kings 17:6; 18:11; Ezra 6:2-4; Esther 1:3, 14, 18-19; Daniel 5:28; 6:8, 12, 15; 8:20.*

MEEKNESS. In OT usage, complete dependence upon God rather than on oneself. The opposite of pride. In the NT the word is used by Jesus in the Beatitudes to indicate one attitude needed to be blessed, and by Paul in the Epistles to show that meekness is becoming to a Christian. In general usage, it is the quality of a person with a gentle and quiet spirit of thoughtful courtesy in dealing with others. *Numbers 12:3; Psalms 10:17; 37:11; Matthew 5:5; II Corinthians 10:1; Ephesians 4:2; James 1:21; 3:13.*

MEGIDDO. An important Canaanite and later Israelite city in north central Palestine overlooking the Valley of Jezreel. It controlled an important mountain pass. King Solomon made Megiddo into a royal chariot city, and archaeologists have uncovered the remains of his fine stables. *Joshua 12:21; 17:11; Judges 1:27; 5:19; I Kings 9:15; II Kings 23:29-30; II Chronicles 35:20-22.*

MELCHIZEDEK. In early OT times, a Canaanite king and priest who prepared a meal for Abraham and blessed him. Since Melchizedek had both royal and priestly authority in the city of Salem (Jerusalem) before the Israelites came, David claimed to be his successor. Melchizedek became the symbol of an ideal priest-king. *Genesis 14:18-20; Psalm 110:4; Hebrews 5:6, 8-10; 6:20; 7:1-4, 10-11, 15-17.*

MENAHEM. King of Israel about 752–742 B.C. He gained the throne by murdering Shallum. He was obliged to pay tribute to Tiglath-pileser III of Assyria. *II Kings 15:13-22.*

MEPHIBOSHETH. Jonathan's lame son and a grandson of King Saul. King David showed great kindness to Mephibosheth and took him into his own household in memory of his friendship with Jonathan. (See *Machir*.) *II Samuel 4:4; 9:1-13; 16:1-4; 19:24-30; 21:7-8.*

MERCY, MERCIFUL. In the OT the continued steadfast love of God by which he keeps his covenant relationship with his people Israel; the quality of having mercy. Human mercy is the quality of kindness and

consideration for the needs of others that God requires of his people. This understanding of mercy is also found in the NT, especially in the Beatitudes where Jesus' words seem to mean that to expect mercy for himself a person must show mercy to others. *Exodus 34:6; II Samuel 24:14; Psalms 23:6; 51:1; 103:4; 145:8; Jeremiah 6:23; Lamentations 2:21; Matthew 5:7; 9:13; 15:22; Luke 10:36-37; II Corinthians 1:3.*

MERCY SEAT. A slab of especially refined gold with a cherub at each end on top of the ark of the covenant. It was reverenced as God's throne, the symbol of his presence in the temple. The mercy seat was sprinkled with blood on the Day of Atonement. *Exodus 25:17-22; 26:34; 37:6-9; Leviticus 16:2-5; Numbers 7:89; I Chronicles 28:11, Hebrews 9:5.*

MEROM, WATERS OF. A body of water, near the Jordan and not far from the Sea of Galilee, where the Israelites led by Joshua defeated a large army of Canaanites. *Joshua 11:1-9.*

MESHACH. See *Shadrach, Meshach, Abednego.*

MESOPOTAMIA. In OT times the land between the Tigris and Euphrates rivers. The borders of Mesopotamia changed many times in its long history. It now lies partly in Syria and partly in Iraq. Much of the culture of the Hebrews came from this region. Abraham came from Haran, an area in northern Mesopotamia known as Paddan-aram, and the Hebrews had connections with this area throughout their history. *Genesis 24:10; Deuteronomy 23:4; Judges 3:8, 10; I Chronicles 19:6; Acts 2:9; 7:2.*

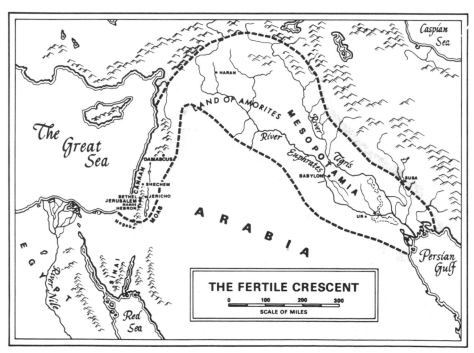

THE FERTILE CRESCENT

MESSIAH. Meaning "anointed one." The word does not appear in the OT. However, the Hebrews throughout their history had looked forward to the coming of an ideal king whom they believed God would send to restore a kingdom to Israel. The title of Messiah was given to Jesus by some who recognized him as the long-awaited king. (See *Holy One.*) *John 1:41; 4:25.*

MICAH. A prophet of the southern kingdom of Judah during the reigns of Jotham, Ahaz, and Hezekiah. Micah must have had a long life in the years between 740 and 687 B.C. At this time Isaiah was preaching in Jerusalem. Micah was from a small village of the Shephelah, low foothills of southwestern Palestine, and he loved the country people and their ways better than the corrupt city dwellers of his day. (See *Micah, Book of.*)

MICAH, BOOK OF. A prophetic book in the OT containing prophecies and warnings of the prophet Micah. There are also a few of what appear to be writings of a later prophet. Having watched the northern kingdom of Israel and its capital Samaria fall to the Assyrians in 722 B.C., Micah warned the people of Judah to return to the law of God and to pure worship of him so that a similar disaster would not befall them.

MICAIAH. A prophet in the ninth century B.C. during the reign of King Ahab of Israel. He was put in prison for speaking the truth to the king in contrast to four hundred false prophets who gave the king favorable answers to his questions concerning a military undertaking at Ramoth-gilead. Ahab was killed there. *I Kings 22:8-28; II Chronicles 18:7-27.*

MICHAEL. A name used to refer to a heavenly being who was the protector of Israel. The Revelation describes Michael as fighting Satan and the rebel angels during the war in heaven. *Daniel 12:1; Jude 1:9; Revelation 12:7-8.*

MICHAL. Daughter of Saul and wife of David. Michal had no children. *I Samuel 14:49; 18:20-27; 19:11-17; 25:44; II Samuel 3:13-16; 6:16-23.*

MICHMASH. A city in the mountains about seven miles northeast of Jerusalem. The rugged mountain area made a kind of natural fortress for this city. The Philistines made their camp in this place and fought with the armies of Israel led by Saul and Jonathan. Later, Nehemiah mentions the men of Michmash (Michmas) as people returned from exile. *I Samuel 13:2, 5, 11, 16-18, 23; 14:5, 31; Ezra 2:27; Nehemiah 7:31; 11:31-35; Isaiah 10:28.*

MIDIAN. Son of Keturah, Abraham's third wife. He was the ancestor of the wandering tribe of Midianites. The "land of Midian" lay in northwestern Arabia on the eastern shore of the Gulf of Aqabah. *Genesis 25:2, 4; Exodus 2:15-16; 3:1; Judges 6:1-14; 7:1-25; I Kings 11:18; Psalm 83:9; Isaiah 9:4; 10:26; 60:6; Habakkuk 3:7.*

MIDIANITES. Riding swift camels, these fierce nomads frequently made raids upon the Israelites in Canaan after the exodus from Egypt. As far as

is known, the Midianites were among the first people to make effective use of the camel, thus increasing their swift striking power. *Genesis 37:28; Judges 6:1-16; 7:1-25.*

MIGHTY MEN. In the OT a title for strong, bold heroes. It was applied to heroes of the past as well as the present, to foreigners as well as to Israelites. "Mighty men" was also used for the mercenaries, or hired soldiers, and warriors of King David. *Genesis 6:4; Joshua 10:2; II Samuel 17:8; 20:7; 23:8-23; I Kings 1:10.*

MIKTAM. The heading of Psalms 16 and 56–60. The meaning is uncertain, but it may mean "to atone" (restore friendly relations with God) or "to cover the sin." Thus these would be psalms of atonement, that is, songs of praise and thanksgiving that someone who has been separated from God by sin has been restored to him. *Psalms 16; 56–60.*

MILETUS. An ancient Greek city on the west coast of Asia Minor. In the days when Paul visited Miletus the port was still active and prominent. Its location made it a natural stopping place for Paul on his way to Jerusalem from Europe. It was close enough to Ephesus so that the church elders from that city were able to visit him at Miletus. The city has been excavated by archaeologists in recent years. *Acts 20:15, 17; II Timothy 4:20.*

MILL, MILLSTONES. A machine made from two hard rough stones used for grinding grain into meal or flour; the stones themselves. One type of mill consisted of a rectangular stone,

slightly hollowed out, upon which a smaller stone, flat on one side, was placed. Grinding was done by pushing the upper, smaller stone back and forth on the larger stone where the grain had been placed. Another type of mill consisted of two round stones fitted together snugly. The top stone often had a hole in the center, through which grain was poured, and a handle for turning the top stone. Both types of mills were used in the home and were usually worked by women. There were also large community mills in which a heavy stone shaped like a wheel was placed on a large, round, lower stone and rolled around by an animal. The upper stone of a mill, called a millstone, was sometimes used as a weapon. *Deuteronomy 24:6; Judges 9:53; Job 41:24; Isaiah 47:2; Jeremiah 25:10; Matthew 18:6; 24:41; Mark 9:42; Luke 17:2; Revelation 18:21-22.*

MILLET. The smallest of grassseeds cultivated for food. It makes poor quality bread and is usually mixed with other grains.

MILLO. A part of the fortifying structure around the city of David. It was probably built on a platform of packed earth. This defense of Jerusalem was started by David but credited to Solomon. *II Samuel 5:9; I Kings 9:14-15, 24; 11:27; I Chronicles 11:8; II Chronicles 32:5.*

MINISTER. As a noun it means "one who serves." In the OT it was used most often as a verb meaning "to serve," especially to serve God in worship and in carrying out sacrifices. In the NT Jesus showed by his own life

the importance of humble service. He said, "I am among you as one who serves." Paul referred to himself as a minister or servant of the gospel. *Exodus 28:43; Numbers 11:28; Ezra 8:15, 17; Isaiah 61:6; Jeremiah 33:21; Joel 1:9; Acts 8:27; Ephesians 3:7; 6:21; Colossians 1:7, 23, 25; I Timothy 4:6.*

Mint

MINT. Mint of several varieties grows wild in the Holy Land. It is extensively used for flavoring. The Jews believed it efficacious in the treatment of many ailments. It was scattered over the floors of the synagogue, its fragrance scenting the air. Along with rue and cummin, mint was important enough to be tithed (Luke 11:42).

MIRACLE. In a broad definition any event in which one sees the supernatural power of God at work. Other words used to mean miracle in the Bible are *signs, wonders, mighty acts* (see John 2:11; 6:14). *Exodus 4:21; 7:9; 15:11; Psalm 105:5; Acts 8:13; 19:11; I Corinthians 12:10; Galatians 3:5.*

MIRIAM. Sister of Moses and Aaron. She is mentioned in several stories with Moses and Aaron. Though she is not named, we are told that the sister of the infant Moses kept watch over the baby in the basket and after his discovery ran to get their own mother for his nurse (see Exodus 2:4, 7-8). Her song of victory when the Israelites crossed the Red Sea is one of the earliest fragments of Hebrew poetry. *Exodus 15:20-21; Numbers 12:1-15; 20:1; Micah 6:4.*

MIZPAH, MISPEH. Meaning "watchtower" or "lookout point." When Jacob and his uncle Laban settled an argument, they erected a pillar called Mizpah (watch post) in memory of Jacob's words, "The Lord watch between you and me, when we are absent one from the other." This has come to be called the Mizpah benediction and is often used in churches today (Genesis 31:49). It was the name of several towns and cities in OT times, the most important of which was on the border between the southern kingdom of Judah and the northern kingdom of Israel. Here archaeologists have discovered what are probably the ruins of the fortifications built by King Asa. This city was a boundary fortress between Judah and Israel. After the fall of Jerusalem to the Babylonians, the area was made a Babylonian province with Mizpah as its capital. Mizpah seems to have become a center of worship also, thus taking the place of Jerusalem as both a political and religious center. *Joshua 11:3, 8; Judges 10:17; 11:11, 29; I Samuel 7:5-16; II Kings 25:23, 25; II Chronicles*

16:6; Nehemiah 3:7, 15, 19; Jeremiah 40:6; 41:3.

MOAB. A high, rolling plateau east of the Dead Sea about three thousand feet above sea level. The Moabites were considered to be descended from Abraham's nephew Lot and so related to the Israelites. They were among those tribes who opposed the Israelites on their way from Egypt to Canaan. From the time of the Exodus until the fall of Jerusalem, Moab was often in conflict with Israel. At one time under King David the Moabites were forced to pay tribute to Israel. A Moabite stone found in 1868 and now in the Louvre in France bears an inscription to King Mesha of Moab, who won a victory over Israel. *Numbers 21:11, 26; 22:1; Deuteronomy 2:8-37; 29:1; 34:1-8; Judges 3:12-14; II Kings 1:1; I Chronicles 18:2; Isaiah 15:1–16:14; Jeremiah 48:1-47; Amos 2:1-3.*

MOLE. The mole is listed among the unclean animals in Leviticus 11:30. Isaiah (2:20) speaks of man's idols being cast "to the moles and the bats." Doubtless the mole was familiar to the Hebrew people, but mole might also mean the mole rat.

MOLE RAT. Though not mentioned in the Bible the mole rat was and is common in Palestine. This leads us to believe that the word translated "mole" in some cases refers to the mole rat. It has much the same habits—burrowing into the ground, feeding on roots and bulbs. It has the same general shape as the mole, though much larger. It, too, has almost sightless eyes and is covered with soft, thick, gray fur.

MOLECH, MOLOCH. A god of the Canaanites to whom children were sacrificed by forcing them to walk through fire. Although it was forbidden by their law, some Israelites also sacrificed their children. Most of these sacrifices took place in the Valley of Hinnom, southwest of Jerusalem. In King Josiah's reign the place of sacrifice was destroyed. *Leviticus 18:21; 20:2-5; I Kings 11:7; II Kings 23:10; Jeremiah 32:35.*

MOLTEN IMAGE. A representation of a god made from melted metal. Among ancient peoples it was the practice to make an image of a god for use in worship. Molten images were made by pouring melted gold, silver, iron, or bronze over a prepared form of wood or clay or into a mold. This practice was forbidden to the Hebrews. *Exodus 34:17; Leviticus 19:4; Deuteronomy 27:15; Nahum 1:14.*

MONEY. Something which is generally accepted as a means of payment for goods. In early Bible times cattle, oil, corn, wine, and wheat were used as payment in barter or exchange for other goods. Later, pieces of copper, silver, and gold molded into various shapes came into use. To make certain full value was being received, the metal was always weighed before it was accepted as payment. When coins came into use they were stamped with the weight of the coin which also became the name of the coin. For example, "shekel" could refer to a coin or to its weight. Many coins of different

nations were in use in NT times, circulating throughout the world. *Genesis 33:19; Exodus 30:13-16; Leviticus 25:37; Numbers 3:48-51; Joshua 24:32; Judges 17:2-4; II Kings 5:26, 12:4-16; Jeremiah 32:9-10; Matthew 22:19; 25:18; Luke 9:3; 19:23; John 12:5-6; Acts 4:37; 8:18.*

MONEY-CHANGER. The term used in ancient times for a man who carried on many of the duties of a modern banker. One of his important services was exchanging coins of one country or province for those of another. In NT times a money-changer was a person who exchanged foreign coins for the half-shekel silver coins minted in Tyre that were used to pay the annual temple tax. Roman and other foreign coins were not acceptable to the Jews because they usually had stamped on them representations of pagan gods. The money-changers received a small fee for their services, but sometimes their charges were excessive. At Passover time money-changers set up their tables in the temple courts. On one of his visits to the temple Jesus drove out the money-changers. *Matthew 21:12; Mark 11:15; John 2:13-15; 17:24.*

MONKEY. Though not found anywhere in biblical lands, monkeys, particularly the baboon, which in Egypt was considered sacred to the god Thoth, were known to the Hebrew people because of their long sojourn in Egypt. As mentioned under *Ape*, several species of primates were common in the court of King Solomon, brought from Africa and India.

MORDECAI. The Jewish hero of the book of Esther. The story tells how he and his cousin, Esther, queen of the Persian king Ahasuerus, uncovered a plot to kill Mordecai and all other Jews in the Persian Empire. *Esther 2:5–10:3.*

MORESHETH. Home of the prophet Micah in the foothills of southwestern Judah. It is now Tell ej-Judeideh. *Jeremiah 26:18; Micah 1:1.*

MORIAH. A rocky hilltop north of Jerusalem where Solomon built the temple. It was said to be the place where Abraham made ready to sacrifice his son Isaac. *Genesis 22:2; II Chronicles 3:1.*

MORNING GLORY. The field variety of the morning glory grows over much of the Holy Land. The long trailing vine is quite often seen in the fields of grain, its pink and white blossoms coloring the grain stalks.

MORTAR. A building material, usually clay mixed with straw and used while damp and soft to bind bricks or stones together. Also, a bowl in which grain, herbs, spices, and dyes were powdered and crushed with a club-shaped implement called a pestle. *Genesis 11:3; Exodus 1:14; Numbers 11:8, Proverbs 27:22; Isaiah 41:25; Nahum 3:14.*

MOSES. Leader of the Hebrew tribes in their escape from Egypt and on their journey to Canaan. In the OT, Moses is considered the most significant figure in the history of Israel. He was prophet, priest, judge, and lawgiver. He was the interpreter of God's

laws by which the people were expected to live in their special covenant relation. The Exodus under Moses' leadership was the beginning of Israel as a people. His life story is told in the first part of the OT known as the Pentateuch. It tells of his birth, when he narrowly escaped death by being hidden in a basket-like boat. It describes his struggles with the pharaoh in Egypt and with the Israelites in the wilderness. Moses died on Mt. Nebo just as he had brought the Hebrews to the border of the Promised Land of Canaan. *See the books of Exodus, Leviticus, Numbers, and Deuteronomy. Psalm 103:7; Matthew 17:3-4, Luke 16:29-31; John 1:17, Acts 7:20-44; Hebrews 11:23-24.*

MOSQUITO. There is no doubt that the Hebrew people were acquainted with the pestiferous mosquito, including the "anophles," carrier of malaria and yellow fever germs. The Hebrew word translated "mosquito" is not too clear, but we can be sure the buzzing and their bites were well known. In fact, a kind of mosquito netting is mentioned in the apochryphal book of Judith where the author mentions one "with purple and gold and emeralds and precious stones" (Judith 10:21).

MOST HOLY PLACE. The innermost room of the tabernacle and temple in which the ark of the covenant was placed. The place where the priests of Aaron ate the offerings not burned was also called a most holy place. (See *Sacrifices and Offerings.*) *Exodus 26:33-34; II Chronicles 3:8, 10; 5:7; Ezekiel 41:4.*

MOTH. Probably the most familiar quotation concerning the moth is the admonition of Jesus: "Lay not up for yourselves treasures on earth where moth and rust corrupt . . ." (Matthew 6:19). As everyone who stores winter clothing in cedar chests and moth balls knows, it is the larvae of the clothes moth, not the adult, which does the damage. Evidently the ancients also had this problem. Job states it definitely when he cries out bitterly, "He [man] as a rotten thing, consumeth, as a garment that is moth eaten" (Job 13:28). There were other kinds of moths, but only the clothes moth is mentioned in the Bible.

MOUND, SIEGE. In OT times a temporary ramp-like structure built outside the wall of a city in order to lay siege to it. From the siege mound arrows and stones could be hurled over the wall into a city by a siege engine, and the wall could be climbed. *II Samuel 20:15; Isaiah 37:33; Jeremiah 6:6; 32:24; Ezekiel 17:17; 21:22.*

MOUNTAIN LILY. Though not too abundant, this member of the amarylis family is found blossoming throughout much of the Middle East. It grows mostly in clay soil. The deep blue flowers are borne on foot-high stems in clusters of three or four.

MOURNING. An expression of grief. Funeral customs in Bible times included tearing one's clothes, sitting in ashes, fasting, wailing, and singing songs of lamentation. Sometimes there were paid professional mourners who sang songs of lament accompanied by musical instruments. *Genesis 37:34;*

50:10-11; I Samuel 25:1; II Samuel 1:11-12; 3:31, 11:27; I Kings 14:13; II Chronicles 35:24; Jeremiah 4: 28; Lamentations 1:4; Amos 5:16; 8:10; Zechariah 12:11-14; Matthew 11:17.

MOUSE. There are over twenty varieties of mice in the Holy Land. The Hebrew word *akbar* is used which was a generic term applying to all species. The Mosaic prohibition against their use as food indicates that the people were familiar with them (Leviticus 11:29). Prominence that seems out of proportion to their size is given the mouse in I Samuel 6. As a guilt offering for their theft of the ark, and which they later decided to return, they were instructed to bring to the Israelites "five golden mice" (I Samuel 6:4) representing the five Philistine lords.

MULE. The mule is mentioned twenty-two times in the Bible, but only in the Old Testament. And only once before King David bade Solomon ride to him on a mule. The breeding of mules, a male donkey mated with a female horse, resulting in an always sterile offspring, was forbidden by Mosaic law (Leviticus 19:19). But mules became so important to the Israelites that this law was often disregarded. Mules, combining the size and strength of the horse with the sure-footedness of the donkey, became popular as a war animal, as a beast of burden, and as a riding animal for royalty. I Kings 1:33; II Samuel 13:29.

MUSICAL INSTRUMENTS. The Bible refers to musical instruments mainly as part of temple worship, but they were also used along with songs and chants at weddings, banquets, and funerals. There was a wide variety of instruments: stringed instruments such as the harp (small enough to be held in the hand) and the lute (gut strings on a wooden frame); wind instruments such as the flute (made of reed pipes), horns (made of an animal horn), and trumpets (of metal); noisemakers such as bells, tambourines, or timbrels (usually played by women for dancing), cymbals, castanets, and gongs. The shophar, or ram's horn, is still used in synagogues today. *Exodus 39:25-26; I Samuel 10:5, I Chronicles 16:42; 25:1; II Chronicles 5:11-13; 29:25-30; Ezra 3:10-11, Nehemiah 12:27, Psalm 150:3-5, Daniel 3:7, 10; Matthew 9:23; I Corinthians 13:1; Revelation 14:2-3.*

Mustard

MUSTARD. Jesus knew whereof he spoke when he referred to the mustard seed as being "among the

least of all seeds" (Matthew 13:32). (Some seeds are smaller.) As he pointed out, it often grows high enough for birds to build nests in it. The yellow blossom variety is most common, but some kinds have white and lilac blooms. The ground seed furnishes the mustard of commerce.

MYRRH (OT). See *Cistus*.

MYRRH (NT). The myrrh included among the three gifts which the magi brought to the Christ child was an aromatic made from the resin of the thorny, bush-like tree. The thick white gum which exudes when the bark is pierced hardens on exposure to the air and becomes reddish in color. It has been used as a spice or as medicine since ancient times. The Hebrews used it as one of the ingredients of the anointing oil for the tabernacle and in the preparation of the dead for burial. Hence Nicodemus brought "a mixture of myrrh and aloes" to be sprinkled over the linen clothes with which he wound the body of Jesus (John 19:39).

MYRTLE. To the Egyptians, Greeks, and the Romans the evergreen myrtle was sacred and used in their worship. While not sacred to the Hebrews it was revered. The tent of the tabernacle was covered with blooming boughs of myrtle. Isaiah mentions it as one of the trees that God "will plant in the wilderness" (Isaiah 41:19). The familiar fifty-fifth chapter of Isaiah closes with the promise that "instead of the brier shall come up the myrtle tree." Sometimes it is a bush, but again it may grow to be a twenty-foot tree. The white blossoms are very fragrant, and the aromatic fruits are dried for perfumes and spices.

MYSTERY. A hidden religious truth. In the NT the word refers to the plan and purpose of God hidden from all except those who see it revealed in the life and ministry of Jesus. *Daniel 2:18-19, 27-28; I Corinthians 15:51; Ephesians 1:9-10; 3:3-4, 9-10; 6:19; Colossians 1:26-27; I Timothy 3:9, 16; Revelation 10:7.*

MYTH. A story told to explain an event or happening which is not understood or a custom or practice the beginning of which has been forgotten. (See *Allegory, Parable*.) *I Timothy 1:4; 4:7; Titus 1:14; II Peter 1:16.*

NAAMAN. Commander of the Syrian army who was cured of his leprosy by Elisha, a Hebrew prophet. *II Kings 5:1-17.*

NABOTH. Owner of a vineyard in Jezreel close to King Ahab's country palace. The king wanted the vineyard and offered to buy it, but Naboth did not wish to sell his land. Hebrew law forbade the king to take away land belonging to the people. Jezebel, Ahab's wife, had a deceitful plan to get the land, and Naboth lost his vineyard and his life. *I Kings 21:1-29; II Kings 9:21-26.*

NADAB. King of Israel about 910–909 B.C., son and successor of Jeroboam I. He was murdered by Baasha, who then succeeded him on the

throne. Also the name of several other men mentioned in the OT. *I Kings 15:25-27.*

NAHASH. Ruler of the Ammonites who was defeated by Saul. This military victory led to Israel's acceptance of Saul as king. *I Samuel 11:1-2; II Samuel 10:2.*

NAHOR. 1. In the OT genealogies the name of the grandfather of Abraham and also of Abraham's brother. *Genesis 11:22-26; 22:20; Joshua 24:2.*

2. The name of a city near Haran in Mesopotamia. *Genesis 24:10.*

NAHUM. A prophet in the southern kingdom Judah in the seventh century B.C. At this time the Babylonian Empire was growing strong. The armies of the Babylonians attacked and defeated the Assyrian capital of Nineveh. Nahum saw the fall of the Assyrian enemy as a great blessing from God to Israel. (See *Nahum, Book of.*)

NAHUM, BOOK OF. A short prophetic book in the OT containing the prophecies of Nahum. Nahum's writing is different from other OT prophets in that he emphasizes the downfall of an enemy rather than the corruption of the Hebrew nation.

NAME. The title by which a person is known. For the Hebrews a person's name was an expression of his character or personality. In the Bible when a name was changed, as from Jacob to Israel or Saul to Paul, it meant a change in character or, as in Abram to Abraham, a change in relationship with God. Many names were given that recalled some particular event or a circumstance attending a person's birth or that expressed gratitude for his birth. Many of the place names in Palestine were established before the Israelites conquered the land and so do not necessarily show Israel's beliefs and practices. Many of these names indicate social or religious customs, the size of the town, the occupation of its inhabitants, or the persons who were important to the place. Such expressions as "the name of the Lord" or "in the name of Christ" mean "by his authority." "For his name's sake" means "according to his nature." *Genesis 25:25-26; 27:36; 32:28; 35:18; I Samuel 4:21; 25:25; I Chronicles 4:9; Psalms 8:1; 76:1; Jeremiah 14:7; Matthew 6:9; Mark 3:17; Acts 3:16; 4:12; Philippians 2:9-10.*

NAOMI. One of the leading characters in the book of Ruth. Naomi returned to Bethlehem after the death of her husband accompanied by her faithful daughter-in-law Ruth, also a widow. Naomi encouraged Ruth to accept the protection of their kinsman Boaz, whom Ruth later married. *Ruth 1:1–4:22.*

NAPHTALI. One of the twelve sons of Jacob from whom the tribe of Naphtali was descended. It was also the name of their territory, which lay west of the Jordan River from Lake Huleh to the southern end of the Sea of Galilee. *Exodus 1:4; Numbers 1:42-43; Joshua 19:32-39; 20:7; Isaiah 9:1; Matthew 4:13, 15.*

NARCISSUS. Our common pollyanna narcissus is one of the common

spring flowers in Bible lands, growing profusely on the plains of Sharon and Jericho. It is quite generally agreed among scholars that this common but fragrant and beautiful flower is the rose of Sharon.

NARD. An expensive, fragrant ointment prepared from the roots and stems of the spikenard which grows in India, Nepal, Bhutan, and the valleys of Tibet. The Romans used the ointment to anoint the head. One pound cost three hundred denarii. A denarius was a day's wages for a laborer and amounted to about twenty cents. *Song of Solomon 1:12; 4:13-14; Mark 14:3; John 12:3.*

Nard

NATHAN. A prophet in the time of David and Solomon. He was the friend and counselor of King David. After David committed his great sin Nathan went to him to accuse him of his crime. This took great courage as kings in those times could have those who displeased them put to death. Nathan also played an important part in having Solomon made king after David's death. According to I Chronicles 29:29 and II Chronicles 9:29, Nathan kept records about the acts of David and Solomon, but these have never been found. *II Samuel 7:1-17; 12:1-15, 24-25; I Kings 1:5-48.*

NATHANAEL. Mentioned only in the Gospel of John as one of the disciples of Jesus. Many believe him to be the apostle called Bartholomew in the other three Gospels. (See *Bartholomew.*) *John 1:45-49; 21:2.*

NATIONS. In biblical times "nations" referred to the whole of mankind divided into kinship groups, not into countries or states as we know them today. Genesis 10 lists seventy different groups of people. Among them were the ancestors of the Hebrews. These peoples were scattered throughout the ancient Near East, and their boundaries constantly changed throughout OT times as they conquered neighboring nations or were conquered by them. Israel felt its importance among the nations because of its covenant with God. This made the Hebrews a holy people among all the nations of the earth. *Genesis 10:1-32; 12:1-3; Exodus 19:3-6; Psalm 106:41; Matthew 24:9; 28:19; Luke 21:24; Revelation 7:9.*

NAVE. The main room of the temple between the vestibule and the inner room. *I Kings 6:3, 5, 17; 7:50; II*

Chronicles 3:4-5, 13; 4:22; Ezekiel 41:1-4, 23-26.

NAZARENE. A native of Nazareth. A NT title for Jesus because he came from the village Nazareth. Early Christians may have been called Nazarenes by Jews who wished to make fun of them. Possibly the members of a Jewish sect whose beliefs were not the traditional Jewish beliefs were also called Nazarenes. *Matthew 2:23; Mark 14:67; Acts 24:5.*

NAZARETH. The village where Jesus lived as a child and where he grew to manhood. It is about fifteen miles from the Sea of Galilee and twenty miles from the Mediterranean. In Jesus' day Nazareth was a small, insignificant village located on a hillside. Modern Nazareth is an important city of nearly twenty thousand people and has a large Christian population. *Matthew 2:23; 21:11; Mark 1:9, 24; 10:47; Luke 2:4-5, 39, 51; 4:16, 34; John 1:45-46; 18:5, 7; 19:19; Acts 2:22; 3:6.*

NAZIRITE. In the OT a person who took a vow of dedication to serve God by following certain rules. For example a Nazirite did not cut his hair or take wine and strong drink. At first the vow was for life, but later one could become a Nazirite for a temporary period. When the vow had been fulfilled, his hair was cut and burned on the altar as an offering. The Nazirite was not a priest but was looked upon as a holy man. *Numbers 6:1-21; Judges 13:5, 7; 16:17; Amos 2:11-12.*

NEBO, MOUNT. A mountain opposite Jericho twelve miles east of the mouth of the Jordan River. In Deuteronomy 32 is recorded a song of Moses, spoken before he climbed this mountain for a view of Canaan. He died there. *Deuteronomy 34:1-5.*

NEBUCHADNEZZAR, NEBUCHADREZZAR (Spelled *Nebuchadrezzar* in the books of Jeremiah and Ezekiel). King of Babylonia 605–562 B.C., whose empire succeeded that of the Assyrians. His marriage to Amyitis of Media united the Medes and the Chaldeans. During his long reign gates and temples were built in Babylon, and enormous walls were constructed around the city. He conquered Syria and Judah. He destroyed Jerusalem and took a large number of Jews into captivity in Babylon. *II Kings 24:1-17; 25:1-30; II Chronicles 36:6-21; Ezra 2:1; Jeremiah 21:2-10; 22:24-25; 27:6-8; and other places in Jeremiah; Ezekiel 26:7; 29:18-19; Daniel 1:1.*

NECO. An Egyptian pharaoh who reigned from 609 to 594 B.C. Neco felt the time was right to expand the Egyptian Empire into Palestine because the power of the Assyrians who had held it so long was weakening. When Neco entered Palestine with his army, Josiah, the king of Judah, tried to stop him but was killed in the effort. Neco seized control of Judah. However, a few years later Nebuchadnezzar, the king of Babylon, defeated Neco and drove him back into Egypt. *II Kings 23:29-35; Jeremiah 46:2.*

NECROMANCY. In OT times a form of reading the future by

communicating with the dead. Such practice was forbidden to the Hebrews. *Deuteronomy 18:10-11.*

NEGEB,THE. A region of the southern part of Canaan with numerous cities and good pastureland. The original inhabitants were the Amalekites. David incorporated the entire Negeb into the kingdom of Judah. After biblical times, due to the devastation of war and the neglect of the vegetation (which helped to hold the moisture in the soil), the Negeb became a desert. Now as a part of modern Israel the land is being restored. *Genesis 12:9; 13:1-3; Numbers 13:29; I Samuel 27:10; Psalm 126:4; Jeremiah 32:44.*

NEHEMIAH. A Jew living in exile in Persia. He was cupbearer to the Persian king Artaxerxes I, who reigned from about 465 to 424 B.C. Nehemiah was grieved at the news that Jerusalem was still in ruins a century and a half after the first exiles had returned there. He received permission from the king to go to Jerusalem to help in the rebuilding of the city and its wall. (See *Nehemiah, Book of*.)

NEHEMIAH, BOOK OF. Originally the book of Ezra and the book of Nehemiah were a single book. They tell of the work of restoring Jerusalem.

NETTLE or ACANTHUS. A wild plant which grows rapidly and is noted for its stinging effect when touched. At least four species are known in Bible lands. Nettles quickly grow up in neglected fields. OT writers often used the word to indicate extreme poverty and the destruction and desolation of an area. *Job 30:7; Proverbs 24:31; Isaiah 34:13, Hosea 9:6; Zephaniah 2:9.*

NETS. Mesh traps woven of twine or cord and used for catching fish, birds, and animals. In Bible times fishing nets were of two types. One was a cone-shaped net with lead weights around the mouth to pull it down under the surface of the water. It was cast by hand. The other was a large dragnet fitted with floats and sinkers that was let out from the beach and hauled ashore in wide semicircles. *Psalm 9:15; Isaiah 51:20; Ezekiel 12:13; Mark 1:16-19; Matthew 13:47; John 21:6-8.*

NETWORK. In the OT a bronze grating on the altar of burnt offering before the tabernacle. Also, a bronze grill or latticework used in connection with the pillars of Solomon's temple. *Exodus 27:4-5; 38:4; I Kings 7:18, 20, 41-42; Jeremiah 52:22-23.*

NEW MOON. The beginning of the month. It was observed as a holy day of rejoicing, special feasting, and sacrifices. *I Samuel 20:24; Ezra 3:5; Nehemiah 10:33; Isaiah 1:13-14; 47:13; Hosea 2:11; Amos 8:4-5; Colossians 2:16.*

NICODEMUS. A member of the Jewish Sanhedrin. He came to Jesus secretly at night to ask questions and hear more of Jesus' teachings. He became a secret follower of Jesus. *John 3:1-9; 7:50-52; 19:38-41.*

NILE. The principal river of Egypt, nearly 3,500 miles long. It rises in the highlands of east central Africa and empties into the Mediterranean Sea. The life of Egypt has always been

dependent upon the annual flooding of the river valley which spreads a rich, muddy soil over the flatlands on both sides of the river banks. In ancient times the annual flood was greeted with celebrations, and the Egyptians considered the river to be a god. *Genesis 41:1-3; Exodus 1:22; Isaiah 23:10; Ezekiel 29:9; Amos 9:5; Nahum 3:8.*

NILE MONITOR. Familiar to the Children of Israel sojourning in Egypt, the Nile monitor is a large sand-colored lizard up to five and six feet in length. Its diet consists largely of smaller lizards, small birds, even tortoises and baby crocodiles that also abound in the Nile.

NINEVEH. Capital city of the Assyrian Empire, located on the east side of the upper Tigris River. One of the oldest and greatest cities of Mesopotamia, Nineveh dates back to prehistoric times. It reached its greatest fame in the eighth century B.C. The Israelites feared and hated Nineveh because it represented the constant threat and oppression of the Assyrians. The Hebrew prophets Nahum and Zephaniah saw its wickedness and proclaimed its destruction. Nineveh was captured and destroyed by the Babylonians in 612 B.C. *Genesis 10:11-12; II Kings 19:36; Jonah 1:2; 3:2-9; 4:11; Nahum 1:1; 2:8; 3:7; Zephaniah 2:13; Luke 11:30, 32.*

NOAH. Hero of the OT story of the Flood. Because of the wickedness and violence of people, God purposed to destroy the earth. He told Noah to build an ark (boat) large enough to hold his entire family and a pair of each kind of animal. Those in the ark were the only survivors of the Great Flood which covered the world. *Genesis 6:5–9:29.*

NUMBERS, BOOK OF. The fourth book of the OT. It continues the history of the people of Israel begun in the book of Exodus. The title refers to a census, or counting, of the tribes described in the opening chapters.

OAK. The veneration of the oak by the ancients was not lost on the Hebrews. Mention of the fact that Deborah was buried beneath an oak (Genesis 35:8) and that Gideon received "an angel of the Lord" under the branches of an oak (Judges 6:11) are instances that indicate it has a special significance. There are several varieties of the tree in Palestine, varying with the altitude and the soil. The expression "as strong as an oak" was as apt a simile when Amos recorded these words (Amos 2:9) as it is today.

OATH. A solemn statement made by an individual and often accompanied by formal words and actions as a guarantee that what he has said or promised is true. The oath was very important in the life of the Hebrew community. Often God was called upon as a witness to an oath (see Psalm 7:3-5), and some symbolic act such as putting a hand on one's head or raising the hands toward heaven was performed. If the statements made with an oath were not true or if the promises

made were not kept, it was a most serious matter. The name of God had been dishonored. Jesus urged that all oaths be omitted and that a person take care to mean what he said in every situation (see Matthew 5:33-37). *Genesis 26:28-29; Leviticus 5:4; II Chronicles 6:22-23; Ezekiel 10:5; James 5:12.*

OBADIAH. A prophet whose visions and oracles are in a book of the OT. (See *Obadiah, Book of.*)

OBADIAH, BOOK OF. A book of prophecy, the shortest in the OT. The date is uncertain, but it was probably written after the destruction of Jerusalem in 586 B.C. It describes the suffering of Jerusalem and the revengeful behavior of the nation of Edom toward Judah at the time of this disaster. The prophet foretold the doom of Edom as punishment for rejoicing in her neighbor's grief. The restoration of Judah is also predicted.

OBED. Son of Ruth and Boaz and grandfather of King David. According to the Gospels of Matthew and Luke he became an ancestor of Jesus. Several men named Obed are mentioned in the OT. *Ruth 4:17, 21-22; I Chronicles 2:12; Matthew 1:5; Luke 3:32.*

OBEISANCE. In the OT the word means "to bow down" or "to touch one's face to the ground" as a sign of submission or as an act of worship or honor. *Genesis 43:28; I Samuel 24:8; II Samuel 15:5; I Chronicles 21:21; II Chronicles 24:17.*

ODOR. Scent or fragrance. In the morning and evening services of worship in OT times the sacrifices and offerings were burned so that the smoke could rise as a pleasant odor before God. In the NT one's acts of love are spoken of in a figure of speech as a fragrant offering to God in the name of Christ (see Ephesians 5:2). *Exodus 29:18, 25, 41; Leviticus 1:9; Numbers 15:24; and other places in Leviticus and Numbers; Ezekiel 6:13.*

OFFERING. In the OT a gift to God given as an act of worship. Gifts included food, drink, incense, money, and animals. These objects represented the worshiper's offering of himself. In the NT, love and service to one's neighbors in the name of Christ are spoken of as offerings. In the early church, offerings of money were often made by Christians of one city to aid Christians in another. *Exodus 35:5-9; Leviticus 3:1-2; Numbers 7:10; and many other references in Leviticus and Numbers; Mark 12:33; Hebrews 7:27; 10:18; I Peter 2:5.*

OFFICER. In biblical use a servant or minister of the king, the army, or the temple. The men sent by the high priest to arrest Jesus were officers of the temple. *Numbers 11:16; Deuteronomy 16:18; 20:5; 29:10; I Chronicles 23:4; Ezra 7:28; Jeremiah 20:1; 41:1; John 7:32, 45-46; 18:3 18, 22.*

OG. King of the land of Bashan, east of the Jordan River; remembered in the old traditions as a giant. His defeat by the Israelites was an important step toward their gaining possession of the land of Canaan. The territory of Bashan became the territory of the tribe of Manasseh. *Numbers 32:33;*

Deuteronomy 1:4; 3:1-11, 13; Joshua 12:4; 13:12, 30-31; Nehemiah 9:22; Psalms 135:11; 136:20.

OIL. A liquid substance containing much fat. Oil was one of the necessities of life in Palestine and was looked upon as a gift from God. Most Palestinian oil was made by pressing olives. The first oil, obtained by putting crushed olives into a basket through which the oil would drain, was the purest and most precious. It was used in many ways in worship. The oil that was forced out by a second, stronger pressure was used for fuel, food, and medicine. *Exodus 27:20; 29:2, 40; Numbers 11:7-8; Deuteronomy 7:13; I Samuel 10:1; I Kings 5:11; 17:12; Ezra 3:7; Jeremiah 31:12; Hosea 2:8; Joel 2:19; Matthew 25:3-8; Mark 6:13; James 5:14.*

OLEANDER. The tall oleander—it may grow as high as twenty feet—is one of the most beautiful shrubs in Palestine when in full bloom. The flowers cover a wide range of colors from white, rose, red to purple. They blossom in the spring and last all summer. It is an evergreen, easily grown. Unfortunately flowers and plant alike are highly poisonous: even the smoke from the burning leaves is wisely avoided.

OLIVE. Asia Minor is believed to be the original home of the olive, which has been cultivated for thousands of years. It was an olive "branch" (twig) that the dove brought back to Noah on the ark. Jesus left the Upper Room and "went out unto the Mount of Olives" (Matthew 26:30).

Olive trees have always been of practical value, the fruit for food, and the oil pressed from the fruit as oil for ancient lamps. And when Samuel took the horn of oil (olive) and poured it over the head of David to anoint him, he was following a ritualistic custom of his race.

OLIVES, MOUNT OF, or OLIVET. A hill east of Jerusalem across the Valley of Kidron. It is part of the main range of mountains that runs through central and southern Palestine. Some of the activities of Jesus during the last week of his life took place on the Mount of Olives. The garden of Gethsemane is located there. It may have been the scene of Jesus' last meeting with his disciples after the resurrection, when he ascended into heaven. *II Samuel 15:30; Zechariah 14:4; Matthew 21:1; 24:3; Mark 11:1-2; 14:26; Luke 19:37; 21:37; Acts 1:12.*

OMEGA. See *Alpha and Omega.*

OMER. In the OT a measure for dry substances equal to a little more than two quarts. *Exodus 16:13-36.*

OMRI. Ruler of the northern kingdom of Israel about 885–874 B.C.; successor of Zimri. Omri was the first of a family called the Omride Dynasty that ruled Israel for many years. He changed the capital from Tirzah to Samaria, which he had built. The name Samaria came to be applied to all the northern kingdom. Several other people mentioned in the OT have the name Omri. *I Kings 16:16-28; Micah 6:16.*

ONESIMUS. A runaway slave probably belonging to Philemon, a

member of the church at Colossae. His story is told in Paul's letter to Philemon. Not only had Onesimus run away from his master, he may have robbed him also. However, after he met Paul and heard the gospel, he was converted and became a most useful (the meaning of his name) servant. The letter expresses Paul's hope that the slave will be freed. Later there was a bishop of the church in Ephesus by the name of Onesimus, and many scholars think that this was the same man. *Colossians 4:7-9; Philemon 1:1-25.*

ONION. The onion, and its culinary cousin, the leek, was widely used for food even before biblical times. In the warm, dry weather of Palestine the cultivated onion grows very large and is very sweet. There are many wild varieties. Some, like the pink onion—the color of the blossom giving it its name—grow in rocky places to a height of three or four feet.

ONYCHA. Mentioned with the sweet spices "stacte [storax] and galbanum" in Exodus 30:34, we know that the onycha was a source of aromatic resin from which is produced labanum. It is a three-foot bush with large flowers having five white petals, each with a spot of scarlet darkening near the center and with stamens and pistil. Also known as the rockrose, it blossoms profusely during the long dry season.

OPHIR. A region of uncertain location chiefly known for its production of fine gold and for a fine-grained, heavy timber from its almug trees. The wood was also called red sandalwood and was used in the making of musical instruments. The scent of the wood was pleasing, and a dye made from it gave a rich red color to silks and woolens. *I Kings 9:28; 10:11; I Chronicles 29:4; II Chronicles 8:18; 9:10; Job 22:24; 28:16; Psalm 45:9; Isaiah 13:12.*

ORACLE. In the OT a speech or a pronouncement given by an inspired prophet, king, or priest as a message from God. An expression used often by the prophets was "Thus says the Lord." *II Samuel 23:1; II Chronicles 24:27; Isaiah 15:1; Nahum 1:1; Malachi 1:1; Romans 3:2.*

ORCHID. Orchids may seem out of place in the Holy Land and the familiar tropical species is not found there. But there are a dozen or more species that are common. The monkey orchid and the earth-wasp orchid are abundant in rocky soil. One of the most common varieties is the Antoilan orchid with rather small pink blossoms, several on a stem and of typical orchid shape. It blooms in March.

ORDINANCE. A law or rule for governing social and religious customs. The term has the same meaning as "commandment." *Exodus 12:14; Leviticus 5:10; I Kings 9:4-5; Psalm 19:9; Isaiah 58:2; Luke 1:6; Ephesians 2:15.*

ORPAH. A sister-in-law of Ruth and daughter-in-law of Naomi. When Naomi returned to Bethlehem, she urged Orpah and Ruth, who were widows, to remain in their own land of Moab because of the difficulties

they would face in a strange land. Orpah obeyed and stayed in Moab while Ruth, in loyal devotion to Naomi, went with her to Bethlehem. *Ruth 1:4-18.*

ORYX. The oryx is a species of antelope, distinguished by its extremely long horns. Most common in Arabia, it was also found in the Holy Land. Isaiah's animal translated "wild bull" in Isaiah 51:20 might well have referred to the oryx.

OSPREY. Spelled "ospray" in the OT (Leviticus 11:13; Deuteronomy 14:12), this is a large fish hawk. Its head, neck, and under parts are white: the back and wings a dark brown with a blackish cast. As it soars high over the water, its keen eyes sight a fish. With wings folded it dives, striking the water feet first, often disappearing beneath the surface for a moment, emerging with a fish clutched in its talons. Then, spreading its broad wings, it flies off to enjoy its catch, after which it returns to fly low over the water to wash its feet.

OSSIFRAGE. See *Lammergier.*

OSTRICH. The ostrich, up to eight feet in height, is the largest bird in the world. It once existed as far north as Syria and so was known to the early Hebrews. Job has much to say about the ostrich, none of it very complimentary (Job 39:13-18). It is true that the bird is not known for its intelligence—but it does not hide its head in the sand when danger threatens! It can run as fast as forty miles an hour and so can outrun most danger, but if forced to fight it can deal terrific blows with its hoof-like toes. It cannot fly. Its cry, likened to the bellowing of a suffering bull, probably is what Micah had in mind when he speaks of "mourning like the ostriches" (Micah 1:8). "Owls" is used in the King James Version, but "ostriches" are doubtless what the prophet meant.

OVEN. In biblical times an outdoor baking device. It was a large round jar of burnt clay with the fire built on pebbles at the bottom. Flat cakes of dough were stuck against the hot inner wall or laid on the pebbles after the fire was down. The fuel was usually dried grass, bushes, or dung. *Exodus 8:3, Leviticus 2:4; Psalm 21:9; Hosea 7:4; Matthew 6:30.*

OVERLAY. In OT times a layer of metal laid over various objects. Parts of the tabernacle, the temple, and the holy furnishing were overlaid with gold, silver, or bronze. King Hezekiah of Judah had to strip away the overlays of precious metal to pay tribute to the king of Assyria. *Exodus 25:11; I Kings 6:20-32; 10:18; II Kings 18:16; I Chronicles 29:4; II Chronicles 3:4, 10; 4:9; 9:17; Isaiah 40:19; Habakkuk 2:19.*

OVERSEER. A taskmaster, supervisor, or foreman of a work gang, a household, or a group performing some special task. *Genesis 39:4-5; 41:34; II Chronicles 2:18; 34:17; Nehemiah 11:9; Isaiah 60:17.*

OWL. In listing the unclean birds in Leviticus 11:17 the writer mentions "the little owl" and "the great owl." This is not strange since there are

many species of owls in the Holy Land. Very likely "little owl" referred to the "scoops owl," only about eight inches long. The large eagle owl might well be the "great owl" with a body up to two feet in length, strong claws, and cruel beak. Owls are nocturnal creatures, spending their daylight hours in ruins and caves (Isaiah 13:21; Jeremiah 50:39).

The owl is the only bird whose eyes are turned forward and cannot be turned in their sockets. In order to see to either side it must turn its head. Its sight and hearing are both very keen.

OX. A domestic animal used in Bible times to pull plows, carts, and threshing sledges. Oxen were used to tread the kernels of grain out from the straw. They were sometimes used in sacrifice. *Exodus 24:5 I Samuel 11:7; Job 1:14; Psalm 106:20; Luke 14:5, 19; I Corinthians 9:9.*

OYSTER. Though the Jews were forbidden to eat oysters, they were familiar with this mollusk because of the pearls found in certain species, plentiful in the adjacent Red Sea and Indian Ocean. Jesus recognized the value of the pearl and used it as an apt symbol of the kingdom of Heaven in the story of the merchant who, when he found one pearl "of great price, went and sold all that he had, and bought it" (Matthew 13:46).

PADDAN-ARAM. In the OT the homeland of the patriarch Abraham, who settled there with his kinsmen after they left Ur. It was located in northern Mesopotamia (now south central Turkey) and included the city of Haran. *Genesis 25:20; 28:2.*

PALESTINE. In modern usage the name for the territory occupied in OT times by the twelve tribes of Israel. The name "Palestine" does not appear in the Bible, and the common Hebrew name for the land was Canaan. This term, however, did not include Transjordan, the land east of the Jordan River. The area referred to as Palestine is bordered roughly by the Mediterranean Sea on the west, the Arabian Desert on the east, the AntiLebanon Mountains on the north, and the Negeb and the Sinai Peninsula on the south. This was the Promised Land given by God to Abraham (see *Canaan*), but it was a challenging land which offered no soft, easy life. The Hebrews were continually aware that God had chosen this place for them to dwell in, and the OT is the record of their response to their surroundings. Their life was influenced by the physical features of the land. These are so varied that almost every kind of terrain can be found somewhere within the 10,000 square miles of territory that make up Palestine. There are rugged mountain ranges, fertile coastal plains, and dry desert regions. Mt. Hermon rises more than 9,000 feet while the surface of the Dead Sea lies 1,300 feet below sea level. The land is set between the sea and the desert but has no favorable harbors on the Mediterranean. The climate is generally one of summer drought and winter rain. The temperatures range from 100 degrees in summer to an average of 40 degrees in Jerusalem in winter. However, there

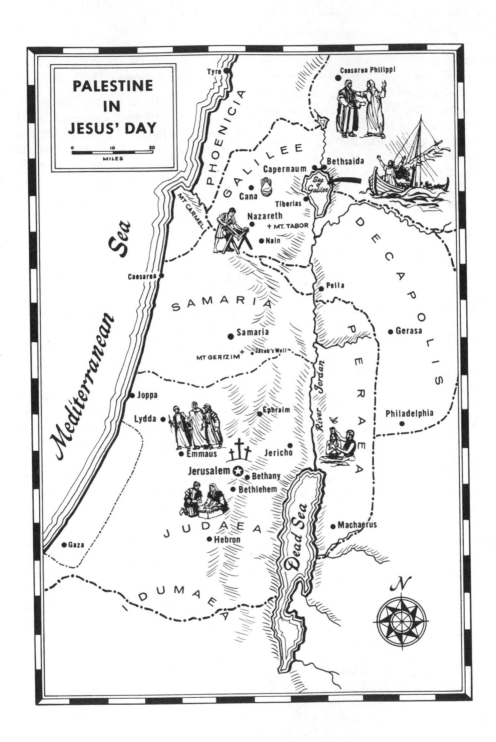

PALESTINE IN JESUS' DAY

0   10   20
MILES

Tyre

PHOENICIA

Caesarea Philippi

GALILEE

Capernaum
Bethsaida
Sea of Galilee

Cana

MT CARMEL

Tiberias

Nazareth
+ MT. TABOR

• Nain

DECAPOLIS

Caesarea

SAMARIA

• Pella

• Samaria

• Gerasa

MT GERIZIM +
Jacob's Well

PERAEA

River Jordan

• Joppa

• Ephraim

• Philadelphia

Lydda •

• Emmaus

† † †

• Jericho

Jerusalem ⭐ • Bethany
• Bethlehem

JUDAEA

Mediterranean Sea

Dead Sea

• Machaerus

• Hebron

• Gaza

IDUMAEA

N

240

is frequent frost. The west wind from the sea brings cooling wind and evening dew so that where there is enough soil crops flourish even in summer. The dreaded sirocco, or east wind that comes scorching from the desert, generally occurs in the fall. The Jordan River flows through the deep Rift Valley and cuts Palestine in half. The gorge is so steep that no cities have ever been built along the river. Palestine also forms a natural passageway between the kingdoms that grew up in the valleys of the Nile and of the Tigris-Euphrates rivers. For this reason Israel and Judah were caught in the constant warfare that went on between these kingdoms as well as those of Asia Minor. All these features combined to produce a vigorous and forceful people whose influence has been felt throughout the world.

PALM TREE. A tall, slender tree with a tuft of branches or leaves at the top. In Bible times it was very useful for its fruit. Dates were an important source of food. Mats were woven from its leaves, and palm fibers provided thread and rigging for boats. In the ancient Near East the palm had religious associations. Carvings on the walls, doors, and other parts of Solomon's Temple represented the palm. The palm tree often appears in the OT as a symbol of the rulers of Israel and as a figure of speech indicating righteousness. Palm Sunday, a Christian festival, received its name from the palm branches waved by the people during Jesus' triumphal entry into Jerusalem. *Exodus 15:27; Leviticus 23:40;* *Deuteronomy 34:3; Judges 1:16; I Kings 6:29, 32, 35; 7:36; II Chronicles 26:15; Nehemiah 8:15; Psalm 92:12; John 12:13; Revelation 7:9.*

PAMPHYLIA. An area along the southern coast of Asia Minor about eighty miles long and twenty miles wide. In NT times it was a Roman province. Paul and Barnabas visited Perga, one of its leading cities, on their first missionary journey. *Acts 2:10; 13:13; 27:5.*

PANNAG. This is a variety of millet which, though not as palatable as wheat or barley, was extensively used for food among the common people, especially in time of famine (Ezekiel 4:9). One stalk may produce thousands of seeds. They are hard and white and are ground into flour (Ezekiel 27:17).

PAPYRUS. A tall reed plant that grows in watery places. It was abundant in lower Egypt and was an important item of export for many centuries. Paper was made from the pith of the inner stalk. It was cut into thin strips that were laid side by side. Other strips were placed across them side by side. An adhesive was used, and the strips were bonded together by pressure. It was then polished with a shell or stone. Papyrus was also used in the making of baskets and small boats. *Job 8:11; Isaiah 18:2.*

PARABLE. A brief story forcefully illustrating a single idea. The word *parable* comes from a verb meaning "to be similar," "to be comparable." Jesus used parables to teach important lessons about God and his kingdom.

PARADISE

He often began them with such phrases as, "With what can we compare . . ." or "The kingdom of heaven is like . . ." or "The kingdom of heaven may be compared to . . . ." (See *Allegory, Fable, Myth.*) *Matthew 13:3-52; Mark 4:30-32; Luke 12:13-21.*

PARADISE. A word meaning "park" or "garden." In NT times the word *paradise* was used to indicate the place of the righteous after death. *Luke 23:43; II Corinthians 12:1-4; Revelation 2:7.*

PARAPET. A railing or low wall built around the edge of a roof to prevent people from falling off. *Deuteronomy 22:8.*

PARCHED GRAIN. Grain prepared by roasting the kernels in a pan or by holding a small bundle of wheat in the fire. In OT times this food was eaten by all people from the highest to the lowest. *Leviticus 2:14, 23:14; Joshua 5:11; Ruth 2:14; I Samuel 17:17; II Samuel 17:28.*

PARCHMENT. A writing material made from the skins of sheep or goats. Gradually it replaced papyrus since it was more lasting. *II Timothy 4:13.*

PARTRIDGE. The partridge is widely distributed throughout the northern hemisphere. There are several kinds in the Holy Land. The most common is the "chuker." It is covered with brightly colored feathers. The sand partridge is less colorful, its buff and brown plumage making it less conspicuous in the wilderness area of Judea. All varieties are hunted for food. Though a fast runner, it tires quickly. Hunters pursue it on horseback until the bird is exhausted, when it may be caught with the bare hands. Perhaps this is what David had in mind when he says that Saul came after him "as when one doth hunt a partridge in the mountains" (I Samuel 26:20).

PASCHAL LAMB. The lamb sacrificed at the Passover festival. Paul used this term to refer to Christ's death and relate it to the Jewish Passover. (See *Passover.*) *I Corinthians 5:7.*

PASSION, THE. A term used for the suffering and death of Jesus. It refers to the last days of Jesus' life and includes such events as the Last Supper, the agony in Gethsemane, the arrest, trial, crucifixion, death, and burial. In the Christian calendar Passion Sunday is the fifth Sunday in Lent. *Acts 1:3.*

PASSOVER, THE. The first of the three great religious festivals in the Jewish year. The Passover and Feast of Unleavened Bread were celebrated in the spring to mark the deliverance of the Israelites from Egyptian slavery. The week-long festival began on the eve of the first day with a family meal of roast lamb (called the Paschal lamb), unleavened bread, and other especially prepared foods. Unleavened bread was eaten for the following seven days. As a boy, Jesus went with his parents to observe the Passover in Jerusalem. The Feast of Unleavened Bread may originally have been a separate celebration which was later combined with the Passover. *Exodus 12:1-20; II Chronicles 30:1-22; 35:1; Ezra 6:19-22; Matthew 26:1-2,*

17-19; Mark 14:12; Luke 22:7-8; John 11:55; 12:1; 13:1.

PASTOR. Meaning "shepherd." In the NT a leader in the early church whose work was closely connected with teaching. *Ephesians 4:11.*

PATMOS. A Greek island about ten miles long and six miles wide composed of rocky, volcanic hills, just off Miletus. The Romans banished political prisoners to small islands such as this. John "the Seer," who wrote the book of Revelation, was exiled on Patmos during a period when the Roman authorities were persecuting Christians. *Revelation 1:9.*

PATRIARCHS. Meaning "fathers." NT term referring to the ancestors of the Israelites. It refers most frequently to Abraham, Isaac, and Jacob. *Acts 2:29; 7:8; Romans 9:5; Hebrews 7:4.*

PAUL THE APOSTLE. A first-century Jew who was changed from a

THE CHURCH AT THE CLOSE OF PAUL'S MINISTRY

persecutor of Christians into the leading missionary of the early Christian church. He called himself an "apostle to the Gentiles" and was the founder of churches in Asia Minor and Greece. His letters to these churches form an important part of the NT. The book of Acts tells of Paul's life and missionary career. "Paul" is the Greek form of his Jewish name "Saul." He was born in Tarsus (in modern Turkey) and inherited Roman citizenship from his family. By trade he may have been a weaver of materials used in making tents, though some scholars think he was a leatherworker. It is not known what happened to Paul after his last journey and imprisonment in Rome. Tradition says that he was put to death by the Emperor Nero about A.D. 64. *Acts 8:1-3; 9:1-25; 13:9-50; 16:9-39; and other places in Acts; Romans 1:1; I Corinthians 1:1; Galatians 1:1.*

PEACOCK. The pomp and glitter of King Solomon's court was greatly enhanced by the gorgeous peacocks brought from India and the tropics by the navy of Hiram, king of Tyre (I Kings 10:22; II Chronicles 9:21). They then spread to other countries in the Mediterranean areas.

The peacock, the male peafowl, with its gleaming colored breast and outspread tail of dazzling colors, has been called the most beautiful bird in the world. It became a symbol of immortality to the early Christians, probably because of the legendary belief that peacock flesh does not decay.

PEKAH. King of the northern kingdom of Israel about 740–732 B.C. He succeeded to the throne by murdering King Pekahiah with the assistance of Rezin, king of Syria. Later Tiglath-pileser, the Assyrian emperor, attacked Syria and Israel, put to death both Rezin and Pekah, and deported the people to other parts of the Assyrian Empire. *II Kings 15:25-37; 16:5; Isaiah 7:1.*

PEKAHIAH. King of the northern kingdom of Israel about 742–740 B.C.; son and successor of Menahem. Pekahiah continued his father's policy of paying tribute to Tiglath-pileser, emperor of Assyria. He was murdered by Pekah with the backing of Rezin, king of Syria. *II Kings 15:23-26.*

PELICAN. The pelican is one of the most curious-looking of birds. The long, flattened beak with a large pouch under the lower mandible, its small head, short legs, and massive body give it a somewhat ludicrous appearance as it awkwardly waddles along on land. But in the air it glides with grace on a wingspan of up to eight feet. Suddenly it dives straight down, landing with a splash and spearing the fish it has sighted.

The pelican's method of feeding its young is peculiar. The mother opens its beak wide and the young pluck food from the mother's crop. This strange procedure led the ancients to believe that the pelican fed its young with its own blood. Thus the pelican became the symbol of mercy in ancient art, perhaps emphasized by the words of the psalmist seeking God's mercy: "I am like a pelican in the wilderness" (Psalm 122:6).

PENNY. A Roman coin of NT times, probably equal to about one fourth of a cent. *Matthew 5:26; 10:29; Mark 12:42; Luke 12:6.*

PENTECOST. Meaning "fiftieth." It was the Greek term for the Jewish Feast of Weeks held fifty days after the Passover. It marked the beginning of the offering of the first fruits of the harvest and came during late May or early June. It was on the day of Pentecost that the Holy Spirit came upon Jesus, disciples gathered together in Jerusalem after he had ascended into heaven. Christians celebrate Pentecost as the birthday of the Christian church. *Acts 2:1; 20:16; I Corinthians 16:8.*

PEOPLE OF GOD. One of the many OT expressions that refer to the special covenant relationship existing between God and the people of Israel. The NT meaning identifies "people of God" with the church grounded upon faith in Jesus Christ. *II Samuel 14:13; Psalm 47:9; Hebrews 4:9; 11:25; I Peter 2:9-10; Revelation 21:3.*

PEOR. Name of a mountain in Moab and of a god worshiped by the Moabite people. *Numbers 23:28; 25:18; 31:16; Joshua 22:17.*

PERDITION. In the Bible a word which refers to death and destruction. *II Samuel 22:5; Psalm 18:4; John 17:12; Revelation 17:8, 11.*

PERFUME. In Bible times sweet-smelling substances used in cosmetics, in preparing the dead for burial, in scenting furniture and clothing, and in incense for worship. *Exodus 30:25; II Chronicles 16:14; Proverbs 27:9; Isaiah 3:20-24.*

PERIZZITE. One of the tribes living in Palestine when the Israelites came. They are named in lists of the population but no information about them is given. *Genesis 13:7; 15:20; 34:30; Deuteronomy 7:1; Joshua 3:10; 17:15; 24:11; Judges 1:4-5; I Kings 9:20; II Chronicles 8:7.*

PERSECUTION. Suffering inflicted upon people because of their beliefs, especially religious beliefs, or because of their race. *Matthew 5:10-12; 13:21; Mark 10:30; Acts 8:1; II Corinthians 12:10; II Timothy 3:11.*

PERSIA. The land now called Iran that lies roughly between the Caspian Sea on the north and the Persian Gulf on the south. After the Persians' defeat of the Babylonians in the sixth century B.C., the great Persian Empire was established from India to Greece, and King Cyrus proclaimed himself "king of the world." His policy of tolerance toward the exiled Jews in Babylon permitted them to go back to Jerusalem and rebuild the walls of the city. Kings of Persia mentioned in the Bible are Cyrus, Darius, and Artaxerxes. (See also *Cyrus.*) *II Chronicles 36:20, 22-23; Ezra 1:1-2, 8; 3:7; 4:3, 5, 7; 6:14; 7:1; Nehemiah 12:22; Daniel 5:25-28; 6:8.*

PESTILENCE. Infectious diseases usually associated with a military siege and probably brought on by a contaminated water supply. In Bible times such disasters were seen as divine punishment. *Exodus 5:3; Leviticus 26:25; Numbers 14:12; Deuteronomy 28:21;*

PETER

Jeremiah 14:12; 27:13; 42:17; 44:13; Luke 21:11.

PETER. Also called Simon, Simon Peter, and Cephas. The most outstanding of Jesus' twelve apostles. His natural leadership qualities made him the spokesman for the Twelve. To Peter, Jesus gave the responsibility of leading the disciples after the resurrection. Peter was a witness to the resurrection and became a strong leader of the early church. *Matthew 4:18-20; 10:2; 14:28-29; 16:16-18; Mark 1:29-30; 14:54, 66-72; Luke 18:28; John 1:41-42; 18:10; Acts 2:14, 37-38; 3:1-12; I Corinthians 9:5; Galatians 2:7-9; II Peter 1:1.*

PETER, FIRST LETTER OF. A book of the NT written by or in the name of Peter the apostle. The letter was probably written for Gentile Christians who were being persecuted in Asia Minor. The letter declares the greatness of the Christian faith and gives instruction for sharing in the suffering of Christ. The letter may have been written about A.D. 70, perhaps during the persecution of the church by the Roman emperor Nero.

PETER, SECOND LETTER OF. The author of this NT book took the name of the apostle Peter to emphasize the importance of his letter. The letter was probably written in the second century A.D. to settle the doubts and false teachings that were confusing the churches.

PHARAOH. A title given to the king of Egypt. It meant "the Great House" and referred to the palace until about 1500 B.C., when it became a title for the person who lived in the royal palace. The pharaoh was considered by the Egyptians to be a god. The land and the people of Egypt belonged to him. The pharaohs in the time of Joseph and of the Exodus cannot be identified with certainty. *Genesis 41:42; Exodus 2:5; 7:10; 12:29-30; I Kings 3:1; 23:29; II Chronicles 12:2-9; Nehemiah 9:10; Psalms 135:9; 136:15; Jeremiah 44:30; Acts 7:13, 21; Romans 9:17.*

PHARAOH'S HEN. This is a small vulture, common in Egypt as the name would imply. But it is also abundant on the plains of Sharon and the hills to the south, especially in the Kedron valley. It is white with black wings. Its large nest is built of sticks, rubbish, and even old rags. It wanders about the village streets eating garbage and refuse that other vultures will not touch.

PHARISEES. A powerful religious party among the Jews in NT times. These men were not priests but laymen who were trained in the law. Their belief in the resurrection after death and their strict way of following the law made them different from the Sadducees, another religious party (see *Sadducees*). The Pharisees expected the royal line of David to be restored and with it the political power of Jerusalem and Israel. The Pharisees opposed Jesus because he did not insist on keeping the law as strictly as they did, and because he did not keep away from sinners. Paul, who became an apostle after the resurrection, was a member of the Pharisees. After he became a Christian, he saw that the law of love as taught by Jesus was more

important than the strict law of the Pharisees. This party continued to oppose Christians and the early church throughout NT times. *Matthew 9:11-13; 12:2-8; 22:15-22; Mark 2:16-17; Luke 11:37-44, 53; John 11:46-48, 57; 18:3-6; Acts 15:5; 23:6-9.*

PHILEMON, LETTER TO. The

eighteenth book of the NT. It was a short letter written by Paul to Philemon, a Colossian Christian, about Philemon's runaway slave, Onesimus. The letter was probably written from Rome about A.D. 62. (See *Onesimus*.)

PHILIP. 1. Philip the apostle came from Bethsaida, which was also the home of Andrew and Peter. It was Philip who brought Nathanael to Jesus. Philip is a Greek name, and this, together with the fact that some Greeks who came looking for Jesus approached him for help, suggests that he probably spoke that language. *Matthew 10:3; Mark 3:18; Luke 6:14; John 1:43-48; 6:5-7; 12:20-22; 14:8-9.*

2. Philip the evangelist. He was one of the Greek-speaking Christians who was given special duties to assist the apostles in the early church in Jerusalem. Following the martyrdom of Stephen, Philip fled to Samaria, where he preached the gospel. *Acts 6:5; 8:4-13; 21:8-9.*

PHILIPPIANS, LETTER TO THE. The eleventh book in the NT; a

letter written by Paul to the church he had started in Philippi. This was his first Christian church in Europe, and his letter shows his loving personal concern for the members. He gave them encouragement and counsel. The letter was probably written when Paul was a prisoner in Rome about A.D. 60–63.

PHILISTINES. The people who occupied Philistia on the southwestern coast of Palestine. Their name came from an Egyptian word meaning "people of the sea." They may originally have come from the island of Crete. Their chief cities were Gath, Gaza, Ashkelon, Ashdod, and Ekron. The Philistines were often at war with the Israelites. They had large armies well equipped with chariots and weapons of iron. *Exodus 15:14; 23:31; Judges 3:3; 14:1-4; 16:23; II Samuel 21:15-19; Psalm 60:8; Isaiah 2:6; Jeremiah 25:20; 47:4.*

PHOENICIA. A long, narrow country on the east coast of the Mediterranean Sea, north of Palestine (modern Lebanon). The irregular coastline provided good harbors, and the people became colonizers and traders and operated ships in the Mediterranean. The cities of Tyre and Sidon were centers of industry and trade (see Ezekiel 27:1-36). The history of Phoenicia goes back very far, and from ancient times Phoenicia was famous for its purple dye. Probably the term *Canaanites* in the OT included the people of Phoenicia, since the word *Canaan* means "the land of the purple." Their worship of Baal influenced the religion of the Israelites when they settled in Canaan. Jesus crossed over to Tyre and Sidon in his ministry (see Matthew 15:21; Mark 7:24). Some of the early Christians settled in Phoenicia to escape persecution. *Obadiah 1:20; Acts 11:19; 15:3; 21:2.*

PHOENIX. Ancient legend gave the phoenix to Christianity as a symbol of the resurrection. It was a mythical bird, said to be very beautiful, quite large, and living five hundred years or more. Then it set its nest on fire and was consumed in the flames, only to rise from the ashes to begin a new life cycle. Some scholars believe that Job was referring to this fantastic creature in the word translated "sand" in Job 29:18. The phoenix is not among the birds mentioned by Job, nor is it mentioned elsewhere in the Bible.

PHRYGIA. In NT times a large area of Asia Minor in what is now Turkey. The Roman authorities divided the area into two parts to be governed by the provinces of Galatia and Asia. Many Jews lived in Phrygia. Paul frequently visited the Phrygian cities of Antioch and Iconium, and Christianity, although persecuted, became strong in Phrygia. *Acts 2:10; 16:6; 18:23.*

PHYLACTERIES. Small leather boxes that were worn bound to the foreheads and arms of the Jewish men at daily prayer. They contained verses from the OT. The head phylactery had four small compartments which contained copies of Exodus 13:1-16 and Deuteronomy 6:4-9; 11:13-21. The hand or arm phylacteries had one compartment. The Greek word for phylactery meant "safeguard," "means of protection." *Matthew 23:5.*

PIGEON. The rock dove of Eurasia is closely related to the turtle dove, but it is a different branch of the family. It has been bred for 5,000 years and the breeding of pigeons is a popular hobby today. The ability of the homing pigeon to find its way back to its loft from a great distance is one of nature's so far unfathomed mysteries. (See *Dove.*)

PILATE, PONTIUS. The Roman governor of Judea A.D. 26–36, and therefore judge in the trial and execution of Jesus. *Matthew 27:2, 11-26, 58-65; Mark 15:1-15; Luke 3:1; 13:1; 23:13-16; John 19:19; Acts 3:13; 4:27; 13:28; I Timothy 6:13.*

PILLAR. In the Bible rough, uncut stone with a rounded top set up as a monument to commemorate an important event or as an object of worship; also, a support column for a roof. *Genesis 28:18; Exodus 23:24; II Samuel 18:18; II Kings 17:10; II Chronicles 14:3; Hosea 3:4; 10:1-2; Micah 5:13.*

PLANE TREE. Tall, stately tree with smooth bark; wide-spreading branches; glossy, vine-like leaves; and spiky, round seedpods. Jacob used branches of this tree in his plot to deceive his uncle Laban. *Genesis 30:37-43; Ezekiel 31:8.*

PLEIADES. A cluster of seven stars. Because of its brilliance it is mentioned in the literature of many peoples throughout the world. *Job 9:9; 38:31; Amos 5:8.*

PLOW, PLOWSHARE. An implement for breaking up the ground. In Bible times the plowshare was a forked stick with a pointed metal tip. It did not dig deep but served only to scratch the ground. Plows with

shafts attached were drawn by oxen. *I Samuel 13:20-21; I Kings 19:19; Proverbs 20:4; Isaiah 2:4; Luke 9:62.*

POMEGRANATE. Growing wild in some sections of the Middle East, the pomegranate is a small tree with reddish bark, shiny green leaves and waxlike blossoms with crinkled, coral-red petals. The ripe fruit is about the size of an orange, maroon, with thick skin and many seeds. The juicy pulp is very palatable.

The popularity of the pomegranate is indicated in the fact that they were used as figures in the decoration of Solomon's Temple (I Kings 7:18, 20). Pomegranate designs were braided into the hem of the ephod of the high priest (Exodus 28:33, 34).

PONTUS. In NT times an area in northern Asia Minor (now in Turkey) that bordered on the Black Sea (then called Euxine Sea). Under Roman rule Pontus became part of the new province of Bithynia and was known as Bithynia and Pontus. Jews from Pontus were in Jerusalem on the day of Pentecost when the Holy Spirit came upon the disciples. *Acts 2:9; 18:2; I Peter 1:1.*

POPPY. The poppy of the orient, the source of opium, was common in the Holy Land long before the Israelites settled there. The "gall" added to the vinegar and offered to Jesus (Matthew 27:34) was the juice of the opium poppy. This gesture may have been intended as an act of mercy since gall is a powerful sleep-inducing narcotic. The rather fragile lavender or white blossoms with a spot of purple at the base belie the sinister nature of the seedpod from which the opium is extracted.

PORCUPINE. This comparatively small insect-eating animal was as familiar to the people of the Bible days as it is today. It was often found in ruins and in deserted habitations. Curled up into a protective ball, its spines were ample protection against roving dogs or inquisitive people. The porcupine does not "throw" its spines, a mistaken notion held by many people. But they are easily pulled out and their barbed ends make removal a painful process. An example of the ambiguity of some of the words in the original Hebrew is evident in Isaiah 14:23 in the word translated "bittern," a kind of bird. Most scholars now believe the word should be translated "porcupine."

POTIPHAR. The Egyptian officer who bought Joseph when he was sold into slavery. Later he had Joseph put into prison. *Genesis 37:36; 39:1.*

POTSHERD. A piece of broken pottery. Potsherds were sometimes used for writing brief notes as we might use a scrap of paper. Potsherd was also a symbol of dryness and utter worthlessness. *Job 2:8; 41:30; Psalm 22:15; Jeremiah 19:2.*

POTTAGE. A thick vegetable soup made with lentils and herbs. Sometimes meat was added. *Genesis 25:29-30, 34; II Kings 4:38-41; Haggai 2:12.*

POTTER. A man who made vessels and dishes from clay. He often used a wheel for shaping the clay into bowls,

jars, lamps and plates. The Hebrews learned to make pottery in Canaan. *I Chronicles 4:23; Isaiah 41:25; Jeremiah 18:1-6; Romans 9:21.*

POUND. In NT times a weight of about twelve ounces; also, a unit of money. *Luke 19:11-27; John 12:3; 19:39.*

PRAETORIUM. In the NT the official residence or palace of a Roman governor. Possibly it was also the barracks and judgment hall. Pilate's temporary residence in Jerusalem during the trial of Jesus may have been Herod's praetorium. The term *praetorian guard* refers to the bodyguard of the Roman emperor. *Matthew 27:27; Mark 15:16; John 18:28, 33; 19:9; Acts 23:35.*

PRAYER. Any attempt to communicate with God. Prayer may be spoken or silent. It may include praise, confession, thanksgiving, repentance, and meditation in behalf of oneself or of another person. The word appears frequently in both OT and NT. Prayer has been at the center of the worship of God from the earliest times. *II Chronicles 7:15; Psalms 65:2; 84:8; 102:1; Proverbs 15:8; Lamentations 3:8; Matthew 6:5-13; 21:22; Mark 12:40; Luke 2:37; Acts 3:1; Philippians 4:6; James 5:15-16; I Peter 4:7.*

PRIESTS AND LEVITES. Those who stand before God as his servants. Under the covenant of Moses the whole nation of Israel was to be a "kingdom" of priests. They were to be a holy people fit to serve God. Their holiness proved to be very imperfect in actual practice. However, the idea of holiness was symbolized in the official priesthood. Among the Israelites the priesthood developed into three divisions—high priest, priest, and Levite, each having its own distinctive functions and privileges. The high priest represented all the people of Israel before God in the sanctuary. He alone could enter the holy of holies once a year to make atonement for the nation's sin. The priests took care of the sanctuary, taught the law, and took part in the sacrifices. The Levites assisted the priests and were responsible for the care of the temple, cleaning the sacred vessels, preparing the cereal offerings, and carrying out the service of praise. They represented the people of Israel as substitutes for the firstborn sons who belonged, by right, to God. In the OT the priesthood began with Moses. He consecrated his brother Aaron and Aaron's sons to be priests. These men were of the tribe of Levi, the traditional priestly tribe. *Exodus 19:6; 28:1; 40-43; I Samuel 1:9; 5:5; I Chronicles 15:14; II Chronicles 34:14; Ezra 3:2; Nehemiah 3:1; Luke 1:5; Acts 4:1, 6; Hebrews 7:23-24; I Peter 2:9.*

PRINCE. A ruler. In the Bible the word was used for a king, military officer, leader, chief of a tribe or of the temple, or any man of noble birth, one worthy of honor. *I Samuel 2:8; 9:15-16; 13:14; II Kings 20:5; Nehemiah 9:32; Isaiah 9:6; Jeremiah 1:18; Hosea 3:4.*

PROCONSUL. In the Roman Empire the administrator of a province. The proconsul usually held office for one year under the authority of the Senate in Rome. *Acts 13:7-8, 12; 18:12-13; 19:38.*

PROFANE. To treat a holy person, place, or institution as if it were not holy; to make unclean or defile a holy name. The Hebrews took great care never to speak the name of God for a foolish or useless purpose. To use it so was to profane or defile his name. *Exodus 20:25; Leviticus 19:12; 21:6; 22:2; Jeremiah 19:4; Malachi 1:12; Matthew 12:5; Acts 24:6; I Corinthians 11:27.*

PROPHET. In the Bible a spokesperson for God. One who was inspired to speak God's message of his purpose and judgment to the people. The prophets saw God at work in all things, even the misfortunes of Israel, and used specific events to proclaim God's will and purpose. Prophecies were often in poetry, parables, stories, or pantomime, which was acting out the prophecy. *Deuteronomy 18:15-18; I Samuel 3:20; 9:9; I Kings 18:1-40; II Kings 19:2-7; Isaiah 37:2; Jeremiah 18:18.*

PROSELYTE. In the NT a person who was converted to the Jewish religion, accepting all its customs and requirements. *Matthew 23:15; Acts 2:10; 6:5.*

PROVERBS, BOOK OF. The twentieth book of the OT. It belongs to the Hebrew writings called Wisdom Literature. The book is made up of brief, wise sayings that give advice on how to live a good and happy life. These sayings were probably collected and some written during the fifth and fourth centuries B.C. King Solomon may have composed some of the proverbs.

PROVINCE. A division of an empire ruled by an appointed official. Judah, for instance, was a province of the Babylonian and Persian Empires after the fall of Jerusalem. Under the Romans in NT times the province was called Judea. All the territory of Asia Minor, Syria, Palestine, Egypt, and other countries, was divided into provinces by the Roman government. *Ezra 4:10; Esther 3:12-14; Acts 23:24; 25:1.*

PRUNING HOOK. In the OT a curved blade attached to a handle and used for removing surplus twigs and trimming vines. *Isaiah 2:4; 18:5; Joel 3:10; Micah 4:3.*

PSALMS. The nineteenth book of the OT. It is a collection of poems, prayers, and hymns for use in public and private worship. These 150 psalms were collected over a long period of time and divided into five sections by the end of the third century B.C. The psalms speak of all the experiences of life. They tell of joy and sorrow, sin and suffering, evil and righteousness. The meanings of the titles are not clear to us today. They may contain directions for the musical performance of these pieces. Jesus often quoted from the psalms.

PURIFICATION. The act of cleansing by washing or by offering a sacrifice after contact with something unclean under Jewish law. *Nehemiah 12:45; Luke 2:22-24; John 2:6; Acts 21:26.*

PURIM. A two-day Jewish festival celebrating the deliverance of the Jews in Persia from Haman's plot to kill them. The story is told in the book of Esther. *Esther 9:23-32.*

PURPLE. A color associated with royalty and wealth. It was the most valuable of ancient dyes and was obtained from a secretion of mollusks found in the Mediterranean Sea. Both Crete and Phoenicia have been associated with the discovery of purple dye. (See *Phoenicia.*) *Exodus 25:4; Lamentations 4:5; Ezekiel 27:7; Luke 16:19; John 19:2, 5; Acts 16:14.*

QUAIL. The quail mentioned in the Bible (Exodus 16:11-13; Numbers 11:31, 32; Psalm 105:40) is not much larger than a robin. Its feathers are brown and black except for those on the belly which are white. Small as it is, the quail is still hunted for food as it was long before the Hebrew immigration to the Holy Land. The deluge of quail mentioned in Numbers 11, "two cubits high on the face of the earth"—no doubt is an exaggeration. But during the fall migration great numbers of them cloud the sky. Unlike other birds, the quail do not migrate en masse. Instead, the migration may be spread over a month or two. Not a particularly good flyer, it covers the migratory route in short distances, often settling on the ground overnight. Often they are so exhausted that they can be caught with bare hands. Nets are sometimes used to capture them.

QUEEN OF HEAVEN. A foreign goddess, an object of worship, particularly for women, in Judah in the time of Jeremiah. It may possibly refer to the goddess Ishtar, who was identified with the Venus star. Jeremiah condemned the Jewish refugees in Egypt for burning incense to the Queen of Heaven. *Jeremiah 7:18; 44:17-19, 25.*

QUIRINIUS. The Roman governor of Syria in NT times. He was appointed by the emperor in A.D. 6. *Luke 2:2.*

QUIVER. A container for carrying arrows. It was usually made of leather, decorated with metal or paint, and carried hung over the shoulder. *Genesis 27:3; Job 39:23; Isaiah 22:6; 49:2; Jeremiah 5:16; Lamentations 3:13.*

RAAMSES. See *Rameses (city).*

RABBAH. Ancient capital city of the Ammonite kingdom, located about twenty-three miles east of the Jordan River. Today it is called Amman and is the capital of the modern country Jordan. Og, the giant king of Bashan, was said to have had his big iron bedstead in Rabbah. David captured Rabbah and organized the Ammonite people into a labor force to work for him. *Deuteronomy 3:11; Joshua 13:25; II Samuel 11:1; 12:27, 29; 17:27; I Chronicles 20:1; Jeremiah 49:2-3; Ezekiel 21:20; 25:5; Amos 1:14.*

RABBI, RABBONI. Hebrew words meaning "master." In the NT either term was a title of respect for a teacher. In modern Judaism a rabbi is ordained, and his office is similar to that of a minister. *Matthew 23:7-8; John*

1:38, 49; 3:2, 26; 4:31; 6:25; 9:2; 11:8; 20:16.

RACHEL. Younger daughter of Laban, second wife of Jacob, and the mother of Joseph and Benjamin. Jacob worked for Laban seven years as a marriage payment for Rachel. At the end of the time Laban tricked Jacob by giving him Leah, the older daughter. Jacob worked seven more years to get Rachel. *Genesis 29:15–30:34; 33:1-2; 35:16-20; Ruth 4:11; I Samuel 10:2; Jeremiah 31:15; Matthew 2:18.*

RAHAB. 1. A woman living in Jericho at the time of the Israelite invasion of Canaan. She hid Joshua's spies in stalks of flax on the roof of her house and allowed them to escape. Joshua spared her life when he took Jericho. *Joshua 2:1-21; 6:17, 23-25; Hebrews 11:31; James 2:25.*

2. The name of a mythical beast representing disorder and chaos. *Job 9:13; 26:12; Psalm 89:10; Isaiah 30:7; 51:9.*

RAINBOW. Called "bow" in the OT. A rainbow is the reflection and refraction of sunlight caused by a curtain of falling rain. It is often seen against a backdrop of retreating clouds and indicates that the storm is over. It is mentioned in the Bible as a sign of God's promise that a flood should never again destroy the world. *Genesis 9:13; Lamentations 2:4; Ezekiel 1:28; Habakkuk 3:9-11; Revelation 10:1.*

RAISIN-CAKES. In Bible times a common food prepared by pressing dried grapes. Because it did not spoil, it was suitable for travelers and for military provisions. *II Samuel 6:19; Isaiah 16:7; Hosea 3:1.*

RAM. A young ram was often used as a sacrificial animal especially at the Feast of the Passover. Very likely it was of the broadtail species of sheep. The horns of the ram were used as trumpets in battle. We read (Joshua 6:4, 5) that "seven priests bearing trumpets of rams' horns" marched around the walls of Jericho, its walls crumbling on the seventh day after a "long blast." Rams' horns were used to hold liquids, such as oil for anointing (I Samuel 16:1).

RAMAH. Also called Ramathaim-zophim, this was a town in the hill country of Ephraim northwest of Jerusalem. It was the home of Samuel and one of the places where he administered justice to Israel. It was to Ramah that the elders of Israel came to ask Samuel for a king. Several other towns with this name are mentioned in the OT. Ramoth-gilead is also called Ramah. (See *Ramoth-gilead.*) *I Samuel 1:19; 2:11; 7:17; 8:4; 15:34; 28:3.*

RAMESES (City). The name of one of the Egyptian store-cities built by the Israelites when they were slaves in Egypt. It is also spelled *Raamses.* Ramses II (1290–1224 B.C.) founded and named the city. It is located in the Egyptian Delta. This was the starting point from which the Israelites began the Exodus. *Exodus 1:11; 12:37; Numbers 33:3-6.*

RAMOTH-GILEAD. An important fortress in Gilead, located in the eastern part of the territory of Gad. It

was a city of refuge. It is often called Ramah. (See *Cities of Refuge.*) *Deuteronomy 4:43; Joshua 21:38; I Kings 4:13; II Kings 8:28; 9:1, 4, 14.*

RAMPART. Outer fortification encircling a city consisting of a broad, sloping embankment usually made of earth. *II Samuel 20:15; Psalm 48:13; Lamentations 2:8; Nahum 3:8; Zechariah 9:3.*

RAT. No doubt the rat was as common, and as abhorred, in biblical times as it is today. The word *rat* does not appear in the Bible, but the word *akbar* included all rodents, rats among them. The unsanitary conditions of the times must have made its obnoxious presence inevitable. The sand rat, native to Egypt and eaten by the Arabs, is the vole.

RAVEN. A large, crow-like bird mentioned in both the OT and NT. It is purplish black and travels in flocks. The raven is a scavenger, eating dead flesh and also attacking small, helpless animals. For this reason it was unclean to the Hebrews and was not to be used for food. *Genesis 8:7; Leviticus 11:15; I Kings 17:4-6; Job 38:41; Psalm 147:9; Proverbs 30:17; Song of Solomon 5:11; Isaiah 34:11; Zephaniah 2:14; Luke 12:24.*

REAP. To harvest grain. In OT times the worker grasped a few stalks and cut them off halfway up the stalk. He used a small sickle made with a head of flint set in a wooden or bone handle. Later the worker probably used a small, curved blade like the sickle of today. *Leviticus 19:9; 23:10, 22; 25:2; I Samuel 8:12; Matthew 6:26; Romans 1:13.*

REBEKAH (NT, REBECCA). Wife of Isaac and mother of Jacob and Esau. Rebekah plotted with Jacob to cheat Esau out of the blessing Isaac intended for him. *Genesis 24:15-67; 25:20-28; 26:7; 27:5-17, 42-46; 29:12; 49:31; Romans 9:10-12.*

RECONCILE, RECONCILIATION. To bring agreement; agreement and harmony between persons who have had a quarrel or a misunderstanding. In the Bible it refers to the restoration of harmony and love between people and God. The NT emphasizes that God in his divine love has brought about a new harmony through the life and death of Jesus Christ. (See *Atonement.*) *I Samuel 29:4; Matthew 5:24; Romans 5:10-11; II Corinthians 5:18-20.*

RECORDER. An official in the royal court of Israel. He advised the king and probably was in charge of keeping the historical records. *II Samuel 8:16; II Kings 18:18, 37; II Chronicles 34:8.*

RED SEA. The arm of the sea which separates Egypt from Arabia. In ancient times the Red Sea included the Indian Ocean, the Persian Gulf, the Gulf of Suez, and the Gulf of Aqabah. The words *sea* and *lake* had the same meaning for the Israelites. The "Red Sea" which the Israelites crossed when fleeing the Egyptians may have been a marshy area or a small lake north of the Gulf of Suez, called the Sea of Reeds. *Exodus 10:19; 15:22; I Kings 9:26; Psalm 136:13-15; Acts 7:36; Hebrews 11:29.*

REDEEM, REDEEMER, REDEMPTION.

Redeem means to reclaim, to get back, or to buy back. *Redeemer* is the person who performs these acts. *Redemption* is the act of reclaiming or liberating or getting back. In OT times firstborn children were considered to belong to God, and a provision was made in Hebrew law to "redeem" them by payment of a fixed sum. It was family law for the nearest relative to buy back, or redeem, a person who had been sold into slavery or to reclaim, buy back, a piece of property lost because of debts. The word *redeem* was used also in reference to God's delivering the Israelites from their slavery in Egypt. "Redeemer" was one of the prophet Isaiah's favorite names for God. In the NT the word *redemption* always implies deliverance or liberation from the power of sin and its effects. Jesus's death was a redemptive act, a deliverance for God's people. *Genesis 48:16; Exodus 6:6; 34:20; Leviticus 25:25, 48-49; Numbers 3:48-49; 18:15-16; Ruth 4:6; Job 19:25; Psalms 19:14; 25:22; 26:11; 107:2-3; 130:7-8; Isaiah 43:1, 14; Jeremiah 32:7-8; Luke 24:21; Galatians 3:13; Ephesians 1:7.*

REED.

The flowering stalk of any of several tall grasses that grow in marshy places. Reeds are sometimes called rushes. The reed had many uses. Measuring rods, pens, baskets, mats, and other things were made of reed. *Genesis:41:2; I Kings 14:15; II Kings 18:21; Job 40:21; Isaiah 42:3; Ezekiel 29:6; 40:5-7; Matthew 11:7; 12:20; 27:29-30; Mark 15:19, 36; Luke 7:24.*

REFINE, REFINING.

To strain or filter out impurities or dross from metals by melting them in large earthenware containers in a hot furnace; the act of purifying. Archaeologists have found Solomon's copper and iron ore furnaces at Ezion-geber. In the Bible "refine" is sometimes used as a figure of speech to describe the way God cleanses or purifies his people. *I Chronicles 28:18; 29:4; Job 28:1; Psalm 12:6; Isaiah 48:10; Jeremiah 9:7; Zechariah 13:9; Malachi 3:3.*

REFUGE.

A place of escape, a stronghold. The word is used to describe God's protection. (See also *Cities of Refuge.*) *Ruth 2:12; Psalms 5:11; 16:1; 36:7; Proverbs 30:5; Jeremiah 16:19; Nahum 1:7.*

REGENERATION.

The act of reforming completely, being made new spiritually. In the NT it is the process by which one changes the direction of his life. The idea is implied in many of Jesus' sayings, but the word occurs only one time. It indicates a complete break with an old way of life and acceptance of Jesus' way. Paul speaks of being a new person in Christ. *Titus 3:5.*

REHOBOAM.

King of Judah from about 931 to 913 B.C., a son and successor of Solomon. Rehoboam was the first king of the southern kingdom after the united kingdom was divided. *I Kings 11:43–12:27; 14:21-31; Matthew 1:7.*

RELIGION.

Found in the NT only, this word refers to service and worship of God through an approved system of beliefs, practices, and patterns

of behavior. *Acts 26:5; I Timothy 2:10; James 1:26-27.*

REMNANT. In the Bible that part of a community which is left after a calamity and which is responsible for the future of the community. The word is used specifically to refer to those Jews who returned to Jerusalem after the Exile. In more general use the word may refer to the small number of people who remained faithful to God when the large number deserted. *Genesis 45:7; Ezra 9:8, 14-15; Isaiah 10:20-22; 11:11, 16; 28:5; 37:31-32; Amos 5:14-15; Micah 5:7-8; Haggai 1:12-14; Zechariah 8:6.*

REPENT, REPENTANCE. In biblical usage to turn away from sin and back to God; the act of doing this. It marks the beginning of a new religious or moral life. In the OT Israel as a nation owed obedience to God, fell under God's judgment when it disobeyed, and could come back into his favor only by turning away from sin. In the NT repentance and faith in God's love and mercy go together. In the early church repentance was considered basic to faith. *Job 42:6; Ezekiel 14:6; Matthew 3:8-11; Luke 3:3; 5:32; 24:47; Acts 2:38; 5:31; 13:24, 19:4; 20:21; II Corinthians 7:10.*

REPHAIM, VALLEY OF. A broad valley or plain near Jerusalem named for the people who lived in Canaan before the Israelites came. They were thought to be a race of giants. The valley is described as being rich in grain. *Deuteronomy 2:11, 20-21; 3:11; Joshua 15:8; 18:16; II Samuel 5:18, 22; I Chronicles 11:15; 14:9; Isaiah 17:5.*

RESURRECTION, THE. In the NT the resurrection is the central fact of the Christian gospel. It is the reality that Jesus was alive after the crucifixion. This was the event that the apostles preached to the world to show that Jesus was the Christ, the son of God. Not only did the resurrection demonstrate Jesus' defeat of death, it also held out to all believers a lively hope for personal resurrection. (See *Eternal Life, Immortality.*) *Matthew 22:23-32; Luke 14:14; John 11:23-27; Acts 1:22; 2:24, 4:2; 24:15; Romans 1:4; 6:5; I Corinthians 15:12-22; I Peter 1:3.*

RESURRECTION PLANT. This plant is sometimes called the rose of Jericho. When withered it closes into a ball, apparently lifeless and blown over the sands "like a rolling thing before the whirlwind" (Isaiah 17:13). Finding moisture, it sends out roots, unrolls and grows again. It is easy to see why early Christians saw it as a symbol of immortality and considered it sacred.

REUBEN. First of the twelve sons of Jacob and the ancestor of the tribe of Reuben. *Genesis 29:32; 37:22-30; 46:8-9; Exodus 6:14.*

REUBENITES. The descendants of Reuben who lived in the land east of the Jordan River. *Joshua 1:12; 12:6; 13:15-23; I Chronicles 5:6, 18.*

REVELATION. Making known the nature and will of God. In the Bible, God is represented as making himself known to people by his actions in history and especially in Jesus Christ. The Bible is a record of this revelation and also one of the ways in which God becomes known

THE
SEVEN CHURCHES of ASIA

0   50   100   150
Miles

PERGAMUM
THYATIRA
SARDIS
SMYRNA   PHILADELPHIA
EPHESUS
LAODICEA
PATMOS

Aegean Sea

PROVINCE

OF

ASIA

Mediterranean Sea

to people. *II Samuel 7:27; Luke 2:32; Romans 16:25; I Corinthians 14:26; Galatians 1:12; Ephesians 1:17; 3:3; I Peter 1:13; Revelation 1:1.*

REVELATION, BOOK OF. The last book in the NT, written probably toward the end of the first century A.D. It was written by an early Christian church leader named John, who was concerned for seven churches in Asia Minor that were probably under his care. It was a time of persecution, and John himself was imprisoned on the Isle of Patmos in the Mediterranean Sea just off Miletus. John wrote his letter in dramatic form using symbols and visions to reassure his readers of God's purpose in history, his saving power, and his final victory over evil.

REZIN. A king of Damascus in the eighth century B.C. With King Pekah of Israel he attacked Judah. (See *Pekah*.) *II Kings 15:37; 16:5-9; Isaiah 7:1, 8.*

RHODES. A Greek island and city in the southeastern part of the Aegean Sea. Paul's ship stopped there on his last journey to Jerusalem. *Ezekiel 27:15; Acts 21:1.*

RIE. In the plague of hail that fell upon Egypt, "the wheat and the rie were not smitten for they were not grown up" (Exodus 9:32). A natural conclusion might be that *rye* was meant. But rie is correct. It is a grain closely resembling wheat, though growing much taller and able to grow and produce in very poor soil. Though the rie flour was much inferior to that of wheat, it was extensively used, the two often being mixed, along with barley (Isaiah 28:25).

RIGHTEOUSNESS. Godliness; being free from wrong or sin; doing what is right. Every person has many relationships with friends, parents, teachers, and others, and with God. Each relationship makes demands on the persons. When God or a person fulfills the demands made on him, then he is, according to the OT, righteous. In the NT righteousness has to do with a "right relationship" with God. God, through Christ, is considered the source of all righteousness. *Genesis 15:1-6; Psalm 118:19; Proverbs 10:2; Isaiah 26:10; Jeremiah 23:6; Matthew 3:15; 5:6; Romans 4:3; II Corinthians 6:4-7; Philippians 3:9; James 1:20; II Peter 2:21.*

ROD. A stick cut from the branch of a tree; a staff. Shepherds and travelers who journeyed by foot used staffs. Rods were also used as poles for carrying burdens and as measuring sticks. A shorter staff, knobbed at one end and often studded with nails or bits of flint, was used as a weapon by soldiers and shepherds. *Exodus 4:2-5, 20; Psalms 2:9; 23:4; 89:32; Proverbs 10:13; 13:24; I Corinthians 4:21; II Corinthians 11:25; Revelation 2:27; 11:1.*

ROMANS, LETTER TO THE. In the NT a letter written by Paul to the Christian church in Rome, probably between A.D. 54 and 57. In the letter Paul wrote a complete and clear account of his understanding of the gospel of Jesus Christ.

ROME, CITY OF. Capital of the world in NT times, located halfway down the west coast of Italy and ten miles up the Tiber River. From Rome there developed the mighty Roman Empire that included the whole Mediterranean world. Christianity came to Rome before A.D. 50. Paul visited the Christian church in Rome, and later he was imprisoned there. There is a strong tradition that Peter visited Rome and that he and Paul were martyred there. *Acts 2:10; 18:2; 19:21; 28:14-16; Romans 1:7, 15; II Timothy 1:17.*

ROOF. The covering of a building. In ancient Middle Eastern homes the roof was flat and covered with a smooth clay. An outside staircase led up to the roof where the family spent a good amount of time. *Joshua 2:6; I Samuel 9:25; II Kings 4:8-10; Mark 2:4.*

ROSE. Wild roses are not too common in Palestine. The thicket rose, a dainty pink-and-white variety, climbs over the rocks of the hill country, blooming in the spring. A tall climbing variety with white blossoms grows in Galilee. The Phoenician rose, a tall bush species with clusters of single white flowers, grows in the higher regions of the Holy Land. The "rose of

Sharon" (Song of Solomon 2:1) is probably a poetic expression.

RUE. One of the herbs which Jesus mentions in his denunciation of obeying the letter of the law only (Luke 11:42) was rue. It is a tall growing plant with clusters of yellow flowers with a knob of green. It was widely used as a disinfectant—its botanical Latin name means "strong smelling"—and also for medicinal purposes. Its strong, unusual taste apparently appealed to the ancients, who used it as a flavoring.

RULER OF SYNAGOGUE. In NT times the leader or president of a synagogue who took charge of the arrangements for the services. *Mark 5:22-42; Luke 13:10-17; Acts 13:14-15; 18:8.*

RUSH. There are many varieties of "rush" growing along the river banks and in the swampy areas of the Holy Land. Any one of these might be indicated in Bildard's query, "Can the rush grow without mire?" (Job 8:11). A common variety is the "bob rush," a grass-like plant growing over four feet high. The leaves are long and slender, cylindrical in shape. They are widely used to make mats and baskets.

RUTH. Meaning "friend, companion." In the OT a Moabite woman who married a Hebrew. At the death of her husband she chose to go with her mother-in-law Naomi instead of returning to her own people. She is mentioned in the genealogy of Jesus in Matthew 1:5. (See *Ruth, Book of.*)

RUTH, BOOK OF. The eighth book of the OT, probably written sometime between 450 and 250 B.C. It is a short story of human kindness and devotion. The story is a good example of the possibility of good will and respect for others no matter what their nationality or religion.

SABBATH. From a word meaning "to cease" or "to be at an end." The Ten Commandments provided that the last day of the seven-day week be a day of rest. From sundown on the eve of the sabbath until sundown on the sabbath all ordinary work and activities stopped. The Hebrew laws setting forth what things could and could not be done were very strict. For example, only very limited travel was permitted (see *Sabbath Day's Journey*). However, the sabbath was a day of joy for the privilege of worshiping God, and there was no fasting on the sabbath. During the times when the temple stood, the official beginning of the sabbath was announced by a trumpet blast. Then special services of worship with prayer and sacrifices were held. Changing the bread of the Presence was a part of the sabbath ritual. After the Exile, services came to be held in the synagogues also. Prayer and readings from the Pentateuch and the prophets were the main features of these services. After the final destruction of the third temple in A.D. 70 the synagogue sabbath services became the most important part of Jewish public worship. During his ministry Jesus took part in these synagogue services. He also gave a

new teaching: "It is lawful to do good on the sabbath." *Exodus 20:8-11; 34:21; 35:2-3; Leviticus 19:3; 25:2-7; 26:34-35; Nehemiah 10:31; Jeremiah 17:19-27; Ezekiel 20:12; 46:1-4; Matthew 12:1-14; Mark 1:21-23; John 19:31; Acts 13:27; 18:4.*

SABBATH DAY'S JOURNEY.
In NT times the distance that one was allowed to travel outside a city on the sabbath, probably about three-fifths of a mile. This interpretation of the OT law (see Exodus 16:29) had been made by the scribes. *Acts 1:12.*

SACKCLOTH. Coarse cloth made of goats' or camels' hair and used for bags. Sackcloth was worn as a sign of mourning, of national disaster, or of repentance. *Genesis 37:34; II Samuel 3:31; II Kings 19:1-2; Nehemiah 9:1; Esther 4:1-4; Psalm 69:11; Isaiah 15:3; 20:2; 37:1-2; 50:3; Jeremiah 4:8; Joel 1:13; Jonah 3:8; Matthew 11:21.*

SACRIFICES AND OFFERINGS.
In the OT something presented to God. A sacrifice involved the killing, burning and sometimes eating of an animal at the altar. An offering could be made of grain, ground flour, fruit, or vegetables. Such things were presented with symbolic gestures such as waving, lifting up, or burning. A sacrifice could be offered for various reasons—as a "gift" to God when asking for protection or for a favor, as an act of thanksgiving, as a tribute or act of devotion to God for his greatness, as a sign of one's repentance for sin, and also as payment of vows or promises made to God. Often the rite of sacrifice was carried out in such a way that it bound God and people together in a sacrificial meal. Part of the animal was offered to God, part eaten by the priests and part eaten by the worshiper. There were extra offerings on sabbaths, seasonal festivals, and holy days. Some of the prophets declared that the people placed too much emphasis on the ritual of the sacrifices and did not realize that the offering represented the worshiper himself. *Exodus 3:18; 40:29; Leviticus 2:1-2; 3:1-5; 7:11-15; 16:5-6, 11, 15-16; 22:21, 23; Numbers 15:3; 28:2-3; 31:50; Deuteronomy 12:5-6; Psalms 50:12-15; 23; 51:16-17; Isaiah 1:11-14; Jeremiah 17:26; Micah 6:6-9.*

SACRILEGE. The abuse or defiling of something sacred or holy. This might involve using holy things for one's own purposes or bringing pagan vessels and idols into the place kept apart for the worship of God. In the second century B.C. a Greek ruler over the Jews set up altars to Greek gods in the Jerusalem temple. *Matthew 24:15; Mark 13:14.*

SADDUCEES. In NT times a priestly religious party of the Jews. The high priest in the temple was chosen from among this group. Well educated and aristocratic, the Sadducees were in the majority in the high council in Jerusalem. The big difference between the Sadducees and the Pharisees, another religious party, was in their interpretation of the law. The Sadducees differed with the Pharisees over the question of the resurrection of the dead (see *Pharisees*). The Sadducees did not believe in

the resurrection of the dead, probably because it was not found in the law. Jesus told them they were wrong and that they did not understand the scriptures or the power of God. *Matthew 3:7; 16:1-12; 22:23; Mark 12:18-27; Luke 20:27-40; Acts 4:1-2; 5:17; 23:6-10.*

SAFFRON. The lavender-colored saffron resembles the crocus, thought larger, and it blooms in the fall. In biblical times, as today, the orange stigmas are the source of the saffron of commerce which is used as a condiment, as perfume, as a coloring ingredient, and in medicines.

SAINT. Meaning "holy" or "set apart" for God's use. In the OT the term is used to describe Israel as God's holy people. In the NT the term is used for members of the Christian church. They were considered the new people of God under the lordship of Jesus Christ. The word was particularly associated with the love Christians showed to one another. *II Chronicles 6:41; Psalms 16:3; 31:23; 37:28; 145:10; Proverbs 2:8; Daniel 7:18; Acts 9:13; 26:10; Romans 1:7; 16:15; I Corinthians 1:2; 6:1-2; Ephesians 2:19; I Timothy 5:10.*

SALAMIS. A principal city of Cyprus situated on the east coast. In the sixth century B.C. the city came under Greek rule. In NT times it was under Roman rule. Paul and Barnabas visited a Jewish colony there. According to tradition, Barnabas was martyred at Salamis. *Acts 13:5.*

SALOME. 1. A Galilean woman who was a follower of Jesus. She was probably the wife of Zebedee and the mother of James and John. She was present at the crucifixion and was one of the women who brought spices to anoint Jesus' body for burial. *Mark 15:40-41; 16:1.*

2. The daughter of Herodias who danced for King Herod Antipas and demanded the head of John the Baptist as her payment. Sources outside the Bible report that her name was Salome. *Matthew 14:6; Mark 6:22.*

SALT. A mineral mined in Bible times from the area around the Dead Sea, or evaporated from its waters. Salt was used as a seasoning and for preserving food and was sprinkled on sacrifices in the temple. It was eaten to seal a covenant or agreement, which bound two people together in loyalty to each other. In OT times it was custom for an army to sow the land they had conquered with salt to prevent any growth of crops. The term is often used in the Bible in figures of speech that reflect both the destructive and life-giving qualities of salt. *Leviticus 2:13; Numbers 18:19; Judges 9:45; Ezra 4:14; 6:9; Job 6:6; Jeremiah 17:6; Matthew 5:13; Mark 9:50; Colossians 4:6.*

SALT SEA. In very early biblical history a name for the lake later called the Dead Sea. It is fed by the Jordan River, but it has no outlet. This lake is over 1,200 feet below sea level and has the highest percentage of salt in any water in the world. Today it is a rich source of valuable minerals; however, there is no plant or animal life in the Dead Sea. Some excavation is at present going on in search for cities

The Bible Companion

that may be under its waters. (See *Sodom, Gomorrah.*) *Genesis 14:3; Numbers 34:3; Deuteronomy 3:17; Joshua 3:16.*

SALVATION, SAVIOR. Meaning the "saving," "redeeming," or "delivering" of something; the person who does this. Salvation is the central theme of the whole Bible. In the OT the history of the people of God, the Hebrews, is the story of their salvation by the acts of God from destruction and ruin. The high point and most important event in this salvation history is the deliverance of the people of Israel from Egypt and God's care for them through the wilderness journey. In the NT, Jesus—whose name means "savior"—is announced as the fulfillment of God's saving of his people. Through Jesus a new people, those who believe that he is the Christ, are saved from the power of sin and death, and a new saving history is begun in the church. *Exodus 14:13; II Samuel 22:3, 36, 47; Nehemiah 9:27; Psalms 27:1; 96:2; Isaiah 12:2-3; Luke 1:47-77; 2:11; John 4:42; Romans 1:16; Ephesians 1:13; Phillippians 2:12; I Timothy 4:10; Hebrews 1:14; II Peter 1:1.*

SALVIA. The "Jerusalem salvia," though of the same botanical family as our familiar red salvia, is quite different in appearance. It has the characteristic square stem of the family, but the blossom stems are spaced so that the individual flowers stand out, resembling tiny orchids, rather than the spike of solid bloom we know. It is thought by some to be the source of the design for the seven-branched candlestick common to the Jews.

SAMARIA. In OT times the capital of the northern kingdom Israel. The city was built by King Omri, and King Ahab continued to enlarge and beautify the city. It was located on a hill in central Palestine about forty-two miles north of Jerusalem. It was a well-planned city with strong fortifications. However, in 722 B.C. it fell to the Assyrians after a siege of three years. The Assyrian king brought people from many other lands to settle in Samaria. The northern kingdom was often called the territory of Samaria. Archaeological excavations have uncovered evidences of many buildings of Omri and Ahab. Potsherds from the time of Jeroboam have also been discovered. On these are written receipts and orders for oil, wine, and barley. *I Kings 16:24, 32; 20:1; 22:10; II Kings 6:24-25; 14:23; 17:1-6, 24-26; 23:19; Ezra 4:8-24; Nehemiah 4:1-9; Jeremiah 31:5; Micah 1:1-7; Acts 1:8; 9:31; 15:3.*

SAMARITANS. The mixed peoples of Samaria. Many of them did not follow the law and worship of the Hebrews. The Samaritans established their center for worship on Mt. Gerizim rather than at Jerusalem. The Jews who returned to Judah from their exile in Babylon found the leaders in Samaria against the rebuilding of Jerusalem and the temple. This was one of the causes of the ill feeling that existed between the Jews and Samaritans in NT times. *II Kings 17:29; Matthew 10:5; Luke 9:52; 17:16; John 4:4-42; Acts 8:25.*

SAMSON. A judge of the Israelite tribe of Dan. He was famous for his

great strength. Samson was dedicated as a Nazirite from birth and kept the vow of not cutting his hair. His long hair was considered to be the secret of his strength. The collection of stories about Samson is based on Hebrew folklore, probably told over and over for generations. The stories give a colorful picture of life in the period of the judges. *Judges 13:2–16:31; Hebrews 11:32.*

SAMUEL. Meaning "name of God." A prophet of the eleventh century B.C. who, as a child, was dedicated to the service of God. He lived in Ramah and was the last judge of Israel. As a prophet Samuel called the Israelites to repent of their idol worship. When the people wished to have a king like other nations, Samuel anointed Saul and later David as king over Israel. *See I Samuel; I Chronicles 6:28; 9:22; 29:29; Jeremiah 15:1; Acts 13:20; Hebrews 11:32.*

SAMUEL, FIRST AND SECOND. The ninth and tenth books of the OT. They report the events of the period from the birth of Samuel through the reigns of Saul and David. Originally the two were one book. The books probably contain the records of several writers who got their material from folklore, historical records, and prophecies. In several instances there are different versions of the same story. The materials were probably compiled into the books in the seventh or sixth century B.C.

SANCTIFICATION, SANCTIFY. The setting apart of something so that it might belong to God; being made clean or acceptable to God. In the OT a person, a priest, or the temple was made holy or set apart for a sacred use. In the NT Christians were sanctified by their faith in Christ and set apart for God by the action of the Holy Spirit. *Exodus 29:43; 31:13; Joshua 3:5; II Kings 10:20; I Chronicles 15:14; II Chronicles 29:17-19; Job 1:5; Isaiah 29:23; Ezekiel 37:28; Joel 1:14; Romans 6:19, 22; I Thessalonians 5:23; Hebrews 2:11; 9:13; I Peter 1:2.*

SANCTUARY. See *High Place.*

SANDALS, SHOES. Flat soles of leather or wood bound to the feet by thongs. Sandals were the usual shoes of people of Bible times. Going without sandals was considered a sign of mourning or poverty. Taking off one's shoes at a holy place was an act of respect. Putting on one's shoes indicated readiness for a journey. Presenting a shoe legally confirmed a business transaction. Shoes were removed at the door of a house and the feet were washed to remove dust and dirt and thus keep the house clean. *Exodus 3:5; 12:11; Ruth 4:7; Amos 8:6; Mark 1:7; 6:9; Luke 10:1, 4; 15:22; Acts 7:33.*

SANHEDRIN. The supreme Jewish council in Jerusalem following the Exile. It was presided over by the high priest and consisted of seventy-one members chosen from among the priests, scribes, Sadducees, and Pharisees. The Sanhedrin had the authority to make laws for the Jews and to judge lawbreakers. Jesus, Peter, John, Stephen, and Paul appeared before this council (see Matthew 26:59; Mark 14:55-63; 15:1; Luke 22:66; John

SARAH, SARAI

11:47-53; Acts 4:13-20; 5:17-29; 6:8-15; 22:30; 24:20).

SARAH, SARAI. Meaning "princess." The wife of Abraham, who in her old age became mother of Isaac. This birth fulfilled God's promise to Abraham. Her name was changed from Sarai to Sarah at the time God gave Abraham his covenant name. *Genesis 11:30; 17:15-21; 18:6-15; 21:1-3; Isaiah 51:2; Romans 4:19; 9:9; Hebrews 11:11; I Peter 3:6.*

SARDIUS. A deep orange-red, semiprecious stone; a variety of chalcedony. It was used in the priest's breastplate. *Exodus 28:17; 39:10.*

SARGON. The name of two kings of Assyria. Little is known about the first, but Sargon II was an able military leader who headed the Assyrian Empire from about 722 to 705 B.C. Shalmaneser V of Assyria began the attack on the city of Samaria. The siege lasted for three years, and apparently he died in the middle of it. Sargon II took over and conquered the city in 722 (see II Kings 17:1-6). He deported most of the people into faraway provinces in Media, where they disappeared. *Isaiah 20:1.*

SATAN. The chief of the devils, the rival of God. In the OT he was the one who accused people and brought them to trial before God. Satan acted only with God's consent and orders. In late OT times Satan was thought to be a destructive angel, taking part in a struggle between good and evil. Satan plays an important part in the poetic drama of Job. In the NT Satan appears as a distinct being. He is represented as the enemy of God who enters into the minds and hearts of people and is responsible for their evil deeds. Other names or expressions for Satan are "the evil one," "the tempter," "the enemy," "the prince of demons," "the ruler of this world," "the accuser," "the devil," "the obstructor," "Belial," "prince of the power of the air," "Beelzebul," and "the great dragon." He also appears as the tempter and opponent of Jesus. *I Chronicles 21:1; Job 1:12-2:7; Zechariah 3:1-2; Matthew 4:1-11; 12:24-28; Mark 1:13; 4:15; Luke 4:1-15; 10:17-18, 22:3, 31; John 13:27; Acts 5:3; Romans 16:20; I Corinthians 7:5; I Thessalonians 2:18.*

SATRAP. A governor of a province in the Persian Empire. *Ezra 8:36; Esther 3:12; 8:9; 9:3; Daniel 3:2, 3; 6:1-7.*

SAUL. 1. The first king of Israel (from about 1020 to 1000 B.C.). At the request of the people, Saul was chosen and anointed by Samuel. Saul was a handsome and commanding figure who was also a good military leader. He challenged and weakened the power of the Philistines and stopped their advance into the central highlands of Israel. In the later years of his reign, as the young David gained fame and favor, Saul was tormented by jealousy and fear until he finally went mad. *I Samuel 9:21; 11:5-15; 13:6-14; 18:6-9; 31:1-6; and many other places in I Samuel; I Chronicles 10:2-14; Isaiah 10:29; Acts 13:21.*

2. The Jewish name of the apostle Paul. (See *Paul the Apostle*.) *Acts 9:1-25.*

SCEPTER. A rod or staff carried by a king as a sign of his authority and

power. Two types of scepters were common in OT times: one a long, slender staff or rod with a decorated head; the other a short-handled club with a heavy head similar to a military weapon. This symbolized the king's striking power. The word is also used as a figure of speech to mean "rule" or "ruler." *Genesis 49:10; Numbers 21:18; Esther 4:11; Psalms 45:6; 110:2; 125:3; Isaiah 14:5; Jeremiah 48:16-17; Ezekiel 19:14; Amos 1:5, 8; Hebrews 1:8.*

SCORPION.

The scorpion has been called "a living fossil" since it is a survivor of the age of the dinosaur. From the many references, from Deuteronomy 8:15 to Revelation 9:3, 10, the scorpion evidently was well known. The most common species in Palestine is the rock scorpion. Its body, from five to seven inches long, is made up of eight segments, the last five forming a tail at the end of which is its poisonous stinger. It has eight eyes and four pairs of legs. The pincers in the upper and lower jaws are used to hold its prey while the poison of its sting gradually paralyzes its victim. It lays eggs which hatch in a very short time, the young living on the mother's back. "If a son . . . shall ask an egg, will he [his father] offer him a scorpion?" (Luke 11:12) is a vivid contrast!

SCOURGING.

Beating with a rod or staff. This was a form of discipline given to slaves and children. Forty strokes was the maximum allowed by law. The leader of a synagogue could use a whip of calfskin to beat anyone who had broken the Jewish law. In NT times it was the Roman practice to scourge all (except Roman citizens) who were condemned to death. Jesus was scourged by Pilate before the crucifixion. *Isaiah 10:26; Matthew 23:34; 27:26; Mark 10:34; 15:15; Luke 18:33; John 19:1; Acts 22:24-29; Hebrews 11:36.*

SCRIBE.

Originally a person who could write. The scribe was important to a king because he could write messages and keep records. The OT scribes became a professional class of men during the Exile. They studied, interpreted, and taught the Jewish law. They came from the families of priests and were probably responsible for gathering together and setting down many of Israel's sacred writings which make up the OT of today. The scribes of NT times were a professional group defending and teaching the law and were important in the Sanhedrin, which was the high council in Jerusalem. Some were members of a religious party called the Pharisees. *I Chronicles 27:32; II Chronicles 34:13; Ezra 4:8-10; 7:6, 11-12, 21; Nehemiah 8:1, 4, 9, 13; 12:26, 36; Psalm 45:1; Jeremiah 8:8; 36:32; Matthew 2:4; 8:19; 13:52; Mark 2:6, 16; 7:1; Luke 20:1, 19; Acts 6:12; 23:9.*

SCRIPTURE.

Meaning "a writing." As it is used in the NT, "scripture" refers to the sacred writings of the Jews, or what is now the OT. Today the Christian Bible, which contains OT and NT, is often called the Scriptures. "Scripture" is sometimes used to refer to a verse or passage from the Bible. *Matthew 22:29; Mark 12:10, 24; Luke 4:21; 24:27, 44-45; John 2:22; 5:39; 19:24, 28; Acts 18:24, 28;*

Romans 15:4; Galatians 3:8; I Timothy 4:13; II Timothy 3:15-17; II Peter 3:15-16.

SCROLL. Meaning "book," a roll of papyrus or parchment, sometimes called the "roll of a book." The scroll was made by fastening the sheets together and rolling them around a rod. Such a roll was usually nine to eleven inches wide and thirty feet long. Writing was done in columns, and the scroll was rolled from right to left as it was read. In 1947 at Qumran, near the Dead Sea, about five hundred scrolls were found in caves. Some of the scrolls contained copies of parts of the OT. One was a complete scroll of Isaiah. The scrolls were the library of a religious group that had lived at Qumran. When the members were forced to leave Qumran about A.D. 70, they stored their parchment scrolls in pottery jars and hid them in the caves. The dry air of the Dead Sea region kept them in good condition. Many of the scrolls are still in the process of being examined and translated. *Ezra 6:2; Isaiah 34:4; Jeremiah 36:2-32; Revelation 5:1-9.*

SCYTHIANS. An ancient wandering tribe of people who came on horseback from the area around the Black Sea. At one time they were allies of Assyria. In the OT they are referred to under the name of Ashkenaz. The threat of their savage raids may have been the reason Zephaniah wrote his book of prophecies and Jeremiah made some of his pronouncements. Paul used the word *Scythian* to mean wild, uncivilized people. *Genesis 10:3; Jeremiah 51:27; Colossians 3:11.*

SEA, MOLTEN. Also called the "bronze sea" and "the sea." It was a large basin about fifteen feet in diameter, made of bronze three inches thick with a brim turned out as a cup. It rested upon twelve bronze oxen set in four groups of threes, facing north east, south, and west. It was located at the entrance of the temple close to the altar. It was a storage place for the water needed by the priests for cleansing the sacrificial vessels and for washing themselves before and after a sacrifice. When the Babylonians captured Jerusalem in 586 B.C., the sea was broken up and carried off to Babylon. *I Kings 7:23-44; II Kings 16:17; 25:13, 16; II Chronicles 4:2-15.*

SEA OF THE ARABAH. A name used in the OT for the Salt Sea, now called the Dead Sea. *Deuteronomy 3:17; 4:49; Joshua 3:16; 12:3; II Kings 14:25.*

SEA OF GALILEE. See *Galilee, Sea of.*

SEA OF GLASS, GLASSY SEA. A sea like crystal in God's throne room. Seen in a vision of John, the seer. This was a symbolic way of showing God's judgment on people's sin and his way of purifying and cleansing people from sin. The vision may have been inspired by the molten sea that had been in the first temple. (See *Sea, Molten.*) *Revelation 4:6; 15:2.*

SEALS. In ancient times bone, metal, stone, or precious gems which had been carved with a design. This design was pressed into a clay or wax to serve as a person's signature. Seals were used to close letters or official documents. A king's seal was one of the

signs of his authority. *I Kings 21:8; Nehemiah 9:38; Esther 8:8; Job 38:14; 41:15; Jeremiah 32:10; Daniel 6:17; John 3:33; Ephesians 1:13.*

SEER. Meaning "one who sees." In the OT it usually referred to a person who had visions and could predict the future. Prophets were sometimes referred to as seers in everyday language. However, prophecy was a more lasting and dependable gift. *I Samuel 9:9-12, 18-19; II Chronicles 12:15; 16:7-10; Isaiah 30:10.*

SEIR. The chief mountain range of Edom. It became the home of Esau and his decendants, the Edomites. "Seir" is also used as a name for the Edomite nation. *Genesis 32:3; 33:14, 16; 36:8-9; Numbers 24:18; Joshua 24:4; Judges 5:4; II Chronicles 25:11-14.*

SELAH. A word of uncertain meaning. Probably a musical direction to the choir or to the musicians. It occurs seventy-one times in thirty-nine psalms. *Psalm 3:2, 4, 8; Habakkuk 3:9, 13.*

SELEUCIA. A coastal city in Syria, it was the port on the Mediterranean for Antioch. From here Paul and Barnabas sailed on their first missionary journey. The modern city of Suediah stands on this site. Excavations of recent times have uncovered houses, a market gate, a Doric temple, and an early fifth-century church. *Acts 13:4.*

SENNACHERIB. King of Assyria and Babylonia from 705 to 681 B.C. He attacked the southern kingdom of Judah and took several of the cities.

King Hezekiah of Judah paid heavy tribute to Sennacherib so that Jerusalem would be spared. When the Assyrians invaded Judah a second time, there was a miraculous deliverance when a plague broke out among the Assyrian troops, killing many of them. Sennacherib was murdered in his capital city, Nineveh. *II Kings 18:13–19:37.*

SEPULCHRE. Meaning "tomb." A natural or an artificial cave used as a burial place. *Genesis 23:6; Nehemiah 2:3-5; 3:16; Psalm 5:9; Matthew 27:61-66; 28:11.*

SERAPHIM. Six-winged heavenly beings seen by the prophet Isaiah in a vision. Like the cherubim they are associated with the glory of God. *Isaiah 6:2-6.*

SERPENT, BRONZE. The figure of a snake made by Moses during the wilderness journey from Egypt to Canaan. There was an invasion of the Israelites' camp by poisonous snakes. This was understood by the people as a judgment from God for their impatience and discontent. Moses put his image of a snake on a pole so that the people could see it. It was a symbol of God's healing power, and those who looked up to it were healed of their bites. *Numbers 21:8-9; John 3:14.*

SERVANT OF THE LORD, THE. One who serves God, as a devoted slave or servant works for a master. In the OT the title was given to the patriarchs, prophets, and some kings. Israel, the nation, was often called the servant of the Lord. In the book of Isaiah the writer speaks of a

SHADES

suffering servant, a servant whose labors cost him pain and humiliation. The servant accepts the suffering willingly and because of this accomplishes the salvation of others. Down through the centuries Christians have recognized in the prophets' descriptions the likeness of Jesus Christ. *Genesis 26:24; Exodus 14:31; Deuteronomy 34:5; Judges 2:8; II Samuel 3:18; II Kings 9:7; Ezra 9:11; Job 1:8; Psalms 89:20; 105:42; Isaiah 41:8; 49:1-6; 52:13–53:10; Amos 3:7; Mark 10:43-45; Philippians 2:5-8.*

SHADES. In the OT a word referring to the ghosts, or spirits, of the dead. Throughout the ancient Near East the spirits of the dead were thought to have power to do harm. The biblical view is that the shades have no power to do good or evil. *Job 26:5; Psalm 88:10; Isaiah 14:9.*

SHADRACH, MESHACH, ABEDNEGO. Three young men who were companions of Daniel in the court of Nebuchadnezzar in Babylon. Their names are Babylonian court names given them when they became favorites of the king. The story was probably written in the second century B.C. when the Jews were suffering under Greek rule. It tells of the blameless lives of these young men, lived according to Hebrew law even in a foreign court, and of their courage and faith which made it possible for them to face death rather than worship the pagan image set up by Nebuchadnezzar. They were put in a fiery furnace but were not harmed by the fire. *Daniel 1:7; 2:49; 3:12-30.*

SHALLUM. King over the northern kingdom of Israel for one month in the year 752 B.C. He gained the throne by murdering King Zechariah, and in turn was murdered by Menahem. The prophet Hosea was preaching in Israel about this time. Several other persons with the name Shallum are mentioned in the OT. *II Kings 15:10, 13-15.*

SHALMANESER. There were five Assyrian kings with this name, but only two are connected with biblical events. Shalmaneser III (858–824 B.C.) was the first Assyrian king to come in contact with the kings of Israel. Though he is not mentioned in the OT, he tried to conquer Israel when Ahab was king and later when Jehu ruled. Shalmaneser V (727–722 B.C.) laid siege to Samaria and forced Hoshea, king of Israel, to pay tribute. Shalmaneser apparently died or was murdered during the siege, and the Assyrian army retreated quickly. His brother, Sargon II, completed the conquest of Samaria. *II Kings 17:3-6; 18:9-10.*

SHAPHAN. Secretary and financial officer to King Josiah. Shaphan brought the "book of the law" that had been found in the temple to the king. Shaphan and his sons helped in the great reform which King Josiah led in the kingdom of Judah in the seventh century B.C. *II Kings 22:3-13; II Chronicles 34:8-20.*

SHARK. Sharks have always been found in the Mediterranean and were familiar to the coastal inhabitants of the Holy Land. Strictly speaking, the shark is not a true fish. It is a "selachian," the

species of marine life which includes the dogfish and the rays.

The "great fish" in the story of Jonah's adventure could have been a shark. The great white shark is capable of swallowing a man, a feat hard to imagine of the whale with its small gullet.

SHARON. A plain about ten miles wide and fifty miles long along the eastern Mediterranean shore extending approximately from Joppa in the south to Mt. Carmel in the north. It was known for its marshes and forests during early Israelite history. Today it is a fertile agricultural area. Recent excavations show that there were some small settlements in Sharon as early as 1200 B.C. The rose of Sharon was a type of crocus growing in the region. *I Chronicles 27:29; Song of Solomon 2:1; Isaiah 33:9; 65:10.*

SHAVING. Removing hair with a razor. Shaving the face and head was not practiced among the Hebrews except in special cases. It was a sign of mourning or shame. It was also done at the completion of a Nazirite vow (see *Nazirite*) or when leprosy of the head was discovered. It was, however, considered proper for Joseph, while living in Egypt, to follow the customs of the Egyptians and to appear before the pharaoh clean-shaven. *Genesis 41:14; Leviticus 13:33; 14:8-9; Numbers 6:18-19; II Samuel 10:4-5; I Chronicles 19:4; Job 1:20.*

SHEATH. The case or covering for a sword or bow. Also called a scabbard. The judgment of God is likened to a sword drawn from the sheath.

I Samuel 17:51; II Samuel 20:8; Jeremiah 47:6; Ezekiel 21:3-5; Habakkuk 3:9; John 18:11.

SHEBA. In OT times an area in southwestern Arabia that was the center of caravan trade. The visit of the queen of Sheba to Solomon may well have been for the purpose of making trade agreements. *I Kings 10:1-13; Psalm 72:15; Jeremiah 6:20; Ezekiel 27:22.*

SHECHEM. An ancient Canaanite city in the hill country near Mt. Gerizim, about forty miles north of Jerusalem. It was associated with the patriarchs and after the conquest of Canaan became an important political and religious center for the Israelites. Later in its history it served for a time as the capital of the northern kingdom of Israel under its first king, Jeroboam. Today it is named Nablus and is inhabited by a community of Samaritans. *Genesis 12:6-7; 33:18-20; Numbers 26:31; Joshua 21:21; 24:1, 32; Judges 9:6; I Kings 12:1, 25; Jeremiah 41:5; Hosea 6:9.*

SHEEP, SHEPHERD. An animal raised for its wool, meat, and milk; the keeper of sheep. Sheep and goats were the main domestic animals of the Hebrews. Sheep represented the chief wealth of early Bible people. The wool and skin were used for cloth, clothing, and sometimes tent coverings. Sheep were important in sacrifices and were burned upon the altar. The shepherd's care of his sheep was often used in the Bible as a figure of speech to show God's love, his mercy, and his compassion for his people and

also to indicate the care religious teachers and leaders should have toward their people, who are like flocks. *II Samuel 12:1-4; Psalm 23:1; Isaiah 40:11; 43:23; 53:6-7; Jeremiah 23:1-4; Ezekiel 34:1-31; Mark 6:34; Luke 15:3-6; John 10:1-18.*

SHEKEL. See *Money.*

SHEM. A son of Noah. According to Genesis, Shem is the ancestor of the Hebrews and of other people who, like the Hebrews, are called Semites (from Shem). *Genesis 6:10; 10:21-32; I Chronicles 1:4; Luke 3:36.*

SHEOL. In the OT a name often used to indicate the place under the earth where the spirits of the dead were supposed to dwell. (See *Abaddon, Gehenna, Hades.*) *Genesis 37:35; 44:29; Deuteronomy 32:22; I Samuel 2:6; Psalm 49:14-15; Isaiah 14:9, 11, 15; Ezekiel 31:15-17.*

SHEPHELAH. Meaning "lowland." In OT times the name for a region of low hills and valleys between the Mediterranean coastal plain and Judean hill country. It was an important agricultural area with an abundance of grain, olives, and grapes. The Shephelah, with well-fortified cities, served as the first line of defense against the Philistines and others attacking the Israelites from the west. *I Kings 10:27; I Chronicles 27:28; II Chronicles 1:15; 9:27; 26:10; 28:18; Jeremiah 32:44.*

SHIBBOLETH. A word meaning "river" or "ear of grain" or "branches." In the OT story of Jephthah it was the password used by the Gileadite sentries at the fords of the Jordan to distinguish between their own people and the enemy Ephraimites. If a person mispronounced the word as "sibboleth," he was recognized as an Ephraimite. *Judges 12:4-6.*

SHILOH. A city of OT times situated in the hill country north of Bethel and east of the main road that ran from Shechem to Jerusalem. At the time of the conquest of Canaan the area was unoccupied. Its remoteness may have been the reason for Joshua's choosing Shiloh as his headquarters. It became an important religious center for the Israelites. Samuel was dedicated there as a child. The ark of the covenant and the tabernacle remained there until the time of Samuel. It was one of the cities of refuge. (See *Cities of Refuge.*) *Joshua 18:1, 8-10; 19:51; 22:9, 12; Judges 21:19; I Samuel 1:3, 24; 4:4; 14:3; Psalm 78:60; Jeremiah 7:12, 14.*

SHINAR. OT name for the territories which came to be known as Babylonia. According to biblical tradition the tower of Babel was built in Shinar. (See *Babel.*) *Genesis 11:2; 14:1, 9; Isaiah 11:11; Daniel 1:2; Zechariah 5:11.*

SHIPS, SAILING. Waterborne vessels; transportation by water using wind power. Because there were no good harbors on the Mediterranean coast of Palestine, and because for a long time the coastal plane was held by the Philistines, the Hebrews did not naturally turn to sea trade as a means of livelihood. In the time of Solomon, however, a fleet of galley

ships was built and sailed out of Ezion-geber on the Gulf of Aqabah. Hiram, king of Tyre, sent Phoenician sailors to train the men for Solomon's fleet. In OT times the Hebrews' contact with ships and sailing was chiefly through the Phoenicians (see Ezekiel 27:1-36). Ships were powered by the force of the wind in sails or by the rowing of teams of slaves. In NT times Paul's missionary journeys were often made by ship. *I Kings 9:26-28; II Chronicles 9:21; Acts 27:6-44; 28:11-16.*

SHITTIM. Meaning "acacia trees." It was a place in the Plains of Moab, northeast of the Dead Sea. It was the last camping spot of the Israelites before crossing the Jordan into Canaan. Shittim was known for its acacia trees, called shittim wood, from which the ark of the covenant was made. *Numbers 25:1; 33:49; Joshua 2:1; 3:1; Hosea 5:2; Micah 6:5.*

SHOWBREAD. See *Bread of the Presence.*

SHRIMP. Well known to the Hebrews along the coastal area, this delicious sea creature was forbidden as food since, without fins or scales, the Mosaic dietary law classed it as unclean.

SHROUD. A linen sheet wound around a dead body in preparing it for burial. *Matthew 27:59; Mark 15:46; Luke 23:53.*

SICKLE. A tool for reaping grain. In early Bible times the blade was made of flint inserted into a curved wooden frame; later it was made of metal with a wooden handle riveted on. *Deuteronomy 16:9; 23:25; Joel 3:13; Mark 4:29.*

SIDON. An ancient Phoenician city on the shores of the Mediterranean about twenty-five miles north of Tyre. These two cities are often mentioned together. Today the city that was Sidon is called Saida. In Bible times it was a commercial city famous for its purple dye industry. Jesus visited the area of Tyre and Sidon during his ministry. Paul stopped there on his way to Rome. *Genesis 10:19; 49:13; Joshua 19:28; Judges 1:31; 10:6; II Samuel 24:6; Jeremiah 25:22; 27:3; 47:4; Ezekiel 28:20-23; Joel 3:4; Matthew 11:21-23; Mark 3:8; Luke 4:26; 6:17; Acts 12:20; 27:3.*

SIEGE. A military blockade. In OT times this method of warfare was used to capture a city or territory. The attackers attempted to cut off a city's water and food supply and to weaken the city walls by tunneling under them or by smashing them with battering rams mounted on siege mounds. A city's ability to withstand a siege depended in large part on its water supply. The siege of Rabbah is the first recorded siege by the Israelites. *Deuteronomy 28:52-53; Joshua 10:31; II Samuel 11:1; 20:15; II Kings 17:5; 25:2; Jeremiah 32:24; 52:4.*

SIEVE. An implement for sifting or cleaning grain after it has been winnowed. In the OT the word was often used as a figure of speech in referring to the day of judgment, when the Lord would "sift the nations." *Isaiah 30:28; Amos 9:9.*

SIGNS AND WONDERS. A combination of words used in the Bible in referring to the acts of God throughout Hebrew history. In the OT the phrase is found mostly in connection with the events surrounding the Israelites' escape from Egypt. In the NT the phrase refers to the miracles of Jesus Christ and the works of the apostles which revealed God's will and purpose. In his ministry Jesus did not use wonders to convince unbelievers, but the wonders were signs to those who did believe. In the faith of the church God's mightiest act was the resurrection. *Deuteronomy 6:20-24; 26:8; Nehemiah 9:10; Psalm 135:9; Jeremiah 32:20; Matthew 24:24; Luke 11:29; John 2:11; 6:26; 11:47; Acts 2:22, 43; 6:8; 14:3; 15:12; Romans 15:19; II Corinthians 12:12; Hebrews 2:4.*

SILAS, SILVANUS. A leading member of the church in Jerusalem. Both the Aramaic form of his name (Silas) and the Latin form (Silvanus) are found in the NT. He was associated with both Paul and Peter in the mission of the early church. *Acts 15:22; 16:19; 17:4, 10, 14; II Corinthians 1:19; I Thessalonians 1:1; I Peter 5:12.*

SILOAM. A pool in Jerusalem which was part of a network of canals, reservoirs, tunnels, and aqueducts built by Hezekiah to supply Jerusalem with water. When Sennacherib's Assyrian armies laid siege to Jerusalem, King Hezekiah kept the water flowing into the city by means of this water system, and Sennacherib failed at the time to capture Jerusalem. By this pool in NT times Jesus healed a man born blind. In 1880 a school boy crawled into Hezekiah's tunnel on a hot day to cool off. He kept on crawling until he came to the spring with which it connected. He fell into the water and found on a wall an inscription which he reported to his schoolmaster. Scholars translated it and found that it explained how the tunnel was dug. *II Kings 20:20; II Chronicles 32:4; Isaiah 7:3; 22:11; John 9:7.*

SILVERSMITH. One who works with silver. In OT times the smith was usually a "founder" who refined the ore and cast it by pouring the liquid metal into casts or molds (see Jeremiah 10:9). He also shaped the silver by beating it. He made musical instruments, decorations, and utensils for the tabernacle and temple. Paul ran into trouble with a guild of silversmiths in Ephesus. *Judges 17:4; Acts 19:24.*

SILVERWEED. This humble plant grows along the dusty wayside, its silvery fern-like leaves pressed flat against the ground, its small yellow flowers giving a bit of color to its drab surroundings.

SIMEON. 1. One of the twelve sons of Jacob and the head of the tribe of Simeon, called Simeonites. The Simeonites at one time occupied territory in central Canaan, but later they merged with the tribe of Judah. *Genesis 29:33; 42:24; Joshua 19:9; Judges 1:3, 17; I Chronicles 2:1; 12:25.*

2. A devout man of Jerusalem who took the baby Jesus in his arms and blessed him when Joseph and Mary

brought the child to the temple to present him to the Lord. *Luke 2:25-35.*

SIMON. 1. One of the twelve apostles. Jesus named him "Peter," or "Cephas," meaning "rock." (See *Peter.) Matthew 4:18; 10:2; 16:16; Mark 3:16; Luke 6:14; 7: 36-50; 22:31; John 1:42; Acts 10:32.*

2. Simon the Cananaean or the Zealot was another of the twelve apostles of Jesus. (See *Cananaean.) Matthew 10:4; Mark 3:18; Luke 6:15; Acts 1:13.*

SIN, TRANSGRESSION, TRESPASS. Distrust or disobedience of God which causes separation from him. In the OT, acts which broke Hebrew law; acts of idol worship, hatred, disobedience, dishonesty, revolt, and the like were sins against God. They were looked upon as defiance of God and rebellion against his rule. The prophets emphasized that their nation's sin brought suffering, military defeat, and finally the exile in Babylon. In the OT relief for the Hebrew nation lay in casting itself completely on God's mercy. The people were urged to repent of their trangressions and to keep God's law more carefully in the future. The NT emphasized that Christ conquered the power of sin through his death on the cross. He preached repentance and, in his life, demonstrated God's forgiveness. The NT made clear that a sinner can come to God through Christ, be judged and forgiven, and be given power to become a new person in Christ. *Genesis 18:20; Exodus 34:6-9; Leviticus 5:14-19; 16:15-16, 21-22; I Kings 8:34-35, 46-51; II Kings 17:7-18; Psalms 51:1-4; 85:2; Isaiah 1:18; Amos 5:12; Matthew 6:14-15; 9:5-6; Mark 2:15; Romans 4:15; 7:15-25; I Corinthians 15:3; Galatians 1:3-5.*

SINAI, MOUNT. Also called Horeb. The mountain near which the Israelites camped on their way from Egypt to Canaan and on which God revealed himself to Moses and entered into a covenant relationship with the Israelites. The exact location of the mountain is uncertain. Tradition identifies it with Jebel Musa in the high mountains of the southern Sinai Peninsula. Some scholars think it was in northwestern Arabia. *Exodus 19:1-25; 24:16; 34:32; Leviticus 25:1; Nehemiah 9:13; Psalm 68:8.*

SLAVERY. The ownership of a person by another. In OT times slavery was a common practice. The main source of a supply of slaves was captives taken in war. Children were sometimes sold into slavery to pay a family's debts, or a man might sell himself into slavery to pay his debts. Among the Hebrews, slaves were used mostly as domestic servants in the households of the rich. The laws of the Hebrews provided for the release of debtors—slaves—every seven years. Slavery continued in NT times and was practiced throughout the Roman Empire. The term *slave* is used in the OT and NT as a figure of speech for those who are owned by or controlled by sin. *Exodus 21:2-6; 20-21; Leviticus 25:38-46; Deuteronomy 16:12; I Kings 9:20-21; Matthew 8:9; Romans 6:17-18; Colossians 3:11; Philemon 1:15-16.*

The Bible Companion

SLEDGE, THRESHING. A machine made of two planks turned up slightly at the front. Sharp stones were set in holes in the bottom, and the machine was weighted with stones or with a driver. These machines were pulled over grain by animals, and the sharp stones collected the straw and separated it from the grain. *II Samuel 24:22; Job 41:30; Isaiah 28:27-28; 41:15; Amos 1:3.*

SLING. A weapon for hurling small stones or clay pellets. It was made of two narrow strips of leather or woven cloth joined by a broader middle section and attached at the center to a pouch-shaped piece of leather for holding a stone. One end was tied to the wrist and the other end held by the hand so that it could be released and the stone thrown after being swung over the head in a circular motion. It was used as a weapon by shepherds as they protected their sheep from wild animals and by soldiers in war. The stones were carried in a bag slung over the shoulder. *Judges 20:16; I Samuel 17:40; 25:29; I Chronicles 12:2; Proverbs 26:8.*

SLOTHFUL, SLUGGARD. Lazy, idle; one who is lazy or idle. In the OT wisdom books there are many wise sayings about the foolishness of living a lazy and idle life. Jesus used the same thought in his parable about the "wicked and slothful servant." *Proverbs 6:6; 10:26; 12:24, 27; 13:4; 15:19; 19:15, 24; 20:4; 21:25; 22:13; 24:30-34; 26:13-16; Ecclesiastes 10:18; Matthew 25:26.*

SMILAX. The prickly smilax of the Holy Land is a close relative of the smilax we know. The very small greenish-white blossoms appear in October and November, followed by brilliant scarlet berries. These remain on the branches, which are used for decoration much as we use sprigs of holly and other berry plants.

SNAIL. Snails of many varieties are common throughout the Middle East. Yet outside the mention of it among the unclean animals (Leviticus 11:30) the only reference is in Psalm 58:8. There the writer speaks of the "snail that melteth away." Among the ancients it was believed that the slimy track left by a crawling snail was substance from its body that in time would be wasted away.

The small marine snail was the source of the important "purple" (actually nearer crimson) dye that colored the robes of Assyrian, Phonecians, and Egyptian royalty as early as 1500 B.C.

SNAKE. From the time of Eve's temptation (Genesis 3:1) the serpent, as the snake is usually called in the Bible, has been a common symbol of evil. The horned viper, or "adder," of the Egyptian and Arabian deserts is mentioned five times: the reference in Psalm 91:13—"Thou shalt tread upon the young lion and the adder"—is familiar to everyone. The bite of the adder is extremely poisonous. So, too, is that of the asp, another name for the cobra. Harmless snakes are plentiful throughout the lands of the Bible. The ancients believed that snakes were

immortal, that with each shedding of the skin, life was renewed.

SNOW. Crystals of frozen water formed from the water vapor of the air. Snow is rare in Palestine. In the hills there are usually three days of snow each year, and there are many snowcapped mountains. There are imaginative passages in the OT telling where snow was stored in nature and describing the cold winds that caused ice, snow, and hail as God's breath. The coldness, cleanness, and beauty of snow were a wonder to the people of Bible times. *II Samuel 23:20; Job 38:22; Psalms 51:7; 147:16-17; Proverbs 25:13; Isaiah 1:18; Jeremiah 18:14.*

SODOM. A city in the time of Abraham that is today thought to be under the waters of the southern end of the Dead Sea. This city and its neighboring city, Gomorrah, were known for their wickedness. They were destroyed by fire, and their destruction was often referred to as a warning for other wicked cities. Scientists, speculating about the cause of the fire, have suggested an earthquake, a volcanic eruption, an explosion of gas, or a stroke of lightning setting fire to oil seeping from the earth. The name Sodom has come to be used for any wicked place. *Genesis 10:19; 13:10-13; 18:16–19:29; Deuteronomy 29:23; Isaiah 1:9; 13:19; Jeremiah 23:14; Amos 4:11; Matthew 10:15.*

SOJOURNER. In the OT a person living in a community and among people not his own. His position is between that of one who is native-born and one who is a stranger

passing through. Among the Hebrews a sojourner had the same rights, privileges, and responsibilities as others in the community but could not own land. The Hebrews had laws that protected the rights of sojourners (and which recalled that the Hebrews themselves had been sojourners, first in Canaan and then in Egypt). *Genesis 23:4; Exodus 2:22; Leviticus 19:10; 24:22; Numbers 9:14; 35:15; Deuteronomy 10:19; 26:11; I Chronicles 29:15; Psalms 39:12; 119:19; Malachi 3:5; Ephesians 2:19.*

SOLOMON. Son of David and Israel's third king (965–931 B.C.). He was famous far and wide for his wisdom. Solomon created a strong central government and undertook an extensive building program. He built the temple in Jerusalem, created a large army, developed a navy, and increased Israel's trade with foreign countries. He taxed the people to support his luxurious court and used forced labor for his building projects. This eventually led to revolt in Israel. He permitted his many foreign wives to worship other gods in Jerusalem. *II Samuel 12:24; I Kings 1:1–12:19; II Chronicles 1:1–9:31; Nehemiah 13:26; Matthew 12:42; Luke 12:27; Acts 7:47.*

SON OF GOD. In the OT a phrase, usually in the plural, used to mean divine beings, angels, or godlike persons. Israel was also called God's son in a special way because God had chosen the nation to be his own people. Just as a son is dependent on and obedient to his father, so Israel was to be dependent on and obedient to God. In the NT the term refers to

Jesus as the special or unique Son of God. The plural "sons of God" in NT use refers to believers in Jesus, whose faith in the Son of God makes them "sons" also. *Genesis 6:2; Deuteronomy 14:1-2; Job 1:6; 38:7; Matthew 4:3, 6; 5:43-45; 27:40, 43; Mark 1:1; 3:11; 5:7; 15:39; Luke 1:35; 4:3, 9, 41; 20:36; John 1:34, 49; 3:16-18; Romans 1:4; 8:14-23.*

SON OF MAN. In the OT a term for a man or human being. In the NT it is a title for Jesus, one which he often used for himself. It refers to Jesus as one who was a son of man but who also was the Son of God, that is, a man but also the Christ. Before the time of Jesus there were writings that used "Son of man" to indicate the coming Messiah. *Numbers 23:19; Job 35:8; Psalms 8:4; 80:17; 144:3; Isaiah 51:12; Ezekiel 2:1, 3; 4:1; 6:1; Matthew 8:20; 12:8, 32, 40; 13:37; 16:13-16, 27-28; 26:63-64; Mark 2:10; 8:31; 9:12; 14:61-62; Luke 22:67-70; 24:7; John 1:51; Acts 7:56.*

SONG OF SOLOMON. An OT book containing a collection of love poems, some of which were intended for use in Hebrew weddings. It is also known as Song of Songs. Biblical scholars agree that Solomon was not the author of this book, though it may have been dedicated to him or have belonged to him (see Song of Solomon 1:1). It was probably edited in the fifth century B.C.

SOOTHSAYER. One who predicts future events by observing various kinds of signs. (See *Divination*.) *II Kings 21:6; Isaiah 2:6; Jeremiah 27:9; Micah 5:12; Acts 16:16-19.*

SORCERY. The use of power that was supposedly gained through the use of charms, magic, or divination. The Israelites were forbidden to practice this sort of witchcraft. (See *Divination*.) *Deuteronomy 18:10; II Kings 17:17; Isaiah 19:3; Galatians 5:20.*

SOUL. In biblical use "soul" meant "life," the "self" or "person." The soul was not considered to be separate from the body. *I Samuel 18:1; Psalms 42:1-11; 49:15; 116:8; 119:81; Isaiah 55:3; Mark 12:30; Acts 2:43; I Peter 2:11, 25.*

SPAN. A measure based on the distance between the end of the thumb and the little finger when the hand is spread. It measures a little more than eight inches. "Span" sometimes refers to length of life. *Exodus 28:16; 39:9; I Samuel 17:4; Isaiah 40:12; Ezekiel 13:13; Luke 12:25.*

SPANISH BROOM. Sometimes called prickly asparagus, the Spanish broom grows in the woods of all the countries of the Mediterranean area. It is a shrub, peculiar with its long grooved stems which are widely used for weaving nets and baskets. The bright yellow flowers along the stems somewhat resemble small orchids.

SPARROW. In picking a bird to represent the humblest of creatures, Jesus chose the sparrow: "Are not two sparrows sold for a farthing? And one of them shall not fall to the ground without your Father [knowing]" (Matthew 10:29). Sparrows are gregarious birds, flocks of them as common in Bible times as today. The psalmist might well have had this fact

in mind when, alone and desolate, he wrote, "I am as a sparrow alone upon a house top" (Psalm 102:7). Though there are instances in the Old Testament where "sparrow" might mean any small bird, there is no doubt that many varieties were as familiar to the ancient Hebrews as to us.

SPEEDWELL. The white and blue speedwell is common throughout the Middle East. It is an early bloomer, three or four inches high, blanketing much of the otherwise winter-barren landscape in early February.

SPICE. The sweet-smelling leaves, roots, and gums of certain vegetables and herbs that were prized for use in cosmetics, sacred oil, incense, perfume, and in preparing a body for burial. In Bible times spices were not generally used in cooking as they are today. *Exodus 25:6; I Kings 10:2; II Chronicles 2:4; 16:14; Ezekiel 27:22; Mark 16:1; John 19:40.*

SPIDER. The spider is named in Isaiah 30:28 as one of the "four things which are little upon the earth, but . . . are exceeding wise." And one must marvel at the "wisdom" of the spider whose web, a trap for insects upon which the spider feeds, is woven according to a definite pattern of its own species. Even the first small web of the newborn spider is an exact miniature of that spun by its parents. The web, a liquid exuded by the spider, hardens on contact with the air and is placed in position by the insect's legs—"the spider taketh hold with her hands" is the way it is expressed in Proverbs 30:28. Not all spiders are weavers but most kinds construct some kind of a web. A few varieties are poisonous.

SPIKENARD. The spikenard which the woman poured over the head of Jesus (Mark 14:3) was indeed "very precious." One pound of spikenard cost three hundred denarii, nearly a year's wages. The spikenard plant is odd in appearance. The lower stems have a hairy covering from which grow the flower stems and leaves. The blossoms are red with a sweet fragrance. But the perfume, for which the plant is best known, comes from the hairy stem. To preserve its fragrance, spikenard is still transported in alabaster boxes as mentioned by Mark.

SPIRIT. In the Bible a term applied to God, gods, bodiless beings, and to the divine element in people. It was sometimes used to indicate God's power in people. Originally meaning "movement of air" or "breath of God," it came to mean also the living force in a person or creature. The phrase the "Spirit of God" referred to God's activity and his power in the world. In the OT it was thought of as inspiring the prophets and leaders. In the NT the Holy Spirit was thought of as God's power in those who had faith in Christ. (See *Holy Spirit.*) *Genesis 1:2; Exodus 35:21; Judges 3:10; I Samuel 10:6-10; II Samuel 13:39; Job 10:12; 27:3; 33:4; Psalms 51:10; 104:30; Isaiah 42:5; Micah 3:8; Zechariah 12:1; Matthew 3:16; 5:3; 12:28, 43-45; Acts 8:7; Romans 8:10; Galatians 4:6.*

SPIT. To expel saliva from the mouth. Among the Hebrews spitting

was a sign of contempt. However, saliva was thought to be useful in healing, and Jesus followed a Jewish belief and practice in the use of saliva to heal. *Numbers 12:14; Deuteronomy 25:9; Job 17:6; Mark 7:33; 8:23; 14:65.*

SPOIL. Loot or plunder taken as a right of conquest. In Bible times warfare involved the right to possess anything belonging to the conquered enemy such as cattle, clothing, metals, and the people themselves. There were rules for dividing the spoil. *Numbers 31:9-11; I Samuel 30:22-25; II Samuel 12:30; I Chronicles 26:27; Psalm 119:162; Proverbs 16:19; Isaiah 3:14; 9:3; 53:12.*

SPONGE. We are apt to forget that sponges belong to the animal kingdom, even though the lowest form of multicelled creatures. There are many varieties, and since they abound in the waters of the Mediterranean Sea the ancient Hebrews doubtless used them, much as we do today. The mention of the sponge soaked with vinegar and pressed to the lips of Jesus on the cross as a stimulant is mentioned in Matthew, Mark, and John.

STACTE. Drops of spicy, gum substance from a number of shrubs and trees used in the holy incense. Flowers of stacte, or the storax shrub, are like snowdrops in shape and are fragrant. *Exodus 30:34-35.*

STAFF. A long pole used by shepherds and travelers for climbing and for defense. (See *Rod.*) *Psalm 23:4; Isaiah 10:15; Zechariah 8:4; Matthew 10:10; Mark 6:8; Hebrews 11:21.*

STANDARD. In OT times a banner or sign of a tribe or an army troop. It was often used as a rallying signal. (See *Banner.*) *Numbers 2:2-3; 10:14; Isaiah 31:9; Jeremiah 4:6.*

STAR OF BETHLEHEM. This is a different plant from the Bethlehem star. Both do belong to the lily family. It is a spring-blooming plant with white six-petaled flowers on the end of six-inch stems. The bulb is sometimes roasted for food or ground into flour. It is strange that such a lovely flower should be called by the rather inelegant name used in II Kings 6:25—"dove dung."

STEADFASTNESS. Patient endurance. In the NT usually related to enduring afflictions, persecutions, and even martyrdom. *Romans 15:4-6; II Thessalonians 1:3-4; James 1:3-4.*

STEPHEN. One of the seven men in the early Christian church selected to serve tables and supervise the giving of help to the poor. These men, called deacons, were chosen at the command of the Twelve who prayed over them and laid hands on them, to appoint them to this work. Stephen became an evangelist, and later he was stoned to death as a result of the opposition of Greek-speaking Jews. He was the first Christian martyr. *Acts 6:5–8:2; 11:19; 22:20.*

STEPPE. In the Bible "steppe" refers to level, unforested land found on and along the edge of the desert east of the Jordan. It received eight to sixteen inches of rain per year. *I Chronicles 6:78; Job 39:6.*

STEWARD. In the Bible an official who was responsible for the affairs of a large household. He directed servants, oversaw meals, and controlled household expenses on behalf of his master. In the NT Christians were spoken of as stewards of God's affairs. Their stewardship involved the use of time, talent, possessions, and themselves in behalf of God. *Genesis 43:19; 44:4; I Chronicles 27:31; 28:1; Isaiah 22:15; Daniel 1:11, 16; Matthew 20:8; Luke 8:3; 16:1-8; John 2:8-9; I Corinthians 4:1; Titus 1:7; I Peter 4:10.*

STIFF-NECKED. A word used in the OT to mean rebellious, stubborn, unteachable. It was originally taken from the way the ox stiffens his neck when he refuses direction. It was used to refer to Israel's refusal to listen to the word of God as delivered by the prophets. *Exodus 32:9; 33:3, 5; 34:9; II Chronicles 30:8; Acts 7:51.*

STOICS. In NT times followers of a school of philosophy of the Greek-Roman world, founded in the fourth century B.C. It takes its name from a porch, a "stoa," which in Athens was an open colonnade where Zeno, the first teacher of this philosophy, taught. Stoic philosophy held that reason can rule all of life, that people can rise above all feelings and conditions. *Acts 17:18.*

STONING. Among the Hebrews a method of execution. Death by stoning was required by OT law for such offenses as adultery, the worship of other gods, and blasphemy. Stoning took place outside the city. Two witnesses to the crime had to cast the first stone. If this first blow did not kill the criminal, all the people joined in stoning him. *Leviticus 24:14; Deuteronomy 17:2-7; I Kings 12:18; 21:13; Matthew 21:35; John 8:5-7; 70:31-33; Acts 7:58-60; 14:5-7.*

STORE-CITIES. Locations where in ancient times warehouses were built for the storage of government supplies of various kinds. Store-cities have been excavated in several places in Egypt. *Exodus 1:11; I Kings 9:19; II Chronicles 17:12-13; 32:27-29; Malachi 3:10.*

STORK. One of the best liked of the birds, the stork's purported association with human childbirth is common the world over. This may have come about originally because of the stork's loyalty to its young, both parents assisting in their incubation and care. The Hebrew word for *stork* means "kindly one" or "loyal one," both titles which one likes to think of as applying to human parents.

The stork is mute; it has no voice box. It communicates by rapidly clapping its bill or through movements of its head, neck, and beak. Feeding on frogs, fish, rodents, and lizards as well as insects, it is on the unclean list.

STRONGHOLD. A fortress chiefly for refuge or defense against military attack. In the Bible "stronghold" is used figuratively to mean God as a refuge for the righteous. *Judges 9:46-49; I Samuel 22:4; II Samuel 5:7; Psalms 9:9; 144:2; Amos 1:10; 6:8.*

STYRAX (also STORAX). The white clusters of drooping white flowers of the styrax are very fragrant. They

The Bible Companion

appear in March or April. The styrax is a shrub that may grow as high as twenty feet on the hills around the Jordan. It is especially abundant in Galilee and is revered by the Palestinians, so much so that it is almost a calamity if one is cut down. Legend says that Moses, on leaving Egypt, made his staff of the styrax. Resin from the plant is used in medicine.

SUCCOTH. 1. Succoth is mentioned as the first stop on the flight of the Israelites from Egypt. *Exodus 12:37; 13:20.*

2. A city in eastern Palestine not far from the Jordan Valley. This town refused to supply bread for Gideon's army. After his military victory Gideon returned to punish the elders of the city for being so inhospitable. *Judges 8:5-17.*

SURETY. In OT times a person who made himself legally responsible for repaying the debts of another. The same term is used figuratively in the Bible, speaking of the relationship of God and Jesus to people. *Genesis 43:9; 44:32; Job 17:3; Proverbs 6:1; Hebrews 7:22.*

SURNAME. A name added to a person's given name. In Bible times it might indicate the family connection, the occupation, or the qualities of a person. *Isaiah 44:5; 45:4; Mark 3:16-17; Acts 1:23; 4:36.*

SWADDLING. A square of cloth used chiefly to wrap a newborn baby to keep him from moving his arms and legs. This custom was followed throughout the period of the OT and the NT. *Job 38:9; Luke 2:7.*

SWALLOW. The swift and graceful flight of the swallow as it darts through the air catching insects was well known to the Israelites. Its habit of building its nest in barns, and even houses, might well have prompted the psalmist to write. "Yea, the sparrow hath found a house, and the swallow a nest for herself where she may lay her young, even thine altars, O Lord of Hosts" (Psalm 84:3).

The swallow, sometimes called "martin," was very likely confused with the swift by the early writers of the Bible. They are very similar in appearance, but not related.

SWAN. Though the swan, common in Egypt, must have been known to the Children of Israel, there is no mention of this graceful long-necked water-bird in the Bible except in the list of unclean birds (Leviticus 11:13, 18).

SWIFT. Often confused with the swallow because of its similar appearance and behavior, the swift is a member of the hummingbird family. It is probably the fastest of flyers with much of its life spent in the air. Its legs are so short that its take-off from the ground is slow. When it alights for the night it clings to a crack or crevice in a cliff, in position for immediate flight.

SWINE. Of all the unclean animals the pig seems to have been singled out as the most loathsome. Even the swineherd, tending the pigs, was looked upon with contempt and was barred from the temple. The prodigal son (Luke 15:11ff) sank as low as he could when he tended swine. It was

so despised that the strictest of the Jews would not even mention the name. They believed that they would be polluted if touched by a pig's bristles.

As with the majority of other injunctions against eating certain flesh, the dietary law of the Hebrews was wise. The swine of ancient times were scavengers, their flesh susceptible to hosts that caused various diseases, not the least of which was trichinosis, which we guard against today. Moslems are also forbidden to eat pork, no doubt for the same reason.

One might wonder why the herd of swine into which Jesus drove the unclean spirit (Matthew 8:32; Mark 5:13; Luke 8:33) since the Jews were forbidden to raise them. This episode took place in the land of the Gerasenes, a non-Jewish community. The Gerasenes kept and ate swine, as did the Egyptians and the Romans.

SYCAMINE. This is the black mulberry tree, the fruit closely resembling large blackberries. Familiar to the Hebrews while in Egypt, it is also known in the Holy Land. Jesus referred to the sycamine tree that "faith as a grain of mustard seed" could move (Luke 17:6).

SYCAMORE. In Palestine a strong, tall tree with dense clusters of mulberry figs smaller and not so sweet as the fruit of the fig tree. This tree is not connected at all with the American sycamore. A "dresser of sycamore trees" pierced the unripe fruit with a sharp instrument to make it edible by allowing insects to escape. The wood

Sycamore

of the tree is porous but enduring. Mummy cases made of it have lasted three thousand years. *I Kings 10:27; I Chronicles 27:28; Psalm 78:47; Isaiah 9:10; Amos 7:14-15; Luke 19:4-7.*

SYNAGOGUE. Place of assembly for worship used by Jewish communities. The word does not appear in the OT, but it is believed that synagogues were first built in the Babylonian exile to give the Jews a place for prayer and instruction. The NT was used by the Jews chiefly for public worship but also for teaching the Scriptures and the law. The reading of the scripture was the most important part of the service, which included a brief talk and prayers. Scrolls of the law and the prophets were kept in the "ark" in the synagogue. In the first century A.D. most cities and towns had a synagogue. The buildings were rectangular and faced toward Jerusalem. Children

went to the synagogue to school. *Matthew 12:9; 13:54; 23:1-6; Mark 5:36; Luke 4:14-39; John 6:59; 16:2; 18:20; Acts 9:2; 13:5; 14:1; 17:1; 18:14.*

SYRIA, SYRIANS. In OT times the same as Aram, an area northeast of Palestine. The Syrians, or Arameans, were an important Semitic people living throughout the area in many scattered tribes and settlements. Damascus was the capital and the center of Syrian power. About 300 B.C. Syria stretched from the Mediterranean to the borders of India. Syria was often at war with the Israelites until it was conquered by the Assyrians. In NT times Syria was a small Roman province. *Judges 10:6; II Samuel 8:5-6; 10:6; I Kings 15:18; II Chronicles 16:2-3, 7; 18:30; 24:23-24; 28:23; Isaiah 7:1-8; Jeremiah 35:11; Amos 1:5; Matthew 4:24; Luke 2:2; Acts 15:23; 18:18; Galatians 1:21.*

TABERNACLE. Meaning "tent" or "dwelling." The tabernacle was also called the "tent of meeting." It was a portable sanctuary for the worship of God. The tabernacle was carried by the Israelites during their wilderness journey from Egypt to Canaan. The ark of the covenant was kept in it, and for the Israelites it was a symbol of the presence of God. The tabernacle was probably kept in several different places in Canaan after the Israelites settled there. It finally was replaced by Solomon's Temple. The tabernacle may have been more simple than the description in Exodus, which was written at a later time. *Exodus 25:1–27:21; 36:1–40:38 (a later description); Numbers 1:50, 53; 3:23-26; 7:1; 9:15, 22; 10:1-28; I Chronicles 6:48; 21:29.*

TABERNACLES, FEAST OF. See *Booths, Feast of.*

TABLE. A piece of furniture made with a flat surface fixed on legs. Several kinds of tables are mentioned in the Bible.

1. The most common use of the table was for eating, though usually only by the wealthy or by royalty. In NT times it was the custom to eat from tables while reclining on couches. For a banquet the tables were often arranged in a U-shape. *II Kings 4:10; Psalm 23:5; Isaiah 21:5; Matthew 15:27; Luke 7:36-38; 22:14-27.*

2. Tables were used in connection with worship in the temple. The bread of the Presence was set out on a table. *Exodus 25:23-30; Ezekiel 40:39-43; Malachi 1:7.*

3. Money-changers in the temple court used tables in their business. *Matthew 21:12.*

4. The "tables" of the testimony or covenant were two stone tablets on which the Ten Commandments were written. *Exodus 24:12; 31:18; 32:15-16; 34:1-4; Deuteronomy 9:9-17; 10:1-5; I Kings 8:9; Hebrews 9:4.*

TABLET. In Bible times a writing surface made from any of a number of materials: stone, wood, metal, or wax. A writing tablet was also made from clay which had been moistened, kneaded, and shaped. Sometimes the word was used in a figure of speech

such as the "tablet of your heart." *Proverbs 3:3; 7:3; Isaiah 8:1; 30:8; Jeremiah 17:1; Habakkuk 2:2; Luke 1:63; II Corinthians 3:3.*

TABOR, MOUNT. A hill in the Valley of Jezreel about twelve miles southwest of the Sea of Galilee. It is mentioned in connection with the judges in Israel. It is traditionally identified with the Mount of Transfiguration, but this is uncertain. Helena, the mother of Constantine, built a church on Mt. Tabor in A.D. 326. A modern road to the top of Mt. Tabor makes it possible to take a bus trip for a view of the valley. It is possible that Jesus came here from nearby Nazareth to see this view. *Joshua 19:22; Judges 4:6, 12, 14; 8:18; Psalm 89:12; Jeremiah 46:18.*

TALENT. In OT times the standard large weight used for payment before coins were made. It probably weighed about seventy-five pounds. Other nations throughout the ancient Near East used talents. In NT times a talent probably represented about a thousand dollars in today's money. *Exodus 25:39; 38:24; II Samuel 12:30; II Kings 5:23; 18:14; II Chronicles 36:3; Matthew 18:23-24; 25:14-28.*

TAMARISK. Possibly influenced by the fact that it was sacred to the Arabs, Abraham planted a tamarisk tree at Beer-sheba (Genesis 21:33). It is a small evergreen with white flowers, flourishing in areas of very low rainfall. Thousands of tamarisk trees have been planted in the desert-dry regions, following the example set by Abraham.

TANNER, TANNING. One who prepared leather from the skins of animals by using lime, juices from certain plants, or the bark or leaves of certain trees; the process of tanning skins. Because tanners handled the skins of dead animals—which according to Hebrew law were unclean—they were unpopular among the Hebrews and had to live outside the cities. The fact that Peter was willing to stay in the house of Simon the tanner indicates that he was ready to change his views about people who were considered outsiders. *Exodus 25:5; 26:14; 35:7; Acts 9:43; 10:6, 32.*

TARES. Jesus' parable of the tares in the wheatfield (Matthew 13:24-30) was so true to life that his listeners could not fail to understand his meaning. The plant referred to is bearded darnel, or rye grass. It so closely resembles the wheat plant during growth that it is difficult to tell the two apart until the grain heads appear, hence the point of Jesus' parable. Winnowing the grain blows away most of the lighter seeds of the tares. Any remaining are disposed of when the grain is shaken in a sieve, the smaller tare seeds falling through the mesh.

TARSHISH. A faraway port of uncertain location, perhaps Spain. In the OT "ships of Tarshish" referred to large seagoing ships regardless of their origin or ports of call. Tarshish also appears in the OT as a personal name. *Genesis 10:4; I Kings 10:22; 22:48; Esther 1:14; Psalm 72:10; Isaiah 2:16; 23:1, 10, 14; 66:19; Jeremiah 10:9; Ezekiel 27:12; Jonah 1:3; 4:2.*

TARSUS. In NT times the capital of the Roman province of Cilicia, located on the southeastern coast of Asia Minor. Tarsus was a prosperous city set in a fertile coastal plain. It was well known for its schools and industries, which included the weaving of linen and the making of tents. Tarsus had a mixed population of Greeks, Romans, and Jews. Because Tarsus was a free Roman city, Paul, who was born there, had Roman citizenship even though he was a Jew. The history of Tarsus dates back to about 3000 B.C. In the modern city of Tarsus in Turkey in 1947, archaeologists excavated a Roman building decorated with mosaics. *Acts 9:11, 30; 11:25; 21:39; 22:3.*

TASKMASTER. See *Overseer.*

TAX. Payment which people are forced to make to support the government, local, national, or foreign. The tax in Bible times was paid in money, treasure, farm products, hours of labor, and so on. In the OT story of Joseph in Egypt there is the report of a tax taken in grain during the seven years of plenty (see Genesis 41:34-35, 47-48). In Israel during the time of the judges there was no army or royal court to support, and therefore no taxes were required. Saul and David supported their armies and courts with tribute and loot taken from the defeated Canaanites around them. Solomon was probably the first to collect a state tax to support the expanding kingdom. He used forced labor to complete the temple (see I Kings 5:13). He also collected toll from caravans and traders passing through his territory (see I Kings 10:14-15).

Throughout their history the Hebrews were often forced to pay tribute to foreign conquerors such as the Assyrians and Babylonians. This tax was usually collected from the defeated king. The Persians developed a system for collecting tax from individuals. In NT times Palestine was under the authority of Rome. There was apparently a systematic enrollment of individuals for the purposes of a head, or poll, tax (see Luke 2:1-3). Under King Herod the Great there was a tax on farm products, a sales tax, and in Jerusalem a house tax. Aside from government taxes the Hebrews throughout their history and into NT times paid a half-shekel fee to support the sanctuary (see Exodus 30:11-16). This tax was called "atonement money." *II Chronicles 24:6-11; II Kings 23:35; Nehemiah 5:4; Ezra 4:13; Matthew 17:24; 22:17, 19; Mark 12:14; Luke 3:12; 19:2; Romans 13:6-7.*

TAX COLLECTOR, TAX OFFICE. An official who collects and keeps account of taxes; the table or booth set up at the gate of the city, on a caravan route, or in the marketplace for collecting taxes. Tax collectors are never popular, and to the Jews of NT times they were especially despised because they represented the foreign authority of Rome. Very often these revenue officers charged too much in order to keep some part of the money for themselves. *Matthew 9:9-11; 11:19; 18:17; Mark 2:14-16; Luke 5:27-30.*

TEACHER. Anyone who instructs. In the OT usually anyone who instructed in and explained the law.

King Jehoshaphat sent his princes out as teachers of the law. Part of the duty of the Levites was to explain the meaning of the law (see Nehemiah 8:7-8). In the NT "teacher" is chiefly a title of respect meaning "master" or "rabbi." It was often applied to Jesus. Some leaders of the early church were also called teachers. *II Chronicles 17:7-9; Isaiah 30:20-21; Luke 2:46; 3:12; 5:17; John 1:38; 3:10; Acts 13:1; I Corinthians 12:28-29; Ephesians 4:11; II Timothy 1:11; James 3:1.*

TEKOA. A city in the hill country of Judah about six miles south of Bethlehem. It was the home of the prophet Amos. It also appears in the OT as a personal name. *II Samuel 14:2-4; II Chronicles 11:5-6; 20:20; Jeremiah 6:1; Amos 1:1.*

TEMPLE, JERUSALEM. The great sacred building constructed in Jerusalem as the religious center of the life of the community of the Hebrews. It was also called the house of the Lord, or the house of God. There are three temples mentioned in the Bible, all built on the same spot. This location is absolutely certain and is occupied today by the famous Muslim "Dome of the Rock." The first temple was built by King Solomon on the land chosen by his father David. He brought in skilled builders from Phoenicia to supervise the work. The building took seven years, and Solomon spared no expense. This first temple was probably completed around 950 B.C. It was destroyed by the Babylonians in 586 B.C. When the people returned to Jerusalem after their exile, they rebuilt the temple, following the basic plan of the original but in a much simpler way. This temple stood for five hundred years. Around 20 B.C. King Herod built a third temple. This is the temple mentioned in the NT and the one that Jesus knew. This was a much-enlarged building set in a complex of other royal houses and surrounded by a system of porches in the Greek style. This building was destroyed about A.D. 70. The basic ground plan for all three temples was the same. Each one had three rooms: the porch or vestibule; the holy place where the golden candlestick, the table holding the bread of the Presence, and the altar of incense were kept; and holy of holies, where the presence of God among his people was symbolized. In this innermost room, the most holy place, there were two enormous cherubim and, until the Exile, the ark of the covenant. In the courtyard outside the temple was the great altar of burnt offering and a spectacular brass basin, called the molten sea, which contained water for the priests to wash themselves and the offerings and vessels. *I Kings 6:1-38; II Chronicles 36:18-19; Ezra 5:14-16; Jeremiah 7:4; 50:28; Habakkuk 2:20; Matthew 4:5; 12:5-6; 21:12-16, 23; Mark 11:11, 15-16; 12:35; John 2:14-21; 10:23-24; Acts 3:1-10; 4:1; 21:28-30; 25:8; 26:21.*

TEN COMMANDMENTS. Meaning "ten words." They summarize the covenant between God and his people, making clear to the Hebrews their duty to God and to one another. In the account in Exodus,

Moses receives this law directly from God, who writes on two tables of stone. This great occasion at Mt. Sinai when God revealed himself to the Hebrews was important in their understanding of themselves as God's people. The longer explanations of the law found in Deuteronomy were probably added at a later time. *Exodus 20:1-17; 34:28; Deuteronomy 4:13; 5:6-22; 10:4.*

TENT OF MEETING. Another name for the tabernacle. (See *Tabernacle.*)

TENTMAKER. Weaver of a felt-like cloth usually made of goats' hair for use in making tents. Some of this cloth was produced in Cilicia, the province in which Tarsus, Paul's native city, was located. It was a tradition among the Jews that every boy should learn a trade no matter what his profession or wealth. Paul's trade may have been tentmaking. Wherever he traveled, he earned his living by working at his trade. Sometimes he lived and worked with others who had the same trade, as in the home of Aquila and Priscilla in Corinth. *Acts 18:3.*

TERAH. Father of Abraham. *Genesis 11:26-32; Joshua 24:2; Luke 3:34.*

TERAPHIM. In OT times small idols made of clay or wood and kept as household gods. *Judges 17:5; 18:14-18; II Kings 23:24; Ezekiel 21:21; Hosea 3:4; Zechariah 10:2.*

TEREBINTH. A strong, sturdy tree of the desert with spreading branches, a heavy trunk, and boughs thick enough to make a good shade from the hot sun. The leaves are coppery green, and red berries hang in clusters. It is sometimes called the turpentine tree. *Isaiah 6:13; Hosea 4:13.*

TERTIUS. A friend of Paul to whom the Apostle's letter to the Romans was dictated. He gives his own name and greeting in the letter. *Romans 16:22.*

TERTULLUS. The prosecutor of Paul before the Roman governor of Judea. He charged that Paul had been a disturber of the peace, a public nuisance, and the leader of the Nazarenes (Christians), who were dangerous extremists. *Acts 24:2-8.*

TESTIMONY. In the Bible, evidence given by a witness to the action and demands of God. In the OT it is often used in connection with the ark or the tabernacle and refers to the Ten Commandments, the special testimony of God's statutes and judgments. In the NT this word refers especially to evidence given by the witnesses to the mighty acts which revealed God's action through Jesus Christ. *Exodus 25:16, 21; 30:36; Numbers 1:50; 17:4-10; Deuteronomy 6:17; Psalms 19:7; 119:2, 24, 36, 59, 125, 152; Isaiah 8:16, 20; Matthew 10:18; Mark 14:55; Luke 21:13; John 1:7, 19; 3:11, 32-33; 5:31; 8:14; Acts 4:33; II Timothy 1:8.*

TETRARCH. Originally the ruler of a fourth part of an area. This exact meaning was lost, however, and in NT times it was the title for a ruler of a part of a Roman province. This title was lower than king and did not

indicate the same authority. The tetrarch is called a king, however, as Herod is in Matthew 14:9. *Matthew 14:1; Luke 3:1; 9:7; Acts 13:1.*

THADDAEUS. One of Jesus' twelve apostles. Possibly this name was given to Judas the son of James to avoid confusion with Judas Iscariot, who betrayed Jesus. According to tradition Thaddaeus helped carry the gospel to Armenia. *Matthew 10:3; Mark 3:18.*

THEOPHILUS. The person to whom the Gospel of Luke and the book of Acts are addressed. Who he was no one knows, but he is the only person to whom NT writings have been dedicated. *Luke 1:3; Acts 1:1.*

THESSALONIANS, FIRST AND SECOND LETTERS TO THE. Two letters written by Paul to the church at Thessalonica. This was a struggling young church which he had started. The first letter was written about A.D. 50 or 51 after Timothy had returned from a visit to Thessalonica and had reported on the church. In the letter Paul expressed his love and concern for the church and gave instructions for these new Christians. The second letter probably was written shortly after the first. It was written to encourage the Thessalonians to stand firm in the face of persecution, to correct a misunderstanding some of them had about the expected return of Christ, and to advise the church on how to discipline lazy members. These two letters are regarded as the earliest writings in the NT.

THESSALONICA. In NT times an important trading city and chief seaport of the Roman province of Macedonia. Today it is known as Salonica and is the second largest city of Greece. In spite of a riot stirred up against him by Thessalonian Jews, Paul established a Christian church largely made up of Gentiles. *Acts 17:1-13; 27:2; Philippians 4:16; I Thessalonians 1:1; II Thessalonians 1:1; II Timothy 4:10.*

THISTLES, THORNS. Wild plants with sharp briers or spines on their stems and leaves. In the hot, rocky soil of Palestine this type of plant could thrive best. The blossoms of one type were a pink-lavender with silvery green leaves; another had golden yellow blossoms. Thistles and thorns were used in figures of speech as symbols of evil choking out the good, and as symbols of worthlessness. Since ancient times thorny bushes have been used as hedges between pieces of ground. Dried thorn bushes have also been used for fuel down through the centuries in Bible lands. *Genesis 3:18; Job 31:40; Proverbs 26:9; Isaiah 9:18; 34:13; Hosea 10:8; Matthew 7:16; 13:7, 22; Mark 4:7, 18; 15:17; John 19:2, 5; Hebrews 6:8.*

THOMAS. Meaning "twin," one of the twelve apostles. He was also known as Didymus among Greek-speaking Christians. Thomas was the only one of the Twelve not present when Jesus appeared to the disciples on the day of the resurrection. Thomas said that he could not believe without proof what the others told him. Later he did see the risen Jesus

The Bible Companion

with his own eyes, but he became most famous for his doubting. However, he was also courageous as was proved by his willingness to accompany Jesus to Jerusalem when he was certain that death awaited them. *Matthew 10:2-3; Mark 3:18; Luke 6:15; John 11:16; 20:24-29; Acts 1:13.*

THRESHING. The process of separating the kernels of grain from the straw. In Bible times the sheaves of grain were laid out on the threshing floor on a flat surface of rock or earth pounded hard—usually in an open place outside a town. The stalks of grain were beaten with a stick or trampled by oxen or by a donkey pulling a threshing sledge over them. *Genesis 50:10-11; Leviticus 26:5; Numbers 15:20; Ruth 3:2; I Samuel 23:1; I Kings 22:10; I Chronicles 21:15-28; Job 41:30; Isaiah 28:27; Jeremiah 51:33; I Corinthians 9:9-10.*

THRONE. In the Bible the ceremonial chair or seat of a king from which he performed his royal duties. The throne was actually a symbol of the kingship. In the OT the ark of the covenant represented the throne of God the king. Sometimes Jerusalem or the temple or the nation was called the "throne of God." *II Samuel 3:10; 7:16; I Kings 10:18-20; 22:19; I Chronicles 22:10; 28:5; Psalms 9:4; 11:4; 47:8; 122:5; Isaiah 6:1; Jeremiah 3:17; 43:10; Matthew 5:34; 25:31; Luke 1:32; Acts 2:30; Hebrews 1:8; Revelation 1:4.*

THUNDER AND LIGHTNING. The loud vibrations and electrical flashes which often accompany storms. In Palestine these natural occurrences are usually in the spring and autumn. They are always awe-inspiring, and the people in Bible times could see divine power demonstrated in them. Some passages in the Bible mention thunder as the voice of God and lightning as the spear or sword of God. Storms often came from the direction of their enemies and suggested to the Israelites the power of God. *Exodus 9:23-34; 19:19; 20:18; I Samuel 12:17-18; Job 26:14; 37:2-5; Psalms 29:3; 104:7; Jeremiah 10:13; John 12:29; Revelation 6:1; 10:3-4.*

THYNE TREE. John, writing from Patmos, mentions "thyne wood" among the merchandise that "the merchants of the earth shall . . . weep over"(Revelation 18:11, 12). Also known as "citronwood," it is a conifer resembling our arbor vitae. The fragrant wood was burned as incense and was highly prized for woodwork as it is almost indestructible.

TIBERIAS. In NT times a city on the west coast of the sea of Galilee. It was built by the tetrarch Herod Antipas about A.D. 25 and was the capital of the tetrarchy of Galilee and Perea. The name Tiberias honored the emperor Tiberius Caesar. During this period it was a name for the Sea of Galilee. *John 6:1, 23; 21:1.*

TIBERIUS CAESAR. The second emperor of the Roman Empire. The adopted son of Augustus, he was named by the Roman Senate to succeed his father. He came to the throne in A.D. 14. In the Gospel of Luke the beginning of the ministry of Jesus is dated as the fifteenth year in the

reign of Tiberius. In other places in the Gospels he is mentioned only by title as Caesar. *Matthew 22:17-21; Mark 12:14-17; Luke 3:1, 20:22-25; 23:2; John 19:12-15.*

TIGLATH-PILESER (III), TIL-GATH-PILNESER. King of Assyria from 745 to 727 B.C. He was a strong ruler and a skillful military leader. His reign ended a time of weakness for Assyria and laid the groundwork for the Assyrian Empire. His conquests included much of Israel and Judah. He deported many of the people to other parts of his empire and exacted tribute from their kings. After a campaign against Babylonia he made himself king of the city of Babylon, taking the name of Pul. *II Kings 15:19-20, 29; 16:7-10; I Chronicles 5:6, 26; II Chronicles 28:20.*

TIGRIS. An important·river in western Asia, which originates in Armenia. It flows through the Mesopotamian plain and joins the Euphrates River forty miles north of the Persian Gulf. It empties into this gulf. Many important ancient cities such as Nineveh, the capital of Assyria, were located on the Tigris. The fertile valley between the Tigris and Euphrates rivers was the land where the Assyrians and Babylonians created great empires. *Daniel 10:4.*

TIMBREL. A musical instrument like a tambourine. *Exodus 15:20; Judges 11:34; I Samuel 18:6; Psalms 68:25; 150:4; Isaiah 24:8; 30:32.*

TIMOTHY. A trusted and faithful worker with Paul who often traveled with Paul on his missionary journeys.

He is mentioned in many of the letters Paul wrote to the early churches. When Paul could not visit a church himself, he often sent Timothy. Paul sent Timothy to Thessalonica, for example, to encourage the Thessalonian Christians who were being persecuted. This gave Paul a direct report on how the young church was getting along. (See *Timothy, First and Second Letters to.*) *Acts 16:1-3; 17:14-15; 18:5; 19:22; 20:4; Romans 16:21; I Corinthians 4:17; 16:10-11; II Corinthians 1:1, 19; Philippians 2:19; Colossians 1:1; I Thessalonians 1:1; Philemon 1:1.*

TIMOTHY, FIRST AND SECOND LETTERS TO. Two letters in the NT which along with the letter to Titus are called the Pastoral Letters. In them a chief pastor is giving practical advice about church matters. Scholars think the two letters were written in the first half of the second century and were probably written in the name of Paul. Some fragments of Paul's writings may be in II Timothy.

TIRZAH. An OT city in Canaan conquered by Joshua. It later became the capital of the northern kingdom Israel from the time of Jeroboam until Omri moved the capital to Samaria. Its location is uncertain. Also, a personal name. *Joshua 12:24; I Kings 14:17; 15:21, 33; 16:17-18, 23-24; II Kings 15:14, 16; Song of Solomon 6:4.*

TITHE. A tenth part. In Bible times a tenth of the produce of the fields, orchards, and flocks was given for the support of the priesthood, for the upkeep of places of worship, and for charity. This was the way in which the

Hebrews acknowledged God's ownership of the land and all that it produced. Jesus criticized people who were careful to tithe only their material possessions but neglected to practice justice and to show love in their relationships. *Genesis 28:22; Leviticus 27:30-32; Numbers 18:21-28; Deuteronomy 12:6-17; 14:22-29; II Chronicles 31:5-6; Nehemiah 10:37-38; 12:44; 13:5, 12; Amos 4:4; Malachi 3:8, 10; Matthew 23:23; Luke 11:42; 18:12; Hebrews 7:4-9.*

TITUS. A Gentile Christian and co-worker with Paul. When Paul first took Titus to Jerusalem, the Jewish Christians insisted that he could not be one of them unless he was circumcised. Paul, however, used Titus' case to demonstrate that the old Jewish law did not apply to Christians who were not Jews. Faith in Jesus Christ was the only requirement. (See *Titus, Letter to.*) *II Corinthians 2:13; 7:6, 13-14; 8:6, 23; 12:17-18; Galatians 2:1-10; II Timothy 4:10.*

TITUS, LETTER TO. A letter in the NT which, like the letters to Timothy, is one of the Pastoral Letters. It is a letter from a chief pastor to the pastor of a church telling how to organize churches and the kind of people to appoint to office. It was probably written in the name of Paul in the first half of the second century.

TOMB. In Bible times a natural or artificial cave cut into the rock of a hillside and used as a burial place for the dead. Shelves or ledges were cut into the walls of the cave, and the bodies were laid on them. In NT times tombs were often sealed with a round, flat stone which was rolled in front of the entrance. Pits, caves, and cisterns were used as tombs by the poor. Since contact with a dead body made a person ceremonially unclean, tombs were whitewashed to warn people to stay away from them. *Genesis 50:5; II Samuel 2:32; Isaiah 22:16; Matthew 8:28; 23:27-29; 27:52-60; Mark 5:2-3; 6:29; 16:2-8; Luke 8:27; John 11:38; 20:11.*

TONGUES, GIFT OF. Also referred to as "speaking in tongues." An emotional experience in which a person considered possessed by the Holy Spirit utters sounds that often cannot be understood. Speaking in tongues was common among the early Christians. The apostle Paul wrote that speaking in tongues was a genuine gift of the Holy Spirit, but warned that it encouraged self-centeredness and disrupted worship. He felt it should be controlled. Speaking in tongues was a part of many religions of the ancient world. *Acts 2:3-11; 10:46; 19:6; I Corinthians 12:10, 28, 30; 13:1; 14:2-33, 39-40.*

TOWER. A high narrow structure, generally higher than things around it. In Bible times towers were a common sight located in cities, pastures, vineyards, and farmlands. Built of brick or stone, they served chiefly for refuge or defense against military attack. Watchtowers were built in vineyards and fields. From here the crops could be guarded against animals and against raiding parties as the crops ripened and were harvested. The word was also used symbolically in referring to God's protective

power. *Genesis 11:4-5; Judges 9:51; II Kings 9:17; 17:9; II Chronicles 14:7; 26:10; 27:4; 32:5; Psalm 61:3; Proverbs 18:10; Isaiah 2:15; Micah 4:8; Matthew 21:33; Mark 12:1; Luke 13:4.*

TRADITION, ORAL; TRADITION OF THE ELDERS. Unwritten memories, stories, customs, beliefs, laws, and other knowledge handed down from one generation to another by word of mouth. Much OT material comes from the oral traditions kept alive among the Hebrews. "Tradition of the elders" refers to the Jewish unwritten law, the purpose of which was to make clear the written law. *Matthew 15:1-6; Mark 7:1-13; Galatians 1:14.*

TRANSGRESSION. Meaning "to go beyond" the limits of the law. In the Bible it means revolt, rebellion, going against the will of God. (See *Sin, Transgresssion, Trespass.*)

TRANSJORDAN. The general term for the area just east of the Jordan River. The area is usually referred to in the Bible as "beyond the Jordan." It included the territories of Ammon, Bashan, Edom, Gilead, and Moab. It is roughly the same as the modern state of Jordan.

TRAPS AND SNARES. Contrivances for catching birds and animals. In Bible times nets, rope nooses, and pits covered with camouflaged nets or brush were used to trap birds and animals. The terms are also used in figures of speech to describe sudden danger, unexpected death, or disaster. *Joshua 23:13; Job 18:8-10; 22:10; Psalms 18:4-5; 69:22; 91:3; 140:5; 142:3; Jeremiah*

18:22; 48:43-44; Ezekiel 12:13; 17:20; Amos 3:5; Luke 21:34; Romans 11:9.

TRESPASS. See *Sin, Transgression, Trespass.*

TRIBE. A group of clans or families held together by bonds of blood and kinship. It was the normal social unit among Semitic nomads, especially among the Israelites before the conquest of Canaan. According to tradition the people of Israel consisted of twelve tribes who were the descendants of Jacob (also called Israel) and his sons. The names of the tribes were also given to the tribal territories they occupied. *Genesis 49:28; Numbers 1:1-54; Joshua 18:11–19:51; II Samuel 5:1; Matthew 19:28; Romans 11:1; Philippians 3:5.*

TRIBULATION. Suffering, distress, and affliction of various kinds. In the NT it especially refers to the suffering of Christians for their faith. *Deuteronomy 4:30-31; Matthew 13:18-21; John 16:33; Acts 14:22; Romans 8:35; 12:12; Revelation 7:14.*

TRIBUNAL. Also called judgment seat. The official place from which the Roman governor heard and judged cases brought before him. *Matthew 27:19; John 19:13; Acts 25:6, 10, 17.*

TRIBUNE. A Roman military officer in charge of a cohort (army division). *Acts 21:31-33; 23:17-22; 24:22; 25:23.*

TRIBUTE. A compulsory contribution in money, goods, or people forced upon a defeated nation by its conquerors. Sometimes a nation paid tribute to obtain military help from another

nation. In the NT it is another word for tax. *Numbers 31:28-41; Judges 3:14-18; II Samuel 8:2, 6; II Chronicles 28:21; Hosea 10:6; Matthew 17:25; Luke 20:22.*

TRIGON. A musical instrument, a triangular lyre or harp. (See *Musical Instruments.*) *Daniel 3:5, 7, 10, 15.*

TROAS. In NT times a city located in northwestern Asia Minor on the shore of the Aegean Sea. Paul visited and preached in Troas several times. It was here that Paul had a vision directing him to preach the gospel in Macedonia (a part of Europe). *Acts 16:8, 11; 20:5-6; II Corinthians 2:12; II Timothy 4:13.*

TRUMPET. A musical instrument. In OT times trumpets were made from animals' horns and were used to muster an army or as the signal that some important occasion was about to begin or some announcement was to be made. Straight trumpets of metal were used in the temple in pairs or for special services in large numbers. (See *Musical Instruments.*) *Judges 3:27; II Chronicles 5:12-13; 29:26-28; Psalms 81:3; 98:6.*

TULIP. It is not strange to find the tulip growing wild in the Holy Land since it is native to nearby Persia. The tulip common in Palestine blooms early in the spring, as tulips do the world over. It is generally a striking red with pointed petals. It is quite generally believed that the tulip, growing profusely on the plain of Sharon, was the "rose of Sharon" mentioned in the Song of Solomon 2:1. The literal translation of the original Hebrew word lends credence to this belief since it indicates that a bulb-growing plant was meant, not a shrub such as a rose.

TUNIC. A kind of coat. In Bible times a long, shirt-like undergarment draped over one shoulder. It was made of wool or linen. *Job 30:18; Matthew 10:10; John 19:23.*

TURBAN. A head covering. A cloth wrapped around the head, usually made of linen. In the OT the priest wore a special turban as part of ceremonial clothing. *Exodus 28:4, 39; Leviticus 8:9; 16:4; Job 29-14; Ezekiel 44:18; Zechariah 3:5.*

TURTLEDOVE or **DOVE**. A small variety of pigeon. It was used in sacrificial offerings. In the OT two turtledoves could be brought by a poor person as a sin offering instead of a larger, more expensive animal. In the NT Mary brought two turtledoves as her offering when the infant Jesus was presented in the temple. The dove has come to be a symbol of the Holy Spirit. *Genesis 15:9; Leviticus 5:7-10; 12:6-8; Numbers 6:10; Psalm 74:18-19; Song of Solomon 2:11-12; Jeremiah 8:7; Matthew 3:16; Mark 1:10; Luke 2:24; 3:22; John 1:32.*

TYCHICUS. A Christian from the Roman province of Asia who associated with Paul on his missionary journeys. Along with Onesimus he carried Paul's letter to the church in Colossae. *Acts 20:4; Ephesians 6:21; Colossians 4:7; II Timothy 4:12; Titus 3:12.*

TYRE. A very old Phoenician city located on the east coast of the Mediterranean Sea. Tyre was important

as a trading and shipping center throughout Bible times. Its chief product was purple dye made from secretions of shellfish. The dye, known as Tyrian purple, was the most famous and precious of dyes in ancient times. Tyre is usually mentioned with Sidon. Today it is an Arab town named Sur. (See *Sidon.*) *Joshua 19:29; II Samuel 5:11:24:7; I Kings 5:1; Isaiah 23:1; Ezekiel 27:2-9; Matthew 11:21-22; Mark 7:24; Acts 21:3-7.*

UNCIRCUMCISED. All
people who failed to keep the law of circumcision. In the OT it referred usually to the Philistines. It was also used as a figure of speech to mean unclean or uncontrolled. In the NT it referred to all Gentiles. *Exodus 6:12, 30; Leviticus 26:41; Judges 14:3; II Samuel 1:20; Jeremiah 9:25-26; Acts 7:51; 11:3; Romans 4:9; I Corinthians 7:18.*

UNCLEAN, UNCLEANNESS.
Not pure according to religious laws. OT laws declared that certain animals, foods, places, objects, and persons were unclean. To come in contact with these, with anything dead, with lepers, with someone who had a bodily discharge, made a person unclean. To be purified he had to go through a cleansing ritual. *Leviticus 5:2-3; Isaiah 6:5; Hosea 9:3; Matthew 23:27; Acts 10:9-16, 18.*

UNICORN. The unicorn, a mythical creature of medieval legend, was said to have the head and body of a horse, the hind legs of an antelope, the tail of a lion, the beard of a goat, and a single, long, sharp, twisted horn projecting from its head. Actually this imaginary animal had no relation to the real animal the writers of the Bible had in mind. But the English translators of the Jewish Scriptures, uncertain as to just what animal was intended in some instances (Numbers 23:22; Job 39:9; Psalm 92:10) called it a "unicorn." Later translations have substituted "wild ox" as the likely subject.

UNLEAVENED BREAD. Bread
or cakes baked without yeast. Among the Hebrews the absence of leaven was a mark of holiness, so all baked grain offerings brought to the altar were baked without yeast. During the seven days of the Feast of Unleavened Bread (the Passover), unleavened bread was eaten (and still is) to remind the Hebrews of the hasty departure their ancestors had made from Egypt, not even stopping to bake leavened bread. *Deuteronomy 16:16; Judges 6:19-21; II Chronicles 30:13; Mark 14:1; Luke 22:1.*

UPPER ROOM. A room in the
upper floor of a house or a room on the roof, usually for guests. In the NT an upper room was the place chosen by Jesus for his last meal with his disciples. *I Kings 17:19; II Kings 1:2; Mark 14:14-15; Luke 22:11-12; Acts 1:12-13; 9:37.*

UR. An ancient city on the Euphrates
River in lower Mesopotamia. It was at one time the capital of the Sumerian Empire. An ancient ziggurat (temple) dedicated to the moon-god Sin has been unearthed at Ur. It is mentioned

in the Bible as the home of Abraham. *Genesis 11:28, 31; 15:7; Nehemiah 9:7.*

URIM AND THUMMIM. In early OT times objects used to determine the will of God. They may have been precious stones or pieces of metal which the priest used in casting lots or in trying to obtain from God answers to questions. The priest kept the stones in a pocket of his breast-piece, worn over the ephod, or priestly garment. He shook them in a container and cast them on the ground in the way dice are thrown. Nothing is known of their origin. *Exodus 28:30; Leviticus 8:8; Numbers 27:21; Deuteronomy 33:8; I Samuel 14:41-42; 28:6; Ezra 2:63.*

UZZAH or UZZA. There are several persons by this name mentioned in the OT. The most notable was the man who drove the oxcart when David arranged to take the ark to Jerusalem. In the story Uzzah was struck dead when he put out his hand to steady the ark. *II Samuel 6:2-7; I Chronicles 13:1-10.*

UZZIAH. King of the southern kingdom of Judah from 792 to 740 B.C., son of King Amaziah. He is also mentioned as Azariah. Azariah may have been his personal name and Uzziah his throne name. He was sixteen years old when he came to the throne. Uzziah was a strong ruler, adding to Judah's defenses and agricultural prosperity. He became a victim of leprosy, and his son Jotham ruled as regent in his stead. The prophets Isaiah, Amos, and Hosea were active during his reign. *II Chronicles 26:1-16, 21-23; II Kings 15:1-3; Isaiah 6:1; Hosea 1:1; Amos 1:1.*

VANITY, VAIN. The quality of being empty or vain; having no real value. In Bible usage, it often refers to pagan gods, which were empty and worthless. *Exodus 20:7; Psalm 89:47; Ecclesiastes 1:2; 6:12; 11:8; 12:8; and many other places in Ecclesiastes; Isaiah 49:4; Acts 14:15.*

VASSAL. One in a subordinate position who has promised loyalty to his overlord. In Bible times a defeated king was often appointed governor by his conquerors and allowed to rule over his own people or territory. He was required to pay tribute to the conquering nation and thus was the vassal of the victorious king. *II Kings 17:3; Lamentations 1:1.*

VEIL. A head covering worn usually by women. It is not certain what these were like, but most scholars agree that they were more for decoration than for concealing the face or person. In the OT story of Rebekah her veil was probably a sign that she was unmarried. *Genesis 24:65; Song of Solomon 4:1; Isaiah 3:23.*

VEIL OF THE TEMPLE or TABERNACLE. The curtain which hung at the entrance to the most holy place in the tabernacle and in the temple. In early OT times when the tabernacle was moved the veil is said to have been used to cover the ark. After the Exile the ark was never restored, and the most holy place

stood empty. In the NT the veil is called the curtain. (See *Curtain of the Temple.*) *Exodus 26:31-35; 30:6; 35:12; 36:35; 39:34; Leviticus 16:2, 12; 24:3; Numbers 4:5; 18:7; II Chronicles 3:14.*

VESTMENTS. Ceremonial garments worn by the priests conducting religious ceremonies. Among the Hebrews they included the *ephod, breastpiece, breeches, robe,* and *turban* (see these terms). *II Kings 10:22; Ezra 3:10.*

VETCH (Vetchling; Fetch). The vetch, or vetchling, of the Holy Land resembles our common variety. There, as here, its slender climbing stem grows in the fields of grain, attaching itself to the stalks. There are several varieties of vetch in Palestine. The "charming vetchling" is especially attractive with small orange-pink blossoms that look like sweet peas. Other varieties are blue.

VILLAGE. A small grouping of houses and other buildings. In OT times, unlike a city, a village had no wall. Villages were often located close to a city, or even built against a city wall. They were dependent upon the cities for markets and for protection in time of war. The village was governed by a council of elders or was sometimes under the control of a nearby city. *Leviticus 25:31; Numbers 32:41-42; Deuteronomy 3:5; Joshua 15:32-62; Nehemiah 12:29; Zechariah 2:4; Matthew 10:11; 21:2; Acts 8:25.*

VINEYARD. A planting of grapevines. In biblical times the vines were usually planted on hillsides since such land was not often used for growing grains. The workman who pruned the vines was called a vinedresser. Olives, figs, and grapes were among the most typical products of Palestine. Grapes were valued because they were the source of wine. In OT times there were various laws governing the use of vineyards. "Vine" and "vineyard" were used in the Bible as figures of speech to mean Israel. In the NT Jesus speaks of himself as a vine and of his followers as branches. Several of his stories have vineyards as their setting. *Exodus 22:5; 23:11; Leviticus 19:10; Deuteronomy 20:6; I Kings 21:7-18; II Kings 5:26; 18:32; 19:29; Nehemiah 9:25; Isaiah 5:1-10; Matthew 20:1-16; 21:28-41; Mark 12:1-9; Luke 20:9-16; John 15:1-7.*

VIPER. There are many kinds of vipers common to the Holy Land, and to much of Europe and Asia. All are poisonous, though some are deadlier than others. "The viper's tongue shall slay him" was the way Job expressed the deadly bite of a viper. Some scholars believe it was the "asp" that Cleopatra permitted to bite her, causing her death.

VISION. In the Bible an experience similar to a dream in which God revealed himself or his will to someone, most often a prophet. *Genesis 15:1; 46:2; Job 4:13; 7:14; Isaiah 1:1; Ezekiel 1:1; 8:3; 11:24; 12:22-24; Matthew 17:9; Acts 9:10-15; 10:3, 17, 19; 11:5; 16:9; II Corinthians 12:1.*

VOLE. Water voles, also called "water rats," are found in Europe and much of Asia. The plague of "mice" that beset the Philistines as punishment for the theft of the ark of the

covenant (I Samuel 6:5) might have been voles. The vole resembles a small muskrat with a short nose, small ears, dark brown color, and is about six inches long with a four-inch tail. It builds an underground system of passages, usually near water, hence its name. It feeds on plant roots underground, so destroying the plant or tree.

VOTIVE OFFERING. A gift to God as a part of a promise made in a vow. *Leviticus 7:16; Deuteronomy 12:17; II Kings 12:18; II Chronicles 15:18.*

VOW. In the Bible a promise or pledge made to God, sometimes as a bargain. In the OT there were many laws which laid down rules for carrying out different kinds of vows, for such promises were very sacred. *Genesis 28:20-22; Numbers 6:21; 21:2; I Samuel 1:11; Psalm 132:2-5; Jonah 1:16; Acts 18:18; 21:23.*

VULTURE. One of the most detested of scavengers, the vulture plays a most important part in nature's plan, feeding on and so disposing of carrion. This fact was well known to the Israelites, and there are many places in the Old Testament in which the vulture is plainly indicated by references to "fowls of the air" that eat dead flesh. (See *Griffin; Lammergier.*) *I Kings 14:11; Psalm 79:2; Proverbs 30:17.*

WAFERS. Thin, unleavened cakes made of flour, sometimes mixed with honey. In the Bible they are usually mentioned in connection with offerings to God, although one reference indicates that they were also part of the everyday diet of the early Hebrews. *Exodus 16:31; 29:2, 23; Leviticus 2:4; 8:26.*

WAISTCLOTH. An inner garment or girdle worn around the waist. It was made of leather or linen. Workmen removed outer garments and wore only the waistcloth when on the job. *Job 12:18; Isaiah 5:27; Jeremiah 13:1-11.*

WALLS. Enclosure of bricks, wood, stone, or other materials for privacy or protection. Stone walls were built around cities for defense against enemy attack. They were usually of great height and thickness with watchtowers and a gate. Sometimes a city had a double wall. The space between the two walls was used for storage or guardrooms. The city gate was the center of community life. Here people bought and sold goods, judges settled disputes, and proclamations and speeches were read. Vineyards and sheepfolds had walls made of piles of loose stones with thorns on the top to prevent thieves and wild animals from stealing the fruits or sheep. *Leviticus 25:31; Joshua 2:15; II Chronicles 8:5; 25:23; Ezra 4:12; Nehemiah 4:3-19; Ezekiel 38:11; Acts 9:25.*

WATCHMAN. In Bible times a sentry or guard. A watchman was placed in the fields and vineyards during the time of the ripening and harvesting of crops. He stayed in a temporary booth or watchtower to frighten away thieves, birds, or

animals. The watchman of a city patrolled the walls of the city at night and from time to time called out that all was well. He was particularly valuable during a time of invasion or siege. *I Samuel 14:16; II Samuel 18:24-27; II Kings 9:17-20; Job 27:18; Psalm 127:1; Song of Solomon 3:3; 5:7; Isaiah 21:6-12; 52:8; Jeremiah 51:12; Hosea 9:8.*

WATER. Liquid that descends from the clouds in rain and is found in springs, lakes, rivers, seas, brooks, and so on. Palestine was a hilly, rocky land where fertility depended upon the annual rainfall. Thus, the Jews came to look upon water as a special blessing from God. They often used "water" as a figure of speech to symbolize God's blessings or goodness; "living water" was fresh, running water. In the NT Jesus referred to himself as living water in a figure of speech to symbolize the new life, the life of God, springing up in people. *Psalms 72:6; 77:17; Isaiah 35:6-7; 41:17-18; Luke 3:16; John 2:7-9; 4:7-15; 7:37-39.*

WATERSKIN. Whole goatskins with the neck and feet tied together to form a container. A poetic figure of speech to describe rain clouds. *Genesis 21:14; Job 38:37.*

WAY. A path, road, or street along which one passes to reach a destination. In the OT a word used to describe the courses of nature and of a person's life. It is also used to describe the paths of good and of evil. In the NT, Christ is referred to as the "Way," and Christianity came to be known as the "Way." *Psalm 1:6;* *Proverbs 16:17; 21:2; 30:18-19; Isaiah 53:6; John 14:4-6; Acts 9:2; 19:9, 23; 22:4; 24:14, 22.*

WEASEL. Though mentioned by name only in Leviticus 11:29 among the unclean animals, the weasel was probably common in the Holy Land. The name of the prophetess consulted by King Josiah when Helkiak found the Book of the Law (I Kings 22:14; II Chronicles 34:22) was "Huldah," a name that definitely means "weasel."

WEEKS, FEAST OF. A harvest celebration among the Hebrews ending the round of festivals that began with Passover. In Palestine, the festival was actually only one day, the fiftieth or last day of a seven-week period (a sabbath of weeks). The seven weeks were counted from the end of the wheat harvest and the beginning of the barley harvest. The first cuttings of the grain were offered in thanksgiving and in recognition that God was the source of the harvest. In NT times the festival was called by the Greek name Pentecost, meaning "fiftieth." After the destruction of the temple in A.D. 70 the Feast of Weeks became a celebration of the giving of the law. For Christians the feast of Pentecost took on a special meaning as the day on which the Holy Spirit came upon the apostles and followers of Jesus as they prayed in Jerusalem. (See *Pentecost.*) *Exodus 34:22; Numbers 28:26; Deuteronomy 16:9-12, 16; II Chronicles 8:13.*

WELL. A source or storage place for water. Because of the scarcity of rainfall, wells have always been

important in the dry Bible lands. *Beer* was the Hebrew word for a well. It was used in the names of many towns and villages where wells were located. The depth and shape of wells varied according to the type of soil and the level of the underground water. Some wells were shallow pits and others, great shafts many feet deep. From these the water was removed in jars or waterskins attached to ropes. Ancient peoples made songs about the wells that told of spirits living in the running waters. A very old Hebrew song of the wells sings of running or living water as the power of the Lord. *Genesis 16:14; 21:30; 26:22; 29:2-3; Numbers 21:16-18; I Samuel 19:22; II Samuel 17:18-21; 23:15-16; Jeremiah 6:7; John 4:6-15.*

WESTERN SEA. A name for the Mediterranean Sea. *Deuteronomy 11:24; 34:2; Joel 2:20; Zechariah 14:8.*

WHALE. The humpback; the fin whale; and the near relative, the dolphin, are found in the Mediterranean Sea. The Hebrew people living along the seacoast no doubt knew of them, even if they seldom saw them. The most familiar of the three or four references to the whale in the Bible is the story of Jonah "in the whale's belly." But as mentioned under *Shark*, "a great fish" is the expression used in Jonah 1:17. The Hebrew word translated "whale" is also translated in the Bible as "monster" or "dragon."

WHEAT. Wheat is the most universal of all grains, so old that there is no record of when or where it originated. Keeping to the custom common today in most European countries, the English translators used "corn" where grain, including wheat, was referred to as was the case in Genesis 41:1, 5-7, when Pharaoh dreamed of seven full ears, then seven thin ears of "corn." Corn was unknown. But there was a variety of wheat with seven "ears" or heads of grain.

WHIRLWIND. A word used in the Bible for several kinds of winds: a high destructive wind, a tornado, or whirling clouds of dust. *II Kings 2:11; Job 38:1; 40:6; Psalm 77:18; Isaiah 17:13; Jeremiah 23:19; Nahum 1:3.*

WIDOW. A woman whose husband has died. Among the Hebrews death before old age was considered a calamity, a judgment for sin, and a wife left in this way was disgraced. She had no right of inheritance. However, if she had no children she would remain with her husband's family and wait for his brother to marry her. She might also return to her own family and remarry (see Ruth 1:8-13). In the early Christian church special consideration was given to widows. *Deuteronomy 24:17-21; 26:12; Psalms 68:5; 94:6; 146:9; Lamentations 1:1; Matthew 22:24; Luke 4:25; 20:47; Acts 6:1; 9:39-41.*

WILDCAT. Although the wildcat is not mentioned by name in the Bible, it has always been quite common in the Holy Land. It measures about two feet to the tip of its bushy tail, stands about two feet high at the shoulders, and may weigh up to fifteen pounds. Its fur is gray with a black stripe down

the middle of the back and across the flanks. Though it occasionally attacks young calves its main fare is birds, mice, and other small animals.

WILDERNESS. A term often used when referring to sandy deserts, rocky plateaus, barren pasturelands, and desolate mountain regions. God's protection of the Israelites during the journey through the wilderness was one of the most important experiences in their history. *Exodus 15:22; Numbers 33:11-16; Deuteronomy 1:19; 8:2; 32:10; Judges 1:16; Isaiah 27:10; 40:3; 41:18; Matthew 3:1; 4:1; John 6:31; Acts 7:36.*

WILLOW TREE. A tree commonly found in Palestine growing in moist places by brooks and rivers. Willow branches along with other branches were used by the Jews in their celebration of the Feast of Booths. *Leviticus 23:40; Job 40:22; Psalm 137:2; Isaiah 15:7; 44:4; Ezekiel 17:5.*

WINEPRESS. A vat in which the juice was pressed from grapes. The vat was usually a hollowed-out limestone rock on a hillside near the vineyard. Grapes were spread over the floor, and barefooted men walked and jumped on the grapes to press out the juice. They shouted while they worked, and their jumping and stomping had a rhythm. All the people joined in their singing, and it was a joyous, happy time. A hole in the rock allowed the juice to trickle down to a lower rock-hewn vat where it was left to settle and ferment into wine. The wine was then put into jars and wineskins. The prophets used word pictures of an abundance of grapes in the winepress to symbolize God's blessing. *Deuteronomy 16:13-14; Nehemiah 13:15; Job 24:11; Isaiah 5:1-2; 16:10; Jeremiah 48:33; Joel 3:13; Micah 6:15; Matthew 21:33; Mark 12:1; Revelation 14:20.*

WINNOW. The process of separating the kernel of the grain from the chaff by fanning or by throwing the cut stalks of grain into the air with a long-handled fork so that the grain seeds would fall back into a pile while the light straw chaff would be carried away by the wind. "Winnowing" is used as a figure of speech for describing the sweeping away of evil. *Ruth 3:2; Isaiah 30:24; 41:16; Jeremiah 15:7; Matthew 25:24-26; Luke 3:17.*

WISE MEN. In ancient times magicians and interpreters of the stars. The courts of the ancient kings of Egypt and Babylonia kept wise men who were authorities on religion and predicted future events. The Hebrews were forbidden to deal in magic and divination. For them a wise man was one who had knowledge of right living. The book of Proverbs contains sayings of wise men and teachers of OT times. Some wise men sat at the gates of cities telling riddles and stories and settling disputes. In the Gospel of Matthew it is reported that wise men came from the East to worship the infant Jesus. These wise men had studied the stars to learn of the birth of Jesus and also how to find him. (See *Magic, Magicians.*) *Genesis 41:8; Exodus 7:11; Isaiah 19:12; Jeremiah 50:35; Daniel 2:12-14, 21, 24, 27; Matthew 2:1-12.*

WITNESS. A person who has firsthand knowledge of a fact or an event. Biblical law required the testimony of two witnesses to establish guilt. If the person was condemned to death, the witnesses themselves threw the first stone. Bearing false witness was a serious crime. In the NT those who testified to the truth of God and those who testified to what they had seen or heard about Jesus were called witnesses. *Exodus 20:16: Deuteronomy 17:6; 19:15-18; Joshua 22:26-27; Judges 11:10; Ruth 4:9-11; Luke 24:48, John 3:11; Acts 1:8, 22; 7:58; 10:39-41; I Timothy 6:12.*

WOLF. The wolf has always been a beast of prey, in the Holy Land as elsewhere. Protecting his sheep from wolves was one of the shepherd's biggest tasks, especially at night. The wolf with its greed and savagery is referred to some thirty times in the Old Testament. Jesus warns against "false prophets which come to you in sheep's clothing, but inwardly are ravening wolves" (Matthew 7:15). And to emphasize the danger that his disciples would encounter he warns, "I send you forth as lambs among wolves" (Luke 10:3). We can be sure they understood what he meant: he was well acquainted with the wolf and the danger it was to the flocks on the hills about Nazareth.

WORD, THE. In the OT God's declaration of his will and his purpose. God's word and his act were the same. For example, the heavens and the earth were created by his word. Throughout the OT history of the Hebrews the word of the Lord was usually received through the prophets. In some places in the NT "the word" still has the OT meaning. In other places it becomes "the Word of Christ," the gospel which he first preached. In the Gospel of John and in Revelation "Word" or "Word of God" is used to mean Jesus Christ himself as God's clearest word to humankind. *Genesis 15:4; Deuteronomy 5:4-5; I Samuel 15:10; Psalm 33:4-6; Isaiah 1:10; Jeremiah 1:2; Ezekiel 1:3; Mark 2:2; 4:14-20, 33; 7:13; Luke 8:11-21; 11:28; John 1:1, 14; 2:22; Acts 4:31; 8:14; 13:7; 16:16; 19:20; I Corinthians 1:18; Colossians 3:16; I John 1:1; Revelation 19:13.*

WORLD, THE. To the ancient Hebrew of the OT, "world" was most often used to mean no more than the familiar lands around the Mediterranean Sea. By NT times the known world was as large as the Roman Empire. "World" was also used to mean not so much lands and nations as all the affairs and doings of people. The word *world* in this sense distinguished the affairs and doings of people from the kingdom of God. The word was sometimes used to refer to the whole created order. (See *Earth.*) *I Samuel 2:8; Psalms 9:8; 24:1-2; 90:2; Isaiah 34:1; Jeremiah 25:26; Nahum 1:5; Matthew 13:22; Mark 14:9; 16:15; Luke 2:1; John 3:16-17; 9:32; 12:19; 14:17, 27; 15:19; Romans 1:8; James 1:27; I John 2:15-16.*

WORM. The worm is mentioned many times in the Bible, although almost always the reference is to the maggot or the catepillar. In an occasional instance, as in Micah 7:17,

earthworms are obviously meant: "They . . . shall move out of their holes like worms of the earth." Earthworms have been common everywhere since the world was young.

WORMWOOD. A variety of shrub with woolly, gray-green leaves. These leaves were used in making medicine and had a very bitter taste. Wormwood extract was poisonous if taken in large quantities. The prophets used it as a figure of speech to describe something that is hard or bitter to accept. "Wormwood" is used as a figure of speech to refer to the results of evil and to the judgment of God. *Jeremiah 9:15; 23:15; Lamentations 3:15, 19; Amos 5:7; 6:12; Revelation 8:10-11.*

WORSHIP. The English word, coming from an Anglo-Saxon word meaning "worthship," means an acknowledgment of worthiness, respect, reverence. In the Bible, worship is an act or attitude intended to recognize the worth of God, to honor him. In OT times worship was expressed with sacrifices and offerings. Psalms and musical instruments were used in the temple services. In later OT times the Jews gathered together in the synagogue for the reading of scripture, for instruction, and for prayers. In the NT, Christian worship centered in the Lord's Supper, in baptism, and in preaching. There was also singing of psalms, reading of scripture, instructions, and prayers. From the earliest times in the Christian church there have been both public or congregational worship and private worship in which an individual participates

alone. *Exodus 34:14; I Samuel 1:3; 15:30; II Samuel 12:20; I Chronicles 16:29; Psalms 22:27; 99:5; Isaiah 36:7; Matthew 4:10; 28:9, 17; Acts 13:2; 17:23; Romans 12:1; I Corinthians 14:25.*

YAHWEH (YHWH). An English-language version of the probable name by which the Hebrews thought of God. For the Hebrews the name of each person represented the person himself. Thus the name of the Holy God represented his power and his holiness (see *God, Names of*). They regarded the name with utmost reverence. It is believed the name would have been pronounced "Yahweh," but it was seldom spoken. In writing it only four letters, translated as YHWH and called the Tetragrammaton, were used. Today in the English versions of the OT "Lord" is often used in places where the name of God is indicated. YHWH or Yahweh rarely appears except in footnotes.

YEAR. A division of time. The oldest calendar of the Israelites was borrowed from the Canaanites. It was an agricultural calendar. The day of cutting the first sheaf of grain was New Year's Day. The year was divided into seven periods of seven weeks plus one extra day in each period, a sacred day. Added to this were two seven-day periods in which were held the Feast of Booths and the Feast of Unleavened Bread. This way of defining time was used until the reign of Solomon. He borrowed the calendar of Tyre, based on the solar

system with 365 days in a normal year. The year began with the autumn equinox—in late September. About 450 B.C. a lunar calendar was adopted which depended on the phases of the moon. In the fourth century B.C. the Jews began to reckon a day as being from sunset to sunset. This lunar calendar developed into the calendar still used today for Jewish religious time-reckoning. *I Kings 6:1; II Chronicles 9:24; 36:21; Psalm 90:9-10; Proverbs 4:10.*

YOKE. A wooden frame placed over the necks of two oxen to harness them together. To the middle of the yoke bar was connected a single shaft which pulled a plow, sled, or cart. Yokes were also put on prisoners of war and slaves. The word was used in the OT as a symbol of slavery. It was used by Paul in the NT to symbolize the bonds in which fellow Christians worked together as a team under Christ. *Numbers 19:2; I Kings 19:19, 21; II Chronicles 10:4; Job 1:3; Jeremiah 27:8; 28:11; Lamentations 1: 14; Matthew 11:29; Galatians 5:1; I Timothy 6:1.*

YOUTH. According to the Bible, the time between a person's infancy and his years of greatest vigor and opportunity but not his years of greatest maturity and judgment. The early years of Israel were called the nation's youth by the prophets. *Job 33:25; Ecclesiates 12:1; Jeremiah 1:6-8, 2:2; Ezekiel 23:19; Hosea 2:15; Acts 26:4; I Timothy 4:12; II Timothy 2:22-26.*

ZACCHAEUS. Chief tax collector of Jericho. The life of this man was changed when he met and talked with Jesus. *Luke 19:1-10.*

ZADOK. The priest of David in Gibeon and later in Jerusalem. After the death of David, Zadok backed Solomon in his struggle against his brother Adonijah for the throne. Until this time Abiathar had been equal in authority with Zadok. Solomon exiled Abiathar and gave Zadok complete charge of the temple. His family continued as the dominant priestly family. *II Samuel 15:24-37; I Kings 1:22-39; 2:35; I Chronicles 16:37-41; Ezekiel 40:46; 43:19; 44:15; 48:11.*

ZEALOT. In NT times a member of a patriotic group of Jews who rebelled against all foreign rulers, especially the Romans. Simon the Zealot, before becoming a disciple of Jesus, had probably been a member of some group like this. *Luke 6:15; Acts 1:13.*

ZEBEDEE. The father of the apostles James and John. He and his sons were in the fishing business with Simon and Andrew at Capernaum and seem to have been prosperous enough to have a fleet of boats and servants. *Matthew 4:21; Mark 1:16-20; Luke 5:10.*

ZEBU. It is quite possible that the "majesty" (Deuteronomy 33:17) and the "beauty" (Jeremiah 46:20), rather strangely applied to the ox, were intended for the zebu which it resembles in some respects. The zebu is known as the East Indian ox. It is a much more majestic and noble-looking animal than the common ox. With its arched hump, massive shoulders, and short horns it was known to the

early Persians, Egyptians, and Babylonians. A close replica of the zebu is the Brahman bull, now common in parts of this country and used for breeding.

ZEBULUN. A son of Jacob and the ancestor of the Israelite tribe by that name whose territory was west of the Sea of Galilee. In the song of Deborah the tribe is mentioned for its bravery. *Genesis 30:20; Numbers 1:30-31; 2:7; 26:26; Judges 4:10; 5:14, 18; 12:11-12; I Chronicles 12:33, 40; Psalm 68:27; Matthew 4:13.*

ZECHARIAH. 1. A prophet about 520 B.C. after the return of some of the exiles to Jerusalem from Babylon. He was concerned with the rebuilding of the temple in Jerusalem. (See *Zechariah, Book of.*) *Ezra 5:1; 6:14; Zechariah 1:1, 7; 7:1, 8.*

2. The name of a king of Israel who ruled for six months in 753 and 752 B.C. and was murdered by Shallum. *II Kings 14:29; 15:8, 11.*

3. The son of the priest Jehoiada. During the reign of Joash in the southern kingdom of Judah he preached against idol worship and announced the judgment of God. The people plotted against him, and Joash ordered him stoned in the temple. In Matthew this Zechariah is identified with the OT prophet, probably through a copyist's mistake. *II Chronicles 24:20-25; Matthew 23:35; Luke 11:51.*

4. Father of John the Baptist. *Luke 1:5-25, 57-79; 3:2.*

ZECHARIAH, BOOK OF. One of the twelve short books of prophecy in the OT. It consists of oracles and visions of the prophet Zechariah after some of the Jews had returned to Jerusalem from exile in Babylon. The last six chapters probably were written by later prophets and added to the collection.

ZEDEKIAH. The last king of the southern kingdom of Judah, from about 597 to 586 B.C. He was placed on the throne by Nebuchadnezzar, king of Babylon, after King Jehoiachin had been sent into exile. Zedekiah rebelled against Nebuchadnezzar, and this led to the attack and destruction of Jerusalem. Zedekiah was taken prisoner. Nebuchadnezzar forced him to watch while his two sons were killed. Then the king's own eyes were put out, and he was led in chains to Babylon. The prophet Jeremiah was active during the reign of Zedekiah. *II Kings 24:17–25:7; II Chronicles 18:10; 36:10-13; Jeremiah 1:3; 27:1-15; 37:1–39:7; 52:1-11.*

ZEPHANIAH. A prophet in the southern kingdom of Judah from around 630 to 625 B.C. His work was done in the reign of King Josiah, who was a great religious leader and did much to encourage faith and worship among his people. (See *Zephaniah, Book of.*)

ZEPHANIAH, BOOK OF. Work of a Judean prophet of the seventh century whose great-great-grandfather was King Hezekiah. Zephaniah prophesied during the reign of King Josiah. In his oracles he denounced idolatry and warned that the day of the Lord would bring judgment on the

Hebrews and on the surrounding nations.

ZERUBBABEL. A Babylonian Jew who returned to Jerusalem after the Exile to become governor under the Persian king Darius I. He resumed the building of the temple about 520 B.C. although a start had been made by the first exiles, who returned around 538 B.C. However, more than twenty years had elapsed without the building's being finished. Zerubbabel was a grandson of Jehoiachin, the exiled king of Judah. *Ezra 3:2-13; 5:1-2; Nehemiah 7:7; 12:1, 47; Haggai 1:1-15.*

ZIKLAG. A town in Judah, north of Beer-sheba. David used it as a base for his raids against the Amalakites before he became king. *I Samuel 27:6; 30:1, 14, 26; II Samuel 1:1; 4:10; I Chronicles 12:1-20; Nehemiah 11:28.*

ZIMRI. King of the northern kingdom of Israel for seven days in 885 B.C. He led a revolt against King Elah and murdered the drunken king, who had remained behind while his army was fighting the Philistines. When word of the king's death reached the army, the men acclaimed Omri, the commander-in-chief, as king. Zimri burned the palace and himself in it when he saw how things had turned against him. *I Kings 16:18-20.*

ZIN, WILDERNESS OF. In the OT a wilderness through which the Israelites passed on their way to Canaan. It was probably a part of the southeastern border of Judah toward the Dead Sea. *Numbers 13:21; 20:1; 27:14; 33:36; 34:3-4; Deuteronomy 32:51; Joshua 15:1, 3.*

ZION. A fortified hill in Jerusalem under the Jebusites. "Zion" was often used as a name for the entire city. After the conquest of Jerusalem by David, Zion was renamed "city of David," and the ark of the covenant was brought there. When the ark was transferred to the temple, the name "city of Zion" was extended to include the temple area. "Daughter of Zion" is a poetic term for Jerusalem and its inhabitants. *II Samuel 5:7; I Kings 8:1; I Chronicles 11:5; II Chronicles 5:2; Psalms 2:6; 69:35; 126:1; Song of Solomon 3:11; Isaiah 10:24; 16:1; 51:11, 16; 52:1, 8; 61:3; Micah 4:2-8; Matthew 21:5; Romans 9:33; 11:26.*

ZIPPORAH. The first wife of Moses and daughter of Jethro. *Exodus 2:16, 21-22; 18:1-4.*

ZOAR. In the OT one of the "five cities of the valley" in the time of Abraham. It was probably located in the area now under water at the southern end of the Dead Sea. Lot, Abraham's nephew, escaped to Zoar when Sodom and Gomorrah were destroyed. Later he left out of fear. *Genesis 13:10; 14:2; 19:20-23, 30; Deuteronomy 34:3; Isaiah 15:5; Jeremiah 48:34.* ◊

A
CONCORDANCE

TO THE
 ## NEW INTERNATIONAL
VERSION

Introduction

This NIV Concordance is a condensation of *The NIV Complete Concordance*, taking over 35,000 references from the latter's 250,000. These 35,000 references have been selected as the most helpful for the average Bible student or layperson.

When determining whether or not to include a verse reference, we gave careful consideration to the passage in which the verse is located. We also encourage you to always consider the larger context of the passage, giving special attention to the flow of the thought from beginning to end. Whenever you look up a verse, your goal should be to discover the intended meaning of the verse in context. Do not use this concordance, or any concordance, merely as a *verse-finder;* it should also be used as a *passage-finder.* The contexts surrounding each entry are longer than those usually found in concordances; but even so, the context excerpts are too brief for study purposes. They serve only to help you locate familiar verses.

In some cases the usual short contextual phrases are ineffective in helping you locate a passage. This is especially true in studying key events in a Bible character's life. Therefore, we have incorporated 260 "block entries" in which we use descriptive phrases that mark the breadth of a passage containing episodes of that person's life. The descriptive phrases replace the brief context surrounding each occurrence of the name.

Often more than one Bible character has the same name. For example, there are more than thirty Zechariahs in the Bible. In these cases we have given the name a block entry, assigning each person a number (1), (2), etc., and have included a descriptive phrase to distinguish each. Insignificant names are not included.

In this concordance there are 1,239 key word entries that have an exhaustive list of every appearance of that word. When this occurs, the word or block entry is marked with an asterisk (*).

This mini-concordance includes some words not found in *The NIV Complete Concordance.* These words include: boy, boy's, boys, daughter, daughters, girl, man, man's, men, men's, people, peoples, woman, and women.

Since this concordance can only serve one translation—the New International Version—it is difficult for readers familiar with the Authorized Version to make the transition from its older, more archaic language to that of the NIV. We have tried, therefore, to make this transition a bit easier by including some forty-four prominent Authorized Version words and linking them to NIV words that have taken their place. We wish to thank Dr. Daniel E. Sauerwein of Multnomah School of the Bible for supplying the data for these additional words.

We pray that this concordance will be used by NIV readers to introduce them to the full scope of God's truth in every book of the Bible.

John R. Kohlenberger III
Edward W. Goodrick

ABBREVIATIONS FOR THE BOOKS OF THE BIBLE

Genesis	Ge	Nahum	Na
Exodus	Ex	Habbakuk	Hab
Leviticus	Lev	Zephaniah	Zep
Numbers	Nu	Haggai	Hag
Deuteronomy	Dt	Zechariah	Zec
Joshua	Jos	Malachi	Mal
Judges	Jdg	Matthew	Mt
Ruth	Ru	Mark	Mk
1 Samuel	1Sa	Luke	Lk
2 Samuel	2Sa	John	Jn
1 Kings	1Ki	Acts	Ac
2 Kings	2Ki	Romans	Ro
1 Chronicles	1Ch	1 Corinthians	1Co
2 Chronicles	2Ch	2 Corinthians	2Co
Ezra	Ezr	Galatians	Gal
Nehemiah	Ne	Ephesians	Eph
Esther	Est	Philippians	Php
Job	Job	Colossians	Col
Psalms	Ps	1 Thessalonians	1Th
Proverbs	Pr	2 Thessalonians	2Th
Ecclesiastes	Ecc	1 Timothy	1Ti
Song of Songs	SS	2 Timothy	2Ti
Isaiah	Isa	Titus	Tit
Jeremiah	Jer	Philemon	Phm
Lamentations	La	Hebrews	Heb
Ezekiel	Eze	James	Jas
Daniel	Da	1 Peter	1Pe
Hosea	Hos	2 Peter	2Pe
Joel	Joel	1 John	1Jn
Amos	Am	2 John	2Jn
Obadiah	Ob	3 John	3Jn
Jonah	Jnh	Jude	Jude
Micah	Mic	Revelation	Rev

AARON

Genealogy of (Ex 6:16-20; Jos 21:4, 10; 1Ch 6: 3-15).

Priesthood of (Ex 28:1; Nu 17; Heb 5:1-4; 7), garments (Ex 28; 39), consecration (Ex 29), ordination (Lev 8).

Spokesman for Moses (Ex 4:14-16, 27-31; 7: 1-2). Supported Moses' hands in battle (Ex 17: 8-13). Built golden calf (Ex 32; Dt 9:20). Talked against Moses (Nu 12). Priesthood opposed (Nu 16); staff budded (Nu 17). Forbidden to enter land (Nu 20:1-12). Death (Nu 20:22-29; 33:38-39).

ABADDON*

Rev   9: 11 whose name in Hebrew is *A*,

ABANDON (ABANDONED)

Dt   4: 31 he will not *a* or destroy you
1Ki   6: 13 and will not *a* my people Israel.''
Ne   9: 19 compassion you did not *a* them
      9: 31 an end to them or *a* them,
Ps   16: 10 you will not *a* me to the grave,
Ac   2: 27 you will not *a* me to the grave,
1Ti   4: 1 in later times some will *a* the faith

ABANDONED (ABANDON)

Ge   24: 27 who has not *a* his kindness
2Co   4: 9 persecuted, but not *a;* struck down,

ABBA*

Mk   14: 36 ''*A*, Father,'' he said, ''everything is
Ro   8: 15 And by him we cry, ''*A*, Father.''
Gal   4: 6 the Spirit who calls out, ''*A*, Father

ABEDNEGO

Deported to Babylon with Daniel (Da 1:1-6). Name changed from Azariah (Da 1:7). Refused defilement by food (Da 1:8-20). Refused idol worship (Da 3:1-12); saved from furnace (Da 3:13-30).

ABEL

Second son of Adam (Ge 4:2). Offered proper sacrifice (Ge 4:4; Heb 11:4). Murdered by Cain (Ge 4:8; Mt 23:35; Lk 11:51; 1Jn 3:12).

ABHOR (ABHORS)

Lev 26: 30 of your idols, and I will *a* you.
Dt   7: 26 Utterly *a* and detest it,
Ps   26: 5 I *a* the assembly of evildoers
    119:163 I hate and *a* falsehood
    139: 21 and *a* those who rise up against you
Am   6: 8 ''I *a* the pride of Jacob
Ro   2: 22 You who *a* idols, do you rob

ABHORS (ABHOR)

Pr   11: 1 The LORD *a* dishonest scales,

ABIATHAR

High priest in days of Saul and David (1Sa 22; 2Sa 15; 1Ki 1-2; Mk 2:26). Escaped Saul's slaughter of priests (1Sa 22:18-23). Supported David in Absalom's revolt (2Sa 15:24-29). Supported Adonijah (1Ki 1:7-42); deposed by Solomon (1Ki 2:22-35; cf. 1Sa 2:31-35).

ABIDE see REMAIN

ABIGAIL

1. Sister of David (1Ch 2:16-17).
2. Wife of Nabal (1Sa 25:30); pled for his life with David (1Sa 25:14-35). Became David's wife after Nabal's death (1Sa 25:36-42); bore him Kileab (2Sa 3:3) also known as Daniel (1Ch 3:1).

ABIHU

Son of Aaron (Ex 6:23; 24:1, 9); killed for offering unauthorized fire (Lev 10; Nu 3:2-4; 1Ch 24:1-2).

ABIJAH

1. Second son of Samuel (1Ch 6:28); a corrupt judge (1Sa 8:1-5).
2. An Aaronic priest (1Ch 24:10; Lk 1:5).
3. Son of Jeroboam I of Israel; died as prophesied by Ahijah (1Ki 14:1-18).
4. Son of Rehoboam; king of Judah who fought Jeroboam I attempting to reunite the kingdom (1Ki 14:31-15:8; 2Ch 12:16-14:1; Mt 1:7).

ABILITY (ABLE)

Ex   35: 34 tribe of Dan, the *a* to teach others.
Dt   8: 18 for it is he who gives you the *a*
Ezr   2: 69 According to their *a* they gave
Mt   25: 15 one talent, each according to his *a*.
Ac   11: 29 disciples, each according to his *a,*
2Co   1: 8 far beyond our *a* to endure,
      8: 3 were able, and even beyond their *a*.

ABIMELECH

1. King of Gerar who took Abraham's wife Sarah, believing her to be his sister (Ge 20). Later made a covenant with Abraham (Ge 21:22-33).
2. King of Gerar who took Isaac's wife Rebekah, believing her to be his sister (Ge 26:1-11). Later made a covenant with Isaac (Ge 26:12-31).
3. Son of Gideon (Jdg 8:31). Attempted to make himself king (Jdg 9).

ABISHAG*

Shunammite virgin; attendant of David in his old age (1Ki 1:1-15; 2:17-22).

ABISHAI

Son of Zeruiah, David's sister (1Sa 26:6; 1Ch 2:16). One of David's chief warriors (1Ch 11: 15-21): against Edom (1Ch 18:12-13), Ammon (2Sa 10), Absalom (2Sa 18), Sheba (2Sa 20). Wanted to kill Saul (1Sa 26), killed Abner (2Sa 2: 18-27; 3:22-39), wanted to kill Shimei (2Sa 16: 5-13; 19:16-23).

ABLE (ABILITY ENABLE ENABLED ENABLES ENABLING)

Nu   14: 16 'The LORD was not *a*
1Ch 29: 14 that we should be *a* to give
2Ch   2: 6 who is *a* to build a temple for them,
Eze   7: 19 and gold will not be *a* to save them
Da   3: 17 the God we serve is *a* to save us
      4: 37 walk in pride he is *a* to humble.
Mt   9: 28 ''Do you believe that I am *a*
Lk   13: 24 will try to enter and will not be *a*
     14: 30 to build and was not *a* to finish.'
     21: 15 none of your adversaries will be *a*
     21: 36 and that you may be *a* to stand
Ac   5: 39 you will not be *a* to stop these men;
Ro   8: 39 will be *a* to separate us
     14: 4 for the Lord is *a* to make him stand
     16: 25 to him who is *a* to establish you
2Co   9: 8 God is *a* to make all grace abound
Eph   3: 8 to him who is *a* to do immeasurably
      6: 13 you may be *a* to stand your ground,
1Ti   3: 2 respectable, hospitable, *a* to teach,
2Ti   1: 12 and am convinced that he is *a*
      2: 24 kind to everyone, *a* to teach,
      3: 15 which are *a* to make you wise
Heb   2: 18 he is *a* to help those who are being
      7: 25 he is *a* to save completely
Jas   3: 2 *a* to keep his whole body in check.
Jude   : 24 To him who is *a* to keep you
Rev   5: 5 He is *a* to open the scroll

ABNER

Cousin of Saul and commander of his army (1Sa 14:50; 17:55-57; 26). Made Ish-Bosheth king after Saul (2Sa 2:8-10), but later defected to David (2Sa 3:6-21). Killed Asahel (2Sa 2:18-32), for which he was killed by Joab and Abishai (2Sa 3: 22-39).

ABOLISH (ABOLISHED ABOLISHING)

Hos   2: 18 I will *a* from the land,
Mt   5: 17 that I have come to *a* the Law

ABOLISHED (ABOLISH)

Gal   5: 11 the offense of the cross has been *a*.

ABOLISHING* (ABOLISH)

Eph   2: 15 by *a* in his flesh the law

ABOMINATION* (ABOMINATIONS)

Da   11: 31 set up the *a* that causes desolation.
     12: 11 *a* that causes desolation is set up,
Mt   24: 15 the holy place 'the *a* that causes
Mk   13: 14 you see 'the *a* that causes

ABOMINATIONS (ABOMINATION)

Da   9: 27 who causes desolation will place *a*

ABOUND (ABOUNDING)

2Co   9: 8 able to make all grace *a* to you,
      9: 8 you will *a* in every good work.
Php   1: 9 that your love may *a* more

ABOUNDING (ABOUND)

Ex   34: 6 slow to anger, *a* in love
Nu   14: 18 *a* in love and forgiving sin
Ne   9: 17 slow to anger and *a* in love.
Ps   86: 5 *a* in love to all who call to you.
     86: 15 slow to anger, *a* in love
    103: 8 slow to anger, *a* in love.
Joel 2: 13 slow to anger and *a* in love,
Jnh   4: 2 slow to anger and *a* in love,

ABRAHAM

Abram, son of Terah (Ge 11:26-27), husband of Sarah (Ge 11:29).

Covenant relation with the LORD (Ge 12:1-3; 13:14-17; 15; 17; 22:15-18; Ex 2:24; Ne 9:8; Ps 105; Mic 7:20; Lk 1:68-75; Ro 4; Heb 6:13-15).

Called from Ur, via Haran, to Canaan (Ge 12: 1; Ac 7:2-4; Heb 11:8-10). Moved to Egypt, nearly lost Sarah to Pharoah (Ge 12:10-20). Divided the land with Lot; settled in Hebron (Ge 13). Saved Lot from four kings (Ge 14:1-16); blessed by Melchizedek (Ge 14:17-20; Heb 7:1-20). Declared righteous by faith (Ge 15:6; Ro 4:3; Gal 3: 6-9). Fathered Ishmael by Hagar (Ge 16).

Name changed from Abram (Ge 17:5; Ne 9:7). Circumcised (Ge 17; Ro 4:9-12). Entertained three visitors (Ge 18); promised a son by Sarah (Ge 18: 9-15; 17:16). Questioned destruction of Sodom and Gomorrah (Ge 18:16-33). Moved to Gerar; nearly lost Sarah to Abimelech (Ge 20). Fathered Isaac by Sarah (Ge 21:1-7; Ac 7:8; Heb 11:11-12); sent away Hagar and Ishmael (Ge 21:8-21; Gal 4: 22-30). Covenant with Abimelech (Ge 21:22-32). Tested by offering Isaac (Ge 22; Heb 11:17-19; Jas 2:21-24). Sarah died; bought field of Ephron for burial (Ge 23). Secured wife for Isaac (Ge 24). Fathered children by Keturah (Ge 25:1-6; 1Ch 1: 32-33). Death (Ge 25:7-11).

Called servant of God (Ge 26:24), friend of God (2Ch 20:7; Isa 41:8; Jas 2:23), prophet (Ge 20:7), father of Israel (Ex 3:15; Isa 51:2; Mt 3:9; Jn 8:39-58).

ABRAM see ABRAHAM

ABSALOM

Son of David by Maacah (2Sa 3:3; 1Ch 3:2). Killed Amnon for rape of his sister Tamar; banished by David (2Sa 13). Returned to Jerusalem; received by David (2Sa 14). Rebelled against David; siezed kingdom (2Sa 15-17). Killed (2Sa 18).

ABSENT

Col   2: 5 though I am *a* from you in body,

ABSOLUTE*

1Ti   5: 2 women as sisters, with *a* purity.

ABSTAIN (ABSTAINS)

Ex   19: 15 *A* from sexual relations.''
Nu   6: 3 he must *a* from wine and other
Ac   15: 20 them to *a* from food polluted
1Pe   2: 11 to *a* from sinful desires,

ABSTAINS* (ABSTAIN)

Ro   14: 6 thanks to God; and he who *a,*

ABUNDANCE (ABUNDANT)

Ge   41: 29 Seven years of great *a* are coming
Job 36: 31 and provides food in *a*.
Ps   66: 12 but you brought us to a place of *a*.
Ecc   5: 12 but the *a* of a rich man
Isa 66: 11 and delight in her overflowing *a*.''
Jer   2: 7 and use an *a* of soap,
Mt   13: 12 given more, and he will have an *a*.
     25: 29 given more, and he will have an *a*.
Lk   12: 15 consist in the *a* of his possessions.''
1Pe   1: 2 Grace and peace be yours in *a*.
2Pe   1: 2 yours in *a* through the knowledge
Jude   : 2 peace and love be yours in *a*.

ABUNDANT (ABUNDANCE)

Dt 28: 11 will grant you *a* prosperity—
    32: 2 like *a* rain on tender plants.
Job 36: 28 and *a* showers fall on mankind.
Ps 68: 9 You gave *a* showers, O God;
    78: 15 gave them water as *a* as the seas;
    132: 15 I will bless her with *a* provisions;
    145: 7 will celebrate your *a* goodness
Pr 12: 11 works his land will have *a* food,
    28: 19 works his land will have *a* food,
Jer 33: 9 and will tremble at the *a* prosperity
Ro 5: 17 who receive God's *a* provision

ABUSIVE

2Ti 3: 2 *a*, disobedient to their parents,

ABYSS*

Lk 8: 31 not to order them to go into the *A*.
Rev 9: 1 the key to the shaft of the *A*.
    9: 2 When he opened the *A*, smoke rose
    9: 2 darkened by the smoke from the *A*.
    9: 11 king over them the angel of the *A*,
    11: 7 up from the *A* will attack them,
    17: 8 and will come up out of the *A*
    20: 1 having the key to the *A*
    20: 3 He threw him into the *A*,

ACCEPT (ACCEPTABLE ACCEPTANCE ACCEPTED ACCEPTS)

Ex 23: 8 "Do not *a* a bribe,
Dt 16: 19 Do not *a* a bribe, for a bribe blinds
Job 42: 8 and I will *a* his prayer and not deal
Pr 10: 8 The wise in heart *a* commands,
    19: 20 Listen to advice and *a* instruction,
Ro 15: 7 *A* one another, then, just
Jas 1: 21 humbly *a* the word planted in you,

ACCEPTABLE (ACCEPT)

Pr 21: 3 is more *a* to the LORD

ACCEPTANCE* (ACCEPT)

Ro 11: 15 what will their *a* be but life
1Ti 1: 15 saying that deserves full *a*:
    4: 9 saying that deserves full *a*

ACCEPTED (ACCEPT)

Ge 4: 7 will you not be *a*? But if you do not
Job 42: 9 and the LORD *a* Job's prayer.
Lk 4: 24 "no prophet is *a* in his home town.
Gal 1: 9 you a gospel other than what you *a*,

ACCEPTS (ACCEPT)

Ps 6: 9 the LORD *a* my prayer.
Jn 13: 20 whoever *a* anyone I send *a* me;
    13: 20 whoever *a* me *a* the one who sent

ACCESS

Ro 5: 2 through whom we have gained *a*
Eph 2: 18 For through him we both have *a*

ACCOMPANIED (ACCOMPANY)

1Co 10: 4 from the spiritual rock that *a* them,
Jas 2: 17 if it is not *a* by action, is dead.

ACCOMPANIES (ACCOMPANY)

2Co 9: 13 obedience that *a* your confession

ACCOMPANY (ACCOMPANIED ACCOMPANIES)

Dt 28: 2 *a* you if you obey the LORD your
Mk 16: 17 these signs will *a* those who believe
Heb 6: 9 your case—things that *a* that salvation.

ACCOMPLISH

Ecc 2: 2 And what does pleasure *a*?"
Isa 44: 28 and will *a* all that I please;
    55: 11 but will *a* what I desire

ACCORD

Nu 24: 13 not do anything of my own *a*,
Jn 10: 18 but I lay it down of my own *a*.
    12: 49 For I did not speak of my own *a*,

ACCOUNT (ACCOUNTABLE)

Ge 2: 4 This is the *a* of the heavens
    5: 1 This is the written *a* of Adam's line
    6: 9 This is the *a* of Noah.
    10: 1 This is the *a* of Shem, Ham

Ge 11: 10 This is the *a* of Shem.
    11: 27 This is the *a* of Terah.
    25: 12 This is the *a* of Abraham's son
    25: 19 This is the *a* of Abraham's son
    36: 1 This is the *a* of Esau (that is, Edom
    36: 9 This is the *a* of Esau the father
    37: 2 This is the *a* of Jacob.
Mt 12: 36 to give *a* on the day of judgment
Lk 16: 2 Give an *a* of your management,
Ro 14: 12 each of us will give an *a* of himself
Heb 4: 13 of him to whom we must give *a*.

ACCOUNTABLE* (ACCOUNT)

Eze 3: 18 and I will hold you *a* for his blood.
    3: 20 and I will hold you *a* for his blood.
    33: 6 but I will hold the watchman *a*
    33: 8 and I will hold you *a* for his blood.
    34: 10 and will hold them *a* for my flock.
Da 6: 2 The satraps were made *a* to them
Jnh 1: 14 Do not hold us *a* for killing
Ro 3: 19 and the whole world held *a* to God.

ACCURATE

Dt 25: 15 You must have *a* and honest
Pr 11: 1 but *a* weights are his delight.

ACCURSED (CURSE)

2Pe 2: 14 experts in greed—an *a* brood!

ACCUSATION (ACCUSE)

1Ti 5: 19 Do not entertain an *a*

ACCUSATIONS (ACCUSE)

2Pe 2: 11 do not bring slanderous *a*

ACCUSE (ACCUSATION ACCUSATIONS ACCUSER ACCUSES ACCUSING)

Pr 3: 30 Do not *a* a man for no reason—
Lk 3: 14 and don't *a* people falsely—

ACCUSER (ACCUSE)

Jn 5: 45 Your *a* is Moses, on whom your
Rev 12: 10 For the *a* of our brothers,

ACCUSES (ACCUSE)

Job 40: 2 Let him who *a* God answer him!"
Rev 12: 10 who *a* them before our God day

ACCUSING (ACCUSE)

Ro 2: 15 and their thoughts now *a*,

ACHAN*

Sin at Jericho caused defeat at Ai; stoned (Jos 7; 22:20; 1Ch 2:7).

ACHE*

Pr 14: 13 Even in laughter the heart may *a*,

ACHIEVE

Isa 55: 11 *a* the purpose for which I sent it.

ACHISH

King of Gath before whom David feigned insanity (1Sa 21:10-15). Later "ally" of David (2Sa 27-29).

ACKNOWLEDGE (ACKNOWLEDGED ACKNOWLEDGES)

Pr 3: 6 in all your ways *a* him,
Jer 3: 13 Only *a* your guilt—
Hos 6: 3 let us press on to *a* him.
Mt 10: 32 *a* him before my Father in heaven.
Lk 12: 8 *a* him before the angels of God.
1Jn 4: 3 spirit that does not *a* Jesus is not

ACKNOWLEDGED (ACKNOWLEDGE)

Lk 7: 29 *a* that God's way was right,

ACKNOWLEDGES* (ACKNOWLEDGE)

Ps 91: 14 for he *a* my name.
Mt 10: 32 "Whoever *a* me before men,
Lk 12: 8 whoever *a* me before men,
1Jn 2: 23 whoever *a* the Son has the Father
    4: 2 Every spirit that *a* that Jesus Christ
    4: 15 If anyone *a* that Jesus is the Son

ACQUIRES (ACQUIRING)

Pr 18: 15 of the discerning *a* knowledge;

ACQUIRING* (ACQUIRES)

Pr 1: 3 for *a* a disciplined and prudent life,

ACQUIT (ACQUITTING)

Ex 23: 7 to death, for I will not *a* the guilty.

ACQUITTING* (ACQUIT)

Dt 25: 1 *a* the innocent and condemning
Pr 17: 15 *A* the guilty and condemning

ACT (ACTION ACTIONS ACTIVE ACTIVITY ACTS)

Ps 119:126 It is time for you to *a*, O LORD;

ACTION (ACT)

2Co 9: 2 has stirred most of them to *a*.
Jas 2: 17 if it is not accompanied by *a*,
1Pe 1: 13 minds for *a*; be self-controlled;

ACTIONS (ACT)

Mt 11: 19 wisdom is proved right by her *a*.''
Gal 6: 4 Each one should test his own *a*.
Tit 1: 16 but by their *a* they deny him.

ACTIVE* (ACT)

Phm 6 I pray that you may be *a*
Heb 4: 12 For the word of God is living and *a*

ACTIVITY (ACT)

Ecc 3: 1 a season for every *a* under heaven:
    3: 17 for there will be a time for every *a*,

ACTS (ACT)

1Ch 16: 9 tell of all his wonderful *a*.
Ps 71: 16 proclaim your mighty *a*,
    71: 24 tell of your righteous *a*
    105: 2 tell of all his wonderful *a*.
    106: 2 Who can proclaim the mighty *a*
    145: 4 they will tell of your mighty *a*.
    145: 12 all men may know of your mighty *a*
    150: 2 Praise him for his *a* of power;
Isa 64: 6 all our righteous *a* are like filthy
Mt 6: 1 not to do your '*a* of righteousness'

ADAM

1. First man (Ge 1:26-2:25; Ro 5:14; 1Ti 2:13). Sin of (Ge 3; Hos 6:7; Ro 5:12-21). Children of (Ge 4:1-5:5). Death of (Ge 5:5; Ro 5:12-21; 1Co 15:22).
2. City (Jos 3:16).

ADD (ADDED)

Dt 4: 2 Do not *a* to what I command you
    12: 32 do not *a* to it or take away from it.
Pr 1: 5 let the wise listen and *a*
    9: 9 he will *a* to his learning.
    30: 6 Do not *a* to his words,
Mt 6: 27 by worrying can *a* a single hour
Lk 12: 25 by worrying can *a* a single hour
Rev 22: 18 God will *a* to him the plagues

ADDED (ADD)

Ecc 3: 14 nothing can be *a* to it and nothing
Ac 2: 47 Lord *a* to their number daily those
Ro 5: 20 The law was *a* so that the trespass
Gal 3: 19 It was *a* because of transgressions

ADDICTED*

Tit 2: 3 to be slanderers or *a* to much wine,

ADMINISTRATION*

1Co 12: 28 with gifts of *a*, and those speaking
Eph 3: 2 Surely you have heard about the *a*
    3: 9 to everyone the *a* of this mystery,

ADMIRABLE*

Php 4: 8 whatever is lovely, whatever is *a*—

ADMIT

Hos 5: 15 until they *a* their guilt.

ADMONISH* (ADMONISHING)

Col 3: 16 and *a* one another with all wisdom,
1Th 5: 12 you in the Lord and who *a* you.

ADMONISHING* (ADMONISH)

Col 1: 28 *a* and teaching everyone

ADONIJAH

1. Son of David by Haggith (2Sa 3:4; 1Ch 3:2). Attempted to be king after David; killed by Solomon's order (1Ki 1-2).

2. Levite; teacher of the Law (2Ch 17:8).

ADOPTED (ADOPTION)

Eph 1: 5 In love he predestined us to be *a*

ADOPTION* (ADOPTED)

Ro 8:23 as we wait eagerly for our *a* as sons,
  9: 4 Theirs is the *a* as sons; theirs

ADORE*

SS 1: 4 How right they are to *a* you!

ADORNMENT* (ADORNS)

1Pe 3: 3 should not come from outward *a*,

ADORNS* (ADORNMENT)

Ps 93: 5 holiness *a* your house
Isa 61:10 as a bride *a* herself with her jewels.
  61:10 bridegroom *a* his head like a priest,

ADULTERER (ADULTERY)

Lev 20:10 both the *a* and the adulteress must
Heb 13: 4 for God will judge the *a*

ADULTERERS (ADULTERY)

1Co 6: 9 idolaters nor *a* nor male prostitutes
1Ti 1:10 for murderers, for *a* and perverts,

ADULTERESS (ADULTERY)

Hos 3: 1 she is loved by another and is an *a*.

ADULTERIES (ADULTERY)

Jer 3: 8 sent her away because of all her *a*.

ADULTEROUS (ADULTERY)

Mk 8:38 in this *a* and sinful generation,
Jas 4: 4 You *a* people, don't you know that

ADULTERY (ADULTERER ADULTERERS ADULTERESS ADULTERIES ADULTEROUS)

Ex 20:14 "You shall not commit *a*.
Dt 5:18 "You shall not commit *a*.'
Mt 5:27 that it was said, 'Do not commit *a*.'
  5:28 lustfully has already committed *a*
  5:32 the divorced woman commits *a*
  15:19 murder, *a*, sexual immorality, theft
  19: 9 marries another woman commits *a*
  18:20 do not commit *a*, do not steal,
Mk 7:21 theft, murder, *a*, greed, malice,
  10:11 marries another woman commits *a*
  10:12 another man, she commits *a*.''
  10:19 do not commit *a*, do not steal,
Lk 16:18 a divorced woman commits *a*.
  16:18 marries another woman commits *a*
  18:20 'Do not commit *a*, do not murder,
Jn 8: 4 woman was caught in the act of *a*.
Rev 18: 3 of the earth committed *a* with her,

ADULTS*

1Co 14:20 but in your thinking be *a*.

ADVANCE (ADVANCED)

Ps 18:29 With your help I can *a*
Php 1:12 has really served to *a* the gospel.

ADVANCED (ADVANCE)

Job 32: 7 *a* years should teach wisdom.'

ADVANTAGE

Ex 22:22 "Do not take *a* of a widow
Dt 24:14 Do not take *a* of a hired man who is
Ro 3: 1 What *a*, then, is there
2Co 11:20 or exploits you or takes *a* of you
1Th 4: 6 should wrong his brother or take *a*

ADVERSITY*

Pr 17:17 and a brother is born for *a*.
Isa 30:20 the Lord gives you the bread of *a*

ADVICE (ADVISERS)

1Ki 12: 8 rejected the *a* the elders
  12:14 he followed the *a* of the young men
2Ch 10: 8 rejected the *a* the elders
Pr 12: 5 but the *a* of the wicked is deceitful.

Pr 12:15 but a wise man listens to *a*.
  19:20 Listen to *a* and accept instruction,
  20:18 Make plans by seeking *a*;

ADVISERS (ADVICE)

Pr 11:14 but many *a* make victory sure.

ADVOCATE*

Job 16:19 my *a* is on high.

AFFLICTED (AFFLICTION)

Job 2: 7 and *a* Job with painful sores
  36: 6 but gives the *a* their rights.
Ps 9:12 he does not ignore the cry of the *a*.
  9:18 nor the hope of the *a* ever perish.
  119:67 Before I was *a* I went astray,
  119:71 It was good for me to be *a*
  119:75 and in faithfulness you have *a* me.
Isa 49:13 will have compassion on his *a* ones.
  53: 4 smitten by him, and *a*.
  53: 7 He was oppressed and *a*,
Na 1:12 Although I have *a* you, O Judah.

AFFLICTION (AFFLICTED AFFLICTIONS)

Dt 16: 3 bread of *a*, because you left Egypt
Ps 107:41 he lifted the needy out of their *a*
Isa 30:20 of adversity and the water of *a*,
  48:10 in the furnace of *a*.
La 3:33 For he does not willingly bring *a*
Ro 12:12 patient in *a*, faithful in prayer.

AFFLICTIONS (AFFLICTION)

Col 1:24 lacking in regard to Christ's *a*,

AFRAID (FEAR)

Ge 3:10 and I was *a* because I was naked;
  26:24 Do not be *a*, for I am with you;
Ex 2:14 Then Moses was *a* and thought,
  3: 6 because he was *a* to look at God.
Dt 1:21 Do not be *a*; do not be discouraged
  1:29 "Do not be terrified; do not be *a*
  20: 1 do not be *a* of them,
  20: 3 Do not be fainthearted or *a*;
2Ki 25:24 "Do not be *a* of the Babylonian
1Ch 13:12 David was *a* of God that day
Ps 27: 1 of whom shall I be *a*?
  56: 3 When I am *a*, / I will trust in you.
  56: 4 in God I trust; I will not be *a*.
Pr 3:24 lie down, you will not be *a*;
Isa 10:24 do not be *a* of the Assyrians,
  12: 2 I will trust and not be *a*.
  44: 8 Do not tremble, do not be *a*.
Jer 1: 8 Do not be *a* of them, for I am
Mt 8:26 You of little faith, why are you so *a*
  10:28 be *a* of the One who can destroy
  10:31 So don't be *a*; you are worth more
Mk 5:36 "Don't be *a*; just believe."
Lk 9:34 and they were *a* as they entered
Jn 14:27 hearts be troubled and do not be *a*.
Ac 27:24 beside me and said, 'Do not be *a*,
Ro 11:20 Do not be arrogant, but be *a*.
Heb 13: 6 Lord is my helper; I will not be *a*.

AGAG (AGAGITE)

King of Amalekites not killed by Saul (1Sa 15).

AGAGITE (AGAG)

Est 8: 3 to the evil plan of Haman the *A*,

AGED (AGES)

Job 12:12 Is not wisdom found among the *a*?
Pr 17: 6 children are a crown to the *a*,

AGES (AGED)

Ro 16:25 the mystery hidden for long *a* past,
Eph 2: 7 that in the coming *a* he might show
  3: 9 which for *a* past was kept hidden
Col 1:26 that has been kept hidden for *a*
Rev 15: 3 King of the *a*.

AGONY

Lk 16:24 because I am in *a* in this fire.'
Rev 16:10 Men gnawed their tongues in *a*

AGREE (AGREEMENT AGREES)

Mt 18:19 on earth *a* about anything you ask
Ro 7:16 want to do, I *a* that the law is good.

Php 4: 2 with Syntyche to *a* with each other

AGREEMENT (AGREE)

2Co 6:16 What *a* is there between the temple

AGREES* (AGREE)

Ac 7:42 This *a* with what is written
  24:14 I believe everything that *a*
1Co 4:17 which *a* with what I teach

AGRIPPA*

Descendant of Herod; king before whom Paul pled his case in Caesarea (Ac 25:13-26:32).

AHAB

1. Son of Omri; king of Israel (1Ki 16:28-22: 40), husband of Jezebel (1Ki 16:31). Promoted Baal worship (1Ki 16:31-33); opposed by Elijah (1Ki 17:1; 18; 21), a prophet (1Ki 20:35-43), Micaiah (1Ki 22:1-28). Defeated Ben-Hadad (1Ki 20). Killed for failing to kill Ben-Hadad and for murder of Naboth (1Ki 20:35-21:40).

2. A false prophet (Jer 29:21-22).

AHAZ

1. Son of Jotham; king of Judah, (2Ki 16; 2Ch 28). Idolatry of (2Ki 16:3-4, 10-18; 2Ch 28:1-4, 22-25). Defeated by Aram and Israel (2Ki 16:5-6; 2Ch 28:5-15). Sought help from Assyria rather than the LORD (2Ki 16:7-9; 2Ch 28:16-21; Isa 7).

2. Benjamite, descendant of Saul (1Ch 8:35-36).

AHAZIAH

1. Son of Ahab; king of Israel (1Ki 22:51-2Ki 1:18; 2Ch 20:35-37). Made an unsuccessful alliance with Jehoshaphat of Judah (2Ch 20:35-37). Died for seeking Baal rather than the LORD (1Ki 1).

2. Son of Jehoram; king of Judah (2Ki 8:25-29; 9:14-29), also called Jehoahaz (2Ch 21:17-22:9; 25:23). Killed by Jehu while visiting Joram (2Ki 9:14-29; 2Ch 22:1-9).

AHIJAH

1Sa 14:18 Saul said to *A*. "Bring the ark
1Ki 14: 2 *A* the prophet is there—the one

AHIMELECH

1. Priest who helped David in his flight from Saul (1Sa 21-22).

2. One of David's warriors (1Sa 26:6).

AHITHOPHEL

One of David's counselors who sided with Absalom (2Sa 15:12, 31-37; 1Ch 27:33-34); committed suicide when his advice was ignored (2Sa 16: 15-17:23).

AI

Jos 7: 4 they were routed by the men of *A*,
  8:28 So Joshua burned *A* and made it

AID

Isa 38:14 troubled; O Lord, come to my *a*!''
Php 4:16 you sent me *a* again and again

AIM

1Co 7:34 Her *a* is to be devoted to the Lord
2Co 13:11 *A* for perfection, listen

AIR

Mt 8:20 and birds of the *a* have nests,
Lk 9:58 and birds of the *a* have nests,
1Co 9:26 not fight like a man beating the *a*.
  14: 9 You will just be speaking into the *a*
Eph 2: 2 of the ruler of the kingdom of the *a*,
1Th 4:17 clouds to meet the Lord in the *a*.

ALABASTER*

Mt 26: 7 came to him with an *a* jar
Mk 14: 3 a woman came with an *a* jar
Lk 7:37 she brought an *a* jar of perfume,

ALARM (ALARMED)

2Co 7:11 indignation, what *a*, what longing,

ALARMED (ALARM)

Mk 13: 7 and rumors of wars, do not be *a*.

2Th 2: 2 not to become easily unsettled or *a*

ALERT*

Jos 8: 4 All of you be on the *a.*
Ps 17: 11 with eyes *a,* to throw me
Isa 21: 7 let him be *a, / fully a.''*
Mk 13: 33 Be *a!* You do not know
Eph 6: 18 be *a* and always keep on praying
1Th 5: 6 but let us be *a* and self-controlled.
1Pe 5: 8 Be self-controlled and *a.*

ALIEN (ALIENATED ALIENS)

Ex 22: 21 ''Do not mistreat an *a*
Lev 24: 22 are to have the same law for the *a*
Ps 146: 9 The Lord watches over the *a*

ALIENATED (ALIEN)

Gal 5: 4 by law have been *a* from Christ;
Col 1: 21 Once you were *a* from God

ALIENS (ALIEN)

Ex 23: 9 know how it feels to be *a,*
1Pe 2: 11 as *a* and strangers in the world,

ALIVE (LIVE)

1Sa 2: 6 Lord brings death and makes *a;*
Lk 24: 23 vision of angels, who said he was *a.*
Ac 1: 3 convincing proofs that he was *a.*
Ro 6: 11 but *a* to God in Christ Jesus.
1Co 15: 22 so in Christ all will be made *a.*
Eph 2: 5 made us *a* with Christ

ALMIGHTY (MIGHT)

Ge 17: 1 ''I am God *A;* walk before me
Ex 6: 3 to Isaac and to Jacob as God *A,*
Ru 1: 20 the *A* has made my life very bitter.
Job 11: 7 Can you probe the limits of the *A?*
    33: 4 the breath of the *A* gives me life.
Ps 89: 8 O Lord God *A,* who is like you?
    91: 1 will rest in the shadow of the *A.*
Isa 6: 3 ''Holy, holy, holy is the Lord *A;*
    45: 13 says the Lord *A.''*
    47: 4 the Lord *A* is his name—
    48: 2 the Lord *A* is his name:
    51: 15 the Lord *A* is his name—
    54: 5 the Lord *A* is his name—
Am 5: 14 the Lord God *A* will be with you,
    5: 15 the Lord God *A* will have mercy
Rev 4: 8 holy is the Lord God *A,* who was,
    19: 6 For our Lord God *A* reigns.

**ALMS see GIVING, (acts of)
RIGHTEOUSNESS**

ALPHA*

Rev 1: 8 ''I am the *A* and the Omega,''
    21: 6 I am the *A* and the Omega,
    22: 13 I am the *A* and the Omega,

ALTAR

Ge 8: 20 Then Noah built an *a* to the Lord
    12: 7 So he built an *a* there to the Lord
    13: 18 where he built an *a* to the Lord.
    22: 9 Abraham built an *a* there
    22: 9 his son Isaac and laid him on the *a,*
    26: 25 Isaac built an *a* there and called
    35: 1 and build an *a* there to God,
Ex 17: 15 Moses built an *a* and called it
    27: 1 ''Build an *a* of acacia wood,
    30: 1 ''Make an *a* of acacia wood
    37: 25 They made the *a* of incense out
Dt 27: 5 an *a* to the Lord your God, an *a*
Jos 8: 30 on Mount Ebal an *a* to the Lord,
    22: 10 built an imposing *a* there
Jdg 6: 24 So Gideon built an *a* to the Lord
    21: 4 the next day they people built an *a*
1Sa 7: 17 he built an *a* there to the Lord.
    14: 35 Then Saul built an *a* to the Lord;
2Sa 24: 25 David built an *a* to the Lord
1Ki 12: 33 sacrifices on the *a* he had built
    13: 2 ''O *a, a!* This is what the Lord
    16: 32 He set up an *a* for Baal
    18: 30 and he repaired the *a* of the Lord
2Ki 16: 11 So Uriah the priest built an *a*
1Ch 21: 26 David built an *a* to the Lord
2Ch 4: 1 made a bronze *a* twenty cubits
    4: 19 the golden *a;* the tables
    15: 8 He repaired the *a* of the Lord
    32: 12 'You must worship before one *a*

2Ch 33: 16 he restored the *a* of the Lord
Ezr 3: 2 to build the *a* of the God of Israel
Isa 6: 6 taken with tongs from the *a.*
Eze 40: 47 the *a* was in front of the temple.
Mt 5: 23 if you are offering your gift at the *a*
Ac 17: 23 found an *a* with this inscription:
Heb 13: 10 We have an *a* from which those
Rev 6: 9 I saw under the *a* the souls

ALTER*

Ps 89: 34 or *a* what my lips have uttered.

ALWAYS

Dt 15: 11 There will *a* be poor people
Ps 16: 8 I have set the Lord *a* before me.
    51: 3 and my sin is *a* before me.
Pr 23: 7 who is *a* thinking about the cost.
Mt 26: 11 The poor you will *a* have with you,
    28: 20 And surely I am with you *a,*
Mk 14: 7 The poor you will *a* have with you,
Jn 12: 8 You will *a* have the poor
1Co 13: 7 *a* protects, *a* trusts, *a* hopes, *a*
Php 4: 4 Rejoice in the Lord *a.*
1Pe 3: 15 be prepared to give an answer

AMALEKITES

Ex 17: 8 *A* came and attacked the Israelites
1Sa 15: 2 'I will punish the *A*

AMASA

Nephew of David (1Ch 2:17). Commander of Absalom's forces (2Sa 17:24-27). Returned to David (2Sa 19:13). Killed by Joab (2Sa 20:4-13).

AMASSES*

Pr 28: 8 *a* it for another, who will be kind

AMAZED

Mt 7: 28 the crowds were *a* at his teaching,
Mk 6: 6 And he was *a* at their lack of faith.
    10: 24 The disciples were *a* at his words.
Ac 2: 7 Utterly *a,* they asked: ''Are not all
    13: 12 for he was *a* at the teaching about

AMAZIAH

1. Son of Joash; king of Judah (2Ki 14; 2Ch 25). Defeated Edom (2Ki 14:7; 2Ch 25:5-13); defeated by Israel for worshiping Edom's gods (2Ki 14:8-14; 2Ch 25:14-24).
2. Idolatrous priest who opposed Amos (Am 7:10-17).

AMBASSADOR* (AMBASSADORS)

Eph 6: 20 for which I am an *a* in chains.

AMBASSADORS (AMBASSADOR)

2Co 5: 20 We are therefore Christ's *a,*

AMBITION*

Ro 15: 20 It has always been my *a*
Gal 5: 20 fits of rage, selfish *a,* dissensions,
Php 1: 17 preach Christ out of selfish *a,*
    2: 3 Do nothing out of selfish *a*
1Th 4: 11 Make it your *a* to lead a quiet life,
Jas 3: 14 and selfish *a* in your hearts,
    3: 16 where you have envy and selfish *a,*

AMENDS

Pr 14: 9 Fools mock at making *a* for sin,

AMNON

Firstborn of David (2Sa 3:2; 1Ch 3:1). Killed by Absalom for raping his sister Tamar (2Sa 13).

AMON

1. Son of Manasseh; king of Judah (2Ki 21:18-26; 1Ch 3:14; 2Ch 33:21-25).
2. Ruler of Samaria under Ahab (1Ki 22:26; 2Ch 18:25).

AMOS

1. Prophet from Tekoa (Am 1:1; 7:10-17).
2. Ancestor of Jesus (Lk 3:25).

ANAK (ANAKITES)

Nu 13: 28 even saw descendants of *A* there.

ANAKITES (ANAK)

Dt 1: 28 We even saw the *A* there.' ''

Dt 2: 10 and numerous, and as tall as the *A.*
    9: 2 ''Who can stand up against the *A?''*

ANANIAS

1. Husband of Sapphira; died for lying to God (Ac 5:1-11).
2. Disciple who baptized Saul (Ac 9:10-19).
3. High priest at Paul's arrest (Ac 22:30-24:1).

ANCESTORS (ANCESTRY)

1Ki 19: 4 I am no better than my *a.''*

ANCESTRY (ANCESTORS)

Ro 9: 5 from them is traced the human *a*

ANCHOR

Heb 6: 19 We have this hope as an *a*

ANCIENT

Da 7: 9 and the *A* of Days took his seat.
    7: 13 He approached the *A* of Days
    7: 22 until the *A* of Days came

ANDREW

Apostle; brother of Simon Peter (Mt 4:18; 10:2; Mk 1:16-18, 29; 3:18; 13:3; Lk 6:14; Jn 1:35-44; 6:8-9; 12:22; Ac 1:13).

ANGEL (ANGELS ARCHANGEL)

Ge 16: 7 The *a* of the Lord found Hagar
    22: 11 But the *a* of the Lord called out
Ex 23: 20 I am sending an *a* ahead of you
Nu 22: 23 When the donkey saw the *a*
Jdg 2: 1 The *a* of the Lord went up
    6: 22 Gideon realized that it was the *a*
    13: 15 Manoah said to the *a* of the Lord
2Sa 24: 16 The *a* of the Lord was then
1Ki 19: 7 The *a* of the Lord came back
2Ki 19: 35 That night the *a* of the Lord went
Ps 34: 7 The *a* of the Lord encamps
Hos 12: 4 He struggled with the *a*
Mt 2: 13 an *a* of the Lord appeared
    28: 2 an *a* of the Lord came
Lk 1: 26 God sent the *a* Gabriel
    2: 9 An *a* of the Lord appeared to them,
    22: 43 An *a* from heaven appeared to him
Ac 6: 15 his face was like the face of an *a.*
    12: 7 Suddenly an *a* of the Lord
2Co 11: 14 Satan himself masquerades as an *a*
Gal 1: 8 or an *a* from heaven should preach

ANGELS (ANGEL)

Ps 91: 11 command his *a* concerning you
Mt 4: 6 command his *a* concerning you,
    13: 39 of the age, and the harvesters are *a.*
    13: 49 The *a* will come and separate
    18: 10 For I tell you that their *a*
    25: 41 prepared for the devil and his *a.*
Lk 4: 10 command his *a* concerning you
    20: 36 for they are like the *a.*
1Co 6: 3 you not know that we will judge *a?*
    13: 1 in the tongues of men and of *a,*
Col 2: 18 and the worship of *a* disqualify you
Heb 1: 4 as much superior to the *a*
    1: 6 ''Let all God's *a* worship him.''
    1: 7 ''He makes his *a* winds,
    1: 14 Are not all *a* ministering spirits
    2: 7 made him a little lower than the *a;*
    2: 9 was made a little lower than the *a,*
    13: 2 some people have entertained *a*
1Pe 1: 12 Even *a* long to look
2Pe 2: 4 For if God did not spare *a*
Jude : 6 *a* who did not keep their positions

ANGER (ANGERED ANGRY)

Ex 15: 7 You unleashed your burning *a;*
    22: 24 My *a* will be aroused, and I will kill
    32: 10 alone so that my *a* may burn
    32: 11 ''why should your *a* burn
    32: 12 Turn from your fierce *a;* relent
    32: 19 his *a* burned and he threw
    34: 6 slow to *a,* abounding in love
Lev 26: 28 then in my *a* I will be hostile
Nu 14: 18 slow to *a,* abounding in love
    25: 11 has turned my *a* away
    32: 10 Lord's *a* was aroused that day
    32: 13 The Lord's *a* burned
Dt 9: 19 I feared the *a* and wrath

ANGERED

Dt   29: 28 In furious *a* and in great wrath
Jdg 14: 19 Burning with *a*, he went up
2Sa 12: 5 David burned with a *a*
2Ki 22: 13 Great is the LORD's *a* that burns
Ne   9: 17 slow to *a* and abounding in love.
Ps   30: 5 For his *a* lasts only a moment,
     78: 38 Time after time he restrained his *a*
     86: 15 slow to *a*, abounding in love
     90: 7 We are consumed by your *a*
    103: 8 slow to *a*, abounding in love.
Pr   15: 1 but a harsh word stirs up *a*.
     29: 11 A fool gives full vent to his *a*,
     30: 33 so stirring up *a* produces strife.''
Jnh   4: 2 slow to *a* and abounding in love,
Eph   4: 26 ''In your *a* do not sin'': Do not let
Jas   1: 20 for man's *a* does not bring about

ANGERED (ANGER)

Pr   22: 24 do not associate with one easily *a*,
1Co 13: 5 it is not easily *a*, it keeps no record

ANGRY (ANGER)

Ps   2: 12 Kiss the Son, lest he be *a*
     95: 10 For forty years I was *a*
Pr   29: 22 An *a* man stirs up dissension,
Mt   5: 22 But I tell you that anyone who is *a*
Jas   1: 19 slow to speak and slow to become *a*

ANGUISH

Ps 118: 5 In my *a* I cried to the LORD,
Jer   4: 19 Oh, my *a*, my *a!*
Zep   1. 13 a day of disuess and *a*,
Lk   21: 25 nations will be in *a* and perplexity
     22: 44 in *a*, he prayed more earnestly,
Ro   9: 2 and unceasing *a* in my heart.

ANIMALS

Ge   1: 24 wild *a*, each according to its kind.''
      7: 16 The *a* going in were male
Dt   14: 4 These are the *a* you may eat: the ox
Job 12: 7 ask the *a*, and they will teach you,
Isa 43: 20 The wild *a* honor me,

ANNOUNCE (ANNOUNCED)

Mt   6: 2 give to the needy, do not *a* it

ANNOUNCED (ANNOUNCE)

Isa 48: 5 before they happened I *a* them
Gal   3: 8 and *a* the gospel in advance

ANNOYANCE*

Pr   12: 16 A fool shows his *a* at once,

ANNUAL*

Ex   30: 10 This *a* atonement must be made
Jdg 21: 19 there is the *a* festival of the LORD
1Sa   1: 21 family to offer the *a* sacrifice
      2: 19 husband to offer the *a* sacrifice.
     20: 6 an *a* sacrifice is being made there
2Ch   8: 13 New Moons and the three *a* feasts
Heb 10: 3 those sacrifices are an *a* reminder

ANOINT (ANOINTED ANOINTING)

Ex   30: 26 use it to *a* the Tent of Meeting,
     30: 30 ''*A* Aaron and his sons
1Sa   9: 16 *A* him leader over my people Israel
     15: 1 to *a* you king over his people Israel
2Ki   9: 3 what the LORD says: I *a* you king
Ps   23: 5 You *a* my head with oil;
Da   9: 24 prophecy and to *a* the most holy.
Jas   5: 14 and *a* him with oil in the name

ANOINTED (ANOINT)

1Ch 16: 22 ''Do not touch my *a* ones;
Ps 105: 15 ''Do not touch my *a* ones;
Isa 61: 1 because the LORD has *a* me
Da   9: 26 the *A* One will be cut off
Lk   4: 18 because he has *a* me
Ac   10: 38 how God *a* Jesus of Nazareth

ANOINTING (ANOINT)

Lev   8: 12 some of the *a* oil on Aaron's head
1Ch 29: 22 *a* him before the LORD to be ruler
Ps   45: 7 by *a* you with the oil of joy.
Heb   1: 9 by *a* you with the oil of joy.''
1Jn   2: 20 you have an *a* from the Holy One,
      2: 27 about all things and as that *a* is real,

ANT* (ANTS)

Pr   6: 6 Go to the *a*, you sluggard;

ANTICHRIST* (ANTICHRISTS)

1Jn   2: 18 have heard that the *a* is coming,
      2: 22 a man is the *a*— he denies
      4: 3 of the *a*, which you have heard is
2Jn   : 7 person is the deceiver and the *a*.

ANTICHRISTS* (ANTICHRIST)

1Jn   2: 18 even now many *a* have come.

ANTIOCH

Ac   11: 26 were first called Christians at *A*.

ANTS* (ANT)

Pr   30: 25 *A* are creatures of little strength,

ANXIETIES* (ANXIOUS)

Lk   21: 34 drunkenness and the *a* of life,

ANXIETY (ANXIOUS)

1Pe   5: 7 Cast all your *a* on him

ANXIOUS (ANXIETIES ANXIETY)

Pr   12: 25 An *a* heart weighs a man down,
Php   4: 6 Do not be *a* about anything,

APOLLOS*

Christian from Alexandria, learned in the Scriptures, instructed by Aquila and Priscilla (Ac 18:24-28). Ministered with Paul at Corinth (Ac 19:1; 1Co 1:12; 3; Tit 3:13).

APOLLYON*

Rev   9: 11 is Abaddon, and in Greek, *A*.

APOSTLE (APOSTLES APOSTLES')

Ro   11: 13 as I am the *a* to the Gentiles,
1Co   9: 1 Am I not an *a*? Have I not seen
2Co 12: 12 The things that mark an *a*— signs,
Gal   2: 8 of Peter as an *a* to the Jews,
1Ti   2: 7 was appointed a herald and an *a*—
2Ti   1: 11 I was appointed a herald and an *a*
Heb   3: 1 *a* and high priest whom we confess.

APOSTLES (APOSTLE)

See also Andrew, Bartholomew, James, John, Judas, Matthew, Matthias, Nathanael, Paul, Peter, Philip, Simon, Thaddaeus, Thomas.
Mk   3: 14 twelve—designating them *a*—
Lk   11: 49 'I will send them prophets and *a*,
Ac   1: 26 so he was added to the eleven *a*—
      2: 43 signs were done by the *a*.
1Co 12: 28 God has appointed first of all *a*,
     15: 9 For I am the least of the *a*
2Co 11: 13 masquerading as *a* of Christ.
Eph   2: 20 built on the foundation of the *a*
      4: 11 It was he who gave some to be *a*,
Rev 21: 14 names of the twelve *a* of the Lamb.

APOSTLES' (APOSTLE)

Ac   5: 2 the rest and put it at the *a'* feet.
      8: 18 at the laying on of the *a'* hands,

APPEAL

Ac   25: 11 I *a* to Caesar!'' After Festus had
Phm   : 9 yet I *a* to you on the basis of love.

APPEAR (APPEARANCE APPEARANCES APPEARED APPEARING APPEARS)

Ge   1: 9 to one place, and let dry ground *a*.''
Lev 16: 2 I *a* in the cloud over the atonement
Mt   24: 30 of the Son of Man will *a* in the sky,
Mk   13: 22 false prophets will *a* and perform
Lk   19: 11 of God was going to *a* at once.
2Co   5: 10 we must all *a* before the judgment
Col   3: 4 also will *a* with him in glory.
Heb   9: 24 now to *a* for us in God's presence.
      9: 28 and he will *a* a second time,

APPEARANCE (APPEAR)

1Sa 16: 7 Man looks at the outward *a*,
Isa 52: 14 his *a* was so disfigured beyond that
     53: 2 in his *a* that we should desire him.
Gal   2: 6 God does not judge by external *a*—

APPEARANCES* (APPEAR)

Jn   7: 24 Stop judging by mere *a*,

APPEARED (APPEAR)

Nu   14: 10 glory of the LORD *a* at the Tent
Mt   1: 20 an angel of the Lord *a* to him
Lk   2: 9 An angel of the Lord *a* to them,
1Co 15: 5 and that he *a* to Peter,
Heb   9: 26 now he has *a* once for all at the end

APPEARING (APPEAR)

1Ti   6: 14 until the *a* of our Lord Jesus Christ,
2Ti   1: 10 through the *a* of our Savior,
      4: 8 to all who have longed for his *a*.
Tit   2: 13 the glorious *a* of our great God

APPEARS (APPEAR)

Mal   3: 2 Who can stand when he *a*?
Col   3: 4 When Christ, who is your life, *a*,
1Pe   5: 4 And when the Chief Shepherd *a*,
1Jn   3: 2 But we know that when he *a*,

APPETITE

Pr   16: 26 The laborer's *a* works for him;
Ecc   6: 7 yet his *a* is never satisfied.
Jer 50: 19 his *a* will be satisfied

APPLES

Pr   25: 11 is like *a* of gold in settings of silver.

APPLY (APPLYING)

Pr   22: 17 *a* your heart to what I teach,
     23: 12 *A* your heart to instruction

APPLYING (APPLY)

Pr   2: 2 and *a* your heart to understanding,

APPOINT (APPOINTED)

Ps   61: 7 *a* your love and faithfulness
1Th   5: 9 For God did not *a* us
Tit   1: 5 and *a* elders in every town,

APPOINTED (APPOINT)

Dt   1: 15 *a* them to have authority over you
Pr   8: 23 I was *a* from eternity,
Da   11: 27 an end will still come at the *a* time.
Hab   2: 3 For the revelation awaits an *a* time;
Jn   15: 16 Chose you and *a* you to go
Ro   9: 9 ''At the *a* time I will return,

APPROACH (APPROACHING)

Ex   24: 2 but Moses alone is to *a* the LORD;
Eph   3: 12 in him we may *a* God with freedom
Heb   4: 16 Let us then *a* the throne of grace

APPROACHING (APPROACH)

Heb 10: 25 all the more as you see the Day *a*.
1Jn   5: 14 is the assurance we have in *a* God:

APPROPRIATE

1Ti   2: 10 *a* for women who profess

APPROVAL (APPROVE)

Jdg 18: 6 Your journey has the LORD's *a*.''
Jn   6: 27 the Father has placed his seal of *a*.''
1Co 11: 19 to show which of you have God's *a*
Gal   1: 10 trying to win the *a* of men,

APPROVE (APPROVAL APPROVED APPROVES)

Ro   2: 18 if you know his will and *a*
      12: 2 and *a* what God's will is—

APPROVED* (APPROVE)

Ro   14: 18 pleasing to God and *a* by men.
     16: 10 Greet Apelles, tested and *a*
2Co 10: 18 who commends himself who is *a*,
1Th   2: 4 as men *a* by God to be entrusted
2Ti   2: 15 to present yourself to God as one *a*,

APPROVES* (APPROVE)

Ro   14: 22 not condemn himself by what he *a*.

APT*

Pr   15: 23 A man finds joy in giving an *a* reply

AQUILA*

Husband of Priscilla; co-worker with Paul, instructor of Apollos (Ac 18; Ro 16:3; 1Co 16:19; 2Ti 4:19).

ARABIA

Gal   1: 17 but I went immediately into *A*
        4: 25 Hagar stands for Mount Sinai in *A*

ARARAT

Ge   8: 4 came to rest on the mountains of *A*.

ARAUNAH

2Sa 24: 16 threshing floor of *A* the Jebusite.

ARBITER* (ARBITRATE)

Lk 12: 14 who appointed me a judge or an *a*

ARBITRATE* (ARBITER)

Job   9: 33 If only there were someone to *a*

ARCHANGEL* (ANGEL)

1Th   4: 16 with the voice of the *a*
Jude   : 9 *a* Michael, when he was disputing

ARCHER

Pr 26: 10 Like an *a* who wounds at random

ARCHIPPUS*

Col   4: 17 Tell *A*: ''See to it that you complete
Phm   : 2 to *A* our fellow soldier

ARCHITECT*

Heb 11: 10 whose *a* and builder is God.

AREOPAGUS*

Ac 17: 19 brought him to a meeting of the *A*,
        17: 22 up in the meeting of the *A*
        17: 34 of the *A*, also a woman named

ARGUE (ARGUMENT ARGUMENTS)

Job 13: 3 and to *a* my case with God.
        13: 8 Will you *a* the case for God?
Pr   25: 9 If you *a* your case with a neighbor,

ARGUMENT (ARGUE)

Heb   6: 16 is said and puts an end to all *a*.

ARGUMENTS (ARGUE)

Isa 41: 21 ''Set forth your *a*,'' says Jacob's
Col   2: 4 you by fine-sounding *a*.
2Ti   2: 23 to do with foolish and stupid *a*,
Tit   3: 9 and *a* and quarrels about the law,

ARK

Ge   6: 14 So make yourself an *a*
Ex   25: 21 and put in the *a* the Testimony,
Dt   10: 5 put the tablets in the *a* I had made,
1Sa   4: 11 The *a* of God was captured,
        7: 2 that the *a* remained at Kiriath
2Sa   6: 17 They brought the *a* of the LORD
1Ki   8: 9 There was nothing in the *a*
1Ch 13: 9 out his hand to steady the *a*,
2Ch 35: 3 ''Put the sacred *a* in the temple that
Heb   9: 4 This *a* contained the gold jar
        11: 7 in holy fear built an *a*
Rev 11: 19 within his temple was seen the *a*

ARM (ARMY)

Nu 11: 23 ''Is the LORD's *a* too short?
Dt   4: 34 hand and an outstretched *a*,
        7: 19 mighty hand and outstretched *a*,
Ps   44: 3 it was your right hand, your *a*,
        98: 1 his right hand and his holy *a*
Jer 27: 5 outstretched *a* I made the earth
1Pe   4: 1 *a* yourselves also with the same

ARMAGEDDON*

Rev 16: 16 that in Hebrew is called *A*.

ARMIES (ARMY)

1Sa 17: 26 Philistine that he should defy the *a*
Rev 19: 14 *a* of heaven were following him,

ARMOR (ARMY)

1Ki 20: 11 on his *a* should not boast like one
Jer 46: 4 put on your *a!*
Ro   13: 12 deeds of darkness and put on the *a*
Eph   6: 11 Put on the full *a* of God
        6: 13 Therefore put on the full *a* of God,

ARMS (ARMY)

Dt   33: 27 underneath are the everlasting *a*.
Ps   18: 32 It is God who *a* me with strength
Pr   31: 17 her *a* are strong for her tasks.
        31: 20 She opens her *a* to the poor
Isa 40: 11 He gathers the lambs in his *a*
Mk   10: 16 And he took the children in his *a*,
Heb 12: 12 strengthen your feeble *a*

ARMY (ARM ARMIES ARMOR ARMS)

Ps   33: 16 No king is saved by the size of his *a*
Joel 2: 2 a large and mighty *a* comes,
        2: 5 like a mighty *a* drawn up for battle.
        2: 11 thunders at the head of his *a;*
Rev 19: 19 the rider on the horse and his *a*.

AROMA

Ge   8: 21 The LORD smelled the pleasing *a*
Ex   29: 18 a pleasing *a*, an offering made
Lev   3: 16 made by fire, a pleasing *a*.
2Co   2: 15 For we are to God the *a* of Christ

AROUSE (AROUSED)

Ro   11: 14 I may somehow *a* my own people

AROUSED (AROUSE)

Ps   78: 58 they *a* his jealousy with their idols.

ARRANGED

1Co 12: 18 But in fact God has *a* the parts

ARRAYED*,

Ps 110: 3 *A* in holy majesty,
Isa 61: 10 and *a* me in a robe of righteousness

ARREST

Mt 10: 19 But when they *a* you, do not worry

ARROGANCE (ARROGANT)

1Sa   2: 3 or let your mouth speak such *a*,
Pr   8: 13 I hate pride and *a*,
Mk   7: 22 lewdness, envy, slander, *a* and folly
2Co 12: 20 slander, gossip, *a* and disorder.

ARROGANT (ARROGANCE)

Ps   5: 5 The *a* cannot stand
       119: 78 May the *a* be put to shame
Pr   17: 7 *A* lips are unsuited to a fool—
        21: 24 a man—''Mocker'' is his name;
Ro   1: 30 God-haters, insolent, *a*
        11: 20 Do not be *a*, but be afraid.
1Ti   6: 17 in this present world not to be *a*

ARROW (ARROWS)

Ps   91: 5 nor the *a* that flies by day,
Pr   25: 18 Like a club or a sword or a sharp *a*

ARROWS (ARROW)

Ps   64: 3 and aim their words like deadly *a*.
        64: 7 But God will shoot them with *a;*
       127: 4 Like *a* in the hands of a warrior
Pr   26: 18 firebrands or deadly *a*
Eph   6: 16 you can extinguish all the flaming *a*

ARTAXERXES

King of Persia; allowed rebuilding of temple under Ezra (Ezr 4; 7), and of walls of Jerusalem under his cupbearer Nehemiah (Ne 2; 5:14; 13:6).

ARTEMIS

Ac 19: 28 ''Great is *A* of the Ephesians!''

ASA

King of Judah (1Ki 15:8-24; 1Ch 3:10; 2Ch 14-16). Godly reformer (2Ch 15); in later years defeated Israel with help of Aram, not the LORD (1Ki 15:16-22; 2Ch 16).

ASAHEL

1. Nephew of David, one of his warriors (2Sa 23:24; 1Ch 2:16; 11:26; 27:7). Killed by Abner (2Sa 2:23); avenged by Joab (2Sa 3:22-39).
2. Levite; teacher (2Ch 17:8).

ASAPH

1. Recorder to Hezekiah (2Ki 18:18, 37; Isa 36: 3, 22).
2. Levitical musician (1Ch 6:39; 15:17-19; 16:

4-7, 37). Sons of (1Ch 25; 2Ch 5:12; 20:14; 29:13; 35:15; Ezr 2:41; 3:10; Ne 7:44; 11:17; 12:27-47). Psalms of (2Ch 29:30; Ps 50; 73-83).

ASCEND* (ASCENDED ASCENDING)

Dt   30: 12 ''Who will *a* into heaven to get it
Ps   24: 3 Who may *a* the hill of the LORD?
Isa 14: 13 ''I will *a* to heaven;
        14: 14 I will *a* above the tops of the clouds
Jn   6: 62 of Man *a* to where he was before!
Ac   2: 34 For David did not *a* to heaven,
Ro   10: 6 'Who will *a* into heaven?' '' (that is,

ASCENDED (ASCEND)

Ps   68: 18 When you *a* on high,
Eph   4: 8 ''When he *a* on high,

ASCENDING (ASCEND)

Ge   28: 12 and the angels of God were *a*
Jn   1: 51 and the angels of God *a*

ASCRIBE*

1Ch 16: 28 *A* to the LORD, O families
        16: 28 *a* to the LORD glory and strength,
        16: 29 *a* to the LORD the glory due his
Job 36: 3 I will *a* justice to my Maker.
Ps   29: 1 *A* to the LORD, O mighty ones,
        29: 1 *a* to the LORD glory and strength,
        29: 2 *A* to the LORD the glory due his
        96: 7 *A* to the LORD, O families
        96: 7 *a* to the LORD glory and strength.
        96: 8 *A* to the LORD the glory due his

ASHAMED (SHAME)

Mk   8: 38 If anyone is *a* of me and my words
Lk   9: 26 If anyone is *a* of me and my words,
Ro   1: 16 I am not *a* of the gospel,
2Ti   1: 8 So do not be *a* to testify about our
        2: 15 who does not need to be *a*

ASHER

Son of Jacob by Zilpah (Ge 30:13; 35:26; 46: 17; Ex 1:4; 1Ch 2:2). Tribe of blessed (Ge 49:20; Dt 33:24-25), numbered (Nu 1:40-41; 26:44-47), allotted land (Jos 19:24-31; Eze 48:2), failed to fully possess (Jdg 1:31-32), failed to support Deborah (Jdg 5:17), supported Gideon (Jdg 6:35; 7:23) and David (1Ch 12:36), 12,000 from (Rev 7: 6).

ASHERAH (ASHERAHS)

Ex   34: 13 and cut down their *A* poles.
1Ki 18: 19 the four hundred prophets of *A*.

ASHERAHS* (ASHERAH)

Jdg   3: 7 and served the Baals and the *A*.

ASHES

Job 42: 6 and repent in dust and *a*.''
Mt 11: 21 ago in sackcloth and *a*.

ASHTORETHS

Jdg   2: 13 and served Baal and the *A*.
1Sa   7: 4 put away their Baals and *A*,

ASLEEP (SLEEP)

1Co 15: 18 who have fallen *a* in Christ are lost.
1Th   4: 13 be ignorant about those who fall *a*,

ASSEMBLY

Ps   1: 5 nor sinners in the *a* of the righteous
        35: 18 I will give you thanks in the great *a*
        82: 1 God presides in the great *a;*
       149: 1 his praise in the *a* of the saints.

ASSIGNED

1Ki   7: 14 and did all the work *a* to him.
Mk 13: 34 with his *a* task, and tells the one
1Co   3: 5 as the Lord has *a* to each his task.
        7: 17 place in life that the Lord *a* to him
2Co 10: 13 to the field God has *a* to us,

ASSOCIATE

Pr   22: 24 do not *a* with one easily angered,
Jn   4: 9 (For Jews do not *a* with Samaritans
Ac 10: 28 law for a Jew to *a* with a Gentile
Ro   12: 16 but be willing to *a* with people
1Co   5: 9 to *a* with sexually immoral people
        5: 11 am writing you that you must not *a*

ASSURANCE (ASSURED)
Heb 10: 22 with a sincere heart in full *a* of faith

ASSURED (ASSURANCE)
Col   4: 12 the will of God, mature and fully *a.*

ASTRAY
Ps 119: 67 Before I was afflicted I went *a,*
Pr   10: 17 ignores correction leads others *a.*
        20: 1 whoever is led *a* by them is not
Isa 53: 6 We all, like sheep, have gone *a,*
Jer 50: 6 their shepherds have led them *a*
Jn   16: 1 you so that you will not go *a.*
1Pe   2: 25 For you were like sheep going *a,*
1Jn 3: 7 do not let anyone lead you *a.*

ASTROLOGERS
Isa 47: 13 Let your *a* come forward,
Da   2: 2 *a* to tell him what he had dreamed.

ATE (EAT)
Ge   3: 6 wisdom, she took some and *a* it.
        27: 25 Jacob brought it to him and he *a;*
2Sa 9: 11 Mephibosheth *a* at David's table
Ps 78: 25 Men *a* the bread of angels;
Jer 15: 16 When your words came, I *a* them;
Eze 3: 3 So I *a* it, and it tasted as sweet
Mt 14: 20 They all *a* and were satisfied,
        15: 37 They all *a* and were satisfied,
Mk   6: 42 They all *a* and were satisfied,
Lk   9: 17 They all *a* and were satisfied.

ATHALIAH
Granddaughter of Omri; wife of Jehoram and mother of Ahaziah; encouraged their evil ways (2Ki 8:18, 27; 2Ch 22:2). At death of Ahaziah she made herself queen, killing all his sons but Joash (2Ki 11:1-3; 2Ch 22:10-12); killed six years later when Joash was revealed (2Ki 11:4-16; 2Ch 23: 1-15).

ATHLETE*
2Ti 2: 5 if anyone competes as an *a.*

ATONE* (ATONEMENT)
Ex 30: 15 to the LORD to *a* for your lives.
2Ch 29: 24 for a sin offering to *a* for all Israel.
Da   9: 24 an end to sin, to *a* for wickedness,

ATONED* (ATONEMENT)
Dt 21: 8 And the bloodshed will be *a* for.
1Sa 3: 14 guilt of Eli's house will never be *a*
Pr 16: 6 faithfulness sin is *a* for;
Isa 6: 7 guilt is taken away and your sin *a*
        22: 14 your dying day this sin will not be *a*
        27: 9 then, will Jacob's guilt be *a* for,

ATONEMENT (ATONE ATONED)
Ex 25: 17 "Make an *a* cover of pure gold—
        30: 10 Once a year Aaron shall make *a*
Lev 17: 11 it is the blood that makes *a*
        23: 27 this seventh month is the Day of *A.*
Nu 25: 13 and made *a* for the Israelites."
Ro   3: 25 presented him as a sacrifice of *a,*
Heb 2: 17 that he might make *a* for the sins

ATTACK
Ps 109: 3 they *a* me without cause.

ATTAINED
Php 3: 16 up to what we have already *a.*
Heb 7: 11 If perfection could have been *a*

ATTENTION (ATTENTIVE)
Pr   4: 1 pay *a* and gain understanding.
        4: 20 My son, pay *a* to what I say;
        5: 1 My son, pay *a* to my wisdom,
        7: 24 pay *a* to what I say.
        22: 17 Pay *a* and listen to the sayings
Ecc 2: 25 Do not pay *a* to every word people
Isa 42: 20 many things, but have paid no *a;*
Tit   1: 14 and will pay no *a* to Jewish myths
Heb 2: 1 We must pay more careful *a,*

ATTENTIVE (ATTENTION)
Ne   1: 11 let your ear be *a* to the prayer
1Pe 3: 12 and his ears are *a* to their prayer,

ATTITUDE (ATTITUDES)
Eph 4: 23 new in the *a* of your minds;
Php 2: 5 Your *a* should be the same
1Pe 4: 1 yourselves also with the same *a,*

ATTITUDES (ATTITUDE)
Heb 4: 12 it judges the thoughts and *a*

ATTRACTIVE
Tit   2: 10 teaching about God our Savior *a.*

AUDIENCE
Pr *29: 26 Many seek an *a* with a ruler,

AUTHORITIES (AUTHORITY)
Ro 13: 1 *a* that exist have been established
        13: 5 it is necessary to submit to the *a,*
        13: 6 for the *a* are God's servants,
Eph 3: 10 and *a* in the heavenly realms,
        6: 12 but against the rulers, against the *a,*
Col   1: 16 thrones or powers or rulers or *a;*
        2: 15 having disarmed the powers and *a,*
Tit   3: 1 people to be subject to rulers and *a,*
1Pe 3: 22 *a* and powers in submission to him.

AUTHORITY (AUTHORITIES)
Mt   7: 29 because he taught as one who had *a*
        9: 6 the Son of Man has *a* on earth
        28: 18 "All *a* in heaven and on earth has
Mk   1: 22 he taught them as one who had *a,*
        2: 10 the Son of Man has *a* on earth
Lk   4: 32 because his message had *a.*
        5: 24 the Son of Man has *a* on earth
Jn 10: 18 *a* to lay it down and *a*
Ac   1: 7 the Father has set by his own *a.*
Ro   7: 1 that the law has *a* over a man only
        13: 1 for there is no *a* except that which
        13: 2 rebels against the *a* is rebelling
1Co 11: 10 to have a sign of *a* on her head.
        15: 24 he has destroyed all dominion, *a*
1Ti 2: 2 for kings and all those in *a,*
        2: 12 to teach or to have *a* over a man;
Tit 2: 15 Encourage and rebuke with all *a.*
Heb 13: 17 your leaders and submit to their *a.*

AUTUMN*
Dt 11: 14 both *a* and spring rains,
Ps 84: 6 the *a* rains also cover it with pools.
Jer 5: 24 who gives *a* and spring rains
Joel 2: 23 both *a* and spring rains, as before.
Jas 5: 7 and how patient he is for the *a*
Jude   : 12 blown along by the wind; *a* trees,

AVENGE (VENGEANCE)
Lev 26: 25 sword upon you to *a* the breaking
Dt 32: 35 It is mine to *a;* I will repay.
        32: 43 for he will *a* the blood
Ro 12: 19 "It is mine to *a;* I will repay,"
Heb 10: 30 "It is mine to *a;* I will repay,"
Rev 6: 10 of the earth and *a* our blood?"

AVENGER (VENGEANCE)
Nu 35: 27 the *a* of blood may kill the accused
Jos 20: 3 find protection from the *a* of blood.
Ps   8: 2 to silence the foe and the *a.*

AVENGES (VENGEANCE)
Ps 94: 1 O LORD, the God who *a.*

AVENGING (VENGEANCE)
1Sa 25: 26 and from *a* yourself with your own
Na   1: 2 The LORD is a jealous and *a* God;

AVOID (AVOIDS)
Pr   4: 15 A it, do not travel on it;
        20: 3 It is to a man's honor to *a* strife,
        20: 19 so *a* a man who talks too much.
Ecc 7: 18 who fears God will *a* all extremes.
1Th 4: 3 you should *a* sexual immorality;
        5: 22 A every kind of evil.
2Ti 2: 16 A godless chatter, because those
Tit   3: 9 But *a* foolish controversies

AVOIDS* (AVOID)
Pr 16: 6 of the LORD a man *a* evil.
        16: 17 The highway of the upright *a* evil;

AWAITS (WAIT)
Pr 15: 10 Stern discipline *a* him who leaves
        28: 22 and is unaware that poverty *a* him.

AWAKE (WAKE)
Ps 17: 15 when I *a,* I will be satisfied
Pr   6: 22 when you *a,* they will speak to you.

AWARD*
2Ti 4: 8 will *a* to me on that day—

AWARE
Ex 34: 29 he was not *a* that his face was
Mt 24: 50 and at an hour he is not *a* of.
Lk 12: 46 and at an hour he is not *a* of.

AWE* (AWESOME OVERAWED)
1Sa 12: 18 So all the people stood in *a*
1Ki 3: 28 they held the king in *a,*
Job 25: 2 "Dominion and *a* belong to God;
Ps 119:120 I stand in *a* of your laws.
Ecc 5: 7 Therefore stand in *a* of God.
Isa 29: 23 will stand in *a* of the God of Israel.
Jer 2: 19 and have no *a* of me,"
        33: 9 they will be in *a* and will tremble
Hab 3: 2 I stand in *a* of your deeds,
Mal 2: 5 and stood in *a* of my name.
Mt   9: 8 they were filled with *a;*
Lk   1: 65 The neighbors were all filled with *a*
        5: 26 They were filled with *a* and said,
        7: 16 They were all filled with *a*
Ac   2: 43 Everyone was filled with *a*
Heb 12: 28 acceptably with reverence and *a,*

AWESOME* (AWE)
Ge 28: 17 and said, "How *a* is this place!
Ex 15: 11 *a* in glory,
        34: 10 among will see how *a* is the work
Dt   4: 34 or by great and *a* deeds,
        7: 21 is among you, is a great and *a* God.
        10: 17 the great God, mighty and *a,*
        10: 21 and *a* wonders you saw
        28: 58 revere this glorious and *a* name—
        34: 12 performed the *a* deeds that Moses
Jdg 13: 6 like an angel of God, very *a.*
2Sa 7: 23 *a* wonders by driving out nations
1Ch 17: 21 *a* wonders by driving out nations
Ne   1: 5 of heaven, the great and *a* God,
        4: 14 and *a,* and fight for your brothers,
        9: 32 the great, mighty and *a* God,
Job 10: 16 again display your power
        37: 22 God comes in *a* majesty.
Ps 45: 4 let your right hand display *a* deeds.
        47: 2 How *a* is the LORD Most High,
        65: 5 us with *a* deeds of righteousness,
        66: 3 to God, "How *a* are your deeds!
        66: 5 how *a* his works in man's behalf!
        68: 35 You are *a,* O God,
        89: 7 he is more *a* than all who surround
        99: 3 praise your great and *a* name—
        106: 22 and *a* deeds by the Red Sea.
        111: 9 holy and *a* is his name.
        145: 6 of the power of your *a* works,
Isa 64: 3 when you did *a* things that we did
Eze 1: 18 Their rims were high and *a,*
        1: 22 expanse, sparkling like ice, and *a.*
Da   2: 31 dazzling statue, *a* in appearance.
        9: 4 "O Lord, the great and *a* God,
Zep 2: 11 The LORD will be *a* to them

AX
Mt   3: 10 The *a* is already at the root
Lk   3: 9 The *a* is already at the root

BAAL
Jdg 6: 25 Tear down your father's altar to *B*
1Ki 16: 32 *B* in the temple of *B* that he built
        18: 25 Elijah said to the prophets of *B,*
        19: 18 knees have not bowed down to *B*
2Ki 10: 28 Jehu destroyed *B* worship in Israel.
Jer 19: 5 places of *B* to burn their sons
Ro 11: 4 have not bowed the knee to *B.*"

BAASHA
King of Israel (1Ki 15:16-16:7; 2Ch 16:1-6).

BABBLER* (BABBLING)
Ac 17: 18 "What is this *b* trying to say?"

BABBLING* (BABBLER)

Mt   6: 7 do not keep on *b* like pagans,

BABIES* (BABY)

Ge 25: 22 The *b* jostled each other within her
Ex   2: 6 "This is one of the Hebrew *b*,"
Lk 18: 15 also bringing *b* to Jesus
Ac   7: 19 them to throw out their newborn *b*
1Pe 2: 2 Like newborn *b*, crave pure

BABY* (BABIES BABY'S)

Ex   2: 6 She opened it and saw the *b*.
     2: 7 women to nurse the *b* for you?''
     2: 9 So the woman took the *b*
     2: 9 "Take this *b* and nurse him for me,
1Ki 3: 17 I had a *b* while she was there
     3: 18 was born, this woman also had a *b*.
     3: 26 give her the living *b!* Don't kill him
     3: 27 Give the living *b* to the first woman
Isa 49: 15 "Can a mother forget the *b*
Lk   1: 41 the *b* leaped in her womb,
     1: 44 the *b* in my womb leaped for joy.
     1: 57 time for Elizabeth to have her *b*,
     2: 6 the time came for the *b* to be born,
     2: 12 You will find a *b* wrapped in strips
     2: 16 the *b*, who was lying in the manger.
Jn 16: 21 but when her *b* is born she forgets

BABY'S* (BABY)

Ex   2: 8 the girl went and got the *b* mother.

BABYLON

Ps 137: 1 By the rivers of *B* we sat and wept
Jer 29: 10 seventy years are completed for *B*,
    51: 37 *B* will be a heap of ruins,
Rev 14: 8 "'Fallen! Fallen is *B* the Great,
    17: 5 MYSTERY *B* THE GREAT

BACKS

2Pe 2: 21 and then to turn their *b*

BACKSLIDING* (BACKSLIDINGS)

Jer 2: 19 your *b* will rebuke you.
     3: 22 I will cure you of *b*.''
    14: 7 For our *b* is great;
    15: 6 "You keep on *b*.
Eze 37: 23 them from all their sinful *b*,

BACKSLIDINGS* (BACKSLIDING)

Jer 5: 6 and their *b* many.

BALAAM

Prophet who attempted to curse Israel (Nu 22-24; Dt 23:4-5; 2Pe 2:15; Jude 11). Killed in Israel's vengeance on Midianites (Nu 31:8; Jos 13:22).

BALAK

Moabite king who hired Balaam to curse Israel (Nu 22-24; Jos 24:9).

BALDHEAD

2Ki 2: 23 "Go on up, you *b!*'' they said.

BALM

Jer 8: 22 Is there no *b* in Gilead?

BANISH (BANISHED)

Jer 25: 10 I will *b* from them the sounds of joy

BANISHED (BANISH)

Dt 30: 4 Even if you have been *b*

BANNER

Ex 17: 15 and called it The LORD is my *B*.
SS   2: 4 and his *b* over me is love.
Isa 11: 10 the Root of Jesse will stand as a *b*

BANQUET

SS   2: 4 He has taken me to the *b* hall,
Lk 14: 13 when you give a *b*, invite the poor,

BAPTISM* (BAPTIZE)

Mt 21: 25 John's *b*— where did it come from?
Mk   1: 4 and preaching the *b* of repentance
    10: 38 baptized with the *b* I am baptized
    10: 39 baptized with the *b* I am baptized
    11: 30 John's *b*— was it from heaven,

Lk   3: 3 preaching a *b* of repentance
    12: 50 But I have a *b* to undergo,
    20: 4 John's *b*— was it from heaven,
Ac   1: 22 beginning from John's *b*
    10: 37 after the *b* that John preached—
    13: 24 and *b* to all the people of Israel.
    18: 25 though he knew only the *b* of John.
    19: 3 did you receive?'' ''John's *b*,''
    19: 3 ''Then what *b* did you receive?''
    19: 4 ''John's *b* was a *b* of repentance.
Ro   6: 4 with him through *b* into death
Eph 4: 5 one Lord, one faith, one *b*;
Col 2: 12 having been buried with him in *b*
1Pe 3: 21 this water symbolizes *b* that now

BAPTISMS* (BAPTIZE)

Heb 6: 2 instruction about *b*, the laying

BAPTIZE* (BAPTISM BAPTISMS BAPTIZED BAPTIZING)

Mt   3: 11 He will *b* you with the Holy Spirit
     3: 11 ''I *b* you with water for repentance.
Mk   1: 8 I *b* you with water, but he will
     1: 8 he will *b* you with the Holy Spirit.''
Lk   3: 16 He will *b* you with the Holy Spirit
     3: 16 John answered them all, ''I *b* you
Jn   1: 25 ''Why then do you *b*
     1: 26 nor the Prophet?'' ''I *b* with water,''
     1: 33 and remain is he who will *b*
     1: 33 me to *b* with water told me,
1Co 1: 14 I am thankful that I did not *b* any
     1: 17 For Christ did not send me to *b*,

BAPTIZED* (BAPTIZE)

Mt   3: 6 they were *b* by him in the Jordan
     3: 13 to the Jordan to be *b* by John.
     3: 14 saying, ''I need to be *b* by you,
     3: 16 as Jesus was *b*, he went out
Mk   1: 5 they were *b* by him in the Jordan.
     1: 9 and was *b* by John in the Jordan.
    10: 38 or be *b* with the baptism I am
    10: 38 with the baptism I am *b* with?''
    10: 39 and be *b* with the baptism I am
    10: 39 with the baptism I am *b* with,
    16: 16 believes and is *b* will be saved,
Lk   3: 7 to the crowds coming out to be *b*
     3: 12 Tax collectors also came to be *b*
     3: 21 were being *b*, Jesus was *b* too.
     7: 29 because they had been *b* by John.
     7: 30 they had not been *b* by John.)
Jn   3: 22 spent some time with them, and *b*.
     3: 23 were constantly coming to be *b*.
     4: 2 in fact it was not Jesus who *b*,
Ac   1: 5 For John *b* with water,
     1: 5 but in a few days you will be *b*
     2: 38 Repent and be *b*, every one of you,
     2: 41 who accepted his message were *b*,
     8: 12 they were *b*, both men and women.
     8: 13 Simon himself believed and was *b*.
     8: 16 they had simply been *b*
     8: 36 Why shouldn't I be *b*?''
     8: 38 into the water and Philip *b* him.
     9: 18 was *b*, and after taking some food,
    10: 47 people from being *b* with water?
    10: 48 So he ordered that they be *b*
    11: 16 what the Lord had said, 'John *b*
    11: 16 you will be *b* with the Holy Spirit.
    16: 15 members of her household were *b*,
    16: 33 he and all his family were *b*.
    18: 8 heard him believed and were *b*.
    19: 5 they were *b* into the name
    22: 16 be *b* and wash your sins away,
Ro   6: 3 *b* into Christ Jesus were *b*
1Co 1: 13 Were you *b* into the name of Paul?
     1: 15 so no one can say that you were *b*
     1: 16 I also *b* the household of Stephanas
     1: 16 I don't remember if I *b* anyone else
    10: 2 They were all *b* into Moses
    12: 13 For we were all *b* by one Spirit
    15: 29 what will those do who are *b*
    15: 29 why are people *b* for them?
Gal 3: 27 all of you who were *b*

BAPTIZING* (BAPTIZE)

Mt   3: 7 coming to where he was *b*,
    28: 19 *b* them in the name of the Father
Mk   1: 4 *b* in the desert region
Jn   1: 28 of the Jordan, where John was *b*.

Jn   1: 31 but the reason I came *b*
     3: 23 also was *b* at Aenon near Salim,
     3: 26 he is *b*, and everyone is going
     4: 1 and *b* more disciples than John,
    10: 40 to the place where John had been *b*

BAR-JESUS*

Ac 13: 6 and false prophet named *B*,

BARABBAS

Mt 27: 26 Then he released *B* to them.

BARAK*

Judge who fought with Deborah against Canaanites (Jdg 4-5; 1Sa 12:11; Heb 11:32).

BARBARIAN*

Col 3: 11 circumcised or uncircumcised, *b*,

BARBS*

Nu 33: 55 allow to remain will become *b*

BARE

Hos 2: 3 as *b* as on the day she was born;
Heb 4: 13 and laid *b* before the eyes of him

BARNABAS*

Disciple, originally Joseph (Ac 4:36), prophet (Ac 13:1), apostle (Ac 14:14). Brought Paul to apostles (Ac 9:27), Antioch (Ac 11:22-29; Gal 2:1-13), on the first missionary journey (Ac 13-14). Together at Jerusalem Council, they separated over John Mark (Ac 15). Later co-workers (1Co 9:6; Col 4:10).

BARREN

Ge 11: 30 Sarai was *b*; she had no children.
    29: 31 her womb, but Rachel was *b*.
Ps 113: 9 He settles the *b* woman
Isa 54: 1 ''Sing, O *b* woman,
Lk   1: 7 children, because Elizabeth was *b*;
Gal 4: 27 ''Be glad, O *b* woman,
Heb 11: 11 and Sarah herself was *b*—

BARTHOLOMEW*

Apostle (Mt 10:3; Mk 3:18; Lk 6:14; Ac 1:13). Possibly also known as Nathanael (Jn 1:45-49; 21:2).

BARUCH

Jeremiah's secretary (Jer 32:12-16; 36; 43:1-6; 45:1-2).

BARZILLAI

1. Gileadite who aided David during Absalom's revolt (2Sa 17:27; 19:31-39).
2. Son-in-law of 1. (Ezr 2:61; Ne 7:63).

BASHAN

Jos 22: 7 Moses had given land in *B*,
Ps 22: 12 strong bulls of *B* encircle me.

BASIN

Ex 30: 18 ''Make a bronze *b*.

BASKET

Ex   2: 3 she got a papyrus *b* for him
Ac   9: 25 him in a *b* through an opening
2Co 11: 33 I was lowered in a *b* from a window

BATCH*

Ro 11: 16 then the whole *b* is holy;
1Co 5: 6 through the whole *b* of dough?
     5: 7 old yeast that you may be a new *b*
Gal 5: 9 through the whole *b* of dough.''

BATH (BATHING)

Jn 13: 10 person who has had a *b* needs only

BATHING (BATH)

2Sa 11: 2 From the roof he saw a woman *b*.

BATHSHEBA*

Wife of Uriah who committed adultery with and became wife of David (2Sa 11), mother of Solomon (2Sa 12:24; 1Ki 1-2; 1Ch 3:5).

BATTLE (BATTLES)

1Sa 17: 47 for the *b* is the LORD's,

2Ch 20: 15 For the b is not yours, but God's.
Ps 24: 8 the LORD mighty in b.
Ecc 9: 11 or the b to the strong,
Isa 31: 4 down to do b on Mount Zion
Eze 13: 5 in the b on the day of the LORD.
Rev 16: 14 them for the b on the great day
20: 8 and Magog—to gather them for b.

BATTLES* (BATTLE)

1Sa 8: 20 to go out before us and fight our b.''
18: 17 and fight the b of the LORD.''
25: 28 because he fights the LORD's b.
2Ch 32: 8 God to help us and to fight our b.''

BEAR (BEARING BEARS BIRTH BIRTHRIGHT BORE BORN CHILDBEARING CHILDBIRTH FIRSTBORN NEWBORN REBIRTH)

Ge 4: 13 punishment is more than I can b.
Ps 38: 4 like a burden too heavy to b.
Isa 11: 7 The cow will feed with the b,
53: 11 and he will b their iniquities.
Da 7: 5 beast, which looked like a b.
Mt 7: 18 A good tree cannot b bad fruit,
Jn 15: 2 branch that does b fruit he prunes
15: 8 glory, that you b much fruit,
15: 16 but I chose you to go and b fruit—
Ro 7: 4 in order that we might b fruit
15: 1 ought to b with the failings
1Co 10: 13 tempted beyond what you can b.
Col 3: 13 B with each other and forgive

BEARD

Lev 19: 27 or clip off the edges of your b.
Isa 50: 6 to those who pulled out my b;

BEARING (BEAR)

Eph 4: 2 b with one another in love.
Col 1: 10 b fruit in every good work,
Heb 13: 13 outside the camp, b the disgrace he

BEARS (BEAR)

1Ki 8: 43 house I have built b your Name.
Ps 68: 19 who daily b our burdens.

BEAST (BEASTS)

Rev 13: 18 him calculate the number of the b,
16: 2 people who had the mark of the b
19: 20 who had received the mark of the b

BEASTS (BEAST)

Da 7: 3 Four great b, each different
1Co 15: 32 If I fought wild b in Ephesus

BEAT (BEATEN BEATING BEATINGS)

Isa 2: 4 They will b their swords
Joel 3: 10 B your plowshares into swords
Mic 4: 3 They will b their swords
1Co 9: 27 I b my body and make it my slave

BEATEN (BEAT)

Lk 12: 47 do what his master wants will be b
12: 48 deserving punishment will be b
2Co 11: 25 Three times I was b with rods,

BEATING (BEAT)

1Co 9: 26 I do not fight like a man b the air.
1Pe 2: 20 if you receive a b for doing wrong

BEATINGS (BEAT)

Pr 19: 29 and b for the backs of fools.

BEAUTIFUL* (BEAUTY)

Ge 6: 2 that the daughters of men were b,
12: 11 ''I know what a b woman you are.
12: 14 saw that she was a very b woman.
24: 16 The girl was very b, a virgin;
26: 7 of Rebekah, because she is b.''
29: 17 Rachel was lovely in form, and b.
49: 21 that bears b fawns.
Nu 24: 5 ''How b are your tents, O Jacob,
Dt 21: 11 among the captives a b woman
Jos 7: 21 saw in the plunder a b robe
1Sa 25: 3 was an intelligent and b woman,
2Sa 11: 2 The woman was very b,
13: 1 the b sister of Absalom son
14: 27 and she became a b woman.
1Ki 1: 3 throughout Israel for a b girl
1Ki 1: 4 The girl was very b; she took care
Est 2: 2 for b young virgins for the king.
2: 3 realm to bring all these b girls
Job 38: 31 ''Can you bind the b Pleiades?
42: 15 land were there found women as b
Ps 48: 2 It is b in its loftiness,
Pr 11: 22 is a b woman who shows no
24: 4 filled with rare and b treasures.
Ecc 3: 11 He has made everything b
SS 1: 8 *Lover* If you do not know, most b
1: 10 Your cheeks are b with earrings,
1: 15 Oh, how b!
1: 15 *Lover* How b you are, my darling!
2: 10 my b one, and come with me.
2: 13 my b one, come with me.''
4: 1 How b you are, my darling!
4: 1 Oh, how b!
4: 7 All b you are, my darling;
5: 9 most b of women?
6: 1 most b of women?
6: 4 *Lover* You are b, my darling,
7: 1 How b your sandaled feet,
7: 6 How b you are and how pleasing,
Isa 4: 2 of the LORD will be b
28: 5 a b wreath
52: 7 How b on the mountains
Jer 3: 19 the most b inheritance
6: 2 so b and delicate.
11: 16 with fruit b in form.
46: 20 ''Egypt is a b heifer,
Eze 7: 20 They were proud of their b jewelry
16: 7 and became the most b of jewels.
16: 12 and a b crown on your head.
16: 13 You became very b and rose
20: 6 and honey, the most b of all lands.
20: 15 and honey, most b of all lands—
23: 42 and b crowns on their heads.
27: 24 traded with you b garments,
31: 3 with b branches overshadowing
31: 9 I made it b
33: 32 who sings love songs with a b voice
Da 4: 12 Its leaves were b, its fruit abundant
4: 21 with b leaves and abundant fruit,
8: 9 to the east and toward the B Land.
11: 16 will establish himself in the B Land
11: 41 He will also invade the B Land.
11: 45 the seas at the b holy mountain.
Zec 9: 17 How attractive and b they will be!
Mt 23: 27 which look b on the outside
26: 10 She has done a b thing to me.
Mk 14: 6 She has done a b thing to me.
Lk 21: 5 temple was adorned with b stones
Ac 3: 2 carried to the temple gate called B,
3: 10 at the temple gate called B,
Ro 10: 15 ''How b are the feet
1Pe 3: 5 in God used to make themselves b.

BEAUTY* (BEAUTIFUL)

Est 1: 11 order to display her b to the people
2: 3 let b treatments be given to them.
2: 9 her with her b treatments
2: 12 months of b treatments prescribed
Ps 27: 4 to gaze upon the b of the LORD
37: 20 LORD's enemies will be like the b
45: 11 The king is enthralled by your b;
50: 2 From Zion, perfect in b,
Pr 6: 25 lust in your heart after her b
31: 30 is deceptive, and b is fleeting;
Isa 3: 24 instead of b, branding.
28: 1 to the fading flower, his glorious b,
28: 4 That fading flower, his glorious b,
33: 17 Your eyes will see the king in his b
53: 2 He had no b or majesty
61: 3 to bestow on them a crown of b
La 2: 15 the perfection of b,
Eze 16: 14 had given you made your b perfect,
16: 14 the nations on account of your b,
16: 15 passed by and your b became his.
16: 15 '' 'But you trusted in your b
16: 25 lofty shrines and degraded your b,
27: 3 ''I am perfect in b.''
27: 4 your builders brought your b
27: 11 they brought your b to perfection.
28: 7 draw their swords against your b
28: 12 full of wisdom and perfect in b.
28: 17 proud on account of your b,
31: 7 It was majestic in b,
31: 8 could match its b.
Jas 1: 11 blossom falls and its b is destroyed.
1Pe 3: 3 Your b should not come
3: 4 the unfading b of a gentle

BED (SICKBED)

Isa 28: 20 The b is too short to stretch out on,
Lk 11: 7 and my children are with me in b.
17: 34 night two people will be in one b;
Heb 13: 4 and the marriage b kept pure,

BEELZEBUB*

Mt 10: 25 of the house has been called B,
12: 24 ''It is only by B, the prince
12: 27 And if I drive out demons by B,
Mk 3: 22 possessed by B! By the prince
Lk 11: 15 ''By B, the prince of demons,
11: 18 claim that I drive out demons by B.
11: 19 Now if I drive out demons by B,

BEER

Pr 20: 1 Wine is a mocker and b a brawler;

BEERSHEBA

Ge 21: 14 and wandered in the desert of B.
Jdg 20: 1 all the Israelites from Dan to B
1Sa 3: 20 to B recognized that Samuel was
2Sa 3: 10 and Judah from Dan to B.''
17: 11 Let all Israel, from Dan to B—
24: 2 the tribes of Israel from Dan to B
24: 15 of the people from Dan to B died.
1Ki 4: 25 from Dan to B, lived in safety,
1Ch 21: 2 count the Israelites from B to Dan.
2Ch 30: 5 throughout Israel, from B to Dan,

BEFALLS*

Pr 12: 21 No harm b the righteous,

BEGGING

Ps 37: 25 or their children b bread.
Ac 16: 9 of Macedonia standing and b him,

BEGINNING

Ge 1: 1 In the b God created the heavens
Ps 102: 25 In the b you laid the foundations
111: 10 of the LORD is the b of wisdom;
Pr 1: 7 of the LORD is the b of knowledge
9: 10 of the LORD is the b of wisdom,
Ecc 3: 11 fathom what God has done from b
Isa 40: 21 Has it not been told you from the b
46: 10 I make known the end from the b,
Mt 24: 8 All these are the b of birth pains.
Lk 1: 3 investigated everything from the b,
Jn 1: 1 In the b was the Word,
1Jn 1: 1 That which was from the b,
Rev 21: 6 and the Omega, the B and the End.
22: 13 and the Last, the B and the End.

BEHAVE (BEHAVIOR)

Ro 13: 13 Let us b decently, as in the daytime

BEHAVIOR (BEHAVE)

1Pe 3: 1 without words by the b of their wives,
3: 16 maliciously against your good b

BEHEMOTH*

Job 40: 15 ''Look at the b,

BELIEVE (BELIEVED BELIEVER BELIEVERS BELIEVES BELIEVING)

Ex 4: 1 ''What if they do not b me
1Ki 10: 7 I did not b these things until I came
2Ch 9: 6 But I did not b what they said
Ps 78: 32 of his wonders, they did not b.
Hab 1: 5 that you would not b,
Mt 18: 6 one of these little ones who b in me
21: 22 If you b, you will receive whatever
27: 42 from the cross, and we will b in him
Mk 1: 15 Repent and b the good news!''
5: 36 ruler, ''Don't be afraid; just b.''
9: 24 ''I do b; help me overcome my
9: 42 one of these little ones who b in me
11: 24 b that you have received it,
15: 32 the cross, that we may see and b.''
16: 16 but whoever does not b will be
16: 17 signs will accompany those who b:
Lk 8: 12 so that they cannot b and be saved.
8: 13 They b for a while, but in the time
8: 50 just b, and she will be healed.''

BELIEVED

Lk　22: 67　you will not *b* me,
　　24: 25　to *b* all that the prophets have
Jn　　1:　7　that through him all men might *b*.
　　　3: 18　does not *b* stands condemned
　　　4: 42　"We no longer *b* just
　　　5: 38　for you do not *b* the one he sent.
　　　5: 46　believed Moses, you would *b* me,
　　　6: 29　to *b* in the one he has sent."
　　　6: 69　We *b* and know that you are
　　　7:　5　his own brothers did not *b* in him.
　　　8: 24　if you do not *b* that I am ˌthe one I
　　　9: 35　"Do you *b* in the Son of Man?"
　　　9: 36　"Tell me so that I may *b* in him."
　　　9: 38　"Lord, I *b*," and he worshiped him.
　　10: 26　you do not *b* because you are not
　　10: 37　Do not *b* me unless I do what my
　　10: 38　you do not *b* me, *b* the miracles,
　　11: 27　"I *b* that you are the Christ,
　　12: 37　they still would not *b* in him.
　　12: 39　For this reason they could not *b*,
　　12: 44　in me, he does not *b* in me only,
　　13: 19　does happen you will *b* that I am
　　14: 10　Don't you *b* that I am in the Father
　　14: 11　*B* me when I say that I am
　　14: 11　or at least *b* on the evidence
　　16: 30　This makes us *b* that you came
　　16: 31　"You *b* at last!" Jesus answered.
　　17:　1　that the world may *b* that you have
　　19: 35　he testifies so that you also may *b*.
　　20: 27　Stop doubting and *b*."
　　20: 31　written that you may *b* that Jesus is
Ac　16: 31　They replied, "*B* in the Lord Jesus,
　　19:　4　the people to *b* in the one coming
　　24: 14　I *b* everything that agrees
　　26: 27　Agrippa, do you *b* the prophets?
Ro　　3: 22　faith in Jesus Christ to all who *b*.
　　　4: 11　he is the father of all who *b*
　　10:　9　*b* in your heart that God raised him
　　10: 10　For it is with your heart that you *b*
　　10: 14　And how can they *b* in the one
　　16: 26　so that all nations might *b*
1Co　1: 21　preached to save those who *b*
Gal　3: 22　might be given to those who *b*.
Php　1: 29　of Christ not only to *b* on him,
1Th　4: 14　We *b* that Jesus died and rose again
2Th　2: 11　delusion so that they will *b* the lie
1Ti　4: 10　and especially of those who *b*.
Tit　　1:　6　a man whose children *b*
Heb 11:　6　comes to him must *b* that he exists
Jas　　1:　6　But when he asks, he must *b*
　　　2: 19　Even the demons that—
　　　2: 19　You *b* that there is one God.
1Pe　2:　7　to you who *b*, this stone is precious
1Jn　3: 23　to *b* in the name of his Son,
　　　4:　1　Dear friends, do not *b* every spirit,
　　　5: 13　things to you who *b* in the name

BELIEVED (BELIEVE)

Ge　15:　6　Abram *b* the Lord, and he
Ex　　4: 31　signs before the people, and they *b*.
Isa　53:　1　Who has *b* our message
Jnh　　3:　5　The Ninevites *b* God.
Lk　　1: 45　is she who has *b* that what the Lord
Jn　　1: 12　to those who *b* in his name,
　　　2: 22　Then they *b* the Scripture
　　　3: 18　because he has not *b* in the name
　　　5: 46　If you *b* Moses, you would believe
　　　7: 39　whom those who *b*
　　11: 40　"Did I not tell you that if you *b*,
　　12: 38　"Lord, who has *b* our message
　　20:　8　He saw and *b*.
　　20: 29　who have not seen and yet have *b*."
Ac　13: 48　were appointed for eternal life *b*.
　　19:　2　the Holy Spirit when you *b*?"
Ro　　4:　3　Scripture say? "Abraham *b* God,
　　10: 14　call on the one they have not *b* in?
　　10: 16　"Lord, who has *b* our message?"
1Co 15:　2　Otherwise, you have *b* in vain.
Gal　3:　6　Consider Abraham: "He *b* God,
2Th　2: 12　who have not *b* the truth
1Ti　3: 16　was *b* on in the world,
2Ti　1: 12　because I know whom I have *b*,
Jas　2: 23　that says, "Abraham *b* God,

BELIEVER* (BELIEVE)

1Ki 18:　3　(Obadiah was a devout *b*
Ac　16:　1　whose mother was a Jewess and a *b*
　　16: 15　"If you consider me a *b* in the Lord

1Co　7: 12　brother has a wife who is not a *b*
　　　7: 13　has a husband who is not a *b*
2Co　6: 15　What does a *b* have in common
1Ti　5: 16　any woman who is a *b* has widows

BELIEVERS* (BELIEVE)

Jn　　4: 41　of his words many more became *b*.
Ac　　1: 15　among the *b* (a group numbering
　　　2: 44　All the *b* were together
　　　4: 32　All the *b* were one in heart
　　　5: 12　And all the *b* used to meet together
　　　9: 41　he called the *b* and the widows
　　10: 45　The circumcised *b* who had come
　　11:　2　the circumcised *b* criticized him
　　15:　2　along with some other *b*,
　　15:　5　Then some of the *b* who belonged
　　15: 23　To the Gentile *b* in Antioch,
　　21: 25　for the Gentile *b*, we have written
1Co　6:　5　to judge a dispute between *b*?
　　14: 22　is for *b*, not for unbelievers.
　　14: 22　not for *b* but for unbelievers,
Gal　6: 10　who belong to the family of *b*.
1Th　1:　7　a model to all the *b* in Macedonia
1Ti　4: 12　set an example for the *b* in speech,
　　　6:　2　benefit from their service are *b*,
Jas　2:　1　*b* in our glorious Lord Jesus Christ,
1Pe　2: 17　Love the brotherhood of *b*,

BELIEVES* (BELIEVE)

Pr　14: 15　A simple man *b* anything,
Mk　9: 23　is possible for him who *b*."
　　11: 23　*b* that what he says will happen,
　　16: 16　Whoever *b* and is baptized will be
Jn　　3: 15　that everyone who *b*
　　　3: 16　that whoever *b* in him shall not
　　　3: 18　Whoever *b* in him is not
　　　3: 36　Whoever *b* in the Son has eternal
　　　5: 24　*b* him who sent me has eternal life
　　　6: 35　and he who *b* in me will never be
　　　6: 40　and *b* in him shall have eternal life,
　　　6: 47　he who *b* has everlasting life.
　　　7: 38　Whoever *b* in me, as the Scripture
　　11: 25　He who *b* in me will live, even
　　11: 26　and *b* in me will never die.
　　12: 44　Jesus cried out, "When a man *b*
　　12: 46　so that no one who *b*
Ac　10: 43　about him that everyone who *b*
　　13: 39　him everyone who *b* is justified
Ro　　1: 16　for the salvation of everyone who *b*
　　10:　4　righteousness for everyone who *b*.
1Jn　5:　1　Everyone who *b* that Jesus is
　　　5:　5　Only he who *b* that Jesus is the Son
　　　5: 10　Anyone who *b* in the Son

BELIEVING* (BELIEVE)

Jn　20: 31　and that by *b* you may have life
Ac　　9: 26　not *b* that he really was a disciple.
1Co　7: 14　sanctified through her *b* husband.
　　　7: 15　A *b* man or woman is not bound
　　　9:　5　right to take a *b* wife along with us,
Gal　3:　2　or by *b* what you heard? Are you
1Ti　6:　2　Those who have *b* masters are not

BELLY

Ge　　3: 14　You will crawl on your *b*
Da　　2: 32　its *b* and thighs of bronze,
Mt　12: 40　three nights in the *b* of a huge fish,

BELONG (BELONGING BELONGS)

Ge　40:　8　"Do not interpretations *b* to God?
Lev 25: 55　for the Israelites *b* to me
Dt　10: 14　Lord your God *b* the heavens,
　　29: 29　The secret things *b*
Job 12: 13　"To God *b* wisdom and power;
　　12: 16　To him *b* strength and victory;
　　25:　2　"Dominion and awe *b* to God;
Ps　47:　9　for the kings of the earth *b* to God;
　　95:　4　and the mountain peaks *b* to him.
　　115: 16　The highest heavens *b*
Jer　5: 10　for these people do not *b*
Jn　　8: 44　You *b* to your father, the devil,
　　15: 19　As it is, you do not *b* to the world,
Ro　　1:　6　called to *b* to Jesus Christ.
　　　7:　4　that you might *b* to another,
　　　8:　9　of Christ, he does not *b* to Christ.
　　14:　8　we live or die, we *b* to the Lord.
1Co　7: 39　but he must *b* to the Lord.
　　15: 23　when he comes, those who *b*

Gal　3: 29　If you *b* to Christ, then you are
　　　5: 24　Those who *b* to Christ Jesus have
1Th　5:　5　We do not *b* to the night
　　　5:　8　But since we *b* to the day, let us be
1Jn　3: 19　then is how we know that we *b*

BELONGING (BELONG)

1Pe　2:　9　a holy nation, a people *b* to God,

BELONGS (BELONG)

Lev 27: 30　*b* to the Lord; it is holy
Dt　　1: 17　of any man, for judgment *b* to God.
Job 41: 11　Everything under heaven *b* to me.
Ps　22: 28　for dominion *b* to the Lord
　　89: 18　Indeed, our shield *b* to the Lord,
　　111: 10　To him *b* eternal praise.
Eze 18:　4　For every living soul *b* to me,
Jn　　8: 47　He who *b* to God hears what God
Ro　12:　5　each member *b* to all the others.
Rev　7: 10　"Salvation *b* to our God,

BELOVED* (LOVE)

Dt　33: 12　"Let the *b* of the Lord rest secure
SS　　5:　9　How is your *b* better than others,
　　　5:　9　*Friends* How is your *b* better
Jer　11: 15　"What is my *b* doing in my temple

BELSHAZZAR

　King of Babylon in days of Daniel (Da 5).

BELT

Ex　12: 11　with your cloak tucked into your *b*,
1Ki 18: 46　and, tucking his cloak into his *b*,
2Ki　4: 29　"Tuck your cloak into your *b*,
　　　9:　1　"Tuck your cloak into your *b*,
Isa　11:　5　Righteousness will be his *b*
Eph　6: 14　with the *b* of truth buckled

BENEFICIAL* (BENEFIT)

1Co　6: 12　for me"—but not everything is *b*.
　　10: 23　but not everything is *b*.

BENEFIT (BENEFICIAL BENEFITS)

Job 22:　2　"Can a man be of *b* to God?
Isa　38: 17　Surely it was for my *b*
Ro　　6: 22　the *b* you reap leads to holiness,
2Co　4: 15　All this is for your *b*,

BENEFITS (BENEFIT)

Ps 103:　2　and forget not all his *b*.
Jn　　4: 38　you have reaped the *b* of their labor

BENJAMIN

　Twelfth son of Jacob by Rachel (Ge 35:16-24; 46:19-21; 1Ch 2:2). Jacob refused to send him to Egypt, but relented (Ge 42-45). Tribe of blessed (Ge 49:27; Dt 33:12), numbered (Nu 1:37; 26:41), allotted land (Jos 18:11-28; Eze 48:23), failed to fully possess (Jdg 1:21), nearly obliterated (Jdg 20-21), sided with Ish-Bosheth (2Sa 2), but turned to David (1Ch 12:2, 29). 12,000 from (Rev 7:8).

BEREANS*

Ac　17: 11　the *B* were of more noble character

BESTOWING* (BESTOWS)

Pr　　8: 21　*b* wealth on those who love me

BESTOWS (BESTOWING)

Ps　84: 11　the Lord *b* favor and honor;

BETHANY

Mk　11:　1　and *B* at the Mount of Olives,

BETHEL

Ge　28: 19　He called that place *B*,

BETHLEHEM

Ru　　1: 19　went on until they came to *B*.
1Sa 16:　1　I am sending you to Jesse of *B*.
2Sa 23: 15　from the well near the gate of *B*!"
Mic　5:　2　"But you, *B* Ephrathah,
Mt　　2:　1　After Jesus was born in *B* in Judea,
　　　2:　6　"'But you, *B*, in the land of Judah,

BETHPHAGE

Mt　21:　1　came to *B* on the Mount of Olives,

BETHSAIDA

Jn 12: 21 who was from *B* in Galilee,

BETRAY (BETRAYED BETRAYS)

Ps 89: 33 nor will I ever *b* my faithfulness.
Pr 25: 9 do not *b* another man's confidence,
Mt 10: 21 "Brother will *b* brother to death,
26: 21 the truth, one of you will *b* me."

BETRAYED (BETRAY)

Mt 27: 4 "for I have *b* innocent blood."

BETRAYS (BETRAY)

Pr 11: 13 A gossip *b* a confidence,
20: 19 A gossip *b* a confidence;

BEULAH*

Isa 62: 4 and your land *B*;

BEWITCHED*

Gal 3: 1 foolish Galatians! Who has *b* you?

BEZALEL

Judahite craftsman in charge of building the tabernacle (Ex 31:1-11; 35:30-39:31).

BIDDING*

Ps 103: 20 you mighty ones who do his *b*,
148: 8 stormy winds that do his *b*,

BILDAD

One of Job's friends (Job 8; 18; 25).

BILHAH

Servant of Rachel, mother of Jacob's sons Dan and Naphtali (Ge 30:1-7; 35:25; 46:23-25).

BIND (BINDS BOUND)

Dt 6: 8 and *b* them on your foreheads.
Pr 3: 3 *b* them around your neck,
6: 21 *B* them upon your heart forever;
7: 3 *B* them on your fingers;
Isa 61: 1 me to *b* up the brokenhearted,
Mt 16: 19 whatever you *b* on earth will be

BINDS (BIND)

Ps 147: 3 and *b* up their wounds.
Isa 30: 26 when the LORD *b* up the bruises

BIRD (BIRDS)

Pr 27: 8 Like a *b* that strays from its nest
Ecc 10: 20 a *b* of the air may carry your words,

BIRDS (BIRD)

Mt 8: 20 and *b* of the air have nests,
Lk 9: 58 and *b* of the air have nests,

BIRTH (BEAR)

Ps 51: 5 Surely I was sinful from *b*,
58: 3 Even from *b* the wicked go astray;
Isa 26: 18 but we gave *b* to wind.
Mt 1: 18 This is how the *b* of Jesus Christ
24: 8 these are the beginning of *b* pains.
Jn 3: 6 Flesh gives *b* to flesh, but the Spirit
1Pe 1: 3 great mercy he has given us new *b*

BIRTHRIGHT (BEAR)

Ge 25: 34 So Esau despised his *b*.

BISHOP see OVERSEER

BITTEN

Nu 21: 8 anyone who is *b* can look at it

BITTER (BITTERNESS EMBITTER)

Ex 12: 8 along with *b* herbs, and bread made
Pr 27: 7 what is *b* tastes sweet.

BITTERNESS (BITTER)

Pr 14: 10 Each heart knows its own *b*,
17: 25 and *b* to the one who bore him.
Ro 3: 14 full of cursing and *b*.''
Eph 4: 31 Get rid of all *b*, rage and anger,

BLACK

Zec 6: 6 The one with the *b* horses is going
Rev 6: 5 and there before me was a *b* horse!

BLAMELESS* (BLAMELESSLY)

Ge 6: 9 *b* among the people of his time,
17: 1 walk before me and be *b*.
Dt 18: 13 You must be *b* before the LORD
2Sa 22: 24 I have been *b* before him
22: 26 to the *b* you show yourself *b*,
Job 1: 1 This man was *b* and upright;
1: 8 one on earth like him; he is *b*
2: 3 one on earth like him; he is *b*
4: 6 and your *b* ways your hope?
8: 20 God does not reject a *b* man
9: 20 if I were *b*, it would pronounce me
9: 21 "Although I am *b*,
9: 22 'He destroys both the *b*
12: 4 though righteous and *b*!
22: 3 gain if your ways were *b*?
31: 6 and he will know that I am *b*—
Ps 15: 2 He whose walk is *b*
18: 23 I have been *b* before him
18: 25 to the *b* you show yourself *b*,
19: 13 Then will I be *b*,
26: 1 for I have led a *b* life;
26: 11 But I lead a *b* life;
37: 18 The days of the *b* are known
37: 37 Consider the *b*, observe the upright
84: 11 from those whose walk is *b*.
101: 2 I will be careful to lead a *b* life—
101: 2 house with *b* heart.
101: 6 he whose walk is *b*
119: 1 Blessed are they whose ways are *b*,
119: 80 May my heart be *b*
Pr 2: 7 a shield to those whose walk is *b*,
2: 21 and the *b* will remain in it;
11: 5 of the *b* makes a straight way
11: 20 in those whose ways are *b*.
19: 1 Better a poor man whose walk is *b*
20: 7 The righteous man leads a *b* life;
28: 6 Better a poor man whose walk is *b*
28: 10 *b* will receive a good inheritance.
28: 18 He whose walk is *b* is kept safe,
Eze 28: 15 You were *b* in your ways
1Co 1: 8 so that you will be *b* on the day
Eph 1: 4 world to be holy and *b* in his sight.
5: 27 any other blemish, but holy and *b*.
Php 1: 10 and *b* until the day of Christ,
2: 15 so that you may become *b* and pure
1Th 2: 10 and *b* we were among you who
3: 13 hearts so that you will be *b*
5: 23 and body be kept *b* at the coming
Tit 1: 6 An elder must be *b*, the husband of
1: 7 he must be *b*— not overbearing,
Heb 7: 26 *b*, pure, set apart from sinners,
2Pe 3: 14 effort to be found spotless, *b*
Rev 14: 5 found in their mouths; they are *b*.

BLAMELESSLY* (BLAMELESS)

Lk 1: 6 commandments and regulations *b*.

BLASPHEME* (BLASPHEMED BLASPHEMER BLASPHEMES BLASPHEMIES BLASPHEMING BLASPHEMOUS BLASPHEMY)

Ex 22: 28 "Do not *b* God or curse the ruler
Ac 26: 11 and I tried to force them to *b*.
1Ti 1: 20 over to Satan to be taught not to *b*.
2Pe 2: 12 these men *b* in matters they do not
Rev 13: 6 He opened his mouth to *b* God,

BLASPHEMED* (BLASPHEME)

Lev 24: 11 of the Israelite woman *b* the Name
2Ki 19: 6 of the king of Assyria have *b* me.
19: 22 Who is it you have insulted and *b*?
Isa 37: 6 of the king of Assyria have *b* me.
37: 23 Who is it you have insulted and *b*?
52: 5 my name is constantly *b*.
Eze 20: 27 your fathers *b* me by forsaking me;
Ac 19: 37 robbed temples nor *b* our goddess.
Ro 2: 24 name is *b* among the Gentiles

BLASPHEMER* (BLASPHEME)

Lev 24: 14 "Take the *b* outside the camp.
24: 23 they took the *b* outside the camp
1Ti 1: 13 I was once a *b* and a persecutor.

BLASPHEMES* (BLASPHEME)

Lev 24: 16 anyone who *b* the name
24: 16 native-born, when he *b* the Name,
Nu 15: 30 native-born or alien, *b* the LORD,

Mk 3: 29 whoever *b* against the Holy Spirit
Lk 12: 10 but anyone who *b* against the Holy

BLASPHEMIES* (BLASPHEME)

Ne 9: 18 or when they committed awful *b*.
9: 26 to you; they committed awful *b*.
Mk 3: 28 and *b* of men will be forgiven them.
Rev 13: 5 and to exercise his authority

BLASPHEMING* (BLASPHEME)

Mt 9: 3 "This fellow is *b*!" Knowing their
Mk 2: 7 He's *b*! Who can forgive sins

BLASPHEMOUS* (BLASPHEME)

Rev 13: 1 and on each head a *b* name.
17: 3 that was covered with *b* names

BLASPHEMY* (BLASPHEME)

Mt 12: 31 and *b* will be forgiven men,
12: 31 the *b* against the Spirit will not be
26: 65 Look, now you have heard the *b*.
26: 65 "He has spoken *b*! Why do we
Mk 14: 64 "You have heard the *b*.
Lk 5: 21 "Who is this fellow who speaks *b*?
Jn 10: 33 replied the Jews, "but for *b*,
10: 36 Why then do you accuse me of *b*
Ac 6: 11 words of *b* against Moses

BLAST*

Ex 15: 8 By the *b* of your nostrils
19: 13 horn sounds a long *b* may they go
19: 16 and a very loud trumpet *b*.
Nu 10: 5 When a trumpet *b* is sounded,
10: 6 At the sounding of a second *b*,
10: 6 The *b* will be the signal
10: 9 sound a *b* on the trumpets.
Jos 6: 5 you hear them sound a long *b*
6: 16 the priests sounded the trumpet *b*,
2Sa 22: 16 at the *b* of breath from his nostrils.
Job 4: 9 at the *b* of his anger they perish.
39: 25 At the *b* of the trumpet he snorts,
Ps 18: 15 the *b* of breath from your nostrils.
98: 6 and the *b* of the ram's horn—
147: 17 Who can withstand his icy *b*?
Isa 27: 8 with his fierce *b* he drives her out,
Eze 22: 20 a furnace to melt it with a fiery *b*,
Am 2: 2 tumult amid war cries and the *b*
Heb 12: 19 to a trumpet *b* or to such a voice

BLEATING*

1Sa 15: 14 "What then is this *b* of sheep

BLEMISH (BLEMISHES)

Lev 22: 21 be without defect or *b*
Eph 5: 27 or wrinkle or any other *b*,
Col 1: 22 without *b* and free from accusation
1Pe 1: 19 a lamb without *b* or defect.

BLEMISHES* (BLEMISH)

2Pe 2: 13 and *b*, reveling in their pleasures
Jude : 12 These men are *b* at your love feasts

BLESS (BLESSED BLESSES BLESSING BLESSINGS)

Ge 12: 3 I will *b* those who *b* you,
32: 26 not let you go unless you *b* me.''
Dt 7: 13 He will love you and *b* you
33: 11 *B* all his skills, O LORD,
Ps 72: 15 and *b* him all day long.
Ro 12: 14 Bless those who persecute you; *b*

BLESSED (BLESS)

Ge 1: 22 God *b* them and said, "Be fruitful
2: 3 And God *b* the seventh day
22: 18 nations on earth will be *b*,
Nu 24: 9 "May those who bless you be *b*
1Ch 17: 27 have *b* it, and it will be *b* forever.''
Ps 1: 1 *B* is the man
2: 12 *B* are all who take refuge in him.
32: 2 *B* is the man
33: 12 *B* is the nation whose God is
40: 4 *B* is the man
41: 1 *B* is he who has regard for the weak
84: 5 *B* are those whose strength is
89: 15 *B* are those who have learned
94: 12 *B* is the man you discipline,
106: 3 *B* are they who maintain justice,
112: 1 *B* is the man who fears the LORD,

Ps 118: 26 *B* is he who comes in the name
   119: 1 *B* are they whose ways are
   119: 2 *B* are they who keep his statutes
   127: 5 *B* is the man
Pr 3: 13 *B* is the man who finds wisdom,
   8: 34 *B* is the man who listens to me,
  28: 20 A faithful man will be richly *b*,
  29: 18 but *b* is he who keeps the law.
  31: 28 Her children arise and call her *b;*
Isa 30: 18 *B* are all who wait for him!
Mal 3: 12 Then all the nations will call you *b*,
   3: 15 But now we call the arrogant *b*.
Mt 5: 3 saying: ''*B* are the poor in spirit,
   5: 4 *B* are those who mourn,
   5: 5 *B* are the meek,
   5: 6 *B* are those who hunger
   5: 7 *B* are the merciful,
   5: 8 *B* are the pure in heart,
   5: 9 *B* are the peacemakers,
   5: 10 *B* are those who are persecuted
   5: 11 ''*B* are you when people insult you,
Lk 1: 48 on all generations will call me *b*,
Jn 12: 13 ''*B* is he who comes in the name
Ac 20: 35 'It is more *b* to give than to receive
Tit 2: 13 while we wait for the *b* hope—
Jas 1: 12 *B* is the man who perseveres
Rev 1: 3 *B* is the one who reads the words
  22: 7 *B* is he who keeps the words
  22: 14 ''*B* are those who wash their robes,

BLESSES (BLESS)

Ps 29: 11 the LORD *b* his people with peace.
Ro 10: 12 and richly *b* all who call on him,

BLESSING (BLESS)

Ge 27: 4 so that I may give you my *b*
Dt 23: 5 turned the curse into a *b* for you,
  33: 1 This is the *b* that Moses the man
Pr 10: 22 The *b* of the LORD brings wealth,
Eze 34: 26 there will be showers of *b*.

BLESSINGS (BLESS)

Dt 11: 29 proclaim on Mount Gerizim the *b*,
Jos 8: 34 all the words of the law—the *b*
Pr 10: 6 *B* crown the head of the righteous,
Ro 15: 27 shared in the Jews' spiritual *b*,

BLIND (BLINDED)

Mt 15: 14 a *b* man leads a *b* man, both will fall
  23: 16 ''Woe to you, *b* guides! You say,
Mk 10: 46 a *b* man, Bartimaeus (that is,
Lk 6: 39 ''Can a *b* man lead a *b* man?
Jn 9: 25 I was *b* but now I see!''

BLINDED (BLIND)

Jn 12: 40 elsewhere: ''He has *b* their eyes
2Co 4: 4 The god of this age has *b* the minds

BLOOD (BLOODSHED BLOODTHIRSTY)

Ge 4: 10 Your brother's *b* cries out to me
   9: 6 ''Whoever sheds the *b* of man,
Ex 12: 13 and when I see the *b*, I will pass
  24: 8 ''This is the *b* of the covenant that
Lev 16: 15 and take its *b* behind the curtain
  17: 11 For the life of a creature is in the *b*,
Dt 12: 23 eat the *b*, because the *b* is the life,
Ps 72: 14 for precious is their *b* in his sight.
Pr 6: 17 hands that shed innocent *b*,
Isa 1: 11 pleasure in the *b* of bulls and lambs
Mt 26: 28 This is my *b* of the covenant,
  27: 24 ''I am innocent of this man's *b*.''
Mk 14: 24 ''This is my *b* of the covenant,
Lk 22: 44 drops of *b* falling to the ground.
Jn 6: 53 of the Son of Man and drink his *b*,
Ac 15: 20 of strangled animals and from *b*.
  20: 26 innocent of the *b* of all men.
Ro 3: 25 of atonement, through faith in his *b*
   5: 9 have now been justified by his *b*,
1Co 11: 25 cup is the new covenant in my *b;*
Eph 1: 7 we have redemption through his *b*,
  2: 13 near through the *b* of Christ.
Col 1: 20 by making peace through his *b*,
Heb 9: 7 once a year, and never without *b*,
   9: 12 once for all by his own *b*,
   9: 20 ''This is the *b* of the covenant,
   9: 22 of *b* there is no forgiveness.
  12: 24 word than the *b* of Abel.

1Pe 1: 19 but with the precious *b* of Christ,
1Jn 1: 7 and the *b* of Jesus, his Son,
Rev 1: 5 has freed us from our sins by his *b*,
   5: 9 with your *b* you purchased men
   7: 14 white in the *b* of the Lamb.
  12: 11 him by the *b* of the Lamb
  19: 13 He is dressed in a robe dipped in *b*,

BLOODSHED (BLOOD)

Jer 48: 10 on him who keeps his sword from *b*
Eze 35: 6 did not hate *b*, *b* will pursue you.
Hab 2: 12 to him who builds a city with *b*

BLOODTHIRSTY* (BLOOD)

Ps 5: 6 *b* and deceitful men
  26: 9 my life with *b* men,
  55: 23 *b* and deceitful men
  59: 2 and save me from *b* men.
  139: 19 Away from me, you *b* men!
Pr 29: 10 *B* men hate a man of integrity

BLOSSOM

Isa 35: 1 the wilderness will rejoice and *b*.

BLOT (BLOTS)

Ex 32: 32 then *b* me out of the book you have
Ps 51: 1 *b* out my transgressions.
Rev 3: 5 I will never *b* out his name

BLOTS (BLOT)

Isa 43: 25 ''I, even I, am he who *b* out

BLOWN

Eph 4: 14 and *b* here and there by every wind
Jas 1: 6 doubts is like a wave of the sea, *b*
Jude : 12 without rain, *b* along by the wind;

BLUSH

Jer 6: 15 they do not even know how to *b*.

BOAST (BOASTS)

1Ki 20: 11 armor should not *b* like one who
Ps 34: 2 My soul will *b* in the LORD;
  44: 8 In God we make our *b* all day long,
Pr 27: 1 Do not *b* about tomorrow,
Jer 9: 23 or the rich man *b* of his riches,
1Co 1: 31 Let him who boasts *b* in the Lord.''
2Co 10: 17 Let him who boasts *b* in the Lord.''
  11: 30 I do not inwardly burn? If I must *b*,
Gal 6: 14 May I never *b* except in the cross
Eph 2: 9 not by works, so that no one can *b*.

BOASTS (BOAST)

Jer 9: 24 but let him who *b* boast about this:

BOAZ

Wealthy Bethlehemite who showed favor to Ruth (Ru 2), married her (Ru 4). Ancestor of David (Ru 4:18-22; 1Ch 2:12-15), Jesus (Mt 1:5-16; Lk 3:23-32).

BODIES (BODY)

Isa 26: 19 their *b* will rise.
Ro 12: 1 to offer your *b* as living sacrifices,
1Co 6: 15 not know that your *b* are members
Eph 5: 28 to love their wives as their own *b*.

BODILY (BODY)

Col 2: 9 of the Deity lives in *b* form,

BODY (BODIES BODILY EMBODIMENT)

Zec 13: 6 What are these wounds on your *b*?'
Mt 10: 28 afraid of those who kill the *b*
  26: 26 saying, ''Take and eat; this is my *b*
  26: 41 spirit is willing, but the *b* is weak.''
Mk 14: 22 saying, ''Take it; this is my *b*.''
Lk 22: 19 saying, ''This is my *b* given for you;
Jn 13: 10 wash his feet; his whole *b* is clean.
Ro 6: 13 Do not offer the parts of your *b*
  12: 4 us has one *b* with many members,
1Co 6: 19 not know that your *b* is a temple
  6: 20 Therefore honor God with your *b*.
  11: 24 ''This is my *b*, which is for you;
  12: 12 The *b* is a unit, though it is made up
  12: 13 baptized into one *b*—
  15: 44 a natural *b*, it is raised a spiritual *b*.
Eph 1: 23 which is his *b*, the fullness
   4: 25 for we are all members of one *b*.

Eph 5: 30 for we are members of his *b*.
Php 1: 20 Christ will be exalted in my *b*,
Col 1: 24 sake of his *b*, which is the church.

BOLD (BOLDNESS)

Ps 138: 3 you made me *b* and stouthearted.
Pr 21: 29 A wicked man puts up a *b* front,
  28: 1 but the righteous are as *b* as a lion.

BOLDNESS* (BOLD)

Lk 11: 8 of the man's *b* he will get up
Ac 4: 29 to speak your word with great *b*.

BONDAGE

Ezr 9: 9 God has not deserted us in our *b*.

BONES

Ge 2: 23 ''This is now bone of my *b*
Ps 22: 14 and all my *b* are out of joint.
  22: 17 I can count all my *b;*
Eze 37: 1 middle of a valley; it was full of *b*.
Jn 19: 36 ''Not one of his *b* will be broken,''

BOOK (BOOKS)

Ex 32: 33 against me I will blot out of my *b*.
Jos 1: 8 Do not let this *B* of the Law depart
2Ki 22: 8 ''I have found the *B* of the Law
2Ch 34: 15 ''I have found the *B* of the Law
Ne 8: 8 They read from the *B* of the Law
Ps 69: 28 May they be blotted out of the *b*
Da 12: 1 name is found written in the *b*—
Jn 20: 30 which are not recorded in this *b*.
Php 4: 3 whose names are in the *b* of life.
Rev 3: 5 never blot out his name from the *b*
  20: 12 *b* was opened, which is the *b*
  20: 15 was not found written in the *b*
  21: 27 written in the Lamb's *b* of life.
  22: 18 him the plagues described in this *b*.

BOOKS* (BOOK)

Ecc 12: 12 Of making many *b* there is no end,
Da 7: 10 and the *b* were opened.
Jn 21: 25 for the *b* that would be written.
Rev 20: 12 the throne, and *b* were opened.
  20: 12 they had done as recorded in the *b*.

BORE (BEAR)

Isa 53: 12 For he *b* the sin of many,
1Pe 2: 24 He himself *b* our sins in his body

BORN (BEAR)

Ecc 3: 2 a time to be *b* and a time to die,
Isa 9: 6 For to us a child is *b*,
  66: 8 Can a country be *b* in a day
Lk 2: 11 of David a Savior has been *b* to you
Jn 3: 3 see kingdom of God unless he is *b* again.
   3: 4 How can a man be *b* when he is old
   3: 5 unless he is *b* of water
   3: 7 at my saying, 'You must be *b* again
   3: 8 it is with everyone *b* of the Spirit.''
1Pe 1: 23 For you have been *b* again,
1Jn 3: 9 because he has been *b* of God.
   4: 7 Everyone who loves has been *b*
   5: 1 believes that Jesus is the Christ is *b*
   5: 4 for everyone *b* of God overcomes
   5: 18 We know that anyone *b*

BORROWER

Pr 22: 7 and the *b* is servant to the lender.

BOTHER (BOTHERING)

Lk 11: 7 one inside answers, 'Don't *b* me.

BOTHERING (BOTHER)

Lk 18: 5 yet because this widow keeps *b* me,

BOUGHT (BUY)

Ac 20: 28 which he *b* with his own blood.
1Co 6: 20 You are not your own; you were *b*
   7: 23 You were *b* at a price; do not
2Pe 2: 1 the sovereign Lord who *b* them—

BOUND (BIND)

Is 56: 3 Let no foreigner who has *b* himself
Mt 16: 19 bind on earth will be *b* in heaven,
  18: 18 bind on earth will be *b* in heaven,
Ro 7: 2 by law a married woman is *b*
1Co 7: 39 A woman is *b* to her husband

Jude : 6 *b* with everlasting chains
Rev 20: 2 and *b* him for a thousand years.

BOUNDARY (BOUNDS)

Nu 34: 3 your southern *b* will start
Pr 23: 10 Do not move an ancient *b* stone
Hos 5: 10 who move *b* stones.

BOUNDS (BOUNDARY)

2Co 7: 4 all our troubles my joy knows no *b*.

BOUNTY*

Ge 49: 26 than the *b* of the age-old hills.
Dt 28: 12 heavens, the storehouse of his *b*,
1Ki 10: 13 he had given her out of his royal *b*.
Ps 65: 11 You crown the year with your *b*,
68: 10 from your *b*, O God, you provided
Jer 31: 12 rejoice in the *b* of the LORD—
31: 14 my people will be filled with my *b*

BOW (BOWED BOWS)

Dt 5: 9 You shall not *b* down to them
1Ki 22: 34 But someone drew his *b* at random
Ps 5: 7 in reverence will I *b* down
44: 6 I do not trust in my *b*,
95: 6 Come, let us *b* down in worship,
138: 2 I will *b* down toward your holy
Isa 44: 19 Shall I *b* down to a block of wood?''
45: 23 Before me every knee will *b*;
Ro 14: 11 'Every knee will *b* before me;
Php 2: 10 name of Jesus every knee should *b*,

BOWED (BOW)

Ps 145: 14 and lifts up all who are *b* down.
146: 8 the LORD lifts up those who are *b*

BOWS (BOW)

Isa 44: 15 he makes an idol and *b* down to it.
44: 17 he *b* down to it and worships.

BOY (BOY'S BOYS)

Ge 21: 17 God heard the *b* crying,
22: 12 not lay a hand on the *b*
Jdg 13: 5 *b* is to be a Nazirite,
1Sa 2: 11 *b* ministered before the LORD.
3: 8 the LORD was calling the *b*.
Isa 7: 16 before the *b* knows enough
Mt 17: 18 demon, and it came out of the *b*
Lk 2: 43 the *b* Jesus stayed behind

BOY'S (BOY)

1Ki 17: 22 the *b* life returned to him
2Ki 4: 34 the *b* body grew warm

BOYS (BOY)

Ge 25: 24 twin *b* in her womb
Ex 1: 18 they let the *b* live.

BRACE*

Job 38: 3 *B* yourself like a man;
40: 7 out of the storm: ''*B* yourself like
Na 2: 1 *b* yourselves,

BRAG*

Am 4: 5 and *b* about your freewill offerings
Ro 2: 17 *b* about your relationship to God;
2: 23 temples? You who *b* about the law,
Jas 4: 16 As it is, you boast and *b*.

BRAIDED

1Ti 2: 9 not with *b* hair or gold or pearls
1Pe 3: 3 as *b* hair and the wearing

BRANCH (BRANCHES)

Isa 4: 2 In that day the *B* of the LORD will
Jer 23: 5 up to David a righteous *B*,
33: 15 I will make a righteous *B* sprout
Zec 3: 8 going to bring my servant, the *B*.
6: 12 is the man whose name is the *B*,
Jn 15: 2 while every *b* that does bear fruit
15: 4 No *b* can bear fruit by itself;

BRANCHES (BRANCH)

Jn 15: 5 ''I am the vine; you are the *b*.
Ro 11: 21 if God did not spare the natural *b*,

BRAVE

2Sa 2: 7 Now then, be strong and *b*,
13: 28 you this order? Be strong and *b*.''

BREACH (BREAK)

Ps 106: 23 stood in the *b* before him

BREACHING (BREAK)

Pr 17: 14 Starting a quarrel is like *b* a dam;

BREAD

Ex 12: 8 and *b* made without yeast.
23: 15 the Feast of Unleavened *B*;
25: 30 Put the *b* of the Presence
Dt 8: 3 that man does not live on *b* alone
Ps 78: 25 Men ate the *b* of angels;
Pr 30: 8 but give me only my daily *b*.
Ecc 11: 1 Cast your *b* upon the waters,
Isa 55: 2 Why spend money on what is not *b*
Mt 4: 3 tell these stones to become *b*.''
4: 4 'Man does not live on *b* alone,
6: 11 Give us today our daily *b*.
26: 26 Jesus took *b*, gave thanks
Mk 14: 22 Jesus took *b*, gave thanks
Lk 4: 3 tell this stone to become *b*.''
4: 4 'Man does not live on *b* alone.' ''
9: 13 ''We have only five loaves of *b*
11: 3 Give us each day our daily *b*.
22: 19 And he took *b*, gave thanks
Jn 6: 33 For the *b* of God is he who comes
6: 35 Jesus declared, ''I am the *b* of life.
6: 41 ''I am the *b* that came
6: 48 I am the *b* of life.
6: 51 I am the living *b* that came
6: 51 This *b* is my flesh, which I will give
21: 13 took the *b* and gave it to them,
1Co 10: 16 And is not the *b* that we break
11: 23 took *b*, and when he had given
11: 26 For whenever you eat this *b*

BREAK (BREACH BREACHING BREAKERS BREAKING BREAKS BROKE BROKEN BROKENNESS)

Nu 30: 2 he must not *b* his word
Jdg 2: 1 'I will never *b* my covenant
Pr 25: 15 and a gentle tongue can *b* a bone.
Isa 42: 3 A bruised reed he will not *b*,
Mal 2: 15 and do not *b* faith with the wife
Mt 12: 20 A bruised reed he will not *b*,
Ac 20: 7 week we came together to *b* bread.
1Co 10: 16 the bread that we *b* a participation
Rev 5: 2 ''Who is worthy to *b* the seals

BREAKERS* (BREAK)

Ps 42: 7 all your waves and *b*
93: 4 mightier than the *b* of the sea—
Jnh 2: 3 all your waves and *b*

BREAKING (BREAK)

Jos 9: 20 fall on us for *b* the oath we swore
Eze 16: 59 oath by *b* the covenant.
17: 18 the oath by *b* the covenant.
Ac 2: 42 to the *b* of bread and to prayer.
Jas 2: 10 at just one point is guilty of *b* all

BREAKS (BREAK)

Jer 23: 29 ''and like a hammer that *b* a rock
1Jn 3: 4 Everyone who sins *b* the law;

BREASTPIECE (BREASTPLATE)

Ex 28: 15 Fashion a *b* for making decisions—

BREASTPLATE* (BREASTPIECE)

Isa 59: 17 He put on righteousness as his *b*,
Eph 6: 14 with the *b* of righteousness in place
1Th 5: 8 putting on faith and love as a *b*,

BREASTS

La 4: 3 Even jackals offer their *b*

BREATH (BREATHED GOD-BREATHED)

Ge 2: 7 into his nostrils the *b* of life,

BREATHED (BREATH)

Ge 2: 7 *b* into his nostrils the breath of life,
Mk 15: 37 With a loud cry, Jesus *b* his last.
Jn 20: 22 And with that he *b* on them

BREEDS*

Pr 13: 10 Pride only *b* quarrels,

BRIBE

Ex 23: 8 ''Do not accept a *b*,
Dt 16: 19 for a *b* blinds the eyes of the wise
27: 25 ''Cursed is the man who accepts a *b*
Pr 6: 35 will refuse the *b*, however great it

BRIDE

Isa 62: 5 as a bridegroom rejoices over his *b*.
Rev 19: 7 and his *b* has made herself ready.
21: 2 as a *b* beautifully dressed
21: 9 I will show you the *b*, the wife
22: 17 The Spirit and the *b* say, ''Come!''

BRIDEGROOM

Ps 19: 5 which is like a *b* coming forth
Mt 25: 1 and went out to meet the *b*.
25: 5 The *b* was a long time in coming,

BRIGHTENS* (BRIGHTNESS)

Pr 16: 15 When a king's face *b*, it means life;
Ecc 8: 1 Wisdom *b* a man's face

BRIGHTER (BRIGHTNESS)

Pr 4: 18 shining ever *b* till the full light

BRIGHTNESS* (BRIGHTENS BRIGHTER)

2Sa 22: 13 Out of the *b* of his presence
23: 4 like the *b* after rain
Ps 18: 12 of the *b* of his presence clouds
Isa 59: 9 for *b*, but we walk in deep shadows.
60: 3 and kings to the *b* of your dawn.
60: 19 will the *b* of the moon shine on you
Da 12: 3 who are wise will shine like the *b*
Am 5: 20 pitch-dark, without a ray of *b*?

BRILLIANCE* (BRILLIANT)

Ac 22: 11 the *b* of the light had blinded me.
Rev 1: 16 was like the sun shining in all its *b*.
21: 11 its *b* was like that of a very precious

BRILLIANT* (BRILLIANCE)

Ecc 9: 11 or wealth to the *b*
Eze 1: 4 and surrounded by *b* light.
1: 27 and *b* light surrounded him.

BRINK*

Pr 5: 14 I have come to the *b* of utter ruin

BRITTLE

Da 2: 42 will be partly strong and partly *b*.

BROAD

Mt 7: 13 and *b* is the road that leads

BROKE (BREAK)

Mt 26: 26 took bread, gave thanks and *b* it,
Mk 14: 22 took bread, gave thanks and *b* it,
Ac 2: 46 They *b* bread in their homes
20: 11 he went upstairs again and *b* bread
1Co 11: 24 when he had given thanks, he *b* it

BROKEN (BREAK)

Ps 34: 20 not one of them will be *b*.
51: 17 The sacrifices of God are a *b* spirit;
Ecc 4: 12 of three strands is not quickly *b*.
Lk 20: 18 on that stone will be *b* to pieces,
Jn 7: 23 the law of Moses may not be *b*,
10: 35 and the Scripture cannot be *b*—
19: 36 ''Not one of his bones will be *b*.''
Ro 11: 20 they were *b* off because of unbelief,

BROKENHEARTED* (HEART)

Ps 34: 18 The LORD is close to the *b*
109: 16 and the needy and the *b*.
147: 3 He heals the *b*
Isa 61: 1 He has sent me to bind up the *b*,

BROKENNESS* (BREAK)

Isa 65: 14 and wail in *b* of spirit.

BRONZE

Ex 27: 2 and overlay the altar with *b*.
30: 18 ''Make a *b* basin, with its *b* stand,
Nu 21: 9 So Moses made a *b* snake
Da 2: 32 and thighs of *b*, its legs of iron,
10: 6 legs like the gleam of burnished *b*,
Rev 1: 15 His feet were like *b* glowing

Rev   2:18 whose feet are like burnished *b*.

BROTHER (BROTHER'S BROTHERHOOD BROTHERLY BROTHERS)

Pr   17:17 and a *b* is born for adversity.
      18:24 a friend who sticks closer than a *b*.
      27:10 neighbor nearby than a *b* far away.
Mt   5:24 and be reconciled to your *b*;
      18:15 "If your *b* sins against you,
Mk   3:35 Whoever does God's will is my *b*
Lk   17:   3 "If your *b* sins, rebuke him,
Ro   14:15 not by your eating destroy your *b*
      14:21 anything else that will cause your *b*
1Co   8:13 if what I eat causes my *b* to fall
2Th   3:   6 away from every *b* who is idle
      3:15 as an enemy, but warn him as a *b*.
Phm   :16 but better than a slave, as a dear *b*.
Jas   2:15 Suppose a *b* or sister is
      4:11 Anyone who speaks against his *b*
1Jn   2:   9 hates his *b* is still in the darkness.
      2:10 Whoever loves his *b* lives
      2:11 But whoever hates his *b* is
      3:10 is anyone who does not love his *b*.
      3:15 who hates his *b* is a murderer,
      3:17 material possessions and sees his *b*
      4:20 For anyone who does not love his *b*
      4:20 yet hates his *b*, he is a liar.
      4:21 loves God must also love his *b*.
      5:16 If anyone sees his *b* commit a sin

BROTHER'S (BROTHER)

Ge   4:   9 "Am I my *b* keeper?" The LORD
Mt   7:   5 remove the speck from your *b* eye.
Ro   14:13 or obstacle in your *b* way.

BROTHERHOOD (BROTHER)

1Pe   2:17 Love the *b* of believers, fear God,

BROTHERLY* (BROTHER)

Ro   12:10 devoted to one another in *b* love.
1Th   4:   9 Now about *b* love we do not need
2Pe   1:   7 and to godliness, *b* kindness;
      1:   7 kindness; and to *b* kindness,

BROTHERS (BROTHER)

Jos   1:14 You are to help your *b*
Ps   133:   1 is when *b* live together in unity!
Pr   6:19 who stirs up dissension among *b*.
Mt   12:49 "Here are my mother and my *b*.
      19:29 everyone who has left houses or *b*
      25:40 one of the least of these *b* of mine,
Mk   3:33 "Who are my mother and my *b*?"
      10:29 or *b* or sisters or mother or father
Lk   21:16 You will be betrayed even by parents,
      22:32 turned back, strengthen your *b*."
Jn   7:   5 his own *b* did not believe in him.
Ac   15:32 to encourage and strengthen the *b*.
Ro   9:   3 off from Christ for the sake of my *b*
1Co   8:12 sin against your *b* in this way
2Co   11:26 and in danger from false *b*.
Gal   2:   4 some false *b* had infiltrated our
1Th   4:10 you do love all the *b*
      5:26 Greet all the *b* with a holy kiss.
1Ti   6:   2 for them because they are *b*.
Heb   2:11 Jesus is not ashamed to call them *b*.
      2:17 to be made like his *b* in every way,
      13:   1 Keep on loving each other as *b*.
1Pe   1:22 you have sincere love for your *b*,
      3:   8 be sympathetic, love as *b*,
1Jn   3:14 death to life, because we love our *b*.
      3:16 to lay down our lives for our *b*.
3Jn   :10 he refuses to welcome the *b*.
Rev   12:10 For the accuser of our *b*,

BROW

Ge   3:19 By the sweat of your *b*

BRUISED (BRUISES)

Isa   42:   3 A *b* reed he will not break,
Mt   12:20 A *b* reed he will not break,

BRUISES (BRUISED)

Isa   30:26 when the LORD binds up the *b*

BRUTAL (BRUTE)

2Ti   3:   3 slanderous, without self-control, *b*,

BRUTE* (BRUTAL)

Ps   73:22 I was a *b* beast before you.
2Pe   2:12 They are like *b* beasts, creatures

BUBBLING*

Pr   18:   4 the fountain of wisdom is a *b* brook.
Isa   35:   7 the thirsty ground *b* springs.

BUCKET*

Isa   40:15 the nations are like a drop in a *b*;

BUCKLED* (BUCKLER)

Eph   6:14 belt of truth *b* around your waist,

BUCKLER* (BUCKLED)

Ps   35:   2 Take up shield and *b*;

BUD (BUDDED)

Isa   27:   6 Israel will *b* and blossom

BUDDED (BUD)

Heb   9:   4 Aaron's staff that had *b*,

BUILD (BUILDER BUILDERS BUILDING BUILDS BUILT REBUILD REBUILT)

2Sa   7:   5 Are you the one to *b* me a house
1Ki   6:   1 he began to *b* the temple
Ecc   3:   3 a time to tear down and a time to *b*,
Mt   16:18 and on this rock I will *b* my church,
Ac   20:32 which can *b* you up and give you
Ro   15:   2 neighbor for his good, to *b* him up.
1Co   14:12 excel in gifts that *b* up the church.
1Th   5:11 one another and *b* each other up,
Jude   :20 *b* yourselves up in your most holy

BUILDER* (BUILD)

1Co   3:10 I laid a foundation as an expert *b*,
Heb   3:   3 the *b* of a house has greater honor
      3:   4 but God is the *b* of everything.
      11:10 whose architect and is God.

BUILDERS (BUILD)

Ps   118:22 The stone the *b* rejected
Mt   21:42 " 'The stone the *b* rejected
Mk   12:10 " 'The stone the *b* rejected
Lk   20:17 " 'The stone the *b* rejected
Ac   4:11 " 'the stone you *b* rejected,
1Pe   2:   7 "The stone the *b* rejected

BUILDING (BUILD)

Ezr   3:   8 to supervise the *b* of the house
Ne   4:17 of Judah who were *b* the wall.
Ro   15:20 so that I would not be *b*
1Co   3:   9 you are God's field, God's *b*.
2Co   5:   1 we have a *b* from God, an eternal
      10:   8 us for *b* you up rather
      13:10 the Lord gave me for *b* you up,
Eph   2:21 him the whole *b* is joined together
      4:29 helpful for *b* others up according

BUILDS (BUILD)

Ps   127:   1 Unless the LORD *b* the house,
Pr   14:   1 The wise woman *b* her house,
1Co   3:10 one should be careful how he *b*.
      3:12 If any man *b* on this foundation
      8:   1 Knowledge puffs up, but love *b* up.
Eph   4:16 grows and *b* itself up in love,

BUILT (BUILD)

1Ki   6:14 So Solomon *b* the temple
Mt   7:24 is like a wise man who *b* his house
Lk   6:49 is like a man who *b* a house
Ac   17:24 does not live in temples *b* by hands.
1Co   3:14 If what he has *b* survives, he will
2Co   5:   1 house, not *b* by human hands.
Eph   2:20 *b* on the foundation of the apostles
      4:12 the body of Christ may be *b* up
Col   2:   7 live in him, rooted and *b* up in him,
1Pe   2:   5 are being *b* into a spiritual house

BULL (BULLS)

Lev   4:   3 bring to the LORD a young *b*

BULLS (BULL)

1Ki   7:25 The Sea stood on twelve *b*,
Heb   10:   4 it is impossible for the blood of *b*

BURDEN (BURDENED BURDENS BURDENSOME)

Ps   38:   4 like a *b* too heavy to bear.
Ecc   1:13 What a heavy *b* God has laid
Mt   11:30 my yoke is easy and my *b* is light."
Ac   15:28 to us not to *b* you with anything
2Co   11:   9 from being a *b* to you in any way,
      12:14 and I will not be a *b* to you,
1Th   2:   9 day in order not to be a *b* to anyone
2Th   3:   8 so that we would not be a *b* to any
Heb   13:17 not a *b*, for that would be

BURDENED* (BURDEN)

Isa   43:23 have not *b* you with grain offerings
      43:24 But you have *b* me with your sins
Mic   6:   3 How have I *b* you? Answer me.
Mt   11:28 all you who are weary and *b*,
2Co   5:   4 in this tent, we groan and are *b*,
Gal   5:   1 do not let yourselves be *b* again
1Ti   5:16 not let the church be *b* with them,

BURDENS (BURDEN)

Ps   68:19 who daily bears our *b*.
Lk   11:46 down with *b* they can hardly carry,
Gal   6:   2 Carry each other's *b*,

BURDENSOME (BURDEN)

1Jn   5:   3 And his commands are not *b*,

BURIED (BURY)

Ru   1:17 die I will die, and there I will be *b*.
Ro   6:   4 *b* with him through baptism
1Co   15:   4 that he was *b*, that he was raised
Col   2:12 having been *b* with him in baptism

BURN (BURNING BURNT)

Dt   7:   5 and *b* their idols in the fire.
Ps   79:   5 long will your jealousy *b* like fire?
1Co   7:   9 to marry than to *b* with passion.

BURNING (BURN)

Ex   27:20 so that the lamps may be kept *b*.
Lev   6:   9 the fire must be kept *b* on the altar.
Ps   18:28 You, O LORD, keep my lamp *b*;
Pr   25:22 you will heap *b* coals on his head,
Ro   12:20 you will heap *b* coals on his head."
Rev   19:20 alive into the fiery lake of *b* sulfur.

BURNISHED*

1Ki   7:45 of the LORD were of *b* bronze.
Eze   1:   7 and gleamed like *b* bronze.
Da   10:   6 and legs like the gleam of *b* bronze,
Rev   2:18 and whose feet are like *b* bronze.

BURNT (BURN)

Ge   8:20 he sacrificed *b* offerings on it.
      22:   2 as a *b* offering on one
Ex   10:25 and *b* offerings to present
      18:12 brought a *b* offering and other
      40:   6 Place the altar of *b* offering in front
Lev   1:   3 " 'If the offering is a *b* offering
Jos   8:31 offered to the LORD *b* offerings
Jdg   6:26 offer the second bull as a *b* offering
      13:16 But if you prepare a *b* offering,
1Ki   3:   4 offered a thousand *b* offerings
      9:25 year Solomon sacrificed *b* offerings
      10:   5 and the *b* offerings he made
Ezr   3:   2 Israel to sacrifice *b* offerings on it,
Eze   43:18 for sacrificing *b* offerings

BURST

Ps   98:   4 *b* into jubilant song with music;
Isa   44:23 *B* into song, you mountains,
      49:13 *b* into song, O mountains!
      52:   9 *B* into songs of joy together,
      54:   1 *b* into song, shout for joy,
      55:12 will *b* into song before you,

BURY (BURIED)

Mt   8:22 and let the dead *b* their own dead."
Lk   9:60 "Let the dead *b* their own dead,

BUSH

Ex   3:   2 the *b* was on fire it did not burn up.
Mk   12:26 the account of the *b*, how God said
Lk   20:37 But in the account of the *b*,
Ac   7:35 who appeared to him in the *b*.

BUSINESS

Ecc   4: 8 a miserable b!
Da   8:27 and went about the king's b.
1Co   5:12 What b is it of mine to judge those
1Th   4:11 to mind your own b and to work
Jas   1:11 even while he goes about his b.

BUSY*

1Ki 18:27 Perhaps he is deep in thought, or b,
     20:40 While your servant was b here
Isa   32: 6 his mind is b with evil:
Hag   1: 9 of you is b with his own house.
2Th   3:11 They are not b; they are
Tit   2: 5 to be b at home, to be kind,

BUSYBODIES*

2Th   3:11 They are not busy; they are b.
1Ti   5:13 b, saying things they ought not to.

BUY (BOUGHT BUYS)

Pr   23:23 B the truth and do not sell it;
Isa   55: 1 Come, b wine and milk
Rev 13:17 so that no one could b or sell

BUYS (BUY)

Pr   31:16 She considers a field and b it;

BYWORD (WORD)

1Ki   9: 7 Israel will then become a b
Ps   44:14 You have made us a b
Joel   2:17 a b among the nations.

CAESAR

Mt   22:21 "Give to C what is Caesar's,

CAIN

Firstborn of Adam (Ge 4:1), murdered brother Abel (Ge 4:1-16; 1Jn 3:12).

CAKE

Hos   7: 8 Ephraim is a flat c not turned over.

CALEB

Judahite who spied out Canaan (Nu 13:6); allowed to enter land because of faith (Nu 13:30-14:38; Dt 1:36). Possessed Hebron (Jdg 14:6-15:19).

CALF

Ex   32: 4 into an idol cast in the shape of a c,
Pr   15:17 than a fattened c with hatred.
Lk   15:23 Bring the fattened c and kill it.
Ac   7:41 made an idol in the form of a c.

CALL (CALLED CALLING CALLS)

1Ki 18:24 I will c on the name of the LORD.
2Ki   5:11 c on the name of the LORD his
1Ch 16: 8 to the LORD, c on his name;
Ps   105: 1 to the LORD, c on his name;
     116:13 and c on the name of the LORD.
     116:17 and c on the name of the LORD.
     145:18 near to all who c on him,
Pr   31:28 children arise and c her blessed;
Isa   5:20 Woe to those who c evil good
      12: 4 to the LORD, c on his name;
      55: 6 c on him while he is near.
      65:24 Before they c I will answer;
Jer   33: 3 'C to me and I will answer you
Zep   3: 9 that all of them may c on the name
Zec   13: 9 They will c on my name
Mt   9:13 come to c the righteous,
Mk   2:17 I have not come to c the righteous,
Lk   5:32 I have not come to c the righteous,
Ac   2:39 all whom the Lord our God will c.''
       9:14 to arrest all who c on your name.''
       9:21 among those who c on this name?
Ro   10:12 and richly blesses all who c on him,
      11:29 gifts and his c are irrevocable.
1Co   1: 2 with all those everywhere who c
1Th   4: 7 For God did not c us to be impure,
2Ti   2:22 along with those who c

CALLED (CALL)

Ge   2:23 she shall be c 'woman,'
       5: 2 he blessed them and c them ''man
      12: 8 and c on the name of the LORD.
      21:33 and there he c upon the name
      26:25 and c on the name of the LORD.
1Sa   3: 5 and said, ''Here I am; you c me.''

2Ch   7:14 if my people, who are c
Ps   34: 6 This poor man c, and the LORD
     116: 4 Then I c on the name of the LORD
Isa   56: 7 for my house will be c
La   3:55 I c on your name, O LORD,
Hos   11: 1 and out of Egypt I c my son.
Mt   1:16 was born Jesus, who is c Christ.
       2:15 ''Out of Egypt I c my son.''
      21:13 '' 'My house will be c a house
Mk   11:17 '' 'My house will be c
Lk   1:32 will be c the Son of the Most High.
       1:35 to be born will be c the Son of God.
Ro   1: 1 c to be an apostle and set apart
       1: 6 among those who are c to belong
       1: 7 loved by God and c to be saints:
       8:28 who have been c according
       8:30 And those he predestined, he also c
1Co   1: 1 c to be an apostle of Christ Jesus
       1: 2 in Christ Jesus and c to be holy,
       1:24 but to those whom God has c,
       1:26 of what you were when you were c.
       7:15 God has c us to live in peace.
       7:17 and to which God has c him.
Gal   1: 6 deserting the one who c you
       1:15 from birth and c me by his grace,
       5:13 You, my brothers, were c to be free
Eph   1:18 the hope to which he has c you,
       4: 4 as you were c to one hope
Col   3:15 of one body you were c to peace.
2Th   2:14 He c you to this through our gospel
1Ti   6:12 life to which you were c
2Ti   1: 9 who has saved us and c us
Heb   9:15 that those who are c may receive
1Pe   1:15 But just as he who c you is holy,
       2: 9 of him who c you out of darkness
       3: 9 to this you were c so that you may
       5:10 who c you to his eternal glory
2Pe   1: 3 of him who c us by his own glory
Jude   : 1 To those who have been c,

CALLING (CALL)

Isa   40: 3 A voice of one c:
Mt   3: 3 ''A voice of one c in the desert,
Mk   1: 3 ''a voice of one c in the desert,
      10:49 Cheer up! On your feet! He's c you
Lk   3: 4 ''A voice of one c in the desert,
Jn   1:23 I am the voice of one c in the desert
Ac   22:16 wash your sins away, c on his name
Eph   4: 1 of the c you have received.
2Th   1:11 may count you worthy of his c,
2Pe   1:10 all the more eager to make your c

CALLOUS* (CALLOUSED)

Ps   17:10 They close up their c hearts,
      73: 7 From their c hearts comes iniquity;
     119:70 Their hearts are c and unfeeling,

CALLOUSED* (CALLOUS)

Isa   6:10 Make the heart of this people c;
Mt   13:15 this people's heart has become c;
Ac   28:27 this people's heart has become c;

CALLS (CALL)

Ps   147: 4 and c them each by name.
Isa   40:26 and c them each by name.
Joel   2:32 And everyone who c
Mt   22:43 speaking by the Spirit, c him 'Lord
Jn   10: 3 He c his own sheep by name
Ac   2:21 And everyone who c
Ro   10:13 ''Everyone who c on the name
1Th   2:12 who c you into his kingdom
       5:24 The one who c you is faithful

CALM (CALMS)

Ps   107:30 They were glad when it grew c,
Isa   7: 4 keep c and don't be afraid.
Eze 16:42 I will be c and no longer angry.

CALMS* (CALM)

Pr   15:18 but a patient man c a quarrel.

CAMEL

Mt   19:24 it is easier for a c to go
      23:24 strain out a gnat but swallow a c.
Mk   10:25 It is easier for a c to go
Lk   18:25 it is easier for a c to go

CAMP (ENCAMPS)

Heb   13:13 outside the c, bearing the disgrace

CANAAN (CANAANITE CANAANITES)

Ge   10:15 C was the father of Sidon his
Lev   14:34 ''When you enter the land of C,
      25:38 of Egypt to give you the land of C
Nu   13: 2 men to explore the land of C,
      33:51 'When you cross the Jordan into C,
Jdg   4: 2 a king of C, who reigned in Hazor.
1Ch   16:18 ''To you I will give the land of C
Ps   105:11 ''To you I will give the land of C
Ac   13:19 He overthrew seven nations in C

CANAANITE (CANAAN)

Ge   10:18 Later the C clans scattered
      28: 1 ''Do not marry a C woman.
Jos   5: 1 all the C kings along the seacoast
Jdg   1:32 lived among the C inhabitants

CANAANITES (CANAAN)

Ex   33: 2 before you and drive out the C,

CANCEL (CANCELED)

Dt   15: 1 seven years you must c debts.

CANCELED (CANCEL)

Mt   18:27 pity on him, c the debt
Lk   7:42 so he c the debts of both.
Col   2:14 having the written code,

CANDLESTICKS see LAMPSTANDS

CANOPY*

2Sa   22:12 He made darkness his c
2Ki   16:18 away the Sabbath c that had been
Ps   18:11 made darkness his covering, his c
Isa   4: 5 over all the glory will be a c.
      40:22 stretches out the heavens like a c,
Jer   43:10 he will spread his royal c

CAPERNAUM

Mt   4:13 Nazareth, he went and lived in C,
Jn   6:59 teaching in the synagogue in C.

CAPITAL

Dt   21:22 guilty of a c offense is put to death

CAPSTONE* (STONE)

Ps   118:22 has become the c;
Zec   4: 7 he will bring out the c to shouts
Mt   21:42 has become the c;
Mk   12:10 has become the c;
Lk   20:17 has become the c'?
Ac   4:11 which has become the c
1Pe   2: 7 has become the c,''

CAPTIVATE* (CAPTIVE)

Pr   6:25 or let her c you with her eyes,

CAPTIVATED* (CAPTIVE)

Pr   5:19 may you ever be c by her love.
       5:20 Why be c, my son, by an adulteress

CAPTIVE (CAPTIVATE CAPTIVATED CAPTIVES CAPTIVITY CAPTURED)

Ac   8:23 full of bitterness and c to sin.''
2Co   10: 5 and we take c every thought
Col   2: 8 See to it that no one takes you c
2Ti   2:26 who has taken them c to do his will.

CAPTIVES (CAPTIVE)

Ps   68:18 you led c in your train;
Isa   61: 1 to proclaim freedom for the c
Eph   4: 8 he led c in his train

CAPTIVITY (CAPTIVE)

Dt   28:41 because they will go into c.
2Ki   25:21 So Judah went into c, away
Jer   30: 3 Israel and Judah back from c
      52:27 So Judah went into c, away
Eze   29:14 I will bring them back from c

CAPTURED

1Sa   4:11 The ark of God was c,
2Sa   5: 7 David c the fortress of Zion,
2Ki   17: 6 the king of Assyria c Samaria

CARCASS

Jdg 14: 9 taken the honey from the lion's c.
Mt 24: 28 there is a c, there the vultures

CARE (CAREFUL CARES CARING)

Ps   8: 4 the son of man that you c for him?
    65: 9 You c for the land and water it;
  144: 3 what is man that you c for him,
Pr 29: 7 The righteous c about justice
Mk 5: 26 deal under the c of many doctors
Lk 10: 34 him to an inn and took c of him.
    18: 4 I don't fear God or c about men,
Jn 21: 16 Jesus said, "Take c of my sheep."
1Ti 3: 5 how can he take c of God's church
    6: 20 what has been entrusted to your c.
Heb 2: 6 the son of man that you c for him?
1Pe 5: 2 of God's flock that is under your c,

CAREFUL* (CARE)

Ge 31: 24 "Be c not to say anything to Jacob,
    31: 29 'Be c not to say anything to Jacob,
Ex 19: 12 'Be c that you do not go up
    23: 13 "Be c to do everything I have said
    34: 12 Be c not to make a treaty
    34: 15 "Be c not to make a treaty
Lev 18: 4 and be c to follow my decrees.
    25: 18 " 'Follow my decrees and be c
    26: 3 and are c to obey my commands,
Dt 2: 4 afraid of you, but be very c.
    4: 9 before you today? Only be c,
    4: 23 Be c not to forget the covenant
    5: 32 So be c to do what the LORD your
    6: 3 be c to obey so that it may go well
    6: 12 be c that you do not forget
    6: 25 And if we are c to obey all this law
    7: 12 attention to these laws and are c
    8: 1 Be c to follow every command I am
    8: 11 Be c that you do not forget
    11: 16 Be c, or you will be enticed
    12: 1 and laws you must be c to follow
    12: 13 Be c not to sacrifice your burnt
    12: 19 Be c not to neglect the Levites
    12: 28 Be c to obey all these regulations I
    12: 30 be c not to be ensnared
    15: 5 are c to follow all these commands
    15: 9 Be c not to harbor this wicked
    17: 10 Be c to do everything they direct
    24: 8 cases of leprous diseases be very c
Jos 1: 7 Be c to obey all the law my servant
    1: 8 so that you may be c
    22: 5 But be very c to keep
    23: 6 be c to obey all that is written
    23: 11 be very c to love the LORD your
1Ki 8: 25 if only your sons are c in all they do
2Ki 10: 31 Yet Jehu was not c to keep the law
    17: 37 You must always be c
    21: 8 if only they will be c
1Ch 22: 13 if you are c to observe the decrees
    28: 8 be c to follow all the commands
2Ch 6: 16 if only your sons are c in all they do
    33: 8 if only they will be c
Ezr 4: 22 Be c not to neglect this matter.
Job 36: 18 Be c that no one entices you
Ps 101: 2 I will be c to lead a blameless life—
Pr 13: 24 he who loves him is c
    27: 23 give c attention to your herds;
Isa 7: 4 Be c, keep calm and don't be afraid.
Jer 17: 21 Be c not to carry a load
    17: 24 But if you are c to obey me,
    22: 4 For if you are c to carry out these
Eze 11: 20 will follow my decrees and be c
    18: 19 has been c to keep all my decrees,
    20: 19 follow my decrees and be c
    20: 21 they were not c to keep my laws—
    36: 27 you to follow my decrees and be c
    37: 24 and be c to keep my decrees.
Mic 7: 5 be c of your words.
Hag 1: 5 "Give c thought to your ways.
    1: 7 "Give c thought to your ways.
    2: 15 give c thought to this from this day
    2: 18 Give c thought: Is there yet any
    2: 18 give c thought to the day
Mt 2: 8 and make a c search for the child.
    6: 1 "Be c not to do your 'acts
    16: 6 "Be c," Jesus said to them.
Mk 8: 15 "Be c," Jesus warned them.
Lk 21: 34 Be c, or your hearts will be weighed

Ro 12: 17 Be c to do what is right in the eyes
1Co 3: 10 each one should be c how he builds
    8: 9 Be c, however, that the exercise
    10: 12 standing firm, be c that you don't
Eph 5: 15 Be very c, then, how you live—
2Ti 4: 2 great patience and c instruction,
Tit 3: 8 may be c to devote themselves
Heb 2: 1 We must pay more c attention,
    4: 1 let us be c that none

CARELESS*

Mt 12: 36 for every c word they have spoken.

CARES* (CARE)

Dt 11: 12 It is a land the LORD your God c
Job 39: 16 she c not that her labor was in vain,
Ps 55: 22 Cast your c on the LORD
    142: 4 no one c for my life.
Pr 12: 10 A righteous man c for the needs
Ecc 5: 3 when there are many c,
Jer 12: 11 because there is no one who c.
    30: 17 Zion for whom no one c.'
Na 1: 7 He c for those who trust in him,
Jn 10: 13 and c nothing for the sheep.
Eph 5: 29 but he feeds and c for it, just
1Pe 5: 7 on him because he c for you.

CARING* (CARE)

1Th 2: 7 like a mother c for her little
1Ti 5: 4 practice by c for their own family

CARNAL see SINFUL, UNSPIRITUAL, WORLDLY

CARPENTER (CARPENTER'S)

Mk 6: 3 does miracles! Isn't this the c?

CARPENTER'S* (CARPENTER)

Mt 13: 55 "Isn't this the c son? Isn't his

CARRIED (CARRY)

Ex 19: 4 and how I c you on eagles' wings
Dt 1: 31 how the LORD your God c you,
Isa 53: 4 and c our sorrows,
    63: 9 he lifted them up and c them
Mt 8: 17 and c our diseases.''
Heb 13: 9 Do not be c away by all kinds
2Pe 1: 21 as they were c along by the Holy
    3: 17 so that you may not be c away

CARRIES (CARRY)

Dt 32: 11 and c them on its pinions.
Isa 40: 11 and c them close to his heart;

CARRY (CARRIED CARRIES CARRYING)

Lev 16: 22 goat will c on itself all their sins
    26: 15 and fail to c out all my commands
Isa 46: 4 I have made you and I will c you;
Lk 14: 27 anyone who does not c his cross
Gal 6: 2 C each other's burdens,
    6: 5 for each one should c his own load.

CARRYING (CARRY)

Jn 19: 17 C his own cross, he went out
1Jn 5: 2 loving God and c out his

CARVED (CARVES)

Nu 33: 52 Destroy all their c images
Mic 5: 13 I will destroy your c images

CARVES* (CARVED)

Dt 27: 15 "Cursed is the man who c an image

CASE

Pr 18: 17 to present his c seems right,
    22: 23 for the LORD will take up their c
    23: 11 he will take up their c against you.

CAST (CASTING)

Ex 34: 17 "Do not make c idols.
Lev 16: 8 He is to c lots for the two goats—
Ps 22: 18 and c lots for my clothing.
    55: 22 C your cares on the LORD
Pr 16: 33 The lot is c into the lap,
Ecc 11: 1 C your bread upon the waters,
Jn 19: 24 and c lots for my clothing.''
1Pe 5: 7 C all your anxiety on him

CASTING (CAST)

Pr 18: 18 C the lot settles disputes
Mt 27: 35 divided up his clothes by c lots.

CATCH (CATCHES CAUGHT)

Lk 5: 4 and let down the nets for a c.''
    5: 10 from now on you will c men.''

CATCHES (CATCH)

Job 5: 13 He c the wise in their craftiness,
1Co 3: 19 "He c the wise in their craftiness'';

CATTLE

Ps 50: 10 and the c on a thousand hills.

CAUGHT (CATCH)

Ge 22: 13 there in a thicket he saw a ram c
2Co 12: 2 who fourteen years ago was c up
1Th 4: 17 and are left will be c up together with them

CAUSE (CAUSES)

Pr 24: 28 against your neighbor without c,
Ecc 8: 3 Do not stand up for a bad c,
Mt 18: 7 of the things that c people to sin!
Ro 14: 21 else that will c your brother
1Co 10: 32 Do not c anyone to stumble,

CAUSES (CAUSE)

Ps 7: 16 The trouble he c recoils on himself;
Isa 8: 14 a stone that c men to stumble
Mt 5: 29 If your right eye c you to sin,
    5: 30 And if your right hand c you to sin,
    18: 6 if anyone c one of these little ones
    18: 8 or your foot c you to sin,
Ro 14: 20 to eat anything that c someone else
1Co 8: 13 if what I eat c my brother to fall
1Pe 2: 8 "A stone that c men to stumble

CAUTIOUS*

Pr 12: 26 A righteous man is c in friendship,

CEASE

Ps 46: 9 He makes wars c to the ends

CELEBRATE*

Ex 10: 9 we are to c a festival to the LORD
    12: 14 generations to come you shall c it
    12: 17 C this day as a lasting ordinance
    12: 17 "C the Feast of Unleavened Bread,
    12: 47 community of Israel must c it.
    12: 48 to c the LORD's Passover must
    23: 14 are to c a festival to me.
    23: 15 "C the Feast of Unleavened Bread;
    23: 16 "C the Feast of Harvest
    23: 16 "C the Feast of Ingathering
    34: 18 "C the Feast of Unleavened Bread.
    34: 22 "C the Feast of Weeks
Lev 23: 39 c the festival to the LORD
    23: 41 C this as a festival to the LORD
    23: 41 for the generations to come; c it
Nu 9: 2 "Have the Israelites c the Passover
    9: 3 C it at the appointed time,
    9: 4 told the Israelites to c the Passover,
    9: 6 of them could not c the Passover
    9: 10 they may still c the LORD's
    9: 11 are to c it on the fourteenth day
    9: 12 When they c the Passover,
    9: 13 on a journey fails to c the Passover,
    9: 14 to c the LORD's Passover must do
    29: 12 C a festival to the LORD
Dt 16: 1 c the Passover of the LORD your
    16: 10 Then c the Feast of Weeks
    16: 13 C the Feast of Tabernacles
    16: 15 For seven days c the Feast
Jdg 16: 23 to Dagon their god and to c,
2Sa 6: 21 the LORD's people Israel—I will c
2Ki 23: 21 "C the Passover to the LORD your
2Ch 30: 1 and c the Passover to the LORD,
    30: 2 decided to c the Passover
    30: 3 able to c it at the regular time
    30: 5 and c the Passover to the LORD.
    30: 13 in Jerusalem to c the Feast
    30: 23 to c the festival seven more days;
Ne 8: 12 of food and to c with great joy.
    12: 27 to c joyfully the dedication
Est 9: 21 to have them c annually
Ps 145: 7 They will c your abundant

Isa 30: 29 as on the night you c a holy festival
Na 1: 15 C your festivals, O Judah,
Zec 14: 16 and to c the Feast of Tabernacles.
14: 18 up to c the Feast of Tabernacles.
14: 19 up to c the Feast of Tabernacles.
Mt 26: 18 I am going to c the Passover
Lk 15: 23 Let's have a feast and c.
15: 24 So they began to c.
15: 29 goat so I could c with my friends.
15: 32 But we had to c and be glad,
Rev 11: 10 will c by sending each other gifts,

CELESTIAL*

2Pe 2: 10 afraid to slander c beings;
Jude : 8 authority and slander c beings.

CENSER (CENSERS)

Lev 16: 12 is to take a c full of burning coals
Rev 8: 3 Another angel, who had a golden c,

CENSERS (CENSER)

Nu 16: 6 Take c and tomorrow put fire

CENTURION

Mt 8: 5 had entered Capernaum, a c came
27: 54 When the c and those
Mk 15: 39 And when the c, who stood there
Lk 7: 3 The c heard of Jesus and sent some
23: 47 The c, seeing what had happened,
Ac 10: 1 a c in what was known
27: 1 handed over to a c named Julius,

CEPHAS* (PETER)

Jn 1: 42 You will be called C'' (which,
1Co 1: 12 another, ''I follow C''; still another,
3: 22 Paul or Apollos or C or the world
9: 5 and the Lord's brothers and C?

CEREMONIAL* (CEREMONY)

Lev 14: 2 at the time of his c cleansing,
15: 13 off seven days for his c cleansing;
Mk 7: 3 they give their hands a c washing,
Jn 2: 6 used by the Jews for c washing,
3: 25 Jew over the matter of c washing.
11: 55 to Jerusalem for their c cleansing
18: 28 to avoid c uncleanness the Jews did
Heb 9: 10 drink and various c washings—
13: 9 not by c foods, which are

CEREMONIALLY* (CEREMONY)

Lev 4: 12 outside the camp to a place c clean,
5: 2 touches anything c unclean—
6: 11 the camp to a place that is c clean.
7: 19 anyone c clean may eat it.
7: 19 touches anything c unclean must
10: 14 Eat them in a c clean place;
11: 4 not have a split hoof; it is c unclean
12: 2 birth to a son will be c unclean
12: 7 and then she will be c clean
13: 3 he shall pronounce him c unclean.
14: 8 with water; then he will be c clean.
15: 28 and after that she will be c clean.
15: 33 lies with a woman who is c unclean.
17: 15 he will be c unclean till evening.
21: 1 must not make himself c unclean
22: 3 of your descendants is c unclean
27: 11 he vowed is a c unclean animal—
Nu 5: 2 who is c unclean because of a dead
6: 7 must not make himself c unclean
8: 6 Israelites and make them c clean.
9: 6 they were c unclean on account
9: 13 But if a man who is c clean
18: 11 household who is c clean may eat
18: 13 household who is c clean may eat
19: 7 but he will be c unclean till evening
19: 9 and put them in a c clean place
19: 18 Then a man who is c clean is
Dt 12: 15 Both the c unclean and the clean
12: 22 Both the c unclean and the clean
14: 7 they are c unclean for you.
15: 22 Both the c unclean and the clean
1Sa 20: 26 to David to make him c unclean—
2Ch 13: 11 the bread on the c clean table
30: 17 for all those who were not c clean
Ezr 6: 20 themselves and were all c clean.
Ne 12: 30 Levites had purified themselves c,
Isa 66: 20 of the LORD in c clean vessels.
Eze 22: 10 period when they are c unclean.

Ac 24: 18 I was c clean when they found me
Heb 9: 13 those who are c unclean sanctify

CEREMONY* (CEREMONIAL CEREMONIALLY)

Ge 50: 11 Egyptians are holding a solemn c
Ex 12: 25 as he promised, observe this c.
12: 26 'What does this c mean to you?'
13: 5 are to observe this c in this month:

CERTAIN (CERTAINTY)

2Pe 1: 19 word of the prophets made more c.

CERTAINTY* (CERTAIN)

Lk 1: 4 so that you may know the c
Jn 17: 8 They knew with c that I came

CERTIFICATE* (CERTIFIED)

Dt 24: 1 and he writes her a c of divorce,
24: 3 and writes her a c of divorce,
Isa 50: 1 ''Where is your mother's c
Jer 3: 8 I gave faithless Israel her c
Mt 5: 31 divorces his wife must give her a c
19: 7 that a man give his wife a c
Mk 10: 4 a man to write a c of divorce

CERTIFIED* (CERTIFICATE)

Jn 3: 33 has accepted it has c that God is

CHAFF

Ps 1: 4 They are like c
35: 5 May they be like c before the wind,
Da 2: 35 became like c on a threshing floor
Mt 3: 12 up the c with unquenchable fire.''

CHAINED (CHAINS)

2Ti 2: 9 But God's word is not c.

CHAINS (CHAINED)

Eph 6: 20 for which I am an ambassador in c.
Col 4: 18 Remember my c.
2Ti 1: 16 and was not ashamed of my c.
Jude 6 with everlasting c for judgment

CHAMPION

Ps 19: 5 like a c rejoicing to run his course.

CHANCE

Ecc 9: 11 but time and c happen to them all.

CHANGE (CHANGED)

1Sa 15: 29 of Israel does not lie or c his mind;
Ps 110: 4 and will not c his mind:
Jer 7: 5 If you really c your ways
Mal 3: 6 ''I the LORD do not c.
Mt 18: 3 unless you c and become like little
Heb 7: 21 and will not c his mind:
Jas 1: 17 who does not c like shifting

CHANGED (CHANGE)

1Sa 10: 6 you will be c into a different person
Hos 11: 8 My heart is c within me;
1Co 15: 51 but we will all be c— in a flash,

CHARACTER*

Ru 3: 11 that you are a woman of noble c.
Pr 12: 4 of noble c is her husband's crown,
31: 10 A wife of noble c who can find?
Ac 17: 11 noble c than the Thessalonians,
Ro 5: 4 perseverance, c; and c, hope.
1Co 15: 33 ''Bad company corrupts good c.''

CHARGE (CHARGES)

Job 34: 13 him in c of the whole world?
Ro 8: 33 Who will bring any c
1Co 9: 18 the gospel I may offer it free of c,
2Co 11: 7 the gospel of God to you free of c?
2Ti 4: 1 I give you this c: Preach the Word;
Phm 18 or owes you anything, c it to me.

CHARGES (CHARGE)

Isa 50: 8 Who then will bring c against me?

CHARIOT (CHARIOTS)

2Ki 2: 11 suddenly a c of fire and horses
Ps 104: 3 He makes the clouds his c
Ac 8: 28 sitting in his c reading the book

CHARIOTS (CHARIOT)

2Ki 6: 17 and c of fire all around Elisha.
Ps 20: 7 Some trust in c and some in horses,
68: 17 The c of God are tens of thousands

CHARITY see LOVE

CHARM* (CHARMING)

Pr 17: 8 bribe is a c to the one who gives it;
31: 30 C is deceptive, and beauty is

CHARMING* (CHARM)

Pr 26: 25 his speech is c, do not believe
SS 1: 16 Oh, how c!

CHASE (CHASES)

Lev 26: 8 Five of you will c a hundred,

CHASES* (CHASE)

Pr 12: 11 he who c fantasies lacks judgment.
28: 19 one who c fantasies will have his

CHASM*

Lk 16: 26 and you a great c has been fixed,

CHATTER* (CHATTERING)

1Ti 6: 20 Turn away from godless c
2Ti 2: 16 Avoid godless c, because those

CHATTERING* (CHATTER)

Pr 10: 8 but a c fool comes to ruin.
10: 10 and a c fool comes to ruin.

CHEAT* (CHEATED CHEATING CHEATS)

Mal 1: 14 ''Cursed is the c who has
1Co 6: 8 you yourselves c and do wrong.

CHEATED* (CHEAT)

Ge 31: 7 yet your father has c me
1Sa 12: 3 Whom have I c? Whom have I
12: 4 ''You have not c or oppressed us,''
Lk 19: 8 if I have c anybody out of anything,
1Co 6: 7 Why not rather be c? Instead,

CHEATING* (CHEAT)

Am 8: 5 and c with dishonest scales,

CHEATS* (CHEAT)

Lev 6: 2 or if he c him, or if he finds lost

CHEEK (CHEEKS)

Mt 5: 39 someone strikes you on the right c,
Lk 6: 29 If someone strikes you on one c,

CHEEKS (CHEEK)

Isa 50: 6 my c to those who pulled out my

CHEERFUL* (CHEERS)

Pr 15: 13 A happy heart makes the face c,
15: 15 but the c heart has a continual feast
15: 30 A c look brings joy to the heart.
17: 22 A c heart is good medicine,
2Co 9: 7 for God loves a c giver.

CHEERS (CHEERFUL)

Pr 12: 25 but a kind word c him up.

CHEMOSH

2Ki 23: 13 for C the vile god of Moab,

CHERISH (CHERISHED CHERISHES)

Ps 17: 14 You still the hunger of those you c;

CHERISHED (CHERISH)

Ps 66: 18 If I had c sin in my heart,

CHERISHES* (CHERISH)

Pr 19: 8 he who c understanding prospers.

CHERUB (CHERUBIM)

Ex 25: 19 Make one c on one end
Eze 28: 14 You were anointed as a guardian c,

CHERUBIM (CHERUB)

Ge 3: 24 side of the Garden of Eden c
1Sa 4: 4 who is enthroned between the c,
2Sa 6: 2 enthroned between the c that are
22: 11 He mounted the c and flew;

1Ki 6: 23 a pair of *c* of olive wood,
2Ki 19: 15 of Israel, enthroned between the *c*,
1Ch 13: 6 who is enthroned between the *c*—
Ps   18: 10 He mounted the *c* and flew;
     80: 1 who sit enthroned between the *c*,
     99: 1 he sits enthroned between the *c*,
Isa 37: 16 of Israel, enthroned between the *c*,
Eze 10: 1 was over the heads of the *c*.

CHEST

Ex 25: 10 "Have them make a *c*
2Ki 12: 9 Jehoiada the priest took a *c*
Da   2: 32 its *c* and arms of silver, its belly
Rev 1: 13 with a golden sash around his *c*.

CHEWS

Lev 11: 3 divided and that *c* the cud.

CHIEF

1Pe 5: 4 And when the *C* Shepherd appears,

CHILD (CHILDISH CHILDREN CHILDREN'S GRANDCHILDREN)

Pr 20: 11 Even a *c* is known by his actions,
    22: 6 Train a *c* in the way he should go,
    22: 15 Folly is bound up in the heart of a *c*
    23: 13 not withhold discipline from a *c;*
    29: 15 *c* left to himself disgraces his mother.
Isa   7: 14 The virgin will be with *c*
     9: 6 For to us a *c* is born,
    11: 6 and a little *c* will lead them.
    66: 13 As a mother comforts her *c*,
Mt   1: 23 "The virgin will be with *c*
    18: 2 He called a little *c* and had him
Lk   1: 42 and blessed is the *c* you will bear!
     1: 80 And the *c* grew and became strong
1Co 13: 11 When I was a *c*, I talked like a *c*,
1Jn 5: 1 who loves the father loves his *c*

CHILDBEARING (BEAR)

Ge   3: 16 greatly increase your pains in *c;*

CHILDBIRTH (BEAR)

Gal 4: 19 the pains of *c* until Christ is formed

CHILDISH* (CHILD)

1Co 13: 11 When I became a man, I put *c* ways

CHILDREN (CHILD)

Ex 20: 5 punishing the *c* for the sin
Dt   4: 9 Teach them to your *c*
     6: 7 Impress them on your *c*.
   11: 19 them to your *c*, talking about them
   14: 1 You are the *c* of the LORD your
   24: 16 nor *c* put to death for their fathers;
   30: 19 so that you and your *c* may live
   32: 46 so that you may command your *c*
Job 1: 5 "Perhaps my *c* have sinned
Ps   8: 2 From the lips of *c* and infants
    78: 5 forefathers to teach their *c*.
Pr 17: 6 Children's *c* are a crown
    20: 7 blessed are his *c* after him.
    31: 28 Her *c* arise and call her blessed;
Joel 1: 3 Tell it to your *c*,
Mal 4: 6 the hearts of the fathers to their *c*,
Mt   7: 11 how to give good gifts to your *c*,
   11: 25 and revealed them to little *c*.
   18: 3 you change and become like little *c*
   19: 14 "Let the little *c* come to me,
   21: 16 "'From the lips of *c* and infants
Mk 9: 37 one of these little *c* in my name
   10: 14 "Let the little *c* come to me,
   10: 16 And he took the *c* in his arms,
   13: 12 *C* will rebel against their parents
Lk 10: 21 and revealed them to little *c*.
   18: 16 "Let the little *c* come to me,
Jn   1: 12 the right to become *c* of God—
Ac   2: 39 The promise is for you and your *c*
Ro 8: 16 with our spirit that we are God's *c*.
1Co 14: 20 Brothers, stop thinking like *c*.
2Co 12: 14 parents, but parents for their *c*.
Eph 6: 1 *C*, obey your parents in the Lord,
     6: 4 do not exasperate your *c;* instead,
Col 3: 20 *C*, obey your parents in everything,
    3: 21 Fathers, do not embitter your *c*,
1Ti 3: 4 and see that his *c* obey him
    3: 12 and must manage his *c* and his
    5: 10 bringing up *c*, showing hospitality,

Heb 2: 13 and the *c* God has given me."
1Jn 3: 1 that we should be called *c* of God!

CHILDREN'S (CHILD)

Isa 54: 13 and great will be your *c* peace.

CHOKE

Mk 4: 19 come in and *c* the word,

CHOOSE (CHOOSES CHOSE CHOSEN)

Dt 30: 19 Now *c* life, so that you
Jos 24: 15 then *c* for yourselves this day
Pr   8: 10 *C* my instruction instead of silver,
   16: 16 to *c* understanding rather
Jn 15: 16 You did not *c* me, but I chose you

CHOOSES (CHOOSE)

Mt 11: 27 to whom the Son *c* to reveal him.
Lk 10: 22 to whom the Son *c* to reveal him."
Jn   7: 17 If any one *c* to do God's will,

CHOSE (CHOOSE)

Ge 13: 11 So Lot *c* for himself the whole plain
Ps   33: 12 the people he *c* for his inheritance.
Jn 15: 16 but I *c* you and appointed you to go
1Co 1: 27 But God *c* the foolish things
Eph 1: 4 he *c* us in him before the creation
2Th 2: 13 from the beginning God *c* you

CHOSEN (CHOOSE)

Isa 41: 8 Jacob, whom I have *c*,
Mt 22: 14 For many are invited, but few are *c*
Lk 10: 42 Mary has *c* what is better,
   23: 35 the Christ of God, the *C* One."
Jn 15: 19 but I have *c* you out of the world.
1Pe 1: 20 He was *c* before the creation
    2: 9 But you are a *c* people, a royal

CHRIST (CHRIST'S CHRISTIAN CHRISTIANS CHRISTS)

Mt   1: 16 was born Jesus, who is called *C*.
   16: 16 Peter answered, "You are the *C*,
   22: 42 "What do you think about the *C*?
Mk 1: 1 of the gospel about Jesus *C*,
    8: 29 Peter answered, "You are the *C*.''
   14: 61 "Are you the *C*, the Son
Lk 9: 20 Peter answered, "The *C* of God."
Jn   1: 41 found the Messiah" (that is, the *C*).
   20: 31 you may believe that Jesus is the *C*,
Ac   2: 36 you crucified, both Lord and *C*."
    5: 42 the good news that Jesus is the *C*.
    9: 22 by proving that Jesus is the *C*.
    9: 34 said to him, "Jesus *C* heals you.
   17: 3 proving that the *C* had to suffer
   18: 28 the Scriptures that Jesus was the *C*.
   26: 23 that the *C* would suffer and,
Ro 1: 4 from the dead: Jesus *C* our Lord.
    3: 22 comes through faith in Jesus *C*
    5: 1 God through our Lord Jesus *C*,
    5: 6 we were still powerless, *C* died
    5: 8 While we were still sinners, *C* died
    5: 11 in God through our Lord Jesus *C*,
    5: 17 life through the one man, Jesus *C*.
    6: 4 as *C* was raised from the dead
    6: 9 that since *C* was raised
    6: 23 life in *C* Jesus our Lord.
    7: 4 to the law through the body of *C*,
    8: 1 for those who are in *C* Jesus,
    8: 9 Spirit of *C*, he does not belong to *C*.
    8: 17 heirs of God and co-heirs with *C*,
    8: 34 Who is he that condemns? *C* Jesus,
    8: 35 us from the love of *C*?
    9: 5 is traced the human ancestry of *C*,
   10: 4 *C* is the end of the law
   12: 5 so in *C* we who are many form one
   13: 14 yourselves with the Lord Jesus *C*,
   14: 9 *C* died and returned to life
   15: 3 For even *C* did not please himself
   15: 5 yourselves as you follow *C* Jesus,
   15: 7 then, just as *C* accepted you,
   16: 18 people are not serving our Lord *C*,
1Co 1: 2 to those sanctified in *C* Jesus
    1: 7 for our Lord Jesus *C* to be revealed.
    1: 13 Is *C* divided? Was Paul crucified
    1: 17 For *C* did not send me to baptize,
    1: 23 but we preach *C* crucified:
    1: 30 of him that you are in *C* Jesus,
    2: 2 except Jesus *C* and him crucified.

1Co 3: 11 one already laid, which is Jesus *C*.
    5: 7 For *C*, our Passover lamb,
    6: 15 bodies are members of *C* himself?
    8: 6 and there is but one Lord, Jesus *C*,
    8: 12 conscience, you sin against *C*.
   10: 4 them, and that rock was *C*.
   11: 1 as I follow the example of *C*.
   11: 3 the head of every man is *C*,
   12: 27 Now you are the body of *C*,
   15: 3 that *C* died for our sins according
   15: 14 And if *C* has not been raised,
   15: 22 so in *C* all will be made alive.
   15: 57 victory through our Lord Jesus *C*.
2Co 1: 5 as the sufferings of *C* flow
    2: 14 us in triumphal procession in *C*
    3: 3 show that you are a letter from *C*,
    3: 14 because only in *C* is it taken away.
    4: 4 light of the gospel of the glory of *C*,
    4: 5 not preach ourselves, but Jesus *C*
    4: 6 of the glory of God in the face of *C*.
    5: 10 before the judgment seat of *C*,
    5: 17 Therefore, if anyone is in *C*,
    6: 15 What harmony is there between *C*
   10: 1 the meekness and gentleness of *C*,
   11: 2 you to one husband, to *C*,
Gal 1: 7 are trying to pervert the gospel of *C*
    2: 4 on the freedom we have in *C* Jesus
    2: 16 but by faith in Jesus *C*.
    2: 17 does that mean that *C* promotes sin
    2: 20 I have been crucified with *C*
    2: 21 *C* died for nothing!'' You foolish
    3: 13 *C* redeemed us from the curse
    3: 16 meaning one person, who is *C*.
    3: 26 of God through faith in *C* Jesus,
    4: 19 of childbirth until *C* is formed
    5: 1 for freedom that *C* has set us free.
    5: 4 by law have been alienated from *C;*
    5: 24 to *C* Jesus have crucified the sinful
    6: 14 in the cross of our Lord Jesus *C*,
Eph 1: 3 with every spiritual blessing in *C*.
    1: 10 together under one head, even *C*.
    1: 20 which he exerted in *C*
    2: 5 made us alive with *C*
    2: 10 created in *C* Jesus
    2: 12 time you were separate from *C*,
    2: 20 with *C* Jesus himself as the chief
    3: 8 the unsearchable riches of *C*,
    3: 17 so that *C* may dwell in your hearts
    4: 7 has been given as *C* apportioned it.
    4: 13 measure of the fullness of *C*.
    4: 15 into him who is the Head, that is, *C*
    4: 32 just as in *C* God forgave you.
    5: 2 as *C* loved us and gave himself up
    5: 21 out of reverence for *C*.
    5: 23 as *C* is the head of the church,
    5: 25 just as *C* loved the church
Php 1: 18 motives or true, *C* is preached.
    1: 21 to live is *C* and to die is gain.
    1: 23 I desire to depart and be with *C*,
    1: 27 worthy of the gospel of *C*.
    1: 29 on behalf of *C* not only to believe
    2: 5 be the same as that of *C* Jesus:
    3: 7 now consider loss for the sake of *C*.
    3: 10 I want to know *C* and the power
    3: 18 as enemies of the cross of *C*.
    4: 19 to his glorious riches in *C* Jesus.
Col 1: 4 heard of your faith in *C* Jesus
    1: 27 which is *C* in you, the hope of glory
    1: 28 may present everyone perfect in *C*.
    2: 2 the mystery of God, namely, *C*,
    2: 6 as you received *C* Jesus as Lord,
    2: 9 For in *C* all the fullness
    2: 13 God made you alive with *C*.
    2: 17 the reality, however, is found in *C*.
    3: 1 then, you have been raised with *C*,
    3: 3 and your life is now hidden with *C*
    3: 15 Let the peace of *C* rule
1Th 5: 9 through our Lord Jesus *C*.
2Th 2: 1 the coming of our Lord Jesus *C*
    2: 14 in the glory of our Lord Jesus *C*.
1Ti 1: 12 I thank *C* Jesus our Lord, who has
    1: 15 *C* Jesus came into the world
    1: 16 *C* Jesus might display his unlimited
    2: 5 the man *C* Jesus, who gave himself
2Ti 1: 9 us in *C* Jesus before the beginning
    1: 10 appearing of our Savior, *C* Jesus,
    2: 1 in the grace that is in *C* Jesus.
    2: 3 us like a good soldier of *C* Jesus.

2Ti 2: 8 Remember Jesus *C*, raised
2: 10 the salvation that is in *C* Jesus,
3: 12 life in *C* Jesus will be persecuted,
3: 15 salvation through faith in *C* Jesus.
4: 1 presence of God and of *C* Jesus,
Tit 2: 13 our great God and Savior, Jesus *C*,
Heb 3: 6 But *C* is faithful as a son
3: 14 to share in *C* if we hold firmly
5: 5 So *C* also did not take
6: 1 the elementary teachings about *C*
9: 11 When *C* came as high priest
9: 14 more, then, will the blood of *C*,
9: 15 For this reason *C* is the mediator
9: 24 For *C* did not enter a man-made
9: 26 Then *C* would have had
9: 28 so *C* was sacrificed once
10: 10 of the body of Jesus *C* once for all.
13: 8 Jesus *C* is the same yesterday
1Pe 1: 2 for obedience to Jesus *C*
1: 3 of Jesus *C* from the dead,
1: 11 he predicted the sufferings of *C*
1: 19 but with the precious blood of *C*,
2: 21 because *C* suffered for you,
3: 15 in your hearts set apart *C* as Lord.
3: 18 For *C* died for sins once for all,
3: 21 you by the resurrection of Jesus *C*,
4: 13 participate in the sufferings of *C*,
4: 14 insulted because of the name of *C*,
2Pe 1: 1 and Savior Jesus *C* have received
1: 16 and coming of our Lord Jesus *C*,
1Jn 1: 1 Jesus *C*, the Righteous One.
2: 22 man who denies that Jesus is the *C*.
3: 16 Jesus *C* laid down his life for us.
3: 23 in the name of his Son, Jesus *C*,
4: 2 that Jesus *C* has come
5: 1 believes that Jesus is the *C* is born
5: 20 even in his Son Jesus *C*.
2Jn : 9 teaching of *C* does not have God;
Jude : 4 deny Jesus *C* our only Sovereign
Rev 1: 1 The revelation of Jesus *C*,
1: 5 from Jesus *C*, who is the faithful
11: 15 kingdom of our Lord and of his *C*,
20: 4 reigned with *C* a thousand years.
20: 6 they will be priests of God and of *C*

CHRIST'S (CHRIST)

1Co 9: 21 from God's law but am under *C* law
2Co 5: 14 For *C* love compels us,
5: 20 We are therefore *C* ambassadors,
12: 9 so that *C* power may rest on me.
Col 1: 22 by *C* physical body through death

CHRISTIAN* (CHRIST)

Ac 26: 28 you can persuade me to be a *C?''*
1Pe 4: 16 as a *C*, do not be ashamed,

CHRISTIANS* (CHRIST)

Ac 11: 26 The disciples were called *C* first

CHRISTS* (CHRIST)

Mt 24: 24 For false *C* and false prophets will
Mk 13: 22 For false *C* and false prophets will

CHURCH

Mt 16: 18 and on this rock I will build my *c*,
18: 17 if he refuses to listen even to the *c*,
Ac 20: 28 Be shepherds of the *c* of God,
1Co 5: 12 of mine to judge those outside the *c*.
14: 4 but he who prophesies edifies the *c*.
14: 12 to excel in gifts that build up the *c*.
14: 26 done for the strengthening of the *c*.
15: 9 because I persecuted the *c* of God.
Gal 1: 13 how intensely I persecuted the *c*
Eph 5: 23 as Christ is the head of the *c*,
Col 1: 18 he is the head of the body, the *c*;
1: 24 the sake of his body, which is the *c*.

CHURNING

Pr 30: 33 For as *c* the milk produces butter,

CIRCLE

Isa 40: 22 enthroned above the *c* of the earth,

CIRCUMCISE (CIRCUMCISED CIRCUMCISION)

Dt 10: 16 *C* your hearts, therefore,

CIRCUMCISED (CIRCUMCISE)

Ge 17: 10 Every male among you shall be *c*.
17: 12 who is eight days old must be *c*,
Jos 5: 3 and *c* the Israelites at Gibeath
Gal 5: 2 that if you let yourselves be *c*,

CIRCUMCISION (CIRCUMCISE)

Ro 2: 25 *C* has value if you observe the law,
2: 29 and *c* is of the heart, by the Spirit,
1Co 7: 19 *C* is nothing and uncircumcision is

CIRCUMSTANCES

Php 4: 11 to be content whatever the *c*.
1Th 5: 18 continually; give thanks in all *c*,

CITIES (CITY)

Lk 19: 17 small matter, take charge of ten *c*.'
19: 19 'You take charge of five *c*.'

CITIZENS (CITIZENSHIP)

Eph 2: 19 but fellow *c* with God's people

CITIZENSHIP* (CITIZENS)

Ac 22: 28 ''I had to pay a big price for my *c*.''
Eph 2: 12 excluded from *c* in Israel
Php 3: 20 But our *c* is in heaven.

CITY (CITIES)

Mt 5: 14 A *c* on a hill cannot be hidden.
Ac 18: 10 I have many people in this *c*.''
Heb 13: 14 here we do not have an enduring *c*,
Rev 21: 2 saw the Holy *C*, the new

CIVILIAN*

2Ti 2: 4 a soldier gets involved in *c* affairs—

CLAIM (CLAIMS RECLAIM)

Pr 25: 6 do not *c* a place among great men;
1Jn 1: 6 If we *c* to have fellowship
1: 8 If we *c* to be without sin, we
1: 10 If we *c* we have not sinned,

CLAIMS (CLAIM)

Jas 2: 14 if a man *c* to have faith
1Jn 2: 6 Whoever *c* to live in him must walk
2: 9 Anyone who *c* to be in the light

CLANGING*

1Co 13: 1 a resounding gong or a *c* cymbal.

CLAP* (CLAPPED CLAPS)

Job 21: 5 *c* your hand over your mouth.
Ps 47: 1 *C* your hands, all you nations;
98: 8 Let the rivers *c* their hands,
Pr 30: 32 *c* your hand over your mouth!
Isa 55: 12 will *c* their hands.
La 2: 15 *c* their hands at you;

CLAPPED* (CLAP)

2Ki 11: 12 and the people *c* their hands
Eze 25: 6 Because you have *c* your hands

CLAPS* (CLAP)

Job 27: 23 It *c* its hands in derision
34: 37 scornfully he *c* his hands among us
Na 3: 19 *c* his hands at your fall,

CLASSIFY*

2Co 10: 12 dare to *c* or compare ourselves

CLAUDIUS

Ac 11: 28 happened during the reign of *C*.)
18: 2 because *C* had ordered all the Jews

CLAY

Isa 45: 9 Does the *c* say to the potter,
64: 8 We are the *c*, you are the potter;
Jer 18: 6 ''Like *c* in the hand of the potter,
La 4: 2 are now considered as pots of *c*,
Da 2: 33 partly of iron and partly of baked *c*.
Ro 9: 21 out of the same lump of *c* some pottery
2Co 4: 7 we have this treasure in jars of *c*
2Ti 2: 20 and *c*; some are for noble purposes

CLEAN (CLEANNESS CLEANSE CLEANSED CLEANSES CLEANSING)

Ge 7: 2 seven of every kind of *c* animal,
Lev 4: 12 the camp to a place ceremonially *c*,
16: 30 you will be *c* from all your sins.

CLEAN

Ps 24: 4 He who has *c* hands and a pure
51: 7 with hyssop, and I will be *c*;
Pr 20: 9 I am *c* and without sin''?
Eze 36: 25 I will sprinkle *c* water on you,
Mt 8: 2 are willing, you can make me *c*.''
12: 44 the house unoccupied, swept *c*
23: 25 You *c* the outside of the cup
Mk 7: 19 Jesus declared all foods ''*c*.''
Jn 13: 10 to wash his feet; his whole body is *c*
15: 3 are already *c* because of the word
Ac 10: 15 impure that God has made *c*.''
Ro 14: 20 All food is *c*, but it is wrong

CLEANNESS (CLEAN)

2Sa 22: 25 according to my *c* in his sight.

CLEANSE (CLEAN)

Ps 51: 2 and *c* me from my sin.
51: 7 *C* me with hyssop, and I will be
Pr 20: 30 Blows and wounds *c* away evil,
Heb 9: 14 *c* our consciences from acts that
10: 22 having our hearts sprinkled to *c* us

CLEANSED (CLEAN)

Heb 9: 22 requires that nearly everything be *c*
2Pe 1: 9 has forgotten that he has been *c*

CLEANSES* (CLEAN)

2Ti 2: 21 If a man *c* himself from the latter,

CLEANSING (CLEAN)

Eph 5: 26 *c* her by the washing with water

CLEFT*

Ex 33: 22 I will put you in a *c* in the rock

CLEVER

Isa 5: 21 and *c* in their own sight.

CLING

Ro 12: 9 Hate what is evil; *c* to what is good.

CLINGS

Ps 63: 8 My soul *c* to you;

CLOAK

Ex 12: 11 with your *c* tucked into your belt,
2Ki 4: 29 ''Tuck your *c* into your belt,
9: 1 ''Tuck your *c* into your belt,
Mt 5: 40 let him have your *c* as well.

CLOSE (CLOSER CLOSES)

2Ki 11: 8 Stay *c* to the king wherever he goes
2Ch 23: 7 Stay *c* to the king wherever he goes
Ps 34: 18 LORD is *c* to the brokenhearted
148: 14 of Israel, the people *c* to his heart.
Isa 40: 11 and carries them *c* to his heart;
Jer 30: 21 himself to be *c* to me?'

CLOSER (CLOSE)

Ex 3: 5 ''Do not come any *c*,'' God said.
Pr 18: 24 there is a friend who sticks *c*

CLOSES (CLOSE)

Pr 28: 27 he who *c* his eyes to them receives

CLOTHE (CLOTHED CLOTHES CLOTHING)

Ps 45: 3 *c* yourself with splendor
Isa 52: 1 *c* yourself with strength.
Ro 13: 14 *c* yourselves with the Lord Jesus
Col 3: 12 *c* yourselves with compassion,
1Pe 5: 5 *C* yourselves with humility

CLOTHED (CLOTHE)

Ps 30: 11 removed my sackcloth and *c* me
104: 1 you are *c* with splendor
Pr 31: 22 she is *c* in fine linen and purple.
31: 25 She is *c* with strength and dignity,
Isa 61: 10 For he has *c* me with garments
Lk 24: 49 until you have been *c* with power
Gal 3: 27 into Christ have *c* yourselves

CLOTHES (CLOTHE)

Dt 8: 4 Your *c* did not wear out
Mt 6: 25 the body more important than *c*?
6: 28 ''And why do you worry about *c*?
27: 35 they divided up his *c* by casting lots
Jn 11: 44 Take off the grave *c* and let him go

CLOTHING (CLOTHE)

Dt 22: 5 A woman must not wear men's *c.*
Job 29:14 I put on righteousness as my *c;*
Ps 22:18 and cast lots for my *c.*
Mt 7:15 They come to you in sheep's *c,*
1Ti 6: 8 But if we have food and *c,*

CLOUD (CLOUDS)

Ex 13:21 them in a pillar of *c* to guide them
1Ki 18:44 *c* as small as a man's hand is rising
Pr 16:15 his favor is like a rain *c* in spring.
Isa 19: 1 See, the LORD rides on a swift *c*
Lk 21:27 of Man coming in a *c* with power
Heb 12: 1 by such a great *c* of witnesses,
Rev 14:14 seated on the *c* was one "like a son

CLOUDS (CLOUD)

Dt 33:26 and on the *c* in his majesty.
Ps 68: 4 extol him who rides on the *c*—
104: 3 He makes the *c* his chariot
Pr 25:14 Like *c* and wind without rain
Da 7:13 coming with the *c* of heaven.
Mt 24:30 of Man coming on the *c* of the sky,
26:64 and coming on the *c* of heaven.''
Mk 13:26 coming in *c* with great power
1Th 4:17 with them in the *c* to meet the Lord
Rev 1: 7 Look, he is coming with the *c,*

CLUB

Pr 25:18 Like a *c* or a sword or a sharp arrow

CO-HEIRS* (INHERIT)

Ro 8:17 heirs of God and *c* with Christ,

COALS

Pr 25:22 you will heap burning *c* on his head
Ro 12:20 you will heap burning *c* on his head

COARSE*

Eph 5: 4 or *c* joking, which are out of place,

CODE*

Ro 2:27 even though you have the written *c*
2:29 by the Spirit, not by the written *c.*
7: 6 not in the old way of the written *c,*
Col 2:14 having canceled the written *c,*

COINS

Mt 26:15 out for him thirty silver *c.*
Lk 15: 8 suppose a woman has ten silver *c*

COLD

Pr 25:25 Like *c* water to a weary soul
Mt 10:42 if anyone gives even a cup of *c* water
24:12 the love of most will grow *c,*

COLLECTION

1Co 16: 1 Now about the *c* for God's people:

COLT

Zec 9: 9 on a *c,* the foal of a donkey.
Mt 21: 5 on a *c,* the foal of a donkey.' ''

COMB

Ps 19:10 than honey from the *c.*

COMFORT* (COMFORTED COMFORTER COMFORTERS COMFORTING COMFORTS)

Ge 5:29 ''He will *c* us in the labor
37:35 and daughters came to *c* him,
Ru 2:13 ''You have given me *c*
1Ch 7:22 and his relatives came to *c* him.
Job 2:11 sympathize with him and *c* him.
7:13 When I think my bed will *c* me
16: 5 *c* from my lips would bring you
36:16 to the *c* of your table laden
Ps 23: 4 rod and your staff, they *c* me.
71:21 and *c* me once again.
119:50 My *c* in my suffering is this:
119:52 and I find *c* in them.
119:76 May your unfailing love be my *c,*
119:82 I say, ''When will you *c* me?''
Isa 40: 1 *C, c* my people,
51: 3 The LORD will surely *c* Zion
51:19 who can *c* you?—
57:18 I will guide him and restore *c*
61: 2 to *c* all who mourn,

Isa 66:13 so will I *c* you;
Jer 16: 7 food to *c* those who mourn
31:13 I will give them *c* and joy instead
La 1: 2 there is none to *c* her.
1: 9 there was none to *c* her.
1:16 No one is near to *c* me,
1:17 but there is no one to *c* her.
1:21 but there is no one to *c* me.
2:13 that I may *c* you,
Eze 16:54 all you have done in giving them *c.*
Na 3: 7 Where can I find anyone to *c* you?''
Zec 1:17 and the LORD will again *c* Zion
10: 2 they give *c* in vain.
Lk 6:24 you have already received your *c.*
Jn 11:19 and Mary to *c* them in the loss
1Co 14: 3 encouragement and *c.*
2Co 1: 3 of compassion and the God of all *c,*
1: 4 so that we can *c* those
1: 4 with the *c* we ourselves have
1: 5 through Christ our *c* overflows.
1: 6 if we are comforted, it is for your *c,*
1: 6 it is for your *c* and salvation;
1: 7 so also you share in our *c.*
2: 7 you ought to forgive and *c* him,
7: 7 also by the *c* you had given him.
Php 2: 1 if any *c* from his love,
Col 4:11 and they have proved a *c* to me.

COMFORTED* (COMFORT)

Ge 24:67 Isaac was *c* after his mother's death
37:35 comfort him, but he refused to be *c.*
2Sa 12:24 Then David *c* his wife Bathsheba,
Job 42:11 They *c* and consoled him
Ps 77: 2 and my soul refused to be *c.*
86:17 have helped me and *c* me.
Isa 12: 1 and you have *c* me.
52: 9 for the LORD has *c* his people,
54:11 lashed by storms and not *c,*
66:13 and you will be *c* over Jerusalem.''
Jer 31:15 and refusing to be *c,*
Mt 2:18 and refusing to be *c,*
5: 4 for they will be *c.*
Lk 16:25 but now he is *c* here and you are
Ac 20:12 man home alive and were greatly *c.*
2Co 1: 6 if we are *c,* it is for your comfort,
7: 6 *c* us by the coming of Titus,

COMFORTER* (COMFORT)

Ecc 4: 1 and they have no *c;*
4: 1 and they have no *c.*
Jer 8:18 O my *C* in sorrow,

COMFORTERS* (COMFORT)

Job 16: 2 miserable *c* are you all!
Ps 69:20 for *c,* but I found none.

COMFORTING* (COMFORT)

Isa 66:11 satisfied at her *c* breasts;
Zec 1:13 *c* words to the angel who talked
Jn 11:31 *c* her, noticed how quickly she got
1Th 2:12 *c* and urging you to live lives

COMFORTS* (COMFORT)

Job 29:25 I was like one who *c* mourners.
Isa 49:13 For the LORD *c* his people
51:12 ''I, even I, am he who *c* you.
66:13 As a mother *c* her child,
2Co 1: 4 who *c* us in all our troubles,
7: 6 But God, who *c* the downcast,

COMMAND (COMMANDED COMMANDING COMMANDENT COMMANDMENTS COMMANDS)

Ex 7: 2 You are to say everything I *c* you,
Nu 14:41 are you disobeying the LORD's *c?*
24:13 to go beyond the *c* of the LORD—
Dt 4: 2 Do not add to what I *c* you
8: 1 to follow every *c* I am giving you
12:32 See that you do all I *c* you;
15:11 I *c* you to be openhanded
30:16 For I *c* you today to love
32:46 so that you may *c* your children
Ps 91:11 For he will *c* his angels concerning
Pr 13:13 but he who respects a *c* is rewarded
Ecc 8: 2 Obey the king's *c,* I say,
Jer 1: 7 you to and say whatever I *c* you.
1:17 and say to them whatever I *c* you.
7:23 Walk in all the ways I *c* you,

Jer 11: 4 Obey me and do everything I *c* you
26: 2 Tell them everything I *c* you;
Joel 2:11 mighty are those who obey his *c.*
Mt 4: 6 He will *c* his angels concerning you
15: 3 why do you break the *c* of God
Lk 4:10 '' 'He will *c* his angels concerning
Jn 14:15 love me, you will obey what I *c.*
15:12 My *c* is this: Love each other
15:14 friends if you do what I *c.*
15:17 This is my *c:* Love each other.
1Co 14:37 writing to you is the Lord's *c.*
Gal 5:14 law is summed up in a single *c:*
1Ti 1: 5 goal of this *c* is love, which comes
6:14 I give you this *c* without spot
6:17 *C* those who are rich
Heb 11: 3 universe was formed at God's *c,*
2Pe 2:21 on the sacred *c* that was passed
3: 2 and the *c* given by our Lord
1Jn 2: 7 I am not writing you a new *c*
3:23 this is his *c:* to believe in the name
4:21 And he has given us this *c:*
2Jn 6 his *c* is that you walk in love.

COMMANDED (COMMAND)

Ge 2:16 And the LORD God *c* the man,
7: 5 Noah did all that the LORD *c* him.
50:12 Jacob's sons did as he had *c* them:
Ex 7: 6 did just as the LORD *c*
19: 7 all the words the LORD had *c* him
Dt 4: 5 laws as the LORD my God *c* me,
6:24 The LORD *c* us to obey all these
Jos 1: 9 Have I not *c* you? Be strong
1:16 Whatever you have *c* us we will do,
2Sa 5:25 So David did as the LORD *c* him,
2Ki 17:13 the entire Law that I *c* your fathers
21: 8 careful to do everything I *c* them
2Ch 33: 8 do everything I *c* them concerning
Ps 33: 9 he *c,* and it stood firm.
78: 5 which he *c* our forefathers
148: 5 for he *c* and they were created.
Mt 28:20 to obey everything I have *c* you.
1Co 9:14 Lord has *c* that those who preach
1Jn 3:23 and to love one another as he *c* us.
2Jn 4 in the truth, just as the Father *c* us.

COMMANDING (COMMAND)

2Ti 2: 4 he wants to please his *c* officer.

COMMANDMENT* (COMMAND)

Jos 22: 5 But be very careful to keep the *c*
Mt 22:36 which is the greatest *c* in the Law?''
22:38 This is the first and greatest *c.*
Mk 12:31 There is no *c* greater than these.''
Lk 23:56 the Sabbath in obedience to the *c.*
Jn 13:34 ''A new *c* I give you: Love one
Ro 7: 8 the opportunity afforded by the *c,*
7: 9 when the *c* came, sin sprang to life
7:10 that the very *c* that was intended
7:11 and through the *c* put me to death.
7:11 the opportunity afforded by the *c,*
7:12 and the *c* is holy, righteous
7:13 through the *c* sin might become
13: 9 and whatever other *c* there may be,
Eph 6: 2 which is the first *c* with a promise
Heb 9:19 Moses had proclaimed every *c*

COMMANDMENTS* (COMMAND)

Ex 20: 6 who love me and keep my *c.*
34:28 of the covenant—the Ten *C.*
Dt 4:13 to you his covenant, the Ten *C.*
5:10 who love me and keep my *c.*
5:22 These are the *c* the LORD
6: 6 These *c* that I give you today are
9:10 were all the *c* the LORD
10: 4 The Ten *C* he had proclaimed
Ecc 12:13 Fear God and keep his *c,*
Mt 5:19 one of the least of these *c*
19:17 If you want to enter life, obey the *c*
22:40 the Prophets hang on these two *c.*''
Mk 10:19 You know the *c:* 'Do not murder,
12:28 ''Of all the *c,* which is the most
Lk 1: 6 observing all the Lord's *c*
18:20 You know the *c:* 'Do not commit
Ro 13: 9 The *c,* ''Do not commit adultery,''
Eph 2:15 in his flesh the law with its *c*
Rev 12:17 those who obey God's *c*
14:12 part of the saints who obey God's *c*

COMMANDS (COMMAND)

Ex 24: 12 and c I have written for their
25: 22 give you all my c for the Israelites.
34: 32 gave them all the c the LORD had
Lev 22: 31 "Keep my c and follow them.
Nu 15: 39 and so you will remember all the c
Dt 7: 9 those who love him and keep his c.
7: 11 Therefore, take care to follow the c
11: 1 decrees, his laws and his c always.
11: 27 the blessing if you obey the c
28: 1 carefully follow all his c I give you
30: 10 LORD your God and keep his c
Jos 22: 5 to walk in all his ways, to obey his c
1Ki 2: 3 and keep his decrees and c,
8: 58 in all his ways and to keep the c,
8: 61 to live by his decrees and obey his c
1Ch 28: 7 unswerving in carrying out my c
29: 19 devotion to keep your c,
2Ch 31: 21 in obedience to the law and the c,
Ne 1: 5 those who love him and obey his c,
Ps 78: 7 but would keep his c.
112: 1 who finds great delight in his c.
119: 10 do not let me stray from your c.
119: 32 I run in the path of your c,
119: 35 Direct me in the path of your c,
119: 47 for I delight in your c
119: 48 I reach out my hands for your c,
119: 73 me understanding to learn your c.
119: 86 All your c are trustworthy;
119: 96 but your c are boundless.
119: 98 Your c make me wiser
119:115 that I may keep the c of my God!
119:127 Because I love your c
119:131 longing for your c.
119:143 but your c are my delight.
119:151 and all your c are true.
119:172 for all your c are righteous.
119:176 for I have not forgotten your c.
Pr 2: 1 and store up my c within you,
3: 1 but keep my c in your heart,
6: 23 For these c are a lamp,
10: 8 The wise in heart accept c.
Isa 48: 18 you had paid attention to my c,
Da 9: 4 all who love him and obey his c,
Mt 5: 19 teaches these c will be called great
Mk 7: 8 You have let go of the c of God
7: 9 way of setting aside the c of God
Jn 14: 21 Whoever has my c and obeys them,
15: 10 If you obey my c, you will remain
Ac 17: 30 but now he c all people everywhere
1Co 7: 19 Keeping God's c is what counts.
1Jn 2: 3 come to know him if we obey his c.
2: 4 but does not do what he c is a liar,
3: 22 we obey his c and do what pleases
3: 24 Those who obey his c live in him,
5: 2 loving God and carrying out his c
5: 3 And his c are not burdensome,
5: 3 This is love for God: to obey his c.
2Jn : 6 that we walk in obedience to his c.

COMMEMORATE

Ex 12: 14 "This is a day you are to c;

COMMEND* (COMMENDABLE COMMENDED COMMENDS)

Ps 145: 4 One generation will c your works
Ecc 8: 15 So I c the enjoyment of life,
Ro 13: 3 do what is right and he will c you.
16: 1 I c to you our sister Phoebe,
2Co 3: 1 beginning to c ourselves again?
4: 2 the truth plainly we c ourselves,
5: 12 trying to c ourselves to you again,
6: 4 as servants of God we c ourselves
10: 12 with some who c themselves.
1Pe 2: 14 and to c those who do right.

COMMENDABLE* (COMMEND)

1Pe 2: 19 For it is c if a man bears up
2: 20 you endure it, this is c before God.

COMMENDED* (COMMEND)

Ne 11: 2 The people c all the men who
Job 29: 11 and those who saw me c me,
Lk 16: 8 master c the dishonest manager
Ac 15: 40 c by the brothers to the grace
2Co 12: 11 I ought to have been c by you,
Heb 11: 2 This is what the ancients were c for
11: 4 By faith he was c as a righteous

Heb 11: 5 he was c as one who pleased God.
11: 39 These were all c for their faith,

COMMENDS* (COMMEND)

Pr 15: 2 of the wise c knowledge,
2Co 10: 18 but the one whom the Lord c.
10: 18 not the one who c himself who is

COMMIT (COMMITS COMMITTED)

Ex 20: 14 "You shall not c adultery.
Dt 5: 18 "You shall not c adultery.
1Sa 7: 3 and c yourselves to the LORD
Ps 31: 5 Into your hands I c my spirit;
37: 5 C your way to the LORD;
Pr 16: 3 C to the LORD whatever you do,
Mt 5: 27 that it was said, 'Do not c adultery.'
5: 32 causes her to c adultery,
19: 18 do not c adultery, do not steal,
Mk 10: 19 do not c adultery, do not steal,
Lk 18: 20 'Do not c adultery, do not murder,
23: 46 into your hands I c my spirit."
Ac 20: 32 I c you to God and to the word
Ro 2: 22 do you c adultery? You who abhor
2: 22 that people should not c adultery,
13: 9 "Do not c adultery,"
1Co 10: 8 We should not c sexual immorality,
Jas 2: 11 do not c adultery but do c murder,
1Pe 4: 19 to God's will should c themselves
Rev 2: 22 I will make those who c adultery

COMMITS (COMMIT)

Pr 6: 32 man who c adultery lacks
29: 22 a hot-tempered one c many sins.
Ecc 8: 12 a wicked man c a hundred crimes
Eze 18: 12 He c robbery.
18: 14 who sees all the sins his father c,
18: 24 from his righteousness and c sin
18: 26 from his righteousness and c sin,
22: 11 you one man c a detestable offense
Mt 5: 32 a woman so divorced c adultery.
19: 9 marries another woman c adultery
Mk 10: 11 marries another woman c adultery
10: 12 another man, she c adultery."
Lk 16: 18 a divorced woman c adultery.
16: 18 marries another woman c adultery,

COMMITTED (COMMIT)

Nu 5: 7 and must confess the sin he has c.
1Ki 8: 61 But your hearts must be fully c
15: 14 Asa's heart was fully c
2Ch 16: 9 those whose hearts are fully c
Mt 5: 28 lustfully has already c adultery
11: 27 "All things have been c to me
Lk 10: 22 "All things have been c to me
Ac 14: 23 c them to the Lord,
14: 26 where they had been c to the grace
1Co 9: 17 I am simply discharging the trust c
2Co 5: 19 And he has c to us the message
1Pe 2: 22 "He c no sin,
Rev 17: 2 the kings of the earth c adultery
18: 3 of the earth c adultery with her,
18: 9 kings of the earth who c adultery

COMMON

Ge 11: 1 had one language and a c speech.
Lev 10: 10 between the holy and the c,
Pr 22: 2 Rich and poor have this in c:
29: 13 the oppressor have this in c:
Ac 2: 44 together and had everything in c.
1Co 10: 13 has seized you except what is c
2Co 6: 14 and wickedness have in c?

COMPANION (COMPANIONS)

Ps 55: 13 my c, my close friend,
55: 20 My c attacks his friends;
Pr 13: 20 but a c of fools suffers harm.
28: 7 a c of gluttons disgraces his father.
29: 3 c of prostitutes squanders his
Rev 1: 9 your brother and c in the suffering

COMPANIONS (COMPANION)

Ps 45: 7 your God, has set you above your c
Pr 18: 24 A man of many c may come to ruin
Heb 1: 9 your God, has set you above your c

COMPANY

Ps 14: 5 present in the c of the righteous.
Pr 21: 16 comes to rest in the c of the dead.

Pr 24: 1 do not desire their c;
Jer 15: 17 I never sat in the c of revelers,
1Co 15: 33 "Bad c corrupts good character."

COMPARE* (COMPARED COMPARING COMPARISON)

Job 28: 17 Neither gold nor crystal can c
28: 19 The topaz of Cush cannot c with it;
39: 13 but they cannot c with the pinions
Ps 86: 8 no deeds can c with yours.
89: 6 skies above can c with the LORD?
Pr 3: 15 nothing you desire can c with her.
8: 11 nothing you desire can c with her.
Isa 40: 18 To whom, then, will you c God?
40: 18 What image will you c him to?
40: 25 "To whom will you c me?
46: 5 "To whom will you c me
La 2: 13 With what can I c you,
Eze 31: 8 c with its branches—
Da 1: 13 Then c our appearance with that
Mt 11: 16 "To what can I c this generation?
Lk 7: 31 I c the people of this generation?
13: 18 What shall I c it to? It is like
13: 20 What shall I c the kingdom of God
2Co 10: 12 and c themselves with themselves,
10: 12 or c ourselves with some who

COMPARED* (COMPARE)

Jdg 8: 2 What have I accomplished c to you
8: 3 What was I able to do c to you?"
Isa 46: 5 you liken me that we may be c?
Eze 31: 2 Who can be c with you in majesty?
31: 18 the trees of Eden be c with you
Php 3: 8 I consider everything a loss c

COMPARING* (COMPARE)

Ro 8: 18 present sufferings are not worth c
2Co 8: 8 the sincerity of your love by c it
Gal 6: 4 without c himself to somebody else

COMPARISON* (COMPARE)

2Co 3: 10 now in c with the surpassing glory.

COMPASSION* (COMPASSIONATE COMPASSIONS)

Ex 33: 19 I will have c on whom I will have c.
Dt 13: 17 he will show you mercy, have c
28: 54 man among you will have no c
30: 3 restore your fortunes and have c
32: 36 and have c on his servants
Jdg 2: 18 for the LORD had c on them
1Ki 3: 26 son was alive was filled with c
2Ki 13: 23 and had c and showed concern
2Ch 30: 9 and your children will be shown c
Ne 9: 19 of your great c you did not
9: 27 and in your great c you gave them
9: 28 in your c you delivered them time
Ps 51: 1 according to your great c
77: 9 Has he in anger withheld his c?"
90: 13 Have c on your servants.
102: 13 You will arise and have c on Zion,
103: 4 and crowns me with love and c.
103: 13 As a father has c on his children,
103: 13 so the LORD has c
116: 5 our God is full of c.
119: 77 Let your c come to me that I may
119:156 Your c is great, O LORD;
135: 14 and have c on his servants.
145: 9 he has c on all he has made.
Isa 13: 18 will they look with c on children.
14: 1 The LORD will have c on Jacob;
27: 11 so their Maker has no c on them,
30: 18 he rises to show you c.
49: 10 He who has c on them will guide
49: 13 and will have c on his afflicted ones
49: 15 and have no c on the child she has
51: 3 and will look with c on all her ruins
54: 7 with deep c I will bring you back.
54: 8 I will have c on you,"
54: 10 says the LORD, who has c on you.
60: 10 in favor I will show you c.
63: 7 to his c and many kindnesses,
63: 15 and c are withheld from us.
Jer 12: 15 I will again have c and will bring
13: 14 c to keep me from destroying them
15: 6 I can no longer show c.
21: 7 show them no mercy or pity or c.'
30: 18 and have c on his dwellings;

Jer 31: 20 I have great *c* for him,''
    33: 26 restore their fortunes and have *c*
    42: 12 I will show you *c* so that he will
    42: 12 so that he will have *c* on you
La   3: 32 he brings grief, he will show *c*.
Eze 9: 5 without showing pity or *c*.
    16: 5 or had *c* enough to do any
    39: 25 and will have *c* on all the people
Hos 2: 19 in love and *c*.
    11: 8 all my *c* is aroused.
    13: 14 ''I will have no *c*,
    14: 3 for in you the fatherless find *c*.''
Am 1: 11 stifling all *c*,
Jnh 3: 9 with *c* turn from his fierce anger
    3: 10 he had *c* on them and did not bring
Mic 7: 19 You will again have *c* on us;
Zec 7: 9 show mercy and *c* to one another.
    10: 6 because I have *c* on them.
Mal 3: 17 as in a *c* a man spares his son who
Mt 9: 36 When he saw the crowds, he had *c*
    14: 14 he had *c* on them and healed their
    15: 32 ''I have *c* for these people;
    20: 34 Jesus had *c* on them and touched
Mk 1: 41 with *c*, Jesus reached out his hand
    6: 34 and saw a large crowd, he had *c*
    8: 2 ''I have *c* for these people;
Lk 15: 20 and was filled with *c* for him;
Ro 9: 15 and I will have *c* on whom I have *c*
2Co 1: 3 the Father of *c* and the God
Php 2: 1 and *c*, then make my joy complete
Col 3: 12 clothe yourselves with *c*, kindness,
Jas 5: 11 The Lord is full of *c* and mercy.

COMPASSIONATE* (COMPASSION)

Ex 22: 27 out to me, I will hear, for I am *c*.
    34: 6 the LORD, the *c* and gracious God
2Ch 30: 9 LORD your God is gracious and *c*.
Ne 9: 17 gracious and *c*, slow to anger
Ps 86: 15 O Lord, are a *c* and gracious God,
   103: 8 The LORD is *c* and gracious,
   111: 4 the LORD is gracious and *c*.
   112: 4 the gracious and *c* and righteous
   145: 8 The LORD is gracious and *c*,
La 4: 10 With their own hands *c* women
Joel 2: 13 for he is gracious and *c*,
Jnh 4: 2 that you are a gracious and *c* God,
Eph 4: 32 Be kind and *c* to one another,
1Pe 3: 8 love as brothers, be *c* and humble.

COMPASSIONS* (COMPASSION)

La 3: 22 for his *c* never fail.

COMPELLED (COMPULSION)

Ac 20: 22 ''And now, *c* by the Spirit,
1Co 9: 16 I cannot boast, for I am *c* to preach.

COMPELS (COMPULSION)

Job 32: 18 and the spirit within me *c* me;
2Co 5: 14 For Christ's love *c* us, because we

COMPETENT* (COMPETENT)

2Co 3: 5 but our *c* comes from God.

COMPETENT* (COMPETENCE)

Ro 15: 14 and *c* to instruct one another.
1Co 6: 2 are you not *c* to judge trivial cases?
2Co 3: 5 Not that we are *c* in ourselves to claim
    3: 6 He has made us *c* as ministers

COMPETES*

1Co 9: 25 Everyone who *c* in the games goes
2Ti 2: 5 Similarly, if anyone *c* as an athlete,
    2: 5 unless he *c* according to the rules.

COMPLACENCY* (COMPLACENT)

Pr 1: 32 and the *c* of fools will destroy them
Eze 30: 9 ships to frighten Cush out of her *c*.

COMPLACENT* (COMPLACENCY)

Isa 32: 9 You women who are so *c*,
    32: 11 Tremble, you *c* women;
Am 6: 1 Woe to you who are *c* in Zion,
Zep 1: 12 and punish those who are *c*.

COMPLAINING*

Php 2: 14 Do everything without *c* or arguing

COMPLETE

Dt 16: 15 your hands, and your joy will be *c*.
Jn 3: 29 That joy is mine, and it is now *c*.
    15: 11 and that your joy may be *c*.
    16: 24 will receive, and your joy will be *c*.
    17: 23 May they be brought to *c* unity
Ac 20: 24 *c* the task the Lord Jesus has given
Php 2: 2 then make my joy *c*
Col 4: 17 to it that you *c* the work you have
Jas 1: 4 so that you may be mature and *c*,
    2: 22 his faith was made *c* by what he did
1Jn 1: 4 We write this to make our joy *c*.
    2: 5 God's love is truly made *c* in him.
    4: 12 and his love is made *c* in us.
    4: 17 love is made *c* among us
2Jn : 12 to face, so that our joy may be *c*.

COMPLIMENTS*

Pr 23: 8 and will have wasted your *c*.

COMPREHEND* (COMPREHENDED)

Job 28: 13 Man does not *c* its worth;
Ecc 8: 17 No one can *c* what goes
    8: 17 he knows, he cannot really *c* it.

COMPREHENDED* (COMPREHEND)

Job 38: 18 Have you *c* the vast expanses

COMPULSION (COMPELLED COMPELS)

2Co 9: 7 not reluctantly or under *c*,

CONCEAL (CONCEALED CONCEALS)

Ps 40: 10 I do not *c* your love and your truth
Pr 25: 2 It is the glory of God to *c* a matter;

CONCEALED (CONCEAL)

Jer 16: 17 nor is their sin *c* from my eyes.
Mt 10: 26 There is nothing *c* that will not be
Mk 4: 22 and whatever is *c* is meant
Lk 8: 17 nothing *c* that will not be known
    12: 2 There is nothing *c* that will not be

CONCEALS* (CONCEAL)

Pr 10: 18 He who *c* his hatred has lying lips,
    28: 13 He who *c* his sins does not prosper,

CONCEIT* (CONCEITED CONCEITS)

Isa 16: 6 her overweening pride and *c*,
Jer 48: 29 her overweening pride and *c*,
Php 2: 3 out of selfish ambition or vain *c*,

CONCEITED* (CONCEIT)

1Sa 17: 28 I know how *c* you are and how
Ro 11: 25 brothers, so that you may not be *c*:
    12: 16 Do not be *c*.
2Co 12: 7 To keep me from becoming *c*
Gal 5: 26 Let us not become *c*, provoking
1Ti 3: 6 or he may become *c* and fall
    6: 4 he is *c* and understands nothing.
2Ti 3: 4 of the good, treacherous, rash, *c*,

CONCEITS* (CONCEIT)

Ps 73: 7 evil *c* of their minds know no

CONCEIVED (CONCEIVES)

Ps 51: 5 from the time my mother *c* me.
Mt 1: 20 what is *c* in her is from the Holy
1Co 2: 9 no mind has *c*
Jas 1: 15 after desire has *c*, it gives birth

CONCEIVES* (CONCEIVED)

Ps 7: 14 *c* trouble gives birth

CONCERN* (CONCERNED)

Ge 39: 6 he did not *c* himself with anything
    39: 8 ''my master does not *c* himself
1Sa 23: 21 ''The LORD bless you for your *c*
2Ki 13: 23 and had compassion and showed *c*
Job 9: 21 I have no *c* for myself;
    19: 4 my error remains my *c* alone.
Ps 131: 1 I do not *c* myself with great matters
Pr 29: 7 but the wicked have no such *c*.
Eze 36: 21 I had *c* for my holy name, which
Ac 15: 14 God at first showed his *c* by taking
    18: 17 But Gallio showed no *c* whatever.
1Co 7: 32 I would like you to be free from *c*,
    12: 25 that its parts should have equal *c*
2Co 7: 7 your deep sorrow, your ardent *c*

2Co 7: 11 what alarm, what longing, what *c*,
    8: 16 of Titus the same *c* I have for you.
   11: 28 of my *c* for all the churches.
Php 4: 10 at last you have renewed your *c*

CONCERNED (CONCERN)

Ex 2: 25 Israelites and was *c* about them.
Ps 142: 4 no one is *c* for me.
Jnh 4: 10 ''You have been *c* about this vine,
    4: 11 Should I not be *c* about that great
1Co 7: 32 An unmarried man is *c* about
    9: 9 Is it about oxen that God is *c*?
Php 4: 10 you have been *c*, but you had no

CONCESSION*

1Co 7: 6 I say this as a *c*, not as a command.

CONDEMN* (CONDEMNATION CONDEMNED CONDEMNING CONDEMNS)

Job 9: 20 innocent, my mouth would *c* me;
    10: 2 I will say to God: Do not *c* me,
    34: 17 Will you *c* the just and mighty One
    34: 29 if he remains silent, who can *c* him?
    40: 8 Would you *c* me to justify yourself?
Ps 94: 21 and *c* the innocent to death.
   109: 7 and may his prayers *c* him.
   109: 31 from those who *c* him.
Isa 50: 9 Who is he that will *c* me?
Mt 12: 41 with this generation and *c* it;
    12: 42 with this generation and *c* it;
    20: 18 They will *c* him to death
Mk 10: 33 They will *c* him to death
Lk 6: 37 Do not *c*, and you will not be
    11: 31 men of this generation and *c* them;
    11: 32 with this generation and *c* it;
Jn 3: 17 Son into the world to *c* the world,
    7: 51 ''Does our law *c* a man
    8: 11 ''Then neither do I *c* you,''
    12: 48 very word which I spoke will *c* him
Ro 2: 27 yet obeys the law will *c* you who,
    14: 3 everything must not *c* the man who
    14: 22 is the man who does not *c* himself
2Co 7: 3 this to *c* you; I have said
1Jn 3: 20 presence whenever our hearts *c* us.
    3: 21 if our hearts do not *c* us,

CONDEMNATION* (CONDEMN)

Jer 42: 18 of *c* and reproach; you will never
   44: 12 and horror, of *c* and reproach.
Ro 3: 8 may result''? Their *c* is deserved. ·
    5: 16 followed one sin and brought *c*,
    5: 18 of one trespass was *c* for all men,
    8: 1 there is now no *c* for those who are
2Pe 2: 3 Their *c* has long been hanging
Jude : 4 certain men whose *c* was written

CONDEMNED* (CONDEMN)

Dt 13: 17 of those *c* things shall be found
Job 32: 3 to refute Job, and yet had *c* him.
Ps 34: 21 the foes of the righteous will be *c*.
    34: 22 will be *c* who takes refuge in him.
    37: 33 let them be *c* when brought to trial.
   79: 11 preserve those *c* to die.
   102: 20 and release those *c* to death.''
Mt 12: 7 you would not have *c* the innocent.
    12: 37 and by your words you will be *c*.''
    23: 33 How will you escape being *c* to hell
    27: 3 betrayed him, saw that Jesus was *c*.
Mk 14: 64 They all *c* him as worthy of death.
    16: 16 whoever does not believe will be *c*.
Lk 6: 37 condemn, and you will not be *c*.
Jn 3: 18 Whoever believes in him is not *c*,
    3: 18 does not believe stands *c* already
    5: 24 has eternal life and will not be *c*;
    5: 29 who have done evil will rise to be *c*.
    8: 10 Has no one *c* you?'' ''No one, sir,''
    16: 11 prince of this world now stands *c*.
Ac 25: 15 against him and asked that he be *c*.
Ro 3: 7 why am I still *c* as a sinner?''
    8: 3 And so he *c* sin in sinful man,
    14: 23 But the man who has doubts is *c*
1Co 4: 9 like men *c* to die in the arena.
    11: 32 disciplined so that we will not be *c*
Gal 1: 8 let him be eternally *c*! As we have
    1: 9 let him be eternally *c*! Am I now
2Th 2: 12 that all will be *c* who have not
Tit 2: 8 of speech that cannot be *c*,

CONDEMNING (continued)

Heb 11: 7 By his faith he c the world
Jas 5: 6 You have c and murdered innocent
5: 12 and your "No," no, or you will be c
2Pe 2: 6 if he c the cities of Sodom
Rev 19: 2 He has c the great prostitute

CONDEMNING* (CONDEMN)

Dt 25: 1 the innocent and c the guilty.
1Ki 8: 32 c the guilty and bringing
Pr 17: 15 the guilty and c the innocent—
Ac 13: 27 yet in c him they fulfilled the words
Ro 2: 1 judge the other, you are c yourself,

CONDEMNS* (CONDEMN)

Job 15: 6 Your own mouth c you, not mine;
Pr 12: 2 but the LORD c a crafty man.
Ro 8: 34 Who is he that c? Christ Jesus,
2Co 3: 9 the ministry that c men is glorious,

CONDITION

Pr 27: 23 Be sure you know the c

CONDUCT (CONDUCTED CONDUCTS)

Pr 10: 23 A fool finds pleasure in evil c,
20: 11 by whether his c is pure and right.
21: 8 but the c of the guilty is upright.
Ecc 6: 8 how to c himself before others?
Jer 4: 18 "Your own c and actions
17: 10 to reward a man according to his c,
Eze 7: 3 I will judge you according to your c
Php 1: 27 c yourselves in a manner worthy
1Ti 3: 15 to c themselves in God's household

CONDUCTED* (CONDUCT)

2Co 1: 12 testifies that we have c ourselves

CONDUCTS* (CONDUCT)

Ps 112: 5 who c his affairs with justice.

CONFESS* (CONFESSED CONFESSES CONFESSING CONFESSION)

Lev 5: 5 he must c in what way he has
16: 21 and c over it all the wickedness
26: 40 "But if they will c their sins
Nu 5: 7 must c the sin he has committed.
1Ki 8: 33 back to you and c your name,
8: 35 toward this place and c your name
2Ch 6: 24 they turn back and c your name,
6: 26 toward this place and c your name
Ne 1: 6 I c the sins we Israelites, including
Ps 32: 5 I said, "I will c
38: 18 I c my iniquity;
Jn 12: 42 they would not c their faith
Ro 10: 9 That if you c with your mouth,
10: 10 it is with your mouth that you c
14: 11 every tongue will c to God.' "
Php 2: 11 every tongue c that Jesus Christ is
Heb 3: 1 and high priest whom we c.
13: 15 the fruit of lips that c his name.
Jas 5: 16 Therefore c your sins to each other
1Jn 1: 9 If we c our sins, he is faithful

CONFESSED* (CONFESS)

1Sa 7: 6 day they fasted and there they c,
Ne 9: 2 in their places and c their sins
Da 9: 4 to the LORD my God and c:
Jn 1: 20 but c freely, "I am not the Christ."
Ac 19: 18 and openly c their evil deeds.

CONFESSES* (CONFESS)

Pr 28. 13 whoever c and renounces them
2Ti 2: 19 and, "Everyone who c the name

CONFESSING* (CONFESS)

Ezr 10: 1 While Ezra was praying and c,
Da 9: 20 c my sin and the sin
Mt 3: 6 C their sins, they were baptized
Mk 1: 5 C their sins, they were baptized

CONFESSION* (CONFESS)

Ezr 10: 11 Now make c to the LORD,
Ne 9: 3 and spent another quarter in c
2Co 9: 13 obedience that accompanies your c
1Ti 6: 12 called when you made your good c
6: 13 Pontius Pilate made the good c,

CONFIDENCE* (CONFIDENT)

Jdg 9: 26 and its citizens put their c in him.
2Ki 18: 19 On what are you basing this c
2Ch 32: 8 And the people gained c
32: 10 On what are you basing your c,
Job 4: 6 Should not your piety be your c
Ps 71: 5 my c since my youth.
Pr 3: 26 for the LORD will be your c
3: 32 but takes the upright into his c.
11: 13 A gossip betrays a c,
20: 19 A gossip betrays a c;
25: 9 do not betray another man's c,
31: 11 Her husband has full c in her
Isa 32: 17 will be quietness and c forever.
36: 4 On what are you basing this c
Jer 17: 7 whose c is in him.
49: 31 which lives in c,"
Eze 29: 16 a source of c for the people of Israel
Mic 7: 5 put no c in a friend.
2Co 2: 3 I had c in all of you, that you would
3: 4 Such c as this is ours
7: 4 I have great c in you; I take great
7: 16 I am glad I can have complete c
8: 22 so because of his great c in you.
Eph 3: 12 God with freedom and c.
Php 3: 3 and who put no c in the flesh—
3: 4 I myself have reasons for such c.
3: 4 reasons to put c in the flesh,
2Th 3: 4 We have c in the Lord that you are
Heb 3: 14 till the end the c we had at first.
4: 16 the throne of grace with c,
10: 19 since we have c to enter the Most
10: 35 So do not throw away your c;
13: 6 So we say with c,
1Jn 3: 21 we have c before God and receive
4: 17 us so that we will have c on the day
5: 14 This is the c we have

CONFIDENT* (CONFIDENCE)

Job 6: 20 because they had been c;
Ps 27: 3 even then will I be c.
27: 13 I am still c of this:
Lk 18: 9 To some who were c
2Co 1: 15 Because I was c of this, I planned
5: 6 Therefore we are always c
5: 8 We are c, I say, and would prefer
9: 4 ashamed of having been so c.
10: 7 If anyone is c that he belongs
Gal 5: 10 I am c in the Lord that you will
Php 1: 6 day until now, being c of this,
2: 24 I am c in the Lord that I myself will
Phm : 21 C of your obedience, I write to you,
Heb 6: 9 we are c of better things
1Jn 2: 28 that when he appears we may be c

CONFIDES*

Ps 25: 14 The LORD c in those who fear him

CONFORM* (CONFORMED CONFORMITY CONFORMS)

Ro 12: 2 Do not c any longer to the pattern
1Pe 1: 14 do not c to the evil desires you had

CONFORMED* (CONFORM)

Eze 5: 7 c to the standards of the nations
11: 12 but have c to the standards
Ro 8: 29 predestined to be c to the likeness

CONFORMITY* (CONFORM)

Eph 1: 11 in c with the purpose of his will,

CONFORMS* (CONFORM)

1Ti 1: 11 to the sound doctrine that c

CONQUEROR* (CONQUERORS)

Mic 1: 15 I will bring a c against you
Rev 6: 2 he rode out as a c bent on conquest.

CONQUERORS (CONQUEROR)

Ro 8: 37 than c through him who loved us.

CONSCIENCE* (CONSCIENCE-STRICKEN CONSCIENCES CONSCIENTIOUS)

Ge 20: 5 I have done this with a clear c
20: 6 I know you did this with a clear c,
1Sa 25: 31 have on his c the staggering burden
Job 27: 6 my c will not reproach me as long

CONSIDERATE (continued)

Ac 23: 1 to God in all good c to this day."
24: 16 to keep my c clear before God
Ro 9: 1 my c confirms it in the Holy Spirit
13: 5 punishment but also because of c.
1Co 4: 4 My c is clear, but that does not
8: 7 since their c is weak, it is defiled.
8: 10 with a weak c sees you who have
8: 12 in this way and wound their weak c
10: 25 without raising questions of c,
10: 27 you without raising questions of c.
10: 28 man who told me and for c' sake—
10: 29 freedom be judged by another's c?
10: 29 the other man's c, I mean,
2Co 1: 12 Our c testifies that we have
4: 2 to every man's c in the sight of God
5: 11 and I hope it is also plain to your c.
1Ti 1: 5 and a good c and a sincere faith.
1: 19 holding on to faith and a good c.
3: 9 truths of the faith with a clear c.
2Ti 1: 3 as my forefathers did, with a clear c
Heb 9: 9 able to clear the c of the worshiper.
10: 22 to cleanse us from a guilty c
13: 18 We are sure that we have a clear c
1Pe 3: 16 and respect, keeping a clear c,
3: 21 the pledge of a good c toward God.

CONSCIENCE-STRICKEN* (CONSCIENCE)

1Sa 24: 5 David was c for having cut
2Sa 24: 10 David was c after he had counted

CONSCIENCES* (CONSCIENCE)

Ro 2: 15 their c also bearing witness,
1Ti 4: 2 whose c have been seared
Tit 1: 15 their minds and c are corrupted.
Heb 9: 14 cleanse our c from acts that lead

CONSCIENTIOUS* (CONSCIENCE)

2Ch 29: 34 for the Levites had been more c

CONSCIOUS*

Ro 3: 20 through the law we become c of sin
1Pe 2: 19 of unjust suffering because he is c

CONSECRATE (CONSECRATED)

Ex 13: 2 "C to me every firstborn male.
40: 9 c it and all its furnishings,
Lev 20: 7 "C yourselves and be holy,
25: 10 C the fiftieth year and proclaim
1Ch 15: 12 fellow Levites are to c yourselves

CONSECRATED (CONSECRATE)

Ex 29: 43 and the place will be c by my glory.
Lev 8: 30 So he c Aaron and his garments
2Ch 7: 16 c this temple so that my Name may
Lk 2: 23 is to be c to the Lord"),
1Ti 4: 5 because it is c by the word of God

CONSENT

1Co 7: 5 except by mutual c and for a time,

CONSIDER (CONSIDERATE CONSIDERED CONSIDERS)

1Sa 12: 24 c what great things he has done
16: 7 "Do not c his appearance
2Ch 19: 6 "C carefully what you do,
Job 37: 14 stop and c God's wonders.
Ps 8: 3 When I c your heavens,
77: 12 and c all your mighty deeds.
107: 43 and c the great love of the LORD.
143: 5 and c what your hands have done.
Pr 6: 6 its ways and be wise!
20: 25 and only later to c his vows.
Ecc 7: 13 C what God has done:
Lk 12: 24 C the ravens: They do not sow
12: 27 about the rest? "C how the lilies
Php 2: 3 but in humility c others better
3: 8 I c everything a loss compared
Heb 10: 24 And let us c how we may spur one
Jas 1: 2 C it pure joy, my brothers,

CONSIDERATE* (CONSIDER)

Tit 3: 2 to be peaceable and c,
Jas 3: 17 then peace-loving, c, submissive,
1Pe 2: 18 only to those who are good and c,
3: 7 in the same way be c as you live

CONSIDERED (CONSIDER)

Job 1: 8 "Have you *c* my servant Job?
      2: 3 "Have you *c* my servant Job?
Ps 44:22 we are *c* as sheep to be slaughtered.
Isa 53: 4 yet we *c* him stricken by God,
Ro 8:36 we are *c* as sheep to be slaughtered

CONSIDERS (CONSIDER)

Pr 31:16 She a *c* field and buys it;
Ro 14: 5 One man *c* one day more sacred
Jas 1:26 If anyone *c* himself religious

CONSIST (CONSISTS)

Lk 12:15 a man's life does not *c*

CONSISTS (CONSIST)

Eph 5: 9 fruit of the light *c* in all goodness,

CONSOLATION

Ps 94:19 your *c* brought joy to my soul.

CONSPIRE

Ps 2: 1 Why do the nations *c*

CONSTANT

Dt 28:66 You will live in *c* suspense,
Pr 19:13 wife is like a *c* dripping.
      27:15 a *c* dripping on a rainy day;
Ac 27:33 "you have been in *c* suspense
Heb 5:14 by *c* use have trained themselves

CONSTRUCTIVE*

1Co 10:23 but not everything is *c*.

CONSULT

Pr 15:12 he will not *c* the wise.
Gal 1:16 I did not *c* any man, nor did I go up

CONSUME (CONSUMES CONSUMING)

Jn 2:17 "Zeal for your house will *c* me."

CONSUMES (CONSUME)

Ps 69: 9 for zeal for your house *c* me,

CONSUMING (CONSUME)

Dt 4:24 For the LORD your God is a *c* fire,
Heb 12:29 and awe, for our "God is a *c* fire."

CONTAIN* (CONTAINED CONTAINS)

1Ki 8:27 the highest heaven, cannot *c* you.
2Ch 2: 6 the highest heavens, cannot *c* him?
      6:18 the highest heavens, cannot *c* you.
Ecc 8: 8 power over the wind to *c* it;
2Pe 3:16 His letters *c* some things that are

CONTAINED (CONTAIN)

Heb 9: 4 This ark *c* the gold jar of manna,

CONTAINS (CONTAIN)

Pr 15: 6 of the righteous *c* great treasure,

CONTAMINATES*

2Co 7: 1 from everything that *c* body

CONTEMPT

Pr 14:31 He who oppresses the poor shows *c*
      17: 5 He who mocks the poor shows *c*
      18: 3 When wickedness comes, so does *c*
Da 12: 2 others to shame and everlasting *c*.
Mal 1: 6 O priests, who show *c* for my name.
Ro 2: 4 Or do you show *c* for the riches
Gal 4:14 you did not treat me with *c*
1Th 5:20 do not treat prophecies with *c*.

CONTEND (CONTENDED CONTENDING CONTENTIOUS)

Ge 6: 3 "My Spirit will not *c*
Ps 35: 1 *C*, O LORD, with those who
Isa 49:25 I will *c* with those who *c* with you,
Jude : 3 you to *c* for the faith that was once

CONTENDED (CONTEND)

Php 4: 3 help these women who have *c*

CONTENDING* (CONTEND)

Php 1:27 *c* as one man for the faith

CONTENT* (CONTENTMENT)

Jos 7: 7 If only we had been *c* to stay
Pr 13:25 The righteous eat to their hearts' *c*,
      19:23 one rests *c*, untouched by trouble.
Ecc 4: 8 yet his eyes were not *c*
Lk 3:14 don't accuse people falsely—be *c*
Php 4:11 to be *c* whatever the circumstances
      4:12 I have learned the secret of being *c*
1Ti 6: 8 and clothing, we will be *c* with that.
Heb 13: 5 and be *c* with what you have,

CONTENTIOUS* (CONTEND)

1Co 11:16 If anyone wants to be *c* about this,

CONTENTMENT* (CONTENT)

Job 36:11 and their years in *c*.
SS 8:10 like one bringing *c*.
1Ti 6: 6 But godliness with *c* is great gain.

CONTEST*

Heb 10:32 in a great *c* in the face of suffering.

CONTINUAL (CONTINUE)

Pr 15:15 but the cheerful heart has a *c* feast.
Eph 4:19 of impurity, with a *c* lust for more.

CONTINUE (CONTINUAL CONTINUES CONTINUING)

1Ki 8:23 servants who *c* wholeheartedly
2Ch 6:14 servants who *c* wholeheartedly
Ps 36:10 *C* your love to those who know you
Ac 13:43 urged them to *c* in the grace of God
Ro 11:22 provided that you *c* in his kindness.
Gal 3:10 Cursed is everyone who does not *c*
Php 2:12 *c* to work out your salvation
Col 1:23 if you *c* in your faith, established
      2: 6 received Christ Jesus as Lord, *c*
1Ti 2:15 if they *c* in faith, love and holiness
2Ti 3:14 *c* in what you have learned
1Jn 2:28 And now, dear children, *c* in him,
      3: 9 born of God will *c* to sin,
      5:18 born of God does not *c* to sin;
2Jn : 9 and does not *c* in the teaching
Rev 22:11 and let him who is holy *c* to be holy
      22:11 let him who does right *c* to do right;

CONTINUES (CONTINUE)

Ps 100: 5 *c* through all generations.
    119:90 Your faithfulness *c*
2Co 10:15 Our hope is that, as your faith *c*
1Jn 3: 6 No one who *c* to sin has

CONTINUING (CONTINUE)

Ro 13: 8 the *c* debt to love one another,

CONTRIBUTION (CONTRIBUTIONS)

Ro 15:26 pleased to make a *c* for the poor

CONTRIBUTIONS (CONTRIBUTION)

2Ch 24:10 all the people brought their *c* gladly
      31:12 they faithfully brought in the *c*.

CONTRITE*

Ps 51:17 a broken and *c* heart,
Isa 57:15 also with him who is *c* and lowly
      57:15 and to revive the heart of the *c*.
      66: 2 he who is humble and *c* in spirit,

CONTROL (CONTROLLED CONTROLS SELF-CONTROL SELF-CONTROLLED)

Pr 29:11 a wise man keeps himself under *c*.
1Co 7: 9 But if they cannot *c* themselves,
      7:37 but has *c* over his own will,
1Th 4: 4 you should learn to *c* his own body

CONTROLLED (CONTROL)

Ps 32: 9 but must be *c* by bit and bridle
Ro 8: 6 but the mind *c* by the Spirit is life
      8: 8 Those *c* by the sinful nature cannot

CONTROLS* (CONTROL)

Job 37:15 you know how God *c* the clouds
Pr 16:32 a man who *c* his temper

CONTROVERSIES*

Ac 26: 3 with all the Jewish customs and *c*.
1Ti 1: 4 These promote *c* rather
      6: 4 He has an unhealthy interest in *c*

CONVERSATION

Col 4: 6 Let your *c* be always full of grace,

Tit 3: 9 But avoid foolish *c* and genealogies

CONVERT

1Ti 3: 6 He must not be a recent *c*,

CONVICT (CONVICTION)

Pr 24:25 with those who *c* the guilty,
Jn 16: 8 he will *c* the world of guilt in regard
Jude :15 and to *c* all the ungodly

CONVICTION* (CONVICT)

1Th 1: 5 the Holy Spirit and with deep *c*.

CONVINCE* (CONVINCED CONVINCING)

Ac 28:23 and tried to *c* them about Jesus

CONVINCED* (CONVINCE)

Ge 45:28 "I'm *c!* My son Joseph is still alive.
Lk 16:31 will not be *c* even if someone rises
Ac 19:26 and hear how this fellow Paul has *c*
      26: 9 "I too was *c* that I ought
      26:26 I am *c* that none of this has escaped
      28:24 Some were *c* by what he said,
Ro 2:19 if you are *c* that you are a guide
      8:38 For I am *c* that neither death
      14: 5 Each one should be fully *c*
      14:14 I am fully *c* that no food is unclean
      15:14 I myself am *c*, my brothers,
1Co 14:24 he will be *c* by all that he is a sinner
2Co 5:14 we are *c* that one died for all,
Php 1:25 *C* of this, I know that I will remain,
2Ti 1:12 and am *c* that he is able
      3:14 have learned and have become *c*

CONVINCING* (CONVINCE)

Ac 1: 3 and gave many *c* proofs that he was

COOLNESS*

Pr 25:13 Like the *c* of snow at harvest time

COPIES (COPY)

Heb 9:23 for the *c* of the heavenly things

COPY (COPIES)

Dt 17:18 for himself on a scroll a *c* of this law
Heb 8: 5 They serve at a sanctuary that is a *c*
      9:24 sanctuary that was only a *c*

CORBAN*

Mk 7:11 received from me is *C*' (that is,

CORD (CORDS)

Jos 2:18 you have tied this scarlet *c*
Ecc 4:12 *c* of three strands is not quickly

CORDS (CORD)

Pr 5:22 the *c* of his sin hold him fast.
Isa 54: 2 lengthen your *c*,
Hos 11: 4 them with *c* of human kindness,

CORINTH

Ac 18: 1 Paul left Athens and went to *C*.
1Co 1: 2 To the church of God in *C*,
2Co 1: 1 To the church of God in *C*,

CORNELIUS*

Roman to whom Peter preached; first Gentile Christian (Ac 10).

CORNER (CORNERS)

Ru 3: 9 "Spread the *c* of your garment
Pr 21: 9 Better to live on a *c* of the roof
      25:24 Better to live on a *c* of the roof
Ac 26:26 because it was not done in a *c*.

CORNERS (CORNER)

Mt 6: 5 on the street *c* to be seen by men.
      22: 9 Go to the street *c* and invite

CORNERSTONE* (STONE)

Job 38: 6 or who laid its *c*—
Isa 28:16 a precious *c* for a sure foundation;
Jer 51:26 rock will be taken from you for a *c*,
Zec 10: 4 From Judah will come the *c*,
Eph 2:20 Christ Jesus himself as the chief *c*.

1Pe 2: 6 a chosen and precious *c*,

CORRECT* (CORRECTED CORRECTING CORRECTION CORRECTIONS CORRECTS)

Job 6: 26 Do you mean to *c* what I say,
40: 2 contends with the Almighty *c* him?
Jer 10: 24 *C* me, Lord, but only with justice
2Ti 4: 2 *c*, rebuke and encourage—

CORRECTED* (CORRECT)

Pr 29: 19 A servant cannot be *c*

CORRECTING* (CORRECT)

2Ti 3: 16 *c* and training in righteousness,

CORRECTION* (CORRECT)

Lev 26: 23 things you do not accept my *c*
Job 36: 10 He makes them listen to *c*
Pr 5: 12 How my heart spurned *c!*
10: 17 whoever ignores *c* leads others
12: 1 but he who hates *c* is stupid.
13: 18 but whoever heeds *c* is honored.
15: 5 whoever heeds *c* shows prudence.
15: 10 he who hates *c* will die.
15: 12 A mocker resents *c;*
15: 32 whoever heeds *c* gains
29: 15 The rod of *c* imparts wisdom,
Jer 2: 30 they did not respond to *c*.
5: 3 crushed them, but they refused *c*.
7: 28 Lord its God or responded to *c*.
Zep 3: 2 she accepts no *c*.
3: 7 you will fear me / and accept *c!*'

CORRECTIONS* (CORRECT)

Pr 6: 23 and the *c* of discipline

CORRECTS* (CORRECT)

Job 5: 17 ''Blessed is the man whom God *c;*
Pr 9: 7 Whoever *c* a mocker invites insult;

CORRUPT (CORRUPTED CORRUPTION CORRUPTS)

Ge 6: 11 Now the earth was *c* in God's sight
Ps 14: 1 They are *c*, their deeds are vile;
14: 3 They have together become *c;*
Pr 4: 24 keep *c* talk far from your lips.
6: 12 who goes about with a *c* mouth,
19: 28 A *c* witness mocks at justice,

CORRUPTED (CORRUPT)

2Co 7: 2 wronged no one, we have *c* no one,
Tit 1: 15 but to those who are *c* and do not

CORRUPTION (CORRUPT)

2Pe 1: 4 escape the *c* in the world caused
2: 20 If they have escaped the *c*

CORRUPTS* (CORRUPT)

Ecc 7: 7 and a bribe *c* the heart.
1Co 15: 33 ''Bad company *c* good character.''
Jas 3: 6 It *c* the whole person, sets

COST (COSTS)

Nu 16: 38 sinned at the *c* of their lives.
Pr 4: 7 Though it *c* all you have, get
7: 23 little knowing it will *c* him his life.
Isa 55: 1 milk without money and without *c*.
Lk 14: 28 and estimate the *c* to see
Rev 21: 6 to drink without *c* from the spring

COSTS (COST)

Pr 6: 31 it *c* him all the wealth of his house.

COUNCIL

Ps 89: 7 In the *c* of the holy ones God is
107: 32 and praise him in the *c* of the elders

COUNSEL (COUNSELOR COUNSELS)

1Ki 22: 5 ''First seek the *c* of the Lord.''
2Ch 18: 4 ''First seek the *c* of the Lord.''
Job 38: 2 ''Who is this that darkens my *c*
42: 3 'Who is this that obscures my *c*
Ps 1: 1 walk in the *c* of the wicked
73: 24 You guide me with your *c*,
107: 11 despised the *c* of the Most High.
Pr 8: 14 *C* and sound judgment are mine;
15: 22 Plans fail for lack of *c*,
27: 9 from his earnest *c*.

Isa 28: 29 wonderful in *c* and magnificent
1Ti 5: 14 So I *c* younger widows to marry,
Rev 3: 18 I *c* you to buy from me gold refined

COUNSELOR (COUNSEL)

Isa 9: 6 Wonderful *C*, Mighty God,
Jn 14: 16 he will give you another *C* to be
14: 26 But the *C*, the Holy Spirit,
15: 26 ''When the *C* comes, whom I will
16: 7 the *C* will not come to you;
Ro 11: 34 Or who has been his *c?*''

COUNSELS (COUNSEL)

Ps 16: 7 I will praise the Lord, who *c* me;

COUNT (COUNTED COUNTING COUNTS)

Ps 22: 17 I can *c* all my bones;
Ro 4: 8 whose sin the Lord will never *c*
6: 11 *c* yourselves dead to sin
2Th 1: 11 that our God may *c* you worthy

COUNTED (COUNT)

Ac 5: 41 because they had been *c* worthy
2Th 1: 5 and as a result you will be *c* worthy

COUNTERFEIT*

2Th 2: 9 displayed in all kinds of *c* miracles,
1Jn 2: 27 not *c*—just as it has taught you,

COUNTING (COUNT)

2Co 5: 19 not *c* men's sins against them.

COUNTRY

Pr 28: 2 When a *c* is rebellious, it has many
29: 4 By justice a king gives a *c* stability,
Isa 66: 8 Can a *c* be born in a day
Lk 15: 13 off for a distant *c* and there
Jn 4: 44 prophet has no honor in his own *c*.)
2Co 11: 26 in danger in the *c*, in danger at sea;
Heb 11: 14 looking for a *c* of their own.

COUNTRYMEN

2Co 11: 26 danger from my own *c*, in danger

COUNTS (COUNT)

Jn 6: 63 The Spirit gives life; the flesh *c*
1Co 7: 19 God's commands is what *c*.
Gal 5: 6 only thing that *c* is faith expressing

COURAGE* (COURAGEOUS)

Jos 2: 11 everyone's *c* failed because of you,
5: 1 and they no longer had the *c*
2Sa 4: 1 he lost *c*, and all Israel became
7: 27 So your servant has found *c*
1Ch 17: 25 So your servant has found *c* to pray
2Ch 15: 8 son of Oded the prophet, he took *c*,
19: 11 Act with *c*, and may the Lord be
Ezr 7: 28 I took *c* and gathered leading men
10: 4 We will support you, so take *c*
Ps 107: 26 in their peril their *c* melted away.
Eze 22: 14 Will your *c* endure or your hands
Da 11: 25 and *c* against the king of the South.
Mt 14: 27 said to them: ''Take *c!*
Mk 6: 50 spoke to them and said, ''Take *c!*
Ac 4: 13 When they saw the *c* of Peter
23: 11 ''Take *c!* As you have testified
27: 22 now I urge you to keep up your *c*,
27: 25 So keep up your *c*, men,
1Co 16: 13 stand firm in the faith; be men of *c;*
Php 1: 20 will have sufficient *c* so that now
Heb 3: 6 if we hold on to our *c* and the hope

COURAGEOUS* (COURAGE)

Dt 31: 6 Be strong and *c*.
31: 7 of all Israel, ''Be strong and *c*,
31: 23 son of Nun: ''Be strong and *c*,
Jos 1: 6 Be strong and *c*, because you will lead these
1: 7 Be strong and very *c*,
1: 9 commanded you? Be strong and *c!*'
1: 18 Only be strong and *c!*''
10: 25 Be strong and *c*.
1Ch 22: 13 Be strong and *c*.
28: 20 ''Be strong and *c*, and do the work.
2Ch 26: 17 priest with eighty other *c* priests
32: 7 with these words: ''Be strong and *c*,

COURSE

Ps 19: 5 a champion rejoicing to run his *c*.
Pr 2: 8 for he guards the *c* of the just
15: 21 of understanding keeps a straight *c*.
16: 9 In his heart a man plans his *c*,
17: 23 to pervert the *c* of justice.
Jas 3: 6 sets the whole *c* of his life on fire,

COURT (COURTS)

Pr 22: 22 and do not crush the needy in *c*,
25: 8 do not bring hastily to *c*,
Mt 5: 25 adversary who is taking you to *c*.
1Co 4: 3 judged by you or by any human *c;*

COURTS (COURT)

Ps 84: 10 Better is one day in your *c*
100: 4 and his *c* with praise.
Am 5: 15 maintain justice in the *c*.
Zec 8: 16 and sound judgment in your *c;*

COURTYARD

Ex 27: 9 ''Make a *c* for the tabernacle.

COUSIN

Col 4: 10 as does Mark, the *c* of Barnabas.

COVENANT (COVENANTS)

Ge 9: 9 ''I now establish my *c* with you
17: 2 I will confirm my *c* between me
Ex 19: 5 if you obey me fully and keep my *c*,
24: 7 Then he took the Book of the *C*
Dt 4: 13 declared to you his *c*, the Ten
29: 1 in addition to the *c* he had made
Jdg 2: 1 'I will never break my *c* with you,
1Sa 23: 18 of them made a *c* before the Lord
1Ki 8: 21 in which is the *c* of the Lord that
8: 23 you who keep your *c* of love
2Ki 23: 2 the words of the Book of the *C*,
1Ch 16: 15 He remembers his *c* forever,
2Ch 6: 14 you who keep your *c* of love
34: 30 the words of the Book of the *C*,
Ne 1: 5 who keeps his *c* of love
Job 31: 1 ''I made a *c* with my eyes
Ps 105: 8 He remembers his *c* forever,
Pr 2: 17 ignored the *c* she made before God
Isa 42: 6 you to be a *c* for the people
61: 8 make an everlasting *c* with them.
Jer 11: 2 ''Listen to the terms of this *c*
31: 31 ''when I will make a new *c*
31: 32 It will not be like the *c*
31: 33 ''This is the *c* I will make
Eze 37: 26 I will make a *c* of peace with them;
Da 9: 27 He will confirm a *c* with many
Hos 6: 7 Like Adam, they have broken the *c*
Mal 2: 14 the wife of your marriage *c*.
3: 1 of the *c*, whom you desire,
Mt 26: 28 blood of the *c*, which is poured out
Mk 14: 24 ''This is my blood of the *c*,
Lk 22: 20 ''This cup is the new *c* in my blood,
1Co 11: 25 ''This cup is the new *c* in my blood;
2Co 3: 6 as ministers of a new *c*—
Gal 4: 24 one *c* is from Mount Sinai
Heb 8: 6 as the *c* of which he is mediator is
8: 8 when I will make a new *c*
9: 15 Christ is the mediator of a new *c*,
12: 24 to Jesus the mediator of a new *c*,

COVENANTS (COVENANT)

Ro 9: 4 theirs the divine glory, the *c*,
Gal 4: 24 for the women represent two *c*.

COVER (COVER-UP COVERED COVERING COVERINGS COVERS)

Ex 25: 17 ''Make an atonement *c* of pure gold
25: 21 Place the *c* on top of the ark
33: 22 and *c* you with my hand
Lev 16: 2 in the cloud over the atonement *c*.
Ps 32: 5 and did not *c* up my iniquity.
91: 4 He will *c* you with his feathers,
Hos 10: 8 say to the mountains, ''*C* us!''
Lk 23: 30 and to the hills, ''*C* us!'' '
1Co 11: 6 If a woman does not *c* her head,
11: 6 shaved off, she should *c* her head,
11: 7 A man ought not to *c* his head,
Jas 5: 20 and *c* over a multitude of sins.

COVER-UP* (COVER)

1Pe 2: 16 but do not use your freedom as a *c*

COVERED (COVER)

Ps 32: 1 whose sins are c.
85: 2 and c all their sins.
Isa 6: 2 With two wings they c their faces,
51: 16 c you with the shadow of my hand
Ro 4: 7 whose sins are c.
1Co 11: 4 with his head c dishonors his head.

COVERING (COVER)

1Co 11: 15 For long hair is given to her as a c.

COVERINGS (COVER)

Ge 3: 7 and made c for themselves.
Pr 31: 22 She makes c for her bed;

COVERS (COVER)

Pr 10: 12 but love c over all wrongs.
17: 9 He who c over an offense promotes
2Co 3: 15 Moses is read, a veil c their hearts.
1Pe 4: 8 love c over a multitude of sins.

COVET* (COVETED COVETING COVETOUS)

Ex 20: 17 You shall not c your neighbor's
20: 17 "You shall not c your neighbor's
34: 24 and no one will c your land
Dt 5: 21 "You shall not c your neighbor's
7: 25 Do not c the silver and gold
Mic 2: 2 They c fields and seize them,
Ro 7: 7 if the law had not said, "Do not c."
13: 9 "Do not steal," "Do not c,"
Jas 4: 2 c, but you cannot have what you

COVETED* (COVET)

Jos 7: 21 weighing fifty shekels, I c them
Ac 20: 33 I have not c anyone's silver or gold

COVETING

Ro 7: 7 what c really was if the law

COVETOUS* (COVET)

Ro 7: 8 in me every kind of c desire.

COWARDLY*

Rev 21: 8 But the c, the unbelieving, the vile,

COWS

Ge 41: 2 of the river there came up seven c,
Ex 25: 5 skins dyed red and hides of sea c,
Nu 4: 6 are to cover this with hides of sea c,
1Sa 6: 7 Hitch the c to the cart,

CRAFTINESS* (CRAFTY)

Job 5: 13 He catches the wise in their c,
1Co 3: 19 "He catches the wise in their c";
Eph 4: 14 and c of men in their deceitful

CRAFTSMAN

Pr 8: 30 Then I was the c at his side.

CRAFTY* (CRAFTINESS)

Ge 3: 1 the serpent was more c than any
1Sa 23: 22 They tell me he is very c.
Job 5: 12 He thwarts the plans of the c,
15: 5 you adopt the tongue of the c.
Pr 7: 10 like a prostitute and with c intent.
12: 2 but the LORD condemns a c man.
14: 17 and a c man is hated.
2Co 12: 16 c fellow that I am, I caught you

CRAVE* (CRAVED CRAVES CRAVING CRAVINGS)

Nu 11: 4 with them began to c other food,
Dt 12: 20 you c meat and say, "I would like
Pr 23: 3 Do not c his delicacies,
23: 6 do not c his delicacies;
31: 4 not for rulers to c beer,
Mic 7: 1 none of the early figs that I c.
1Pe 2: 2 newborn babies, c pure spiritual

CRAVED* (CRAVE)

Nu 11: 34 the people who had c other food.
Ps 78: 18 by demanding the food they c.
78: 29 for he had given them what they c,
78: 30 turned from the food they c,

CRAVES* (CRAVE)

Pr 13: 4 The sluggard c and gets nothing,

Pr 21: 10 The wicked man c evil;
21: 26 All day long he c for more,

CRAVING* (CRAVE)

Job 20: 20 he will have no respite from his c;
Ps 106: 14 In the desert they gave in to their c;
Pr 10: 3 but he thwarts the c of the wicked.
13: 2 the unfaithful have a c for violence.
21: 25 The sluggard's c will be the death
Jer 2: 24 sniffing the wind in her c—

CRAVINGS* (CRAVE)

Ps 10: 3 He boasts of the c of his heart;
Eph 2: 3 gratifying the c of our sinful nature
1Jn 2: 16 in the world—the c of sinful man,

CRAWL

Ge 3: 14 You will c on your belly

CREATE* (CREATED CREATES CREATING CREATION CREATOR)

Ps 51: 10 C in me a pure heart, O God,
Isa 4: 5 Then the LORD will c over all
45: 7 I bring prosperity and c disaster;
45: 7 I form the light and c darkness,
45: 18 he did not c it to be empty,
65: 17 "Behold, I will c / new heavens
65: 18 for I will c Jerusalem to be a delight
65: 18 forever in what I will c,
Jer 31: 22 The LORD will c a new thing
Mal 2: 10 one Father? Did not one God c us?
Eph 2: 15 His purpose was to c

CREATED* (CREATE)

Ge 1: 1 In the beginning God c the heavens
1: 21 God c the great creatures of the sea
1: 27 So God c man in his own image,
1: 27 in the image of God he c him;
1: 27 male and female he c them.
2: 4 and the earth when they were c.
5: 1 When God c man, he made him
5: 2 He c them male and female;
5: 2 when they were c, he called them
6: 7 whom I have c, from the face
Dt 4: 32 from the day God c man
Ps 89: 12 You c the north and the south;
89: 47 what futility you have c all men!
102: 18 a people not yet c may praise
104: 30 you send your Spirit, / they are c,
139: 13 For you c my inmost being;
148: 5 for he commanded and they were c
Isa 40: 26 Who c all these?
41: 20 that the Holy One of Israel has c it.
42: 5 he who c the heavens and stretched
43: 1 he who c you, O Jacob,
43: 7 whom I c for my glory,
45: 8 I, the LORD, have c it.
45: 12 and c mankind upon it.
45: 18 he who c the heavens,
48: 7 They are c now, and not long ago;
54: 16 And it is I who have c the destroyer
54: 16 "See, it is I who c the blacksmith
57: 16 the breath of man that I have c."
Eze 21: 30 In the place where you were c,
28: 13 the day you were c they were
28: 15 ways from the day you were c
Mk 13: 19 when God c the world, until now—
Ro 1: 25 and served c things rather
1Co 11: 9 neither was man c for woman,
Eph 2: 10 c in Christ Jesus to do good works,
3: 9 hidden in God, who c all things.
4: 24 c to be like God in true
Col 1: 16 For by him all things were c:
1: 16 all things were c by him
1Ti 4: 3 which God c to be received
4: 4 For everything God c is good,
Heb 12: 27 c things—so that what cannot be
Jas 1: 18 a kind of firstfruits of all he c.
Rev 4: 11 and by your will they were c
4: 11 for you c all things,
10: 6 who c the heavens and all that is

CREATES* (CREATE)

Am 4: 13 c the wind,

CREATING* (CREATE)

Ge 2: 3 the work of c that he had done.
Isa 57: 19 c praise on the lips of the mourners

CREATION* (CREATE)

Hab 2: 18 he who makes it trusts in his own c;
Mt 13: 35 hidden since the c of the world."
25: 34 for you since the c of the world.
Mk 10: 6 of c God 'made them male
16: 15 and preach the good news to all c.
Jn 17: 24 me before the c of the world.
Ro 1: 20 For since the c of the world God's
8: 19 The c waits in eager expectation
8: 20 For the c was subjected
8: 21 in hope that the c itself will be
8: 22 that the whole c has been groaning
8: 39 depth, nor anything else in all c,
2Co 5: 17 he is a new c; the old has gone,
Gal 6: 15 anything; what counts is a new c.
Eph 1: 4 us in him before the c of the world
Col 1: 15 God, the firstborn over all c.
Heb 4: 3 finished since the c of the world.
4: 13 Nothing in all c is hidden
9: 11 that is to say, not a part of this c.
9: 26 times since the c of the world.
1Pe 1: 20 chosen before the c of the world,
2Pe 3: 4 as it has since the beginning of c."
Rev 3: 14 true witness, the ruler of God's c.
13: 8 slain from the c of the world.
17: 8 life from the c of the world will be

CREATOR* (CREATE)

Ge 14: 19 C of heaven and earth.
14: 22 God Most High, C of heaven
Dt 32: 6 Is he not your Father, your C,
Ecc 12: 1 Remember your C
Isa 27: 11 and their C shows them no favor.
40: 28 the C of the ends of the earth.
43: 15 Israel's C, your King."
Mt 19: 4 the beginning the C 'made them
Ro 1: 25 created things rather than the C—
Col 3: 10 in knowledge in the image of its C.
1Pe 4: 19 themselves to their faithful C

CREATURE (CREATURES)

Lev 17: 11 For the life of a c is in the blood,
17: 14 the life of every c is its blood.
Ps 136: 25 and who gives food to every c.
Eze 1: 15 beside each c with its four faces.
Rev 4: 7 The first living c was like a lion,

CREATURES (CREATURE)

Ge 6: 19 bring into the ark two of all living c,
8: 21 again will I destroy all living c,
Ps 104: 24 the earth is full of your c.
Eze 1: 5 was what looked like four living c.

CREDIT (CREDITED CREDITOR CREDITS)

Lk 6: 33 what c is that to you? Even
Ro 4: 24 to whom God will c righteousness
1Pe 2: 20 it to your c if you receive a beating

CREDITED (CREDIT)

Ge 15: 6 and he c it to him as righteousness.
Ps 106: 31 This was c to him as righteousness
Eze 18: 20 of the righteous man will be c
Ro 4: 3 and it was c to him as righteousness
4: 4 his wages are not c to him as a gift,
4: 5 his faith is c as righteousness.
4: 9 saying that Abraham's faith was c
4: 23 The words "it was c
Gal 3: 6 and it was c to him as righteousness
Php 4: 17 for what may be c to your account.
Jas 2: 23 and it was c to him as righteousness

CREDITOR (CREDIT)

Dt 15: 2 Every c shall cancel the loan he has

CREDITS (CREDIT)

Ro 4: 6 whom God c righteousness apart

CRETANS (CRETE)

Tit 1: 12 "C are always liars, evil brutes,

CRETE (CRETANS)

Ac 27: 12 harbor in C, facing both southwest

CRIED (CRY)

Ex 2: 23 groaned in their slavery and c out,
14: 10 They were terrified and c out
Nu 20: 16 but when we c out to the LORD,

Jos 24: 7 But they c to the LORD for help,
Jdg 3: 9 But when they c out to the LORD,
3: 15 Again the Israelites c out
4: 3 they c to the LORD for help.
6: 6 the Israelites that they c out
10: 12 Maonites oppressed you and you c
1Sa 7: 9 He c out to the LORD
12: 8 they c out to the LORD for help,
12: 10 They c out to the LORD and said,
Ps 18: 6 I c to my God for help.

CRIMINALS

Lk 23: 32 both c, were also led out with him

CRIMSON

Isa 1: 18 though they are red as c,
63: 1 with his garments stained c?

CRIPPLED

2Sa 9: 3 of Jonathan; he is c in both feet.''
Mk 9: 45 better for you to enter life c

CRISIS*

1Co 7: 26 of the present c, I think that it is

CRITICISM*

2Co 8: 20 We want to avoid any c

CROOKED*

Dt 32: 5 but a warped and c generation.
2Sa 22: 27 to the c you show yourself shrewd.
Ps 18: 26 to the c you show yourself shrewd.
125: ¶ But those who turn to c ways
Pr 2: 15 whose paths are c
5: 6 her paths are c, but she knows it
8: 8 none of them is c or perverse.
10: 9 he who takes c paths will be found
Ecc 7: 13 what he has made c?
Isa 59: 8 have turned them into c roads;
La 3: 9 he has made my paths c.
Lk 3: 5 The c roads shall become straight,
Php 2: 15 children of God without fault in a c

CROP (CROPS)

Mt 13: 8 where it produced a c— a hundred,
21: 41 share of the c at harvest time.''

CROPS (CROP)

Pr 3: 9 with the firstfruits of all your c;
10: 5 He who gathers c in summer is
28: 3 like a driving rain that leaves no c.
2Ti 2: 6 the first to receive a share of the c.

CROSS (CROSSED CROSSING)

Dt 4: 21 swore that I would not c the Jordan
12: 10 But you will c the Jordan
Mt 10: 38 and anyone who does not take his c
16: 24 and take up his c and follow me.
Mk 8: 34 and take up his c and follow me.
Lk 9: 23 take up his c daily and follow me.
14: 27 anyone who does not carry his c
Jn 19: 17 Carrying his own c, he went out
Ac 2: 23 to death by nailing him to the c.
1Co 1: 17 lest the c of Christ be emptied
1: 18 the message of the c is foolishness
Gal 5: 11 offense of the c has been abolished.
6: 12 persecuted for the c of Christ.
6: 14 in the c of our Lord Jesus Christ,
Eph 2: 16 both of them to God through the c,
Php 2: 8 even death on a c!
3: 18 as enemies of the c of Christ.
Col 1: 20 through his blood, shed on the c.
2: 14 he took it away, nailing it to the c.
2: 15 triumphing over them by the c.
Heb 12: 2 set before him endured the c,

CROSSED (CROSS)

Jos 4: 7 When it c the Jordan, the waters
Jn 5: 24 he has c over from death to life.

CROSSING (CROSS)

Ge 48: 14 he was the younger, and c his arms,

CROSSROADS (ROAD)

Jer 6: 16 ''Stand at the c and look;

CROUCHING

Ge 4: 7 sin is c at your door; it desires

CROWD (CROWDS)

Ex 23: 2 Do not follow the c in doing wrong.

CROWDS (CROWD)

Mt 9: 36 he saw the c, he had compassion

CROWED (CROWS)

Mt 26: 74 the man!'' Immediately a rooster c.

CROWN (CROWNED CROWNS)

Pr 4: 9 present you with a c of splendor.''
10: 6 Blessings c the head
12: 4 noble character is her husband's c,
16: 31 Gray hair is a c of splendor;
17: 6 Children's children are a c
Isa 35: 10 everlasting joy will c their heads.
51: 11 everlasting joy will c their heads.
61: 3 to bestow on them a c of beauty
62: 3 You will be a c of splendor
Eze 16: 12 and a beautiful c on your head.
Zec 9: 16 like jewels in a c.
Mt 27: 29 and then twisted together a c of thorns
Mk 15: 17 then twisted together a c of thorns
Jn 19: 2 The soldiers twisted together a c
19: 5 When Jesus came out wearing the c
1Co 9: 25 it to get a c that will last forever.
9: 25 it to get a c that will not last;
Php 4: 1 and long for, my joy and c,
1Th 2: 19 or the c in which we will glory
2Ti 2: 5 he does not receive the victor's c
4: 8 store for me the c of righteousness.
Jas 1: 12 he will receive the c
1Pe 5: 4 you will receive the c
Rev 2: 10 and I will give you the c of life.
3: 11 so that no one will take your c.
14: 14 a son of man'' with a c of gold

CROWNED* (CROWN)

Ps 8: 5 and c him with glory and honor.
Pr 14: 18 the prudent are c with knowledge.
SS 3: 11 crown with which his mother c him
Heb 2: 7 you c him with glory and honor
2: 9 now c with glory and honor

CROWNS (CROWN)

Ps 103: 4 and c me with love and compassion
149: 4 he c the humble with salvation.
Pr 11: 26 blessing c him who is willing to sell.
Rev 4: 4 and had c of gold on their heads.
4: 10 They lay their c before the throne
12: 3 ten horns and seven c on his heads.
19: 12 and on his head are many c.

CROWS (CROWED)

Mt 26: 34 this very night, before the rooster c

CRUCIFIED* (CRUCIFY)

Mt 20: 19 to be mocked and flogged and c.
26: 2 of Man will be handed over to be c
27: 26 and handed him over to be c.
27: 35 When they had c him, they divided
27: 38 Two robbers were c with him,
27: 44 same way the robbers who were c
28: 5 looking for Jesus, who was c.
Mk 15: 14 and handed him over to be c.
15: 24 And they c him.
15: 25 the third hour when they c him.
15: 27 They c two robbers with him,
15: 32 Those c with him also heaped
16: 6 for Jesus the Nazarene, who was c.
Lk 23: 23 insistently demanded that he be c.
23: 33 c him, along with the criminals—
24: 7 be c and on the third day be raised
24: 20 sentenced to death, and they c him;
Jn 19: 16 him over to them to be c.
19: 18 Here they c him, and with him two
19: 20 for the place where Jesus was c was
19: 23 When the soldiers c Jesus,
19: 32 of the first man who had been c
19: 41 At the place where Jesus was c,
Ac 2: 36 whom you c, both Lord and Christ
4: 10 whom you c but whom God raised
Ro 6: 6 For we know that our old self was c
1Co 1: 13 Is Christ divided? Was Paul c
1: 23 but we preach Christ c: a stumbling
2: 2 except Jesus Christ and him c.
2: 8 they would not have c the Lord
2Co 13: 4 to be sure, he was c in weakness,

Gal 2: 20 I have been c with Christ
3: 1 Christ was clearly portrayed as c.
5: 24 Christ Jesus have c the sinful
6: 14 which the world has been c
Rev 11: 8 where also their Lord was c.

CRUCIFY* (CRUCIFIED CRUCIFYING)

Mt 23: 34 Some of them you will kill and c;
27: 22 They all answered, ''C him!'' ''Why
27: 23 they shouted all the louder, ''C him
27: 31 Then they led him away to c him.
Mk 15: 13 ''C him!'' they shouted.
15: 14 they shouted all the louder, ''C him
15: 20 Then they led him out to c him.
Lk 23: 21 they kept shouting, ''C him! C him
Jn 19: 6 they shouted, ''C! C!''
19: 6 ''You take him and c him.
19: 10 either to free you or to c you?''
19: 15 Crucify him!'' ''Shall I c your king
19: 15 away! Take him away! C him!''

CRUCIFYING* (CRUCIFY)

Heb 6: 6 to their loss they are c the Son

CRUSH (CRUSHED)

Ge 3: 15 he will c your head,
Isa 53: 10 it was the LORD's will to c him
Ro 16: 20 The God of peace will soon c Satan

CRUSHED (CRUSH)

Ps 34: 18 and saves those who are c in spirit.
Pr 17: 22 but a c spirit dries up the bones.
18: 14 but a c spirit who can bear?
Isa 53: 5 he was c for our iniquities;
2Co 4: 8 not c; perplexed, but not in despair;

CRY (CRIED)

Ex 2: 23 c for help because of their slavery
Ps 5: 2 Listen to my c for help,
34: 15 and his ears are attentive to their c;
40: 1 he turned to me and heard my c.
130: 1 Out of the depths I c to you,
Pr 21: 13 to the c of the poor,
La 2: 18 c out to the Lord.
Hab 2: 11 The stones of the wall will c out,
Lk 19: 40 keep quiet, the stones will c out.''

CUNNING

2Co 11: 3 deceived by the serpent's c,
Eph 4: 14 and by the c and craftiness of men

CUP

Ps 23: 5 my c overflows.
Isa 51: 22 from that c, the goblet of my wrath,
51: 22 the c that made you stagger;
Mt 10: 42 if anyone gives even a c of cold water
20: 22 ''Can you drink the c I am going
23: 25 You clean the outside of the c
23: 26 First clean the inside of the c
26: 27 Then he took the c, gave thanks
26: 39 may this c be taken from me.
26: 42 possible for this c to be taken away
Mk 9: 41 anyone who gives you a c of water
10: 38 ''Can you drink the c I drink
10: 39 ''You will drink the c I drink
14: 23 Then he took the c, gave thanks
14: 36 Take this c from me.
Lk 11: 39 Pharisees clean the outside of the c
22: 17 After taking the c, he gave thanks
22: 20 after the supper he took the c,
22: 20 ''This c is the new covenant
22: 42 if you are willing, take this c
Jn 18: 11 I not drink the c the Father has
1Co 10: 16 Is not the c of thanksgiving
10: 21 the c of the Lord and the c
11: 25 after supper he took the c, saying,
11: 25 ''This c is the new covenant

CUPBEARER

Ge 40: 1 the c and the baker of the king
Ne 1: 11 I was c to the king.

CURE (CURED)

Jer 17: 9 and beyond c.
30: 15 your pain that has no c?
Hos 5: 13 But he is not able to c you,
Lk 9: 1 out all demons and to c diseases,

CURED (CURE)

Mt 11: 5 those who have leprosy are c,
Lk 6: 18 troubled by evil spirits were c,

CURSE (ACCURSED CURSED CURSES CURSING)

Ge 4: 11 Now you are under a c
     8: 21 "Never again will I c the ground
   12: 3 and whoever curses you I will c;
Dt 11: 26 before you today a blessing and a c
   11: 28 the c if you disobey the commands
   21: 23 hung on a tree is under God's c.
   23: 5 turned the c into a blessing for you,
Job 1: 11 he will surely c you to your face."
   2: 5 he will surely c you to your face."
   2: 9 C God and die!" He replied,
Ps 109: 28 They may c, but you will bless;
Pr 3: 33 The LORD's c is on the house
   24: 24 peoples will c him and nations
Mal 2: 2 and I will c your blessings.
Lk 6: 28 bless those who c you, pray
Ro 12: 14 persecute you; bless and do not c.
Gal 3: 10 on observing the law are under a c,
   3: 13 of the law by becoming a c for us,
Jas 3: 9 with it we c men, who have been
Rev 22: 3 No longer will there be any c.

CURSED (CURSE)

Ge 3: 17 "C is the ground because of you;
Dt 27: 15 "C is the man who carves an image
   27: 16 "C is the man who dishonors his
   27: 17 "C is the man who moves his
   27: 18 "C is the man who leads the blind
   27: 19 C is the man who withholds justice
   27: 20 "C is the man who sleeps
   27: 21 "C is the man who has sexual
   27: 22 "C is the man who sleeps
   27: 23 "C is the man who sleeps
   27: 24 "C is the man who kills his
   27: 25 "C is the man who accepts a bribe
   27: 26 "C is the man who does not uphold
Jer 17: 5 "C is the one who trusts in man,
Mal 1: 14 "C is the cheat who has
Ro 9: 3 I could wish that I myself were c
1Co 4: 12 When we are c, we bless;
   12: 3 "Jesus be c," and no one can say,
Gal 3: 10 "C is everyone who does not
   3: 13 C is everyone who is hung on a tree

CURSES (CURSE)

Ex 21: 17 "Anyone who c his father
Lev 20: 9 " 'If anyone c his father or mother,
Nu 5: 23 is to write these c on a scroll
Jos 8: 34 the blessings and the c— just
Pr 20: 20 If a man c his father or mother,
   28: 27 to them receives many c.
Mt 15: 4 and 'Anyone who c his father
Mk 7: 10 and, 'Anyone who c his father

CURSING (CURSE)

Ps 109: 18 He wore c as his garment;
Ro 3: 14 "Their mouths are full of c
Jas 3: 10 the same mouth come praise and c.

CURTAIN

Ex 26: 31 "Make a c of blue, purple
   26: 33 The c will separate the Holy Place
Mt 27: 51 At that moment the c
Mk 15: 38 The c of the temple was torn in two
Lk 23: 45 the c of the temple was torn in two.
Heb 6: 19 the inner sanctuary behind the c,
   9: 3 Behind the second c was a room
   10: 20 opened for us through the c,

CUSTOM

Job 1: 5 This was Job's regular c.
Mk 10: 1 and as was his c, he taught them.
Lk 4: 16 into the synagogue, as was his c.
Ac 17: 2 As his c was, Paul went

CUT

Lev 19: 27 " 'Do not c the hair at the sides
   21: 5 of their beards or c their bodies.
1Ki 3: 25 "C the living child in two
Isa 51: 1 to the rock from which you were c
   53: 8 For he was c off from the land
Da 2: 45 of the rock c out of a mountain,
   9: 26 the Anointed One will be c off

Mt 3: 10 not produce good fruit will be c
   24: 22 If those days had not been c short,
1Co 11: 6 for a woman to have her hair c

CYMBAL* (CYMBALS)

1Co 13: 1 a resounding gong or a clanging c.

CYMBALS (CYMBAL)

1Ch 15: 16 instruments: lyres, harps and c.
2Ch 5: 12 dressed in fine linen and playing c,
Ps 150: 5 praise him with resounding c.

CYRUS

Persian king who allowed exiles to return (2Ch 36:22-Ezr 1:8), to rebuild temple (Ezr 5:13-6:14), as appointed by the LORD (Isa 44:28-45:13).

DAGON

Jdg 16: 23 offer a great sacrifice to D their god
1Sa 5: 2 Dagon's temple and set it beside D.

DAMASCUS

Ac 9: 3 As he neared D on his journey,

DAN

1. Son of Jacob by Bilhah (Ge 30:4-6; 35:25; 46:23). Tribe of blessed (Ge 49:16-17; Dt 33:22), numbered (Nu 1:39; 26:43), allotted land (Jos 19: 40-48; Eze 48:1), failed to fully possess (Jdg 1: 34-35), failed to support Deborah (Jdg 5:17), possessed Laish/Dan (Jdg 18).
2. Northernmost city in Israel (Ge 14:14; Jdg 18; 20:1).

DANCE (DANCED DANCING)

Ecc 3: 4 a time to mourn and a time to d,
Mt 11: 17 and you did not d;

DANCED (DANCE)

2Sa 6: 14 d before the LORD
Mk 6: 22 of Herodias came in and d,

DANCING (DANCE)

Ps 30: 11 You turned my wailing into d;
   149: 3 Let them praise his name with d

DANGER

Pr 22: 3 A prudent man sees d
   27: 12 The prudent see d and take refuge,
Mt 5: 22 will be in d of the fire of hell.
Ro 8: 35 famine or nakedness or d or sword?
2Co 11: 26 I have been in d from rivers,

DANIEL

1. Hebrew exile to Babylon, name changed to Belteshazzar (Da 1:6-7). Refused to eat unclean food (Da 1:8-21). Interpreted Nebuchadnezzar's dreams (Da 2; 4), writing on the wall (Da 5). Thrown into lion's den (Da 6). Visions of (Da 7-12).
2. Son of David (1Ch 3:1).

DARIUS

1. King of Persia (Ezr 4:5), allowed rebuilding of temple (Ezr 5-6).
2. Mede who conquered Babylon (Da 5:31).

DARK (DARKENED DARKENS DARKNESS)

Job 34: 22 There is no d place, no deep
Ps 18: 9 d clouds were under his feet.
Pr 31: 15 She gets up while it is still d;
SS 1: 5 Do not stare at me because I am d,
Jn 12: 35 in the d does not know where he is
Ro 2: 19 a light for those who are in the d,
2Pe 1: 19 as to a light shining in a d place,

DARKENED (DARK)

Joel 2: 10 the sun and moon are d,
Mt 24: 29 " 'the sun will be d,
Ro 1: 21 and their foolish hearts were d.
Eph 4: 18 They are d in their understanding

DARKENS (DARK)

Job 38: 2 "Who is this that d my counsel

DARKNESS (DARK)

Ge 1: 2 d was over the surface of the deep,
   1: 4 he separated the light from the d.

Ex 10: 22 and total d covered all Egypt
   20: 21 approached the thick d where God
2Sa 22: 29 The LORD turns my d into light.
Ps 18: 28 my God turns my d into light.
   91: 6 the pestilence that stalks in the d,
   112: 4 Even in d light dawns
   139: 12 even the d will not be dark to you;
Pr 4: 19 the way of the wicked is like deep d
Isa 5: 20 and light for d,
   42: 16 I will turn the d into light
   45: 7 I form the light and create d,
   58: 10 then your light will rise in the d,
   61: 1 and release from d,
Joel 2: 31 The sun will be turned to d
Mt 4: 16 the people living in d
   6: 23 how great is that d! "No one can
Lk 11: 34 are bad, your body also is full of d.
   23: 44 and d came over the whole land
Jn 1: 5 The light shines in the d,
   3: 19 but men loved d instead of light
Ac 2: 20 The sun will be turned to d
2Co 4: 6 who said, "Let light shine out of d
   6: 14 fellowship can light have with d?
Eph 5: 8 For you were once d, but now you
   5: 11 to do with the fruitless deeds of d,
1Pe 2: 9 out of d into his wonderful light.
2Pe 2: 17 Blackest d is reserved for them.
1Jn 1: 5 in him there is no d at all.
   2: 9 but hates his brother is still in the d.
Jude 6 in d, bound with everlasting chains
   13 for whom blackest d has been

DASH

Ps 2: 9 you will d them to pieces like

DAUGHTER (DAUGHTERS)

Ex 1: 10 she took him to Pharaoh's d
Jdg 11: 48 to commemorate the d of Jephthah
Est 2: 7 Mordecai had taken her as his own d
Ps 9: 14 praises in the gates of the D of Zion
   137: 8 O D of Babylon, doomed
Isa 62: 11 "Say to the D of Zion,
Zec 9: 9 Shout, D of Jerusalem!
Mk 5: 34 "D, your faith has healed you.
   7: 29 the demon has left your d.

DAUGHTERS (DAUGHTER)

Ge 6: 2 the d of men were beautiful,
   19: 36 Lot's d became pregnant
Nu 36: 10 Zelophehad's d did as the LORD
Joel 2: 28 sons and d will prophesy,

DAVID

Son of Jesse (Ru 4:17-22; 1Ch 2:13-15), ancestor of Jesus (Mt 1:1-17; Lk 3:31). Wives and children (1Sa 18; 25:39-44; 2Sa 3:2-5; 5:13-16; 11:27; 1Ch 3:1-9). Anointed king by Samuel (1Sa 16:1-13). Musician to Saul (1Sa 16:14-23; 18:10). Killed Goliath (1Sa 17). Relation with Jonathan (1Sa 18:1-4; 19-20; 23:16-18; 2Sa 1). Disfavor of Saul (1Sa 18: 6-23:29). Spared Saul's life (1Sa 24; 26). Among Philistines (1Sa 21:10-14; 27-30). Lament for Saul and Jonathan (2Sa 1). Anointed king of Judah (2Sa 2:1-11). Conflict with house of Saul (2Sa 2-4). Anointed king of Israel (2Sa 5:1-4; 1Ch 11:1-3). Conquered Jerusalem (2Sa 6; 1Ch 13; 15-16). The LORD promised eternal dynasty (2Sa 7; 1Ch 17; Ps 132). Showed kindness to Mephibosheth (2Sa 9). Adultery with Bathsheba, murder of Uriah (2Sa 11-12). Son Amnon raped daughter Tamar; killed by Absalom (2Sa 13). Absalom's revolt (2Sa 14-17); death (2Sa 18). Sheba's revolt (2Sa 20). Victories: Philistines (2Sa 5:17-25; 1Ch 14:8-17; 2Sa 21:15-22; 1Ch 20:4-8), Ammonites (2Sa 10; 1Ch 19), various (2Sa 8; 1Ch 18). Mighty men (2Sa 23:8-39; 1Ch 11-12). Punished for numbering army (2Sa 24; 1Ch 21). Appointed Solomon king (1Ki 1: 28-2:9). Prepared for building of temple (1Ch 22-29). Last words (2Sa 23:1-7). Death (1Ki 2:10-12; 1Ch 29:28).

Psalmist (Mt 22:43-45), musician (Am 6:5), prophet (2Sa 23:2-7; Ac 1:16; 2:30).

Psalms of: 2 (Ac 4:25), 3-32, 34-41, 51-65, 68-70, 86, 95 (Heb 4:7), 101, 103, 108-110, 122, 124, 131, 133, 138-145.

DAWN (DAWNED DAWNS)

Ps 37: 6 your righteousness shine like the *d*,
Pr 4: 18 is like the first gleam of *d*,
Isa 14: 12 O morning star, son of the *d*!
Am 4: 13 he who turns *d* to darkness,
5: 8 who turns blackness into *d*

DAWNED (DAWN)

Isa 9: 2 a light has *d*.
Mt 4: 16 a light has *d*."

DAWNS* (DAWN)

Ps 65: 8 where morning *d* and evening
112: 4 in darkness light *d* for the upright,
Hos 10: 15 When that day *d*,
2Pe 1: 19 until the day *d* and the morning

DAY (DAYS)

Ge 1: 5 God called the light "*d*"
1: 5 and there was morning—the first *d*
1: 8 there was morning—the second *d*.
1: 13 there was morning—the third *d*.
1: 19 there was morning—the fourth *d*.
1: 23 there was morning—the fifth *d*.
1: 31 there was morning—the sixth *d*.
2: 2 so on the seventh *d* he rested
8: 22 *d* and night
Ex 16: 30 the people rested on the seventh *d*.
20: 8 "Remember the Sabbath *d*
Lev 16: 30 on this *d* atonement will be made
23: 28 because it is the *D* of Atonement,
Nu 14: 14 before them in a pillar of cloud by *d*
Jos 1: 8 meditate on it *d* and night,
2Ki 7: 9 This is a *d* of good news
25: 30 *D* by *d* the king gave Jehoiachin
1Ch 16: 23 proclaim his salvation *d* after *d*.
Ne 8: 18 *D* after *d*, from the first *d*
Ps 84: 10 Better is one *d* in your courts
96: 2 proclaim his salvation *d* after *d*.
118: 24 This is the *d* the LORD has made;
Pr 27: 1 not know what a *d* may bring forth.
Isa 13: 9 a cruel *d*, with wrath and fierce
Jer 46: 10 But that *d* belongs to the Lord,
50: 31 "for your *d* has come,
Eze 30: 2 "Alas for that *d*!"
Joel 1: 15 "Alas for that *d*!
2: 31 and dreadful *d* of the LORD.
Am 3: 14 On the *d* I punish Israel for her sins
5: 20 Will not the *d* of the LORD be
Ob : 15 "The *d* of the LORD is near
Zep 1: 14 The great *d* of the LORD is near—
Zec 2: 11 joined with the LORD in that *d*
14: 1 A *d* of the LORD is coming
14: 7 It will be a unique *d*,
Mal 4: 5 dreadful *d* of the LORD comes.
Mt 24: 38 up to the *d* Noah entered the ark;
Lk 11: 3 Give us each *d* our daily bread.
17: 24 in his *d* will be like the lightning,
Ac 5: 42 *D* after *d*, in the temple courts
17: 11 examined the Scriptures every *d*
17: 17 as in the marketplace *d* by *d*
Ro 14: 5 man considers every *d* alike.
1Co 5: 5 his spirit saved on the *d* of the Lord
2Co 4: 16 we are being renewed *d* by *d*.
11: 25 I spent a night and a *d*
1Th 5: 2 for you know very well that the *d*
5: 4 so that this *d* should surprise you
2Th 2: 2 saying that the *d* of the Lord has
Heb 7: 27 need to offer sacrifices *d* after *d*,
2Pe 3: 8 With the Lord a *d* is like
3: 10 *d* of the Lord will come like a thief.
Rev 6: 17 For the great *d* of their wrath has
16: 14 on the great *d* of God Almighty.

DAYS (DAY)

Dt 17: 19 he is to read it all the *d* of his life
32: 7 Remember the *d* of old;
Ps 23: 6 all the *d* of my life,
34: 12 and desires to see many good *d*,
39: 5 have made my *d* a mere
90: 10 The length of our *d* is seventy years
90: 12 Teach us to number our *d* aright,
103: 15 As for man, his *d* are like grass,
128: 5 all the *d* of your life;
Pr 31: 12 all the *d* of her life.
Ecc 9: 9 all the *d* of this meaningless life
12: 1 Creator in the *d* of your youth,
Isa 38: 20 all the *d* of our lives
Da 7: 9 and the Ancient of *D* took his seat.
7: 13 He approached the Ancient of *D*
7: 22 until the Ancient of *D* came
Hos 3: 5 and to his blessings in the last *d*.
Joel 2: 29 I will pour out my Spirit in those *d*.
Mic 4: 1 In the last *d*
Lk 19: 43 The *d* will come upon you
Ac 2: 17 by the prophet Joel: " 'In the last *d*,
2Ti 3: 1 will be terrible times in the last *d*.
Heb 1: 2 in these last *d* he has spoken to us
2Pe 3: 3 that in the last *d* scoffers will come,

DAZZLING*

Da 2: 31 *d* statue, awesome in appearance.
Mk 9: 3 His clothes became *d* white,

DEACON* (DEACONS)

1Ti 3: 12 A *d* must be the husband of

DEACONS* (DEACON)

Php 1: 1 together with the overseers and *d*:
1Ti 3: 8 *D*, likewise, are to be men worthy
3: 10 against them, let them serve as *d*.

DEAD (DIE)

Lev 17: 15 who eats anything found *d*
Dt 18: 11 or spiritist or who consults the *d*.
Isa 8: 19 Why consult the *d* on behalf
Mt 8: 22 and let the *d* bury their own *d*."
28: 7 'He has risen from the *d*
Lk 15: 24 For this son of mine was *d*
24: 46 rise from the *d* on the third day,
Ro 6: 11 count yourselves *d* to sin
1Co 15: 29 do who are baptized for the *d*?
Eph 2: 1 you were *d* in your transgressions
1Th 4: 16 and the *d* in Christ will rise first.
Jas 2: 17 is not accompanied by action, is *d*.
2: 26 so faith without deeds is *d*.
Rev 14: 13 Blessed are the *d* who die
20: 12 And I saw the *d*, great and small,

DEADENED* (DIE)

Jn 12: 40 and *d* their hearts,

DEAR* (DEARER)

2Sa 1: 26 you were very *d* to me.
Ps 102: 14 For her stones are *d*
Jer 31: 20 Is not Ephraim my *d* son,
Jn 2: 4 "*D* woman, why do you involve me
19: 26 he said to his mother, "*D* woman,
Ac 15: 25 to you with our *d* friends Barnabas
Ro 16: 5 Greet my *d* friend Epenetus,
16: 9 in Christ, and my *d* friend Stachys.
16: 12 Greet my *d* friend Persis, another
1Co 4: 14 but to warn you, as my *d* children.
10: 14 my *d* friends, flee from idolatry.
15: 58 Therefore, my *d* brothers,
2Co 7: 1 we have these promises, *d* friends,
12: 19 and everything we do, *d* friends,
Gal 4: 19 My *d* children, for whom I am
Eph 6: 21 the *d* brother and faithful servant
Php 2: 12 my *d* friends, as you have always
4: 1 firm in the Lord, *d* friends!
Col 1: 7 Epaphras, our *d* fellow servant,
4: 7 He is a *d* brother, a faithful
4: 9 our faithful and *d* brother,
4: 14 Our *d* friend Luke, the doctor,
1Th 2: 8 because you had become so *d* to us.
1Ti 6: 2 their service are believers, and *d*
2Ti 1: 2 To Timothy, my *d* son: Grace,
Phm : 1 To Philemon our *d* friend
: 16 He is very *d* to me but
: 16 better than a slave, as a *d* brother.
Heb 6: 9 we speak like this, *d* friends,
Jas 1: 16 Don't be deceived, my *d* brothers.
1: 19 My *d* brothers, take note of this:
2: 5 thoughts? Listen, my *d* brothers:
1Pe 2: 11 *D* friends, I urge you, as aliens
4: 12 *D* friends, do not be surprised
2Pe 3: 1 *D* friends, this is now my second
3: 8 not forget this one thing, *d* friends:
3: 14 *d* friends, since you are looking
3: 15 just as our *d* brother Paul
3: 17 *d* friends, since you already know
1Jn 2: 1 My *d* children, I write this to you
2: 7 *D* friends, I am not writing you
2: 12 I write to you, *d* children,
2: 13 I write to you, *d* children,
1Jn 2: 18 *D* children, this is the last hour;
2: 28 *d* children, continue in him,
3: 2 *D* friends, now we are children
3: 7 *D* children, do not let anyone lead
3: 18 love of God be in him? *D* children,
3: 21 *D* friends, if our hearts do not
4: 1 *D* friends, do not believe every
4: 4 *d* children, are from God
4: 7 *D* friends, let us love one another,
4: 11 *D* friends, since God so loved us,
5: 21 *D* children, keep yourselves
2Jn : 5 *d* lady, I am not writing you a new
3Jn : 1 The elder, To my *d* friend Gaius,
: 2 *D* friend, I pray that you may enjoy
: 5 *D* friend, you are faithful
: 11 *D* friend, do not imitate what is evil
Jude : 3 *D* friends, although I was very
: 17 But, *d* friends, remember what
: 20 *d* friends, build yourselves up

DEARER* (DEAR)

Phm : 16 dear to me but even *d* to you,

DEATH (DIE)

Ex 21: 12 kills him shall surely be put to *d*.
Nu 35: 16 the murderer shall be put to *d*.
Dt 30: 19 set before you life and *d*,
Ru 1: 17 if anything but *d* separates you
2Ki 4: 40 O man of God, there is *d* in the pot
Job 26: 6 *D* is naked before God;
Ps 23: 4 the valley of the shadow of *d*,
44: 22 for your sake we face *d* all day long
89: 48 What man can live and not see *d*,
116: 15 is the *d* of his saints.
Pr 8: 36 all who hate me love *d*."
11: 19 he who pursues evil goes to his *d*.
14: 12 but in the end it leads to *d*.
15: 11 *D* and Destruction lie open
16: 25 but in the end it leads to *d*.
18: 21 tongue has the power of life and *d*,
19: 18 do not be a willing party to his *d*.
23: 14 and save his soul from *d*.
Ecc 7: 2 for *d* is the destiny of every man;
Isa 25: 8 he will swallow up *d* forever.
53: 12 he poured out his life unto *d*,
Eze 18: 23 pleasure in the *d* of the wicked?
18: 32 pleasure in the *d* of anyone,
33: 11 pleasure in the *d* of the wicked,
Hos 13: 14 Where, O *d*, are your plagues?
Jn 5: 24 he has crossed over from *d* to life.
Ro 4: 25 delivered over to *d* for our sins
5: 12 and in this way *d* came to all men,
5: 14 *d* reigned from the time of Adam
6: 3 Jesus were baptized into his *d*?
6: 23 For the wages of sin is *d*,
7: 24 me from this body of *d*?
8: 13 put to *d* the misdeeds of the body,
8: 36 your sake we face *d* all day long;
1Co 15: 21 For since *d* came through a man,
15: 26 The last enemy to be destroyed is *d*
15: 55 Where, O *d*, is your sting?"
2Ti 1: 10 who has destroyed *d* and has
Heb 2: 14 him who holds the power of *d*—
1Jn 5: 16 There is a sin that leads to *d*.
Rev 1: 18 And I hold the keys of *d* and Hades
2: 11 hurt at all by the second *d*.
20: 6 The second *d* has no power
20: 14 The lake of fire is the second *d*.
20: 14 Then *d* and Hades were thrown
21: 4 There will be no more *d*
21: 8 This is the second *d*."

DEBAUCHERY*

Ro 13: 13 not in sexual immorality and *d*,
2Co 12: 21 and *d* in which they have indulged.
Gal 5: 19 impurity and *d*; idolatry
Eph 5: 18 drunk on wine, which leads to *d*.
1Pe 4: 3 living in *d*, lust, drunkenness,

DEBORAH*

1. Prophetess who led Israel to victory over Canaanites (Jdg 4-5).
2. Rebekah's nurse (Ge 35:8).

DEBT* (DEBTOR DEBTORS DEBTS)

Dt 15: 3 must cancel any *d* your brother
24: 6 the upper one—as security for a *d*,
1Sa 22: 2 or in *d* or discontented gathered

Job 24: 9 of the poor is seized for a *d*.
Mt 18:25 that he had be sold to repay the *d*.
18:27 canceled the *d* and let him go.
18:30 into prison until he could pay the *d*.
18:32 'I canceled all that *d* of yours
Lk 7:43 who had the bigger *d* canceled.''
Ro 13: 8 Let no *d* remain outstanding,
13: 8 continuing *d* to love one another,

DEBTOR* (DEBT)

Isa 24: 2 for *d* as for creditor.

DEBTORS* (DEBT)

Hab 2: 7 Will not your *d* suddenly arise?
Mt 6:12 as we also have forgiven our *d*.
Lk 16: 5 called in each one of his master's *d*.

DEBTS* (DEBT)

Dt 15: 1 seven years you must cancel *d*.
15: 2 time for canceling *d* has been
15: 9 the year for canceling *d*, is near,''
31:10 in the year for canceling *d*,
2Ki 4: 7 ''Go, sell the oil and pay your *d*.
Ne 10:31 the land and will cancel all *d*.
Pr 22:26 or puts up security for *d*;
Mt 6:12 Forgive us our *d*,
Lk 7:42 so he canceled the *d* of both.

DECAY*

Ps 16:10 will you let your Holy One see *d*.
49: 9 and not see *d*.
49:14 their forms will *d* in the grave,
Pr 12: 4 a disgraceful wife is like *d*
Isa 5:24 so their roots will *d*
Hab 3:16 *d* crept into my bones,
Ac 2:27 will you let your Holy One see *d*
2:31 to the grave, nor did his body see *d*.
13:34 never to *d*, is stated in these words:
13:35 will not let your Holy One see *d*.'
13:37 raised from the dead did not see *d*.
Ro 8:21 liberated from its bondage to *d*

DECEIT (DECEIVE)

Ps 5: 9 with their tongue they speak *d*.
Isa 53: 9 nor was any *d* in his mouth.
Da 8:25 He will cause *d* to prosper,
Zep 3:13 nor will *d* be found in their mouths.
Mk 7:22 greed, malice, *d*, lewdness, envy,
Ac 13:10 You are full of all kinds of *d*
Ro 1:29 murder, strife, *d* and malice.
3:13 their tongues practice *d*.''
1Pe 2: 1 yourselves of all malice and all *d*,
2:22 and no *d* was found in his mouth.''

DECEITFUL (DECEIVE)

Jer 17: 9 The heart is *d* above all things
Hos 10: 2 Their heart is *d*,
2Co 11:13 men are false apostles, *d* workmen,
Eph 4:14 of men in their *d* scheming.
4:22 is being corrupted by its *d* desires;
1Pe 3:10 and his lips from *d* speech.
Rev 21:27 who does what is shameful or *d*,

DECEITFULNESS* (DECEIVE)

Ps 119:118 for their *d* is in vain.
Mt 13:22 and the *d* of wealth choke it,
Mk 4:19 the *d* of wealth and the desires
Heb 3:13 of you may be hardened by sin's *d*.

**DECEIVE (DECEIT DECEITFUL
DECEITFULNESS DECEIVED DECEIVER
DECEIVERS DECEIVES DECEIVING
DECEPTION DECEPTIVE)**

Lev 19:11 '' 'Do not *d* one another.
Pr 14: 5 A truthful witness does not *d*,
24:28 or use your lips to *d*.
Jer 37: 9 Do not *d* yourselves, thinking,
Zec 13: 4 garment of hair in order to *d*.
Mt 24: 5 'I am the Christ,' and will *d* many.
24:11 will appear and *d* many people.
24:24 and miracles to *d* even the elect—
Mk 13: 6 'I am he,' and will *d* many.
13:22 and miracles to *d* the elect—
Ro 16:18 and flattery they *d* the minds
1Co 3:18 Do not *d* yourselves.
Eph 5: 6 Let no one *d* you with empty words
Col 2: 4 this so that no one may *d* you
2Th 2: 3 Don't let anyone *d* you in any way,

Jas 1:22 to the word, and so *d* yourselves.
1Jn 1: 8 we *d* ourselves and the truth is not
Rev 20: 8 and will go out to *d* the nations

DECEIVED (DECEIVE)

Ge 3:13 ''The serpent *d* me, and I ate.''
Lk 21: 8 ''Watch out that you are not *d*.
1Co 6: 9 the kingdom of God? Do not be *d*:
2Co 11: 3 Eve was *d* by the serpent's cunning
Gal 6: 7 Do not be *d*: God cannot be
1Ti 2:14 And Adam was not the one *d*;
2Ti 3:13 to worse, deceiving and being *d*.
Tit 3: 3 *d* and enslaved by all kinds
Jas 1:16 Don't be *d*, my dear brothers.
Rev 13:14 he *d* the inhabitants of the earth.
20:10 And the devil, who *d* them,

DECEIVER (DECEIVE)

Mt 27:63 while he was still alive that *d* said,
2Jn : 7 Any such person is the *d*

DECEIVERS* (DECEIVE)

Ps 49: 5 when wicked *d* surround me—
Tit 1:10 and *d*, especially those
2Jn : 7 Many *d*, who do not acknowledge

DECEIVES (DECEIVE)

Pr 26:19 is a man who *d* his neighbor
Mt 24: 4 ''Watch out that no one *d* you.
Mk 13: 5 ''Watch out that no one *d* you.
Gal 6: 3 when he is nothing, he *d* himself.
2Th 2:10 sort of evil that *d* those who are
Jas 1:26 he *d* himself and his religion is

DECEIVING* (DECEIVE)

Lev 6: 2 by *d* his neighbor about something
1Ti 4: 1 follow *d* spirits and things taught
2Ti 3:13 go from bad to worse, *d*
Rev 20: 3 him from *d* the nations anymore

DECENCY* (DECENTLY)

1Ti 2: 9 women to dress modestly, with *d*

DECENTLY* (DECENCY)

Ro 13:13 Let us behave *d*, as in the daytime,

DECEPTION (DECEIVE)

Pr 14: 8 but the folly of fools is *d*.
26:26 His malice may be concealed by *d*,
Mt 27:64 This last *d* will be worse
2Co 4: 2 we do not use *d*, nor do we distort

DECEPTIVE (DECEIVE)

Pr 11:18 The wicked man earns *d* wages,
31:30 Charm is *d*, and beauty is fleeting;
Jer 7: 4 Do not trust in *d* words and say,
Col 2: 8 through hollow and *d* philosophy,

DECIDED (DECISION)

2Co 9: 7 man should give what he has *d*

DECISION (DECIDED)

Ex 28:29 heart on the breastpiece of *d*
Joel 3:14 multitudes in the valley of *d*!

DECLARE (DECLARED DECLARING)

1Ch 16:24 *D* his glory among the nations,
Ps 19: 1 The heavens *d* the glory of God;
96: 3 *D* his glory among the nations,
Isa 42: 9 and new things I *d*;

DECLARED (DECLARE)

Mk 7:19 Jesus *d* all foods ''clean.'')
Ro 2:13 the law who will be *d* righteous.
3:20 no one will be *d* righteous

DECLARING (DECLARE)

Ps 71: 8 *d* your splendor all day long.
Ac 2:11 we hear them *d* the wonders

DECREE (DECREED DECREES)

Ex 15:25 There the LORD made a *d*
1Ch 16:17 He confirmed it to Jacob as a *d*,
Ps 2: 7 I will proclaim the *d* of the LORD:
7: 6 Awake, my God; *d* justice.
81: 4 this is a *d* for Israel,
148: 6 he gave a *d* that will never pass
Da 4:24 and this is the *d* the Most High has
Lk 2: 1 Augustus issued a *d* that a census

Ro 1:32 know God's righteous *d* that those

DECREED (DECREE)

Ps 78: 5 He *d* statutes for Jacob
Jer 40: 2 LORD your God *d* this disaster
La 3:37 happen if the Lord has not *d* it?
Da 9:24 ''Seventy 'sevens' are *d*
9:26 and desolations have been *d*.
Lk 22:22 Son of Man will go as it has been *d*,

DECREES (DECREE)

Ge 26: 5 my commands, my *d* and my laws
Ex 15:26 to his commands and keep all his *d*,
18:16 inform them of God's *d* and laws.''
18:20 Teach them the *d* and laws,
Lev 10:11 Israelites all the *d* the LORD has
18: 4 and be careful to follow my *d*.
18: 5 Keep my *d* and laws,
18:26 you must keep my *d* and my laws.
Ps 119:12 teach me your *d*.
119:16 I delight in your *d*;
119:48 and I meditate on your *d*.
119:112 My heart is set on keeping your *d*

DEDICATE (DEDICATED DEDICATION)

Nu 6:12 He must *d* himself to the LORD
Pr 20:25 for a man to *d* something rashly

DEDICATED (DEDICATE)

Lev 21:12 he has been *d* by the anointing oil
Nu 6: 9 thus defiling the hair he has *d*,
6:18 shave off the hair that he *d*.
18: 6 *d* to the LORD to do the work
1Ki 8:63 and all the Israelites *d* the temple
2Ch 29:31 ''You have now *d* yourselves
Ne 3: 1 They *d* it and set its doors in place,

DEDICATION (DEDICATE)

Nu 6:19 shaved off the hair of his *d*,
Jn 10:22 came the Feast of *D* at Jerusalem.
1Ti 5:11 sensual desires overcome their *d*

DEED (DEEDS)

Jer 32:10 and sealed the *d*, had it witnessed,
32:16 After I had given the *d* of purchase
Col 3:17 you do, whether in word or *d*,
2Th 2:17 and strengthen you in every good *d*

DEEDS (DEED)

Dt 3:24 or on earth who can do the *d*
4:34 or by great and awesome *d*,
34:12 the awesome *d* that Moses
1Sa 2: 3 and by him *d* are weighed.
1Ch 16:24 his marvelous *d* among all peoples.
Job 34:25 Because he takes note of their *d*,
Ps 26: 7 and telling of all your wonderful *d*.
45: 4 right hand display awesome *d*.
65: 5 with awesome *d* of righteousness,
66: 3 ''How awesome are your *d*!
71:17 day I declare your marvelous *d*.
72:18 who alone does marvelous *d*,
73:28 I will tell of all your *d*.
75: 1 men tell of your wonderful *d*.
77:11 I will remember the *d* of the LORD
77:12 and consider all your mighty *d*.
78: 4 the praiseworthy *d* of the LORD,
78: 7 and would not forget his *d*
86: 8 no *d* can compare with yours.
86:10 you are great and do marvelous *d*;
88:12 or your righteous *d* in the land
90:16 May your *d* be shown
92: 4 For you make me glad by your *d*,
96: 3 his marvelous *d* among all peoples.
107: 8 and his wonderful *d* for men,
107:15 and his wonderful *d* for men,
107:21 and his wonderful *d* for men,
107:24 his wonderful *d* in the deep.
107:31 and his wonderful *d* for men,
111: 3 Glorious and majestic are his *d*,
145: 6 and I will proclaim your great *d*.
Jer 32:19 purposes and mighty are your *d*.
Hab 3: 2 I stand in awe of your *d*, O LORD.
Mt 5:16 that they may see your good *d*
Lk 1:51 He has performed mighty *d*
23:41 we are getting what our *d* deserve.
Ac 26:20 prove their repentance by their *d*.
1Ti 6:18 rich in good *d*, and to be generous
Heb 10:24 on toward love and good *d*.

Jas   2: 14 claims to have faith but has no *d?*
       2: 18 Show me your faith without *d,*
       2: 20 faith without *d* is useless?
       2: 26 so faith without *d* is dead.
1Pe   2: 12 they may see your good *d*
Rev   2: 19 I know your *d,* your love and faith,
       2: 23 each of you according to your *d.*
       3: 1 I know your *d;* you have
       3: 2 I have not found your *d* complete
       3: 8 I know your *d.*
       3: 15 I know your *d,* that you are neither
      14: 13 for their *d* will follow them.''
      15: 3 ''Great and marvelous are your *d,*

DEEP (DEPTH DEPTHS)

Ge   1: 2 was over the surface of the *d,*
       8: 2 Now the springs of the *d*
Ps   42: 7 *D* calls to *d*
Lk   5: 4 to Simon, ''Put out into *d* water,
1Co   2: 10 all things, even the *d* things
1Ti   3: 9 hold of the *d* truths of the faith

DEER

Ps   42: 1 As the *d* pants for streams of water,

DEFAMED*

Isa   48: 11 How can I let myself be *d?*

DEFEATED

1Co   6: 7 have been completely *d* already.

DEFEND (DEFENDED DEFENDER DEFENDING DEFENDS DEFENSE)

Ps   72: 4 He will *d* the afflicted
      74: 22 Rise up, O God, and *d* your cause;
      82: 2 ''How long will you *d* the unjust
      82: 3 *D* the cause of the weak
     119:154 *D* my cause and redeem me;
Pr   31: 9 *d* the rights of the poor and needy
Isa   1: 17 *D* the cause of the fatherless,
       1: 23 They do not *d* the cause
Jer   5: 28 they do not *d* the rights of the poor.
      50: 34 He will vigorously *d* their cause

DEFENDED (DEFEND)

Jer   22: 16 He *d* the cause of the poor

DEFENDER (DEFEND)

Ex   22: 2 He is not guilty of bloodshed;
Ps   68: 5 to the fatherless, a *d* of widows,
Pr   23: 11 for their *D* is strong;

DEFENDING (DEFEND)

Ps   10: 18 *d* the fatherless and the oppressed,
Ro   2: 15 now accusing, now even *d* them.)
Php   1: 7 or *d* and confirming the gospel.

DEFENDS* (DEFEND)

Dt   10: 18 He *d* the cause of the fatherless
      33: 7 With his own hands he *d* his cause.
Isa   51: 22 your God, who *d* his people:

DEFENSE (DEFEND)

Ps   35: 23 Awake, and rise to my *d!*
Php   1: 16 here for the *d* of the gospel.
1Jn   2: 1 speaks to the Father in our *d*—

DEFERRED*

Pr   13: 12 Hope *d* makes the heart sick,

DEFIED

1Sa   17: 45 armies of Israel, whom you have *d.*
1Ki   13: 26 the man of God who *d* the word

DEFILE (DEFILED)

Da   1: 8 Daniel resolved not to *d* himself
Rev   14: 4 are those who did not *d* themselves

DEFILED (DEFILE)

Isa   24: 5 The earth is *d* by its people;

DEFRAUD

Lev   19: 13 Do not *d* your neighbor or rob him.
Mk   10: 19 do not *d,* honor your father

DEITY*

Col   2: 9 of the *D* lives in bodily form,

DELAY

Ecc   5: 4 vow to God, do not *d* in fulfilling it.
Isa   48: 9 my own name's sake I *d* my wrath;
Heb   10: 37 is coming will come and will not *d.*
Rev   10: 6 and said, ''There will be no more *d!*

DELICACIES

Ps   141: 4 let me not eat of their *d.*
Pr   23: 3 Do not crave his *d,*
      23: 6 do not crave his *d;*

DELICIOUS*

Pr   9: 17 food eaten in secret is *d!*''

DELIGHT* (DELIGHTED DELIGHTFUL DELIGHTING DELIGHTS)

Lev   26: 31 and I will take no *d* in the pleasing
Dt   30: 9 The LORD will again *d* in you
1Sa   2: 1 for I *d* in your deliverance.
      15: 22 ''Does the LORD *d*
Ne   1: 11 the prayer of your servants who *d*
Job   22: 26 Surely then you will find *d*
      27: 10 Will he find *d* in the Almighty?
Ps   1: 2 But his *d* is in the law of the LORD
      16: 3 in whom is all my *d.*
      35: 9 and *d* in his salvation.
      35: 27 those who *d* in my vindication
      37: 4 *D* yourself in the LORD
      43: 4 to God, my joy and my *d.*
      51: 16 You do not *d* in sacrifice,
      51: 19 whole burnt offerings to *d* you;
      62: 4 they take *d* in lies.
      68: 30 Scatter the nations who *d* in war.
     111. 2 by all who *d* in them.
     112: 1 who finds great *d* in his commands.
     119: 16 I *d* in your decrees;
     119: 24 Your statutes are my *d;*
     119: 35 for there I find *d.*
     119: 47 for I *d* in your commands
     119: 70 but I *d* in your law.
     119: 77 for your law is my *d.*
     119: 92 If your law had not been my *d,*
     119:143 but your commands are my *d.*
     119:174 and your law is my *d.*
     147: 10 nor his *d* in the legs of a man;
     149: 4 For the LORD takes *d*
Pr   1: 22 How long will mockers *d*
       2: 14 who *d* in doing wrong
       8: 30 I was filled with *d* day after day,
      11: 1 but accurate weights are his *d.*
      29: 17 he will bring *d* to your soul.
Ecc   2: 10 My heart took *d* in all my work,
SS   1: 4 We rejoice and *d* in you;
       2: 3 I *d* to sit in his shade,
Isa   5: 7 are the garden of his *d.*
      11: 3 he will *d* in the fear of the LORD.
      13: 17 and have no *d* in gold.
      32: 14 the *d* of donkeys, a pasture
      42: 1 my chosen one in whom I *d;*
      55: 2 and your soul will *d* in the richest
      58: 13 if you call the Sabbath a *d*
      61: 10 I *d* greatly in the LORD;
      62: 4 for the LORD will take *d* in you,
      65: 18 for I will create Jerusalem to be a *d*
      65: 19 and take *d* in my people;
      66: 3 their souls *d* in their abominations;
      66: 11 in her overflowing abundance.''
Jer   9: 24 for in these I *d,*''
      15: 16 they were my joy and my heart's *d,*
      31: 20 the child in whom I *d?*
      49: 25 the town in which I *d?*
Eze   24: 16 away from you the *d* of your eyes.
      24: 21 in which you take pride, the *d*
      24: 25 and glory, the *d* of their eyes,
Hos   7: 3 the king with their wickedness,
Mic   1: 16 for the children in whom you *d;*
       7: 18 but *d* to show mercy.
Zep   3: 17 He will take great *d* in you,
Mt   12: 18 the one I love, in whom I *d;*
Mk   12: 37 large crowd listened to him with *d.*
Lk   1: 14 He will be a joy and *d* to you,
Ro   7: 22 in my inner being I *d* in God's law;
1Co   13: 6 Love does not *d* in evil
2Co   12: 10 for Christ's sake, I *d* in weaknesses,
Col   2: 5 and *d* to see how orderly you are

DELIGHTED (DELIGHT)

2Sa   22: 20 he rescued me because he *d* in me.

1Ki   10: 9 who has *d* in you and placed you
2Ch   9: 8 who has *d* in you and placed you
Ps   18: 19 he rescued me because he *d* in me.
Lk   13: 17 but the people were *d* with all

DELIGHTFUL* (DELIGHT)

Ps   16: 6 surely I have a *d* inheritance.
SS   1: 2 for your love is more *d* than wine.
       4: 10 How *d* is your love, my sister,
Mal   3: 12 for yours will be a *d* land,''

DELIGHTING* (DELIGHT)

Pr   8: 31 and *d* in mankind.

DELIGHTS (DELIGHT)

Est   6: 6 for the man the king *d* to honor?''
Ps   22: 8 since he *d* in him.''
      35: 27 who *d* in the well-being
      36: 8 from your river of *d.*
      37: 23 if the LORD *d* in man's way
     147: 11 the LORD *d* in those who fear him,
Pr   3: 12 as a father the son he *d* in.
      10: 23 of understanding *d* in wisdom.
      11: 20 he *d* in those whose ways are
      12: 22 but he *d* in men who are truthful.
      14: 35 A king *d* in a wise servant,
      18: 2 but *d* in airing his own opinions.
      23: 24 he who has a wise son *d* in him.
Col   2: 18 Do not let anyone who *d*

DELILAH*

Woman who betrayed Samson (Jdg 16:4-22).

DELIVER (DELIVERANCE DELIVERED DELIVERER DELIVERS)

Dt   32: 39 and no one can *d* out of my hand.
Ps   22: 8 Let him *d* him,
      72: 12 For he will *d* the needy who cry out
      79: 9 *d* us and atone for our sins
     109: 21 of the goodness of your love, *d* me.
     119:170 *d* me according to your promise.
Mt   6: 13 but *d* us from the evil one.'
2Co   1: 10 hope that he will continue to *d* us,

DELIVERANCE (DELIVER)

1Sa   2: 1 for I delight in your *d.*
Ps   3: 8 From the LORD comes *d.*
      32: 7 and surround me with songs of *d.*
      33: 17 A horse is a vain hope for *d;*
Ob   : 17 But on Mount Zion will be *d;*

DELIVERED (DELIVER)

Ps   34: 4 he *d* me from all my fears.
     107: 6 and he *d* them from their distress.
     116: 8 have *d* my soul from death,
Da   12: 1 written in the book—will be *d.*
Ro   4: 25 He was *d* over to death for our sins

DELIVERER* (DELIVER)

Jdg   3: 9 for them a *d,* Othniel son of Kenaz,
       3: 15 and he gave them a *d*— Ehud,
2Sa   22: 2 is my rock, my fortress and my *d;*
2Ki   13: 5 The LORD provided a *d* for Israel,
Ps   18: 2 is my rock, my fortress and my *d;*
      40: 17 You are my help and my *d;*
      70: 5 You are my help and my *d;*
     140: 7 O Sovereign LORD, my strong *d,*
     144: 2 my stronghold and my *d,*
Ac   7: 35 sent to be their ruler and *d*
Ro   11: 26 ''The *d* will come from Zion;

DELIVERS (DELIVER)

Ps   34: 17 he *d* them from all their troubles.
      34: 19 but the LORD *d* him from them all
      37: 40 The LORD helps them and *d* them
      37: 40 he *d* them from the wicked

DELUSION*

2Th   2: 11 God sends them a powerful *d*

DEMAND (DEMANDED)

Lk   6: 30 belongs to you, do not *d* it back.

DEMANDED (DEMAND)

Lk   12: 20 This very night your life will be *d*
      12: 48 been given much, much will be *d;*

DEMETRIUS

Ac   19: 24 A silversmith named *D,* who made

DEMON* (DEMONS)

Mt 9: 33 And when the *d* was driven out,
    11: 18 and they say, 'He has a *d.*'
    17: 18 Jesus rebuked the *d*, and it came
Mk 7: 26 to drive the *d* out of her daughter.
    7: 29 the *d* has left your daughter.''
    7: 30 lying on the bed, and the *d* gone.
Lk 4: 33 there was a man possessed by a *d*,
    4: 35 Then the *d* threw the man
    7: 33 wine, and you say, 'He has a *d.*'
    8: 29 driven by the *d* into solitary places.
    9: 42 the *d* threw him to the ground
    11: 14 When the *d* left, the man who had
    11: 14 was driving out a *d* that was mute.
Jn 8: 49 ''I am not possessed by a *d*,''
    10: 21 Can a *d* open the eyes of the blind
    10: 21 sayings of a man possessed by a *d*.

DEMON-POSSESSED* (DEMON-POSSESSION)

Mt 4: 24 those suffering severe pain, the *d*,
    8: 16 many who were *d* were brought
    8: 28 two *d* men coming
    8: 33 what had happened to the *d* men.
    9: 32 man who was *d* and could not talk
    12: 22 they brought him a *d* man who was
Mk 1: 32 brought to Jesus all the sick and *d*.
    5: 16 what had happened to the *d* man—
    5: 18 the man who had been *d* begged
Lk 8: 27 met by a *d* man from the town.
    8: 36 the people how the *d* man had been
Jn 7: 20 ''You are *d*,'' the crowd answered.
    8: 48 that you are a Samaritan and *d*?''
    8: 52 ''Now we know that you are *d!*
    10: 20 Many of them said, ''He is *d*
Ac 19: 13 Jesus over those who were *d*.

DEMON-POSSESSION* (DEMON-POSSESSED)

Mt 15: 22 is suffering terribly from *d*.''

DEMONS* (DEMON)

Dt 32: 17 to *d*, which are not God—
Ps 106: 37 and their daughters to *d*.
Mt 7: 22 and in your name drive out *d*
    8: 31 *d* begged Jesus, ''If you drive us
    9: 34 prince of *d* that he drives out *d*.''
    10: 8 who have leprosy, drive out *d*.
    12: 24 of *d*, that this fellow drives out
    12: 24 that this fellow drives out *d*.''
    12: 27 And if I drive out *d* by Beelzebub,
    12: 28 if I drive out *d* by the Spirit of God,
Mk 1: 34 He also drove out many *d*,
    1: 34 but he would not let the *d* speak
    1: 39 their synagogues and driving out *d*.
    3: 15 to have authority to drive out *d*.
    3: 22 the prince of *d* he is driving out *d*.''
    5: 12 The *d* begged Jesus, ''Send us
    5: 15 possessed by the legion of *d*,
    6: 13 They drove out many *d*
    9: 38 ''we saw a man driving out *d*
    16: 9 out of whom he had driven seven *d*
    16: 17 In my name they will drive out *d*;
Lk 4: 41 *d* came out of many people,
    8: 2 from whom seven *d* had come out;
    8: 30 because many *d* had gone into him.
    8: 32 The *d* begged Jesus to let them go
    8: 33 When the *d* came out of the man,
    8: 35 from whom the *d* had gone out,
    8: 38 from whom the *d* had gone out
    9: 1 and authority to drive out all *d*
    9: 49 ''we saw a man driving out *d*
    10: 17 the *d* submit to us in your name.''
    11: 15 the prince of *d*, he is driving out *d*.''
    11: 18 you claim that I drive out *d*
    11: 19 Now if I drive out *d* by Beelzebub,
    11: 20 if I drive out *d* by the finger of God,
    13: 32 'I will drive out *d* and heal people
Ro 8: 38 neither angels nor *d*, neither
1Co 10: 20 of pagans are offered to *d*,
    10: 20 you to be participants with *d*.
    10: 21 of the Lord and the cup of *d* too;
    10: 21 the Lord's table and the table of *d*.
1Ti 4: 1 spirits and things taught by *d*.
Jas 2: 19 Good! Even the *d* believe that—
Rev 9: 20 they did not stop worshiping *d*,
    16: 14 of *d* performing miraculous signs,

Rev 18: 2 She has become a home for *d*

DEMONSTRATE* (DEMONSTRATES DEMONSTRATION)

Ro 3: 25 He did this to *d* his justice,
    3: 26 he did it to *d* his justice

DEMONSTRATES* (DEMONSTRATE)

Ro 5: 8 God *d* his own love for us in this:

DEMONSTRATION* (DEMONSTRATE)

1Co 2: 4 but with a *d* of the Spirit's power,

DEN

Da 6: 16 and threw him into the lions' *d*.
Mt 21: 13 you are making it a '*d* of robbers.' ''
Mk 11: 17 you have made it 'a *d* of robbers.' ''
Lk 19: 46 but you have made it 'a *d* of robbers

DENARII* (DENARIUS)

Mt 18: 28 who owed him a hundred *d*.
Lk 7: 41 One owed him five hundred *d*,

DENARIUS (DENARII)

Mt 20: 2 agreed to pay them a *d* for the day
Mk 12: 15 Bring me a *d* and let me look at it.''

DENIED (DENY)

Mt 26: 70 But he *d* it before them all.
Mk 14: 68 But he *d* it.
Lk 22: 57 But he *d* it.
Jn 18: 25 He *d* it, saying, ''I am not.''
1Ti 5: 8 he has *d* the faith and is worse
Rev 3: 8 my word and have not *d* my name.

DENIES (DENY)

1Jn 2: 22 It is the man who *d* that Jesus is
    2: 23 No one who *d* the Son has

DENY (DENIED DENIES DENYING)

Ex 23: 6 ''Do not *d* justice to your poor
Job 27: 5 till I die, I will not *d* my integrity.
Isa 5: 23 but *d* justice to the innocent.
La 3: 35 to *d* a man his rights
Am 2: 7 and *d* justice to the oppressed.
Mt 16: 24 he must *d* himself and take up his
Mk 8: 34 he must *d* himself and take up his
Lk 9: 23 he must *d* himself and take up his
    22: 34 you will *d* three times that you
Ac 4: 16 miracle, and we cannot *d* it.
Tit 1: 16 but by their actions they *d* him.
Jas 3: 14 do not boast about it or *d* the truth.
Jude   : 4 *d* Jesus Christ our only Sovereign

DENYING* (DENY)

Eze 22: 29 mistreat the alien, *d* them justice.
2Ti 3: 5 a form of godliness but *d* its power.
2Pe 2: 1 *d* the sovereign Lord who bought

DEPART (DEPARTED DEPARTS DEPARTURE)

Ge 49: 10 The scepter will not *d* from Judah,
Job 1: 21 and naked I will *d*.
Mt 25: 41 '*D* from me, you who are cursed,
Php 1: 23 I desire to *d* and be with Christ,

DEPARTED (DEPART)

1Sa 4: 21 ''The glory has *d* from Israel''—
Ps 119:102 I have not *d* from your laws,

DEPARTS (DEPART)

Ecc 5: 15 and as he comes, so he *d*.

DEPARTURE (DEPART)

Lk 9: 31 spoke about his *d*, which he was
2Ti 4: 6 and the time has come for my *d*.
2Pe 1: 15 after my *d* you will always be able

DEPEND

Ps 62: 7 My salvation and my honor *d*

DEPOSES*

Da 2: 21 he sets up kings and *d* them.

DEPOSIT

Mt 25: 27 money on *d* with the bankers,
Lk 19: 23 didn't you put my money on *d*,
2Co 1: 22 put his Spirit in our hearts as a *d*,
    5: 5 and has given us the Spirit as a *d*,

Eph 1: 14 who is a *d* guaranteeing our
2Ti 1: 14 Guard the good *d* that was

DEPRAVED* (DEPRAVITY)

Eze 16: 47 ways you soon became more *d*
    23: 11 and prostitution she was more *d*
Ro 1: 28 he gave them over to a *d* mind,
Php 2: 15 fault in a crooked and *d* generation,
2Ti 3: 8 oppose the truth—men of *d* minds,

DEPRAVITY* (DEPRAVED)

Ro 1: 29 of wickedness, evil, greed and *d*.
2Pe 2: 19 they themselves are slaves of *d*—

DEPRIVE

Dt 24: 17 Do not *d* the alien or the fatherless
Pr 18: 5 or to *d* the innocent of justice.
    31: 5 *d* all the oppressed of their rights.
Isa 10: 2 to *d* the poor of their rights
    29: 21 with false testimony *d* the innocent
La 3: 36 to *d* a man of justice—
1Co 7: 5 Do not *d* each other
    9: 15 die than have anyone *d* me

DEPTH (DEEP)

Ro 8: 39 any powers, neither height nor *d*,
    11: 33 the *d* of the riches of the wisdom

DEPTHS (DEEP)

Ps 130: 1 Out of the *d* I cry to you, O LORD;

DERIDES*

Pr 11: 12 who lacks judgment *d* his neighbor,

DERIVES*

Eph 3: 15 in heaven and on earth *d* its name.

DESCEND (DESCENDED DESCENDING)

Ro 10: 7 ''or 'Who will *d* into the deep?' ''

DESCENDED (DESCEND)

Eph 4: 9 except that he also *d* to the lower,
Heb 7: 14 For it is clear that our Lord *d*

DESCENDING (DESCEND)

Ge 28: 12 of God were ascending and *d* on it.
Mt 3: 16 the Spirit of God *d* like a dove
Mk 1: 10 and the Spirit of on him like a dove.
Jn 1: 51 and *d* on the Son of Man.''

DESECRATING*

Ne 13: 17 you are doing—*d* the Sabbath day?
    13: 18 against Israel by *d* the Sabbath.''
Isa 56: 2 who keeps the Sabbath without *d* it
    56: 6 who keep the Sabbath without *d* it
Eze 44: 7 *d* my temple while you offered me

DESERT

Nu 32: 13 wander in the *d* forty years,
Dt 8: 16 He gave you manna to eat in the *d*,
    29: 5 years that I led you through the *d*,
Ne 9: 19 you did not abandon them in the *d*.
Ps 78: 19 ''Can God spread a table in the *d*?
    78: 52 led them like sheep through the *d*.
Pr 21: 19 Better to live in a *d*
Isa 32: 2 like streams of water in the *d*
    32: 15 and the *d* becomes a fertile field,
    35: 6 and streams in the *d*.
    43: 20 because I provide water in the *d*
Mk 1: 3 ''a voice of one calling in the *d*,
    1: 13 and he was in the *d* forty days,
Rev 12: 6 fled into the *d* to a place prepared

DESERTED (DESERTS)

Ezr 9: 9 our God has not *d* us
Mt 26: 56 all the disciples *d* him and fled.
2Ti 1: 15 in the province of Asia has *d* me,

DESERTING (DESERTS)

Gal 1: 6 are so quickly *d* the one who called

DESERTS (DESERTED DESERTING)

Zec 11: 17 who *d* the flock!

DESERVE* (DESERVED DESERVES)

Ge 40: 15 to *d* being put in a dungeon.''
Lev 26: 21 times over, as your sins *d*.
Jdg 20: 10 it can give them what they *d*
1Sa 26: 16 you and your men *d* to die,

DESERVED

1Ki 2: 26 You *d* to die, but I will not put you
Ps 28: 4 bring back upon them what they *d.*
  94: 2 pay back to the proud what they *d.*
  103: 10 he does not treat us as our sins *d*
Pr 3: 27 from those who *d* it,
Ecc 8: 14 men who get what the righteous *d,*
  8: 14 men who get what the wicked *d,*
Isa 66: 6 repaying his enemies all they *d.*
Jer 14: 16 out on them the calamity they *d.*
  17: 10 according to what his deeds *d.''*
  21: 14 I will punish you as your deeds *d,*
  32: 19 to his conduct and as his deeds *d.*
  49: 12 ''If those who do not *d*
La 3: 64 Pay them back what they *d,*
Eze 16: 59 I will deal with you as you *d,*
Zec 1: 6 to us what our ways and practices *d*
Mt 8: 8 I do not *d* to have you come
  22: 8 those I invited did not *d* to come.
Lk 7: 6 for I do not *d* to have you come
  23: 15 he has done nothing to *d* death.
  23: 41 for we are getting what our deeds *d*
Ro 1: 32 those who do such things *d* death,
1Co 15: 9 even *d* to be called an apostle,
  16: 18 Such men *d* recognition.
2Co 11: 15 end will be what their actions *d.*
Rev 16: 6 blood to drink as they *d.''*

DESERVED* (DESERVE)

2Sa 19: 28 descendants *d* nothing
Ezr 9: 13 less than our sins have *d* ·
Job 33: 27 but I did not get what I *d.*
Ac 23: 29 charge against him that *d* death
Ro 3: 8 Their condemnation is *d.*

DESERVES* (DESERVE)

Nu 35: 31 the life of a murderer, who *d* to die.
Dt 25: 2 If the guilty man *d* to be beaten,
  25: 2 the number of lashes his crime *d,*
Jdg 9: 16 and if you have treated him as he *d*
2Sa 12: 5 The man who did this *d* to die!
Job 34: 11 upon him what his conduct *d.*
Jer 51: 6 he will pay her what she *d.*
Lk 7: 4 ''This man *d* to have you do this,
  10: 7 for the worker *d* his wages.
Ac 26: 31 is not doing anything that *d* death
1Ti 1: 15 saying that *d* full acceptance
  4: 9 saying that *d* full acceptance
  5: 18 and ''The worker *d* his wages.''
Heb 10: 29 severely do you think a man *d*

DESIGNATED

Lk 6: 13 also *d* apostles: Simon (whom he
Heb 5: 10 and was *d* by God to be high priest

DESIRABLE* (DESIRE)

Ge 3: 6 and also *d* for gaining wisdom,
Pr 22: 1 A good name is more *d*
Jer 3: 19 and give you a *d* land,

DESIRE* (DESIRABLE DESIRED DESIRES)

Ge 3: 16 Your *d* will be for your husband,
Dt 5: 21 You shall not set your *d*
1Sa 9: 20 to whom is all the *d* of Israel turned
2Sa 19: 38 anything you *d* from me I will do
  23: 5 and grant me my every *d?*
1Ch 29: 18 keep this *d* in the hearts
2Ch 1: 11 ''Since this is your heart's *d*
  9: 8 and his *d* to uphold them forever,
Job 13: 3 But I *d* to speak to the Almighty
  21: 14 We have no *d* to know your ways.
Ps 10: 17 O LORD, the *d* of the afflicted;
  20: 4 May he give you the *d*
  21: 2 You have granted him the *d*
  27: 12 me over to the *d* of my foes,
  40: 6 Sacrifice and offering you did not *d*
  40: 8 I *d* to do your will, O my God;
  40: 14 may all who *d* my ruin
  41: 2 him to the *d* of his foes.
  51: 6 Surely you *d* truth
  70: 2 may all who *d* my ruin
  73: 25 earth has nothing I *d* besides you
Pr 3: 15 nothing you *d* can compare
  8: 11 and nothing you *d* can compare
  10: 24 what the righteous *d* will be
  11: 23 The *d* of the righteous ends only
  12: 12 The wicked *d* the plunder
  17: 16 since he has no *d* to get wisdom?

Pr 24: 1 do not *d* their company;
Ecc 12: 5 and *d* no longer is stirred.
SS 6: 12 my *d* set me among the royal
  7: 10 and his *d* is for me.
Isa 26: 8 are the *d* of our hearts.
  53: 2 appearance that we should *d* him.
  55: 11 but will accomplish what I *d*
Eze 24: 25 delight of their eyes, their heart's *d,*
Hos 6: 6 For I *d* mercy, not sacrifice,
Mic 7: 3 the powerful dictate what they *d—*
Mal 3: 1 whom you *d,* will come,'' says
Mt 9: 13 learn what this means: 'I *d* mercy,
  12: 7 what these words mean, 'I *d* mercy,
Jn 8: 44 want to carry out your father's *d.*
Ro 7: 8 in me every kind of covetous *d.*
  7: 18 For I have the *d* to do what is good,
  9: 16 depend on man's *d* or effort,
  10: 1 my heart's *d* and prayer to God
1Co 12: 31 But eagerly *d* the greater gifts.
  14: 1 and eagerly *d* spiritual gifts,
2Co 8: 10 but also to have the *d* to do so.
  8: 13 Our *d* is not that others might be
Php 1: 23 I *d* to depart and be with Christ,
Heb 10: 5 Sacrifice and offering you did not *d,*
  10: 8 and sin offerings you did not *d,*
  13: 18 *d* to live honorably in every way.
Jas 1: 14 by his own evil *d,* he is dragged
  1: 15 Then, after *d* has conceived,
2Pe 2: 10 of those who follow the corrupt *d*

DESIRED (DESIRE)

Hag 2: 7 and the *d* of all nations will come,
Lk 22: 15 ''I have eagerly *d* to eat this

DESIRES* (DESIRE)

Ge 4: 7 at your door; it *d* to have you,
  41: 16 will give Pharaoh the answer he *d.''*
2Sa 3: 21 rule over all that your heart *d.''*
1Ki 11: 37 rule over all that your heart *d;*
Job 17: 11 and so are the *d* of my heart.
  31: 16 ''If I have denied the *d* of the poor
Ps 34: 12 and *d* to see many good days,
  37: 4 he will give you the *d* of your heart.
  103: 5 He satisfies my *d* with good things,
  140: 8 do not grant the wicked their *d,*
  145: 16 satisfy the *d* of every living thing.
  145: 19 He fulfills the *d* of those who fear
Pr 11: 6 the unfaithful are trapped by evil *d.*
  13: 4 *d* of the diligent are fully satisfied.
  19: 22 What a man *d* is unfailing love;
Ecc 6: 2 so that he lacks nothing his heart *d,*
SS 2: 7 or awaken love / until it so *d.*
  3: 5 or awaken love / until it so *d.*
  8: 4 or awaken love / until it so *d.*
Hab 2: 4 his *d* are not upright—
Mk 4: 19 and the *d* for other things come in
Ro 1: 24 over in the sinful *d* of their hearts
  6: 12 body so that you obey its evil *d.*
  8: 5 set on what that nature *d;*
  8: 5 set on what the Spirit *d.*
  13: 14 to gratify the *d* of the sinful nature.
Gal 5: 16 and you will not gratify the *d*
  5: 17 the sinful nature *d* what is contrary
  5: 24 nature with its passions and *d.*
Eph 2: 3 and following its *d* and thoughts.
  4: 22 being corrupted by its deceitful *d;*
Col 3: 5 impurity, lust, evil *d* and greed,
1Ti 3: 1 an overseer, he *d* a noble task.
  5: 11 their sensual *d* overcome their
  6: 9 and harmful *d* that plunge men
2Ti 2: 22 Flee the evil *d* of youth,
  3: 6 are swayed by all kinds of evil *d,*
  4: 3 Instead, to suit their own *d,*
Jas 1: 20 about the righteous life that God *d.*
  4: 1 from your *d* that battle within you?
1Pe 1: 14 conform to the evil *d* you had
  2: 11 to abstain from sinful *d,* which war
  4: 2 of his earthly life for evil human *d,*
2Pe 1: 4 in the world caused by evil *d.*
  2: 18 to the lustful *d* of sinful human
  3: 3 and following their own evil *d.*
1Jn 2: 17 The world and its *d* pass away,
Jude : 16 they follow their own evil *d;*
  : 18 will follow their own ungodly *d.''*

DESOLATE (DESOLATION)

Isa 54: 1 are the children of the *d* woman
Gal 4: 27 are the children of the *d* woman

DESOLATION (DESOLATE)

Da 11: 31 up the abomination that causes *d.*
  12: 11 abomination that causes *d* is set up,
Mt 24: 15 'the abomination that causes *d,'*

DESPAIR (DESPAIRED)

Isa 61: 3 instead of a spirit of *d.*
2Co 4: 8 perplexed, but not in *d;* persecuted,

DESPAIRED* (DESPAIR)

2Co 1: 8 ability to endure, so that we *d*

DESPERATE*

2Sa 12: 18 He may do something *d.''*
Ps 60: 3 have shown your people *d* times;
  79: 8 for we are in *d* need.
  142: 6 for I am in *d* need;

DESPISE (DESPISED DESPISES)

2Sa 12: 9 Why did you *d* the word
Job 5: 17 so do not *d* the discipline
  36: 5 God is mighty, but does not *d* men;
  42: 6 Therefore I *d* myself
Ps 51: 17 O God, you will not *d.*
  102: 17 he will not *d* their plea.
Pr 1: 7 but fools *d* wisdom and discipline.
  3: 11 do not *d* the LORD's discipline
  6: 30 Men do not *d* a thief if he steals
  23: 22 do not *d* your mother
Jer 14: 21 of your name do not *d* us;
Am 5: 10 and *d* him who tells the truth.
  5: 21 ''I hate, I *d* your religious feasts;
Mt 6: 24 devoted to the one and *d* the other.
Lk 16: 13 devoted to the one and *d* the other.
1Co 11: 22 Or do you *d* the church of God
Tit 2: 15 Do not let anyone *d* you.
2Pe 2: 10 of the sinful nature and *d* authority.

DESPISED (DESPISE)

Ge 25: 34 So Esau *d* his birthright.
Ps 22: 6 by men and *d* by the people.
Pr 12: 8 but men with warped minds are *d.*
Isa 53: 3 He was *d* and rejected by men,
  53: 3 he was *d,* and we esteemed him not
1Co 1: 28 of this world and the *d* things—

DESPISES (DESPISE)

Pr 14: 21 He who *d* his neighbor sins,
  15: 20 but a foolish man *d* his mother.
  15: 32 who ignores discipline *d* himself,
Zec 4: 10 ''Who of you *d* the day of small things?

DESTINED (DESTINY)

Lk 2: 34 ''This child is *d* to cause the falling
1Co 2: 7 and that God *d* for our glory
Col 2: 22 These are all *d* to perish with use,
1Th 3: 3 know quite well that we were *d*
Heb 9: 27 Just as man is *d* to die once,
1Pe 2: 8 which is also what they were *d* for.

DESTINY* (DESTINED PREDESTINED)

Job 8: 13 Such is the *d* of all who forget God;
Ps 73: 17 then I understood their final *d.*
Ecc 7: 2 for death is the *d* of every man;
  9: 2 share a common *d—* the righteous
  9: 3 the sun: The same *d* overtakes all.
Isa 65: 11 and fill bowls of mixed wine for *D,*
Php 3: 19 Their *d* is destruction, their god is

DESTITUTE

Ps 102: 17 to the prayer of the *d;*
Pr 31: 8 for the rights of all who are *d.*
Heb 11: 37 *d,* persecuted and mistreated—

DESTROY (DESTROYED DESTROYING DESTROYS DESTRUCTION DESTRUCTIVE)

Ge 6: 17 floodwaters on the earth to *d* all life
  9: 11 will there be a flood to *d* the earth.''
Pr 1: 32 complacency of fools will *d* them;
Mt 10: 28 of the One who can *d* both soul
Mk 14: 58 'I will *d* this man-made temple
Lk 4: 34 to *d* us? I know who you are—
Jn 10: 10 only to steal and kill and *d;*
Ac 8: 3 But Saul began to *d* the church.
Rev 11: 18 destroying those who *d* the earth.''

DESTROYED (DESTROY)

Dt   8: 19 you today that you will surely be *d*.
Job 19: 26 And after my skin has been *d*,
Pr   6: 15 he will suddenly be *d*—
     11: 3 the unfaithful are *d*
     21: 28 listens to him will be *d* forever.
     29: 1 will suddenly be *d*—
Isa 55: 13 which will not be *d*.''
Da   2: 44 up a kingdom that will never be *d*,
      6: 26 his kingdom will not be *d*,
1Co   5: 5 so that the sinful nature may be *d*
      8: 11 for whom Christ died, is *d*
     15: 24 Father after he has *d* all dominion,
     15: 26 The last enemy to be *d* is death.
2Co   4: 9 abandoned; struck down, but not *d*.
      5: 1 if the earthly tent we live in is *d*,
Gal   5: 15 or you will be *d* by each other.
Eph   2: 14 the two and has *d* the barrier,
2Ti   1: 10 who has *d* death and has brought
Heb 10: 39 of those who shrink back and are *d*,
2Pe   2: 12 born only to be caught and *d*,
      3: 10 the elements will be *d* by fire,
      3: 11 Since everything will be *d*
Jude : 5 later *d* those who did not believe.
      : 11 have been *d* in Korah's rebellion.

DESTROYING (DESTROY)

Jer 23: 1 ''Woe to the shepherds who are *d*

DESTROYS (DESTROY)

Pr   6: 32 whoever does so *d* himself.
     11: 9 mouth the godless *d* his neighbor,
     18: 9 is brother to one who *d*.
     28: 24 he is partner to him who *d*.
Ecc   9: 18 but one sinner *d* much good.
1Co   3: 17 If anyone *d* God's temple,

DESTRUCTION (DESTROY)

Nu 32: 15 and you will be the cause of their *d*
Pr   16: 18 Pride goes before *d*,
     17: 19 he who builds a high gate invites *d*.
     24: 22 for those two will send sudden *d*
Hos 13: 14 Where, O grave, is your *d*?
Mt   7: 13 broad is the road that leads to *d*,
Lk   6: 49 it collapsed and its *d* was complete
Jn   17: 12 except the one doomed to *d*
Ro   9: 22 of his wrath—prepared for *d*?
Gal   6: 8 from that nature will reap *d*;
Php   3: 19 Their destiny is *d*, their god is their
1Th   5: 3 *d* will come on them suddenly,
2Th   1: 9 punished with everlasting *d*
      2: 3 is revealed, the man doomed to *d*.
1Ti   6: 9 that plunge men into ruin and *d*.
2Pe   2: 1 bringing swift *d* on themselves.
      2: 3 and their *d* has not been sleeping.
      3: 7 of judgment and *d* of ungodly men.
      3: 12 That day will bring about the *d*
      3: 16 other Scriptures, to their own *d*.
Rev 17: 8 out of the Abyss and go to his *d*.
     17: 11 to the seven and is going to his *d*.

DESTRUCTIVE (DESTROY)

2Pe   2: 1 will secretly introduce *d* heresies,

DETERMINED (DETERMINES)

Job 14: 5 Man's days are *d*;
Isa 14: 26 This is the plan *d* for the whole
Da 11: 36 for what has been *d* must take place
Ac 17: 26 and he *d* the times set for them

DETERMINES* (DETERMINED)

Ps 147: 4 He *d* the number of the stars
Pr   16: 9 but the LORD *d* his steps.
1Co 12: 11 them to each one, just as he *d*.

DETEST (DETESTABLE DETESTED DETESTS)

Lev 11: 10 in the water—you are to *d*.
Pr   8: 7 for my lips *d* wickedness.
     13: 19 but fools *d* turning from evil.
     16: 12 Kings *d* wrongdoing,
     24: 9 and men *d* a mocker.
     29: 27 The righteous *d* the dishonest;
     29: 27 the wicked *d* the upright.

DETESTABLE (DETEST)

Pr   6: 16 seven that are *d* to him:
     21: 27 The sacrifice of the wicked is *d*—

Pr   28: 9 even his prayers are *d*.
Isa   1: 13 Your incense is *d* to me.
     41: 24 he who chooses you is *d*.
     44: 19 Shall I make a *d* thing
Jer 44: 4 'Do not do this *d* thing that I hate!'
Eze   8: 13 doing things that are even more *d*.''
Lk   16: 15 among men is *d* in God's sight.
Tit   1: 16 They are *d*, disobedient
1Pe   4: 3 orgies, carousing and *d* idolatry.

DETESTED* (DETEST)

Zec 11: 8 The flock *d* me, and I grew weary

DETESTS* (DETEST)

Dt 22: 5 LORD your God *d* anyone who
     23: 18 the LORD your God *d* them both.
     25: 16 LORD your God *d* anyone who
Pr   3: 32 for the LORD *d* a perverse man
     11: 20 The LORD *d* men
     12: 22 The LORD *d* lying lips,
     15: 8 The LORD *d* the sacrifice
     15: 9 The LORD *d* the way
     15: 26 The LORD *d* the thoughts
     16: 5 The LORD *d* all the proud of heart
     17: 15 the LORD *d* them both.
     20: 10 the LORD *d* them both.
     20: 23 The LORD *d* differing weights,

DEVIATE*

2Ch   8: 15 They did not *d* from the king's

DEVICES*

Ps 81: 12 to follow their own *d*.

DEVIL* (DEVIL'S)

Mt   4: 1 the desert to be tempted by the *d*.
      4: 5 the *d* took him to the holy city
      4: 8 took him to a very high mountain
      4: 11 the *d* left him, and angels came
     13: 39 the enemy who sows them is the *d*.
     25: 41 the eternal fire prepared for the *d*
Lk   4: 2 forty days he was tempted by the *d*.
      4: 3 *d* said to him, ''If you are the Son
      4: 5 The *d* led him up to a high place
      4: 9 The *d* led him to Jerusalem
      4: 13 When the *d* had finished all this
      8: 12 then the *d* comes and takes away
Jn   6: 70 of you is a *d*!'' (He meant Judas,
      8: 44 You belong to your father, the *d*,
     13: 2 the *d* had already prompted Judas
Ac   10: 38 were under the power of the *d*,
     13: 10 ''You are a child of the *d*
Eph   4: 27 and do not give the *d* a foothold.
1Ti   3: 6 under the same judgment as the *d*.
2Ti   2: 26 and escape from the trap of the *d*,
Heb   2: 14 the *d*—and free those who all their
Jas   3: 15 but is earthly, unspiritual, of the *d*.
      4: 7 Resist the *d*, and he will flee
1Pe   5: 8 Your enemy the *d* prowls
1Jn   3: 8 because the *d* has been sinning
      3: 8 who does what is sinful is of the *d*,
      3: 10 and who the children of the *d* are:
Jude : 9 with the *d* about the body of Moses
Rev 12: 9 *d* will put some of you in prison
     12: 9 that ancient serpent called the *d*
     12: 12 the *d* has gone down to you!
     20: 2 that ancient serpent, who is the *d*,
     20: 10 And the *d*, who deceived them,

DEVIL'S* (DEVIL)

Eph   6: 11 stand against the *d* schemes.
1Ti   3: 7 into disgrace and into the *d* trap.
1Jn   3: 8 was to destroy the *d* work.

DEVILS see DEMONS

DEVIOUS*

Pr   2: 15 and who are *d* in their ways.
      14: 2 he whose ways are *d* despises him.
      21: 8 The way of the guilty is *d*,

DEVOTE* (DEVOTED DEVOTING DEVOTION DEVOUT)

1Ch 22: 19 Now *d* your heart and soul
2Ch 31: 4 Levites so they could *d* themselves
Job 11: 13 ''Yet if you *d* your heart to him
Jer 30: 21 for who is he who will *d* himself
Mic   4: 13 You will *d* their ill-gotten gains
1Co   7: 5 so that you may *d* yourselves

Col   4: 2 *D* yourselves to prayer, being
1Ti   1: 4 nor to *d* themselves to myths
      4: 13 *d* yourself to the public reading
Tit   3: 8 may be careful to *d* themselves
      3: 14 people must learn to *d* themselves

DEVOTED (DEVOTE)

1Ki 11: 4 and his heart was not fully *d*
Ezr   7: 10 For Ezra had *d* himself to the study
Ps 86: 2 Guard my life, for I am *d* to you.
Mt   6: 24 or he will be *d* to the one
Mk   7: 11 from me is Corban' (that is, a gift *d*
Ac   2: 42 They *d* themselves
     18: 5 Paul *d* himself exclusively
Ro   12: 10 Be *d* to one another
1Co   7: 34 Her aim is to be *d* to the Lord
     16: 15 and they have *d* themselves
2Co   7: 12 for yourselves how *d* to us you are.

DEVOTING* (DEVOTE)

1Ti   5: 10 *d* herself to all kinds of good deeds.

DEVOTION* (DEVOTE)

2Ki 20: 3 and with wholehearted *d* and have
1Ch 28: 9 and serve him with wholehearted *d*
     29: 3 in my *d* to the temple
     29: 19 son Solomon the wholehearted *d*
2Ch 32: 32 and his acts of *d* are written
     35: 26 of Josiah's reign and his acts of *d*,
Job   6: 14 despairing man should have the *d*
     15: 4 and hinder *d* to God.
Isa 38: 3 and with wholehearted *d* and have
Jer   2: 2 '' 'I remember the *d* of your youth,
Eze 33: 31 With their mouths they express *d*,
1Co   7: 35 way in undivided *d* to the Lord.
2Co 11: 3 from your sincere and pure *d*

DEVOUR (DEVOURED DEVOURING DEVOURS)

2Sa   2: 26 ''Must the sword *d* forever?
Mk   12: 40 They *d* widows' houses
1Pe   5: 8 lion looking for someone to *d*.

DEVOURED (DEVOUR)

Jer 30: 16 But all who devour you will be *d*;

DEVOURING (DEVOUR)

Gal   5: 15 keep on biting and *d* each other,

DEVOURS (DEVOUR)

2Sa 11: 25 the sword *d* one as well as another.
Pr   21: 20 but a foolish man *d* all he has.

DEVOUT* (DEVOTE)

1Ki 18: 3 (Obadiah was a *d* believer
Isa 57: 1 *d* men are taken away,
Lk   2: 25 Simeon, who was righteous and *d*.
Ac   10: 2 his family were *d* and God-fearing;
     10: 7 a soldier who was one of his attendants
     13: 43 and *d* converts to Judaism followed
     22: 12 He was a *d* observer of the law

DEW

Jdg   6: 37 If there is *d* only on the fleece

DICTATED

Jer 36: 4 and while Jeremiah *d* all the words

DIE (DEAD DEADENED DEATH DIED DIES DYING)

Ge   2: 17 when you eat of it you will surely *d*
      3: 3 you must not touch it, or you will *d*
      3: 4 will not surely *d*,'' the serpent said
Ex   11: 5 Every firstborn son in Egypt will *d*,
Ru   1: 17 Where you *d* I will *d*, and there I
2Ki 14: 6 each is to *d* for his own sins.''
Job   2: 9 Curse God and *d*!'' He replied,
Pr   5: 23 He will *d* for lack of discipline,
     10: 21 but fools *d* for lack of judgment.
     15: 10 he who hates correction will *d*.
     23: 13 with the rod, he will not *d*.
Ecc   3: 2 a time to be born and a time to *d*,
Isa 22: 13 ''for tomorrow we *d*!''
     66: 24 their worm will not *d*, nor will their
Jer 31: 30 everyone will *d* for his own sin;
Eze   3: 18 that wicked man will *d* for his sin,
      3: 19 he will *d* for his sin; but you will

Eze 3: 20 block before him, he will *d*.
18: 4 soul who sins is the one who will *d*.
18: 20 soul who sins is the one who will *d*.
18: 31 Why will you *d*, O house of Israel?
33: 8 'O wicked man, you will surely *d*,'
Mt 26: 52 ''for all who draw the sword will *d*.
Mk   9: 48 '' 'their worm does not *d*,
Jn   8: 21 and you will *d* in your sin.
11: 26 and believes in me will never *d*.
Ro   5: 7 Very rarely will anyone *d*
14: 8 and if we *d*, we *d* to the Lord.
1Co 15: 22 in Adam all *d*, so in Christ all will
15: 31 I *d* every day—I mean that,
15: 32 for tomorrow we *d*.''
Php 1: 21 to live is Christ and to *d* is gain.
Heb 9: 27 Just as man is destined to *d* once,
1Pe 2: 24 so that we might *d* to sins
Rev 14: 13 Blessed are the dead who *d*

DIED (DIE)

1Ki 16: 18 So he *d*, because of the sins he had
1Ch 1: 51 Hadad also *d*.
10: 13 Saul *d* because he was unfaithful
Lk 16: 22 ''The time came when the beggar *d*
Ro   5: 6 we were still powerless, Christ *d*
5: 8 we were still sinners, Christ *d*
6: 2 By no means! We *d* to sin;
6: 7 anyone who has *d* has been freed
6: 8 if we *d* with Christ, we believe that
6: 10 The death he *d*, he *d* to sin once
14: 9 Christ *d* and returned to life
14: 15 brother for whom Christ *d*.
1Co 8: 11 for whom Christ *d*, is destroyed
15: 3 that Christ *d* for our sins according
2Co 5: 14 *d* for all, and therefore all *d*.
5: 15 he *d* for all, that those who live
Col 2: 20 Since you *d* with Christ
3: 3 For you *d*, and your life is now
1Th 4: 14 We believe that Jesus *d*
5: 10 He *d* for us so that, whether we are
2Ti 2: 11 If we *d* with him,
Heb 9: 15 now that he has *d* as a ransom
9: 17 in force only when somebody has *d*
1Pe 3: 18 For Christ *d* for sins once for all,
Rev 2: 8 who *d* and came to life again.

DIES (DIE)

Job 14: 14 If a man *d*, will he live again?
Pr 11: 7 a wicked man *d*, his hope perishes;
26: 20 without gossip a quarrel *d* down.
Jn 11: 25 in me will live, even though he *d*;
12: 24 But if it *d*, it produces many seeds.
Ro   7: 2 but if her husband *d*, she is released
14: 7 and none of us *d* to himself alone.
1Co 7: 39 But if her husband *d*, she is free
15: 36 does not come to life unless it *d*.

DIFFERENCE* (DIFFERENT)

2Sa 19: 35 Can I tell the *d* between what is
2Ch 12: 8 so that they may learn the *d*
Eze 22: 26 they teach that there is no *d*
44: 23 are to teach my people the *d*
Ro   3: 22 There is no *d*, for all have sinned
10: 12 For there is no *d* between Jew
Gal 2: 6 whatever they were makes no *d*

DIFFERENCES* (DIFFERENT)

1Co 11: 19 to be *d* among you to show which

DIFFERENT* (DIFFERENCE DIFFERENCES DIFFERING DIFFERS)

Lev 19: 19 '' 'Do not mate *d* kinds of animals.
Nu 14: 24 my servant Caleb has a *d* spirit
1Sa 10: 6 you will be changed into a *d* person
Est 1: 7 each one *d* from the other,
3: 8 Their customs are *d* from those
Da   7: 3 Four great beasts, each *d*
7: 7 It was *d* from all the former beasts,
7: 19 which was *d* from all the others
7: 23 It will be *d* from all the other
7: 24 them another king will arise, *d*
11: 29 but this time the outcome will be *d*
Mk 16: 12 Jesus appeared in a *d* form
Ro 12: 6 We have *d* gifts, according
1Co 4: 7 For who makes you *d*
12: 4 There are *d* kinds of gifts,
12: 5 There are *d* kinds of service,
12: 6 There are *d* kinds of working,

1Co 12: 10 speaking in *d* kinds of tongues,
12: 28 and those speaking in *d* kinds
2Co 11: 4 or a *d* gospel from the one you
11: 4 or if you receive a *d* spirit
Gal 1: 6 and are turning to a *d* gospel—
4: 1 he is no *d* from a slave,
Heb 7: 13 are said belonged to a *d* tribe,
Jas 2: 25 and sent them off in a *d* direction?

DIFFERING* (DIFFERENT)

Dt 25: 13 Do not have two *d* weights
25: 14 Do not have two *d* measures
Pr 20: 10 Differing weights and *d* measures
20: 10 *D* weights and differing measures
20: 23 The LORD detests *d* weights,

DIFFERS* (DIFFERENT)

1Co 15: 41 and star *d* from star in splendor.

DIFFICULT (DIFFICULTIES)

Ex 18: 22 but have them bring every *d* case
Dt 30: 11 commanding you today is not too *d*
2Ki 2: 10 ''You have asked a *d* thing,''
Eze 3: 5 of obscure speech and *d* language,
Ac 15: 19 that we should not make it *d*

DIFFICULTIES* (DIFFICULT)

Dt 31: 17 and *d* will come upon them,
31: 21 when many disasters and *d* come
2Co 12: 10 in hardships, in persecutions, in *d*.

DIGNITY

Pr 31: 25 She is clothed with strength and *d*;

DIGS

Pr 26: 27 If a man *d* a pit, he will fall into it;

DILIGENCE (DILIGENT)

Ezr 5: 8 The work is being carried on with *d*
Heb 6: 11 to show this same *d* to the very end

DILIGENT (DILIGENCE)

Pr 10: 4 but *d* hands bring wealth.
12: 24 *D* hands will rule,
12: 27 the *d* man prizes his possessions.
13: 4 of the *d* are fully satisfied.
21: 5 The plans of the *d* lead to profit
1Ti 4: 15 Be *d* in these matters; give yourself

DINAH*

Only daughter of Jacob, by Leah (Ge 30:21; 46: 15). Raped by Shechem; avenged by Simeon and Levi (Ge 34).

DINE

Pr 23: 1 When you sit to *d* with a ruler,

DIOTREPHES*

3Jn   : 9 but *D*, who loves to be first,

DIRECT (DIRECTED DIRECTIVES DIRECTS)

Ge 18: 19 so that he will *d* his children
Dt 17: 10 to do everything they *d* you to do.
Ps 119: 35 *D* me in the path of your
119:133 *D* my footsteps according
Jer 10: 23 it is not for man to *d* his steps.
2Th 3: 5 May the Lord *d* your hearts
1Ti 5: 17 The elders who *d* the affairs

DIRECTED (DIRECT)

Ge 24: 51 master's son, as the LORD has *d*.''
Nu 16: 40 as the LORD *d* him through Moses
Dt   2: 1 Sea, as the LORD had *d* me.
6: 1 laws the LORD your God *d* me
Jos 11: 9 did to them as the LORD had *d*:
11: 23 just as the LORD had *d* Moses,
Pr 20: 24 A man's steps are *d* by the LORD.
Jer 13: 2 as the LORD *d*, and put it
Ac   7: 44 It had been made as God *d* Moses,
Tit 1: 5 elders in every town, as I *d* you.

DIRECTIVES* (DIRECT)

1Co 11: 17 In the following *d* I have no praise

DIRECTS (DIRECT)

Ps 42: 8 By day the LORD *d* his love,
Isa 48: 17 who *d* you in the way you should

DIRGE*

Mt 11: 17 we sang a *d*,
Lk   7: 32 we sang a *d*,

DISABLED*

Jn   5: 3 number of *d* people used to lie—
Heb 12: 13 so that the lame may not be *d*,

DISAGREEMENT*

Ac 15: 39 had such a sharp *d* that they parted

DISAPPEAR (DISAPPEARED DISAPPEARS)

Mt   5: 18 will by any means *d* from the Law
Lk 16: 17 earth to *d* than for the least stroke
Heb 8: 13 is obsolete and aging will soon *d*.
2Pe 3: 10 The heavens will *d* with a roar;

DISAPPEARED (DISAPPEAR)

1Ki 20: 40 busy here and there, the man *d*.''

DISAPPEARS (DISAPPEAR)

1Co 13: 10 perfection comes, the imperfect *d*.

DISAPPOINT* (DISAPPOINTED)

Ro   5: 5 And hope does not *d* us,

DISAPPOINTED (DISAPPOINT)

Ps 22: 5 in you they trusted and were not *d*.

DISAPPROVE*

Pr 24: 18 or the LORD will see and *d*

DISARMED*

Col 2: 15 And having *d* the powers

DISASTER

Ex 32: 12 and do not bring *d* on your people.
Ps 57: 1 wings until the *d* has passed.
Pr   1: 26 I in turn will laugh at your *d*;
3: 25 Have no fear of sudden *d*
6: 15 Therefore *d* will overtake him
16: 4 even the wicked for a day of *d*.
17: 5 over *d* will not go unpunished.
27: 10 house when *d* strikes you—
Isa 45: 7 I bring prosperity and create *d*;
Jer 17: 17 you are my refuge in the day of *d*.
Eze 7: 5 An unheard-of *d* is coming.

DISCERN (DISCERNED DISCERNING DISCERNMENT)

Ps 19: 12 Who can *d* his errors?
139: 3 You *d* my going out and my lying
Php 1: 10 you may be able to *d* what is best

DISCERNED (DISCERN)

1Co 2: 14 because they are spiritually *d*.

DISCERNING (DISCERN)

1Ki 3: 9 So give your servant a *d* heart
3: 12 I will give you a wise and *d* heart,
Pr   1: 5 and let the *d* get guidance—
8: 9 To the *d* all of them are right;
10: 13 on the lips of the *d*,
14: 6 knowledge comes easily to the *d*.
14: 33 in the heart of the *d*
15: 14 The *d* heart seeks knowledge,
16: 21 The wise in heart are called *d*,
17: 24 A *d* man keeps wisdom in view,
17: 28 and if he holds his tongue.
18: 15 heart of the *d* acquires knowledge;
19: 25 rebuke a *d* man, and he will gain
28: 7 He who keeps the law is a *d* son,

DISCERNMENT (DISCERN)

Ps 119:125 I am your servant; give me *d*
Pr   3: 21 preserve sound judgment and *d*,
17: 10 A rebuke impresses a man of *d*
28: 11 a poor man who has *d* sees

DISCHARGED* (DISCHARGING)

Ecc 8: 8 As no one is *d* in time of war,

DISCHARGING* (DISCHARGED)

1Co 9: 17 I am simply *d* the trust committed

DISCIPLE (DISCIPLES DISCIPLES')

Mt 10: 42 these little ones because he is my *d*,
Lk 14: 26 his own life—he cannot be my *d*.

Lk 14: 27 and follow me cannot be my *d*.
    14: 33 everything he has cannot be my *d*.
Jn 13: 23 of them, the *d* whom Jesus loved,
    19: 26 and the *d* whom he loved standing
    21: 7 Then the *d* whom Jesus loved said
    21: 20 saw that the *d* whom Jesus loved

DISCIPLES (DISCIPLE)

Mt 10: 1 He called his twelve *d* to him
    26: 56 Then all the *d* deserted him
    28: 19 Therefore go and make *d*
Mk 3: 7 withdrew with his *d* to the lake,
    16: 20 Then the *d* went out and preached
Lk 6: 13 he called his *d* to him and chose
Jn 2: 11 and his *d* put their faith in him.
    6: 66 many of his *d* turned back
    8: 31 to my teaching, you are really my *d*
    12: 16 At first his *d* did not understand all
    13: 35 men will know that you are my *d*
    15: 8 showing yourselves to be my *d*.
    20: 20 The *d* were overjoyed
Ac 6: 1 the number of *d* was increasing,
    11: 26 The *d* were called Christians first
    14: 22 strengthening the *d*
    18: 23 Phrygia, strengthening all the *d*.

DISCIPLES' (DISCIPLE)

Jn 13: 5 and began to wash his *d* feet,

DISCIPLINE* (DISCIPLINED DISCIPLINES SELF-DISCIPLINE)

Dt 4: 36 made you hear his voice to *d* you.
    11: 2 and experienced the *d*
    21: 18 listen to them when they *d* him,
Job 5: 17 so do not despise the *d*
Ps 6: 1 or *d* me in your wrath.
    38: 1 or *d* me in your wrath.
    39: 11 You rebuke and *d* men for their sin;
    94: 12 Blessed is the man you *d*, O LORD
Pr 1: 2 for attaining wisdom and *d*,
    1: 7 but fools despise wisdom and *d*.
    3: 11 do not despise the LORD's *d*
    5: 12 You will say, ''How I hated *d!*
    5: 23 He will die for lack of *d*,
    6: 23 and the corrections of *d*
    10: 17 He who heeds *d* shows the way
    12: 1 Whoever loves *d* loves knowledge,
    13: 18 He who ignores *d* comes to poverty
    13: 24 who loves him is careful to *d* him.
    15: 5 A fool spurns his father's *d*,
    15: 10 Stern *d* awaits him who leaves
    15: 32 He who ignores *d* despises himself,
    19: 18 *D* your son, for in that there is hope
    22: 15 the rod of *d* will drive it far
    23: 13 Do not withhold *d* from a child;
    23: 23 get wisdom, *d* and understanding.
    29: 17 *D* your son, and he will give you
Jer 17: 23 would not listen or respond to *d*.
    30: 11 I will *d* you but only with justice;
    32: 33 would not listen or respond to *d*.
    46: 28 I will *d* you but only with justice;
Hos 5: 2 I will *d* all of them.
Heb 12: 5 do not make light of the Lord's *d*,
    12: 7 as *d;* God is treating you
    12: 8 (and everyone undergoes *d*),
    12: 11 No *d* seems pleasant at the time,
Rev 3: 19 Those whom I love I rebuke and *d*.

DISCIPLINED* (DISCIPLINE)

Pr 1: 3 for acquiring a *d* and prudent life,
Isa 26: 16 when you *d* them,
Jer 31: 18 and I have been *d*.
    31: 18 'You *d* me like an unruly calf,
1Co 11: 32 we are being *d* so that we will not
Tit 1: 8 upright, holy and *d*.
Heb 12: 7 For what son is not *d* by his father?
    12: 8 you are not *d* (and everyone
    12: 9 all had human fathers who *d* us
    12: 10 Our fathers *d* us for a little while

DISCIPLINES* (DISCIPLINE)

Dt 8: 5 so the LORD your God *d* you.
    8: 5 your heart that as a man *d* his son,
Ps 94: 10 Does he who *d* nations not punish?
Pr 3: 12 the LORD *d* those he loves,
Heb 12: 6 because the Lord *d* those he loves,
    12: 10 but God *d* us for our good,

DISCLOSED

Lk 8: 17 is nothing hidden that will not be *d*,
Col 1: 26 and generations, but is now *d*
Heb 9: 8 Holy Place had not yet been *d*

DISCORD

Gal 5: 20 idolatry and witchcraft; hatred, *d*,

DISCOURAGED* (DISCOURAGEMENT)

Nu 32: 9 they *d* the Israelites
Dt 1: 21 Do not be afraid; do not be *d*.''
    31: 8 Do not be afraid; do not be *d*.''
Jos 1: 9 Do not be terrified; do not be *d*,
    8: 1 ''Do not be afraid; do not be *d*.
    10: 25 ''Do not be afraid; do not be *d*.
1Ch 22: 13 Do not be afraid or *d*.
    28: 20 or *d*, for the LORD God,
2Ch 20: 15 or *d* because of this vast army.
    20: 17 Do not be afraid; do not be *d*.
    32: 7 or *d* because of the king of Assyria
Job 4: 5 to you, and you are *d;*
Isa 42: 4 he will not falter or be *d*
Eph 3: 13 to be *d* because of my sufferings
Col 3: 21 children, or they will become *d*.

DISCOURAGEMENT* (DISCOURAGED)

Ex 6: 9 of their *d* and cruel bondage.

DISCOVERED

2Ki 23: 24 book that Hilkiah the priest had *d*

DISCREDIT* (DISCREDITED)

Ne 6: 13 would give me a bad name to *d* me.
Job 40: 8 ''Would you *d* my justice?

DISCREDITED (DISCREDIT)

2Co 6: 3 so that our ministry will not be *d*.

DISCRETION*

1Ch 22: 12 May the LORD give you *d*
Pr 1: 4 knowledge and *d* to the young—
    2: 11 *D* will protect you,
    5: 2 that you may maintain *d*
    8: 12 I possess knowledge and *d*.
    11: 22 a beautiful woman who shows no *d*.

DISCRIMINATED*

Jas 2: 4 have you not *d* among yourselves

DISEASE (DISEASES)

Mt 4: 23 and healing every *d* and sickness
    9: 35 and healing every *d* and sickness.
    10: 1 and to heal every *d* and sickness.

DISEASES (DISEASE)

Ps 103: 3 and heals all my *d;*
Mt 8: 17 and carried our *d*.''
Mk 3: 10 those with *d* were pushing forward
Lk 9: 1 drive out all demons and to cure *d*,

DISFIGURE* (DISFIGURED)

Mt 6: 16 for they *d* their faces

DISFIGURED (DISFIGURE)

Isa 52: 14 his appearance was so *d*

DISGRACE (DISGRACEFUL DISGRACES)

Ps 44: 15 My *d* is before me all day long,
    52: 1 you who are a *d* in the eyes of God?
    74: 21 not let the oppressed retreat in *d;*
Pr 6: 33 Blows and *d* are his lot,
    11: 2 When pride comes, then comes *d*,
    14: 34 but sin is a *d* to any people.
    19: 26 is a son who brings shame and *d*.
Mt 1: 19 want to expose her to public *d*,
Ac 5: 41 of suffering *d* for the Name.
1Co 11: 6 and if it is a *d* for a woman
    11: 14 it is a *d* to him, but that
1Ti 3: 7 so that he will not fall into *d*
Heb 6: 6 and subjecting him to public *d*.
    11: 26 He regarded *d* for the sake
    13: 13 the camp, bearing the *d* he bore.

DISGRACEFUL (DISGRACE)

Pr 10: 5 during harvest is a *d* son.
    12: 4 a *d* wife is like decay in his bones.
    17: 2 wise servant will rule over a *d* son,

1Co 14: 35 for it is *d* for a woman to speak

DISGRACES (DISGRACE)

Pr 28: 7 of gluttons *d* his father.
    29: 15 but a child left to himself *d* his mother

DISGUISES*

Pr 26: 24 A malicious man *d* himself

DISH

Pr 19: 24 sluggard buries his hand in the *d;*
Mt 23: 25 the outside of the cup and *d*,

DISHONEST*

Ex 18: 21 trustworthy men who hate *d* gain
Lev 19: 35 '' 'Do not use *d* standards
1Sa 8: 3 They turned aside after *d* gain
Pr 11: 1 The LORD abhors *d* scales,
    13: 11 *D* money dwindles away,
    20: 23 and *d* scales do not please him.
    29: 27 The righteous detest the *d;*
Jer 22: 17 are set only on *d* gain,
Eze 28: 18 By your many sins and *d* trade
Hos 12: 7 The merchant uses *d* scales;
Am 8: 5 and cheating with *d* scales,
Mic 6: 11 Shall I acquit a man with *d* scales,
Lk 16: 8 master commended the *d* manager
    16: 10 whoever is *d* with very little will
    16: 10 with very little will also be *d*
1Ti 3: 8 wine, and not pursuing *d* gain.
Tit 1: 7 not violent, not pursuing *d* gain.
    1: 11 and that for the sake of *d* gain.

DISHONOR* (DISHONORED DISHONORS)

Lev 18: 7 '' 'Do not *d* your father.
    18: 8 wife; that would *d* your father.
    18: 10 daughter; that would *d* you.
    18: 14 '' 'Do not *d* your father's brother
    18: 16 that would *d* your brother.
    20: 19 for that would *d* a close relative;
Dt 22: 30 he must not *d* his father's bed.
Pr 30: 9 and so *d* the name of my God.
Jer 14: 21 do not *d* your glorious throne.
    20: 11 their *d* will never be forgotten.
La 2: 2 princes down to the ground in *d*.
Eze 22: 10 are those who *d* their fathers' bed;
Jn 8: 49 I honor my Father and you *d* me.
Ro 2: 23 do you *d* God by breaking the law?
1Co 15: 43 it is sown in *d*, it is raised in glory;
2Co 6: 8 through glory and *d*, bad report

DISHONORED* (DISHONOR)

Lev 20: 11 father's wife, he has *d* his father.
    20: 17 He has *d* his sister and will be held
    20: 20 with his aunt, he has *d* his uncle.
    20: 21 of impurity; he has *d* his brother.
Dt 21: 14 as a slave, since you have *d* her.
Ezr 4: 14 proper for us to see the king *d*,
1Co 4: 10 You are honored, we are *d!*

DISHONORS* (DISHONOR)

Dt 27: 16 Cursed is the man who *d* his father
    27: 20 for he *d* his father's bed.''
Job 20: 3 hear a rebuke that *d* me,
Mic 7: 6 For a son *d* his father,
1Co 11: 4 with his head covered *d* his head.
    11: 5 her head uncovered *d* her head—

DISILLUSIONMENT*

Ps 7: 14 conceives trouble gives birth to *d*.

DISMAYED

Isa 28: 16 the one who trusts will never be *d*.
    41: 10 do not be *d*, for I am your God.

DISOBEDIENCE* (DISOBEY)

Jos 22: 22 in rebellion or *d* to the LORD,
Jer 43: 7 So they entered Egypt in *d*
Ro 5: 19 as through the *d* of the one man
    11: 30 mercy as a result of their *d*,
    11: 32 to *d* so that he may have mercy
2Co 10: 6 ready to punish every act of *d*,
Heb 2: 2 and received its just punishment,
    4: 6 go in, because of their *d*.
    4: 11 fall by following their example of *d*.

DISOBEDIENT* (DISOBEY)

Ne   9: 26 "But they were *d* and rebelled
Lk   1: 17 and the *d* to the wisdom
Ac   26: 19 I was not *d* to the vision
Ro   10: 21 hands to a *d* and obstinate people."
    11: 30 as you who were at one time *d*
    11: 31 so they too have now become *d*
Eph   2: 2 now at work in those who are *d*.
    5: 6 comes on those who are *d*.
    5: 12 to mention what the *d* do in secret.
2Ti   3: 2 proud, abusive, *d* to their parents,
Tit   1: 6 to the charge of being wild and *d*.
    1: 16 *d* and unfit for doing anything
    3: 3 At one time we too were foolish, *d*,
Heb   11: 31 killed with those who were *d*.

DISOBEY* (DISOBEDIENCE DISOBEDIENT DISOBEYED DISOBEYING DISOBEYS)

Dt   11: 28 the curse if you *d* the commands
2Ch   24: 20 'Why do you *d* the LORD's
Est   3: 3 Why do you *d* the king's command
Jer   42: 13 and so *d* the LORD your God,
Ro   1: 30 they *d* their parents; they are
1Pe   2: 8 because they *d* the message—

DISOBEYED* (DISOBEY)

Nu   14: 22 and in the desert but who *d* me
    27: 14 both of you *d* my command
Jdg   2: 2 Yet you have *d* me.
Ne   9: 29 arrogant and *d* your commands.
Isa   24: 5 they have *d* the laws,
Jer   43: 4 and all the people *d* the LORD's
Lk   15: 29 for you and never *d* your orders.
Heb   3: 18 rest if not to those who *d?*
1Pe   3: 20 the spirits in prison who *d* long ago

DISOBEYING* (DISOBEY)

Nu   14: 41 "Why are you *d* the LORD's

DISOBEYS* (DISOBEY)

Eze   33: 12 man will not save him when he *d*,

DISORDER

1Co   14: 33 For God is not a God of *d*
2Co   12: 20 slander, gossip, arrogance and *d*,
Jas   3: 16 there you find *d* and every evil

DISOWN (DISOWNS)

Pr   30: 9 I may have too much and *d* you
Mt   10: 33 I will *d* him before my Father
    26: 35 to die with you, I will never *d* you."
2Ti   2: 12 If we *d* him,

DISOWNS (DISOWN)

Lk   12: 9 he who *d* me before men will be

DISPENSATION see ADMINISTRATION, TRUST

DISPLACES

Pr   30: 23 a maidservant who *d* her mistress.

DISPLAY (DISPLAYED DISPLAYS)

Ps   45: 4 your right hand *d* awesome deeds.
Eze   39: 21 I will *d* my glory among the nations
Ro   9: 17 that I might *d* my power in you
1Co   4: 9 on *d* at the end of the procession,
1Ti   1: 16 Christ Jesus might *d* his unlimited

DISPLAYED (DISPLAY)

Jn   9: 3 work of God might be *d* in his life.
2Th   2: 9 the work of Satan *d* in all kinds

DISPLAYS (DISPLAY)

Isa   44: 23 he *d* his glory in Israel.

DISPLEASE (DISPLEASED)

1Th   2: 15 They *d* God and are hostile

DISPLEASED (DISPLEASE)

2Sa   11: 27 David had done *d* the LORD.

DISPUTABLE* (DISPUTE)

Ro   14: 1 passing judgment on *d* matters.

DISPUTE (DISPUTABLE DISPUTES DISPUTING)

Pr   17: 14 before a *d* breaks out.
1Co   6: 1 If any of you has a *d* with another,

DISPUTES (DISPUTE)

Pr   18: 18 Casting the lot settles *d*

DISPUTING (DISPUTE)

1Ti   2: 8 in prayer, without anger or *d*.

DISQUALIFIED*

1Co   9: 27 I myself will not be *d* for the prize.

DISREPUTE*

2Pe   2: 2 will bring the way of truth into *d*.

DISSENSION* (DISSENSIONS)

Pr   6: 14 he always stirs up *d*.
    6: 19 and a man who stirs up *d*
    10: 12 Hatred stirs up *d*,
    15: 18 A hot-tempered man stirs up *d*,
    16: 28 A perverse man stirs up *d*,
    28: 25 A greedy man stirs up *d*,
    29: 22 An angry man stirs up *d*,
Ro   13: 13 debauchery, not in *d* and jealousy.

DISSENSIONS* (DISSENSION)

Gal   5: 20 selfish ambition, *d*, factions

DISSIPATION*

Lk   21: 34 will be weighed down with *d*,
1Pe   4: 4 with them into the same flood of *d*,

DISTINCTION

Ac   15: 9 He made no *d* between us

DISTINGUISH (DISTINGUISHING)

1Ki   3: 9 and to *d* between right and wrong.
Heb   5: 14 themselves to *d* good from evil.

DISTINGUISHING

1Co   12: 10 the *d* between spirits,

DISTORT

Ac   20: 30 and *d* the truth in order
2Co   4: 2 nor do we *d* the word of God.
2Pe   3: 16 ignorant and unstable people *d*,

DISTRACTED*

Lk   10: 40 But Martha was *d* by all

DISTRESS (DISTRESSED)

2Ch   15: 4 in their *d* they turned to the LORD
Ps   18: 6 In my *d* I called to the LORD;
    81: 7 In your *d* you called and I rescued
    120: 1 I call on the LORD in my *d*,
Jnh   2: 2 "In my *d* I called to the LORD,
Mt   24: 21 For then there will be great *d*,
Jas   1: 27 after orphans and widows in their *d*

DISTRESSED (DISTRESS)

Lk   12: 50 how *d* I am until it is completed!
Ro   14: 15 If your brother is *d*

DIVIDE (DIVIDED DIVIDING DIVISION DIVISIONS DIVISIVE)

Ps   22: 18 They *d* my garments among them

DIVIDED (DIVIDE)

Mt   12: 25 household *d* against itself will not
Lk   23: 34 they *d* up his clothes by casting lots
1Co   1: 13 Is Christ *d?* Was Paul crucified

DIVIDING (DIVIDE)

Eph   2: 14 destroyed the barrier, the *d* wall
Heb   4: 12 it penetrates even to *d* soul

DIVINATION

Lev   19: 26 " 'Do not practice *d* or sorcery.

DIVINE

Ro   1: 20 his eternal power and *d* nature—
2Co   10: 4 they have *d* power
2Pe   1: 4 you may participate in the *d* nature

DIVISION (DIVIDE)

Lk   12: 51 on earth? No, I tell you, but *d*.
1Co   12: 25 so that there should be no *d*

DIVISIONS (DIVIDE)

Ro   16: 17 to watch out for those who cause *d*
1Co   1: 10 another so that there may be no *d*
    11: 18 there are *d* among you,

DIVISIVE* (DIVIDE)

Tit   3: 10 Warn a *d* person once,

DIVORCE* (DIVORCED DIVORCES)

Dt   22: 19 he must not *d* her as long as he lives
    22: 29 He can never *d* her as long
    24: 1 and he writes her a certificate of *d*,
    24: 3 and writes her a certificate of *d*,
Isa   50: 1 is your mother's certificate of *d*
Jer   3: 8 faithless Israel her certificate of *d*
Mal   2: 16 "I hate," says the LORD God
Mt   1: 19 he had in mind to *d* her quietly.
    5: 31 must give her a certificate of *d*.'
    19: 3 for a man to *d* his wife for any
    19: 7 man give his wife a certificate of *d*
    19: 8 permitted you to *d* your wives
Mk   10: 2 Is it lawful for a man to *d* his wife?"
    10: 4 a man to write a certificate of *d*
1Co   7: 11 And a husband must not *d* his wife.
    7: 12 to live with him, he must not *d* her.
    7: 13 to live with her, she must not *d* him
    7: 27 Are you married? Do not seek a *d*.

DIVORCED* (DIVORCE)

Lev   21: 7 or *d* from their husbands,
    21: 14 not marry a widow, a *d* woman,
    22: 13 daughter becomes a widow or is *d*,
Nu   30: 9 or *d* woman will be binding on her.
Dt   24: 4 then her first husband, who *d* her,
1Ch   8: 8 after he had *d* his wives Hushim
Eze   44: 22 not marry widows or *d* women;
Mt   5: 32 marries the *d* woman commits adultery.
Lk   16: 18 who marries a *d* woman commits

DIVORCES* (DIVORCE)

Jer   3: 1 "If a man *d* his wife
Mt   5: 31 'Anyone who *d* his wife must give
    5: 32 tell you that anyone who *d* his wife,
    19: 9 tell you that anyone who *d* his wife,
Mk   10: 11 "Anyone who *d* his wife
    10: 12 And if she *d* her husband
Lk   16: 18 "Anyone who *d* his wife

DOCTOR

Mt   9: 12 "It is not the healthy who need a *d*,

DOCTRINE* (DOCTRINES)

1Ti   1: 10 to the sound *d* that conforms
    4: 16 Watch your life and *d* closely.
2Ti   4: 3 men will not put up with sound *d*.
Tit   1: 9 can encourage others by sound *d*
    2: 1 is in accord with sound *d*.

DOCTRINES* (DOCTRINE)

1Ti   1: 3 not to teach false *d* any longer
    6: 3 If anyone teaches false *d*

DOEG*

Edomite; Saul's head shepherd; responsible for murder of priests at Nob (1Sa 21:7; 22:6-23; Ps 52).

DOG (DOGS)

Pr   26: 11 As a *d* returns to its vomit,
Ecc   9: 4 a live *d* is better off than a dead lion
2Pe   2: 22 "A *d* returns to its vomit," and,

DOGS (DOG)

Mt   7: 6 "Do not give *d* what is sacred;
    15: 26 bread and toss it to their *d*."

DOMINION

Job   25: 2 "*D* and awe belong to God;
Ps   22: 28 for *d* belongs to the LORD

DONKEY

Nu   22: 30 *d* said to Balaam, "Am I not your
Zec   9: 9 gentle and riding on a *d*,
Mt   21: 5 gentle and riding on a *d*,
2Pe   2: 16 for his wrongdoing by a *d*—

DOOR (DOORS)

Job   31: 32 for my *d* was always open

Ps 141: 3 keep watch over the *d* of my lips.
Mt 6: 6 close the *d* and pray to your Father
7: 7 and the *d* will be opened to you.
Ac 14:27 how he had opened the *d* of faith
1Co 16: 9 a great *d* for effective work has
2Co 2:12 found that the Lord had opened a *d*
Rev 3:20 I stand at the *d* and knock.

DOORFRAMES
Dt 6: 9 Write them on the *d* of your houses

DOORKEEPER
Ps 84:10 I would rather be a *d* in the house

DOORS (DOOR)
Ps 24: 7 be lifted up, you ancient *d,*

DORCAS
Ac 9:36 is *D)*, who was always doing good

DOUBLE
2Ki 2: 9 "Let me inherit a *d* portion
1Ti 5:17 church well are worthy of *d* honor,

DOUBLE-EDGED (EDGE)
Heb 4:12 Sharper than any *d* sword,
Rev 1:16 of his mouth came a sharp *d* sword.
2:12 of him who has the sharp, *d* sword.

DOUBLE-MINDED* (MIND)
Ps 119:113 I hate *d* men,
Jas 1: 8 he is a *d* man, unstable
4: 8 and purify your hearts, you *d.*

DOUBT (DOUBTING DOUBTS)
Mt 14:31 he said, "why did you *d?*"
21:21 if you have faith and do not *d,*
Mk 11:23 and does not *d* in his heart
Jas 1: 6 he must believe and not *d,*
Jude : 22 Be merciful to those who *d;*

DOUBTING* (DOUBT)
Jn 20:27 Stop *d* and believe."

DOUBTS* (DOUBT)
Lk 24:38 and why do *d* rise in your minds?
Ro 14:23 the man who has *d* is condemned
Jas 1: 6 he who *d* is like a wave of the sea,

DOVE (DOVES)
Ge 8: 8 Then he sent out a *d* to see
Mt 3:16 Spirit of God descending like a *d*

DOVES (DOVE)
Lev 12: 8 is to bring two *d* or two young
Mt 10:16 as snakes and as innocent as *d.*
Lk 2:24 "a pair of *d* or two young pigeons."

DOWNCAST
Ps 42: 5 Why are you *d,* O my soul?
2Co 7: 6 But God, who comforts the *d,*

DOWNFALL
Hos 14: 1 Your sins have been your *d!*

DRAGON
Rev 12: 7 and his angels fought against the *d,*
13: 2 The *d* gave the beast his power
20: 2 He seized the *d,* that ancient

DRAW (DRAWING DRAWS)
Mt 26:52 "for all who *d* the sword will die
Jn 12:32 up from the earth, will *d* all men
Heb 10:22 let us *d* near to God

DRAWING (DRAW)
Lk 21:28 because your redemption is *d* near

DRAWS (DRAW)
Jn 6:44 the Father who sent me *d* him,

DREAD (DREADFUL)
Ps 53: 5 they were, overwhelmed with *d,*

DREADFUL (DREAD)
Mt 24:19 How *d* it will be in those days
Heb 10:31 It is a *d* thing to fall into the hands

DREAM
Joel 2:28 your old men will *d* dreams,
Ac 2:17 your old men will *d* dreams.

DRESS
1Ti 2: 9 I also want women to *d* modestly,

DRIFT*
Heb 2: 1 so that we do not *d* away.

DRINK (DRINKING DRINKS DRUNK DRUNKARD DRUNKARD'S DRUNKARDS DRUNKENNESS)
Ex 29:40 of a hin of wine as a *d* offering.
Nu 6: 3 He must not *d* grape juice
Jdg 7: 5 from those who kneel down to *d.*"
2Sa 23:15 that someone would get me a *d*
Pr 5:15 *D* water from your own cistern,
Mt 20:22 "Can you *d* the cup I am going to *d*
26:27 saying, "*D* from it, all of you.
Mk 16:18 and when they *d* deadly poison,
Lk 12:19 Take life easy; eat, *d* and be merry
Jn 7:37 let him come to me and *d.*
18:11 Shall I not *d* the cup the Father has
1Co 10: 4 and drank the same spiritual *d;*
12:13 were all given the one Spirit to *d.*
Php 2:17 being poured out like a *d* offering
2Ti 4: 6 being poured out like a *d* offering,
Rev 14:10 too, will *d* of the wine of God's fury
21: 6 to *d* without cost from the spring

DRINKING (DRINK)
Ro 14:17 God is not a matter of eating and *d,*

DRINKS (DRINK)
Isa 5:22 and champions at mixing *d,*
Jn 4:13 "Everyone who *d* this water will be
6:54 and *d* my blood has eternal life,
1Co 11:27 or *d* the cup of the Lord

DRIPPING
Pr 19:13 wife is like a constant *d.*
27:15 a constant *d* on a rainy day;

DRIVE (DRIVES)
Ex 23:30 Little by little I will *d* them out
Nu 33:52 *d* out all the inhabitants of the land
Jos 13:13 Israelites did not *d* out the people
23:13 will no longer *d* out these nations
Pr 22:10 *D* out the mocker, and out goes
Mt 10: 1 authority to *d* out evil spirits
Jn 6:37 comes to me I will never *d* away.

DRIVES (DRIVE)
Mt 12:26 If Satan *d* out Satan, he is divided
1Jn 4:18 But perfect love *d* out fear,

DROP (DROPS)
Pr 17:14 so *d* the matter before a dispute
Isa 40:15 Surely the nations are like a *d*

DROPS (DROP)
Lk 22:44 his sweat was like *d* of blood falling

DROSS
Ps 119:119 of the earth you discard like *d;*
Pr 25: 4 Remove the *d* from the silver,

DROUGHT
Jer 17: 8 It has no worries in a year of *d*

DROWNED
Ex 15: 4 are *d* in the Red Sea.
Mt 18: 6 and to be *d* in the depths of the sea.
Heb 11:29 tried to do so, they were *d.*

DROWSINESS*
Pr 23:21 and *d* clothes them in rags.

DRUNK (DRINK)
1Sa 1:13 Eli thought she was *d* and said
Ac 2:15 men are not *d,* as you suppose.
Eph 5:18 Do not get *d* on wine, which leads

DRUNKARD (DRINK)
Mt 11:19 and a *d,* a friend of tax collectors
1Co 5:11 or a slanderer, a *d* or a swindler.

DRUNKARD'S* (DRINK)
Pr 26: 9 Like a thornbush in a *d* hand

DRUNKARDS (DRINK)
Pr 23:21 for *d* and gluttons become poor,
1Co 6:10 nor the greedy nor *d* nor slanderers

DRUNKENNESS (DRINK)
Lk 21:34 weighed down with dissipation, *d*
Ro 13:13 and *d,* not in sexual immorality
Gal 5:21 factions and envy; *d,* orgies,
1Ti 3: 3 not given to *d,* not violent
1Pe 4: 3 living in debauchery, lust, *d,* orgies,

DRY
Ge 1: 9 place, and let *d* ground appear."
Ex 14:16 go through the sea on *d* ground.
Jos 3:17 the crossing on *d* ground.
Isa 53: 2 and like a root out of *d* ground.
Eze 37: 4 '*D* bones, hear the word

DULL
Isa 6:10 make their ears *d*
2Co 3:14 But their minds were made *d,*

DUMB
Mk 7:37 the deaf hear and the *d* speak."
1Co 12: 2 and led astray to *d* idols.

DUST
Ge 2: 7 man from the *d* of the ground
3:19 for *d* you are
Job 42: 6 and repent in *d* and ashes."
Ps 22:15 you lay me in the *d* of death.
103: 14 he remembers that we are *d.*
Ecc 3:20 all come from *d,* and to all return.
Mt 10:14 shake the *d* off your feet
1Co 15:47 was of the *d* of the earth,

DUTIES (DUTY)
2Ti 4: 5 discharge all the *d* of your ministry

DUTY (DUTIES)
Ecc 12:13 for this is the whole *d* of man.
Ac 23: 1 I have fulfilled my *d* to God
1Co 7: 3 husband should fulfill his marital *d*

DWELL (DWELLING DWELLINGS DWELLS DWELT)
Ex 25: 8 for me, and I will *d* among them.
2Sa 7: 5 the one to build me a house to *d* in?
1Ki 8:27 "But will God really *d* on earth?
Ps 23: 6 I will *d* in the house of the LORD
37: 3 *d* in the land and enjoy safe pasture
61: 4 I long to *d* in your tent forever
Pr 8:12 wisdom, *d* together with prudence;
Isa 33:14 of us can *d* with the consuming fire
43:18 do not *d* on the past.
Jn 5:38 nor does his word *d* in you,
Eph 3:17 so that Christ may *d* in your hearts
Col 1:19 to have all his fullness *d* in him,
3:16 the word of Christ *d* in you richly

DWELLING (DWELL)
Lev 26:11 I will put my *d* place among you,
Dt 26:15 from heaven, your holy *d* place,
Ps 90: 1 Lord, you have been our *d* place
2Co 5: 2 to be clothed with our heavenly *d,*
Eph 2:22 to become a *d* in which God lives

DWELLINGS (DWELL)
Lk 16: 9 will be welcomed into eternal *d.*

DWELLS (DWELL)
Ps 46: 4 holy place where the Most High *d.*
91: 1 He who *d* in the shelter

DWELT (DWELL)
Dt 33:16 of him who *d* in the burning bush.

DYING (DIE)
Ro 7: 6 by *d* to what once bound us,
2Co 6: 9 yet regarded as unknown; *d,*

EAGER
Pr 31:13 and works with *e* hands.
Ro 8:19 The creation waits in *e* expectation
1Co 14:12 Since you are *e* to have spiritual

1Co 14: 39 my brothers, be *e* to prophesy,
Tit   2: 14 a people that are his very own, *e*
1Pe   5: 2 greedy for money, but *e* to serve;

EAGLE (EAGLE'S EAGLES)

Dt 32: 11 like an *e* that stirs up its nest
Eze   1: 10 each also had the face of an *e*.
Rev   4: 7 the fourth was like a flying *e*.
      12: 14 given the two wings of a great *e*,

EAGLE'S (EAGLE)

Ps 103: 5 my youth is renewed like the *e*.

EAGLES (EAGLE)

Isa 40: 31 They will soar on wings like *e*;

EAR (EARS)

Ex 21: 6 and pierce his *e* with an awl.
Ps   5: 1 Give *e* to my words, O LORD.
Pr   2: 2 turning your *e* to wisdom
1Co   2: 9 no *e* has heard,
      12: 16 if the *e* should say, "Because I am
Rev   2: 7 He who has an *e*, let him hear what

EARN (EARNED EARNINGS)

2Th   3: 12 down and *e* the bread they eat.

EARNED (EARN)

Pr 31: 31 Give her the reward she has *e*,

EARNEST see DEPOSIT

EARNESTNESS

2Co   7: 11 what *e*, what eagerness
       8: 7 in complete *e* and in your love

EARNINGS (EARN)

Pr 31: 16 out of her *e* she plants a vineyard.

EARRING (EARRINGS)

Pr 25: 12 Like an *e* of gold or an ornament

EARRINGS (EARRING)

Ex 32: 2 Take off the gold *e* that your wives,

EARS (EAR)

Job 42: 5 My *e* had heard of you
Ps 34: 15 and his *e* are attentive to their cry;
Pr 21: 13 If a man shuts his *e* to the cry
      26: 17 Like one who seizes a dog by the *e*
Isa   6: 10 hear with their *e*,
Mt 11: 15 He who has *e*, let him hear.
2Ti   4: 3 to say what their itching *e* want
1Pe   3: 12 his *e* are attentive to their prayer.

EARTH (EARTH'S EARTHLY)

Ge   1: 1 God created the heavens and the *e*.
       1: 2 Now the *e* was formless and empty.
       7: 24 The waters flooded the *e*
     14: 19 Creator of heaven and *e*.
1Ki   8: 27 "But will God really dwell on *e*?
Job 26: 7 he suspends the *e* over nothing.
Ps 24: 1 is the LORD's, and everything
     46: 6 he lifts his voice, the *e* melts.
     90: 2 or you brought forth the *e*
     97: 5 before the Lord of all the *e*.
   102: 25 you laid the foundations of the *e*,
   108: 5 and let your glory be over all the *e*.
Pr   8: 26 before he made the *e* or its fields
Isa   6: 3 the whole *e* is full of his glory."
     24: 20 The *e* reels like a drunkard,
     37: 16 You have made heaven and *e*.
     40: 22 enthroned above the circle of the *e*,
     51: 6 the *e* will wear out like a garment
     54: 5 he is called the God of all the *e*.
     55: 9 the heavens are higher than the *e*,
     65: 17 new heavens and a new *e*.
     66: 1 and the *e* is my footstool.
Jer 10: 10 When he is angry, the *e* trembles;
     23: 24 "Do not I fill heaven and *e*?"
     33: 25 and the fixed laws of heaven and *e*,
Hab   2: 20 let all the *e* be silent before him."
Mt   5: 5 for they will inherit the *e*.
      5: 35 or by the *e*, for it is his footstool;
      6: 10 done on *e* as it is in heaven.
     16: 19 bind on *e* will be bound
     24: 35 Heaven and *e* will pass away,
     28: 18 and on *e* has been given to me.
Lk   2: 14 on *e* peace to men

Jn   12: 32 when I am lifted up from the *e*,
Ac   4: 24 "you made the heaven and the *e*
      7: 49 and the *e* is my footstool.
1Co 10: 26 The *e* is the Lord's, and everything
Eph   3: 15 in heaven and on *e* derives its name
Php   2: 10 in heaven and on *e* and under the *e*,
Heb   1: 10 you laid the foundations of the *e*,
2Pe   3: 13 to a new heaven and a new *e*,
Rev   8: 7 A third of the *e* was burned up,
     12: 12 But woe to the *e* and the sea,
     20: 11 *E* and sky fled from his presence,
     21: 1 I saw a new heaven and a new *e*,
     21: 1 and the first *e* had passed away,

EARTH'S (EARTH)

Job 38: 4 when I laid the *e* foundation?

EARTHENWARE

Pr 26: 23 Like a coating of glaze over *e*

EARTHLY (EARTH)

Eph   4: 9 descended to the lower, *e* regions?
Php   3: 19 Their mind is on *e* things.
Col   3: 2 on things above, not on *e* things.
      3: 5 whatever belongs to your *e* nature:

EARTHQUAKE (EARTHQUAKES)

Eze 38: 19 at that time there shall be a great *e*
Mt 28: 2 There was a violent *e*, for an angel
Rev   6: 12 There was a great *e*.

EARTHQUAKES (EARTHQUAKE)

Mt 24: 7 There will be famines and *e*

EASE

Pr   1: 33 and be at *e*, without fear of harm."

EASIER (EASY)

Lk 16: 17 It is *e* for heaven and earth
     18: 25 it is *e* for a camel to go

EAST

Ge   2: 8 God had planted a garden in the *e*.
Ps 103: 12 as far as the *e* is from the west,
Eze 43: 2 God of Israel coming from the *e*.
Mt   2: 1 Magi from the *e* came to Jerusalem
      2: 2 We saw his star in the *e*

EASY (EASIER)

Mt 11: 30 For my yoke is *e* and my burden is

EAT (ATE EATEN EATER EATING EATS)

Ge   2: 16 "You are free to *e* from any tree
      2: 17 but you must not *e* from the tree
      3: 19 you will *e* your food
Ex 12: 11 *E* in haste; it is the LORD's
Lev 11: 2 these are the ones you may *e*:
     17: 12 "None of you may *e* blood.
Dt   8: 16 He gave you manna to *e*
     14: 4 These are the animals you may *e*:
Jdg 14: 14 "Out of the eater, something to *e*;
2Sa 9: 7 and you will always *e* at my table."
Pr 31: 27 and does not *e* the bread of idleness
Isa 55: 1 come, buy and *e!*
     65: 25 and the lion will *e* straw like the ox,
Eze 3: 1 *e* what is before you, *e* this scroll;
Mt 14: 16 You give them something to *e*."
     15: 2 wash their hands before they *e!*"
     26: 26 "Take and *e*; this is my body."
Mk 14: 14 where I may *e* the Passover
Lk 10: 8 and are welcomed, *e* what is set
     12: 19 Take life easy; *e*, drink
     12: 22 what you will *e*; or about your body
Jn   4: 32 to *e* that you know nothing about."
      6: 31 bread from heaven to *e*.'
      6: 52 can this man give us his flesh to *e*?"
Ac 10: 13 Kill and *e*.'
Ro 14: 2 faith allows him to *e* everything.
     14: 15 is distressed because of what you *e*,
     14: 20 to *e* anything that causes someone
     14: 21 It is better not to *e* meat
1Co 5: 11 With such a man do not even *e*
      8: 13 if what I *e* causes my brother to fall
     10: 25 *E* anything sold in the meat market
     10: 27 *e* whatever is put before you
     10: 31 So whether you *e* or drink
     11: 26 For whenever you *e* this bread

2Th   3: 10 man will not work, he shall not *e*."
Rev   2: 7 the right to *e* from the tree of life,
      3: 20 I will come in and *e* with him,

EATEN (EAT)

Ge   3: 11 Have you *e* from the tree that I
Ac 10: 14 "I have never *e* anything impure
Rev 10: 10 when I had *e* it, my stomach turned

EATER (EAT)

Isa 55: 10 for the sower and bread for the *e*,

EATING (EAT)

Ex 34: 28 and forty nights without *e* bread
Ro 14: 15 not by your *e* destroy your brother
     14: 17 kingdom of God is not a matter of *e*
     14: 23 because his *e* is not from faith;
1Co 8: 4 about *e* food sacrificed to idols:
      8: 10 you who have this knowledge *e*
Jude   : 12 *e* with you without the slightest

EATS (EAT)

1Sa 14: 24 "Cursed be any man who *e* food
Lk 15: 2 "This man welcomes sinners and *e*
Jn   6: 51 If a man *e* of this bread, he will live
      6: 54 Whoever *e* my flesh and drinks my
Ro 14: 2 faith is weak, *e* only vegetables.
     14: 3 man who *e* everything must not
     14: 6 He who *e* meat, *e* to the Lord,
     14: 23 has doubts is condemned if he *e*,
1Co 11: 27 whoever *e* the bread or drinks

EBAL

Dt 11: 29 and on Mount *E* the curses.
Jos   8: 30 Joshua built on Mount *E* an altar

EBENEZER

1Sa   7: 12 He named it *E*, saying, "Thus far

EDEN

Ge   2: 8 in *E*; and there he put the man
Eze 28: 13 You were in *E*,

EDGE (DOUBLE-EDGED)

Mt   9: 20 and touched the *e* of his cloak.

EDICT

Heb 11: 23 they were not afraid of the king's *e*.

EDIFICATION (EDIFIED EDIFIES)

Ro 14: 19 leads to peace and to mutual *e*.

EDIFIED* (EDIFICATION)

1Co 14: 5 so that the church may be *e*.
     14: 17 but the other man is not *e*.

EDIFIES* (EDIFICATION)

1Co 14: 4 but he who prophesies *e* the church
     14: 4 speaks in a tongue *e* himself.

EDOM

Ge 36: 1 the account of Esau (that is, *E*).
     36: 8 *E*) settled in the hill country of Seir
Isa 63: 1 is this coming from *E*,
Ob   : 1 Sovereign LORD says about *E*—

EDUCATED*

Ac   7: 22 Moses was *e* in all the wisdom

EFFECT* (EFFECTIVE)

Job 41: 26 sword that reaches him has no *e*,
Isa 32: 17 *e* of righteousness will be quietness
Ac   7: 53 put into *e* through angels
1Co 15: 10 his grace to me was not without *e*.
Gal 3: 19 put into *e* through angels
Eph 1: 10 put into *e* when the times will have
Heb 9: 17 it never takes *e* while the one who
      9: 18 put into *e* without blood.

EFFECTIVE* (EFFECT)

1Co 16: 9 a great door for *e* work has opened
Jas   5: 16 a righteous man is powerful and *e*.

EFFORT*

Ecc 2: 19 into which I have poured my *e*,
Da   6: 14 and made every *e* until sundown
Lk 13: 24 "Make every *e* to enter
Jn   5: 44 yet make no *e* to obtain the praise
Ro   9: 16 depend on man's desire or *e*.

Ro 14: 19 make every *e* to do what leads
Gal   3: 3 to attain your goal by human *e?*
Eph   4: 3 Make every *e* to keep the unity
1Th   2: 16 to all men in their *e* to keep us
      2: 17 intense longing we made every *e*
Heb   4: 11 make every *e* to enter that rest,
     12: 14 make every *e* to live in peace
2Pe   1: 5 make every *e* to add
      1: 15 And I will make every *e* to see that
      3: 14 make every *e* to be found spotless,

EGG

Lk 11: 12 for an *e*, will give him a scorpion?

EGLON

1. Fat king of Moab killed by Ehud (Jdg 3: 12-30).
2. City in Canaan (Jos 10).

EGYPT (EGYPTIANS)

Ge 12: 10 went down to *E* to live there
    37: 28 Ishmaelites, who took him to *E.*
    42: 3 went down to buy grain from *E.*
    45: 20 the best of all *E* will be yours.' ''
    46: 6 and all his offspring went to *E.*
    47: 27 Now the Israelites settled in *E*
Ex   3: 11 and bring the Israelites out of *E?*''
    12: 40 lived in *E* was 430 years.
    12: 41 all the Lord's divisions left *E.*
    32: 1 Moses who brought us up out of *E,*
Nu 11: 18 We were better off in *E!''*
    14: 4 choose a leader and go back to *E.''*
    24: 8 ''God brought them out of *E;*
Dt   6: 21 ''We were slaves of Pharaoh in *E,*
1Ki   4: 30 greater than all the wisdom of *E.*
    10: 28 horses were imported from *E*
    11: 40 but Jeroboam fled to *E,*
    14: 25 king of *E* attacked Jerusalem.
2Ch 35: 20 Neco king of *E* went to fight
    36: 3 The king of *E* dethroned him
Isa 19: 23 a highway from *E* to Assyria.
Hos 11: 1 and out of *E* I called my son.
Mt   2: 15 ''Out of *E* I called my son.''
Heb 11: 27 By faith he left *E,* not fearing
Rev 11: 8 is figuratively called Sodom and *E,*

EGYPTIANS (EGYPT)

Nu 14: 13 ''Then the *E* will hear about it!

EHUD

Left-handed judge who delivered Israel from Moabite king, Eglon (Jdg 3:12-30).

EKRON

1Sa   5: 10 So they sent the ark of God to *E.*

ELAH

Son of Baasha; king of Israel (1Ki 16:6-14).

ELATION

Pr 28: 12 righteous triumph, there is great *e;*

ELDER* (ELDERLY ELDERS)

Isa   3: 2 the soothsayer and *e,*
1Ti   5: 19 an accusation against an *e*
Tit   1: 6 *e* must be blameless, the husband
1Pe   5: 1 among you, I appeal as a fellow *e,*
2Jn   : 1 The *e,* To the chosen lady
3Jn   : 1 The *e,* To my dear friend Gaius.

ELDERLY* (ELDER)

Lev 19: 32 show respect for the *e*

ELDERS (ELDER)

1Ki 12: 8 rejected the advice the *e* gave him
Mt 15: 2 break the tradition of the *e?*
Mk   7: 3 holding to the tradition of the *e.*
     7: 5 to the tradition of the *e* instead
Ac 11: 30 gift to the *e* by Barnabas
    14: 23 and Barnabas appointed *e* for them
    15: 2 the apostles and *e* about this
    15: 4 the church and the apostles and *e,*
    15: 6 and *e* met to consider this question.
    15: 22 and *e,* with the whole church,
    15: 23 The apostles and *e,* your brothers,
    16: 4 and *e* in Jerusalem for the people
    20: 17 to Ephesus for the *e* of the church.
    21: 18 and all the *e* were present.

Ac 23: 14 They went to the chief priests and *e*
    24: 1 to Caesarea with some of the *e*
1Ti   4: 14 when the body of *e* laid their hands
     5: 17 The *e* who direct the affairs
Tit   1: 5 and appoint *e* in every town,
Jas   5: 14 He should call the *e* of the church
1Pe   5: 1 To the *e* among you, I appeal
Rev   4: 4 seated on them were twenty-four *e.*
     4: 10 the twenty-four *e* fall

ELEAZAR

Third son of Aaron (Ex 6:23-25). Succeeded Aaron as high priest (Nu 20:26; Dt 10:6). Allotted land to tribes (Jos 14:1). Death (Jos 24:33).

ELECT* (ELECTION)

Mt 24: 22 the sake of the *e* those days will be
    24: 24 miracles to deceive even the *e—*
    24: 31 and they will gather his *e*
Mk 13: 20 sake of the *e,* whom he has chosen,
    13: 22 and miracles to deceive the *e—*
    13: 27 gather his *e* from the four winds,
Ro 11: 7 it did not obtain, but the *e* did.
1Ti   5: 21 and Christ Jesus and the *e* angels,
2Ti   2: 10 everything for the sake of the *e,*
1Pe   1: 1 To God's *e,* strangers in the world,

ELECTION* (ELECT)

Ro   9: 11 God's purpose in *e* might stand:
    11: 28 but as far as *e* is concerned,
2Pe   1: 10 to make your calling and *e* sure.

ELEMENTARY* (ELEMENTS)

Heb   5: 12 someone to teach you the *e* truths
     6: 1 us leave the *e* teachings about

ELEMENTS* (ELEMENTARY)

2Pe   3: 10 the *e* will be destroyed by fire,
     3: 12 and the *e* will melt in the heat.

ELEVATE*

2Co 11: 7 to *e* you by preaching the gospel

ELI

High priest in youth of Samuel (1Sa 1-4). Blessed Hannah (1Sa 1:12-18); raised Samuel (1Sa 2:11-26). Prophesied against because of wicked sons (1Sa 2:27-36). Death of Eli and sons (1Sa 4:11-22).

ELIHU

One of Job's friends (Job 32-37).

ELIJAH

Prophet; predicted famine in Israel (1Ki 17:1; Jas 5:17). Fed by ravens (1Ki 17:2-6). Raised Sidonian widow's son (1Ki 17:7-24). Defeated prophets of Baal at Carmel (1Ki 18:16-46). Ran from Jezebel (1Ki 19:1-9). Prophesied death of Azariah (2Ki 1). Succeeded by Elishah (1Ki 19: 19-21; 2Ki 2:1-18). Taken to heaven in whirlwind (2Ki 2:11-12).
Return prophesied (Mal 4:5-6); equated with John the Baptist (Mt 17:9-13; Mk 9:9-13; Lk 1: 17). Appeared with Moses in transfiguration of Jesus (Mt 17:1-8; Mk 9:1-8).

ELIMELECH

Ru   1: 3 Now *E,* Naomi's husband, died,

ELIPHAZ

1. Firstborn of Esau (Ge 36).
2. One of Job's friends (Job 4-5; 15; 22).

ELISHA

Prophet; successor of Elijah (1Ki 19:16-21); inherited his cloak (2Ki 2:1-18). Purified bad water (2Ki 2:19-22). Cursed young men (2Ki 2: 23-25). Aided Israel's defeat of Moab (2Ki 3). Provided widow with oil (2Ki 4:1-7). Raised Shunammite woman's son (2Ki 4:8-37). Purified food (2Ki 4:38-41). Fed 100 men (2Ki 4:42-44). Healed Naaman's leprosy (2Ki 5). Made axhead float (2Ki 6:1-7). Captured Arameans (2Ki 6:8-23). Political adviser to Israel (2Ki 6:24-8:6; 9: 1-3; 13:14-19), Damascus (2Ki 8:7-15). Death (2Ki 13:20).

ELIZABETH*

Mother of John the Baptist, relative of Mary (Lk 1:5-58).

ELKANAH

Husband of Hannah, father of Samuel (1Sa 1-2).

ELOI*

Mt 27: 46 ''*E, E, lama sabachthani?''—*
Mk 15: 34 ''*E, E, lama sabachthani?''—*

ELOQUENCE* (ELOQUENT)

1Co   2: 1 come with *e* or superior wisdom

ELOQUENT* (ELOQUENCE)

Ex   4: 10 ''O Lord, I have never been *e,*

ELYMAS

Ac 13: 8 *E* the sorcerer (for that is what his

EMBEDDED*

Ecc 12: 11 sayings like firmly *e* nails—

EMBERS

Pr 26: 21 As charcoal to *e* and as wood to fire

EMBITTER* (BITTER)

Col   3: 21 Fathers, do not *e* your children,

EMBODIMENT* (BODY)

Ro   2: 20 have in the law the *e* of knowledge

EMPTIED (EMPTY)

1Co   1: 17 the cross of Christ be *e* of its power.

EMPTY (EMPTIED)

Ge   1: 2 Now the earth was formless and *e,*
Job 26: 7 the northern skies over *e* space;
Isa 45: 18 he did not create it to be *e,*
    55: 11 It will not return to me *e,*
Jer   4: 23 and it was formless and *e;*
Lk   1: 53 but has sent the rich away *e.*
Eph   5: 6 no one deceive you with *e* words,
1Pe   1: 18 from the *e* way of life handed
2Pe   2: 18 For they mouth *e,* boastful words

ENABLE (ABLE)

Lk   1: 74 to *e* us to serve him without fear
Ac   4: 29 *e* your servants to speak your word

ENABLED* (ABLE)

Lev 26: 13 *e* you to walk with heads held high.
Ru   4: 13 And the Lord *e* her to conceive,
Jn   6: 65 unless the Father has *e* him.''
Ac   2: 4 other tongues as the Spirit *e* them.
     7: 10 and *e* him to gain the goodwill
Heb 11: 11 was *e* to become a father

ENABLES (ABLE)

Php   3: 21 by the power that *e* him

ENABLING* (ABLE)

Ac 14: 3 the message of his grace by *e* them

ENCAMPS* (CAMP)

Ps 34: 7 The angel of the Lord *e*

ENCOURAGE* (ENCOURAGED ENCOURAGEMENT ENCOURAGES ENCOURAGING)

Dt   1: 38 *E* him, because he will lead Israel
     3: 28 and *e* and strengthen him,
2Sa 11: 25 Say this to *e* Joab.''
    19: 7 Now go out and *e* your men.
Job 16: 5 But my mouth would *e* you;
Ps 10: 17 you *e* them, and you listen
    64: 5 They *e* each other in evil plans,
Isa   1: 17 *e* the oppressed.
Jer 29: 8 to the dreams you *e* them to have.
Ac 15: 32 to *e* and strengthen the brothers.
Ro 12: 8 if it is encouraging, let him *e;*
Eph   6: 22 how we are, and that he may *e* you.
Col   4: 8 and that he may *e* your hearts.
1Th   3: 2 to strengthen and *e* you
     4: 18 Therefore *e* each other
     5: 11 Therefore *e* one another
     5: 14 those who are idle, *e* the timid,
2Th   2: 17 *e* your hearts and strengthen you

2Ti 4: 2 rebuke and e— with great patience
Tit 1: 9 so that he can e others
     2: 6 e the young men to be
    2: 15 E and rebuke with all authority.
Heb 3: 13 But e one another daily, as long
    10: 25 but let us e one another—

ENCOURAGED* (ENCOURAGE)

Jdg 7: 11 you will be e to attack the camp.''
   20: 22 But the men of Israel e one another
2Ch 22: 3 for his mother e him
    32: 6 and e them with these words:
    35: 2 and e them in the service
Eze 13: 22 you e the wicked not to turn
Ac   9: 31 It was strengthened; and e
   11: 23 and e them all to remain true
   16: 40 met with the brothers and e them.
   18: 27 the brothers e him and wrote
   27: 36 They were all e and ate some food
   28: 15 men Paul thanked God and was e.
Ro   1: 12 and I may be mutually e
1Co 14: 31 everyone may be instructed and e.
2Co 4: 4 I am greatly e; in all our troubles
    7: 13 By all this we are e.
Php 1: 14 brothers in the Lord have been e
Col 2: 2 My purpose is that they may be e
1Th 3: 7 persecution we were e about you
Heb 6: 18 offered to us may be greatly e.

ENCOURAGEMENT* (ENCOURAGE)

Ac   4: 36 Barnabas (which means Son of E),
  13: 15 a message of e for the people,
   20: 2 speaking many words of e
Ro 15: 4 e of the Scriptures we might have
   15: 5 and e give you a spirit of unity
1Co 14: 3 to men for their strengthening, e
2Co 7: 13 to our own e, we were especially
Php 2: 1 If you have any e from being united
2Th 2: 16 and by his grace gave us eternal e
Phm   7 love has given me great joy and e,
Heb 12: 5 word of e that addresses you

ENCOURAGES* (ENCOURAGE)

Isa 41: 7 The craftsman e the goldsmith,

ENCOURAGING* (ENCOURAGE)

Ac 14: 22 e them to remain true to the faith.
   15: 31 and were glad for its e message.
   20: 1 for the disciples and, after e them,
Ro 12: 8 if it is e, let him encourage;
1Th 2: 12 e, comforting and urging you
1Pe 5: 12 you and testifying that this is

ENCROACH

Pr 23: 10 or e on the fields of the fatherless,

END (ENDS)

Ps 119: 33 then I will keep them to the e.
  119:112 to the very e.
Pr   1: 19 Such is the e of all who go
    5: 4 but in the e she is bitter as gall,
    5: 11 At the e of your life you will groan,
   14: 12 but in the e it leads to death.
   14: 13 and joy may e in grief.
   16: 25 but in the e it leads to death.
   19: 20 and in the e you will be wise.
   20: 21 will not be blessed at the e.
   23: 32 In the e it bites like a snake
   25: 8 for what will you do in the e
   28: 23 in the e gain more favor
   29: 21 he will bring grief in the e.
Ecc 3: 11 done from beginning to e.
    7: 8 The e of a matter is better
   12: 12 making many books there is no e.
Eze 7: 2 The e! The e has come
Mt 10: 22 firm to the e will be saved.
   24: 13 firm to the e will be saved.
   24: 14 nations, and then the e will come.
Lk 21: 9 but the e will not come right away
Ro 10: 4 Christ is the e of the law
1Co 15: 24 the e will come, when he hands
Rev 21: 6 Omega, the Beginning and the E.
   22: 13 the Last, the Beginning and the E.

ENDS (END)

Ps 19: 4 their words to the e of the world.
Pr 20: 17 he e up with a mouth full of gravel.
Isa 49: 6 salvation to the e of the earth.''

Isa 62: 11 proclamation to the e of the earth:
Ac 13: 47 salvation to the e of the earth.' ''
Ro 10: 18 their words to the e of the world.''

ENDURANCE* (ENDURE)

Ro 15: 4 through e and the encouragement
   15: 5 May the God who gives e
2Co 1: 6 which produces in you patient e
    6: 4 in great e; in troubles, hardships
Col 1: 11 might so that you may have great e
1Th 1: 3 and your e inspired by hope
1Ti 6: 11 faith, love, e and gentleness.
2Ti 3: 10 patience, love, e, persecutions,
Tit 2: 2 and sound in faith, in love and in e.
Rev 1: 9 and patient e that are ours in Jesus,
   13: 10 This calls for patient e
   14: 12 This calls for patient e on the part

ENDURE (ENDURANCE ENDURED ENDURES ENDURING)

Ps 72: 17 May his name e forever;
Pr 12: 19 Truthful lips e forever,
   27: 24 for riches do not e forever,
Ecc 3: 14 everything God does will e forever;
Da   2: 44 to an end, but it will itself e forever.
Mal 3: 2 who can e the day of his coming?
1Co 4: 12 when we are persecuted, we e it;
2Co 1: 8 far beyond our ability to e.
2Ti 2: 3 E hardship with us like a good
    2: 10 Therefore I e everything
    2: 12 if we e, / we will also reign
    4: 5 head in all situations, e hardship,
Heb 12: 7 E hardship as discipline; God is
1Pe 2: 20 a beating for doing wrong and e it?
    2: 20 suffer for doing good and you e it,
Rev 3: 10 kept my command to e patiently,

ENDURED* (ENDURE)

Ps 123: 3 for we have e much contempt.
  123: 4 We have e much ridicule
  132: 1 and all the hardships he e.
Ac 13: 18 and e their conduct forty years
2Ti 3: 11 and Lystra, the persecutions I e.
Heb 12: 2 set before him e the cross,
   12: 3 him who e such opposition
Rev 2: 3 and have e hardships for my name,

ENDURES (ENDURE)

Ps 102: 12 renown e through all generations.
  112: 9 his righteousness e forever;
  136: 1 His love e forever.
Da   9: 15 made for yourself a name that e
2Co 9: 9 his righteousness e forever.''

ENDURING (ENDURE)

2Th 1: 4 persecutions and trials you are e.
1Pe 1: 23 through the living and e word

ENEMIES (ENEMY)

Ps 23: 5 in the presence of my e.
  110: 1 hand until I make your e
Pr 16: 7 his e live at peace with him.
Isa 59: 18 wrath to his e
Mic 7: 6 a man's e are the members
Mt   5: 44 Love your e and pray
   10: 36 a man's e will be the members
Lk   6: 27 Love your e, do good
    6: 35 But love your e, do good to them,
   20: 43 hand until I make your e
Ro   5: 10 For if, when we were God's e,
1Co 15: 25 reign until he has put all his e
Php 3: 18 many live as e of the cross of Christ
Heb 1: 13 hand until I make your e
   10: 13 for his e to be made his footstool.

ENEMY (ENEMIES ENMITY)

Pr 24: 17 Do not gloat when your e falls;
   25: 21 If your e is hungry, give him food
   27: 6 but an e multiplies kisses
   29: 24 of a thief is his own e;
Lk 10: 19 to overcome all the power of the e;
Ro 12: 20 ''If your e is hungry, feed him;
1Co 15: 26 The last e to be destroyed is death.
1Ti 5: 14 and to give the e no opportunity
1Pe 5: 8 Your e the devil prowls

ENERGY*

Col 1: 29 struggling with all his e, which

ENGRAVED

Isa 49: 16 I have e you on the palms
2Co 3: 7 which was e in letters on stone,

ENHANCES*

Ro   3: 7 my falsehood e God's truthfulness

ENJOY (JOY)

Dt   6: 2 and so that you may e long life.
Ps 37: 3 dwell in the land and e safe pasture.
Pr 28: 16 ill-gotten gain will e a long life.
Ecc 3: 22 better for a man than to e his work,
Eph 6: 3 and that you may e long life
Heb 11: 25 rather than to e the pleasures of sin
3Jn   2 I pray that you may e good health

ENJOYMENT (JOY)

Ecc 4: 8 and why am I depriving myself of e
1Ti 6: 17 us with everything for our e.

ENLARGE (ENLARGES)

2Co 9: 10 e the harvest of your righteousness.

ENLARGES (ENLARGE)

Dt 33: 20 Blessed is he who e Gad's domain!

ENLIGHTENED* (LIGHT)

Eph 1: 18 that the eyes of your heart may be e
Heb 6: 4 for those who have once been e.

ENMITY* (ENEMY)

Ge   3: 15 And I will put e

ENOCH

  1. Son of Cain (Ge 4:17-18).
  2. Descendant of Seth; walked with God and taken by him (Ge 5:18-24; Heb 11:5). Prophet (Jude 14).

ENSLAVED (SLAVE)

Gal 4: 9 Do you wish to be e by them all
Tit 3: 3 and e by all kinds of passions

ENSNARE (SNARE)

Pr   5: 22 of a wicked man e him;
Ecc 7: 26 but the sinner she will e.

ENSNARED* (SNARE)

Dt   7: 25 for yourselves, or you will be e by it
   12: 30 be careful not to be e
Ps   9: 16 the wicked are e by the work
Pr   6: 2 e by the words of your mouth,
   22: 25 and get yourself e.

ENTANGLED (ENTANGLES)

2Pe 2: 20 and are again e in it and overcome,

ENTANGLES* (ENTANGLED)

Heb 12: 1 and the sin that so easily e,

ENTER (ENTERED ENTERING ENTERS ENTRANCE)

Ps 95: 11 ''They shall never e my rest.''
  100: 4 E his gates with thanksgiving
Pr   2: 10 for wisdom will e your heart,
Mt   5: 20 will certainly not e the kingdom
    7: 13 ''E through the narrow gate.
    7: 21 Lord,' will e the kingdom of heaven
   18: 3 you will never e the kingdom
   18: 8 It is better for you to e life maimed
   19: 17 to e life, obey the commandments
   19: 23 man to e the kingdom of heaven.
Mk 9: 43 It is better for you to e life maimed
    9: 45 It is better for you to e life crippled
    9: 47 for you to e the kingdom of God
   10: 15 like a little child will never e it.''
   10: 23 is for the rich to e the kingdom
Lk 13: 24 will try to e and will not be able to.
   13: 24 ''Make every effort to e
   18: 17 like a little child will never e it.''
   18: 24 is for the rich to e the kingdom
Jn   3: 5 he cannot e the kingdom of God.
Heb 3: 11 'They shall never e my rest.' ''
    4: 11 make every effort to e that rest.

ENTERED (ENTER)

Ps 73: 17 me till I e the sanctuary of God;
Eze 4: 14 meat has ever e my mouth.''

Ac 11: 8 or unclean has ever e my mouth.'
Ro 5: 12 as sin e the world through one man,
Heb 9: 12 but he e the Most Holy Place once

ENTERING (ENTER)

Mt 21: 31 the prostitutes are e the kingdom
Lk 11: 52 have hindered those who were e.''
Heb 4: 1 the promise of e his rest still stands,

ENTERS (ENTER)

Mk 7: 18 you see that nothing that e a man
Jn 10: 2 The man who e by the gate is

**ENTERTAIN* (ENTERTAINED
ENTERTAINMENT)**

Jdg 16: 25 ''Bring out Samson to e us.''
Mt 9: 4 ''Why do you e evil thoughts
1Ti 5: 19 Do not e an accusation
Heb 13: 2 Do not forget to e strangers,

ENTERTAINED* (ENTERTAIN)

Ac 28: 7 and for three days e us hospitably.
Heb 13: 2 so doing some people have e angels

ENTERTAINMENT* (ENTERTAIN)

Da 6: 18 without any e being brought to him

ENTHRALLED*

Ps 45: 11 The king is e by your beauty;

ENTHRONED* (THRONE)

1Sa 4: 4 who is e between the cherubim.
2Sa 6: 2 who is e between the cherubim that
2Ki 19: 15 of Israel, e between the cherubim,
1Ch 13: 6 who is e between the cherubim—
Ps 2: 4 The One e in heaven laughs;
9: 11 to the LORD, e in Zion;
22: 3 Yet you are e as the Holy One;
29: 10 The LORD sits e over the flood;
29: 10 the LORD is e as King forever.
55: 19 God, who is e forever,
61: 7 May he be e in God's presence
80: 1 who sit e between the cherubim,
99: 1 he sits e between the cherubim,
102: 12 But you, O LORD, sit e forever;
113: 5 the One who sits e on high,
132: 14 here I will sit e, for I have desired it
Isa 14: 13 I will sit e on the mount
37: 16 of Israel, e between the cherubim,
40: 22 He sits e above the circle
52: 2 rise up, sit e, O Jerusalem.

ENTHRONES* (THRONE)

Job 36: 7 he e them with kings

ENTHUSIASM*

2Co 8: 17 he is coming to you with much e
9: 2 and your e has stirred most of them

ENTICE* (ENTICED ENTICES)

Pr 1: 10 My son, if sinners e you,
2Pe 2: 18 they e people who are just escaping
Rev 2: 14 who taught Balak to e the Israelites

ENTICED* (ENTICE)

Dt 4: 19 do not be e into bowing
11: 16 or you will be e to turn away
2Ki 17: 21 Jeroboam e Israel away
Job 31: 9 If my heart has been e by a woman,
31: 27 so that my heart was secretly e
Jas 1: 14 desire, he is dragged away and e.

ENTICES* (ENTICE)

Dt 13: 6 your closest friend secretly e you,
Job 36: 18 Be careful that no one e you
Pr 16: 29 A violent man e his neighbor

ENTIRE

Gal 5: 14 The e law is summed up

ENTRANCE (ENTER)

Mt 27: 60 stone in front of the e to the tomb
Mk 15: 46 a stone against the e of the tomb.
16: 3 away from the e of the tomb?''
Jn 11: 38 cave with a stone laid across the e.
20: 1 had been removed from the e.

ENTRUST (TRUST)

Jn 2: 24 Jesus would not e himself to them,

2Ti 2: 2 the presence of many witnesses e

ENTRUSTED (TRUST)

Jer 13: 20 Where is the flock that was e to you
Jn 5: 22 but has e all judgment to the Son,
Ro 3: 2 they have been e with the very
6: 17 of teaching to which you were e.
1Co 4: 1 as those e with the secret things
1Th 2: 4 by God to be e with the gospel.
1Ti 1: 11 of the blessed God, which he e
6: 20 guard what has been e to your care.
2Ti 1: 12 able to guard what I have e to him
1: 14 Guard the good deposit that was e
Tit 1: 3 light through the preaching e to me
1: 7 Since an overseer is e
1Pe 2: 23 he e himself to him who judges
5: 3 not lording it over those e to you,
Jude : 3 once for all e to the saints.

ENVIES

Jas 4: 5 spirit he caused to live in us e

ENVIOUS (ENVY)

Dt 32: 21 I will make them e
Pr 24: 19 or be e of the wicked,
Ro 10: 19 ''I will make you e

ENVOY

Pr 13: 17 but a trustworthy e brings healing.

ENVY (ENVIOUS ENVYING)

Pr 3: 31 Do not e a violent man
14: 30 but e rots the bones.
23: 17 Do not let your heart e sinners,
24: 1 Do not e wicked men,
Mk 7: 22 malice, deceit, lewdness, e, slander
Ro 1: 29 They are full of e, murder, strife,
11: 14 arouse my own people to e
1Co 13: 4 It does not e, it does not boast,
Gal 5: 21 factions and e; drunkenness, orgies
Php 1: 15 that some preach Christ out of e
1Ti 6: 4 and quarrels about words that result in
e,
Tit 3: 3 lived in malice and e, being hated
Jas 3: 14 But if you harbor bitter e
3: 16 where you have e and selfish
1Pe 2: 1 e, and slander of every kind.

ENVYING* (ENVY)

Gal 5: 26 provoking and e each other.

EPHAH

Eze 45: 11 The e and the bath are

EPHESUS

Ac 18: 19 at E, where Paul left Priscilla
19: 1 the interior and arrived at E.
Eph 1: 1 To the saints in E, the faithful
Rev 2: 1 the angel of the church in E write:

EPHRAIM

1. Second son of Joseph (Ge 41:52; 46:20).
Blessed as firstborn by Jacob (Ge 48). Tribe of
numbered (Nu 1:33; 26:37), blessed (Dt 33:17),
allotted land (Jos 16:4-9; Eze 48:5), failed to fully
possess (Jos 16:10; Jdg 1:29).
2. Synonymous with Northern Kingdom (Isa 7:
17; Hos 5).

EQUAL (EQUALITY EQUITY)

Dt 33: 25 and your strength will e your days.
1Sa 9: 2 without e among the Israelites—
Isa 40: 25 who is my e?'' says the Holy One.
46: 5 you compare me or count me e?
Da 1: 19 and he found none e to Daniel,
Jn 5: 18 making himself e with God.
1Co 12: 25 that its parts should have e concern
2Co 2: 16 And who is e to such a task?

EQUALITY* (EQUAL)

2Co 8: 13 pressed, but that there might be e.
8: 14 Then there will be e, as it is written:
Php 2: 6 did not consider e

EQUIP* (EQUIPPED)

Heb 13: 21 e you with everything good

EQUIPPED (EQUIP)

2Ti 3: 17 man of God may be thoroughly e

EQUITY* (EQUAL)

Ps 96: 10 he will judge the peoples with e.
98: 9 and the peoples with e.
99: 4 you have established e;

ERODES*

Job 14: 18 ''But as a mountain e and crumbles

ERROR (ERRORS)

Jas 5: 20 Whoever turns a sinner from the e
2Pe 2: 18 escaping from those who live in e.

ERRORS* (ERROR)

Ps 19: 12 Who can discern his e?
Ecc 10: 4 calmness can lay great e to rest.

ESAU

Firstborn of Isaac, twin of Jacob (Ge 25:21-
26). Also called Edom (Ge 25:30). Sold Jacob his
birthright (Ge 25:29-34); lost blessing (Gen 27).
Married Hittites (Ge 26:34), Ishmaelites (Ge 28:
6-9). Reconciled to Jacob (Gen 33). Genealogy
(Ge 36). The LORD chose Jacob over Esau (Mal 1:
2-3), but gave Esau land (Dt 2:2-12). Descendants
eventually obliterated (Ob 1-21; Jer 49:7-22).

**ESCAPE (ESCAPED ESCAPES
ESCAPING)**

Ps 68: 20 from the Sovereign LORD comes e
Pr 11: 9 through knowledge the righteous e.
Ro 2: 3 think you will e God's judgment?
1Th 5: 3 woman, and they will not e.
2Ti 2: 26 and e from the trap of the devil,
Heb 2: 3 how shall we e if we ignore such
12: 25 If they did not e when they refused
2Pe 1: 4 and e the corruption in the world

ESCAPED (ESCAPE)

2Pe 2: 20 If they have e the corruption

ESCAPES (ESCAPE)

Pr 12: 13 but a righteous man e trouble.

ESCAPING (ESCAPE)

1Co 3: 15 only as one e through the flames.
2Pe 2: 18 they entice people who are just e

**ESTABLISH (ESTABLISHED
ESTABLISHES)**

Ge 6: 18 But I will e my covenant with you,
17: 21 But my covenant I will e with Isaac
2Sa 7: 11 The LORD himself will e a house
1Ki 9: 5 I will e your royal throne
1Ch 28: 7 I will e his kingdom forever
Ps 90: 17 e the work of our hands for us—
Isa 26: 12 LORD, you e peace for us;
Ro 10: 3 God and sought to e their own,
16: 25 able to e you by my gospel
Heb 10: 9 sets aside the first to e the second.

ESTABLISHED (ESTABLISH)

Ge 9: 17 the sign of the covenant I have e
Ex 6: 4 also e my covenant with them
Pr 16: 12 a throne is e through righteousness.

ESTABLISHES (ESTABLISH)

Job 25: 2 he e order in the heights of heaven.
Isa 42: 4 till he e justice on earth.

ESTATE

Ps 136: 23 who remembered us in our low e

ESTEEMED

Pr 22: 1 to be e is better than silver or gold.
Isa 53: 3 he was despised, and we e him not.

ESTHER

Jewess, originally named Hadassah, who lived
in Persia; cousin of Mordecai (Est 2:7). Chosen
queen of Xerxes (Est 2:8-18). Persuaded by Mordecai to foil Haman's plan to exterminate the Jews
(Est 3-4). Revealed Haman's plans to Xerxes,
resulting in Haman's death (Est 7), the Jews' pres-
ervation (Est 8-9), Mordecai's exaltation (Est 8:
15; 9:4; 10). Decreed celebration of Purim (Est 9:
18-32).

ETERNAL* (ETERNALLY ETERNITY)

Ge   21:33 the name of the LORD, the *E* God.
Dt   33:27 The *e* God is your refuge,
1Ki 10:   9 of the LORD's *e* love for Israel,
Ps   16:11 with *e* pleasures at your right hand,
    21:   6 you have granted him *e* blessings
    111: 10 To him belongs *e* praise.
    119: 89 Your word, O LORD, is *e;*
    119:160 all your righteous laws are *e.*
Ecc 12:   5 Then man goes to his *e* home
Isa 26:   4 LORD, the LORD, is the Rock *e.*
    47:   7 the *e* queen!''
Jer   10:10 he is the living God, the *e* King.
Da   4:   3 His kingdom is an *e* kingdom;
    4:34 His dominion is an *e* dominion,
Hab 3:   6 His ways are *e.*
Mt   18:   8 two feet and be thrown into *e* fire.
    19:16 good thing must I do to get *e* life?''
    19:29 as much and will inherit *e* life.
    25:41 into the *e* fire prepared for the devil
    25:46 but the righteous to *e* life.''
    25:46 they will go away to *e* punishment,
Mk   3:29 be forgiven; he is guilty of an *e* sin.''
    10:17 ''what must I do to inherit *e* life?''
    10:30 and in the age to come, *e* life,
Lk   10:25 ''what must I do to inherit *e* life?''
    16:   9 will be welcomed into *e* dwellings.
    18:18 what must I do to inherit *e* life?''
    18:30 and, in the age to come, *e* life.''
Jn   3:15 believes in him may have *e* life.
    3:16 him shall not perish but have *e* life.
    3:36 believes in the Son has *e* life,
    4:14 spring of water welling up to *e* life.''
    4:36 now he harvests the crop for *e* life,
    5:24 believes him who sent me has *e* life
    5:39 that by them you possess *e* life.
    6:27 but for food that endures to *e* life,
    6:40 believes in him shall have *e* life,
    6:54 and drinks my blood has *e* life,
    6:68 You have the words of *e* life.
    10:28 I give them *e* life, and they shall
    12:25 in this world will keep it for *e* life.
    12:50 that his command leads to *e* life.
    17:   2 all people that he might give *e* life
    17:   3 this is *e* life: that they may know
Ac   13:46 yourselves worthy of *e* life,
    13:48 were appointed for *e* life believed.
Ro   1:20 his *e* power and divine nature—
    2:   7 and immortality, he will give *e* life.
    5:21 righteousness to bring *e* life
    6:22 to holiness, and the result is *e* life.
    6:23 but the gift of God is *e* life
    16:26 by the command of the *e* God,
2Co 4:17 for us an *e* glory that far outweighs
    4:18 temporary, but what is unseen is *e.*
    5:   1 from God, an *e* house in heaven,
Gal 6:   8 from the Spirit will reap *e* life.
Eph 3:11 to his *e* purpose which he
2Th 2:16 his grace gave us *e* encouragement
1Ti   1:16 believe on him and receive *e* life.
    1:17 Now to the King *e*, immortal,
    6:12 Take hold of the *e* life
2Ti   2:10 is in Christ Jesus, with *e* glory.
Tit   1:   2 resting on the hope of *e* life,
    3:   7 heirs having the hope of *e* life.
Heb 5:   9 he became the source of *e* salvation
    6:   2 of the dead, and *e* judgment.
    9:12 having obtained *e* redemption.
    9:14 through the *e* Spirit offered himself
    9:15 the promised *e* inheritance—
    13:20 of the *e* covenant brought back
1Pe 5:10 you to his *e* glory in Christ,
2Pe 1:   1 into the *e* kingdom of our Lord
1Jn 1:   2 and we proclaim to you the *e* life,
    2:25 what he promised us—even *e* life.
    3:15 know that no murderer has *e* life
    5:11 God has given us *e* life,
    5:13 you may know that you have *e* life.
    5:20 He is the true God and *e* life.
Jude   :   7 who suffer the punishment of *e* fire.
    : 21 Christ to bring you to *e* life.
Rev 14:   6 and he had the *e* gospel to proclaim

ETERNALLY* (ETERNAL)

Gal   1:   8 let him be *e* condemned! As we
    1:   9 let him be *e* condemned! Am I now

ETERNITY* (ETERNAL)

Ps   93:   2 you are from all *e.*
Pr   8:23 I was appointed from *e,*
Ecc   3:11 also set *e* in the hearts of men;

ETHIOPIAN*

Jer   13:23 Can the *E* change his skin
Ac   8:27 and on his way he met an *E* eunuch

EUNUCH (EUNUCHS)

Ac   8:27 on his way he met an Ethiopian *e,*

EUNUCHS (EUNUCH)

Isa 56:   4 ''To the *e* who keep my Sabbaths,
Mt   19:12 For some are *e* because they were

EUTYCHUS*

Ac   20:   9 was a young man named *E,*

EVANGELIST* (EVANGELISTS)

Ac   21:   8 stayed at the house of Philip the *e,*
2Ti   4:   5 hardship, do the work of an *e,*

EVANGELISTS* (EVANGELIST)

Eph   4:11 some to be prophets, some to be *e,*

EVE*

Ge   3:20 Adam named his wife *E,*
    4:   1 Adam lay with his wife *E,*
2Co 11:   3 as *E* was deceived by the serpent's
1Ti   2:13 For Adam was formed first, then *E*

EVEN-TEMPERED* (TEMPER)

Pr   17:27 and a man of understanding is *e.*

EVENING

Ge   1:   5 there was *e,* and there was morning

EVER (EVERLASTING FOREVER FOREVERMORE)

Ex   15:18 LORD will reign for *e* and *e.''*
Dt   8:19 If you *e* forget the LORD your
1Ki   3:12 anyone like you, nor will there *e* be.
Job   4:   7 were the upright *e* destroyed?
Ps   5:11 let them *e* sing for joy.
    10:16 The LORD is King for *e* and *e;*
    21:   4 length of days, for *e* and *e.*
    25:   3 will *e* be put to shame,
    25:15 My eyes are *e* on the LORD,
    26:   3 for your love is *e* before me,
    45:   6 O God, will last for *e* and *e;*
    45:17 nations will praise you for *e* and *e.*
    46:   1 an *e-* present help in trouble.
    48:14 For this God is our God for *e* and *e;*
    52:   8 God's unfailing love for *e* and *e.*
    61:   8 will I *e* sing praise to your name
    71:   6 I will *e* praise you.
    84:   4 they are *e* praising you.
    89:33 nor will I *e* betray my faithfulness.
    111:   8 They are steadfast for *e* and *e,*
    119: 44 your law, for *e* and *e.*
    119: 98 for they are *e* with me.
    132: 12 sit on your throne for *e* and *e.''*
    145:   1 I will praise your name for *e* and *e.*
    145:   2 and extol your name for *e* and *e.*
    145: 21 his holy name for *e* and *e.*
Pr   4:18 shining *e* brighter till the full light
    5:19 may you *e* be captivated
Isa 66:   8 Who has *e* heard of such a thing?
    66:   8 Who has *e* seen such things?
Jer   7:   7 I gave your forefathers for *e* and *e.*
    25:   5 and your fathers for *e* and *e.*
    31:36 the descendants of Israel *e* cease
Da   2:20 be to the name of God for *e* and *e;*
    7:18 it forever—yes, for *e* and *e.'*
    12:   3 like the stars for *e* and *e.*
Mic   4:   5 our God for *e* and *e.*
Mt   13:14 you will be *e* seeing but never
    13:14 '' 'You will be *e* hearing
Mk   4:12 *e* hearing but never understanding;
Jn   1:18 No one has *e* seen God,
Gal   1:   5 to whom be glory for *e* and *e.*
Eph   3:21 all generations, for *e* and *e!*
Php   4:20 and Father be glory for *e* and *e.*
1Ti   1:17 be honor and glory for *e* and *e.*
2Ti   4:18 To him be glory for *e* and *e.*
Heb   1:   8 O God, will last for *e* and *e,*
    13:21 to whom be glory for *e* and *e.*

EVIDENCE (EVIDENT)

1Pe   4:11 the glory and the power for *e* and *e.*
    5:11 To him be the power for *e* and *e.*
1Jn   4:12 No one has *e* seen God;
Rev 1:   6 him be glory and power for *e* and *e!*
    1:18 and behold I am alive for *e* and *e!*
    21:27 Nothing impure will *e* enter it,
    22:   5 And they will reign for *e* and *e.*

EVER-INCREASING* (INCREASE)

Ro   6:19 to impurity and to *e* wickedness,
2Co 3:18 into his likeness with *e* glory,

EVERLASTING* (EVER)

Ge   9:16 and remember the *e* covenant
    17:   7 an *e* covenant between me and you
    17:   8 I will give as an *e* possession to you
    17:13 in your flesh is to be an *e* covenant.
    17:19 an *e* covenant for his descendants
    48:   4 *e* possession to your descendants
Nu   18:19 It is an *e* covenant of salt
Dt   33:15 and the fruitfulness of the *e* hills;
    33:27 and underneath are the *e* arms.
2Sa 23:   5 made with me an *e* covenant,
1Ch 16:17 to Israel as an *e* covenant:
    16:36 from *e* to *e*
    29:10 from *e* to *e.*
Ezr   9:12 to your children as an *e* inheritance
Ne   9:   5 your God, who is from *e* to *e.''*
Ps   41:13 from *e* to *e.*
    52:   5 God will bring you down to *e* ruin;
    74:   3 toward these *e* ruins,
    78:66 he put them to *e* shame.
    90:   2 from *e* to *e* you are God.
    103: 17 But from *e* to *e*
    105: 10 to Israel as an *e* covenant:
    106: 48 from *e* to *e.*
    119:142 Your righteousness is *e*
    139: 24 and lead me in the way *e.*
    145: 13 Your kingdom is an *e* kingdom,
Isa 9:   6 Father, Prince of Peace.
    24:   5 and broken the *e* covenant.
    30:   8 it may be an *e* witness.
    33:14 Who of us can dwell with *e* burning
    35:10 *e* joy will crown their heads.
    40:28 The LORD is the *e* God,
    45:17 the LORD with an *e* salvation;
    45:17 to ages *e.*
    51:11 *e* joy will crown their heads.
    54:   8 but with *e* kindness
    55:   3 I will make an *e* covenant with you,
    55:13 for an *e* sign,
    56:   5 I will give them an *e* name
    60:15 I will make you the *e* pride
    60:19 for the LORD will be your *e* light,
    60:20 the LORD will be your *e* light,
    61:   7 and *e* joy will be theirs.
    61:   8 and make an *e* covenant with them.
    63:12 to gain for himself *e* renown,
Jer   5:22 an *e* barrier it cannot cross.
    23:40 I will bring upon you *e* disgrace—
    23:40 shame that will not be forgotten.''
    25:   9 of horror and scorn, and an *e* ruin.
    31:   3 ''I have loved you with an *e* love;
    32:40 I will make an *e* covenant with
    50:   5 the LORD in an *e* covenant
Eze 16:60 and I will establish an *e* covenant
    37: 26 with them; it will be an *e* covenant
Da   7:14 dominion is an *e* dominion that will
    7:27 His kingdom will be an *e* kingdom,
    9:24 to bring in *e* righteousness,
    12:   2 others to shame and *e* contempt.
    12:   2 some to *e* life, others to shame
Mic 6:   2 you *e* foundations of the earth.
Hab 1:12 O LORD, are you not from *e?*
Jn   6:47 the truth, he who believes has *e* life.
2Th 1:   9 punished with *e* destruction
Jude   :   6 bound with *e* chains for judgment

EVIDENCE (EVIDENT)

Jn   14:11 on the *e* of the miracles themselves.
Ac   11:23 and saw the *e* of the grace of God,
2Th 1:   5 All this is *e* that God's judgment is
Jas   2:20 do you want *e* that faith

EVIDENT (EVIDENCE)

Php   4:   5 Let your gentleness be *e* to all.

EVIL (EVILDOER EVILDOERS EVILS)

Ge   2:   9 of the knowledge of good and *e*.
     3:   5 be like God, knowing good and *e*.''
     6:   5 of his heart was only *e* all the time.
Ex 32:22 how prone these people are to *e*.
Jdg 2:11 Then the Israelites did *e* in the eyes
     3:   7 The Israelites did *e* in the eyes
    3:12 Once again the Israelites did *e*
     4:   1 the Israelites once again did *e*
     6:   1 Again the Israelites did *e*
    10:   6 Again the Israelites did *e*
    13:   1 Again the Israelites did *e*
1Ki 11:   6 So Solomon did *e* in the eyes
    16:25 But Omri did *e* in the eyes
2Ki 15:24 Pekahiah did *e* in the eyes
Job   1:   1 he feared God and shunned *e*.
     1:   8 a man who fears God and shuns *e*.''
    34:10 Far be it from God to do *e*,
    36:21 Beware of turning to *e*,
Ps   5:   4 not a God who takes pleasure in *e*;
    23:   4 I will fear no *e*,
    34:13 keep your tongue from *e*
    34:14 Turn from *e* and do good;
    34:16 is against those who do *e*,
    37:   1 Do not fret because of *e* men
    37:   8 do not fret—it leads only to *e*.
    37:27 Turn from *e* and do good;
    49:   5 fear when *e* days come,
    51:   4 and done what is *e* in your sight,
    97:10 those who love the LORD hate *e*,
   101:   4 I will have nothing to do with *e*.
   141:   4 not my heart be drawn to what is *e*,
Pr   4:27 keep your foot from *e*.
     8:13 To fear the LORD is to hate *e*;
    10:23 A fool finds pleasure in *e* conduct,
    11:19 he who pursues *e* goes to his death.
    11:27 *e* comes to him who searches for it.
    14:16 man fears the LORD and shuns *e*,
    17:13 If a man pays back *e* for good,
    20:30 Blows and wounds cleanse away *e*,
    24:19 Do not fret because of *e* men
    24:20 for the *e* man has no future hope,
    26:23 are fervent lips with an *e* heart.
    28:   5 *E* men do not understand justice,
    29:   6 An *e* man is snared by his own sin,
Ecc 12:14 whether it is good or *e*.
Isa   5:20 Woe to those who call *e* good
    13:11 I will punish the world for its *e*,
    55:   7 and the *e* man his thoughts.
Jer   4:14 wash the *e* from your heart
    18:   8 nation I warned repents of its *e*,
    18:11 So turn from your *e* ways,
Eze 33:11 Turn! Turn from your *e* ways!
    33:13 he will die for the *e* he has done.
    33:15 and does no *e*, he will surely live;
Am   5:13 for the times are *e*.
Hab   1:13 Your eyes are too pure to look on *e*;
Zec   8:17 do not plot *e* against your neighbor,
Mt   5:45 He causes his sun to rise on the *e*
     6:13 but deliver us from the *e* one.'
     7:11 If you, then, though you are *e*,
    12:34 you who are *e* say anything good?
    12:35 and the *e* man brings *e* things out
    12:35 out of the *e* stored up in him.
    12:43 "When an *e* spirit comes out
    15:19 out of the heart come *e* thoughts,
Mk   7:21 come *e* thoughts, sexual
Lk   6:45 and the *e* man brings *e* things out
    11:13 If you then, though you are *e*,
Jn   3:19 of light because their deeds were *e*.
     3:20 Everyone who does *e* hates
    17:15 you protect them from the *e* one.
Ro   1:30 they invent ways of doing *e*;
     2:   8 who reject the truth and follow *e*,
     2:   9 for every human being who does *e*;
     3:   8 "Let us do *e* that good may result"?
     6:12 body so that you obey its *e* desires.
     7:19 no, the *e* I do not want to do—
     7:21 to do good, *e* is right there with me.
    12:   9 Hate what is *e*; cling
    12:17 Do not repay anyone *e* for *e*.
    12:21 Do not be overcome by *e*,
    14:16 good to be spoken of as *e*.
    16:19 and innocent about what is *e*.
1Co 13:   6 Love does not delight in *e*
    14:20 In regard to *e* be infants,
Eph   5:16 because the days are *e*.

Eph   6:12 forces of *e* in the heavenly realms.
     6:16 all the flaming arrows of the *e* one.
Col   3:   5 impurity, lust, *e* desires and greed,
1Th   5:22 Avoid every kind of *e*.
2Th   3:   3 and protect you from the *e* one.
1Ti   6:10 of money is a root of all kinds of *e*.
2Ti   2:22 Flee the *e* desires of youth,
     3:   6 are swayed by all kinds of *e* desires,
     3:13 while *e* men and impostors will go
Heb   5:14 to distinguish good from *e*.
Jas   1:13 For God cannot be tempted by *e*,
     1:21 and the *e* that is so prevalent,
     3:   6 a world of *e* among the parts
     3:   8 It is a restless *e*, full
1Pe   2:16 your freedom as a cover-up for *e*;
     3:   9 Do not repay *e* with *e* or insult
     3:10 must keep his tongue from *e*
     3:17 for doing good than for doing *e*.
1Jn   2:13 you have overcome the *e* one.
     2:14 and you have overcome the *e* one.
     3:12 who belonged to the *e* one
     5:18 and the *e* one cannot harm him.
     5:19 is under the control of the *e* one.
3Jn   : 11 do not imitate what is *e*

EVILDOER* (EVIL)

2Sa   3:39 the LORD repay the *e* according
Ps 101:   8 I will cut off every *e*
Mal   4:   1 and every *e* will be stubble,

EVILDOERS* (EVIL)

1Sa 24:13 saying goes, 'From *e* come evil
Job   8:20 or strengthen the hands of *e*.
    34:   8 He keeps company with *e*;
    34:22 where *e* can hide.
Ps   14:   4 Will *e* never learn—
    14:   6 You *e* frustrate the plans
    26:   5 I abhor the assembly of *e*
    36:12 See how the *e* lie fallen—
    53:   4 Will the *e* never learn—
    59:   2 Deliver me from *e*
    64:   2 from that noisy crowd of *e*.
    92:   7 and all *e* flourish,
    92:   9 all *e* will be scattered.
    94:   4 all the *e* are full of boasting.
    94:16 will take a stand for me against *e*?
  119:115 Away from me, you *e*,
   125:   5 the LORD will banish with the *e*.
   141:   4 deeds with men who are *e*;
   141:   5 ever against the deeds of *e*;
   141:   9 from the traps set by *e*.
Pr   21:15 but terror to *e*.
Isa   1:   4 a brood of *e*,
    31:   2 against those who help *e*.
Jer   23:14 They strengthen the hands of *e*,
Hos 10:   9 the *e* in Gibeah?
Mal   3:15 Certainly the *e* prosper, and
Mt   7:23 you *e*!' "Therefore everyone who
Lk 13:27 Away from me, all you *e*!'
    18:11 *e*, adulterers—or even like this tax

EVILS* (EVIL)

Mk   7:23 All these *e* come from inside

EWE

2Sa 12:   3 one little *e* lamb he had bought.

EXACT*

Ge 43:21 the *e* weight—in the mouth
Est   4:   7 including the *e* amount
Mt   2:   7 from them the *e* time the star had
Jn   4:53 realized that this was the *e* time
Ac 17:26 the *e* places where they should live.
Heb   1:   3 the *e* representation of his being,

EXALT* (EXALTED EXALTS)

Ex 15:   2 my father's God, and I will *e* him.
Jos   3:   7 begin to *e* you in the eyes
1Sa   2:10 and *e* the horn of his anointed.''
1Ch 25:   5 the promises of God to *e* him.
    29:12 power to *e* and give strength to all.
Job 19:   5 If indeed you would *e* yourselves
Ps   30:   1 I will *e* you, O LORD,
    34:   3 let us *e* his name together.
    35:26 may all who *e* themselves over me
    37:34 He will *e* you to possess the land;
    38:16 *e* themselves over me
    75:   6 or from the desert can *e* a man.

Ps 89:17 and by your favor you *e* our horn.
    99:   5 *E* the LORD our God
    99:   9 *E* the LORD our God
   107: 32 Let them *e* him in the assembly
   118: 28 you are my God, and I will *e* you.
   145:   1 I will *e* you, my God the King;
Pr   4:   8 Esteem her, and she will *e* you;
    25:   6 Do not *e* yourself in the king's
Isa 24:15 *e* the name of the LORD, the God
    25:   1 I will *e* you and praise your name,
Eze 29:15 and will never again *e* itself
Da   4:37 *e* and glorify the King of heaven,
    11:36 He will *e* and magnify himself
    11:37 but will *e* himself above them all.
Hos 11:   7 he will by no means *e* them.
2Th   2:   4 will *e* himself over everything that is

EXALTED* (EXALT)

Ex 15:   1 for he is highly *e*.
    15:21 for he is highly *e*.
Nu 24:   7 their kingdom will be *e*.
Jos   4:14 That day the LORD *e* Joshua
2Sa   5:12 and had *e* his kingdom for the sake
    22:47 *E* be God, the Rock, my Savior!
    22:49 You *e* me above my foes;
    23:   1 of the man *e* by the Most High,
1Ch 14:   2 that his kingdom had been highly *e*
    17:17 as though I were the most *e* of men,
    29:11 you are *e* as head over all.
    29:25 The LORD highly *e* Solomon
Ne   9:   5 and may it be *e* above all blessing
Job 24:24 For a little while they are *e*,
    36:22 "God is *e* in his power.
    37:23 beyond our reach and *e* in power;
Ps 18:46 *E* be God my Savior!
    18:48 You *e* me above my foes;
    21:13 Be *e*, O LORD, in your strength;
    27:   6 Then my head will be *e*
    35:27 they always say, "The LORD be *e*,
    40:16 "The LORD be *e*!''
    46:10 I will be *e* among the nations,
    46:10 I will be *e* in the earth.''
    47:   9 he is greatly *e*.
    57:   5 Be *e*, O God, above the heavens;
    57:11 Be *e*, O God, above the heavens;
    70:   4 "Let God be *e*!''
    89:13 hand is strong, your right hand *e*.
    89:19 I have *e* a young man
    89:24 through my name his horn will be *e*.
    89:27 the most *e* of the kings of the earth.
    89:42 You have *e* the right hand
    92:   8 But you, O LORD, are *e* forever.
    92:10 You have *e* my horn like that
    97:   9 you are *e* far above all gods.
    99:   2 he is *e* over all the nations.
   108:   5 Be *e*, O God, above the heavens,
   113:   4 The LORD is *e* over all the nations
   138:   2 for you have *e* above all things
   148:13 for his name alone is *e*;
Pr 11:11 of the upright a city is *e*,
    30:32 have played the fool and *e* yourself,
Isa   2:11 The LORD alone will be *e*
     2:12 for all that is *e*
     2:17 The LORD alone will be *e*
     5:16 the LORD Almighty will be *e*
     6:   1 *e*, and the train of his robe filled
    12:   4 and proclaim that his name is *e*.
    24:   4 the *e* of the earth languish.
    33:   5 The LORD is *e*, for he dwells
    33:10 "Now will I be *e*;
    52:13 be raised and lifted up and highly *e*.
Jer 17:12 A glorious throne, *e*
La   2:17 he has *e* the horn of your foes.
Eze 21:26 The lowly will be *e* and the *e* will be
Hos 13:   1 he was *e* in Israel.
Mic   6:   6 and bow down before the *e* God?
Mt 23:12 whoever humbles himself will be *e*.''
Lk 14:11 he who humbles himself will be *e*.''
   18:14 he who humbles himself will be *e*.''
Ac   2:33 *E* to the right hand of God,
     5:31 God *e* him to his own right hand
Php   1:20 always Christ will be *e* in my body,
     2:   9 Therefore God *e* him
Heb   7:26 from sinners, *e* above the heavens.

EXALTS* (EXALT)

1Sa   2:   7 he humbles and he *e*.
Job 36:   7 and *e* them forever.

Ps 75: 7 He brings one down, he *e* another.
Pr 14: 34 Righteousness *e* a nation,
Mt 23: 12 For whoever *e* himself will be
Lk 14: 11 For everyone who *e* himself will be
     18: 14 For everyone who *e* himself will be

EXAMINE (EXAMINED EXAMINES)

Ps 11: 4 his eyes *e* them.
     17: 3 you probe my heart and *e* me
     26: 2 *e* my heart and my mind;
Jer 17: 10 and *e* the mind,
     20: 12 Almighty, you who *e* the righteous
La   3: 40 Let us *e* our ways and test them,
1Co 11: 28 A man ought to *e* himself
2Co 13: 5 *E* yourselves to see whether you

EXAMINED (EXAMINE)

Job 13: 9 Would it turn out well if he *e* you?
Ac 17: 11 *e* the Scriptures every day to see

EXAMINES (EXAMINE)

Ps 11: 5 The LORD *e* the righteous,
Pr   5: 21 he *e* all his paths.

EXAMPLE* (EXAMPLES)

2Ki 14: 3 In everything he followed the *e*
Ecc 9: 13 also saw under the sun this *e*
Eze 14: 8 and make him an *e* and a byword.
Jn 13: 15 have set you an *e* that you should
Ro   7: 2 as long as he lives? For *e*,
1Co 11: 1 Follow my *e*, as I follow
     11: 1 as I follow the *e* of Christ.
Gal 3: 15 let me take up an *e* from everyday life.
Php 3: 17 Join with others in following my *e*,
2Th 3: 7 how you ought to follow our *e*.
1Ti 1: 16 as an *e* for those who would believe
     4: 12 set an *e* for the believers in speech,
Tit 2: 7 In everything set them an *e*
Heb 4: 11 fall by following their *e*
Jas   5: 4 Or take ships as an *e*.
     5: 10 as an *e* of patience in the face
1Pe 2: 21 leaving you an *e*, that you should
2Pe 2: 6 made them an *e* of what is going
Jude : 7 as an *e* of those who suffer

EXAMPLES* (EXAMPLE)

1Co 10: 6 Now these things occurred as *e*
     10: 11 as *e* and were written down
1Pe 5: 3 to you, but being *e* to the flock.

EXASPERATE*

Eph 6: 4 Fathers, do not *e* your children;

EXCEL* (EXCELLENT)

Ge 49: 4 as the waters, you will no longer *e*,
1Co 14: 12 to *e* in gifts that build up the church
2Co 8: 7 But just as you *e* in everything—
     8: 7 also *e* in this grace of giving.

EXCELLENT (EXCEL)

1Co 12: 31 now I will show you the most *e* way
Php 4: 8 if anything is *e* or praiseworthy—
1Ti 3: 13 have served well gain an *e* standing
Tit 3: 8 These things are *e* and profitable

EXCESSIVE

Eze 18: 8 or take *e* interest.
2Co 2: 7 not be overwhelmed by *e* sorrow.

EXCHANGE (EXCHANGED)

Mt 16: 26 Or what can a man give in *e*
Mk 8: 37 Or what can a man give in *e*
2Co 6: 13 As a fair *e*—I speak

EXCHANGED (EXCHANGE)

Ps 106: 20 They *e* their Glory
Jer 2: 11 But my people have *e* their Glory
Hos 4: 7 they *e* their Glory
Ro 1: 23 *e* the glory of the immortal God
     1: 25 They *e* the truth of God for a lie,
     1: 26 their women *e* natural relations

EXCLAIM

Ps 35: 10 My whole being will *e*,

EXCUSE* (EXCUSES)

Ps 25: 3 who are treacherous without *e*.
Lk 14: 18 Please *e* me.'
     14: 19 Please *e* me.'

Jn 15: 22 they have no *e* for their sin.
Ro 1: 20 so that men are without *e*,
     2: 1 You, therefore, have no *e*,

EXCUSES* (EXCUSE)

Lk 14: 18 "But they all alike began to make *e*.

EXERTED*

Eph 1: 20 which he *e* in Christ

EXHORT*

1Ti 5: 1 but *e* him as if he were your father.

EXILE

2Ki 17: 23 taken from their homeland into *e*
     25: 11 into *e* the people who remained

EXISTED* (EXISTS)

2Pe 3: 5 ago by God's word the heavens *e*

EXISTS (EXISTED)

Heb 2: 10 and through whom everything *e*,
     11: 6 to him must believe that he *e*

EXPANSE

Ge 1: 7 So God made the *e* and separated
     1: 8 God called the *e* "sky."

EXPECT (EXPECTATION EXPECTED EXPECTING)

Mt 24: 44 at an hour when you do not *e* him.
Lk 12: 40 at an hour when you do not *e* him."
Php 1: 20 I eagerly and hope that I will

EXPECTATION (EXPECT)

Ro 8: 19 waits in eager *e* for the sons
Heb 10: 27 but only a fearful *e* of judgment

EXPECTED (EXPECT)

Pr 11: 7 all he *e* from his power comes
Hag 1: 9 "You *e* much, but see, it turned out

EXPECTING (EXPECT)

Lk 6: 35 and lend to them without *e*

EXPEL* (EXPELLED)

1Co 5: 13 *E* the wicked man from among you

EXPELLED (EXPEL)

Eze 28: 16 and I *e* you, O guardian cherub,

EXPENSE (EXPENSIVE)

1Co 9: 7 Who serves as a soldier at his own *e*

EXPENSIVE* (EXPENSE)

Mt 26: 7 jar of very *e* perfume,
Mk 14: 3 jar of very *e* perfume,
Lk 7: 25 those who wear *e* clothes
Jn 12: 3 a pint of pure nard, an *e* perfume;
1Ti 2: 9 or gold or pearls or *e* clothes,

EXPERT

1Co 3: 10 I laid a foundation as an *e* builder,

EXPLAINING (EXPLAINS)

Ac 17: 3 *e* and proving that the Christ had

EXPLAINS* (EXPLAINING)

Ac 8: 31 he said, "unless someone *e* it to me

EXPLOIT* (EXPLOITED EXPLOITING EXPLOITS)

Pr 22: 22 Do not *e* the poor because they are
Isa 58: 3 and *e* all your workers.
2Co 12: 17 Did I *e* you through any
     12: 18 Titus did not *e* you, did he?
2Pe 2: 3 greed these teachers will *e* you

EXPLOITED* (EXPLOIT)

2Co 7: 2 no one, we have *e* no one.

EXPLOITING* (EXPLOIT)

Jas 2: 6 Is it not the rich who are *e* you?

EXPLOITS (EXPLOIT)

2Co 11: 20 or *e* you or takes advantage of you

EXPLORE

Nu 13: 2 "Send some men to *e* the land

EXPOSE (EXPOSED)

1Co 4: 5 will *e* the motives of men's hearts.
Eph 5: 11 of darkness, but rather *e* them.

EXPOSED (EXPOSE)

Jn 3: 20 for fear that his deeds will be *e*.
Eph 5: 13 everything *e* by the light becomes

EXPRESS (EXPRESSING)

Ro 8: 26 us with groans that words cannot *e*.

EXPRESSING* (EXPRESS)

1Co 2: 13 *e* spiritual truths in spiritual words.
Gal 5: 6 thing that counts is faith *e* itself

EXTENDS (EXTENT)

Pr 31: 20 and *e* her hands to the needy.
Lk 1: 50 His mercy *e* to those who fear him,

EXTENT (EXTENDS)

Jn 13: 1 he now showed them the full *e*

EXTERNAL

Gal 2: 6 judge by *e* appearance—

EXTINGUISH (EXTINGUISHED)

Eph 6: 16 which you can *e* all the flaming

EXTINGUISHED (EXTINGUISH)

2Sa 21: 17 the lamp of Israel will not be *e*."

EXTOL*

Job 36: 24 Remember to *e* his work,
Ps 34: 1 I will *e* the LORD at all times;
     68: 4 *e* him who rides on the clouds—
     95: 2 and *e* him with music and song.
   109: 30 mouth I will greatly *e* the LORD;
   111: 1 I will *e* the LORD with all my heart
   115: 18 it is we who *e* the LORD,
   117: 1 *e* him, all you peoples.
   145: 2 and *e* your name for ever and ever.
   145: 10 your saints will *e* you.
   147: 12 *E* the LORD, O Jerusalem;

EXTORT*

Lk 3: 14 "Don't *e* money and don't accuse

EXTRAORDINARY*

Ac 19: 11 God did *e* miracles through Paul,

EXTREME (EXTREMES)

2Co 8: 2 and their *e* poverty welled up

EXTREMES* (EXTREME)

Ecc 7: 18 who fears God will avoid all *e*.

EXULT

Ps 89: 16 they *e* in your righteousness.
Isa 45: 25 will be found righteous and will *e*.

EYE (EYES)

Ge 3: 6 good for food and pleasing to the *e*,
Ex 21: 24 you are to take life for life, *e* for *e*,
Dt 19: 21 life for life, *e* for *e*, tooth for tooth,
Ps 94: 9 Does he who formed the *e* not see?
Mt 5: 29 If your right *e* causes you to sin,
     5: 38 '*E* for *e*, and tooth for tooth.'
     6: 22 "The *e* is the lamp of the body.
     7: 3 of sawdust in your brother's *e*
1Co 2: 9 "No *e* has seen,
     12: 16 I am not an *e*, I do not belong
     15: 52 of an *e*, at the last trumpet.
Eph 6: 6 favor when their *e* is on you,
Col 3: 22 not only when their *e* is on you
Rev 1: 7 and every *e* will see him,

EYES (EYE)

Nu 15: 39 the lusts of your own hearts and *e*.
     33: 55 remain will become barbs in your *e*
Dt 11: 12 the *e* of the LORD your God are
     12: 25 right in the *e* of the LORD.
     16: 19 for a bribe blinds the *e* of the wise
Jos 23: 13 on your backs and thorns in your *e*
1Sa 15: 17 you were once small in your own *e*,
1Ki 10: 7 I came and saw with my own *e*,
2Ki 9: 30 heard about it, she painted her *e*,
2Ch 16: 9 For the *e* of the LORD range
Job 31: 1 "I made a covenant with my *e*

Job 36: 7 He does not take his *e*
Ps 25:15 My *e* are ever on the LORD,
36: 1 God before his *e.*
101: 6 My *e* will be on the faithful
118: 23 and it is marvelous in our *e.*
119: 18 Open my *e* that I may see
119: 37 my *e* away from worthless things;
121: 1 I lift up my *e* to the hills—
123: 1 I lift up my *e* to you,
139: 16 your *e* saw my unformed body.
141: 8 But my *e* are fixed on you,
Pr 3: 7 Do not be wise in your own *e;*
4:25 Let your *e* look straight ahead,
15: 3 The *e* of the LORD are everywhere
17:24 a fool's *e* wander to the ends
Isa 6: 5 and my *e* have seen the King,
33:17 Your *e* will see the king
42: 7 to open *e* that are blind,
Jer 24: 6 My *e* will watch over them
Hab 1:13 Your *e* are too pure to look on evil;
Mt 6:22 If your *e* are good, your whole
21:42 and it is marvelous in our *e'?*
Lk 16:15 ones who justify yourselves in the *e*
24:31 Then their *e* were opened
Jn 4:35 open your *e* and look at the fields!
Ac 1: 9 he was taken up before their very *e,*
2Co 4:18 So we fix our *e* not on what is seen,
8:21 not only in the *e* of the Lord but
Eph 1:18 also that the *e* of your heart may be
Heb 12: 2 Let us fix our *e* on Jesus, the author
Jas 2: 5 poor in the *e* of the world to be rich
1Pe 3:12 For the *e* of the Lord are
Rev 7:17 wipe away every tear from their *e.''*
21: 4 He will wipe every tear from their *e*

EYEWITNESSES* (WITNESS)

Lk 1: 2 by those who from the first were *e*
2Pe 1:16 but we were *e* of his majesty.

EZEKIEL*

Priest called to be prophet to the exiles (Eze 1-3). Symbolically acted out destruction of Jerusalem (Eze 4-5; 12; 24).

EZRA*

Priest and teacher of the Law who led a return of exiles to Israel to reestablish temple and worship (Ezr 7-8). Corrected intermarriage of priests (Ezr 9-10). Read Law at celebration of Feast of Tabernacles (Ne 8). Participated in dedication of Jerusalem's walls (Ne 12).

FACE (FACES)

Ge 32:30 ''It is because I saw God *f* to *f,*
Ex 3: 6 Moses hid his *f,* because he was
33:11 would speak to Moses *f* to *f,*
33:20 But,'' he said, ''you cannot see my *f*
34:29 was not aware that his *f* was radiant
Nu 6:25 the LORD make his *f* shine
12: 8 With him I speak *f* to *f,*
14:14 O LORD, have been seen *f* to *f,*
Dt 5: 4 The LORD spoke to you *f* to *f* out
31:17 I will hide my *f* from them,
34:10 whom the LORD knew *f* to *f,*
Jdg 6:22 the angel of the LORD *f* to *f!''*
2Ki 14: 8 challenge: ''Come, meet me *f* to *f.''*
1Ch 16:11 seek his *f* always.
2Ch 7:14 and seek my *f* and turn
25:17 of Israel: ''Come, meet me *f* to *f.''*
Ezr 9: 6 and disgraced to lift up my *f* to you,
Ps 4: 6 Let the light of your *f* shine upon us
27: 8 Your *f,* LORD, I will seek.
31:16 Let your *f* shine on your servant;
44: 3 and the light of your *f,*
44:22 Yet for your sake we *f* death all day
51: 9 Hide your *f* from my sins
67: 1 and make his *f* shine upon us; *Selah*
80: 3 make your *f* shine upon us,
105: 4 seek his *f* always.
119:135 Make your *f* shine
SS 2:14 and your *f* is lovely.
Isa 50: 7 Therefore have I set my *f* like flint,
50: 8 Let us *f* each other!
54: 8 I hid my *f* from you for a moment,
Jer 32: 4 and will speak with him *f* to *f*
34: 3 and he will speak with you *f* to *f.*
Eze 1:10 Each of the four had the *f* of a man,
20:35 *f* to *f,* I will execute judgment

Mt 17: 2 His *f* shone like the sun,
18:10 angels in heaven always see the *f*
Lk 9:29 the appearance of his *f* changed,
Ro 8:36 ''For your sake we *f* death all day
1Co 13:12 reflection; then we shall see *f* to *f.*
2Co 3: 7 could not look steadily at the *f*
4: 6 the glory of God in the *f* of Christ.
10: 1 who am ''timid'' when *f* to *f*
1Pe 3:12 but the *f* of the Lord is
2Jn 12 to visit you and talk with you *f* to *f,*
3Jn 14 see you soon, and we will talk *f* to *f.*
Rev 1:16 His *f* was like the sun shining
22: 4 They will see his *f,* and his name

FACES (FACE)

2Co 3:18 who with unveiled *f* all reflect

FACTIONS

2Co 12:20 outbursts of anger, *f,* slander,
Gal 5:20 selfish ambition, dissensions, *f*

FADE (FADING)

Jas 1:11 the rich man will *f* away
1Pe 5: 4 of glory that will never *f* away.

FADING (FADE)

2Co 3: 7 *f* though it was, will not
3:11 if what was *f* away came with glory,
3:13 at it while the radiance was *f* away.

FAIL (FAILED FAILING FAILINGS FAILS FAILING)

Lev 26:15 and *f* to carry out all my commands
1Ki 2: 4 you will never *f* to have a man
1Ch 28:20 He will not *f* you or forsake you
2Ch 34:33 they did not *f* to follow the LORD,
Ps 89:28 my covenant with him will never *f.*
Pr 15:22 Plans *f* for lack of counsel,
Isa 51: 6 my righteousness will never *f.*
La 3:22 for his compassions never *f.*
Lk 22:32 Simon, that your faith may not *f.*
2Co 13: 5 unless, of course, you *f* the test?

FAILED (FAIL)

Jos 23:14 has been fulfilled; not one has *f.*
1Ki 8:56 Not one word has *f*
Ps 77: 8 Has his promise *f* for all time?
Ro 9: 6 as though God's word had *f.*
2Co 13: 6 discover that we have not *f* the test.

FAILING (FAIL)

1Sa 12:23 sin against the LORD by *f* to pray

FAILINGS (FAIL)

Ro 15: 1 ought to bear with the *f* of the weak

FAILS (FAIL)

Jer 14: 6 their eyesight *f*
Joel 1:10 the oil *f.*
1Co 13: 8 Love never *f.*

FAILURE* (FAIL)

1Th 2: 1 that our visit to you was not a *f.*

FAINT

Isa 40:31 they will walk and not be *f.*

FAINTHEARTED* (HEART)

Dt 20: 3 Do not be *f* or afraid; do not be
20: 8 shall add, ''Is any man afraid or *f?*

FAIR (FAIRNESS)

Pr 1: 3 doing what is right and just and *f;*
Col 4: 1 slaves with what is right and *f,*

FAIRNESS* (FAIR)

Pr 29:14 If a king judges the poor with *f,*

FAITH* (FAITHFUL FAITHFULLY FAITHFULNESS FAITHLESS)

Ex 21: 8 because he has broken *f* with her.
Dt 32:51 both of you broke *f* with me
Jos 22:16 'How could you break *f*
Jdg 9:16 and in good *f* when you made
9:19 and in good *f* toward Jerub-Baal
1Sa 14:33 ''You have broken *f,''* he said.
2Ch 20:20 have *f* in the LORD your God
20:20 have *f* in his prophets and you will
Isa 7: 9 If you do not stand firm in your *f,*

Isa 26: 2 the nation that keeps *f.*
Hab 2: 4 but the righteous will live by his *f—*
Mal 2:10 by breaking *f* with one another?
2:11 one another? Judah has broken *f.*
2:14 because you have broken *f* with her
2:15 and do not break *f* with the wife
2:16 in your spirit, and do not break *f.*
Mt 6:30 O you of little *f?* So do not worry,
8:10 anyone in Israel with such great *f.*
8:26 He replied, ''You of little *f,*
9: 2 When Jesus saw their *f,* he said
9:22 he said, ''your *f* has healed you.''
9:29 According to your *f* will it be done
13:58 there because of their lack of *f.*
14:31 of little *f,''* he said, ''why did you
15:28 ''Woman, you have great *f!*
16: 8 Jesus asked, ''You of little *f,*
17:20 if you have *f* as small as a mustard
17:20 ''Because you have so little *f.*
21:21 if you have *f* and do not doubt,
24:10 many will turn away from the *f*
Mk 2: 5 When Jesus saw their *f,* he said
4:40 still have no *f?''* They were
5:34 ''Daughter, your *f* has healed you.
6: 6 he was amazed at their lack of *f.*
10:52 said Jesus, ''your *f* has healed you.''
11:22 ''Have *f* in God,'' Jesus answered.
16:14 he rebuked them for their lack of *f*
Lk 5:20 When Jesus saw their *f,* he said,
7: 9 I have not found such great *f*
7:50 the woman, ''Your *f* has saved you;
8:25 ''Where is your *f?''* he asked his
8:48 ''Daughter, your *f* has healed you.
12:28 will he clothe you, O you of little *f!*
17: 5 ''Increase our *f!''* He replied,
17: 6 ''If you have *f* as small
17:19 your *f* has made you well.''
18: 8 will he find *f* on the earth?''
18:42 your sight; your *f* has healed you.''
22:32 Simon, that your *f* may not fail.
Jn 2:11 and his disciples put their *f* in him.
7:31 in the crowd put their *f* in him.
8:30 he spoke, many put their *f* in him.
11:45 had seen what Jesus did, put their *f*
12:11 to Jesus and putting their *f* in him.
12:42 they would not confess their *f*
14:12 anyone who has *f* in me will do
Ac 3:16 By *f* in the name of Jesus, this man
3:16 that comes through him that has
6: 5 full of *f* and of the Holy Spirit,
6: 7 of priests became obedient to the *f.*
11:24 full of the Holy Spirit and *f,*
13: 8 to turn the proconsul from the *f.*
14: 9 saw that he had *f* to be healed
14:22 them to remain true to the *f,*
14:27 the door of *f* to the Gentiles.
15: 9 for he purified their hearts by *f.*
16: 5 were strengthened in the *f*
20:21 and have *f* in our Lord Jesus.
24:24 as he spoke about *f* in Christ Jesus.
26:18 those who are sanctified by *f*
27:25 for I have *f* in God that it will
Ro 1: 5 to the obedience that comes from *f.*
1: 8 because your *f* is being reported all
1:12 encouraged by each other's *f.*
1:17 is by *f* from first to last,
1:17 ''The righteous will live by *f.''*
3: 3 What if some did not have *f?*
3: 3 lack of *f* nullify God's faithfulness?
3:22 comes through *f* in Jesus Christ
3:25 a sacrifice of atonement, through *f*
3:26 one who justifies those who have *f*
3:27 the law? No, but on that of *f.*
3:28 by *f* apart from observing the law.
3:30 through that same *f.*
3:30 will justify the circumcised by *f*
3:31 nullify the law by this *f?* Not at all!
4: 5 his *f* is credited as righteousness.
4: 9 that Abraham's *f* was credited
4:11 had by *f* while he was still
4:12 of the *f* that our father Abraham
4:13 the righteousness that comes by *f.*
4:14 *f* has no value and the promise is
4:16 Therefore, the promise comes by *f,*
4:16 are of the *f* of Abraham.
4:19 Without weakening in his *f,*
4:20 but was strengthened in his *f*
5: 1 we have been justified through *f,*

Ro 5: 2 access by *f* into this grace
     9:30 a righteousness that is by *f;*
     9:32 Because they pursued it not by *f*
    10: 6 the righteousness that is by *f* says:
    10: 8 the word of *f* we are proclaiming:
    10:17 *f* comes from hearing the message,
    11:20 of unbelief, and you stand by *f.*
    12: 3 measure of *f* God has given you.
    12: 6 let him use it in proportion to his *f.*
    14: 1 Accept him whose *f* is weak,
    14: 2 One man's *f* allows him
    14: 2 but another man, whose *f* is weak,
    14:23 because his eating is not from *f;*
    14:23 that does not come from *f* is sin.
1Co 2: 5 so that your *f* might not rest
    12: 9 to another *f* by the same Spirit,
    13: 2 and if I have a *f* that can move
    13:13 And now these three remain: *f,*
    15:14 is useless and so is your *f.*
    15:17 has not been raised, your *f* is futile;
    16:13 stand firm in the *f;* be men
2Co 1:24 Not that we lord it over your *f,*
     1:24 because it is by *f* you stand firm.
     4:13 With that same spirit of *f* we
     5: 7 We live by *f,* not by sight.
     8: 7 in *f,* in speech, in knowledge,
    10:15 as your *f* continues to grow,
    13: 5 to see whether you are in the *f;*
Gal 1:23 now preaching the *f* he once tried
     2:16 Jesus that we may be justified by *f*
     2:16 but by *f* in Jesus Christ.
     2:16 have put our *f* in Christ Jesus that
     2:20 I live by *f* in the Son of God,
     3: 8 would justify the Gentiles by *f,*
     3: 9 So those who have *f* are blessed
     3: 9 along with Abraham, the man of *f.*
     3:11 "The righteous will live by *f.*"
     3:12 based on *f;* on the contrary,
     3:14 by *f* we might receive the promise
     3:22 being given through *f*
     3:23 Before this *f* came, we were held
     3:23 up until *f* should be revealed.
     3:24 that we might be justified by *f.*
     3:25 that *f* has come, we are no longer
     3:26 of God through *f* in Christ Jesus,
     5: 5 But by *f* we eagerly await
     5: 6 that counts is *f* expressing itself
Eph 1:15 ever since I heard about your *f*
     2: 8 through *f*— and this not
     3:12 through *f* in him we may approach
     3:17 dwell in your hearts through *f.*
     4: 5 one Lord, one *f,* one baptism;
     4:13 up until we all reach unity in the *f*
     6:16 to all this, take up the shield of *f,*
     6:23 love with *f* from God the Father
Php 1:25 for your progress and joy in the *f.*
     1:27 as one man for the *f* of the gospel
     2:17 and service coming from your *f,*
     3: 9 comes from God and is by *f.*
     3: 9 that which is through *f* in Christ—
Col 1: 4 heard of your *f* in Christ Jesus
     1: 5 the *f* and love that spring
     1:23 continue in your *f,* established
     2: 5 and how firm your *f* in Christ is.
     2: 7 in the *f* as you were taught,
     2:12 him through your *f* in the power
1Th 1: 3 Father your work produced by *f,*
     1: 8 your *f* in God has become known
     3: 2 and encourage you in your *f,*
     3: 5 I sent to find out about your *f,*
     3: 6 brought good news about your *f*
     3: 7 about you because of your *f.*
     3:10 supply what is lacking in your *f.*
     5: 8 on *f* and love as a breastplate,
2Th 1: 3 because your *f* is growing more
     1: 4 and *f* in all the persecutions
     1:11 and every act prompted by your *f.*
     3: 2 evil men, for not everyone has *f.*
1Ti 1: 2 To Timothy my true son in the *f:*
     1: 4 than God's work—which is by *f.*
     1: 5 a good conscience and a sincere *f.*
     1:14 along with the *f* and love that are
     1:19 and so have shipwrecked their *f.*
     1:19 on to *f* and a good conscience.
     2: 7 of the true *f* to the Gentiles.
     2:15 if they continue in *f,* love
     3: 9 of the *f* with a clear conscience.
     3:13 assurance in their *f* in Christ Jesus.

1Ti 4: 1 later times some will abandon the *f*
     4: 6 brought up in the truths of the *f*
     4:12 in life, in love, in *f* and in purity.
     5: 8 he has denied the *f* and is worse
     6:10 have wandered from the *f*
     6:11 pursue righteousness, godliness, *f,*
     6:12 Fight the good fight of the *f.*
     6:21 so doing have wandered from the *f.*
2Ti 1: 5 been reminded of your sincere *f,*
     1:13 with *f* and love in Christ Jesus.
     2:18 and they destroy the *f* of some.
     2:22 and pursue righteousness, *f,*
     3: 8 as far as the *f* is concerned,
     3:10 my purpose, *f,* patience, love,
     3:15 wise for salvation through *f*
     4: 7 finished the race, I have kept the *f.*
Tit 1: 1 Christ for the *f* of God's elect
     1: 2 a *f* and knowledge resting
     1: 4 my true son in our common *f:*
     1:13 so that they will be sound in the *f*
     2: 2 self-controlled, and sound in *f,*
     3:15 Greet those who love us in the *f.*
Phm : 5 because I hear about your *f*
      : 6 may be active in sharing your *f.*
Heb 4: 2 heard did not combine it with *f.*
     4:14 firmly to the *f* we profess.
     6: 1 and of *f* in God, instruction about
     6:12 but to imitate those who through *f*
    10:22 heart in full assurance of *f,*
    10:38 But my righteous one will live by *f.*
    11: 1 *f* is being sure of what we hope for
    11: 3 By *f* we understand that
    11: 4 And by *f* he still speaks, even
    11: 4 By *f* Abel offered God a better
    11: 4 By *f* he was commended
    11: 5 By *f* Enoch was taken from this life
    11: 6 And without *f* it is impossible
    11: 7 By his *f* he condemned the world
    11: 7 By *f* Noah, when warned about
    11: 7 the righteousness that comes by *f.*
    11: 8 By *f* Abraham, when called to go
    11: 9 By *f* he made his home
    11:11 By *f* Abraham, even though he was
    11:13 living by *f* when they died.
    11:17 By *f* Abraham, when God tested
    11:20 By *f* Isaac blessed Jacob
    11:21 By *f* Jacob, when he was dying,
    11:22 By *f* Joseph, when his end was near
    11:23 By *f* Moses' parents hid him
    11:24 By *f* Moses, when he had grown up
    11:27 By *f* he left Egypt, not fearing
    11:28 By *f* he kept the Passover
    11:29 By *f* the people passed
    11:30 By *f* the walls of Jericho fell,
    11:31 By *f* the prostitute Rahab,
    11:33 through *f* conquered kingdoms,
    11:39 were all commended for their *f,*
    12: 2 the author and perfecter of our *f,*
    12: 7 way of life and imitate their *f.*
Jas 1: 3 of your *f* develops perseverance.
     2: 5 the eyes of the world to be rich in *f*
     2:14 has no deeds? Can such *f* save him?
     2:14 if a man claims to have *f*
     2:17 In the same way, *f* by itself,
     2:18 I will show you my *f* by what I do.
     2:18 Show me your *f* without deeds.
     2:18 "You have *f;* I have deeds."
     2:20 do you want evidence that *f*
     2:22 You see that his *f* and his actions
     2:22 and his *f* was made complete
     2:24 by what he does and not by *f* alone.
     2:26 so *f* without deeds is dead.
     5:15 in *f* will make the sick person well;
1Pe 1: 5 who through *f* are shielded
     1: 7 These have come so that your *f*—
     1: 9 you are receiving the goal of your *f,*
     1:21 and so your *f* and hope are in God.
     5: 9 Resist him, standing firm in the *f,*
2Pe 1: 1 Jesus Christ have received a *f*
     1: 5 effort to add to your *f* goodness;
1Jn 5: 4 overcome the world, even our *f.*
Jude : 3 to contend for the *f* that was once
      : 20 up in your most holy *f*
Rev 2:13 You did not renounce your *f* in me,
     2:19 your love and *f,* your service

FAITHFUL* (FAITH)
Nu 12: 7 he is *f* in all my house.

Dt 7: 9 your God is God; he is the *f* God,
    32: 4 A *f* God who does no wrong,
1Sa 2:35 I will raise up for myself a *f* priest,
2Sa 20:19 We are the peaceful and *f* in Israel.
    22:26 "To the *f* you show yourself *f,*
1Ki 3: 6 because he was *f* to you
2Ch 31:18 were *f* in consecrating themselves.
    31:20 and *f* before the LORD his God.
Ne 9: 8 You found his heart *f* to you,
Ps 12: 1 the *f* have vanished
    18:25 To the *f* you show yourself *f,*
    25:10 of the LORD are loving and *f*
    31:23 The LORD preserves the *f,*
    33: 4 he is *f* in all he does.
    37:28 and will not forsake his *f* ones.
    78: 8 whose spirits were not *f* to him.
    78:37 they were not *f* to his covenant.
    89:19 to your *f* people you said:
    89:24 My *f* love will be with him,
    89:37 the *f* witness in the sky."
    97:10 for he guards the lives of his *f* ones
   101: 6 My eyes will be on the *f* in the land,
   111: 7 The works of his hands are *f*
   145:13 The LORD is *f* to all his promises
   146: 6 the LORD, who remains *f* forever.
Pr 2: 8 and protects the way of his *f* ones.
    20: 6 but a *f* man who can find?
    28:20 A *f* man will be richly blessed,
    31:26 and *f* instruction is on her tongue.
Isa 1:21 See how the *f* city has become
     1:26 the *F* City."
    49: 7 because of the LORD, who is *f,*
    55: 3 my *f* love promised to David.
Jer 42: 5 *f* witness against us if we do not act
Eze 43:11 so that they may be *f* to its design
    48:11 who were *f* in serving me
Hos 11:12 even against the *f* Holy One.
Zec 8: 8 I will be *f* and righteous to them
Mt 24:45 Who then is the *f* and wise servant,
    25:21 'Well done, good and *f* servant!
    25:21 You have been *f* with a few things;
    25:23 You have been *f* with a few things;
    25:23 'Well done, good and *f* servant!
Lk 12:42 then is the *f* and wise manager,
Ro 12:12 patient in affliction, *f* in prayer.
1Co 1: 9 his Son Jesus Christ our Lord, is *f.*
     4: 2 been given a trust must prove *f.*
     4:17 my son whom I love, who is *f*
    10:13 And God is *f;* he will not let you be
2Co 1:18 no"? But as surely as God is *f,*
Eph 1: 1 in Ephesus, the *f* in Christ Jesus:
     6:21 the dear brother and *f* servant
Col 1: 2 and *f* brothers in Christ at Colosse:
     1: 7 who is a *f* minister of Christ
     4: 7 a *f* minister and fellow servant
     4: 9 He is coming with Onesimus, our *f*
1Th 5:24 The one who calls you is *f*
2Th 3: 3 the Lord is *f,* and he will strengthen
1Ti 1:12 he considered me *f,* appointing me
     5: 9 has been *f* to her husband,
2Ti 2:13 he will remain *f,*
Heb 2:17 and *f* high priest in service to God.
     3: 2 He was *f* to the one who appointed
     3: 2 as Moses was *f* in all God's house.
     3: 5 Moses was *f* as a servant
     3: 6 But Christ is *f* as a son
     8: 9 because they did not remain *f*
    10:23 for he who promised is *f.*
    11:11 he considered him *f* who had made
1Pe 4:19 themselves to their *f* Creator
     5:12 whom I regard as a *f* brother,
1Jn 1: 9 he is *f* and just and will forgive us
3Jn : 5 you are *f* in what you are doing
Rev 1: 5 who is the *f* witness, the firstborn
     2:10 Be *f,* even to the point of death,
     2:13 the days of Antipas, my *f* witness,
     3:14 the words of the Amen, the *f*
    14:12 commandments and remain *f*
    17:14 his called, chosen and *f* followers."
    19:11 whose rider is called *F* and True.

FAITHFULLY* (FAITH)
Dt 11:13 if you obey the commands I am
Jos 2:14 *f* when the LORD gives us the land
1Sa 12:24 and serve him *f* with all your heart;
1Ki 2: 4 and *f* walk *f* before me
2Ki 20: 3 how I have walked before you *f*
    22: 7 because they are acting *f.*"

FAITHFULNESS

2Ch 19: 9 must serve *f* and wholeheartedly
31: 12 they *f* brought in the contributions,
31: 15 and Shecaniah assisted him *f*
32: 1 all that Hezekiah had so *f* done,
34: 12 The men did the work *f.*
Ne 9: 33 you have acted *f,* while we did
13: 14 so *f* done for the house of my God
Isa 38: 3 how I have walked before you *f*
Jer 23: 28 one who has my word speak it *f.*
Eze 18: 9 and *f* keeps my laws.
44: 15 and who *f* carried out the duties
1Pe 4: 10 *f* administering God's grace

FAITHFUL* (FAITH)

Ge 24: 27 not abandoned his kindness and *f*
24: 49 if you will show kindness and *f*
32: 10 and *f* you have shown your servant.
47: 29 you will show me kindness and *f.*
Ex 34: 6 *f,* maintaining love to thousands,
Jos 24: 14 the LORD and serve him with all *f.*
1Sa 26: 23 man for his righteousness and
2Sa 2: 6 now show you kindness and *f.*
15: 20 May kindness and *f* be with you.''
Ps 30: 9 Will it proclaim your *f?*
36: 5 your *f* to the skies.
40: 10 I speak of your *f* and salvation.
54: 5 in your *f* destroy them.
57: 3 God sends his love and his *f.*
57: 10 your *f* reaches to the skies.
61: 7 appoint your love and *f*
71: 22 the harp for your *f,* O my God;
85: 10 Love and *f* meet together;
85: 11 *F* springs from the earth,
86: 15 to anger, abounding in love and *f*
88: 11 your *f* in Destruction?
89: 1 mouth I will make your *f* known
89: 2 that you established your *f*
89: 5 your *f* too, in the assembly
89: 8 and your *f* surrounds you.
89: 14 love and *f* go before you.
89: 33 nor will I ever betray my *f,*
89: 49 which in your *f* you swore to David
91: 4 his *f* will be your shield
92: 2 and your *f* at night,
98: 3 and his *f* to the house of Israel;
100: 5 *f* continues through all
108: 4 your *f* reaches to the skies.
111: 8 done in *f* and uprightness.
115: 1 because of your love and *f.*
117: 2 the *f* of the LORD endures forever.
119: 75 and in *f* you have afflicted me.
119: 90 *f* continues through all
138: 2 name for your love and your *f,*
143: 1 in your *f* and righteousness
Pr 3: 3 Let love and *f* never leave you;
14: 22 plan what is good find love and *f.*
16: 6 Through love and *f* sin is atoned for
20: 28 Love and *f* keep a king safe;
Isa 11: 5 and *f* the sash around his waist.
16: 5 in *f* a man will sit on it—
25: 1 for in perfect *f*
38: 18 cannot hope for your *f.*
38: 19 about your *f.*
42: 3 In *f* he will bring forth justice;
61: 8 In my *f* I will reward them
La 3: 23 great is your *f.*
Hos 2: 20 I will betroth you in *f.*
4: 1 ''There is no *f,* no love,
Mt 23: 23 of the law—justice, mercy and *f.*
Ro 3: 3 lack of faith nullify God's *f?*
Gal 5: 22 patience, kindness, goodness, *f,*
3Jn : 3 and tell about your *f* to the truth
Rev 13: 10 and *f* on the part of the saints.

FAITHLESS* (FAITH)

Ps 78: 57 fathers they were disloyal and *f,*
101: 3 The deeds of *f* men I hate;
119:158 I look on the *f* with loathing.
Pr 14: 14 The *f* will be fully repaid
Jer 3: 6 you seen what *f* Israel has done?
3: 8 I gave *f* Israel her certificate
3: 11 ''*F* Israel is more righteous
3: 12 *f* Israel,' declares the LORD.
3: 14 *f* people,'' declares the LORD.
3: 22 ''Return, *f* people;
12: 1 Why do all the *f* live at ease?
Ro 1: 31 they are senseless, *f,* heartless,
2Ti 2: 13 if we are *f,*

FALL (FALLEN FALLING FALLS)

Ps 37: 24 though he stumble, he will not *f,*
55: 22 he will never let the righteous *f.*
69: 9 of those who insult you *f* on me.
145: 14 The LORD upholds all those who *f*
Pr 11: 28 Whoever trusts in his riches will *f,*
Isa 40: 7 The grass withers and the flowers *f,*
Mt 7: 25 yet it did not *f,* because it had its
Lk 10: 18 ''I saw Satan *f* like lightning
11: 17 a house divided against itself will *f.*
23: 30 say to the mountains, ''*F* on us!''
Ro 3: 23 and *f* short of the glory of God,
Heb 6: 6 if they *f* away, to be brought back

FALLEN (FALL)

2Sa 1: 19 How the mighty have *f!*
Isa 14: 12 How you have *f* from heaven,
1Co 11: 30 and a number of you have *f* asleep.
15: 6 though some have *f* asleep.
15: 18 who have *f* asleep in Christ are lost.
15: 20 of those who have *f* asleep.
Gal 5: 4 you have *f* away from grace.
1Th 4: 15 precede those who have *f* asleep.

FALLING (FALL)

Jude : 24 able to keep you from *f*

FALLS (FALL)

Pr 11: 14 For lack of guidance a nation *f,*
24: 17 Do not gloat when your enemy *f;*
28: 14 he who hardens his heart *f*
Mt 13: 21 of the word, he quickly *f* away.
21: 44 He who *f* on this stone will be
Jn 12: 24 a kernel of wheat *f* to the ground
Ro 14: 4 To his own master he stands or *f.*

FALSE (FALSEHOOD FALSELY)

Ex 20: 16 ''You shall not give *f* testimony
23: 1 ''Do not spread *f* reports.
23: 7 Have nothing to do with a *f* charge
Dt 5: 20 ''You shall not give *f* testimony
Pr 12: 17 but a *f* witness tells lies.
13: 5 The righteous hate what is *f,*
14: 5 but a *f* witness pours out lies.
14: 25 but a *f* witness is deceitful.
19: 5 A *f* witness will not go unpunished,
19: 9 A *f* witness will not go unpunished,
21: 28 A *f* witness will perish,
25: 18 is the man who gives *f* testimony
Isa 44: 25 who foils the signs of *f* prophets
Jer 23: 16 they fill you with *f* hopes.
Mt 7: 15 ''Watch out for *f* prophets.
15: 19 theft, *f* testimony, slander.
19: 18 not steal, do not give *f* testimony,
24: 11 and many *f* prophets will appear
24: 24 For *f* Christs and *f* prophets will
Mk 10: 19 do not give *f* testimony, do not
13: 22 For *f* Christs and *f* prophets will
Lk 6: 26 their fathers treated the *f* prophets.
18: 20 not steal, do not give *f* testimony,
Jn 1: 47 in whom there is nothing *f.*''
1Co 15: 15 found to be *f* witnesses about God,
2Co 11: 13 For such men are *f* apostles,
11: 26 and in danger from *f* brothers.
Gal 2: 4 some *f* brothers had infiltrated our
Php 1: 18 whether from *f* motives or true,
Col 2: 18 anyone who delights in *f* humility
2: 23 their *f* humility and their harsh
1Ti 1: 3 not to teach *f* doctrines any longer
6: 3 If anyone teaches *f* doctrines
2Pe 2: 1 also *f* prophets among the people,
2: 1 there will be *f* teachers among you.
1Jn 4: 1 many *f* prophets have gone out
Rev 16: 13 out of the mouth of the *f* prophet.
19: 20 with him the *f* prophet who had
20: 10 and the *f* prophet had been thrown.

FALSEHOOD* (FALSE)

Job 21: 34 left of your answers but *f!*''
31: 5 ''If I have walked in *f*
Ps 52: 3 *f* rather than speaking the truth.
119:163 I hate and abhor *f*
Pr 30: 8 Keep *f* and lies far from me;
Isa 28: 15 and *f* our hiding place.''
Ro 3: 7 ''If my *f* enhances God's
Eph 4: 25 each of you must put off *f*
1Jn 4: 6 Spirit of truth and the spirit of *f.*
Rev 22: 15 everyone who loves and practices *f*

FALSELY (FALSE)

Lev 19: 12 '' 'Do not swear *f* by my name
Mt 5: 11 *f* say all kinds of evil against you
Lk 3: 14 and don't accuse people *f—*
1Ti 6: 20 ideas of what is *f* called knowledge,

FALTER*

Pr 24: 10 If you *f* in times of trouble,
Isa 42: 4 he will not *f* or be discouraged

FAME

Jos 9: 9 of the *f* of the LORD your God.
Isa 66: 19 islands that have not heard of my *f*
Hab 3: 2 LORD, I have heard of your *f;*

FAMILIES (FAMILY)

Ps 68: 6 God sets the lonely in *f,*

FAMILY (FAMILIES)

Pr 15: 27 greedy man brings trouble to his *f,*
31: 15 she provides food for her *f*
Mk 5: 19 to your *f* and tell them how much
Lk 9: 61 go back and say good-by to my *f.*''
12: 52 in one *f* divided against each other,
Ac 10: 2 He and all his *f* were devout
16: 33 and all his *f* were baptized.
16: 34 he and his whole *f.*
1Ti 3: 4 He must manage his own *f* well
3: 5 how to manage his own *f,*
5: 4 practice by caring for their own *f*
5: 8 and especially for his immediate *f.*

FAMINE

Ge 12: 10 Now there was a *f* in the land,
26: 1 Now there was a *f* in the land—
41: 30 seven years of *f* will follow them.
Ru 1: 1 the judges ruled, there was a *f*
1Ki 18: 2 Now the *f* was severe in Samaria,
Am 8: 11 but a *f* of hearing the words
Ro 8: 35 or persecution or *f* or nakedness

FAN*

2Ti 1: 6 you to *f* into flame the gift of God,

FANTASIES*

Ps 73: 20 you will despise them as *f.*
Pr 12: 11 but he who chases *f* lacks judgment
28: 19 one who chases *f* will have his fill

FAST (FASTING)

Dt 10: 20 Hold *f* to him and take your oaths
11: 22 in all his ways and to hold *f* to him
13: 4 serve him and hold *f* to him.
30: 20 to his voice, and hold *f* to him.
Jos 22: 5 to hold *f* to him and to serve him
23: 8 to hold *f* to the LORD your God,
2Ki 18: 6 He held *f* to the LORD
Ps 119: 31 I hold *f* to your statutes, O LORD;
139: 10 your right hand will hold me *f.*
Mt 6: 16 ''When you *f,* do not look somber
1Pe 5: 12 Stand *f* in it.

FASTING (FAST)

Ps 35: 13 and humbled myself with *f.*
Ac 13: 2 were worshiping the Lord and *f,*
14: 23 and *f,* committed them to the Lord

FATHER (FATHER'S FATHERED FATHERLESS FATHERS FOREFATHERS)

Ge 2: 24 this reason a man will leave his *f*
17: 4 You will be the *f* of many nations.
Ex 20: 12 ''Honor your *f* and your mother.
21: 15 ''Anyone who attacks his *f*
21: 17 ''Anyone who curses his *f*
Lev 18: 7 '' 'Do not dishonor your *f*
19: 3 you must respect his mother and *f,*
20: 9 '' 'If anyone curses his *f* or mother,
Dt 1: 31 carried you, as a *f* carries his son,
5: 16 ''Honor your *f* and your mother,
21: 18 son who does not obey his *f*
32: 6 Is he not your *F,* your Creator,
2Sa 7: 14 I will be his *f,* and he will be my son
1Ch 17: 13 I will be his *f,* and he will be my son
22: 10 will be my son, and I will be his *f.*
28: 6 to be my son, and I will be his *f.*
Job 38: 28 Does the rain have a *f?*
Ps 2: 7 today I have become your *F.*
27: 10 Though my *f* and mother forsake

FATHER'S (continued)

Ps 68: 5 A *f* to the fatherless, a defender
89: 26 to me, 'You are my *F*,
103: 13 As a *f* has compassion
Pr 3: 12 as a *f* the son he delights in.
10: 1 A wise son brings joy to his *f*.
17: 21 there is no joy for the *f* of a fool.
17: 25 A foolish son brings grief to his *f*
23: 22 Listen to your *f*, who gave you life,
23: 24 *f* of a righteous man has great joy;
28: 7 of gluttons disgraces his *f*.
28: 24 He who robs his *f* or mother
29: 3 loves wisdom brings joy to his *f*,
Isa 9: 6 Everlasting *F*, Prince of Peace.
45: 10 Woe to him who says to his *f*,
63: 16 But you are our *F*,
Jer 2: 27 They say to wood, 'You are my *f*,'
3: 19 I thought you would call me '*F*'
31: 9 because I am Israel's *f*,
Eze 18: 19 the son not share the guilt of his *f*?'
Mic 7: 6 For a son dishonors his *f*,
Mal 1: 6 If I am a *f*, where is the honor due
2: 10 we not all one *F*? Did not one God
Mt 3: 9 'We have Abraham as our *f*.'
5: 16 and praise your *F* in heaven.
6: 9 '' 'Our *F* in heaven,
6: 26 yet your heavenly *F* feeds them.
10: 37 ''Anyone who loves his *f*
11: 27 no one knows the *F* except the Son
15: 4 'Honor your *f* and mother'
18: 10 the face of my *F* in heaven.
19: 5 this reason a man will leave his *f*
19: 19 honor your *f* and mother,'
19: 29 or brothers or sisters or *f* or mother
23: 9 And do not call anyone on earth '*f*,'
Mk 7: 10 'Honor your *f* and your mother,' and,
Lk 9: 59 ''Lord, first let me go and bury my *f*
12: 53 *f* against son and son against *f*,
14: 26 and does not hate his *f* and mother,
18: 20 honor your *f* and mother.' ''
23: 34 Jesus said, ''*F*, forgive them,
Jn 3: 35 The *F* loves the Son and has placed
4: 21 you will worship the *F* neither
5: 17 ''My *F* is always at his work
5: 18 he was even calling God his own *F*,
5: 20 For the *F* loves the Son
6: 44 the *F* who sent me draws him,
6: 46 No one has seen the *F*
8: 19 ''You do not know me or my *F*,''
8: 28 speak just what the *F* has taught me
8: 41 The only *F* we have is God himself
8: 42 God were your *F*, you would love
8: 44 You belong to your *f*, the devil,
10: 17 reason my *F* loves me is that I lay
10: 30 I and the *F* are one.''
10: 38 and understand that the *F* is in me,
14: 6 No one comes to the *F*
14: 9 who has seen me has seen the *F*.
14: 28 for the *F* is greater than I.
15: 9 ''As the *F* has loved me,
15: 23 He who hates me hates my *F*
20: 17 'I am returning to my *F* and your *F*,
Ac 13: 33 today I have become your *F*.'
Ro 4: 11 he is the *f* of all who believe
4: 16 He is the *f* of us all.
8: 15 And by him we cry, ''*Abba*, *F*.''
1Co 4: 15 for in Christ Jesus I became your *f*
2Co 6: 18 ''I will be a *F* to you,
Eph 5: 31 this reason a man will leave his *f*
6: 2 ''Honor your *f* and mother''—
Php 2: 11 to the glory of God the *F*.
Heb 1: 5 today I have become your *F*''?
12: 7 what son is not disciplined by his *f*?
1Jn 1: 3 And our fellowship is with the *F*
2: 15 the love of the *F* is not in him.
2: 22 he denies the *F* and the Son.

FATHER'S (FATHER)

Pr 13: 1 A wise son heeds his *f* instruction,
15: 5 A fool spurns his *f* discipline,
19: 13 A foolish son is his *f* ruin,
Mt 16: 27 going to come in his *F* glory
Lk 2: 49 had to be in my *F* house?''
Jn 2: 16 How dare you turn my *F* house
10: 29 can snatch them out of my *F* hand.
14: 2 In my *F* house are many rooms;
15: 8 to my *F* glory, that you bear much

FATHERED (FATHER)

Dt 32: 18 You deserted the Rock, who *f* you;

FATHERLESS (FATHER)

Dt 10: 18 He defends the cause of the *f*
14: 29 the *f* and the widows who live
24: 17 Do not deprive the alien or the *f*
24: 19 Leave it for the alien, the *f*
26: 12 the alien, the *f* and the widow,
Ps 68: 5 A father to the *f*, a defender
82: 3 Defend the cause of the weak and *f*
Pr 23: 10 or encroach on the fields of the *f*,

FATHERS (FATHER)

Ex 20: 5 for the sin of the *f* to the third
Jer 31: 29 'The *f* have eaten sour grapes,
Mal 4: 6 the hearts of the children to their *f*;
Lk 1: 17 the hearts of the *f* to their children
11: 11 ''Which of you *f*, if your son asks
Jn 4: 20 Our *f* worshiped on this mountain,
1Co 4: 15 you do not have many *f*,
Eph 6: 4 *F*, do not exasperate your children;
Col 3: 21 *F*, do not embitter your children,
Heb 12: 9 all had human *f* who disciplined us

FATHOM* (FATHOMED)

Job 11: 7 ''Can you *f* the mysteries of God?
Ps 145: 3 his greatness no one can *f*.
Ecc 3: 11 yet they cannot *f* what God has
Isa 40: 28 and his understanding no one can *f*
1Co 13: 2 and can *f* all mysteries and all

FATHOMED* (FATHOM)

Job 5: 9 performs wonders that cannot be *f*.
9: 10 performs wonders that cannot be *f*.

FATTENED

Pr 15: 17 than a *f* calf with hatred.
Lk 15: 23 Bring the *f* calf and kill it.

FAULT (FAULTS)

1Sa 29: 3 I have found no *f* in him.''
Mt 18: 15 and show him his *f*, just
Php 2: 15 of God without *f* in a crooked
Jas 1: 5 generously to all without finding *f*,
Jude : 24 his glorious presence without *f*

FAULTFINDERS*

Jude : 16 These men are grumblers and *f*;

FAULTLESS*

Pr 8: 9 they are *f* to those who have
Php 3: 6 as for legalistic righteousness, *f*.
Jas 1: 27 Father accepts as pure and *f* is this:

FAULTS* (FAULT)

Job 10: 6 that you must search out my *f*
Ps 19: 12 Forgive my hidden *f*.

FAVOR (FAVORITISM)

Ge 4: 4 The Lord looked with *f* on Abel
6: 8 But Noah found *f* in the eyes
Ex 33: 12 and you have found *f* with me.'
34: 9 if I have found *f* in your eyes,''
Lev 26: 9 ''I will look on you with *f*
Nu 11: 15 if I have found *f* in your eyes—
Jdg 6: 17 ''If now I have found *f* in your eyes,
1Sa 2: 26 in *f* with the Lord and with men.
2Sa 2: 6 and I too will show you the same *f*
2Ki 13: 4 Jehoahaz sought the Lord's *f*,
2Ch 33: 12 In his distress he sought the *f*
Est 7: 3 ''If I have found *f* with you, O king,
Ps 90: 17 May the *f* of the Lord our God rest
Pr 8: 35 and receives *f* from the Lord.
18: 22 and receives *f* from the Lord.
19: 6 Many curry *f* with a ruler,
Isa 61: 2 proclaim the year of the Lord's *f*
Zec 11: 7 I called one *F* and the other Union,
Lk 1: 30 Mary, you have found *f* with God.
2: 14 to men on whom his *f* rests.''
2: 52 and in *f* with God and men.
4: 19 to proclaim the year of the Lord's *f*
2Co 6: 2 now is the time of God's *f*,

FAVORITISM* (FAVOR)

Ex 23: 3 and do not show *f* to a poor man
Lev 19: 15 to the poor or *f* to the great,
Ac 10: 34 true it is that God does not show *f*

Ro 2: 11 For God does not show *f*.
Eph 6: 9 and there is no *f* with him.
Col 3: 25 for his wrong, and there is no *f*.
1Ti 5: 21 and to do nothing out of *f*.
Jas 2: 1 Lord Jesus Christ, don't show *f*.
2: 9 But if you show *f*, you sin

**FEAR (AFRAID FEARED FEARS
FRIGHTENED GOD-FEARING)**

Dt 6: 13 *F* the Lord your God, serve him
10: 12 but to *f* the Lord your God,
31: 12 and learn to *f* the Lord your God
31: 13 and learn to *f* the Lord your God
Jos 4: 24 you might always *f* the Lord
24: 14 ''Now *f* the Lord and serve him
1Sa 12: 14 If you *f* the Lord and serve
12: 24 But be sure to *f* the Lord
2Sa 23: 3 when he rules in the *f* of God,
2Ch 19: 7 let the *f* of the Lord be upon you.
26: 5 who instructed him in the *f* of God.
Job 1: 9 ''Does Job *f* God for nothing?''
Ps 2: 11 Serve the Lord with *f*
19: 9 The *f* of the Lord is pure,
23: 4 I will *f* no evil,
27: 1 whom shall I *f*?
33: 8 Let all the earth *f* the Lord;
34: 7 around those who *f* him,
34: 9 *F* the Lord, you his saints,
46: 2 Therefore we will not *f*,
86: 11 that I may *f* your name.
90: 11 great as the *f* that is due you.
91: 5 You will not *f* the terror of night,
111: 10 *f* of the Lord is the beginning
118: 4 Let those who *f* the Lord say:
128: 1 Blessed are all who *f* the Lord,
145: 19 of those who *f* him;
147: 11 delights in those who *f* him,
Pr 1: 7 *f* of the Lord is the beginning
1: 33 at ease, without *f* of harm.''
8: 13 To *f* the Lord is to hate evil;
9: 10 *f* of the Lord is the beginning
10: 27 The *f* of the Lord adds length
14: 27 The *f* of the Lord is a fountain
15: 33 *f* of the Lord teaches a man
16: 6 through the *f* of the Lord a man
19: 23 The *f* of the Lord leads to life:
22: 4 Humility and the *f* of the Lord
29: 25 *F* of man will prove to be a snare,
31: 21 she has no *f* for her household;
Ecc 12: 13 *F* God and keep his
Isa 11: 3 delight in the *f* of the Lord.
33: 6 the *f* of the Lord is the key
35: 4 ''Be strong, do not *f*;
41: 10 So do not *f*, for I am with you;
41: 13 and says to you, Do not *f*;
43: 1 ''*F* not, for I have redeemed you;
51: 7 Do not *f* the reproach of men
54: 14 you will have nothing to *f*.
Jer 17: 8 It does not *f* when heat comes;
Lk 12: 5 I will show you whom you should *f*:
2Co 5: 11 we know what it is to *f* the Lord,
Php 2: 12 to work out your salvation with *f*
1Jn 4: 18 But perfect love drives out *f*,
Jude : 23 to others show mercy, mixed with *f*
Rev 14: 7 ''*F* God and give him glory,

FEARED (FEAR)

Job 1: 1 he *f* God and shunned evil.
Ps 76: 7 You alone are to be *f*.
Mal 3: 16 those who *f* the Lord talked

FEARS (FEAR)

Job 1: 8 a man who *f* God and shuns evil.''
2: 3 a man who *f* God and shuns evil.
Ps 34: 4 he delivered me from all my *f*.
112: 1 is the man who *f* the Lord,
Pr 14: 16 A wise man *f* the Lord
14: 26 He who *f* the Lord has a secure
31: 30 a woman who *f* the Lord is
2Co 7: 5 conflicts on the outside, *f* within.
1Jn 4: 18 The one who *f* is not made perfect

FEAST (FEASTING FEASTS)

Pr 15: 15 the cheerful heart has a continual *f*.
2Pe 2: 13 pleasures while they *f* with you.

FEASTING (FEAST)

Pr 17: 1 than a house full of *f*, with strife.

FEASTS (FEAST)

Am 5:21 "I hate, I despise your religious *f;*
Jude : 12 men are blemishes at your love *f,*

FEATHERS

Ps 91: 4 He will cover you with his *f,*

FEEBLE

Job 4: 3 you have strengthened *f* hands.
Isa 35: 3 Strengthen the *f* hands,
Heb 12: 12 strengthen your *f* arms

FEED (FEEDS)

Jn 21:15 Jesus said, "*F* my lambs."
21:17 Jesus said, "*F* my sheep.
Ro 12:20 "If your enemy is hungry, *f* him;
Jude : 12 shepherds who *f* only themselves.

FEEDS (FEED)

Pr 15:14 but the mouth of a fool *f* on folly.
Mt 6:26 yet your heavenly Father *f* them.
Jn 6:57 so the one who *f* on me will live

FEEL

Jdg 16:26 me where I can *f* the pillars that
Ps 115: 7 they have hands, but cannot *f,*

FEET (FOOT)

Ru 3: 8 discovered a woman lying at his *f.*
Ps 8: 6 you put everything under his *f;*
22:16 have pierced my hands and my *f.*
40: 2 he set my *f* on a rock
56:13 and my *f* from stumbling,
66: 9 and kept our *f* from slipping,
73: 2 as for me, my *f* had almost slipped;
110: 1 a footstool for your *f."*
119:105 Your word is a lamp to my *f*
Pr 4:26 Make level paths for your *f*
Isa 52: 7 are the *f* of those who bring good
Da 2:33 its *f* partly of iron and partly
Na 1:15 the *f* of one who brings good news,
Mt 10:14 shake the dust off your *f*
22:44 enemies under your *f."*
Lk 1:79 to guide our *f* into the path of peace
20:43 a footstool for your *f."*
24:39 Look at my hands and my *f.*
Jn 13: 5 and began to wash his disciples' *f,*
13:14 also should wash one another's *f.*
Ro 3:15 "Their *f* are swift to shed blood;
10:15 "How beautiful are the *f*
16:20 will soon crush Satan under your *f.*
1Co 12:21 And the head cannot say to the *f,*
15:25 has put all his enemies under his *f.*
Eph 1:22 God placed all things under his *f*
1Ti 5:10 washing the *f* of the saints,
Heb 1:13 a footstool for your *f"?*
2: 8 and put everything under his *f."*
12:13 "Make level paths for your *f,"*
Rev 1:15 His *f* were like bronze glowing

FEIGNED*

1Sa 21:13 So he *f* insanity in their presence;

FELIX

Governor before whom Paul was tried (Ac 23: 23-24:27).

FELLOWSHIP

Ex 20:24 burnt offerings and *f* offerings,
Lev 3: 1 If someone's offering is a *f* offering,
1Co 1: 9 who has called you into *f*
5: 2 out of your *f* the man who did this?
2Co 6:14 what *f* can light have with darkness
13:14 and the *f* of the Holy Spirit be
Gal 2: 9 and Barnabas the right hand of *f*
Php 2: 1 if any *f* with the Spirit,
3:10 the *f* of sharing in his sufferings,
1Jn 1: 3 And our *f* is with the Father
1: 3 so that you also may have *f* with us.
1: 6 claim to have *f* with him yet walk
1: 7 we have *f* with one another,

FEMALE

Ge 1:27 male and *f* he created them.
5: 2 He created them male and *f*
Mt 19: 4 Creator 'made them male and *f,'*
Mk 10: 6 God 'made them male and *f.'*
Gal 3:28 *f,* for you are all one in Christ Jesus

FEROCIOUS

Mt 7:15 but inwardly they are *f* wolves.

FERTILE (FERTILIZE)

Isa 32:15 and the desert becomes a *f* field,
Jer 2: 7 I brought you into a *f* land

FERTILIZE* (FERTILE)

Lk 13: 8 and I'll dig around it and *f* it.

FERVOR*

Ac 18:25 and he spoke with great *f*
Ro 12:11 but keep your spiritual *f,* serving

FESTIVAL

1Co 5: 8 Therefore let us keep the *F,*
Col 2:16 or with regard to a religious *f,*

FESTUS

Successor of Felix; sent Paul to Caesar (Ac 25-26).

FEVER

Job 30:30 my body burns with *f.*
Mt 8:14 mother-in-law lying in bed with a *f.*
Lk 4:38 was suffering from a high *f,*
Jn 4:52 "The *f* left him yesterday
Ac 28: 8 suffering from *f* and dysentery.

FIELD (FIELDS)

Ge 4: 8 Abel, "Let's go out to the *f.*"
Lev 19: 9 reap to the very edges of your *f*
19:19 Do not plant your *f* with two kinds
Pr 31:16 She considers a *f* and buys it;
Isa 40: 6 glory is like the flowers of the *f.*
Mt 6:28 See how the lilies of the *f* grow.
6:30 how God clothes the grass of the *f,*
13:38 *f* is the world, and the good seed
13:44 is like treasure hidden in a *f.*
Lk 14:18 I have just bought a *f,* and I must go
1Co 3: 9 you are God's *f,* God's building.
1Pe 1:24 glory is like the flowers of the *f;*

FIELDS (FIELD)

Ru 2: 2 go to the *f* and pick up the leftover
Lk 2: 8 were shepherds living out in the *f*
Jn 4:35 open your eyes and look at the *f!*

FIG (FIGS SYCAMORE-FIG)

Ge 3: 7 so they sewed *f* leaves together
Jdg 9:10 "Next, the trees said to the *f* tree,
1Ki 4:25 man under his own vine and *f* tree.
Pr 27:18 He who tends a *f* tree will eat its
Mic 4: 4 and under his own *f* tree,
Zec 3:10 to sit under his vine and *f* tree,'
Mt 21:19 Seeing a *f* tree by the road,
Lk 13: 6 "A man had a *f* tree, planted
Jas 3:12 brothers, can a *f* tree bear olives,
Rev 6:13 drop from a *f* tree when shaken

FIGHT (FIGHTING FIGHTS FOUGHT)

Ex 14:14 The LORD will *f* for you; you need
Dt 1:30 going before you, will *f* for you,
3:22 the LORD your God himself will *f*
Ne 4:20 Our God will *f* for us!"
Ps 35: 1 *f* against those who *f* against me.
Jn 18:36 my servants would *f*
1Co 9:26 I do not *f* like a man beating the air.
2Co 10: 4 The weapons we *f*
1Ti 1:18 them you may *f* the good *f,*
6:12 Fight the good *f* of the faith.
2Ti 4: 7 fought the good *f,* I have finished

FIGHTING (FIGHT)

Jos 10:14 Surely the LORD was *f* for Israel!

FIGHTS (FIGHT)

Jos 23:10 the LORD your God *f* for you,
1Sa 25:28 because he *f* the LORD's battles.
Jas 4: 1 What causes *f* and quarrels

FIGS (FIG)

Lk 6:44 People do not pick *f*
Jas 3:12 grapevine bear *f?* Neither can a salt

FILL (FILLED FILLING FILLS FULL FULLNESS FULLY)

Ge 1:28 and increase in number; *f* the earth
Ps 16:11 you will *f* me with joy
81:10 wide your mouth and I will *f* it.
Pr 28:19 who chases fantasies will have his *f*
Hag 2: 7 and I will *f* this house with glory,'
Jn 6:26 you ate the loaves and had your *f.*
Ac 2:28 you will *f* me with joy
Ro 15:13 the God of hope *f* you with all joy

FILLED (FILL)

Ex 31: 3 I have *f* him with the Spirit of God,
35:31 he has *f* him with the Spirit of God,
Dt 34: 9 son of Nun was *f* with the spirit
1Ki 8:10 the cloud *f* the temple
8:11 glory of the LORD *f* his temple.
2Ch 5:14 of the LORD *f* the temple of God.
7: 1 the glory of the LORD *f* the temple
Ps 72:19 may the whole earth be *f*
119: 64 The earth is *f* with your love,
Isa 6: 4 and the temple was *f* with smoke.
Eze 10: 3 and a cloud *f* the inner court.
10: 4 The cloud *f* the temple,
43: 5 the glory of the LORD *f* the temple
Hab 2:14 For the earth will be *f*
3: 3 and his praise *f* the earth.
Mt 5: 6 for they will be *f.*
Lk 1:15 and he will be *f* with the Holy Spirit
1:41 and Elizabeth was *f* with the Holy
1:67 His father Zechariah was *f*
2:40 and became strong; he was *f*
Jn 12: 3 the house was *f* with the fragrance
Ac 2: 2 *f* the whole house where they were
2: 4 All of them were *f*
4: 8 Then Peter, *f* with the Holy Spirit,
4:31 they were all *f* with the Holy Spirit
9:17 and be *f* with the Holy Spirit."
13: 9 called Paul, *f* with the Holy Spirit,
Eph 5:18 Instead, be *f* with the Spirit.
Php 1:11 with the fruit of righteousness
Rev 15: 8 And the temple was *f* with smoke

FILLING (FILL)

Eze 44: 4 the glory of the LORD *f* the temple

FILLS (FILL)

Nu 14:21 of the LORD *f* the whole earth,
Ps 107: 9 and the hungry with good things.
Eph 1:23 fullness of him who *f* everything

FILTH (FILTHY)

Isa 4: 4 The Lord will wash away the *f*
Jas 1:21 rid of all moral *f* and the evil that is

FILTHY (FILTH)

Isa 64: 6 all our righteous acts are like *f* rags;
Col 3: 8 and *f* language from your lips.
2Pe 2: 7 by the *f* lives of lawless men

FINAL (FINALITY)

Ps 73:17 then I understood their *f* destiny.

FINALITY* (FINAL)

Ro 9:28 on earth with speed and *f."*

FINANCIAL*

1Ti 6: 5 that godliness is a means to *f* gain.

FIND (FINDS FOUND)

Nu 32:23 be sure that your sin will *f* you out.
Dt 4:29 you will *f* him if you look for him
1Sa 23:16 and helped him *f* strength in God.
Job 23: 3 If only I knew where to *f* him;
Ps 36: 7 *f* refuge in the shadow
62: 5 *F* rest, O my soul, in God alone;
91: 4 under his wings you will *f* refuge;
Pr 8:17 and those who seek me *f* me.
14:22 those who plan what is good *f* love
20: 6 but a faithful man who can *f?*
24:14 if you *f* it, there is a future hope
31:10 A wife of noble character who can *f*
Jer 6:16 and you will *f* rest for your souls.
29:13 and *f* me when you seek me
Mt 7: 7 seek and you will *f;* knock
11:29 and you will *f* rest for your souls.
16:25 loses his life for me will *f* it.
22: 9 invite to the banquet anyone you *f.'*

Lk 11: 9 seek and you will *f*; knock
   18: 8 will he *f* faith on the earth?''
Jn 10: 9 come in and go out, and *f* pasture.

FINDS (FIND)

Ps 62: 1 My soul *f* rest in God alone;
   112: 1 who *f* great delight
   119:162 like one who *f* great spoil.
Pr 3: 13 Blessed is the man who *f* wisdom,
   8: 35 For whoever *f* me *f* life
   11: 27 He who seeks good *f* good will,
   18: 22 He who *f* a wife *f* what is good
Mt 7: 8 he who seeks *f*; and to him who
   10: 39 Whoever *f* his life will lose it,
Lk 11: 10 he who seeks *f*; and to him who
   12: 37 whose master *f* them watching
   12: 43 servant whom the master *f* doing
   15: 4 go after the lost sheep until he *f* it?
   15: 8 and search carefully until she *f* it?

FINE-SOUNDING* (SOUND)

Col 2: 4 may deceive you by *f* arguments.

FINGER

Ex 8: 19 to Pharaoh, ''This is the *f* of God.''
   31: 18 of stone inscribed by the *f* of God.
Dt 9: 10 two stone tablets inscribed by the *f*
Lk 11: 20 But if I drive out demons by the *f*
   16: 24 to dip the tip of his *f* in water
Jn 8: 6 to write on the ground with his *f*.
   20: 25 and put my *f* where the nails were,

FINISH (FINISHED)

Jn 4: 34 him who sent me and to *f* his work.
   5: 36 that the Father has given me to *f*.
Ac 20: 24 if only I may *f* the race
2Co 8: 11 Now *f* the work, so that your eager
Jas 1: 4 Perseverance must *f* its work

FINISHED (FINISH)

Ge 2: 2 seventh day God had *f* the work he
Jn 19: 30 the drink, Jesus said, ''It is *f*.''
2Ti 4: 7 I have *f* the race, I have kept

FIRE

Ex 3: 2 in flames of *f* from within a bush.
   13: 21 in a pillar of *f* to give them light,
Lev 6: 12 *f* on the altar must be kept burning;
   9: 24 *F* came out from the presence
1Ki 18: 38 Then the *f* of the LORD fell
2Ki 2: 11 suddenly a chariot of *f*
Isa 5: 24 as tongues of *f* lick up straw
   30: 27 and his tongue is a consuming *f*.
Jer 23: 29 my word like *f*,'' declares
Da 3: 25 four men walking around in the *f*,
Zec 3: 2 stick snatched from the *f*?''
Mal 3: 2 For he will be like a refiner's *f*
Mt 3: 11 you with the Holy Spirit and with *f*.
   3: 12 the chaff with unquenchable *f*.''
   5: 22 will be in danger of the *f* of hell.
   18: 8 and be thrown into eternal *f*.
   25: 41 into the eternal *f* prepared
Mk 9: 43 where the *f* never goes out.
   9: 48 and the *f* is not quenched.'
   9: 49 Everyone will be salted with *f*.
Lk 3: 16 you with the Holy Spirit and with *f*.
   12: 49 I have come to bring *f* on the earth,
Ac 2: 3 to be tongues of *f* that separated
1Co 3: 13 It will be revealed with *f*.
1Th 5: 19 Do not put out the Spirit's *f*;
Heb 12: 29 for our ''God is a consuming *f*.''
Jas 3: 5 set on *f* by a small spark.
   3: 6 also is a *f*, a world of evil
2Pe 3: 10 the elements will be destroyed by *f*,
Jude : 7 suffer the punishment of eternal *f*.
   : 23 snatch others from the *f*
Rev 1: 14 and his eyes were like blazing *f*.
   20: 14 The lake of *f* is the second death.

FIRM*

Ex 14: 13 Stand *f* and you will see
   15: 8 surging waters stood *f* like a wall;
Jos 3: 17 the covenant of the LORD stood *f*
2Ch 20: 17 stand *f* and see the deliverance
Ezr 9: 8 giving us a *f* place in his sanctuary,
Job 11: 15 you will stand *f* and without fear.
   36: 5 he is mighty, and *f* in his purpose.
   41: 23 they are *f* and immovable.

Ps 20: 8 but we rise up and stand *f*.
   30: 7 you made my mountain stand *f*;
   33: 9 he commanded, and it stood *f*.
   33: 11 of the LORD stand *f* forever,
   37: 23 he makes his steps *f*;
   40: 2 and gave me a *f* place to stand.
   75: 3 it is I who hold its pillars *f*.
   78: 13 made the water stand *f* like a wall.
   89: 2 that your love stands *f* forever,
   89: 4 and make your throne *f*
   93: 5 Your statutes stand *f*;
   119: 89 it stands *f* in the heavens.
Pr 4: 26 and take only ways that are *f*.
   10: 25 but the righteous stand *f* forever.
   12: 7 the house of the righteous stands *f*.
Isa 7: 9 If you do not stand *f* in your faith,
   22: 17 about to take *f* hold of you
   22: 23 drive him like a peg into a *f* place;
   22: 25 into the *f* place will give way;
Eze 13: 5 so that it will stand *f* in the battle
Zec 8: 23 nations will take *f* hold of one Jew
Mt 10: 22 he who stands *f* to the end will be
   24: 13 he who stands *f* to the end will be
Mk 13: 13 he who stands *f* to the end will be
Lk 21: 19 By standing *f* you will save
1Co 10: 12 So, if you think you are standing *f*,
   15: 58 my dear brothers, stand *f*.
   16: 13 on your guard; stand *f* in the faith,
2Co 1: 7 for you is *f*, because we know that
   1: 21 who makes both us and you stand *f*
   1: 24 because it is by faith you stand *f*.
Gal 5: 1 Stand *f*, then, and do not let
Eph 6: 14 Stand *f* then, with the belt
Php 1: 27 I will know that you stand *f*
   4: 1 that is how you should stand *f*
Col 1: 23 in your faith, established and *f*,
   2: 5 and how *f* your faith in Christ is.
   4: 12 that you may stand *f* in all the will
1Th 3: 8 since you are standing *f* in the Lord
2Th 2: 15 stand *f* and hold to the teachings
1Ti 6: 19 a *f* foundation for the coming age,
2Ti 2: 19 God's solid foundation stands *f*,
Heb 6: 19 an anchor for the soul, *f* and secure
Jas 5: 8 You too, be patient and stand *f*,
1Pe 5: 9 Resist him, standing *f* in the faith,
   5: 10 make you strong, *f* and steadfast.

FIRMAMENT see EXPANSE, HEAVENS, SKIES

FIRST

Ge 1: 5 and there was morning—the *f* day.
   13: 4 and where he had *f* built an altar.
Ex 34: 19 *f* offspring of every womb belongs
1Ki 22: 5 ''F seek the counsel of the LORD.''
Pr 18: 17 *f* to present his case seems right,
Isa 44: 6 I am the *f* and I am the last;
   48: 12 I am the *f* and I am the last.
Mt 5: 24 *F* go and be reconciled
   6: 33 But seek *f* his kingdom
   7: 5 *f* take the plank out
   19: 30 But many who are *f* will be last,
   20: 16 last will be *f*, and the *f* will be last.''
   20: 27 wants to be *f* must be your slave—
   22: 38 This is the *f* and greatest
   23: 26 *F* clean the inside of the cup
Mk 9: 35 to be *f*, he must be the very last,
   10: 31 are *f* will be last, and the last *f*.''
   10: 44 wants to be *f* must be slave
   13: 10 And the gospel must *f* be preached
Lk 13: 30 will be *f*, and *f* who will be last.''
Jn 8: 7 let him be the *f* to throw a stone
Ac 11: 26 disciples were called Christians *f*
Ro 1: 16 *f* for the Jew, then for the Gentile.
   1: 17 is by faith from *f* to last,
   2: 9 *f* for the Jew, then for the Gentile;
   2: 10 *f* for the Jew, then for the Gentile.
1Co 12: 28 in the church God has appointed *f*
   15: 45 ''The *f* man Adam became a living
2Co 8: 5 they gave themselves *f* to the Lord
Eph 6: 2 which is the *f* commandment
1Th 4: 16 and the dead in Christ will rise *f*.
1Ti 2: 13 For Adam was formed *f*, then Eve.
Heb 10: 9 He sets aside the *f*
Jas 3: 17 comes from heaven is *f* of all pure;
1Jn 4: 19 We love because he *f* loved us.
3Jn : 9 but Diotrephes, who loves to be *f*,
Rev 1: 17 I am the *F* and the Last.

Rev 2: 4 You have forsaken your *f* love.
   22: 13 and the Omega, the *F* and the Last,

FIRSTBORN (BEAR)

Ex 11: 5 Every *f* son in Egypt will die,
   34: 20 Redeem all your *f* sons.
Ps 89: 27 I will also appoint him my *f*,
Lk 2: 7 and she gave birth to her *f*, a son.
Ro 8: 29 that he might be the *f*
Col 1: 15 image of the invisible God, the *f*
   1: 18 and the *f* from among the dead,
Heb 1: 6 when God brings his *f*
   12: 23 of the *f*, whose names are written
Rev 1: 5 who is the faithful witness, the *f*

FIRSTFRUITS

Ex 23: 16 the Feast of Harvest with the *f*
   23: 19 ''Bring the best of the *f* of your soil
Ro 8: 23 who have the *f* of the Spirit,
1Co 15: 23 Christ, the *f*; then, when he comes,
Rev 14: 4 offered as *f* to God and the Lamb.

FISH (FISHERS)

Ge 1: 26 let them rule over the *f* of the sea
Jnh 1: 17 But the LORD provided a great *f*
Mt 7: 10 asks for a *f*, will give him a snake?
   12: 40 three nights in the belly of a huge *f*,
   14: 17 loaves of bread and two *f*.''
Mk 6: 38 they said, ''Five—and two *f*.''
Lk 5: 6 of *f* that their nets began to break.
   9: 13 loaves of bread and two *f*—
Jn 6: 9 small barley loaves and two small *f*,
   21' 5 haven't you any *f*?'' ''No,''
   21: 11 It was full of large *f*, 153, but

FISHERMEN

Mk 1: 16 a net into the lake, for they were *f*.

FISHERS (FISH)

Mt 4: 19 ''and I will make you *f* of men.''
Mk 1: 17 ''and I will make you *f* of men.''

FISHHOOK*

Job 41: 1 pull in the leviathan with a *f*

FISTS

Mt 26: 67 and struck him with their *f*.

FIT (FITTING)

Jdg 17: 6 no king; everyone did as he saw *f*.
   21: 25 no king; everyone did as he saw *f*.

FITTING* (FIT)

Ps 33: 1 it is *f* for the upright to praise him.
   147: 1 how pleasant and *f* to praise him!
Pr 10: 32 of the righteous know what is *f*,
   19: 10 It is not *f* for a fool to live in luxury
   26: 1 honor is not *f* for a fool.
1Co 14: 40 everything should be done in a *f*
Col 3: 18 to your husbands, as is *f* in the Lord
Heb 2: 10 sons to glory, it was *f* that God,

FIX* (FIXED)

Dt 11: 18 *F* these words of mine
Job 14: 3 Do you *f* your eye on such a one?
Pr 4: 25 *f* your gaze directly before you.
Isa 46: 8 ''Remember this, *f* it in mind,
Am 9: 4 I will *f* my eyes upon them
2Co 4: 18 we *f* our eyes not on what is seen,
Heb 3: 1 heavenly calling, *f* your thoughts
   12: 2 Let us *f* our eyes on Jesus,

FIXED* (FIX)

2Ki 8: 11 stared at him with a *f* gaze
Job 38: 10 when I *f* limits for it
Ps 141: 8 my eyes are *f* on you, O Sovereign
Pr 8: 28 *f* securely the fountains of the deep
Jer 33: 25 and night and day *f* laws of heaven
Lk 16: 26 and you a great chasm has been *f*,

FLAME (FLAMES FLAMING)

2Ti 1: 6 you to fan into *f* the gift of God,

FLAMES (FLAME)

1Co 3: 15 only as one escaping through the *f*.
   13: 3 and surrender my body to the *f*,

FLAMING (FLAME)

Eph 6: 16 you can extinguish all the *f* arrows

FLANK
Eze 34: 21 Because you shove with *f*

FLASH
1Co 15: 52 in a *f*, in the twinkling of an eye,

FLATTER* (FLATTERING FLATTERS FLATTERY)
Job 32: 21 nor will I *f* any man;
Ps   78: 36 But then they would *f* him
Jude   : 16 *f* others for their own advantage.

FLATTERING* (FLATTER)
Ps   12: 2 their *f* lips speak with deception.
     12: 3 May the LORD cut off all *f* lips
Pr   26: 28 and a *f* mouth works ruin.
     28: 23 than he who has a *f* tongue.
Eze 12: 24 or *f* divinations among the people

FLATTERS* (FLATTER)
Ps   36: 2 For in his own eyes he *f* himself
Pr   29: 5 Whoever *f* his neighbor

FLATTERY* (FLATTER)
Job 32: 22 for if I were skilled in *f*,
Da   11: 32 With *f* he will corrupt those who
Ro   16: 18 and *f* they deceive the minds
1Th   2: 5 You know we never used *f*,

FLAWLESS*
2Sa 22: 31 the word of the LORD is *f*.
Job 11: 4 You say to God, 'My beliefs are *f*
Ps   12: 6 And the words of the LORD are *f*,
     18: 30 the word of the LORD is *f*.
Pr   30: 5 "Every word of God is *f*;
SS   5: 2 my dove, my *f* one.

FLEE (FLEES)
Ps 139: 7 Where can I *f* from your presence?
1Co   6: 18 *F* from sexual immorality.
     10: 14 my dear friends, *f* from idolatry.
1Ti   6: 11 But you, man of God, *f* from all this
2Ti   2: 22 *F* the evil desires of youth,
Jas   4: 7 Resist the devil, and he will *f*

FLEECE
Jdg   6: 37 I will place a wool *f*

FLEES (FLEE)
Pr   28: 1 The wicked man *f* though no one

FLEETING*
Job 14: 2 like a *f* shadow, he does not endure
Ps   39: 4 let me know how *f* is my life.
     89: 47 Remember how *f* is my life.
    144: 4 his days are like a *f* shadow.
Pr   21: 6 is a *f* vapor and a deadly snare.
     31: 30 Charm is deceptive, and beauty is *f*

FLESH see also BODY, MANKIND, PEOPLE, SINFUL (nature)
Ge   2: 23 and *f* of my *f*;
     2: 24 and they will become one *f*.
2Ch 32: 8 With him is only the arm of *f*,
Job 19: 26 yet in my *f* I will see God;
Eze 11: 19 of stone and give them a heart of *f*.
     36: 26 of stone and give you a heart of *f*.
Mt   19: 5 and the two will become one *f* ?
Mk 10: 8 and the two will become one *f*.'
Jn   1: 14 The Word became *f* and lived for a
     6: 51 This bread is my *f*, which I will give
1Co   6: 16 "The two will become one *f*."
     15: 39 All *f* is not the same: Men have one
Eph   5: 31 and the two will become one *f*."
     6: 12 For our struggle is not against *f*
Php   3: 2 do evil, those mutilators of the *f*.
1Jn   4: 2 come in the *f* is from God,
Jude   : 23 the clothing stained by corrupted *f*.

FLIGHT
Dt   32: 30 or two put ten thousand to *f*.

FLINT
Isa   50: 7 Therefore have I set my face like *f*.
Zec   7: 12 They made their hearts as hard as *f*

FLIRTING*
Isa   3: 16 *f* with their eyes,

FLOCK (FLOCKS)
Ps   77: 20 You led your people like a *f*
     78: 52 he brought his people out like a *f*;
     95: 7 the *f* under his care.
Isa   40: 11 He tends his *f* like a shepherd.
Jer   10: 21 and all their *f* is scattered.
     23: 2 "Because you have scattered my *f*
     31: 10 watch over his *f* like a shepherd.'
Eze 34: 2 not shepherds take care of the *f*?
Zec   11: 17 who deserts the *f*!
Mt   26: 31 the sheep of the *f* will be scattered.'
Lk   12: 32 little *f*, for your Father has been
Jn   10: 16 shall be one *f* and one shepherd.
Ac   20: 28 all the *f* of which the Holy Spirit
1Co   9: 7 Who tends a *f* and does not drink
1Pe   2: 2 Be shepherds of God's *f* that is
     5: 3 but being examples to the *f*.

FLOCKS (FLOCK)
Lk   2: 8 keeping watch over their *f* at night.

FLOG (FLOGGED FLOGGING)
Pr   19: 25 *F* a mocker, and the simple will
Ac   22: 25 to *f* a Roman citizen who hasn't

FLOGGED (FLOG)
Jn   19: 1 Pilate took Jesus and had him *f*.
Ac   5: 40 the apostles in and had them *f*.
     16: 23 After they had been severely *f*,
2Co 11: 23 frequently, been *f* more severely,

FLOGGING (FLOG)
Heb 11: 36 *f*, while still others were chained

FLOOD (FLOODGATES)
Ge   7: 7 ark to escape the waters of the *f*.
Mal   2: 13 You *f* the LORD's altar with tears.
Mt   24: 38 For in the days before the *f*,
2Pe   2: 5 world when he brought the *f*

FLOODGATES (FLOOD)
Ge   7: 11 the *f* of the heavens were opened.
Mal   3: 10 see if I will not throw open the *f*

FLOOR
Jas   2: 3 or "Sit on the *f* by my feet,"

FLOUR
Lev   2: 1 his offering is to be of fine *f*.
Nu   7: 13 filled with fine *f* mixed with oil
     28: 9 of an ephah of fine *f* mixed with oil.

FLOURISH (FLOURISHES FLOURISHING)
Ps   72: 7 In his days the righteous will *f*
     92: 7 and all evildoers *f*,
     92: 12 The righteous will *f* like a palm tree
Pr   14: 11 but the tent of the upright will *f*.

FLOURISHES (FLOURISH)
Pr   12: 12 but the root of the righteous *f*.

FLOURISHING (FLOURISH)
Ps   52: 8 *f* in the house of God;

FLOW (FLOWING)
Nu   13: 27 and it does *f* with milk and honey!
Jn   7: 38 streams of living water will *f*

FLOWER (FLOWERS)
Job 14: 2 up like a *f* and withers away;
Ps 103: 15 he flourishes like a *f* of the field;
Jas   1: 10 he will pass away like a wild *f*.

FLOWERS (FLOWER)
Isa   40: 6 and all their glory is like the *f*
     40: 7 The grass withers and the *f* fall,
1Pe   1: 24 and all their glory is like the *f*

FLOWING (FLOW)
Ex   3: 8 a land *f* with milk and honey—
     33: 3 Go up to the land *f* with milk
Nu   16: 14 us into a land *f* with milk
Jos   5: 6 a land *f* with milk and honey.
Ps 107: 33 *f* springs into thirsty ground,
    107: 35 the parched ground into *f* springs;
Jer   32: 22 a land *f* with milk and honey.
Eze 20: 6 a land *f* with milk and honey,

Rev 22: 1 *f* from the throne of God

FLUTE
Ps 150: 4 praise him with the strings and *f*,
Mt   11: 17 " 'We played the *f* for you,
1Co 14: 7 that make sounds, such as the *f*

FOAL*
Zec   9: 9 on a colt, the *f* of a donkey.
Mt   21: 5 on a colt, the *f* of a donkey.' "

FOILS*
Ps   33: 10 The LORD *f* the plans
Isa   44: 25 who *f* the signs of false prophets

FOLDING* (FOLDS)
Pr   6: 10 a little *f* of the hands to rest—
     24: 33 a little *f* of the hands to rest—

FOLDS (FOLDING)
Ecc   4: 5 The fool *f* his hands

FOLLOW (FOLLOWED FOLLOWING FOLLOWS)
Ex   23: 2 Do not *f* the crowd in doing wrong.
Lev 18: 4 and be careful to *f* my decrees.
Dt   5: 1 Learn them and be sure to *f* them.
     17: 19 *f* carefully all the words of this law
1Ki   11: 6 he did not *f* the LORD completely,
2Ch 34: 33 they did not fail to *f* the LORD,
Ps   23: 6 Surely goodness and love will *f* me
   119:166 and I *f* your commands.
Mt   4: 19 *f* me," Jesus said, "and I will make
     8: 19 I will *f* you wherever you go."
     8: 22 But Jesus told him, "*F* me,
     16: 24 and take up his cross and *f* me.
     19: 27 "We have left everything to *f* you!
Lk   9: 23 take up his cross daily and *f* me.
     9: 61 Still another said, "I will *f* you,
Jn   10: 4 his sheep *f* him because they know
     10: 5 But they will never *f* a stranger;
     10: 27 I know them, and they *f* me.
     12: 26 Whoever serves me must *f* me;
     21: 19 Then he said to him, "*F* me!"
1Co   1: 12 One of you says, "I *f* Paul";
     11: 1 *F* my example, as I follow
     14: 1 *F* the way of love and eagerly
2Th   3: 9 ourselves a model for you to *f*.
1Pe   2: 21 that you should *f* in his steps.
Rev 14: 4 They *f* the Lamb wherever he goes.

FOLLOWED (FOLLOW)
Nu   32: 11 they have not *f* me wholeheartedly,
Dt   1: 36 he *f* the LORD wholeheartedly."
Jos   14: 14 he *f* the LORD, the God of Israel,
2Ch 10: 14 he *f* the advice of the young men
Mt   4: 20 once they left their nets and *f* him.
     9: 9 and Matthew got up and *f* him.
     26: 58 But Peter *f* him at a distance,
Lk   18: 43 he received his sight and *f* Jesus,

FOLLOWING (FOLLOW)
Ps 119: 14 I rejoice in *f* your statutes
Php   3: 17 Join with others in *f* my example,
1Ti   1: 18 by *f* them you may fight the good

FOLLOWS (FOLLOW)
Jn   8: 12 Whoever *f* me will never walk

FOLLY (FOOL)
Pr   14: 29 a quick-tempered man displays *f*.
     19: 3 A man's own *f* ruins his life,
Ecc 10: 1 so a little *f* outweighs wisdom
Mk   7: 22 envy, slander, arrogance and *f*.
2Ti   3: 9 their *f* will be clear to everyone.

FOOD (FOODS)
Ge   1: 30 I give every green plant for *f*."
Pr   12: 9 to be somebody and have no *f*.
     12: 11 his land will have abundant *f*,
     20: 13 you will have *f* to spare.
     20: 17 *F* gained by fraud tastes sweet
     21: 20 of the wise are stores of choice *f*
     22: 9 for he shares his *f* with the poor.
     23: 3 for that *f* is deceptive.
     23: 6 Do not eat the *f* of a stingy man,
     25: 21 If your enemy is hungry, give him *f*
     31: 14 bringing her *f* from afar.

FOODS (continued)

Pr　31: 15 she provides *f* for her family
Isa 58:　7 not to share your *f* with the hungry
Eze 18:　7 but gives his *f* to the hungry
Da　　1:　8 to defile himself with the royal *f*
Mt　　3:　4 His *f* was locusts and wild honey.
　　　　6: 25 Is not life more important than *f*,
Jn　　4: 32 "I have *f* to eat that you know
　　　　4: 34 have brought him *f*?" "My *f*,"
　　　　6: 27 Do not work for *f* that spoils,
　　　　6: 55 my flesh is real *f* and my blood is
Ac　15: 20 to abstain from *f* polluted by idols,
Ro　14: 14 fully convinced that no *f* is unclean
1Co　8:　1 Now about *f* sacrificed to idols:
　　　　8:　8 But *f* does not bring us near to God
2Co 11: 27 and have often gone without *f*:
1Ti　　6:　8 But if we have *f* and clothing,
Heb　5: 14 But solid *f* is for the mature,
Jas　　2: 15 sister is without clothes and daily *f*

FOODS (FOOD)

Mk　　7: 19 Jesus declared all *f* "clean.")

FOOL (FOLLY FOOL'S FOOLISH FOOLISHNESS FOOLS)

1Sa 25: 25 his name is *F*, and folly goes
Ps　14:　1 The *f* says in his heart,
Pr　10: 10 and a chattering *f* comes to ruin.
　　10: 18 and whoever spreads slander is a *f*.
　　12: 15 The way of a *f* seems right to him,
　　12: 16 A *f* shows his annoyance at once,
　　14: 16 but a *f* is hotheaded and reckless.
　　15:　5 A *f* spurns his father's discipline,
　　17: 12 than a *f* in his folly.
　　17: 16 use is money in the hand of a *f*,
　　17: 21 To have a *f* for a son brings grief;
　　17: 28 Even a *f* is thought wise
　　18:　2 A *f* finds no pleasure
　　20:　3 but every *f* is quick to quarrel.
　　23:　9 Do not speak to a *f*,
　　24:　7 Wisdom is too high for a *f*:
　　26:　4 Do not answer a *f* according
　　26:　5 Answer a *f* according to his folly,
　　26:　7 is a proverb in the mouth of a *f*.
　　26: 11 so a *f* repeats his folly.
　　26: 12 for a *f* than for him.
　　27: 22 Though you grind a *f* in a mortar,
　　28: 26 He who trusts in himself is a *f*,
　　29: 11 A *f* gives full vent to his anger,
　　29: 20 for a *f* than for him.
Mt　　5: 22 But anyone who says, 'You *f*!'
Lk　12: 20 "But God said to him, 'You *f*!'
1Co　3: 18 he should become a "*f*"
2Co 11: 21 I am speaking as a *f*—I

FOOL'S (FOOL)

Pr　14:　3 A *f* talk brings a rod to his back.
　　18:　7 A *f* mouth is his undoing.

FOOLISH (FOOL)

Pr　10:　1 but a *f* son grief to his mother.
　　14:　1 her own hands the *f* one tears hers
　　15: 20 but a *f* man despises his mother.
　　17: 25 A *f* son brings grief to his father
　　19: 13 A *f* son is his father's ruin,
Mt　　7: 26 practice is like a *f* man who built
　　25:　2 of them were *f* and five were wise.
Lk　11: 40 You *f* people! Did not the one who
　　24: 25 He said to them, "How *f* you are,
1Co　1: 20 Has not God made *f* the wisdom
　　　1: 27 God chose the *f* things of the world
Gal　　3:　1 died for nothing!" You *f* Galatians!
Eph　5:　4 should there be obscenity, *f* talk
　　　5: 17 Therefore do not be *f*,
Tit　　3:　9 But avoid *f* controversies

FOOLISHNESS (FOOL)

1Co　1: 18 of the cross is *f* to those who are
　　　1: 21 through the *f* of what was preached
　　　1: 23 block to Jews and *f* to Gentiles,
　　　1: 25 For the *f* of God is wiser
　　　2: 14 for they are *f* to him, and he cannot
　　　3: 19 of this world is *f* in God's sight.

FOOLS (FOOL)

Pr　　1:　7 but *f* despise wisdom and discipline
　　　3: 35 but *f* he holds up to shame.
　　12: 23 but the heart of *f* blurts out folly.
　　13: 19 but *f* detest turning from evil.

Pr　13: 20 but a companion of *f* suffers harm.
　　14:　9 *F* mock at making amends for sin,
　　14: 24 but the folly of *f* yields folly.
Ecc　7:　5 than to listen to the song of *f*.
　　　7:　6 so is the laughter of *f*.
　　10:　6 *F* are put in many high positions,
Mt　23: 17 You blind *f*! Which is greater:
Ro　　1: 22 they became *f* and exchanged
1Co　4: 10 We are *f* for Christ, but you are

FOOT (FEET FOOTHOLD)

Jos　　1:　3 every place where you set your *f*,
Ps 121:　3 He will not let your *f* slip—
Pr　　3: 23 and your *f* will not stumble;
　　　4: 27 keep your *f* from evil.
　　25: 17 Seldom set *f* in your neighbor's
Isa　　1:　6 From the sole of your *f* to the top
Mt　18:　8 or your *f* causes you to sin,
Lk　　4: 11 so that you will not strike your *f*
1Co 12: 15 If the *f* should say, "Because I am
Rev 10:　2 He planted his right *f* on the sea

FOOTHOLD* (FOOT)

Ps　69:　2 where there is no *f*.
　　73:　2 I had nearly lost my *f*.
Eph　4: 27 and do not give the devil a *f*.

FOOTSTEPS (STEP)

Ps 119:133 Direct my *f* according

FOOTSTOOL

Ps　99:　5 and worship at his *f*;
　　110:　1 a *f* for your feet."
Isa　66:　1 and the earth is my *f*.
Mt　　5: 35 for it is his *f*; or by Jerusalem,
Ac　　7: 49 and the earth is my *f*.
Heb　1: 13 a *f* for your feet"?
　　10: 13 for his enemies to be made his *f*.

FORBEARANCE*

Ro　　3: 25 because in his *f* he had left the sins

FORBID

1Co 14: 39 and do not *f* speaking in tongues.
1Ti　　4:　3 They *f* people to marry

FORCE (FORCED FORCEFUL FORCES FORCING)

Jn　　6: 15 to come and make him king by *f*,
Ac　26: 11 and I tried to *f* them to blaspheme.
Gal　　2: 14 that you *f* Gentiles

FORCED (FORCE)

Mt　27: 32 and they *f* him to carry the cross.
Phm　　14 do will be spontaneous and not *f*.

FORCEFUL* (FORCE)

Mt　11: 12 forcefully advancing, and *f* men lay
2Co 10: 10 "His letters are weighty and *f*,

FORCES (FORCE)

Mt　　5: 41 If someone *f* you to go one mile,
Eph　6: 12 against the spiritual *f* of evil

FORCING (FORCE)

Lk　16: 16 and everyone is *f* his way into it.

FOREFATHERS (FATHER)

Heb　1:　1 spoke to our *f* through the prophets
1Pe　1: 18 handed down to you from your *f*,

FOREHEAD (FOREHEADS)

Ex　13:　9 a reminder on your *f* that the law
　　13: 16 on your *f* that the LORD brought
1Sa 17: 49 and struck the Philistine on the *f*.
Rev 13: 16 a mark on his right hand or on his *f*,

FOREHEADS (FOREHEAD)

Dt　　6:　8 hands and bind them on your *f*.
Rev　9:　4 not have the seal of God on their *f*.
　　14:　1 his Father's name written on their *f*

FOREIGN (FOREIGNER FOREIGNERS)

Ge　35:　2 "Get rid of the *f* gods you have
2Ch 14:　3 He removed the *f* altars
　　33: 15 He got rid of the *f* gods
Isa　28: 11 with *f* lips and strange tongues

FOREIGNER (FOREIGN)

Lk　17: 18 give praise to God except this *f*?"
1Co 14: 11 I am a *f* to the speaker,

FOREIGNERS (FOREIGN)

Eph　2: 12 *f* to the covenants of the promise,
　　　2: 19 you are no longer *f* and aliens,

FOREKNEW* (KNOW)

Ro　　8: 29 For those God *f* he
　　11:　2 not reject his people, whom he *f*.

FOREKNOWLEDGE* (KNOW)

Ac　　2: 23 to you by God's set purpose and *f*;
1Pe　1:　2 to the *f* of God the Father,

FORESAW*

Gal　　3:　8 Scripture *f* that God would justify

FOREST

Jas　　3:　5 Consider what a great *f* is set

FOREVER (EVER)

Ge　　3: 22 the tree of life and eat, and live *f*."
　　　6:　3 Spirit will not contend with man *f*,
Ex　　3: 15 This is my name *f*, the name
2Sa　7: 26 so that your name will be great *f*.
1Ki　2: 33 may there be the LORD's peace *f*."
　　　9:　3 by putting my Name there *f*.
1Ch 16: 15 He remembers his covenant *f*,
　　16: 34 his love endures *f*.
　　16: 41 "for his love endures *f*."
　　17: 24 and that your name will be great *f*.
2Ch　5: 13 his love endures *f*."
　　20: 21 for his love endures *f*."
Ps　　9:　7 The LORD reigns *f*;
　　23:　6 dwell in the house of the LORD *f*.
　　28:　9 be their shepherd and carry them *f*.
　　29: 10 the LORD is enthroned as King *f*.
　　33: 11 the plans of the LORD stand firm *f*
　　37: 28 They will be protected *f*,
　　44:　8 and we will praise your name *f*.
　　61:　4 I long to dwell in your tent *f*
　　72: 19 Praise be to his glorious name *f*;
　　73: 26 and my portion *f*.
　　77:　8 Has his unfailing love vanished *f*?
　　79: 13 will praise you *f*;
　　81: 15 and their punishment would last *f*.
　　86: 12 I will glorify your name *f*.
　　89:　1 of the LORD's great love *f*;
　　92:　8 But you, O LORD, are exalted *f*.
　　100:　5 is good and his love endures *f*;
　　102: 12 But you, O LORD, sit enthroned *f*;
　　104: 31 of the LORD endure *f*;
　　107:　1 his love endures *f*.
　　110:　4 "You are a priest *f*,
　　111:　3 and his righteousness endures *f*.
　　112:　6 man will be remembered *f*.
　　117:　2 of the LORD endures *f*.
　　118:　1 his love endures *f*.
　　119:111 Your statutes are my heritage *f*;
　　119:152 that you established them to last *f*.
　　136:　1 His love endures *f*.
　　146:　6 the LORD, who remains faithful *f*.
Pr　10: 25 but the righteous stand firm *f*.
　　27: 24 for riches do not endure *f*,
Isa　25:　8 he will swallow up death *f*.
　　26:　4 Trust in the LORD *f*,
　　32: 17 will be quietness and confidence *f*.
　　40:　8 but the word of our God stands *f*."
　　51:　6 But my salvation will last *f*,
　　51:　8 But my righteousness will last *f*,
　　57: 15 he who lives *f*, whose name is holy:
　　59: 21 from this time on and *f*,"
Jer　33: 11 his love endures *f*."
Eze 37: 26 put my sanctuary among them *f*.
Da　　2: 44 to an end, but it will itself endure *f*.
　　　3:　9 live *f*! You have issued a decree,
Jn　　6: 51 eats of this bread, he will live *f*.
　　14: 16 Counselor to be with you *f*—
Ro　　9:　5 who is God over all, *f* praised!
　　16: 27 to the only wise God be glory *f*
1Co　1:　8 blameless on the day of our Lord
1Th　4: 17 And so we will be with the Lord *f*.
Heb　5:　6 "You are a priest *f*,
　　　7: 17 "You are a priest *f*,
　　　7: 24 Jesus lives *f*, he has a permanent
　　13:　8 same yesterday and today and *f*.

1Pe 1: 25 but the word of the Lord stands *f*."
1Jn 2: 17 who does the will of God lives *f*.
2Jn : 2 lives in us and will be with us *f*:

FOREVERMORE (EVER)

Ps 113: 2 both now and *f*.

FORFEIT

Mk 8: 36 the whole world, yet *f* his soul?
Lk 9: 25 and yet lose or *f* his very self?

FORGAVE (FORGIVE)

Ps 32: 5 and you *f*
65: 3 you *f* our transgressions
78: 38 you *f* their iniquities
Eph 4: 32 just as in Christ God *f* you.
Col 2: 13 He *f* us all our sins, having
3: 13 Forgive as the Lord *f* you.

FORGET (FORGETS FORGETTING FORGOT FORGOTTEN)

Dt 4: 23 Be careful not to *f* the covenant
6: 12 that you do not *f* the Lord,
2Ki 17: 38 Do not *f* the covenant I have made
Ps 9: 17 all the nations that *f* God.
10: 12 Do not *f* the helpless.
50: 22 "Consider this, you who *f* God,
78: 7 and would not *f* his deeds
103: 2 and *f* not all his benefits.
119: 93 I will never *f* your precepts,
137: 5 may my right hand *f* its skill.
Pr 3: 1 My son, do not *f* my teaching,
4: 5 do not *f* my words or swerve
Isa 49: 15 "Can a mother *f* the baby
51: 13 that you *f* the Lord your Maker,
Jer 2: 32 Does a maiden *f* her jewelry,
23: 39 I will surely *f* you and cast you out
Heb 6: 10 he will not *f* your work
13: 2 Do not *f* to entertain strangers,
13: 16 And do not *f* to do good
2Pe 3: 8 But do not *f* this one thing.

FORGETS (FORGET)

Jn 16: 21 her baby is born she *f* the anguish
Jas 1: 24 immediately *f* what he looks like.

FORGETTING* (FORGET)

Php 3: 13 *F* what is behind and straining
Jas 1: 25 to do this, not *f* what he has heard,

FORGIVE* (FORGAVE FORGIVENESS FORGIVES FORGIVING)

Ge 50: 17 I ask you to *f* your brothers the sins
50: 17 please *f* the sins of the servants
Ex 10: 17 Now *f* my sin once more
23: 21 he will not *f* your rebellion.
32: 32 But now, please *f* their sin—
34: 9 *f* our wickedness and our sin,
Nu 14: 19 with your great love, *f* the sin
Dt 29: 20 will never be willing to *f* him;
Jos 24: 19 He will not *f* your rebellion
1Sa 15: 25 *f* my sin and come back with me,
25: 28 Please *f* your servant's offense.
1Ki 8: 30 place, and when you hear, *f*.
8: 34 and *f* the sin of your people Israel
8: 36 and *f* the sin of your servants,
8: 39 *F* and act; deal with each man
8: 50 *f* all the offenses they have
8: 50 *f* your people, who have sinned
2Ki 5: 18 But may the Lord *f* your servant
5: 18 may the Lord *f* your servant
24: 4 and the Lord was not willing to *f*.
2Ch 6: 21 place; and when you hear, *f*.
6: 25 and *f* the sin of your people Israel
6: 27 and *f* the sin of your servants,
6: 30 *F*, and deal with each man
6: 39 *f* your people, who have sinned
7: 14 will *f* their sin and will heal their
Job 7: 21 and *f* my sins?
Ps 19: 12 *F* my hidden faults.
25: 11 *f* my iniquity, though it is great.
79: 9 deliver us and *f* our sins
Isa 2: 9 do not *f* them.
Jer 5: 1 I will *f* this city.
5: 7 "Why should I *f* you?
18: 23 Do not *f* their crimes
31: 34 "For I will *f* their wickedness
33: 8 and will *f* all their sins of rebellion

Jer 36: 3 then I will *f* their wickedness
50: 20 for I will *f* the remnant I spare.
Da 9: 19 O Lord, listen! O Lord, *f*! O Lord,
Hos 1: 6 that I should at all *f* them.
14: 2 "*F* all our sins
Am 7: 2 *f*! How can Jacob survive?
Mt 6: 12 *F* us our debts,
6: 14 For if you *f* men when they sin
6: 14 heavenly Father will also *f* you.
6: 15 But if you do not *f* men their sins,
6: 15 your Father will not *f* your sins.
9: 6 authority on earth to *f* sins..
18: 21 many times shall I *f* my brother
18: 35 you *f* your brother from your heart
Mk 2: 7 Who can *f* sins but God alone?"
2: 10 authority on earth to *f* sins
11: 25 anything against anyone, *f* him,
11: 25 in heaven may *f* you your sins."
Lk 5: 21 Who can *f* sins but God alone?"
5: 24 authority on earth to *f* sins..
6: 37 *F*, and you will be forgiven.
11: 4 *F* us our sins,
11: 4 *f* everyone who sins against us.
17: 3 rebuke him, and if he repents, *f* him
17: 4 and says, 'I repent,' *f* him."
23: 34 Jesus said, "Father, *f* them,
Jn 20: 23 If you *f* anyone his sins, they are
20: 23 if you do not *f* them, they are not
Ac 8: 22 Perhaps he will *f* you
2Co 2: 7 you ought to *f* and comfort him,
2: 10 If you *f* anyone, I also *f* him.
2: 10 if there was anything to *f*—
12: 13 a burden to you? *F* me this wrong!
Col 3: 13 and *f* whatever grievances you may
3: 13 *F* as the Lord forgave you.
Heb 8: 12 For I will *f* their wickedness
1Jn 1: 9 and just and will *f* us our sins

FORGIVENESS* (FORGIVE)

Ps 130: 4 But with you there is *f*;
Mt 26: 28 out for many for the *f* of sins.
Mk 1: 4 of repentance for the *f* of sins.
Lk 1: 77 salvation through the *f* of their sins,
3: 3 of repentance for the *f* of sins.
24: 47 and *f* of sins will be preached
Ac 5: 31 that he might give repentance and *f*
10: 43 believes in him receives *f* of sins
13: 38 that through Jesus the *f*
26: 18 so that they may receive *f* of sins
Eph 1: 7 through his blood, the *f* of sins,
Col 1: 14 in whom we have redemption, the *f*
Heb 9: 22 the shedding of blood there is no *f*.

FORGIVES* (FORGIVE)

Ps 103: 3 He *f* all my sins
Mic 7: 18 pardons sin and *f* the transgression
Lk 7: 49 "Who is this who even *f* sins?"

FORGIVING* (FORGIVE)

Ex 34: 7 and *f* wickedness, rebellion and sin.
Nu 14: 18 abounding in love and *f* sin
Ne 9: 17 But you are a *f* God, gracious
Ps 86: 5 You are *f* and good, O Lord,
99: 8 you were to Israel a *f* God,
Da 9: 9 The Lord our God is merciful and *f*
Eph 4: 32 to one another, *f* each other,

FORGOT (FORGET)

Dt 32: 18 you the God who gave you birth.
Ps 78: 11 They *f* what he had done,
106: 13 But they soon *f* what he had done

FORGOTTEN (FORGET)

Job 11: 6 God has even *f* some of your sin.
Ps 44: 20 If we had *f* the name of our God
Isa 17: 10 You have *f* God your Savior;
Hos 8: 14 Israel has *f* his Maker
Lk 12: 6 Yet not one of them is *f* by God.
2Pe 1: 9 and has *f* that he has been cleansed

FORM (FORMED)

Isa 52: 14 *f* marred beyond human likeness—
2Ti 3: 5 having a *f* of godliness

FORMED (FORM)

Ge 2: 7 —the Lord God *f* the man
2: 19 Now the Lord God had *f* out
Ps 103: 14 for he knows how we are *f*,

Ecc 11: 5 or how the body is *f* in a mother's
Isa 29: 16 Shall what is *f* say to him who *f* it,
45: 18 but *f* it to be inhabited—
49: 5 he who *f* me in the womb
Jer 1: 5 "Before I *f* you in the womb I knew
Ro 9: 20 "Shall what is *f* say to him who *f* it,
Gal 4: 19 of childbirth until Christ is *f* in you,
1Ti 2: 13 For Adam was *f* first, then Eve.
Heb 11: 3 understand that the universe was *f*
2Pe 3: 5 and the earth was *f* out of water

FORMLESS*

Ge 1: 2 Now the earth was *f* and empty,
Jer 4: 23 and it was *f* and empty;

FORNICATION see IMMORALITY, UNFAITHFULNESS

FORSAKE (FORSAKEN)

Dt 31: 6 he will never leave you nor *f* you."
Jos 1: 5 I will never leave you nor *f* you.
24: 16 "Far be it from us to *f* the Lord
2Ch 15: 2 but if you *f* him, he will *f* you.
Ps 27: 10 Though my father and mother *f* me
94: 14 he will never *f* his inheritance.
Isa 55: 7 Let the wicked *f* his way
Heb 13: 5 never will I *f* you."

FORSAKEN (FORSAKE)

Ps 22: 1 my God, why have you *f* me?
37: 25 I have never seen the righteous *f*
Mt 27: 46 my God, why have you *f* me?"
Rev 2: 4 You have *f* your first love.

FORTRESS

2Sa 22: 2 "The Lord is my rock, my *f*
Ps 18: 2 The Lord is my rock, my *f*
31: 2 a strong *f* to save me.
59: 16 for you are my *f*,
71: 3 for you are my rock and my *f*.
Pr 14: 26 who fears the Lord has a secure *f*.

FORTUNE-TELLING*

Ac 16: 16 deal of money for her owners by *f*.

FORTY

Ge 7: 4 on the earth for *f* days and *f* nights,
18: 29 "What if only *f* are found there?"
Ex 16: 35 The Israelites ate manna *f* years,
24: 18 on the mountain *f* days and *f* nights
Nu 14: 34 For *f* years—one year for each
Jos 14: 7 I was *f* years old when Moses
1Sa 4: 18 He had led Israel *f* years.
2Sa 5: 4 king, and he reigned *f* years.
1Ki 19: 8 he traveled *f* days and *f* nights
2Ki 12: 1 and he reigned in Jerusalem *f* years
2Ch 9: 30 in Jerusalem over all Israel *f* years.
Eze 29: 12 her cities will lie desolate *f* years
Jnh 3: 4 "*F* more days and Nineveh will be
Mt 4: 2 After fasting *f* days and *f* nights,

FOUGHT (FIGHT)

1Co 15: 32 If I *f* wild beasts in Ephesus
2Ti 4: 7 I have *f* the good fight, I have

FOUND (FIND)

2Ki 22: 8 "I have *f* the Book of the Law
1Ch 28: 9 If you seek him, he will be *f* by you;
2Ch 15: 15 sought God eagerly, and he was *f*
Isa 55: 6 Seek the Lord while he may be *f*;
65: 1 I was *f* by those who did not seek
Da 5: 27 on the scales and *f* wanting.
Mt 1: 18 she was *f* to be with child
Lk 15: 6 with me; I have *f* my lost sheep.'
15: 9 with me; I have *f* my lost coin.'
15: 24 is alive again; he was lost and is *f*.'
Ac 4: 12 Salvation is *f* in no one else,
Ro 10: 20 "I was *f* by those who did not seek
Jas 2: 8 If you really keep the royal law *f*
Rev 5: 4 no one was *f* who was worthy

FOUNDATION (FOUNDATIONS FOUNDED)

Isa 28: 16 a precious cornerstone for a sure *f*;
Mt 7: 25 because it had its *f* on the rock.
Lk 14: 29 For if he lays the *f* and is not able
Ro 15: 20 building on someone else's *f*.
1Co 3: 10 I laid a *f* as an expert builder,
3: 11 For no one can lay any *f* other

FOUNDATIONS

Eph　2: 20 built on the *f* of the apostles
1Ti　3: 15 the pillar and *f* of the truth.
2Ti　2: 19 God's solid *f* stands firm,
Heb　6: 1 not laying again the *f* of repentance

FOUNDATIONS (FOUNDATION)

Ps 102: 25 In the beginning you laid the *f*
Heb　1: 10 O Lord, you laid the *f* of the earth,

FOUNDED (FOUNDATION)

Jer　10: 12 he *f* the world by his wisdom
Heb　8: 6 and it is *f* on better promises.

FOUNTAIN

Ps　36: 9 For with you is the *f* of life;
Pr　14: 27 The fear of the LORD is a *f* of life,
　　　18: 4 the *f* of wisdom is a bubbling brook.
Zec 13: 1 "On that day a *f* will be opened

FOX (FOXES)

Lk　13: 32 He replied, "Go tell that *f*,

FOXES (FOX)

SS　2: 15 the little *f*
Mt　8: 20 "*F* have holes and birds

FRAGRANCE (FRAGRANT)

Ex　30: 38 it to enjoy its *f* must be cut
Jn　12: 3 filled with the *f* of the perfume.
2Co　2: 14 us spreads everywhere the *f*
　　　2: 16 of death; to the other, the *f* of life.

FRAGRANT (FRAGRANCE)

Eph　5: 2 as a *f* offering and sacrifice to God.
Php　4: 18 They are a *f* offering, an acceptable

FREE (FREED FREEDOM FREELY)

Ge　2: 16 "You are *f* to eat from any tree
Ps 118: 5 and he answered by setting me *f*.
　　119: 32 for you have set my heart *f*.
　　146: 7 The LORD sets prisoners *f*,
Pr　6: 3 then do this, my son, to *f* yourself,
Jn　8: 32 and the truth will set you *f*."
　　8: 36 if the Son sets you *f*, you will be *f*
Ro　6: 18 You have been set *f* from sin
　　8: 2 of life set me *f* from the law of sin
1Co 12: 13 whether Jews or Greeks, slave or *f*
Gal　3: 28 slave nor *f*, male nor female,
　　5: 1 for freedom that Christ has set us *f*.
1Pe　2: 16 free men, but do not use your freedom

FREED (FREE)

Ps 116: 16 you have *f* me from my chains.
Ro　6: 7 anyone who has died has been *f*
Rev　1: 5 has *f* us from our sins by his blood,

FREEDOM (FREE)

Ps 119: 45 I will walk about in *f*,
Isa　61: 1 to proclaim *f* for the captives
Lk　4: 18 me to proclaim *f* for the prisoners
Ro　8: 21 into the glorious *f* of the children
1Co　7: 21 although if you can gain your *f*,
2Co　3: 17 the Spirit of the Lord is, there is *f*.
Gal　2: 4 ranks to spy on the *f* we have
　　5: 13 But do not use your *f* to indulge
Jas　1: 25 into the perfect law that gives *f*,
1Pe　2: 16 but do not use your *f* as a cover-up

FREELY (FREE)

Isa　55: 7 and to our God, for he will *f* pardon
Mt　10: 8 Freely you have received, *f* give.
Ro　3: 24 and are justified *f* by his grace
Eph　1: 6 which he has *f* given us

FRESH

Jas　3: 11 Can both *f* water and salt water

FRET*

Ps　37: 1 Do not *f* because of evil men
　　37: 7 do not *f* when men succeed
　　37: 8 do not *f* — it leads only to evil.
Pr　24: 19 Do not *f* because of evil men

FRICTION

1Ti　6: 5 and constant *f* between men

FRIEND (FRIENDS FRIENDSHIP)

Ex　33: 11 as a man speaks with his *f*.
2Ch 20: 7 descendants of Abraham your *f*?

Pr　17: 17 A *f* loves at all times,
　　18: 24 there is a *f* who sticks closer
　　27: 6 Wounds from a *f* can be trusted
　　27: 10 Do not forsake your *f* and the *f*
Isa　41: 8 you descendants of Abraham my *f*,
Mt　11: 19 a *f* of tax collectors and "sinners." '
Lk　11: 8 him the bread because he is his *f*,
Jn　19: 12 "If you let this man go, you are no *f*
Jas　2: 23 and he was called God's *f*.
　　4: 4 Anyone who chooses to be a *f*

FRIENDS (FRIEND)

Pr　16: 28 and a gossip separates close *f*.
　　17: 9 the matter separates close *f*.
Zec 13: 6 given at the house of my *f*.'
Jn　15: 13 that he lay down his life for his *f*.
　　15: 14 You are my *f* if you do what I

FRIENDSHIP (FRIEND)

Jas　4: 4 don't you know that *f*

FRIGHTENED (FEAR)

Php　1: 28 gospel without being *f* in any way
1Pe　3: 14 fear what they fear; do not be *f*."

FROGS

Ex　8: 2 plague your whole country with *f*.
Rev 16: 13 three evil spirits that looked like *f*;

FRUIT (FRUITFUL)

Jdg　9: 11 'Should I give up my *f*, so good
Ps　1: 3 which yields its *f* in season
Pr　11: 30 The *f* of the righteous is a tree
　　12: 14 From the *f* of his lips a man is filled
　　27: 18 He who tends a fig tree will eat its *f*
Isa　11: 1 from his roots a Branch will bear *f*.
　　27: 6 and fill all the world with *f*.
　　32: 17 The *f* of righteousness will be peace
Jer　17: 8 and never fails to bear *f*."
Hos 10: 12 reap the *f* of unfailing love,
　　14: 2 that we may offer the *f* of our lips.
Am　8: 1 showed me: a basket of ripe *f*.
Mt　3: 8 Produce *f* in keeping
　　3: 10 does not produce good *f* will be cut
　　7: 16 By their *f* you will recognize them.
　　7: 17 good *f*, but a bad tree bears bad *f*.
　　7: 20 by their *f* you will recognize them.
　　12: 33 a tree good and its *f* will be good,
Lk　3: 9 does not produce good *f* will be cut
　　6: 43 nor does a bad tree bear good *f*.
　　13: 6 and he went to look for *f* on it,
Jn　15: 2 branch in me that bears no *f*,
　　15: 16 and bear *f* — that will last,
Ro　7: 4 in order that we might bear *f*
Gal　5: 22 But the *f* of the Spirit is love, joy,
Php　1: 11 with the *f* of righteousness that
Col　1: 10 bearing *f* in every good work,
Heb 13: 15 the *f* of lips that confess his name.
Jas　3: 17 and good *f*, impartial and sincere.
Jude　: 12 autumn trees, without *f*
Rev 22: 2 of *f*, yielding its *f* every month.

FRUITFUL (FRUIT)

Ge　1: 22 "Be *f* and increase in number
　　9: 1 "Be *f* and increase in number
　　35: 11 be *f* and increase in number.
Ex　1: 7 the Israelites were *f* and multiplied
Ps 128: 3 Your wife will be like a *f* vine
Jn　15: 2 prunes so that it will be even more *f*.
Php　1: 22 This will mean *f* labor for me.

FRUITLESS*

Eph　5: 11 to do with the *f* deeds of darkness,

FRUSTRATION

Ro　8: 20 For the creation was subjected to *f*,

FUEL

Isa　44: 19 "Half of it I used for *f*;

FULFILL (FULFILLED FULFILLMENT FULFILLS)

Nu　23: 19 Does he promise and not *f*?
Ps　61: 8 and *f* my vows day after day.
　　116: 14 I will *f* my vows to the LORD
　　138: 8 The LORD will *f* his purpose,
Ecc　5: 5 than to make a vow and not *f* it.
Isa　46: 11 far-off land, a man to *f* my purpose.

Jer　33: 14 'when I will *f* the gracious promise
Mt　1: 22 place to *f* what the Lord had said
　　3: 15 us to do this to *f* all righteousness."
　　4: 14 *f* what was said
　　5: 17 come to abolish them but to *f* them.
　　8: 17 This was to *f* what was spoken
　　12: 17 This was to *f* what was spoken
　　21: 4 place to *f* what was spoken
Jn　12: 38 This was to *f* the word
　　13: 18 But this is to *f* the scripture:
　　15: 25 But this is to *f* what is written
1Co　7: 3 husband should *f* his marital duty

FULFILLED (FULFILL)

Jos 21: 45 of Israel failed; every one was *f*.
　　23: 14 Every promise has been *f*;
Pr　13: 12 but a longing *f* is a tree of life.
　　13: 19 A longing *f* is sweet to the soul,
Mt　2: 15 so was *f* what the Lord had said
　　2: 17 the prophet Jeremiah was *f*:
　　2: 23 So was *f* what was said
　　13: 14 In them is *f* the prophecy of Isaiah:
　　13: 35 So was *f* what was spoken
　　26: 54 would the Scriptures be *f* that say it
　　26: 56 of the prophets might be *f*."
　　27: 9 by Jeremiah the prophet was *f*:
Mk　13: 4 that they are all about to be *f*?''
　　14: 49 But the Scriptures must be *f*."
Lk　4: 21 "Today this scripture is *f*
　　18: 31 about the Son of Man will be *f*.
　　24: 44 Everything must be *f* that is
Jn　18: 9 words he had spoken would be *f*:
　　19: 24 the Scripture might be *f* which said,
　　19: 28 and so that the Scripture would be *f*
　　19: 36 so that the Scripture would be *f*:
Ac　1: 16 to be *f* which the Holy Spirit spoke
Ro　13: 8 loves his fellowman has *f* the law.
Jas　2: 23 And the scripture was *f* that says,

FULFILLMENT (FULFILL)

Ro　13: 10 Therefore love is the *f* of the law.

FULFILLS (FULFILL)

Ps　57: 2 to God, who *f* his purpose, for me.
　　145: 19 He *f* the desires of those who fear

FULL (FILL)

2Ch 24: 10 them into the chest until it was *f*.
Ps 127: 5 whose quiver is *f* of them.
Pr　27: 7 He who is *f* loathes honey,
　　31: 11 Her husband has *f* confidence
Isa　6: 3 the whole earth is *f* of his glory.''
　　11: 9 for the earth will be *f*
Lk　4: 1 Jesus, *f* of the Holy Spirit,
Jn　10: 10 may have life, and have it to the *f*.
Ac　6: 3 known to be *f* of the Spirit
　　6: 5 a man *f* of faith and of the Holy
　　7: 55 But Stephen, *f* of the Holy Spirit,
　　11: 24 *f* of the Holy Spirit and faith,

FULL-GROWN* (GROW)

Jas　1: 15 when it is *f*, gives birth to death.

FULLNESS* (FILL)

Dt　33: 16 gifts of the earth and its *f*
Jn　1: 16 From the *f* of his grace we have all
Ro　11: 12 greater riches will their *f* bring!
Eph　1: 23 the *f* of him who fills everything
　　3: 19 to the measure of all the *f* of God.
　　4: 13 to the whole measure of the *f*
Col　1: 19 to have all his *f* dwell in him,
　　1: 25 to you the word of God in its *f* —
　　2: 9 in Christ all the *f* of the Deity lives
　　2: 10 and you have been given *f* in Christ

FULLY (FILL)

1Ki　8: 61 your hearts must be *f* committed
2Ch 16: 9 whose hearts are *f* committed
Ps 119: 4 that are to be *f* obeyed.
　　119:138 they are *f* trustworthy.
Pr　13: 4 of the diligent are *f* satisfied.
Lk　6: 40 everyone who is *f* trained will be
Ro　4: 21 being *f* persuaded that God had
　　14: 5 Each one should be *f* convinced
1Co 13: 12 shall know *f*, even as I am *f* known.
　　15: 58 Always give yourselves *f*
2Ti　4: 17 the message might be *f* proclaimed

FURIOUS (FURY)

Dt 29: 28 In *f* anger and in great wrath
Jer 32: 37 where I banish them in my *f* anger

FURNACE

Isa 48: 10 in the *f* of affliction.
Da 3: 6 be thrown into a blazing *f.*"
Mt 13: 42 will throw them into the fiery *f.*

FURY (FURIOUS)

Isa 14: 6 and in *f* subdued nations
Jer 21: 5 and a mighty arm in anger and *f*
Rev 14: 10 will drink of the wine of God's *f.*
       16: 19 with the wine of the *f* of his wrath
       19: 15 the winepress of the *f* of the wrath

FUTILE (FUTILITY)

Mal 3: 14 You have said, 'It is *f* to serve God.
1Co 3: 20 that the thoughts of the wise are *f.*"

FUTILITY (FUTILE)

Eph 4: 17 in the *f* of their thinking.

FUTURE

Ps 37: 37 there is a *f* for the man of peace.
Pr 23: 18 There is surely a *f* hope for you,
Ecc 7: 14 anything about his *f.*
      8: 7 Since no man knows the *f,*
Jer 29: 11 plans to give you hope and a *f.*
      31: 17 So there is hope for your *f.*"
Ro 8: 38 neither the present nor the *f,*
1Co 3: 22 life or death or the present or the *f*

GABRIEL*

Angel who interpreted Daniel's visions (Da 8: 16-26; 9:20-27); announced births of John (Lk 1: 11-20), Jesus (Lk 1:26-38).

GAD

1. Son of Jacob by Zilpah (Ge 30:9-11; 35:26; 1Ch 2:1). Tribe of blessed (Ge 49:19; Dt 33:20-21), numbered (Nu 1:25; 26:18), allotted land east of the Jordan (Nu 32; 34:14; Jos 18:7; 22), west (Eze 48:27-28), 12,000 from (Rev 7:5).

2. Prophet; seer of David (1Sa 22:5; 2Sa 24: 11-19; 1Ch 29:29).

GAIN (GAINED GAINS)

Ex 14: 17 And I will *g* glory through Pharaoh
Ps 60: 12 With God we will *g* the victory,
Pr 4: 1 pay attention and *g* understanding.
      8: 5 You who are simple, *g* prudence;
      28: 16 he who hates ill-gotten *g* will enjoy
      28: 23 in the end *g* more favor
Isa 63: 12 to *g* for himself everlasting renown
Da 2: 8 that you are trying to *g* time,
Mk 8: 36 it for a man to *g* the whole world,
Lk 9: 25 it for a man to *g* the whole world,
      21: 19 standing firm you will *g* life.
1Co 13: 3 but have not love, I *g* nothing.
Php 1: 21 to live is Christ and to die is *g.*
      3: 8 that I may *g* Christ and be found
1Ti 3: 13 have served well *g* an excellent
      6: 5 godliness is a means to financial *g.*
      6: 6 with contentment is great *g.*

GAINED (GAIN)

Jer 32: 20 have *g* the renown that is still yours
Ro 5: 2 through whom we have *g* access

GAINS (GAIN)

Pr 3: 13 the man who *g* understanding,
      11: 16 A kindhearted woman *g* respect,
      15: 32 heeds correction *g* understanding.
      29: 23 but a man of lowly spirit *g* honor.
Mt 16: 26 for a man if he *g* the whole world,

GALILEE

Isa 9: 1 but in the future he will honor *G*
Mt 4: 15 *G* of the Gentiles—
      26: 32 I will go ahead of you into *G.*"
      28: 10 Go and tell my brothers to go to *G;*

GALL

Mt 27: 34 mixed with *g;* but after tasting it,

GALLIO

Ac 18: 12 While *G* was proconsul of Achaia,

GALLOWS

Est 7: 10 Haman on the *g* he had prepared

GAMALIEL

Ac 5: 34 But a Pharisee named *G,* a teacher

GAMES

1Co 9: 25 in the *g* goes into strict training.

GAP

Eze 22: 30 stand before me in the *g* on behalf

GAPE*

Ps 35: 21 They *g* at me and say, "Aha! Aha!

GARDEN (GARDENER)

Ge 2: 8 the LORD God had planted a *g*
      2: 15 put him in the *G* of Eden to work it
SS 4: 12 You are a *g* locked up, my sister,
Isa 58: 11 You will be like a well-watered *g,*
Jer 31: 12 They will be like a well-watered *g.*
Eze 28: 13 the *g* of God;
      31: 9 Eden in the *g* of God.

GARDENER (GARDEN)

Jn 15: 1 true vine and my Father is the *g.*

GARLAND*

Pr 1: 9 They will be a *g* to grace your head
      4: 9 She will set a *g* of grace

GARMENT (GARMENTS)

Ps 102: 26 they will all wear out like a *g.*
Isa 50: 9 They will all wear out like a *g;*
      51: 6 the earth will wear out like a *g*
      61: 3 and a *g* of praise
Mt 9: 16 of unshrunk cloth on an old *g.*
Jn 19: 23 This *g* was seamless, woven
Heb 1: 11 they will all wear out like a *g.*

GARMENTS (GARMENT)

Ge 3: 21 The LORD God made *g* of skin
Ex 28: 2 Make sacred *g* for your brother
Lev 16: 23 and take off the linen *g* he put
      16: 24 holy place and put on his regular *g.*
Isa 61: 10 me with *g* of salvation
      63: 1 with his *g* stained crimson?
Joel 2: 13 and not your *g.*
Zec 3: 4 and I will put rich *g* on you."
Jn 19: 24 "They divided my *g* among them

GATE (GATES)

Ps 118: 20 This is the *g* of the LORD
Pr 31: 23 husband is respected at the city *g,*
      31: 31 works bring her praise at the city *g.*
Mt 7: 13 For wide is the *g* and broad is
      7: 13 "Enter through the narrow *g.*
Jn 10: 1 not enter the sheep pen by the *g,*
      10: 2 enters by the *g* is the shepherd
      10: 7 "I tell you the truth, I am the *g*
      10: 9 I am the *g;* whoever enters
Heb 13: 12 also suffered outside the city *g*
Rev 21: 21 each *g* made of a single pearl.

GATES (GATE)

Ps 24: 7 Lift up your heads, O you *g;*
      24: 9 Lift up your heads, O you *g;*
      100: 4 Enter his *g* with thanksgiving
      118: 19 Open for me the *g* of righteousness
Isa 60: 11 Your *g* will always stand open,
      60: 18 and your *g* Praise.
      62: 10 Pass through, pass through the *g!*
Mt 16: 18 the *g* of Hades will not overcome it
Rev 21: 12 On the *g* were written the names
      21: 21 The twelve *g* were twelve pearls,
      21: 25 On no day will its *g* ever be shut,
      22: 14 may go through the *g* into the city.

GATH

1Sa 17: 23 the Philistine champion from *G,*
2Sa 1: 20 "Tell it not in *G,*
Mic 1: 10 Tell it not in *G;*

GATHER (GATHERED GATHERS)

Ps 106: 47 and *g* us from the nations,
Isa 11: 12 and *g* the exiles of Israel;
Jer 3: 17 and all nations will *g* in Jerusalem
      23: 3 "I myself will *g* the remnant

GATHER (continued)

Jer 31: 10 who scattered Israel will *g* them
Zep 2: 1 *G* together, *g* together,
      3: 20 At that time I will *g* you;
Zec 14: 2 I will *g* all the nations to Jerusalem
Mt 12: 30 he who does not *g* with me scatters
      13: 30 then *g* the wheat and bring it
      23: 37 longed to *g* your children together,
      24: 31 and they will *g* his elect
      25: 26 *g* where I have not scattered seed?
Mk 13: 27 and *g* his elect from the four winds,
Lk 3: 17 and to *g* the wheat into his barn,
      11: 23 and he who does not *g* with me,
      13: 34 longed to *g* your children together,

GATHERED (GATHER)

Ex 16: 18 and how *g* little did not have too
Pr 30: 4 Who has *g* up the wind
Mt 25: 32 All the nations will be *g* before him
2Co 8: 15 and he who *g* little did not have too
2Th 2: 1 Lord Jesus Christ and our being *g*
Rev 16: 16 Then they *g* the kings together

GATHERS (GATHER)

Ps 147: 2 he *g* the exiles of Israel.
Pr 10: 5 He who *g* crops in summer is a wise
Isa 40: 11 He *g* the lambs in his arms
Mt 23: 37 a hen *g* her chicks under her wings,

GAVE (GIVE)

Ge 2: 20 man *g* names to all the livestock,
      3: 6 She also *g* some to her husband,
      14: 20 Abram *g* him a tenth of everything.
      28: 4 the land God *g* to Abraham."
      35: 12 The land I *g* to Abraham
      39: 23 *g* him success in whatever he did.
      47: 11 *g* them property in the best part
Ex 4: 11 to him, "Who *g* man his mouth?
      31: 18 he *g* him the two tablets
Dt 2: 12 did in the land the LORD *g* them
      2: 36 The LORD our God *g* us all
      3: 12 I *g* the Reubenites and the Gadites
      3: 13 I *g* to the half tribe of Manasseh.
      3: 15 And I *g* Gilead to Makir.
      3: 16 Gadites I *g* the territory extending
      8: 16 He *g* you manna to eat in the desert
      26: 9 us to this place and *g* us this land,
      32: 8 the Most High *g* the nations their
Jos 11: 23 and he *g* it as an inheritance
      13: 14 tribe of Levi he *g* no inheritance,
      14: 13 *g* him Hebron as his inheritance.
      21: 44 The LORD *g* them rest
      24: 13 I *g* you a land on which you did not
1Sa 27: 6 So on that day Achish *g* him Ziklag
2Sa 12: 8 I *g* you the house of Israel
1Ki 4: 29 God *g* Solomon wisdom
      5: 12 The LORD *g* Solomon wisdom,
Ezr 2: 69 According to their ability they *g*
Ne 9: 15 In their hunger you *g* them bread
      9: 20 You *g* your good Spirit
      9: 22 You *g* them kingdoms and nations,
      9: 27 compassion you *g* them deliverers,
Job 1: 21 LORD *g* and the LORD has taken
      42: 10 prosperous again and *g* him twice
Ps 69: 21 and *g* me vinegar for my thirst.
      135: 12 he *g* their land as an inheritance,
Ecc 12: 7 the spirit returns to God who *g* it.
Eze 3: 2 and he *g* me the scroll to eat.
Mt 1: 25 And he *g* him the name Jesus.
      25: 35 and you *g* me something to drink,
      25: 42 and you *g* me nothing to drink,
      26: 26 Jesus took bread, *g* thanks
      27: 50 in a loud voice, he *g* up his spirit.
Mk 6: 7 *g* them authority over evil spirits.
Jn 1: 12 he *g* the right to become children
      3: 16 so loved the world that he *g* his one
      17: 4 by completing the work you *g* me
      17: 6 you *g* them to me and they have
      19: 30 bowed his head and *g* up his spirit.
Ac 1: 3 *g* many convincing proofs that he
      2: 45 they *g* to anyone as he had need.
      11: 17 *g* them the same gift as he *g* us,
Ro 1: 24 Therefore God *g* them
      1: 26 God *g* them over to shameful lusts.
      1: 28 he *g* them over to a depraved mind,
      8: 32 not spare his own Son, but *g* him up
2Co 5: 18 *g* us the ministry of reconciliation:
      8: 3 For I testify that they *g* as much
      8: 5 they *g* themselves first to the Lord

GAZE

Gal 1: 4 who *g* himself for our sins
    2: 20 who loved me and *g* himself for me
Eph 4: 8 and *g* gifts to men.''
    5: 2 as Christ loved us and *g* himself up
    5: 25 and *g* himself up for her
2Th 2: 16 and by his grace *g* us eternal
1Ti 2: 6 who *g* himself as a ransom
Tit 2: 14 who *g* himself for us to redeem us
1Jn 3: 24 We know it by the Spirit he *g* us.

GAZE

Ps 27: 4 to *g* upon the beauty of the LORD
Pr 4: 25 fix your *g* directly before you.

GEDALIAH

Governor of Judah appointed by Nebuchadnezzar (2Ki 25:22-26; Jer 39-41).

GEHAZI*

Servant of Elisha (2Ki 4:12-5:27; 8:4-5).

GENEALOGIES

1Ti 1: 4 themselves to myths and endless *g.*
Tit 3: 9 avoid foolish controversies and *g*

GENERATION (GENERATIONS)

Ex 3: 15 am to be remembered from *g* to *g.*
Nu 32: 13 until the whole *g* of those who had
Dt 1: 35 of this evil *g* shall see the good land
Jdg 2: 10 After that whole *g* had been
Ps 24: 6 Such is the *g* of those who seek him
    48: 13 tell of them to the next *g.*
    71: 18 I declare your power to the next *g,*
    78: 4 we will tell the next *g*
    102: 18 Let this be written for a future *g,*
    112: 2 the *g* of the upright will be blessed
    145: 4 One *g* will commend your works
La 5: 19 your throne endures from *g* to *g.*
Da 4: 3 his dominion endures from *g* to *g.*
    4: 34 his kingdom endures from *g* to *g.*
Joel 1: 3 and their children to the next *g.*
Mt 12: 39 adulterous *g* asks for a miraculous
    17: 17 ''O unbelieving and perverse *g,*''
    23: 36 all this will come upon this *g.*
    24: 34 this *g* will certainly not pass away
Mk 9: 19 ''O unbelieving *g,*'' Jesus replied,
    13: 30 this *g* will certainly not pass away
Lk 1: 50 who fear him, from *g* to *g.*
    11: 29 Jesus said, ''This is a wicked *g.*
    11: 30 will the Son of Man be to this *g.*
    11: 50 Therefore this *g* will be held
    21: 32 this *g* will certainly not pass away
Ac 2: 40 Save yourselves from this corrupt *g*
Php 2: 15 fault in a crooked and depraved *g,*

GENERATIONS (GENERATION)

Ge 9: 12 a covenant for all *g* to come:
    17: 7 after you for the *g* to come,
    17: 9 after you for the *g* to come,
Ex 20: 6 a thousand *g* of those
    31: 13 and you for the *g* to come,
Dt 7: 9 covenant of love to a thousand *g*
    32: 7 consider the *g* long past.
1Ch 16: 15 he commanded, for a thousand *g,*
Job 8: 8 ''Ask the former *g*
Ps 22: 30 future *g* will be told about the Lord
    33: 11 of his heart through all *g.*
    45: 17 your memory through all *g;*
    89: 1 faithfulness known through all *g.*
    90: 1 throughout all *g.*
    100: 5 continues through all *g.*
    102: 12 your renown endures through all *g.*
    105: 8 he commanded, for a thousand *g,*
    119: 90 continues through all *g;*
    135: 13 renown, O LORD, through all *g.*
    145: 13 dominion endures through all *g.*
    146: 10 your God, O Zion, for all *g.*
Pr 27: 24 and a crown is not secure for all *g.*
Isa 41: 4 forth the *g* from the beginning?
    51: 8 my salvation through all *g.*''
Lk 1: 48 now on all *g* will call me blessed,
Eph 3: 5 not made known to men in other *g*
    3: 21 in Christ Jesus throughout all *g,*
Col 1: 26 been kept hidden for ages and *g,*

GENEROSITY* (GENEROUS)

2Co 8: 2 poverty welled up in rich *g.*
    9: 11 and through us your *g* will result

2Co 9: 13 and for your *g* in sharing with them

GENEROUS* (GENEROSITY)

Ps 37: 26 They are always *g* and lend freely;
    112: 5 Good will come to him who is *g*
Pr 11: 25 A *g* man will prosper;
    22: 9 A *g* man will himself be blessed,
Mt 20: 15 Or are you envious because I am *g?*
2Co 9: 5 Then it will be ready as a *g* gift,
    9: 5 for the *g* gift you had promised.
    9: 11 way so that you can be *g*
1Ti 6: 18 and to be *g* and willing to share.

GENTILE (GENTILES)

Ac 21: 25 As for the *G* believers, we have
Ro 1: 16 first for the Jew, then for the *G.*
    2: 9 first for the Jew, then for the *G;*
    2: 10 first for the Jew, then for the *G.*
    10: 12 difference between Jew and *G*—

GENTILES (GENTILE)

Isa 42: 6 and a light for the *G,*
    49: 6 also make you a light for the *G,*
    49: 22 ''See, I will beckon to the *G,*
Lk 2: 32 a light for revelation to the *G*
    21: 24 on by the *G* until the times
Ac 9: 15 to carry my name before the *G*
    10: 45 been poured out even on the *G.*
    11: 18 granted the *G* repentance unto life
    13: 16 and you *G* who worship God,
    13: 46 of eternal life, we now turn to the *G*
    13: 47 I have made you a light for the *G,*
    14: 27 opened the door of faith to the *G.*
    15: 14 by taking from the *G* a people
    18: 6 From now on I will go to the *G.*''
    22: 21 I will send you far away to the *G.*'''
    26: 20 and in all Judea, to the *G* also,
    28: 28 salvation has been sent to the *G.*
Ro 2: 14 when *G,* who do not have the law,
    3: 9 and *G* alike are all under sin.
    3: 29 Is he not the God of *G* too? Yes,
    9: 24 from the Jews but also from the *G?*
    11: 11 to the *G* to make Israel envious.
    11: 12 their loss means riches for the *G,*
    11: 13 as I am the apostle to the *G.*
    15: 9 I will praise you among the *G;*
    15: 9 so that the *G* may glorify God
1Co 1: 23 block to Jews and foolishness to *G,*
Gal 1: 16 I might preach him among the *G,*
    2: 2 gospel that I preach among the *G.*
    2: 8 my ministry as an apostle to the *G.*
    2: 9 agreed that we should go to the *G,*
    3: 8 that God would justify the *G*
    3: 14 to the *G* through Christ Jesus,
Eph 3: 6 the gospel the *G* are heirs together
    3: 8 to the *G* the unsearchable riches
Col 1: 27 among the *G* the glorious riches
1Ti 2: 7 a teacher of the true faith to the *G.*
2Ti 4: 17 and all the *G* might hear it.

GENTLE* (GENTLENESS)

Dt 28: 54 Even the most *g* and sensitive man
    28: 56 The most *g* and sensitive woman
    28: 56 and *g* that she would not venture
2Sa 18: 5 Be *g* with the young man Absalom
1Ki 19: 12 And after the fire came a *g* whisper
Job 41: 3 Will he speak to you with *g* words?
Pr 15: 1 A *g* answer turns away wrath,
    25: 15 and a *g* tongue can break a bone.
Jer 11: 19 I had been like a *g* lamb led
Zec 9: 9 *g* and riding on a donkey,
Mt 11: 29 for I am *g* and humble in heart,
    21: 5 *g* and riding on a donkey,
Ac 27: 13 When a *g* south wind began
1Co 4: 21 or in love and with a *g* spirit?
Eph 4: 2 Be completely humble and *g;*
1Th 2: 7 but we were *g* among you,
1Ti 3: 3 not violent but *g,* not quarrelsome,
1Pe 3: 4 the unfading beauty of a *g*

GENTLENESS* (GENTLE)

2Co 10: 1 By the meekness and *g* of Christ,
Gal 5: 23 faithfulness, *g* and self-control.
Php 4: 5 Let your *g* be evident to all.
Col 3: 12 kindness, humility, *g* and patience.
1Ti 6: 11 faith, love, endurance and *g.*
1Pe 3: 15 But do this with *g* and respect,

GENUINE*

2Co 6: 8 *g,* yet regarded as impostors;
Php 2: 20 who takes a *g* interest
1Pe 1: 7 may be proved *g* and may result

GERIZIM

Dt 27: 12 on Mount *G* to bless the people:

GERSHOM

Ex 2: 22 and Moses named him *G,* saying,

GETHSEMANE*

Mt 26: 36 disciples to a place called *G,*
Mk 14: 32 They went to a place called *G,*

GHOST see also SPIRIT

Lk 24: 39 a *g* does not have flesh and bones,

GIBEON

Jos 10: 12 ''O sun, stand still over *G,*

GIDEON*

Judge, also called Jerub-Baal; freed Israel from
Midianites (Jdg 6-8; Heb 11:32). Given sign of
fleece (Jdg 8:36-40).

GIFT (GIFTED GIFTS)

Pr 18: 16 A *g* opens the way for the giver
    21: 14 A *g* given in secret soothes anger,
Ecc 3: 13 in all his toil—this is the *g* of God.
Mt 5: 23 if you are offering your *g*
Jn 4: 10 ''If you knew the *g* of God
Ac 1: 4 wait for the *g* my Father promised,
    2: 38 And you will receive the *g*
    11: 17 So if God gave them the same *g*
Ro 6: 23 but the *g* of God is eternal life
    12: 6 If a man's *g* is prophesying,
1Co 7: 7 each man has his own *g* from God;
2Co 8: 12 the *g* is acceptable according
    9: 15 be to God for his indescribable *g!*
Eph 2: 8 it is the *g* of God—not by works,
1Ti 4: 14 not neglect your *g,* which was
2Ti 1: 6 you to fan into flame the *g* of God,
Heb 6: 4 who have tasted the heavenly *g,*
Jas 1: 17 and perfect *g* is from above,
1Pe 3: 7 with you of the gracious *g* of life,
    4: 10 should use whatever *g* he has
Rev 22: 17 let him take the free *g* of the water

GIFTED* (GIFT)

1Co 14: 37 he is a prophet or spiritually *g.*

GIFTS (GIFT)

Ps 76: 11 bring *g* to the One to be feared.
    112: 9 He has scattered abroad his *g*
Pr 25: 14 of *g* he does not give.
Mt 2: 11 and presented him with *g* of gold
    7: 11 Father in heaven give good *g*
    7: 11 to give good *g* to your children,
Lk 11: 13 to give good *g* to your children,
Ac 10: 4 and *g* to the poor have come up
Ro 11: 29 for God's *g* and his call are
    12: 6 We have different *g,* according
1Co 12: 1 Now about spiritual *g,* brothers,
    12: 4 There are different kinds of *g,*
    12: 28 those with *g* of administration,
    12: 30 all work miracles? Do all have *g*
    12: 31 But eagerly desire the greater *g.*
    14: 1 and eagerly desire spiritual *g,*
    14: 12 eager to have spiritual *g,*
    14: 12 excel in *g* that build up the church.
2Co 9: 9 ''He has scattered abroad his *g*
Eph 4: 8 and gave *g* to men.''
Heb 2: 4 and *g* of the Holy Spirit distributed
    9: 9 indicating that the *g* and sacrifices

GILEAD

1Ch 27: 21 the half-tribe of Manasseh in *G:*
Jer 8: 22 Is there no balm in *G?*
    46: 11 ''Go up to *G* and get balm,

GILGAL

Jos 5: 9 So the place has been called *G*

GIRD*

Ps 45: 3 *G* your sword upon your side,

GIRL

Ge 24: 16 *g* was very beautiful, a virgin;
2Ki 5: 2 a young *g* from Israel.
Mk 5: 41 Little *g*, I say to you, get up!

GIVE (GAVE GIVEN GIVER GIVES GIVING LIFE-LONG)

Ge 28: 4 you and your descendants the blessing *g* to Abraham
28: 22 that you *g* me I will *g* you a tenth.''
Ex 20: 16 ''You shall not *g* false testimony
30: 15 The rich are not to *g* more
Nu 6: 26 and *g* you peace.'' '
Dt 5: 20 ''You shall not *g* false testimony
15: 10 *G* generously to him and do
15: 14 *G* to him as the LORD your God
1Sa 1: 11 then I will *g* him to the LORD
1: 28 So now I *g* him to the LORD.
2Ch 15: 7 be strong and do not *g* up,
Pr 21: 26 but the righteous *g* without sparing
23: 26 My son, *g* me your heart
25: 21 if he is thirsty, *g* him water to drink
30: 8 but *g* me only my daily bread.
31: 31 *G* her the reward she has earned,
Ecc 3: 6 a time to search and a time to *g* up,
Isa 42: 8 I will not *g* my glory to another
Eze 36: 26 I will *g* you a new heart
Mt 6: 11 *G* us today our daily bread.
7: 11 know how to *g* good gifts
10: 8 Freely you have received, freely *g*.
16: 19 I will *g* you the keys
22: 21 ''*G* to Caesar what is Caesar's,
Mk 8: 37 Or what can a man *g* in exchange
10: 19 not steal, do not *g* false testimony,
Lk 6: 38 *G*, and it will be given to you.
11: 3 *G* us each day our daily bread.
11: 13 Father in heaven *g* the Holy Spirit
14: 33 who does not *g* up everything he
Jn 10: 28 I *g* them eternal life, and they shall
13: 34 ''A new commandment I *g* you:
14: 16 he will *g* you another Counselor
14: 27 I do not *g* to you as the world gives.
14: 27 leave with you; my peace I *g* you.
17: 2 people that he might *g* eternal life
Ac 20: 35 blessed to *g* than to receive.' ''
Ro 2: 7 immortality, he will *g* eternal life.
8: 32 with him, graciously *g* us all things
12: 8 let him *g* generously;
13: 7 *G* everyone what you owe him:
14: 12 each of us will *g* an account
2Co 9: 7 Each man should *g* what he has
Gal 2: 5 We did not *g* in to them
6: 9 reap a harvest if we do not *g* up.
Heb 10: 25 Let us not *g* up meeting together,
Rev 14: 7 ''Fear God and *g* him glory,

GIVEN (GIVE)

Nu 8: 16 are to be *g* wholly to me.
Dt 26: 11 things the LORD your God has *g*
Job 3: 23 Why is life *g* to a man
Ps 115: 16 but the earth he has *g* to man.
Isa 9: 6 to us a son is *g*,
Mt 6: 33 and all these things will be *g* to you
7: 7 ''Ask and it will be *g* to you;
13: 12 Whoever has will be *g* more.
22: 30 people will neither marry nor be *g*
25: 29 everyone who has will be *g* more,
Lk 6: 38 Give, and it will be *g* to you.
8: 10 kingdom of God has been *g* to you,
11: 9 Ask and it will be *g* to you;
22: 19 saying, ''This is my body *g* for you;
Jn 3: 27 man can receive only what is *g* him
15: 7 you wish, and it will be *g* you.
17: 24 I want those you have *g* me to be
17: 24 the glory you have *g* me
18: 11 the cup the Father has *g* me?''
Ac 5: 32 whom God has *g* to those who
20: 24 the task the Lord Jesus has *g* me—
Ro 5: 5 the Holy Spirit, whom he has *g* us.
1Co 4: 2 those who have been *g* a trust must
11: 24 and when he had *g* thanks,
12: 13 we were all *g* the one Spirit to drink
2Co 5: 5 and has *g* us the Spirit as a deposit,
Gal 2: 7 they saw that I had been *g* the task
Eph 1: 6 which he has freely *g* us
4: 7 to each one of us grace has been *g*
1Ti 4: 14 was *g* you through a prophetic

1Jn 4: 13 because he has *g* us of his Spirit.

GIVER* (GIVE)

Pr 18: 16 A gift opens the way for the *g*
2Co 9: 7 for God loves a cheerful *g*.

GIVES (GIVE)

Job 35: 10 who *g* songs in the night,
Ps 119:130 The entrance of your words *g* light;
Pr 3: 34 but *g* grace to the humble.
11: 24 One man *g* freely, yet gains
14: 30 A heart at peace *g* life to the body,
15: 30 good news *g* health to the bones.
19: 6 of a man who *g* gifts.
25: 26 is a righteous man who *g* way
28: 27 He who *g* to the poor will lack
29: 4 justice a king *g* a country stability,
Isa 40: 29 He *g* strength to the weary
Hab 2: 15 ''Woe to him who *g* drink
Mt 10: 42 And if anyone *g* a cup of cold water
Jn 5: 21 even so the Son *g* life to whom he is
6: 63 The Spirit *g* life; the flesh counts
1Co 15: 57 He *g* us the victory
2Co 3: 6 the letter kills, but the Spirit *g* life.
1Th 4: 8 who *g* you his Holy Spirit.
Jas 1: 25 into the perfect law that *g* freedom,
4: 6 but *g* grace to the humble.''
1Pe 5: 5 but *g* grace to the humble.''

GIVING (GIVE)

Ne 8: 8 *g* the meaning so that the people
Est 9: 19 a day for *g* presents to each other.
Ps 19: 8 *g* joy to the heart.
Pr 15: 23 A man finds joy in *g* an apt reply—
Mt 6: 4 so that your *g* may be in secret.
24: 38 marrying and *g* in marriage,
Ac 15: 8 them by *g* the Holy Spirit to them,
2Co 8: 7 also excel in this grace of *g*.
Php 4: 15 shared with me in the matter of *g*

GLAD* (GLADDENS GLADNESS)

Ex 4: 14 his heart will be *g* when he sees you
Jos 22: 33 They were *g* to hear the report
Jdg 8: 25 ''We'll be *g* to give them.''
18: 20 household?'' Then the priest was *g*.
1Sa 19: 5 and you saw it and were *g*.
2Sa 1: 20 daughters of the Philistines be *g*,
1Ki 8: 66 *g* in heart for all the good things
1Ch 16: 31 heavens rejoice, let the earth be *g*;
2Ch 7: 10 and *g* in heart for the good things
Ps 5: 11 let all who take refuge in you be *g*;
9: 2 I will be *g* and rejoice in you;
14: 7 let Jacob rejoice and Israel be *g*!
16: 9 Therefore my heart is *g*
21: 6 made him *g* with the joy
31: 7 I will be *g* and rejoice in your love,
32: 11 Rejoice in the LORD and be *g*,
40: 16 rejoice and be *g* in you;
45: 8 music of the strings makes you *g*.
46: 4 whose streams make *g* the city
48: 11 the villages of Judah are *g*
53: 6 let Jacob rejoice and Israel be *g*!
58: 10 The righteous will be *g*
67: 4 May the nations be *g* and sing
68: 3 But may the righteous be *g*
69: 32 The poor will see and be *g*—
70: 4 rejoice and be *g* in you;
90: 14 for joy and be *g* all our days.
90: 15 Make us *g* for as many days
92: 4 For you make me *g* by your deeds,
96: 11 heavens rejoice, let the earth be *g*;
97: 1 LORD reigns, let the earth be *g*;
97: 8 and the villages of Judah are *g*
105: 38 Egypt was *g* when they left,
107: 30 They were *g* when it grew calm,
118: 24 let us rejoice and be *g* in it.
149: 2 of Zion be *g* in their King.
Pr 23: 15 then my heart will be *g*;
23: 25 May your father and mother be *g*;
29: 6 a righteous one can sing and be *g*.
Ecc 8: 15 sun than to eat and drink and be *g*.
Isa 25: 9 let us rejoice and be *g*
35: 1 and the parched land will be *g*;
65: 18 But be *g* and rejoice forever
66: 10 with Jerusalem and be *g*
Jer 20: 15 who made him very *g*, saying,
31: 13 Then maidens will dance and be *g*,
41: 13 were with him, they were *g*.

Jer 50: 11 ''Because you rejoice and are *g*,
La 4: 21 be *g*, O Daughter of Edom,
Joel 2: 21 be *g* and rejoice.
2: 23 Be *g*, O people of Zion,
Hab 1: 15 and so he rejoices and is *g*.
Zep 3: 14 Be *g* and rejoice with all your heart
Zec 2: 10 and be *g*, O Daughter of Zion.
8: 19 will become joyful and *g* occasions
10: 7 their hearts will be *g* as with wine.
Mt 5: 12 be *g*, because great is your reward
Lk 15: 32 But we had to celebrate and be *g*,
Jn 4: 36 and the reaper may be *g* together.
8: 56 my day; he saw it and was *g*.''
11: 15 for your sake I am *g* I was not there
14: 28 you would be *g* that I am going
Ac 2: 26 Therefore my heart is *g*
2: 46 together with *g* and sincere hearts,
11: 23 he was *g* and encouraged them all
13: 48 they were *g* and honored the word
15: 3 news made all the brothers very *g*.
15: 31 were *g* for its encouraging message.
1Co 16: 17 was *g* when Stephanas, Fortunatus
2Co 2: 2 who is left to make me *g*
7: 16 I am *g* I can have complete
13: 9 We are *g* whenever we are weak
Gal 4: 27 ''Be *g*, O barren woman,
Php 2: 17 I am *g* and rejoice with all of you.
2: 18 So you too should be *g* and rejoice
2: 28 you see him again you may be *g*
Rev 19: 7 Let us rejoice and be *g*

GLADDENS* (GLAD)

Ps 104: 15 wine that *g* the heart of man,

GLADNESS* (GLAD)

2Ch 29: 30 So they sang praises with *g*
Est 8: 16 a time of happiness and joy, *g*
8: 17 there was joy and *g*
Job 3: 22 who are filled with *g*
Ps 35: 27 shout for joy and *g*;
45: 15 They are led in with joy and *g*;
51: 8 Let me hear joy and *g*;
65: 12 the hills are clothed with *g*.
100: 2 Worship the LORD with *g*;
Ecc 5: 20 God keeps him occupied with *g*
9: 7 Go, eat your food with *g*,
Isa 16: 10 *g* are taken away from the orchards
35: 10 *G* and joy will overtake them,
51: 3 Joy and *g* will be found in her,
51: 11 *G* and joy will overtake them,
61: 3 the oil of joy / instead of mourning,
Jer 7: 34 and *g* and to the voices of bride
16: 9 and *g* and to the voices of bride
25: 10 from them the sounds of joy and *g*,
31: 13 I will turn their mourning into *g*;
33: 11 once more the sounds of joy and *g*,
48: 33 Joy and *g* are gone
Joel 1: 16 joy and *g*

GLAZE*

Pr 26: 23 of *g* over earthenware

GLEAM*

Pr 4: 18 of the righteous is like the first *g*
Da 10: 6 legs like the *g* of burnished bronze,

GLOAT (GLOATS)

Pr 24: 17 Do not *g* when your enemy falls;

GLOATS* (GLOAT)

Pr 17: 5 whoever *g* over disaster will not go

GLORIES* (GLORY)

1Pe 1: 11 and the *g* that would follow.

GLORIFIED* (GLORY)

Isa 66: 5 'Let the LORD be *g*,
Eze 39: 13 day I am *g* will be a memorable day
Da 4: 34 and *g* him who lives forever.
Jn 7: 39 since Jesus had not yet been *g*.
11: 4 glory so that God's Son may be *g*
12: 16 after Jesus was *g* did they realize
12: 23 come for the Son of Man to be *g*.
12: 28 ''I have *g* it, and will glorify it again
13: 31 Son of Man *g* and God is in him.
13: 32 If God is *g* in him, God will glorify
Ac 3: 13 our fathers, has *g* his servant Jesus.
Ro 1: 21 they neither *g* him as God

Ro 8:30 those he justified, he also *g*.
2Th 1:10 comes to be *g* in his holy people
　　 1:12 of our Lord Jesus may be *g* in you,
1Pe 1:21 him from the dead and *g* him,

GLORIFIES* (GLORY)

Lk 1:46 My soul *g* the Lord
Jn 8:54 as your God, is the one who *g* me.

GLORIFY* (GLORY)

Ps 34: 3 *G* the LORD with me;
　　 63: 3 my lips will *g* you.
　　 69:30 and *g* him with thanksgiving.
　　 86:12 I will *g* your name forever.
Isa 60:13 and I will *g* the place of my feet.
Da 4:37 and exalt and *g* the King of heaven,
Jn 14:13 Jesus replied, "If I *g* myself,
　　 12:28 glorified it, and will *g* it again."
　　 12:28 *g* your name!" Then a voice came
　　 13:32 God will *g* the Son in himself,
　　 13:32 in himself, and will *g* him at once.
　　 17: 1 *G* your Son, that your Son may
　　 17: 1 your Son, that your Son may *g* you.
　　 17: 5 *g* me in your presence
　　 21:19 death by which Peter would *g* God.
Ro 15: 6 and mouth you may *g* the God
　　 15: 9 so that the Gentiles may *g* God
1Pe 2:12 and *g* God on the day he visits us.
Rev 16: 9 they refused to repent and *g* him.

GLORIFYING* (GLORY)

Lk 2:20 *g* and praising God

GLORIOUS* (GLORY)

Dt 28:58 not revere this *g* and awesome
　　 33:29 and your *g* sword.
1Ch 29:13 and praise your *g* name.
Ne 9: 5 "Blessed be your *g* name,
Ps 16: 3 they are the *g* ones
　　 45:13 All *g* is the princess
　　 66: 2 make his praise *g*.
　　 72:19 Praise be to his *g* name forever;
　　 87: 3 *G* things are said of you,
　　 111: 3 *G* and majestic are his deeds,
　　 145: 5 of the *g* splendor of your majesty,
　　 145:12 the *g* splendor of your kingdom.
Isa 3: 8 defying his *g* presence.
　　 4: 2 the LORD will be beautiful and *g*,
　　 11:10 and his place of rest will be *g*.
　　 12: 5 for he has done *g* things;
　　 28: 1 to the fading flower, his *g* beauty,
　　 28: 4 That fading flower, his *g* beauty,
　　 28: 5 will be a *g* crown,
　　 42:21 to make his law great and *g*.
　　 60: 7 and I will adorn my *g* temple.
　　 63:12 who sent his *g* arm of power
　　 63:14 to make for yourself a *g* name.
　　 63:15 from your lofty throne, holy and *g*.
　　 64:11 *g* temple, where our fathers praised
Jer 13:18 for your *g* crowns
　　 14:21 do not dishonor your *g* throne,
　　 17:12 A *g* throne, exalted
　　 48:17 how broken the *g* staff!'
Mt 19:28 the Son of Man sits on his *g* throne,
Lk 9:31 appeared in *g* splendor, talking
Ac 2:20 of the great and *g* day of the Lord.
Ro 8:21 and brought into the *g* freedom
2Co 3: 8 of the Spirit be even more *g*?
　　 3: 9 how much more *g* is the ministry
　　 3: 9 ministry that condemns men is *g*,
　　 3:10 For what was *g* has no glory now
Eph 1: 6 to the praise of his *g* grace,
　　 1:17 *g* Father, may give you the Spirit
　　 1:18 the riches of his *g* inheritance
　　 3:16 of his *g* riches he may strengthen
Php 3:21 so that they will be like his *g* body,
　　 4:19 to his *g* riches in Christ Jesus.
Col 1:11 all power according to his *g* might
　　 1:27 among the Gentiles the *g* riches
1Ti 1:11 to the *g* gospel of the blessed God,
Tit 2:13 the *g* appearing of our great God
Jas 2: 1 believers in our *g* Lord Jesus Christ
1Pe 1: 8 with an inexpressible and *g* joy,
Jude : 24 before his *g* presence without fault

GLORIOUSLY* (GLORY)

Isa 24:23 and before its elders, *g*.

GLORY (GLORIES GLORIFIED GLORIFIES GLORIFY GLORIFYING GLORIOUS GLORIOUSLY)

Ex 14: 4 But I will gain *g* for myself
　　 14:17 And I will gain *g* through Pharaoh
　　 15:11 awesome in *g*,
　　 16:10 and there was the *g* of the LORD
　　 24:16 and the *g* of the LORD settled
　　 33:18 Moses said, "Now show me your *g*
　　 40:34 and the *g* of the LORD filled
Nu 14:21 the *g* of the LORD fills the whole
Dt 5:24 LORD our God has shown us his *g*
Jos 7:19 "My son, give *g* to the LORD,
'1Sa 4:21 "The *g* has departed from Israel"—
1Ch 16:10 *G* in his holy name;
　　 16:24 Declare his *g* among the nations,
　　 16:28 ascribe to the LORD *g*
　　 29:11 and the *g* and the majesty
Ps 8: 1 You have set your *g*
　　 8: 5 and crowned him with *g* and honor
　　 19: 1 The heavens declare the *g* of God;
　　 24: 7 that the King of *g* may come in.
　　 26: 8 the place where your *g* dwells.
　　 29: 1 ascribe to the LORD *g*
　　 29: 9 And in his temple all cry, "*G*!"
　　 57: 5 let your *g* be over all the earth.
　　 66: 2 Sing the *g* of his name;
　　 72:19 the whole earth be filled with his *g*.
　　 96: 3 Declare his *g* among the nations,
　　 102:15 of the earth will revere your *g*.
　　 108: 5 and let your *g* be over all the earth.
　　 149: 9 This is the *g* of all his saints.
Pr 19:11 it is to his *g* to overlook an offense.
　　 25: 2 It is the *g* of God to conceal
Isa 4: 5 over all the *g* will be a canopy.
　　 6: 3 the whole earth is full of his *g*."
　　 24:16 "*G* to the Righteous One."
　　 26:15 You have gained *g* for yourself;
　　 35: 2 they will see the *g* of the LORD,
　　 40: 5 the *g* of the LORD will be revealed
　　 42: 8 I will not give my *g* to another
　　 42:12 Let them give *g* to the LORD
　　 43: 7 whom I created for my *g*,
　　 44:23 he displays his *g* in Israel.
　　 48:11 I will not yield my *g* to another.
　　 66:18 and they will come and see my *g*.
　　 66:19 They will proclaim my *g*
Eze 1:28 the likeness of the *g* of the LORD.
　　 10: 4 the radiance of the *g* of the LORD.
　　 43: 2 and the land was radiant with his *g*.
　　 44: 4 and saw the *g* of the LORD filling
Hab 2:14 knowledge of the *g* of the LORD,
　　 3: 3 His *g* covered the heavens
Zec 2: 5 'and I will be its *g* within.'
Mt 16:27 in his Father's *g* with his angels,
　　 24:30 of the sky, with power and great *g*.
　　 25:31 sit on his throne in heavenly *g*,
　　 25:31 the Son of Man comes in his *g*,
Mk 8:38 in his Father's *g* with the holy
　　 13:26 in clouds with great power and *g*.
Lk 2: 9 and the *g* of the Lord shone
　　 2:14 saying, "*G* to God in the highest,
　　 9:26 and in the *g* of the Father
　　 9:26 of him when he comes in his *g*
　　 9:32 they saw his *g* and the two men
　　 19:38 in heaven and *g* in the highest!"
　　 21:27 in a cloud with power and great *g*.
　　 24:26 these things and then enter his *g*?"
Jn 1:14 We have seen his *g*, the *g* of the One
　　 2:11 He thus revealed his *g*,
　　 8:50 I am not seeking *g* for myself;
　　 8:54 myself, my *g* means nothing.
　　 11: 4 for God's *g* so that God's Son may
　　 11:40 you would see the *g* of God?"
　　 12:41 he saw Jesus' *g* and spoke about
　　 14:13 so that the Son may bring *g*
　　 15: 8 is to my Father's *g*, that you bear
　　 16:14 He will bring *g* to me by taking
　　 17: 4 I have brought you *g* on earth
　　 17: 5 presence with the *g* I had with you
　　 17:10 *g* has come to me through them.
　　 17:22 given them the *g* that you gave
　　 17:24 to see my *g*, the *g* you have given
Ac 2: 2 The God of *g* appeared
　　 7:55 up to heaven and saw the *g* of God,
Ro 1:23 exchanged the *g* of the immortal
　　 2: 7 by persistence in doing good seek *g*

Ro 2:10 then for the Gentile; but *g*,
　　 3: 7 truthfulness and so increases his *g*,
　　 3:23 and fall short of the *g* of God,
　　 4:20 in his faith and gave *g* to God,
　　 8:17 that we may also share in his *g*.
　　 8:18 with the *g* that will be revealed
　　 9: 4 theirs the divine *g*, the covenants,
　　 9:23 riches of his *g* known to the objects
　　 9:23 whom he prepared in advance for *g*
　　 11:36 To him be the *g* forever! Amen.
　　 15:17 Therefore I *g* in Christ Jesus
　　 16:27 to the only wise God be *g* forever
1Co 2: 7 for our *g* before time began.
　　 10:31 whatever you do, do it all for the *g*
　　 11: 7 but the woman is the *g* of man.
　　 11: 7 since he is the image and *g* of God;
　　 11:15 it is her *g*? For long hair is given
　　 15:43 it is raised in *g*; it is sown
2Co 1:20 spoken by us to the *g* of God.
　　 3: 7 in letters on stone, came with *g*,
　　 3: 7 the face of Moses because of its *g*,
　　 3:10 comparison with the surpassing *g*.
　　 3:10 what was glorious has no *g* now
　　 3:11 how much greater is the *g*
　　 3:11 what was fading away came with *g*,
　　 3:18 faces all reflect the Lord's *g*,
　　 3:18 likeness with ever-increasing *g*,
　　 4: 4 of the gospel of the *g* of Christ,
　　 4: 6 of the knowledge of the *g* of God
　　 4:15 to overflow to the *g* of God.
　　 4:17 us an eternal *g* that far outweighs
Gal 1: 5 to whom be *g* for ever and ever.
Eph 1:12 might be for the praise of his *g*.
　　 1:14 to the praise of his *g*.
　　 3:13 for you, which are your *g*.
　　 3:21 to him be *g* in the church
Php 1:11 to the *g* and praise of God.
　　 2:11 to the *g* of God the Father.
　　 3: 3 of God, who *g* in Christ Jesus,
　　 4:20 and Father be *g* for ever and ever.
Col 1:27 Christ in you, the hope of *g*.
　　 3: 4 also will appear with him in *g*.
1Th 2:12 you into his kingdom and *g*.
　　 2:19 in which we will *g* in the presence
　　 2:20 Indeed, you are our *g* and joy.
2Th 2:14 in the *g* of our Lord Jesus Christ.
1Ti 1:17 be honor and *g* for ever and ever.
　　 3:16 was taken up in *g*.
2Ti 2:10 is in Christ Jesus, with eternal *g*.
　　 4:18 To him be *g* for ever and ever.
Heb 1: 3 The Son is the radiance of God's *g*
　　 2: 7 you crowned him with *g* and honor
　　 2: 9 now crowned with *g* and honor
　　 2:10 In bringing many sons to *g*,
　　 5: 5 take upon himself the *g*
　　 9: 5 the ark were the cherubim of the *G*,
　　 13:21 to whom be *g* for ever and ever.
1Pe 1: 7 *g* and honor when Jesus Christ is
　　 1:24 and all their *g* is like the flowers
　　 4:11 To him be the *g* and the power
　　 4:13 overjoyed when his *g* is revealed.
　　 4:14 for the Spirit of *g* and of God rests
　　 5: 1 will share in the *g* to be revealed:
　　 5: 4 of *g* that will never fade away.
　　 5:10 you to his eternal *g* in Christ,
2Pe 1: 3 of him who called us by his own *g*
　　 1:17 and *g* from God the Father
　　 1:17 came to him from the Majestic *G*,
　　 3:18 To him be *g* both now and forever!
Jude : 25 to the only God our Savior be *g*,
Rev 1: 6 to him be *g* and power for ever
　　 4: 9 the living creatures give *g*,
　　 4:11 to receive *g* and honor and power,
　　 5:12 and honor and *g* and praise!"
　　 5:13 and honor and *g* and power,
　　 7:12 Praise and *g*
　　 11:13 and gave *g* to the God of heaven.
　　 14: 7 "Fear God and give him *g*,
　　 15: 4 and bring *g* to your name?
　　 15: 8 with smoke from the *g* of God
　　 19: 1 *g* and power belong to our God,
　　 19: 7 and give him *g*!
　　 21:11 It shone with the *g* of God,
　　 21:23 for the *g* of God gives it light,
　　 21:26 *g* and honor of the nations will be

GLOWING

Eze 8: 2 was as bright as *g* metal.

Rev 1: 15 His feet were like bronze *g*

GLUTTONS* (GLUTTONY)

Pr 23: 21 for drunkards and *g* become poor,
28: 7 of *g* disgraces his father.
Tit 1: 12 always liars, evil brutes, lazy *g*."

GLUTTONY* (GLUTTONS)

Pr 23: 2 throat if you are given to *g*.

GNASHING

Mt 8: 12 where there will be weeping and *g*

GNAT* (GNATS)

Mt 23: 24 You strain out a *g* but swallow

GNATS (GNAT)

Ex 8: 16 of Egypt will become *g*."

GOADS

Ecc 12: 11 The words of the wise are like *g*.
Ac 26: 14 hard for you to kick against the *g*.'

GOAL*

Lk 13: 32 on the third day I will reach my *g*.'
2Co 5: 9 So we make it our *g* to please him,
Gal 3: 3 to attain your *g* by human effort?
Php 3: 14 on toward the *g* to win the prize
1Ti 1: 5 The *g* of this command is love,
1Pe 1: 9 for you are receiving the *g*

GOAT (GOATS SCAPEGOAT)

Ge 15: 9 "Bring me a heifer, a *g* and a ram,
30: 32 and every spotted or speckled *g*.
37: 31 slaughtered a *g* and dipped
Ex 26: 7 Make curtains of *g* hair for the tent
Lev 16: 9 shall bring the *g* whose lot falls
Nu 7: 16 one male *g* for a sin offering;
Isa 11: 6 the leopard will lie down with the *g*
Da 8: 5 suddenly a *g* with a prominent

GOATS (GOAT)

Nu 7: 17 five male *g* and five male lambs
Mt 25: 32 separates the sheep from the *g*.
Heb 10: 4 of bulls and *g* to take away sins.

GOD (GOD'S GODLINESS GODLY GODS)

Ge 1: 1 In the beginning *G* created
1: 2 and the Spirit of *G* was hovering
1: 3 And *G* said, "Let there be light,"
1: 7 So *G* made the expanse
1: 9 And *G* said, "Let the water
1: 11 Then *G* said, "Let the land produce
1: 20 And *G* said, "Let the water teem
1: 21 So *G* created the great creatures
1: 25 *G* made the wild animals according
1: 26 Then *G* said, "Let us make man
1: 27 So *G* created man in his own image
1: 31 *G* saw all that he had made,
2: 3 And *G* blessed the seventh day
2: 7 And the Lord *G* formed the man
2: 8 the Lord *G* had planted a garden
2: 18 The Lord *G* said, "It is not good
2: 22 Then the Lord *G* made a woman
3: 1 to the woman, "Did *G* really say,
3: 5 you will be like *G*, knowing good
3: 8 from the Lord *G* among the trees
3: 9 But the Lord *G* called to the man
3: 21 The Lord *G* made garments
3: 22 Lord *G* said, "The man has now
3: 23 So the Lord *G* banished him
5: 1 When *G* created man, he made him
5: 22 Enoch walked with *G* 300 years
5: 24 because *G* took him away.
6: 2 sons of *G* saw that the daughters
6: 9 of his time, and he walked with *G*.
6: 12 *G* saw how corrupt the earth had
8: 1 But *G* remembered Noah
9: 1 Then *G* blessed Noah and his sons,
9: 6 for in the image of *G*
9: 16 everlasting covenant between *G*
14: 18 He was priest of *G* Most High,
14: 19 Blessed be Abram by *G* Most High,
16: 13 "You are the *G* who sees me,"
17: 1 "I am *G* Almighty; walk before me
17: 7 to be your *G* and the *G*
21: 4 him, as *G* commanded him.

Ge 21: 6 "*G* has brought me laughter,
21: 20 *G* was with the boy as he grew up.
21: 22 *G* is with you in everything you do.
21: 33 name of the Lord, the Eternal *G*.
22: 1 Some time later *G* tested Abraham.
22: 8 "*G* himself will provide the lamb
22: 12 Now I know that you fear *G*,
25: 11 Abraham's death, *G* blessed his
28: 12 and the angels of *G* were ascending
28: 17 other than the house of *G*;
31: 42 But *G* has seen my hardship
31: 50 remember that *G* is a witness
32: 1 and the angels of *G* met him.
32: 28 because you have struggled with *G*
32: 30 "It is because I saw *G* face to face,
33: 11 for *G* has been gracious to me
35: 1 and build an altar there to *G*,
35: 5 and the terror of *G* fell
35: 10 *G* said to him, "Your name is Jacob
35: 11 *G* said to him, "I am *G* Almighty;
41: 51 *G* has made me forget all my
41: 52 *G* has made me fruitful in the land
50: 20 but *G* intended it for good
50: 24 But *G* will surely come to your aid

Ex 2: 24 *G* heard their groaning
3: 5 "Do not come any closer," *G* said.
3: 6 because he was afraid to look at *G*.
3: 12 And *G* said, "I will be with you.
3: 14 what shall I tell them?" *G* said
4: 27 he met Moses at the mountain of *G*
6: 7 own people, and I will be your *G*.
8: 10 is no one like the Lord our *G*.
10: 16 sinned against the Lord your *G*
13: 18 So *G* led the people
15: 2 He is my *G*, and I will praise him,
16: 12 that I am the Lord your *G*.' "
17: 9 with the staff of *G* in my hands."
18: 5 camped near the mountain of *G*.
19: 3 Then Moses went up to *G*,
20: 1 And *G* spoke all these words:
20: 2 the Lord your *G*, who brought
20: 5 the Lord your *G*, am a jealous *G*,
20: 7 the name of the Lord your *G*,
20: 10 a Sabbath to the Lord your *G*.
20: 12 the Lord your *G* is giving you.
20: 19 But do not have *G* speak to us
20: 20 the fear of *G* will be with you
22: 20 "Whoever sacrifices to any *g* other
22: 28 "Do not blaspheme *G*
23: 19 to the house of the Lord your *G*.
31: 18 inscribed by the finger of *G*,
34: 6 the compassionate and gracious *G*,
34: 14 name is Jealous, is a jealous *G*.

Lev 2: 13 salt of the covenant of your *G* out
11: 44 the Lord your *G*; consecrate
18: 21 not profane the name of your *G*.
19: 2 the Lord your *G*, am holy.
20: 7 because I am the Lord your *G*.
21: 6 They must be holy to their *G*
22: 33 out of Egypt to be your *G*.
26: 12 walk among you and be your *G*,

Nu 15: 40 and will be consecrated to your *G*.
22: 18 the command of the Lord my *G*.
22: 38 I must speak only what *G* puts
23: 19 *G* is not a man, that he should lie.
25: 13 zealous for the honor of his *G*

Dt 1: 17 for judgment belongs to *G*.
1: 21 the Lord your *G* has given you
1: 30 The Lord your *G*, who is going
3: 22 Lord your *G* himself will fight
3: 24 For what *g* is there in heaven
4: 24 is a consuming fire, a jealous *G*.
4: 29 there you seek the Lord your *G*,
4: 31 the Lord your *G* is a merciful *G*;
4: 39 heart this day that the Lord is *G*
5: 9 the Lord your *G*, am a jealous *G*,
5: 11 the name of the Lord your *G*,
5: 12 the Lord your *G* has commanded
5: 14 a Sabbath to the Lord your *G*.
5: 15 the Lord your *G* brought you out
5: 16 the Lord your *G* has commanded
5: 16 the Lord your *G* is giving you.
5: 24 Lord our *G* has shown us his
5: 26 of the living *G* speaking out of fire,
6: 2 them may fear the Lord your *G*
6: 4 Lord our *G*, the Lord is one.
6: 5 Love the Lord your *G*
6: 13 the Lord your *G*, serve him only

Dt 6: 16 Do not test the Lord your *G*
7: 6 holy to the Lord your *G*.
7: 9 your *G* is *G*; he is the faithful *G*,
7: 12 the Lord your *G* will keep his
7: 19 Lord your *G* will do the same
7: 21 is a great and awesome *G*.
8: 5 the Lord your *G* disciplines you.
8: 11 do not forget the Lord your *G*,
8: 18 But remember the Lord your *G*,
9: 10 inscribed by the finger of *G*.
10: 12 but to fear the Lord your *G*,
10: 14 the Lord your *G* belong
10: 17 For the Lord your *G* is *G* of gods
10: 21 He is your praise; he is your *G*,
11: 1 Love the Lord your *G*
11: 13 to love the Lord your *G*
12: 12 rejoice before the Lord your *G*,
12: 28 in the eyes of the Lord your *G*.
13: 3 The Lord your *G* is testing you
13: 4 the Lord your *G* you must
15: 6 the Lord your *G* will bless you
15: 19 the Lord your *G* every firstborn
16: 11 rejoice before the Lord your *G*,
16: 17 the Lord your *G* has blessed you.
18: 13 before the Lord your *G*.
18: 15 The Lord your *G* will raise up
19: 9 to love the Lord your *G*
22: 5 the Lord your *G* detests anyone
23: 5 the Lord your *G* loves you.
23: 14 the Lord your *G* moves about
23: 21 a vow to the Lord your *G*,
25: 16 the Lord your *G* detests anyone
26: 5 declare before the Lord your *G*;
29: 13 that he may be your *G*
29: 29 belong to the Lord our *G*,
30: 2 return to the Lord your *G*
30: 4 the Lord your *G* will gather you
30: 6 The Lord your *G* will circumcise
30: 16 today to love the Lord your *G*,
30: 20 you may love the Lord your *G*,
31: 6 for the Lord your *G* goes
32: 3 Oh, praise the greatness of our *G*!
32: 4 A faithful *G* who does no wrong,
33: 27 The eternal *G* is your refuge,

Jos 1: 9 for the Lord your *G* will be
14: 8 the Lord my *G* wholeheartedly.
14: 9 the Lord my *G* wholeheartedly.'
14: 14 the *G* of Israel, wholeheartedly.
22: 5 to love the Lord your *G*,
22: 22 The Mighty One, *G*, the Lord!
22: 34 Between Us that the Lord is *G*.
23: 8 to hold fast to the Lord your *G*,
23: 11 careful to love the Lord your *G*.
23: 14 the Lord your *G* gave you has
23: 15 of the Lord your *G* has come true
24: 19 He is a holy *G*; he is a jealous *G*.
24: 23 to the Lord, the *G* of Israel.

Jdg 5: 3 to the Lord, the *G* of Israel.
16: 28 O *G*, please strengthen me just

Ru 1: 16 be my people and your *G* my *G*.
2: 12 by the Lord, the *G* of Israel,

1Sa 2: 2 there is no Rock like our *G*.
2: 3 for the Lord is a *G* who knows,
2: 25 another man, *G* may mediate
10: 26 men whose hearts *G* had touched.
12: 12 the Lord your *G* was your king.
16: 15 spirit from *G* is tormenting you.
17: 26 defy the armies of the living *G*?"
17: 36 defied the armies of the living *G*.
17: 45 the *G* of the armies of Israel,
17: 46 world will know that there is a *G*
23: 16 and helped him find strength in *G*.
28: 15 and *G* has turned away from me.
30: 6 strength in the Lord his *G*.

2Sa 7: 22 and there is no *G* but you,
7: 23 on earth that *G* went out to redeem
14: 14 But *G* does not take away life;
21: 14 *G* answered prayer in behalf
22: 3 my *G* is my rock, in whom I take
22: 31 "As for *G*, his way is perfect;
22: 32 And who is the Rock except our *G*
22: 33 It is *G* who arms me with strength
22: 47 Exalted be *G*, the Rock, my Savior!

1Ki 2: 3 what the Lord your *G* requires:
4: 29 *G* gave Solomon wisdom
5: 5 for the Name of the Lord my *G*,
8: 23 there is no *G* like you in heaven
8: 27 "But will *G* really dwell on earth?

1Ki 8: 60 may know that the LORD is *G*
    8: 61 committed to the LORD our *G*,
   10: 24 to hear the wisdom *G* had put
   15: 30 he provoked the LORD, the *G*
   18: 21 If the LORD is *G*, follow him;
   18: 36 it be known today that you are *G*
   18: 37 are *G*, and that you are turning
   20: 28 a *g* of the hills and not a *g*
2Ki 5: 15 "Now I know that there is no *G*
   18: 5 in the LORD, the *G* of Israel.
   19: 15 *G* of Israel, enthroned
   19: 19 Now, O LORD our *G*, deliver us
1Ch 12: 18 for your *G* will help you."
   13: 2 if it is the will of the LORD our *G*,
   16: 35 Cry out, "Save us, O *G* our Savior,
   17: 20 and there is no *G* but you,
   17: 24 the *G* over Israel, is Israel's *G!*'
   21: 8 said to *G*, "I have sinned greatly
   22: 1 house of the LORD *G* is to be here,
   22: 19 soul to seeking the LORD your *G*.
   28: 2 for the footstool of our *G*,
   28: 9 acknowledge the *G* of your father,
   28: 20 for the LORD *G*, my *G*, is with you
   29: 1 not for man but for the LORD *G*.
   29: 2 provided for the temple of my *G*—
   29: 3 of my *G* I now give my personal
   29: 10 *G* of our father Israel,
   29: 13 Now, our *G*, we give you thanks,
   29: 16 O LORD our *G*, as for all this
   29: 17 my *G*, that you test the heart
   29: 18 *G* of our fathers Abraham,
2Ch 2: 4 for the Name of the LORD my *G*
   5: 14 of the LORD filled the temple of *G*
   6: 4 be to the LORD, the *G* of Israel,
   6: 14 there is no *G* like you in heaven
   6: 18 "But will *G* really dwell on earth
   10: 15 for this turn of events was from *G*,
   13: 12 *G* is with us; he is our leader.
   15: 3 was without the true *G*,
   15: 12 the *G* of their fathers,
   15: 15 They sought *G* eagerly,
   18: 13 I can tell him only what my *G* says
   19: 3 have set your heart on seeking *G*.'
   19: 7 with the LORD our *G* there is no
   20: 6 are you not the *G* who is in heaven?
   20: 20 Have faith in the LORD your *G*
   25: 8 for *G* has the power to help
   26: 5 sought the LORD, *G* gave him
   30: 9 for the LORD your *G* is gracious
   30: 19 who sets his heart on seeking *G*—
   31: 21 he sought his *G* and worked
   32: 31 *G* left him to test him
   33: 12 the favor of the LORD his *G*
   34: 33 fail to follow the LORD, the *G*
Ezr 6: 21 to seek the LORD, the *G* of Israel.
   7: 18 accordance with the will of your *G*.
   7: 23 Whatever the *G* of heaven has
   8: 22 "The gracious hand of our *G* is
   8: 31 The hand of our *G* was on us,
   9: 6 "O my *G*, I am too ashamed
   9: 9 our *G* has not deserted us
   9: 13 our *G*, you have punished us less
   9: 15 *G* of Israel, you are righteous!
Ne 1: 5 the great and awesome *G*,
   5: 9 fear of our *G* to avoid the reproach
   5: 15 for *G* I did not act like that.
   7: 2 feared *G* more than most men do.
   8: 8 from the Book of the Law of *G*,
   8: 18 from the Book of the Law of *G*.
   9: 5 and praise the LORD your *G*,
   9: 17 But you are a forgiving *G*,
   9: 31 you are a gracious and merciful *G*.
   9: 32 the great, mighty and awesome *G*,
   10: 29 oath to follow the Law of *G* given
   10: 39 not neglect the house of our *G*."
   12: 43 *G* had given them great joy.
   13: 11 Why is the house of *G* neglected?''
   13: 26 He was loved by his *G*,
   13: 31 Remember me with favor, O my *G*.
Job 1: 1 he feared *G* and shunned evil.
   1: 22 by charging *G* with wrongdoing.
   2: 10 Shall we accept good from *G*,
   4: 17 a mortal be more righteous than *G?*
   5: 17 is the man whom *G* corrects;
   8: 3 Does *G* pervert justice?
   8: 20 "Surely *G* does not reject
   9: 2 a mortal be righteous before *G?*
   11: 7 Can you fathom the mysteries of *G*

Job 12: 13 "To *G* belong wisdom and power;
   16: 7 Surely, O *G*, you have worn me out
   19: 26 yet in my flesh I will see *G;*
   21: 19 '*G* stores up a man's punishment
   21: 22 Can anyone teach knowledge to *G*,
   22: 12 "Is not *G* in the heights of heaven?
   22: 13 Yet you say, 'What does *G* know?
   22: 21 "Submit to *G* and be at peace
   25: 2 "Dominion and awe belong to *G;*
   25: 4 can a man be righteous before *G?*
   26: 6 Death is naked before *G;*
   30: 20 O *G*, but you do not answer;
   31: 6 let *G* weigh me in honest scales
   31: 14 do when *G* confronts me?
   32: 13 let *G* refute him, not man.'
   33: 6 I am just like you before *G;*
   33: 14 For *G* does speak—now one way,
   33: 26 He prays to *G* and finds favor
   34: 10 Far be it from *G* to do evil,
   34: 12 is unthinkable that *G* would do
   34: 23 *G* has no need to examine men
   34: 33 Should *G* then reward you
   36: 5 "*G* is mighty, but does not despise
   36: 26 is *G*— beyond our understanding!
   37: 22 *G* comes in awesome majesty.
Ps 5: 4 You are not a *G* who takes pleasure
   7: 11 *G* is a righteous judge,
   10: 14 O *G*, do see trouble and grief;
   14: 5 for *G* is present in the company
   18: 2 my *G* is my rock, in whom I take
   18: 28 my *G* turns my darkness into light.
   18: 30 As for *G*, his way is perfect;
   18: 31 And who is the Rock except our *G*
   18: 32 It is *G* who arms me with strength
   18: 46 Exalted be *G* my Savior!
   19: 1 The heavens declare the glory of *G;*
   22: 1 *G*, my *G*, why have you forsaken
   22: 10 womb you have been my *G*.
   27: 9 O *G* my Savior.
   29: 3 the *G* of glory thunders,
   31: 5 redeem me, O LORD, the *G*
   31: 14 I say, "You are my *G*.''
   33: 12 the nation whose *G* is the LORD,
   35: 24 righteousness, O LORD my *G;*
   37: 31 The law of his *G* is in his heart;
   40: 3 a hymn of praise to our *G*.
   40: 8 I desire to do your will, O my *G;*
   42: 1 so my soul pants for you, O *G*.
   42: 2 thirsts for *G*, for the living *G*.
   42: 5 Put your hope in *G*,
   42: 8 a prayer to the *G* of my life.
   42: 11 Put your hope in *G*,
   43: 4 to *G*, my joy and my delight.
   44: 8 In *G* we make our boast all day
   45: 6 O *G*, will last for ever and ever;
   45: 7 therefore *G*, your *G*, has set you
   46: 1 *G* is our refuge and strength,
   46: 5 *G* will help her at break of day.
   46: 10 "Be still, and know that I am *G;*
   47: 1 shout to *G* with cries of joy.
   47: 6 Sing praises to *G*, sing praises;
   47: 7 For *G* is the King of all the earth;
   48: 9 Within your temple, O *G*,
   49: 7 or give to *G* a ransom for him—
   50: 2 *G* shines forth.
   50: 3 Our *G* comes and will not be silent;
   51: 1 Have mercy on me, O *G*,
   51: 10 Create in me a pure heart, O *G*,
   51: 17 O *G*, you will not despise.
   53: 2 any who seek *G*.
   54: 4 Surely *G* is my help;
   55: 19 *G*, who is enthroned forever,
   56: 4 In *G*, whose word I praise,
   56: 10 In *G*, whose word I praise,
   56: 13 that I may walk before *G*
   57: 3 *G* sends his love and his
   57: 7 My heart is steadfast, O *G*,
   59: 17 are my fortress, my loving *G*.
   62: 1 My soul finds rest in *G* alone;
   62: 7 my honor depend on *G;*
   62: 8 for *G* is our refuge.
   62: 11 One thing *G* has spoken,
   63: 1 O *G*, you are my *G*,
   65: 5 O *G* our Savior,
   66: 1 Shout with joy to *G*, all the earth!
   66: 3 Say to *G*, "How awesome are your
   66: 5 Come and see what *G* has done,
   66: 16 listen, all you who fear *G;*

Ps 66: 20 Praise be to *G*,
   68: 4 Sing to *G*, sing praise to his name,
   68: 6 *G* sets the lonely in families,
   68: 20 Our *G* is a *G* who saves;
   68: 24 has come into view, O *G*,
   68: 35 You are awesome, O *G*,
   69: 5 You know my folly, O *G;*
   70: 1 Hasten, O *G*, to save me;
   70: 4 "Let *G* be exalted!"
   70: 5 come quickly to me, O *G*.
   71: 17 my youth, O *G*, you have taught
   71: 18 do not forsake me, O *G*,
   71: 19 reaches to the skies, O *G*,
   71: 22 harp for your faithfulness, O my *G;*
   73: 17 me till I entered the sanctuary of *G;*
   73: 26 but *G* is the strength of my heart
   76: 11 Make vows to the LORD your *G*
   77: 13 What *g* is so great as our God?
   77: 14 You are the *G* who performs
   78: 19 Can *G* spread a table in the desert?
   79: 9 Help us, O *G* our Savior,
   81: 1 Sing for joy to *G* our strength;
   82: 1 *G* presides in the great assembly;
   84: 2 out for the living *G*.
   84: 10 a doorkeeper in the house of my *G*
   84: 11 For the LORD *G* is a sun
   86: 12 O Lord my *G*, with all my heart;
   86: 15 a compassionate and gracious *G*,
   87: 3 O city of *G: Selah*
   89: 7 of the holy ones *G* is greatly feared;
   90: 2 to everlasting you are *G*.
   91: 2 my *G*, in whom I trust.''
   94: 22 my *G* the rock in whom I take
   95: 7 for he is our *G*
   99: 8 you were to Israel a forgiving *G*,
   99: 9 Exalt the LORD our *G*
   100: 3 Know that the LORD is *G*.
   108: 1 My heart is steadfast, O *G*,
   113: 5 Who is like the LORD our *G*,
   115: 3 Our *G* is in heaven;
   116: 5 our *G* is full of compassion.
   123: 2 look to the LORD our *G*,
   136: 2 Give thanks to the *G* of gods.
   136: 26 Give thanks to the *G* of heaven.
   139: 17 to me are your thoughts, O *G!*
   139: 23 Search me, O *G*, and know my
   143: 10 for you are my *G;*
   144: 2 He is my loving *G* and my fortress,
   147: 1 is to sing praises to our *G*,
Pr 3: 4 in the sight of *G* and man.
   14: 31 to the needy honors *G*.
   25: 2 of *G* to conceal a matter;
   30: 5 "Every word of *G* is flawless;
Ecc 2: 26 *G* gives wisdom, knowledge
   3: 11 cannot fathom what *G* has done
   3: 13 in all his toil—this is the gift of *G*.
   3: 14 *G* does it, so men will revere him.
   5: 4 When you make a vow to *G*,
   5: 19 in his work—this is a gift of *G*.
   8: 12 who are reverent before *G*.
   11: 5 cannot understand the work of *G*,
   12: 7 the spirit returns to *G* who gave it.
   12: 13 Fear *G* and keep his
Isa 1: 4 the holy *G* will show himself holy
   9: 6 Wonderful Counselor, Mighty *G*,
   12: 2 Surely *G* is my salvation;
   25: 9 "Surely this is our *G;*
   28: 11 *G* will speak to this people,
   29: 23 will stand in awe of the *G* of Israel.
   30: 18 For the LORD is a *G* of justice.
   35: 4 your *G* will come,
   37: 16 you alone are *G* over all
   40: 1 says your *G*.
   40: 3 a highway for our *G*.
   40: 8 the word of our *G* stands forever.''
   40: 18 then, will you compare *G?*
   40: 28 The LORD is the everlasting *G*,
   41: 10 not be dismayed, for I am your *G*.
   41: 13 For I am the LORD, your *G*,
   43: 10 Before me no *g* was formed,
   44: 6 apart from me there is no *G*.
   44: 15 he also fashions a *g* and worships it;
   45: 18 he is *G;*
   48: 17 "I am the LORD your *G*,
   52: 7 "Your *G* reigns!''
   52: 12 *G* of Israel will be your rear guard.
   55: 7 to our *G*, for he will freely pardon.
   57: 21 says my *G*, "for the wicked."

Isa 59: 2 you from your *G;*
60: 19 and your *G* will be your glory.
61: 2 and the day of vengeance of our *G,*
61: 10 my soul rejoices in my *G.*
62: 5 so will your *G* rejoice over you.
Jer 7: 23 I will be your *G* and you will be my
10: 10 But the LORD is the true *G;*
10: 12 But *G* made the earth by his power;
23: 23 "Am I only a *G* nearby,"
23: 36 distort the words of the living *G,*
31: 33 I will be their *G,*
32: 27 "I am the LORD, the *G*
42: 6 for we will obey the LORD our *G.*"
51: 10 what the LORD our *G* has done.'
51: 56 For the LORD is a *G* of retribution
Eze 28: 13 the garden of *G;*
34: 31 and I am your *G,* declares
Da 2: 28 there is a *G* in heaven who reveals
3: 17 the *G* we serve is able to save us
3: 29 for no other *g* can save in this way
6: 16 "May your *G,* whom you serve
9: 4 O Lord, the great and awesome *G,*
10: 12 to humble yourself before your *G,*
11: 36 things against the *G* of gods.
Hos 1: 9 my people, and I am not your *G.*
1: 10 will be called 'sons of the living *G.'*
4: 6 you have ignored the law of your *G*
6: 6 acknowledgment of *G* rather
9: 8 The prophet, along with my *G,*
12: 6 and wait for your *G* always.
Joel 2: 13 Return to the LORD your *G,*
2: 23 rejoice in the LORD your *G,*
Am 4: 12 prepare to meet your *G,* O Israel."
4: 13 the LORD *G* Almighty is his name
Jnh 4: 6 Get up and call on your *g!*
4: 2 a gracious and compassionate *G,*
Mic 6: 8 and to walk humbly with your *G.*
7: 7 I wait for *G* my Savior,
7: 18 Who is a *G* like you,
Na 1: 2 LORD is a jealous and avenging *G;*
Hab 3: 18 I will be joyful in *G* my Savior.
Zep 3: 17 The LORD your *G* is with you,
Zec 14: 5 Then the LORD my *G* will come,
Mal 2: 10 Father? Did not one *G* create us?
2: 16 says the LORD *G* of Israel,
3: 8 Will a man rob *G?* Yet you rob me.
Mt 1: 23 which means, "*G* with us."
4: 4 comes from the mouth of *G.'*"
4: 7 'Do not put the Lord your *G*
4: 10 'Worship the Lord your *G,*
5: 8 for they will see *G.*
6: 24 You cannot serve both *G*
19: 6 Therefore what *G* has joined
19: 26 but with *G* all things are possible."
22: 21 and to *G* what is God's."
22: 32 He is not the *G* of the dead
22: 37 "'Love the Lord your *G*
27: 46 which means, "My *G,* my *G,*
Mk 2: 7 Who can forgive sins but *G* alone?"
7: 13 Thus you nullify the word of *G*
10: 6 of creation *G* 'made them male
10: 9 Therefore what *G* has joined
10: 18 "No one is good—except *G* alone.
10: 27 all things are possible with *G.*"
11: 22 "Have faith in *G,*" Jesus answered.
12: 17 and to *G* what is God's."
12: 29 the Lord our *G,* the Lord is one.
12: 30 Love the Lord your *G*
15: 34 which means, "My *G,* my *G,*
16: 19 he sat at the right hand of *G.*
Lk 1: 30 Mary, you have found favor with *G.*
1: 37 For nothing is impossible with *G.*"
1: 47 my spirit rejoices in *G* my Savior,
2: 14 "Glory to *G* in the highest,
2: 52 and in favor with *G* and men.
4: 8 'Worship the Lord your *G*
5: 21 Who can forgive sins but *G* alone?"
8: 39 tell how much *G* has done for you."
10: 9 'The kingdom of *G* is near you.'
10: 27 "'Love the Lord your *G*
13: 18 "What is the kingdom of *G* like?
18: 19 "No one is good—except *G* alone.
18: 27 with men is possible with *G.*"
20: 25 and to *G* what is God's."
20: 38 He is not the *G* of the dead,
22: 69 at the right hand of the mighty *G.*"
Jn 1: 1 was with *G,* and the Word was *G.*
1: 18 ever seen *G,* but *G* the One and Only,

Jn 1: 29 Lamb of *G,* who takes away the sin
3: 16 "For *G* so loved the world that he
3: 34 the one whom *G* has sent speaks
4: 24 *G* is spirit, and his worshipers must
5: 44 praise that comes from the only *G?*
6: 29 answered, "The work of *G* is this:
7: 17 my teaching comes from *G* or
8: 42 to them, "If *G* were your Father,
8: 47 belongs to *G* hears what *G* says.
11: 40 you would see the glory of *G?*"
13: 3 from *G* and was returning to *G;*
13: 31 of Man glorified and *G* is glorified
14: 1 Trust in *G;* trust also in me.
17: 3 the only true *G,* and Jesus Christ,
20: 17 your Father, to my *G* and your *G*
20: 28 "My Lord and my *G!*"
20: 31 the Son of *G,* and that
Ac 2: 11 wonders of *G* in our own tongues!"
2: 24 But *G* raised him from the dead,
2: 33 Exalted to the right hand of *G,*
2: 36 *G* has made this Jesus, whom you
3: 15 but *G* raised him from the dead.
3: 19 Repent, then, and turn to *G,*
4: 31 and spoke the word of *G* boldly.
5: 4 You have not lied to men but to *G*
5: 29 "We must obey *G* rather than men!
5: 31 *G* exalted him to his own right
5: 32 whom *G* has given
7: 55 to heaven and saw the glory of *G,*
8: 21 your heart is not right before *G.*
11: 9 anything impure that *G* has made
12: 24 But the word of *G* continued
13: 32 What *G* promised our fathers he
15: 10 to test *G* by putting on the necks
17: 23 TO AN UNKNOWN *G.*
17: 30 In the past *G* overlooked such
20: 27 to you the whole will of *G.*
20: 32 "Now I commit you to *G*
24: 16 keep my conscience clear before *G*
Ro 1: 16 the power of *G* for the salvation
1: 17 a righteousness from *G* is revealed,
1: 18 The wrath of *G* is being revealed
1: 24 Therefore *G* gave them
1: 26 *G* gave them over to shameful lusts
2: 11 For *G* does not show favoritism.
2: 16 when *G* will judge men's secrets
3: 4 Let *G* be true, and every man a liar.
3: 19 world held accountable to *G.*
3: 23 and fall short of the glory of *G,*
3: 29 Is *G* the *G* of Jews only? Is he not
4: 3 say? "Abraham believed *G,*
4: 6 to whom *G* credits righteousness
4: 17 the *G* who gives life to the dead
4: 24 to whom *G* will credit
5: 1 we have peace with *G*
5: 5 because *G* has poured out his love
5: 8 *G* demonstrates his own love for us
6: 22 and have become slaves to *G,*
6: 23 but the gift of *G* is eternal life
8: 7 the sinful mind is hostile to *G.*
8: 17 heirs of *G* and co-heirs with Christ,
8: 28 in all things *G* works for the good
9: 14 What then shall we say? Is *G* unjust
9: 18 Therefore *G* has mercy
10: 9 in your heart that *G* raised him
11: 2 *G* did not reject his people,
11: 22 the kindness and sternness of *G:*
11: 32 For *G* has bound all men
13: 1 exist have been established by *G.*
14: 12 give an account of himself to *G.*
16: 20 of peace will soon crush Satan
1Co 1: 18 are being saved it is the power of *G.*
1: 20 Has not *G* made foolish
1: 25 For the foolishness of *G* is wiser
1: 27 But *G* chose the foolish things
2: 9 what *G* has prepared
2: 11 of *G* except the Spirit of *G.*
3: 6 watered it, but *G* made it grow.
3: 17 God's temple, *G* will destroy
6: 20 Therefore honor *G* with your body.
7: 7 each man has his own gift from *G;*
7: 15 *G* has called us to live in peace.
7: 20 was in when *G* called him.
7: 24 each man, as responsible to *G,*
8: 3 man who loves *G* is known by *G.*
8: 8 food does not bring us near to *G;*
10: 13 *G* is faithful; he will not let you be
10: 31 do it all for the glory of *G.*

1Co 12: 24 But *G* has combined the members
14: 33 For *G* is not a *G* of disorder
15: 24 over the kingdom to *G* the Father
15: 28 so that *G* may be all in all.
15: 34 are some who are ignorant of *G—*
15: 57 be to *G!* He gives us the victory
2Co 1: 9 rely on ourselves but on *G.*
2: 14 be to *G,* who always leads us
2: 15 For we are to *G* the aroma of Christ
2: 17 we do not peddle the word of *G*
3: 5 but our competence comes from *G.*
4: 2 nor do we distort the word of *G.*
4: 7 this all-surpassing power is from *G*
5: 5 Now it is *G* who has made us
5: 19 that *G* was reconciling the world
5: 20 though *G* were making his appeal
5: 21 *G* made him who had no sin
6: 16 we are the temple of the living *G.*
9: 7 for *G* loves a cheerful giver.
9: 8 *G* is able to make all grace abound
10: 13 to the field *G* has assigned to us,
Gal 2: 6 *G* does not judge by external
3: 5 Does *G* give you his Spirit
3: 6 Abraham: "He believed *G,*
3: 11 justified before *G* by the law,
3: 26 You are all sons of *G* through faith
6: 7 not be deceived: *G* cannot be
Eph 1: 22 *G* placed all things under his feet
2: 8 it is the gift of *G*— not by works,
2: 10 which *G* prepared in advance for us
2: 22 in which *G* lives by his Spirit.
4: 6 one baptism; one *G* and Father
4: 24 to be like *G* in true righteousness
5: 1 Be imitators of *G,* therefore,
6: 6 doing the will of *G* from your heart.
Php 2: 6 Who, being in very nature *G,*
2: 9 Therefore *G* exalted him
2: 13 for it is *G* who works in you to will
4: 7 peace of *G,* which transcends all
4: 19 And my *G* will meet all your needs
Col 1: 19 For *G* was pleased
2: 13 *G* made you alive with Christ.
1Th 2: 4 trying to please men but *G,*
2: 13 but as it actually is, the word of *G,*
3: 9 How can we thank *G* enough
4: 7 For *G* did not call us to be impure,
4: 9 taught by *G* to love each other.
5: 9 For *G* did not appoint us
1Ti 2: 5 one mediator between *G* and men,
4: 4 For everything *G* created is good,
5: 4 for this is pleasing to *G.*
2Ti 1: 6 you to fan into flame the gift of *G,*
2: 19 which *G,* who does not lie,
Tit 2: 13 glorious appearing of our great *G*
Heb 1: 1 In the past *G* spoke
3: 4 but *G* is the builder of everything.
4: 4 "And on the seventh day *G* rested
4: 12 For the word of *G* is living
6: 10 *G* is not unjust; he will not forget
6: 18 in which it is impossible for *G* to lie
7: 19 by which we draw near to *G.*
7: 25 come to *G* through him,
10: 22 draw near to *G* with a sincere heart
10: 31 to fall into the hands of the living *G*
11: 5 commended as one who pleased *G.*
11: 6 faith it is impossible to please *G,*
12: 7 as discipline; *G* is treating you
12: 10 but *G* disciplines us for our good,
12: 29 for our "*G* is a consuming fire."
13: 15 offer to *G* a sacrifice of praise—
Jas 1: 12 crown of life that *G* has promised
1: 13 For *G* cannot be tempted by evil,
1: 27 Religion that *G* our Father accepts
2: 19 You believe that there is one *G.*
2: 23 "Abraham believed *G,*
4: 4 the world becomes an enemy of *G.*
4: 6 "*G* opposes the proud
4: 8 Come near to *G* and he will come
1Pe 1: 23 the living and enduring word of *G.*
2: 20 this is commendable before *G.*
3: 18 the unrighteous, to bring you to *G.*
4: 11 it with the strength *G* provides,
5: 5 because, "*G* opposes the proud
2Pe 1: 21 but men spoke from *G*
2: 4 For if *G* did not spare angels
1Jn 1: 5 *G* is light; in him there is no
2: 17 the will of *G* lives forever.
3: 1 we should be called children of *G!*

1Jn 3: 9 born of *G* will continue to sin,
    3: 10 we know who the children of *G* are
    3: 20 For *G* is greater than our hearts,
    4: 7 for love comes from *G.*
    4: 8 not know *G,* because *G* is love.
    4: 9 This is how *G* showed his love
    4: 11 Dear friends, since *G* so loved us,
    4: 12 No one has ever seen *G;*
    4: 15 *G* lives in him and he in *G.*
    4: 16 *G* is love.
    4: 20 ''I love *G,*'' yet hates his brother,
    4: 21 Whoever loves *G* must
    5: 2 that we love the children of *G:*
    5: 3 love for *G:* to obey his commands.
    5: 4 born of *G* overcomes the world.
    5: 10 does not believe *G* has made him
    5: 14 have in approaching *G;*
    5: 18 born of *G* does not continue to sin;
Rev 4: 8 holy is the Lord *G* Almighty,
    7: 12 be to our *G* for ever and ever.
    7: 17 *G* will wipe away every tear
   11: 16 fell on their faces and worshiped *G,*
   15: 3 Lord *G* Almighty.
   17: 17 For *G* has put it into their hearts
   19: 6 For our Lord *G* Almighty reigns.
   21: 3 Now the dwelling of *G* is with men,
   21: 23 for the glory of *G* gives it light,

GOD-BREATHED* (BREATH)

2Ti 3: 16 All Scripture is *G* and is useful

GOD-FEARING* (FEAR)

Ecc 8: 12 that it will go better with *G* men,
Ac   2: 5 staying in Jerusalem *G* Jews
   10: 2 all his family were devout and *G;*
   10: 22 He is a righteous and *G* man,
   13: 26 of Abraham, and you *G* Gentiles.
   13: 50 But the Jews incited the *G* women
   17: 4 as did a large number of *G* Greeks
   17: 17 with the Jews and the *G* Greeks,

GOD-HATERS* (HATE)

Ro   1: 30 They are gossips, slanderers, *G,*

GOD'S (GOD)

2Ch 20: 15 For the battle is not yours, but *G.*
Job 37: 14 stop and consider *G* wonders.
Ps 52: 8 I trust in *G* unfailing love
   69: 30 I will praise *G* name in song
Mk 3: 35 Whoever does *G* will is my brother
Jn   7: 17 If any one chooses to do *G* will,
   10: 36 'I am *G* Son'? Do not believe me
Ro   2: 3 think you will escape *G* judgment?
   2: 4 not realizing that *G* kindness leads
   3: 3 lack of faith nullify *G* faithfulness?
   7: 22 in my inner being I delight in *G* law
   9: 16 or effort, but on *G* mercy.
  11: 29 for *G* gifts and his call are
  12: 2 and approve what *G* will is—
  12: 13 Share with *G* people who are
  13: 6 for the authorities are *G* servants,
1Co 7: 19 Keeping *G* commands is what
2Co 6: 2 now is the time of *G* favor,
Eph 1: 7 riches of *G* grace that he lavished
1Th 4: 3 It is *G* will that you should be holy;
   5: 18 for this is *G* will for you
1Ti 6: 1 so that *G* name and our teaching
2Ti 2: 19 *G* solid foundation stands firm,
Tit   1: 7 overseer is entrusted with *G* work,
Heb 1: 3 The Son is the radiance of *G* glory
   9: 24 now to appear for us in *G* presence.
  11: 3 was formed at *G* command,
1Pe 2: 15 For it is *G* will that
   3: 4 which is of great worth in *G* sight.
1Jn 2: 5 *G* love is truly made complete

GODLESS

Job 20: 5 the joy of the *g* lasts but a moment.
1Ti 6: 20 Turn away from *g* chatter

GODLINESS (GOD)

1Ti 2: 2 and quiet lives in all *g* and holiness.
   4: 8 but *g* has value for all things,
   6: 5 and who think that *g* is a means
   6: 6 *g* with contentment is great gain.
   6: 11 and pursue righteousness, *g,* faith,
2Pe 1: 6 and to perseverance, *g;*

GODLY (GOD)

Ps   4: 3 that the LORD has set apart the *g*
2Co 7: 10 *G* sorrow brings repentance that
   11: 2 jealous for you with a *g* jealousy.
2Ti 3: 12 everyone who wants to live a *g* life
2Pe 3: 11 You ought to live holy and *g* lives

GODS (GOD)

Ex 20: 3 ''You shall have no other *g*
Dt   5: 7 ''You shall have no other *g*
1Ch 16: 26 For all the *g* of the nations are idols
Ps 82: 6 ''I said, 'You are ''*g*'';
Jn 10: 34 have said you are *g*'? If he called
Ac 19: 26 He says that man-made *g* are no *g*

GOG

Eze 38: 18 When *G* attacks the land of Israel,
Rev 20: 8 *G* and Magog—to gather them

GOLD

1Ki 20: 3 'Your silver and *g* are mine.
Job 22: 25 then the Almighty will be your *g,*
   23: 10 tested me, I will come forth as *g.*
   28: 15 cannot be bought with the finest *g.*
   31: 24 ''If I have put my trust in *g*
Ps 19: 10 They are more precious than *g,*
 119:127 more than *g,* more than pure *g,*
Pr   3: 14 and yields better returns than *g.*
  22: 1 esteemed is better than silver or *g.*
Hag 2: 8 The silver is mine and the *g* is mine
Mt   2: 11 and presented him with gifts of *g*
Rev 3: 18 to buy from me *g* refined in the fire,

GOLGOTHA*

Mt 27: 33 to a place called *G* (which means
Mk 15: 22 to the place called *G* (which means
Jn 19: 17 (which in Aramaic is called *G*).

GOLIATH

Philistine giant killed by David (1Sa 17; 21:9).

GOMORRAH

Ge 19: 24 sulfur on Sodom and *G*—
Mt 10: 15 and *G* on the day of judgment
2Pe 2: 6 and *G* by burning them to ashes,
Jude   : 7 *G* and the surrounding towns gave

GOOD

Ge   1: 4 God saw that the light was *g,*
   1: 10 And God saw that it was *g.*
   1: 12 And God saw that it was *g.*
   1: 18 And God saw that it was *g.*
   1: 21 And God saw that it was *g.*
   1: 25 And God saw that it was *g.*
   1: 31 he had made, and it was very *g.*
   2: 9 and the tree of the knowledge of *g*
   2: 9 pleasing to the eye and *g* for food.
   2: 18 ''It is not *g* for the man to be alone.
   3: 22 become like one of us, knowing *g*
  50: 20 but God intended it for *g*
2Ch 7: 3 ''He is *g; /* his love endures
   31: 20 doing what was *g* and right
Job 2: 10 Shall we accept *g* from God,
Ps   14: 1 there is no one who does *g.*
   34: 8 Taste and see that the LORD is *g;*
   34: 14 Turn from evil and do *g;*
   37: 3 Trust in the LORD and do *g.*
   37: 27 Turn from evil and do *g;*
   52: 9 for your name is *g.*
   53: 3 there is no one who does *g,*
   84: 11 no *g* thing does he withhold
   86: 5 You are forgiving and *g,* O Lord
  100: 5 For the LORD is *g* and his love
  103: 5 satisfies my desires with *g* things,
  112: 5 *G* will come to him who is
  119: 68 You are *g,* and what you do is *g;*
  133: 1 How *g* and pleasant it is
  145: 9 The LORD is *g* to all;
  147: 1 How *g* it is to sing praises
Pr   3: 4 you will win favor and a *g* name
   3: 27 Do not withhold *g*
  11: 27 He who seeks *g* finds will,
  13: 22 A *g* man leaves an inheritance
  14: 22 those who plan what is *g* find love
  15: 3 on the wicked and the *g.*
  15: 23 and how *g* is a timely word!
  15: 30 *g* news gives health to the bones.
  17: 22 A cheerful heart is *g* medicine,

Pr 18: 22 He who finds a wife finds what is *g*
   19: 2 It is not *g* to have zeal
   22: 1 A *g* name is more desirable
   31: 12 She brings him *g,* not harm,
Ecc 12: 14 whether it is *g* or evil.
Isa   5: 20 Woe to those who call evil *g*
   40: 9 You who bring *g* tidings
   52: 7 the feet of those who bring *g* news,
   61: 1 me to preach *g* news to the poor.
Jer   6: 16 ask where the *g* way is,
   13: 23 Neither can you do *g*
   32: 39 the *g* of their children after them.
Eze 34: 14 I will tend them in a *g* pasture,
Mic 6: 8 has showed you, O man, what is *g.*
Na   1: 15 the feet of one who brings *g* news,
Mt   5: 45 sun to rise on the evil and the *g,*
   7: 11 Father in heaven give *g* gifts
   7: 17 Likewise every *g* tree bears *g* fruit,
   7: 18 A *g* tree cannot bear bad fruit,
  12: 35 The *g* man brings *g* things out
  13: 8 Still other seed fell on *g* soil,
  13: 24 is like a man who sowed *g* seed
  13: 48 and collected the *g* fish in baskets,
  19: 17 ''There is only One who is *g.*
  22: 10 both *g* and bad, and the wedding
  25: 21 'Well done, *g* and faithful servant!
Mk   1: 15 Repent and believe the *g* news!''
   3: 4 lawful on the Sabbath: to do *g*
   4: 8 Still other seed fell on *g* soil.
   8: 36 What *g* is it for a man
  10: 18 ''No one is *g*— except God alone.
  16: 15 preach the *g* news to all creation.
Lk   2: 10 I bring you *g* news
   3: 9 does not produce *g* fruit will be
   6: 27 do to those who hate you,
   6: 43 nor does a bad tree bear *g* fruit.
   6: 45 The *g* man brings *g* things out
   8: 8 Still other seed fell on *g* soil.
   9: 25 What *g* is it for a man
  14: 34 ''Salt is *g,* but if it loses its saltiness,
  18: 19 ''No one is *g*— except God alone.
  19: 17 '' 'Well done, my *g* servant!'
Jn 10: 11 ''I am the *g* shepherd.
Ro   3: 12 there is no one who does *g,*
   7: 12 is holy, righteous and *g.*
   7: 16 want to do, I agree that the law is *g.*
   7: 18 I have the desire to do what is *g,*
   8: 28 for the *g* of those who love him,
  10: 15 feet of those who bring *g* news!''
  12: 2 his *g,* pleasing and perfect will.
  12: 9 Hate what is evil; cling to what is *g.*
  13: 4 For he is God's servant to do you *g*
  16: 19 you to be wise about what is *g.*
1Co 7: 1 It is *g* for a man not to marry.
  10: 24 should seek his own *g,* but the *g*
  15: 33 Bad company corrupts *g* character
2Co 9: 8 you will abound in every *g* work.
Gal 4: 18 provided the purpose is *g,*
   6: 9 us not become weary in doing *g,*
   6: 10 as we have opportunity, let us do *g*
Eph 2: 10 in Christ Jesus to do *g* works,
   6: 8 everyone for whatever *g* he does,
Php 1: 6 that he who began a *g* work
Col   1: 6 bearing fruit in every *g* work,
1Th 5: 21 Hold on to the *g.*
1Ti 3: 7 have a *g* reputation with outsiders,
   4: 4 For everything God created is *g,*
   6: 12 Fight the *g* fight of the faith.
   6: 18 them to do *g,* to be rich in *g* deeds,
2Ti 3: 17 equipped for every *g* work.
   4: 7 I have fought the *g* fight, I have
Tit   1: 8 loves what is *g,* who is
   2: 7 an example by doing what is *g.*
   2: 14 his very own, eager to do what is *g.*
Heb 5: 14 to distinguish *g* from evil.
  10: 24 on toward love and *g* deeds.
  12: 10 but God disciplines us for our *g,*
  13: 16 do not forget to do *g* and to share
Jas   4: 17 who knows the *g* he ought to do
1Pe 2: 3 you have tasted that the Lord is *g.*
   2: 12 Live such *g* lives among the pagans
   2: 18 not only to those who are *g*
   3: 17 to suffer for doing *g*

GOODS

Ecc 5: 11 As *g* increase,

GORGE

Pr 23: 20 or *g* themselves on meat,

GOSHEN

Ge 45: 10 You shall live in the region of *G*
Ex   8: 22 differently with the land of *G*.

GOSPEL

Ro   1: 16 I am not ashamed of the *g*,
    15: 16 duty of proclaiming the *g* of God,
    15: 20 to preach the *g* where Christ was
1Co 1: 17 to preach the *g*— not with words
     9: 12 rather than hinder the *g* of Christ.
     9: 14 who preach the *g* should receive
     9: 16 Woe to me if I do not preach the *g!*
    15: 1 you of the *g* I preached to you,
    15: 2 By this *g* you are saved,
2Co 4: 4 light of the *g* of the glory of Christ,
     9: 13 your confession of the *g*
Gal 1: 7 a different *g*— which is really no *g*
Eph 6: 15 comes from the *g* of peace.
Php 1: 27 in a manner worthy of the *g*
Col 1: 23 This is the *g* that you heard
1Th 2: 4 by God to be entrusted with the *g*.
2Th 1: 8 do not obey the *g* of our Lord Jesus
2Ti 1: 10 immortality to light through the *g*.
Rev 14: 6 he had the eternal *g* to proclaim

GOSSIP*

Pr 11: 13 A *g* betrays a confidence,
    16: 28 and a *g* separates close friends.
    18: 8 of a *g* are like choice morsels;
    20: 19 A *g* betrays a confidence,
    26: 20 without a *g* a quarrel dies down.
    26: 22 of a *g* are like choice morsels;
2Co 12: 20 slander, *g*, arrogance and disorder.

GOVERN (GOVERNMENT)

Ge   1: 16 the greater light to *g* the day
Job 34: 17 Can he who hates justice *g*?
Ro 12: 8 it is leadership, let him *g* diligently;

GOVERNMENT (GOVERN)

Isa 9: 6 and the *g* will be on his shoulders.

GRACE* (GRACIOUS)

Ps 45: 2 lips have been anointed with *g*,
Pr   1: 9 will be a garland to *g* your head
     3: 22 an ornament to *g* your neck.
     3: 34 but gives *g* to the humble.
     4: 9 She will set a garland of *g*
Isa 26: 10 Though *g* is shown to the wicked,
Jnh 2: 8 forfeit the *g* that could be theirs.
Zec 12: 10 of Jerusalem a spirit of *g*
Lk   2: 40 and the *g* of God was upon him.
Jn   1: 14 who came from the Father, full of *g*
     1: 16 of his *g* we have all received one
     1: 17 *g* and truth came through Jesus
Ac   4: 33 and much *g* was upon them all.
     6: 8 a man full of God's *g* and power,
    11: 23 saw the evidence of the *g* of God,
    13: 43 them to continue in the *g* of God.
    14: 3 message of his *g* by enabling them
    14: 26 they had been committed to the *g*
    15: 11 We believe it is through the *g*
    15: 40 by the brothers to the *g* of the Lord
    18: 27 to those who by *g* had believed.
    20: 24 testifying to the gospel of God's *g*.
    20: 32 to God and to the word of his *g*,
Ro   1: 5 we received *g* and apostleship
     1: 7 *G* and peace to you
     3: 24 and are justified freely by his *g*
     4: 16 be by *g* and may be guaranteed
     5: 2 access by faith into this *g*
     5: 15 came by the *g* of the one man,
     5: 15 how much more did God's *g*
     5: 17 God's abundant provision of *g*
     5: 20 where sin increased, *g* increased all
     5: 21 also *g* might reign
     6: 1 on sinning so that *g* may increase?
     6: 14 you are not under law, but under *g*.
     6: 15 we are not under law but under *g*?
    11: 5 there is a remnant chosen by *g*.
    11: 6 if by *g*, then it is no longer by works
    11: 6 if it were, *g* would no longer be *g*.
    12: 3 For by the *g* given me I say
    12: 6 according to the *g* given us.
    15: 15 because of the *g* God gave me

Ro 16: 20 The *g* of our Lord Jesus be
1Co 1: 3 *G* and peace to you
     1: 4 of his *g* given you in Christ Jesus.
     3: 10 By the *g* God has given me,
    15: 10 But by the *g* of God I am what I am
    15: 10 but the *g* of God that was with me.
    15: 10 his *g* to me was not without effect.
    16: 23 The *g* of the Lord Jesus be with you
2Co 1: 2 *G* and peace to you
     1: 12 wisdom but according to God's *g*.
     4: 15 so that the *g* that is reaching more
     6: 1 not to receive God's *g* in vain.
     8: 1 to know about the *g* that God has
     8: 6 also to completion this act of *g*
     8: 7 also excel in this *g* of giving.
     8: 9 For you know the *g*
     9: 8 able to make all *g* abound to you,
     9: 14 of the surpassing *g* God has given
    12: 9 "My *g* is sufficient for you,
    13: 14 May the *g* of the Lord Jesus Christ,
Gal 1: 3 *G* and peace to you
     1: 6 the one who called you by the *g*
     1: 15 from birth and called me by his *g*,
     2: 9 when they recognized the *g* given
     2: 21 I do not set aside the *g* of God,
     3: 18 God in his *g* gave it to Abraham
     5: 4 you have fallen away from *g*.
     6: 18 The *g* of our Lord Jesus Christ be
Eph 1: 2 *G* and peace to you
     1: 6 to the praise of his glorious *g*,
     1: 7 riches of God's *g* that he lavished
     2: 5 it is by *g* you have been saved.
     2: 7 the incomparable riches of his *g*,
     2: 8 For it is by *g* you have been saved,
     3: 2 of God's *g* that was given to me
     3: 7 by the gift of God's *g* given me
     3: 8 God's people, this *g* was given me:
     4: 7 to each one of us *g* has been given
     6: 24 *G* to all who love our Lord Jesus
Php 1: 2 *G* and peace to you
     1: 7 all of you share in God's *g* with me.
     4: 23 The *g* of the Lord Jesus Christ be
Col 1: 2 *G* and peace to you
     1: 6 understood God's *g* in all its truth.
     4: 6 conversation be always full of *g*,
     4: 18 *G* be with you.
1Th 1: 1 and the Lord Jesus Christ: *G*
     5: 28 The *g* of our Lord Jesus Christ be
2Th 1: 2 *G* and peace to you
     1: 12 according to the *g* of our God
     2: 16 and by his *g* gave us eternal
     3: 18 The *g* of our Lord Jesus Christ be
1Ti 1: 2 my true son in the faith: *G*,
     1: 14 The *g* of our Lord was poured out
     6: 21 *G* be with you.
2Ti 1: 2 To Timothy, my dear son: *G*,
     1: 9 This *g* was given us in Christ Jesus
     1: 9 because of his own purpose and *g*.
     2: 1 be strong in the *g* that is
     4: 22 *G* be with you.
Tit 1: 4 *G* and peace from God the Father
     2: 11 For the *g* of God that brings
     3: 7 having been justified by his *g*,
     3: 15 *G* be with you all.
Phm   3 *G* to you and peace
       25 The *g* of the Lord Jesus Christ be
Heb 2: 9 that by the *g* of God he might taste
     4: 16 find *g* to help us in our time of need
     4: 16 the throne of *g* with confidence,
    10: 29 and who has insulted the Spirit of *g*
    12: 15 See to it that no one misses the *g*
    13: 9 hearts to be strengthened by *g*,
    13: 25 *G* be with you all.
Jas 4: 6 but gives *g* to the humble.''
     4: 6 But he gives us more *g*. That is why
1Pe 1: 2 *G* and peace be yours in abundance
     1: 10 who spoke of the *g* that was
     1: 13 fully on the *g* to be given you
     4: 10 faithfully administering God's *g*
     5: 5 but gives *g* to the humble.''
     5: 10 The God of all *g*, who called you
     5: 12 and testifying that this is the true *g*
2Pe 1: 2 *G* and peace be yours in abundance
     3: 18 But grow in the *g* and knowledge
2Jn   3 and will be with us forever: *G*,
Jude   4 who change the *g* of our God
Rev 1: 4 *G* and peace to you
    22: 21 The *g* of the Lord Jesus be

GRACIOUS (GRACE)

Ex 34: 6 the compassionate and *g* God,
Nu   6: 25 and be *g* to you;
Ne   9: 17 But you are a forgiving God, *g*
Ps 67: 1 May God be *g* to us and bless us
Pr 22: 11 a pure heart and whose speech is *g*
Isa 30: 18 Yet the LORD longs to be *g* to you

GRAIN

Lev 2: 1 When someone brings a *g* offering
Lk 17: 35 women will be grinding *g* together;
1Co 9: 9 ox while it is treading out the *g*.''

GRANDCHILDREN (CHILD)

1Ti 5: 4 But if a widow has children or *g*,

GRANDMOTHER (MOTHER)

2Ti 1: 5 which first lived in your *g* Lois

GRANT (GRANTED)

Ps 20: 5 May the LORD *g* all your requests
    51: 12 *g* me a willing spirit, to sustain me.

GRANTED (GRANT)

Pr 10: 24 what the righteous desire will be *g*.
Mt 15: 28 great faith! Your request is *g*.''
Php 1: 29 For it has been *g* to you on behalf

GRAPES

Nu 13: 23 branch bearing a single cluster of *g*.
Jer 31: 29 'The fathers have eaten sour *g*,
Eze 18: 2 '' 'The fathers eat sour *g*,
Mt   7: 16 Do people pick *g* from thornbushes
Rev 14: 18 and gather the clusters of *g*

GRASPED

Php 2: 6 with God something to be *g*,

GRASS

Ps 103: 15 As for man, his days are like *g*,
Isa 40: 6 ''All men are like *g*,
Mt   6: 30 If that is how God clothes the *g*
1Pe 1: 24 ''All men are like *g*,

GRASSHOPPERS

Nu 13: 33 We seemed like *g* in our own eyes,

GRATIFY* (GRATITUDE)

Ro 13: 14 think about how to *g* the desires
Gal 5: 16 and you will not *g* the desires

GRATITUDE (GRATIFY)

Col 3: 16 and spiritual songs with *g*

GRAVE (GRAVES)

Nu 19: 16 who touches a human bone or a *g*,
Dt 34: 6 day no one knows where his *g* is.
Ps   5: 9 Their throat is an open *g*;
    49: 15 will redeem my life from the *g*;
Pr   7: 27 Her house is a highway to the *g*,
Hos 13: 14 Where, O *g*, is your destruction?
Jn 11: 44 ''Take off the *g* clothes
Ac   2: 27 you will not abandon me to the *g*.

GRAVES (GRAVE)

Eze 37: 12 I am going to open your *g*
Jn   5: 28 are in their *g* will hear his voice
Ro   3: 13 ''Their throats are open *g*;

GRAY

Pr 16: 31 *G* hair is a crown of splendor;
    20: 29 *g* hair the splendor of the old.

GREAT (GREATER GREATEST GREATNESS)

Ge 12: 2 I will make your name *g*,
    12: 2 ''I will make you into a *g* nation
Ex 32: 11 out of Egypt with *g* power
Nu 14: 19 In accordance with your *g* love,
Dt   4: 32 so *g* as this ever happened,
    10: 17 the *g* God, mighty and awesome,
    29: 28 in *g* wrath the LORD uprooted
Jos 7: 9 do for your own *g* name?''
Jdg 16: 5 you the secret of his *g* strength
2Sa 7: 22 ''How *g* you are, O Sovereign
    22: 36 you stoop down to make me *g*.
    24: 14 for his mercy is *g*; but do not let me
1Ch 17: 19 made known all these *g* promises.

Ps 18: 35 you stoop down to make me *g*.
   19: 11 in keeping them there is *g* reward.
   47: 2 the *g* King over all the earth!
   57: 10 For *g* is your love, reaching
   68: 11 and *g* was the company
   89: 1 of the LORD's *g* love forever;
   103: 11 so *g* is his love for those who fear
   107: 1 consider the *g* love of the LORD.
   108: 4 For *g* is your love, higher
   117: 2 For *g* is his love toward us,
   119:165 *G* peace have they who love your
   145: 3 *G* is the LORD and most worthy
Pr 22: 1 is more desirable than *g* riches;
   23: 24 of a righteous man has *g* joy;
Isa 42: 21 to make his law *g* and glorious.
Jer 27: 5 With my *g* power and outstretched
   32: 19 *g* are your purposes and mighty are
La 3: 23 *g* is your faithfulness.
Da 9: 4 ''O Lord, the *g* and awesome God,
Joel 2: 11 The day of the LORD is *g;*
   2: 20 Surely he has done *g* things.
Zep 1: 14 ''The *g* day of the LORD is near—
Mal 1: 11 My name will be *g*
   4: 5 the prophet Elijah before that *g*
Mt 20: 26 whoever wants to become *g*
Mk 10: 43 whoever wants to become *g*
Lk 6: 23 because *g* is your reward in heaven.
   6: 35 Then your reward will be *g*,
   21: 27 in a cloud with power and *g* glory.
Eph 1: 19 and his incomparably *g* power
   2: 4 But because of his *g* love for us,
1Ti 6: 6 with contentment is *g* gain.
Tit 2: 13 glorious appearing of our *g* God
Heb 2: 3 if we ignore such a *g* salvation?
1Jn 3: 1 How *g* is the love the Father has
Rev 6: 17 For the *g* day of their wrath has
   20: 11 Then I saw a *g* white throne

GREATER (GREAT)

Mt 11: 11 there has not risen anyone *g*
   12: 6 I tell you that one *g*
   12: 41 and now one *g* than Jonah is here.
   12: 42 now one *g* than Solomon is here.
Mk 12: 31 There is no commandment *g*
Jn 1: 50 You shall see *g* things than that.''
   3: 30 He must become *g;* I must become
   14: 12 He will do even *g* things than these
   15: 13 *G* love has no one than this,
1Co 12: 31 But eagerly desire the *g* gifts.
2Co 3: 11 how much *g* is the glory
Heb 3: 3 the builder of a house has *g* honor
   3: 3 worthy of *g* honor than Moses,
   7: 7 lesser person is blessed by the *g*.
   11: 26 as of *g* value than the treasures
1Jn 3: 20 For God is *g* than our hearts,
   4: 4 is in you is *g* than the one who is

GREATEST (GREAT)

Mt 22: 38 is the first and *g* commandment.
   23: 11 *g* among you will be your servant.
Lk 9: 48 least among you all—he is the *g*.''
1Co 13: 13 But the *g* of these is love.

GREATNESS* (GREAT)

Ex 15: 7 In the *g* of your majesty
Dt 3: 24 to show to your servant your *g*
   32: 3 Oh, praise the *g* of our God!
1Ch 29: 11 O LORD, is the *g* and the power
2Ch 9: 6 half the *g* of your wisdom was told
Est 10: 2 account of the *g* of Mordecai
Ps 145: 3 his *g* no one can fathom.
   150: 2 praise him for his surpassing *g*.
Isa 63: 1 forward in the *g* of his strength?
Eze 38: 23 I will show my *g* and my holiness,
Da 4: 22 your *g* has grown until it reaches
   5: 18 and *g* and glory and splendor.
   7: 27 and *g* of the kingdoms
Mic 5: 4 will live securely, for then his *g*
Lk 9: 43 And they were all amazed at the *g*
Php 3: 8 compared to the surpassing *g*

GREED (GREEDY)

Lk 12: 15 on your guard against all kinds of *g*
Ro 1: 29 full of wickedness, evil, *g*
Eph 5: 3 or of any kind of impurity, or of *g*,
Col 3: 5 evil desires and *g*, which is idolatry.
2Pe 2: 14 experts in *g*— an accursed brood!

GREEDY (GREED)

Pr 15: 27 A *g* man brings trouble
1Co 6: 10 nor thieves nor the *g* nor drunkards
Eph 5: 5 No immoral, impure or *g* person—
1Pe 5: 2 not *g* for money, but eager to serve;

GREEK (GREEKS)

Gal 3: 28 There is neither Jew nor *G*,
Col 3: 11 Here there is no *G* or Jew,

GREEKS (GREEK)

1Co 1: 22 miraculous signs and *G* look

GREEN

Ps 23: 2 makes me lie down in *g* pastures,

GREW (GROW)

Lk 1: 80 And the child *g* and became strong
   2: 52 And Jesus *g* in wisdom and stature,
Ac 9: 31 by the Holy Spirit, it *g* in numbers,
   16: 5 in the faith and *g* daily in numbers.

GRIEF (GRIEFS GRIEVANCES GRIEVE GRIEVED)

Ps 10: 14 O God, do see trouble and *g;*
Pr 10: 1 but a foolish son *g* to his mother.
   14: 13 and joy may end in *g*.
   17: 21 To have a fool for a son brings *g;*
Ecc 1: 18 the more knowledge, the more *g*.
La 3: 32 Though he brings *g*, he will show
Jn 16: 20 but your *g* will turn to joy.
1Pe 1: 6 had to suffer *g* in all kinds of trials.

GRIEFS* (GRIEF)

1Ti 6: 10 pierced themselves with many *g*.

GRIEVANCES* (GRIEF)

Col 3: 13 forgive whatever *g* you may have

GRIEVE (GRIEF)

Eph 4: 30 do not *g* the Holy Spirit of God,
1Th 4: 13 or to *g* like the rest of men,

GRIEVED (GRIEF)

Isa 63: 10 and *g* his Holy Spirit.

GRINDING

Lk 17: 35 women will be *g* grain together;

GROAN (GROANING GROANS)

Ro 8: 23 *g* inwardly as we wait eagerly
2Co 5: 4 For while we are in this tent, we *g*

GROANING (GROAN)

Ex 2: 24 God heard their *g* and he
Eze 21: 7 'Why are you *g?*' you shall say,
Ro 8: 22 that the whole creation has been *g*

GROANS (GROAN)

Ro 8: 26 with *g* that words cannot express.

GROUND

Ge 1: 10 God called the dry *g* ''land,''
   3: 17 ''Cursed is the *g* because of you;
   4: 10 blood cries out to me from the *g*.
Ex 3: 5 where you are standing is holy *g*.''
   15: 19 walked through the sea on dry *g*.
Isa 53: 2 and like a root out of dry *g*.
Mt 10: 29 fall to the *g* apart from the will
   25: 25 and hid your talent in the *g*.
Jn 8: 6 to write on the *g* with his finger.
Eph 6: 13 you may be able to stand your *g*,

GROW (FULL-GROWN GREW GROWING GROWS)

Pr 13: 11 by little makes it *g*.
   20: 13 not love sleep or you will *g* poor;
Isa 40: 31 they will run and not *g* weary,
Mt 6: 28 See how the lilies of the field *g*.
1Co 3: 6 watered it, but God made it *g*.
2Pe 3: 18 But *g* in the grace and knowledge

GROWING (GROW)

Col 1: 6 this gospel is bearing fruit and *g*,
   1: 10 *g* in the knowledge of God,
2Th 1: 3 your faith is *g* more and more,

GROWS (GROW)

Eph 4: 16 *g* and builds itself up in love,

Col 2: 19 *g* as God causes it to grow.

GRUMBLE (GRUMBLED GRUMBLERS GRUMBLING)

1Co 10: 10 And do not *g*, as some of them did
Jas 5: 9 Don't *g* against each other,

GRUMBLED (GRUMBLE)

Ex 15: 24 So the people *g* against Moses,
Nu 14: 29 and who has *g* against me.

GRUMBLERS* (GRUMBLE)

Jude : 16 These men are *g* and faultfinders;

GRUMBLING (GRUMBLE)

Jn 6: 43 ''Stop *g* among yourselves,''
1Pe 4: 9 to one another without *g*.

GUARANTEE (GUARANTEEING)

Heb 7: 22 Jesus has become the *g*

GUARANTEEING* (GUARANTEE)

2Co 1: 22 as a deposit, *g* what is to come.
   5: 5 as a deposit, *g* what is to come.
Eph 1: 14 who is a deposit *g* our inheritance

GUARD (GUARDS)

1Sa 2: 9 He will *g* the feet of his saints.
Ps 141: 3 Set a *g* over my mouth, O LORD;
Pr 2: 11 and understanding will *g* you.
   4: 13 *g* it well, for it is your life.
   4: 23 Above all else, *g* your heart,
   7: 2 *g* my teachings as the apple
Isa 52: 12 the God of Israel will be your rear *g*
Mk 13: 33 Be on *g!* Be alert! You do not know
Lk 12: 1 ''Be on your *g* against the yeast
   12: 15 Be on your *g* against all kinds
Ac 20: 31 So be on your *g!* Remember that
1Co 16: 13 Be on your *g;* stand firm in the faith
Php 4: 7 will *g* your hearts and your minds
1Ti 6: 20 *g* what has been entrusted
2Ti 1: 14 *G* the good deposit that was

GUARDS (GUARD)

Pr 13: 3 He who *g* his lips *g* his life,
   19: 16 who obeys instructions *g* his life,
   21: 23 He who *g* his mouth and his tongue
   22: 5 he who *g* his soul stays far

GUIDANCE (GUIDE)

Pr 1: 5 and let the discerning get *g*—
   11: 14 for lack of *g* a nation falls,
   24: 6 for waging war you need *g*,

GUIDE (GUIDANCE GUIDED GUIDES)

Ex 13: 21 of cloud to *g* them on their way
   15: 13 In your strength you will *g* them
Ne 9: 19 cease to *g* them on their path,
Ps 25: 5 *g* me in your truth and teach me,
   43: 3 let them *g* me;
   48: 14 he will be our *g* even to the end.
   67: 4 and *g* the nations of the earth.
   73: 24 You *g* me with your counsel,
   139: 10 even there your hand will *g* me,
Pr 4: 11 I *g* you in the way of wisdom
   6: 22 When you walk, they will *g* you;
Isa 58: 11 The LORD will *g* you always;
Jn 16: 13 comes, he will *g* you into all truth.

GUIDED (GUIDE)

Ps 107: 30 he *g* them to their desired haven.

GUIDES (GUIDE)

Ps 23: 3 He *g* me in paths of righteousness
   25: 9 He *g* the humble in what is right
Pr 11: 3 The integrity of the upright *g* them,
   16: 23 A wise man's heart *g* his mouth,
Mt 23: 16 ''Woe to you, blind *g!* You say,
   23: 24 You blind *g!* You strain out a gnat

GUILT (GUILTY)

Lev 5: 15 It is a *g* offering.
Ps 32: 5 the *g* of my sin.
   38: 4 My *g* has overwhelmed me
Isa 6: 7 your *g* is taken away and your sin
Jer 2: 22 the stain of your *g* is still before me
Eze 18: 19 'Why does the son not share the *g*

GUILTY (GUILT)

Ex 34: 7 does not leave the *g* unpunished;
Mk 3: 29 Spirit will never be forgiven; he is *g*
Jn 8: 46 Can any of you prove me *g* of sin?
1Co 11: 27 in an unworthy manner will be *g*
Heb 10: 2 and would no longer have felt *g*
10: 22 to cleanse us from a *g* conscience
Jas 2: 10 at just one point is *g* of breaking all

HABAKKUK*

Prophet to Judah (Hab 1:1; 3:1).

HABIT

1Ti 5: 13 they get into the *h* of being idle
Heb 10: 25 as some are in the *h* of doing,

HADAD

Edomite adversary of Solomon (1Ki 11:14-25).

HADES*

Mt 16: 18 the gates of *H* will not overcome it.
Rev 1: 18 And I hold the keys of death and *H*
6: 8 *H* was following close behind him.
20: 13 and *H* gave up the dead that were
20: 14 *H* were thrown into the lake of fire.

HAGAR

Servant of Sarah, wife of Abraham, mother of Ishmael (Ge 16:1-6; 25:12). Driven away by Sarah while pregnant (Ge 16:5-16); after birth of Isaac (Ge 21:9-21; Gal 4:21-31).

HAGGAI*

Post-exilic prophet who encouraged rebuilding of the temple (Ezr 5:1; 6:14; Hag 1-2).

HAIL

Ex 9: 19 the *h* will fall on every man
Rev 8: 7 and there came *h* and fire mixed

HAIR (HAIRS HAIRY)

Lev 19: 27 '' 'Do not cut the *h* at the sides
Nu 6: 5 he must let the *h* of his head grow
Pr 16: 31 Gray *h* is a crown of splendor;
20: 29 gray *h* the splendor of the old.
Lk 7: 44 and wiped them with her *h*.
21: 18 But not a *h* of your head will perish
Jn 11: 2 and wiped his feet with her *h*.
12: 3 and wiped his feet with her *h*.
1Co 11: 6 for a woman to have her *h* cut
11: 6 she should have her *h* cut off;
11: 14 that if a man has long *h*,
11: 15 For long *h* is given to her
11: 15 but that if a woman has long *h*,
1Ti 2: 9 not with braided *h* or gold or pearls
1Pe 3: 3 as braided *h* and the wearing
Rev 1: 14 and *h* were white like wool,

HAIRS (HAIR)

Mt 10: 30 even the very *h* of your head are all
Lk 12: 7 the very *h* of your head are all

HAIRY (HAIR)

Ge 27: 11 ''But my brother Esau is a *h* man,

HALF

Ex 30: 13 This *h* shekel is an offering
Jos 8: 33 *H* of the people stood in front
1Ki 3: 25 give *h* to one and *h* to the other.''
10: 7 Indeed, not even *h* was told me;
Est 5: 3 Even up to *h* the kingdom,
Da 7: 25 him for a time, times and *h* a time.
Mk 6: 23 up to *h* my kingdom.''

HALF-TRIBE (TRIBE)

Nu 32: 33 and the *h* of Manasseh son

HALLELUJAH*

Rev 19: 1 3, 4, 6.

HALLOWED* (HOLY)

Mt 6: 9 *h* be your name,
Lk 11: 2 *h* be your name,

HALT

Job 38: 11 here is where your proud waves *h*'?

HALTER*

Pr 26: 3 for the horse, a *h* for the donkey,

HAM

Son of Noah (Ge 5:32; 1Ch 1:4), father of Canaan (Ge 9:18; 10:6-20; 1Ch 1:8-16). Saw Noah's nakedness (Ge 9:20-27).

HAMAN

Agagite nobleman honored by Xerxes (Est 3: 1-2). Plotted to exterminate the Jews because of Mordecai (Est 3:3-15). Forced to honor Mordecai (Est 5-6). Plot exposed by Esther (Est 5:1-8; 7: 1-8). Hanged (Est 7:9-10).

HAMPERED*

Pr 4: 12 you walk, your steps will not be *h;*

HAND (HANDED HANDFUL HANDS OPENHANDED)

Ge 24: 2 ''Put your *h* under my thigh.
47: 29 put your *h* under my thigh
Ex 13: 3 out of it with a mighty *h*.
15: 6 Your right *h*, O LORD,
33: 22 and cover you with my *h*
Dt 12: 7 in everything you have put your *h*
1Ki 8: 42 and your mighty *h* and your
13: 4 But the *h* he stretched out
1Ch 29: 14 you only what comes from your *h*.
29: 16 it comes from your *h*, and all
2Ch 6: 15 with your *h* you have fulfilled it—
Ne 4: 17 materials did their work with one *h*
Job 40: 4 I put my *h* over my mouth.
Ps 16: 8 Because he is at my right *h*,
32: 4 your *h* was heavy upon me;
37: 24 the LORD upholds him with his *h*.
44: 3 it was your right *h*, your arm,
45: 9 at your right *h* is the royal bride
63: 8 your right *h* upholds me.
75: 8 In the *h* of the LORD is a cup
91: 7 ten thousand at your right *h*,
98: 1 his right *h* and his holy arm
109: 31 at the right *h* of the needy one,
110: 1 ''Sit at my right *h*
137: 5 may my right *h* forget its skill.
139: 10 even there your *h* will guide me,
145: 16 You open your *h*
Pr 27: 16 or grasping oil with the *h*.
Ecc 5: 15 that he can carry in his *h*.
9: 10 Whatever your *h* finds to do,
Isa 11: 8 the young child put his *h*
40: 12 the waters in the hollow of his *h*,
41: 13 who takes hold of your right *h*
44: 5 still another will write on his *h*,
48: 13 My own *h* laid the foundations
64: 8 we are all the work of your *h*.
La 3: 3 he has turned his *h* against me
Da 10: 10 *h* touched me and set me trembling
Jnh 4: 11 people who cannot tell their right *h*
Hab 3: 4 rays flashed from his *h*,
Mt 5: 30 if your right *h* causes you to sin,
6: 3 know what your right *h* is doing,
12: 10 a man with a shriveled *h* was there.
18: 8 If your *h* or your foot causes you
22: 44 ''Sit at my right *h*
26: 64 at the right *h* of the Mighty One
Mk 3: 1 a man with a shriveled *h* was there.
9: 43 If your *h* causes you to sin, cut it off
12: 36 ''Sit at my right *h*
16: 19 and he sat at the right *h* of God.
Lk 6: 6 there whose right *h* was shriveled.
20: 42 ''Sit at my right *h*
22: 69 at the right *h* of the mighty God.''
Jn 10: 28 one can snatch them out of my *h*.
20: 27 Reach out your *h* and put it
Ac 7: 55 Jesus standing at the right *h* of God
1Co 12: 15 I am not a *h*, I do not belong
Heb 1: 13 ''Sit at my right *h*
Rev 13: 16 to receive a mark on his right *h*

HANDED (HAND)

Da 7: 25 The saints will be *h* over to him
1Ti 1: 20 whom I have *h* over to Satan

HANDFUL (HAND)

Ecc 4: 6 Better one *h* with tranquillity

HANDLE (HANDLES)

Col 2: 21 ''Do not *h!* Do not taste! Do not

HANDLES (HANDLE)

2Ti 2: 15 who correctly *h* the word of truth.

HANDS (HAND)

Ge 27: 22 but the *h* are the *h* of Esau.''
Ex 17: 11 As long as Moses held up his *h*,
29: 10 his sons shall lay their *h* on its head
Dt 6: 8 Tie them as symbols on your *h*
Jdg 7: 6 lapped with their *h* to their mouths.
2Ki 11: 12 and the people clapped their *h*
2Ch 6: 4 who with his *h* has fulfilled what he
22: 16 they have pierced my *h*
24: 4 He who has clean *h* and a pure
31: 5 Into your *h* I commit my spirit;
31: 15 My times are in your *h;*
47: 1 Clap your *h*, all you nations;
63: 4 and in your name I will lift up my *h*
Pr 10: 4 Lazy *h* make a man poor,
21: 25 because his *h* refuse to work.
31: 13 and works with eager *h*.
31: 20 and extends her *h* to the needy.
Ecc 10: 18 if his *h* are idle, the house leaks.
Isa 35: 3 Strengthen the feeble *h*,
49: 16 you on the palms of my *h;*
55: 12 will clap their *h*.
65: 2 All day long I have held out my *h*
La 3: 41 Let us lift up our hearts and our *h*
Lk 23: 46 into your *h* I commit my spirit.''
Ac 6: 6 who prayed and laid their *h*
8: 18 at the laying on of the apostles' *h*,
13: 3 they placed their *h* on them
19: 6 When Paul placed his *h* on them,
28: 8 placed his *h* on him and healed him
1Th 4: 11 and to work with your *h*,
1Ti 2: 8 to lift up holy *h* in prayer,
4: 14 body of elders laid their *h* on you.
5: 22 hasty in the laying on of *h*,
2Ti 1: 6 you through the laying on of my *h*.
Heb 6: 2 the laying on of *h*, the resurrection

HANDSOME*

Ge 39: 6 Now Joseph was well-built and *h*,
1Sa 16: 12 a fine appearance and *h* features.
17: 42 ruddy and *h*, and he despised him.
2Sa 14: 25 praised for his *h* appearance
1Ki 1: 6 also very *h* and was born next
SS 1: 16 *Beloved* How *h* you are, my lover!
Eze 23: 6 all of them *h* young men,
23: 12 horsemen, all *h* young men.
23: 23 with them, *h* young men,
Da 1: 4 without any physical defect, *h*.
Zec 11: 13 the *h* price at which they priced me

HANG (HANGED HANGING HUNG)

Mt 22: 40 and the Prophets *h* on these two

HANGED (HANG)

Mt 27: 5 Then he went away and *h* himself.

HANGING (HANG)

Ac 10: 39 They killed him by *h* him on a tree,

HANNAH*

Wife of Elkanah, mother of Samuel (1Sa 1). Prayer at dedication of Samuel (1Sa 2:1-10). Blessed (1Sa 2:18-21).

HAPPIER (HAPPY)

Mt 18: 13 he is *h* about that one sheep
1Co 7: 40 she is *h* if she stays as she is—

HAPPINESS* (HAPPY)

Dt 24: 5 bring *h* to the wife he has married.
Est 8: 16 For the Jews it was a time of *h*
Job 7: 7 my eyes will never see *h* again.
Ecc 2: 26 gives wisdom, knowledge and *h*,
Mt 25: 21 Come and share your master's *h!*'
25: 23 Come and share your master's *h!*'

HAPPY* (HAPPIER HAPPINESS)

Ge 30: 13 The women will call me *h*.''
30: 13 Then Leah said, ''How *h* I am!
1Ki 4: 20 they drank and they were *h*.
10: 8 How *h* your men must be!
10: 8 men must be! How *h* your officials,

HARD

2Ch 9: 7 How *h* your men must be!
    9: 7 men must be! How *h* your officials,
Est 5: 9 Haman went out that day *h*
    5: 14 the king to the dinner and be *h.''*
Ps 10: 6 I'll always be *h* and never have
    68: 3 may they be *h* and joyful.
  113: 9 as a *h* mother of children.
  137: 8 *h* is he who repays you
Pr 15: 13 A *h* heart makes the face cheerful,
Ecc 3: 12 better for men than to be *h*
    5: 19 to accept his lot and be *h*
    7: 14 When times are good, be *h;*
    11: 9 Be *h,* young man, while you are
Jnh 4: 6 Jonah was very *h* about the vine.
Zec 8: 19 and glad occasions and *h* festivals
1Co 7: 30 those who are *h,* as if they were not
2Co 7: 9 yet now I am *h,* not because you
    7: 13 delighted to see how *h* Titus was,
Jas 5: 13 Is anyone *h?* Let him sing songs

HARD (HARDEN HARDENED HARDENING HARDENS HARDER HARDSHIP HARDSHIPS)

Ge 18: 14 Is anything too *h* for the LORD?
1Ki 10: 1 came to test him with *h* questions.
Pr 14: 23 All *h* work brings a profit,
Jer 32: 17 Nothing is too *h* for you.
Zec 7: 12 They made their hearts as *h* as flint
Mt 19: 23 it is *h* for a rich man
Mk 10: 5 your hearts were *h* that Moses
Jn 6: 60 disciples said, ''This is a *h* teaching.
Ac 20: 35 of *h* work we must help the weak,
    26: 14 It is *h* for you to kick
Ro 16: 12 woman who has worked very *h*
1Co 4: 12 We work *h* with our own hands.
2Co 6: 5 imprisonments and riots; in *h* work
1Th 5: 12 to respect those who work *h*
Rev 2: 2 your *h* work and your

HARDEN

Ex 4: 21 I will *h* his heart so that he will not
Ps 95: 8 do not *h* your hearts as you did
Ro 9: 18 he hardens whom he wants to *h.*
Heb 3: 8 do not *h* your hearts

HARDENED (HARD)

Ex 10: 20 But the LORD *h* Pharaoh's heart,

HARDENING* (HARD)

Ro 11: 25 Israel has experienced a *h* in part
Eph 4: 18 in them due to the *h* of their hearts.

HARDENS* (HARD)

Pr 28: 14 he who *h* his heart falls into trouble
Ro 9: 18 and he *h* whom he wants to harden.

HARDER (HARD)

1Co 15: 10 No, I worked *h* than all of them—
2Co 11: 23 I have worked much *h,* been

HARDHEARTED* (HEART)

Dt 15: 7 do not be *h* or tightfisted

HARDSHIP (HARD)

Ro 8: 35 Shall trouble or *h* or persecution
2Ti 2: 3 Endure *h* with us like a good
    4: 5 endure *h,* do the work
Heb 12: 7 Endure *h* as discipline; God is

HARDSHIPS (HARD)

Ac 14: 22 go through many *h* to enter
2Co 6: 4 in troubles, *h* and distresses;
  12: 10 in insults, in *h,* in persecutions,
Rev 2: 3 and have endured *h* for my name,

HARLOT see PROSTITUTE

HARM (HARMS)

1Ch 16: 22 do my prophets no *h.''*
Ps 105: 15 do my prophets no *h.''*
  121: 6 the sun will not *h* you by day,
Pr 3: 29 not plot *h* against your neighbor,
  12: 21 No *h* befalls the righteous,
  31: 12 She brings him good, not *h,*
Jer 10: 5 they can do no *h*
  29: 11 to prosper you and not to *h* you,
Ro 13: 10 Love does no *h* to its neighbor.
1Co 11: 17 for your meetings do more *h*
1Jn 5: 18 the evil one cannot *h* him.

HARMONY*

Zec 6: 13 there will be *h* between the two.'
Ro 12: 16 Live in *h* with one another.
2Co 6: 15 What *h* is there between Christ
1Pe 3: 8 live in *h* with one another;

HARMS* (HARM)

Pr 8: 36 whoever fails to find me *h* himself;

HARP (HARPS)

Ge 4: 21 the father of all who play the *h*
1Sa 16: 23 David would take his *h* and play.
Ps 33: 2 Praise the LORD with the *h;*
  98: 5 with the *h* and the sound of singing
  150: 3 praise him with the *h* and lyre,
Rev 5: 8 Each one had a *h* and they were

HARPS (HARP)

Ps 137: 2 we hung our *h,*

HARSH

Pr 15: 1 but a *h* word stirs up anger.
Col 2: 23 and their *h* treatment of the body,
    3: 19 and do not be *h* with them.
1Pe 2: 18 but also to those who are *h.*
Jude : 15 of all the *h* words ungodly sinners

HARVEST (HARVESTERS)

Ge 8: 22 seedtime and *h,*
Ex 23: 16 the Feast of *H* with the firstfruits
Dt 16: 15 God will bless you in all your *h*
Pr 10: 5 during *h* is a disgraceful son.
Jer 8: 20 ''The *h* is past,
Joel 3: 13 for the *h* is ripe.
Mt 9: 37 *h* is plentiful but the workers are
Lk 10: 2 He told them, ''The *h* is plentiful,
Jn 4: 35 at the fields! They are ripe for *h.*
1Co 9: 11 if we reap a material *h* from you?
2Co 9: 10 the *h* of your righteousness.
Gal 6: 9 at the proper time we will reap a *h*
Heb 12: 11 it produces a *h* of righteousness
Jas 3: 18 in peace raise a *h* of righteousness.
Rev 14: 15 for the *h* of the earth is ripe.''

HARVESTERS (HARVEST)

Ru 2: 3 to glean in the fields behind the *h.*

HASTE (HASTEN HASTY)

Ex 12: 11 it in *h; it is the LORD's Passover.
Pr 21: 5 as surely as *h* leads to poverty.
  29: 20 Do you see a man who speaks in *h?*

HASTEN (HASTE)

Ps 70: 1 *H,* O God, to save me;
  119: 60 I will *h* and not delay

HASTY* (HASTE)

Pr 19: 2 nor to be *h* and miss the way.
Ecc 5: 2 do not be *h* in your heart
1Ti 5: 22 Do not be *h* in the laying

HATE (GOD-HATERS HATED HATES HATING HATRED)

Lev 19: 17 '' 'Do not *h* your brother
Ps 5: 5 you *h* all who do wrong.
  36: 2 too much to detect or *h* his sin.
  45: 7 righteousness and *h* wickedness;
  97: 10 those who love the LORD *h* evil,
  119:104 therefore I *h* every wrong path.
  119:163 I *h* and abhor falsehood
  139: 21 Do I not *h* those who *h* you,
Pr 8: 13 To fear the LORD is to *h* evil;
    9: 8 rebuke a mocker or he will *h* you;
  13: 5 The righteous *h* what is false,
  25: 17 too much of you, and he will *h* you.
  29: 10 Bloodthirsty men *h* a man
Ecc 3: 8 a time to love and a time to *h,*
Isa 61: 8 I *h* robbery and iniquity.
Eze 35: 6 Since you did not *h* bloodshed,
Am 5: 15 *H* evil, love good;
Mal 2: 16 ''I *h* divorce,'' says the LORD God
Mt 5: 43 your neighbor and *h* your enemy.'
  10: 22 All men will *h* you because of me,
Lk 6: 22 Blessed are you when men *h* you,
  6: 27 do good to those who *h* you,
  14: 26 does not *h* his father and mother,
Ro 12: 9 *H* what is evil; cling to what is good

HATED (HATE)

Mal 1: 3 loved Jacob, but Esau I have *h,*
Jn 15: 18 keep in mind that it *h* me first.
Ro 9: 13 ''Jacob I loved, but Esau I *h.''*
Eph 5: 29 no one ever *h* his own body,
Heb 1: 9 righteousness and *h* wickedness;

HATES (HATE)

Pr 6: 16 There are six things the LORD *h,*
  13: 24 He who spares the rod *h* his son,
  15: 27 but he who *h* bribes will live.
  26: 28 A lying tongue *h* those it hurts,
Jn 3: 20 Everyone who does evil *h* the light,
  12: 25 while the man who *h* his life
1Jn 2: 9 his brother is still in the darkness.
  4: 20 ''I love God,'' yet *h* his brother,

HATING (HATE)

Jude : 23 *h* even the clothing stained

HATRED (HATE)

Pr 10: 12 *H* stirs up dissension,
  15: 17 than a fattened calf with *h.*
Jas 4: 4 with the world is *h* toward God?

HAUGHTY

Pr 6: 17 detestable to him: / *h* eyes,
  16: 18 a *h* spirit before a fall.

HAVEN

Ps 107: 30 he guided them to their desired *h.*

HAY

1Co 3: 12 costly stones, wood, *h* or straw,

HEAD (HEADS HOTHEADED)

Ge 3: 15 he will crush your *h,*
Nu 6: 5 no razor may be used on his *h.*
Jdg 16: 17 If my *h* were shaved, my strength
1Sa 9: 2 a *h* taller than any of the others.
2Sa 18: 9 Absalom's *h* got caught in the tree.
Ps 23: 5 You anoint my *h* with oil;
  133: 2 is like precious oil poured on the *h,*
Pr 10: 6 Blessings crown the *h*
  25: 22 will heap burning coals on his *h,*
Isa 59: 17 and the helmet of salvation on his *h*
Eze 33: 4 his blood will be on his own *h.*
Mt 8: 20 of Man has no place to lay his *h.''*
Jn 19: 2 crown of thorns and put it on his *h.*
Ro 12: 20 will heap burning coals on his *h.''*
1Co 11: 3 and the *h* of Christ is God.
  11: 5 her *h* uncovered dishonors her *h*—
  12: 21 And the *h* cannot say to the feet,
Eph 1: 22 him to be *h* over everything
  5: 23 For the husband is the *h* of the wife
Col 1: 18 And he is the *h* of the body,
2Ti 4: 5 keep your *h* in all situations,
Rev 14: 14 with a crown of gold on his *h*
  19: 12 and on his *h* are many crowns.

HEADS (HEAD)

Lev 26: 13 you to walk with *h* held high.
Ps 22: 7 they hurl insults, shaking their *h:*
  24: 7 Lift up your *h,* O you gates;
Isa 35: 10 everlasting joy will crown their *h.*
  51: 11 everlasting joy will crown their *h.*
Mt 27: 39 shaking their *h* and saying,
Lk 21: 28 stand up and lift up your *h,*
Ac 18: 6 ''Your blood be on your own *h!*
Rev 4: 4 and had crowns of gold on their *h.*

HEAL* (HEALED HEALING HEALS)

Nu 12: 13 please *h* her!'' The LORD replied
Dt 32: 39 I have wounded and I will *h,*
2Ki 20: 5 and seen your tears; I will *h* you.
  20: 8 the sign that the LORD will *h* me
2Ch 7: 14 their sin and will *h* their land.
Job 5: 18 he injures, but his hands also *h.*
Ps 6: 2 *h* me, for my bones are in agony.
  41: 4 *h* me, for I have sinned against you
Ecc 3: 3 a time to kill and a time to *h,*
Isa 19: 22 he will strike them and *h* them.
  19: 22 respond to their pleas and *h* them.
  57: 18 seen his ways, but I will *h* him;
  57: 19 ''And I will *h* them.''
Jer 17: 14 *H* me, O LORD, and I will be
  30: 17 and *h* your wounds,'
  33: 6 I will *h* my people and will let them

HEALED

La 2: 13 Who can *h* you?
Hos 5: 13 not able to *h* your sores.
      6: 1 but he will *h* us;
      7: 1 whenever I wound *h* Israel,
     14: 4 "I will *h* their waywardness
Na 3: 19 Nothing can *h* your wound;
Zec 11: 16 or seek the young, or *h* the injured,
Mt 8: 7 said to him, "I will go and *h* him."
     10: 1 to *h* every disease and sickness.
     10: 8 *H* the sick, raise the dead,
     12: 10 "Is it lawful to *h* on the Sabbath?"
     13: 15 and turn, and I would *h* them.'
     17: 16 but they could not *h* him."
Mk 3: 2 if he would *h* him on the Sabbath.
      6: 5 on a few sick people and *h* them.
Lk 4: 23 to me: 'Physician, *h* yourself!
      5: 17 present for him to *h* the sick.
      6: 7 to see if he would *h* on the Sabbath.
      7: 3 him to come and *h* his servant.
      8: 43 years, but no one could *h* her.
      9: 2 kingdom of God and to *h* the sick.
     10: 9 *H* the sick who are there
     13: 32 and *h* people today and tomorrow,
     14: 3 "Is it lawful to *h* on the Sabbath
Jn 4: 47 begged him to come and *h* his son,
     12: 40 nor turn—and I would *h* them."
Ac 4: 30 Stretch out your hand to *h*
     28: 27 and turn, and I would *h* them.'

HEALED* (HEAL)

Ge 20: 17 to God, and God *h* Abimelech,
Ex 21: 19 and see that he is completely *h*.
Lev 13: 37 hair has grown in it, the itch is *h*.
     14: 3 If the person has been *h*
Jos 5: 8 were in camp until they were *h*.
1Sa 6: 3 you will be *h*, and you will know
2Ki 2: 21 LORD says: 'I have *h* this water.
2Ch 30: 20 heard Hezekiah and *h* the people.
Ps 30: 2 and you *h* me.
    107: 20 He sent forth his word and *h* them;
Isa 6: 10 and turn and be *h*."
     53: 5 and by his wounds we are *h*.
Jer 14: 19 us so that we cannot be *h*?
     17: 14 Heal me, O LORD, and I will be *h*;
     51: 8 perhaps she can be *h*.
     51: 9 but she cannot be *h*;
     51: 9 " 'We would have *h* Babylon,
Eze 34: 4 the weak or *h* the sick
Hos 11: 3 it was I who *h* them.
Mt 4: 24 and the paralyzed, and he *h* them.
      8: 8 the word, and my servant will be *h*.
      8: 13 his servant was *h* at that very hour.
      8: 16 with a word and *h* all the sick.
      9: 21 If I only touch his cloak, I will be *h*
      9: 22 he said, "your faith has *h* you."
      9: 22 woman was *h* from that moment.
     12: 15 him, and he *h* all their sick,
     12: 22 Jesus *h* him, so that he could both
     14: 14 on them and *h* their sick.
     14: 36 and all who touched him were *h*.
     15: 28 And her daughter was *h*
     15: 30 laid them at his feet; and he *h* them
     17: 18 and he was *h* from that moment.
     19: 2 followed him, and he *h* them there.
     21: 14 to him at the temple, and he *h* them.
Mk 1: 34 and Jesus *h* many who had various
      3: 10 For he had *h* many, so that those
      5: 23 hands on her so that she will be *h*
      5: 28 If I just touch his clothes, I will be *h*
      5: 34 "Daughter, your faith has *h* you.
      6: 13 people with oil and *h* them.
      6: 56 and all who touched him were *h*.
     10: 52 said Jesus, "your faith has *h* you."
Lk 4: 40 hands on each one, he *h* them.
      5: 15 and to be *h* of their sicknesses.
      6: 18 and to be *h* of their diseases.
      7: 7 the word, and my servant will be *h*.
      8: 47 and how she had been instantly *h*.
      8: 48 "Daughter, your faith has *h* you.
      8: 50 just believe, and she will be *h*."
      9: 11 and *h* those who needed healing.
      9: 42 *h* the boy and gave him back
     13: 14 Jesus had *h* on the Sabbath,
     13: 14 So come and be *h* on those days,
     14: 4 he *h* him and sent him away.
     17: 15 when he saw he was *h*, came back,
     18: 42 your sight; your faith has *h* you."
     22: 51 touched the man's ear and *h* him.

Jn 5: 10 said to the man who had been *h*,
      5: 13 man who was *h* had no idea who it
Ac 4: 9 and are asked how he was *h*,
      4: 10 stands before you *h*.
      4: 14 who had been *h* standing there
      4: 22 man who was miraculously *h* was
      5: 16 evil spirits, and all of them were *h*.
      8: 7 paralytics and cripples were *h*.
     14: 9 saw that he had faith to be *h*
     28: 8 placed his hands on him and *h* him.
Heb 12: 13 may not be disabled, but rather *h*.
Jas 5: 16 for each other so that you may be *h*
1Pe 2: 24 by his wounds you have been *h*.
Rev 13: 3 but the fatal wound had been *h*.
     13: 12 whose fatal wound had been *h*.

HEALING* (HEAL)

2Ch 28: 15 food and drink, and *h* balm.
Pr 12: 18 but the tongue of the wise brings *h*.
     13: 17 but a trustworthy envoy brings *h*.
     15: 4 The tongue that brings *h* is a tree
     16: 24 sweet to the soul and *h* to the bones
Isa 58: 8 and your *h* will quickly appear;
Jer 8: 15 for a time of *h*
      8: 22 Why then is there no *h*
     14: 19 for a time of *h*
     30: 12 your injury beyond *h*.
     30: 13 no *h* for you.
     33: 6 I will bring health and *h* to it;
     46: 11 there is no *h* for you.
Eze 30: 21 It has not been bound up for *h*
     47: 12 for food and their leaves for *h*."
Mal 4: 2 rise with *h* in its wings.
Mt 4: 23 and *h* every disease and sickness
      9: 35 and *h* every disease and sickness
Lk 6: 19 coming from him and *h* them all.
      9: 6 gospel and *h* people everywhere.
      9: 11 and healed those who needed *h*.
Jn 7: 23 angry with me for *h* the whole man
Ac 3: 16 him that has given this complete *h*
     10: 38 *h* all who were under the power
1Co 12: 9 to another gifts of *h*
     12: 28 also those having gifts of *h*,
     12: 30 Do all have gifts of *h*? Do all speak
Rev 22: 2 are for the *h* of the nations.

HEALS* (HEAL)

Ex 15: 26 for I am the LORD who *h* you."
Lev 13: 18 a boil on his skin and it *h*,
Ps 103: 3 and *h* all my diseases;
    147: 3 He *h* the brokenhearted
Isa 30: 26 and *h* the wounds he inflicted.
Ac 9: 34 said to him, "Jesus Christ *h* you.

HEALTH* (HEALTHIER HEALTHY)

1Sa 25: 6 And good *h* to all that is yours!
     25: 6 Good *h* to you and your household
Ps 38: 3 of your wrath there is no *h*
     38: 7 there is no *h* in my body.
Pr   3: 8 This will bring *h* to your body
      4: 22 and *h* to a man's whole body.
     15: 30 and good news gives *h* to the bones
Isa 38: 16 You restored me to *h*
Jer 30: 17 But I will restore you to *h*
     33: 6 I will bring *h* and healing to it;
3Jn   2 I pray that you may enjoy good *h*

HEALTHIER* (HEALTH)

Da 1: 15 end of the ten days they looked *h*

HEALTHY* (HEALTH)

Ge 41: 5 Seven heads of grain, *h* and good,
     41: 7 of grain swallowed up the seven *h*,
Ps 73: 4 their bodies are *h* and strong.
Zec 11: 16 or heal the injured, or feed the *h*,
Mt   9: 12 "It is not the *h* who need a doctor,
Mk   2: 17 "It is not the *h* who need a doctor,
Lk   5: 31 "It is not the *h* who need a doctor,

HEAP

Pr 25: 22 you will *h* burning coals
Ro 12: 20 you will *h* burning coals

HEAR (HEARD HEARING HEARS)

Ex 15: 14 The nations will *h* and tremble;
     22: 17 I will *h*, for I am compassionate.
Nu 14: 13 Then the Egyptians will *h* about it!
Dt   1: 16 *H* the disputes between your

Dt   4: 36 heaven he made you *h* his voice
      6: 4 *H*, O Israel: The LORD our God,
     19: 20 The rest of the people will *h* of this
     31: 13 must *h* it and learn
Jos 7: 9 of the country will *h* about this
1Ki 8: 30 *H* the supplication of your servant
2Ki 19: 16 O LORD, and *h*; open your eyes,
2Ch 7: 14 then will I *h* from heaven
Job 31: 35 ("Oh, that I had someone to *h* me!
Ps 94: 9 he who implanted the ear not *h*?
     95: 7 Today, if you *h* his voice,
Ecc 7: 21 or you may *h* your servant cursing
Isa 21: 3 I am staggered by what I *h*,
     29: 18 that day the deaf will *h* the words
     30: 21 your ears will *h* a voice behind you,
     51: 7 *H* me, you who know what is right,
     59: 1 nor his ear too dull to *h*.
     65: 24 while they are still speaking I will *h*
Jer 5: 21 who have ears but do not *h*:
Eze 33: 7 so *h* the word I speak and give
     37: 4 'Dry bones, *h* the word
Mt 11: 5 the deaf *h*, the dead are raised,
     11: 15 He who has ears, let him *h*.
     13: 17 and to *h* what you *h* but did not *h* it
Mk 12: 29 answered Jesus, "*H*,
Lk   7: 22 the deaf *h*, the dead are raised,
Jn   8: 47 reason you do not *h* is that you do
Ac   3: 7 he wanted to *h* the word of the Lord.
     13: 44 gathered to *h* the word of the Lord.
     17: 32 "We want to *h* you again
Ro   2: 13 is not those who the law who are
     10: 14 they *h* without someone preaching
2Ti 4: 3 what their itching ears want to *h*.
Heb 3: 7 "Today, if you *h* his voice,
Rev 1: 3 and blessed are those who *h* it

HEARD (HEAR)

Ex   2: 24 God *h* their groaning and he
Dt   4: 32 has anything like it ever been *h* of?
2Sa 7: 22 as we have *h* with our own ears.
Job 42: 5 My ears had *h* of you
Isa 40: 21 Have you not *h*?
     40: 28 Have you not *h*?
     66: 8 Who has ever *h* of such a thing?
Jer 18: 13 Who has ever *h* anything like this?
Da 10: 12 your words were *h*, and I have
     12: 8 I *h*, but I did not understand.
Hab 3: 16 I *h* and my heart pounded,
Mt   5: 21 "You have *h* that it was said
      5: 27 "You have *h* that it was said,
      5: 33 you have *h* that it was said
      5: 38 "You have *h* that it was said,
      5: 43 "You have *h* that it was said,
Lk 12: 3 in the dark will be *h* in the daylight,
Jn   8: 26 and what I have *h* from him I tell
Ac   2: 6 because each one *h* them speaking
1Co 2: 9 no ear has *h*,
2Co 12: 4 He *h* inexpressible things,
1Th 2: 13 word of God, which you *h* from us,
2Ti 1: 13 What you *h* from me, keep
Jas 1: 25 not forgetting what he has *h*,
Rev 22: 8 am the one who *h* and saw these

HEARING (HEAR)

Isa 6: 9 Be ever *h*, but never understanding
Mt 13: 14 will be ever *h* but never
Mk   4: 12 ever *h* but never understanding;
Ac 28: 26 will be ever *h* but never
Ro 10: 17 faith comes from *h* the message,
1Co 12: 17 where would the sense of *h* be?

HEARS (HEAR)

Jn   5: 24 whoever *h* my word and believes
1Jn 5: 14 according to his will, he *h* us.
Rev 3: 20 If anyone *h* my voice and opens

HEART (BROKENHEARTED FAINT-HEARTED HARDHEARTED HEART'S HEARTACHE HEARTS KINDHEARTED SIMPLEHEARTED STOUTHEARTED WHOLEHEARTED WHOLEHEARTEDLY)

Ge   6: 5 of his *h* was only evil all the time.
Ex   4: 21 But I will harden his *h*
     25: 2 each man whose *h* prompts him
     35: 21 and whose *h* moved him come
Lev 19: 17 Do not hate your brother in your *h*.
Dt   4: 9 or let them slip from your *h* as long

Dt   4: 29 if you look for him with all your *h*
       6: 5 LORD your God with all your *h*
      10: 12 LORD your God with all your *h*
      11: 13 and to serve him with all your *h*
      13: 3 you love him with all your *h*
      15: 10 and do so without a grudging *h;*
      26: 16 observe them with all your *h*
      29: 18 you today whose *h* turns away
      30: 2 and obey him with all your *h*
      30: 6 you may love him with all your *h*
      30: 10 LORD your God with all your *h*
Jos   22: 5 and to serve him with all your *h*
      23: 14 You know with all your *h*
1Sa   10: 9 God changed Saul's *h.*
      12: 20 serve the LORD with all your *h.*
      12: 24 serve him faithfully with all your *h;*
      13: 14 sought out a man after his own *h*
      14: 7 I am with you *h* and soul."
      16: 7 but the LORD looks at the *h.*"
      17: 32 "Let no one lose *h* on account
1Ki   2: 4 faithfully before me with all their *h*
       3: 9 So give your servant a discerning *h*
       3: 12 give you a wise and discerning *h,*
       8: 48 back to you with all their *h*
       9: 3 and my *h* will always be there.
       9: 4 walk before me in integrity of *h*
      10: 24 the wisdom God had put in his *h.*
      11: 4 and his *h* was not fully devoted
      14: 8 and followed me with all his *h,*
      15: 14 Asa's *h* was fully committed
2Ki   22: 19 Because your *h* was responsive
      23: 3 with all his *h* and all his soul,
1Ch   28: 9 for the LORD searches every *h*
2Ch   6: 38 back to you with all their *h*
       7: 16 and my *h* will always be there.
      15: 12 of their fathers, with all their *h*
      15: 17 Asa's *h* was fully committed
      17: 6 His *h* was devoted to the ways
      22: 9 sought the LORD with all his *h.*"
      34: 31 with all his *h* and all his soul,
      36: 13 stiff-necked and hardened his *h*
Ezr   1: 5 everyone whose *h* God had moved
Ne   4: 6 the people worked with all their *h.*
Job   11: 27 How my *h* yearns within me!
      22: 22 and lay up his words in your *h.*
      37: 1 "At this my *h* pounds
Ps   9: 1 you, O LORD, with all my *h;*
      14: 1 The fool says in his *h,*
      16: 9 Therefore my *h* is glad
      19: 14 and the meditation of my *h*
      20: 4 he give you the desire of your *h*
      24: 4 who has clean hands and a pure *h,*
      26: 2 examine my *h* and my mind;
      37: 4 will grant you the desires of your *h.*
      37: 31 The law of his God is in his *h;*
      44: 21 since he knows the secrets of the *h*
      45: 1 My *h* is stirred by a noble theme
      51: 10 Create in me a pure *h,* O God,
      51: 17 a broken and contrite *h,*
      53: 1 The fool says in his *h,*
      66: 18 If I had cherished sin in my *h,*
      73: 1 to those who are pure in *h.*
      73: 26 My flesh and my *h* may fail,
      86: 11 give me an undivided *h,*
      90: 12 that we may gain a *h* of wisdom.
      97: 11 and joy on the upright in *h.*
     108: 1 My *h* is steadfast, O God;
     109: 22 and my *h* is wounded within me.
     111: 1 will extol the LORD with all my *h*
     112: 7 his *h* is steadfast, trusting
     112: 8 His *h* is secure, he will have no fear
     119: 2 and seek him with all their *h.*
     119: 10 I seek you with all my *h;*
     119: 11 I have hidden your word in my *h*
     119: 30 I have set my *h* on your laws.
     119: 32 for you have set my *h* free.
     119: 34 and obey it with all my *h.*
     119: 36 Turn my *h* toward your statutes
     119: 58 sought your face with all my *h;*
     119: 69 I keep your precepts with all my *h.*
     119:111 they are the joy of my *h.*
     119:112 My *h* is set on keeping your
     119:145 I call with all my *h;* answer me,
     125: 4 to those who are upright in *h.*
     138: 1 you, O LORD, with all my *h;*
     139: 23 Search me, O God, and know my *h*
Pr   2: 2 applying your *h* to understanding,
       3: 1 but keep my commands in your *h,*

Pr   3: 3 write them on the tablet of your *h.*
       3: 5 Trust in the LORD with all your *h*
       4: 4 hold of my words with all your *h;*
       4: 21 keep them within your *h;*
       4: 23 Above all else, guard your *h,*
       6: 21 Bind them upon your *h* forever;
       7: 3 write them on the tablet of your *h.*
      10: 8 The wise in *h* accept commands,
      13: 12 Hope deferred makes the *h* sick,
      14: 13 Even in laughter the *h* may ache,
      14: 30 A *h* at peace gives life to the body,
      15: 13 A happy *h* makes the face cheerful,
      15: 15 the cheerful *h* has a continual feast.
      15: 28 *h* of the righteous weighs its
      15: 30 A cheerful look brings joy to the *h,*
      16: 23 A wise man's *h* guides his mouth,
      17: 22 A cheerful *h* is good medicine,
      20: 9 can say, "I have kept my *h* pure;
      22: 11 He who loves a pure *h*
      22: 17 apply your *h* to what I teach,
      22: 18 when you keep them in your *h*
      23: 15 My son, if your *h* is wise,
      23: 19 and keep your *h* on the right path.
      23: 26 My son, give me your *h*
      24: 17 stumbles, do not let your *h* rejoice,
      27: 19 so a man's *h* reflects the man.
Ecc   5: 2 do not be hasty in your *h*
       8: 5 wise *h* will know the proper time
      11: 10 banish anxiety from your *h*
SS   3: 1 I looked for the one my *h* loves;
       4: 9 You have stolen my *h,* my sister,
       5: 2 *Beloved* I slept but my *h* was awake
       5: 4 my *h* began to pound for him.
       8: 6 Place me like a seal over your *h,*
Isa   6: 10 Make the *h* of this people callous
      40: 11 and carries them close to his *h;*
      57: 15 and to revive the *h* of the contrite.
      66: 14 you see this, your *h* will rejoice
Jer   3: 15 give you shepherds after my own *h,*
       4: 14 wash the evil from your *h*
       9: 26 of Israel is uncircumcised in *h.*"
      17: 9 The *h* is deceitful above all things
      20: 9 is in my *h* like a fire,
      24: 7 I will give them a *h* to know me,
      29: 13 when you seek me with all your *h.*
      32: 39 I will give them singleness of *h*
      32: 41 them in this land with all my *h.*
      51: 46 Do not lose *h* or be afraid
Eze   11: 19 I will give them an undivided *h*
      18: 31 and get a new *h* and a new spirit.
      36: 26 I will give you a new *h*
      44: 7 foreigners uncircumcised in *h*
Da   7: 4 the *h* of a man was given to it.
Joel   2: 12 "return to me with all your *h,*
       2: 13 Rend your *h*
Zep   3: 14 Be glad and rejoice with all your *h,*
Mt   5: 8 Blessed are the pure in *h,*
       5: 28 adultery with her in his *h.*
       6: 21 treasure is, there your *h* will be
      11: 29 for I am gentle and humble in *h,*
      12: 34 of the *h* the mouth speaks.
      13: 15 For this people's *h* has become
      15: 18 out of the mouth come from the *h,*
      15: 19 For out of the *h* come evil thoughts
      18: 35 forgive your brother from your *h.*"
      22: 37 the Lord your God with all your *h*
Mk   11: 23 and does not doubt in his *h*
      12: 30 the Lord your God with all your *h*
      12: 33 To love him with all your *h,*
Lk   2: 19 and pondered them in her *h.*
       2: 51 treasured all these things in her *h.*
       6: 45 out of the good stored up in his *h,*
       6: 45 overflow of his *h* his mouth speaks.
       8: 15 for those with a noble and good *h,*
      10: 27 the Lord your God with all your *h*
      12: 34 treasure is, there your *h* will be
Jn   12: 27 "Now my *h* is troubled,
Ac   1: 24 "Lord, you know everyone's *h.*
       2: 37 they were cut to the *h*
       4: 32 All the believers were one in *h*
       8: 21 your *h* is not right before God.
      15: 8 who knows the *h,* showed that he
      16: 14 The Lord opened her *h* to respond
      28: 27 For this people's *h* has become
Ro   1: 9 with my whole *h* in preaching
       2: 29 is circumcision of the *h,*
      10: 9 in your *h* that God raised him
      10: 10 is with your *h* that you believe

Ro   15: 6 with one *h* and mouth you may
1Co   14: 25 the secrets of his *h* will be laid bare.
2Co   2: 4 anguish of *h* and with many tears,
       4: 1 this ministry, we do not lose *h.*
       4: 16 Therefore we do not lose *h.*
       9: 7 give what he has decided in his *h*
Eph   1: 18 eyes of your *h* may be enlightened
       5: 19 make music in your *h* to the Lord,
       6: 5 and with sincerity of *h,* just
       6: 6 doing the will of God from your *h.*
Php   1: 7 since I have you in my *h;* for
Col   2: 2 is that they may be encouraged in *h*
       3: 22 but with sincerity of *h*
       3: 23 work at it with all your *h,*
1Ti   5: 1 which comes from a pure *h*
       3: 1 If anyone sets his *h*
2Ti   2: 22 call on the Lord out of a pure *h.*
Phm   : 12 who is my very *h*— back to you.
       : 20 in the Lord; refresh my *h* in Christ.
Heb   4: 12 the thoughts and attitudes of the *h.*
1Pe   1: 22 one another deeply, from the *h.*

HEART'S* (HEART)

2Ch   1: 11 "Since this is your *h* desire
Jer   15: 16 they were my joy and my *h* delight,
Eze   24: 25 delight of their eyes, their *h* desire,
Ro   10: 1 my *h* desire and prayer to God

HEARTACHE* (HEART)

Pr   15: 13 but *h* crushes the spirit.

HEARTLESS*

La   4: 3 but my people have become *h*
Ro   1: 31 they are senseless, faithless, *h,*

HEARTS (HEART)

Lev   26: 41 their uncircumcised *h* are humbled
Dt   6: 6 are to be upon your *h.*
      10: 16 Circumcise your *h,* therefore,
      11: 18 Fix these words of mine in your *h*
      30: 6 your God will circumcise your *h*
Jos   11: 20 himself who hardened their *h*
      24: 23 and yield your *h* to the LORD,
1Sa   7: 3 to the LORD with all your *h,*
      10: 26 valiant men whose *h* God had
2Sa   15: 6 and so he stole the *h* of the men
1Ki   8: 39 for you alone know the *h* of all men
       8: 61 your *h* must be fully committed
      18: 37 are turning their *h* back again."
1Ch   29: 18 and keep their *h* loyal to you.
2Ch   6: 30 (for you alone know the *h* of men),
      11: 16 tribe of Israel who set their *h*
      29: 31 all whose *h* were willing brought
Ps   7: 9 who searches minds and *h,*
      33: 21 In him our *h* rejoice,
      62: 8 pour out your *h* to him,
      95: 8 do not harden your *h* as you did
Ecc   3: 11 also set eternity in the *h* of men;
Isa   26: 8 are the desire of our *h.*
      29: 13 but their *h* are far from me.
      35: 4 say to those with fearful *h,*
      51: 7 people who have my law in your *h;*
      63: 17 harden our *h* so we do not revere
      65: 14 out of the joy of their *h,*
Jer   4: 4 circumcise your *h,*
      12: 2 but far from their *h*
      17: 1 on the tablets of their *h*
      31: 33 and write it on their *h.*
Mal   4: 6 He will turn the *h* of the fathers
Mt   15: 8 but their *h* are far from me.
Mk   6: 52 the loaves; their *h* were hardened.
       7: 6 but their *h* are far from me.
       7: 21 out of men's *h,* come evil thoughts,
Lk   1: 17 to turn the *h* of the fathers
      16: 15 of men, but God knows your *h.*
      24: 32 "Were not our *h* burning within us
Jn   5: 42 not have the love of God in your *h.*
      14: 1 "Do not let your *h* be troubled.
      14: 27 Do not let your *h* be troubled
Ac   7: 51 with uncircumcised *h* and ears!
      11: 23 true to the Lord with all their *h*
      15: 9 for he purified their *h* by faith.
      28: 27 understand with their *h*
Ro   1: 21 and their foolish *h* were darkened.
       2: 15 of the law are written on their *h,*
       5: 5 love into our *h* by the Holy Spirit,
       8: 27 who searches our *h* knows
1Co   4: 5 will expose the motives of men's *h.*

2Co 1: 22 put his Spirit in our *h* as a deposit,
    3: 2 written on our *h,* known
    3: 3 but on tablets of human *h.*
    4: 6 shine in our *h* to give us the light
    6: 11 and opened wide our *h* to you.
    6: 13 to my children—open wide your *h*
    7: 2 Make room for us in our *h.*
Gal 4: 6 the Spirit of his Son into our *h,*
Eph 3: 17 dwell in your *h* through faith.
Php 4: 7 will guard your *h* and your minds
Col 3: 1 set your *h* on things above,
    3: 15 the peace of Christ rule in your *h,*
    3: 16 with gratitude in your *h* to God.
1Th 2: 4 men but God, who tests our *h.*
    3: 13 May he strengthen your *h*
2Th 2: 17 encourage your *h* and strengthen
Phm : 7 have refreshed the *h* of the saints.
Heb 3: 8 do not harden your *h*
    8: 10 and write them on their *h.*
    10: 16 I will put my laws in their *h,*
    10: 22 having our *h* sprinkled
Jas 4: 8 purify your *h,* you double-minded.
2Pe 1: 19 the morning star rises in your *h.*
1Jn 3: 20 For God is greater than our *h,*

HEAT

Ps 19: 6 nothing is hidden from its *h.*
2Pe 3: 12 and the elements will melt in the *h.*

HEATHEN see GENTILES, NATIONS

HEAVEN (HEAVENLY HEAVENS HEAVENWARD)

Ge 14: 19 Creator of *h* and earth.
    28: 12 with its top reaching to *h,*
Ex 16: 4 rain down bread from *h* for you.
    20: 22 that I have spoken to you from *h:*
Dt 26: 15 from *h,* your holy dwelling place,
    30: 12 "Who will ascend into *h* to get it
1Ki 8: 27 the highest *h,* cannot contain you.
    8: 30 Hear from *h,* your dwelling place,
    22: 19 the host of *h* standing around him
2Ki 2: 1 up to *h* in a whirlwind,
    19: 15 You have made *h* and earth.
2Ch 7: 14 then will I hear from *h*
Isa 14: 12 How you have fallen from *h,*
    66: 1 *H* is my throne,
Da 7: 13 coming with the clouds of *h.*
Mt 3: 2 for the kingdom of *h* is near."
    3: 16 At that moment *h* was opened,
    4: 17 for the kingdom of *h* is near."
    5: 12 because great is your reward in *h,*
    5: 19 great in the kingdom of *h.*
    6: 9 " 'Our Father in *h,*
    6: 10 done on earth as it is in *h.*
    6: 20 up for yourselves treasures in *h,*
    7: 21 Lord,' will enter the kingdom of *h,*
    16: 19 bind on earth will be bound in *h,*
    18: 3 will never enter the kingdom of *h.*
    18: 18 bind on earth will be bound in *h,*
    19: 14 the kingdom of *h* belongs to such
    19: 21 and you will have treasure in *h.*
    19: 23 man to enter the kingdom of *h.*
    23: 13 the kingdom of *h* in men's faces.
    24: 35 *H* and earth will pass away,
    26: 64 and coming on the clouds of *h.*"
    28: 18 "All authority in *h*
Mk 1: 10 he saw *h* being torn open
    10: 21 and you will have treasure in *h.*
    13: 31 *H* and earth will pass away,
    14: 62 and coming on the clouds of *h.*"
    16: 19 he was taken up into *h*
Lk 3: 21 *h* was opened and the Holy Spirit
    10: 18 saw Satan fall like lightning from *h.*
    10: 20 that your names are written in *h.*"
    12: 33 in *h* that will not be exhausted,
    15: 7 in *h* over one sinner who repents
    18: 22 and you will have treasure in *h.*
    21: 33 *H* and earth will pass away,
    24: 51 left them and was taken up into *h.*
Jn 3: 13 No one has ever gone into *h*
    6: 38 down from *h* not to do my will
    12: 28 Then a voice came from *h,*
Ac 1: 11 has been taken from you into *h,*
    7: 49 the prophet says: " '*H* is my
    7: 55 looked up to *h* and saw the glory
    9: 3 a light from *h* flashed around him.
    26: 19 disobedient to the vision from *h.*

Ro 10: 6 'Who will ascend into *h?*' " (that is,
1Co 15: 47 the earth, the second man from *h.*
2Co 5: 1 an eternal house in *h,* not built
    12: 2 ago was caught up to the third *h.*
Eph 1: 10 to bring all things in *h*
Php 2: 10 *h* and on earth and under the earth,
    3: 20 But our citizenship is in *h.*
Col 1: 16 things in *h* and on earth, visible
    4: 1 that you also have a Master in *h.*
1Th 1: 10 and to wait for his Son from *h,*
    4: 16 himself will come down from *h,*
Heb 1: 3 hand of the Majesty in *h.*
    8: 5 and shadow of what is in *h.*
    9: 24 he entered *h* itself, now to appear
    12: 23 whose names are written in *h.*
1Pe 1: 4 spoil or fade—kept in *h* for you,
    3: 22 who has gone into *h* and is
2Pe 3: 13 we are looking forward to a new *h*
Rev 5: 13 Then I heard every creature in *h*
    11: 19 God's temple in *h* was opened,
    12: 7 And there was war in *h.*
    15: 5 this I looked and in *h* the temple,
    19: 1 of a great multitude in *h* shouting:
    19: 11 I saw *h* standing open and there
    21: 1 Then I saw a new *h* and a new earth
    21: 10 coming down out of *h* from God.

HEAVENLY (HEAVEN)

Ps 8: 5 him a little lower than the *h* beings
2Co 5: 2 to be clothed with our *h* dwelling,
Eph 1: 3 in the *h* realms with every spiritual
    1: 20 at his right hand in the *h* realms,
2Ti 4: 18 bring me safely to his *h* kingdom.
Heb 12: 22 to the *h* Jerusalem, the city

HEAVENS (HEAVEN)

Ge 1: 1 In the beginning God created the *h*
    11: 4 with a tower that reaches to the *h,*
Dt 33: 26 who rides on the *h* to help you
1Ki 8: 27 The *h,* even the highest heaven,
2Ch 2: 6 since the *h,* even the highest
Ezr 9: 6 and our guilt has reached to the *h.*
Ne 9: 6 You made the *h,* even the highest
Job 11: 8 They are higher than the *h*—
    38: 33 Do you know the laws of the *h?*
Ps 8: 3 When I consider your *h,*
    19: 1 The *h* declare the glory of God;
    33: 6 of the LORD were the *h* made,
    57: 5 Be exalted, O God, above the *h;*
    102: 25 the *h* are the work of your hands.
    103: 11 as high as the *h* are above the earth,
    108: 4 is your love, higher than the *h;*
    115: 16 The highest *h* belong to the LORD
    119: 89 it stands firm in the *h.*
    135: 6 in the *h* and on the earth,
    139: 8 If I go up to the *h,* you are there;
    148: 1 Praise the LORD from the *h,*
Isa 40: 26 Lift your eyes and look to the *h:*
    45: 8 "You *h* above, rain
    51: 6 Lift up your eyes to the *h,*
    55: 9 "As the *h* are higher than the earth,
    65: 17 new *h* and a new earth.
Jer 31: 37 if the *h* above can be measured
    32: 17 you have made the *h* and the earth
Eze 1: 1 *h* were opened and I saw visions
Da 12: 3 shine like the brightness of the *h,*
Joel 2: 30 I will show wonders in the *h*
Mt 24: 31 from one end of the *h* to the other.
Mk 13: 27 of the earth to the ends of the *h.*
Eph 4: 10 who ascended higher than all the *h,*
Heb 4: 14 priest who has gone through the *h,*
    7: 26 from sinners, exalted above the *h.*
2Pe 3: 5 ago by God's word the *h* existed
    3: 10 The *h* will disappear with a roar;

HEAVENWARD (HEAVEN)

Php 3: 14 for which God has called me *h*

HEAVIER (HEAVY)

Pr 27: 3 provocation by a fool is *h* than both

HEAVY (HEAVIER)

1Ki 12: 4 and the *h* yoke he put on us,
Ecc 1: 13 What a burden God has laid
Isa 47: 6 you laid a very *h* yoke.
Mt 23: 4 They tie up *h* loads and put them

HEBREW (HEBREWS)

Ge 14: 13 and reported this to Abram the *H.*
2Ki 18: 26 speak to us in *H* in the hearing
Php 3: 5 tribe of Benjamin, a *H* of Hebrews;

HEBREWS (HEBREW)

Ex 9: 1 of the *H,* says: "Let my people go,
2Co 11: 22 Are they *H?* So am I.

HEBRON

Ge 13: 18 near the great trees of Mamre at *H,*
    23: 2 died at Kiriath Arba (that is, *H)*
Jos 14: 13 and gave him *H* as his inheritance.
    20: 7 *H)* in the hill country of Judah.
    21: 13 the priest they gave *H* (a city
2Sa 2: 11 king in *H* over the house

HEDGE

Job 1: 10 "Have you not put a *h* around him

HEED (HEEDS)

Ecc 7: 5 It is better to *h* a wise man's rebuke

HEEDS (HEED)

Pr 13: 1 wise son *h* his father's instruction,
    13: 18 whoever *h* correction is honored.
    15: 5 whoever *h* correction shows
    15: 32 whoever *h* correction gains

HEEL

Ge 3: 15 and you will strike his *h.*"

HEIR (INHERIT)

Gal 4: 7 God has made you also an *h.*
Heb 1: 2 whom he appointed *h* of all things,

HEIRS (INHERIT)

Ro 8: 17 then we are *h*— *h* of God
Gal 3: 29 and according to the promise.
Eph 3: 6 gospel the Gentiles are *h* together
1Pe 3: 7 as *h* with you of the gracious gift

HELD (HOLD)

Ex 17: 11 As long as Moses *h* up his hands,
Dt 4: 4 but all of you who *h* fast
2Ki 18: 6 He *h* fast to the LORD
SS 3: 4 I *h* him and would not let him go
Isa 65: 2 All day long I have *h* out my hands
Ro 10: 21 day long I have *h* out my hands
Col 2: 19 and *h* together by its ligaments

HELL*

Mt 5: 22 will be in danger of the fire of *h.*
    5: 29 body to be thrown into *h.*
    5: 30 for your whole body to go into *h.*
    10: 28 destroy both soul and body in *h.*
    18: 9 and be thrown into the fire of *h.*
    23: 15 as much a son of *h* as you are.
    23: 33 you escape being condemned to *h?*
Mk 9: 43 than with two hands to go into *h,*
    9: 45 have two feet and be thrown into *h.*
    9: 47 two eyes and be thrown into *h,*
Lk 12: 5 has power to throw you into *h.*
    16: 23 In *h,* where he was in torment,
Jas 3: 6 and is itself set on fire by *h.*
2Pe 2: 4 but sent them to *h,* putting them

HELMET

Isa 59: 17 and the *h* of salvation on his head;
Eph 6: 17 Take the *h* of salvation
1Th 5: 8 and the hope of salvation as a *h.*

HELP (HELPED HELPER HELPFUL HELPING HELPLESS HELPS)

Ex 23: 5 leave it there; be sure you *h* him
Lev 25: 35 *h* him as you would an alien
Dt 33: 26 who rides on the heavens to *h* you
2Ch 16: 12 even in his illness he did not seek *h*
Ps 18: 6 I cried to my God for *h.*
    30: 2 my God, I called to you for *h*
    33: 20 he is our *h* and our shield.
    46: 1 an ever-present *h* in trouble.
    72: 12 the afflicted who have no one to *h.*
    79: 9 *H* us, O God our Savior,
    108: 12 for the *h* of man is worthless.
    115: 9 he is their *h* and shield.
    121: 1 where does my *h* come from?
Ecc 4: 10 his friend can *h* him up.

Isa 41: 10 I will strengthen you and *h* you;
Jnh 2: 2 depths of the grave I called for *h*,
Mk 9: 24 *h* me overcome my unbelief!''
Lk 11: 46 will not lift one finger to *h* them.
Ac 16: 9 Come over to Macedonia and *h* us
    18: 27 he was a great *h* to those who
    20: 35 of hard work we must *h* the weak,
    26: 22 I have had God's *h* to this very day,
1Co 1: 28 those able to *h* others, those
2Co 9: 2 For I know your eagerness to *h*,
1Ti 5: 16 she should *h* them and not let

HELPED (HELP)

1Sa 7: 12 ''Thus far has the LORD *h* us.''

HELPER (HELP)

Ge 2: 18 I will make a *h* suitable for him.''
Ps 10: 14 you are the *h* of the fatherless.
Heb 13: 6 Lord is my *h*; I will not be afraid.

HELPFUL (HELP)

Eph 4: 29 only what is *h* for building others

HELPING (HELP)

Ac 9: 36 always doing good and *h* the poor.
1Ti 5: 10 *h* those in trouble and devoting

HELPLESS (HELP)

Ps 10: 12 Do not forget the *h*.
Mt 9: 36 because they were harassed and *h*,

HELPS (HELP)

Ro 8: 26 the Spirit *h* us in our weakness.

HEN

Mt 23: 37 as a *h* gathers her chicks
Lk 13: 34 as a *h* gathers her chicks

HERALD

1Ti 2: 7 for this purpose I was appointed a *h*
2Ti 1: 11 of this gospel I was appointed a *h*

HERBS

Ex 12: 8 with bitter *h*, and bread made

HERITAGE (INHERIT)

Ps 61: 5 you have given me the *h*
    119:111 Your statutes are my *h* forever;
    127: 3 Sons are a *h* from the LORD,

HEROD

1. King of Judea who tried to kill Jesus (Mt 2; Lk 1:5).
2. Son of 1. Tetrarch of Galilee who arrested and beheaded John the Baptist (Mt 14:1-12; Mk 6:14-29; Lk 3:1, 19-20; 9:7-9); tried Jesus (Lk 23: 6-15).
3. Grandson of 1. King of Judea who killed James (Ac 12:2); arrested Peter (Ac 12:3-19). Death (Ac 12:19-23).

HERODIAS

Wife of Herod the Tetrarch who persuaded her daughter to ask for John the Baptist's head (Mt 14: 1-12; Mk 6:14-29).

HEWN

Isa 51: 1 the quarry from which you were *h*;

HEZEKIAH

King of Judah. Restored the temple and worship (2Ch 29-31). Sought the LORD for help against Assyria (2Ki 18-19; 2Ch 32:1-23; Isa 36-37). Illness healed (2Ki 20:1-11; 2Ch 32:24-26; Isa 38). Judged for showing Babylonians his treasures (2Ki 20:12-21; 2Ch 32:31; Isa 39).

HID (HIDE)

Ge 3: 8 and they *h* from the LORD God
Ex 2: 2 she *h* him for three months.
Jos 6: 17 because she *h* the spies we sent.
1Ki 18: 13 I *h* a hundred of the LORD's
2Ch 22: 11 she *h* the child from Athaliah
Isa 54: 8 I *h* my face from you for a moment,
Mt 13: 44 When a man found it, he *h* it again,
    25: 25 and *h* your talent in the ground.
Heb 11: 23 By faith Moses' parents *h* him

HIDDEN (HIDE)

1Sa 10: 22 has *h* himself among the baggage.''
Job 28: 11 and brings *h* things to light.
Ps 19: 12 Forgive my *h* faults.
    78: 2 I will utter *h* things, things from of old—
    119: 11 I have *h* your word in my heart
Pr 2: 4 and search for it as for *h* treasure,
    27: 5 rebuke than *h* love.
Isa 59: 2 your sins have *h* his face from you,
Da 2: 22 He reveals deep and *h* things;
Mt 5: 14 A city on a hill cannot be *h*.
    10: 26 or *h* that will not be made known.
    11: 25 because you have *h* these things
    13: 35 I will utter things *h*
    13: 44 of heaven is like treasure *h*
Mk 4: 22 For whatever is *h* is meant
Ro 16: 25 of the mystery *h* for long ages past,
1Co 2: 7 a wisdom that has been *h*
Eph 3: 9 for ages past was kept *h* in God,
Col 1: 26 the mystery that has been kept *h*
    2: 3 in whom are *h* all the treasures
    3: 3 and your life is now *h* with Christ

HIDE (HID HIDDEN HIDING)

Dt 31: 17 I will *h* my face from them,
Ps 17: 8 *h* me in the shadow of your wings
    27: 5 he will *h* me in the shelter
    143: 9 for I *h* myself in you.
Isa 53: 3 one from whom men *h* their faces

HIDING (HIDE)

Ps 32: 7 You are my *h* place;
Pr 28: 12 to power, men go into *h*.

HIGH

Ge 14: 18 He was priest of God Most *H*.
    14: 22 God Most *H*, Creator of heaven
Ps 21: 7 the unfailing love of the Most *H*
    82: 6 you are all sons of the Most *H*.'
Isa 14: 14 I will make myself like the Most *H*
Da 4: 17 know that the Most *H* is sovereign
Mk 5: 7 Jesus, Son of the Most *H* God?
Heb 7: 1 and priest of God Most *H*.

HIGHWAY

Isa 40: 3 a *h* for our God.

HILL (HILLS)

Ps 24: 3 ascend the *h* of the LORD?
Isa 40: 4 every mountain and *h* made low;
Mt 5: 14 A city on a *h* cannot be hidden.
Lk 3: 5 every mountain and *h* made low.

HILLS (HILL)

1Ki 20: 23 ''Their gods are gods of the *h*.
Ps 50: 10 and the cattle on a thousand *h*.
    121: 1 I lift up my eyes to the *h*—
Hos 10: 8 and to the *h*, ''Fall on us!''
Lk 23: 30 and to the *h*, ''Cover us!'''
Rev 17: 9 The seven heads are seven *h*

HINDER (HINDERED HINDERS)

1Sa 14: 6 Nothing can *h* the LORD
Mt 19: 14 come to me, and do not *h* them,
1Co 9: 12 anything rather than *h* the gospel
1Pe 3: 7 so that nothing will *h* your prayers.

HINDERED (HINDER)

Lk 11: 52 and you have *h* those who were

HINDERS (HINDER)

Heb 12: 1 let us throw off everything that *h*

HINT*

Eph 5: 3 even a *h* of sexual immorality,

HIP

Ge 32: 32 socket of Jacob's *h* was touched

HIRAM

King of Tyre; helped David build his palace (2Sa 5:11-12; 1Ch 14:1); helped Solomon build the temple (1Ki 5; 2Ch 2) and his navy (1Ki 9: 10-27; 2Ch 8).

HIRED

Lk 15: 15 and *h* himself out to a citizen

Jn 10: 12 *h* hand is not the shepherd who

HOARDED (HOARDS)

Ecc 5: 13 wealth *h* to the harm of its owner,
Jas 5: 3 You have *h* wealth in the last days.

HOARDS (HOARDED)

Pr 11: 26 People curse the man who *h* grain,

HOLD (HELD HOLDS)

Ex 20: 7 LORD will not *h* anyone guiltless
Lev 19: 13 '' 'Do not *h* back the wages
Dt 5: 11 LORD will not *h* anyone guiltless
    11: 22 in all his ways and to *h* fast to him
    13: 4 serve him and *h* fast to him.
    30: 20 listen to his voice, and *h* fast to him
Jos 22: 5 to *h* fast to him and to serve him
2Ki 4: 16 ''you will *h* a son in your arms.''
Ps 18: 16 from on high and took *h* of me;
    73: 23 you *h* me by my right hand.
Pr 4: 4 ''Lay *h* of my words
Isa 41: 13 who takes *h* of your right hand
    54: 2 do not *h* back;
Eze 3: 18 and I will *h* you accountable
    3: 20 and I will *h* you accountable
    33: 6 I will *h* the watchman accountable
Zec 8: 23 nations will take firm *h* of one Jew
Mk 11: 25 if you *h* anything against anyone,
Jn 20: 17 Jesus said, ''Do not *h* on to me,
Php 2: 16 as you *h* out the word of life—
    3: 12 but I press on to take *h* of that
Col 1: 17 and in him all things *h* together;
1Th 5: 21 *H* on to the good.
1Ti 6: 12 Take *h* of the eternal life
Heb 10: 23 Let us *h* unswervingly

HOLDS (HOLD)

Pr 10: 19 but he who *h* his tongue is wise.
    17: 28 and discerning if he *h* his tongue.

HOLES

Hag 1: 6 to put them in a purse with *h* in it.''
Mt 8: 20 ''Foxes have *h* and birds

HOLINESS* (HOLY)

Ex 15: 11 majestic in *h*,
Dt 32: 51 because you did not uphold my *h*
1Ch 16: 29 the LORD in the splendor of his *h*.
2Ch 20: 21 him for the splendor of his *h*
Ps 29: 2 in the splendor of his *h*.
    89: 35 Once for all, I have sworn by my *h*
    93: 5 *h* adorns your house
    96: 9 in the splendor of his *h*;
Isa 29: 23 they will acknowledge the *h*
    35: 8 it will be called the Way of *H*.
Eze 36: 23 I will show the *h* of my great name.
    38: 23 I will show my greatness and my *h*.
Am 4: 2 LORD has sworn by his *h*:
Lk 1: 75 fear in *h* and righteousness
Ro 1: 4 the Spirit of *h* was declared
    6: 19 to righteousness leading to *h*.
    6: 22 the benefit you reap leads to *h*.
1Co 1: 30 our righteousness, *h*
2Co 1: 12 in the *h* and sincerity that are
    7: 1 perfecting *h* out of reverence
Eph 4: 24 God in true righteousness and *h*.
1Ti 2: 2 quiet lives in all godliness and *h*.
    2: 15 love and *h* with propriety.
Heb 12: 10 that we may share in his *h*.
    12: 14 without *h* no one will see the Lord.

HOLY (HALLOWED HOLINESS)

Ge 2: 3 the seventh day and made it *h*,
Ex 3: 5 you are standing is *h* ground.''
    16: 23 a *h* Sabbath to the LORD.
    19: 6 kingdom of priests and a *h* nation.
    20: 8 the Sabbath day by keeping it *h*.
    26: 33 Place from the Most *H* Place.
    26: 33 curtain will separate the *H* Place
    28: 36 seal: *H* TO THE LORD.
    29: 37 Then the altar will be most *h*.
    30: 10 It is most *h* to the LORD.''
    30: 29 them so they will be most *h*.
    31: 13 I am the LORD, who makes you *h*.
    40: 9 all its furnishings, and it will be *h*.
Lev 10: 3 I will show myself *h*;
    10: 10 must distinguish between the *h*
    10: 13 in a *h* place, because it is your share

Lev 11: 44 and be *h*, because I am *h*.
   11: 45 therefore be *h*, because I am *h*.
   19: 2 'Be *h* because I, the LORD your
   19: 8 he has desecrated what is *h*
   19: 24 the fourth year all its fruit will be *h*,
   20: 3 and profaned my *h* name.
   20: 7 " 'Consecrate yourselves and be *h*,
   20: 8 I am the LORD, who makes you *h*.
   20: 26 You are to be *h* to me because I,
   21: 6 They must be *h* to their God
   21: 8 Consider them *h*, because I
   22: 9 am the LORD, who makes them *h*.
   22: 32 Do not profane my *h* name.
   25: 12 For it is a jubilee and is to be *h*
   27: 9 gate to the LORD becomes *h*.
Nu 4: 15 they must not touch the *h* things
   6: 5 He must be *h* until the period
   20: 12 as h in the sight of the Israelites,
   20: 13 and where he showed himself *h*
Dt 5: 12 the Sabbath day by keeping it *h*,
   23: 14 Your camp must be *h*,
   26: 15 from heaven, your *h* dwelling place
   33: 2 He came with myriads of *h* ones
Jos 5: 15 place where you are standing is *h*."
   24: 19 He is a *h* God; he is a jealous God.
1Sa 2: 2 "There is no one *h* like the LORD;
   6: 20 of the LORD, this *h* God?
   21: 5 even on missions that are not *h*.
2Ki 4: 9 often comes our way is a *h* man
1Ch 16: 10 Glory in his *h* name;
   16: 35 may give thanks to your *h* name,
   29: 3 I have provided for this *h* temple:
2Ch 30: 27 heaven, his *h* dwelling place.
Ezr 9: 2 and have mingled the *h* race
Ne 11: 1 the *h* city, while the remaining nine
Job 6: 10 not denied the words of the *H* One.
Ps 2: 6 King on Zion, my *h* hill."
   11: 4 The LORD is in his *h* temple;
   16: 10 will not let your *H* One see decay.
   22: 3 you are enthroned as the *H* One;
   24: 3 Who may stand in his *h* place?
   30: 4 praise his *h* name.
   77: 13 Your ways, O God, are *h*.
   78: 54 to the border of his *h* land,
   99: 3 he is *h*.
   99: 5 he is *h*.
   99: 9 for the LORD our God is *h*.
   105: 3 Glory in his *h* name;
   111: 9 *h* and awesome is his name.
Pr 9: 10 of the *H* One is understanding.
Isa 5: 16 the *h* God will show himself *h*
   3 *H*, *h*, *h* is the LORD Almighty;
   8: 13 is the one you are to regard as *h*,
   29: 23 they will keep my name *h*;
   40: 25 who is my equal?" says the *H* One.
   43: 3 the *H* One of Israel, your Savior;
   54: 5 *H* One of Israel is your Redeemer;
   57: 15 who lives forever, whose name is *h*:
   58: 13 and the LORD's *h* day honorable,
Jer 17: 22 but keep the Sabbath day *h*,
Eze 20: 41 I will show myself *h* among you
   22: 26 to my law and profane my *h* things;
   28: 22 and show myself *h* within her.
   28: 25 I will show myself *h* among them
   36: 20 nations they profaned my *h* name.
   38: 16 when I show myself *h* through you
   44: 23 the difference between the *h*
Da 9: 24 prophecy and to anoint the most *h*.
Hab 2: 20 But the LORD is in his *h* temple;
Zec 14: 5 and all the *h* ones with him.
   14: 20 On that day *H* TO THE LORD
Mt 24: 15 in the *h* place 'the abomination
Mk 1: 24 the *H* One of God!" 'Be quiet!"
Lk 1: 35 the *h* one to be born will be called
   1: 49 *h* is his name.
   4: 34 the *H* One of God!" 'Be quiet!"
Jn 6: 69 and know that you are the *H* One
Ac 2: 27 will you let your *H* One see decay.
   13: 35 will not let your *H* One see decay.'
Ro 1: 2 prophets in the *H* Scriptures
   7: 12 and the commandment is *h*,
   11: 16 if the root is *h*, so are the branches.
   12: 1 as living sacrifices, *h* and pleasing
1Co 1: 2 in Christ Jesus and called to be *h*,
   7: 14 be unclean, but as it is, they are *h*.
Eph 1: 4 the creation of the world to be *h*
   2: 21 and rises to become a *h* temple
   3: 5 by the Spirit to God's *h* apostles

Eph 5: 3 improper for God's *h* people.
   5: 26 up for her to make her *h*,
Col 1: 22 death to present you *h* in his sight,
1Th 2: 10 and so is God, of how *h*,
   3: 13 and *h* in the presence of our God
   3: 13 comes with all his *h* ones.
   4: 7 us to be impure, but to live a *h* life.
2Th 1: 10 to be glorified in his *h* people
1Ti 2: 8 to lift up *h* hands in prayer,
2Ti 1: 9 saved us and called us to a *h* life—
   2: 21 for noble purposes, made *h*,
   3: 15 you have known the *h* Scriptures,
Tit 1: 8 upright, *h* and disciplined.
Heb 2: 11 Both the one who makes men *h*
   7: 26 one who is *h*, blameless, pure,
   10: 1 we have been made *h*
   10: 14 those who are being made *h*.
   10: 19 to enter the Most *H* Place
   12: 14 in peace with all men and to be *h*;
   13: 12 gate to make the people *h*
1Pe 1: 15 But just as he who called you is *h*,
   1: 16 is written: "Be *h*, because I am *h*."
   2: 5 house to be a *h* priesthood,
   2: 9 a royal priesthood, a *h* nation,
   3: 5 For this is the way the *h* women
2Pe 3: 11 You ought to live *h* and godly lives
Jude : 14 upon thousands of his *h* ones
Rev 3: 7 are the words of him who is *h*
   4: 8 "*H*, *h*, *h* is the Lord God
   15: 4 For you alone are *h*.
   20: 6 and *h* are those who have part
   22: 11 let him who is *h* continue to be *h*."

HOME (HOMES)

Dt 6: 7 Talk about them when you sit at *h*
   11: 19 about them when you sit at *h*
   20: 5 Let him go *h*, or he may die
   24: 5 is to be free to stay at *h*
Ru 1: 11 "Return *h*, my daughters.
2Sa 7: 10 them so that they can have a *h*
1Ch 16: 43 and David returned *h* to bless his
Ps 84: 3 Even the sparrow has found a *h*,
   113: 9 settles the barren woman in her *h*
Pr 3: 33 but he blesses the *h* of the righteous
   27: 8 is a man who strays from his *h*.
Ecc 12: 5 Then man goes to his eternal *h*
Eze 36: 8 for they will soon come *h*.
Mic 2: 2 They defraud a man of his *h*,
Mt 1: 24 and took Mary *h* as his wife.
Mk 10: 29 "no one who has left *h* or brothers
Lk 10: 38 named Martha opened her *h*
Jn 14: 23 to him and make our *h* with him.
   19: 27 this disciple took her into his *h*.
Ac 16: 15 baptized, she invited us to her *h*.
Tit 2: 5 to be busy at *h*, to be kind,

HOMELESS*

1Co 4: 11 we are brutally treated, we are *h*.

HOMES (HOME)

Ne 4: 14 daughters, your wives and your *h*.''
Isa 32: 18 in secure *h*,
Mk 10: 30 as much in this present age *(h*,
1Ti 5: 14 to manage their *h* and to give

HOMETOWN

Mt 13: 57 "Only in his *h*
Lk 4: 24 "no prophet is accepted in his *h*.

HOMOSEXUAL*

1Co 6: 9 male prostitutes nor *h* offenders

HONEST (HONESTY)

Lev 19: 36 Use *h* scales and *h* weights,
Dt 25: 15 and *h* weights and measures,
Job 31: 6 let God weigh me in *h* scales
Pr 12: 17 truthful witness gives *h* testimony,

HONESTY (HONEST)

2Ki 12: 15 they acted with complete *h*.

HONEY (HONEYCOMB)

Ex 3: 8 a land flowing with milk and *h*—
Jdg 14: 8 a swarm of bees and some *h*,
1Sa 14: 26 they saw the *h* oozing out,
Ps 19: 10 than *h* from the comb.
   119:103 sweeter than *h* to my mouth!
Pr 25: 16 If you find *h*, eat just enough—

SS 4: 11 milk and *h* are under your tongue.
Isa 7: 15 and *h* when he knows enough
Eze 3: 3 it tasted as sweet as *h* in my mouth.
Mt 3: 4 His food was locusts and wild *h*.
Rev 10: 9 mouth it will be as sweet as *h*.''

HONEYCOMB (HONEY)

SS 4: 11 Your lips drop sweetness as the *h*,
   5: 1 I have eaten my *h* and my honey;

HONOR (HONORABLE HONORABLY HONORED HONORS)

Ex 20: 12 "*H* your father and your mother,
Nu 20: 12 trust in me enough to *h* me
   25: 13 he was zealous for the *h* of his God
Dt 5: 16 "*H* your father and your mother,
Jdg 4: 9 going about this, the *h* will not be
1Sa 2: 8 and has them inherit a throne of *h*.
   2: 30 Those who *h* me I will *h*,
1Ch 29: 12 Wealth and *h* come from you;
2Ch 1: 11 or *h*, nor for the death
   18: 1 had great wealth and *h*,
Est 6: 6 for the man the king delights to *h*
Ps 8: 5 and crowned him with glory and *h*.
   45: 11 *h* him, for he is your lord.
   84: 11 the LORD bestows favor and *h*;
Pr 3: 9 *H* the LORD with your wealth,
   3: 35 The wise inherit *h*,
   15: 33 and humility comes before *h*.
   18: 12 but humility comes before *h*.
   20: 3 It is to a man's *h* to avoid strife,
   25: 27 is it honorable to seek one's own *h*.
Isa 29: 13 and *h* me with their lips,
Jer 33: 9 and *h* before all nations
Mt 13: 57 own house is a prophet without *h*.''
   15: 4 '*H* your father and mother'
   15: 8 These people *h* me with their lips,
   19: 19 *h* your father and mother,'
   23: 6 they love the place of *h* at banquets
Mk 6: 4 own house is a prophet without *h*.''
Lk 14: 8 do not take the place of *h*,
Jn 5: 23 that all may *h* the Son just
   7: 18 does so to gain *h* for himself,
   12: 26 My Father will *h* the one who
Ro 12: 10 *H* one another above yourselves.
1Co 6: 20 Therefore *h* God with your body.
Eph 6: 2 "*H* your father and mother''—
1Ti 5: 17 well are worthy of double *h*,
Heb 2: 7 you crowned him with glory and *h*
Rev 4: 9 *h* and thanks to him who sits

HONORABLE (HONOR)

1Th 4: 4 body in a way that is holy and *h*,

HONORABLY (HONOR)

Heb 13: 18 and desire to live *h* in every way.

HONORED (HONOR)

Ps 12: 8 when what is vile is *h* among men.
Pr 13: 18 but whoever heeds correction is *h*.
Da 4: 34 I *h* and glorified him who lives
1Co 12: 26 if one part is *h*, every part rejoices
Heb 13: 4 Marriage should be *h* by all,

HONORS (HONOR)

Ps 15: 4 but *h* those who fear the LORD,
Pr 14: 31 to the needy *h* God.

HOOF

Ex 10: 26 not a *h* is to be left behind.

HOOKS

Isa 2: 4 and their spears into pruning *h*.
Joel 3: 10 and your pruning *h* into spears.
Mic 4: 3 and their spears into pruning *h*.

HOPE (HOPES)

Job 13: 15 Though he slay me, yet will I *h*
Ps 25: 3 No one whose *h* is in you
   33: 17 A horse is a vain *h* for deliverance;
   33: 18 on those whose *h* is
   42: 5 Put your *h* in God,
   62: 5 my *h* comes from him.
   119: 74 for I have put my *h* in your word.
   130: 5 and in his word I put my *h*.
   130: 7 O Israel, put your *h* in the LORD,
   146: 5 whose *h* is in the LORD his God,
   147: 11 who put their *h* in his unfailing love

Pr 13: 12 *H* deferred makes the heart sick,
23: 18 There is surely a future *h* for you,
Isa 40: 31 but those who *h* in the LORD
Jer 29: 11 plans to give you *h* and a future.
La 3: 21 and therefore I have *h:*
Zec 9: 12 to your fortress, O prisoners of *h;*
Ro 5: 4 character; and character, *h.*
8: 20 in *h* that the creation itself will be
8: 24 But *h* that is seen is no *h* at all.
8: 25 if we *h* for what we do not yet have,
12: 12 Be joyful in *h,* patient in affliction,
15: 4 of the Scriptures we might have *h.*
15: 13 May the God of *h* fill you
1Co 13: 13 now these three remain: faith, *h*
15: 19 for this life we have *h* in Christ,
Eph 2: 12 without *h* and without God
Col 1: 27 Christ in you, the *h* of glory.
1Th 1: 3 and your endurance inspired by *h*
5: 8 and the *h* of salvation as a helmet.
1Ti 4: 10 that we have put our *h*
6: 17 but to put their *h* in God,
Tit 1: 2 resting on the *h* of eternal life,
2: 13 while we wait for the blessed *h*—
Heb 6: 19 We have this *h* as an anchor
10: 23 unswervingly to the *h* we profess,
11: 1 faith is being sure of what we *h* for
1Jn 3: 3 Everyone who has this *h*

HOPES (HOPE)

1Co 13: 7 always *h,* always perseveres.

HORN (HORNS)

Ex 19: 13 when the ram's *h* sounds a long
27: 2 Make a *h* at each of the four
Da 7: 8 This *h* had eyes like the eyes

HORNS (HORN)

Da 7: 24 ten *h* are ten kings who will come
Rev 5: 6 He had seven *h* and seven eyes,
12: 3 and ten *h* and seven crowns
13: 1 He had ten *h* and seven heads,
17: 3 and had seven heads and ten *h.*

HORRIBLE (HORROR)

Jer 5: 30 "A *h* and shocking thing

HORROR (HORRIBLE)

Jer 2: 12 and shudder with great *h,*"

HORSE

Ps 147: 10 not in the strength of the *h,*
Pr 26: 3 A whip for the *h,* a halter
Zec 1: 8 before me was a man riding a red *h*
Rev 6: 2 and there before me was a white *h!*
6: 4 Come!" Then another *h* came out,
6: 5 and there before me was a black *h!*
6: 8 and there before me was a pale *h!*
19: 11 and there before me was a white *h,*

HOSANNA

Mt 21: 9 "*H* in the highest!"
Mk 11: 9 "*H!*"
Jn 12: 13 "*H!*"

HOSEA

Prophet whose wife and family pictured the unfaithfulness of Israel (Hos 1-3).

HOSHEA (JOSHUA)

1. Original name of Joshua (Nu 13:16).
2. Last king of Israel (2Ki 15:30; 17:1-6).

HOSPITABLE* (HOSPITALITY)

1Ti 3: 2 self-controlled, respectable, *h.*
Tit 1: 8 Rather he must be *h,* one who loves

HOSPITABLY* (HOSPITALITY)

Ac 28: 7 and for three days entertained us *h.*

HOSPITALITY* (HOSPITABLE HOSPITALITY)

Ro 12: 13 Practice *h.*
16: 23 whose *h* I and the whole church
1Ti 5: 10 as bringing up children, showing *h,*
1Pe 4: 9 Offer *h* to one another
3Jn : 8 therefore to show *h* to such men

HOSTILE (HOSTILITY)

Ro 8: 7 the sinful mind is *h* to God.

HOSTILITY (HOSTILE)

Eph 2: 14 wall of *h,* by abolishing
2: 16 by which he put to death their *h.*

HOT

1Ti 4: 2 have been seared as with a *h* iron.
Rev 3: 15 that you are neither cold nor *h.*

HOT-TEMPERED (TEMPER)

Pr 15: 18 A *h* man stirs up dissension,
19: 19 A *h* man must pay the penalty;
22: 24 Do not make friends with a *h* man,
29: 22 and a *h* one commits many sins.

HOTHEADED (HEAD)

Pr 14: 16 but a fool is *h* and reckless.

HOUR

Ecc 9: 12 knows when his *h* will come:
Mt 6: 27 you by worrying can add a single *h*
Lk 12: 40 the Son of Man will come at an *h*
Jn 12: 23 The *h* has come for the Son of Man
12: 27 for this very reason I came to this *h*

HOUSE (HOUSEHOLD HOUSEHOLDS HOUSES HOUSETOPS STOREHOUSE)

Ex 12: 22 the door of his *h* until morning.
20: 17 shall not covet your neighbor's *h.*
Nu 12: 7 he is faithful in all my *h.*
Dt 5: 21 desire on your neighbor's *h*
2Sa 7: 11 LORD himself will establish a *h*
1Ch 17: 23 and his *h* be established forever.
Ne 10: 39 "We will not neglect the *h*
Ps 23: 6 I will dwell in the *h* of the LORD
27: 4 dwell in the *h* of the LORD
69: 9 for zeal for your *h* consumes me,
84: 10 a doorkeeper in the *h* of my God
122: 1 "Let us go to the *h* of the LORD."
127: 1 Unless the LORD builds the *h,*
Pr 7: 27 Her *h* is a highway to the grave,
21: 9 than share a *h* with a quarrelsome
Isa 56: 7 a *h* of prayer for all nations."
Jer 7: 11 Has this *h,* which bears my Name,
18: 2 "Go down to the potter's *h.*
Eze 33: 7 made you a watchman for the *h*
Joel 3: 18 will flow out of the LORD's *h*
Zec 13: 6 given at the *h* of my friends.'
Mt 7: 24 is like a wise man who built his *h*
10: 11 and stay at his *h* until you leave.
12: 29 can anyone enter a strong man's *h*
21: 13 My *h* will be called a *h* of prayer,'
Mk 3: 25 If a *h* is divided against itself,
11: 17 " 'My *h* will be called
Lk 6: 48 He is like a man building a *h,*
10: 7 Do not move around from *h* to *h.*
11: 17 a *h* divided against itself will fall.
11: 24 'I will return to the *h* I left.'
15: 8 sweep the *h* and search carefully
19: 9 Today salvation has come to this *h,*
Jn 2: 16 How dare you turn my Father's *h*
2: 17 "Zeal for your *h* will consume me."
12: 3 the *h* was filled with the fragrance
14: 2 In my Father's *h* are many rooms;
Ac 20: 20 you publicly and from *h* to *h.*
Ro 16: 5 the church that meets at their *h.*
Heb 3: 3 the builder of a *h* has greater honor
1Pe 2: 5 built into a spiritual *h* to be a holy

HOUSEHOLD (HOUSE)

Ex 12: 3 lamb for his family, one for each *h.*
Jos 24: 15 my *h,* we will serve the LORD."
Pr 31: 21 it snows, she has no fear for her *h;*
31: 27 over the affairs of her *h*
Mic 7: 6 are the members of his own *h.*
Mt 10: 36 will be the members of his own *h.'*
12: 25 or *h* divided against itself will not
Ac 16: 31 you will be saved—you and your *h*
Eph 2: 19 people and members of God's *h,*
1Ti 3: 12 manage his children and his *h* well.
3: 15 to conduct themselves in God's *h.*

HOUSEHOLDS (HOUSE)

Tit 1: 11 because they are ruining whole *h*

HOUSES (HOUSE)

Ex 12: 27 passed over the *h* of the Israelites
Mt 19: 29 everyone who has left *h* or brothers

HOVERING* (HOVERS)

Ge 1: 2 of God was *h* over the waters.
Isa 31: 5 Like birds *h* overhead,

HOVERS* (HOVERING)

Dt 32: 11 and *h* over its young,

HULDAH*

Prophetess inquired by Hilkiah for Josiah (2Ki 22; 2Ch 34:14-28).

HUMAN (HUMANITY)

Lev 24: 17 If anyone takes the life of a *h* being,
Isa 52: 14 his form marred beyond *h* likeness
Jn 8: 15 You judge by *h* standards;
Ro 1: 3 as to his *h* nature was a descendant
9: 5 from them is traced the *h* ancestry
1Co 1: 17 not with words of *h* wisdom,
1: 26 of you were wise by *h* standards;
2: 13 not in words taught us by *h* wisdom
2Co 3: 3 of stone but on tablets of *h* hearts.
Gal 3: 3 to attain your goal by *h* effort?
2Pe 2: 18 lustful desires of sinful *h* nature,

HUMANITY* (HUMAN)

Heb 2: 14 he too shared in their *h* so that

HUMBLE (HUMBLED HUMBLES HUMILIATE HUMILIATED HUMILITY)

Nu 12: 3 (Now Moses was a very *h* man,
2Ch 7: 14 will *h* themselves and pray
Ps 18: 27 You save the *h*
25: 9 He guides the *h* in what is right
149: 4 he crowns the *h* with salvation.
Pr 3: 34 but gives grace to the *h.*
Isa 66: 2 he who is *h* and contrite in spirit,
Mt 11: 29 for I am gentle and *h* in heart,
Eph 4: 2 Be completely *h* and gentle;
Jas 4: 6 but gives grace to the *h.'*
4: 10 *H* yourselves before the Lord,
1Pe 5: 5 but gives grace to the *h.'*
5: 6 *H* yourselves,

HUMBLED (HUMBLE)

Mt 23: 12 whoever exalts himself will be *h,*
Lk 14: 11 who exalts himself will be *h,*
Php 2: 8 he *h* himself

HUMBLES* (HUMBLE)

1Sa 2: 7 he *h* and he exalts.
Isa 26: 5 He *h* those who dwell on high,
Mt 18: 4 whoever *h* himself like this child is
23: 12 whoever *h* himself will be exalted.
Lk 14: 11 he who *h* himself will be exalted."
18: 14 he who *h* himself will be exalted."

HUMILIATE* (HUMBLE)

Pr 25: 7 than for him to *h* you
1Co 11: 22 and *h* those who have nothing?

HUMILIATED (HUMBLE)

Jer 31: 19 I was ashamed and *h*
Lk 14: 9 *h,* you will have to take the least

HUMILITY* (HUMBLE)

Ps 45: 4 of truth, *h* and righteousness;
Pr 11: 2 but with *h* comes wisdom.
15: 33 and *h* comes before honor,
18: 12 but *h* comes before honor.
22: 4 *H* and the fear of the LORD
Zep 2: 3 Seek righteousness, seek *h;*
Ac 20: 19 I served the Lord with great *h*
Php 2: 3 but in *h* consider others better
Col 2: 18 let anyone who delights in false *h*
2: 23 their false *h* and their harsh
3: 12 *h,* gentleness and patience.
Tit 3: 2 and to show true *h* toward all men.
Jas 3: 13 in the *h* that comes from wisdom.
1Pe 5: 5 Clothe yourselves with *h*

HUNG (HANG)

Dt 21: 23 anyone who is *h* on a tree is
Mt 18: 6 him to have a large millstone *h*
Lk 19: 48 all the people *h* on his words.
Gal 3: 13 "Cursed is everyone who is *h*

HUNGER (HUNGRY)

Ne 9: 15 In their *h* you gave them bread

Pr   6: 30 to satisfy his *h* when he is starving.
Mt   5: 6 Blessed are those who *h*
Lk   6: 21 Blessed are you who *h* now,
2Co   6: 5 sleepless nights and *h;* in purity,
     11: 27 I have known *h* and thirst
Rev   7: 16 Never again will they *h;*

HUNGRY (HUNGER)

Job 24: 10 carry the sheaves, but still go *h.*
Ps 107: 9 and fills the *h* with good things.
    146: 7 and gives food to the *h.*
Pr   19: 15 and the shiftless man goes *h.*
     25: 21 If your enemy is *h*, give him food
     27: 7 to the *h* even what is bitter tastes
Isa 58: 7 not to share your food with the *h*
     58: 10 spend yourselves in behalf of the *h*
Eze 18: 7 but gives his food to the *h*
     18: 16 but gives his food to the *h*
Mt   15: 32 I do not want to send them away *h,*
     25: 35 For I was *h* and you gave me
     25: 42 For I was *h* and you gave me
Lk   1: 53 He has filled the *h* with good things
Jn   6: 35 comes to me will never go *h,*
Ro   12: 20 "If your enemy is *h*, feed him;
1Co   4: 11 To this very hour we go *h*
Php   4: 12 whether well fed or *h,*

HUR

Ex   17: 12 Aaron and *H* held his hands up—

HURL

Mic   7: 19 *h* all our iniquities into the depths

HURT (HURTS)

Ecc   8: 9 it over others to his own *h.*
Mk   16: 18 deadly poison, it will not *h* them
Rev   2: 11 He who overcomes will not be *h*

HURTS* (HURT)

Ps   15: 4 even when it *h,*
Pr   26: 28 A lying tongue hates those it *h,*

HUSBAND (HUSBAND'S HUSBANDS)

Pr   31: 11 Her *h* has full confidence in her
     31: 23 Her *h* is respected at the city gate,
     31: 28 her *h* also, and he praises her:
Isa 54: 5 For your Maker is your *h—*
Jer   3: 14 the LORD, "for I am your *h.*
      3: 20 like a woman unfaithful to her *h,*
Jn   4: 17 "I have no *h,*" she replied.
Ro   7: 2 a married woman is bound to her *h*
1Co   7: 2 and each woman her own *h.*
      7: 3 The *h* should fulfill his marital duty
      7: 10 wife must not separate from her *h.*
      7: 11 And a *h* must not divorce his wife.
      7: 13 And if a woman has a *h* who is not
      7: 14 For the unbelieving *h* has been
      7: 39 A woman is bound to her *h* as long
      7: 39 But if her *h* dies, she is
2Co 11: 2 I promised you to one *h*, to Christ,
Gal   4: 27 woman than of her who has a *h.*"
Eph   5: 23 For the *h* is the head of the wife
      5: 33 and the wife must respect her *h.*
1Ti   3: 2 the *h* of but one wife, temperate,
      3: 12 A deacon must be the *h* of
      5: 9 has been faithful to her *h,*
Tit   1: 6 An elder must be blameless, the *h*

HUSBANDMAN see GARDENER

HUSBAND'S (HUSBAND)

Dt   25: 5 Her *h* brother shall take her
Pr   12: 4 of noble character is her *h* crown,
1Co   7: 4 the *h* body does not belong

HUSBANDS (HUSBAND)

Eph   5: 22 submit to your *h* as to the Lord.
      5: 25 *H*, love your wives, just
      5: 28 *h* ought to love their wives
Col   3: 18 submit to your *h*, as is fitting
      3: 19 *H*, love your wives and do not be
Tit   2: 4 the younger women to love their *h*
      2: 5 and to be subject to their *h,*
1Pe   3: 1 same way be submissive to your *h*
      3: 7 *H*, in the same way be considerate

HUSHAI

Wise man of David who frustrated Ahithophel's advice and foiled Absalom's revolt (2Sa 15:

32-37; 16:15-17:16; 1Ch 27:33).

HYMN* (HYMNS)

Ps   40: 3 a *h* of praise to our God.
Mt   26: 30 they had sung a *h*, they went out
Mk   14: 26 they had sung a *h*, they went out
1Co 14: 26 everyone has a *h*, or a word

HYMNS* (HYMN)

Ac   16: 25 Silas were praying and singing *h*
Ro   15: 9 I will sing *h* to your name."
Eph   5: 19 to one another with psalms, *h*
Col   3: 16 *h* and spiritual songs with gratitude

HYPOCRISY* (HYPOCRITE HYPOCRITES HYPOCRITICAL)

Mt   23: 28 but on the inside you are full of *h*
Mk   12: 15 we?" But Jesus knew their *h.*
Lk   12: 1 yeast of the Pharisees, which is *h.*
Gal   2: 13 The other Jews joined him in his *h,*
      2: 13 by their *h* even Barnabas was led
1Pe   2: 1 *h*, envy, and slander of every kind.

HYPOCRITE* (HYPOCRISY)

Mt   7: 5 You *h*, first take the plank out
Lk   6: 42 You *h*, first take the plank out

HYPOCRITES* (HYPOCRISY)

Ps   26: 4 nor do I consort with *h;*
Mt   6: 2 as the *h* do in the synagogues
      6: 5 when you pray, do not be like the *h*
      6: 16 do not look somber as the *h* do,
     15: 7 You *h!* Isaiah was right
     22: 18 their evil intent, said, "You *h,*
     23: 13 of the law and Pharisees, you *h!*
     23: 15 of the law and Pharisees, you *h!*
     23: 23 of the law and Pharisees, you *h!*
     23: 25 of the law and Pharisees, you *h!*
     23: 27 you *h!* You are like whitewashed
     23: 29 of the law and Pharisees, you *h!*
     24: 51 and assign him a place with the *h,*
Mk   7: 6 when he prophesied about you *h;*
Lk   12: 56 *H!* You know how
     13: 15 The Lord answered him, "You *h!*

HYPOCRITICAL* (HYPOCRISY)

1Ti   4: 2 teachings come through *h* liars,

HYSSOP

Ex   12: 22 Take a bunch of *h*, dip it
Ps   51: 7 with *h*, and I will be clean;
Jn   19: 29 the sponge on a stalk of the *h* plant,

ICHABOD

1Sa   4: 21 She named the boy *I*, saying,

IDLE* (IDLENESS IDLERS)

Dt   32: 47 They are not just *i* words for you—
Job 11: 3 Will your *i* talk reduce men
Ecc 10: 18 If his hands are *i*, the house leaks.
     11: 6 at evening let not your hands be *i.*
Isa 58: 13 as you please or speaking *i* words,
Col   2: 18 mind puffs him up with *i* notions.
1Th   5: 14 those who are *i*, encourage
2Th   3: 6 away from every brother who is *i*
      3: 7 We were not *i* when we were
      3: 11 We hear that some among you are *i*
1Ti   5: 13 they get into the habit of being *i*

IDLENESS* (IDLE)

Pr   31: 27 and does not eat the bread of *i.*

IDLERS* (IDLE)

1Ti   5: 13 And not only do they become *i,*

IDOL (IDOLATER IDOLATERS IDOLATRY IDOLS)

Ex   20: 4 make for yourself an *i* in the form
     32: 4 made it into an *i* cast in the shape
Isa 40: 19 As for an *i*, a craftsman casts it,
     41: 7 He nails down the *i*
     44: 15 he makes an *i* and bows down to it.
     44: 17 From the rest he makes a god, his *i;*
Hab   2: 18 "Of what value is an *i,*
1Co   8: 4 We know that an *i* is nothing at all

IDOLATER* (IDOL)

1Co   5: 11 an *i* or a slanderer, a drunkard
Eph   5: 5 greedy person—such a man is an *i*

IDOLATERS (IDOL)

1Co   5: 10 or the greedy and swindlers, or *i.*
      6: 9 Neither the sexually immoral nor *i*

IDOLATRY (IDOL)

1Sa 15: 23 and arrogance like the evil of *i.*
1Co 10: 14 my dear friends, flee from *i.*
Gal   5: 20 and debauchery; *i* and witchcraft;
Col   3: 5 evil desires and greed, which is *i.*
1Pe   4: 3 orgies, carousing and detestable *i.*

IDOLS (IDOL)

Dt   32: 16 angered him with their detestable *i.*
Ps   78: 58 aroused his jealousy with their *i.*
Isa 44: 9 All who make *i* are nothing,
Eze 23: 39 sacrificed their children to their *i,*
Ac   15: 20 to abstain from food polluted by *i,*
     21: 25 abstain from food sacrificed to *i,*
1Co   8: 1 Now about food sacrificed to *i:*
1Jn   5: 21 children, keep yourselves from *i.*
Rev   2: 14 to sin by eating food sacrificed to *i*

IGNORANT (IGNORE)

1Co 15: 34 for there are some who are *i* of God
Heb   5: 2 to deal gently with those who are *i*
1Pe   2: 15 good you should silence the *i* talk
2Pe   3: 16 which *i* and unstable people distort

IGNORE (IGNORANT IGNORED IGNORES)

Dt   22: 1 do not *i* it but be sure
Ps   9: 12 he does not *i* the cry of the afflicted
Heb   2: 3 if we *i* such a great salvation?

IGNORED (IGNORE)

Hos   4: 6 you have *i* the law of your God,
1Co 14: 38 he ignores this, he himself will be *i.*

IGNORES* (IGNORE)

Pr   10: 17 whoever *i* correction leads others
     13: 18 He who *i* discipline comes
     15: 32 he who *i* discipline despises
1Co 14: 38 If he *i* this, he himself will be

ILL (ILLNESS)

Mt   4: 24 brought to him all who were *i*

ILL-GOTTEN

Pr   1: 19 the end of all who go after *i* gain;
     10: 2 *I* treasures are of no value,

ILL-TEMPERED* (TEMPER)

Pr   21: 19 than with a quarrelsome and *i* wife.

ILLEGITIMATE

Heb 12: 8 then you are *i* children

ILLNESS (ILL)

2Ki   8: 9 "Will I recover from this *i?*"
2Ch 16: 12 even in his *i* he did not seek help
Ps   41: 3 and restore him from his bed of *i.*
Isa 38: 9 king of Judah after his *i*

ILLUMINATED*

Rev 18: 1 and the earth was *i* by his splendor.

IMAGE (IMAGES)

Ge   1: 26 "Let us make man in our *i,*
      1: 27 So God created man in his own *i,*
      9: 6 for in the *i* of God
Dt   27: 15 "Cursed is the man who carves an *i*
Isa 40: 18 What *i* will you compare him to?
Da   3: 1 King Nebuchadnezzar made an *i*
1Co 11: 7 since he is the *i* and glory of God;
2Co   4: 4 glory of Christ, who is the *i* of God.
Col   1: 15 He is the *i* of the invisible God,
      3: 10 in knowledge in the *i* of its Creator.
Rev 13: 14 them to set up an *i* in honor

IMAGES (IMAGE)

Ps   97: 7 All who worship *i* are put to shame,
Jer 10: 14 His *i* are a fraud;
Ro   1: 23 of the immortal God for *i* made

IMAGINATION (IMAGINE)

Eze 13: 2 who prophesy out of their own *i:*

IMAGINE (IMAGINATION)
Eph   3: 20 more than all we ask or i,

IMITATE (IMITATORS)
1Co   4: 16 Therefore I urge you to i me.
Heb   6: 12 but to i those who through faith
        13: 7 of their way of life and i their faith.
3Jn   : 11 do not i what is evil but what is

IMITATORS* (IMITATE)
Eph   5: 1 Be i of God, therefore,
1Th   1: 6 You became i of us and of the Lord
        2: 14 became i of God's churches

IMMANUEL*
Isa   7: 14 birth to a son, and will call him I.
        8: 8 O I!''
Mt   1: 23 and they will call him I''—

IMMORAL* (IMMORALITY)
Pr   6: 24 keeping you from the i woman,
1Co   5: 9 to associate with sexually i people
        5: 10 the people of this world who are i,
        5: 11 but is sexually i or greedy,
        6: 9 Neither the sexually i nor idolaters
Eph   5: 5 No i, impure or greedy person—
Heb 12: 16 See that no one is sexually i,
        13: 4 the adulterer and all the sexually i.
Rev 21: 8 the murderers, the sexually i,
        22: 15 the sexually i, the murderers,

IMMORALITY* (IMMORAL)
Nu   25: 1 in sexual i with Moabite women,
Jer   3: 9 Because Israel's i mattered so little
Mt   15: 19 murder, adultery, sexual i, theft,
Mk   7: 21 sexual i, theft, murder, adultery,
Ac   15: 20 from sexual i, from the meat
        15: 29 animals and from sexual i.
        21: 25 animals and from sexual i.''
Ro   13: 13 not in sexual i and debauchery,
1Co   5: 1 reported that there is sexual i
        6: 13 The body is not meant for sexual i,
        6: 18 Flee from sexual i.
        7: 2 But since there is so much i,
        10: 8 We should not commit sexual i,
Gal   5: 19 sexual i, impurity and debauchery;
Eph   5: 3 must not be even a hint of sexual i,
Col   3: 5 sexual i, impurity, lust, evil desires
1Th   4: 3 that you should avoid sexual i;
Jude   : 4 grace of our God into a license for i
        : 7 gave themselves up to sexual i
Rev   2: 14 and by committing sexual i.
        2: 20 misleads my servants into sexual i
        2: 21 given her time to repent of her i.
        9: 21 their sexual i or their thefts.

IMMORTAL* (IMMORTALITY)
Ro   1: 23 glory of the i God for images made
1Ti   1: 17 Now to the King eternal, i,
        6: 16 who alone is i and who lives

IMMORTALITY* (IMMORTAL)
Pr   12: 28 along that path is i
Ro   2: 7 honor and i, he will give eternal life
1Co 15: 53 and the mortal with i.
        15: 54 with i, then the saying that is
2Ti   1: 10 and i to light through the gospel.

IMPARTIAL*
Jas   3: 17 and good fruit, i and sincere.

IMPARTS*
Pr   29: 15 The rod of correction i wisdom,

IMPERFECT*
1Co 13: 10 perfection comes, the i disappears.

IMPERISHABLE
1Co 15: 42 it is raised i; it is sown in dishonor,
        15: 50 nor does the perishable inherit the i
1Pe   1: 23 not of perishable seed, but of i,

IMPLANTED*
Ps   94: 9 Does he who i the ear not hear?

IMPLORE*
Mal   1: 9 ''Now I God to be gracious to us.
2Co   5: 20 We i you on Christ's behalf:

IMPORTANCE* (IMPORTANT)
1Co 15: 3 passed on to you as of first i:

IMPORTANT (IMPORTANCE)
Mt   6: 25 Is not life more i than food,
        23: 23 have neglected the more i matters
Mk   12: 29 ''The most i one,'' answered Jesus,
        12: 33 as yourself is more i than all burnt
Php   1: 18 The i thing is that in every way,

IMPOSSIBLE
Mt   17: 20 Nothing will be i for you.''
        19: 26 ''With man this is i,
Mk   10: 27 ''With man this is i, but not
Lk   1: 37 For nothing is i with God.''
        18: 27 ''What is i with men is possible
Ac   2: 24 it was i for death to keep its hold
Heb   6: 4 It is i for those who have once been
        6: 18 things in which it is i for God to lie,
        10: 4 because it is i for the blood of bulls
        11: 6 without faith it is i to please God.

IMPOSTORS
2Ti   3: 13 and i will go from bad to worse,

IMPRESS* (IMPRESSES)
Dt   6: 7 I them on your children.

IMPRESSES* (IMPRESS)
Pr   17: 10 A rebuke i a man of discernment

IMPROPER*
Eph   5: 3 these are i for God's holy people.

IMPURE (IMPURITY)
Ac   10: 15 not call anything i that God has
Eph   5: 5 No immoral, i or greedy person—
1Th   2: 3 spring from error or i motives,
        4: 7 For God did not call us to be i,
Rev 21: 27 Nothing i will ever enter it,

IMPURITY (IMPURE)
Ro   1: 24 hearts to sexual i for the degrading
Gal   5: 19 sexual immorality, i
Eph   4: 19 as to indulge in every kind of i,
        5: 3 or of any kind of i, or of greed,
Col   3: 5 i, lust, evil desires and greed,

INCENSE
Ex   30: 1 altar of acacia wood for burning i.
        40: 5 Place the gold altar of i in front
Ps 141: 2 my prayer be set before you like i;
Mt   2: 11 him with gifts of gold and of i
Heb   9: 4 which had the golden altar of i
Rev   5: 8 were holding golden bowls full of i,
        8: 4 The smoke of the i, together

INCLINATION (INCLINES)
Ge   6: 5 and that every i of the thoughts

INCLINES* (INCLINATION)
Ecc 10: 2 The heart of the wise i to the right,

INCOME
Ecc   5: 10 wealth is never satisfied with his i.
1Co 16: 2 sum of money in keeping with his i,

INCOMPARABLE*
Eph   2: 7 ages he might show the i riches

INCREASE (EVER-INCREASING INCREASED INCREASES INCREASING)
Ge   1: 22 ''Be fruitful and i in number
        3: 16 ''I will greatly i your pains
        8: 17 be fruitful and i in number upon it
Ps   62: 10 though your riches i,
Pr   22: 16 oppresses the poor to i his wealth
Isa   9: 7 Of the i of his government
Mt   24: 12 Because of the i of wickedness,
Lk   17: 5 said to the Lord, ''I our faith!''
Ac   12: 24 But the word of God continued to i
Ro   5: 20 added so that the trespass might i.
1Th   3: 12 May the Lord make your love i

INCREASED (INCREASE)
Ac   6: 7 of disciples in Jerusalem i rapidly,
Ro   5: 20 But where sin i, grace i all the more

INCREASES (INCREASE)
Pr   24: 5 and a man of knowledge i strength;

INCREASING (INCREASE)
Ac   6: 1 when the number of disciples was i,
2Th   1: 3 one of you has for each other is i.
2Pe   1: 8 these qualities in i measure,

INCREDIBLE*
Ac   26: 8 of you consider it i that God raises

INDECENT
Ro   1: 27 Men committed i acts

INDEPENDENT*
1Co 11: 11 however, woman is not i of man,
        11: 11 of man, nor is man i of woman.

INDESCRIBABLE*
2Co   9: 15 Thanks be to God for his i gift!

INDESTRUCTIBLE*
Heb   7: 16 on the basis of the power of an i life

INDIGNANT
Mk   10: 14 When Jesus saw this, he was i.

INDISPENSABLE*
1Co 12: 22 seem to be weaker are i,

INEFFECTIVE*
2Pe   1: 8 they will keep you from being i

INEXPRESSIBLE*
2Co 12: 4 He heard i things, things that man
1Pe   1: 8 are filled with an i and glorious joy,

INFANCY* (INFANTS)
2Ti   3: 15 from i you have known the holy

INFANTS (INFANCY)
Ps   8: 2 From the lips of children and i
Mt   21: 16 '' 'From the lips of children and i
1Co   3: 1 but as worldly—mere i in Christ.
        14: 20 In regard to evil be i,
Eph   4: 14 Then we will no longer be i,

INFIRMITIES*
Isa 53: 4 Surely he took up our i
Mt   8: 17 ''He took up our i

INFLAMED
Ro   1: 27 were i with lust for one another.

INFLUENTIAL*
1Co   1: 26 not many were i; not many were

INHABITANTS (INHABITED)
Nu   33: 55 '' ''But if you do not drive out the i
Rev   8: 13 Woe! Woe to the i of the earth,

INHABITED (INHABITANTS)
Isa 45: 18 but formed it to be i—

INHERIT (CO-HEIRS HEIR HEIRS HERITAGE INHERITANCE)
Dt   1: 38 because he will lead Israel to i it.
Jos   1: 6 people to i the land I swore
Ps   37: 11 But the meek will i the land
        37: 29 the righteous will i the land
Zec   2: 12 The LORD will i Judah
Mt   5: 5 for they will i the earth.
        19: 29 as much and will i eternal life.
Mk   10: 17 ''what must I do to i eternal life?''
Lk   10: 25 ''what must I do to i eternal life?''
        18: 18 what must I do to i eternal life?''
1Co   6: 9 the wicked will not i the kingdom
        15: 50 blood cannot i the kingdom of God
Rev 21: 7 He who overcomes will i all this,

INHERITANCE (INHERIT)
Lev 20: 24 I will give it to you as an i,
Dt   4: 20 to be the people of his i,
        10: 9 The LORD is their i, as the LORD
Jos   14: 3 two-and-a-half tribes their i east
Ps   16: 6 surely I have a delightful i.
        33: 12 the people he chose for his i.
        136: 21 and gave their land as an i,
Pr   13: 22 A good man leaves an i

Mt 25: 34 blessed by my Father; take your *i*,
Eph 1: 14 who is a deposit guaranteeing our *i*
5: 5 has any *i* in the kingdom of Christ
Col 1: 12 you to share in the *i* of the saints
3: 24 you know that you will receive an *i*
Heb 9: 15 receive the promised eternal *i*—
1Pe 1: 4 and into an *i* that can never perish,

INIQUITIES (INIQUITY)

Ps 78: 38 he atoned for their *i*
103: 10 or repay us according to our *i*.
Isa 53: 5 he was crushed for our *i*;
53: 11 and he will bear their *i*.
59: 2 But your *i* have separated
Mic 7: 19 and hurl all our *i* into the depths

INIQUITY (INIQUITIES)

Ps 25: 11 forgive my *i*, though it is great.
32: 5 and did not cover up my *i*.
51: 2 Wash away all my *i*
51: 9 and blot out all my *i*.
Isa 53: 6 the *i* of us all.

INJURED

Eze 34: 16 will bind up the *i* and strengthen
Zec 11: 16 or heal the *i*, or feed the healthy,

INJUSTICE

2Ch 19: 7 the LORD our God there is no *i*

INK

2Co 3: 3 not with *i* but with the Spirit

INN*

Lk 2: 7 there was no room for them in the *i*
10: 34 took him to an *i* and took care

INNOCENT

Ex 23: 7 do not put an *i* or honest person
Dt 25: 1 acquitting the *i* and condemning
Pr 6: 17 hands that shed *i* blood,
17: 26 It is not good to punish an *i* man,
Mt 10: 16 shrewd as snakes and as *i* as doves.
27: 4 "for I have betrayed *i* blood."
27: 24 "I am *i* of this man's blood," he said.
Ac 20: 26 declare to you today that I am *i*
Ro 16: 19 what is good, and *i* about what is
1Co 4: 4 but that does not make me *i*.

INQUIRE

Isa 8: 19 should not a people *i* of their God?

INSCRIPTION

Mt 22: 20 And whose *i*?" "Caesar's,"
2Ti 2: 19 with this *i*: "The Lord knows those

INSIGHT

1Ki 4: 29 Solomon wisdom and very great *i*,
Ps 119: 99 have more *i* than all my teachers,
Pr 5: 1 listen well to my words of *i*,
21: 30 There is no wisdom, no *i*, no plan
Php 1: 9 more in knowledge and depth of *i*,
2Ti 2: 7 for the Lord will give you *i*

INSOLENT

Ro 1: 30 God-haters, *i*, arrogant

INSPIRED*

Hos 9: 7 the *i* man a maniac
1Th 1: 3 and your endurance *i* by hope

INSTALLED

Ps 2: 6 "I have *i* my King

INSTINCT* (INSTINCTS)

2Pe 2: 12 are like brute beasts, creatures of *i*,
Jude : 10 things they do understand by *i*,

INSTINCTS* (INSTINCT)

Jude : 19 who follow mere natural *i*

INSTITUTED

Ro 13: 2 rebelling against what God has *i*,
1Pe 2: 13 to every authority *i* among men:

INSTRUCT (INSTRUCTED INSTRUCTION INSTRUCTIONS INSTRUCTOR)

Ps 32: 8 I will *i* you and teach you

Ps 105: 22 to *i* his princes as he pleased
Pr 9: 9 *I* a wise man and he will be wiser
Ro 15: 14 and competent to *i* one another.
1Co 2: 16 that he may *i* him?"
14: 19 to *i* others than ten thousand words
2Ti 2: 25 who oppose him he must gently *i*,

INSTRUCTED (INSTRUCT)

2Ch 26: 5 who *i* him in the fear of God.
Pr 21: 11 a wise man is *i*, he gets knowledge.
Isa 50: 4 LORD has given me an *i* tongue;
Mt 13: 52 who has been *i* about the kingdom
1Co 14: 31 in turn so that everyone may be *i*

INSTRUCTION (INSTRUCT)

Pr 1: 8 Listen, my son, to your father's *i*
4: 1 Listen, my sons, to a father's *i*;
4: 13 Hold on to *i*, do not let it go;
8: 10 Choose my *i* instead of silver,
8: 33 Listen to my *i* and be wise;
13: 1 A wise son heeds his father's *i*,
13: 13 He who scorns *i* will pay for it,
16: 20 Whoever gives heed to *i* prospers,
16: 21 and pleasant words promote *i*.
19: 20 Listen to advice and accept *i*,
23: 12 Apply your heart to *i*
1Co 14: 6 or prophecy or word of *i*?
14: 26 or a word of *i*, a revelation,
Eph 6: 4 up in the training and *i* of the Lord.
1Th 4: 8 he who rejects this *i* does not reject
2Th 3: 14 If anyone does not obey our *i*
1Ti 1: 18 I give you this *i* in keeping
6: 3 to the sound *i* of our Lord Jesus
2Ti 4: 2 with great patience and careful *i*.

INSTRUCTIONS (INSTRUCT)

1Ti 3: 14 I am writing you these *i* so that,

INSTRUCTOR (INSTRUCT)

Gal 6: 6 share all good things with his *i*.

INSTRUMENT* (INSTRUMENTS)

Eze 33: 32 beautiful voice and plays an *i* well,
Ac 9: 15 This man is my chosen *i*
2Ti 2: 21 he will be an *i* for noble purposes,

INSTRUMENTS (INSTRUMENT)

Ro 6: 13 as *i* of wickedness, but rather offer

INSULT (INSULTED INSULTS)

Pr 9: 7 corrects a mocker invites *i*;
12: 16 but a prudent man overlooks an *i*.
Mt 5: 11 Blessed are you when people *i* you,
Lk 6: 22 when they exclude you and *i* you
1Pe 3: 9 evil with evil or *i* with *i*,

INSULTED (INSULT)

Heb 10: 29 and who has *i* the Spirit of grace?
Jas 2: 6 love him? But you have *i* the poor.
1Pe 4: 14 If you are *i* because of the name

INSULTS (INSULT)

Ps 22: 7 they hurl *i*, shaking their heads:
69: 9 the *i* of those who insult you fall
Pr 22: 10 quarrels and *i* are ended.
Mk 15: 29 passed by hurled *i* at him,
Jn 9: 28 Then they hurled *i* at him and said,
Ro 15: 3 "The *i* of those who insult you have
2Co 12: 10 in *i*, in hardships, in persecutions,
1Pe 2: 23 When they hurled their *i* at him,

INTEGRITY*

Dt 9: 5 or your *i* that you are going
1Ki 9: 4 if you walk before me in *i* of heart
1Ch 29: 17 the heart and are pleased with *i*.
Ne 7: 2 because he was a man of *i*
Job 2: 3 And he still maintains his *i*,
2: 9 "Are you still holding on to your *i*?
6: 29 reconsider, for my *i* is at stake.
27: 5 till I die, I will not deny my *i*.
Ps 7: 8 according to my *i*, O Most High.
25: 21 May *i* and uprightness protect me,
41: 12 In my *i* you uphold me
78: 72 David shepherded them with *i*
Pr 10: 9 The man of *i* walks securely,
11: 3 The *i* of the upright guides them,
13: 6 Righteousness guards the man of *i*,
17: 26 or to flog officials for their *i*.

Pr 29: 10 Bloodthirsty men hate a man of *i*
Isa 45: 23 my mouth has uttered in all *i*
59: 4 no one pleads his case with *i*.
Mt 22: 16 "we know you are a man of *i*
Mk 12: 14 we know you are a man of *i*.
Tit 2: 7 your teaching show *i*, seriousness

INTELLIGENCE (INTELLIGENT)

Isa 29: 14 the *i* of the intelligent will vanish."
1Co 1: 19 *i* of the intelligent I will frustrate."

INTELLIGENT (INTELLIGENCE)

Isa 29: 14 the intelligence of the *i* will vanish

INTELLIGIBLE

1Co 14: 19 I would rather speak five *i* words

INTENDED

Ge 50: 20 place of God? You *i* to harm me,

INTENSE

1Th 2: 17 out of our *i* longing we made every
Rev 16: 9 They were seared by the *i* heat

INTERCEDE (INTERCEDES INTERCEDING INTERCESSION INTERCESSOR)

Heb 7: 25 he always lives to *i* for them.

INTERCEDES* (INTERCEDE)

Ro 8: 26 but the Spirit himself *i* for us
8: 27 because the Spirit *i* for the saints

INTERCEDING* (INTERCEDE)

Ro 8: 34 hand of God and is also *i* for us.

INTERCESSION* (INTERCEDE)

Isa 53: 12 and made *i* for the transgressors.
1Ti 2: 1 *i* and thanksgiving be made

INTERCESSOR* (INTERCEDE)

Job 16: 20 My *i* is my friend

INTEREST (INTERESTS)

Lev 25: 36 Do not take *i* of any kind from him,
Dt 23: 20 You may charge a foreigner *i*,
Mt 25: 27 would have received it back with *i*.
Php 2: 20 who takes a genuine *i*

INTERESTS (INTEREST)

1Co 7: 34 his wife—and his *i* are divided.
Php 2: 4 only to your own *i*, but also to the *i*
2: 21 everyone looks out for his own *i*,

INTERFERE*

Ezr 6: 7 Do not *i* with the work

INTERMARRY (MARRY)

Dt 7: 3 Do not *i* with them.
Ezr 9: 14 and *i* with the peoples who commit

INTERPRET (INTERPRETATION INTERPRETER INTERPRETS)

Ge 41: 15 "I had a dream, and no one can *i* it.
Mt 16: 3 you cannot *i* the signs of the times.
1Co 12: 30 Do all *i*? But eagerly desire
14: 13 pray that he may *i* what he says.
14: 27 one at a time, and someone must *i*.

INTERPRETATION (INTERPRET)

1Co 12: 10 and to still another the *i* of tongues.
14: 26 a revelation, a tongue or an *i*.
2Pe 1: 20 about by the prophet's own *i*.

INTERPRETER (INTERPRET)

1Co 14: 28 If there is no *i*, the speaker should

INTERPRETS (INTERPRET)

1Co 14: 5 he *i*, so that the church may be

INVADED

2Ki 17: 5 king of Assyria *i* the entire land,
24: 1 king of Babylon *i* the land,

INVENT* (INVENTED)

Ro 1: 30 boastful; they *i* ways of doing evil;

INVENTED* (INVENT)

2Pe 1: 16 We did not follow cleverly *i* stories

INVESTIGATED

Lk 1: 3 I myself have carefully *i* everything

INVISIBLE*

Ro 1: 20 of the world God's *i* qualities—
Col 1: 15 He is the image of the *i* God,
1: 16 and on earth, visible and *i*,
1Ti 1: 17 immortal, *i*, the only God,
Heb 11: 27 because he saw him who is *i*.

INVITE (INVITED INVITES)

Mt 22: 9 *i* to the banquet anyone you find.'
25: 38 did we see you a stranger and *i* you
Lk 14: 12 do not *i* your friends, your brothers
14: 13 you give a banquet, *i* the poor,

INVITED (INVITE)

Zep 1: 7 he has consecrated those he has *i*.
Mt 22: 3 For many are *i*, but few are chosen
25: 35 I was a stranger and you *i* me in,
Lk 14: 10 But when you are *i*, take the lowest
Rev 19: 9 'Blessed are those who are *i*

INVITES (INVITE)

Pr 18: 6 and his mouth *i* a beating.
1Co 10: 27 If some unbeliever *i* you to a meal

INVOLVED

2Ti 2: 4 a soldier gets *i* in civilian affairs—

IRON

2Ki 6: 6 threw it there, and made the *i* float.
Ps 2: 9 will rule them with an *i* scepter;
Pr 27: 17 As *i* sharpens *i*,
Da 2: 33 and thighs of bronze, its legs of *i*,
1Ti 4: 2 have been seared as with a hot *i*.
Rev 2: 27 He will rule them with an *i* scepter;
12: 5 all the nations with an *i* scepter.
19: 15 He will rule them with an *i* scepter

IRRELIGIOUS*

1Ti 1: 9 and sinful, the unholy and *i;*

IRREVOCABLE*

Ro 11: 29 for God's gifts and his call are *i*.

ISAAC

Son of Abraham by Sarah (Ge 17:19; 21:1-7; 1Ch 1:28). Abrahamic covenant perpetuated through (Ge 17:21; 26:2-5). Offered up by Abraham (Ge 22; Heb 11:17-19). Rebekah taken as wife (Ge 24). Inherited Abraham's estate (Ge 25: 5). Fathered Esau and Jacob (Ge 25:19-26; 1Ch 1: 34). Nearly lost Rebekah to Abimelech (Ge 26: 1-11). Covenant with Abimelech (Ge 26:12-31). Tricked into blessing Jacob (Ge 27). Death (Ge 35:27-29). Father of Israel (Ex 3:6; Dt 29:13; Ro 9:10).

ISAIAH

Prophet to Judah (Isa 1:1). Called by the LORD (Isa 6). Announced judgment to Ahaz (Isa 7), deliverance from Assyria to Hezekiah (2Ki 19; Isa 36-37), deliverance from death to Hezekiah (2Ki 20:1-11; Isa 38). Chronicler of Judah's history (2Ch 26:22; 32:32).

ISCARIOT see JUDAS

ISH-BOSHETH*

Son of Saul who attempted to succeed him as king (2Sa 2:8-4:12; 1Ch 8:33).

ISHMAEL

Son of Abraham by Hagar (Ge 16; 1Ch 1:28). Blessed, but not son of covenant (Ge 17:18-21; Gal 4:21-31). Sent away by Sarah (Ge 21:8-21). Children (Ge 25:12-18; 1Ch 1:29-31). Death (Ge 25:17).

ISLAND

Rev 1: 9 was on the *i* of Patmos
16: 20 Every *i* fled away

ISRAEL (ISRAEL'S ISRAELITE ISRAELITES)

1. Name given to Jacob (see JACOB).
2. Corporate name of Jacob's descendants; often specifically Northern Kingdom.

Ex 28: 11 Engrave the names of the sons of *I*
28: 29 of the sons of *I* over his heart
Nu 24: 17 a scepter will rise out of *I*.
Dt 6: 4 Hear, O *I:* The LORD our God,
10: 12 O *I*, what does the LORD your
Jos 4: 22 *I* crossed the Jordan on dry ground
Jdg 17: 6 In those days *I* had no king;
Ru 2: 12 of *I*, under whose wings you have
1Sa 3: 20 *I* from Dan to Beersheba
4: 21 "The glory has departed from *I'*—
14: 23 So the LORD rescued *I* that day,
15: 26 has rejected you as king over *I!*"
17: 46 will know that there is a God in *I*.
18: 16 But all *I* and Judah loved David,
2Sa 5: 2 'You will shepherd my people *I*,
5: 3 they anointed David king over *I*.
14: 25 In all *I* there was not a man
1Ki 1: 35 I have appointed him ruler over *I*
10: 9 of the LORD's eternal love for *I*,
18: 17 "Is that you, you troubler of *I?*"
19: 18 Yet I reserve seven thousand in *I*—
2Ki 5: 8 know that there is a prophet in *I*."
1Ch 17: 22 made your people *I* your very own
21: 1 incited David to take a census of *I*.
29: 25 Solomon in the sight of all *I*
2Ch 9: 8 of the love of your God for *I*
Ps 73: 1 Surely God is good to *I*,
81: 8 if you would but listen to me, O *I!*
98: 3 his faithfulness to the house of *I*;
99: 8 you were to *I* a forgiving God,
Isa 11: 12 and gather the exiles of *I*;
27: 6 *I* will bud and blossom
44: 21 O *I*, I will not forget you.
46: 13 my splendor to *I*.
Jer 2: 3 *I* was holy to the LORD,
23: 6 and *I* will live in safety.
31: 2 I will come to give rest to *I*."
31: 10 'He who scattered *I* will gather
31: 31 covenant with the house of *I*
33: 17 sit on the throne of the house of *I*,
Eze 3: 17 you a watchman for the house of *I*;
33: 7 you a watchman for the house of *I*;
34: 2 prophesy against the shepherds of *I*
37: 28 that I the LORD make *I* holy,
39: 23 of *I* went into exile for their sin,
Da 9: 20 my sin and the sin of my people *I*
Hos 11: 1 "When *I* was a child, I loved him,
Am 4: 12 prepare to meet your God, O *I*."
7: 11 and *I* will surely go into exile,
8: 2 "The time is ripe for my people *I*;
9: 14 I will bring back my exiled people *I*
Mic 5: 2 one who will be ruler over *I*,
Zep 3: 13 The remnant of *I* will do no wrong;
Zec 11: 14 brotherhood between Judah and *I*.
Mal 1: 5 even beyond the borders of *I!*'
Mt 2: 6 be the shepherd of my people *I*.'
10: 6 Go rather to the lost sheep of *I*.
15: 24 only to the lost sheep of *I*.''
Mk 12: 29 'Hear, O *I*, the Lord our God,
Lk 22: 30 judging the twelve tribes of *I*.
Ac 1: 6 going to restore the kingdom to *I?*''
9: 15 and before the people of *I*.
Ro 9: 4 of my own race, the people of *I*.
9: 6 all who are descended from *I* are *I*.
9: 31 but *I*, who pursued a law
11: 7 What *I* sought so earnestly it did
11: 26 And so all *I* will be saved,
Gal 6: 16 who follow this rule, even to the *I*
Eph 2: 12 excluded from citizenship in *I*,
3: 6 Gentiles are heirs together with *I*,
Heb 8: 8 covenant with the house of *I*
Rev 7: 4 144,000 from all the tribes of *I*.
21: 12 the names of the twelve tribes of *I*.

ISRAEL'S (ISRAEL)

Jdg 10: 16 he could bear *I* misery no longer.
2Sa 23: 1 *I* singer of songs;
Isa 44: 6 *I* King and Redeemer, the LORD
Jer 3: 9 Because *I* immorality mattered
31: 9 because I am *I* father,
Jn 3: 10 "You are *I* teacher," said Jesus,

ISRAELITE (ISRAEL)

Ex 16: 1 The whole *I* community set out
35: 29 All the *I* men and women who
Nu 8: 16 offspring from every *I* woman.
20: 1 the whole *I* community arrived
20: 22 The whole *I* community set out

Jn 1: 47 "Here is a true *I*, in whom there is
Ro 11: 1 I am an *I* myself, a descendant

ISRAELITES (ISRAEL)

Ex 1: 7 the *I* were fruitful and multiplied
2: 23 The *I* groaned in their slavery
3: 9 the cry of the *I* has reached me,
12: 35 The *I* did as Moses instructed
12: 37 The *I* journeyed from Rameses
14: 22 and the *I* went through the sea
16: 12 I have heard the grumbling of the *I*.
16: 35 The *I* ate manna forty years,
24: 17 To the *I* the glory of the LORD
28: 30 decisions for the *I* over his heart
29: 45 Then I will dwell among the *I*
31: 16 The *I* are to observe the Sabbath,
33: 5 "Tell the *I*, 'You are a stiff-necked
39: 42 The *I* had done all the work just
Lev 22: 32 be acknowledged as holy by the *I*.
25: 46 rule over your fellow *I* ruthlessly.
25: 55 for the *I* belong to me as servants.
Nu 2: 32 These are the *I*, counted according
6: 23 'This is how you are to bless the *I*.
9: 2 "Have the *I* celebrate the Passover
9: 17 the *I* set out; wherever the cloud
10: 12 Then the *I* set out from the Desert
14: 2 All the *I* grumbled against Moses
20: 12 as holy in the sight of the *I*,
21: 6 they bit the people and many *I* died
26: 65 had told those *I* they would surely
27: 12 and see the land I have given the *I*.
33: 3 The *I* set out from Rameses
35: 10 "Speak to the *I* and say to them:
Dt 33: 1 on the *I* before his death.
Jos 1: 2 about to give to them—to the *I*.
5: 6 The *I* had moved about
7: 1 the *I* acted unfaithfully in regard
8: 32 Then in the presence of the *I*,
18: 1 of the *I* gathered at Shiloh
21: 3 the *I* gave the Levites the following
22: 9 of Manasseh left the *I* at Shiloh
Jdg 2: 11 Then the *I* did evil in the eyes
3: 12 Once again the *I* did evil
4: 1 the *I* once again did evil in the eyes
6: 1 Again the *I* did evil in the eyes
10: 6 Again the *I* did evil in the eyes
13: 1 Again the *I* did evil in the eyes
1Sa 17: 2 Saul and the *I* assembled
1Ki 8: 63 and all the *I* dedicated the temple
9: 22 did not make slaves of any of the *I*;
12: 1 for all the *I* had gone there
12: 17 But as for the *I* who were living
2Ki 17: 24 towns of Samaria to replace the *I*.
1Ch 9: 2 in their own towns were some *I*,
10: 1 fought against Israel; the *I* fled
11: 4 and all the *I* marched to Jerusalem,
2Ch 7: 6 and all the *I* were standing.
Ne 1: 6 the sins we *I*, including myself
Jer 16: 14 who brought the *I* up out of Egypt,'
Hos 1: 10 "Yet the *I* will be like the sand
3: 1 Love her as the LORD loves the *I*,
Am 4: 5 boast about them, you *I*,
Mic 5: 3 return to join the *I*.
Ro 9: 27 the number of the *I* be like the sand
10: 1 for the *I* is that they may be saved.
10: 16 But not all the *I* accepted the good
2Co 11: 22 Are they *I?* So am I.

ISSACHAR

Son of Jacob by Leah (Ge 30:18; 35:23; 1Ch 2: 1). Tribe of blessed (Ge 49:14-15; Dt 33:18-19), numbered (Nu 1:29; 26:25), allotted land (Jos 19: 17-23; Eze 48:25), assisted Deborah (Jdg 5:15), 12,000 from (Rev 7:7).

ISSUING*

Da 9: 25 From the *i* of the decree to restore

ITALY

Ac 27: 1 decided that we would sail for *I*,
Heb 13: 24 from *I* send you their greetings.

ITCHING*

2Ti 4: 3 to say what their *i* ears want to hear

ITHAMAR

Son of Aaron (Ex 6:23; 1Ch 6:3). Duties at tabernacle (Ex 38:21; Nu 4:21-33; 7:8).

ITTAI

2Sa 15: 19 The king said to *I* the Gittite,

IVORY

1Ki 10: 22 silver and *i*, and apes and baboons.
22: 39 the palace he built and inlaid with *i*

JABBOK

Ge 32: 22 and crossed the ford of the *J*.
Dt 3: 16 and out to the *J* River,

JABESH

1Sa 11: 1 And all the men of *J* said to him,
31: 12 wall of Beth Shan and went to *J*,
1Ch 10: 12 and his sons and brought them to *J*.

JABESH GILEAD

Jdg 21: 8 that no one from *J* had come to
2Sa 2: 4 the men of *J* who had buried Saul,
1Ch 10: 11 the inhabitants of *J* heard

JACOB

Second son of Isaac, twin of Esau (Ge 26: 21-26; 1Ch 1:34). Bought Esau's birthright (Ge 26:29-34); tricked Isaac into blessing him (Ge 27: 1-37). Fled to Haran (Ge 28:1-5). Abrahamic covenant perpetuated through (Ge 28:13-15; Mal 1:2). Vision at Bethel (Ge 28:10-22). Served Laban for Rachel and Leah (Ge 29:1-30). Children (Ge 29: 31-30:24; 35:16-26; 1Ch 2-9). Flocks increased (Ge 30:25-43). Returned to Canaan (Ge 31). Wrestled with God; name changed to Israel (Ge 32:22-32). Reconciled to Esau (Ge 33). Returned to Bethel (Ge 35:1-15). Favored Joseph (Ge 37:3). Sent sons to Egypt during famine (Ge 42-43). Settled in Egypt (Ge 46). Blessed Ephraim and Manasseh (Ge 48). Blessed sons (Ge 49:1-28; Heb 11:21). Death (Ge 49:29-33). Burial (Ge 50:1-14).

JAEL*

Woman who killed Canaanite general, Sisera (Jdg 4:17-22; 5:24-27).

JAIR

Judge from Gilead (Jdg 10:3-5).

JAIRUS*

Synagogue ruler whose daughter Jesus raised (Mk 5:22-43; Lk 8:41-56).

JAMES

1. Apostle; brother of John (Mt 4:21-22; 10:2; Mk 3:17; Lk 5:1-10). At transfiguration (Mt 17: 1-13; Mk 9:1-13; Lk 9:28-36). Killed by Herod (Ac 12:2).
2. Apostle; son of Alphaeus (Mt 10:3; Mk 3:18; Lk 6:15).
3. Brother of Jesus (Mt 13:55; Mk 6:3; Lk 24: 10; Gal 1:19) and Judas (Jude 1). With believers before Pentecost (Ac 1:13). Leader of church at Jerusalem (Ac 12:17; 15; 21:18; Gal 2:9, 12). Author of epistle (Jas 1:1).

JAPHETH

Son of Noah (Ge 5:32; 1Ch 1:4-5). Blessed (Ge 9:18-28). Sons of (Ge 10:2-5).

JAR (JARS)

Ge 24: 14 let down your *j* that I may have
1Ki 17: 14 'The *j* of flour will not be used up
Jer 19: 1 ''Go and buy a clay *j* from a potter.
Lk 8: 16 hides it in a *j* or puts it under a bed.

JARS (JAR)

Jn 2: 6 Nearby stood six stone water *j*,
2Co 4: 7 we have this treasure in *j* of clay

JASPER

Ex 28: 20 row a chrysolite, an onyx and a *j*.
Eze 28: 13 chrysolite, onyx and *j*,
Rev 4: 3 sat there had the appearance of *j*
21: 19 The first foundation was *j*,

JAVELIN

1Sa 17: 45 me with sword and spear and *j*,

JAWBONE

Jdg 15: 15 Finding a fresh *j* of a donkey,

JEALOUS (JEALOUSY)

Ex 20: 5 the Lord your God, am a *j* God,
34: 14 whose name is Jealous, is a *j* God.
Dt 4: 24 God is a consuming fire, a *j* God.
6: 15 is a *j* God and his anger will burn
32: 21 They made me *j* by what is no god
Jos 24: 19 He is a holy God; he is a *j* God.
Eze 16: 38 of my wrath and *j* anger.
16: 42 my *j* anger will turn away from you
23: 25 I will direct my *j* anger against you,
36: 6 in my *j* wrath because you have
Joel 2: 18 the Lord will be *j* for his land
Na 1: 2 Lord is a *j* and avenging God;
Zep 3: 8 consumed by the fire of my *j* anger.
Zec 1: 14 I am very *j* for Jerusalem and Zion,
8: 2 ''I am very *j* for Zion; I am burning
2Co 11: 2 I am *j* for you with a godly jealousy

JEALOUSY (JEALOUS)

Ps 79: 5 How long will your *j* burn like fire?
Pr 6: 34 for *j* arouses a husband's fury,
27: 4 but who can stand before *j*?
SS 8: 6 its *j* unyielding as the grave.
Zep 1: 18 In the fire of his *j*
Zec 8: 2 I am burning with *j* for her.''
Ro 13: 13 debauchery, not in dissension and *j*
1Co 3: 3 For since there is *j* and quarreling
10: 22 trying to arouse the Lord's *j*?
2Co 11: 2 I am jealous for you with a godly *j*.
12: 20 *j*, outbursts of anger, factions,
Gal 5: 20 hatred, discord, *j*, fits of rage,

JECONIAH see JEHOIACHIN

JEERS*

Heb 11: 36 Some faced *j* and flogging,

JEHOAHAZ

1. Son of Jehu; king of Israel (2Ki 13:1-9).
2. Son of Josiah; king of Judah (2Ki 23:31-34; 2Ch 36:1-4).

JEHOASH

1. See JOASH.
2. Son of Jehoahaz; king of Israel. Defeat of Aram prophesied by Elisha (2Ki 13:10-25). Defeated Amaziah in Jerusalem (2Ki 14:1-16; 2Ch 25:17-24).

JEHOIACHIN

Son of Jehoiakim; king of Judah exiled by Nebuchadnezzar (2Ki 24:8-17; 2Ch 36:8-10; Jer 22:24-30; 24:1). Raised from prisoner status (2Ki 25:27-30; Jer 52:31-34).

JEHOIADA

Priest who sheltered Joash from Athaliah (2Ki 11-12; 2Ch 22:11-24:16).

JEHOIAKIM

Son of Jehoahaz; made king of Judah by Pharaoh Neco (2Ki 23:34-24:6; 2Ch 36:4-8; Jer 22: 18-23). Burned scroll of Jeremiah's prophecies (Jer 36).

JEHORAM

1. Son of Jehoshaphat; king of Judah (2Ki 8: 16-24). Prophesied against by Elijah; killed by the Lord (2Ch 21).
2. See JORAM.

JEHOSHAPHAT

Son of Asa; king of Judah. Strengthened his kingdom (2Ch 17). Joined with Ahab against Aram (2Ki 22; 2Ch 18). Established judges (2Ch 19). Joined with Joram against Moab (2Ki 3; 2Ch 20).

JEHOVAH see LORD‡

JEHU

1. Prophet against Baasha (2Ki 16:1-7).
2. King of Israel. Anointed by Elijah to obliterate house of Ahab (1Ki 19:16-17); anointed by servant of Elisha (2Ki 9:1-13). Killed Joram and Ahaziah (2Ki 9:14-29; 2Ch 22:7-9), Jezebel (2Ki 9:30-37), relatives of Ahab (2Ki 10:1-17), ministers of Baal (2Ki 10:18-29). Death (2Ki 10:30-36).

JEPHTHAH

Judge from Gilead who delivered Israel from Ammon (Jdg 10:6-12:7). Made rash vow concerning his daughter (Jdg 11:30-40).

JEREMIAH

Prophet to Judah (Jer 1:1-3). Called by the Lord (Jer 1). Put in stocks (Jer 20:1-3). Threatened for prophesying (Jer 11:18-23; 26). Opposed by Hananiah (Jer 28). Scroll burned (Jer 36). Imprisoned (Jer 37). Thrown into cistern (Jer 38). Forced to Egypt with those fleeing Babylonians (Jer 43).

JERICHO

Nu 22: 1 along the Jordan across from *J*.
Jos 3: 16 the people crossed over opposite *J*.
5: 10 camped at Gilgal on the plains of *J*,
Lk 10: 30 going down from Jerusalem to *J*,
Heb 11: 30 By faith the walls of *J* fell,

JEROBOAM

1. Official of Solomon; rebelled to become first king of Israel (1Ki 11:26-40; 12:1-20; 2Ch 10). Idolatry (1Ki 12:25-33); judgment for (1Ki 13-14; 2Ch 13).
2. Son of Jehoash; king of Israel (1Ki 14:23-29).

JERUB-BAAL see GIDEON

JERUSALEM

Jos 10: 1 of *J* heard that Joshua had taken Ai
15: 8 of the Jebusite city (that is, *J*).
Jdg 1: 8 The men of Judah attacked *J* also
1Sa 17: 54 head and brought it to *J*,
2Sa 5: 5 and in *J* he reigned over all Israel
5: 6 and his men marched to *J*
9: 13 And Mephibosheth lived in *J*,
11: 1 But David remained in *J*.
15: 29 took the ark of God back to *J*
24: 16 stretched out his hand to destroy *J*,
1Ki 3: 1 the Lord, and the wall around *J*.
9: 15 the wall of *J*, and Hazor, Megiddo
9: 19 whatever he desired to build in *J*,
10: 26 cities and also with him in *J*.
10: 27 as common in *J* as stones,
11: 7 of *J*, Solomon built a high place
11: 13 my servant and for the sake of *J*,
11: 36 always have a lamp before me in *J*,
11: 42 Solomon reigned in *J*
12: 27 at the temple of the Lord in *J*,
14: 21 and he reigned seventeen years in *J*
14: 25 Shishak king of Egypt attacked *J*.
15: 2 and he reigned in *J* three years.
15: 10 and he reigned in *J* forty-one years.
22: 42 he reigned in *J* twenty-five years.
2Ki 8: 17 and he reigned in *J* eight years.
8: 26 and he reigned in *J* one year.
12: 1 and he reigned in *J* forty years.
12: 17 Then he turned to attack *J*.
14: 2 he reigned in *J* twenty-nine years.
14: 13 Then Jehoash went to *J*
15: 2 and he reigned in *J* fifty-two years.
15: 33 and he reigned in *J* sixteen years.
16: 2 and he reigned in *J* sixteen years.
16: 5 Israel marched up to fight against *J*
18: 2 he reigned in *J* twenty-nine years.
18: 17 Lachish to King Hezekiah at *J*.
19: 31 For out of *J* will come a remnant,
21: 1 and he reigned in *J* fifty-five years.
21: 12 going to bring such disaster on *J*
21: 19 and he reigned in *J* two years.
22: 1 he reigned in *J* thirty-one years.
23: 27 and I will reject *J*, the city I chose,
23: 31 and he reigned in *J* three months.
23: 36 and he reigned in *J* eleven years.
24: 8 and he reigned in *J* three months.
24: 10 king of Babylon advanced on *J*
24: 14 He carried into exile all *J*:
24: 18 and he reigned in *J* eleven years.
24: 20 anger that all this happened to *J*
25: 1 king of Babylon marched against *J*
25: 9 royal palace and all the houses of *J*.
1Ch 11: 4 and all the Israelites marched to *J*,
21: 16 sword in his hand extended over *J*.
2Ch 1: 4 he had pitched a tent for it in *J*.
3: 1 the Lord in *J* on Mount Moriah,

2Ch 6: 6 now I have chosen *J* for my Name
9: 1 she came to *J* to test him
20: 15 and all who live in Judah and *J!*
20: 27 and *J* returned joyfully to *J*,
29: 8 Lord has fallen on Judah and *J*;
36: 19 and broke down the wall of *J*;
Ezr 1: 2 a temple for him at *J* in Judah.
2: 1 to Babylon (they returned to *J*
3: 1 people assembled as one man in *J*
4: 12 up to us from you have gone to *J*
4: 24 of God in *J* came to a standstill
6: 12 or to destroy this temple in *J*,
7: 8 Ezra arrived in *J* in the fifth month
9: 9 a wall of protection in Judah and *J*.
10: 7 for all the exiles to assemble in *J*.
Ne 1: 2 the exile, and also about *J*.
1: 3 The wall of *J* is broken down,
2: 11 to *J*, and after staying there three
2: 17 Come, let us rebuild the wall of *J*,
2: 20 you have no share in *J* or any claim
3: 8 They restored *J* as far as the Broad
4: 8 fight against *J* and stir up trouble
11: 1 leaders of the people settled in *J*,
12: 27 At the dedication of the wall of *J*,
12: 43 in *J* could be heard far away.
Ps 51: 18 build up the walls of *J*.
79: 1 they have reduced *J* to rubble.
122: 2 in your gates, O *J*.
122: 3 *J* is built like a city
122: 6 Pray for the peace of *J*:
125: 2 As the mountains surround *J*,
128: 5 may you see the prosperity of *J*,
137: 5 If I forget you, O *J*,
147: 2 The Lord builds up *J*;
147: 12 Extol the Lord, O *J*;
SS 6: 4 lovely as *J*,
Isa 1: 1 and *J* that Isaiah son of Amoz saw
2: 1 saw concerning Judah and *J*.
3: 1 is about to take from *J* and Judah
3: 8 *J* staggers,
4: 3 recorded among the living in *J*,
8: 14 And for the people of *J* he will be
27: 13 Lord on the holy mountain in *J*.
31: 5 the Lord Almighty will shield *J*;
33: 20 your eyes will see *J*,
40: 2 Speak tenderly to *J*,
40: 9 You who bring good tidings to *J*,
52: 1 O *J*, the holy city.
52: 2 rise up, sit enthroned, O *J*.
62: 6 on your walls, O *J*;
62: 7 give him no rest till he establishes *J*
65: 18 for I will create *J* to be a delight
Jer 2: 2 and proclaim in the hearing of *J*:
3: 17 time they will call *J* The Throne
4: 5 and proclaim in *J* and say:
4: 14 O *J*, wash the evil from your heart
5: 1 "Go up and down the streets of *J*,
6: 6 and build siege ramps against *J*.
8: 5 Why does *J* always turn away?
9: 11 "I will make *J* a heap of ruins,
13: 27 Woe to you, O *J*!
23: 14 And among the prophets of *J*
24: 1 into exile from *J* to Babylon
26: 18 *J* will become a heap of rubble,
32: 2 of Babylon was then besieging *J*,
33: 10 the streets of *J* that are deserted,
39: 1 This is how *J* was taken: In
51: 50 and think on *J*."
52: 14 broke down all the walls around *J*.
La 1: 7 *J* remembers all the treasures
Eze 14: 21 send against *J* my four dreadful
16: 2 confront *J* with her detestable
Da 6: 10 the windows opened toward *J*.
9: 2 of *J* would last seventy years.
9: 12 done like what has been done to *J*.
9: 25 and rebuild *J* until the Anointed
Joel 3: 1 restore the fortunes of Judah and *J*,
3: 16 and thunder from *J*;
3: 17 *J* will be holy;
Am 2: 5 will consume the fortresses of *J*."
Ob : 11 and cast lots for *J*.
Mic 1: 5 Is it not *J*?
4: 2 the word of the Lord from *J*.
Zep 3: 16 On that day they will say to *J*,
Zec 1: 14 'I am very jealous for *J* and Zion,
1: 17 comfort Zion and choose *J*.' "
2: 2 He answered me, "To measure *J*,
2: 4 '*J* will be a city without walls

Zec 8: 3 I will return to Zion and dwell in *J*.
8: 8 I will bring them back to live in *J*;
8: 15 determined to do good again to *J*
8: 22 powerful nations will come to *J*
9: 9 Shout, Daughter of *J!*
9: 10 and the war-horses from *J*,
12: 3 I will make *J* an immovable rock
12: 10 the inhabitants of *J* a spirit of grace
14: 2 the nations to *J* to fight against it;
14: 8 living water will flow out from *J*,
14: 16 that have attacked *J* will go up
Mt 16: 21 to his disciples that he must go to *J*
20: 18 said to them, "We are going up to *J*
21: 10 When Jesus entered *J*, the whole
23: 37 "O *J*, *J*, you who kill the prophets
Mk 10: 33 "We are going up to *J*," he said,
Lk 2: 22 Mary took him to *J* to present him
2: 41 Every year his parents went to *J*
2: 43 the boy Jesus stayed behind in *J*,
4: 9 The devil led him to *J*
9: 31 about to bring to fulfillment at *J*.
9: 51 Jesus resolutely set out for *J*,
13: 34 die outside *J*.' "O *J*, *J*,
18: 31 told them, "We are going up to *J*,
19: 41 As he approached *J* and saw
21: 20 "When you see *J* surrounded
21: 24 *J* will be trampled
24: 47 name to all nations, beginning at *J*.
Jn 4: 20 where we must worship is in *J*."
Ac 1: 4 this command: "Do not leave *J*,
1: 8 and you will be my witnesses in *J*,
6: 7 of disciples in *J* increased rapidly,
20: 22 by the Spirit, I am going to *J*.
23: 11 As you have testified about me in *J*
Ro 15: 19 So from *J* all the way
Gal 4: 25 corresponds to the present city of *J*
4: 26 But the *J* that is above is free,
Heb 12: 22 to the heavenly *J*, the city
Rev 3: 12 the new *J*, which is coming
21: 2 I saw the Holy City, the new *J*,
21: 10 and showed me the Holy City, *J*,

JESSE

Father of David (Ru 4:17-22; 1Sa 16; 1Ch 2: 12-17).

JESUS

LIFE: Genealogy (Mt 1:1-17; Lk 3:21-37). Birth announced (Mt 1:18-25; Lk 1:26-45). Birth (Mt 2:1-12; Lk 2:1-40). Escape to Egypt (Mt 2: 13-23). As a boy in the temple (Lk 2:41-52). Baptism (Mt 3:13-17; Mk 1:9-11; Lk 3:21-22; Jn 1:32-34). Temptation (Mt 4:1-11; Mk 1:12-13; Lk 4:1-13). Ministry in Galilee (Mt 4:12-18:35; Mk 1:14-9:50; Lk 4:14-13:9; Jn 1:35-2:11; 4; 6). Transfiguration (Mt 17:1-8; Mk 9:2-8; Lk 9:28-36), on the way to Jerusalem (Mt 19-20; Mk 10; Lk 13:10-19:27), in Jerusalem (Mt 21-25; Mk 11-13; Lk 19:28-21:38; Jn 2:12-3:36; 5; 7-12). Last supper (Mt 26:17-35; Mk 14:12-31; Lk 22:1-38; Jn 13-17). Arrest and trial (Mt 26:36-27:31; Mk 14:43-15:20; Lk 22:39-23:25; Jn 18:1-19:16). Crucifixion (Mt 27:32-66; Mk 15:21-47; Lk 23: 26-55; Jn 19:28-42). Resurrection and appearances (Mt 28; Mk 16; Lk 24; Jn 20-21; Ac 1:1-11; 7:56; 9:3-6; 1Co 15:1-8; Rev 1:1-20).

MIRACLES. Healings: official's son (Jn 4:43-54), demoniac in Capernaum (Mk 1:23-26; Lk 4: 33-35), Peter's mother-in-law (Mt 8:14-17; Mk 1: 29-31; Lk 4:38-39), leper (Mt 8:2-4; Mk 1:40-45; Lk 5:12-16), paralytic (Mt 9:1-8; Mk 2:1-12; Lk 5: 17-26), cripple (Jn 5:1-9), shriveled hand (Mt 12: 10-13; Mk 3:1-5; Lk 6:6-11), centurion's servant (Mt 8:5-13; Lk 7:1-10), widow's son raised (Lk 7: 11-17), demoniac (Mt 12:22-23; Lk 11:14), Gadarene demoniacs (Mt 8:28-34; Mk 5:1-20; Lk 8: 26-39), woman's bleeding and Jairus' daughter (Mt 9:18-26; Mk 5:21-43; Lk 8:40-56), blind man (Mt 9:27-31), mute man (Mt 9:32-33), Canaanite woman's daughter (Mt 15:21-28; Mk 7:24-30), deaf man (Mk 7:31-37), blind man (Mk 8:22-26), demoniac boy (Mt 17:14-18; Mk 9:14-29; Lk 9: 37-43), ten lepers (Lk 17:11-19), man born blind (Jn 9:1-7), Lazarus raised (Jn 11), crippled woman (Lk 13:11-17), man with dropsy (Lk 14:1-6), two blind men (Mt 20:29-34; Mk 10:46-52; Lk 18: 35-43), Malchus' ear (Lk 22:50-51). Other Miracles: water to wine (Jn 2:1-11), catch of fish (Lk

5:1-11), storm stilled (Mt 8:23-27; Mk 4:37-41; Lk 8:22-25), 5,000 fed (Mt 14:15-21; Mk 6:35-44; Lk 9:10-17; Jn 6:1-14), walking on water (Mt 14: 25-33; Mk 6:48-52; Jn 6:15-21), 4,000 fed (Mt 15: 32-39; Mk 8:1-9), money from fish (Mt 17:24-27), fig tree cursed (Mt 21:18-22; Mk 11:12-14), catch of fish (Jn 21:1-14).

MAJOR TEACHING: Sermon on the Mount (Mt 5-7; Lk 6:17-49), to Nicodemus (Jn 3), to Samaritan woman (Jn 4), Bread of Life (Jn 6: 22-59), at Feast of Tabernacles (Jn 7-8), woes to Pharisees (Mt 23; Lk 11:37-54), Good Shepherd (Jn 10:1-18), Olivet Discourse (Mt 24-25; Mk 13; Lk 21:5-36), Upper Room Discourse (Jn 13-16).

PARABLES: Sower (Mt 13:3-23; Mk 4:3-25; Lk 8:5-18), seed's growth (Mk 4:26-29), wheat and weeds (Mt 13:24-30, 36-43), mustard seed (Mt 13:31-32; Mk 4:30-32), yeast (Mt 13:33-35; Mk 4:33-34), hidden treasure (Mt 13:44), valuable pearl (Mt 13:45-46), net (Mt 13:47-51), house owner (Mt 13:52), good Samaritan (Lk 10:25-37), unmerciful servant (Mt 18:15-35), lost sheep (Mt 18:10-14; Lk 15:4-7), lost coin (Lk 15:8-10), prodigal son (Lk 15:11-32), dishonest manager (Lk 16:1-13), rich man and Lazarus (Lk 16:19-31), persistent widow (Lk 18:1-8), Pharisee and tax collector (Lk 18:9-14), payment of workers (Mt 20:1-16), tenants and the vineyard (Mt 21: 28-46; Mt 12:1-12; Lk 20:9-19), wedding banquet (Mt 22:1-14), faithful servant (Mt 24:45-51), ten virgins (Mt 25:1-13), talents (Mt 25:1-30; Lk 19: 12-27).

DISCIPLES see APOSTLES. Call of (Jn 1: 35-51; Mt 4:18-22; 9:9; Mk 1:16-20; 2:13-14; Lk 5:1-11, 27-28). Named Apostles (Mk 3:13-19; Lk 6:12-16). Twelve sent out (Mt 10; Mk 6:7-11; Lk 9:1-5). Seventy sent out (Lk 10:1-24). Defection of (Jn 6:60-71; Mt 26:56; Mk 14:50-52). Final commission (Mt 28:16-20; Jn 21:15-23; Ac 1:3-8).

Ac 2: 32 God has raised this *J* to life,
9: 5 "I am *J*, whom you are persecuting
9: 34 said to him, "*J* Christ heals you.
15: 11 of our Lord *J* that we are saved,
16: 31 "Believe in the Lord *J*,
20: 24 the task the Lord *J* has given me—
Ro 3: 24 redemption that came by Christ *J*.
5: 17 life through the one man, *J* Christ.
8: 1 for those who are in Christ *J*,
1Co 1: 7 for our Lord *J* Christ to be revealed
2: 2 except *J* Christ and him crucified.
6: 11 in the name of the Lord *J* Christ
8: 6 and there is but one Lord, *J* Christ,
12: 3 and no one can say, "*J* is Lord,"
2Co 4: 5 not preach ourselves, but *J* Christ
13: 5 Do you not realize that Christ *J* is
Gal 2: 16 but by faith in *J* Christ.
3: 28 for you are all one in Christ *J*.
5: 6 in Christ *J* neither circumcision
6: 17 bear on my body the marks of *J*.
Eph 1: 5 as his sons through *J* Christ,
2: 10 created in Christ *J*
2: 20 with Christ *J* himself as the chief
Php 1: 6 until the day of Christ *J*.
2: 5 be the same as that of Christ *J*:
2: 10 name of *J* every knee should bow,
Col 3: 17 do it all in the name of the Lord *J*,
1Th 1: 10 whom he raised from the dead—*J*,
4: 14 We believe that *J* died
5: 23 at the coming of our Lord *J* Christ.
2Th 1: 7 when the Lord *J* is revealed
2: 1 the coming of our Lord *J* Christ
1Ti 1: 15 Christ *J* came into the world
2Ti 1: 10 appearing of our Savior, Christ *J*,
2: 3 us like a good soldier of Christ *J*.
3: 12 life in Christ *J* will be persecuted,
Tit 2: 13 our great God and Savior, *J* Christ,
Heb 2: 9 But we see *J*, who was made a little
2: 11 So *J* is not ashamed to call them
3: 1 fix your thoughts on *J*, the apostle
3: 3 *J* has been found worthy
4: 14 through the heavens, *J* the Son
6: 20 where *J*, who went before us,
7: 22 *J* has become the guarantee
7: 24 but because *J* lives forever,
8: 6 But the ministry *J* has received is
12: 2 Let us fix our eyes on *J*, the author
12: 24 to *J* the mediator of a new

1Pe 1: 3 the resurrection of *J* Christ
2Pe 1: 16 and coming of our Lord *J* Christ,
1Jn 1: 7 and the blood of *J*, his Son,
   2: 1 *J* Christ, the Righteous One.
   2: 6 to live in him must walk as *J* did.
   4: 15 anyone acknowledges that *J* is
Rev 1: 1 The revelation of *J* Christ,
  22: 16 *J*, have sent my angel
  22: 20 Come, Lord *J*.

JETHRO

Father-in-law and adviser of Moses (Ex 3:1; 18). Also known as Reuel (Ex 2:18).

JEW (JEWS JEWS' JUDAISM)

Est 2: 5 of Susa a *J* of the tribe of Benjamin,
Zec 8: 23 of one *J* by the hem of his robe
Ac 21: 39 "I am a *J*, from Tarsus in Cilicia,
Ro 1: 16 first for the *J*, then for the Gentile.
  2: 28 A man is not a *J* if he is only one
  10: 12 there is no difference between *J*
1Co 9: 20 To the Jews I became like a *J*,
Gal 2: 14 "You are a *J*, yet you live like
  3: 28 There is neither *J* nor Greek,
Col 3: 11 Here there is no Greek or *J*,

JEWEL (JEWELRY JEWELS)

Pr 20: 15 that speak knowledge are a rare *j*.
SS 4: 9 with one *j* of your necklace.
Rev 21: 11 of a very precious *j*,

JEWELRY (JEWEL)

Ex 35: 22 and brought gold *j* of all kinds:
Jer 2: 32 Does a maiden forget her *j*,
Eze 16: 11 you with *j*: I put bracelets
1Pe 3: 3 wearing of gold *j* and fine clothes.

JEWELS (JEWEL)

Isa 54: 12 your gates of sparkling *j*,
  61: 10 as a bride adorns herself with her *j*.
Zec 9: 16 like *j* in a crown.

JEWS (JEW)

Ne 4: 1 He ridiculed the *J*,
Est 3: 13 kill and annihilate all the *J*—
  4: 14 and deliverance for the *J* will arise
Mt 2: 2 who has been born king of the *J*?
  27: 11 "Are you the king of the *J*?" "Yes,
Jn 4: 9 (For *J* do not associate
  4: 22 for salvation is from the *J*.
  19: 3 saying, "Hail, king of the *J*!"
Ac 20: 21 I have declared to both *J*
Ro 3: 29 Is God the God of *J* only?
  9: 24 not only from the *J* but
  15: 27 they owe it to the *J* to share
1Co 1: 22 *J* demand miraculous signs
  9: 20 To the *J* I became like a Jew,
  12: 13 whether *J* or Greeks, slave or free
Gal 2: 8 of Peter as an apostle to the *J*,
Rev 2: 9 slander of those who say they are *J*
  3: 9 claim to be *J* though they are not,

JEWS' (JEW)

Ro 15: 27 shared in the *J* spiritual blessings,

JEZEBEL

Sidonian wife of Ahab (1Ki 16:31). Promoted Baal worship (1Ki 16:32-33). Killed prophets of the LORD (1Ki 18:4, 13). Opposed Elijah (1Ki 19:1-2). Had Naboth killed (1Ki 21). Death prophesied (1Ki 21:17-24). Killed by Jehu (2Ki 9:30-37).

JEZREEL

2Ki 9: 36 at *J* dogs will devour Jezebel's flesh
  10: 7 and sent them to Jehu in *J*.
Hos 1: 4 house of Jéhu for the massacre at *J*,

JOAB

Nephew of David (1Ch 2:16). Commander of his army (2Sa 8:16). Victorious over Ammon (2Sa 10; 1Ch 19), Rabbah (2Sa 11; 1Ch 20), Jerusalem (1Ch 11:6), Absalom (2Sa 18), Sheba (2Sa 20). Killed Abner (2Sa 3:22-39), Amasa (2Sa 20:1-13). Numbered David's army (2Sa 24; 1Ch 21). Sided with Adonijah (1Ki 1:17, 19). Killed by Benaiah (1Ki 2:5-6, 28-35).

JOASH

Son of Ahaziah; king of Judah. Sheltered from Athaliah by Jehoiada (2Ki 11; 2Ch 22:10-23:21). Repaired temple (2Ki 12; 2Ch 24).

JOB

Wealthy man from Uz; feared God (Job 1:1-5). Righteousness tested by disaster (Job 1:6-22), personal affliction (Job 2). Maintained innocence in debate with three friends (Job 3-31), Elihu (Job 32-37). Rebuked by the LORD (Job 38-41). Vindicated and restored to greater stature by the LORD (Job 42). Example of righteousness (Eze 14:14, 20).

JOCHEBED*

Mother of Moses and Aaron (Ex 6:20; Nu 26: 59).

JOEL

Prophet (Joel 1:1; Ac 2:16).

JOHN

1. Son of Zechariah and Elizabeth (Lk 1). Called the Baptist (Mt 3:1-12; Mk 1:2-8). Witness to Jesus (Mt 3:11-12; Mk 1:7-8; Jn 3:15-18; Jn 1: 6-35; 3:27-30; 5:33-36). Doubts about Jesus (Mt 11:2-6; Lk 7:18-23). Arrest (Mt 4:12; Mk 1:14). Execution (Mt 14:1-12; Mk 6:14-29; Lk 9:7-9). Ministry compared to Elijah (Mt 11:7-19; Mk 9: 11-13; Lk 7:24-35).
2. Apostle; brother of James (Mt 4:21-22; 10: 2; Mk 3:17; Lk 5:1-10). At transfiguration (Mt 17: 1-13; Mk 9:1-13; Lk 9:28-36). Desire to be greatest (Mk 10:35-45). Leader of church at Jerusalem (Ac 4:1-3; Gal 2:9). Elder who wrote epistles (2Jn 1; 3Jn 1). Prophet who wrote Revelation (Rev 1: 1; 22:8).
3. Cousin of Barnabas, co-worker with Paul, (Ac 12:12-13:13; 15:37), see MARK.

JOIN (JOINED JOINS)

Ne 10: 29 all these now *j* their brothers
Pr 23: 20 Do not *j* those who drink too much
  24: 21 and do not *j* with the rebellious,
Jer 3: 18 of Judah will *j* the house of Israel,
Eze 37: 17 *j* them together into one stick
Da 11: 34 who are not sincere will *j* them.
Ro 15: 30 to *j* me in my struggle by praying
2Ti 1: 8 *j* with me in suffering for the gospel

JOINED (JOIN)

Zec 2: 11 "Many nations will be *j*
Mt 19: 6 Therefore what God has *j* together,
Mk 10: 9 Therefore what God has *j* together,
Ac 1: 14 They all *j* together constantly
Eph 2: 21 him the whole building is *j* together
  4: 16 *j* and held together

JOINS (JOIN)

1Co 16: 16 and to everyone who *j* in the work,

JOINT (JOINTS)

Ps 22: 14 and all my bones are out of *j*.

JOINTS (JOINT)

Heb 4: 12 even to dividing soul and spirit, *j*

JOKING*

Ge 19: 14 his sons-in-law thought he was *j*.
Pr 26: 19 and says, "I was only *j*!"
Eph 5: 4 or coarse *j*, which are out of place.

JONAH

Prophet in days of Jeroboam II (2Ki 14:25). Called to Nineveh; fled to Tarshish (Jnh 1:1-3). Cause of storm; thrown into sea (Jnh 1:4-16). Swallowed by fish (Jnh 1:17). Prayer (Jnh 2). Preached to Nineveh (Jnh 3). Attitude reproved by the LORD (Jnh 4). Sign of (Mt 12:39-41; Lk 11: 29-32).

JONATHAN

Son of Saul (1Sa 13:16; 1Ch 8:33). Valiant warrior (1Sa 13-14). Relation to David (1Sa 18: 1-4; 19-20; 23:16-18). Killed at Gilboa (1Sa 31). Mourned by David (2Sa 1).

JOPPA

Ezr 3: 7 logs by sea from Lebanon to *J*,
Jnh 1: 3 to *J*, where he found a ship bound
Ac 9: 43 Peter stayed in *J* for some time

JORAM

1. Son of Ahab; king of Israel. Fought with Jehoshaphat against Moab (2Ki 3). Killed with Ahaziah by Jehu (2Ki 8:25-29; 9:14-26; 2Ch 22: 5-9).
2. See JEHORAM.

JORDAN

Ge 13: 10 plain of the *J* was well watered,
Nu 22: 1 and camped along the *J*
  34: 12 boundary will go down along the *J*
Dt 3: 27 you are not going to cross this *J*.
Jos 1: 2 get ready to cross the *J* River
  3: 11 go into the *J* ahead of you.
  3: 17 ground in the middle of the *J*,
  4: 22 Israel crossed the *J* on dry ground.'
2Ki 2: 7 and Elisha had stopped at the *J*.
  2: 13 and stood on the bank of the *J*.
  5: 10 wash yourself seven times in the *J*,
  6: 4 They went to the *J* and began
Ps 114: 3 the *J* turned back;
Isa 9: 1 along the *J*— The people walking
Jer 12: 5 manage in the thickets by the *J*?
Mt 3: 6 baptized by him in the *J* River.
  4: 15 the way to the sea, along the *J*,
Mk 1: 9 and was baptized by John in the *J*.

JOSEPH

1. Son of Jacob by Rachel (Ge 30:24; 1Ch 2:2). Favored by Jacob, hated by brothers (Ge 37:3-4). Dreams (Ge 37:5-11). Sold by brothers (Ge 37: 12-36). Served Potiphar; imprisoned by false accusation (Ge 39). Interpreted dreams of Pharaoh's servants (Ge 40), of Pharaoh (Ge 41:4-40). Made greatest in Egypt (Ge 41:41-57). Sold grain to brothers (Ge 42-45). Brought Jacob and sons to Egypt (Ge 46-47). Sons Ephraim and Manasseh blessed (Ge 48). Blessed (Ge 49:22-26; Dt 33: 13-17). Death (Ge 50:22-26; 2 Ex 13:19; Heb 11: 22). 12,000 from (Rev 7:8).
2. Husband of Mary, mother of Jesus (Mt 1: 16-24; 2:13-19; Lk 1:27; 2; Jn 1:45).
3. Disciple from Arimathea, who gave his tomb for Jesus' burial (Mt 27:57-61; Mk 15:43-47; Lk 24:50-52).
4. Original name of Barnabas (Ac 4:36).

JOSHUA (HOSHEA)

1. Son of Nun; name changed from Hoshea (Nu 13:8, 16; 1Ch 7:27). Fought Amalekites under Moses (Ex 17:9-14). Servant of Moses on Sinai (Ex 24:13; 32:17). Spied Canaan (Nu 13). With Caleb, allowed to enter land (Nu 14:6, 30). Succeeded Moses (Dt 1:38; 31:1-18; 33:9).
Charged Israel to conquer Canaan (Jos 1). Crossed Jordan (Jos 3-4). Circumcised sons of wilderness wanderings (Jos 5). Conquered Jericho (Jos 6), Ai (Jos 7-8), five kings at Gibeon (Jos 10: 1-28), southern Canaan (Jos 10:29-43), northern Canaan (Jos 11-12). Defeated at Ai (Jos 7). Deceived by Gibeonites (Jos 9). Renewed covenant (Jos 8:30-35; 24:1-27). Divided land among tribes (Jos 13-22). Last words (Jos 23). Death (Jos 24: 28-31).
2. High priest during rebuilding of temple (Hag 1-2; Zec 3:1-9; 6:11).

JOSIAH

Son of Amon; king of Judah (2Ki 21:26; 1Ch 3: 14). Prophesied (1Ki 13:2). Book of Law discovered during his reign (2Ki 22; 2Ch 34:14-31). Reforms (2Ki 23:1-25; 2Ch 34:1-13; 35:1-19). Killed by Pharaoh Neco (2Ki 23:29-30; 2Ch 35: 20-27).

JOTHAM

1. Son of Gideon (Jdg 9).
2. Son of Azariah (Uzziah); king of Judah (2Ki 15:32-38; 2Ch 26:21-27:9).

JOURNEY

Dt 1: 33 who went ahead of you on your *j*,
  2: 7 over your *j* through this vast desert

Jdg 18: 6 Your *j* has the LORD's approval."
Ezr 8:21 and ask him for a safe *j* for us
Job 16:22 before I go on the *j* of no return.
Isa 35: 8 The unclean will not *j* on it;
Mt 25:14 it will be like a man going on a *j*,
Ro 15:24 to have you assist me on my *j* there

JOY* (ENJOY ENJOYMENT JOYFUL JOYOUS OVERJOYED REJOICE REJOICES REJOICING)

Ge 31:27 so I could send you away with *j*
Lev 9:24 shouted for *j* and fell facedown.
Dt 16:15 and your *j* will be complete.
Jdg 9:19 may Abimelech be your *j*,
1Ch 12:40 and sheep, for there was *j* in Israel.
  16:27 strength and *j* in his dwelling place.
  16:33 sing for *j* before the LORD,
  29:17 with *j* how willingly your people
  29:22 drank with great *j* in the presence
2Ch 30:26 There was great *j* in Jerusalem,
Ezr 3:12 while many others shouted for *j*.
  3:13 of the shouts of *j* from the sound
  6:16 of the house of God with *j*.
  6:22 with *j* by changing the attitude
  6:22 *j* the Feast of Unleavened Bread,
Ne 8:10 for the *j* of the LORD is your
  8:12 and to celebrate with great *j*,
  8:17 And their *j* was very great.
  12:43 God had given them great *j*.
Est 8:16 a time of happiness and *j*,
  8:17 there was *j* and gladness
  9:17 and made it a day of feasting and *j*.
  9:18 and made it a day of feasting and *j*.
  9:19 as a day of *j* and feasting,
  9:22 and *j* and giving presents of food
  9:22 their sorrow was turned into *j*
Job 3: 7 may no shout of *j* be heard in it.
  6:10 my *j* in unrelenting pain—
  8:21 and your lips with shouts of *j*.
  9:25 they fly away without a glimpse of *j*
  10:20 from me so I can have a moment's *j*
  20: 5 the *j* of the godless lasts
  33:26 he sees God's face and shouts for *j*;
  38: 7 and all the angels shouted for *j*?
Ps 4: 7 have filled my heart with greater *j*
  5:11 let them ever sing for *j*.
  16:11 me with *j* in your presence,
  19: 8 giving *j* to the heart.
  20: 5 We will shout for *j*
  21: 1 How great is his *j* in the victories
  21: 6 with the *j* of your presence.
  27: 6 will I sacrifice with shouts of *j*;
  28: 7 My heart leaps for *j*
  30:11 sackcloth and clothed me with *j*,
  33: 3 play skillfully, and shout for *j*.
  35:27 shout for *j* and gladness;
  42: 4 with shouts of *j* and thanksgiving
  43: 4 to God, my *j* and my delight.
  45: 7 by anointing you with the oil of *j*.
  45:15 They are led in with *j* and gladness;
  47: 1 shout to God with cries of *j*.
  47: 5 God has ascended amid shouts of *j*,
  48: 2 the *j* of the whole earth.
  51: 8 Let me hear *j* and gladness;
  51:12 to me the *j* of your salvation
  65: 8 you call forth songs of *j*.
  65:13 they shout for *j* and sing.
  66: 1 Shout with *j* to God, all the earth!
  67: 4 the nations be glad and sing for *j*,
  71:23 My lips will shout for *j*
  81: 1 Sing for *j* to God our strength;
  86: 4 Bring *j* to your servant,
  89:12 Hermon sing for *j* at your name.
  90:14 for *j* and be glad all our days.
  92: 4 I sing for *j* at the works
  94:19 your consolation brought *j*
  95: 1 let us sing for *j* to the LORD;
  96:12 the trees of the forest will sing for *j*;
  97:11 and *j* on the upright in heart.
  98: 4 for *j* to the LORD, all the earth,
  98: 6 shout for *j* before the LORD.
  98: 8 the mountains sing together for *j*;
  100: 1 for *j* to the LORD, all the earth.
  105:43 his chosen ones with shouts of *j*;
  106: 5 share in the *j* of your nation
  107:22 and tell of his works with songs of *j*
  118:15 Shouts of *j* and victory
  119:111 they are the *j* of my heart.

Ps 126: 2 our tongues with songs of *j*.
 126: 3 and we are filled with *j*.
 126: 5 will reap with songs of *j*.
 126: 6 will return with songs of *j*,
 132: 9 may your saints sing for *j*."
 132:16 and her saints will ever sing for *j*.
 137: 3 tormentors demanded songs of *j*;
 137: 6 my highest *j*.
 149: 5 and sing for *j* on their beds.
Pr 10: 1 A wise son brings *j* to his father,
  10:28 The prospect of the righteous is *j*,
  11:10 wicked perish, there are shouts of *j*.
  12:20 but *j* for those who promote peace.
  14:10 and no one else can share its *j*.
  14:13 and *j* may end in grief.
  15:20 A wise son brings *j* to his father,
  15:23 A man finds *j* in giving an apt reply
  15:30 A cheerful look brings *j*
  17:21 there is no *j* for the father of a fool.
  21:15 it brings *j* to the righteous
  23:24 of a righteous man has great *j*;
  27: 9 incense bring *j* to the heart,
  27:11 my son, and bring *j* to my heart;
  29: 3 A man who loves wisdom brings *j*
Ecc 8:15 Then *j* will accompany him
  11: 9 let your heart give you *j* in the days
Isa 9: 3 and increased their *j*.
  12: 3 With *j* you will draw water
  12: 6 Shout aloud and sing for *j*,
  16: 9 shouts of *j* over your ripened fruit
  16:10 *J* and gladness are taken away
  22:13 But see, there is *j* and revelry,
  24:11 all *j* turns to gloom,
  24:14 raise their voices, they shout for *j*;
  26:19 wake up and shout for *j*.
  35: 2 will rejoice greatly and shout for *j*.
  35: 6 the mute tongue shout for *j*.
  35:10 Gladness and *j* will overtake them,
  35:10 everlasting *j* will crown their heads
  42:11 Let the people of Sela sing for *j*;
  44:23 Sing for *j*, O heavens,
  48:20 Announce this with shouts of *j*
  49:13 Shout for *j*, O heavens;
  51: 3 *J* and gladness will be found in her,
  51:11 Gladness and *j* will overtake them,
  51:11 everlasting *j* will crown their heads
  52: 8 together they shout for *j*.
  52: 9 Burst into songs of *j* together,
  54: 1 burst into song, shout for *j*,
  55:12 You will go out in *j*
  56: 7 give them *j* in my house of prayer.
  58:14 then you will find your *j*
  60: 5 heart will throb and swell with *j*;
  60:15 and the *j* of all generations.
  61: 7 and everlasting *j* will be theirs.
  65:14 out of the *j* of their hearts,
  65:18 and its people a *j*.
  66: 5 that we may see your *j*!"
Jer 7:34 will bring an end to the sounds of *j*
  15:16 they were my *j* and my heart's
  16: 9 will bring an end to the sounds of *j*
  25:10 banish from them the sounds of *j*,
  31: 7 "Sing with *j* for Jacob;
  31:12 shout for *j* on the heights of Zion;
  31:13 give them comfort and *j* instead
  33: 9 this city will bring me renown, *j*,
  33:11 be heard once more the sounds of *j*
  48:33 *J* and gladness are gone
  48:33 no one treads them with shouts of *j*
  48:33 they are not shouts of *j*
  51:48 will shout for *j* over Babylon,
La 2:15 the *j* of the whole earth?"
  5:15 *J* is gone from our hearts;
Eze 7: 7 not *j*, upon the mountains.
  24:25 their *j* and glory, the delight
Joel 1:12 Surely the *j* of mankind
  1:16 *j* and gladness
Mt 13:20 and at once receives it with *j*.
  13:44 in his *j* went and sold all he had
  28: 8 afraid yet filled with *j*,
Mk 4:16 and at once receive it with *j*.
Lk 1:14 He will be a *j* and delight to you,
  1:44 the baby in my womb leaped for *j*.
  1:58 great mercy, and they shared her *j*.
  2:10 news of great *j* that will be
  6:23 "Rejoice in that day and leap for *j*,
  8:13 the word with *j* when they hear it,
  10:17 The seventy-two returned with *j*

Lk 10:21 full of *j* through the Holy Spirit,
  24:41 still did not believe it because of *j*
  24:52 returned to Jerusalem with great *j*.
Jn 3:29 That *j* is mine, and it is now
  3:29 full of *j* when he hears
  15:11 and that your *j* may be complete.
  15:11 this so that my *j* may be in you
  16:20 but your grief will turn to *j*.
  16:21 because of her *j* that a child is born
  16:22 and no one will take away your *j*.
  16:24 and your *j* will be complete.
  17:13 measure of my *j* within them.
Ac 2:28 with *j* in your presence.'
  8: 8 So there was great *j* in that city.
  13:52 And the disciples were filled with *j*
  14:17 and fills your hearts with *j*."
  16:34 he was filled with *j* because he had come
Ro 14:17 peace and *j* in the Holy Spirit,
  15:13 the God of hope fill you with all *j*
  15:32 will I may come to you with *j*
  16:19 so I am full of *j* over you;
2Co 1:24 but we work with you for your *j*,
  2: 3 that you would all share my *j*.
  7: 4 our troubles my *j* knows no
  7: 4 so that my *j* was greater than ever.
  8: 2 their overflowing *j* and their
Gal 4:15 What has happened to all your *j*?
  5:22 *j*, peace, patience, kindness,
Php 1: 4 I always pray with *j*
  1:25 for your progress and *j* in the faith,
  1:26 being with you again your *j*
  2: 2 then make my *j* complete
  2:29 him in the Lord with great *j*,
  4: 1 and long for, my *j* and crown,
1Th 1: 6 with the *j* given by the Holy Spirit.
  2:19 For what is our hope, our *j*,
  2:20 Indeed, you are our glory and *j*.
  3: 9 you in return for all the *j* we have
2Ti 1: 4 so that I may be filled with *j*.
Phm : 7 Your love has given me great *j*
Heb 1: 9 by anointing you with the oil of *j*."
  12: 2 for the *j* set before him endured
  13:17 them so that their work will be a *j*,
Jas 1: 2 Consider it pure *j*, my brothers,
  4: 9 to mourning and your *j* to gloom.
1Pe 1: 8 with an inexpressible and glorious *j*
1Jn 1: 4 this to make our *j* complete.
2Jn : 4 It has given me great *j* to find some
  : 12 so that our *j* may be complete.
3Jn : 3 It gave me great *j* to have some
  : 4 I have no greater *j*
Jude : 24 without fault and with great *j*—

JOYFUL* (JOY)

Dt 16:14 Be *j* at your Feast—you, your sons
1Sa 18: 6 with *j* songs and with tambourines
1Ki 8:66 *j* and glad in heart
1Ch 15:16 as singers to sing *j* songs,
2Ch 7:10 *j* and glad in heart
Ps 68: 3 may they be happy and *j*.
  100: 2 come before him with *j* songs.
Ecc 9: 7 and drink your wine with a *j* heart,
Isa 24: 8 the *j* harp is silent.
Jer 31: 4 and go out to dance with the *j*.
Hab 3:18 I will be *j* in God my Savior.
Zec 8:19 and tenth months will become *j*
  10: 7 Their children will see it and be *j*;
Ro 12:12 Be *j* in hope, patient in affliction,
1Th 5:16 Be *j* always; pray continually;
Heb 12:22 thousands of angels in *j* assembly,

JOYOUS* (JOY)

Est 8:15 the city of Susa held a *j* celebration.

JUBILANT

Ps 96:12 let the fields be *j*, and everything
  98: 4 burst into *j* song with music;

JUBILEE

Lev 25:11 The fiftieth year shall be a *j* for you;

JUDAH (JUDEA)

1. Son of Jacob by Leah (Ge 29:35; 35:23; 1Ch 2:1). Did not want to kill Joseph (Ge 37:26-27). Among Canaanites, fathered Perez by Tamar (Ge 38). Tribe of blessed as ruling tribe (Ge 49:8-12; Dt 33:7), numbered (Nu 1:27; 26:22), allotted

land (Jos 15; Eze 48:7), failed to fully possess (Jos 15:63; Jdg 1:1-20).
 2. Name used for people and land of Southern Kingdom.
Ru 1: 7 take them back to the land of *J*.
2Sa 2: 4 king over the house of *J*.
Isa 1: 1 The vision concerning *J*
   3: 8 *J* is falling;
Jer 13: 19 All *J* will be carried into exile,
  30: 3 bring my people Israel and *J* back
Hos 1: 7 I will show love to the house of *J*;
Zec 10: 4 From *J* will come the cornerstone,
Mt 2: 6 least among the rulers of *J*;
Heb 7: 14 that our Lord descended from *J*,
  8: 8 and with the house of *J*.
Rev 5: 5 of the tribe of *J*, the Root of David,

JUDAISM (JEW)

Ac 13: 43 devout converts to *J* followed Paul
Gal 1: 13 of my previous way of life in *J*,
  1: 14 advancing in *J* beyond many Jews

JUDAS

 1. Apostle; son of James (Lk 6:16; Jn 14:22; Ac 1:13). Probably also called Thaddaeus (Mt 10:3; Mk 3:18).
 2. Brother of James and Jesus (Mt 13:55; Mk 6:3), also called Jude (Jude 1).
 3. Christian prophet (Ac 15:22-32).
 4. Apostle, also called Iscariot, who betrayed Jesus (Mt 10:4; 26:14-56; Mk 3:19; 14:10-50; Lk 6:16; 22:3-53; Jn 6:71; 12:4; 13:2-30; 18:2-11). Suicide of (Mt 27:3-5; Ac 1:16-25).

JUDE see JUDAS

JUDEA (JUDAH)

Mt 2: 1 born in Bethlehem in *J*,
  24: 16 are in *J* flee to the mountains.
Lk 3: 1 Pontius Pilate was governor of *J*,
Ac 1: 8 and in all *J* and Samaria,
  9: 31 Then the church throughout *J*,
1Th 2: 14 imitators of God's churches in *J*,

JUDGE (JUDGED JUDGES JUDGING JUDGMENT JUDGMENTS)

Ge 16: 5 May the Lord *j* between you
  18: 25 Will not the *J* of all the earth do
Lev 19: 15 but *j* your neighbor fairly.
Dt 1: 16 between your brothers and *j* fairly.
  17: 12 man who shows contempt for the *j*
  32: 36 The Lord will *j* his people
Jdg 2: 18 Whenever the Lord raised up a *j*
1Sa 2: 10 the Lord will *j* the ends
  3: 13 that I would *j* his family forever
  7: 15 *j* over Israel all the days of his life.
  24: 12 May the Lord *j* between you
1Ki 8: 32 *J* between your servants,
1Ch 16: 33 for he comes to *j* the earth.
2Ch 6: 23 *J* between your servants, repaying
  19: 7 *J* carefully, for with the Lord our
Job 9: 15 plead with my *J* for mercy.
Ps 7: 8 *J* me, O Lord, according
  7: 8 let the Lord *j* the peoples.
  7: 11 God is a righteous *j*,
  9: 8 He will *j* the world in righteousness
  50: 6 for God himself is *j*.
  51: 4 and justified when you *j*.
  75: 2 it is I who *j* uprightly.
  76: 9 when you, O God, rose up to *j*,
  82: 8 Rise up, O God, *j* the earth.
  94: 2 Rise up, O *J* of the earth;
  96: 10 he will *j* the peoples with equity.
  96: 13 He will *j* the world in righteousness
  98: 9 He will *j* the world in righteousness
  110: 6 He will *j* the nations, heaping up
Pr 31: 9 Speak up and *j* fairly.
Isa 2: 4 He will *j* between the nations
  3: 13 he rises to *j* the people.
  11: 3 He will not *j* by what he sees
  33: 22 For the Lord is our *j*,
Jer 11: 20 Almighty, you who *j* righteously
Eze 7: 3 I will *j* you according
  7: 27 by their own standards I will *j* them
  18: 30 O house of Israel, I will *j* you,
  20: 36 so I will *j* you, declares
  22: 2 "Son of man, will you *j* her?
  34: 17 I will *j* between one sheep
Joel 3: 12 sit to *j* all the nations on every side.

Mic 3: 11 Her leaders *j* for a bribe,
  4: 3 He will *j* between many peoples
Mt 7: 1 Do not *j*, or you too will be judged.
Lk 6: 37 "Do not *j*, and you will not be
  18: 2 there was a *j* who neither feared
Jn 5: 27 And he has given him authority to *j*
  5: 30 By myself I can do nothing; I *j* only
  8: 16 But if I do *j*, my decisions are right,
  12: 47 For I did not come to *j* the world,
  12: 48 There is a *j* for the one who rejects
Ac 10: 42 as *j* of the living and the dead.
  17: 31 a day when he will *j* the world
Ro 2: 16 day when God will *j* men's secrets
  3: 6 how could God *j* the world?
  14: 10 then, why do you *j* your brother?
1Co 4: 3 indeed, I do not even *j* myself.
  4: 5 Therefore *j* nothing
  6: 2 And if you are to *j* the world,
  6: 2 that the saints will *j* the world?
Gal 2: 6 not *j* by external appearance—
Col .2: 16 Therefore do not let anyone *j* you
2Ti 4: 1 who will *j* the living and the dead,
  4: 8 which the Lord, the righteous *J*,
Heb 10: 30 "The Lord will *j* his people."
  12: 23 come to God, the *j* of all men,
  13: 4 for God will *j* the adulterer
Jas 4: 12 There is only one Lawgiver and *J*,
  4: 12 who are you to *j* your neighbor?
1Pe 4: 5 to him who is ready to *j* the living
Rev 20: 4 who had been given authority to *j*.

JUDGED (JUDGE)

Mt 7: 1 "Do not judge, or you too will be *j*.
1Co 4: 3 I care very little if I am *j* by you
  10: 29 For why should my freedom be *j*
  11: 31 But if we *j* ourselves, we would not
  14: 24 all that he is a sinner and will be *j*
Jas 3: 1 who teach will be *j* more strictly.
Rev 20: 12 The dead were *j* according

JUDGES (JUDGE)

Jdg 2: 16 Then the Lord raised up *j*,
Job 9: 24 he blindfolds its *j*.
Ps 58: 11 there is a God who *j* the earth."
  75: 7 But it is God who *j*:
Pr 29: 14 If a king *j* the poor with fairness,
Jn 5: 22 Moreover, the Father *j* no one,
1Co 4: 4 It is the Lord who *j* me.
Heb 4: 12 it *j* the thoughts and attitudes
1Pe 1: 17 on a Father who *j* each man's work
  2: 23 himself to him who *j* justly.
Rev 19: 11 With justice he *j* and makes war.

JUDGING (JUDGE)

Ps 9: 4 on your throne, *j* righteously.
Pr 24: 23 To show partiality in *j* is not good:
Isa 16: 5 one who in *j* seeks justice
Mt 19: 28 *j* the twelve tribes of Israel.
Jn 7: 24 Stop *j* by mere appearances.

JUDGMENT (JUDGE)

Nu 33: 4 for the Lord had brought *j*
Dt 1: 17 of any man, for *j* belongs to God.
  32: 41 and my hand grasps it in *j*,
1Sa 25: 33 May you be blessed for your good *j*
Ps 1: 5 the wicked will not stand in the *j*,
  9: 7 he has established his throne for *j*.
  76: 8 From heaven you pronounced *j*,
  82: 1 he gives *j* among the "gods";
  119: 66 Teach me knowledge and good *j*,
  143: 2 Do not bring your servant into *j*,
Pr 3: 21 preserve sound *j* and discernment,
  6: 32 man who commits adultery lacks *j*;
  8: 14 Counsel and sound *j* are mine;
  10: 21 but fools die for lack of *j*.
  11: 12 man who lacks *j* derides his
  12: 11 but he who chases fantasies lacks *j*.
  17: 18 A man lacking in *j* strikes hands
  18: 1 he defies all sound *j*.
  28: 16 A tyrannical ruler lacks *j*,
Ecc 12: 14 God will bring every deed into *j*,
Isa 3: 14 The Lord enters into *j*
  28: 6 justice to him who sits in *j*,
  53: 8 By oppression and *j* he was taken
  66: 16 the Lord will execute *j*
Jer 2: 35 But I will pass *j* on you
  25: 31 he will bring *j* on all mankind
  51: 18 when their *j* comes, they will

Eze 11: 10 and I will execute *j* on you
Da 7: 22 pronounced *j* in favor of the saints
Am 7: 4 Sovereign Lord was calling for *j*
Zec 8: 16 and sound *j* in your courts;
Mal 3: 5 "So I will come near to you for *j*.
Mt 5: 21 who murders will be subject to *j*.'
  5: 22 with his brother will be subject to *j*.
  10: 15 on the day of *j* than for that town.
  11: 24 on the day of *j* than for you."
  12: 36 have to give account on the day of *j*
  12: 41 up at the *j* with this generation
Jn 5: 22 but has entrusted all *j* to the Son,
  5: 30 as I hear, and my *j* is just,
  7: 24 appearances, and make a right *j*."
  8: 26 "I have much to say in *j* of you.
  9: 39 "For *j* I have come into this world,
  12: 31 Now is the time for *j* on this world;
  16: 8 to sin and righteousness and *j*:
  16: 11 in regard to *j*, because the prince
Ac 24: 25 self-control and the *j* to come,
Ro 2: 1 you who pass *j* on someone else,
  2: 2 Now we know that God's *j*
  5: 16 The *j* followed one sin
  12: 3 rather think of yourself with sober *j*,
  14: 10 stand before God's *j* seat.
  14: 13 Therefore let us stop passing *j*
1Co 7: 40 In my *j*, she is happier if she stays
  11: 29 body of the Lord eats and drinks *j*
2Co 5: 10 appear before the *j* seat of Christ,
2Th 1: 5 is evidence that God's *j* is right,
1Ti 3: 6 fall under the same *j* as the devil.
  5: 12 Thus they bring *j* on themselves,
Heb 6: 2 of the dead, and eternal *j*.
  9: 27 to die once, and after that to face *j*,
  10: 27 but only a fearful expectation of *j*
Jas 2: 13 *j* without mercy will be shown
  4: 11 are not keeping it, but sitting in *j*
1Pe 4: 17 For it is time for *j* to begin
2Pe 2: 9 the unrighteous for the day of *j*,
  3: 7 being kept for the day of *j*
1Jn 4: 17 have confidence on the day of *j*,
Jude 6 bound with everlasting chains for *j*
Rev 14: 7 because the hour of his *j* has come.

JUDGMENTS (JUDGE)

Jer 1: 16 I will pronounce my *j* on my people
Da 9: 11 and sworn *j* written in the Law
Hos 6: 5 my *j* flashed like lightning
Ro 11: 33 How unsearchable his *j*,
1Co 2: 15 spiritual man makes *j* about all
Rev 16: 7 true and just are your *j*."

JUG

1Sa 26: 12 and water *j* near Saul's head,
1Ki 17: 12 of flour in a jar and a little oil in a *j*.

JUST* (JUSTICE JUSTIFICATION JUSTIFIED JUSTIFIES JUSTIFY JUSTIFYING JUSTLY)

Ge 18: 19 Lord by doing what is right and *j*.
Dt 2: 12 *j* as Israel did in the land
  6: 3 *j* as the Lord, the God
  27: 3 and honey, *j* as the Lord,
  30: 9 *j* as he delighted in your fathers,
  32: 4 and all his ways are *j*
  32: 4 upright and *j* is he.
  32: 47 They are not *j* idle words for you—
  32: 50 *j* as your brother Aaron died
2Sa 8: 15 doing what was *j* and right
1Ch 18: 14 doing what was *j* and right
2Ch 12: 6 and said, "The Lord is *j*."
Ne 9: 13 and laws that are *j* and right,
  9: 33 you have been *j*; you have acted
Job 34: 17 Will you condemn the *j*
  35: 2 Elihu said: "Do you think this is *j*?
Ps 37: 28 For the Lord loves the *j*
  37: 30 and his tongue speaks what is *j*.
  99: 4 what is *j* and right.
  111: 7 of his hands are faithful and *j*;
  119: 121 I have done what is righteous and *j*;
Pr 1: 3 doing what is right and *j* and fair;
  2: 8 for he guards the course of the *j*
  2: 9 will understand what is right and *j*
  8: 8 All the words of my mouth are *j*;
  8: 15 and rulers make laws that are *j*;
  12: 5 The plans of the righteous are *j*,
  21: 3 To do what is right and *j*
Isa 32: 7 even when the plea of the needy is *j*

Isa 58: 2 They ask me for *j* decisions
Jer 4: 2 if in a truthful, *j* and righteous way
22: 3 what the LORD says: Do what is *j*
22: 15 He did what was right and *j*,
23: 5 do what is *j* and right in the land.
33: 15 he will do what is *j* and right
Eze 18: 5 who does what is *j* and right.
18: 19 Since the son has done what is *j*
18: 21 and does what is *j* and right,
18: 25 'The way of the Lord is not *j*.'
18: 27 and does what is *j* and right,
18: 29 'The way of the Lord is not *j*.'
33: 14 and does what is *j* and right—
33: 16 He has done what is *j* and right;
33: 17 But it is their way that is not *j*.
33: 17 'The way of the Lord is not *j*.'
33: 19 and does what is *j* and right,
33: 20 'The way of the Lord is not *j*.'
45: 9 and oppression and do what is *j*
Da 4: 37 does is right and all his ways are *j*.
Jn 5: 30 as I hear, and my judgment is *j*,
Ro 3: 26 as to be *j* and the one who justifies
2Th 1: 6 God is *j*: He will pay back trouble
Heb 2: 2 received its *j* punishment,
1Jn 1: 9 and *j* will forgive us our sins
Rev 15: 3 *J* and true are your ways,
16: 5 "You are *j* in these judgments,
16: 7 true and *j* are your judgments."
19: 2 for true and *j* are his judgments.

JUSTICE* (JUST)
Ge 49: 16 "Dan will provide *j* for his people
Ex 23: 2 do not pervert *j* by siding
23: 6 "Do not deny *j* to your poor people
Lev 19: 15 " 'Do not pervert *j*; do not show
Dt 16: 19 Do not pervert *j* or show partiality.
16: 20 Follow *j* and *j* alone,
24: 17 the alien or the fatherless of *j*,
27: 19 Cursed is the man who withholds *j*
1Sa 8: 3 accepted bribes and perverted *j*.
2Sa 15: 4 and I would see that he gets *j*.''
15: 6 came to the king asking for *j*.
1Ki 3: 11 for discernment in administering *j*,
3: 28 wisdom from God to administer *j*.
7: 7 the Hall of *J*, where he was to judge
10: 9 to maintain *j* and righteousness.''
2Ch 9: 8 to maintain *j* and righteousness.''
Ezr 7: 25 and judges to administer *j*
Est 1: 13 experts in matters of law and *j*.
Job 8: 3 Does God pervert *j*?
9: 19 matter of *j*, who will summon him?
19: 7 though I call for help, there is no *j*.
27: 2 as God lives, who has denied me *j*,
29: 14 *j* was my robe and my turban.
31: 13 "If I have denied *j*
34: 5 but God denies me *j*.
34: 12 that the Almighty would pervert *j*.
34: 17 Can he who hates *j* govern?
36: 3 I will ascribe *j* to my Maker.
36: 17 *j* have taken hold of you.
37: 23 in his *j* and great righteousness,
40: 8 "Would you discredit my *j*?
Ps 7: 6 Awake, my God; decree *j*.
9: 8 he will govern the peoples with *j*.
9: 16 The LORD is known by his *j*;
11: 7 he loves *j*;
33: 5 LORD loves righteousness and *j*;
36: 6 your *j* like the great deep.
37: 6 *j* of your cause like the noonday
45: 6 a scepter of *j* will be the scepter
72: 1 Endow the king with your *j*, O God
72: 2 your afflicted ones with *j*.
89: 14 *j* are the foundation of your throne;
97: 2 *j* are the foundation of his throne.
99: 4 The King is mighty, he loves *j*—
101: 1 I will sing of your love and *j*;
103: 6 and *j* for all the oppressed.
106: 3 Blessed are they who maintain *j*,
112: 5 who conducts his affairs with *j*.
140: 12 I know that the LORD secures *j*
Pr 8: 20 along the paths of *j*,
16: 10 and his mouth should not betray *j*.
17: 23 to pervert the course of *j*.
18: 5 or to deprive the innocent of *j*.
19: 28 A corrupt witness mocks at *j*,
21: 15 When *j* is done, it brings joy
28: 5 Evil men do not understand *j*,
29: 4 By *j* a king gives a country stability

Pr 29: 7 The righteous care about *j*
29: 26 from the LORD that man gets *j*.
Ecc 3: 16 place of *j*— wickedness was there.
5: 8 poor oppressed in a district, and *j*
Isa 1: 17 Seek *j*,
1: 21 She once was full of *j*;
1: 27 Zion will be redeemed with *j*,
5: 7 he looked for *j*, but saw bloodshed;
5: 16 Almighty will be exalted by his *j*,
5: 23 but deny *j* to the innocent.
9: 7 it with *j* and righteousness
10: 2 and withhold *j* from the oppressed of my people
11: 4 with *j* he will give decisions
16: 5 one who in judging seeks *j*
28: 6 He will be a spirit of *j*
28: 17 I will make *j* the measuring line
29: 21 deprive the innocent of *j*.
30: 18 For the LORD is a God of *j*.
32: 1 and rulers will rule with *j*.
32: 16 *J* will dwell in the desert
33: 5 with *j* and righteousness.
42: 1 and he will bring *j* to the nations.
42: 3 In faithfulness he will bring forth *j*;
42: 4 till he establishes *j* on earth.
51: 4 my *j* will become a light
51: 5 my arm will bring *j* to the nations.
56: 1 "Maintain *j*
59: 4 No one calls for *j*;
59: 8 there is no *j* in their paths.
59: 9 So *j* is far from us,
59: 11 We look for *j*, but find none;
59: 14 So *j* is driven back,
59: 15 that there was no *j*.
61: 8 "For I, the LORD, love *j*;
Jer 9: 24 *j* and righteousness on earth,
10: 24 Correct me, LORD, but only with *j*
12: 1 I speak with you about your *j*:
21: 12 " 'Administer *j* every morning;
30: 11 I will discipline you but only with *j*,
46: 28 I will discipline you but only with *j*;
La 3: 36 to deprive a man of *j*—
Eze 22: 7 mistreat the alien, denying them *j*.
34: 16 I will shepherd the flock with *j*.
Hos 2: 19 you in righteousness and *j*,
12: 6 maintain love and *j*,
Am 2: 7 and deny *j* to the oppressed.
5: 7 You who turn *j* into bitterness
5: 12 and you deprive the poor of *j*
5: 15 maintain *j* in the courts.
5: 24 But let *j* roll on like a river,
6: 12 But you have turned *j* into poison
Mic 3: 1 Should you not know *j*,
3: 8 and with *j* and might,
3: 9 who despise *j*
Hab 1: 4 and *j* never prevails.
1: 4 so that *j* is perverted.
Zep 3: 5 by morning he dispenses his *j*,
Zec 7: 9 'Administer true *j*; show mercy
Mal 2: 17 or "Where is the God of *j*?"
3: 5 and deprive aliens of *j*,
Mt 12: 18 he will proclaim *j* to the nations.
12: 20 till he leads *j* to victory.
23: 23 important matters of the law—*j*,
Lk 11: 42 you neglect *j* and the love of God.
18: 3 'Grant me *j* against my adversary.'
18: 5 I will see that she gets *j*,
18: 7 And will not God bring about *j*
18: 8 he will see that they get *j*,
Ac 8: 33 humiliation he was deprived of *j*.
17: 31 with *j* by the man he has appointed.
28: 4 *J* has not allowed him to live."
Ro 3: 25 He did this to demonstrate his *j*,
3: 26 it to demonstrate his *j*
2Co 7: 11 what readiness to see *j* done.
Heb 11: 33 administered *j*, and gained what
Rev 19: 11 With *j* he judges and makes war.

JUSTIFICATION* (JUST)
Eze 16: 52 for you have furnished some *j*
Ro 4: 25 and was raised to life for our *j*.
5: 16 many trespasses and brought *j*.
5: 18 of righteousness was *j* that brings

JUSTIFIED* (JUST)
Ps 51: 4 and *j* when you judge.
Lk 18: 14 rather than the other, went home *j*
Ac 13: 39 from everything you could not be *j*

Ac 13: 39 him everyone who believes is *j*
Ro 3: 24 and are *j* freely by his grace
3: 28 For we maintain that a man is *j*
4: 2 If, in fact, Abraham was *j* by works,
5: 1 since we have been *j* through faith,
5: 9 Since we have now been *j*
8: 30 those he called, he also *j*; those he *j*.
10: 10 heart that you believe and are *j*.
1Co 6: 11 you were *j* in the name
Gal 2: 16 in Christ Jesus that we may be *j*
2: 16 observing the law no one will be *j*.
2: 16 sinners' know' that a man is not *j*
2: 17 "If, while we seek to be *j* in Christ,
3: 11 Clearly no one is *j* before God
3: 24 to Christ that we might be *j* by faith
5: 4 to be *j* by law have been alienated
Tit 3: 7 so that, having been *j* by his grace,
Jas 2: 24 You see that a person is *j*

JUSTIFIES* (JUST)
Ro 3: 26 one who *j* those who have faith
4: 5 but trusts God who *j* the wicked,
8: 33 God has chosen? It is God who *j*.

JUSTIFY* (JUST)
Est 7: 4 such distress would *j* disturbing
Job 40: 8 you condemn me to *j* yourself?
Isa 53: 11 my righteous servant will *j* many,
Lk 10: 29 But he wanted to *j* himself,
16: 15 "You are the ones who *j* yourselves
Ro 3: 30 who will *j* the circumcised by faith
Gal 3: 8 that God would *j* the Gentiles

JUSTIFYING* (JUST)
Job 32: 2 angry with Job for *j* himself rather

JUSTLY* (JUST)
Ps 58: 1 Do you rulers indeed speak *j*?
67: 4 for you rule the peoples *j*
Jer 7: 5 and deal with each other *j*,
Mic 6: 8 To act *j* and to love mercy
Lk 23: 41 We are punished *j*,
1Pe 2: 23 himself to him who judges *j*.

KADESH
Nu 20: 1 of Zin, and they stayed at *K*.
Dt 1: 46 And so you stayed in *K* many days

KADESH BARNEA
Nu 32: 8 I sent them from *K* to look over

KEBAR
Eze 1: 1 among the exiles by the *K* River,

KEDORLAOMER
Ge 14: 17 Abram returned from defeating *K*

KEEP (KEEPER KEEPING KEEPS KEPT)
Ge 31: 49 "May the LORD *k* watch
Ex 15: 26 his commands and *k* all his
20: 6 and *k* my commandments.
Lev 15: 31 You must *k* the Israelites separate
Nu 6: 24 and *k* you;
Dt 4: 2 but *k* the commands of the LORD
6: 17 Be sure to *k* the commands
7: 9 who love him and *k* his commands.
7: 12 your God will *k* his covenant
11: 1 your God and *k* his requirements,
13: 4 *K* his commands and obey him;
30: 10 your God and *k* his commands
30: 16 and to *k* his commands, decrees
Jos 22: 5 careful to *k* the commandment
1Ki 8: 58 and to *k* the commands,
2Ki 17: 19 Judah did not *k* the commands
23: 3 the LORD and *k* his commands,
1Ch 29: 18 and *k* their hearts loyal to you.
2Ch 6: 14 you who *k* your covenant of love
34: 31 the LORD and *k* his commands,
Job 14: 16 but not *k* track of my sin.
Ps 18: 28 You, O LORD, *k* my lamp burning
19: 13 *K* your servant also from willful
78: 10 they did not *k* God's covenant
119: 2 Blessed are they who *k* his statutes
119: 9 can a young man *k* his way pure?
121: 7 The LORD will *k* you
141: 3 *k* watch over the door of my lips.
Pr 4: 21 *k* them within your heart;
4: 24 *k* corrupt talk far from your lips.

Pr 30: 8 *K* falsehood and lies far from me;
Ecc 3: 6 a time to *k* and a time
12: 11 and *k* his commandments,
Isa 26: 3 You will *k* in perfect peace
42: 6 I will *k* you and will make you
58: 13 "If you *k* your feet
Jer 16: 11 forsook me and did not *k* my law.
Eze 20: 19 and be careful to *k* my laws.
Mt 10: 10 for the worker is worth his *k*.
Lk 12: 35 and *k* your lamps burning,
17: 33 tries to *k* his life will lose it,
Jn 10: 24 How long will you *k* us in suspense
12: 25 in this world will *k* it for eternal life
Ac 2: 24 for death to *k* its hold on him.
18: 9 "Do not be afraid; *k* on speaking,
Ro 7: 19 want to do—this I *k* on doing.
12: 11 but *k* your spiritual fervor,
14: 22 you believe about these things *k*
16: 17 *K* away from them.
1Co 1: 8 He will *k* you strong to the end,
2Co 12: 7 To *k* me from becoming conceited
Gal 5: 25 let us *k* in step with the Spirit.
Eph 4: 3 Make every effort to *k* the unity
2Th 3: 6 to *k* away from every brother who
1Ti 5: 22 *K* yourself pure.
2Ti 4: 5 *k* your head in all situations,
Heb 9: 20 God has commanded you to *k*.''
13: 5 *K* your lives free from the love
Jas 1: 26 and yet does not *k* a tight rein
2: 8 If you really *k* the royal law found
3: 2 able to *k* his whole body in check.
2Pe 1: 8 will *k* you from being ineffective
Jude : 21 *K* yourselves in God's love
: 24 able to *k* you from falling
Rev 3: 10 also *k* you from the hour
22: 9 of all who *k* the words of this book.

KEEPER (KEEP)

Ge 4: 9 I my brother's *k*?'' The LORD

KEEPING (KEEP)

Ex 20: 8 the Sabbath day by *k* it holy,
Dt 5: 12 the Sabbath day by *k* it holy,
13: 18 *k* all his commands that I am
Ps 19: 11 in *k* them there is great reward.
119:112 My heart is set on *k* your decrees
Pr 15: 3 *k* watch on the wicked
Mt 3: 8 Produce fruit in *k* with repentance.
Lk 2: 8 *k* watch over their flocks at night.
1Co 7: 19 *K* God's commands is what counts.
2Co 8: 5 and then in us in *k* with God's will.
Jas 4: 11 you are not *k* it, but sitting
1Pe 3: 16 and respect, *k* a clear conscience,
2Pe 3: 9 Lord is not slow in *k* his promise,

KEEPS (KEEP)

Ne 1: 5 who *k* his covenant of love
Ps 15: 4 who *k* his oath
Pr 12: 23 A prudent man *k* his knowledge
15: 21 of understanding *k* a straight
17: 28 a fool is thought wise if he *k* silent,
29: 11 a wise man *k* himself under control
Isa 56: 2 who *k* the Sabbath
Da 9: 4 who *k* his covenant of love
Am 5: 13 Therefore the prudent man *k* quiet
Jn 7: 19 Yet not one of you *k* the law.
8: 51 if a man *k* my word, he will never
1Co 13: 5 is not easily angered, it *k* no record
Jas 2: 10 For whoever *k* the whole law
Rev 22: 7 Blessed is he who *k* the words

KEILAH

1Sa 23: 13 that David had escaped from *K*,

KEPT (KEEP)

Ex 12: 42 Because the LORD *k* vigil that
Dt 7: 8 and *k* the oath he swore
2Ki 18: 6 he *k* the commands the LORD had
Ne 9: 8 You have *k* your promise
Ps130: 3 If you, O LORD, *k* a record of sins,
Isa 38: 17 In your love you *k* me
Mt 19: 20 these I have *k*,'' the young man
2Co 11: 9 I have *k* myself from being
2Ti 4: 7 finished the race, I have *k* the faith.
1Pe 1: 4 spoil or fade—*k* in heaven for you,

KERNEL

Mk 4: 28 then the full *k* in the head.

Jn 12: 24 a *k* of wheat falls to the ground

KEY (KEYS)

Isa 33: 6 the fear of the LORD is the *k*
Rev 20: 1 having the *k* to the Abyss

KEYS* (KEY)

Mt 16: 19 I will give you the *k* of the kingdom
Rev 1: 18 And I hold the *k* of death

KICK*

Ac 26: 14 for you to *k* against the goads.'

KILL (KILLED KILLS)

Ecc 3: 3 a time to *k* and a time to heal,
Mt 10: 28 *k* the body but cannot *k* the soul.
17: 23 They will *k* him, and on the third
Mk 9: 31 will *k* him, and after three days
10: 34 spit on him, flog him and *k* him.

KILLED (KILL)

Ge 4: 8 his brother Abel and *k* him.
Ex 2: 12 he *k* the Egyptian and hid him
13: 15 the LORD *k* every firstborn
Nu 35: 11 who has *k* someone accidentally
1Sa 17: 50 down the Philistine and *k* him.
Ne 9: 26 They *k* your prophets, who had
Hos 6: 5 I *k* you with the words
Lk 11: 48 they *k* the prophets, and you build
Ac 3: 15 You *k* the author of life,

KILLS (KILL)

Ex 21: 12 *k* him shall surely be put to death.
Lev 24: 21 but whoever *k* a man must be put
2Co 3: 6 for the letter *k*, but the Spirit gives

KIND (KINDNESS KINDNESSES KINDS)

Ge 1: 24 animals, each according to its *k*.''
2Ch 10: 7 "If you will be *k* to these people
Pr 11: 17 A *k* man benefits himself,
12: 25 but a *k* word cheers him up.
14: 21 blessed is he who is *k* to the needy.
14: 31 whoever is *k* to the needy honors
19: 17 He who is *k* to the poor lends
Da 4: 27 by being *k* to the oppressed.
Lk 6: 35 because he is *k* to the ungrateful
1Co 13: 4 Love is patient, love is *k*.
15: 35 With what *k* of body will they
Eph 4: 32 Be *k* and compassionate
1Th 5: 15 but always try to be *k* to each other
2Ti 2: 24 instead, he must be *k* to everyone,
Tit 2: 5 to be busy at home, to be *k*,

KINDHEARTED* (HEART)

Pr 11: 16 A *k* woman gains respect,

KINDNESS (KIND)

Ge 24: 12 and show *k* to my master Abraham
32: 10 I am unworthy of all the *k*
39: 21 he showed him *k* and granted him
Jdg 8: 35 failed to show *k* to the family
Ru 2: 20 has not stopped showing his *k*
2Sa 2: 6 to whom I can show God's *k*?''
22: 51 he shows unfailing *k*
Ps 18: 50 he shows unfailing *k*
141: 5 righteous man strike me—it is a *k*;
Isa 54: 8 but with everlasting *k*
Jer 9: 24 I am the LORD, who exercises *k*,
Hos 11: 4 I led them with cords of human *k*,
Ac 14: 17 He has shown *k* by giving you rain
Ro 11: 22 Consider therefore the *k*
2Co 6: 6 understanding, patience and *k*;
Gal 5: 22 peace, patience, *k*, goodness,
Eph 2: 7 expressed in his *k* to us
Col 3: 12 yourselves with compassion, *k*,
Tit 3: 4 But when the *k* and love
2Pe 1: 7 brotherly *k*; and to brotherly *k*,

KINDNESSES* (KIND)

Ps 106: 7 did not remember your many *k*,
Isa 63: 7 I will tell of the *k* of the LORD,
63: 7 to his compassion and many *k*.

KINDS (KIND)

Ge 1: 12 bearing seed according to their *k*
1Co 12: 4 There are different *k* of gifts,
1Ti 6: 10 of money is a root of all *k* of evil.

1Pe 1: 6 had to suffer grief in all *k* of trials.

KING (KING'S KINGDOM KINGDOMS KINGS)

1. Kings of Judah and Israel: see Saul, David, Solomon.
2. Kings of Judah: see Rehoboam, Abijah, Asa, Jehoshaphat, Jehoram, Ahaziah, Athaliah (Queen), Joash, Amaziah, Azariah (Uzziah), Jotham, Ahaz, Hezekiah, Manasseh, Amon, Josiah, Jehoahaz, Jehoiakim, Jehoiachin, Zedekiah.
3. Kings of Israel: see Jeroboam I, Nadab, Baasha, Elah, Zimri, Tibni, Omri, Ahab, Ahaziah, Joram, Jehu, Jehoahaz, Jehoash, Jeroboam II, Zechariah, Shallum, Menahem, Pekah, Pekahiah, Hoshea.

Ex 1: 8 a new *k*, who did not know about
Dt 17: 14 "Let us set a *k* over us like all
Jdg 17: 6 In those days Israel had no *k*;
1Sa 8: 5 now appoint a *k* to lead us,
11: 15 as *k* in the presence of the LORD.
12: 12 the LORD your God was your *k*.
2Sa 2: 4 and there they anointed David *k*
1Ki 1: 30 Solomon your son shall be *k*
Ps 2: 6 "I have installed my *K*
24: 7 that the *K* of glory may come in.
44: 4 You are my *K* and my God,
47: 7 For God is the *K* of all the earth;
Isa 32: 1 See, a *k* will reign in righteousness
Jer 30: 9 and David their *k*,
Hos 3: 5 their God and David their *k*.
Mic 2: 13 *k* will pass through before them,
Zec 9: 9 See, your *k* comes to you,
Mt 2: 2 is the one who has been born *k*
27: 11 "Are you the *k* of the Jews?'' "Yes,
Lk 19: 38 "Blessed is the *k* who comes
23: 3 "Are you the *k* of the Jews?'' "Yes,
23: 38 THE *K* OF THE JEWS.
Jn 1: 49 of God; you are the *K* of Israel.''
12: 13 "Blessed is the *K* of Israel!''
Ac 17: 7 saying that there is another *k*,
1Ti 1: 17 Now to the *K* eternal, immortal,
6: 15 the *K* of kings and Lord of lords,
Heb 7: 1 This Melchizedek was *k* of Salem
1Pe 2: 13 to the *k*, as the supreme authority,
2: 17 of believers, fear God, honor the *k*.
Rev 15: 3 *K* of the ages.
17: 14 he is Lord of lords and *K* of kings—
19: 16 *K* OF KINGS AND LORD

KING'S (KING)

Pr 21: 1 The *k* heart is in the hand
Ecc 8: 3 in a hurry to leave the *k* presence.

KINGDOM (KING)

Ex 19: 6 you will be for me a *k* of priests
Dt 17: 18 When he takes the throne of his *k*,
2Sa 7: 12 body, and I will establish his *k*.
1Ki 11: 31 to tear the *k* out of Solomon's hand
1Ch 17: 11 own sons, and I will establish his *k*.
29: 11 Yours, O LORD, is the *k*;
Ps 45: 6 justice will be the scepter of your *k*.
103: 19 and his *k* rules over all.
145: 11 They will tell of the glory of your *k*
Eze 29: 14 There they will be a lowly *k*.
Da 2: 39 "After you, another *k* will rise,
4: 3 His *k* is an eternal *k*;
7: 27 His *k* will be an everlasting *k*,
Ob : 21 And the *k* will be the LORD's.
Mt 3: 2 Repent, for the *k* of heaven is near
4: 17 Repent, for the *k* of heaven is near
4: 23 preaching the good news of the *k*,
5: 3 for theirs is the *k* of heaven.
5: 10 for theirs is the *k* of heaven.
5: 19 great in the *k* of heaven.
5: 19 least in the *k* of heaven,
5: 20 you will certainly not enter the *k*
6: 10 your *k* come,
6: 33 But seek first his *k* and his
7: 21 Lord,' will enter the *k* of heaven,
8: 11 Isaac and Jacob in the *k* of heaven.
8: 12 the subjects of the *k* will be thrown
9: 35 preaching the good news of the *k*,
10: 7 preach this message: 'The *k*
11: 11 least in the *k* of heaven is greater
11: 12 the *k* of heaven has been forcefully
12: 25 "Every *k* divided against itself will
12: 26 How then can his *k* stand?

Mt 12: 28 then the *k* of God has come
13: 11 knowledge of the secrets of the *k*
13: 19 hears the message about the *k*
13: 24 ''The *k* of heaven is like a man who
13: 31 *k* of heaven is like a mustard seed,
13: 33 ''The *k* of heaven is like yeast that
13: 38 stands for the sons of the *k*.
13: 41 of his *k* everything that causes sin
13: 43 the sun in the *k* of their Father.
13: 44 the *k* of heaven is like treasure hidden
13: 45 the *k* of heaven is like a merchant
13: 47 of heaven is like a net that was let
13: 52 has been instructed about the *k*
16: 19 the keys of the *k* of heaven;
16: 28 the Son of Man coming in his *k*.''
18: 1 the greatest in the *k* of heaven?''
18: 3 you will never enter the *k*
18: 4 the greatest in the *k* of heaven.
18: 23 the *k* of heaven is like a king who
19: 12 because of the *k* of heaven.
19: 14 for the *k* of heaven belongs to such
19: 23 man to enter the *k* of heaven.
19: 24 for a rich man to enter the *k* of God
20: 1 ''For the *k* of heaven is like
20: 21 the other at your left in your *k*.''
21: 31 the prostitutes are entering the *k*
21: 43 ''Therefore I tell you that the *k*
22: 2 ''The *k* of heaven is like a king who
23: 13 You shut the *k* of heaven
24: 7 rise against nation, and *k* against *k*.
24: 14 gospel of the *k* will be preached
25: 1 ''At that time the *k*
25: 34 the *k* prepared for you
26: 29 anew with you in my Father's *k*.''
Mk 1: 15 ''The *k* of God is near.
3: 24 If a *k* is divided against itself,
3: 24 against itself, that *k* cannot stand.
4: 11 ''The secret of the *k*
4: 26 ''This is what the *k* of God is like.
4: 30 ''What shall we say the *k*
6: 23 I will give you, up to half my *k*.''
9: 1 before they see the *k* of God come
9: 47 better for you to enter the *k* of God
10: 14 for the *k* of God belongs to such
10: 15 anyone who will not receive the *k*
10: 23 for the rich to enter the *k* of God!''
10: 24 how hard it is to enter the *k* of God
10: 25 for a rich man to enter the *k* of God
11: 10 ''Blessed is the coming *k*
12: 34 ''You are not far from the *k* of God
13: 8 rise against nation, and *k* against *k*.
14: 25 day when I drink it anew in the *k*
15: 43 who was himself waiting for the *k*
Lk 1: 33 Jacob forever; his *k* will never
4: 43 of God to the other towns
6: 20 for yours is the *k* of God.
7: 28 in the *k* of God is greater than he.''
8: 1 proclaiming the good news of the *k*
8: 10 knowledge of the secrets of the *k*
9: 2 out to preach the *k* of God
9: 11 spoke to them about the *k* of God,
9: 27 before they see the *k* of God.''
9: 60 you go and proclaim the *k* of God
9: 62 fit for service in the *k* of God.''
10: 9 'The *k* of God is near you.'
10: 11 sure of this: The *k* of God is near.'
11: 2 your *k* come.
11: 17 ''Any *k* divided against itself will
11: 18 himself, how can his *k* stand?
11: 20 then the *k* of God has come to you.
12: 31 seek his *k*, and these things will be
12: 32 has been pleased to give you the *k*.
13: 18 ''What is the *k* of God like?
13: 20 What shall I compare the *k* of God
13: 28 all the prophets in the *k* of God,
13: 29 places at the feast in the *k* of God
14: 15 eat at the feast in the *k* of God.''
16: 16 the good news of the *k*
17: 20 when the *k* of God would come,
17: 20 *k* of God does not come visibly,
17: 21 because the *k* of God is within you
18: 16 for the *k* of God belongs to such
18: 17 anyone who will not receive the *k* of
18: 24 for the rich to enter the *k* of God!
18: 25 for a rich man to enter the *k* of God
18: 29 for the sake of the *k* of God will fail
19: 11 and the people thought that the *k*
21: 10 rise against nation, and *k* against *k*.

Lk 21: 31 you know that the *k* of God is near.
22: 16 until it finds fulfillment in the *k*
22: 18 the vine until the *k* of God comes.''
22: 29 And I confer on you a *k*, just
22: 30 and drink at my table in my *k*
23: 42 me when you come into your *k*.''
23: 51 he was waiting for the *k* of God.
Jn 3: 3 no one can see the *k* of God.
3: 5 no one can enter the *k* of God.
18: 36 now my *k* is from another place.''
18: 36 ''My *k* is not of this world.
Ac 1: 3 and spoke about the *k* of God.
1: 6 going to restore the *k* to Israel?''
8: 12 he preached the good news of the *k*
14: 22 hardships to enter the *k* of God,''
19: 8 arguing persuasively about the *k*
20: 25 about preaching the *k* will ever see
28: 23 and declared to them the *k* of God
28: 31 hindrance he preached the *k*
Ro 14: 17 For the *k* of God is not a matter
1Co 4: 20 For the *k* of God is not a matter
6: 9 the wicked will not inherit the *k*
6: 10 swindlers will inherit the *k* of God.
15: 24 hands over the *k* to God the Father
15: 50 blood cannot inherit the *k* of God,
Gal 5: 21 live like this will not inherit the *k*
Eph 2: 2 and of the ruler of the *k* of the air,
5: 5 has any inheritance in the *k*
Col 1: 12 of the saints in the *k* of light.
1: 13 and brought us into the *k*
4: 11 among my fellow workers for the *k*
1Th 2: 12 who calls you into his *k* and glory.
2Th 1: 5 will be counted worthy of the *k*
2Ti 4: 1 in view of his appearing and his *k*,
4: 18 bring me safely to his heavenly *k*.
Heb 1: 8 will be the scepter of your *k*.
12: 28 we are receiving a *k* that cannot be
Jas 2: 5 to inherit the *k* he promised those
2Pe 1: 11 into the eternal *k* of our Lord
Rev 1: 6 has made us to be a *k* and priests
1: 9 companion in the suffering and *k*
5: 10 You have made them to be a *k*
11: 15 of the world has become the *k*
11: 15 ''The *k* of the world has become
12: 10 the power and the *k* of our God,
16: 10 his *k* was plunged into darkness.
17: 12 who have not yet received a *k*,

KINGDOMS (KING)

2Ki 19: 15 God over all the *k* of the earth.
19: 19 so that all *k* on earth may know
2Ch 20: 6 rule over all the *k* of the nations.
Ps 68: 32 Sing to God, O *k* of the earth,
Isa 37: 16 God over all the *k* of the earth.
37: 20 so that all *k* on earth may know
Eze 29: 15 It will be the lowliest of *k*
37: 22 or be divided into two *k*.
Da 4: 17 Most High is sovereign over the *k*
7: 17 great beasts are four *k* that will rise
Zep 3: 8 to gather the *k*

KINGS (KING)

Ps 2: 2 The *k* of the earth take their stand
47: 9 for the *k* of the earth belong to God
68: 29 *k* will bring you gifts.
72: 11 All *k* will bow down to him
110: 5 he will crush *k* on the day
149: 8 to bind their *k* with fetters,
Pr 16: 12 *K* detest wrongdoing,
Isa 24: 21 and the *k* on the earth below.
52: 15 and *k* will shut their mouths
60: 11 their *k* led in triumphal procession.
Da 2: 21 he sets up *k* and deposes them.
7: 24 ten horns are ten *k* who will come
Lk 21: 12 and you will be brought before *k*
1Co 4: 8 You have become *k*—
1Ti 2: 2 for *k* and all those in authority,
6: 15 the King of *k* and Lord of lords,
Rev 1: 5 and the ruler of the *k* of the earth.
17: 14 he is Lord of lords and King of *k*—
19: 16 KING OF *K* AND LORD

KINSMAN-REDEEMER (REDEEM)

Ru 3: 9 over me, since you are a *k*.''
4: 14 day has not left you without a *k*.

KISS (KISSED KISSES)

Ps 2: 12 *K* the Son, lest he be angry
Pr 24: 26 is like a *k* on the lips.
SS 1: 2 *Beloved* Let him *k* me
8: 1 I would *k* you,
Lk 22: 48 the Son of Man with a *k*?''
Ro 16: 16 Greet one another with a holy *k*.
1Co 16: 20 Greet one another with a holy *k*.
2Co 13: 12 Greet one another with a holy *k*.
1Th 5: 26 Greet all the brothers with a holy *k*
1Pe 5: 14 Greet one another with a kiss of love.

KISSED (KISS)

Mk 14: 45 Judas said, ''Rabbi!'' and *k* him.
Lk 7: 38 *k* them and poured perfume

KISSES* (KISS)

Pr 27: 6 but an enemy multiplies *k*.
SS 1: 2 with the *k* of his mouth—

KNEE (KNEES)

Isa 45: 23 Before me every *k* will bow;
Ro 14: 11 'Every *k* will bow before me;
Php 2: 10 name of Jesus every *k* should bow,

KNEEL (KNELT)

Est 3: 2 But Mordecai would not *k* down
Ps 95: 6 let us *k* before the LORD our
Eph 3: 14 For this reason I *k*

KNEES (KNEE)

1Ki 19: 18 all whose *k* have not bowed
Isa 35: 3 steady the *k* that give way;
Da 6: 10 times a day he got down on his *k*
Lk 5: 8 he fell at Jesus' *k* and said,
Heb 12: 12 your feeble arms and weak *k*.

KNELT* (KNEEL)

1Ki 1: 16 Bathsheba bowed low and *k*
2Ch 6: 13 and then *k* down before the whole
7: 3 they *k* on the pavement
29: 29 everyone present with him *k* down
Est 3: 2 officials at the king's gate *k* down
Mt 8: 2 and *k* before him and said,
9: 18 a ruler came and *k* before him
15: 25 The woman came and *k* before him
17: 14 a man approached Jesus and *k*
27: 29 *k* in front of him and mocked him.
Lk 22: 41 down and prayed, ''Father,
Ac 20: 36 he *k* down with all of them
21: 5 there on the beach we *k* to pray.

KNEW (KNOW)

2Ch 33: 13 Manasseh *k* that the LORD is God
Job 23: 3 If only I *k* where to find him;
Pr 24: 12 ''But we *k* nothing about this,''
Jer 1: 5 you in the womb I *k* you,
Jnh 4: 2 I *k* that you are a gracious
Mt 7: 23 tell them plainly, 'I never *k* you.
12: 25 Jesus *k* their thoughts
Jn 2: 24 himself to them, for he *k* all men.
14: 7 If you really *k* me, you would know

KNIFE

Ge 22: 10 and took the *k* to slay his son.
Pr 23: 2 and put a *k* to your throat

KNOCK* (KNOCKS)

Mt 7: 7 *k* and the door will be opened
Lk 11: 9 *k* and the door will be opened
Rev 3: 20 I am! I stand at the door and *k*.

KNOCKS (KNOCK)

Mt 7: 8 and to him who *k*, the door will be

KNOW (FOREKNEW FOREKNOWLEDGE KNEW KNOWING KNOWLEDGE KNOWN KNOWS)

Ge 22: 12 Now I *k* that you fear God,
Ex 6: 7 you will *k* that I am the LORD
14: 4 and the Egyptians will *k* that I am
33: 13 teach me your ways so I may *k* you
Dt 7: 9 *K* therefore that the LORD your
18: 21 ''How can we *k* when a message
Jos 4: 24 of the earth might *k* that the hand
23: 14 You *k* with all your heart
1Sa 17: 46 the whole world will *k* that there is
1Ki 8: 39 heart (for you alone *k* the hearts

Job 11: 6 *K* this: God has even forgotten
19: 25 I *k* that my Redeemer lives,
42: 3 things too wonderful for me to *k*.
Ps 9: 10 Those who *k* your name will trust
46: 10 ''Be still, and *k* that I am God;
100: 3 *K* that the LORD is God.
139: 1 and you *k* me.
139: 23 Search me, O God, and *k* my heart;
145: 12 so that all men may *k*
Pr 27: 1 for you do not *k* what a day may
30: 4 Tell me if you *k!*
Ecc 8: 5 wise heart will *k* the proper time
Isa 29: 15 ''Who sees us? Who will *k?*''
40: 21 Do you not *k?*
Jer 6: 15 they do not even *k* how to blush.
22: 16 Is that not what it means to *k* me?''
24: 7 I will give them a heart to *k* me,
31: 34 his brother, saying, '*K* the LORD,'
33: 3 unsearchable things you do not *k*.'
Eze 2: 5 they will *k* that a prophet has been
6: 10 they will *k* that I am the LORD;
Da 11: 32 people who *k* their God will firmly
Mt 6: 3 let your left hand *k* what your right
7: 11 *k* how to give good gifts
9: 6 But so that you may *k* that the Son
22: 29 you do not *k* the Scriptures
24: 42 you do not *k* on what day your
26: 74 ''I don't *k* the man!'' Immediately
Mk 12: 24 you do not *k* the Scriptures
Lk 1: 4 so that you may *k* the certainty
11: 13 *k* how to give good gifts
12: 48 But the one who does not *k*
13: 25 'I don't *k* you or where you come
21: 31 you *k* that the kingdom of God is
23: 34 for they do not *k* what they are
Jn 1: 26 among you stands one you do not *k*
3: 11 we speak of what we *k*,
4: 22 we worship what we do *k*,
4: 42 and we *k* that this man really is
6: 69 and *k* that you are the Holy One
7: 28 You do not *k* him, but I *k* him
8: 14 for I *k* where I came from
8: 19 ''You do not *k* me or my Father,''
8: 32 Then you will *k* the truth,
8: 55 Though you do not *k* him, I *k* him.
9: 25 One thing I do *k*.
10: 4 him because they *k* his voice.
10: 14 I *k* my sheep and my sheep *k* me—
10: 27 I *k* them, and they follow me.
12: 35 the dark does not *k* where he is
13: 17 Now that you *k* these things,
13: 35 All men will *k* that you are my
14: 17 you *k* him, for he lives with you
15: 21 for they do not *k* the One who sent
16: 30 we can see that you *k* all things
17: 3 that they may *k* you, the only true
17: 23 to let the world *k* that you sent me
21: 15 he said, ''you *k* that I love you.''
21: 24 We *k* that his testimony is true.
Ac 1: 7 ''It is not for you to *k* the times
1: 24 ''Lord, you *k* everyone's heart.
Ro 3: 17 and the way of peace they do not *k*
6: 3 Or don't you *k* that all
6: 6 For we *k* that our old self was
6: 16 Don't you *k* that when you offer
7: 14 We *k* that the law is spiritual;
7: 18 I *k* that nothing good lives in me,
8: 22 We *k* that the whole creation has
8: 26 We do not *k* what we ought to pray
8: 28 we *k* that in all things God works
1Co 1: 21 through its wisdom did not *k* him,
2: 2 For I resolved to *k* nothing
3: 16 Don't you *k* that you yourselves
5: 6 Don't you *k* that a little yeast
6: 2 Do you not *k* that the saints will
6: 15 Do you not *k* that he who unites
6: 16 Do you not *k* that your bodies are
6: 19 Do you not *k* that your body is
7: 16 How do you *k*, wife, whether you
8: 2 does not yet *k* as he ought to *k*.
9: 13 Don't you *k* that those who work
9: 24 Do you not *k* that
13: 9 For we *k* in part and we prophesy
13: 12 Now I *k* in part; then I shall *k* fully,
15: 58 because you *k* that your labor
2Co 5: 1 we *k* that if the earthly tent we live
5: 11 we *k* what it is to fear the Lord,
8: 9 For you *k* the grace

Gal 1: 11 you to *k*, brothers, that the gospel I
2: 16 not 'Gentile sinners' *k* that a man
Eph 1: 17 so that you may *k* him better.
1: 18 in order that you may *k* the hope
6: 8 you *k* that the Lord will reward
6: 9 since you *k* that he who is both
Php 3: 10 I want to *k* Christ and the power
4: 12 I *k* what it is to be in need,
Col 2: 2 order that they may *k* the mystery
4: 1 because you *k* that you
4: 6 so that you may *k* how
1Th 3: 4 *k* quite well that we were
5: 2 for you *k* very well that the day
2Th 1: 8 punish those who do not *k* God
1Ti 1: 7 they do not *k* what they are talking
3: 5 (If anyone does not *k* how
3: 15 you will *k* how people ought
2Ti 1: 12 because I *k* whom I have believed,
2: 23 you *k* they produce quarrels.
4: 14 you *k* those from whom you
Heb 8: 11 because they will all *k* me,
11: 8 he did not *k* where he was going.
Jas 1: 3 because you *k* that the testing
3: 1 you *k* that we who teach will be
4: 4 don't you *k* that friendship
4: 14 *k* what will happen tomorrow.
1Pe 1: 18 For you *k* that it was not
2Pe 1: 12 even though you *k* them
1Jn 2: 3 We *k* that we have come
2: 4 The man who says, ''I *k* him,''
2: 5 This is how we *k* we are in him:
2: 11 he does not *k* where he is going,
2: 20 and all of you *k* the truth.
2: 29 you *k* that everyone who does
3: 1 not *k* us is that it did not *k* him.
3: 2 But we *k* that when he appears,
3: 10 This is how we *k* who the children
3: 14 We *k* that we have passed
3: 16 This is how we *k* what love is:
3: 19 then is how we *k* that we belong
3: 24 We *k* it by the Spirit he gave us.
4: 8 does not love does not *k* God,
4: 13 We *k* that we live in him
4: 16 so we *k* and rely on the love God
5: 2 This is how we *k* that we love
5: 13 so that you may *k* that you have
5: 15 And if we *k* that he hears us—
5: 18 We *k* that anyone born
5: 20 We *k* also that the Son
Rev 2: 2 I *k* your deeds, your hard work
2: 9 I *k* your afflictions and your
2: 19 I *k* your deeds, your love and faith,
3: 3 you will not *k* at what time I will
3: 15 I *k* your deeds, that you are neither

KNOWING (KNOW)

Ge 3: 5 and you will be like God, *k* good
3: 22 now become like one of us, *k* good
Jn 19: 28 *k* that all was now completed,
Php 3: 8 of *k* Christ Jesus my Lord,
Phm : 21 *k* that you will do even more
Heb 13: 2 entertained angels without *k* it.

KNOWLEDGE (KNOW)

Ge 2: 9 the tree of the *k* of good and evil.
2: 17 eat from the tree of the *k* of good
2Ch 1: 10 and *k*, that I may lead this people,
Job 21: 22 ''Can anyone teach *k* to God,
38: 2 counsel with words without *k?*
42: 3 obscures my counsel without *k?*'
Ps 19: 2 night after night they display *k*.
73: 11 Does the Most High have *k?*''
94: 10 Does he who teaches man lack *k?*
119: 66 Teach me *k* and good judgment,
139: 6 Such *k* is too wonderful for me,
Pr 1: 4 *k* and discretion to the young—
1: 7 of the LORD is the beginning of *k*,
2: 5 and find the *k* of God.
2: 6 from his mouth come *k*
2: 10 and *k* will be pleasant to your soul.
3: 20 by his *k* the deeps were divided,
8: 10 *k* rather than choice gold,
8: 12 I possess *k* and discretion.
9: 10 *k* of the Holy One is understanding
10: 14 Wise men store up *k*,
12: 1 Whoever loves discipline loves *k*,
12: 23 A prudent man keeps his *k*
13: 16 Every prudent man acts out of *k*,

Pr 14: 6 *k* comes easily to the discerning.
15: 7 The lips of the wise spread *k*;
15: 14 The discerning heart seeks *k*,
17: 27 A man of *k* uses words
18: 15 heart of the discerning acquires *k*;
19: 2 to have zeal without *k*,
19: 25 discerning man, and he will gain *k*.
20: 15 lips that speak *k* are a rare jewel.
23: 12 and your ears to words of *k*.
24: 4 through *k* its rooms are filled
Ecc 7: 12 but the advantage of *k* is this:
Isa 11: 2 the Spirit of *k* and of the fear
11: 9 full of the *k* of the LORD
40: 14 Who was it that taught him *k*
Jer 3: 15 who will lead you with *k*
Hos 4: 6 are destroyed from lack of *k*.
Hab 2: 14 filled with the *k* of the glory
Mal 2: 7 lips of a priest ought to preserve *k*,
Mt 13: 11 The *k* of the secrets of the kingdom
Lk 8: 10 The *k* of the secrets of the kingdom
11: 52 you have taken away the key to *k*.
Ac 18: 24 with a thorough *k* of the Scriptures
Ro 1: 28 worthwhile to retain the *k* of God,
10: 2 but their zeal is not based on *k*.
11: 33 riches of the wisdom and *k* of God!
1Co 8: 1 *K* puffs up, but love builds up.
8: 11 Christ died, is destroyed by your *k*.
12: 8 to another the message of *k*
13: 2 can fathom all mysteries and all *k*,
13: 8 where there is *k*, it will pass away.
2Co 2: 14 everywhere the fragrance of the *k*
4: 6 light of the *k* of the glory of God
8: 7 in *k*, in complete earnestness
11: 6 a trained speaker, but I do have *k*.
Eph 3: 19 to know this love that surpasses *k*
4: 13 and in the *k* of the Son of God
Php 1: 9 and more in *k* and depth of insight,
Col 1: 9 God to fill you with the *k* of his will
1: 10 every good work, growing in the *k*
2: 3 all the treasures of wisdom and *k*.
3: 10 which is being renewed in *k*
1Ti 2: 4 and to come to a *k* of the truth.
6: 20 ideas of what is falsely called *k*,
Tit 1: 1 and the *k* of the truth that leads
Heb 10: 26 after we have received the *k*
2Pe 1: 5 and to goodness, *k*; and to *k*,
3: 18 grow in the grace and *k* of our Lord

KNOWN (KNOW)

Ex 6: 3 the LORD I did not make myself *k*
Ps 16: 11 You have made *k* to me the path
89: 1 I will make your faithfulness *k*
98: 2 LORD has made his salvation *k*
105: 1 make *k* among the nations what he
119: 168 for all my ways are *k* to you.
Pr 20: 11 Even a child is *k* by his actions,
Isa 12: 4 make *k* among the nations what he
46: 10 *k* the end from the beginning,
61: 9 Their descendants will be *k*
Eze 38: 23 I will make myself *k* in the sight
39: 7 ''I will make *k* my holy name
Mt 10: 26 or hidden that will not be made *k*.
24: 43 of the house had *k* at what time
Lk 19: 42 had only *k* on this day what would
Jn 15: 15 from my Father I have made *k*
16: 14 from what is mine and making it *k*
17: 26 I have made you *k* to them,
Ac 2: 28 You have made *k* to me the paths
Ro 1: 19 since what may be *k* about God is
3: 21 apart from law, has been made *k*,
9: 22 his wrath and make his power *k*,
11: 34 ''Who has the mind of the Lord?
15: 20 the gospel where Christ was not *k*,
16: 26 and made *k* through the prophetic
1Co 2: 16 ''For who has the *k* the mind
8: 3 But the man who loves God is *k*
13: 12 know fully, even as I am fully *k*.
2Co 3: 2 written on our hearts, *k*
Gal 4: 9 or rather are *k* by God—
Eph 3: 5 which was not made *k* to men
6: 19 will fearlessly make *k* the mystery
2Ti 3: 15 infancy you have *k* the holy
2Pe 2: 21 than to have *k* it and then

KNOWS (KNOW)

1Sa 2: 3 for the LORD is a God who *k*,
Est 4: 14 And who *k* but that you have come
Job 23: 10 But he *k* the way that I take;

Ps   44: 21 since my *k* the secrets of the heart?
      94: 11 The LORD *k* the thoughts of man;
     103: 14 for he *k* how we are formed,
Ecc   8: 7 Since no man *k* the future,
      8: 17 Even if a wise man claims he *k*,
      9: 12 no man *k* when his hour will come:
Isa 29: 16 "He *k* nothing"?
Jer   9: 24 that he understands and *k* me,
Mt   6: 8 for your Father *k* what you need
     11: 27 No one *k* the Son
     24: 36 "No one *k* about that day or hour,
Lk   12: 47 "That servant who *k* his master's
     16: 15 of men, but God *k* your hearts.
Ac   1: 8 who *k* the heart, showed that he
Ro   8: 27 who searches our hearts *k* the mind
1Co   2: 11 who among men *k* the thoughts
      8: 2 who thinks he *k* something does
2Ti   2: 19 The Lord *k* those who are his," and
Jas   4: 17 who *k* the good he ought to do
1Jn   3: 6 and whoever *k* God listens to us;
      4: 7 born of God and *k* God.

KOHATHITE (KOHATHITES)

Nu   3: 29 The *K* clans were to camp

KOHATHITES (KOHATHITE)

Nu   3: 28 The *K* were responsible
      4: 15 *K* are to carry those things that are

KORAH

Levite who led rebellion against Moses and Aaron (Nu 16; Jude 11).

KORAZIN

Mt   11: 21 "Woe to you, *K*! Woe to you,

LABAN

Brother of Rebekah (Ge 24:29), father of Rachel and Leah (Ge 29:16). Received Abraham's servant (Ge 24:29-51). Provided daughters as wives for Jacob in exchange for Jacob's service (Ge 29:1-30). Provided flocks for Jacob's service (Ge 30:25-43). After Jacob's departure, pursued and covenanted with him (Ge 31).

LABOR (LABORING)

Ex   1: 11 to oppress them with forced *l*,
     20: 9 Six days you shall *l* and do all your
Dt   5: 13 Six days you shall *l* and do all your
Ps 127: 1 its builders *l* in vain.
    128: 2 You will eat the fruit of your *l*;
Pr   12: 24 but laziness ends in slave *l*.
Isa 54: 1 you who were never in *l*;
     55: 2 and your *l* on what does not satisfy
Mt   6: 28 They do not *l* or spin.
Jn   4: 38 have reaped the benefits of their *l*."
1Co   3: 8 rewarded according to his own *l*.
     15: 58 because you know that your *l*
Gal   4: 11 you who have no *l* pains;
Php   2: 16 day of Christ that I did not run or *l*
Rev 14: 13 "they will rest from their *l*,

LABORING* (LABOR)

2Th   3: 8 *l* and toiling so that we would not

LACK (LACKED LACKING LACKS)

Ps   34: 9 for those who fear him *l* nothing.
Pr   5: 23 He will die for *l* of discipline,
     10: 21 but fools die for *l* of judgment.
     11: 14 For *l* of guidance a nation falls,
     15: 22 Plans fail for *l* of counsel,
     28: 27 to the poor will *l* nothing,
Mk   6: 6 he was amazed at their *l* of faith.
     16: 14 he rebuked them for their *l* of faith
Ro   3: 3 Will their *l* of faith nullify God's
1Co   1: 7 you do not *l* any spiritual gift
      7: 5 because of your *l* of self-control.
Col   2: 23 *l* any value in restraining sensual

LACKED (LACK)

Dt   2: 7 and you have not *l* anything.
Ne   9: 21 them in the desert; they *l* nothing,
1Co 12: 24 honor to the parts that *l* it,

LACKING (LACK)

Pr   17: 18 A man *l* in judgment strikes hands
Ro   12: 11 Never be *l* in zeal, but keep your
Jas   1: 4 and complete, not *l* anything.

LACKS (LACK)

Pr   6: 32 who commits adultery *l* judgment;
     11: 12 man who *l* judgment derides his
     12: 11 he who chases fantasies *l* judgment
     15: 21 delights a man who *l* judgment,
     24: 30 of the man who *l* judgment;
     25: 28 is a man who *l* self-control.
     28: 16 A tyrannical ruler *l* judgment,
     31: 11 and *l* nothing of value.
Eze 34: 8 because my flock *l* a shepherd
Jas   1: 5 any of you *l* wisdom, he should ask

LAID (LAY)

Isa 53: 6 and the LORD has *l* on him
Mk   6: 29 took his body and *l* it in a tomb.
Lk   6: 48 and the foundation on rock.
Ac   6: 6 and *l* their hands on them.
1Co   3: 11 other than the one already *l*,
1Ti   4: 14 body of elders *l* their hands on you.
1Jn   3: 16 Jesus Christ *l* down his life for us.

LAKE

Mt   8: 24 a furious storm came up on the *l*,
     14: 25 out to them, walking on the *l*.
Mk   4: 1 into a boat and sat in it out on the *l*,
Lk   8: 33 down the steep bank into the *l*
Jn   6: 25 him on the other side of the *l*,
Rev 19: 20 into the fiery *l* of burning sulfur.
     20: 14 The *l* of fire is the second death.

LAMB (LAMB'S LAMBS)

Ge   22: 8 "God himself will provide the *l*
Ex   12: 21 and slaughter the Passover *l*.
Nu   9: 11 are to eat the *l*, together
2Sa 12: 4 he took the ewe *l* that belonged
Isa 11: 6 The wolf will live with the *l*,
     53: 7 he was led like a *l* to the slaughter,
Mk   14: 12 to sacrifice the Passover *l*,
Jn   1: 29 *L* of God, who takes away the sin
Ac   8: 32 as a *l* before the shearer is silent,
1Co   5: 7 our Passover *l*, has been sacrificed.
1Pe   1: 19 a *l* without blemish or defect.
Rev   5: 6 Then I saw a *L*, looking
      5: 12 "Worthy is the *L*, who was slain,
      7: 14 white in the blood of the *L*.
     14: 4 They follow the *L* wherever he
     15: 3 of God and the song of the *L*:
     17: 14 but the *L* will overcome them
     19: 9 to the wedding supper of the *L*!"
     21: 23 gives it light, and the *L* is its lamp.

LAMB'S (LAMB)

Rev 21: 27 written in the *L* book of life.

LAMBS (LAMB)

Lk   10: 3 I am sending you out like *l*
Jn   21: 15 Jesus said, "Feed my *l*."

LAME

Isa 33: 23 even the *l* will carry off plunder.
     35: 6 Then will the *l* leap like a deer,
Mt   11: 5 The blind receive sight, the *l* walk,
     15: 31 the *l* walking and the blind seeing.
Lk   14: 21 the crippled, the blind and the *l*.'

LAMENT

2Sa   1: 17 took up this *l* concerning Saul
Eze 19: 1 Take up a *l* concerning the princes

LAMP (LAMPS LAMPSTAND LAMPSTANDS)

2Sa 22: 29 You are my *l*, O LORD;
Ps   18: 28 You, O LORD, keep my *l* burning;
    119:105 Your word is a *l* to my feet
    132: 17 and set up a *l* for my anointed one.
Pr   6: 23 For these commands are a *l*,
     20: 27 *l* of the LORD searches the spirit
     31: 18 and her *l* does not go out at night.
Mt   6: 22 "The eye is the *l* of the body.
Lk   8: 16 "No one lights a *l* and hides it
Rev 21: 23 gives it light, and the Lamb is its *l*.
     22: 5 They will not need the light of a *l*

LAMPS (LAMP)

Mt   25: 1 be like ten virgins who took their *l*
Lk   12: 35 for service and keep your *l* burning.
Rev   4: 5 the throne, seven *l* were blazing.

LAMPSTAND (LAMP)

Ex   25: 31 "Make a *l* of pure gold
Zec   4: 2 "I see a solid gold *l* with a bowl
      4: 11 on the right and the left of the *l*?"
Heb   9: 2 In its first room were the *l*,
Rev   2: 5 and remove your *l* from its place.

LAMPSTANDS (LAMP)

2Ch   4: 7 He made ten gold *l* according
Rev   1: 12 when I turned I saw seven golden *l*,
      1: 20 and of the seven golden *l* is this:

LAND (LANDS)

Ge   1: 10 God called the dry ground "*l*,"
      1: 11 "Let the *l* produce vegetation:
      1: 24 "Let the *l* produce living creatures
     12: 1 and go to the *l* I will show you.
     12: 7 To your offspring I will give this *l*."
     13: 15 All the *l* that you see I will give
     15: 18 "To your descendants I give this *l*.
     50: 24 out of this *l* to the *l* he promised
Ex   3: 8 a *l* flowing with milk and honey—
      6: 8 to the *l* I swore with uplifted hand
     33: 3 Go up to the *l* flowing with milk
Lev 25: 23 *l* must not be sold permanently,
Nu   14: 8 us into that *l*, a *l* flowing with milk
     35: 33 Do not pollute the *l* where you are.
Dt   1: 8 See, I have given you this *l*.
      8: 7 God is bringing you into a good *l*—
     11: 10 The *l* you are entering to take
     28: 21 you from the *l* you are entering
     29: 19 will bring disaster on the watered *l*
     34: 1 LORD showed him the whole *l*—
Jos 13: 2 "This is the *l* that remains:
     14: 3 Levites received no share of the *l*
     14: 9 *l* on which your feet have walked
2Sa 21: 14 answered prayer in behalf of the *l*.
2Ki 17: 5 of Assyria invaded the entire *l*,
     24: 1 king of Babylon invaded the *l*,
     25: 21 into captivity, away from her *l*.
2Ch   7: 3 their sin and will heal their *l*.
      7: 20 then I will uproot Israel from my *l*,
     36: 21 The *l* enjoyed its sabbath rests;
Ezr   9: 11 entering to possess is a *l* polluted
Ne   9: 36 in the *l* you gave our forefathers
Ps   37: 11 But the meek will inherit the *l*
     37: 29 the righteous will inherit the *l*
    136: 21 and gave their *l* as an inheritance,
    142: 5 my portion in the *l* of the living."
Pr   2: 21 For the upright will live in the *l*,
     12: 11 who works his *l* will have abundant
Isa   6: 13 though a tenth remains in the *l*,
     53: 8 cut off from the *l* of the living;
Jer   2: 7 but you came and defiled my *l*
Eze 36: 24 and bring you back into your own *l*.

LANDS (LAND)

Ps 111: 6 giving them the *l* of other nations.
Eze 20: 6 honey, the most beautiful of all *l*.
Zec 10: 9 in distant *l* they will remember me.

LANGUAGE (LANGUAGES)

Ge   11: 1 Now the whole world had one *l*
     11: 9 there the LORD confused the *l*
Ps   19: 3 There is no speech or *l*
Jn   8: 44 When he lies, he speaks his native *l*
Ac   2: 6 heard them speaking in his own *l*.
Col   3: 8 slander, and filthy *l* from your lips.
Rev   5: 9 from every tribe and *l* and people
      7: 9 every nation, tribe, people and *l*,
     14: 6 to every nation, tribe, *l* and people.

LANGUAGES (LANGUAGE)

Zec   8: 23 "In those days ten men from all *l*

LAODICEA

Rev   3: 14 the angel of the church in *L* write:

LAP

Jdg   7: 5 "Separate those who *l* the water

LASHES

Pr   17: 10 more than a hundred *l* a fool.
2Co 11: 24 from the Jews the forty *l* minus one

LAST (LASTING LASTS LATTER)

Ex   14: 24 During the *l* watch of the night
2Sa 23: 1 These are the *l* words of David:

LASTING

Isa 2: 2 and Jerusalem: In the *l* days
    41: 4 and with the *l*— I am he.''
    44: 6 I am the first and I am the *l*;
    48:12 I am the first and I am the *l*.
Hos 3: 5 and to his blessings in the *l* days.
Mic 4: 1 In the *l* days
Mt 19:30 But many who are first will be *l*.
    20: 8 beginning with the *l* ones hired
    21:37 *L* of all, he sent his son to them.
Mk 9:35 must be the very *l*, and the servant
    10:31 are first will be *l*, and the *l* first.''
    15:37 a loud cry, Jesus breathed his *l*.
Jn 6:40 and I will raise him up at the *l* day.''
    15:16 and bear fruit—fruit that will *l*.
Ac 2:17 '' 'In the *l* days, God says,
Ro 1:17 is by faith from first to *l*,
1Co 15:26 *l* enemy to be destroyed is death.
    15:52 of an eye, at the *l* trumpet.
2Ti 3: 1 will be terrible times in the *l* days.
2Pe 3: 3 in the *l* days scoffers will come,
Jude   : 18 ''In the *l* times there will be
Rev 1:17 I am the First and the *L*.
    22:13 the First and the *L*, the Beginning

LASTING (LAST)

Ex 12:14 to the LORD—a *l* ordinance.
Lev 24: 8 of the Israelites, as a *l* covenant.
Nu 25:13 have a covenant of a *l* priesthood,
Heb 10:34 had better and *l* possessions.

LASTS (LAST)

Ps 30: 5 For his anger *l* only a moment,
2Co 3:11 greater is the glory of that which *l*!

LATTER (LAST)

Job 42:12 The LORD blessed the *l* part
Mt 23:23 You should have practiced the *l*,
Php 1:16 I do so in love, knowing that I am

LAUGH (LAUGHED LAUGHS LAUGHTER)

Ps 59: 8 But you, O LORD, *l* at them;
Pr 31:25 she can *l* at the days to come.
Ecc 3: 4 a time to weep and a time to *l*,
Lk 6:21 for you will *l*.
    6:25 Woe to you who *l* now,

LAUGHED (LAUGH)

Ge 17:17 Abraham fell facedown; he *l*
    18:12 So Sarah *l* to herself as she thought,

LAUGHS (LAUGH)

Ps 2: 4 The One enthroned in heaven *l*;
    37:13 but the Lord *l* at the wicked.

LAUGHTER (LAUGH)

Ge 21: 6 Sarah said, ''God has brought me *l*.
Ps 126: 2 Our mouths were filled with *l*,
Pr 14:13 Even in *l* the heart may ache,
Jas 4: 9 Change your *l* to mourning

LAVISHED

Eph 1: 8 of God's grace that he *l* on us
1Jn 3: 1 great is the love the Father has *l*

LAW (LAWFUL LAWGIVER LAWS)

Lev 24:22 are to have the same *l* for the alien
Nu 6:13 '' 'Now this is the *l* for the Nazirite
Dt 1: 5 Moses began to expound this *l*,
    6:25 to obey all this *l* before the LORD
    27:26 of this *l* by carrying them out.''
    31:11 you shall read this *l* before them
    31:26 ''Take this Book of the *L*
Jos 1: 7 to obey all the *l* my servant Moses
    1: 8 of the *L* depart from your mouth;
    22: 5 and the *l* that Moses the servant
2Ki 22: 8 of the *L* in the temple of the LORD
2Ch 6:16 walk before me according to my *l*,
    17: 9 the Book of the *L* of the LORD;
    34:14 of the *L* of the LORD that had
Ezr 7: 6 versed in the *L* of Moses.
Ne 8: 2 Ezra the priest brought the *L*
    8: 8 from the Book of the *L* of God,
Ps 1: 2 and on his *l* he meditates day
    19: 7 The *l* of the LORD is perfect,
    37:31 The *l* of his God is in his heart;
    40: 8 your *l* is within my heart.''
    119: 18 wonderful things in your *l*.

Ps 119: 70 but I delight in your *l*.
    119: 72 *l* from your mouth is more precious
    119: 77 for your *l* is my delight.
    119: 97 Oh, how I love your *l*!
    119:163 but I love your *l*.
    119:165 peace have they who love your *l*,
Pr 28: 9 If anyone turns a deaf ear to the *l*,
    29:18 but blessed is he who keeps the *l*.
Isa 2: 3 The *l* will go out from Zion,
    8:20 To the *l* and to the testimony!
    42:21 to make his *l* great and glorious.
Jer 2: 8 deal with the *l* did not know me;
    8: 8 for we have the *l* of the LORD,''
    31:33 ''I will put my *l* in their minds
Mic 4: 2 The *l* will go out from Zion,
Hab 1: 7 they are a *l* to themselves
Zec 7:12 as flint and would not listen to the *l*
Mt 5:17 that I have come to abolish the *L*
    7:12 sums up the *L* and the Prophets.
    22:36 greatest commandment in the *L*?''
    22:40 All the *L* and the Prophets hang
    23:23 more important matters of the *l*—
Lk 11:52 ''Woe to you experts in the *l*,
    16:17 stroke of a pen to drop out of the *L*.
    24:44 me in the *L* of Moses.
Jn 1:17 For the *l* was given through Moses;
Ac 13:39 justified from by *l* of Moses.
Ro 2:12 All who sin apart from the *l* will
    2:15 of the *l* are written on their hearts,
    2:20 you have in the *l* the embodiment
    2:25 value if you observe the *l*,
    3:19 we know that whatever the *l* says,
    3:20 in his sight by observing the *l*;
    3:21 apart from *l*, has been made known
    3:28 by faith apart from observing the *l*.
    3:31 Not at all! Rather, we uphold the *l*.
    4:13 It was not through *l* that Abraham
    4:15 worthless, because *l* brings wrath.
    4:16 not only to those who are of the *l*
    5:13 for before the *l* was given,
    5:20 *l* was added so that the trespass
    6:14 because you are not under *l*,
    6:15 we are not under *l* but under grace?
    7: 1 that the *l* has authority
    7: 4 also died to the *l* through the body
    7: 5 aroused by the *l* were at work
    7: 6 released from the *l* so that we serve
    7: 7 then? Is the *l* sin? Certainly not!
    7: 8 For apart from *l*, sin is dead.
    7:12 *l* is holy, and the commandment is
    7:14 We know that the *l* is spiritual;
    7:22 my inner being I delight in God's *l*;
    7:25 in my mind am a slave to God's *l*,
    8: 2 because through Christ Jesus the *l*
    8: 3 For what the *l* was powerless to do
    8: 4 of the *l* might be fully met in us.
    8: 7 It does not submit to God's *l*,
    9: 4 covenants, the receiving of the *l*,
    9:31 who pursued a *l* of righteousness,
    10: 4 Christ is the end of the *l*
    13: 8 his fellowman has fulfilled the *l*.
    13:10 love is the fulfillment of the *l*.
1Co 6: 6 goes to *l* against another—
    9: 9 For it is written in the *L* of Moses:
    9:20 the *l* I became like one under the *l*
    9:21 I became like one not having the *l*
    15:56 and the power of sin is the *l*.
Gal 2:16 justified by observing the *l*,
    2:19 For through the *l* I died to the *l*
    3: 2 the Spirit by observing the *l*,
    3: 5 you because you observe the *l*,
    3:10 on observing the *l* are under a curse
    3:11 justified before God by the *l*,
    3:13 curse of the *l* by becoming a curse
    3:17 The *l*, introduced 430 years later,
    3:19 then, was the purpose of the *l*?
    3:21 Is the *l*, therefore, opposed
    3:23 we were held prisoners by the *l*,
    3:24 So the *l* was put in charge to lead us
    4:21 you who want to be under the *l*,
    5: 3 obligated to obey the whole *l*.
    5: 4 justified by *l* have been alienated
    5:14 The entire *l* is summed up
    5:18 by the Spirit, you are not under *l*.
    6: 2 and in this way you will fulfill the *l*
Eph 2:15 flesh the *l* with its commandments
Php 3: 9 of my own that comes from the *l*,
1Ti 1: 8 We know that the *l* is good

Heb 7:12 there must also be a change of the *l*.
    7:19 (for the *l* made nothing perfect),
    10: 1 The *l* is only a shadow
Jas 1:25 intently into the perfect *l* that gives
    2: 8 If you really keep the royal *l* found
    2:10 For whoever keeps the whole *l*
    4:11 or judges him speaks against the *l*
1Jn 3: 4 Everyone who sins breaks the *l*;

LAWFUL (LAW)

Mt 12:12 Therefore it is *l* to do good

LAWGIVER* (LAW)

Isa 33:22 the LORD is our *l*,
Jas 4:12 There is only one *L* and Judge,

LAWLESS (LAWLESSNESS)

2Th 2: 8 And then the *l* one will be revealed
Heb 10:17 ''Their sins and *l* acts

LAWLESSNESS* (LAWLESS)

2Th 2: 3 and the man of *l* is revealed,
    2: 7 power of *l* is already at work;
1Jn 3: 4 sins breaks the law; in fact, sin is *l*.

LAWS (LAW)

Ex 21: 1 ''These are the *l* you are to set
Lev 25:18 and be careful to obey my *l*,
Dt 4: 1 and *l* I am about to teach you.
    30:16 decrees and *l*; then you will live
Ps 119: 30 I have set my heart on your *l*.
    119: 43 for I have put my hope in your *l*.
    119:120 I stand in awe of your *l*.
    119:164 for your righteous *l*.
    119:175 and may your *l* sustain me.
Eze 36:27 and be careful to keep my *l*.
Heb 8:10 I will put my *l* in their minds
    10:16 I will put my *l* in their hearts,

LAWSUITS

Hos 10: 4 therefore *l* spring up
1Co 6: 7 The very fact that you have *l*

LAY (LAID LAYING LAYS)

Ex 29:10 and his sons shall *l* their hands
Lev 1: 4 He is to *l* his hand on the head
    4:15 the community are to *l* their hands
Nu 8:10 the Israelites are to *l* their hands
    27:18 whom is the spirit, and *l* your hand
1Sa 26: 9 Who can *l* a hand on the LORD's
Job 1:12 on the man himself do not *l* a finger
    22:22 and *l* up his words in your heart.
Ecc 10: 4 calmness can *l* great errors to rest.
Isa 28:16 ''See, I *l* a stone in Zion,
Mt 8:20 of Man has no place to *l* his head.''
    28: 6 Come and see the place where he *l*.
Mk 6: 5 *l* his hands on a few sick people
Lk 9:58 of Man has no place to *l* his head.''
Jn 10:15 and I *l* down my life for the sheep.
    10:18 but I *l* it down of my own accord.
    15:13 that he *l* down his life
Ac 8:19 on whom I *l* my hands may receive
Ro 9:33 I *l* in Zion a stone that causes men
1Co 3:11 no one can *l* any foundation other
1Pe 2: 6 ''See, I *l* a stone in Zion,
1Jn 3:16 And we ought to *l* down our lives
Rev 4:10 They *l* their crowns

LAYING (LAY)

Lk 4:40 and *l* his hands on each one,
Ac 8:18 at the *l* on of the apostles' hands,
1Ti 5:22 Do not be hasty in the *l* on of hands
2Ti 1: 6 is in you through the *l*
Heb 6: 1 not *l* again the foundation
    6: 2 instruction about baptisms, the *l*

LAYS (LAY)

Jn 10:11 The good shepherd *l* down his life

LAZARUS

   1. Poor man in Jesus' parable (Lk 16:19-31).
   2. Brother of Mary and Martha whom Jesus raised from the dead (Jn 11:1-12:19).

LAZINESS* (LAZY)

Pr 12:24 but *l* ends in slave labor.
    19:15 *L* brings on deep sleep.

LAZY* (LAZINESS)

Ex   5: 8 They are *l*; that is why they are
       5: 17 Pharaoh said, ''*L*, that's what you
       5: 17 ''Lazy, that's what you are—*l!*'
Pr   10: 4 *L* hands make a man poor,
      12: 27 The *l* man does not roast his game,
      26: 15 he is too *l* to bring it back
Ecc 10: 18 If a man is *l*, the rafters sag;
Mt   25: 26 replied, 'You wicked, *l* servant!
Tit   1: 12 liars, evil brutes, *l* gluttons.''
Heb   6: 12 We do not want you to become *l*,

LEAD (LEADER LEADERS LEADERSHIP LEADS LED)

Ex   15: 13 ''In your unfailing love you will *l*
Nu   14: 8 with us, he will *l* us into that land,
Dt   31: 2 and I am no longer able to *l* you.
Jos   1: 6 because you will *l* these people
1Sa   8: 5 now appoint a king to *l* us,
2Ch   1: 9 knowledge, that I may *l* this people
Ps   27: 11 *l* me in a straight path
      61: 2 *l* me to the rock that is higher
     139: 24 and *l* me in the way everlasting.
     143: 10 *l* me on level ground.
Pr   4: 11 and *l* you along straight paths.
Ecc   5: 6 Do not let your mouth *l* you
Isa 11: 6 and a little child will *l* them.
      49: 10 and leads them beside springs of water.
Da   12: 3 those who *l* many to righteousness,
Mt   6: 13 And *l* us not into temptation,
Lk   11: 4 And *l* us not into temptation. ''
Gal   3: 24 So the law was put in charge to *l* us
1Th   4: 11 it your ambition to *l* a quiet life,
1Jn   3: / do not let anyone / you astray.
Rev   7: 17 he will *l* them to springs

LEADER (LEAD)

1Sa   7: 6 Samuel was *l* of Israel at Mizpah.
      10: 1 Has not the LORD anointed you *l*
      12: 2 I have been your *l* from my youth
      13: 14 and appointed him *l* of his people,

LEADERS (LEAD)

Heb 13: 7 Remember your *l*, who spoke
      13: 17 Obey your *l* and submit

LEADERSHIP* (LEAD)

Nu   33: 1 by divisions under the *l* of Moses
Ps 109: 8 may another take his place of *l*.
Ac   1: 20 '' `May another take his place of *l*.'
Ro   12: 8 if it is *l*, let him govern diligently;

LEADS (LEAD)

Dt   27: 18 is the man who *l* the blind astray
Ps   23: 2 he *l* me beside quiet waters,
      37: 8 do not fret—it *l* only to evil.
      68: 6 he *l* forth the prisoners
Pr   2: 18 For her house *l* down to death
      10: 17 ignores correction *l* others astray.
      14: 23 but mere talk *l* only to poverty.
      16: 25 but in the end it *l* to death.
      19: 23 The fear of the LORD *l* to life:
      20: 7 blameless life; man *l* a blameless life;
      21: 5 as surely as haste *l* to poverty.
Isa 40: 11 he gently *l* those that have young.
Mt   7: 13 and broad is the road that *l*
      12: 20 till he *l* justice to victory.
      15: 14 If a blind man *l* a blind man,
Jn   10: 3 sheep by name and *l* them out.
Ro   6: 16 which *l* to death, or to obedience,
       6: 22 the benefit you reap *l* to holiness,
      14: 19 effort to do what *l* to peace
2Co   2: 14 always *l* us in triumphal procession
       7: 10 sorrow brings repentance that *l*
Tit   1: 1 of the truth that *l* to godliness—

LEAH

Wife of Jacob (Ge 29:16-30); bore six sons and one daughter (Ge 29:31-30:21; 34:1; 35:23).

LEAN (LEANED)

Pr   3: 5 *l* not on your own understanding;

LEANED (LEAN)

Ge   47: 31 as he *l* on the top of his staff.
Jn   21: 20 (This was the one who had *l* back
Heb 11: 21 as he *l* on the top of his staff.

LEAP (LEAPED LEAPS)

Isa 35: 6 Then will the lame *l* like a deer,
Mal   4: 2 *l* like calves released from the stall.
Lk   6: 23 ''Rejoice in that day and *l* for joy,

LEAPED (LEAP)

Lk   1: 41 heard Mary's greeting, the baby *l*

LEAPS (LEAP)

Ps   28: 7 My heart *l* for joy

LEARN (LEARNED LEARNING LEARNS)

Dt   4: 10 so that they may *l* to revere me
       5: 1 *L* them and be sure to follow them.
      31: 12 and *l* to fear the LORD your God
Ps 119: 7 as I *l* your righteous laws.
Isa   1: 17 *l* to do right!
      26: 9 of the world *l* righteousness.
Mt   11: 29 yoke upon you and *l* from me,
Jn   14: 31 world must *l* that I love the Father
1Th   4: 4 that each of you should *l*
1Ti   2: 11 A woman should *l* in quietness
       5: 4 these should *l* first of all

LEARNED (LEARN)

Ps 119:152 Long ago I *l* from your statutes
Mt   11: 25 things from the wise and *l*,
Php   4: 9 Whatever you have *l* or received
       4: 11 for I have *l* to be content whatever
2Ti   3: 14 continue in what you have *l*
Heb   5: 8 he *l* obedience from what he

LEARNING (LEARN)

Pr   1: 5 let the wise listen and add to their *l*,
       9: 9 man and he will add to his *l*.
Isa 44: 25 who overthrows the *l* of the wise
Jn   7: 15 ''How did this man get such *l*
2Ti   3: 7 always *l* but never able

LEARNS (LEARN)

Jn   6: 45 and *l* from him comes to me.

LEATHER

2Ki   1: 8 and with a *l* belt around his waist.''
Mt   3: 4 and he had a *l* belt around his waist

LEAVES

Ge   3: 7 so they sewed fig *l* together
Eze 47: 12 for food and their *l* for healing.''
Rev 22: 2 the *l* of the tree are for the healing

LEBANON

Dt   11: 24 from the desert to *L*,
1Ki   4: 33 from the cedar of *L*

LED (LEAD)

Ex   3: 1 and he *l* the flock to the far side
Dt   8: 2 the LORD your God *l* you all
1Ki 11: 3 and his wives *l* him astray.
2Ch 26: 16 his pride *l* to his downfall.
Ne   13: 26 he was *l* into sin by foreign women.
Ps   68: 18 you *l* captives in your train;
      78: 52 he *l* them like sheep
Pr   7: 21 persuasive words she *l* him astray;
      20: 1 whoever is *l* astray
Isa 53: 7 he was *l* like a lamb to the slaughter
Jer 11: 19 I had been like a gentle lamb *l*
Am   2: 10 and I *l* you forty years in the desert
Mt   4: 1 Then Jesus was *l* by the Spirit
      27: 31 they *l* him away to crucify him.
Lk   4: 1 was *l* by the Spirit in the desert,
Ac   8: 32 ''He was *l* like a sheep
Ro   8: 14 those who are *l* by the Spirit
2Co   7: 9 your sorrow *l* you to repentance.
Gal   5: 18 But if you are *l* by the Spirit,
Eph   4: 8 he *l* captives in his train

LEEKS*

Nu   11: 5 melons, *l*, onions and garlic,

LEFT

Dt   28: 14 or to the *l*, following other gods
Jos   1: 7 turn from it to the right or to the *l*,
      23: 6 aside to the right or to the *l*.
2Ki 22: 2 aside to the right or to the *l*,
Pr   4: 27 Do not swerve to the right or the *l*;
Isa 30: 21 turn to the right or to the *l*,
Mt   6: 3 do not let your *l* hand know what

Mt   25: 33 on his right and the goats on his *l*.

LEGALISTIC*

Php   3: 6 as for *l* righteousness, faultless.

LEGION

Mk   5: 9 ''My name is *L*,'' he replied,

LEND (LENDER LENDS MONEYLENDER)

Lev 25: 37 You must not *l* him money
Dt   15: 8 freely *l* him whatever he needs.
Ps   37: 26 are always generous and *l* freely;
Eze 18: 8 He does not *l* at usury
Lk   6: 34 if you *l* to those from whom you

LENDER (LEND)

Pr   22: 7 and the borrower is servant to the *l*.
Isa 24: 2 for borrower as for *l*,

LENDS (LEND)

Ps   15: 5 who *l* his money without usury
     112: 5 to him who is generous and *l* freely,
Pr   19: 17 to the poor *l* to the LORD,

LENGTH (LONG)

Ps   90: 10 The *l* of our days is seventy years—
Pr   10: 27 The fear of the LORD adds *l* to life

LENGTHY* (LONG)

Mk   12: 40 and for a show make *l* prayers.
Lk   20: 47 and for a show make *l* prayers.

LEOPARD

Isa 11: 6 the *l* will lie down with the goat,
Da   7: 6 beast, one that looked like a *l*.
Rev 13: 2 The beast I saw resembled a *l*,

LEPROSY (LEPROUS)

Nu   12: 10 toward her and saw that she had *l*;
2Ki   5: 1 was a valiant soldier, but he had *l*.
       7: 3 men with *l* at the entrance
2Ch 26: 21 King Uzziah had *l*
Mt   11: 5 those who have *l* are cured,
Lk   17: 12 ten men who had *l* met him.

LEPROUS (LEPROSY)

Ex   4: 6 and when he took it out, it was *l*,

LETTER (LETTERS)

Mt   5: 18 not the smallest *l*, not the least
2Co   3: 2 You yourselves are our *l*, written
       3: 6 for the *l* kills, but the Spirit gives
2Th   3: 14 not obey our instruction in this *l*,

LETTERS (LETTER)

2Co   3: 7 which was engraved in *l* on stone,
      10: 10 ''His *l* are weighty and forceful,
2Pe   3: 16 His *l* contain some things that are

LEVEL

Ps 143: 10 lead me on *l* ground.
Pr   4: 26 Make *l* paths for your feet
Isa 26: 7 The path of the righteous is *l*;
      40: 4 the rough ground shall become *l*,
Jer 31: 9 on a *l* path where they will not
Heb 12: 13 ''Make *l* paths for your feet,''

LEVI (LEVITE LEVITES LEVITICAL)

1. Son of Jacob by Leah (Ge 29:34; 46:11; 1Ch 2:1). With Simeon avenged rape of Dinah (Ge 34). Tribe of blessed (Ge 49:5-7; Dt 33:8-11), chosen as priests (Nu 3-4), numbered (Nu 3:39; 26:62), allotted cities, but not land (Nu 18: 35; Dt 10:9; Jos 13:14; 21), land (Eze 48:8-22), 12,000 from (Rev 7:7).
2. See MATTHEW.

LEVIATHAN

Job 41: 1 pull in the *l* with a fishhook
Ps   74: 1 you who crushed the heads of *L*
Isa 27: 1 *L* the gliding serpent,

LEVITE (LEVI)

Dt   26: 12 you shall give it to the *L*, the alien,
Jdg 19: 1 a *L* who lived in a remote area

LEVITES (LEVI)

Nu   1: 53 The *L* are to be responsible

LEVITICAL

Nu   3:12 "I have taken the L
      8: 6 "Take the L from among the other
   18:21 I give to the L all the tithes in Israel
   35: 7 must give the L forty-eight towns,
2Ch 31: 2 assigned the priests and L
Mal   3: 3 he will purify the L and refine them

LEVITICAL (LEVI)

Heb 7:11 attained through the L priesthood

LEWDNESS

Mk 7:22 malice, deceit, l, envy, slander,

LIAR* (LIE)

Dt 19:18 and if the witness proves to be a l,
Job 34: 6 I am considered a l;
Pr 17: 4 l pays attention to a malicious
   19:22 better to be poor than a l.
   30: 6 will rebuke you and prove you a l.
Mic 2:11 If a l and deceiver comes and says,
Jn   8:44 for he is a l and the father of lies.
    8:55 I did not, I would be a l like you,
Ro   3: 4 Let God be true, and every man a l.
1Jn 1:10 we make him out to be a l
    2: 4 not do what he commands is a l,
    2:22 Who is the l? It is the man who
    4:20 yet hates his brother, he is a l.
    5:10 God has made him out to be a l,

LIARS* (LIE)

Ps 63:11 the mouths of l will be silenced.
  116:11 "All men are l."
Isa 57: 4 the offspring of l?
Mic 6:12 her people are l
1Ti 1:10 for slave traders and l and perjurers
    4: 2 come through hypocritical l,
Tit 1:12 "Cretans are always l, evil brutes,
Rev 3: 9 though they are not, but are l—
   21: 8 magic arts, the idolaters and all l—

LIBERATED*

Ro   8:21 that the creation itself will be l

LICENSE

Jude   : 4 of our God into a l for immorality

LICK

Ps 72: 9 and his enemies will l the dust.
Isa 49:23 they will l the dust at your feet.
Mic 7:17 They will l dust like a snake,

LIE (LIAR LIARS LIED LIES LYING)

Lev 18:22 " 'Do not l with a man
   19:11 " 'Do not l
Nu 23:19 God is not a man, that he should l,
Dt   6: 7 when you l down and when you get
   25: 2 the judge shall make him l down
1Sa 15:29 the Glory of Israel does not l
Ps   4: 8 I will l down and sleep in peace,
   23: 2 me l down in green pastures,
  89:35 and I will not l to David—
Pr   3:24 when you l down, you will not be
Isa 11: 6 leopard will l down with the goat,
   28:15 for we have made a l our refuge
Jer   9: 5 They have taught their tongues to l
   23:14 They commit adultery and live a l.
Eze 13: 6 are false and their divinations a l.
   34:14 they will l down in good grazing
Ro   1:25 exchanged the truth of God for a l,
Col   3: 9 Do not l to each other,
2Th 2:11 so that they will believe the l
Tit   1: 2 which God, who does not l,
Heb 6:18 which it is impossible for God to l,
1Jn 2:21 because no l comes from the truth.
Rev 14: 5 No l was found in their mouths;

LIED (LIE)

Ac   5: 4 You have not l to men but to God."

LIES (LIE)

Lev 6: 3 finds lost property and l about it,
Ps   5: 6 You destroy those who tell l;
   10: 7 His mouth is full of curses and l
   12: 2 Everyone l to his neighbor;
  34:13 and your lips from speaking l.
  58: 3 they are wayward and speak l.
 144: 8 whose mouths are full of l,
Pr   6:19 a false witness who pours out l

Pr 12:17 but a false witness tells l.
   19: 5 he who pours out l will not go free.
   19: 9 and he who pours out l will perish.
   29:12 If a ruler listens to l,
   30: 8 Keep falsehood and l far from me;
Isa 59: 3 Your lips have spoken l.
Jer   5:31 The prophets prophesy l,
    9: 3 like a bow, to shoot l;
   14:14 "The prophets are prophesying l
Hos 11:12 Ephraim has surrounded me with l,
Jn   8:44 for he is a liar and the father of l.

LIFE (LIVE)

Ge   1:30 everything that has the breath of l
    2: 7 into his nostrils the breath of l,
    2: 9 of the garden were the tree of l
    6:17 to destroy all l under the heavens,
    9: 5 for the l of his fellow man.
    9:11 Never again will all l be cut
Ex 21: 6 Then he will be his servant for l.
   21:23 you are to take l for l, eye for eye,
   23:26 I will give you a full l span.
Lev 17:14 the l of every creature is its blood.
   24:17 " 'If anyone takes the l
   24:18 must make restitution—l for l.
Nu 35:31 a ransom for the l of a murderer,
Dt   4:42 one of these cities and save his l.
   12:23 because the blood is the l,
   19:21 Show no pity: l for l, eye for eye,
   30:15 I set before you today l
   30:19 Now choose l, so that you
   30:20 For the LORD is your l,
   32:39 I put to death and I bring to l,
   32:47 words for you—they are your l.
1Sa 19: 5 He took his l in his hands
Job 2: 6 hands; but you must spare his l."
   33: 4 of the Almighty gives me l.
   33:30 that the light of l may shine on him.
Ps 16:11 known to me the path of l;
   17:14 this world whose reward is in this l.
   23: 6 all the days of my l,
   27: 1 LORD is the stronghold of my l—
   34:12 Whoever of you loves l
   36: 9 For with you is the fountain of l;
   39: 4 let me know how fleeting is my l.
   41: 2 will protect him and preserve his l;
   49: 7 No man can redeem the l
   49: 8 the ransom for a l is costly,
   63: 3 Because your love is better than l,
   69:28 they be blotted out of the book of l
   91:16 With long l will I satisfy him
 104:33 I will sing to the LORD all my l;
 119:25 preserve my l according to your word
Pr   1: 3 a disciplined and prudent l,
    3: 2 will prolong your l many years
    3:18 of l to those who embrace her;
    4:23 for it is the wellspring of l.
    6:23 are the way to l,
    6:26 adulteress preys upon your very l.
    7:23 little knowing it will cost him his l.
    8:35 For whoever finds me finds l
   10:11 of the righteous is a fountain of l,
   10:27 of the LORD adds length to l,
   11:30 of the righteous is a tree of l,
   13: 3 He who guards his lips guards his l,
   13:12 but a longing fulfilled is a tree of l.
   13:14 of the wise is a fountain of l,
   14:27 of the LORD is a fountain of l,
   15: 4 that brings healing is a tree of l,
   16:22 Understanding is a fountain of l
   19: 3 A man's own folly ruins his l,
   19:23 The fear of the LORD leads to l:
   21:21 finds l, prosperity and honor.
Isa 53:10 LORD makes his l a guilt offering,
   53:11 he will see the light of l,
   53:12 he poured out his l unto death,
Jer 10:23 that a man's l is not his own;
La   3:58 you redeemed my l.
Eze 18:27 and right, he will save his l.
   37: 5 enter you, and you will come to l.
Da 12: 2 some to everlasting l, others
Jnh 2: 6 you brought my l up from the pit,
Mal 2: 5 a covenant of l and peace,
Mt   6:25 Is not l more important than food,
    7:14 and narrow the road that leads to l,
   10:39 Whoever finds his l will lose it,
   16:21 and on the third day be raised to l.
   16:25 wants to save his l will lose it,

Mt 18: 8 better for you to enter l maimed
   19:16 thing must I do to get eternal l?"
   19:29 as much and will inherit eternal l.
   20:28 to give his l as a ransom for many."
   25:46 but the righteous to eternal l."
Mk 8:35 but whoever loses his l for me
    9:43 better for you to enter l maimed
   10:17 "what must I do to inherit eternal l
   10:30 and in the age to come, eternal l.
   10:45 to give his l as a ransom for many."
Lk   6: 9 to save l or to destroy it?"
    9:22 and on the third day be raised to l."
    9:24 wants to save his l will lose it,
   12:15 a man's l does not consist
   12:22 do not worry about your l,
   12:25 can add a single hour to his l?
   14:26 even his own l— he cannot be my
   17:33 tries to keep his l will lose it,
   21:19 standing firm you will gain l.
Jn   1: 4 In him was l, and that l was
    3:15 believes in him may have eternal l.
    3:36 believes in the Son has eternal l,
    4:14 of water welling up to eternal l."
    5:21 raises the dead and gives them l,
    5:24 him who sent me has eternal l
    5:26 For as the Father has l in himself,
    5:39 that by them you possess eternal l.
    5:40 refuse to come to me to have l.
    6:27 for food that endures to eternal l,
    6:33 down from heaven and gives l
    6:35 Jesus declared, "I am the bread of l
    6:40 believes in him shall have eternal l,
    6:47 he who believes has everlasting l.
    6:48 I am the bread of l.
    6:51 give for the l of the world."
    6:53 and drink his blood, you have no l
    6:63 The Spirit gives l; the flesh counts
    6:68 You have the words of eternal l.
    8:12 but will have the light of l."
   10:10 I have come that they may have l,
   10:15 and I lay down my l for the sheep.
   10:17 loves me is that I lay down my l—
   10:28 I give them eternal l, and they shall
   11:25 "I am the resurrection and the l.
   12:25 The man who loves his l will lose it,
   12:50 his command leads to eternal l.
   13:37 I will lay down my l for you."
   14: 6 am the way and the truth and the l.
   15:13 lay down his l for his friends.
   17: 2 people that he might give eternal l
   17: 3 Now this is eternal l: that they may
   20:31 that by believing you may have l
Ac   2:32 God has raised this Jesus to l,
    3:15 You killed the author of l,
   11:18 the Gentiles repentance unto l."
   13:48 appointed for eternal l believed.
Ro   2: 7 immortality, he will give eternal l.
    4:25 was raised to l for our justification.
    5:10 shall we be saved through his l!
    5:18 was justification that brings l
    5:21 righteousness to bring eternal l
    6: 4 the Father, we too may live a new l
    6:13 have been brought from death to l;
    6:22 holiness, and the result is eternal l.
    6:23 but the gift of God is eternal l
    8: 6 mind controlled by the Spirit is l
    8:11 also give l to your mortal bodies
    8:38 convinced that neither death nor l,
1Co 15:19 If only for this l we have hope
   15:36 What you sow does not come to l
2Co 2:16 to the other, the fragrance of l.
    3: 6 letter kills, but the Spirit gives l.
    4:10 so that the l of Jesus may
    5: 4 is mortal may be swallowed up by l.
Gal 2:20 The l I live in the body, I live
    3:21 had been given that could impart l,
    6: 8 from the Spirit will reap eternal l.
Eph 4: 1 I urge you to live a l worthy
Php 2:16 as you hold out the word of l—
    4: 3 whose names are in the book of l.
Col   1:10 order that you may live a l worthy
    3: 3 your l is now hidden with Christ
1Th 4:12 so that your daily l may win
1Ti 1:16 on him and receive eternal l.
    4: 8 for both the present l and the l
    4:12 in l, in love, in faith and in purity.
    4:16 Watch your l and doctrine closely.
    6:12 Take hold of the eternal l

1Ti 6: 19 hold of the *l* that is truly *l*.
2Ti 1: 9 saved us and called us to a holy *l*—
      1: 10 destroyed death and has brought *l*
      3: 12 to live a godly *l* in Christ Jesus will
Tit   1: 2 hope on the hope of eternal *l*,
      3: 7 heirs having the hope of eternal *l*.
Heb 7: 16 of the power of an indestructible *l*.
Jas 1: 12 crown of *l* that God has promised
      3: 13 Let him show it by his good *l*,
1Pe 3: 7 with you of the gracious gift of *l*,
      3: 10 ''Whoever would love *l*
      4: 2 rest of his earthly *l* for evil human
2Pe 1: 3 given us everything we need for *l*
1Jn 1: 1 proclaim concerning the Word of *l*.
      2: 25 he promised us—even eternal *l*.
      3: 14 we have passed from death to *l*,
      3: 16 Jesus Christ laid down his *l* for us.
      5: 11 has given us eternal *l*, and this *l* is
      5: 20 He is the true God and eternal *l*.
Jude   : 21 Christ to bring you to eternal *l*.
Rev 2: 7 the right to eat from the tree of *l*,
      2: 8 who died and came to *l* again.
      2: 10 and I will give you the crown of *l*.
      3: 5 name from the book of *l*,
     13: 8 written in the book of *l* belonging
     17: 8 in the book of *l* from the creation
    20: 12 was opened, which is the book of *l*.
    20: 15 not found written in the book of *l*
    21: 6 from the spring of the water of *l*.
    21: 27 written in the Lamb's book of *l*.
    22: 1 me the river of the water of *l*,
    22: 2 side of the river stood the tree of *l*,
    22: 14 may have the right to the tree of *l*
    22: 17 take the free gift of the water of *l*.
    22: 19 from him his share in the tree of *l*

LIFE-GIVING (GIVE)

Pr 15: 31 He who listens to a *l* rebuke
1Co 15: 45 being''; the last Adam, a *l* spirit.

LIFETIME (LIVE)

Ps 30: 5 but his favor lasts a *l*;
Lk 16: 25 in your *l* you received your good

LIFT (LIFTED LIFTING LIFTS)

Ps   3: 3 you bestow glory on me and *l*
    28: 2 as I *l* up my hands
    63: 4 in your name I will *l* up my hands.
    91: 12 they will *l* you up in their hands,
  121: 1 I *l* up my eyes to the hills—
  123: 1 I *l* up my eyes to you,
  134: 2 *L* up your hands in the sanctuary
  143: 8 for to you I *l* up my soul.
Isa 40: 9 *l* up your voice with a shout,
La   2: 19 *L* up your hands to him
    3: 41 Let us *l* up our hearts and our
Mt   4: 6 they will *l* you up in their hands,
Lk 21: 28 stand up and *l* up your heads,
1Ti 2: 8 everywhere to *l* up holy hands
Jas 4: 10 the Lord, and he will *l* you up.
1Pe 5: 6 that he may *l* you up in due time.

LIFTED (LIFT)

Ne   8: 6 and all the people *l* their hands
Ps 24: 7 be *l* up, you ancient doors,
    40: 2 He *l* me out of the slimy pit,
    41: 9 has *l* up his heel against me.
Isa 52: 13 *l* up and highly exalted.
    63: 9 he *l* them up and carried them
Jn   3: 14 Moses *l* up the snake in the desert,
    8: 28 ''When you have *l* up the Son
    12: 32 when I am *l* up from the earth,
    12: 34 'The Son of Man must be *l* up'?
    13: 18 shares my bread has *l* up his heel

LIFTING (LIFT)

Ps 141: 2 may the *l* up of my hands be like

LIFTS (LIFT)

Ps 113: 7 and *l* the needy from the ash heap;

LIGAMENT* (LIGAMENTS)

Eph 4: 16 held together by every supporting *l*

LIGAMENTS* (LIGAMENT)

Col 2: 19 held together by its *l* and sinews,

LIGHT (ENLIGHTENED LIGHTS)

Ge   1: 3 ''Let there be *l*,'' and there was *l*.
Ex 13: 21 in a pillar of fire to give them *l*,
    25: 37 it so that they *l* the space in front
2Sa 22: 29 *L*ord turns my darkness into *l*.
Job 38: 19 ''What is the way to the abode of *l*?
Ps   4: 6 Let the *l* of your face shine upon us
    18: 28 my God turns my darkness into *l*.
    19: 8 giving *l* to the eyes.
    27: 1 *L*ord is my *l* and my salvation—
    36: 9 in your *l* we see *l*.
    56: 13 God in the *l* of life.
    76: 4 You are resplendent with *l*,
    89: 15 who walk in the *l* of your presence,
  104: 2 He wraps himself in *l*
  119:105 and a *l* for my path.
  119:130 The unfolding of your words gives *l*;
  139: 12 for darkness is as *l* to you.
Pr   4: 18 till the full *l* of day.
Isa   2: 5 let us walk in the *l* of the *L*ord.
    9: 2 have seen a great *l*;
    42: 6 and a *l* for the Gentiles,
    45: 7 I form the *l* and create darkness,
    49: 6 also make you a *l* for the Gentiles,
    53: 11 he will see the *l* of life,
    60: 1 ''Arise, shine, for your *l* has come,
    60: 19 *L*ord will be your everlasting *l*,
Eze 1: 27 and brilliant *l* surrounded him.
Mic 7: 8 the *L*ord will be my *l*.
Mt   4: 16 have seen a great *l*;
    5: 14 ''You are the *l* of the world.
    5: 15 it gives *l* to everyone in the house.
    5: 16 let your *l* shine before men,
    6: 22 your whole body will be full of *l*.
    11: 30 yoke is easy and my burden is *l*.''
    17: 2 his clothes became as white as the *l*
    24: 29 and the moon will not give its *l*;
Mk 13: 24 and the moon will not give its *l*;
Lk   2: 32 a *l* for revelation to the Gentiles
    8: 16 those who come in can see the *l*.
    11: 33 those who come in may see the *l*.
Jn   1: 4 and that life was the *l* of men.
    1: 5 The *l* shines in the darkness,
    1: 7 witness to testify concerning that *l*,
    1: 9 The true *l* that gives *l*
    3: 19 but men loved darkness instead of *l*
    3: 20 Everyone who does evil hates the *l*,
    8: 12 he said, ''I am the *l* of the world.
    9: 5 in the world, I am the *l* of the world
    12: 35 Walk while you have the *l*,
    12: 46 I have come into the world as a *l*,
Ac 13: 47 ''I have made you a *l*
Ro 13: 12 darkness and put on the armor of *l*.
2Co 4: 6 made his *l* shine in our hearts
    6: 14 Or what fellowship can *l* have
    11: 14 masquerades as an angel of *l*.
Eph 5: 8 but now you are *l* in the Lord.
1Th 5: 5 You are all sons of the *l*
1Ti 6: 16 and who lives in unapproachable *l*,
1Pe 2: 9 of darkness into his wonderful *l*.
2Pe 1: 19 as to a *l* shining in a dark place,
1Jn 1: 5 God is *l*; in him there is no
    1: 7 But if we walk in the *l*,
    2: 9 Anyone who claims to be in the *l*
Rev 21: 23 for the glory of God gives it *l*,
    22: 5 for the Lord God will give them *l*.

LIGHTNING

Ex 9: 23 and *l* flashed down to the ground.
    20: 18 and *l* and heard the trumpet
Ps 18: 12 with hailstones and bolts of *l*.
Eze 1: 13 it was bright, and *l* flashed out of it.
Da 10: 6 his face like *l*, his eyes like flaming
Mt 24: 27 For as the *l* that comes from the east
    28: 3 His appearance was like *l*,
Lk 10: 18 ''I saw Satan fall like *l* from heaven.
Rev 4: 5 From the throne came flashes of *l*,

LIGHTS (LIGHT)

Ge   1: 14 ''Let there be *l* in the expanse
Lk   8: 16 No one *l* a lamp and hides it in a jar

LIKE-MINDED* (MIND)

Php 2: 2 make my joy complete by being *l*,

LIKENESS

Ge   1: 26 man in our image, in our *l*,
Ps 17: 15 I will be satisfied with seeing your *l*

Isa 52: 14 his form marred beyond human *l*—
Ro   8: 3 Son in the *l* of sinful man
    8: 29 to be conformed to the *l* of his Son,
2Co 3: 18 his *l* with ever-increasing glory,
Php 2: 7 being made in human *l*.
Jas 3: 9 who have been made in God's *l*.

LILIES (LILY)

Lk 12: 27 ''Consider how the *l* grow.

LILY (LILIES)

SS   2: 1 a *l* of the valleys.
    2: 2 *Lover* Like a *l* among thorns

LIMIT

Ps 147: 5 his understanding has no *l*.
Jn   3: 34 him God gives the Spirit without *l*.

LINEN

Lev 16: 4 He is to put on the sacred *l* tunic,
Pr 31: 22 she is clothed in fine *l* and purple.
    31: 24 She makes *l* garments
Mk 15: 46 So Joseph bought some *l* cloth,
Jn 20: 6 He saw the strips of *l* lying there,
Rev 15: 6 shining *l* and wore golden sashes
    19: 8 Fine *l*, bright and clean,

LINGER

Hab 2: 3 Though it *l*, wait for it;

LION (LION'S LIONS')

Jdg 14: 6 power so that he tore the *l* apart
1Sa 17: 34 When a *l* or a bear came
Isa 11: 7 and the *l* will eat straw like the ox.
    65: 25 and the *l* will eat straw like the ox,
Eze 1: 10 right side each had the face of a *l*,
    10: 14 the third the face of a *l*,
Da   7: 4 ''The first was like a *l*,
1Pe 5: 8 around like a roaring *l* looking
Rev 4: 7 The first living creature was like a *l*
    5: 5 See, the *L* of the tribe of Judah,

LION'S (LION)

Ge 49: 9 You are a *l* cub, O Judah;

LIONS' (LION)

Da   6: 7 shall be thrown into the *l* den.

LIPS

Ps   8: 2 From the *l* of children and infants
    34: 1 his praise will always be on my *l*.
    40: 9 I do not seal my *l*,
    63: 3 my *l* will glorify you.
  119:171 May my *l* overflow with praise,
  140: 3 the poison of vipers is on their *l*.
  141: 3 keep watch over the door of my *l*.
Pr 10: 13 on the *l* of the discerning,
    10: 18 who conceals his hatred has lying *l*,
    10: 32 *l* of the righteous know what is
    12: 22 The *L*ord detests lying *l*,
    13: 3 He who guards his *l* guards his soul
    14: 7 will not find knowledge on his *l*.
    24: 26 is like a kiss on the *l*.
    26: 23 are fervent *l* with an evil heart.
    27: 2 someone else, and not your own *l*.
Isa 6: 5 For I am a man of unclean *l*,
    28: 11 with foreign *l* and strange tongues
    29: 13 and honor me with their *l*,
Mal 2: 7 ''For the *l* of a priest ought
Mt 15: 8 These people honor me with their *l*
    21: 16 '' 'From the *l* of children
Lk   4: 22 words that came from his *l*.
Ro   3: 13 ''The poison of vipers is on their *l*.''
Col 3: 8 and filthy language from your *l*.
Heb 13: 15 the fruit of *l* that confess his name.
1Pe 3: 10 and his *l* from deceitful speech.

LISTEN (LISTENED LISTENING LISTENS)

Dt 18: 15 You must *l* to him.
    30: 20 *l* to his voice, and hold fast to him.
1Ki 4: 34 came to *l* to Solomon's wisdom,
2Ki 21: 9 But the people did not *l*.
Pr   1: 5 let the wise *l* and add
Ecc 5: 1 Go near to *l* rather
Eze 2: 5 And whether they *l* or fail to *l*—
Mt 12: 42 earth to *l* to Solomon's wisdom,
Mk 9: 7 *L* to him!'' Suddenly,

LISTENED

Jn 10: 27 My sheep *l* to my voice; I know
Ac 3: 22 you must *l* to everything he tells
Jas 1: 19 Everyone should be quick to *l*,
1: 22 Do not merely *l* to the word,
1Jn 4: 6 not from God does not *l* to us.

LISTENED (LISTEN)

Ne 8: 3 And all the people *l* attentively
Isa 66: 4 when I spoke, no one *l*.
Da 9: 6 We have not *l* to your servants

LISTENING (LISTEN)

1Sa 3: 9 Speak, LORD, for your servant is *l*
Pr 18: 13 He who answers before *l*—
Lk 10: 39 at the Lord's feet *l* to what he said.

LISTENS (LISTEN)

Pr 12: 15 but a wise man *l* to advice.
Lk 10: 16 "He who *l* to you *l*
1Jn 4: 6 and whoever knows God *l* to us;

LIVE (ALIVE LIFE LIFETIME LIVES LIVING)

Ge 3: 22 tree of life and eat, and *l* forever."
Ex 20: 12 so that you may *l* long
33: 20 for no one may see me and *l*."
Nu 21: 8 who is bitten can look at it and *l*."
Dt 5: 24 we have seen that a man can *l*
6: 2 as you *l* by keeping all his decrees
8: 3 to teach you that man does not *l*
Job 14: 14 If a man dies, will he *l* again?
Ps 15: 1 Who may *l* on your holy hill?
24: 1 the world, and all who *l* in it;
26: 8 I love the house where you *l*,
119:175 Let me *l* that I may praise you,
Pr 21: 9 Better to *l* on a corner of the roof
21: 19 Better to *l* in a desert
Ecc 9: 4 a dog is better off than a dead lion
Isa 26: 19 But your dead will *l*;
55: 3 hear me, that your soul may *l*.
Eze 17: 19 LORD says: As surely as I *l*,
20: 11 for the man who obeys them will *l*
37: 3 can these bones *l?*" I said,
Am 5: 6 Seek the LORD and *l*,
Hab 2: 4 but the righteous will *l* by his faith
Zec 2: 11 I will *l* among you and you will
Mt 4: 4 'Man does not *l* on bread alone,
Lk 4: 4 'Man does not *l* on bread alone.' "
Jn 14: 19 Because I *l*, you also will *l*
Ac 17: 24 does not *l* in temples built by hands
17: 28 'For in him we *l* and move
Ro 1: 17 "The righteous will *l* by faith."
2Co 5: 7 We *l* by faith, not by sight.
6: 16 "I will *l* with them and walk
Gal 2: 20 The life I *l* in the body, I *l* by faith
3: 11 "The righteous will *l* by faith."
5: 25 Since we *l* by the Spirit, let us keep
Eph 4: 17 that you must no longer *l*
Php 1: 21 to *l* is Christ and to die is gain.
Col 1: 10 order that you may *l* a life worthy
1Th 4: 1 we instructed you how to *l* in order
5: 13 *L* in peace with each other.
1Ti 2: 2 that we may *l* peaceful
2Ti 3: 12 who wants to *l* a godly life
Tit 2: 12 and to *l* self-controlled, upright
Heb 10: 38 But my righteous one will *l* by faith
12: 14 Make every effort to *l* in peace
1Pe 1: 17 your lives as strangers here
3: 8 *l* in harmony with one another;

LIVES (LIVE)

Ge 45: 7 and to save your *l* by a great
Job 19: 25 I know that my Redeemer *l*,
Pr 1: 19 it takes away the *l*
Isa 57: 15 he who *l* forever, whose name is
Da 3: 28 to give up their *l* rather than serve
Jn 14: 17 for he *l* with you and will be in you.
Ro 6: 10 but the life he *l*, he *l* to God.
7: 18 I know that nothing good *l* in me,
8: 9 if the Spirit of God *l* in you.
14: 7 For none of us *l* to himself alone
1Co 3: 16 and that God's Spirit *l* in you?
Gal 2: 20 I no longer live, but Christ *l* in me.
1Th 2: 8 only the gospel of God but our *l*
1Ti 2: 2 quiet *l* in all godliness and holiness.
Tit 2: 12 and godly *l* in this present age,
Heb 7: 24 but because Jesus *l* forever,
13: 5 Keep your *l* free from the love

LIVING (LIVE)

Ge 2: 7 and the man became a *l* being.
1Sa 17: 26 defy the armies of the *l* God?"
Isa 53: 8 cut off from the land of the *l;*
Jer 2: 13 the spring of *l* water,
Eze 1: 5 what looked like four *l* creatures.
Zec 14: 8 On that day *l* water will flow out
Mt 22: 32 the God of the dead but of the *l*."
Jn 4: 10 he would have given you *l* water."
6: 51 I am the *l* bread that came
7: 38 streams of *l* water will flow
Ro 8: 11 Jesus from the dead is *l* in you,
12: 1 to offer your bodies as *l* sacrifices,
1Co 9: 14 the gospel should receive their *l*
Heb 4: 12 For the word of God is *l* and active.
10: 20 and *l* way opened for us
10: 31 to fall into the hands of the *l* God.
1Pe 1: 23 through the *l* and enduring word
Rev 1: 18 I am the *L* One; I was dead,
4: 6 the throne, were four *l* creatures,
7: 17 to springs of *l* water.

LOAD (LOADS)

Gal 6: 5 for each one should carry his own *l*.

LOADS (LOAD)

Mt 23: 4 They tie up heavy *l* and put them

LOAF (LOAVES)

1Co 10: 17 for we all partake of the one *l*.

LOAVES (LOAF)

Mk 6: 41 Taking the five *l* and the two fish
8: 6 When he had taken the seven *l*
Lk 11: 5 'Friend, lend me three *l* of bread,

LOCKED

Jn 20: 26 the doors were *l*, Jesus came
Gal 3: 23 *l* up until faith should be revealed.

LOCUSTS

Ex 10: 4 I will bring *l* into your country
Joel 2: 25 you for the years the *l* have eaten—
Mt 3: 4 His food was *l* and wild honey.
Rev 9: 3 And out of the smoke *l* came

LOFTY

Ps 139: 6 too *l* for me to attain.
Isa 57: 15 is what the high and *l* One says—

LONELY

Ps 68: 6 God sets the *l* in families,
Lk 5: 16 Jesus often withdrew to *l* places

LONG (LENGTH LENGTHY LONGED LONGING LONGINGS LONGS)

Ex 17: 11 As *l* as Moses held up his hands,
Nu 6: 5 the hair of his head grow *l*.
1Ki 18: 21 "How *l* will you waver
Ps 119: 97 I meditate on it all day *l*.
119:174 I *l* for your salvation, O LORD.
Hos 7: 13 I *l* to redeem them
Am 5: 18 Why do you *l* for the day
Mt 25: 5 The bridegroom was a *l* time
Jn 9: 4 As *l* as it is day, we must do
1Co 11: 14 that if a man has *l* hair,
Eph 3: 18 to grasp how wide and *l* and high
Php 1: 8 God can testify how I *l* for all
1Pe 1: 12 Even angels *l* to look

LONGED (LONG)

Mt 13: 17 righteous men *l* to see what you see
23: 37 how often I have *l*
Lk 13: 34 how often I have *l*
2Ti 4: 8 to all who have *l* for his appearing.

LONGING* (LONG)

Dt 28: 65 with *l*, and a despairing heart.
Job 7: 2 Like a slave *l* for the evening
Ps 119: 20 My soul is consumed with *l*
119: 81 with *l* for your salvation,
119:131 *l* for your commands.
143: 7 my spirit faints with *l*.

LONGINGS* (LONG)

1Pe 3: 2 the purity and reverence of your *l*.
2Pe 3: 11 You ought to live holy and godly *l*
1Jn 3: 16 to lay down our *l* for our brothers.
4: 16 Whoever *l* in love *l* in God,

LONGS* (LONG)

Ps 38: 9 All my *l* lie open before you,
112: 10 the *l* of the wicked will come

LONGS* (LONG)

Ps 63: 1 my body *l* for you,
Isa 26: 9 in the morning my spirit *l* for you.
30: 18 Yet the LORD *l* to be gracious
Php 2: 26 For he *l* for all of you and is

LOOK (LOOKED LOOKING LOOKS)

Ge 19: 17 "Flee for your lives! Don't *l* back,
Ex 3: 6 because he was afraid to *l* at God.
Nu 21: 8 anyone who is bitten can *l* at it
32: 8 Kadesh Barnea to *l* over the land.
Dt 4: 29 you will find him if you *l* for him
1Sa 16: 7 The LORD does not *l*
Job 31: 1 not to *l* lustfully at a girl.
Ps 34: 5 Those who *l* to him are radiant;
105: 4 *L* to the LORD and his strength;
113: 6 who stoops down to *l*
123: 2 As the eyes of slaves *l* to the hand
Pr 1: 28 they will *l* for me but will not find
4: 25 Let your eyes *l* straight ahead,
15: 30 A cheerful *l* brings joy to the heart,
Isa 17: 7 In that day men will *l*
31: 1 do not *l* to the Holy One of Israel,
40: 26 Lift your eyes and *l* to the heavens:
60: 5 Then you will *l* and be radiant,
Jer 3: 3 Yet you have the brazen *l*
6: 16 "Stand at the crossroads and *l;*
Eze 34: 11 for my sheep and *l* after them.
Hab 1: 13 Your eyes are too pure to *l* on evil;
Zec 12: 10 They will *l* on me, the one they
Mt 18: 10 "See that you do not *l* down on one
18: 12 go to *l* for the one that wandered
23: 27 which *l* beautiful on the outside
Mk 13: 21 *'L*, here is the Christ!' or, *'L*,
Lk 6: 41 "Why do you *l* at the speck
24: 39 *L* at my hands and my feet.
Jn 1: 36 he said, *"L*, the Lamb of God!"
4: 35 open your eyes and *l* at the fields!
19: 37 "They will *l* on the one they have
Ro 14: 10 why do you *l* down on your brother
Php 2: 4 Each of you should *l* not only
1Ti 4: 12 Don't let anyone *l* down on you
Jas 1: 27 to *l* after orphans and widows
1Pe 1: 12 long to *l* into these things.
2Pe 3: 12 as you *l* forward to the day of God

LOOKED (LOOK)

Ge 19: 26 Lot's wife *l* back, and she became
Ex 2: 25 So God *l* on the Israelites
1Sa 6: 19 because they had *l* into the ark
SS 3: 1 I *l* for the one my heart loves;
Eze 22: 30 "I *l* for a man among them who
34: 6 and no one searched or *l* for them.
44: 4 I *l* and saw the glory
Da 7: 9 "As I *l*,
10: 5 I *l* up and there before me was
Hab 3: 6 he *l*, and made the nations tremble.
Mt 25: 36 I was sick and you *l* after me,
Lk 18: 9 and *l* down on everybody else,
22: 61 The Lord turned and *l* straight
1Jn 1: 1 which we have *l* at and our hands

LOOKING (LOOK)

Ps 69: 3 *l* for my God.
119: 82 My eyes fail, *l* for your promise;
119:123 My eyes fail, *l* for your salvation,
Mk 16: 6 "You are *l* for Jesus the Nazarene,
2Co 10: 7 *l* only on the surface
Php 4: 17 Not that I am *l* for a gift,
1Th 2: 6 We were not *l* for praise from men,
2Pe 3: 13 with his promise we are *l* forward
Rev 5: 6 I saw a Lamb, *l* as if it had been

LOOKS (LOOK)

1Sa 16: 7 Man *l* at the outward appearance,
Ezr 8: 22 is on everyone who *l* to him,
Ps 104: 32 He *l* at the earth, and it trembles;
   138: 6 on high, he *l* upon the holy,
Pr 27: 18 he who *l* after his master will be
Eze 34: 12 As a shepherd *l* after his scattered
Mt 5: 28 But I tell you that anyone who *l*
   16: 4 and adulterous generation *l*
Lk 9: 62 and *l* back is fit for service
Jn 6: 40 Father's will is that everyone who *l*
   12: 45 When he *l* at me, he sees the one
Php 2: 21 For everyone *l* out
Jas 1: 25 But the man who *l* intently

LOOSE

Isa 33: 23 Your rigging hangs *l*:
Mt 16: 19 and whatever you *l* on earth will be
   18: 18 and whatever you *l* on earth will be

LORD† (LORD'S† LORDED LORDING)

Ge 18: 27 been so bold as to speak to the *L*,
Ex 15: 17 O *L*, your hands established.
Nu 16: 13 now you also want to *l* it over us?
Dt 10: 17 God of gods and *L* of lords,
Jos 3: 13 the *L* of all the earth—set foot
1Ki 3: 10 *L* was pleased that Solomon had
Ne 4: 14 Remember the *L*, who is great
Job 28: 28 'The fear of the *L*— that is wisdom,
Ps 37: 13 but the *L* laughs at the wicked,
   38: 22 O *L* my Savior.
   54: 4 the *L* is the one who sustains me.
   62: 12 and that you, O *L*, are loving.
   69: 6 O *L*, the LORD Almighty;
   86: 5 You are kind and forgiving, O *L*,
   86: 8 gods there is none like you, O *L*;
   89: 49 O *L*, where is your former great
   110: 1 The LORD says to my *L*:
   110: 5 The *L* is at your right hand;
   130: 3 O *L*, who could stand?
   135: 5 that our *L* is greater than all gods.
   136: 3 Give thanks to the *L* of lords:
   147: 5 Great is our *L* and mighty in power
Isa 6: 1 I saw the *L* seated on a throne,
Da 2: 47 and the *L* of kings and a revealer
   9: 4 "O *L*, the great and awesome God,
   9: 7 "*L*, you are righteous,
   9: 9 The *L* our God is merciful
   9: 19 O *L*, listen! O *L*, forgive! O *L*,
Mt 3: 3 'Prepare the way for the *L*,
   4: 7 'Do not put the *L* your God
   4: 10 'Worship the *L* your God,
   7: 21 "Not everyone who says to me, '*L*,
   9: 38 Ask the *L* of the harvest, therefore,
   12: 8 Son of Man is *L* of the Sabbath."
   20: 25 of the Gentiles *l* it over them,
   21: 9 comes in the name of the *L*!"
   22: 37 " 'Love the *L* your God
   22: 44 For he says, " 'The *L* said to my *L*:
   23: 39 comes in the name of the *L*.' "
Mk 1: 3 'Prepare the way for the *L*,
   12: 11 *L* has done this,
   12: 29 the *L* our God, the *L* is one.
   12: 30 Love the *L* your God
Lk 2: 9 glory of the *L* shone around them,
   6: 5 The Son of Man is *L* of the Sabbath
   6: 46 "Why do you call me, '*L*, *L*,'
   10: 27 " 'Love the *L* your God
   11: 1 one of his disciples said to him, "*L*,
   24: 34 The *L* has risen and has appeared
Jn 1: 23 'Make straight the way for the *L*.' "
Ac 2: 21 on the name of the *L* will be saved.'
   2: 25 " 'I saw the *L* always before me.
   2: 34 " 'The *L* said to my *L*:
   8: 16 into the name of the *L* Jesus.
   9: 5 "Who are you, *L*?" Saul asked.
   10: 36 through Jesus Christ, who is *L*
   11: 23 true to the *L* with all their hearts.
   16: 31 replied, "Believe in the *L* Jesus,
Ro 4: 24 in him who raised Jesus our *L*,
   5: 11 In God through our *L* Jesus Christ,
   6: 23 life in Christ Jesus our *L*.
   8: 39 of God that is in Christ Jesus our *L*.
   10: 9 with your mouth, "Jesus is *L*,"
   10: 13 on the name of the *L* will be saved

Ro 10: 16 *L*, who has believed our message?"
   11: 34 Who has known the mind of the *L*?
   12: 11 your spiritual fervor, serving the *L*.
   13: 14 yourselves with the *L* Jesus Christ,
   14: 4 for the *L* is able to make him stand.
   14: 8 we live to the *L*; and if we die,
1Co 1: 31 Let him who boasts boast in the *L*."
   3: 5 the *L* has assigned to each his task.
   4: 5 time; wait till the *L* comes.
   6: 13 for the *L*, and the *L* for the body.
   6: 14 By his power God raised the *L*
   7: 32 affairs—how he can please the *L*.
   7: 34 to be devoted to the *L* in both body
   7: 35 in undivided devotion to the *L*.
   7: 39 but he must belong to the *L*.
   8: 6 and there is but one *L*, Jesus Christ,
   10: 9 We should not test the *L*,
   11: 23 For I received from the *L* what I
   12: 3 "Jesus is *L*," except by the Holy
   15: 57 victory through our *L* Jesus Christ.
   15: 58 fully to the work of the *L*,
   16: 22 If anyone does not love the *L*—
2Co 1: 24 Not that we *l* it over your faith,
   2: 12 found that the *L* had opened a door
   3: 17 Now the *L* is the Spirit,
   4: 5 but Jesus Christ as *L*, and ourselves
   5: 6 in the body we are away from the *L*
   5: 8 they gave themselves first to the *L*
   8: 21 not only in the eyes of the *L* but
   10: 17 Let him who boasts boast in the *L*."
   10: 18 but the one whom the *L* commends
   13: 10 the authority the *L* gave me
Gal 6: 14 in the cross of our *L* Jesus Christ,
Eph 4: 5 one *L*, one faith, one baptism;
   5: 8 but now you are light in the *L*.
   5: 10 and find out what pleases the *L*.
   5: 19 make music in your heart to the *L*,
   5: 22 submit to your husbands as to the *L*
   6: 1 obey your parents in the *L*,
   6: 7 as if you were serving the *L*,
   6: 8 know that the *L* will reward
   6: 10 in the *L* and in his mighty power.
Php 2: 11 confess that Jesus Christ is *L*,
   3: 1 my brothers, rejoice in the *L*!
   3: 8 of knowing Christ Jesus my *L*,
   4: 1 you should stand firm in the *L*,
   4: 4 Rejoice in the *L* always.
   4: 5 The *L* is near.
Col 1: 10 you may live a life worthy of the *L*
   2: 6 as you received Christ Jesus as *L*,
   3: 13 Forgive as the *L* forgave you.
   3: 17 do it all in the name of the *L* Jesus,
   3: 18 your husbands, as is fitting in the *L*
   3: 20 in everything, for this pleases the *L*
   3: 23 as working for the *L*, not for men,
   3: 24 It is the *L* Christ you are serving.
   3: 24 receive an inheritance from the *L*
   4: 17 work you have received in the *L*."
1Th 3: 8 since you are standing firm in the *L*
   3: 12 May the *L* make your love increase
   4: 1 and urge you in the *L* Jesus
   4: 6 The *L* will punish men
   4: 15 who are left till the coming of the *L*
   5: 2 day of the *L* will come like a thief
   5: 23 at the coming of our *L* Jesus Christ.
2Th 1: 7 when the *L* Jesus is revealed
   1: 12 of our *L* Jesus may be glorified
   2: 1 the coming of our *L* Jesus Christ,
   2: 8 whom the *L* Jesus will overthrow
   3: 3 *L* is faithful, and he will strengthen
   3: 5 May the *L* direct your hearts
1Ti 6: 15 the King of kings and *L* of lords,
2Ti 1: 8 ashamed to testify about our *L*,
   2: 19 "The *L* knows those who are his,"
   4: 8 which the *L*, the righteous Judge,
   4: 17 But the *L* stood at my side
Heb 1: 10 O *L*, you laid the foundations
   10: 30 "The *L* will judge his people."
   12: 14 holiness no one will see the *L*.
   13: 6 *L* is my helper; I will not be afraid.
Jas 3: 9 With the tongue we praise our *L*
   4: 10 Humble yourselves before the *L*,
   5: 11 The *L* is full of compassion
1Pe 1: 25 the word of the *L* stands forever."
   2: 3 you have tasted that the *L* is good.
   3: 12 eyes of the *L* are on the righteous

1Pe 3: 15 in your hearts set apart Christ as *L*.
2Pe 1: 11 into the eternal kingdom of our *L*
   1: 16 and coming of our *L* Jesus Christ,
   2: 1 the sovereign *L* who bought
   2: 9 then the *L* knows how
   3: 9 The *L* is not slow in keeping his
   3: 18 and knowledge of our *L* and Savior
Jude : 14 the *L* is coming with thousands
Rev 4: 8 holy, holy is the *L* God Almighty,
   4: 11 "You are worthy, our *L* and God,
   11: 15 has become the kingdom of our *L*
   17: 14 he is *L* of lords and King of kings—
   19: 16 KINGS AND *L* OF LORDS.
   22: 5 for the *L* God will give them light.
   22: 20 Come, *L* Jesus.

LORD'S† (LORD†)

Lk 1: 38 "I am the *L* servant," Mary
Ac 11: 21 The *L* hand was with them,
   21: 14 and said, "The *L* will be done."
1Co 7: 32 is concerned about the *L* affairs—
   10: 26 "The earth is the *L*, and everything
   11: 26 you proclaim the *L* death
2Co 3: 18 faces all reflect the *L* glory,
Eph 5: 17 but understand what the *L* will is.
2Ti 2: 24 And the *L* servant must not quarrel
Heb 12: 5 light of the *L* discipline,
Jas 4: 15 you ought to say, "If it is the *L* will,
   5: 8 because the *L* coming is near.
1Pe 2: 13 Submit yourselves for the *L* sake

LORDED* (LORD†)

Ne 5: 15 Their assistants also *l* it

LORDING* (LORD†)

1Pe 5: 3 not *l* it over those entrusted to you,

LORD‡ (LORD'S‡)

Ge 2: 4 When the *L* God made the earth
   2: 7 And the *L* God formed the man
   2: 22 Then the *L* God made a woman
   3: 21 The *L* God made garments of skin
   3: 23 So the *L* God banished him
   4: 4 The *L* looked with favor on Abel
   4: 26 began to call on the name of the *L*.
   6: 7 So the *L* said, "I will wipe mankind
   7: 16 Then the *L* shut him in.
   9: 26 Blessed be the *L*, the God of Shem!
   11: 9 there the *L* confused the language
   12: 1 *L* had said to Abram, "Leave your
   15: 6 Abram believed the *L*,
   15: 18 On that day the *L* made a covenant
   17: 1 the *L* appeared to him and said,
   18: 1 The *L* appeared to Abraham
   18: 14 Is anything too hard for the *L*?
   18: 19 way of the *L* by doing what is right
   21: 1 Now the *L* was gracious to Sarah
   22: 14 that place "The *L* will Provide."
   24: 1 the *L* had blessed him in every way
   26: 2 The *L* appeared to Isaac and said,
   28: 13 There above it stood the *L*,
   31: 49 "May the *L* keep watch
   39: 2 The *L* was with Joseph
   39: 21 in the prison, the *L* was with him;
Ex 3: 2 the angel of the *L* appeared to him
   4: 11 Is it not I, the *L*? Now go;
   4: 31 heard that the *L* was concerned
   6: 2 also said to Moses, "I am the *L*.
   9: 12 the *L* hardened Pharaoh's heart
   12: 27 'It is the Passover sacrifice to the *L*,
   12: 43 The *L* said to Moses and Aaron,
   13: 9 For the *L* brought you out of Egypt
   13: 21 By day the *L* went ahead of them
   14: 13 the deliverance the *L* will bring
   14: 30 That day the *L* saved Israel
   15: 3 The *L* is a warrior;
   15: 11 among the gods is like you, O *L*?
   15: 26 for I am the *L*, who heals you."
   16: 12 know that I am the *L* your God.' "
   16: 23 day of rest, a holy Sabbath to the *L*
   17: 15 and called it The *L* is my Banner.
   19: 8 will do everything the *L* has said."
   19: 20 The *L* descended to the top
   20: 2 "I am the *L* your God, who
   20: 5 the *L* your God, am a jealous God,
   20: 7 for the *L* will not hold anyone

‡This entry represents the translation of the Hebrew name for God, *Yahweh*, always indicated in the NIV by LORD. For Lord, see the concordance entries **LORD†** and **LORD'S†**.

Ex 20: 10 a Sabbath to the *L* your God.
20: 11 in six days the *L* made the heavens
20: 12 in the land the *L* your God is giving
23: 25 Worship the *L* your God,
24: 3 "Everything the *L* has said we will
24: 12 The *L* said to Moses, "Come up
24: 16 and the glory of the *L* settled
25: 1 The *L* said to Moses, "Tell
28: 36 HOLY TO THE *L*.
30: 11 Then the *L* said to Moses,
31: 13 so you may know that I am the *L*,
31: 18 When the *L* finished speaking
33: 11 The *L* would speak to Moses face
33: 19 And the *L* said, "I will cause all my
34: 1 *L* said to Moses, "Chisel out two
34: 6 proclaiming, "The *L*, the *L*,
34: 10 awesome is the work that I, the *L*,
34: 29 because he had spoken with the *L*
40: 34 glory of the *L* filled the tabernacle.
40: 38 So the cloud of the *L* was
Lev 8: 36 did everything the *L* commanded
9: 23 and the glory of the *L* appeared
10: 2 and they died before the *L*.
19: 2 'Be holy because I, the *L* your God,
20: 8 I am the *L*, who makes you holy.
20: 26 to be holy to me because I, the *L*,
23: 40 and rejoice before the *L* your God
Nu 6: 24 Say to them: " ' ' 'The *L* bless you
8: 5 *L* said to Moses: "Take the Levites
11: 1 hardships in the hearing of the *L*,
14: 14 O *L*, have been seen face to face,
14: 18 you have declared: 'The *L* is slow
14: 21 glory of the *L* fills the whole earth,
21: 6 Then the *L* sent venomous snakes
22: 31 Then the *L* opened Balaam's eyes,
23: 12 "Must I not speak what the *L* puts
30: 2 When a man makes a vow to the *L*
32: 12 followed the *L* wholeheartedly.'
Dt 1: 21 and take possession of it as the *L*,
2: 7 forty years the *L* your God has
4: 29 there you seek the *L* your God,
5: 6 And he said: "I am the *L* your God,
5: 9 the *L* your God, am a jealous God,
6: 4 The *L* our God, the *L* is one.
6: 5 Love the *L* your God
6: 16 Do not test the *L* your God
6: 25 law before the *L* our God,
7: 1 When the *L* your God brings you
7: 6 holy to the *L* your God.
7: 8 But it was because the *L* loved you
7: 9 that the *L* your God is God;
7: 12 then the *L* your God will keep his
8: 5 so the *L* your God disciplines you.
9: 10 The *L* gave me two stone tablets
10: 12 but to fear the *L* your God,
10: 14 To the *L* your God belong
10: 17 For the *L* your God is God of gods
10: 20 Fear the *L* your God and serve him
10: 22 now the *L* your God has made you
11: 1 Love the *L* your God and keep his
11: 13 to love the *L* your God
16: 1 the Passover of the *L* your God,
17: 15 the king the *L* your God choses.
28: 1 If you fully obey the *L* your God
28: 15 if you do not obey the *L* your God
29: 1 covenant the *L* commanded Moses
29: 29 things belong to the *L* our God,
30: 4 from there the *L* your God will
30: 6 *L* your God will circumcise your
30: 10 if you obey the *L* your God
30: 16 today to love the *L* your God
30: 20 For the *L* is your life, and he will
31: 6 for the *L* your God goes with you;
34: 5 of the *L* died there in Moab,
Jos 10: 14 a day when the *L* listened to a man.
22: 5 to love the *L* your God, to walk
23: 11 careful to love the *L* your God
24: 15 my household, we will serve the *L*
24: 18 We will serve the *L*,
Jdg 2: 12 They forsook the *L*, the God
Ru 1: 8 May the *L* show kindness to you,
4: 13 And the *L* enabled her to conceive,
1Sa 1: 11 him to the *L* for all the days
1: 15 I was pouring out my soul to the *L*.
1: 28 So now I give him to the *L*.
2: 2 "There is no one holy like the *L*;
2: 25 but if a man sins against the *L*,
2: 26 in favor with the *L* and with men.

1Sa 3: 9 *L*, for your servant is listening.' "
3: 19 The *L* was with Samuel
7: 12 "Thus far has the *L* helped us."
9: 17 sight of Saul, the *L* said to him,
11: 15 as king in the presence of the *L*.
12: 18 all the people stood in awe of the *L*
12: 22 his great name the *L* will not reject
12: 24 But be sure to fear the *L*
13: 14 the *L* has sought out a man
14: 6 Nothing can hinder the *L*
15: 22 "Does the *L* delight
16: 13 Spirit of the *L* came upon David
17: 45 you in the name of the *L* Almighty,
2Sa 6: 14 danced before the *L*
7: 22 How great you are, O Sovereign *L*!
8: 6 *L* gave David victory everywhere
12: 7 This is what the *L*, the God
22: 2 "The *L* is my rock, my fortress
22: 29 You are my lamp, O *L*;
22: 31 the word of the *L* is flawless.
1Ki 1: 30 today what I swore to you by the *L*,
1: 3 and observe what the *L* your God
3: 7 O *L* my God, you have made your
5: 5 for the Name of the *L* my God,
5: 12 The *L* gave Solomon wisdom,
8: 11 the glory of the *L* filled his temple.
8: 23 toward heaven and said: "O *L*,
8: 61 fully committed to the *L* our God,
9: 3 The *L* said to him: "I have heard
10: 9 Praise be to the *L* your God,
15: 14 committed to the *L* all his life.
18: 21 If the *L* is God, follow him;
18: 36 "O *L*, God of Abraham, Isaac
18: 39 "The *L*— he is God! The *L*—
21: 23 also concerning Jezebel the *L* says:
2Ki 13: 23 But the *L* was gracious to them
17: 18 So the *L* was very angry with Israel
18: 5 Hezekiah trusted in the *L*,
19: 1 and went into the temple of the *L*.
20: 11 *L* made the shadow go back the ten
21: 12 Therefore this is what the *L*,
22: 2 right in the eyes of the *L*
22: 8 of the Law in the temple of the *L*."
23: 3 to follow the *L* and keep his
23: 21 the Passover to the *L* your God,
23: 25 a king like him who turned to the *L*
24: 2 The *L* sent Babylonian, Aramean,
24: 4 and the *L* was not willing to forgive
1Ch 10: 13 because he was unfaithful to the *L*;
11: 3 with them at Hebron before the *L*,
11: 9 the *L* Almighty was with him.
13: 6 from there the ark of God the *L*, who
16: 8 Give thanks to the *L*, call
16: 11 Look to the *L* and his strength;
16: 14 He is the *L* our God;
16: 23 Sing to the *L*, all the earth;
17: 1 covenant of the *L* is under a tent."
21: 24 take for the *L* what is yours,
22: 5 to be built for the *L* should be
22: 11 build the house of the *L* your God,
22: 13 and laws that the *L* gave Moses
22: 16 Now begin the work, and the *L* be
22: 19 soul to seeking the *L* your God.
25: 7 and skilled in music for the *L*—
28: 9 for the *L* searches every heart
28: 20 for the *L* God, my God, is with you
29: 1 not for man but for the *L* God.
29: 11 O *L*, is the greatness and the power
29: 18 O *L*, God of our fathers Abraham,
29: 25 The *L* highly exalted Solomon
2Ch 1: 1 for the *L* his God was with him
5: 13 to give praise and thanks to the *L*.
5: 14 the glory of the *L* filled the temple
6: 16 "Now *L*, God of Israel, keep
6: 41 O *L* God, and come
6: 42 O *L* God, do not reject your
7: 1 the glory of the *L* filled the temple.
7: 12 the *L* appeared to him at night
7: 21 'Why has the *L* done such a thing
9: 8 as king to rule for the *L* your God.
13: 12 do not fight against the *L*,
14: 2 right in the eyes of the *L* his God.
15: 14 to the *L* with loud acclamation,
16: 9 of the *L* range throughout the earth
17: 9 the Book of the Law of the *L*;
18: 13 said, "As surely as the *L* lives,
19: 6 judging for man but for the *L*,
19: 9 wholeheartedly in the fear of the *L*.

2Ch 20: 15 This is what the *L* says to you:
20: 20 Have faith in the *L* your God
20: 21 appointed men to sing to the *L*
26: 5 As long as he sought the *L*,
26: 16 He was unfaithful to the *L* his God,
29: 30 to praise the *L* with the words
30: 9 for the *L* your God is gracious
31: 20 and faithful before the *L* his God.
32: 8 with us is the *L* our God to help us
34: 14 Law of the *L* that had been given
34: 31 to follow the *L* and keep his
Ezr 3: 10 foundation of the temple of the *L*,
7: 6 for the hand of the *L* his God was
7: 10 observance of the Law of the *L*,
9: 5 hands spread out to the *L* my God
9: 8 the *L* our God has been gracious
9: 15 O *L*, God of Israel, you are
Ne 5: 1 Then I said: "O *L*, God of heaven,
8: 1 which the *L* had commanded
9: 6 You alone are the *L*.
Job 1: 6 to present themselves before the *L*,
1: 21 *L* gave and the *L* has taken away;
38: 1 the *L* answered Job out
42: 9 and the *L* accepted Job's prayer.
42: 12 The *L* blessed the latter part
Ps 1: 2 But his delight is in the law of the *L*
1: 6 For the *L* watches over the way
4: 6 of your face shine upon us, O *L*.
4: 8 for you alone, O *L*,
5: 3 Morning by morning, O *L*,
6: 1 O *L*, do not rebuke me
8: 1 O *L*, our Lord,
9: 9 The *L* is a refuge for the oppressed,
9: 19 Arise, O *L*, let not man triumph;
10: 16 The *L* is King for ever and ever;
12: 6 And the words of the *L* are flawless
16: 5 *L*, you have assigned me my
16: 8 I have set the *L* always before me.
18: 1 I love you, O *L*, my strength.
18: 6 In my distress I called to the *L*;
18: 30 the word of the *L* is flawless.
19: 7 The law of the *L* is perfect,
19: 14 O *L*, my Rock and my Redeemer.
20: 5 May the *L* grant all your requests.
20: 7 in the name of the *L* our God.
22: 8 let the *L* rescue him.
23: 1 The *L* is my shepherd, I shall lack
23: 6 I will dwell in the house of the *L*
24: 3 Who may ascend the hill of the *L*?
24: 8 The *L* strong and mighty,
25: 10 All the ways of the *L* are loving
27: 1 The *L* is my light and my salvation
27: 4 to gaze upon the beauty of the *L*
27: 6 I will sing and make music to the *L*.
29: 1 Ascribe to the *L*, O mighty ones,
29: 4 The voice of the *L* is powerful;
30: 4 Sing to the *L*, you saints of his;
31: 5 redeem me, O *L*, the God of truth.
32: 2 whose sin the *L* does not count
33: 1 joyfully to the *L*, you righteous;
33: 6 of the *L* were the heavens made,
33: 12 is the nation whose God is the *L*,
33: 18 But the eyes of the *L* are
34: 1 I will extol the *L* at all times;
34: 3 Glorify the *L* with me;
34: 4 I sought the *L*, and he answered me
34: 7 The angel of the *L* encamps
34: 8 Taste and see that the *L* is good;
34: 9 Fear the *L*, you his saints,
34: 15 The eyes of the *L* are
34: 18 The *L* is close to the brokenhearted
37: 4 Delight yourself in the *L*
37: 5 Commit your way to the *L*;
39: 4 "Show me, O *L*, my life's end
40: 1 I waited patiently for the *L*;
40: 5 Many, O *L* my God,
46: 8 Come and see the works of the *L*,
47: 2 How awesome is the *L* Most High,
48: 1 Great is the *L*, and most worthy
50: 1 The Mighty One, God, the *L*,
55: 22 Cast your cares on the *L*
59: 8 But you, O *L*, laugh at them;
68: 4 his name is the *L*—
68: 18 O *L* God, might dwell there.
68: 20 from the Sovereign *L* comes escape
69: 31 This will please the *L* more
72: 18 Praise be to the *L* God, the God
75: 8 In the hand of the *L* is a cup

Ps 78: 4 the praiseworthy deeds of the *L,*
84: 8 my prayer, O *L* God Almighty;
84: 11 For the *L* God is a sun and shield;
85: 7 Show us your unfailing love, O *L,*
86: 11 Teach me your way, O *L,*
87: 2 the *L* loves the gates of Zion
89: 5 heavens praise your wonders, O *L,*
89: 8 O *L* God Almighty, who is like you
91: 2 I will say of the *L,* "He is my refuge
92: 1 It is good to praise the *L*
92: 4 by your deeds, O *L;*
92: 13 planted in the house of the *L,*
93: 1 The *L* reigns, he is robed in majesty
93: 5 house for endless days, O *L.*
94: 1 O *L,* the God who avenges,
94: 12 is the man you discipline, O *L,*
94: 18 your love, O *L,* supported me.
95: 1 Come, let us sing for joy to the *L;*
95: 3 For the *L* is the great God,
95: 6 let us kneel before the *L* our Maker
96: 1 Sing to the *L* a new song;
96: 5 but the *L* made the heavens.
96: 8 to the *L* the glory due his name;
96: 9 Worship the *L* in the splendor
96: 13 they will sing before the *L,*
97: 1 The *L* reigns, let the earth be glad;
97: 9 O *L,* are the Most High
98: 1 Sing to the *L* a new song;
98: 2 *L* has made his salvation known
98: 4 Shout for joy to the *L,* all the earth,
99: 1 The *L* reigns,
99: 2 Great is the *L* in Zion;
99: 5 Exalt the *L* our God
99: 9 Exalt the *L* our God
100: 1 Shout for joy to the *L,* all the earth.
100: 2 Worship the *L* with gladness;
100: 3 Know that the *L* is God.
100: 5 For the *L* is good and his love
101: 1 to you, O *L,* I will sing praise.
102: 12 But you, O *L,* sit enthroned forever
103: 1 Praise the *L,* O my soul;
103: 8 The *L* is compassionate
103: 19 The *L* has established his throne
104: 1 O *L* my God, you are very great;
104: 24 How many are your works, O *L!*
104: 33 I will sing to the *L* all my life;
105: 4 Look to the *L* and his strength;
105: 7 He is the *L* our God;
106: 2 proclaim the mighty acts of the *L*
107: 1 Give thanks to the *L,* for he is good
107: 8 to the *L* for his unfailing love
107: 21 to the *L* for his unfailing love
107: 43 and consider the great love of the *L*
108: 3 I will praise you, O *L,*
109: 26 Help me, O *L* my God;
110: 1 The *L* says to my Lord:
110: 4 The *L* has sworn
111: 2 Great are the works of the *L;*
111: 4 *L* is gracious and compassionate.
111: 10 The fear of the *L* is the beginning
112: 1 Blessed is the man who fears the *L,*
113: 1 Praise, O servants of the *L,*
113: 2 Let the name of the *L* be praised,
113: 4 *L* is exalted over all the nations,
113: 5 Who is like the *L* our God,
115: 1 Not to us, O *L,* not to us
115: 18 it is we who extol the *L,*
116: 12 How can I repay the *L*
116: 15 Precious in the sight of the *L*
117: 1 Praise the *L,* all you nations;
118: 1 Give thanks to the *L,* for he is good
118: 5 In my anguish I cried to the *L,*
118: 8 It is better to take refuge in the *L*
118: 18 The *L* has chastened me severely,
118: 23 the *L* has done this,
118: 24 This is the day the *L* has made;
118: 26 comes in the name of the *L.*
119: 1 to the law of the *L.*
119: 64 with your love, O *L,*
119: 89 Your word, O *L,* is eternal;
119:126 It is time for you to act, O *L;*
119:159 O *L,* according to your love.
120: 1 I call on the *L* in my distress,
121: 2 My help comes from the *L,*
121: 5 The *L* watches over you—
121: 8 the *L* will watch over your coming
122: 1 "Let us go to the house of the *L."*
123: 2 so our eyes look to the *L* our God,

Ps 124: 1 If the *L* had not been on our side—
124: 8 Our help is in the name of the *L,*
125: 2 so the *L* surrounds his people
126: 3 The *L* has done great things for us,
126: 4 Restore our fortunes, O *L,*
127: 1 Unless the *L* builds the house,
127: 3 Sons are a heritage from the *L,*
128: 1 Blessed are all who fear the *L,*
130: 1 O *L;* O Lord, hear my voice.
130: 3 If you, O *L,* kept a record of sins,
130: 5 I wait for the *L,* my soul waits,
131: 3 O Israel, put your hope in the *L*
132: 1 O *L,* remember David
132: 13 For the *L* has chosen Zion,
133: 3 For there the *L* bestows his
134: 3 May the *L,* the Maker of heaven
135: 4 For the *L* has chosen Jacob
135: 6 The *L* does whatever pleases him,
136: 1 Give thanks to the *L,* for he is good
137: 4 How can we sing the songs of the *L*
138: 1 I will praise you, O *L,*
138: 8 The *L* will fulfill his purpose
139: 1 O *L,* you have searched me
140: 1 Rescue me, O *L,* from evil men;
141: 1 O *L,* I call to you; come quickly
141: 3 Set a guard over my mouth, O *L;*
142: 1 I cry to you, O *L;*
143: 9 Rescue me from my enemies, O *L,*
144: 3 O *L,* what is man that you care
145: 3 Great is the *L* and most worthy
145: 8 *L* is gracious and compassionate,
145: 9 The *L* is good to all;
145: 17 The *L* is righteous in all his ways
145: 18 The *L* is near to all who call on him
146: 5 whose hope is in the *L* his God,
146: 7 The *L* sets prisoners free,
147: 2 The *L* builds up Jerusalem;
147: 7 Sing to the *L* with thanksgiving;
147: 11 *L* delights in those who fear him,
147: 12 Extol the *L,* O Jerusalem;
148: 1 Praise the *L* from the heavens,
148: 7 Praise the *L* from the earth,
149: 4 For the *L* takes delight
150: 1 Praise the *L.*
150: 6 that has breath praise the *L.*
Pr 1: 7 The fear of the *L* is the beginning
1: 29 and did not choose to fear the *L,*
2: 5 will understand the fear of the *L*
2: 6 For the *L* gives wisdom.
3: 5 Trust in the *L* with all your heart
3: 7 fear the *L* and shun evil.
3: 9 Honor the *L* with your wealth,
3: 12 the *L* disciplines those he loves,
3: 19 By wisdom the *L* laid the earth's
5: 21 are in full view of the *L,*
6: 16 There are six things the *L* hates,
8: 13 To fear the *L* is to hate evil;
9: 10 "The fear of the *L* is the beginning
10: 27 The fear of the *L* adds length to life
11: 1 The *L* abhors dishonest scales,
12: 22 The *L* detests lying lips,
14: 2 whose walk is upright fears the *L.*
14: 26 He who fears the *L* has a secure
14: 27 The fear of the *L* is a fountain
15: 3 The eyes of the *L* are everywhere,
15: 16 Better a little with the fear of the *L*
15: 33 of the *L* teaches a man wisdom,
16: 2 but motives are weighed by the *L.*
16: 3 Commit to the *L* whatever you do,
16: 4 The *L* works out everything
16: 5 The *L* detests all the proud of heart
16: 9 but the *L* determines his steps.
16: 33 but its every decision is from the *L.*
18: 10 The name of the *L* is a strong tower
18: 22 and receives favor from the *L.*
19: 14 but a prudent wife is from the *L.*
19: 17 to the poor lends to the *L,*
19: 23 The fear of the *L* leads to life:
20: 10 The *L* detests them both.
21: 2 but the *L* weighs the heart.
21: 3 to the *L* than sacrifice.
21: 30 that can succeed against the *L.*
21: 31 but victory rests with the *L.*
22: 2 The *L* is the Maker of them all.
22: 23 for the *L* will take up their case
23: 17 for the fear of the *L.*
24: 18 or the *L* will see and disapprove
24: 21 Fear the *L* and the king, my son,

Pr 25: 22 and the *L* will reward you.
28: 14 is the man who always fears the *L,*
29: 26 from the *L* that man gets justice.
30: 7 "Two things I ask of you, O *L;*
31: 30 a woman who fears the *L* is
Isa 2: 3 up to the mountain of the *L,*
2: 10 the ground from dread of the *L*
3: 17 the *L* will make their scalps bald."
4: 2 of the *L* will be beautiful
5: 16 the *L* Almighty will be exalted
6: 3 holy, holy is the *L* Almighty;
9: 7 The zeal of the *L* Almighty
11: 2 The Spirit of the *L* will rest on him
11: 9 full of the knowledge of the *L*
12: 2 The *L,* the *L,* is my strength
18: 7 of the Name of the *L* Almighty.
24: 1 the *L* is going to lay waste the earth
25: 1 O *L,* you are my God;
25: 6 this mountain the *L* Almighty will
25: 8 The Sovereign *L* will wipe away
26: 4 Trust in the *L* forever,
26: 8 *L,* walking in the way of your laws,
26: 13 O *L,* our God, other lords
26: 21 the *L* is coming out of his dwelling
27: 1 he *L* will punish with his sword,
27: 12 In that day the *L* will thresh
28: 5 In that day the *L* Almighty
29: 6 the *L* Almighty will come
29: 15 to hide their plans from the *L,*
30: 18 For the *L* is a God of justice.
30: 26 when the *L* binds up the bruises
30: 27 the Name of the *L* comes from afar
30: 30 The *L* will cause men
33: 2 O *L,* be gracious to us,
33: 6 the fear of the *L* is the key
33: 22 For the *L* is our judge,
34: 2 The *L* is angry with all nations;
35: 2 they will see the glory of the *L,*
35: 10 the ransomed of the *L* will return.
38: 7 to you that the *L* will do what he
40: 3 the way for the *L;*
40: 5 the glory of the *L* will be revealed,
40: 7 the breath of the *L* blows on them.
40: 10 the Sovereign *L* comes with power,
40: 14 Whom did the *L* consult
40: 28 The *L* is the everlasting God,
40: 31 but those who hope in the *L*
41: 14 will help you," declares the *L,*
41: 20 that the hand of the *L* has done this
42: 6 the *L,* have called you
42: 8 "I am the *L;* that is my name!
42: 13 The *L* will march out like a mighty
42: 21 It pleased the *L*
43: 3 For I am the *L,* your God,
43: 11 I, even I, am the *L,*
44: 6 "This is what the *L* says—
44: 24 I am the *L,*
45: 5 I am the *L,* and there is no other;
45: 7 I, the *L,* do all these things.
45: 21 Was it not I, the *L?*
48: 17 "I am the *L* your God,
50: 4 Sovereign *L* has given me
50: 10 Who among you fears the *L*
51: 1 and who seek the *L;*
51: 11 The ransomed of the *L* will return.
51: 15 the *L* Almighty is his name.
53: 1 the arm of the *L* been revealed?
53: 6 and the *L* has laid on him
53: 10 and the will of the *L* will prosper
54: 5 the *L* Almighty is his name—
55: 6 Seek the *L* while he may be found;
55: 7 to the *L,* and he will have mercy
56: 6 who bind themselves to the *L*
58: 8 of the *L* will be your rear guard.
58: 11 The *L* will guide you always;
59: 1 the arm of the *L* is not too short
60: 1 the glory of the *L* rises upon you.
60: 16 Then you will know that I, the *L,*
60: 20 the *L* will be your everlasting light,
61: 1 Spirit of the Sovereign *L* is on me,
61: 3 a planting of the *L.*
61: 10 I delight greatly in the *L;*
61: 11 so the Sovereign *L* will make
62: 4 for the *L* will take delight in you,
63: 7 I will tell of the kindnesses of the *L,*
64: 8 Yet, O *L,* you are our Father.
66: 15 See, the *L* is coming with fire,
Jer 1: 9 Then the *L* reached out his hand

Jer 2: 19 when you forsake the *L* your God
3: 25 sinned against the *L* our God,
4: 4 Circumcise yourselves to the *L*,
8: 7 the requirements of the *L*.
9: 24 I am the *L*, who exercises kindness,
10: 6 No one is like you, O *L*;
10: 10 But the *L* is the true God;
12: 1 You are always righteous, O *L*,
14: 7 O *L*, do something for the sake
14: 20 O *L*, we acknowledge our
16: 15 will say, 'As surely as the *L* lives,
16: 19 O *L*, my strength and my fortress,
17: 7 is the man who trusts in the *L*,
17: 10 ''I the *L* search the heart
20: 11 *L* is with me like a mighty warrior;
23: 6 The *L* Our Righteousness.
24: 7 heart to know me, that I am the *L*.
28: 9 as one truly sent by the *L* only
31: 11 For the *L* will ransom Jacob
31: 22 The *L* will create a new thing
31: 34 his brother, saying, 'Know the *L*,'
32: 27 I am the *L*, the God of all mankind.
33: 16 The *L* Our Righteousness.'
36: 6 the words of the *L* that you wrote
40: 3 now the *L* has brought it about;
42: 3 Pray that the *L* your God will tell
42: 4 I will tell you everything the *L* says
42: 6 we will obey the *L* our God,
50: 4 go in tears to seek the *L* their God.
51: 10 '' 'The *L* has vindicated us;
51: 56 For the *L* is a God of retribution;
La 3: 24 to myself, ''The *L* is my portion;
3: 25 *L* is good to those whose hope is
3: 40 and let us return to the *L*.
Eze 1: 3 the word of the *L* came
1: 28 of the likeness of the glory of the *L*.
4: 14 Sovereign *L!* I have never defiled
10: 4 Then the glory of the *L* rose
15: 7 you will know that I am the *L*.
30: 3 the day of the *L* is near—
36: 23 nations will know that I am the *L*,
37: 4 'Dry bones, hear the word of the *L!*'
43: 4 glory of the *L* entered the temple
44: 4 LORD filling the temple of the *L*,
Da 9: 2 to the word of the *L* given
Hos 1: 7 horsemen, but by the *L* their God.''
2: 20 and you will acknowledge the *L*.
3: 1 as the *L* loves the Israelites,
3: 5 They will come trembling to the *L*
6: 1 ''Come, let us return to the *L*.
6: 3 Let us acknowledge the *L*;
10: 12 for it is time to seek the *L*,
12: 5 the *L* is his name of renown!
14: 1 O Israel, to the *L* your God.
Joel 1: 1 The word of the *L* that came
1: 15 For the day of the *L* is near;
2: 1 for the day of the *L* is coming.
2: 11 The day of the *L* is great;
2: 13 Return to the *L* your God,
2: 23 rejoice in the *L* your God,
2: 31 the great and dreadful day of the *L*.
2: 32 on the name of the *L* will be saved;
3: 14 For the day of the *L* is near
3: 16 the *L* will be a refuge for his people,
Am 4: 13 the *L* God Almighty is his name.
5: 6 Seek the *L* and live,
5: 15 Perhaps the *L* God Almighty will
5: 18 long for the day of the *L*?
7: 15 *L* took me from tending the flock
8: 12 searching for the word of the *L*,
9: 5 The Lord, the *L* Almighty,
Ob : 15 ''The day of the *L* is near
Jnh 1: 3 But Jonah ran away from the *L*
1: 4 the *L* sent a great wind on the sea,
1: 17 But the *L* provided a great fish
2: 9 Salvation comes from the *L*.''
4: 2 He prayed to the *L*, ''O *L*,
4: 2 Then the *L* God provided a vine
Mic 1: 1 The word of the *L* given to Micah
4: 2 up to the mountain of the *L*,
5: 4 flock in the strength of the *L*,
6: 2 For the *L* has a case
6: 8 And what does the *L* require of you
7: 7 as for me, I watch in hope for the *L*,
Na 1: 2 The *L* takes vengeance on his foes
1: 3 The *L* is slow to anger
Hab 2: 14 knowledge of the glory of the *L*,
2: 20 But the *L* is in his holy temple;

Hab 3: 2 I stand in awe of your deeds, O *L*.
Zep 1: 1 The word of the *L* that came
1: 7 for the day of the *L* is near.
3: 17 The *L* your God is with you,
Hag 1: 1 the word of the *L* came
1: 8 and be honored,'' says the *L*.
2: 23 that day,' declares the *L* Almighty,
Zec 1: 1 the word of the *L* came
1: 17 and the *L* will again comfort Zion
3: 1 standing before the angel of the *L*,
4: 6 by my Spirit,' says the *L* Almighty.
6: 12 and build the temple of the *L*.
8: 21 the *L* and seek the *L* Almighty.
9: 16 The *L* their God will save them
14: 5 Then the *L* my God will come,
14: 9 The *L* will be king
14: 16 the *L* Almighty, and to celebrate
Mal 1: 1 The word of the *L* to Israel
3: 6 ''I the *L* do not change.
4: 5 and dreadful day of the *L* comes.

LORD'S‡ (LORD‡)

Ex 4: 14 the *L* anger burned against Moses
12: 11 Eat it in haste; it is the *L* Passover.
34: 34 he entered the *L* presence
Lev 23: 4 '' 'These are the *L* appointed feasts,
Nu 9: 23 At the *L* command they encamped
14: 41 you disobeying the *L* command?
32: 13 The *L* anger burned against Israel
Dt 6: 18 is right and good in the *L* sight,
10: 13 and to observe the *L* commands
32: 9 For the *L* portion is his people,
Jos 21: 45 Not one of all the *L* good promises
1Sa 24: 10 because he is the *L* anointed.'
1Ki 10: 9 Because of the *L* eternal love
Ps 24: 1 The earth is the *L*, and everything
32: 10 but the *L* unfailing love
89: 1 of the *L* great love forever;
103: 17 *L* love is with those who fear him,
118: 15 ''The *L* right hand has done mighty
Pr 3: 11 do not despise the *L* discipline
19: 21 but it is the *L* purpose that prevails.
Isa 24: 14 west they acclaim the *L* majesty.
30: 9 to listen to the *L* instruction.
49: 4 Yet what is due me is in the *L* hand
53: 10 Yet it was the *L* will to crush him
55: 13 This will be for the *L* renown,
61: 2 to proclaim the year of the *L* favor
62: 3 of splendor in the *L* hand,
Jer 25: 17 So I took the cup from the *L* hand
48: 10 lax in doing the *L* work!
51: 7 was a gold cup in the *L* hand;
La 3: 22 of the *L* great love we are not
Eze 7: 19 them in the day of the *L* wrath.
Joel 3: 18 will flow out of the *L* house
Ob : 21 And the kingdom will be the *L*.
Mic 4: 1 of the *L* temple will be established
6: 2 O mountains, the *L* accusation;
Hab 2: 16 from the *L* right hand is coming
Zep 2: 3 sheltered on the day of the *L* anger.

LOSE (LOSES LOSS LOST)

Dt 1: 28 Our brothers have made us *l* heart.
1Sa 17: 32 ''Let no one *l* heart on account
Isa 7: 4 Do not *l* heart because of these two
Mt 10: 39 Whoever finds his life will *l* it,
Lk 9: 25 and yet *l* or forfeit his very self?
Jn 6: 39 that I shall *l* none of all that he has
2Co 4: 1 this ministry, we do not *l* heart.
4: 16 Therefore we do not *l* heart.
Heb 12: 3 will not grow weary and *l* heart.
12: 5 do not *l* heart when he rebukes you
2Jn : 8 that you do not *l* what you have

LOSES (LOSE)

Mt 5: 13 But if the salt *l* its saltiness,
Lk 15: 4 you has a hundred sheep and *l* one
15: 8 has ten silver coins and *l* one.

LOSS (LOSE)

Ro 11: 12 and their *l* means riches
1Co 3: 15 he will suffer *l*; he himself will be
Php 3: 8 I consider everything a *l* compared

LOST (LOSE)

Ps 73: 2 I had nearly *l* my foothold.
Jer 50: 6 ''My people have been *l* sheep;
Eze 34: 4 the strays or searched for the *l*.

Eze 34: 16 for the *l* and bring back the strays.
Mt 18: 14 any of these little ones should be *l*.
Lk 15: 4 go after the *l* sheep until he finds it?
15: 6 with me; I have found my *l* sheep.'
15: 9 with me; I have found my *l* coin.'
15: 24 is alive again; he was *l* and is found
19: 10 to seek and to save what was *l*.''
Php 3: 8 for whose sake I have *l* all things.

LOT (LOTS)

Nephew of Abraham (Ge 11:27; 12:5). Chose to live in Sodom (Ge 13). Rescued from four kings (Ge 14). Rescued from Sodom (Ge 19:1-29; 2Pe 2:7). Fathered Moab and Ammon by his daughters (Ge 19:30-38).

Est 3: 7 the *l*) in the presence of Haman
9: 24 the *l*) for their ruin and destruction.
Pr 16: 33 The *l* is cast into the lap,
18: 18 Casting the *l* settles disputes
Ecc 3: 22 his work, because that is his *l*.
Ac 1: 26 Then they cast lots, and the *l* fell

LOTS (LOT)

Jos 18: 10 Joshua then cast *l* for them
Ps 22: 18 and cast *l* for my clothing.
Joel 3: 3 They cast *l* for my people
Ob : 11 and cast *l* for Jerusalem,
Mt 27: 35 divided up his clothes by casting *l*.
Ac 1: 26 Then they cast *l*, and the lot fell

LOVE* (BELOVED LOVED LOVELY LOVER LOVER'S LOVERS LOVES LOVING LOVING-KINDNESS)

Ge 20: 13 'This is how you can show your *l*
22: 2 your only son Isaac, whom you *l*,
29: 18 Jacob was in *l* with Rachel and said
29: 20 days to live because of his *l* for her.
29: 32 Surely my husband will *l* me now.''
Ex 15: 13 ''In your unfailing *l* you will lead
20: 6 showing *l* to a thousand generations who *l* me
21: 5 'I *l* my master and my wife
34: 6 abounding in *l* and faithfulness,
34: 7 maintaining *l* to thousands,
Lev 19: 18 but *l* your neighbor as yourself.
19: 34 *L* him as yourself,
Nu 14: 18 abounding in *l* and forgiving sin
14: 19 In accordance with your great *l*,
Dt 5: 10 showing *l* to thousands who *l* me
6: 5 *L* the LORD your God
7: 9 generations of those who *l* him
7: 9 keeping his covenant of *l*
7: 12 God will keep his covenant of *l*
7: 13 He will *l* you and bless you
10: 12 to walk in all his ways, to *l* him,
10: 19 you are to *l* those who are aliens,
11: 1 *L* the LORD your God
11: 13 to *l* the LORD your God
11: 22 to *l* the LORD your God,
13: 3 you *l* him with all your heart
13: 6 wife you *l*, or your closest friend
19: 9 to the LORD your God
21: 15 the son of the wife he does not *l*,
21: 16 the son of the wife he does not *l*.
30: 6 so that you may *l* him
30: 16 today to *l* the LORD your God,
30: 20 and that you may *l* the LORD your God
33: 3 Surely it is you who *l* the people;
Jos 22: 5 to *l* the LORD your God, to walk
23: 11 careful to *l* the LORD your God.
Jdg 5: 31 may they who *l* you be like the sun
14: 16 You hate me! You don't really *l* me
16: 4 he fell in *l* with a woman
16: 15 ''How can you say, 'I *l* you,'
1Sa 18: 20 Saul's daughter Michal was in *l*
20: 17 had David reaffirm his oath out of *l*
2Sa 1: 26 Your *l* for me was wonderful,
7: 15 But my *l* will never be taken away
13: 1 son of David fell in *l* with Tamar,
13: 4 said to him, ''I'm in *l* with Tamar,
16: 17 ''Is this the *l* you show your friend?
19: 6 You *l* those who hate you
19: 6 hate you and hate those who *l* you.
1Ki 3: 3 Solomon showed his *l*
8: 23 you who keep your covenant of *l*
10: 9 of the LORD's eternal *l* for Israel,
11: 2 Solomon held fast to them in *l*.
1Ch 16: 34 his *l* endures forever.

1Ch 16: 41 "for his *l* endures forever."
17: 13 I will never take my *l* away
2Ch 5: 13 his *l* endures forever."
6: 14 you who keep your covenant of *l*
6: 42 Remember the great *l* promised
7: 3 his *l* endures forever."
7: 6 saying, "His *l* endures forever."
9: 8 Because of the *l* of your God
19: 2 and *l* those who hate the LORD?
20: 21 for his *l* endures forever."
Ezr 3: 11 his *l* to Israel endures forever."
Ne 1: 5 covenant of *l* with those who *l* him
9: 17 slow to anger and abounding in *l*.
9: 32 who keeps his covenant of *l*,
13: 22 to me according to your great *l*.
Job 15: 34 of those who *l* bribes.
19: 19 those I *l* have turned against me.
37: 13 or to water his earth and show his *l*.
Ps 4: 2 How long will you *l* delusions
5: 11 that those who *l* your name may
6: 4 save me because of your unfailing *l*.
11: 5 wicked and those who *l* violence
13: 5 But I trust in your unfailing *l*;
17: 7 Show the wonder of your great *l*,
18: 1 I *l* you, O LORD, my strength.
21: 7 through the unfailing *l*
23: 6 Surely goodness and *l* will follow
25: 6 O LORD, your great mercy and *l*,
25: 7 according to your *l* remember me,
26: 3 for your *l* is ever before me,
26: 8 I *l* the house where you live,
31: 7 I will be glad and rejoice in your *l*,
31: 16 save me in your unfailing *l*.
31: 21 for he showed his wonderful *l*
31: 23 *L* the LORD, all his saints!
32: 10 but the LORD's unfailing *l*
33: 5 the earth is full of his unfailing *l*.
33: 18 whose hope is in his unfailing *l*,
33: 22 May your unfailing *l* rest upon us,
36: 5 Your *l*, O LORD, reaches
36: 7 How priceless is your unfailing *l*!
36: 10 Continue your *l* to those who know
40: 10 I do not conceal your *l*
40: 11 may your *l* and your truth always
40: 16 may those who *l* your salvation
42: 8 By day the LORD directs his *l*,
44: 26 of your unfailing *l*.
45: 7 You *l* righteousness and hate
48: 9 we meditate on your unfailing *l*.
51: 1 according to your unfailing *l*;
52: 3 You *l* evil rather than good,
52: 4 You *l* every harmful word,
52: 8 I trust in God's unfailing *l*
57: 3 God sends his *l* and his faithfulness
57: 10 For great is your *l*, reaching
59: 16 in the morning I will sing of your *l*;
60: 5 that those you may be delivered.
61: 7 appoint your *l* and faithfulness
63: 3 Because your *l* is better than life,
66: 20 or withheld his *l* from me!
69: 13 in your great *l*, O God,
69: 16 out of the goodness of your *l*;
69: 36 and those who *l* his name will dwell
70: 4 may those who *l* your salvation
77: 8 Has his unfailing *l* vanished forever
85: 7 Show us your unfailing *l*, O LORD
85: 10 *L* and faithfulness meet together;
86: 5 abounding in *l* to all who call
86: 13 For great is your *l* toward me;
86: 15 abounding in *l* and faithfulness.
88: 11 Is your *l* declared in the grave,
89: 1 of the LORD's great *l* forever;
89: 2 declare that your *l* stands firm
89: 14 *l* and faithfulness go before you.
89: 24 My faithful *l* will be with him,
89: 28 I will maintain my *l* to him forever,
89: 33 but I will not take my *l* from him,
89: 49 where is your former great *l*,
90: 14 with your unfailing *l*,
92: 2 to proclaim your *l* in the morning
94: 18 your *l*, O LORD, supported me.
97: 10 Let those who *l* the LORD hate
98: 3 He has remembered his *l*
100: 5 is good and his *l* endures forever;
101: 1 I will sing of your *l* and justice;
103: 4 crowns me with *l* and compassion.
103: 8 slow to anger, abounding in *l*.
103: 11 so great is his *l* for those who fear

Ps 103: 17 LORD's *l* is with those who fear
106: 1 his *l* endures forever.
106: 45 and out of his great *l* he relented.
107: 1 his *l* endures forever.
107: 8 to the LORD for his unfailing *l*
107: 15 to the LORD for his unfailing *l*
107: 21 to the LORD for his unfailing *l*
107: 31 to the LORD for his unfailing *l*
107: 43 consider the great *l* of the LORD.
108: 4 For great is your *l*, higher
108: 6 that those you *l* may be delivered.
109: 21 out of the goodness of your *l*,
109: 26 save me in accordance with your *l*.
115: 1 because of your *l* and faithfulness.
116: 1 I *l* the LORD, for he heard my
117: 2 For great is his *l* toward us,
118: 1 his *l* endures forever.
118: 2 "His *l* endures forever."
118: 3 "His *l* endures forever."
118: 4 "His *l* endures forever."
118: 29 his *l* endures forever.
119: 41 May your unfailing *l* come to me,
119: 47 because I *l* them.
119: 48 for your commandments, which I *l*,
119: 64 The earth is filled with your *l*,
119: 76 May your unfailing *l* be my
119: 88 my life according to your *l*,
119: 97 Oh, how I *l* your law!
119:113 but I *l* your law.
119:119 therefore I *l* your statutes.
119:124 your servant according to your *l*
119:127 Because I *l* your commands
119:132 to those who *l* your name.
119:149 in accordance with your *l*;
119:159 O LORD, according to your *l*.
119:159 See how I *l* your precepts;
119:163 but I *l* your law.
119:165 peace have they who *l* your law,
119:167 for I *l* them greatly.
122: 6 "May those who *l* you be secure.
130: 7 for with the LORD is unfailing *l*
136: 1 -26 His *l* endures forever.
138: 2 for your *l* and your faithfulness,
138: 8 your *l*, O LORD, endures forever
143: 8 of your unfailing *l*,
143: 12 In your unfailing *l*, silence my
145: 8 slow to anger and rich in *l*.
145: 20 over all who *l* him,
147: 11 who put their hope in his unfailing *l*
Pr 1: 22 you simple ones *l* your simple
3: 3 Let *l* and faithfulness never leave
4: 6 *l* her, and she will watch over you.
5: 19 you ever be captivated by her *l*.
7: 18 let's drink deep of *l* till morning;
7: 18 let's enjoy ourselves with *l*!
8: 17 I *l* those who *l* me,
8: 21 wealth on those who *l* me
8: 36 all who hate me *l* death."
9: 8 rebuke a wise man and he will *l* you
10: 12 but *l* covers over all wrongs.
14: 22 Those who plan what is good find *l*
15: 17 of vegetables where there is *l*
16: 6 Through *l* and faithfulness sin is
17: 9 over an offense promotes *l*,
18: 21 and those who *l* it will eat its fruit.
19: 22 What a man desires is unfailing *l*;
20: 6 claims to have unfailing *l*,
20: 13 Do not *l* sleep or you will grow
20: 28 *L* and faithfulness keep a king safe;
20: 28 through *l* his throne is made secure
21: 21 who pursues righteousness and *l*
27: 5 rebuke than hidden *l*.
Ecc 3: 8 a time to *l* and a time to hate,
9: 1 but no man knows whether *l*
9: 6 Their *l*, their hate
9: 9 life with your wife, whom you *l*,
SS 1: 2 for your *l* is more delightful
1: 3 No wonder the maidens *l* you!
1: 4 we will praise your *l* more
1: 7 you whom I *l*, where you graze
2: 4 and his banner over me is *l*.
2: 5 for I am faint with *l*.
2: 7 Do not arouse or awaken *l*
3: 5 Do not arouse or awaken *l*
4: 10 How delightful is your *l*, my sister,
4: 10 How much more pleasing is your *l*
5: 8 Tell him I am faint with *l*.
7: 6 O *l*, with your delights!

SS 7: 12 there I will give you my *l*.
8: 4 Do not arouse or awaken *l*
8: 6 for *l* is as strong as death,
8: 7 Many waters cannot quench *l*;
8: 7 all the wealth of his house for *l*,
Isa 1: 23 they all *l* bribes
5: 1 I will sing for the one I *l*
16: 5 In a throne will be established;
38: 17 In your *l* you kept me
43: 4 and because I *l* you,
54: 10 yet my unfailing *l* for you will not
55: 3 my faithful *l* promised to David.
56: 6 to *l* the name of the LORD,
56: 10 they *l* to sleep.
57: 8 a pact with those whose beds you *l*,
61: 8 "For I, the LORD, *l* justice;
63: 9 In his *l* and mercy he redeemed
66: 10 all you who *l* her;
Jer 2: 25 I *l* foreign gods,
2: 33 How skilled you are at pursuing *l*!
5: 31 and my people *l* it this way.
12: 7 I will give the one I *l*
14: 10 "They greatly *l* to wander;
16: 5 my *l* and my pity from this people
31: 3 you with an everlasting *l*;
32: 18 You show *l* to thousands
33: 11 his *l* endures forever."
La 3: 22 of the LORD's great *l* we are not
3: 32 so great is his unfailing *l*.
Eze 16: 8 saw that you were old enough for *l*,
23: 17 of *l*, and in their lust they defiled
33: 32 more than one who sings *l* songs
Da 9: 4 covenant of *l* with all who *l* him
Hos 1: 6 for I will no longer show *l*
1: 7 Yet I will show *l* to the house
2: 4 I will not show my *l* to her children
2: 19 in *l* and compassion.
2: 23 I will show my *l* to the one I called
3: 1 Go, show your *l* to your wife again,
3: 1 and *l* the sacred raisin cakes."
3: 1 *L* her as the LORD loves
4: 1 "There is no faithfulness, no *l*,
4: 18 their rulers dearly *l* shameful ways.
6: 4 Your *l* is like the morning mist,
9: 1 you *l* the wages of a prostitute
9: 15 I will no longer *l* them;
10: 12 reap the fruit of unfailing *l*,
11: 4 with ties of *l*;
12: 6 maintain *l* and justice,
14: 4 and *l* them freely,
Joel 2: 13 slow to anger and abounding in *l*,
Am 4: 5 for this is what you *l* to do,"
5: 15 Hate evil, *l* good;
Jnh 4: 2 slow to anger and abounding in *l*,
Mic 3: 2 you who hate good and *l* evil;
6: 8 To act justly and to *l* mercy
Zep 3: 17 he will quiet you with his *l*,
Zec 8: 17 and do not *l* to swear falsely.
8: 19 Therefore *l* truth and peace."
Mt 3: 17 "This is my Son, whom I *l*;
5: 43 'L* your neighbor and hate your
5: 44 *L* your enemies and pray
5: 46 you *l* those who *l* you, what reward
6: 5 for they *l* to pray standing
6: 24 he will hate the one and *l* the other,
12: 18 the one I *l*, in whom I delight;
17: 5 "This is my Son, whom I *l*;
19: 19 and 'l* your neighbor as yourself.' "
22: 37 " 'L* the Lord your God
22: 39 'L* your neighbor as yourself.'
23: 6 they *l* the place of honor
23: 7 they *l* to be greeted
24: 12 the *l* of most will grow cold,
Mk 1: 11 "You are my Son, whom I *l*;
9: 7 "This is my Son, whom I *l*.
12: 30 *L* the Lord your God
12: 31 'L* your neighbor as yourself.'
12: 33 To *l* him with all your heart,
12: 33 and to *l* your neighbor
Lk 3: 22 "You are my Son, whom I *l*;
6: 27 who hear me: *L* your enemies,
6: 32 Even 'sinners' *l* those who *l* them.
6: 32 you *l* those who *l* you, what credit
6: 35 *l* your enemies, do good to them,
7: 42 which of them will *l* him more?"
10: 27 and, 'L* your neighbor as yourself
10: 27 " 'L* the Lord your God
11: 42 you neglect justice and the *l* of God

Lk 11: 43 you *l* the most important seats
     16: 13 he will hate the one and *l* the other,
     20: 13 whom I *l*; perhaps they will respect
     20: 46 *l* to be greeted in the marketplaces
Jn   5: 42 I know that you do not have the *l*
      8: 42 were your Father, you would *l* me,
     11:   3 "Lord, the one you *l* is sick."
     13:   1 them the full extent of his *l*.
     13: 34 I give you: *L* one another.
     13: 34 so you must *l* one another.
     13: 35 disciples if you *l* one another."
     14: 15 "If you *l* me, you will obey what I
     14: 21 I too will *l* him and show myself
     14: 23 My Father will *l* him, and we will
     14: 24 He who does not *l* me will not obey
     14: 31 world must learn that I *l* the Father
     15:   9 Now remain in my *l*.
     15: 10 commands and remain in his *l*.
     15: 10 you will remain in my *l*,
     15: 12 *L* each other as I have loved you.
     15: 13 Greater *l* has no one than this,
     15: 17 This is my command: *L* each other.
     15: 19 to the world, it would *l* you
     17: 26 known in order that the *l* you have
     21: 15 do you truly *l* me more than these
     21: 15 he said, "you know that I *l* you."
     21: 16 Yes, Lord, you know that I *l* you.
     21: 16 do you truly *l* me?" He answered,
     21: 17 all things; you know that I *l* you."
     21: 17 "Do you *l* me?" He said, "Lord,
     21: 17 "Simon son of John, do you *l* me?"
Ro   5:   5 because God has poured out his *l*
      5:   8 God demonstrates his own *l* for us
      8: 28 for the good of those who *l* him,
      8: 35 us from the *l* of Christ?
      8: 39 us from the *l* of God that is
     12:   9 *L* must be sincere.
     12: 10 to one another in brotherly *l*.
     13:   8 continuing debt to *l* one another,
     13:   9 "*L* your neighbor as yourself."
     13: 10 Therefore *l* is the fulfillment
     13: 10 *L* does no harm to its neighbor.
     14: 15 you are no longer acting in *l*.
     15: 30 and by the *l* of the Spirit,
     16:   8 Greet Ampliatus, whom I *l*
1Co 2:   9 prepared for those who *l* him"—
      4: 17 my son whom I *l*, who is faithful
      4: 21 or in *l* and with a gentle spirit?
      8:   1 Knowledge puffs up, but *l* builds up
     13:   1 have not *l*, I am only a resounding
     13:   2 but have not *l*, I am nothing.
     13:   3 but have not *l*, I gain nothing.
     13:   4 Love is patient, *l* is kind.
     13:   4 *L* is patient, love is kind.
     13:   6 *L* does not delight in evil
     13:   8 *L* never fails.
     13: 13 But the greatest of these is *l*.
     13: 13 three remain: faith, hope and *l*.
     14:   1 way of *l* and eagerly desire spiritual
     16: 14 Do everything in *l*.
     16: 22 If anyone does not *l* the Lord—
     16: 24 My *l* to all of you in Christ Jesus.
2Co 2:   4 to let you know the depth of my *l*
      2:   8 therefore, to reaffirm your *l* for him
      5: 14 For Christ's *l* compels us,
      6:   6 in the Holy Spirit and in sincere *l*;
      8:   7 complete earnestness and in your *l*
      8:   8 sincerity of your *l* by comparing it
      8: 24 show these men the proof of your *l*
     11: 11 Why? Because I do not *l* you?
     12: 15 If I *l* you more, will you *l* me less?
     13: 11 And the God of *l* and peace will be
     13: 14 of the Lord Jesus Christ, and the *l*
Gal 5:   6 is faith expressing itself through *l*.
      5: 13 rather, serve one another in *l*.
      5: 14 "*L* your neighbor as yourself."
      5: 22 But the fruit of the Spirit is *l*, joy,
Eph 1:   4 In *l* he predestined us
      1: 15 and your *l* for all the saints,
      2:   4 But because of his great *l* for us,
      3: 17 being rooted and established in *l*,
      3: 18 and high and deep is the *l* of Christ,
      3: 19 and to know this *l* that surpasses
      4:   2 bearing with one another in *l*.
      4: 15 Instead, speaking the truth in *l*,
      4: 16 grows and builds itself up in *l*,
      5:   2 loved children and live a life of *l*,
      5: 25 *l* your wives, just as Christ loved

Eph 5: 28 husbands ought to *l* their wives
      5: 33 each one of you also must *l* his wife
      6: 23 *l* with faith from God the Father
      6: 24 Christ with an undying *l*.
      6: 24 to all who *l* our Lord Jesus Christ
Php 1:   9 that your *l* may abound more
      1: 16 so in *l*, knowing that I am put here
      2:   1 from his *l*, if any fellowship
      2:   2 having the same *l*, being one
      4:   1 you whom I *l* and long for,
Col   1:   4 of the *l* you have for all the saints—
      1:   5 *l* that spring from the hope that is
      1:   8 also told us of your *l* in the Spirit.
      2:   2 in heart and united in *l*,
      3: 14 And over all these virtues put on *l*,
      3: 19 *l* your wives and do not be harsh
1Th 1:   3 your labor prompted by *l*,
      3:   6 good news about your faith and *l*.
      3: 12 May the Lord make your *l* increase
      4:   9 about brotherly *l* we do not need
      4:   9 taught by God to *l* each other.
      4: 10 you do *l* all the brothers
      5:   8 on faith and *l* as a breastplate,
      5: 13 them in the highest regard in *l*
2Th 1:   3 and the *l* every one of you has
      2: 10 because they refused to *l* the truth
      3:   5 direct your hearts into God's *l*
1Ti   1:   5 The goal of this command is *l*,
      1: 14 and *l* that are in Christ Jesus.
      2: 15 *l* and holiness with propriety.
      4: 12 in life, in *l*, in faith and in purity.
      6: 10 For the *l* of money is a root
      6: 11 faith, *l*, endurance and gentleness.
2Ti   1:   7 of power, of *l* and of self-discipline.
      1: 13 with faith and *l* in Christ Jesus.
      2: 22 and pursue righteousness, faith, *l*
      3:   3 unholy, without *l*, unforgiving,
      3: 10 faith, patience, *l*, endurance,
Tit   2:   2 in faith, in *l* and in endurance.
      2:   4 women to *l* their husbands
      3:   4 and *l* of God our Savior appeared,
      3: 15 Greet those who *l* us in the faith.
Phm :   5 and your *l* for all the saints.
      :   7 Your *l* has given me great joy
      :   9 yet I appeal to you on the basis of *l*.
Heb 6: 10 and the *l* you have shown him
     10: 24 may spur one another on toward *l*
     13:   5 free from the *l* of money
Jas   1: 12 promised to those who *l* him.
      2:   5 he promised those who *l* him?
      2:   8 "*L* your neighbor as yourself,"
1Pe 1:   8 you have not seen him, you *l* him;
      1: 22 the truth so that you have sincere *l*
      1: 22 *l* one another deeply,
      2: 17 *L* the brotherhood of believers,
      3:   8 be sympathetic, *l* as brothers,
      3: 10 "Whoever would *l* life
      4:   8 Above all, *l* each other deeply,
      4:   8 *l* covers over a multitude of sins.
      5: 14 Greet one another with a kiss of *l*.
2Pe 1:   7 and to brotherly kindness, *l*.
      1: 17 "This is my Son, whom I *l*;
1Jn   2:   5 God's *l* is truly made complete
      2: 15 Do not *l* the world or anything
      2: 15 the *l* of the Father is not in him.
      3:   1 How great is the *l* the Father has
      3: 10 anyone who does not *l* his brother.
      3: 11 We should *l* one another.
      3: 14 Anyone who does not *l* remains
      3: 14 because we *l* our brothers.
      3: 16 This is how we know what *l* is:
      3: 17 how can the *l* of God be in him?
      3: 18 let us not *l* with words or tongue
      3: 23 to *l* one another as he commanded
      4:   7 Dear friends, let us *l* one another,
      4:   7 for *l* comes from God.
      4:   8 Whoever does not *l* does not know
      4:   8 not know God, because God is *l*.
      4:   9 This is how God showed his *l*
      4: 10 This is *l*: not that we loved God,
      4: 11 we also ought to *l* one another.
      4: 12 and his *l* is made complete in us.
      4: 12 seen God; but if we *l* one another,
      4: 16 God is *l*.
      4: 16 Whoever lives in *l* lives in God,
      4: 16 and rely on the *l* God has for us.
      4: 17 *L* is made complete among us
      4: 18 But perfect *l* drives out fear,

1Jn 4: 18 There is no fear in *l*.
      4: 18 who fears is not made perfect in *l*.
      4: 19 We *l* because he first loved us.
      4: 20 If anyone says, "I *l* God,"
      4: 20 anyone who does not *l* his brother.
      4: 20 whom he has seen, cannot *l* God,
      4: 21 loves God must also *l* his brother.
      5:   2 we know that we *l* the children
      5:   3 This is *l* for God: to obey his
2Jn   :   1 whom I *l* in the truth—
      :   3 will be with us in truth and *l*.
      :   5 I ask that we *l* one another.
      :   6 his command is that you walk in *l*.
      :   6 this is *l*: that we walk in obedience
3Jn   :   1 To my dear friend Gaius, whom I *l*
      :   6 have told the church about your *l*.
Jude   :   2 peace and *l* be yours in abundance.
      : 12 men are blemishes at your *l* feasts,
      : 21 Keep yourselves in God's *l*
Rev 2:   4 You have forsaken your first *l*.
      2: 19 I know your deeds, your *l* and faith
      3: 19 Those whom I *l* I rebuke
     12: 11 they did not *l* their lives so much

LOVED* (LOVE)

Ge 24: 67 she became his wife, and he *l* her;
     25: 28 *l* Esau, but Rebekah *l* Jacob.
     29: 30 and he *l* Rachel more than Leah.
     29: 31 the LORD saw that Leah was not *l*,
     29: 33 the LORD heard that I am not *l*,
     34:   3 and he *l* the girl and spoke tenderly
     37:   3 Now Israel *l* Joseph more than any
     37:   4 saw that their father *l* him more
Dt   4: 37 Because he *l* your forefathers
      7:   8 But it was because the LORD *l* you
     10: 15 on your forefathers and *l* them,
1Sa 1:   5 a double portion because he *l* her,
     18:   1 in spirit with David, and he *l* him
     18:   3 with David because he *l* him
     18: 16 But all Israel and Judah *l* David,
     18: 28 that his daughter Michal *l* David,
     20: 17 because he *l* him as he *l* himself.
2Sa 1: 23 in life they were *l* and gracious,
     12: 24 The LORD *l* him; and
     12: 25 and because the LORD *l* him,
     13: 15 hated her more than he had *l* her.
1Ki 11:   1 *l* many foreign women
2Ch 11: 21 Rehoboam *l* Maacah daughter
     26: 10 in the fertile lands, for he *l* the soil.
Ne 13: 26 He was *l* by his God, and God
Ps 44:   3 light of your face, for you *l* them.
     47:   4 the pride of Jacob, whom he *l*.
     78: 68 Mount Zion, which he *l*.
     88: 18 taken my companions and *l* ones
    109: 17 He *l* to pronounce a curse—
Isa 5:   1 My *l* one had a vineyard
Jer 2:   2 how as a bride you *l* me
      8:   2 which they have *l* and served
     31:   3 "I have *l* you with an everlasting
Eze 16: 37 those you *l* as well as those you
Hos 2:   1 and of your sisters, 'My *l* one.'
      2: 23 to the one I called 'Not my *l* one.'
      3:   1 though she is *l* by another
      9: 10 became as vile as the thing they *l*.
     11:   1 "When Israel was a child, I *l* him,
Mal 1:   2 "But you ask, 'How have you *l* us?'
      1:   2 "I have *l* you,'' says the LORD.
      1:   2 "Yet I have *l* Jacob, but Esau I
Mk 10: 21 Jesus looked at him and *l* him.
     12:   6 left to send, a son, whom he *l*.
Lk   7: 47 been forgiven—for she *l* much.
     16: 14 The Pharisees, who *l* money,
Jn   3: 16 so *l* the world that he gave his one
      3: 19 but men *l* darkness instead of light
     11:   5 Jesus *l* Martha and her sister
     11: 36 "See how he *l* him!" But some
     12: 43 for they *l* praise from men more
     13:   1 Having *l* his own who were
     13: 23 the disciple whom Jesus *l*,
     13: 34 As I have *l* you, so you must love
     14: 21 He who loves me will be *l*
     14: 28 If you *l* me, you would be glad that
     15:   9 the Father has *l* me, so have I *l* you.
     15: 12 Love each other as I have *l* you.
     16: 27 loves you because you have *l* me
     17: 23 have *l* them even as you have *l* me.
     17: 24 you *l* me before the creation
     19: 26 the disciple whom he *l* standing

Jn 20: 2 one Jesus *l*, and said, ''They have
     21: 7 the disciple whom Jesus *l* said
     21:20 whom Jesus *l* was following
Ro   1: 7 To all in Rome who are *l* by God
      8:37 conquerors through him who *l* us.
      9:13 ''Jacob I *l*, but Esau I hated.''
      9:25 her 'my *l* one' who is not my *l* one,''
    11:28 they are *l* on account
Gal 2:20 who *l* me and gave himself for me.
Eph 5: 1 as dearly *l* children and live a life
      5: 2 as Christ *l* us and gave himself up
      5:25 just as Christ *l* the church
Col 3:12 and dearly *l*, clothe yourselves
1Th 1: 4 For we know, brothers *l* by God,
      2: 8 We *l* you so much that we were
2Th 2:13 for you, brothers *l* by the Lord,
      2:16 who *l* us and by his grace gave us
2Ti 4:10 for Demas, because he *l* this world,
Heb 1: 9 You have *l* righteousness
2Pe 2:15 who *l* the wages of wickedness.
1Jn 4:10 This is love: not that we *l* God,
      4:10 but that he *l* us and sent his Son
      4:11 Dear friends, since God so *l* us,
      4:19 We love because he first *l* us.
Jude   : 1 who are *l* by God the Father
Rev 3: 9 and acknowledge that I have *l* you.

LOVELY* (LOVE)

Ge 29:17 but Rachel was *l* in form,
Est 1:11 and nobles, for she was *l* to look at.
      2: 7 was *l* in form and features,
Ps 84: 1 How *l* is your dwelling place,
SS 1: 5 Dark am I, yet *l*,
      2:14 and your face is *l*.
      4: 3 your mouth is *l*.
      5:16 he is altogether *l*.
      6: 4 *l* as Jerusalem,
Am 8:13 *l* young women and strong young
Php 4: 8 whatever is *l*, whatever is

LOVER* (LOVE)

SS 1:13 My *l* is to me a sachet of myrrh
      1:14 My *l* is to me a cluster
      1:16 How handsome you are, my *l!*
      2: 3 is my *l* among the young men.
      2: 8 Listen! My *l!*
      2: 9 My *l* is like a gazelle or a young
      2:10 My *l* spoke and said to me,
      2:16 *Beloved* My *l* is mine and I am his;
      2:17 turn, my *l*,
      4:16 Let my *l* come into his garden
      5: 2 Listen! My *l* is knocking:
      5: 4 My *l* thrust his hand
      5: 5 I arose to open for my *l*,
      5: 6 I opened for my *l*,
      5: 6 but my *l* had left; he was gone.
      5: 8 if you find my *l*,
      5:10 *Beloved* My *l* is radiant and ruddy,
      5:16 This is my *l*, this my friend,
      6: 1 Where has your *l* gone,
      6: 1 Which way did your *l* turn,
      6: 2 *Beloved* My *l* has gone
      6: 3 I am my lover's and my *l* is mine;
      7: 9 May the wine go straight to my *l*,
      7:10 I belong to my *l*,
      7:11 my *l*, let us go to the countryside,
      7:13 that I have stored up for you, my *l*.
      8: 5 leaning on her *l?*
      8:14 *Beloved* Come away, my *l*,
1Ti 3: 3 not quarrelsome, not a *l* of money.

LOVER'S* (LOVE)

SS 6: 3 I am my *l* and my lover is mine;

LOVERS* (LOVE)

SS 5: 1 drink your fill, O *l*.
Jer 3: 1 as a prostitute with many *l—*
      3: 2 the roadside you sat waiting for *l*,
      4:30 Your *l* despise you;
La   1: 2 Among all her *l*
Eze 16:33 but you give gifts to all your *l*,
    16:36 in your promiscuity with your *l*,
    16:37 I am going to gather all your *l*,
    16:39 Then I will hand you over to your *l*,
    16:41 and you will no longer pay your *l*.
    23: 5 she lusted after her *l*, the Assyrians
    23: 9 I handed her over to her *l*,
    23:20 There she lusted after her *l*,

Eze 23:22 I will stir up your *l* against you,
Hos 2: 5 She said, 'I will go after my *l*,
      2: 7 She will chase after her *l*
      2:10 lewdness before the eyes of her *l*;
      2:12 she said were her pay from her *l*;
      2:13 and went after her *l*,
      8: 9 Ephraim has sold herself to *l*.
2Ti 3: 2 People will be *l* of themselves,
      3: 2 *l* of money, boastful, proud,
      3: 3 without self-control, brutal, not *l*
      3: 4 *l* of pleasure rather than *l* of God—

LOVES* (LOVE)

Ge 44:20 sons left, and his father *l* him.'
Dt 10:18 and *l* the alien, giving him food
    15:16 because he *l* you and your family
    21:15 and he *l* one but not the other,
    21:16 son of the wife he *l* in preference
    23: 5 because the Lord your God *l* you
    28:54 wife he *l* or his surviving children,
    28:56 will begrudge the husband she *l*
    33:12 and the one the Lord *l* rests
Ru 4:15 who *l* you and who is better to you
2Ch 2:11 ''Because the Lord *l* his people,
Ps 11: 7 he *l* justice;
    33: 5 The Lord *l* righteousness
    34:12 Whoever of you *l* life
    37:28 For the Lord *l* the just
    87: 2 the Lord *l* the gates of Zion
    91:14 Because he *l* me,'' says the Lord,
    99: 4 The King is mighty, he *l* justice—
  119:140 and your servant *l* them.
   127: 2 for he grants sleep to those he *l*.
   146: 8 the Lord *l* the righteous.
Pr 3:12 the Lord disciplines those he *l*,
    12: 1 Whoever *l* discipline *l* knowledge,
    13:24 he who *l* him is careful
    15: 9 he *l* those who pursue
    17:17 A friend *l* at all times,
    17:19 He who *l* a quarrel *l* sin;
    19: 8 He who gets wisdom *l* his own soul
    21:17 He who *l* pleasure will become
    21:17 whoever *l* wine and oil will never
    22:11 He who *l* a pure heart and whose
    29: 3 A man who *l* wisdom brings joy
Ecc 5:10 Whoever *l* money never has
      5:10 whoever *l* wealth is never satisfied
SS 3: 1 I looked for the one my heart *l*.
      3: 2 I will search for the one my heart *l*.
      3: 3 ''Have you seen the one my heart *l*
      3: 4 when I found the one my heart *l*.
Hos 3: 1 as the Lord *l* the Israelites,
    10:11 that *l* to thresh;
    12: 7 he *l* to defraud.
Mal 2:11 the sanctuary the Lord *l*,
Mt 10:37 anyone who *l* his son or daughter
    10:37 ''Anyone who *l* his father
Lk 7: 5 because he *l* our nation
      7:47 has been forgiven little *l* little.''
Jn 3:35 Father *l* the Son and has placed
      5:20 For the Father *l* the Son
    10:17 reason my Father *l* me is that I lay
    12:25 The man who *l* his life will lose it,
    14:21 He who *l* me will be loved
    14:21 obeys them, he is the one who *l* me.
    14:23 Jesus replied, ''If anyone *l* me,
    16:27 the Father himself *l* you
Ro 13: 8 for he who *l* his fellowman has
1Co 8: 3 But the man who *l* God is known
2Co 9: 7 for God *l* a cheerful giver.
Eph 1: 6 has freely given us in the One he *l*.
      5:28 He who *l* his wife *l* himself.
      5:33 must love his wife as he *l* himself,
Col 1:13 us into the kingdom of the Son he *l*,
Tit 1: 8 one who *l* what is good, who is
Heb 12: 6 the Lord disciplines those he *l*,
1Jn 2:10 Whoever *l* his brother lives
      2:15 If anyone *l* the world, the love
      4: 7 Everyone who *l* has been born
      4:21 Whoever *l* God must also love his
      5: 1 who *l* the father *l* his child
3Jn   : 9 but Diotrephes, who *l* to be first,
Rev 1: 5 To him who *l* us and has freed us
    20: 9 camp of God's people, the city he *l*.
    22:15 and everyone who *l* and practices

LOVING* (LOVE)

Ps 25:10 All the ways of the Lord are *l*

Ps 59:10 my *l* God.
    59:17 O God, are my fortress, my *l* God.
    62:12 and that you, O Lord, are *l*.
  144: 2 He is my *l* God and my fortress,
  145:13 and *l* toward all he has made.
  145:17 and *l* toward all he has made.
Pr 5:19 A *l* doe, a graceful deer—
Heb 13: 1 Keep on *l* each other as brothers.
1Jn 5: 2 by *l* God and carrying out his

LOVING-KINDNESS* (LOVE)

Jer 31: 3 I have drawn you with *l*.

LOWER

Ps 8: 5 You made him a little *l*
2Co 11: 7 a sin for me to *l* myself in order
Heb 2: 7 You made him a little *l*

LOWING

1Sa 15:14 What is this *l* of cattle that I hear?''

LOWLY

Job 5:11 The *l* he sets on high,
Ps 138: 6 on high, he looks upon the *l*,
Pr 29:23 but a man of *l* spirit gains honor.
Isa 57:15 also with him who is contrite and *l*
Eze 21:26 I will be exalted and the exalted
1Co 1:28 He chose the *l* things of this world

LOYAL

1Ch 29:18 and keep their hearts *l* to you.
Ps 78: 8 whose hearts were not *l* to God,

LUKE*

    Co-worker with Paul (Col 4:14; 2Ti 4:11; Phm 24).

LUKEWARM*

Rev 3:16 So, because you are *l*— neither hot

LUST (LUSTED LUSTS)

Pr 6:25 Do not *l* in your heart
Eze 20:30 and *l* after their vile images?
Col 3: 5 sexual immorality, impurity, *l*,
1Th 4: 5 not in passionate *l* like the heathen,
1Pe 4: 3 in debauchery, *l*, drunkenness,
1Jn 2:16 the *l* of his eyes and the boasting

LUSTED (LUST)

Eze 23: 5 she *l* after her lovers, the Assyrians

LUSTS* (LUST)

Nu 15:39 yourselves by going after the *l*
Ro 1:26 God gave them over to shameful *l*.

LUXURY

Jas 5: 5 You have lived on earth in *l*

LYDIA'S*

Ac 16:40 went to *L* house, where they met

LYING (LIE)

Pr 6:17 a *l* tongue,
    12:22 The Lord detests *l* lips,
    21: 6 A fortune made by a *l* tongue
    26:28 A *l* tongue hates those it hurts,

MACEDONIA

Ac 16: 9 ''Come over to *M* and help us.''

MAD

Dt 28:34 The sights you see will drive you *m*

MADE (MAKE)

Ge 1: 7 So God *m* the expanse
      1:16 God *m* two great lights—
      1:16 He also *m* the stars.
      1:25 God *m* the wild animals according
      1:31 God saw all that he had *m*,
      2:22 Then the Lord God *m* a woman
      6: 6 was grieved that he had *m* man
      9: 6 has God *m* man.
    15:18 that the Lord *m* a covenant
Ex 20:11 six days the Lord *m* the heavens
    20:11 the Sabbath day and *m* it holy.
    24: 8 the covenant that the Lord has *m*
    32: 4 *m* it into an idol cast in the shape
Lev 16:34 Atonement is to be *m* once a year
Dt 32: 6 who *m* you and formed you?

Jos 24: 25 On that day Joshua *m* a covenant
2Ki 19: 15 You have *m* heaven and earth.
2Ch 2: 12 the God of Israel, who *m* heaven
Ne 9: 6 You *m* the heavens,
 9: 10 You a name for yourself,
Ps 33: 6 of the LORD were the heavens *m*,
 95: 5 The sea is his, for he *m* it,
 96: 5 but the LORD *m* the heavens.
 100: 3 It is he who *m* us, and we are his;
 118: 24 This is the day the LORD has *m*;
 136: 7 who *m* the great lights—
 139: 14 I am fearfully and wonderfully *m*;
Ecc 3: 11 He has *m* everything beautiful
Isa 43: 7 whom I formed and *m*.''
 45: 12 It is I who *m* the earth
 45: 18 he who fashioned and *m* the earth,
 66: 2 Has not my hand *m* all these things
Jer 10: 12 But God *m* the earth by his power;
 27: 5 and outstretched arm I *m* the earth
 32: 17 you have *m* the heavens
 33: 2 LORD says, he who *m* the earth,
 51: 15 "He *m* the earth by his power;
Eze 3: 17 I have *m* you a watchman
 33: 7 I have *m* you a watchman
Am 5: 8 (he who *m* the Pleiades and Orion,
Jnh 1: 9 who *m* the sea and the land.''
Mk 2: 27 "The Sabbath was *m* for man,
Jn 1: 3 Through him all things were *m*;
Ac 17: 24 "The God who *m* the world
1Co 3: 6 watered it, but God *m* it grow.
Heb 1: 2 through whom he *m* the universe.
Jas 3: 9 who have been *m* in God's likeness
Rev 14: 7 Worship him who *m* the heavens,

MAGDALENE

Lk 8: 2 Mary (called *M*) from whom seven

MAGI

Mt 2: 1 *M* from the east came to Jerusalem

MAGIC (MAGICIANS)

Eze 13: 20 I am against your *m* charms
Rev 21: 8 those who practice *m* arts,
 22: 15 those who practice *m* arts,

MAGICIANS (MAGIC)

Ex 7: 11 the Egyptian *m* also did the same
Da 2: 2 So the king summoned the *m*,

MAGNIFICENCE* (MAGNIFICENT)

1Ch 22: 5 for the LORD should be of great *m*

MAGNIFICENT (MAGNIFICENCE)

1Ki 8: 13 I have indeed built a *m* temple
Isa 28: 29 in counsel and *m* in wisdom.
Mk 13: 1 stones! What *m* buildings!''

MAGOG

Eze 38: 2 of the land of *M*, the chief prince
 39: 6 I will send fire on *M*
Rev 20: 8 and *M*— to gather them for battle.

MAIDEN (MAIDENS)

Pr 30: 19 and the way of a man with a *m*.
Isa 62: 5 As a young man marries a *m*,
Jer 2: 32 Does a *m* forget her jewelry,

MAIDENS (MAIDEN)

SS 1: 3 No wonder the *m* love you!

MAIMED

Mt 18: 8 It is better for you to enter life *m*

MAINTAIN (MAINTAINING)

Ps 82: 3 *m* the rights of the poor
 106: 3 Blessed are they who *m* justice,
Hos 12: 6 *m* love and justice,
Am 5: 15 *m* justice in the courts.
Ro 3: 28 For we *m* that a man is justified

MAINTAINING* (MAINTAIN)

Ex 34: 7 faithfulness, *m* love to thousands,

MAJESTIC* (MAJESTY)

Ex 15: 6 was *m* in power.
 15: 11 *m* in holiness.
Job 37: 4 he thunders with his *m* voice.
Ps 8: 1 how *m* is your name in all the earth
 8: 9 how *m* is your name in all the earth

Ps 29: 4 the voice of the LORD is *m*.
 68: 15 of Bashan are *m* mountains;
 76: 4 more *m* than mountains rich
 111: 3 Glorious and *m* are his deeds,
SS 6: 4 *m* as troops with banners.
 6: 10 *m* as the stars in procession?
Isa 30: 30 men to hear his *m* voice
Eze 37: 1 It was *m* in beauty,
2Pe 1: 17 came to him from the *M* Glory,

MAJESTY* (MAJESTIC)

Ex 15: 7 In the greatness of your *m*
Dt 5: 24 has shown us his glory and his *m*,
 11: 2 his *m*, his mighty hand, his
 33: 17 In *m* he is like a firstborn bull;
 33: 26 and on the clouds in his *m*.
1Ch 16: 27 Splendor and *m* are before him;
 29: 11 and the *m* and the splendor,
Est 1: 4 the splendor and glory of his *m*.
 7: 3 if it pleases your *m*, grant me my
Job 37: 22 God comes in awesome *m*.
 40: 10 and clothe yourself in honor and *m*
Ps 21: 5 on him splendor and *m*.
 45: 3 with splendor and *m*.
 45: 4 In your *m* ride forth victoriously
 68: 34 whose *m* is over Israel,
 93: 1 The LORD reigns, he is robed in *m*
 93: 1 the LORD is robed in *m*
 96: 6 Splendor and *m* are before him;
 104: 1 clothed with splendor and *m*.
 110: 3 Arrayed in holy *m*,
 145: 12 of the glorious splendor of your *m*,
Isa 2: 10 and the splendor of his *m*!
 2: 19 and the splendor of his *m*,
 2: 21 and the splendor of his *m*,
 24: 14 west they acclaim the LORD's *m*.
 26: 10 and regard not the *m* of the LORD.
 53: 2 or *m* to attract us to him,
Eze 31: 2 can be compared with you in *m*?
 31: 18 with you in splendor and *m*?
Da 4: 30 and for the glory of my *m*?''
Mic 5: 4 in the *m* of the name
Zec 6: 13 and he will be clothed with *m*
Ac 19: 27 will be robbed of her divine *m*.''
 25: 26 to write to His *M* about him.
2Th 1: 9 and from the *m* of his power
Heb 1: 3 hand of the *M* in heaven.
 8: 1 of the throne of the *M* in heaven,
2Pe 1: 16 but we were eyewitnesses of his *m*.
Jude 25 only God our Savior be glory, *m*,

MAKE (MADE MAKER MAKERS MAKES MAKING MAN-MADE)

Ge 1: 26 "Let us *m* man in our image,
 2: 18 I will *m* a helper suitable for him.''
 6: 14 yourself an ark of cypress wood;
 12: 2 "I will *m* you into a great nation
Ex 22: 3 thief must *m* restitution,
 25: 9 *M* this tabernacle and all its
 25: 40 See that you *m* them according
Nu 6: 25 the LORD *m* his face shine
2Sa 7: 9 Now I will *m* your name great,
Job 7: 17 "What is man that you *m* so much
Ps 4: 8 *m* me dwell in safety.
 20: 4 and *m* all your plans succeed.
 108: 1 I will *m* music with all my soul.
 110: 1 hand until I *m* your enemies
 119:165 and nothing can *m* them stumble.
Pr 3: 6 and he will *m* your paths straight.
 4: 26 *M* level paths for your feet
 20: 18 *M* plans by seeking advice;
Isa 14: 14 I will *m* myself like the Most High
 29: 16 "He did not *m* me''?
 55: 3 I will *m* an everlasting covenant
 61: 8 and *m* an everlasting covenant
Jer 31: 31 "when I will *m* a new covenant
Eze 37: 26 I will *m* a covenant of peace
Mt 3: 3 *m* straight paths for him.' ''
 28: 19 and *m* disciples of all nations,
Mk 1: 17 "and I will *m* you fishers of men.''
Lk 13: 24 "*M* every effort to enter
 14: 23 country lanes and *m* them come in,
Ro 14: 19 *m* every effort to do what leads
2Co 5: 9 So we *m* it our goal to please him,
Eph 4: 3 *M* every effort to keep the unity
Col 4: 5 *m* the most of every opportunity.
1Th 4: 11 *M* it your ambition
Heb 4: 11 *m* every effort to enter that rest,

Heb 8: 5 it that you *m* everything according
 12: 14 *M* every effort to live in peace
2Pe 1: 5 *m* every effort to add
 3: 14 *m* every effort to be found spotless,

MAKER* (MAKE)

Job 4: 17 Can a man be more pure than his *M*
 9: 9 He is the *M* of the Bear and Orion,
 32: 22 my *M* would soon take me away.
 35: 10 no one says, 'Where is God my *M*,
 36: 3 I will ascribe justice to my *M*.
 40: 19 yet his *M* can approach him
Ps 95: 6 kneel before the LORD our *M*;
 115: 15 the *M* of heaven and earth.
 121: 2 the *M* of heaven and earth.
 124: 8 the *M* of heaven and earth.
 134: 3 the *M* of heaven and earth,
 146: 6 the *M* of heaven and earth,
 149: 2 Let Israel rejoice in their *M*;
Pr 14: 31 poor shows contempt for their *M*,
 17: 5 poor shows contempt for their *M*;
 22: 2 The LORD is the *M* of them all.
Ecc 11: 5 the *M* of all things.
Isa 17: 7 that day men will look to their *M*
 27: 11 so their *M* has no compassion
 45: 9 to him who quarrels with his *M*,
 45: 11 the Holy One of Israel, and its *M*:
 51: 13 that you forget the LORD your *M*,
 54: 5 For your *M* is your husband—
Jer 10: 16 for he is the *M* of all things,
 51: 19 for he is the *M* of all things,
Hos 8: 14 Israel has forgotten his *M*

MAKERS* (MAKE)

Isa 45: 16 All the *m* of idols will be put

MAKES (MAKE)

Ps 23: 2 *m* me lie down in green pastures,
Pr 13: 12 Hope deferred *m* the heart sick,
1Co 3: 7 but only God, who *m* things grow.

MAKING (MAKE)

Ps 19: 7 *m* wise the simple.
Ecc 12: 12 Of *m* many books there is no end,
Jn 5: 18 *m* himself equal with God.
Eph 5: 16 *m* the most of every opportunity,

MALACHI*

Mal 1: 1 of the LORD to Israel through *M*.

MALE

Ge 1: 27 *m* and female he created them.
Ex 13: 2 to me every firstborn *m*.
Nu 8: 16 the first *m* offspring
Mt 19: 4 the Creator 'made them *m*
Gal 3: 28 slave nor free, *m* nor female,

MALICE (MALICIOUS)

Mk 7: 22 adultery, greed, *m*, deceit,
Ro 1: 29 murder, strife, deceit and *m*.
1Co 5: 8 the yeast of *m* and wickedness,
Eph 4: 31 along with every form of *m*.
Col 3: 8 *m*, slander, and filthy language
1Pe 2: 1 rid yourselves of all *m*

MALICIOUS (MALICE)

Pr 26: 24 A *m* man disguises himself
1Ti 3: 11 not *m* talkers but temperate
 6: 4 *m* talk, evil suspicions

MALIGN

Tit 2: 5 so that no one will *m* the word

MAMMON see MONEY, WEALTH

MAN (MAN'S MANKIND MEN MEN'S WOMAN WOMEN)

Ge 1: 26 "Let us make *m* in our image,
 2: 7 God formed the *m* from the dust
 2: 8 *m* became a living being
 2: 15 God took the *m* and put
 2: 18 for the *m* to be alone
 2: 20 *m* gave names to all the
 2: 23 she was taken out of *m*.
 2: 25 *m* and his wife were both
 3: 9 God called to the *m*,
 3: 22 *m* has now become like
 4: 1 I have brought forth a *m*.
 6: 3 not contend with *m* forever,

Ge 6: 6 grieved that he had made *m*
9: 6 Whoever sheds the blood of *m*,
Dt 8: 3 *m* does not live on bread
1Sa 13: 14 a *m* after his own heart
15: 29 he is not a *m* that he
16: 7 at the things *m* looks at.
Job 14: 1 *M* born of woman is of few
14: 14 If a *m* dies, will he live
Ps 1: 1 Blessed is the *m* who does
8: 4 what is *m* that you are
32: 2 Blessed is the *m* whose sin
40: 4 Blessed is the *m* who makes
84: 12 blessed is the *m* who trusts
103: 15 As for *m*, his days are
112: 1 Blessed is the *m* who fears
119: 9 can a young *m* keep his
127: 5 Blessed is the *m* whose quiver
144: 3 what is *m* that you care
Pr 3: 13 Blessed is the *m* who finds
9: 9 Instruct a wise *m*
14: 12 that seems right to a *m*,
30: 19 way of a *m* with a maiden.
Isa 53: 3 a *m* of sorrows,
Jer 17: 5 the one who trusts in *m*,
17: 7 blessed is the *m* who trusts
Eze 22: 30 I looked for a *m*
Mt 4: 4 *M* does not live on bread
19: 5 a *m* will leave his father
Mk 8: 36 What good is it for a *m*
Lk 4: 4 'M does not live on bread
Ro 5: 12 entered the world through one *m*
1Co 2: 15 spiritual *m* makes judgments
3: 12 If any *m* builds on this
7: 1 good for a *m* not to marry.
7: 2 each *m* should have his own
11: 3 head of every *m* is Christ,
11: 3 head of woman is *m*
13: 11 When I became a *m*,
15: 21 death came through a *m*,
15: 45 first *m* Adam became a
15: 47 the second *m* from heaven
2Co 12: 2 I know a *m* in Christ
Eph 2: 15 create in himself one new *m*
5: 31 a *m* will leave his father
Php 2: 8 found in appearance as a *m*,
1Ti 2: 5 the *m* Christ Jesus,
2: 11 have authority over a *m*;
2Ti 3: 17 that the *m* of God may be
Heb 2: 6 what is *m* that you are
9: 27 as *m* is destined to die

MAN'S (MAN)

Pr 20: 24 A *m* steps are directed by
Jer 10: 23 a *m* life is not his own;
1Co 1: 25 is wiser than *m* wisdom,

MAN-MADE (MAKE)

Heb 9: 11 perfect tabernacle that is not *m*,
9: 24 not enter a *m* sanctuary that was

MANAGE (MANAGER)

Jer 12: 5 how will you *m* in the thickets
1Ti 3: 4 He must *m* his own family well
3: 12 one wife and must *m* his children
5: 14 to *m* their homes and to give

MANAGER (MANAGE)

Lk 12: 42 Who then is the faithful and wise *m*
16: 1 a rich man whose *m* was accused

MANASSEH

1. Firstborn of Joseph (Ge 41:51; 46:20). Blessed by Jacob but not firstborn (Ge 48). Tribe of blessed (Dt 33:17), numbered (Nu 1:35; 26:34), half allotted land east of Jordan (Nu 32; Jos 13: 8-33), half west (Jos 16; Eze 48:4), failed to fully possess (Jos 16:10; Jdg 1:27), 12,000 from (Rev 7:6).
2. Son of Hezekiah; king of Judah (2Ki 21: 1-18; 2Ch 33:1-20). Judah exiled for his detestable sins (2Ki 21:10-15). Repentance (2Ch 33:12-19).

MANDRAKES

Ge 30: 14 give me some of your son's *m*.''

MANGER

Lk 2: 12 in strips of cloth and lying in a *m*.''

MANIFESTATION*

1Co 12: 7 to each one the *m* of the Spirit is

MANKIND (MAN)

Ge 6: 7 I will wipe *m*, whom I have created
Ps 33: 13 and sees all *m*;
Pr 8: 31 and delighting in *m*.
Ecc 7: 29 God made *m* upright,
Isa 40: 5 and all *m* together will see it.
45: 12 and created *m* upon it.
Jer 32: 27 ''I am the LORD, the God of all *m*.
Zec 2: 13 Be still before the LORD, all *m*,
Lk 3: 6 And all *m* will see God's salvation

MANNA

Ex 16: 31 people of Israel called the bread *m*.
Dt 8: 16 He gave you *m* to eat in the desert,
Jn 6: 49 Your forefathers ate the *m*
Rev 2: 17 I will give some of the hidden *m*.

MANNER

1Co 11: 27 in an unworthy *m* will be guilty
Php 1: 27 conduct yourselves in a *m* worthy

MANSIONS*

Ps 49: 14 far from their princely *m*.
Isa 5: 9 the fine *m* left without occupants.
Am 3: 15 and the *m* will be demolished,''
5: 11 though you have built stone *m*,

MARCH

Jos 6: 4 *m* around the city seven times,
Isa 42: 13 LORD will *m* out like a mighty

MARITAL* (MARRY)

Ex 21: 10 of her food, clothing and *m* rights.
Mt 5: 32 except for *m* unfaithfulness,
19: 9 except for *m* unfaithfulness,
1Co 7: 3 husband should fulfill his *m* duty

MARK (MARKS)

Cousin of Barnabas (Col 4:10; 2Ti 4:11; Phm 24; 1Pe 5:13), see JOHN.
Ge 4: 15 Then the LORD put a *m* on Cain
Rev 13: 16 to receive a *m* on his right hand

MARKET (MARKETPLACE MARKETPLACES)

Jn 2: 16 turn my Father's house into a *m*!''

MARKETPLACE (MARKET)

Lk 7: 32 are like children sitting in the *m*

MARKETPLACES (MARKET)

Mt 23: 7 they love to be greeted in the *m*

MARKS (MARK)

Jn 20: 25 Unless I see the nail *m* in his hands
Gal 6: 17 bear on my body the *m* of Jesus.

MARRED

Isa 52: 14 his form *m* beyond human likeness

MARRIAGE (MARRY)

Mt 22: 30 neither marry nor be given in *m*;
24: 38 marrying and giving in *m*,
Ro 7: 2 she is released from the law of *m*.
Heb 13: 4 by all, and the *m* bed kept pure,

MARRIED (MARRY)

Dt 24: 5 happiness to the wife he has *m*.
Ezr 10: 10 you have *m* foreign women,
Pr 30: 23 an unloved woman who is *m*,
Mt 1: 18 pledged to be *m* to Joseph,
Mk 12: 23 since the seven were *m* to her?''
Ro 7: 2 by law a *m* woman is bound
1Co 7: 27 Are you *m*? Do not seek a divorce.
7: 33 But a *m* man is concerned about
7: 36 They should get *m*.

MARRIES (MARRY)

Mt 5: 32 anyone who *m* the divorced woman
19: 9 and *m* another woman commits
Lk 16: 18 the man who *m* a divorced woman

MARROW

Heb 4: 12 joints and *m*; it judges the thoughts

MARRY (INTERMARRY MARITAL MARRIAGE MARRIED MARRIES)

Dt 25: 5 brother shall take her and *m* her
Mt 22: 30 resurrection people will neither *m*
1Co 7: 1 It is good for a man not to *m*.
7: 9 control themselves, they should *m*,
7: 28 if you do *m*, you have not sinned;
1Ti 4: 3 They forbid people to *m*
5: 14 So I counsel younger widows to *m*,

MARTHA*

Sister of Mary and Lazarus (Lk 10:38-42; Jn 11; 12:2).

MARVELED* (MARVELOUS)

Lk 2: 33 mother *m* at what was said about
2Th 1: 10 and to be *m* at among all those who

MARVELING* (MARVELOUS)

Lk 9: 43 While everyone was *m*

MARVELOUS* (MARVELED MARVELING)

1Ch 16: 24 his *m* deeds among all peoples.
Job 37: 5 God's voice thunders in *m* ways;
Ps 71: 17 to this day I declare your *m* deeds.
72: 18 who alone does *m* deeds.
86: 10 For you are great and do *m* deeds;
96: 3 his *m* deeds among all peoples.
98: 1 for he has done *m* things;
118: 23 and it is *m* in our eyes.
Isa 25: 1 you have done *m* things,
Zec 8: 6 but will it seem *m* to me?''
8: 6 ''It may seem *m* to the remnant
Mt 21: 42 and it is *m* in our eyes'?
Mk 12: 11 and it is *m* in our eyes'?''
Rev 15: 1 in heaven another great and *m* sign
15: 3 ''Great and *m* are your deeds,

MARY

1. Mother of Jesus (Mt 1:16-25; Lk 1:27-56; 2: 1-40). With Jesus at temple (Lk 2:41-52), at the wedding in Cana (Jn 2:1-5), questioning his sanity (Mk 3:21), at the cross (Jn 19:25-27). Among disciples after Ascension (Ac 1:14).
2. Magdalene; former demoniac (Lk 8:2). Helped support Jesus' ministry (Lk 8:1-3). At the cross (Mt 27:56; Mk 15:40; Jn 19:25), burial (Mt 27:61; Mk 15:47). Saw angel after resurrection (Mt 28:1-10; Mk 16:1-9; Lk 24:1-12); also Jesus (Jn 20:1-18).
3. Sister of Martha and Lazarus (Jn 11). Washed Jesus' feet (Jn 12:1-8).

MASQUERADES*

2Co 11: 14 for Satan himself *m* as an angel

MASTER (MASTER'S MASTERED MASTERS MASTERY)

Ge 4: 7 to have you, but you must *m* it.''
Hos 2: 16 you will no longer call me 'my *m*.'
Mal 1: 6 If I am a *m*, where is the respect
Mt 10: 24 nor a servant above his *m*.
23: 8 for you have only one *M*
24: 46 that servant whose *m* finds him
25: 21 ''His *m* replied, 'Well done,
25: 23 ''His *m* replied, 'Well done,
Ro 6: 14 For sin shall not be your *m*,
14: 4 To his own *m* he stands or falls.
Col 4: 1 you know that you also have a *M*
2Ti 2: 21 useful to the *M* and prepared

MASTER'S (MASTER)

Mt 25: 21 Come and share your *m* happiness

MASTERED* (MASTER)

1Co 6: 12 but I will not be *m* by anything.
2Pe 2: 19 a slave to whatever has *m* him.

MASTERS (MASTER)

Pr 25: 13 he refreshes the spirit of his *m*.
Mt 6: 24 ''No one can serve two *m*.
Lk 16: 13 ''No servant can serve two *m*.
Eph 6: 5 obey your earthly *m* with respect
6: 9 And *m*, treat your slaves
Col 3: 22 obey your earthly *m* in everything;
4: 1 *M*, provide your slaves
1Ti 6: 1 should consider their *m* worthy

1Ti 6: 2 who have believing *m* are not
Tit 2: 9 subject to their *m* in everything,
1Pe 2: 18 to your *m* with all respect,

MASTERY* (MASTER)

Ro 6: 9 death no longer has *m* over him.

MAT

Mk 2: 9 'Get up, take your *m* and walk'?
Ac 9: 34 Get up and take care of your *m*.''

MATCHED*

2Co 8: 11 do it may be *m* by your completion

MATTHEW*

Apostle; former tax collector (Mt 9:9-13; 10:3;
Mk 3:18; Lk 6:15; Ac 1:13). Also called Levi (Mk
2:14-17; Lk 5:27-32).

MATTHIAS

Ac 1: 26 the lot fell to *M;* so he was added

MATURE* (MATURITY)

Lk 8: 14 and pleasures, and they do not *m*.
1Co 2: 6 a message of wisdom among the *m*,
Eph 4: 13 of the Son of God and become *m*,
Php 3: 15 of us who are *m* should take such
Col 4: 12 firm in all the will of God, *m*
Heb 5: 14 But solid food is for the *m*,
Jas 1: 4 work so that you may be *m*

MATURITY* (MATURE)

Heb 6: 1 about Christ and go on to *m*,

MEAL

Pr 15: 17 Better a *m* of vegetables where
1Co 10: 27 some unbeliever invites you to a *m*
Heb 12: 16 for a single *m* sold his inheritance

MEANING

Ne 8: 8 and giving the *m* so that the people

MEANINGLESS

Ecc 1: 2 ''*M! M!*'' says the Teacher.
1Ti 1: 6 from these and turned to *m* talk.

MEANS

1Co 9: 22 by all possible *m* I might save some

MEASURE (MEASURED MEASURES)

Ps 71: 15 though I know not its *m*.
Eze 45: 3 In the sacred district, *m*
Zec 2: 2 He answered me, ''To *m* Jerusalem
Lk 6: 38 A good *m*, pressed
Eph 3: 19 to the *m* of all the fullness of God.
    4: 13 to the whole *m* of the fullness
Rev 11: 1 ''Go and *m* the temple of God

MEASURED (MEASURE)

Isa 40: 12 Who has *m* the waters
Jer 31: 37 if the heavens above can be *m*

MEASURES (MEASURE)

Dt 25: 14 Do not have two differing *m*
Pr 20: 10 Differing weights and differing *m*

MEAT

Pr 23: 20 or gorge themselves on *m*,
Ro 14: 6 He who eats *m*, eats to the Lord,
   14: 21 It is better not to eat *m*
1Co 8: 13 I will never eat *m* again,
   10: 25 *m* market without raising questions

MEDDLER* (MEDDLES)

1Pe 4: 15 kind of criminal, or even as a *m*.

MEDDLES* (MEDDLER)

Pr 26: 17 is a passer-by who *m*

MEDIATOR

1Ti 2: 5 and one *m* between God and men,
Heb 8: 6 of which he is *m* is superior
    9: 15 For this reason Christ is the *m*
   12: 24 to Jesus the *m* of a new covenant,

MEDICINE*

Pr 17: 22 A cheerful heart is good *m*,

MEDITATE* (MEDITATED MEDITATES MEDITATION)

Ge 24: 63 out to the field one evening to *m*,
Jos 1: 8 from your mouth; *m* on it day
Ps 48: 9 we *m* on your unfailing love.
   77: 12 I will *m* on all your works
  119: 15 I *m* on your precepts
  119: 23 your servant will *m*
  119: 27 then I will *m* on your wonders.
  119: 48 and I *m* on your decrees.
  119: 78 but I will *m* on your precepts.
  119: 97 I *m* on it all day long.
  119: 99 for I *m* on your statutes.
  119:148 that I may *m* on your promises.
  143: 5 I *m* on all your works
  145: 5 I will *m* on your wonderful works.

MEDITATED* (MEDITATE)

Ps 39: 3 and as I *m*, the fire burned;

MEDITATES* (MEDITATE)

Ps 1: 2 and on his law he *m* day and night.

MEDITATION* (MEDITATE)

Ps 19: 14 of my mouth and the *m* of my heart
  104: 34 May my *m* be pleasing to him,

MEDIUM

Lev 20: 27 '' 'A man or woman who is a *m*

MEEK* (MEEKNESS)

Ps 37: 11 But the *m* will inherit the land
Zep 3: 12 the *m* and humble,
Mt 5: 5 Blessed are the *m*,

MEEKNESS* (MEEK)

2Co 10: 1 By the *m* and gentleness of Christ,

MEET (MEETING MEETINGS MEETS)

Ps 42: 2 When can I go and *m* with God?
  85: 10 Love and faithfulness *m* together;
Am 4: 12 prepare to *m* your God, O Israel.''
1Co 11: 34 when you *m* together it may not
1Th 4: 17 them in the clouds to *m* the Lord

MEETING (MEET)

Ex 40: 34 the cloud covered the Tent of *M*,
Heb 10: 25 Let us not give up *m* together,

MEETINGS* (MEET)

1Co 11: 17 for your *m* do more harm

MEETS (MEET)

Heb 7: 26 Such a high priest *m* our need—

MELCHIZEDEK

Ge 14: 18 *M* king of Salem brought out bread
Ps 110: 4 in the order of *M*.''
Heb 7: 11 in the order of *M*, not in the order

MELT (MELTS)

2Pe 3: 12 and the elements will *m* in the heat.

MELTS (MELT)

Am 9: 5 he who touches the earth and it *m*,

MEMBER (MEMBERS)

Ro 12: 5 each *m* belongs to all the others.

MEMBERS (MEMBER)

Mic 7: 6 a man's enemies are the *m*
Mt 10: 36 a man's enemies will be the *m*
Ro 7: 23 law at work in the *m* of my body,
  12: 4 of us has one body with many *m*,
1Co 6: 15 not know that your bodies are
  12: 24 But God has combined the *m*
Eph 3: 6 together of one body,
   4: 25 for we are all *m* of one body,
   5: 30 for we are *m* of his body.
Col 3: 15 as *m* of one body you were called

MEMORABLE* (MEMORY)

Eze 39: 13 day I am glorified will be a *m* day

MEMORIES* (MEMORY)

1Th 3: 6 us that you always have pleasant *m*

MEMORY (MEMORABLE MEMORIES)

Pr 10: 7 *m* of the righteous will be
Mt 26: 13 she has done will also be told, in *m*

MEN (MAN)

Ge 6: 2 daughter of *m* were beautiful,
   6: 4 heroes of old, *m* of renown
Ps 9: 20 nations know they are but *m*.
  11: 4 He observes the sons of *m;*
Mt 4: 19 will make you fishers of *m*
   5: 16 your light shine before *m*
   6: 14 if you forgive *m* when
  10: 32 acknowledges me before *m*
  12: 31 blasphemy will be forgiven *m*,
  12: 36 *m* will have to give account
  23: 5 is done for *m* to see:
Mk 7: 7 are but rules taught by *m*.
Lk 6: 22 Blessed are you when *m*
   6: 26 Woe to you when all *m*
Jn 1: 4 life was the light of *m*.
   2: 24 for he knew all *m*.
   3: 19 *m* loved darkness instead
  12: 32 will draw all *m* to myself
  13: 35 all *m* will know that you
Ac 5: 29 obey God rather than *m!*
Ro 1: 18 wickedness of *m*
   1: 27 indecent acts with other *m*,
   5: 12 death came to all *m*,
1Co 2: 11 among *m* knows the thoughts
   3: 3 acting like mere *m?*
   3: 21 no more boasting about *m!*
   9: 22 all things to all *m*
  13: 1 tongues of *m* and of angels
  16: 13 be *m* of courage;
  16: 18 Such *m* deserve recognition.
2Co 5: 11 we try to persuade *m*.
   8: 21 but also in the eyes of *m*.
Gal 1: 1 sent not from *m* nor
   1: 10 to win approval of *m*, or
Eph 4: 8 and gave gifts to *m*.
1Th 2: 4 as approved by God
   2: 13 not as the word of *m*,
1Ti 2: 4 wants all *m* to be saved
   2: 6 as a ransom for all *m*—
   4: 10 the Savior of all *m*
   5: 2 younger *m* as brothers
2Ti 2: 2 entrust to reliable *m*
Tit 2: 11 has appeared to all *m*.
Heb 5: 1 is selected from among *m*
   7: 28 high priests *m* who are weak;
2Pe 1: 21 but *m* spoke from God
Rev 21: 3 dwelling of God is with *m*,

MEN'S (MAN)

2Ki 19: 18 fashioned by *m* hands.
2Ch 32: 19 the work of *m* hands.
1Co 2: 5 not rest on *m* wisdom,

MENAHEM*

King of Israel (2Ki 15:17-22).

MENE

Da 5: 25 that was written: *M*, *M*,

MEPHIBOSHETH

Son of Jonathan shown kindness by David (2Sa
4:4; 9; 21:7). Accused of siding with Absalom
(2Sa 16:1-4; 19:24-30).

MERCHANT

Pr 31: 14 She is like the *m* ships,
Mt 13: 45 of heaven is like a *m* looking

MERCIFUL (MERCY)

Dt 4: 31 the LORD your God is a *m* God;
Ne 9: 31 for you are a gracious and *m* God.
Ps 77: 9 Has God forgotten to be *m?*
  78: 38 Yet he was *m;*
Jer 3: 12 for I am *m*,' declares the LORD,
Da 9: 9 The Lord our God is *m*
Mt 5: 7 Blessed are the *m*,
Lk 1: 54 remembering to be *m*
   6: 36 Be *m*, just as your Father is *m*.
Heb 2: 17 in order that he might become a *m*
Jas 2: 13 to anyone who has not been *m*.
Jude : 22 Be *m* to those who doubt; snatch

MERCY (MERCIFUL)

Ex 33: 19 *m* on whom I will have *m*,
2Sa 24: 14 of the LORD, for his *m* is great;
1Ch 21: 13 for his *m* is very great;
Ne   9: 31 But in your great *m* you did not put
Ps 25: 6 O LORD, your great *m* and love,
      28: 6 for he has heard my cry for *m*.
      57: 1 Have *m* on me, O God, have *m*
Pr 28: 13 renounces them finds *m*.
Isa 63: 9 and *m* he redeemed them;
Da   9: 18 but because of your great *m*.
Hos 6: 6 For I desire *m*, not sacrifice,
Am   5: 15 LORD God Almighty will have *m*
Mic 6: 8 To act justly and to love *m*
      7: 18 but delight to show *m*.
Hab 3: 2 in wrath remember *m*.
Zec 7: 9 show *m* and compassion
Mt 5: 7 for they will be shown *m*.
      9: 13 learn what this means: 'I desire *m*,
     12: 7 'I desire *m*, not sacrifice,' you
     18: 33 Shouldn't you have had *m*
     23: 23 justice, *m* and faithfulness.
Lk   1: 50 His *m* extends to those who fear
Ro   9: 15 "I will have *m* on whom I have *m*,
      9: 18 Therefore God has *m*
     11: 32 so that he may have *m* on them all.
     12: 1 brothers, in view of God's *m*,
     12: 8 if it is showing *m*, let him do it
Eph 2: 4 who is rich in *m*, made us alive
1Ti 1: 13 I was shown *m* because I acted
      1: 16 for that very reason I was shown *m*
Tit 3: 5 we had done, but because of his *m*.
Heb 4: 16 so that we may receive *m*
Jas 2: 13 judgment without *m* will be shown
      2: 13 *M* triumphs over judgment!
      3: 17 submissive, full of *m* and good fruit
      5: 11 full of compassion and *m*.
1Pe 1: 3 In his great *m* he has given us new
      2: 10 once you had not received *m*,
Jude : 23 to others show *m*, mixed with fear

MERRY

Lk 12: 19 Take life easy; eat, drink and be *m*

MESHACH

Hebrew exiled to Babylon; name changed from
Mishael (Da 1:6-7). Refused defilement by food
(Da 1:8-20). Refused to worship idol (Da 3:1-18);
saved from furnace (Da 3:19-30).

MESSAGE (MESSENGER)

Isa 53: 1 Who has believed our *m*
Jn 12: 38 "Lord, who has believed our *m*
Ac   5: 20 "and tell the people the full *m*
     10: 36 You know the *m* God sent
     17: 11 for they received the *m*
Ro 10: 16 who has believed our *m*?"
     10: 17 faith comes from hearing the *m*,
1Co 1: 18 For the *m* of the cross is
      2: 4 My *m* and my preaching were not
2Co 5: 19 to us the *m* of reconciliation.
2Th 3: 1 pray for us that the *m*
Tit 1: 3 firmly to the trustworthy *m*
Heb 4: 2 the *m* they heard was of no value
1Pe 2: 8 because they disobey the *m*—

MESSENGER (MESSAGE)

Pr 25: 13 is a trustworthy *m*
Mal 3: 1 I will send my *m*, who will prepare
Mt 11: 10 " 'I will send my *m* ahead of you,
2Co 12: 7 a *m* of Satan, to torment me.

MESSIAH*

Jn   1: 41 "We have found the *M*" (that is,
      4: 25 "I know that *M*" (called Christ) "is

METHUSELAH

Ge   5: 27 Altogether, *M* lived 969 years,

MICAH

1. Idolater from Ephraim (Jdg 17-18).
2. Prophet from Moresheth (Jer 26:18-19; Mic
1:1).

MICAIAH

Prophet of the LORD who spoke against Ahab
(1Ki 22:1-28; 2Ch 18:1-27).

MICHAEL

Archangel (Jude 9); warrior in angelic realm,
protector of Israel (Da 10:13, 21; 12:1; Rev 12:7).

MICHAL

Daughter of Saul, wife of David (1Sa 14:49;
18:20-28). Warned David of Saul's plot (1Sa 19).
Saul gave her to Paltiel (1Sa 25:44); David re-
trieved her (2Sa 3:13-16). Criticized David for
dancing before the ark (2Sa 6:16-23); 1Ch 15:29).

MIDIAN

Ex   2: 15 Pharaoh and went to live in *M*,
Jdg 7: 2 me to deliver *M* into their hands.

MIDWIVES

Ex   1: 17 The *m*, however, feared God

MIGHT (ALMIGHTY MIGHTIER MIGHTY)

Jdg 16: 30 Then he pushed with all his *m*,
2Sa 6: 5 with all their *m* before the LORD,
      6: 14 before the LORD with all his *m*,
2Ch 20: 6 Power and *m* are in your hand,
Ps 21: 13 we will sing and praise your *m*.
      54: 1 vindicate me by your *m*.
Isa 63: 15 Where are your zeal and your *m*?
Mic 3: 8 and with justice and *m*,
Zec 4: 6 'Not by *m* nor by power,
Col 1: 11 power according to his glorious *m*
1Ti 6: 16 To him be honor and *m* forever.

MIGHTIER (MIGHT)

Ps 93. 4 *M* than the thunder

MIGHTY (MIGHT)

Ge 49: 24 of the hand of the *M* One of Jacob,
Ex   6: 1 of my *m* hand he will drive them
     13: 3 out of it with a *m* hand.
Dt   5: 15 out of there with a *m* hand
      7: 8 he brought you out with a *m* hand
     10: 17 the great God, *m* and awesome,
     34: 12 one has ever shown the *m* power
2Sa 1: 19 How the *m* have fallen!
     23: 8 the names of David's *m* men:
Ne   9: 32 the great, *m* and awesome God,
Job 36: 5 God is *m*, but does not despise men
Ps 24: 8 The LORD strong and *m*,
     45: 3 upon your side, O *m* one;
     50: 1 The *M* One, God, the LORD,
     62: 7 he is my *m* rock, my refuge.
     68: 33 who thunders with *m* voice.
     71: 16 proclaim your *m* acts,
     77: 12 and consider all your *m* deeds.
     77: 15 With your *m* arm you redeemed
     89: 8 You are *m*, O LORD,
     93: 4 the LORD on high is *m*.
     99: 4 The King is *m*, he loves justice—
    110: 2 LORD will extend your *m* scepter
    118: 15 right hand has done *m* things!
    136: 12 with a *m* hand and outstretched
    145: 4 may tell of your *m* acts,
    145: 12 all men may know of your *m* acts
    147: 5 Great is our Lord and *m* in power;
SS   8: 6 like a *m* flame.
Isa 9: 6 Wonderful Counselor, *M* God,
     60: 16 your Redeemer, the *M* One
     63: 1 *m* to save."
Jer 10: 6 and your name is *m* in power.
     20: 11 with me like a *m* warrior;
     32: 19 your purposes and *m* are your
Eze 20: 33 I will rule over you with a *m* hand
Zep 3: 17 he is *m* to save.
Mt 26: 64 at the right hand of the *M* One
Eph 1: 19 like the working of his *m* strength,
      6: 10 in the Lord and in his *m* power.
1Pe 5: 6 therefore, under God's *m* hand,

MILE*

Mt   5: 41 If someone forces you to go one *m*,

MILK

Ex   3: 8 a land flowing with *m* and honey—
     23: 19 a young goat in its mother's *m*.
Pr 30: 33 as churning the *m* produces butter,
Isa 55: 1 Come, buy wine and *m*
1Co 3: 2 I gave you *m*, not solid food,
Heb 5: 12 You need *m*, not solid food!

1Pe 2: 2 babies, crave pure spiritual *m*,

MILLSTONE (STONE)

Lk 17: 2 sea with a *m* tied around his neck

MIND (DOUBLE-MINDED LIKE-MINDED MINDED MINDFUL MINDS)

Nu 23: 19 that he should change his *m*.
Dt 28: 65 LORD will give you an anxious *m*,
1Sa 15: 29 Israel does not lie or change his *m*;
1Ch 28: 9 devotion and with a willing *m*,
2Ch 30: 12 the people to give them unity of *m*
Ps 26: 2 examine my heart and my *m*;
    110: 4 and will not change his *m*:
Isa 26: 3 him whose *m* is steadfast,
Jer 17: 10 and examine the *m*,
Mt 22: 37 all your soul and with all your *m*.'
Mk 12: 30 with all your *m* and with all your
Lk 10: 27 your strength and with all your *m*';
Ac   4: 32 believers were one in heart and *m*.
Ro   1: 28 he gave them over to a depraved *m*
      7: 25 I myself in my *m* am a slave
      8: 6 The *m* of sinful man is death,
      8: 7 the sinful *m* is hostile to God.
     12: 2 by the renewing of your *m*.
     14: 13 make up your *m* not
1Co 1: 10 you may be perfectly united in *m*
      2: 9 no *m* has conceived
     14: 14 spirit prays, but my *m* is unfruitful.
2Co 13: 11 be of one *m*, live in peace.
Php 3: 19 Their *m* is on earthly things.
Col 2: 18 and his unspiritual *m* puffs him up
1Th 4: 11 to *m* your own business
Heb 7: 21 and will not change his *m*:

MINDED* (MIND)

1Pe 4: 7 be clear *m* and self-controlled

MINDFUL* (MIND)

Ps   8: 4 what is man that you are *m* of him,
Lk   1: 48 God my Savior, for he has been *m*
Heb 2: 6 What is man that you are *m* of him,

MINDS (MIND)

Dt 11: 18 of mine in your hearts and *m*;
Ps   7: 9 who searches *m* and hearts,
Jer 31: 33 "I will put my law in their *m*
Lk 24: 38 and why do doubts rise in your *m*?
     24: 45 Then he opened their *m*
Ro   8: 5 to the sinful nature have their *m* set
2Co 4: 4 god of this age has blinded the *m*
Eph 4: 23 new in the attitude of your *m*;
Col 3: 2 Set your *m* on things above,
Heb 8: 10 I will put my laws in their *m*
     10: 16 and I will write them on their *m*."
1Pe 1: 13 prepare your *m* for action;
Rev 2: 23 I am he who searches hearts and *m*.

MINISTER (MINISTERING MINISTERS MINISTRY)

Ps 101: 6 will *m* to me.
1Ti 4: 6 you will be a good *m*

MINISTERING (MINISTER)

Heb 1: 14 Are not all angels *m* spirits sent

MINISTERS (MINISTER)

2Co 3: 6 as *m* of a new covenant—

MINISTRY (MINISTER)

Ac   6: 4 to prayer and the *m* of the word."
Ro 11: 13 I make much of my *m*
2Co 4: 1 God's mercy we have this *m*,
      5: 18 gave us the *m* of reconciliation:
      6: 3 so that our *m* will not be
Gal 2: 8 who was at work in the *m* of Peter
2Ti 4: 5 discharge all the duties of your *m*.
Heb 8: 6 But the *m* Jesus has received is

MIRACLE* (MIRACLES MIRACULOUS)

Ex   7: 9 'Perform a *m*,' then say to Aaron,
Mk   9: 39 "No one who does a *m*
Lk 23: 8 hoped to see him perform some *m*.
Jn   7: 21 "I did one *m*, and you are all
Ac   4: 16 they have done an outstanding *m*.

MIRACLES* (MIRACLE)

1Ch 16: 12 his *m*, and the judgments he
Ne   9: 17 to remember the *m* you performed
Job 5: 9 *m* that cannot be counted.
      9: 10 *m* that cannot be counted.
Ps 77: 11 I will remember your *m* of long ago
     77: 14 You are the God who performs *m;*
     78: 12 He did *m* in the sight
    105: 5 his *m*, and the judgments he
    106: 7 they gave no thought to your *m;*
    106: 22 *m* in the land of Ham
Mt   7: 22 out demons and perform many *m?'*
     11: 20 most of his *m* had been performed,
     11: 21 If the *m* that were performed
     11: 23 If the *m* that were performed
     13: 58 And he did not do many *m* there
     24: 24 and perform great signs and *m?*
Mk   6: 2 does *m!* Isn't this the carpenter?
      6: 5 He could not do any *m* there,
     13: 22 and *m* to deceive the elect—
Lk 10: 13 For if the *m* that were performed
     19: 37 for all the *m* they had seen:
Jn   7: 3 disciples may see the *m* you do.
     10: 25 *m* I do in my Father's name speak
     10: 32 "I have shown you many great *m*
     10: 38 do not believe me, believe the *m*,
     14: 11 the evidence of the *m* themselves.
     15: 24 But now they have seen these *m*,
Ac   2: 22 accredited by God to you by *m*,
      8: 13 by the great signs and *m* he saw.
     19: 11 God did extraordinary *m*
Ro 15: 19 by the power of signs and *m*,
1Co 12: 28 third teachers, then workers of *m*,
     12: 29 Are all teachers? Do all work *m?*
2Co 12: 12 and *m*— were done among you
Gal 3: 5 work *m* among you because you
2Th 2: 9 in all kinds of counterfeit *m*,
Heb 2: 4 it by signs, wonders and various *m*,

MIRACULOUS (MIRACLE)

Dt 13: 1 and announces to you a *m* sign
Mt 12: 39 generation asks for a *m* sign!
     13: 54 this wisdom and these *m* powers?"
Jn   2: 11 This, the first of his *m* signs,
      2: 23 people saw the *m* signs he was
      3: 2 could perform the *m* signs you are
      4: 48 "Unless you people see *m* signs
      7: 31 will he do more *m* signs
      9: 16 "How can a sinner do such *m* signs
     12: 37 Jesus had done all these *m* signs
     20: 30 Jesus did many other *m* signs
Ac   2: 43 *m* signs were done by the apostles.
      5: 12 apostles performed many *m* signs
1Co 1: 22 Jews demand *m* signs and Greeks
     12: 10 to another *m* powers,

MIRE

Ps 40: 2 out of the mud and *m;*
Isa 57: 20 whose waves cast up *m* and mud.

MIRIAM

Sister of Moses and Aaron (Nu 26:59). Led
dancing at Red Sea (Ex 15:20-21). Struck with
leprosy for criticizing Moses (Nu 12). Death (Nu
20:1).

MIRROR

1Co 13: 12 but a poor reflection as in a *m;*
Jas 1: 23 a man who looks at his face in a *m*

MISDEEDS*

Ps 99: 8 though you punished their *m*.
Ro   8: 13 put to death the *m* of the body,

MISERY

Ex   3: 7 "I have indeed seen the *m*
Jdg 10: 16 he could bear Israel's *m* no longer.
Hos 5: 15 in their *m* they will earnestly seek
Ro   3: 16 ruin and *m* mark their ways,
Jas 5: 1 of the *m* that is coming upon you.

MISFORTUNE

Ob   : 12 brother in the day of his *m*,

MISLEAD (MISLED)

Isa 47: 10 wisdom and knowledge *m* you

MISLED (MISLEAD)

1Co 15: 33 Do not be *m*: "Bad company

MISS (MISSES)

Pr 19: 2 nor to be hasty and *m* the way.

MISSES (MISS)

Heb 12: 15 See to it that no one *m* the grace

MIST

Hos 6: 4 Your love is like the morning *m*,
Jas 4: 14 You are a *m* that appears for a little

MISTREAT (MISTREATED)

Ex 22: 21 "Do not *m* an alien or oppress him,
Eze 22: 29 and needy and *m* the alien,
Lk   6: 28 pray for those who *m* you.

MISTREATED (MISTREAT)

Eze 22: 7 *m* the fatherless and the widow.
Heb 11: 25 to be *m* along with the people
     11: 37 destitute, persecuted and *m*—
     13: 3 who are *m* as if you yourselves

MISUSE* (MISUSES)

Ex 20: 7 "You shall not *m* the name
Dt   5: 11 "You shall not *m* the name
Ps 139: 20 your adversaries *m* your name.

MISUSES* (MISUSE)

Ex 20: 7 anyone guiltless who *m* his name.
Dt   5: 11 anyone guiltless who *m* his name.

MIXED (MIXING)

Da   2: 41 even as you saw iron *m* with clay.

MIXING (MIXED)

Isa 5: 22 and champions at *m* drinks,

MOAB (MOABITESS)

Ge 19: 37 she named him *M;* he is the father
Dt 34: 6 He buried him in *M*, in the valley
Ru   1: 1 live for a while in the country of *M.*
Isa 15: 1 An oracle concerning *M:*
Jer 48: 16 "The fall of *M* is at hand;
Am   2: 1 "For three sins of *M*,

MOABITESS (MOAB)

Ru   1: 22 accompanied by Ruth the *M*.

MOAN

Ps 90: 9 we finish our years with a *m*.

MOCK (MOCKED MOCKER MOCKERS MOCKING MOCKS)

Ps 22: 7 All who see me *m* me;
    119: 51 The arrogant *m* me
Pr   1: 26 I will *m* when calamity overtakes
     14: 9 Fools *m* at making amends for sin,
Mk 10: 34 who will *m* him and spit on him,

MOCKED (MOCK)

Ps 89: 51 with which they have *m* every step
Mt 27: 29 knelt in front of him and *m* him.
     27: 41 of the law and the elders *m* him.
Gal 6: 7 not be deceived: God cannot be *m*.

MOCKER (MOCK)

Pr   9: 7 corrects a *m* invites insult;
      9: 12 if you are a *m*, you alone will suffer
     20: 1 Wine is a *m* and beer a brawler;
     22: 10 Drive out the *m*, and out goes strife

MOCKERS (MOCK)

Ps   1: 1 or sit in the seat of *m*.
Pr 29: 8 *M* stir up a city,

MOCKING (MOCK)

Isa 50: 6 face from *m* and spitting.

MOCKS (MOCK)

Pr 17: 5 He who *m* the poor shows
     30: 17 "The eye that *m* a father,

MODEL*

Eze 28: 12 "'You were the *m* of perfection,
1Th 1: 7 And so you became a *m*
2Th 3: 9 to make ourselves a *m* for you

MODESTY*

1Co 12: 23 are treated with special *m*,

MOLDED*

Job 10: 9 Remember that you *m* me like clay

MOLDY

Jos 9: 5 of their food supply was dry and *m*.

MOLECH

Lev 20: 2 of his children to *M* must be put
1Ki 11: 33 and *M* the god of the Ammonites,

MOMENT (MOMENTARY)

Job 20: 5 the joy of the godless lasts but a *m*.
Ps   2: 12 for his wrath can flare up in a *m*.
     30: 5 For his anger lasts only a *m*,
Pr 12: 19 but a lying tongue lasts only a *m*.
Isa 54: 7 "For a brief *m* I abandoned you,
     66: 8 or a nation be brought forth in a *m?*
Gal 2: 5 We did not give in to them for a *m*,

MOMENTARY* (MOMENT)

2Co 4: 17 and *m* troubles are achieving

MONEY

Pr 13: 11 Dishonest *m* dwindles away,
Ecc 5: 10 Whoever loves *m* never has *m*
Isa 55: 1 and you who have no *m*,
Mt   6: 24 You cannot serve both God and *M*.
     27: 5 Judas threw the *m* into the temple
Lk   3: 14 "Don't extort and don't accuse
      9: 3 no bread, no *m*, no extra tunic.
     16: 13 You cannot serve both God and *M*
Ac   5: 2 part of the *m* for himself,
1Co 16: 2 set aside a sum of *m* in keeping
1Ti 3: 3 not quarrelsome, not a lover of *m*.
      6: 10 For the love of *m* is a root
2Ti 3: 2 lovers of *m*, boastful, proud,
Heb 13: 5 free from the love of *m*
1Pe 5: 2 not greedy for *m*, but eager to serve

MONEYLENDER* (LEND)

Ex 22: 25 not be like a *m;* charge him no
Lk   7: 41 men owed money to a certain *m*.

MONTH (MONTHS)

Ex 12: 2 This *m* is to be for you the first
Eze 47: 12 Every *m* they will bear,
Rev 22: 2 of fruit, yielding its fruit every *m*.

MONTHS (MONTH)

Gal 4: 10 and *m* and seasons and years!
Rev 11: 2 trample on the holy city for 42 *m*.
     13: 5 his authority for forty-two *m*.

MOON

Jos 10: 13 and the *m* stopped,
Ps   8: 3 the *m* and the stars,
     74: 16 you established the sun and *m*.
     89: 37 be established forever like the *m*,
    104: 19 The *m* marks off the seasons,
    121: 6 nor the *m* by night.
    136: 9 the *m* and stars to govern the night;
    148: 3 Praise him, sun and *m*,
SS   6: 10 fair as the *m*, bright as the sun,
Joel 2: 31 and the *m* to blood
Hab 3: 11 and *m* stood still in the heavens
Mt 24: 29 and the *m* will not give its light;
Ac   2: 20 and the *m* to blood
1Co 15: 41 *m* another and the stars another;
Col 2: 16 a New *M* celebration or a Sabbath
Rev 6: 12 the whole *m* turned blood red,
     21: 23 city does not need the sun or the *m*

MORAL*

Jas 1: 21 rid of all *m* filth and the evil that is

MORDECAI

Benjamite exile who raised Esther (Est 2:5-15).
Exposed plot to kill Xerxes (Est 2:19-23). Refused
to honor Haman (Est 3:1-6; 5:9-14). Charged Es-
ther to foil Haman's plot against the Jews (Est 4).
Xerxes forced Haman to honor Mordecai (Est 6).
Mordecai exalted (Est 8-10). Established Purim
(Est 9:18-32).

MORIAH*

Ge   22:   2 and go to the region of *M*.
2Ch   3:   1 LORD in Jerusalem on Mount *M*,

MORNING

Ge   1:   5 and there was *m*— the first day.
Dt   28: 67 In the *m* you will say, ''If only it
2Sa 23:   4 he is like the light of *m* at sunrise
Ps   5:   3 In the *m*, O LORD,
Pr   27: 14 blesses his neighbor early in the *m*,
Isa 14: 12 O *m* star, son of the dawn!
La   3: 23 They are new every *m*;
2Pe   1: 19 and the *m* star rises in your hearts.
Rev   2: 28 I will also give him the *m* star.
     22: 16 of David, and the bright *M* Star.''

MORTAL

Ge   6:   3 for he is *m*; his days will be
Job 10:   4 Do you see as a *m* sees?
Ro   8: 11 also give life to your *m* bodies
1Co 15: 53 and the *m* with immortality.
2Co   5:   4 that what is *m* may be swallowed

MOSES

Levite; brother of Aaron (Ex 6:20; 1Ch 6:3).
Put in basket into Nile; discovered and raised by
Pharaoh's daughter (Ex 2:1-10). Fled to Midian
after killing Egyptian (Ex 2:11-15). Married to
Zipporah, fathered Gershom (Ex 2:16-22).
     Called by the LORD to deliver Israel (Ex 3-4).
Pharaoh's resistance (Ex 5). Ten plagues (Ex 7-
11). Passover and Exodus (Ex 12-13). Led Israel
through Red Sea (Ex 14). Song of deliverance (Ex
15:1-21). Brought water from rock (Ex 17:1-7).
Raised hands to defeat Amalekites (Ex 17:8-16).
Delegated judges (Ex 18; Dt 1:9-18).
     Received Law at Sinai (Ex 19-23; 25-31; Jn 1:
17). Announced Law to Israel (Ex 19:7-8; 24; 35).
Broke tablets because of golden calf (Ex 32; Dt 9).
Saw glory of the LORD (Ex 33-34). Supervised
building of tabernacle (Ex 36-40). Set apart Aaron
and priests (Lev 8-9). Numbered tribes (Nu 1-4;
26). Opposed by Aaron and Miriam (Nu 12). Sent
spies into Canaan (Nu 13). Announced forty years
of wandering for failure to enter land (Nu 14).
Opposed by Korah (Nu 16). Forbidden to enter
land for striking rock (Nu 20:1-13; Dt 1:37). Lifted bronze snake for healing (Nu 21:4-9; Jn 3:14).
Final address to Israel (Dt 1-33). Succeeded by
Joshua (Nu 27:12-23; Dt 34). Death (Dt 34:5-12).
     ''Law of Moses'' (1Ki 2:3; Ezr 3:2; Mk 12:26;
Lk 24:44). ''Book of Moses'' (2Ch 25:12; Ne 13:
1). ''Song of Moses'' (Ex 15:1-21; Rev 15:3).
''Prayer of Moses'' (Ps 90).

MOTH

Mt   6: 19 where *m* and rust destroy,

MOTHER (GRANDMOTHER
MOTHER-IN-LAW MOTHER'S)

Ge   2: 24 and *m* be united to his wife,
     3: 20 because she would become the *m*
Ex   20: 12 ''Honor your father and your *m*,
Lev 20:   9 '' ''If anyone curses his father or *m*,
Dt   5: 16 ''Honor your father and *m*
     21: 18 who does not obey his father and *m*
     27: 16 who dishonors his father or his *m*.''
Jdg   5:   7 arose a *m* in Israel.
1Sa   2: 19 Each year his *m* made him a little
Ps 113:   9 as a happy *m* of children.
Pr   10:   1 but a foolish son grief to his *m*.
     23: 22 do not despise your *m*
     23: 25 May your father and *m* be glad;
     29: 15 a child left to himself disgraces his *m*.
     30: 17 that scorns obedience to a *m*,
     31:   1 an oracle his *m* taught him:
Isa 49: 15 ''Can a *m* forget the baby
     66: 13 As a *m* comforts her child,
Jer 20: 17 with my *m* as my grave,
Mic   7:   6 a daughter rises up against her *m*,
Mt   10: 35 a daughter against her *m*,
     10: 37 or *m* more than me is not worthy
     12: 48 he replied, ''Who is my *m*,
     15:   4 'Honor your father and *m*'
     19:   5 and *m* and be united to his wife.
     19: 19 honor your father and *m*,'
Mk   7: 10 'Honor your father and your *m*,' and,
     10: 19 honor your father and *m*.' ''

Lk   11: 27 ''Blessed is the *m* who gave you
     12: 53 daughter and daughter against *m*,
     18: 20 honor your father and *m*.' ''
Jn   19: 27 to the disciple, ''Here is your *m*.''
Gal   4: 26 is above is free, and she is our *m*.
Eph   5: 31 and *m* and be united to his wife,
     6:   2 ''Honor your father and *m*''—
1Th   2:   7 like a *m* caring for her little
2Ti   1:   5 and in your *m* Eunice and,

MOTHER-IN-LAW (MOTHER)

Ru   2: 19 Ruth told her *m* about the one
Mt   10: 35 a daughter-in-law against her *m*—

MOTHER'S (MOTHER)

Job   1: 21 ''Naked I came from my *m* womb,
Pr   1:   8 and do not forsake your *m* teaching
Ecc   5: 15 from his *m* womb,
     11:   5 the body is formed in a *m* womb,
Jn   3:   4 time into his *m* womb to be born!''

MOTIVE* (MOTIVES)

1Ch 28:   9 and understands every *m*

MOTIVES* (MOTIVE)

Pr   16:   2 but *m* are weighed by the LORD.
1Co   4:   5 will expose the *m* of men's hearts.
Php   1: 18 whether from false *m* or true,
1Th   2:   3 spring from error or impure *m*,
Jas   4:   3 because you ask with wrong *m*,

MOUNT (MOUNTAIN MOUNTAINS
MOUNTAINTOPS)

Ps   89:   9 when its waves *m* up, you still them
Isa 14: 13 enthroned on the *m* of assembly,
Eze 28: 14 You were on the holy *m* of God;
Zec 14:   4 stand on the *M* of Olives,

MOUNTAIN (MOUNT)

Ge   22: 14 ''On the *m* of the LORD it will be
Ex   24: 18 And he stayed on the *m* forty days
Dt   5:   4 face to face out of the fire on the *m*.
Job 14: 18 ''But as a *m* erodes and crumbles
Ps   48:   1 in the city of our God, his holy *m*.
Isa 40:   4 every *m* and hill made low;
Mic   4:   2 let us go up to the *m* of the LORD,
Mt   4:   8 the devil took him to a very high *m*
     17: 20 say to this *m*, 'Move from here
Mk   9:   2 with him and led them up a high *m*,
Lk   3:   5 every *m* and hill made low.
Jn   4: 21 the Father neither on this *m*
2Pe   1: 18 were with him on the sacred *m*.

MOUNTAINS (MOUNT)

Ps   36:   6 righteousness is like the mighty *m*,
     46:   2 the *m* fall into the heart of the sea,
     90:   2 Before the *m* were born
Isa 52:   7 How beautiful on the *m*
     54: 10 Though the *m* be shaken
     55: 12 the *m* and hills
Eze 34:   6 My sheep wandered over all the *m*
Mt   24: 16 are in Judea flee to the *m*.
Lk   23: 30 they will say to the *m*, ''Fall on us!''
1Co 13:   2 if I have a faith that can move *m*,
Rev   6: 16 They called to the *m* and the rocks,

MOUNTAINTOPS (MOUNT)

Isa 42: 11 let them shout from the *m*.

MOURN (MOURNING MOURNS)

Ecc   3:   4 a time to *m* and a time to dance,
Isa 61:   2 to comfort all who *m*,
Mt   5:   4 Blessed are those who *m*,
Ro   12: 15 *m* with those who *m*.

MOURNING (MOURN)

Isa 61:   3 instead of *m*,
Jer 31: 13 I will turn their *m* into gladness;
Rev 21:   4 There will be no more death or *m*

MOURNS (MOURN)

Zec 12: 10 as one *m* for an only child,

MOUTH (MOUTHS)

Nu   22: 38 only what God puts in my *m*.''
Dt   8:   3 comes from the *m* of the LORD.
     18: 18 I will put my words in his *m*,
     30: 14 it is in your *m* and in your heart

Jos   1:   8 of the Law depart from your *m*;
2Ki   4: 34 *m* to *m*, eyes to eyes, hands
Ps   10:   7 His *m* is full of curses and lies
     17:   3 resolved that my *m* will not sin.
     19: 14 May the words of my *m*
     37: 30 *m* of the righteous man utters
     40:   3 He put a new song in my *m*,
     71:   8 My *m* is filled with your praise,
     119:103 sweeter than honey to my *m*!
     141:   3 Set a guard over my *m*, O LORD;
Pr   2:   6 and from his *m* come knowledge
     4: 24 Put away perversity from your *m*;
     10: 11 The *m* of the righteous is a fountain
     10: 31 *m* of the righteous brings forth
     16: 23 A wise man's heart guides his *m*,
     26: 28 and a flattering *m* works ruin.
     27:   2 praise you, and not your own *m*;
Ecc   5:   2 Do not be quick with your *m*,
SS   1:   2 with the kisses of his *m*—
     5: 16 His *m* is sweetness itself;
Isa 29: 13 come near to me with their *m*
     40:   5 For the *m* of the LORD has spoken
     45: 23 my *m* has uttered in all integrity
     51: 16 I have put my words in your *m*
     53:   7 so he did not open his *m*.
     55: 11 my word that goes out from my *m*:
     59: 21 *m* will not depart from your *m*,
Eze   3:   2 So I opened my *m*, and he gave me
Mal   2:   7 and from his *m* men should seek
Mt   4:   4 comes from the *m* of God.' ''
     12: 34 overflow of the heart the *m* speaks.
     15: 11 into a man's *m* does not make him
     15: 18 out of the *m* come from the heart,
Lk   6: 45 overflow of his heart his *m* speaks.
Ro   10:   9 That if you confess with your *m*,
     15:   6 and *m* you may glorify the God
1Pe   2: 22 and no deceit was found in his *m*.''
Rev   1: 16 and out of his *m* came a sharp
     2: 16 them with the sword of my *m*.
     3: 16 I am about to spit you out of my *m*.
     19: 15 Out of his *m* comes a sharp sword

MOUTHS (MOUTH)

Ps   78: 36 would flatter him with their *m*,
Eze 33: 31 With their *m* they express devotion
Ro   3: 14 ''Their *m* are full of cursing
Eph   4: 29 talk come out of your *m*,
Jas   3:   3 bits into the *m* of horses

MOVE (MOVED MOVES)

Dt   19: 14 Do not *m* your neighbor's
Pr   23: 10 Do not *m* an ancient boundary
Ac   17: 28 and *m* and have our being.'
1Co 13:   2 have a faith that can *m* mountains,
     15: 58 Let nothing *m* you.

MOVED (MOVE)

Ex   35: 21 and whose heart *m* him came
2Ch 36: 22 the LORD *m* the heart
Ezr   1:   5 everyone whose heart God had *m*
Ps   93:   1 it cannot be *m*.
Jn   11: 33 he was deeply *m* in spirit
Col   1: 23 not *m* from the hope held out

MOVES (MOVE)

Dt   23: 14 For the LORD your God *m* about

MUD (MUDDIED)

Ps   40:   2 out of the *m* and mire;
Isa 57: 20 whose waves cast up mire and *m*.
Jn   9:   6 made some *m* with the saliva,
2Pe   2: 22 back to her wallowing in the *m*.''

MUDDIED (MUD)

Pr   25: 26 Like a *m* spring or a polluted well
Eze 32: 13 or *m* by the hoofs of cattle.

MULBERRY*

Lk   17:   6 you can say to this *m* tree,

MULTITUDE (MULTITUDES)

Isa 31:   1 who trust in the *m* of their chariots
Jas   5: 20 and cover over a *m* of sins.
1Pe   4:   8 love covers over a *m* of sins.
Rev   7:   9 me was a great *m* that no one could
     19:   1 of a great *m* in heaven shouting:

MULTITUDES (MULTITUDE)

Ne   9: 6 and the *m* of heaven worship you.
Da 12: 2 *M* who sleep in the dust
Joel 3: 14 *M*, *m* in the valley of decision!

MURDER (MURDERED MURDERER MURDERERS)

Ex 20: 13 ''You shall not *m*.
Dt   5: 17 ''You shall not *m*.
Pr 28: 17 A man tormented by the guilt of *m*
Mt   5: 21 'Do not *m*, and anyone who
     15: 19 *m*, adultery, sexual immorality,
Ro   1: 29 *m*, strife, deceit and malice.
     13: 9 ''Do not *m*,'' ''Do not steal,''
Jas   2: 11 adultery,'' also said, ''Do not *m*.''

MURDERED (MURDER)

Mt 23: 31 of those who *m* the prophets.
Ac   7: 52 now you have betrayed and *m* him
1Jn   3: 12 to the evil one and *m* his brother.

MURDERER (MURDER)

Nu 35: 16 he is a *m*; the *m* shall be put
Jn   8: 44 He was a *m* from the beginning,
1Jn   3: 15 who hates his brother is a *m*,

MURDERERS (MURDER)

1Ti   1: 9 for *m*, for adulterers and perverts,
Rev 21: 8 the *m*, the sexually immoral,
     22: 15 the sexually immoral, the *m*,

MUSIC* (MUSICAL MUSICIAN MUSICIANS)

Ge 31: 27 singing to the *m* of tambourines
Jdg   5: 3 I will make *m* to the LORD,
1Ch   6: 31 put in charge of the *m* in the house
      6: 32 They ministered with *m*
     25: 6 fathers for the *m* of the temple
     25: 7 and skilled in *m* for the LORD—
Ne 12: 27 and with the *m* of cymbals,
Job 21: 12 They sing to the *m* of tambourine
Ps 27: 6 and make *m* to the LORD.
     33: 2 make *m* to him on the ten-stringed
     45: 8 the *m* of the strings makes you glad
     57: 7 I will sing and make *m*.
     81: 2 Begin the *m*, strike the tambourine,
     87: 7 As they make *m* they will sing,
     92: 1 and make *m* to your name,
     92: 3 to the *m* of the ten-stringed lyre
     95: 2 and extol him with *m* and song.
     98: 4 burst into jubilant song with *m*;
     98: 5 make *m* to the LORD
    108: 1 make *m* with all my soul.
    144: 9 the ten-stringed lyre I will make *m*
    147: 7 make *m* to our God on the harp.
    149: 3 make *m* to him with tambourine
Isa 30: 32 will be to the *m* of tambourines
La   5: 14 young men have stopped their *m*.
Eze 26: 13 *m* of your harps will be heard no
Da   3: 5 lyre, harp, pipes and all kinds of *m*,
      3: 7 and all kinds of *m*, all the peoples,
      3: 10 and all kinds of *m* must fall down
      3: 15 lyre, harp, pipes and all kinds of *m*,
Am   5: 23 to the *m* of your harps.
Hab   3: 19 For the director of *m*.
Lk 15: 25 came near the house, he heard *m*
Eph   5: 19 make *m* in your heart to the Lord,
Rev 18: 22 The *m* of harpists and musicians,

MUSICAL* (MUSIC)

1Ch 15: 16 accompanied by *m* instruments
     23: 5 with the *m* instruments I have
2Ch   7: 6 with the LORD's *m* instruments,
     23: 13 with *m* instruments were leading
     34: 12 skilled in playing *m* instruments—
Ne 12: 36 with *m* instruments prescribed
Am   6: 5 and improvise on *m* instruments.

MUSICIAN* (MUSIC)

1Ch   6: 33 Heman, the *m*, the son of Joel,

MUSICIANS* (MUSIC)

1Ki 10: 12 to make harps and lyres for the *m*.
1Ch 15: 19 Those who were *m*, heads
     15: 19 The *m* Heman, Asaph
2Ch   5: 12 All the Levites who were *m*—
      9: 11 to make harps and lyres for the *m*,
     35: 15 The *m*, the descendants of Asaph,

Ps 68: 25 are the singers, after them the *m*;
Rev 18: 22 The music of harpists and *m*,

MUSTARD

Mt 13: 31 kingdom of heaven is like a *m* seed,
     17: 20 you have faith as small as a *m* seed,
Mk   4: 31 It is like a *m* seed, which is

MUTILATORS*

Php 3: 2 those men who do evil, those *m*

MUTUAL* (MUTUALLY)

Ro 14: 19 leads to peace and to *m* edification.
1Co 7: 5 by *m* consent and for a time,

MUTUALLY* (MUTUAL) ·

Ro   1: 12 and I may be *m* encouraged

MUZZLE*

Dt 25: 4 Do not *m* an ox while it is treading
Ps 39: 1 I will put a *m* on my mouth
1Co 9: 9 ''Do not *m* an ox while it is
1Ti   5: 18 ''Do not *m* the ox while it is

MYRRH

Ps 45: 8 All your robes are fragrant with *m*
SS   1: 13 My lover is to me a sachet of *m*
Mt   2: 11 of gold and of incense and of *m*.
Mk 15: 23 offered him wine mixed with *m*,
Jn 19: 39 Nicodemus brought a mixture of *m*
Rev 18: 13 of incense, *m* and frankincense,

MYSTERIES* (MYSTERY)

Job 11: 7 ''Can you fathom the *m* of God?
Da   2: 28 a God in heaven who reveals *m*,
      2: 29 of *m* showed you what is going
      2: 47 Lord of kings and a revealer of *m*,
1Co 13: 2 can fathom all *m* and all knowledge
     14: 2 he utters *m* with his spirit.

MYSTERY* (MYSTERIES)

Da   2: 18 God of heaven concerning this *m*,
      2: 19 the night the *m* was revealed
      2: 27 to the king the *m* he has asked
      2: 30 this *m* has been revealed to me,
      2: 47 for you were able to reveal this *m*.''
      4: 9 and no *m* is too difficult for you.
Ro 11: 25 you to be ignorant of this *m*,
     16: 25 to the revelation of the *m* hidden
1Co 15: 51 I tell you a *m*: We will not all sleep,
Eph   1: 9 to us the *m* of his will according
      3: 3 the *m* made known to me
      3: 4 insight into the *m* of Christ,
      3: 6 This *m* is that through the gospel
      3: 9 the administration of this *m*,
      5: 32 This is a profound *m*—
      6: 19 I will fearlessly make known the *m*
Col   1: 26 the *m* that has been kept hidden
      1: 27 the glorious riches of this *m*,
      2: 2 in order that they may know the *m*
      4: 3 so that we may proclaim the *m*
1Ti   3: 16 the *m* of godliness is great:
Rev 1: 20 *m* of the seven stars that you saw
     10: 7 the *m* of God will be accomplished,
     17: 5 written on her forehead: *M*
     17: 7 explain to you the *m* of the woman

MYTHS*

1Ti   1: 4 nor to devote themselves to *m*
      4: 7 Have nothing to do with godless *m*
2Ti   4: 4 from the truth and turn aside to *m*.
Tit   1: 14 will pay no attention to Jewish *m*

NAAMAN

Aramean general whose leprosy was cleansed by Elisha (2Ki 5).

NABAL

Wealthy Carmelite the LORD killed for refusing to help David (1Sa 25). David married Abigail, his widow (1Sa 25:39-42).

NABOTH*

Jezreelite killed by Jezebel for his vineyard (1Ki 21). Ahab's family destroyed for this (1Ki 21:17-24; 2Ki 9:21-37).

NADAB

1. Firstborn of Aaron (Ex 6:23); killed with

Abihu for offering unauthorized fire (Lev 10; Nu 3:4).
2. Son of Jeroboam I; king of Israel (1Ki 15: 25-32).

NAHUM

Prophet against Nineveh (Na 1:1).

NAIL* (NAILING)

Jn 20: 25 ''Unless I see the *n* marks

NAILING* (NAIL)

Ac   2: 23 him to death by *n* him to the cross.
Col   2: 14 he took it away, *n* it to the cross.

NAIVE

Ro 16: 18 they deceive the minds of *n* people.

NAKED

Ge   2: 25 The man and his wife were both *n*,
Job 1: 21 *N* I came from my mother's womb,
Isa 58: 7 when you see the *n*, to clothe him,
2Co 5: 3 are clothed, we will not be found *n*.

NAME (NAMES)

Ge   2: 19 man to see what he would *n* them;
      4: 26 to call on the *n* of the LORD.
     11: 4 so that we may make a *n*
     12: 2 I will make your *n* great,
     32: 29 Jacob said, ''Please tell me your *n*.''
Ex   3: 15 This is my *n* forever, the *n*
     20: 7 ''You shall not misuse the *n*
     34: 14 for the LORD, whose *n* is Jealous,
Lev 24: 11 Israelite woman blasphemed the *N*
Dt   5: 11 ''You shall not misuse the *n*
     12: 11 choose as a dwelling for his *N*—
     18: 5 minister in the LORD's *n* always.
     25: 6 carry on the *n* of the dead brother
     28: 58 this glorious and awesome *n*—
Jos   7: 9 do for your own great *n*?''
Jdg 13: 17 ''What is your *n*, so that we may
1Sa 12: 22 of his great *n* the LORD will not
2Sa 6: 2 which is called by the *N*, the name
      7: 9 Now I will make your *n* great,
1Ki 5: 5 will build the temple for my *N*.'
      8: 29 you said, 'My *N* shall be there,'
1Ch 17: 8 I will make your *n* like the names
2Ch 7: 14 my people, who are called by my *n*,
Ne   9: 10 You made a *n* for yourself,
Ps   8: 1 how majestic is your *n*
      9: 10 Those who know your *n* will trust
     20: 7 in the *n* of the LORD our God.
     29: 2 to the LORD the glory due his *n*;
     34: 3 let us exalt his *n* together.
     44: 20 If we had forgotten the *n*
     66: 2 Sing the glory of his *n*;
     68: 4 Sing to God, sing praise to his *n*,
     79: 9 for the glory of your *n*;
     96: 8 to the LORD the glory due his *n*;
    103: 1 my inmost being, praise his holy *n*.
    115: 1 but to your *n* be the glory,
    138: 2 your *n* and your word.
    145: 1 I will praise your *n* for ever
    147: 4 and calls them each by *n*.
Pr   3: 4 you will win favor and a good *n*
     18: 10 *n* of the LORD is a strong tower;
     22: 1 A good *n* is more desirable
     30: 4 What is his *n*, and the *n* of his son?
Ecc 7: 1 A good *n* is better
SS   1: 3 your *n* is like perfume poured out.
Isa 12: 4 thanks to the LORD, call on his *n*;
     26: 8 your *n* and renown
     40: 26 and calls them each by *n*.
     42: 8 ''I am the LORD; that is my *n*!
     56: 5 I will give them an everlasting *n*
     57: 15 who lives forever, whose *n* is holy:
     63: 14 to make for yourself a glorious *n*.
Jer 14: 7 do something for the sake of your *n*
     15: 16 for I bear your *n*,
Eze 20: 9 of my *n* I did what would keep it
     20: 14 of my *n* I did what would keep it
     20: 22 of my *n* I did what would keep it
Da 12: 1 everyone whose *n* is found written
Hos 12: 5 the LORD is his *n* of renown!
Joel 2: 32 on the *n* of the LORD will be saved
Mic 5: 4 in the majesty of the *n*
Zep 3: 9 call on the *n* of the LORD
Zec 6: 12 is the man whose *n* is the Branch,

Zec 14: 9 one LORD, and his *n* the only *n*.
Mal 1: 6 O priests, who show contempt for my *n*.
Mt 1:21 and you are to give him the *n* Jesus,
6: 9 hallowed be your *n*,
18:20 or three come together in my *n*,
24: 5 For many will come in my *n*,
28:19 them in the *n* of the Father
Mk 9:41 gives you a cup of water in my *n*
Lk 11: 2 hallowed be your *n*,
Jn 10: 3 He calls his own sheep by *n*
14:13 I will do whatever you ask in my *n*,
16:24 asked for anything in my *n*.
Ac 2:21 on the *n* of the Lord will be saved.'
4:12 for there is no other *n*
Ro 10:13 "Everyone who calls on the *n*
Php 2: 9 him the *n* that is above every *n*,
2:10 at the *n* of Jesus every knee should
Col 3:17 do it all in the *n* of the Lord Jesus,
Heb 1: 4 as the *n* he has inherited is superior
Jas 5:14 him with oil in the *n* of the Lord.
1Jn 5:13 believe in the *n* of the Son of God
Rev 2:17 stone with a new *n* written on it,
3: 5 I will never blot out his *n*
3:12 I will also write on him my new *n*.
19:13 and his *n* is the Word of God.
20:15 If anyone's *n* is not found written

NAMES (NAME)

Ex 28: 9 engrave on them the *n* of the sons
Lk 10:20 but rejoice that your *n* are written
Php 4: 3 whose *n* are in the book of life.
Heb 12:23 whose *n* are written in heaven.
Rev 21:27 but only those whose *n* are written

NAOMI

Wife of Elimelech, mother-in-law of Ruth (Ru 1:2, 4). Left Bethlehem for Moab during famine (Ru 1:1). Returned a widow, with Ruth (Ru 1: 6-22). Advised Ruth to seek marriage with Boaz (Ru 2:17-3:4). Cared for Ruth's son Obed (Ru 4: 13-17).

NAPHTALI

Son of Jacob by Bilhah (Ge 30:8; 35:25; 1Ch 2: 2). Tribe of blessed (Ge 49:21; Dt 33:23), numbered (Nu 1:43; 26:50), allotted land (Jos 19:32-39; Eze 48:3), failed to fully possess (Jdg 1:33), supported Deborah (Jdg 4:10; 5:18), David (1Ch 12:34), 12,000 from (Rev 7:6).

NARROW

Mt 7:13 "Enter through the *n* gate.
7:14 and *n* the road that leads to life,

NATHAN

Prophet and chronicler of Israel's history (1Ch 29:29; 2Ch 9:29). Announced the Davidic covenant (2Sa 7; 1Ch 17). Denounced David's sin with Bathsheba (2Sa 12). Supported Solomon (1Ki 1).

NATHANAEL*

Apostle (Jn 1:45-49; 21:2). Probably also called Bartholomew (Mt 10:3).

NATION (NATIONS)

Ge 12: 2 "I will make you into a great *n*
Ex 19: 6 a kingdom of priests and a holy *n*.'
Dt 4: 7 What other *n* is so great
Jos 5: 8 And after the whole *n* had been
2Sa 7:23 one *n* on earth that God went out
Ps 33:12 Blessed is the *n* whose God is
Pr 11:14 For lack of guidance a *n* falls,
14:34 Righteousness exalts a *n*,
Isa 1: 4 will not take up sword
26: 2 that the righteous *n* may enter,
60:12 For the *n* or kingdom that will not
65: 1 To a *n* that did not call on my name
66: 8 a *n* be brought forth in a moment?
Mic 4: 3 will not take up sword
Mt 24: 7 *N* will rise against *n*,
Mk 13: 8 *N* will rise against *n*,
1Pe 2: 9 a royal priesthood, a holy *n*,
Rev 5: 9 and language and people and *n*.
7: 9 from every *n*, tribe, people
14: 6 to every *n*, tribe, language

NATIONS (NATION)

Ge 17: 4 You will be the father of many *n*.
18:18 and all *n* on earth will be blessed
Ex 19: 5 of all *n* you will be my treasured
Lev 20:26 apart from the *n* to be my own.
Dt 7: 1 drives out before you many *n*—
15: 6 You will rule over many *n*
Jdg 3: 1 These are the *n* the LORD left
2Ch 20: 6 rule over all the kingdoms of the *n*.
Ne 1: 8 I will scatter you among the *n*,
Ps 2: 1 Why do the *n* conspire
2: 8 I will make the *n* your inheritance,
9: 5 You have rebuked the *n*
22:28 and he rules over the *n*.
46:10 I will be exalted among the *n*,
47: 8 God reigns over the *n*;
66: 7 his eyes watch the *n*—
67: 2 your salvation among all *n*.
68:30 Scatter the *n* who delight in war.
72:17 All *n* will be blessed through him,
96: 3 Declare his glory among the *n*,
99: 2 he is exalted over all the *n*.
106: 35 but they mingled with the *n*
110: 6 He will judge the *n*, heaping up
113: 4 The LORD is exalted over all the *n*
Isa 2: 2 and all *n* will stream to it.
11:10 the *n* will rally to him,
12: 4 among the *n* what he has done,
40:15 Surely the *n* are like a drop
42: 1 and he will bring justice to the *n*.
51: 4 justice will become a light to the *n*.
52:15 so will he sprinkle many *n*,
56: 7 a house of prayer for all *n*.''
60: 3 *N* will come to your light,
66:18 and gather all *n* and tongues,
Jer 1: 5 you as a prophet to the *n*.''
3:17 and all *n* will gather in Jerusalem
31:10 "Hear the word of the LORD, O *n*;
33: 9 and honor before all *n*
46:28 I completely destroy all the *n*
Eze 22: 4 you an object of scorn to the *n*
34:13 I will bring them out from the *n*
36:23 *n* will know that I am the LORD,
37:22 and they will never again be two *n*
39:21 I will display my glory among the *n*
Hos 7: 8 "Ephraim mixes with the *n*;
Joel 2:17 a byword among the *n*,
3: 2 I will gather all *n*
Am 9:12 and all the *n* that bear my name,''
Zep 3: 8 I have decided to assemble the *n*,
Hag 2: 7 and the desired of all *n* will come,
Zec 8:13 an object of cursing among the *n*,
8:23 *n* will take firm hold of one Jew
9:10 He will proclaim peace to the *n*.
14: 2 I will gather all the *n* to Jerusalem
Mt 12:18 he will proclaim justice to the *n*.
24: 9 and you will be hated by all *n*
24:14 whole world as a testimony to all *n*,
25:32 All the *n* will be gathered
28:19 and make disciples of all *n*,
Mk 11:17 a house of prayer for all *n*'?
Ac 4:25 ''Why do the *n* rage
Ro 15:12 who will arise to rule over the *n*;
Gal 3: 8 All *n* will be blessed through you.''
1Ti 3:16 was preached among the *n*,
Rev 15: 4 All *n* will come
21:24 The *n* will walk by its light,
22: 2 are for the healing of the *n*.

NATURAL (NATURE)

Ro 6:19 you are weak in your *n* selves.
1Co 15:44 If there is a *n* body, there is

NATURE (NATURAL)

Ro 1:20 his eternal power and divine *n*—
7:18 lives in me, that is, in my sinful *n*.
8: 4 do not live according to the sinful *n*
8: 5 to the sinful *n* have their minds set
8: 8 by the sinful *n* cannot please God.
13:14 to gratify the desires of the sinful *n*.
Gal 5:13 freedom to indulge the sinful *n*;
5:19 The acts of the sinful *n* are obvious:
5:24 Jesus have crucified the sinful *n*
Php 2: 6 Who, being in very *n* God,
Col 3: 5 whatever belongs to your earthly *n*
2Pe 1: 4 you may participate in the divine *n*

NAZARENE* (NAZARETH)

Mt 2:23 prophets: ''He will be called a *N*.''
Mk 14:67 ''You also were with that *N*, Jesus,''
16: 6 ''You are looking for Jesus the *N*,
Ac 24: 5 He is a ringleader of the *N* sect and

NAZARETH (NAZARENE)

Mt 4:13 Leaving *N*, he went and lived
Lk 4:16 to *N*, where he had been brought
Jn 1:46 ''*N*! Can anything good come

NAZIRITE

Nu 6: 2 of separation to the LORD as a *N*,
Jdg 13: 7 because the boy will be a *N* of God

NEBO

Dt 34: 1 Then Moses climbed Mount *N*

NEBUCHADNEZZAR

Babylonian king. Subdued and exiled Judah (2Ki 24-25; 2Ch 36; Jer 39). Dreams interpreted by Daniel (Da 2; 4). Worshiped God (Da 3:28-29; 4:34-37).

NECESSARY*

Ac 1:21 Therefore it is *n* to choose one
Ro 13: 5 it is *n* to submit to the authorities,
2Co 9: 5 I thought it *n* to urge the brothers
Php 1:24 it is more *n* for you that I remain
2:25 But I think it is *n* to send back
Heb 8: 3 and so it was *n* for this one
9:16 it is *n* to prove the death
9:23 It was *n*, then, for the copies

NECK (STIFF-NECKED)

Pr 3:22 an ornament to grace your *n*.
6:21 fasten them around your *n*.
Mt 18: 6 a large millstone hung around his *n*

NECO

Pharaoh who killed Josiah (2Ki 23:29-30; 2Ch 35:20-22), deposed Jehoahaz (2Ki 23:33-35; 2Ch 36:3-4).

NEED (NEEDS NEEDY)

1Ki 8:59 Israel according to each day's *n*,
Ps 79: 8 for we are in desperate *n*.
116: 6 when I was in great *n*, he saved me.
142: 1 for I am in desperate *n*.''
Mt 6: 8 for your Father knows what you *n*
Lk 15:14 country, and he began to be in *n*.
Ac 2:45 they gave to anyone as he had *n*.
Ro 12:13 with God's people who are in *n*.
1Co 12:21 say to the hand, ''I don't *n* you!''
Eph 4:28 something to share with those in *n*.
1Ti 5: 3 to those widows who are really in *n*
Heb 4:16 grace to help us in our time of *n*.
1Jn 3:17 sees his brother in *n* but has no pity

NEEDLE

Mt 19:24 go through the eye of a *n*

NEEDS (NEED)

Isa 58:11 he will satisfy your *n*
Php 2:25 sent to take care of my *n*,
4:19 God will meet all your *n* according
Jas 2:16 does nothing about his physical *n*,

NEEDY (NEED)

Dt 15:11 toward the poor and *n* in your land.
1Sa 2: 8 and lifts the *n* from the ash heap;
Ps 35:10 and *n* from those who rob them.''
69:33 The LORD hears the *n*
72:12 he will deliver the *n* who cry out,
140: 12 and upholds the cause of the *n*.
Pr 14:21 blessed is he who is kind to the *n*.
14:31 to the *n* honors God.
22:22 and do not crush the *n* in court,
31: 9 defend the rights of the poor and *n*
31:20 and extends her hands to the *n*.
Mt 6: 2 ''So when you give to the *n*,

NEGLECT* (NEGLECTED)

Dt 12:19 Be careful not to *n* the Levites
14:27 not the Levites living
Ezr 4:22 Be careful not to *n* this matter.
Ne 10:39 We will not *n* the house of our God
Est 6:10 Do not *n* anything you have

Ps 119: 16 I will not *n* your word.
Lk 11: 42 you *n* justice and the love of God.
Ac 6: 2 for us to *n* the ministry of the word
1Ti 4: 14 Do not *n* your gift, which was

NEGLECTED (NEGLECT)

Mt 23: 23 But you have *n* the more important

NEHEMIAH

Cupbearer of Artaxerxes (Ne 2:1); governor of Israel (Ne 8:9). Returned to Jerusalem to rebuild walls (Ne 2-6). With Ezra, reestablished worship (Ne 8). Prayer confessing nation's sin (Ne 9). Dedicated wall (Ne 12).

NEIGHBOR'S (NEIGHBOR)

Ex 20: 16 give false testimony against your *n*.
20: 17 or anything that belongs to your *n*
Lev 19: 13 Do not defraud your *n* or rob him.
19: 17 Rebuke your *n* frankly
19: 18 but love your *n* as yourself.
Ps 15: 3 who does his *n* no wrong
Pr 3: 29 Do not plot harm against your *n*,
11: 12 who lacks judgment derides his *n*,
14: 21 He who despises his *n* sins,
16: 29 A violent man entices his *n*
24: 28 against your *n* without cause,
25: 18 gives false testimony against his *n*.
27: 10 better a *n* nearby than a brother far
27: 14 If a man loudly blesses his *n*
29: 5 Whoever flatters his *n*
Jer 31: 34 No longer will a man teach his *n*,
Zec 8: 17 do not plot evil against your *n*,
Mt 5: 43 Love your *n* and hate your enemy.'
19: 19 and 'love your *n* as yourself.' ''
Mk 12: 31 The second is this: 'Love your *n*
Lk 10: 27 and, 'Love your *n* as yourself.' ''
10: 29 who is my *n*?'' In reply Jesus said:
Ro 13: 9 "Love your *n* as yourself."
13: 10 Love does no harm to its *n*
15: 2 Each of us should please his *n*
Gal 5: 14 "Love your *n* as yourself."
Eph 4: 25 and speak truthfully to his *n*,
Heb 8: 11 No longer will a man teach his *n*,
Jas 2: 8 "Love your *n* as yourself,"

NEIGHBOR'S (NEIGHBOR)

Ex 20: 17 You shall not covet your *n* wife,
Dt 5: 21 not set your desire on your *n* house
19: 14 not move your *n* boundary stone
27: 17 who moves his *n* boundary stone.''
Pr 25: 17 Seldom set foot in your *n* house—

NESTS

Mt 8: 20 and birds of the air have *n*,

NET (NETS)

Pr 1: 17 How useless to spread a *n*
Hab 1: 15 he catches them in his *n*,
Mt 13: 47 of heaven is like a *n* that was let
Jn 21: 6 "Throw your *n* on the right side

NETS (NET)

Ps 141: 10 Let the wicked fall into their own *n*
Mt 4: 20 At once they left their *n*
Lk 5: 4 and let down the *n* for a catch.''

NEVER-FAILING*

Am 5: 24 righteousness like a *n* stream!

NEW

Ps 40: 3 He put a *n* song in my mouth,
98: 1 Sing to the LORD a *n* song,
Ecc 1: 9 there is nothing *n* under the sun.
Isa 42: 9 and *n* things I declare;
62: 2 you will be called by a *n* name
65: 17 *n* heavens and a *n* earth.
66: 22 ''As the *n* heavens and the *n* earth
Jer 31: 31 ''when I will make a *n* covenant
La 3: 23 They are *n* every morning;
Eze 11: 19 undivided heart and put a *n* spirit
18: 31 and get a *n* heart and a *n* spirit.
36: 26 give you a *n* heart and put a *n* spirit
Zep 3: 5 and every *n* day he does not fail,
Mt 9: 17 Neither do men pour *n* wine
Mk 16: 17 they will speak in *n* tongues;
Lk 5: 39 after drinking old wine wants the *n*
22: 20 ''This cup is the *n* covenant

Jn 13: 34 ''A *n* commandment I give you:
Ac 5: 20 the full message of this *n* life.''
Ro 6: 4 the Father, we too may live a *n* life.
1Co 5: 7 old yeast that you may be a *n* batch
11: 25 ''This cup is the *n* covenant
2Co 3: 6 as ministers of a *n* covenant—
5: 17 he is a *n* creation; the old has gone,
Gal 6: 15 what counts is a *n* creation.
Eph 4: 23 to be made *n* in the attitude
4: 24 and to put on the *n* self, created
Col 3: 10 and have put on the *n* self,
Heb 8: 8 when I will make a *n* covenant
9: 15 is the mediator of a *n* covenant,
10: 20 by a *n* and living way opened for us
12: 24 Jesus the mediator of a *n* covenant,
1Pe 1: 3 great mercy he has given us *n* birth
2Pe 3: 13 to a *n* heaven and a *n* earth,
1Jn 2: 8 Yet I am writing you a *n* command;
Rev 2: 17 stone with a *n* name written on it,
3: 12 the *n* Jerusalem, which is coming
21: 1 I saw a *n* heaven and a *n* earth,

NEWBORN (BEAR)

1Pe 2: 2 Like *n* babies, crave pure spiritual

NEWS

2Ki 7: 9 This is a day of good *n*
Ps 112: 7 He will have no fear of bad *n*;
Pr 15: 30 good *n* gives health to the bones.
25: 25 is good *n* from a distant land.
Isa 52: 7 the feet of those who bring good *n*,
61: 1 me to preach good *n* to the poor.
Na 1: 15 the feet of one who brings good *n*,
Mt 4: 23 preaching the good *n*
9: 35 preaching the good *n*
11: 5 the good *n* is preached to the poor.
Mk 1: 15 Repent and believe the good *n!*''
16: 15 preach the good *n* to all creation.
Lk 1: 19 and to tell you this good *n*.
2: 10 I bring you good *n*
3: 18 and preached the good *n* to them.
4: 43 ''I must preach the good *n*
8: 1 proclaiming the good *n*
16: 16 the good *n* of the kingdom
Ac 5: 42 proclaiming the good *n* that Jesus
10: 36 telling the good *n* of peace
14: 7 continued to preach the good *n*.
14: 21 They preached the good *n*
17: 18 preaching the good *n* about Jesus
Ro 10: 15 feet of those who bring good *n!*''

NICODEMUS*

Pharisee who visted Jesus at night (Jn 3). Argued fair treatment of Jesus (Jn 7:50-52). With Joseph, prepared Jesus for burial (Jn 19:38-42).

NIGHT (NIGHTS NIGHTTIME)

Ge 1: 5 and the darkness he called ''*n*.''
1: 16 and the lesser light to govern the *n*.
Ex 13: 21 and by *n* in a pillar of fire
14: 24 During the last watch of the *n*,
Dt 28: 66 filled with dread both *n* and day,
Jos 1: 8 and *n*, so that you may be careful
Job 35: 10 who gives songs in the *n*,
Ps 1: 2 on his law he meditates day and *n*.
19: 2 *n* after *n* they display knowledge.
42: 8 at *n* his song is with me—
63: 6 of you through the watches of the *n*
77: 6 I remembered my songs in the *n*.
90: 4 or like a watch in the *n*.
91: 5 You will not fear the terror of *n*,
119:148 through the watches of the *n*
121: 6 nor the moon by *n*.
136: 9 the moon and stars to govern the *n*;
Pr 31: 18 and her lamp does not go out at *n*.
Isa 21: 11 Watchman, what is left of the *n*?''
58: 10 and your will become like the *n*
Jer 33: 20 and my covenant with the *n*,
Lk 2: 8 watch over their flocks at *n*.
6: 12 and spent the *n* praying to God.
Jn 3: 2 He came to Jesus at *n* and said,
9: 4 *N* is coming, when no one can work
1Th 5: 2 Lord will come like a thief in the *n*.
5: 5 We do not belong to the *n*
Rev 21: 25 for there will be no *n* there.

NIGHTS (NIGHT)

Jnh 1: 17 the fish three days and three *n*.

Mt 4: 2 After fasting forty days and forty *n*
12: 40 three *n* in the belly of a huge fish,
2Co 6: 5 in hard work, sleepless *n*

NIGHTTIME* (NIGHT)

Zec 14: 7 or *n*— a day known to the LORD.

NIMROD

Ge 10: 9 ''Like *N*, a mighty hunter

NINEVEH

Jnh 1: 2 ''Go to the great city of *N*
Na 1: 1 An oracle concerning *N*.
Mt 12: 41 The men of *N* will stand up

NOAH

Righteous man (Eze 14:14, 20) called to build ark (Ge 6-8; Heb 11:7; 1Pe 3:20; 2Pe 2:5). God's covenant with (Ge 9:1-17). Drunkenness of (Ge 9: 18-23). Blessed sons, cursed Canaan (Ge 9:24-27).

NOBLE

Ru 3: 11 you are a woman of *n* character.
Ps 45: 1 My heart is stirred by a *n* theme
Pr 12: 4 of *n* character is her husband's
31: 10 A wife of *n* character who can find?
31: 29 ''Many women do *n* things,
Isa 32: 8 But the *n* man makes *n* plans,
Lk 8: 15 good soil stands for those with a *n*
Ro 9: 21 of clay some pottery for *n* purposes
Php 4: 8 whatever is *n*, whatever is right,
2Ti 2: 20 some are for *n* purposes

NOSTRILS

Ge 2: 7 and breathed into his *n* the breath
Ex 15: 8 By the blast of your *n*
Ps 18: 15 at the blast of breath from your *n*.

NOTE

Ac 4: 13 and they took *n* that these men had
Php 3: 17 take *n* of those who live according

NOTHING

2Sa 24: 24 offerings that cost me *n*.''
Ne 9: 21 in the desert; they lacked *n*,
Jer 32: 17 *N* is too hard for you
Jn 15: 5 apart from me you can do *n*.

NOURISH

Pr 10: 21 The lips of the righteous *n* many,

NULLIFY

Mt 15: 6 Thus you *n* the word of God
Ro 3: 31 Do we, then, *n* the law by this faith

OATH

Ex 33: 1 up to the land I promised on *o*
Nu 30: 2 or takes an *o* to obligate himself
Dt 6: 18 promised on *o* to your forefathers,
7: 8 and kept the *o* he swore
29: 12 you this day and sealing with an *o*,
Ps 95: 11 So I declared on *o* in my anger,
119:106 I have taken an *o* and confirmed it,
132: 11 The LORD swore an *o* to David,
Ecc 8: 2 because you took an *o* before God.
Mt 5: 33 'Do not break your *o*, but keep
Heb 7: 20 And it was not without an *o!*

OBADIAH

1. Believer who sheltered 100 prophets from Jezebel (1Ki 18:1-16).
2. Prophet against Edom (Ob 1).

OBEDIENCE* (OBEY)

Ge 49: 10 and the *o* of the nations is his.
Jdg 2: 17 of *o* to the LORD's commands.
1Ch 21: 19 So David went up in *o*
2Ch 31: 21 in *o* to the law and the commands,
Pr 30: 17 that scorns *o* to a mother,
Lk 23: 56 Sabbath in *o* to the commandment.
Ac 21: 24 but that you yourself are living in *o*
Ro 1: 5 to the *o* that comes from faith.
5: 19 also through the *o* of the one man
6: 16 to *o*, which leads to righteousness?
16: 19 Everyone has heard about your *o*,
2Co 9: 13 for the *o* that accompanies your
10: 6 once your *o* is complete.
Phm : 21 Confident of your *o*, I write to you,

Heb 5: 8 he learned *o* from what he suffered
1Pe 1: 2 for *o* to Jesus Christ and sprinkling
2Jn : 6 that we walk in *o* to his commands.

OBEDIENT* (OBEY)

Dt 30: 17 heart turns away and you are not *o*,
Isa 1: 19 If you are willing and *o*,
Lk 2: 51 with them and was *o* to them.
Ac 6: 7 of priests became *o* to the faith.
2Co 2: 9 if you would stand the test and be *o*
     7: 15 he remembers that you were all *o*,
     10: 5 thought to make it *o* to Christ.
Php 2: 8 and became *o* to death—
Tit 3: 1 to be *o*, to be ready
1Pe 1: 14 As *o* children, do not conform

OBEY (OBEDIENCE OBEDIENT OBEYED OBEYING OBEYS)

Ex 12: 24 ''*O* these instructions as a lasting
     19: 5 Now if you *o* me fully and keep my
     24: 7 the LORD has said; we will *o*.''
Lev 18: 4 You must *o* my laws and be careful
     25: 18 and be careful to *o* my laws,
Nu 15: 40 remember to *o* all my commands
Dt 5: 27 We will listen and *o*.''
     6: 3 careful to *o* so that it may go well
     6: 24 us to *o* all these decrees
     11: 13 if you faithfully *o* the commands I
     12: 28 to *o* all these regulations I am
     13: 4 Keep his commands and *o* him;
     21: 18 son who does not *o* his father
     28: 1 If you fully *o* the LORD your God
     28: 15 if you do not *o* the LORD your God
     30: 2 and *o* him with all your heart
     30: 10 if you *o* the LORD your God
     30: 14 and in your heart so you may *o* it.
     32: 46 children to *o* carefully all the words
Jos 1: 7 to *o* all the law my servant Moses
     22: 5 in all his ways, to *o* his commands,
     24: 24 the LORD our God and *o* him.''
1Sa 15: 22 To *o* is better than sacrifice,
1Ki 8: 61 by his decrees and *o* his commands
2Ki 17: 13 that I commanded your fathers to *o*
2Ch 34: 31 and to *o* the words of the covenant
Ne 1: 5 who love him and *o* his commands,
Ps 103: 8 and remember to *o* his precepts.
     103: 20 who *o* his word.
     119: 17 I will *o* your word.
     119: 34 and *o* it with all my heart.
     119: 57 I have promised to *o* your words.
     119: 67 but now I *o* your word.
     119:100 for I *o* your precepts.
     119:129 therefore I *o* them.
     119:167 I *o* your statutes,
Pr 5: 13 I would not *o* my teachers
Jer 7: 23 I gave them this command: *O* me,
     11: 4 '*O* me and do everything I
     11: 7 and again, saying, ''*O* me.''
     42: 6 we will *o* the LORD our God,
Da 9: 4 who love him and *o* his commands,
Mt 8: 27 the winds and the waves *o* him!''
     19: 17 to enter life, *o* the commandments
     28: 20 to *o* everything I have commanded
Lk 11: 28 hear the word of God and *o* it.''
Jn 14: 15 you will *o* what I command.
     14: 23 loves me, he will *o* my teaching.
     14: 24 not love me will not *o* my teaching.
     15: 10 If you *o* my commands, you will
Ac 5: 29 ''We must *o* God rather than men!
     5: 32 given to those who *o* him.''
Ro 2: 13 it is those who *o* the law who will
     6: 12 body so that you *o* its evil desires.
     6: 16 slaves to the one whom you *o*—
     6: 16 yourselves to someone to *o* him
     15: 18 in leading the Gentiles to *o* God
     16: 26 nations might believe and *o* him—
Gal 5: 3 obligated to *o* the whole law.
Eph 6: 1 *o* your parents in the Lord,
     6: 5 *o* your earthly masters with respect
Col 3: 20 *o* your parents in everything,
     3: 22 *o* your earthly masters
2Th 3: 14 anyone does not *o* our instruction
1Ti 3: 4 and see that his children *o* him
Heb 5: 9 eternal salvation for all who *o* him
     13: 17 *O* your leaders and submit
1Pe 4: 17 for those who do not *o* the gospel
1Jn 3: 24 Those who *o* his commands live
     5: 3 love for God: to *o* his commands

Rev 12: 17 those who *o* God's commandments
     14: 12 the saints who *o* God's

OBEYED (OBEY)

Ge 22: 18 blessed, because you have *o* me.''
Jos 1: 17 we fully *o* Moses, so we will obey
Ps 119: 4 that are to be fully *o*.
Da 9: 10 we have not *o* the LORD our God
Jnh 3: 3 Jonah *o* the word of the LORD
Mic 5: 15 the nations that have not *o* me.''
Jn 15: 10 as I have *o* my Father's commands
     15: 20 If they *o* my teaching, they will
     17: 6 and they have *o* your word.
Ac 7: 53 through angels but have not *o* it.''
Ro 6: 17 you wholeheartedly *o* the form
Php 2: 12 as you have always *o*— not only
Heb 11: 8 *o* and went, even though he did not
1Pe 3: 6 who *o* Abraham and called him her

OBEYING (OBEY)

1Sa 15: 22 as in *o* the voice of the LORD?
Ps 119: 5 steadfast in *o* your decrees!
Gal 5: 7 and kept you from *o* the truth?
1Pe 1: 22 purified yourselves by *o* the truth

OBEYS (OBEY)

Lev 18: 5 for the man who *o* them will live
Pr 19: 16 He who *o* instructions guards his
Eze 20: 11 for the man who *o* them will live
Jn 14: 21 has my commands and *o* them,
Ro 2: 27 and yet *o* the law will condemn you
1Jn 2: 5 if anyone *o* his word, God's love is

OBLIGATED (OBLIGATION)

Ro 1: 14 I am *o* both to Greeks
Gal 5: 3 himself be circumcised that he is *o*

OBLIGATION (OBLIGATED)

Ro 8: 12 Therefore, brothers, we have an *o*

OBSCENITY*

Eph 5: 4 Nor should there be *o*, foolish talk

OBSCURES*

Job 42: 3 'Who is this that *o* my counsel

OBSERVE (OBSERVING)

Ex 31: 13 'You must *o* my Sabbaths.
Lev 25: 2 the land itself must *o* a sabbath
Dt 4: 6 *O* them carefully, for this will show
     5: 12 ''*O* the Sabbath day
     8: 6 *O* the commands of the LORD
     11: 22 If you carefully *o* all these
     26: 16 carefully *o* them with all your heart
Ps 37: 37 the blameless, *o* the upright;

OBSERVING (OBSERVE)

Ro 3: 27 principle? On that of *o* the law?
Gal 2: 16 a man is not justified by *o* the law,
     3: 2 you receive the Spirit by *o* the law,
     3: 10 All who rely on *o* the law are

OBSOLETE

Heb 8: 13 he has made the first one *o*;

OBSTACLE* (OBSTACLES)

Ro 14: 13 or *o* in your brother's way.

OBSTACLES (OBSTACLE)

Ro 16: 17 put *o* in your way that are contrary

OBSTINATE

Isa 65: 2 hands to an *o* people,
Ro 10: 21 to a disobedient and *o* people.''

OBTAIN (OBTAINED OBTAINS)

Ro 11: 7 sought so earnestly it did not *o*,
2Ti 2: 10 they too may *o* the salvation that

OBTAINED (OBTAIN)

Ro 9: 30 not pursue righteousness, have *o* it,
Php 3: 12 Not that I have already *o* all this,
Heb 9: 12 having *o* eternal redemption.

OBTAINS* (OBTAIN)

Pr 12: 2 A good man *o* favor

OBVIOUS*

Mt 6: 18 so that it will not be *o*

Gal 5: 19 The acts of the sinful nature are *o*:
1Ti 5: 24 The sins of some men are *o*,
     5: 25 In the same way, good deeds are *o*,

OCCASIONS

Eph 6: 18 in the Spirit on all *o* with all kinds

OFFENDED (OFFENSE)

Pr 18: 19 An *o* brother is more unyielding

OFFENDERS* (OFFENSE)

1Co 6: 9 nor homosexual *o* nor thieves

OFFENSE (OFFENDED OFFENDERS OFFENSES OFFENSIVE)

Pr 17: 9 over an *o* promotes love,
     19: 11 it is to his glory to overlook an *o*.
Gal 5: 11 In that case the *o* of the cross has

OFFENSES (OFFENSE)

Isa 44: 22 swept away your *o* like a cloud,
     59: 12 For our *o* are many in your sight,
Eze 18: 30 Repent! Turn away from all your *o*;
     33: 10 ''Our *o* and sins weigh us down,

OFFENSIVE (OFFENSE)

Ps 139: 24 See if there is any *o* way in me,

OFFER (OFFERED OFFERING OFFERINGS OFFERS)

Ps 4: 5 *O* right sacrifices
     66: 2 *o* him glory and praise!
Ro 6: 13 Do not *o* the parts of your body
     12: 1 to *o* your bodies as living sacrifices,
Heb 9: 25 he enter heaven to *o* himself again
     13: 15 therefore, let us continually *o*

OFFERED (OFFER)

Isa 50: 6 I *o* my back to those who beat me,
1Co 9: 13 share in what is *o* on the altar?
     10: 20 of pagans are *o* to demons,
Heb 7: 27 once for all when he *o* himself.
     9: 14 the eternal Spirit *o* himself
     11: 4 By faith Abel *o* God a better
     11: 17 when God tested him, *o* Isaac
Jas 5: 15 prayer *o* in faith will make the sick

OFFERING (OFFER)

Ge 4: 3 of the soil as an *o* to the LORD.
     22: 2 a burnt *o* on one of the mountains I
     22: 8 provide the lamb for the burnt *o*,
Ex 29: 24 before the LORD as a wave *o*.
     29: 40 quarter of a hin of wine as a drink *o*.
Lev 1: 3 If the *o* is a burnt *o* from the herd,
     2: 4 '' 'If you bring a grain *o* baked
     3: 1 '' 'If someone's *o* is a fellowship *o*,
     4: 3 a sin *o* for the sin he has committed
     5: 15 It is a guilt *o*.
     7: 37 ordination *o* and the fellowship *o*,
     9: 24 and consumed the burnt *o*
     22: 18 to fulfill a vow or as a freewill *o*,
     22: 21 a vow or as a freewill *o*,
1Sa 1: 9 And Saul offered up the burnt *o*.
1Ch 21: 26 from heaven on the altar of burnt *o*.
2Ch 7: 1 and consumed the burnt *o*
Ps 40: 6 Sacrifice and *o* you did not desire,
     116: 17 I will sacrifice a thank *o* to you
Isa 53: 10 the LORD makes his life a guilt *o*,
Mt 5: 23 if you are *o* your gift at the altar
Ro 8: 3 likeness of sinful man to be a sin *o*.
Eph 5: 2 as a fragrant *o* and sacrifice to God.
Php 2: 17 I am being poured out like a drink *o*
     4: 18 are a fragrant *o*, an acceptable
2Ti 4: 6 being poured out like a drink *o*,
Heb 10: 5 ''Sacrifice and *o* you did not desire,
1Pe 2: 5 *o* spiritual sacrifices acceptable

OFFERINGS (OFFER)

1Sa 15: 22 Does the LORD delight in burnt *o*
2Ch 35: 7 and goats for the Passover *o*,
Isa 1: 13 Stop bringing meaningless *o*!
Hos 6: 6 of God rather than burnt *o*.
Mal 3: 8 'In this and *o*.
Mk 12: 33 is more important than all burnt *o*
Heb 10: 8 First he said, ''Sacrifices and *o*,

OFFERS (OFFER)

Heb 10: 11 and again he *o* the same sacrifices,

OFFICER (OFFICIALS)

2Ti   2:   4 wants to please his commanding *o.*

OFFICIALS (OFFICER)

Ex   5: 21 a stench to Pharaoh and his *o.*
Pr   17: 26 or to flog *o* for their integrity.
    29: 12 all his *o* become wicked.

OFFSPRING

Ge   3: 15 and between your *o* and hers;
    12:   7 "To your *o* I will give this land."
    13: 16 I will make your *o* like the dust
    26:   4 and through your *o* all nations
    28: 14 blessed through you and your *o.*
Ex   13:   2 The first *o* of every womb
Ru   4: 12 Through the *o* the LORD gives
Isa   44:   3 I will pour out my Spirit on your *o,*
    53: 10 he will see his *o* and prolong his
Ac   3: 25 'Through your *o* all peoples
    17: 28 own poets have said, 'We are his *o.'*
    17: 29 "Therefore since we are God's *o,*
Ro   4: 18 said to him, "So shall your *o* be."
    9:   8 who are regarded as Abraham's *o.*

OG

Nu   21: 33 *O* king of Bashan and his whole
Ps 136: 20 and *O* king of Bashan—

OIL

Ex   29:   7 Take the anointing *o* and anoint
    30: 25 It will be the sacred anointing *o.*
Dt   14: 23 tithe of your grain, new wine and *o,*
1Sa 10:   1 Then Samuel took a flask of *o*
    16: 13 So Samuel took the horn of *o*
1Ki 17: 16 and the jug of *o* did not run dry,
2Ki   4:   6 Then the *o* stopped flowing.
Ps   23:   5 You anoint my head with *o;*
    45:   7 by anointing you with the *o* of joy.
    104: 15 *o* to make his face shine,
    133:   2 It is like precious *o* poured
Pr   21: 17 loves wine and *o* will never be
Isa   1:   6 or soothed with *o.*
    61:   3 the *o* of gladness
Mt   25:   3 but did not take any *o* with them.
Heb   1:   9 by anointing you with the *o* of joy.''

OLIVE (OLIVES)

Ge   8: 11 beak was a freshly plucked *o* leaf!
Jdg   9:   8 said to the *o* tree, 'Be our king.'
Jer   11: 16 LORD called you a thriving *o* tree
Zec   4:   3 Also there are two *o* trees by it,
Ro   11: 17 and you, though a wild *o* shoot,
    11: 24 of an *o* tree that is wild by nature,
Rev 11:   4 These are the two *o* trees

OLIVES (OLIVE)

Zec 14:   4 stand on the Mount of *O,*
Mt   24:   3 sitting on the Mount of *O,*
Jas   3: 12 a fig tree bear *o,* or a grapevine bear

OMEGA

Rev   1:   8 "I am the Alpha and the *O,*"
    21:   6 I am the Alpha and the *O,*
    22: 13 I am the Alpha and the *O,*

OMIT*

Jer 26:   2 I command you; do not *o* a word.

OMRI

King of Israel (1Ki 16:21-26).

ONESIMUS*

Col   4:   9 He is coming with *O,* our faithful
Phm   : 10 I appeal to you for my son *O,*

ONESIPHORUS*

2Ti   1: 16 mercy to the household of *O,*
    4: 19 Aquila and the household of *O.*

ONIONS*

Nu   11:   5 melons, leeks, *o* and garlic.

ONYX

Ex   28:   9 "Take two *o* stones and engrave
    28: 20 in the fourth row a chrysolite, an *o*

OPENHANDED* (HAND)

Dt   15:   8 Rather be *o* and freely lend him

Dt   15: 11 you to be *o* toward your brothers

OPINIONS*

1Ki 18: 21 will you waver between two *o?*
Pr   18:   2 but delights in airing his own *o.*

OPPONENTS (OPPOSE)

Pr   18: 18 and keeps strong *o* apart.

OPPORTUNE (OPPORTUNITY)

Lk   4: 13 he left him until an *o* time.

OPPORTUNITY* (OPPORTUNE)

1Sa 18: 21 "Now you have a second *o*
Jer 46: 17 he has missed his *o.'*
Mt   26: 16 watched for an *o* to hand him over.
Mk 14: 11 So he watched for an *o* to hand him
Lk   22:   6 and watched for an *o* to hand Jesus
Ac   25: 16 and has had an *o* to defend himself
Ro   7:   8 seizing the *o* afforded
    7: 11 seizing the *o* afforded
1Co 16: 12 but he will go when he has the *o.*
2Co   5: 12 are giving you an *o* to take pride
    11: 12 from under those who want an *o*
Gal   6: 10 as we have *o,* let us do good
Eph   5: 16 making the most of every *o,*
Php   4: 10 but you had no *o* to show it.
Col   4:   5 make the most of every *o.*
1Ti   5: 14 to give the enemy no *o* for slander.
Heb 11: 15 they would have had *o* to return.

OPPOSE (OPPONENTS OPPOSED OPPOSES OPPOSING OPPOSITION)

Ex   23: 22 and will *o* those who *o* you.
1Sa   2: 10 those who *o* the LORD will be
Job 23: 13 he stands alone, and who can *o* him
Ac   11: 17 I to think that I could *o* God?''
2Ti   2: 25 Those who *o* him he must gently
Tit   1:   9 doctrine and refute those who *o* it.
    2:   8 so that those who *o* you may be

OPPOSED (OPPOSE)

Gal   2: 11 to Antioch, I *o* him to his face,
    3: 21 therefore, *o* to the promises of God

OPPOSES (OPPOSE)

Jas   4:   6 "God *o* the proud
1Pe   5:   5 because, "God *o* the proud

OPPOSING (OPPOSE)

1Ti   6: 20 the *o* ideas of what is falsely called

OPPOSITION (OPPOSE)

Heb 12:   3 Consider him who endured such *o*

OPPRESS (OPPRESSED OPPRESSES OPPRESSION OPPRESSOR)

Ex   1: 11 masters over them to *o* them
    22: 21 "Do not mistreat an alien or *o* him,
Isa   3:   5 People will *o* each other—
Eze 22: 29 they *o* the poor and needy
Da   7: 25 the Most High and *o* his saints
Am   5: 12 You *o* the righteous and take bribes
Zec   7: 10 Do not *o* the widow
Mal   3:   5 who *o* the widows

OPPRESSED (OPPRESS)

Jdg   2: 18 as they groaned under those who *o*
Ps   9:   9 The LORD is a refuge for the *o,*
    82:   3 the rights of the poor and *o.*
    146:   7 He upholds the cause of the *o*
Pr   16: 19 in spirit and among the *o*
    31:   5 and deprive all the *o* of their rights.
Isa   1: 17 encourage the *o.*
    53:   7 He was *o* and afflicted,
    58: 10 and satisfy the needs of the *o,*
Zec 10:   2 *o* for lack of a shepherd.
Lk   4: 18 to release the *o,*

OPPRESSES (OPPRESS)

Pr   14: 31 He who *o* the poor shows contempt
    22: 16 He who *o* the poor
Eze 18: 12 He *o* the poor and needy.

OPPRESSION (OPPRESS)

Ps   12:   5 "Because of the *o* of the weak
    72: 14 He will rescue them from *o*
    119:134 Redeem me from the *o* of men,
Isa 53:   8 By *o* and judgment he was taken

Isa   58:   9 "If you do away with the yoke of *o,*

OPPRESSOR (OPPRESS)

Ps   72:   4 he will crush the *o.*
Isa   51: 13 For where is the wrath of the *o?*
Jer   22:   3 hand of his *o* the one who has been

ORDAINED

Ps   8:   2 you have *o* praise
    111:   9 he *o* his covenant forever—
    139: 16 All the days *o* for me
Eze 28: 14 for so I *o* you.
Hab   1: 12 you have *o* them to punish.
Mt   21: 16 you have *o* praise'?''

ORDER (ORDERLY ORDERS)

Nu   9: 23 They obeyed the LORD's *o,*
Ps 110:   4 in the *o* of Melchizedek."
Heb   5: 10 priest in the *o* of Melchizedek.
    9: 10 until the time of the new *o.*
Rev 21:   4 for the old *o* of things has passed

ORDERLY (ORDER)

1Co 14: 40 done in a fitting and *o* way.
Col   2:   5 and delight to see how *o* you are

ORDERS (ORDER)

Mk   1: 27 He even gives *o* to evil spirits
    3: 12 But he gave them strict *o* not
    9:   9 Jesus gave them *o* not

ORDINARY

Ac   4: 13 that they were unschooled, *o* men,

ORGIES*

Ro   13: 13 not in *o* and drunkenness,
Gal   5: 21 drunkenness, *o,* and the like.
1Pe   4:   3 *o,* carousing and detestable

ORIGIN (ORIGINATE ORIGINS)

2Pe   1: 21 For prophecy never had its *o*

ORIGINATE* (ORIGIN)

1Co 14: 36 Did the word of God *o* with you?

ORIGINS* (ORIGIN)

Mic   5:   2 whose *o* are from of old,

ORNAMENT* (ORNAMENTED)

Pr   3: 22 an *o* to grace your neck.
    25: 12 of gold or an *o* of fine gold

ORNAMENTED (ORNAMENT)

Ge 37:   3 and he made a richly *o* robe for him

ORPHAN* (ORPHANS)

Ex   22: 22 advantage of a widow or an *o.*

ORPHANS (ORPHAN)

Jn   14: 18 will not leave you as *o;* I will come
Jas   1: 27 to look after *o* and widows

OTHNIEL

Nephew of Caleb (Jos 15:15-19; Jdg 1:12-15).
Judge who freed Israel from Aram (Jdg 3:7-11).

OUTBURSTS*

2Co 12: 20 jealousy, *o* of anger, factions,

OUTCOME

Heb 13:   7 Consider the *o* of their way of life
1Pe   4: 17 what will the *o* be for those who do

OUTNUMBER

Ps 139: 18 they would *o* the grains of sand.

OUTSIDERS*

Col   4:   5 wise in the way you act toward *o;*
1Th   4: 12 daily life may win the respect of *o,*
1Ti   3:   7 also have a good reputation with *o,*

OUTSTANDING

SS   5: 10 *o* among ten thousand.
Ro   13:   8 no debt remain *o,*

OUTSTRETCHED

Ex   6:   6 and will redeem you with an *o* arm
Dt   4: 34 by a mighty hand and an *o* arm,
    5: 15 with a mighty hand and an *o* arm.

OUTWEIGHS

1Ki 8: 42 your mighty hand and your *o* arm
Ps 136: 12 with a mighty hand and *o* arm;
Jer 27: 5 and *o* arm I made the earth
       32: 17 by your great power and *o* arm.
Eze 20: 33 an *o* arm and with outpoured wrath

OUTWEIGHS (WEIGH)

2Co 4: 17 an eternal glory that far *o* them all.

OUTWIT*

2Co 2: 11 in order that Satan might not *o* us.

OVERAWED* (AWE)

Ps 49: 16 Do not be *o* when a man grows rich

OVERBEARING*

Tit 1: 7 not *o*, not quick-tempered,

OVERCAME (OVERCOME)

Rev 3: 21 as I *o* and sat down with my Father
      12: 11 They *o* him

OVERCOME (OVERCAME OVERCOMES)

Mt 16: 18 and the gates of Hades will not *o* it.
Mk   9: 24 I do believe; help me *o* my unbelief
Lk 10: 19 to *o* all the power of the enemy;
Jn 16: 33 But take heart! I have *o* the world.''
Ro 12: 21 Do not be *o* by evil, but *o* evil
2Pe 2: 20 and are again entangled in it and *o*,
1Jn 2: 13 because you have *o* the evil one.
      4: 4 are from God and have *o* them,
      5: 4 is the victory that has *o* the world,
Rev 17: 14 but the Lamb will *o* them

OVERCOMES* (OVERCOME)

1Jn 5: 4 born of God *o* the world.
      5: 5 Who is it that *o* the world?
Rev 2: 7 To him who *o*, I will give the right
      2: 11 He who *o* will not be hurt at all
      2: 17 To him who *o*, I will give some
      2: 26 To him who *o* and does my will
      3: 5 He who *o* will, like them, be
      3: 12 Him who *o* I will make a pillar
      3: 21 To him who *o*, I will give the right
     21: 7 He who *o* will inherit all this,

OVERFLOW (OVERFLOWING OVERFLOWS)

Ps 65: 11 and your carts *o* with abundance.
   119:171 May my lips *o* with praise,
La   1: 16 and my eyes *o* with tears.
Mt 12: 34 out of the *o* of the heart the mouth
Lk   6: 45 out of the *o* of his heart his mouth
Ro   5: 5 Jesus Christ, *o* to them? Many! Again,
      15: 13 so that you may *o* with hope
2Co 4: 15 to *o* to the glory of God.
1Th 3: 12 *o* for each other and for everyone

OVERFLOWING (OVERFLOW)

Pr   3: 10 then your barns will be filled to *o*,
2Co 8: 2 their *o* joy and their extreme
      9: 12 *o* in many expressions of thanks
Col 2: 7 as you were taught, and *o*

OVERFLOWS* (OVERFLOW)

Ps 23: 5 my cup *o*.
2Co 1: 5 also through Christ our comfort *o*.

OVERJOYED* (JOY)

Da   6: 23 The king was *o* and gave orders
Mt   2: 10 they saw the star, they were *o*.
Jn 20: 20 The disciples were *o*
Ac 12: 14 she was so *o* she ran back
1Pe 4: 13 so that you may be *o*

OVERLOOK

Pr 19: 11 it is to his glory to *o* an offense.

OVERSEER* (OVERSEERS)

Pr   6: 7 no *o* or ruler,
1Ti 3: 1 anyone sets his heart on being an *o*,
      3: 2 Now the *o* must be above reproach,
Tit 1: 7 Since an *o* is entrusted
1Pe 2: 25 returned to the Shepherd and *O*

OVERSEERS* (OVERSEER)

Ac 20: 28 the Holy Spirit has made you *o*.
Php 1: 1 together with the *o* and deacons:

1Pe 5: 2 as *o*— not because you must,

OVERSHADOW* (OVERSHADOWING)

Lk   1: 35 power of the Most High will *o* you.

OVERSHADOWING (OVERSHADOW)

Ex 25: 20 wings spread upward, *o* the cover
Heb 9: 5 the glory, *o* the atonement cover.

OVERTHROW (OVERTHROWS)

2Th 2: 8 whom the Lord Jesus will *o*

OVERTHROWS (OVERTHROW)

Pr 13: 6 but wickedness *o* the sinner.
Isa 44: 25 who *o* the learning of the wise

OVERWHELMED (OVERWHELMING)

2Sa 22: 5 the torrents of destruction *o* me.
1Ki 10: 5 temple of the LORD, she was *o*.
Ps 38: 4 My guilt has *o* me
      65: 3 When we were *o* by sins,
Mt 26: 38 ''My soul is *o* with sorrow
Mk   7: 37 People were *o* with amazement.
      9: 15 they were *o* with wonder
2Co 2: 7 so that he will not be *o*

OVERWHELMING (OVERWHELMED)

Pr 27: 4 Anger is cruel and fury *o*,
Isa 10: 22 *o* and righteous.
      28: 15 When an *o* scourge sweeps by,

OWE

Ro 13: 7 If you *o* taxes, pay taxes; if revenue
Phm   : 19 to mention that you *o* me your very

OWNER'S (OWNERSHIP)

Isa 1: 3 the donkey his *o* manger,

OWNERSHIP* (OWNER'S)

2Co 1: 22 He anointed us, set his seal of *o*

OX (OXEN)

Dt 25: 4 Do not muzzle an *o*
Isa 11: 7 and the lion will eat straw like the *o*
Eze 1: 10 and on the left the face of an *o*;
Lk 13: 15 of you on the Sabbath untie his *o*
1Co 9: 9 ''Do not muzzle an *o*
1Ti 5: 18 ''Do not muzzle the *o*
Rev 4: 7 second was like an *o*, the third had

OXEN (OX)

1Ki 19: 20 Elisha then left his *o* and ran
Lk 14: 19 ''I have just bought five yoke of *o*,

PAGAN (PAGANS)

Mt 18: 17 as you would a *p* or a tax collector.
Lk 12: 30 For the *p* world runs

PAGANS* (PAGAN)

Isa 2: 6 and clasp hands with *p*.
Mt   5: 47 Do not even *p* do that? Be perfect,
      6: 7 do not keep on babbling like *p*,
      6: 32 For the *p* run after all these things,
1Co 5: 1 that does not occur even among *p*:
     10: 20 but the sacrifices of *p* are offered
     12: 2 You know that when you were *p*
1Pe 2: 12 such good lives among the *p* that,
      4: 3 in the past doing what *p* choose
3Jn   : 7 receiving no help from the *p*.

PAID (PAY)

Isa 40: 2 that her sin has been *p* for,
Zec 11: 12 So they *p* me thirty pieces of silver.

PAIN (PAINFUL PAINS)

Ge   3: 16 with *p* you will give birth
      6: 6 and his heart was filled with *p*.
Job 6: 10 my joy in unrelenting *p*—
      33: 19 may be chastened on a bed of *p*
Jer 4: 19 I writhe in *p*.
      15: 18 Why is my *p* unending
Mt   4: 24 suffering severe *p*,
Jn 16: 21 woman giving birth to a child has *p*
1Pe 2: 19 up under the *p* of unjust suffering
Rev 21: 4 or mourning or crying or *p*,

PAINFUL (PAIN)

Ge   3: 17 through *p* toil you will eat of it
      5: 29 and *p* toil of our hands caused

Job 6: 25 How *p* are honest words!
Eze 28: 24 neighbors who are *p* briers
2Co 2: 1 I would not make another *p* visit
Heb 12: 11 seems pleasant at the time, but *p*.
1Pe 4: 12 at the *p* trial you are suffering,

PAINS (PAIN)

Ge   3: 16 ''I will greatly increase your *p*
Mt 24: 8 these are the beginning of birth *p*.
Ro   8: 22 as in the *p* of childbirth right up
Gal 4: 19 again in the *p* of childbirth
1Th 5: 3 as labor *p* on a pregnant woman,

PAIRS

Ge   7: 8 *P* of clean and unclean animals,

PALACE (PALACES)

2Sa 7: 2 ''Here I am, living in a *p* of cedar,
Jer 22: 6 is what the LORD says about the *p*
     22: 13 ''Woe to him who builds his *p*

PALACES (PALACE)

Mt 11: 8 wear fine clothes are in kings' *p*.
Lk   7: 25 and indulge in luxury are in *p*.

PALE

Isa 29: 22 no longer will their faces grow *p*.
Jer 30: 6 every face turned deathly *p*?
Da 10: 8 my face turned deathly *p*
Rev 6: 8 and there before me was a *p* horse!

PALM (PALMS)

Jn 12: 13 They took *p* branches and went out
Rev 7: 9 and were holding *p* branches

PALMS (PALM)

Isa 49: 16 you on the *p* of my hands;

PAMPERS*

Pr 29: 21 If a man *p* his servant from youth,

PANIC

Dt 20: 3 or give way to *p* before them.
1Sa 14: 15 It was a *p* sent by God.
Eze 7: 7 there is *p*, not joy,
Zec 14: 3 by the LORD with great *p*.

PANTS

Ps 42: 1 As the deer *p* for streams of water,

PARABLES

    See also JESUS: Parables
Ps 78: 2 I will open my mouth in *p*,
Mt 13: 35 ''I will open my mouth in *p*,
Lk   8: 10 but to others I speak in *p*, so that,

PARADISE*

Lk 23: 43 today you will be with me in *p*.''
2Co 12: 4 God knows—was caught up to *p*.
Rev 2: 7 of life, which is in the *p* of God.

PARALYTIC

Mt   9: 2 Some men brought to him a *p*,
Mk   2: 3 bringing to him a *p*, carried by four
Ac   9: 33 a *p* who had been bedridden

PARCHED

Ps 143: 6 my soul thirsts for you like a *p* land.

PARCHMENTS*

2Ti 4: 13 and my scrolls, especially the *p*.

PARDON* (PARDONED PARDONS)

2Ch 30: 18 *p* everyone who sets his heart
Job 7: 21 Why do you not *p* my offenses
Isa 55: 7 and to our God, for he will freely *p*.
Joel 3: 21 I will *p*.''

PARDONED* (PARDON)

Nu 14: 19 as you have *p* them from the time
Joel 3: 21 bloodguilt, which I have not *p*.

PARDONS* (PARDON)

Mic 7: 18 who *p* sin and forgives

PARENTS

Pr 17: 6 and *p* are the pride of their children
     19: 14 wealth are inherited from *p*,
Mt 10: 21 children will rebel against their *p*

PARTAKE

Lk 18: 29 left home or wife or brothers or *p*
   21: 16 You will be betrayed even by *p*, brothers
Jn 9: 3 Neither this man nor his *p* sinned,''
Ro 1: 30 they disobey their *p*; they are
2Co 12: 14 for their *p*, but *p* for their children.
Eph 6: 1 Children, obey your *p* in the Lord,
Col 3: 20 obey your *p* in everything,
1Ti 5: 4 repaying their *p* and grandparents,
2Ti 3: 2 disobedient to their *p*, ungrateful,

PARTAKE*

1Co 10: 17 for we all *p* of the one loaf.

PARTIAL* (PARTIALITY)

Pr 18: 5 It is not good to be *p* to the wicked

PARTIALITY (PARTIAL)

Lev 19: 15 do not show *p* to the poor
Dt 1: 17 Do not show *p* in judging;
   10: 17 who shows no *p* and accepts no
   16: 19 Do not pervert justice or show *p*.
2Ch 19: 7 our God there is no injustice or *p*
Job 32: 21 I will show *p* to no one,
   34: 19 who shows no *p* to princes
Pr 24: 23 To show *p* in judging is not good:
Mal 2: 9 have shown *p* in matters of the law
Lk 20: 21 and that you do not show *p*
1Ti 5: 21 keep these instructions without *p*,

PARTICIPANTS (PARTICIPATE)

1Co 10: 20 you to be *p* with demons.

PARTICIPATE (PARTICIPANTS PARTICIPATION)

1Pe 4: 13 rejoice that you *p* in the sufferings
2Pe 1: 4 that through them you may *p*

PARTICIPATION (PARTICIPATE)

1Co 10: 16 is not the bread that we break a *p*

PARTNER (PARTNERS PARTNERSHIP)

Pr 2: 17 who has left the *p* of her youth
Mal 2: 14 though she is your *p*, the wife
1Pe 3: 7 them with respect as the weaker *p*

PARTNERS (PARTNER)

Eph 5: 7 Therefore do not be *p* with them.

PARTNERSHIP* (PARTNER)

Php 1: 5 because of your *p* in the gospel

PASS (PASSED PASSER-BY PASSING)

Ex 12: 13 and when I see the blood, I will *p*
   33: 19 goodness to *p* in front of you,
1Ki 9: 8 all who *p* by will be appalled
   19: 11 for the Lord is about to *p* by.''
Ps 90: 10 for they quickly *p*, and we fly away.
   105: 19 till what he foretold came to *p*,
Isa 31: 5 he will '*p* over' it and will rescue it
   43: 2 When you *p* through the waters,
   62: 10 *P* through, *p* through the gates!
Jer 22: 8 ''People from many nations will *p*
La 1: 12 to you, all you who *p* by?
Da 7: 14 dominion that will not *p* away,
Am 5: 17 for I will *p* through your midst,''
Mt 24: 34 will certainly not *p* away
   24: 35 Heaven and earth will *p* away,
Mk 13: 31 Heaven and earth will *p* away,
Lk 21: 33 Heaven and earth will *p* away,
1Co 13: 8 there is knowledge, it will *p* away.
Jas 1: 10 he will *p* away like a wild flower.
1Jn 2: 17 The world and its desires *p* away,

PASSED (PASS)

Ge 15: 17 a blazing torch appeared and *p*
Ex 33: 22 you with my hand until I have *p* by.
2Ch 21: 20 He *p* away, to no one's regret,
Ps 57: 1 wings until the disaster has *p*.
Lk 10: 32 saw him, *p* by on the other side.
1Co 15: 3 For what I received I *p* on to you
Heb 11: 29 By faith the people *p*

PASSER-BY* (PASS)

Pr 26: 10 is he who hires a fool or any *p*.
   26: 17 is a *p* who meddles

PASSING (PASS)

1Co 7: 31 world in its present form is *p* away.

1Jn 2: 8 because the darkness is *p*

PASSION* (PASSIONATE PASSIONS)

Hos 7: 6 Their *p* smolders all night;
1Co 7: 9 better to marry than to burn with *p*.

PASSIONATE* (PASSION)

1Th 4: 5 not in *p* lust like the heathen,

PASSIONS* (PASSION)

Ro 7: 5 the sinful *p* aroused
Gal 5: 24 crucified the sinful nature with its *p*
Tit 2: 12 to ungodliness and worldly *p*,
   3: 3 and enslaved by all kinds of *p*

PASSOVER

Ex 12: 11 Eat it in haste; it is the Lord's *P*.
Nu 9: 2 Have the Israelites celebrate the *P*
Dt 16: 1 celebrate the *P* of the Lord your
Jos 5: 10 the Israelites celebrated the *P*.
2Ki 23: 21 ''Celebrate the *P* to the Lord
Ezr 6: 19 the exiles celebrated the *P*.
Mk 14: 12 customary to sacrifice the *P* lamb,
Lk 22: 1 called the *P*, was approaching,
1Co 5: 7 our *P* lamb, has been sacrificed.
Heb 11: 28 he kept the *P* and the sprinkling

PAST

Isa 43: 18 do not dwell on the *p*.
   65: 16 For the *p* troubles will be forgotten
Ro 15: 4 in the *p* was written to teach us,
   16: 25 the mystery hidden for long ages *p*,
Eph 3: 9 which for ages *p* was kept hidden
Heb 1: 1 In the *p* God spoke

PASTORS*

Eph 4: 11 and some to be *p* and teachers,

PASTURE (PASTURES)

Ps 37: 3 dwell in the land and enjoy safe *p*.
   95: 7 and we are the people of his *p*,
   100: 3 we are his people, the sheep of his *p*
Jer 50: 7 against the Lord, their true *p*,
Eze 34: 13 I will *p* them on the mountains
Zec 11: 4 '*P* the flock marked for slaughter.
Jn 10: 9 come in and go out, and find *p*.

PASTURES (PASTURE)

Ps 23: 2 He makes me lie down in green *p*,

PATCH

Jer 10: 5 Like a scarecrow in a melon *p*,
Mt 9: 16 No one sews a *p* of unshrunk cloth

PATH (PATHS)

Ps 16: 11 known to me the *p* of life;
   27: 11 lead me in a straight *p*
   119: 32 I run in the *p* of your commands,
   119:105 and a light for my *p*.
Pr 2: 9 and fair—every good *p*.
   12: 28 along that *p* is immortality.
   15: 10 awaits him who leaves the *p*;
   15: 19 the *p* of the upright is a highway.
   15: 24 The *p* of life leads upward
   21: 16 from the *p* of understanding
Isa 26: 7 The *p* of the righteous is level;
Jer 31: 9 on a level *p* where they will not
Mt 13: 4 fell along the *p*, and the birds came
Lk 1: 79 to guide our feet into the *p* of peace
2Co 6: 3 no stumbling block in anyone's *p*.

PATHS (PATH)

Ps 23: 3 He guides me in *p* of righteousness
   25: 4 teach me your *p*;
Pr 2: 13 who leave the straight *p*
   3: 6 and he will make your *p* straight.
   4: 11 and lead you along straight *p*.
   4: 26 Make level *p* for your feet
   5: 21 and he examines all his *p*.
   8: 20 along the *p* of justice,
   22: 5 In the *p* of the wicked lie thorns
Isa 2: 3 so that we may walk in his *p*.''
Jer 6: 16 ask for the ancient *p*,
Mic 4: 2 so that we may walk in his *p*.''
Mt 3: 3 make straight *p* for him.' ''
Ac 2: 28 to me the *p* of life;
Ro 11: 33 and his *p* beyond tracing out!
Heb 12: 13 ''Make level *p* for your feet,''

PATIENCE* (PATIENT)

Pr 19: 11 A man's wisdom gives him *p*;
   25: 15 Through a *p* a ruler can be persuaded
Ecc 7: 8 and *p* is better than pride.
Isa 7: 13 Is it not enough to try the *p* of men?
   7: 13 Will you try the *p* of my God also?
Ro 2: 4 and *p*, not realizing that God's
   9: 22 bore with great *p* the objects
2Co 6: 6 understanding, *p* and kindness;
Gal 5: 22 joy, peace, *p*, kindness, goodness,
Col 1: 11 may have great endurance and *p*,
   3: 12 humility, gentleness and *p*.
1Ti 1: 16 Jesus might display his unlimited *p*
2Ti 3: 10 my purpose, faith, *p*, love,
   4: 2 with great *p* and careful instruction
Heb 6: 12 *p* inherit what has been promised.
Jas 5: 10 as an example of *p* in the face
2Pe 3: 15 that our Lord's *p* means salvation,

PATIENT* (PATIENCE PATIENTLY)

Ne 9: 30 For many years you were *p*
Job 6: 11 What prospects, that I should be *p*?
Pr 14: 29 A man has great understanding,
   15: 18 but a *p* man calms a quarrel.
   16: 32 Better a *p* man than a warrior,
Mt 18: 26 'Be *p* with me,' he begged,
   18: 29 'Be *p* with me,' and I will pay you
Ro 12: 12 Be joyful in hope, *p* in affliction,
1Co 13: 4 Love is *p*, love is kind.
2Co 1: 6 produces in you *p* endurance
Eph 4: 2 humble and gentle; be *p*,
1Th 5: 14 help the weak, be *p* with everyone.
Jas 5: 7 Be *p*, then, brothers,
   5: 7 and how *p* he is for the autumn
   5: 8 You too, be *p* and stand firm,
2Pe 3: 9 He is *p* with you, not wanting
Rev 1: 9 *p* endurance that are ours in Jesus,
   13: 10 This calls for *p* endurance
   14: 12 This calls for *p* endurance

PATIENTLY* (PATIENT)

Ps 37: 7 still before the Lord and wait *p*
   40: 1 I waited *p* for the Lord;
Isa 38: 13 I waited *p* till dawn,
Hab 3: 16 Yet I will wait *p* for the day
Ac 26: 3 I beg you to listen to me *p*.
Ro 8: 25 we do not yet have, we wait for it *p*.
Heb 6: 15 after waiting *p*, Abraham received
1Pe 3: 20 ago when God waited *p* in the days
Rev 3: 10 kept my command to endure *p*,

PATTERN

Ex 25: 40 according to the *p* shown you
Ro 5: 14 who was a *p* of the one to come.
   12: 2 longer to the *p* of this world,
2Ti 1: 13 keep as the *p* of sound teaching,
Heb 8: 5 according to the *p* shown you

PAUL

Also called Saul (Ac 13:9). Pharisee from Tarsus (Ac 9:11; Php 3:5). Apostle (Gal 1). At stoning of Stephen (Ac 8:1). Persecuted Church (Ac 9:1-2; Gal 1:13). Vision of Jesus on road to Damascus (Ac 9:4-9; 26:12-18). In Arabia (Gal 1:17). Preached in Damascus; escaped death through the wall in a basket (Ac 9:19-25). In Jerusalem; sent back to Tarsus (Ac 9:26-30).

Brought to Antioch by Barnabas (Ac 11:22-26). First missionary journey to Cyprus and Galatia (Ac 13-14). Stoned at Lystra (Ac 14:19-20). At Jerusalem council (Ac 15). Split with Barnabas over Mark (Ac 15:36-41).

Second missionary journey with Silas (Ac 16-20). Called to Macedonia (Ac 16:6-10). Freed from prison in Philippi (Ac 16:16-40). In Thessalonica (Ac 17:1-9). Speech in Athens (Ac 17:16-33). In Corinth (Ac 18). In Ephesus (Ac 19). Return to Jerusalem (Ac 20). Farewell to Ephesian elders (Ac 20:13-38). Arrival in Jerusalem (Ac 21:1-26). Arrested (Ac 21:27-36). Addressed crowds (Ac 22), Sanhedrin (Ac 23:1-11). Transferred to Caesarea (Ac 23:12-35). Trial before Felix (Ac 24), Festus (Ac 25:1-12). Before Agrippa (Ac 25:13-26:32). Voyage to Rome; shipwreck (Ac 27). Arrival in Rome (Ac 28).

Epistles: Romans, 1 and 2 Corinthians, Galatians, Ephesians, Philippians, Colossians, 1 and 2 Thessalonians, 1 and 2 Timothy, Titus, Philemon.

PAVEMENT

Jn 19: 13 as The Stone *P* (which

PAY (PAID PAYMENT PAYS REPAID REPAY REPAYING)

Lev 26: 43 They will *p* for their sins
Dt   7: 12 If you *p* attention to these laws
Pr   4: 1 *p* attention and gain understanding
    4: 20 My son, *p* attention to what I say;
    5: 1 My son, *p* attention to my wisdom,
    6: 31 if he is caught, he must *p* sevenfold,
    19: 19 man must *p* the penalty;
    22: 17 *p* attention and listen
    24: 29 I'll *p* that man back for what he did
Eze 40: 4 and *p* attention to everything I am
Zec 11: 12 give me my *p*; but if not, keep it.''
Mt 20: 2 He agreed to *p* them a denarius
    22: 16 you *p* no attention to who they are.
    22: 17 Is it right to *p* taxes to Caesar
Lk   3: 14 falsely—be content with your *p*.''
    19: 8 I will *p* back four times the amount
Ro 13: 6 This is also why you *p* taxes,
2Pe 1: 19 you will do well to *p* attention to it,

PAYMENT (PAY)

Ps 49: 8 no *p* is ever enough—
Php 4: 18 I have received full *p* and

PAYS (PAY)

Pr 17: 13 If a man *p* back evil for good,
1Th 5: 15 sure that nobody *p* back wrong

PEACE (PEACEABLE PEACEFUL PEACEMAKERS)

Lev 26: 6 '' 'I will grant *p* in the land,
Nu   6: 26 and give you *p*.' ' '
    25: 12 him I am making my covenant of *p*
Dt 20: 10 make its people an offer of *p*.
Jdg 3: 11 So the land had *p* for forty years,
    3: 30 and the land had *p* for eighty years.
    5: 31 Then the land had *p* forty years.
    6: 24 and called it The LORD is *P*.
    8: 28 the land enjoyed *p* forty years.
1Sa 7: 14 And there was *p* between Israel
2Sa 10: 19 they made *p* with the Israelites
1Ki 2: 33 may there be the LORD's *p* forever
    22: 44 also at *p* with the king of Israel.
2Ki 9: 17 come in *p*?' '' The horseman rode
1Ch 19: 19 they made *p* with David
    22: 9 and I will grant Israel *p*
2Ch 14: 1 and in his days the country was at *p*
    20: 30 kingdom of Jehoshaphat was at *p*,
Job 3: 26 I have no *p*, no quietness;
    22: 21 to God and be at *p* with him;
Ps 29: 11 LORD blesses his people with *p*.
    34: 14 seek *p* and pursue it.
    37: 11 and enjoy great *p*.
    37: 37 there is a future for the man of *p*.
    85: 10 righteousness and *p* kiss each other
    119:165 Great *p* have they who love your
    120: 7 I am a man of *p*;
    122: 6 Pray for the *p* of Jerusalem:
    147: 14 He grants *p* to your borders
Pr 12: 20 but joy for those who promote *p*.
    14: 30 A heart at *p* gives life to the body,
    16: 7 his enemies live at *p* with him.
    17: 1 Better a dry crust with *p* and quiet
Ecc 3: 8 a time for war and a time for *p*.
Isa 9: 6 Everlasting Father, Prince of *P*.
    14: 7 All the lands are at rest and at *p*;
    26: 3 You will keep in perfect *p*
    32: 17 The fruit of righteousness will be *p*;
    48: 18 your *p* would have been like a river,
    48: 22 ''There is no *p*,'' says the LORD,
    52: 7 who proclaim *p*,
    53: 5 punishment that brought us *p* was
    54: 10 nor my covenant of *p* be removed,''
    55: 12 and be led forth in *p*;
    57: 2 enter into *p*;
    57: 19 *P*, *p*, to those far and near,''
    57: 21 ''There is no *p*,'' says my God,
    59: 8 The way of *p* they do not know;
Jer 6: 14 '*P*, *p*,' they say,
    8: 11 '*P*, *p*,' . . . there is no *p*.
    30: 10 Jacob will again have *p*
    46: 27 Jacob will again have *p*
Eze 13: 10 ''*P*,'' when there is no *p*,
    34: 25 '' 'I will make a covenant of *p*

Eze 37: 26 I will make a covenant of *p*
Mic 5: 5 And he will be their *p*.
Zec 8: 19 Therefore love truth and *p*.''
    9: 10 He will proclaim *p* to the nations.
Mal 2: 5 a covenant of life and *p*,
    2: 6 He walked with me in *p*
Mt 10: 34 I did not come to bring *p*,
Mk 9: 50 and be at *p* with each other.''
Lk 1: 79 to guide our feet into the path of *p*
    2: 14 on earth *p* to men on whom his
    19: 38 ''*P* in heaven and glory
Jn 14: 27 *P* I leave with you; my *p*
    16: 33 so that in me you may have *p*.
Ro 1: 7 and *p* to you from God our Father
    2: 10 and *p* for everyone who does good:
    5: 1 we have *p* with God
    8: 6 by the Spirit is life and *p*;
    12: 18 on you, live at *p* with everyone.
    14: 19 effort to do what leads to *p*
1Co 7: 15 God has called us to live in *p*.
    14: 33 a God of disorder but of *p*.
2Co 13: 11 be of one mind, live in *p*.
Gal 5: 22 joy, *p*, patience, kindness,
Eph 2: 14 he himself is our *p*, who has made
    2: 15 thus making *p*, and in this one body
    2: 17 and *p* to those who were near.
    6: 15 comes from the gospel of *p*.
Php 4: 7 the *p* of God, which transcends all
Col 1: 20 by making *p* through his blood,
    3: 15 Let the *p* of Christ rule
    3: 15 of one body you were called to *p*.
1Th 5: 3 While people are saying, ''*P*
    5: 13 Live in *p* with each other.
    5: 23 the God of *p*, sanctify you through
2Th 3: 16 the Lord of *p* himself give you *p*
2Ti 2: 22 righteousness, faith, love and *p*,
Heb 7: 2 ''king of Salem'' means ''king of *p*.''
    12: 11 *p* for those who have been trained
    12: 14 effort to live in *p* with all men
    13: 20 May the God of *p*, who
1Pe 3: 11 he must seek *p* and pursue it.
2Pe 3: 14 blameless and at *p* with him.
Rev 6: 4 power to take *p* from the earth

PEACEABLE* (PEACE)

Tit 3: 2 to slander no one, to be *p*

PEACEFUL (PEACE)

1Ti 2: 2 that we may live *p* and quiet lives

PEACE-LOVING

Jas 3: 17 then *p*, considerate

PEACEMAKERS* (PEACE)

Mt 5: 9 Blessed are the *p*,
Jas 3: 18 *P* who sow in peace raise a harvest

PEARL* (PEARLS)

Rev 21: 21 each gate made of a single *p*.

PEARLS (PEARL)

Mt 7: 6 do not throw your *p* to pigs.
    13: 45 like a merchant looking for fine *p*.
1Ti 2: 9 or gold or *p* or expensive clothes,
Rev 21: 21 The twelve gates were twelve *p*,

PEDDLE*

2Co 2: 17 we do not *p* the word of God

PEG

Jdg 4: 21 She drove the *p* through his temple

PEKAH

King of Israel (2Ki 16:25-31; Isa 7:1).

PEKAHIAH*

Son of Menahem; king of Israel (2Ki 16:22-26).

PEN

Ps 45: 1 my tongue is the *p*
Mt 5: 18 letter, not the least stroke of a *p*.
Jn 10: 1 who does not enter the sheep *p*

PENETRATES*

Heb 4: 12 it *p* even to dividing soul and spirit,

PENNIES* (PENNY)

Lk 12: 6 not five sparrows sold for two *p*?

PENNY* (PENNIES)

Mt 5: 26 out until you have paid the last *p*.
    10: 29 Are not two sparrows sold for a *p*?
Mk 12: 42 worth only a fraction of a *p*.
Lk 12: 59 out until you have paid the last *p*.''

PENTECOST*

Ac 2: 1 of *P* came, they were all together
    20: 16 if possible, by the day of *P*.
1Co 16: 8 I will stay on at Ephesus until *P*,

PEOPLE (PEOPLES)

Ge 11: 6 as one *p* speaking the same
Ex 5: 1 Let my *p* go,
    6: 7 take you as my own *p*,
    8: 23 between my *p* and your *p*.
    15: 13 the *p* you have redeemed.
    19: 8 The *p* all responded together,
    24: 3 Moses went and told the *p*
    32: 1 When the *p* saw that Moses
    32: 9 they are a stiff-necked *p*.
    33: 13 this nation is your *p*.
Lev 9: 7 for yourself and the *p*:
    16: 24 the burnt offering for the *p*,
    26: 12 and you will be my *p*.
Nu 11: 11 burden of all these *p* on
    14: 11 treat me with contempt?
    14: 19 forgive the sin of these *p*,
    22: 5 A *p* has come out of Egypt
Dt 4: 6 a wise and understanding *p*.
    4: 20 the *p* of his inheritance,
    5: 28 what this *p* said to you.
    7: 6 a *p* holy to the LORD
    26: 18 that you are his *p*,
    31: 7 you must go with this *p*
    31: 16 these *p* will soon prostitute
    32: 9 the LORD's portion is his *p*,
    32: 43 atonement for his land and *p*.
    33: 29 a people saved by the LORD?
Jos 1: 6 you will lead this *p*
    24: 24 the *p* said to Joshua,
Jdg 2: 7 *p* served the LORD throughout
Ru 1: 16 Your *p* will be my *p*
1Sa 8: 7 the *p* are saying to you;
    12: 22 LORD will not reject his *p*,
2Sa 5: 2 will shepherd my *p* Israel
    7: 10 provide a place for my *p*
1Ki 3: 8 among the *p* you have chosen,
    8: 30 your *p* Israel when they pray
    8: 56 has given rest to his *p*
    18: 39 when all the *p* saw this,
2Ki 23: 3 all the *p* pledged themselves
1Ch 17: 21 to redeem *p* for himself
    29: 17 how willingly your *p* who are
2Ch 2: 11 Because the LORD loves his *p*,
    7: 5 *p* dedicated the temple
    7: 14 if my *p*, who are called
    30: 6 ''*P* of Israel, return to
    36: 16 was aroused against his *p*
Ezr 2: 1 These are the *p* of the
    3: 1 *p* assembled as one man
Ne 1: 10 your *p*, whom you redeemed
    4: 6 *p* worked with all their heart
    8: 1 *p* assembled as one man
Est 3: 6 to destroy all Mordecai's *p*,
Job 2: 2 Doubtless you are the *p*,
Ps 29: 11 gives strength to his *p*;
    33: 12 *p* he chose for his inheritance
    50: 4 that he may judge his *p*
    53: 6 restores the fortunes of his *p*,
    81: 13 If my *p* would but listen
    94: 14 LORD will not reject his *p*;
    95: 7 we are the *p* of his pasture,
    95: 10 a *p* whose hearts go astray,
    125: 2 the LORD surrounds his *p*
    135: 14 LORD will vindicate his *p*
    144: 15 *p* whose God is the LORD.
Pr 14: 34 sin is a disgrace to any *p*.
    29: 2 righteous thrive, the *p* rejoice
    29: 18 the *p* cast off restraint
Isa 1: 3 my *p* do not understand.
    1: 4 a *p* loaded with guilt,
    5: 13 my *p* will go into exile
    6: 10 the heart of this *p* calloused;
    9: 2 the *p* walking in darkness
    12: 12 will assemble the scattered *p*
    19: 25 Blessed be Egypt my *p*,

Isa 25: 8 remove the disgrace of his *p*
29: 13 These *p* come near to me
40: 1 Comfort, comfort my *p*
40: 7 Surely the *p* are grass.
42: 6 a covenant for the *p*
49: 13 the LORD comforts his *p*
51: 4 "Listen to me, my *p;*
52: 6 my *p* will know my name;
53: 8 for the transgression of my *p*
60: 21 will all your *p* be righteous
62: 12 will be called The Holy P,
65: 23 they will be a *p* blessed
Jer 2: 11 my *p* have exchanged their
2: 13 *p* have committed two sins:
2: 32 my *p* have forgotten me,
4: 22 My *p* are fools;
5: 14 Because the *p* have spoken
5: 31 my *p* love it this way
7: 16 do not pray for this *p*
18: 15 my *p* have forgotten me;
25: 7 They will be my *p,*
30: 3 I will bring my *p* Israel
Eze 13: 23 I will save my *p* from
36: 8 fruit for my *p* Israel,
36: 28 you will be my *p,*
36: 38 be filled with flocks of *p.*
37: 13 Then you, my *p,* will know
38: 14 *p* Israel are living in safety
39: 7 name among my *p* Israel.
Da 7: 27 saints, the *p* of the Most High.
8: 24 mighty men and the holy *p*
9: 19 your *p* bear your name
9: 24 are decreed for your *p*
9: 26 *p* of the ruler who will come
10: 14 will happen to your *p*
11: 32 *p* who know their God will
12: 1 prince who protects your *p.*
Hos 1: 10 'You are not my *p,*'
2: 23 'You are my *p';*
4: 14 a *p* without understanding
Joel 2: 18 and take pity on his *p.*
3: 16 be a refuge for his *p,*
Am 9: 14 back my exiled *p* Israel;
Mic 6: 2 a case against his *p;*
7: 14 Shepherd your *p* with
Hag 1: 12 remnant of the *p* obeyed
Zec 2: 11 and will become my *p,*
8: 7 I will save my *p*
13: 9 will say, 'They are my *p,*'
Mk 7: 6 *p* honor me with their lips
8: 27 "Who do *p* say I am?"
Lk 1: 17 make ready a *p* prepared
1: 68 and has redeemed his *p.*
2: 10 joy that will be for all the *p.*
21: 23 and wrath against this *p.*
Jn 11: 50 one man die for the *p*
18: 14 if one man died for the *p.*
Ac 15: 14 from the Gentiles a *p*
18: 10 have many *p* in this city.
Ro 9: 25 will call them 'my *p,*'
11: 1 Did God reject his *p?*
15: 10 O Gentiles, with his *p.*"
2Co 6: 16 and they will be my *p.*"
Tit 2: 14 a *p* that are his very own,
Heb 2: 17 for the sins of the *p.*
4: 9 a Sabbath-rest for the *p*
5: 3 for the sins of the *p.*
10: 30 Lord will judge his *p.*
11: 25 mistreated along with the *p*
13: 12 to make the *p* holy
1Pe 2: 9 you are a chosen *p,*
2: 10 Once you were not a *p,*
2: 10 you are the *p* of God;
2Pe 2: 1 false prophets among the *p,*
3: 11 kind of *p* ought you to be ?
Rev 18: 4 "Come out of her, my *p,*
21: 3 They will be his *p,*

PEOPLES (PEOPLE)

Ge 17: 16 kings of *p* will come from her
25: 23 two *p* from within you will
27: 29 and *p* bow down to you
28: 3 become a community of *p.*
48: 4 you a community of *p.*
Dt 14: 2 of all the *p* on the face of
28: 10 Then all the *p* on earth
32: 8 set up boundaries for the *p*
Jos 4: 24 all the *p* of the earth might

1Ki 8: 43 all the *p* of the earth may
2Ch 7: 20 of ridicule among all *p.*
Ps 9: 8 he will govern the *p*
67: 5 may all the *p* praise you.
87: 6 in the register of the *p:*
96: 10 he will judge the *p*
Isa 2: 4 settle disputes for many *p.*
17: 12 Oh, the uproar of the *p*—
25: 6 of rich food for all *p,*
34: 1 pay attention, you *p!*
55: 4 him a witness to the *p,*
Jer 10: 3 customs of the *p* are worthless
Da 7: 14 all *p,* nations and men
Mic 4: 1 and *p* will stream to it.
4: 3 will judge between many *p*
5: 7 in the midst of many *p*
Zep 3: 9 purify the lips of the *p,*
3: 20 among all the *p* of the
Zec 8: 20 Many *p* and the inhabitants
12: 2 all the surrounding *p* reeling.
Rev 10: 11 prophesy again about many *p,*
17: 15 the prostitute sits, are *p,*

PEOR

Nu 25: 3 joined in worshiping the Baal of P.
Dt 4: 3 who followed the Baal of P,

PERCEIVE (PERCEIVING)

Ps 139: 2 you *p* my thoughts from afar.
Pr 24: 12 not he who weighs the heart *p* it?

PERCEIVING* (PERCEIVE)

Isa 6: 9 be ever seeing, but never *p.*'
Mt 13: 14 you will be ever seeing but never *p.*
Mk 4: 12 may be ever seeing but never *p,*
Ac 28: 26 you will be ever seeing but never *p*

PERFECT* (PERFECTER PERFECTING PERFECTION)

Dt 32: 4 He is the Rock, his works are *p,*
2Sa 22: 31 "As for God, his way is *p;*
22: 33 and makes my way *p.*
Job 36: 4 one *p* in knowledge is with you.
37: 16 of him who is *p* in knowledge?
Ps 18: 30 As for God, his way is *p;*
18: 32 and makes my way *p.*
19: 7 The law of the LORD is *p,*
50: 2 From Zion, *p* in beauty,
64: 6 "We have devised a *p* plan!"
SS 6: 9 but my dove, my *p* one, is unique,
Isa 25: 1 for in *p* faithfulness
26: 3 You will keep in *p* peace
Eze 16: 14 had given you made your beauty *p,*
27: 3 "I am *p* in beauty."
28: 12 full of wisdom and *p* in beauty.
Mt 5: 48 Do not even pagans do that? Be *p,*
5: 48 as your heavenly Father is *p.*
19: 21 answered, "If you want to be *p,*
Ro 12: 2 his good, pleasing and *p* will.
2Co 12: 9 for my power is made *p*
Php 3: 12 or have already been made *p,*
Col 1: 28 so that we may present everyone *p*
3: 14 binds them all together in *p* unity.
Heb 2: 10 the author of their salvation *p*
5: 9 what he suffered and, once made *p,*
7: 19 useless (for the law made nothing *p*
7: 28 who has been made *p* forever.
9: 11 and more *p* tabernacle that is not
10: 1 make *p* those who draw
10: 14 he has made *p* forever those who
11: 40 with us would they be made *p.*
12: 23 spirits of righteous men made *p,*
Jas 1: 17 Every good and *p* gift is from above
1: 25 into the *p* law that gives freedom,
1Jn 3: 2 he is a *p* man, able
4: 18 But *p* love drives out fear,
4: 18 The one who fears is not made *p*

PERFECTER* (PERFECT)

Heb 12: 2 the author and *p* of our faith,

PERFECTING* (PERFECT)

2Co 7: 1 *p* holiness out of reverence for God

PERFECTION* (PERFECT)

Ps 119: 96 To all *p* I see a limit;
La 2: 15 the *p* of beauty,
Eze 27: 4 builders brought your beauty to *p.*

Eze 27: 11 they brought your beauty to *p.*
28: 12 " 'You were the model of *p,*
1Co 13: 10 but when *p* comes, the imperfect
2Co 13: 9 and our prayer is for your *p.*
13: 11 Aim for *p,* listen to my appeal,
Heb 7: 11 If *p* could have been attained

PERFORM (PERFORMED PERFORMS)

Ex 3: 20 with all the wonders that I will *p*
2Sa 7: 23 to *p* great and awesome wonders
Jn 3: 2 no one could *p* the miraculous

PERFORMED (PERFORM)

Mt 11: 21 If the miracles that were *p*
Jn 10: 41 John never *p* a miraculous

PERFORMS (PERFORM)

Ps 77: 14 You are the God who *p* miracles;

PERFUME

Ecc 7: 1 A good name is better than fine *p,*
SS 1: 3 your name is like *p* poured out.
Mk 14: 3 jar of very expensive *p,*

PERIL

2Co 1: 10 us from such a deadly *p,*

PERISH (PERISHABLE PERISHED PERISHES PERISHING)

Ge 6: 17 Everything on earth will *p.*
Est 4: 16 And if I *p,* I *p.*"
Ps 1: 6 but the way of the wicked will *p.*
37: 20 But the wicked will *p:*
73: 27 Those who are far from you will *p;*
102: 26 They will *p,* but you remain;
Pr 11: 10 when the wicked *p,* there are
19: 9 and he who pours out lies will *p.*
21: 28 A false witness will *p,*
28: 28 when the wicked *p,* the righteous
Isa 28: 18 who forsake the LORD will *p.*
29: 14 the wisdom of the wise will *p,*
60: 12 that will not serve you will *p;*
Zec 11: 9 the dying die, and the perishing *p.*
Lk 13: 3 unless you repent, you too will all *p*
13: 5 unless you repent, you too will all *p*
21: 18 But not a hair of your head will *p.*
Jn 3: 16 whoever believes in him shall not *p*
10: 28 eternal life, and they shall never *p;*
Ro 2: 12 apart from the law will also *p* apart
Col 2: 22 These are all destined to *p* with use,
2Th 2: 10 They *p* because they refused
Heb 1: 11 They will *p,* but you remain;
1Pe 1: 4 into an inheritance that can never *p*
2Pe 3: 9 not wanting anyone to *p,*

PERISHABLE (PERISH)

1Co 15: 42 The body that is sown is *p,*
1Pe 1: 18 not with *p* things such
1: 23 not of *p* seed, but of imperishable,

PERISHED (PERISH)

Ps 119: 92 I would have *p* in my affliction.

PERISHES (PERISH)

Job 8: 13 so *p* the hope of the godless.
1Pe 1: 7 which *p* even though refined by fire

PERISHING (PERISH)

1Co 1: 18 foolishness to those who are *p,*
2Co 2: 15 being saved and those who are *p.*
4: 3 it is veiled to those who are *p.*

PERJURERS* (PERJURY)

Mal 3: 5 and *p,* against those who defraud
1Ti 1: 10 for slave traders and liars and *p*—

PERJURY* (PERJURERS)

Jer 7: 9 murder, commit adultery and *p.*

PERMANENT

Heb 7: 24 lives forever, he has a *p* priesthood.

PERMISSIBLE (PERMIT)

1Co 6: 12 "Everything is *p* for me"—
10: 23 "Everything is *p*"— but not

PERMIT (PERMISSIBLE PERMITTED)

Hos 5: 4 "Their deeds do not *p* them
1Ti 2: 12 I do not *p* a woman to teach

PERMITTED (PERMIT)

Mt 19: 8 Moses *p* you to divorce your wives
2Co 12: 4 things that man is not *p* to tell.

PERSECUTE (PERSECUTED PERSECUTION PERSECUTIONS)

Ps 119: 86 for men *p* me without cause.
Mt   5: 11 *p* you and falsely say all kinds
      5: 44 and pray for those who *p* you,
Jn 15: 20 they persecuted me, they will *p* you
Ac   9: 4 why do you *p* me?'' ''Who are you,
Ro 12: 14 Bless those who *p* you; bless

PERSECUTED (PERSECUTE)

Mt   5: 10 Blessed are those who are *p*
      5: 12 same way they *p* the prophets who
Jn 15: 20 If they *p* me, they will persecute
1Co 4: 12 when we are *p*, we endure it;
      15: 9 because I *p* the church of God.
2Co 4: 9 in despair; *p*, but not abandoned;
1Th 3: 4 kept telling you that we would be *p*.
2Ti 3: 12 life in Christ Jesus will be *p*,
Heb 11: 37 destitute, *p* and mistreated—

PERSECUTION (PERSECUTE)

Mt 13: 21 When trouble or *p* comes
Ro   8: 35 or hardship or *p* or famine

PERSECUTIONS (PERSECUTE)

Mk 10: 30 and with them, *p)* and in the age
2Co 12: 10 in hardships, in *p*, in difficulties.
2Th 1: 4 faith in all the *p* and trials you are
2Ti 3: 11 love, endurance, *p*, sufferings—

PERSEVERANCE* (PERSEVERE)

Ro   5: 3 we know that suffering produces *p;*
      5: 4 *p*, character; and character, hope.
2Co 12: 12 were done among you with great *p*.
2Th 1: 4 churches we boast about your *p*
      3: 5 into God's love and Christ's *p*.
Heb 12: 1 run with *p* the race marked out
Jas 1: 4 *P* must finish its work
      1: 4 the testing of your faith develops *p*.
      5: 11 You have heard of Job's *p*
2Pe 1: 6 *p;* and to *p*, godliness;
Rev 2: 2 your hard work and your *p*.
      2: 19 and faith, your service and *p*,

PERSEVERE* (PERSEVERANCE PERSEVERED PERSEVERES PERSEVERING)

1Ti 4: 16 *P* in them, because if you do,
Heb 10: 36 You need to *p* so that

PERSEVERED* (PERSEVERE)

Heb 11: 27 he *p* because he saw him who is
Jas 5: 11 consider blessed those who have *p*.
Rev 2: 3 You have *p* and have endured

PERSEVERES* (PERSEVERE)

1Co 13: 7 trusts, always hopes, always *p*.
Jas 1: 12 Blessed is the man who *p*

PERSEVERING* (PERSEVERE)

Lk   8: 15 retain it, and by *p* produce a crop.

PERSIANS

Da   6: 15 law of the Medes and *P* no decree

PERSISTENCE*

Ro   2: 7 To those who by *p*

PERSUADE (PERSUADED PERSUASIVE)

Ac 18: 4 trying to *p* Jews and Greeks.
2Co 5: 11 is to fear the Lord, we try to *p* men.

PERSUADED (PERSUADE)

Ro   4: 21 being fully *p* that God had power

PERSUASIVE (PERSUADE)

1Co 2: 4 not with wise and *p* words,

PERVERSION* (PERVERT)

Lev 18: 23 sexual relations with it; that is a *p*.
      20: 12 What they have done is a *p;*
Ro   1: 27 the due penalty for their *p*.
Jude   : 7 up to sexual immorality and *p*.

PERVERT (PERVERSION PERVERTED PERVERTS)

Ex 23: 2 do not *p* justice by siding
Dt 16: 19 Do not *p* justice or show partiality.
Job 34: 12 that the Almighty would *p* justice.
Pr 17: 23 to *p* the course of justice.
Gal 1: 7 are trying to *p* the gospel of Christ.

PERVERTED (PERVERT)

1Sa 8: 3 and accepted bribes and *p* justice.

PERVERTS* (PERVERT)

1Ti 1: 10 for murderers, for adulterers and *p*,

PESTILENCE (PESTILENCES)

Ps 91: 6 nor the *p* that stalks in the darkness

PESTILENCES (PESTILENCE)

Lk 21: 11 famines and *p* in various places,

PETER

Apostle, brother of Andrew, also called Simon (Mt 10:2; Mk 3:16; Lk 6:14; Ac 1:13), and Cephas (Jn 1:42). Confession of Christ (Mt 16:13-20; Mk 8:27-30; Lk 9:18-27). At transfiguration (Mt 17:1-8; Mk 9:2-8; Lk 9:28-36; 2Pe 1:16-18). Caught fish with coin (Mt 17:24-27). Denial of Jesus predicted (Mt 26:31-35; Mk 14:27-31; Lk 22:31-34; Jn 13:31-38). Denied Jesus (Mt 26:69-75; Mk 14:66-72; Lk 22:54-62; Jn 18:15-27). Commissioned by Jesus to shepherd his flock (Jn 21:15-23). Speech at Pentecost (Ac 2). Healed beggar (Ac 3:1-10). Speech at temple (Ac 3:11-26), before Sanhedrin (Ac 4:1-22). In Samaria (Ac 8:14-25). Sent by vision to Cornelius (Ac 10). Announced salvation of Gentiles in Jerusalem (Ac 11; 15). Freed from prison (Ac 12). Inconsistency at Antioch (Gal 2:11-21). At Jerusalem Council (Ac 15). Epistles: 1-2 Peter.

PETITION (PETITIONS)

1Ch 16: 4 to make *p*, to give thanks,
Php 4: 6 by prayer and *p*, with thanksgiving,

PETITIONS (PETITION)

Heb 5: 7 he offered up prayers and *p*

PHANTOM*

Ps 39: 6 Man is a mere *p* as he goes to

PHARAOH (PHARAOH'S)

Ge 12: 15 her to *P*, and she was taken
      41: 14 So *P* sent for Joseph, and he was
Ex 14: 4 glory for myself through *P*
      14: 17 And I will gain glory through *P*

PHARAOH'S (PHARAOH)

Ex   7: 3 But I will harden *P* heart, and

PHARISEE (PHARISEES)

Ac 23: 6 brothers, I am a *P*, the son of a *P*.
Php 3: 5 in regard to the law, a *P;* as for zeal,

PHARISEES (PHARISEE)

Mt   5: 20 surpasses that of the *P*
      16: 6 guard against the yeast of the *P*
      23: 13 of the law and *P*, you hypocrites!
Jn   3: 1 a man of the *P* named Nicodemus,

PHILADELPHIA

Rev 3: 7 the angel of the church in *P* write:

PHILEMON*

Phm   : 1 To *P* our dear friend and fellow

PHILIP

1. Apostle (Mt 10:3; Mk 3:18; Lk 6:14; Jn 1:43-48; 14:8; Ac 1:13).
2. Deacon (Ac 6:1-7); evangelist in Samaria (Ac 8:4-25), to Ethiopian (Ac 8:26-40).

PHILIPPI

Ac 16: 12 From there we traveled to *P*,
Php 1: 1 To all the saints in Christ Jesus at *P*

PHILISTINE (PHILISTINES)

Jos 13: 3 of the five *P* rulers in Gaza,
1Sa 14: 1 let's go over to the *P* outpost
      17: 26 is this uncircumcised *P* that he

1Sa 17: 37 me from the hand of this *P*.''

PHILISTINES (PHILISTINE)

Jdg 10: 7 them into the hands of the *P*
      13: 1 the hands of the *P* for forty years.
      16: 5 The rulers of the *P* went to her
1Sa 4: 1 at Ebenezer, and the *P* at Aphek.
      5: 8 together all the rulers of the *P*
      13: 23 a detachment of *P* had gone out
      17: 1 the *P* gathered their forces for war
      23: 1 the *P* are fighting against Keilah
      27: 1 is to escape to the land of the *P*.
      31: 1 Now the *P* fought against Israel;
2Sa 5: 17 When the *P* heard that David had
      8: 1 David defeated the *P* and subdued
      21: 15 there was a battle between the *P*
2Ki 18: 8 he defeated the *P*, as far as Gaza
Am   1: 8 Ekron till the last of the *P* is dead,''

PHILOSOPHER* (PHILOSOPHY)

1Co 1: 20 Where is the *p* of this age?

PHILOSOPHY* (PHILOSOPHER)

Col 2: 8 through hollow and deceptive *p*,

PHINEHAS

Nu 25: 7 When *P* son of Eleazar, the son
Ps 106: 30 But *P* stood up and intervened,

PHOEBE*

Ro 16: 1 I commend to you our sister *P*,

PHYLACTERIES*

Mt 23: 5 They make their *p* wide

PHYSICAL

Ro   2: 28 merely outward and *p*.
Col 1: 22 by Christ's *p* body through death
1Ti 4: 8 For *p* training is of some value,
Jas 2: 16 but does nothing about his *p* needs,

PICK (PICKED)

Mk 16: 18 they will *p* up snakes

PICKED (PICK)

Lk 14: 7 noticed how the guests *p* the places
Jn   5: 9 he *p* up his mat and walked.

PIECE (PIECES)

Jn 19: 23 woven in one *p* from top to bottom.

PIECES (PIECE)

Ge 15: 17 and passed between the *p*.
Jer 34: 18 and then walked between its *p*.
Zec 11: 12 So they paid me thirty *p* of silver.
Mt 14: 20 of broken *p* that were left over.

PIERCE (PIERCED)

Ex 21: 6 and *p* his ear with an awl.
Pr 12: 18 Reckless words *p* like a sword,
Lk   2: 35 a sword will *p* your own soul too.''

PIERCED (PIERCE)

Ps 22: 16 they have *p* my hands and my feet.
      40: 6 but my ears you have *p;*
Isa 53: 5 But he was *p* for our transgressions,
Zec 12: 10 look on me, the one they have *p*,
Jn 19: 37 look on the one they have *p*.''
Rev 1: 7 even those who *p* him;

PIG'S (PIGS)

Pr 11: 22 Like a gold ring in a *p* snout

PIGEONS

Lev 5: 11 afford two doves or two young *p*,
Lk   2: 24 ''a pair of doves or two young *p*.''

PIGS (PIG'S)

Mt   7: 6 do not throw your pearls to *p*.
Mk   5: 11 A large herd of *p* was feeding on

PILATE

Governor of Judea. Questioned Jesus (Mt 27:1-26; Mk 15:15; Lk 22:66-23:25; Jn 18:28-19:16); sent to Herod (Lk 23:6-12); consented to his crucifixion when crowds chose Barabbas (Mt 27:15-26; Mk 15:6-15; Lk 23:13-25; Jn 19:1-10).

PILLAR (PILLARS)

Ge 19: 26 and she became a *p* of salt.
Ex 13: 21 ahead of them in a *p* of cloud
1Ti   3: 15 the *p* and foundation of the truth.
Rev   3: 12 who overcomes I will make a *p*

PILLARS (PILLAR)

Gal   2: 9 and John, those reputed to be *p*,

PINIONS

Dt 32: 11 and carries them on its *p*.

PISGAH

Dt   3: 27 Go up to the top of *P* and look west

PIT

Ps   7: 15 falls into the *p* he has made.
     40: 2 He lifted me out of the slimy *p*,
    103: 4 he redeems my life from the *p*
Pr 23: 27 for a prostitute is a deep *p*
     26: 27 If a man digs a *p*, he will fall into it;
Isa 24: 17 Terror and *p* and snare await you,
     38: 17 me from the *p* of destruction;
Mt 15: 14 a blind man, both will fall into a *p*.''

PITCH

Ge   6: 14 and coat it with *p* inside and out.
Ex   2: 3 and coated it with tar and *p*.

PITIED (PITY)

1Co 15: 19 we are to be *p* more than all men.

PITY (PITIED)

Ps 72: 13 He will take *p* on the weak
Ecc   4: 10 But *p* the man who falls
Lk 10: 33 when he saw him, he took *p* on him

PLAGUE (PLAGUED PLAGUES)

2Ch   6: 28 ''When famine or *p* comes
Ps 91: 6 nor the *p* that destroys at midday.

PLAGUED* (PLAGUE)

Ps 73: 5 they are not *p* by human ills.
     73: 14 All day long I have been *p*;

PLAGUES (PLAGUE)

Hos 13: 14 Where, O death, are your *p*?
Rev 21: 9 full of the seven last *p* came
     22: 18 to him the *p* described in this book.

PLAIN

Isa 40: 4 the rugged places a *p*.
Ro   1: 19 what may be known about God is *p*

PLAN (PLANNED PLANS)

Ex 26: 30 according to the *p* shown you
Job 42: 2 no *p* of yours can be thwarted.
Pr 14: 22 those who *p* what is good find love
     21: 30 is no wisdom, no insight, no *p*
Am   3: 7 nothing without revealing his *p*
Eph   1: 11 predestined according to the *p*

PLANK

Mt   7: 3 attention to the *p* in your own eye?
Lk   6: 41 attention to the *p* in your own eye?

PLANNED (PLAN)

Ps 40: 5 The things you *p* for us
Isa 14: 24 ''Surely, as I have *p*, so it will be,
     23: 9 The LORD Almighty *p* it,
     46: 11 what I have *p*, that will I do.
Heb 11: 40 God had *p* something better for us

PLANS (PLAN)

Ps 20: 4 and make all your *p* succeed.
     33: 11 *p* of the LORD stand firm forever,
Pr 15: 22 *P* fail for lack of counsel,
     16: 3 and your *p* will succeed.
     19: 21 Many are the *p* in a man's heart,
     20: 18 Make *p* by seeking advice;
Isa 29: 15 to hide their *p* from the LORD,
     30: 1 those who carry out *p* that are not
     32: 8 But the noble man makes noble *p*,
2Co   1: 17 Or do I make my *p* in a worldly

PLANT (PLANTED PLANTING PLANTS)

Am   9: 15 I will *p* Israel in their own land,
Mt 15: 13 ''Every *p* that my heavenly Father

PLANTED (PLANT)

Ge   2: 8 the LORD God had *p* a garden
Ps   1: 3 He is like a tree *p* by streams
Jer 17: 8 He will be like a tree *p* by the water
Mt 15: 13 Father has not *p* will be pulled
     21: 33 was a landowner who *p* a vineyard.
Lk 13: 6 ''A man had a fig tree, *p*
1Co   3: 6 I *p* the seed, Apollos watered it,
Jas   1: 21 humbly accept the word *p* in you,

PLANTING (PLANT)

Isa 61: 3 a *p* of the LORD

PLANTS (PLANT)

Pr 31: 16 out of her earnings she *p* a vineyard
1Co   3: 7 So neither he who *p* nor he who
      9: 7 Who *p* a vineyard and does not eat

PLATTER

Mk   6: 25 head of John the Baptist on a *p*.''

PLAY (PLAYED)

1Sa 16: 23 David would take his harp and *p*.
Isa 11: 8 The infant will *p* near the hole

PLAYED (PLAY)

Lk   7: 32 '' 'We *p* the flute for you,
1Co 14: 7 anyone know what tune is being *p*

PLEA (PLEAD PLEADED PLEADS)

1Ki   8: 28 to your servant's prayer and his *p*
Ps 102: 17 he will not despise their *p*.
La   3: 56 You heard my *p*: ''Do not close

PLEAD (PLEA)

Isa   1: 17 *p* the case of the widow.

PLEADED (PLEA)

2Co 12: 8 Three times I *p* with the Lord

PLEADS (PLEA)

Job 16: 21 on behalf of a man he *p* with God

PLEASANT (PLEASE)

Ge 49: 15 and how *p* is his land,
Ps 16: 6 for me in *p* places;
    133: 1 How good and *p* it is
    135: 3 sing praise to his name, for that is *p*
    147: 1 how *p* and fitting to praise him!
Pr   2: 10 knowledge will be *p* to your soul.
      3: 17 Her ways are *p* ways,
     16: 21 and *p* words promote instruction.
     16: 24 *P* words are a honeycomb,
Isa 30: 10 Tell us *p* things,
1Th   3: 6 that you always have *p* memories
Heb 12: 11 No discipline seems *p* at the time,

PLEASANTNESS* (PLEASE)

Pr 27: 9 the *p* of one's friend springs

PLEASE (PLEASANT PLEASANTNESS PLEASED PLEASES PLEASING PLEASURE PLEASURES)

Ps 69: 31 This will *p* the LORD more
Pr 20: 23 and dishonest scales do not *p* him.
Isa 46: 10 and I will do all that I *p*.
Jer   6: 20 your sacrifices do not *p* me.''
      27: 5 and I give it to anyone I *p*.
Jn   5: 30 for I seek not to *p* myself
Ro   8: 8 by the sinful nature cannot *p* God.
     15: 1 of the weak and not to *p* ourselves.
     15: 2 Each of us should *p* his neighbor
1Co   7: 32 affairs—how he can *p* the Lord.
     10: 33 I try to *p* everybody in every way.
2Co   5: 9 So we make it our goal to *p* him.
Gal   1: 10 or of God? Or am I trying to *p* men
      1: 10 the one who sows to *p* the Spirit,
Col   1: 10 and may *p* him in every way:
1Th   2: 4 We are not trying to *p* men
      2: 4 but to *p* God,
      4: 1 how to live in order to *p* God,
2Ti   2: 4 wants to *p* his commanding officer.
Tit   2: 9 to try to *p* them, not to talk back
Heb 11: 6 faith it is impossible to *p* God,

PLEASED (PLEASE)

Dt 28: 63 as it *p* the LORD to make you
1Sa 12: 22 LORD was *p* to make you his own.
1Ki   3: 10 The Lord was *p* that Solomon had
1Ch 29: 17 that you test the heart and are *p*
Mic   6: 7 Will the LORD be *p*
Mal   1: 10 I am not *p* with you,'' says
Mt   3: 17 whom I love; with him I am well *p*
     17: 5 whom I love; with him I am well *p*.
Mk   1: 11 whom I love; with you I am well *p*
Lk   3: 22 whom I love; with you I am well *p*
1Co   1: 21 God was *p* through the foolishness
Col   1: 19 For God was *p* to have all his
Heb 10: 6 you were not *p*.
     10: 8 nor were you *p* with them''
     10: 38 I will not be *p* with him.''
     11: 5 commended as one who *p* God.
     13: 16 for with such sacrifices God is *p*.
2Pe   1: 17 whom I love; with him I am well *p*

PLEASES (PLEASE)

Job 23: 13 He does whatever he *p*.
Ps 115: 3 he does whatever *p* him.
    135: 6 The LORD does whatever *p* him,
Pr 15: 8 but the prayer of the upright *p* him.
     21: 1 it like a watercourse wherever he *p*.
Ecc   2: 26 To the man who *p* him, God gives
      7: 26 man who *p* God will escape her,
Da   4: 35 He does as he *p*
Jn   3: 8 The wind blows wherever it *p*.
      8: 29 for I always do what *p* him.
Eph   5: 10 truth) and find out what *p* the Lord
Col   3: 20 in everything, for this *p* the Lord.
1Ti   2: 3 This is good, and *p* God our Savior,
1Jn   3: 22 his commands and do what *p* him.

PLEASING (PLEASE)

Ge   2: 9 trees that were *p* to the eye
Lev   1: 9 an aroma *p* to the LORD.
Ps 19: 14 be *p* in your sight,
    104: 34 May my meditation be *p* to him,
Pr 15: 26 but those of the pure are *p* to him.
     16: 7 When a man's ways are *p*
SS   1: 3 *P* is the fragrance of your perfumes
      4: 10 How much more *p* is your love
      7: 6 How beautiful you are and how *p*,
Ro 12: 1 *p* to God—this is your spiritual
     14: 18 Christ in this way is *p* to God
Php   4: 18 an acceptable sacrifice, *p* to God.
1Ti   5: 4 grandparents, for this is *p* to God.
Heb 13: 21 may he work in us what is *p* to him,

PLEASURE (PLEASE)

Ps   5: 4 You are not a God who takes *p*
     51: 16 you do not take *p* in burnt offerings
    147: 10 His *p* is not in the strength
Pr 10: 23 A fool finds *p* in evil conduct,
     18: 2 A fool finds no *p* in understanding
     21: 17 He who loves *p* will become poor;
Isa   1: 11 I have no *p* in it.
Jer   6: 10 they find no *p* in it.
Eze 18: 23 Do I take any *p* in the death
     18: 32 For I take no *p* in the death
     33: 11 I take no *p* in the death
Lk 10: 21 Father, for this was your good *p*.
Eph   1: 5 in accordance with his *p* and will—
      1: 9 of his will according to his good *p*,
1Ti   5: 6 the widow who lives for *p* is dead
2Ti   3: 4 lovers of *p* rather than lovers
2Pe   2: 13 Their idea of *p* is to carouse

PLEASURES* (PLEASE)

Ps 16: 11 with eternal *p* at your right hand.
Lk   8: 14 and *p*, and they do not mature.
Tit   3: 3 by all kinds of passions and *p*.
Heb 11: 25 rather than to enjoy the *p* of sin
Jas   4: 3 may spend what you get on your *p*.
2Pe   2: 13 reveling in their *p* while they feast

PLEDGE

Dt 24: 17 take the cloak of the widow as a *p*.
1Pe   3: 21 but the *p* of a good conscience

PLEIADES

Job 38: 31 ''Can you bind the beautiful *P*?
Am   5: 8 (he who made the *P* and Orion,

PLENTIFUL (PLENTY)

Mt 9: 37 harvest is *p* but the workers are
Lk 10: 2 harvest is *p*, but the workers are

PLENTY (PLENTIFUL)

2Co 8: 14 the present time your *p* will supply
Php 4: 12 whether living in *p* or in want.

PLOT (PLOTS)

Est 2: 22 Mordecai found out about the *p*
Ps 2: 1 and the peoples *p* in vain?
Pr 3: 29 not *p* harm against your neighbor,
Zec 8: 17 do not *p* evil against your neighbor,
Ac 4: 25 and the peoples *p* in vain?

PLOTS (PLOT)

Pr 6: 14 who *p* evil with deceit in his heart

PLOW (PLOWMAN PLOWSHARES)

Lk 9: 62 ''No one who puts his hand to the *p*

PLOWMAN (PLOW)

1Co 9: 10 because when the *p* plows

PLOWSHARES (PLOW)

1Sa 13: 20 to the Philistines to have their *p*,
Isa 2: 4 They will beat their swords into *p*
Joel 3: 10 Beat your *p* into swords
Mic 4: 3 They will beat their swords into *p*

PLUCK

Mk 9: 47 your eye causes you to sin, *p* it out.

PLUNDER (PLUNDERED)

Ex 3: 22 And so you will *p* the Egyptians.''
Est 3: 13 of Adar, and to *p* their goods.
8: 11 to *p* the property of their enemies.
9: 10 did not lay their hands on the *p*.
Pr 22: 23 and will *p* those who *p* them.
Isa 3: 14 the *p* from the poor is

PLUNDERED (PLUNDER)

Eze 34: 8 lacks a shepherd and so has been *p*

PLUNGE

1Ti 6: 9 and harmful desires that *p* men
1Pe 4: 4 think it strange that you do not *p*

PODS

Lk 15: 16 with the *p* that the pigs were eating,

POINT

Mt 4: 5 on the highest *p* of the temple.
26: 38 with sorrow to the *p* of death.
Jas 2: 10 yet stumbles at just one *p* is guilty
Rev 2: 10 Be faithful, even to the *p* of death,

POISON

Ps 140: 3 the *p* of vipers is on their lips.
Mk 16: 18 and when they drink deadly *p*,
Ro 3: 13 ''The *p* of vipers is on their lips.''
Jas 3: 8 It is a restless evil, full of deadly *p*.

POLE (POLES)

Nu 21: 8 ''Make a snake and put it up on a *p*;
Dt 16: 21 not set up any wooden Asherah *p*

POLES (POLE)

Ex 25: 13 Then make *p* of acacia wood

POLISHED

Isa 49: 2 he made me into a *p* arrow

POLLUTE* (POLLUTED POLLUTES)

Nu 35: 33 '' 'Do not *p* the land where you are.
Jude : 8 these dreamers *p* their own bodies,

POLLUTED* (POLLUTE)

Ezr 9: 11 entering to possess is a land *p*
Pr 25: 26 Like a muddied spring or a *p* well
Ac 15: 20 to abstain from food *p* by idols,
Jas 1: 27 oneself from being *p* by the world.

POLLUTES* (POLLUTE)

Nu 35: 33 Bloodshed *p* the land,

PONDER (PONDERED)

Ps 64: 9 and *p* what he has done.
119: 95 but I will *p* your statutes.

PONDERED (PONDER)

Ps 111: 2 they are *p* by all who delight
Lk 2: 19 up all these things and *p* them

POOR (POVERTY)

Lev 19: 10 Leave them for the *p* and the alien.
23: 22 Leave them for the *p* and the alien.
27: 8 If anyone making the vow is too *p*
Dt 15: 4 there should be no *p* among you,
15: 7 is a *p* man among your brothers
15: 11 There will always be *p* people
24: 12 If the man is *p*, do not go to sleep
24: 14 advantage of a hired man who is *p*
Job 5: 16 So the *p* have hope,
24: 4 force all the *p* of the land
Ps 14: 6 frustrate the plans of the *p*,
34: 6 This *p* man called, and the LORD
35: 10 You rescue the *p* from those too
40: 17 Yet I am *p* and needy;
68: 10 O God, you provided for the *p*.
82: 3 maintain the rights of the *p*
112: 9 scattered abroad his gifts to the *p*,
113: 7 He raises the *p* from the dust
140: 12 the LORD secures justice for the *p*
Pr 10: 4 Lazy hands make a man *p*,
13: 7 to be *p*, yet has great wealth.
14: 20 The *p* are shunned
14: 31 oppresses the *p* shows contempt
17: 5 who mocks the *p* shows contempt
19: 1 Better a *p* man whose walk is
19: 17 to the *p* lends to the LORD,
19: 22 better to be *p* than a liar.
20: 13 not love sleep or you will grow *p*;
21: 13 to the cry of the *p*,
21: 17 who loves pleasure will become *p*;
22: 2 Rich and *p* have this in common:
22: 9 for he shares his food with the *p*.
22: 22 not exploit the *p* because they are *p*
28: 6 Better a *p* man whose walk is
28: 27 to the *p* will lack nothing,
29: 7 care about justice for the *p*,
31: 9 defend the rights of the *p*
31: 20 She opens her arms to the *p*
Ecc 4: 13 Better a *p* but wise youth
Isa 3: 14 the plunder from the *p* is
10: 2 to deprive the *p* of their rights
14: 30 of the *p* will find pasture,
25: 4 You have been a refuge for the *p*,
32: 7 schemes to destroy the *p* with lies,
61: 1 me to preach good news to the *p*.
Jer 22: 16 He defended the cause of the *p*
Eze 18: 12 He oppresses the *p* and needy.
Am 2: 7 They trample on the heads of the *p*
4: 1 you women who oppress the *p*
5: 11 You trample on the *p*
Zec 7: 10 or the fatherless, the alien or the *p*.
Mt 5: 3 saying: ''Blessed are the *p* in spirit,
11: 5 the good news is preached to the *p*.
19: 21 your possessions and give to the *p*,
26: 11 The *p* you will always have
Mk 12: 42 But a *p* widow came and put
14: 7 The *p* you will always have
Lk 4: 18 me to preach good news to the *p*.
6: 20 ''Blessed are you who are *p*,
11: 41 is inside the dish, to the *p*,
14: 13 invite the *p*, the crippled, the lame,
21: 2 also saw a *p* widow put
Jn 12: 8 You will always have the *p*
Ac 9: 36 doing good and helping the *p*.
10: 4 and gifts to the *p* have come up
24: 17 to bring my people gifts for the *p*
Ro 15: 26 for the *p* among the saints
1Co 13: 3 If I give all I possess to the *p*
2Co 6: 10 sorrowful, yet always rejoicing; *p*,
8: 9 yet for your sakes he became *p*,
Gal 2: 10 continue to remember the *p*,
Jas 2: 2 and a *p* man in shabby clothes
2: 5 not God chosen those who are *p*
2: 6 But you have insulted the *p*.

POPULATION*

Pr 14: 28 A large *p* is a king's glory,

PORTION

Nu 18: 29 as the LORD's *p* the best
Dt 32: 9 For the LORD's *p* is his people,
1Sa 1: 5 But to Hannah he gave a double *p*

PORTRAIT

Lk 20: 24 Whose *p* and inscription are on it?''

PORTRAYED

Gal 3: 1 very eyes Jesus Christ was clearly *p*

POSITION (POSITIONS)

Ro 12: 16 to associate with people of low *p*.
Jas 1: 9 ought to take pride in his high *p*.
2Pe 3: 17 and fall from your secure *p*.

POSITIONS (POSITION)

2Ch 20: 17 Take up your *p*; stand firm
Jude : 6 the angels who did not keep their *p*

POSSESS (POSSESSED POSSESSING POSSESSION POSSESSIONS)

Nu 33: 53 for I have given you the land to *p*.
Dt 4: 14 you are crossing the Jordan to *p*.
Pr 8: 12 I *p* knowledge and discretion.
Jn 5: 39 that by them you *p* eternal life.

POSSESSED (POSSESS)

Jn 10: 21 the sayings of a man *p* by a demon.

POSSESSING* (POSSESS)

2Co 6: 10 nothing, and yet *p* everything.

POSSESSION (POSSESS)

Ge 15: 7 to give you this land to take *p* of it
Ex 6: 8 I will give it to you as a *p*.
19: 5 nations you will be my treasured *p*.
Nu 13: 30 ''We should go up and take *p*
Dt 7: 6 to be his people, his treasured *p*.
Jos 1: 11 take *p* of the land the LORD your
Ps 2: 8 the ends of the earth your *p*.
135: 4 Israel to be his treasured *p*.
Eph 1: 14 of those who are God's *p*—

POSSESSIONS (POSSESS)

Mt 19: 21 go, sell your *p* and give to the poor,
Lk 11: 21 guards his own house, his *p* are safe
12: 15 consist in the abundance of his *p*.''
19: 8 now I give half of my *p* to the poor,
Ac 4: 32 any of his *p* was his own,
2Co 12: 14 what I want is not your *p* but you.
Heb 10: 34 yourselves had better and lasting *p*.
1Jn 3: 17 If anyone has material *p*

POSSIBLE

Mt 19: 26 but with God all things are *p*.''
26: 39 if it is *p*, may this cup be taken
Mk 9: 23 ''Everything is *p* for him who
10: 27 all things are *p* with God.''
14: 35 prayed that if *p* the hour might pass
Ro 12: 18 If it is *p*, as far as it depends on you,
1Co 6: 5 Is it *p* that there is nobody
9: 19 to everyone, to win as many as *p*
9: 22 by all *p* means I might save some.

POT (POTSHERD POTTER POTTER'S POTTERY)

2Ki 4: 40 there is death in the *p*!''
Jer 18: 4 But the *p* he was shaping

POTIPHAR*

Egyptian who bought Joseph (Ge 37:36), set him over his house (Ge 39:1-6), sent him to prison (Ge 39:7-30).

POTSHERD (POT)

Isa 45: 9 a *p* among the potsherds

POTTER (POT)

Isa 29: 16 Can the pot say of the *p*,
45: 9 Does the clay say to the *p*,
64: 8 We are the clay, you are the *p*;
Jer 18: 6 ''Like clay in the hand of the *p*,
Zec 11: 13 it to the *p*''— the handsome price
Ro 9: 21 Does not the *p* have the right

POTTER (continued - right column)

2Ki 2: 9 ''Let me inherit a double *p*
Ps 73: 26 and my *p* forever.
119: 57 You are my *p*, O LORD;
Isa 53: 12 Therefore I will give him a *p*
Jer 10: 16 He who is the *P* of Jacob is not like
La 3: 24 to myself, ''The LORD is my *p*;
Zec 2: 12 LORD will inherit Judah as his *p*

POTTER'S (POT)

Mt 27: 7 to use the money to buy the *p* field

POTTERY (POT)

Ro 9:21 of clay some *p* for noble purposes

POUR (POURED POURS)

Ps 62: 8 *p* out your hearts to him,
Isa 44: 3 I will *p* out my Spirit
Eze 20: 8 So I said I would *p* out my wrath
    39:29 for I will *p* out my Spirit
Joel 2:28 I will *p* out my Spirit on all people.
Zec 12:10 I will *p* out on the house of David
Mal 3:10 *p* out so much blessing that you
Ac 2:17 I will *p* out my Spirit on all people.

POURED (POUR)

Ps 22:14 I am *p* out like water,
Isa 32:15 till the Spirit is *p* upon us
Mt 26:28 which is *p* out for many
Lk 22:20 in my blood, which is *p* out for you.
Ac 2:33 and has *p* out what you now see
    10:45 of the Holy Spirit had been *p* out
Ro 5: 5 because God has *p* out his love
Php 2:17 even if I am being *p* out like a drink
2Ti 4: 6 I am already being *p* out like
Tit 3: 6 whom he *p* out on us generously
Rev 16: 2 and *p* out his bowl on the land,

POURS (POUR)

Lk 5:37 And no one *p* new wine

POVERTY* (POOR)

Dt 28:48 and thirst, in nakedness and dire *p*,
1Sa 2: 7 The LORD sends *p* and wealth;
Pr 6:11 will come on you like a bandit
    10:15 but *p* is the ruin of the poor.
    11:24 withholds unduly, but comes to *p*.
    13:18 who ignores discipline comes to *p*
    14:23 but mere talk leads only to *p*.
    21: 5 as surely as haste leads to *p*.
    22:16 to the rich—both come to *p*.
    24:34 *p* will come on you like a bandit
    28:19 fantasies will have his fill of *p*.
    28:22 and is unaware that *p* awaits him.
    30: 8 give me neither *p* nor riches,
    31: 7 let them drink and forget their *p*
Ecc 4:14 born in *p* within his kingdom.
Mk 12:44 out of her *p*, put in everything—
Lk 21: 4 she out of her *p* put in all she had
2Co 8: 2 and their extreme *p* welled up
    8: 9 through his *p* might become rich.
Rev 2: 9 I know your afflictions and your *p*

POWER (POWERFUL POWERS)

Ex 15: 6 was majestic in *p*.
    32:11 out of Egypt with great *p*
Dt 8:17 "My *p* and the strength
    34:12 one has ever shown the mighty *p*
1Sa 10: 6 LORD will come upon you in *p*,
    10:10 Spirit of God came upon him in *p*,
    11: 6 Spirit of God came upon him in *p*,
    16:13 the LORD came upon David in *p*.
1Ch 29:11 LORD, is the greatness and the *p*
2Ch 20: 6 *P* and might are in your hand,
    32: 7 for there is a greater *p* with us
Job 9: 4 wisdom is profound, his *p* is vast.
    36:22 "God is exalted in his *p*.
    37:23 beyond our reach and exalted in *p*;
Ps 20: 6 with the saving *p* of his right hand.
    63: 2 and beheld your *p* and your glory.
    66: 3 So great is your *p*
    68:34 Proclaim the *p* of God,
    77:14 you display your *p*
    89:13 Your arm is endued with *p*;
    145: 6 of the *p* of your awesome works,
    147: 5 Great is our Lord and mighty in *p*;
    150: 2 Praise him for his acts of *p*;
Pr 3:27 when it is in your *p* to act.
    18:21 The tongue has the *p* of life
    24: 5 A wise man has great *p*,
Isa 11: 2 the Spirit of counsel and of *p*,
    40:10 the Sovereign LORD comes with *p*,
    40:26 of his great *p* and mighty strength,
    63:12 who sent his glorious arm of *p*
Jer 10: 6 and your name is mighty in *p*.
    10:12 But God made the earth by his *p*;
    27: 5 With my great *p* and outstretched

Jer 32:17 and the earth by your great *p*
Hos 13:14 from the *p* of the grave;
Na 1: 3 to anger and great in *p*;
Zec 4: 6 nor by *p*, but by my Spirit,'
Mt 22:29 do not know the Scriptures or the *p*
    24:30 on the clouds of the sky, with *p*
Lk 1:35 and the *p* of the Most High will
    4:14 to Galilee in the *p* of the Spirit,
    9: 1 he gave them *p* and authority
    10:19 to overcome all the *p* of the enemy;
    24:49 clothed with *p* from on high.''
Ac 1: 8 you will receive *p* when the Holy
    4:28 They did what your *p* and will had
    4:33 With great *p* the apostles
    10:38 with the Holy Spirit and *p*,
    26:18 and from the *p* of Satan to God,
Ro 1:16 it is the *p* of God for the salvation
    1:20 his eternal *p* and divine nature—
    4:21 fully persuaded that God had *p*
    9:17 that I might display my *p* in you
    15:13 overflow with hope by the *p*
    15:19 through the *p* of the Spirit.
1Co 1:17 cross of Christ be emptied of its *p*.
    1:18 to us who are being saved it is the *p*
    2: 4 a demonstration of the Spirit's *p*,
    6:14 By his *p* God raised the Lord
    15:24 all dominion, authority and *p*.
    15:56 of death is sin, and the *p*
2Co 4: 7 to show that this all-surpassing *p* is
    6: 7 in truthful speech and in the *p*
    10: 4 they have divine *p*
    12: 9 for my *p* is made perfect
    13: 4 weakness, yet he lives by God's *p*.
Eph 1:19 and his incomparably great *p*
    3:16 you with *p* through his Spirit
    3:20 according to his *p* that is at work
    6:10 in the Lord and in his mighty *p*.
Php 3:10 and the *p* of his resurrection
    3:21 by the *p* that enables him
Col 1:11 strengthened with all *p* according
    2:10 who is the head over every *p*
1Th 1: 5 also with *p*, with the Holy Spirit
2Ti 1: 7 but a spirit of *p*, of love
    3: 5 form of godliness but denying its *p*.
Heb 2:14 might destroy him who holds the *p*
    7:16 of the *p* of an indestructible life.
1Pe 1: 5 by God's *p* until the coming
2Pe 1: 3 His divine *p* has given us
Jude 25 and authority, through Jesus
Rev 4:11 to receive glory and honor and *p*,
    5:12 to receive *p* and wealth
    11:17 you have taken your great *p*
    19: 1 and glory and *p* belong to our God,
    20: 6 The second death has no *p*

POWERFUL (POWER)

2Ch 27: 5 Jotham grew *p* because he walked
Est 9: 4 and he became more and more *p*.
Ps 29: 4 The voice of the LORD is *p*;
Jer 32:18 *p* God, whose name is the LORD
Zec 8:22 *p* nations will come to Jerusalem
Mk 1: 7 ''After me will come one more *p*
Lk 24:19 in word and deed before God
2Th 1: 7 in blazing fire with his *p* angels.
Heb 1: 3 sustaining all things by his *p* word.
Jas 5:16 The prayer of a righteous man is *p*

POWERLESS

Ro 5: 6 when we were still *p*, Christ died
    8: 3 For what the law was *p* to do

POWERS (POWER)

Da 4:35 pleases with the *p* of heaven
Ro 8:38 nor any *p*, neither height nor depth
1Co 12:10 to another miraculous *p*,
Eph 6:12 against the *p* of this dark world
Col 1:16 whether thrones or *p* or rulers
    2:15 And having disarmed the *p*
Heb 6: 5 and the *p* of the coming age,
1Pe 3:22 and *p* in submission to him.

PRACTICE (PRACTICED PRACTICES)

Lev 19:26 '' 'Do not *p* divination or sorcery.
Ps 119:56 This has been my *p*:
Eze 33:31 but they do not put them into *p*.
Mt 7:24 into *p* is like a wise man who built
    23: 3 for they do not *p* what they preach.
Lk 8:21 hear God's word and put it into *p*.''

Ro 12:13 *P* hospitality.
Php 4: 9 or seen in me—put it into *p*.
1Ti 5: 4 to put their religion into *p* by caring

PRACTICED (PRACTICE)

Mt 23:23 You should have *p* the latter,

PRACTICES (PRACTICE)

Ps 101: 7 No one who *p* deceit
Mt 5:19 but whoever *p* and teaches these
Col 3: 9 taken off your old self with its *p*

PRAISE (PRAISED PRAISES PRAISEWORTHY PRAISING)

Ex 15: 2 He is my God, and I will *p* him,
Dt 10:21 He is your *p*; he is your God,
    26:19 declared that he will set you in *p*,
    32: 3 Oh, *p* the greatness of our God!
Ru 4:14 said to Naomi: ''*P* be to the LORD,
2Sa 22: 4 to the LORD, who is worthy of *p*,
    22:47 The LORD lives! *P* be to my Rock
1Ch 16:25 is the LORD and most worthy of *p*;
    16:35 that we may glory in your *p*.''
    23: 5 four thousand are to *p* the LORD
    29:10 ''*P* be to you, O LORD,
2Ch 5:13 they raised their voices in *p*
    20:21 and to *p* him for the splendor
    29:30 to *p* the LORD with the words
Ezr 3:10 took their places to *p* the LORD,
Ne 9: 5 and *p* the LORD your God,
Ps 8: 2 you have ordained *p*
    9: 1 I will *p* you, O LORD,
    16: 7 I will *p* the LORD, who counsels
    26: 7 proclaiming aloud your *p*
    30: 4 *p* his holy name.
    33: 1 it is fitting for the upright to *p* him.
    34: 1 his *p* will always be on my lips.
    40: 3 a hymn of *p* to our God.
    42: 5 for I will yet *p* him,
    43: 5 for I will yet *p* him,
    45:17 the nations will *p* you for ever
    47: 7 sing to him a psalm of *p*.
    48: 1 the LORD, and most worthy of *p*,
    51:15 and my mouth will declare your *p*.
    56: 4 In God, whose word I *p*,
    57: 9 I will *p* you, O Lord,
    63: 4 I will *p* you as long as I live,
    65: 1 *P* awaits you, O God, in Zion;
    66: 2 make his *p* glorious.
    66: 8 *P* our God, O peoples,
    68:19 *P* be to the Lord, to God our Savior
    68:26 *p* the LORD in the assembly
    69:30 I will *p* God's name in song
    69:34 Let heaven and earth *p* him,
    71: 8 My mouth is filled with your *p*,
    71:14 I will *p* you more and more.
    71:22 I will *p* you with the harp
    74:21 the poor and needy *p* your name.
    86:12 I will *p* you, O Lord my God,
    89: 5 The heavens *p* your wonders,
    92: 1 It is good to *p* the LORD
    96: 2 Sing to the LORD, *p* his name;
    100: 4 and his courts with *p*;
    101: 1 to you, O LORD, I will sing *p*.
    102:18 not yet created may *p* the LORD:
    103: 1 *P* the LORD, O my soul;
    103:20 *P* the LORD, you his angels,
    104: 1 *P* the LORD, O my soul.
    105: 2 Sing to him, sing *p* to him;
    106: 1 *P* the LORD.
    108: 3 I will *p* you, O LORD,
    111: 1 *P* the LORD.
    113: 1 *P* the LORD.
    117: 1 *P* the LORD, all you nations;
    119:175 Let me live that I may *p* you,
    135: 1 *P* the LORD.
    135:20 you who fear him, *p* the LORD.
    138: 1 I will *p* you, O LORD,
    139:14 I *p* you because I am fearfully
    144: 1 *P* be to the LORD my Rock,
    145: 3 is the LORD and most worthy of *p*;
    145:10 All you have made will *p* you,
    145:21 Let every creature *p* his holy name
    146: 1 *P* the LORD, O my soul.
    147: 1 how pleasant and fitting to *p* him!
    148: 1 *P* the LORD from the heavens,
    148:13 Let them *p* the name of the LORD,
    149: 1 his *p* in the assembly of the saints.

Ps 149:   6 May the *p* of God be
149:   9 *P* the Lord.
150:   2 *p* him for his surpassing greatness.
150:   6 that has breath *p* the Lord.
Pr 27:   2 Let another *p* you, and not your
27: 21 man is tested by the *p* he receives.
31: 31 let her works bring her *p*
SS   1:   4 we will *p* your love more than wine
Isa 12:   1 "I will *p* you, O Lord.
42: 10 his *p* from the ends of the earth,
61:   3 and a garment of *p*
Jer 33:   9 *p* and honor before all nations
Da   2: 20 "*P* be to the name of God for ever
4: 37 *p* and exalt and glorify the King
Mt   5: 16 and *p* your Father in heaven.
21: 16 you have ordained *p*'?"
Lk 19: 37 to *p* God in loud voices
Jn   5: 44 effort to obtain the *p* that comes
12: 43 for they loved *p* from men more
Ro   2: 29 Such a man's *p* is not from men,
15:   7 in order to bring *p* to God.
2Co   1:   3 *P* be to the God and Father
Eph   1:   3 *P* be to the God and Father
1:   6 to the *p* of his glorious grace,
1: 12 might be for the *p* of his glory.
1: 14 to the *p* of his glory.
1Th   2:   6 We were not looking for *p*
Heb 13: 15 offer to God a sacrifice of *p*—
Jas   3:   9 With the tongue we *p* our Lord
5: 13 happy? Let him sing songs of *p*.
Rev   5: 13 be *p* and honor and glory
7: 12 *P* and glory

PRAISED (PRAISE)

1Ch 29: 10 David *p* the Lord in the presence
Ne   8:   6 Ezra *p* the Lord, the great God;
Job   1: 21 may the name of the Lord be *p*."
Ps 113:   2 Let the name of the Lord be *p*,
Pr 31: 30 who fears the Lord is to be *p*.
Isa 63:   7 the deeds for which he is to be *p*,
Da   2: 19 Then Daniel *p* the God of heaven
4: 34 Then I *p* the Most High; I honored
Lk 18: 43 the people saw it, they also *p* God.
23: 47 seeing what had happened, *p* God
Ro   9:   5 who is God over all, forever *p*!
Gal   1: 24 And they *p* God because of me.
1Pe   4: 11 that in all things God may be *p*

PRAISES (PRAISE)

2Sa 22: 50 I will sing *p* to your name.
Ps   18: 49 I will sing *p* to your name.
47:   6 Sing *p* to God, sing *p*;
147:   1 How good it is to sing *p* to our God,
Pr 31: 28 her husband also, and he *p* her:
1Pe   2:   9 that you may declare the *p*

PRAISEWORTHY* (PRAISE)

Ps 78:   4 the *p* deeds of the Lord,
Php   4:   8 if anything is excellent or *p*—

PRAISING (PRAISE)

Lk   2: 13 *p* God and saying, "Glory to God
2: 20 *p* God for all the things they had
Ac   2: 47 *p* God and enjoying the favor
10: 46 speaking in tongues and *p* God.
1Co 14: 16 If you are *p* God with your spirit,

PRAY (PRAYED PRAYER PRAYERS PRAYING PRAYS)

Dt   4:   7 is near us whenever we *p* to him?
1Sa 12: 23 the Lord by failing to *p* for you.
1Ki   8: 30 when they *p* toward this place.
2Ch   7: 14 will humble themselves and *p*
Ezr   6: 10 and *p* for the well-being of the king
Job 42:   8 My servant Job will *p* for you,
Ps   5:   2 for to you I *p*.
32:   6 let everyone who is godly *p*
122:   6 *P* for the peace of Jerusalem:
Jer 29:   7 *P* to the Lord for it,
29: 12 upon me and come and *p* to me,
42:   3 *P* that the Lord your God will
Mt   5: 44 and *p* for those who persecute you,
6:   5 "And when you *p*, do not be like
6:   9 "This, then, is how you should *p*:
14: 23 up on a mountainside by himself to *p*.
19: 13 hands on them and *p* for them.
26: 36 Sit here while I go over there and *p*
Lk   6: 28 *p* for those who mistreat you.

Lk 11:   1 us to *p*, just as John taught his
18:   1 them that they should always *p*
22: 40 "*P* that you will not fall
Jn 17: 20 I *p* also for those who will believe
Ro   8: 26 do not know what we ought to *p* for,
1Co 14: 13 in a tongue should *p* that he may
Eph   1: 18 I *p* also that the eyes
3: 16 I *p* that out of his glorious riches he
6: 18 and *p* in the Spirit on all occasions
Col   1: 10 we *p* this in order that you may live
4:   3 *p* for us, too, that God may open
1Th   5: 17 Be joyful always; *p* continually;
2Th   1: 11 in mind, we constantly *p* for you,
Jas   5: 13 one of you in trouble? He should *p*.
5: 16 *p* for each other so that you may be
1Pe   4:   7 self-controlled so that you can *p*.
Jude   : 20 up in your most holy faith and *p*

PRAYED (PRAY)

1Sa   1: 27 I *p* for this child, and the Lord
1Ki 18: 36 Elijah stepped forward and *p*:
19:   4 under it and *p* that he might die.
2Ki   6: 17 And Elisha *p*, "O Lord,
2Ch 30: 18 But Hezekiah *p* for them, saying,
Ne   4:   9 we *p* to our God and posted a guard
Job 42: 10 After Job had *p* for his friends,
Da   6: 10 got down on his knees and *p*,
9:   4 I *p* to the Lord my God
Jnh   2:   1 From inside the fish Jonah *p*
Mt 26: 39 with his face to the ground and *p*,
Mk   1: 35 off to a solitary place, where he *p*.
14: 35 *p* that if possible the hour might
Lk 22: 41 knelt down and *p*, "Father,
Jn 17:   1 he looked toward heaven and *p*:
Ac   4: 31 After they *p*, the place where they
6:   6 who *p* and laid their hands on them
8: 15 they *p* for them that they might
13:   3 So after they had fasted and *p*,

PRAYER (PRAY)

2Ch 30: 27 for their *p* reached heaven,
Ezr   8: 23 about this, and he answered our *p*.
Ps   4:   1 be merciful to me and hear my *p*.
6:   9 the Lord accepts my *p*.
17:   1 Give ear to my *p*—
17:   6 give ear to me and hear my *p*.
65:   2 O you who hear *p*,
66: 20 who has not rejected my *p*
86:   6 Hear my *p*, O Lord,
Pr 15:   8 but the *p* of the upright pleases him
15: 29 but he hears the *p* of the righteous.
Isa 56:   7 a house of *p* for all nations."
Mt 21: 13 house will be called a house of *p*,'
21: 22 receive whatever you ask for in *p*."
Mk   9: 29 This kind can come out only by *p*."
11: 24 whatever you ask for in *p*,
Jn 17: 15 My *p* is not that you take them out
Ac   1: 14 all joined together constantly in *p*,
2: 42 to the breaking of bread and to *p*.
6:   4 and will give our attention to *p*
10: 31 has heard your *p* and remembered
16: 13 expected to find a place of *p*.
Ro 12: 12 patient in affliction, faithful in *p*.
1Co   7:   5 you may devote yourselves to *p*.
2Co 13:   9 and our *p* is for your perfection.
Php   1:   9 this is my *p*: that your love may
4:   6 but in everything, by *p* and petition
Col   4:   2 yourselves to *p*, being watchful
1Ti   2:   8 to lift up holy hands in *p*,
4:   5 by the word of God and *p*.
Jas   5: 15 *p* offered in faith will make the sick
1Pe   3: 12 and his ears are attentive to their *p*,

PRAYERS (PRAY)

1Ch   5: 20 He answered their *p*, because they
Isa   1: 15 even if you offer many *p*,
Mk 12: 40 and for a show make lengthy *p*.
2Co   1: 11 as you help us by your *p*.
Eph   6: 18 on all occasions with all kinds of *p*
1Ti   2:   1 then, first of all, that requests, *p*,
1Pe   3:   7 so that nothing will hinder your *p*.
Rev   5:   8 which are the *p* of the saints.
8:   3 with the *p* of all the saints,

PRAYING (PRAY)

Ge 24: 45 "Before I finished *p* in my heart,
1Sa   1: 12 As she kept on *p* to the Lord,
Mk 11: 25 And when you stand *p*,

Lk   3: 21 as he was *p*, heaven was opened
6: 12 and spent the night *p* to God.
9: 29 As he was *p*, the appearance
Jn 17:   9 I am not *p* for the world,
Ac   9: 11 from Tarsus named Saul, for he is *p*
16: 25 and Silas were *p* and singing hymns
Ro 15: 30 in my struggle by *p* to God for me.
Eph   6: 18 always keep on *p* for all the saints.

PRAYS (PRAY)

1Co 14: 14 my spirit *p*, but my mind is

PREACH (PREACHED PREACHING)

Isa 61:   1 me to *p* good news to the poor.
Mt 10:   7 As you go, *p* this message:
23:   3 they do not practice what they *p*.
Mk 16: 15 and *p* the good news to all creation.
Lk   4: 18 me to *p* good news to the poor.
Ac   9: 20 At once he began to *p*
16: 10 us to *p* the gospel to them.
Ro   1: 15 am so eager to *p* the gospel
10: 15 how can they *p* unless they are sent
15: 20 to *p* the gospel where Christ was
1Co   1: 17 to *p* the gospel—not with words
1: 23 wisdom, but we *p* Christ crucified:
9: 14 that those who *p* the gospel should
9: 16 Woe to me if I do not *p* the gospel!
2Co   4:   5 For we do not *p* ourselves,
10: 16 so that we can *p* the gospel
Gal   1:   8 from heaven should *p* a gospel
2Ti   4:   2 I give you this charge: *P* the Word;

PREACHED (PREACH)

Mt 24: 14 gospel of the kingdom will be *p*
Mk   6: 12 and *p* that people should repent.
13: 10 And the gospel must first be *p*
14:   9 wherever the gospel is *p*
Ac   8:   4 had been scattered *p* the word
28: 31 hindrance he *p* the kingdom
1Co   9: 27 so that after I have *p* to others,
15:   1 you of the gospel I *p* to you,
2Co 11:   4 other than the Jesus we *p*,
Gal   1:   8 other than the one we *p* to you,
Eph   2: 17 *p* peace to you who were far away
Php   1: 18 false motives or true, Christ is *p*.
1Ti   3: 16 was *p* among the nations,
1Pe   1: 25 this is the word that was *p* to you.
3: 19 and *p* to the spirits in prison who

PREACHING (PREACH)

Lk   9:   6 *p* the gospel and healing people
Ac 18:   5 devoted himself exclusively to *p*,
Ro 10: 14 hear without someone *p* to them?
1Co   2:   4 and my *p* were not with wise
9: 18 in *p* the gospel I may offer it free
Gal   1:   9 If anybody is *p* to you a gospel
1Ti   4: 13 the public reading of Scripture, to *p*
5: 17 especially those whose work is *p*

PRECEDE*

1Th   4: 15 will certainly not *p* those who have

PRECEPTS*

Dt 33: 10 He teaches your *p* to Jacob
Ps   19:   8 The *p* of the Lord are right,
103: 18 and remember to obey his *p*.
105: 45 that they might keep his *p*
111:   7 all his *p* are trustworthy.
111: 10 who follow his *p* have good
119:   4 You have laid down *p*
119: 15 I meditate on your *p*
119: 27 understand the teaching of your *p*;
119: 40 How I long for your *p*!
119: 45 for I have sought out your *p*.
119: 56 I obey your *p*.
119: 63 to all who follow your *p*.
119: 69 I keep your *p* with all my heart.
119: 78 but I will meditate on your *p*.
119: 87 but I have not forsaken your *p*.
119: 93 I will never forget your *p*,
119: 94 I have sought out your *p*.
119: 100 for I obey your *p*.
119: 104 I gain understanding from your *p*;
119: 110 but I have not strayed from your *p*.
119: 128 because I consider all your *p* right,
119: 134 that I may obey your *p*.
119: 141 I do not forget your *p*.
119: 159 See how I love your *p*;

PRECIOUS (continued)

Ps 119:168 I obey your *p* and your statutes,
  119:173 for I have chosen your *p*.

PRECIOUS

Ps 19: 10 They are more *p* than gold,
  72: 14 for *p* is their blood in his sight.
  116: 15 *P* in the sight of the LORD
  119: 72 from your mouth is more *p* to me
  139: 17 How *p* to me are your thoughts,
Pr   8: 11 for wisdom is more *p* than rubies.
Isa 28: 16 a *p* cornerstone for a sure
1Pe 1: 19 but with the *p* blood of Christ,
   2: 4 but chosen by God and *p* to him—
   2: 6 a chosen and *p* cornerstone,
2Pe 1: 1 Christ have received a faith as *p*
   1: 4 us his very great and *p* promises,

PREDESTINED* (DESTINY)

Ro   8: 29 *p* to be conformed to the likeness
   8: 30 And those he *p*, he also called;
Eph 1: 5 In love he *p* us to be adopted
   1: 11 having been *p* according

PREDICTED (PREDICTION)

1Sa 28: 17 The LORD has done what he *p*
Ac   7: 52 killed those who *p* the coming
1Pe 1: 11 when he *p* the sufferings of Christ

PREDICTION* (PREDICTED PREDICTIONS)

Jer 28: 9 only if his *p* comes true.''

PREDICTIONS (PREDICTION)

Isa 44: 26 and fulfills the *p* of his messengers,

PREGNANT

Ex 21: 22 who are fighting hit a *p* woman
Mt 24: 19 be in those days for *p* women
1Th 5: 3 as labor pains on a *p* woman,

PREPARE (PREPARED)

Ps 23: 5 You *p* a table before me
Isa 25: 6 the LORD Almighty will *p*
  40: 3 ''In the desert *p*
Am   4: 12 *p* to meet your God, O Israel.''
Mal 3: 1 who will *p* the way before me.
Mt   3: 3 '*P* the way for the Lord,
Jn 14: 2 there to *p* a place for you.
Eph 4: 12 to *p* God's people for works
1Pe 1: 13 Therefore, *p* your minds for action;

PREPARED (PREPARE)

Ex 23: 20 to bring you to the place I have *p*.
Mt 25: 34 the kingdom *p* for you
Ro   9: 22 of his wrath—*p* for destruction?
1Co 2: 9 what God has *p* for those who love
Eph 2: 10 which God *p* in advance for us
2Ti 2: 21 and *p* to do any good work.
   4: 2 be *p* in season and out of season;
1Pe 3: 15 Always be *p* to give an answer

PRESCRIBED

Ezr 7: 23 Whatever the God of heaven has *p*,

PRESENCE (PRESENT)

Ex 25: 30 Put the bread of the *P* on this table
  33: 14 The LORD replied, ''My *P* will go
Nu   4: 7 ''Over the table of the *P* they are
1Sa 6: 20 in the *p* of the LORD, this
  21: 6 of the *P* that had been removed
2Sa 22: 13 Out of the brightness of his *p*
2Ki 17: 23 LORD removed them from his *p*,
  23: 27 also from my *p* as I removed Israel,
Ezr 9: 15 one of us can stand in your *p*.''
Ps 16: 11 you will fill me with joy in your *p*,
  21: 6 with the joy of your *p*.
  23: 5 in the *p* of my enemies.
  31: 20 the shelter of your *p* you hide them
  41: 12 and set me in your *p* forever.
  51: 11 Do not cast me from your *p*
  52: 9 in the *p* of your saints.
  89: 15 who walk in the light of your *p*,
  90: 8 our secret sins in the light of your *p*
  114: 7 O earth, at the *p* of the Lord,
  139: 7 Where can I flee from your *p*?
Isa 26: 17 so were we in your *p*, O LORD,
Jer 5: 22 ''Should you not tremble in my *p*?
Eze 38: 20 of the earth will tremble at my *p*.

Hos 6: 2 that we may live in his *p*.
Na   1: 5 The earth trembles at his *p*,
Mal 3: 16 in his *p* concerning those who
Ac   2: 28 you will fill me with joy in your *p*.'
1Th 3: 9 have in the *p* of our God
   3: 13 and holy in the *p* of our God
2Th 1: 9 and shut out from the *p* of the Lord
Heb 9: 24 now to appear for us in God's *p*.
1Jn 3: 19 rest in his *p* whenever our hearts
Jude : 24 before his glorious *p* without fault

PRESENT (PRESENCE)

Ps 46: 1 an ever *p* help in trouble.
1Co 7: 22 life or death or the *p* or the future—
   7: 26 of the *p* crisis, I think that it is good
2Co 11: 2 so that I might *p* you as a pure
Eph 5: 27 and to *p* her to himself
1Ti 4: 8 holding promise for both the *p* life
2Ti 2: 15 Do your best to *p* yourself to God
Jude : 24 and to *p* you before his glorious

PRESERVE

Lk 17: 33 and whoever loses his life will *p* it.

PRESS (PRESSED PRESSURE)

Php 3: 12 but I *p* on to take hold of that
   3: 14 I *p* on toward the goal

PRESSED (PRESS)

Lk   6: 38 *p* down, shaken together

PRESSURE (PRESS)

2Co 1: 8 We were under great *p*, far
  11: 28 I face daily the *p* of my concern

PREVAILS

1Sa 2: 9 ''It is not by strength that one *p*;
Pr 19: 21 but it is the LORD's purpose that *p*

PRICE (PRICELESS)

Job 28: 18 the *p* of wisdom is beyond rubies.
1Co 6: 20 your own; you were bought at a *p*.
   7: 23 bought at a *p*; do not become slaves

PRICELESS* (PRICE)

Ps 36: 7 How *p* is your unfailing love!

PRIDE (PROUD)

Pr   8: 13 I hate *p* and arrogance,
  11: 2 When *p* comes, then comes
  13: 10 *P* only breeds quarrels,
  16: 18 *P* goes before destruction,
  29: 23 A man's *p* brings him low,
Isa 25: 11 God will bring down their *p*
Da   4: 37 And those who walk in *p* he is able
Am   8: 7 The LORD has sworn by the *P*
2Co 5: 12 giving you an opportunity to take *p*
   7: 4 in you; I take great *p* in you.
   8: 24 and the reason for our *p* in you,
Gal 6: 4 Then he can take *p* in himself,
Jas 1: 9 ought to take *p* in his high position.

PRIEST (PRIESTHOOD PRIESTLY PRIESTS)

Ge 14: 18 He was *p* of God Most High,
Nu   5: 10 to the *p* will belong to the *p*.' ''
2Ch 13: 9 and seven rams may become a *p*
Ps 110: 4 ''You are a *p* forever,
Heb 2: 17 faithful high *p* in service to God,
   3: 1 and high *p* whom we confess.
   4: 14 have a great high *p* who has gone
   4: 15 do not have a high *p* who is unable
   5: 6 ''You are a *p* forever,
   6: 20 He has become a high *p* forever,
   7: 3 Son of God he remains a *p* forever.
   7: 15 clear if another *p* like Melchizedek
   7: 26 Such a high *p* meets our need—
   8: 1 We do have such a high *p*,
  10: 11 Day after day every *p* stands
  13: 11 The high *p* carries the blood

PRIESTHOOD (PRIEST)

Heb 7: 24 lives forever, he has a permanent *p*.
1Pe 2: 5 into a spiritual house to be a holy *p*,
   2: 9 you are a chosen people, a royal *p*,

PRIESTLY (PRIEST)

Ro 15: 16 to the Gentiles with the *p* duty

PRIESTS (PRIEST)

Ex 19: 6 you will be for me a kingdom of *p*
Lev 21: 1 ''Speak to the *p*, the sons of Aaron,
Eze 42: 13 where the *p* who approach
  46: 2 *p* are to sacrifice his burnt offering
Mal 1: 6 O *p*, who show contempt for my name.
Rev 5: 10 to be a kingdom and *p*
  20: 6 but they will be *p* of God

PRIME

Isa 38: 10 recovery: I said, ''In the *p* of my life

PRINCE (PRINCES PRINCESS)

Isa 9: 6 Everlasting Father, *P* of Peace.
Eze 34: 24 and my servant David will be *p*
  37: 25 my servant will be their *p* forever.
Da   8: 25 stand against the *P* of princes.
Jn 12: 31 now the *p* of this world will be
Ac   5: 31 as *P* and Savior that he might give

PRINCES (PRINCE)

Ps 118: 9 than to trust in *p*.
  148: 11 you *p* and all rulers on earth,
Isa 40: 23 He brings *p* to naught

PRINCESS* (PRINCE)

Ps 45: 13 All glorious is the *p*

PRISCILLA*

Wife of Aquila; co-worker with Paul (Ac 18; Ro 16:3; 1Co 16:19; 2Ti 4:19); instructor of Apollos (Ac 18:24-28).

PRISON (PRISONER PRISONERS)

Ps 66: 11 You brought us into *p*
  142: 7 Set me free from my *p*,
Isa 42: 7 to free captives from *p*
Mt 25: 36 I was in *p* and you came to visit me
2Co 11: 23 been in *p* more frequently,
Heb 11: 36 others were chained and put in *p*.
  13: 3 Remember those in *p*
1Pe 3: 19 spirits in *p* who disobeyed long ago
Rev 20: 7 Satan will be released from his *p*

PRISONER (PRISON)

Ro   7: 23 and making me a *p* of the law of sin
Gal 3: 22 declares that the whole world is a *p*
Eph 3: 1 the *p* of Christ Jesus for the sake

PRISONERS (PRISON)

Ps 68: 6 he leads forth the *p* with singing;
  79: 11 groans of the *p* come before you;
  107: 10 *p* suffering in iron chains,
  146: 7 The LORD sets *p* free,
Zec 9: 12 to your fortress, O *p* of hope;
Lk   4: 18 me to proclaim freedom for the *p*
Gal 3: 23 we were held *p* by the law,

PRIVILEGE*

2Co 8: 4 pleaded with us for the *p* of sharing

PRIZE*

1Co 9: 24 Run in such a way as to get the *p*.
   9: 24 but only one gets the *p*? Run
   9: 27 will not be disqualified for the *p*.
Php 3: 14 on toward the goal to win the *p*
Col 2: 18 of angels disqualify you for the *p*.

PROBE

Job 11: 7 Can you *p* the limits
Ps 17: 3 Though you *p* my heart

PROCEDURE

Ecc 8: 6 For there is a proper time and *p*

PROCESSION

Ps 68: 24 Your *p* has come into view, O God,
  118: 27 boughs in hand, join in the festal *p*
1Co 4: 9 on display at the end of the *p*,
2Co 2: 14 us in triumphal *p* in Christ

PROCLAIM (PROCLAIMED PROCLAIMING PROCLAIMS PROCLAMATION)

Ex 33: 19 and I will *p* my name, the LORD,
Lev 25: 10 and *p* liberty throughout the land
Dt 30: 12 and *p* it to us so we may obey it?''
2Sa 1: 20 *p* it not in the streets of Ashkelon,

1Ch 16: 23 *p* his salvation day after day.
Ne 8: 15 and that they should *p* this word
Ps 2: 7 I will *p* the decree of the LORD:
 9: 11 *p* among the nations what he has
 19: 1 the skies *p* the work of his hands.
 22: 31 They will *p* his righteousness
 40: 9 I *p* righteousness in the great
 50: 6 the heavens *p* his righteousness,
 64: 9 they will *p* the works of God
 68: 34 *P* the power of God,
 71: 16 I will come and *p* your mighty acts,
 92: 2 to *p* your love in the morning
 96: 2 *p* his salvation day after day.
 97: 6 The heavens *p* his righteousness,
 106: 2 Who can *p* the mighty acts
 118: 17 will *p* what the LORD has done.
 145: 6 and I will *p* your great deeds.
Isa 12: 4 and *p* that his name is exalted.
 42: 12 and *p* his praise in the islands.
 52: 7 who *p* salvation,
 61: 1 to *p* freedom for the captives
 66: 19 They will *p* my glory
Jer 7: 2 house and there *p* this message:
 50: 2 lift up a banner and *p* it;
Hos 5: 9 I *p* what is certain.
Zec 9: 10 He will *p* peace to the nations.
Mt 10: 27 in your ear, *p* from the roofs.
 12: 18 and he will *p* justice to the nations.
Lk 4: 18 me to *p* freedom for the prisoners
 9: 60 you go and *p* the kingdom of God.''
Ac 17: 23 unknown I am going to *p*
 20: 27 hesitated to *p* to you the whole will
1Co 11: 26 you *p* the Lord's death
Col 1. 28 We *p* him, admonishing
 4: 4 Pray that I may *p* it clearly,
1Jn 1: 1 this we *p* concerning the Word

PROCLAIMED (PROCLAIM)

Ex 9: 16 and that my name might be *p*
 34: 5 there with him and *p* his name,
Ps 68: 11 was the company of those who *p* it:
Ro 15: 19 I have fully *p* the gospel of Christ.
Col 1: 23 that has been *p* to every creature
2Ti 4: 17 me the message might be fully *p*

PROCLAIMING (PROCLAIM)

Ps 26: 7 *p* aloud your praise
 92: 15 *p*, ''The LORD is upright;
Ac 5: 42 and *p* the good news that Jesus is
Ro 10: 8 the word of faith we are *p:*

PROCLAIMS (PROCLAIM)

Dt 18: 22 If what a prophet *p* in the name

PROCLAMATION (PROCLAIM)

Isa 62: 11 The LORD has made *p*

PRODUCE (PRODUCES)

Mt 3: 8 *P* fruit in keeping with repentance.
 3: 10 tree that does not *p* good fruit will

PRODUCES (PRODUCE)

Pr 30: 33 so stirring up anger *p* strife.''
Ro 5: 3 that suffering *p* perseverance;
Heb 12: 11 it *p* a harvest of righteousness

PROFANE (PROFANED)

Lev 19: 12 and so *p* the name of your God.
 22: 32 Do not *p* my holy name.
Mal 2: 10 Why do we *p* the covenant

PROFANED (PROFANE)

Eze 36: 20 the nations they *p* my holy name,

PROFESS*

1Ti 2: 10 for women who *p* to worship God.
Heb 4: 14 let us hold firmly to the faith we *p*.
 10: 23 unswervingly to the hope we *p*,

PROFIT (PROFITABLE)

Pr 14: 23 All hard work brings a *p*,
 21: 5 The plans of the diligent lead to *p*
Isa 44: 10 which can *p* him nothing?
2Co 2: 17 not peddle the word of God for *p*.
Php 3: 7 was to my *p* I now consider loss

PROFITABLE* (PROFIT)

Pr 3: 14 for she is more *p* than silver

Pr 31: 18 She sees that her trading is *p*,
Tit 3: 8 These things are excellent and *p*

PROFOUND

Job 9: 4 His wisdom is *p*, his power is vast.
Ps 92: 5 how *p* your thoughts!
Eph 5: 32 This is a *p* mystery—but I am

PROGRESS

Php 1: 25 continue with all of you for your *p*
1Ti 4: 15 so that everyone may see your *p*.

PROLONG*

Dt 5: 33 *p* your days in the land that you
Ps 85: 5 Will you *p* your anger
Pr 3: 2 for they will *p* your life many years
Isa 53: 10 will see his offspring and *p* his days,
La 4: 22 he will not *p* your exile.

PROMISE (PROMISED PROMISES)

Nu 23: 19 Does he *p* and not fulfill?
Jos 23: 14 Every *p* has been fulfilled;
2Sa 7: 25 keep forever the *p* you have made
1Ki 8: 20 The LORD has kept the *p* he made
 8: 24 You have kept your *p*
Ne 5: 13 man who does not keep this *p*.
 9: 8 have kept your *p* because you are
Ps 77: 8 Has his *p* failed for all time?
 119: 41 your salvation according to your *p;*
 119: 50 Your *p* preserves my life.
 119: 58 to me according to your *p*.
 119:162 I rejoice in your *p*
Ac 2: 39 The *p* is for you and your children
Ro 4: 13 offspring received the *p* that he
 4: 20 unbelief regarding the *p* of God,
Gal 3: 14 that by faith we might receive the *p*
Eph 2: 12 foreigners to the covenants of the *p*
1Ti 4: 8 holding *p* for both the present life
Heb 6: 13 When God made his *p* to Abraham
 11: 11 him faithful who had made the *p*.
2Pe 3: 9 Lord is not slow in keeping his *p*,
 3: 13 with his *p* we are looking forward

PROMISED (PROMISE)

Ge 21: 1 did for Sarah what he had *p*.
 24: 7 who spoke to me and *p* me on oath,
Ex 3: 17 And I have *p* to bring you up out
Nu 10: 29 for the LORD has *p* good things
Dt 15: 6 your God will bless you as he has *p*,
 26: 18 his treasured possession as he *p*,
2Sa 7: 28 and you have *p* these good things
1Ki 9: 5 I *p* David your father when I said,
2Ch 6: 15 with your mouth you have *p*
Ps 119: 57 I have *p* to obey your words.
Lk 24: 49 to send you what my Father has *p;*
Ac 1: 4 but wait for the gift my Father *p*,
 13: 32 What God *p* our fathers he has
Ro 4: 21 power to do what he had *p*.
Tit 1: 2 *p* before the beginning of time,
Heb 10: 23 for he who *p* is faithful.
 10: 36 you will receive what he has *p*.
Jas 1: 12 the crown of life that God has *p*
 2: 5 the kingdom he *p* those who love
2Pe 3: 4 ''Where is this 'coming' he *p?*
1Jn 2: 25 And this is what he *p* us—

PROMISES (PROMISE)

Jos 21: 45 one of all the LORD's good *p*
 23: 14 of all the good *p* the LORD your
1Ki 8: 56 failed of all the good *p* he gave
1Ch 17: 19 and made known all these great *p*.
Ps 85: 8 he *p* peace to his people, his saints
 106: 12 Then they believed his *p*
 119:140 Your *p* have been thoroughly
 119:148 that I may meditate on your *p*.
 145: 13 The LORD is faithful to all his *p*
Ro 9: 4 the temple worship and the *p*.
2Co 1: 20 matter how many *p* God has made,
 7: 1 Since we have these *p*, dear friends,
Heb 8: 6 and it is founded on better *p*.
2Pe 1: 4 us his very great and precious *p*,

PROMOTE (PROMOTES)

Pr 12: 20 but joy for those who *p* peace.
 16: 21 and pleasant words *p* instruction.
1Ti 1: 4 These *p* controversies rather

PROMOTES (PROMOTE)

Pr 17: 9 over an offense *p* love,

PROMPTED

1Th 1: 3 your labor *p* by love, and your
2Th 1: 11 and every act *p* by your faith.

PRONOUNCE (PRONOUNCED)

1Ch 23: 13 to *p* blessings in his name forever.

PRONOUNCED (PRONOUNCE)

1Ch 16: 12 miracles, and the judgments he *p*,

PROOF (PROVE)

Ac 17: 31 He has given *p* of this to all men
2Co 8: 24 Therefore show these men the *p*

PROPER

Ps 104: 27 give them their food at the *p* time.
 145: 15 give them their food at the *p* time.
Ecc 5: 18 Then I realized that it is good and *p*
 8: 5 the wise heart will know the *p* time
Mt 24: 45 give them their food at the *p* time?
Lk 1: 20 which will come true at their *p* time
1Co 11: 13 Is it *p* for a woman to pray to God
Gal 6: 9 at the *p* time we will reap a harvest
1Ti 2: 6 the testimony given in its *p* time.
1Pe 2: 17 Show *p* respect to everyone:

PROPERTY

Heb 10: 34 the confiscation of your *p*,

PROPHECIES (PROPHESY)

1Co 13: 8 where there are *p*, they will cease;
1Th 5. 20 do not treat *p* with contempt.

PROPHECY (PROPHESY)

Da 9: 24 to seal up vision and *p*
1Co 12: 10 miraculous powers, to another *p*,
 13: 2 of *p* and can fathom all mysteries
 14: 1 gifts, especially the gift of *p*.
 14: 6 or *p* or word of instruction?
 14: 22 *p*, however, is for believers,
2Pe 1: 20 you must understand that no *p*
Rev 22: 18 the words of the *p* of this book:

PROPHESIED (PROPHESY)

Nu 11: 25 the Spirit rested on them, they *p*,
1Sa 19: 24 and also *p* in Samuel's presence.
Jn 11: 51 that year he *p* that Jesus would
Ac 19: 6 and they spoke in tongues and *p*.
 21: 9 four unmarried daughters who *p*.

PROPHESIES (PROPHESY)

Jer 28: 9 the prophet who *p* peace will be
Eze 12: 27 and he *p* about the distant future.'
1Co 11: 4 *p* with his head covered dishonors
 14: 3 But everyone who *p* speaks to men

PROPHESY (PROPHECIES PROPHECY PROPHESIED PROPHESIES PROPHESYING PROPHET PROPHET'S PROPHETESS PROPHETS)

1Sa 10: 6 and you will *p* with them;
Eze 13: 2 Say to those who *p*
 13: 17 daughters of your people who *p* out
 34: 2 *p* against the shepherds of Israel;
 37: 4 ''*P* to these bones and say to them,
Joel 2: 28 Your sons and daughters will *p*,
Mt 7: 22 Lord, did we not *p* in your name,
Ac 2: 17 Your sons and daughters will *p*,
1Co 13: 9 know in part and we *p* in part,
 14: 39 my brothers, be eager to *p*,
Rev 11: 3 and they will *p* for 1,260 days,

PROPHESYING (PROPHESY)

1Ch 25: 1 and Jeduthun for the ministry of *p*,
Ro 12: 6 If a man's gift is *p*, let him use it

PROPHET (PROPHESY)

Ex 7: 1 your brother Aaron will be your *p*.
Nu 12: 6 ''When a *p* of the LORD is
Dt 13: 1 If a *p*, or one who foretells
 18: 18 up for them a *p* like you
 18: 22 If what a *p* proclaims in the name
1Sa 3: 20 that Samuel was attested as a *p*
 9: 9 because the *p* of today used
1Ki 1: 8 son of Jehoiada, Nathan the *p*,

PROPHET'S

1Ki 18: 36 the *p* Elijah stepped forward
2Ki 5: 8 and he will know that there is a *p*
6: 12 "but Elisha, the *p* who is in Israel,
20: 1 The *p* Isaiah son of Amoz went
2Ch 35: 18 since the days of the *p* Samuel;
36: 12 himself before Jeremiah the *p*,
Ezr 5: 1 Haggai the *p* and Zechariah the,
Eze 2: 5 they will know that a *p* has been
33: 33 they will know that a *p* has been
Hos 9: 7 the *p* is considered a fool,
Am 7: 14 "I was neither a *p* nor a prophet's
Hab 1: 1 that Habakkuk the *p* received.
Hag 1: 1 came through the *p* Haggai
Zec 1: 1 to the *p* Zechariah son of Berekiah,
13: 4 that day every *p* will be ashamed
Mal 4: 5 I will send you the *p* Elijah
Mt 10: 41 Anyone who receives a *p*
11: 9 what did you go out to see? A *p?*
12: 39 except the sign of the *p* Jonah.
Lk 1: 76 will be called a *p* of the Most High;
4: 24 "no *p* is accepted in his hometown.
7: 16 A great *p* has appeared among us,"
24: 19 "He was a *p*, powerful in word
Jn 1: 21 "Are you the *P?*" He answered,
Ac 3: 22 'God will send you a *p* like me
21: 10 a *p* named Agabus came
1Co 14: 37 If anybody thinks he is a *p*
Rev 16: 13 and out of the mouth of the false *p*.

PROPHET'S (PROPHESY)

2Pe 1: 20 about by the *p* own interpretation.

PROPHETESS (PROPHESY)

Ex 15: 20 Then Miriam the *p*, Aaron's sister,
Jdg 4: 4 a *p*, the wife of Lappidoth,
Isa 8: 3 I went to the *p*, and she conceived
Lk 2: 36 a *p*, Anna, the daughter of Phanuel,

PROPHETS (PROPHESY)

Nu 11: 29 that all the LORD's people were *p*
1Sa 10: 11 Is Saul also among the *p?*"
28: 6 him by dreams or Urim or *p*.
1Ki 19: 10 put your *p* to death with the sword.
1Ch 16: 22 do my *p* no harm."
Ps 105: 15 do my *p* no harm."
Jer 23: 9 Concerning the *p;*
23: 30 "I am against the *p* who steal
Eze 13: 2 prophesy against the *p*
Mt 5: 17 come to abolish the Law or the *P;*
7: 12 for this sums up the Law and the *P.*
7: 15 "Watch out for false *p*.
22: 40 and the *P* hang on these two
23: 37 you who kill the *p* and stone those
24: 24 false Christs and false *p* will appear
26: 56 of the *p* might be fulfilled."
Lk 10: 24 For I tell you that many *p*
11: 49 'I will send them *p* and apostles,
24: 25 believe all that the *p* have spoken!
24: 44 me in the Law of Moses, the *P*
Ac 3: 24 "Indeed, all the *p* from Samuel on,
10: 43 All the *p* testify about him that
13: 1 the church at Antioch there were *p*
26: 22 nothing beyond what the *p*
28: 23 the Law of Moses and from the *P.*
Ro 1: 2 through his *p* in the Holy
3: 21 to which the Law and the *P* testify.
11: 3 they have killed your *p*
1Co 12: 28 second *p*, third teachers, then
12: 29 Are all *p?* Are all teachers?
14: 32 The spirits of *p* are subject
Eph 2: 20 foundation of the apostles and *p*,
3: 5 Spirit to God's holy apostles and *p*.
4: 11 some to be *p*, some
Heb 1: 1 through the *p* at many times
1Pe 1: 10 Concerning this salvation, the *p*,
2Pe 1: 19 word of the *p* made more certain,
3: 2 spoken in the past by the holy *p*
1Jn 4: 1 because many false *p* have gone out
Rev 11: 10 these two *p* had tormented those
18: 20 Rejoice, saints and apostles and *p!*

PROPITIATION see (atoning) SACRIFICE

PROPORTION

Dt 16: 10 by giving a freewill offering in *p*
16: 17 Each of you must bring a gift in *p*

PROPRIETY*

1Ti 2: 9 with decency and *p*,
2: 15 in faith, love and holiness with *p*.

PROSPECT*

Pr 10: 28 The *p* of the righteous is joy,

PROSPER (PROSPERED PROSPERITY PROSPEROUS PROSPERS)

Dt 5: 33 so that you may live and *p*
28: 63 pleased the LORD to make you *p*
29: 9 that you may *p* in everything you
1Ki 2: 3 so that you may *p* in all you do
Ezr 6: 14 and *p* under the preaching
Pr 11: 10 When the righteous *p*, the city
11: 25 A generous man will *p;*
17: 20 A man of perverse heart does not *p*
28: 13 who conceals his sins does not *p*,
28: 25 he who trusts in the LORD will *p*.
Isa 53: 10 of the LORD will *p* in his hand.
Jer 12: 1 Why does the way of the wicked *p?*

PROSPERED (PROSPER)

Ge 39: 2 was with Joseph and he *p*,
2Ch 14: 7 So they built and *p*.
31: 21 And so he *p*.

PROSPERITY (PROSPER)

Dt 28: 11 will grant you abundant *p—*
30: 15 I set before you today life and *p*,
Job 36: 11 will spend the rest of their days in *p*
Ps 73: 3 when I saw the *p* of the wicked.
122: 9 I will seek your *p*.
128: 2 blessings and *p* will be yours.
Pr 3: 2 and bring you *p*.
13: 21 but *p* is the reward of the righteous.
21: 21 finds life, *p* and honor.
Isa 45: 7 I bring *p* and create disaster;

PROSPEROUS (PROSPER)

Dt 30: 9 your God will make you most *p*
Jos 1: 8 Then you will be *p* and successful.
Job 42: 10 the LORD made him *p* again

PROSPERS (PROSPER)

Ps 1: 3 Whatever he does *p*.
Pr 16: 20 gives heed to instruction *p*,
19: 8 he who cherishes understanding *p*.

PROSTITUTE (PROSTITUTES PROSTITUTION)

Lev 20: 6 and spiritists to *p* himself
Nu 15: 39 and not *p* yourselves by going
Jos 2: 1 the house of a *p* named Rahab
Pr 6: 26 for the *p* reduces you to a loaf
7: 10 like a *p* and with crafty intent.
23: 27 for a *p* is a deep pit
Eze 16: 15 and used your fame to become a *p*.
23: 7 a *p* to all the elite of the Assyrians
Hos 3: 3 you must not be a *p* or be intimate
1Co 6: 15 of Christ and unite them with a *p?*
6: 16 with a *p* is one with her in body?
Rev 17: 1 you the punishment of the great *p*,

PROSTITUTES (PROSTITUTE)

Pr 29: 3 of *p* squanders his wealth.
Mt 21: 31 and the *p* are entering the kingdom
Lk 15: 30 property with *p* comes home,
1Co 6: 9 male *p* nor homosexual offenders

PROSTITUTION (PROSTITUTE)

Eze 16: 16 where you carried on your *p*.
23: 3 engaging in *p* from their youth.
Hos 4: 10 engage in *p* but not increase,

PROSTRATE

Dt 9: 18 again I fell *p* before the LORD
1Ki 18: 39 they fell *p* and cried, "The LORD

PROTECT (PROTECTED PROTECTION PROTECTS)

Dt 23: 14 about in your camp to *p* you
Ps 25: 21 integrity and uprightness *p* me,
32: 7 you will *p* me from trouble
40: 11 your truth always *p* me.
41: 2 The LORD will *p* him
91: 14 I will *p* him, for he acknowledges
140: 1 *p* me from men of violence,

PROTECTED (PROTECT)

Pr 2: 11 Discretion will *p* you,
4: 6 forsake wisdom, and she will *p* you;
Jn 17: 11 *p* them by the power of your name
17: 15 that you *p* them from the evil one.
2Th 3: 3 and *p* you from the evil one.

PROTECTED (PROTECT)

Jos 24: 17 He *p* us on our entire journey
1Sa 30: 23 He has *p* us and handed
Ps 37: 28 They will be *p* forever,
Jn 17: 12 I *p* them and kept them safe

PROTECTION (PROTECT)

Ezr 9: 9 he has given us a wall of *p* in Judah
Ps 5: 11 Spread your *p* over them,

PROTECTS (PROTECT)

Ps 116: 6 The LORD *p* the simplehearted;
Pr 2: 8 and *p* the way of his faithful ones.
1Co 13: 7 It always *p*, always trusts,

PROUD (PRIDE)

Ps 31: 23 but the *p* he pays back in full.
101: 5 has haughty eyes and a *p* heart,
138: 6 but the *p* he knows from afar.
Pr 3: 34 He mocks *p* mockers
16: 5 The LORD detests all the *p*
16: 19 than to share plunder with the *p*.
18: 12 his downfall a man's heart is *p*,
21: 4 Haughty eyes and a *p* heart,
Isa 2: 12 store for all the *p* and lofty,
Ro 12: 16 Do not be *p*, but be willing
1Co 13: 4 it does not boast, it is not *p*.
2Ti 3: 2 lovers of money, boastful, *p*,
Jas 4: 6 "God opposes the *p*
1Pe 5: 5 because, "God opposes the *p*

PROVE (PROOF PROVED PROVING)

Pr 29: 25 Fear of man will *p* to be a snare,
Jn 8: 46 Can any of you *p* me guilty of sin?
Ac 26: 20 their repentance by their deeds.
1Co 4: 2 been given a trust must *p* faithful.

PROVED (PROVE)

Ps 51: 4 so that you are *p* right
Mt 11: 19 wisdom is *p* right by her actions."
Ro 3: 4 "So that you may be *p* right
1Pe 1: 7 may be *p* genuine and may result

PROVIDE (PROVIDED PROVIDES PROVISION)

Ge 22: 8 "God himself will *p* the lamb
22: 14 that place "The LORD will *P*."
Isa 43: 20 because I *p* water in the desert
61: 3 and *p* for those who grieve in Zion
1Co 10: 13 *p* a way out so that you can stand
1Ti 5: 8 If anyone does not *p*
Tit 3: 14 in order that they may *p*

PROVIDED (PROVIDE)

Ps 68: 10 O God, you *p* for the poor.
111: 9 He *p* redemption for his people;
Jnh 1: 17 But the LORD *p* a great fish
4: 6 Then the LORD God *p* a vine
4: 7 dawn the next day God *p* a worm,
4: 8 God *p* a scorching east wind,
Gal 4: 18 to be zealous, *p* the purpose is good
Heb 1: 3 After he had *p* purification for sins,

PROVIDES (PROVIDE)

Ps 111: 5 He *p* food for those who fear him;
Pr 31: 15 she *p* food for her family
Eze 18: 7 and *p* clothing for the naked.
1Ti 6: 17 who richly *p* us with everything
1Pe 4: 11 it with the strength God *p*,

PROVING* (PROVE)

Ac 9: 22 by *p* that Jesus is the Christ.
17: 3 and *p* that the Christ had to suffer
18: 28 *p* from the Scriptures that Jesus

PROVISION (PROVIDE)

Ro 5: 17 who receive God's abundant *p*

PROVOKED

Ecc 7: 9 Do not be quickly *p* in your spirit,
Jer 32: 32 Judah have *p* me by all the evil they

PROWLS

1Pe　5: 8 Your enemy the devil *p*

PRUDENCE* (PRUDENT)

Pr　1: 4 for giving *p* to the simple,
　　8: 5 You who are simple, gain *p;*
　　8:12 "I, wisdom, dwell together with *p;*
　15: 5 whoever heeds correction shows *p.*
　19:25 and the simple will learn *p;*

PRUDENT* (PRUDENCE)

Pr　1: 3 acquiring a disciplined and *p* life,
　12:16 but a *p* man overlooks an insult.
　12:23 A *p* man keeps his knowledge
　13:16 Every *p* man acts out of knowledge
　14: 8 The wisdom of the *p* is
　14:15 a *p* man gives thought to his steps.
　14:18 the *p* are crowned with knowledge.
　19:14 but a *p* wife is from the LORD.
　22: 3 *p* man sees danger and takes
　27:12 The *p* see danger and take refuge,
Jer　49: 7 Has counsel perished from the *p?*
Am　5:13 Therefore the *p* man keeps quiet

PRUNES (PRUNING)

Jn　15: 2 that does bear fruit he *p*

PRUNING (PRUNES)

Isa　2: 4 and their spears into *p* hooks.
Joel　3:10 and your *p* hooks into spears.

PSALMS

Eph　5:19 Speak to one another with *p,*
Col　3:16 and as you sing *p,* hymns

PUBLICLY

Ac　20:20 have taught you *p* and from house
1Ti　5:20 Those who sin are to be rebuked *p,*

PUFFS

1Co　8: 1 Knowledge *p* up, but love builds up

PULLING

2Co 10: 8 building you up rather than *p* you

PUNISH (PUNISHED PUNISHES PUNISHMENT)

Ge　15:14 But I will *p* the nation they serve
Ex　32:34 I will *p* them for their sin."
Pr　17:26 It is not good to *p* an innocent man,
　23:13 if you *p* him with the rod, he will
Isa　13:11 I will *p* the world for its evil,
Jer　2:19 Your wickedness will *p* you;
　21:14 I will *p* you as your deeds deserve,
Zep　1:12 and *p* those who are complacent,
Ac　7: 7 But I will *p* the nation they serve
2Th　1: 8 He will *p* those who do not know
1Pe　2:14 by him to *p* those who do wrong

PUNISHED (PUNISH)

Ezr　9:13 you have *p* us less than our sins
Ps　99: 8 though you *p* their misdeeds.
La　3:39 complain when *p* for his sins?
Mk　12.40 Such men will be *p* most severely.''
Lk　23:41 the same sentence? We are *p* justly,
2Th　1: 9 be *p* with everlasting destruction
Heb 10:29 to be *p* who has trampled the Son

PUNISHES (PUNISH)

Heb 12: 6 and he *p* everyone he accepts

PUNISHMENT (PUNISH)

Isa　53: 5 the *p* that brought us peace was
Jer　4:18 This is your *p.*
Mt　25:46 Then they will go away to eternal *p*
Lk　12:48 and does things deserving *p* will be
　21:22 For this is the time of *p*
Ro　13: 4 wrath to bring *p* on the wrongdoer.
Heb　2: 2 disobedience received its just *p,*
2Pe　2: 9 while continuing their *p.*

PURCHASED

Ps　74: 2 Remember the people you *p* of old,
Rev　5: 9 with your blood you *p* men for God

PURE (PURIFICATION PURIFIED PURIFIES PURIFY PURITY)

2Sa 22:27 to the *p* you show yourself *p,*
Job　14: 4 Who can bring what is *p*
Ps　19: 9 The fear of the LORD is *p,*
　24: 4 who has clean hands and a *p* heart,
　51:10 Create in me a *p* heart, O God,
　119: 9 can a young man keep his way *p?*
Pr　15:26 those of the *p* are pleasing to him.
　20: 9 can say, "I have kept my heart *p;*
Isa　52:11 Come out from it and be *p,*
Hab　1:13 Your eyes are too *p* to look on evil;
Mt　5: 8 Blessed are the *p* in heart,
2Co 11: 2 I might present you as a *p* virgin
Php　4: 8 whatever is *p,* whatever is lovely,
1Ti　1: 5 which comes from a *p* heart
　5:22 Keep yourself *p.*
2Ti　2:22 call on the Lord out of a *p* heart.
Tit　1:15 To the *p,* all things are *p,*
　2: 5 to be self-controlled and *p,*
Heb　7:26 blameless, *p,* set apart from sinners
　13: 4 and the marriage bed kept *p,*
Jas　1:27 that God our Father accepts as *p*
　3:17 comes from heaven is first of all *p;*
1Jn　3: 3 him purifies himself, just as he is *p.*

PURGE

Pr　20:30 and beatings *p* the inmost being.

PURIFICATION (PURE)

Heb　1: 3 After he had provided *p* for sins,

PURIFIED (PURE)

Ac　15: 9 for he *p* their hearts by faith.
1Pe　1:22 Now that you have *p* yourselves

PURIFIES* (PURE)

1Jn　1: 7 of Jesus, his Son, *p* us from all sin.
　3: 3 who has this hope in him *p* himself,

PURIFY (PURE)

Nu　19:12 He must *p* himself with the water
2Co　7: 1 us *p* ourselves from everything that
Tit　2:14 to *p* for himself a people that are
Jas　4: 8 you sinners, and *p* your hearts,
1Jn　1: 9 and *p* us from all unrighteousness.

PURIM

Est　9:26 Therefore these days were called P

PURITY* (PURE)

Hos　8: 5 long will they be incapable of *p?*
2Co　6: 6 in *p,* understanding, patience
1Ti　4:12 in life, in love, in faith and in *p.*
　5: 2 as sisters, with absolute *p.*
1Pe　3: 2 when they see the *p* and reverence

PURPLE

Pr　31:22 she is clothed in fine linen and *p.*
Mk　15:17 They put a *p* robe on him, then

PURPOSE (PURPOSED PURPOSES)

Ex　9:16 I have raised you up for this very *p,*
Job　36: 5 he is mighty, and firm in his *p.*
Pr　19:21 but it is the LORD's *p* that prevails
Isa　46:10 I say: My *p* will stand,
　55:11 and achieve the *p* for which I sent it
Ac　2:23 handed over to you by God's set *p*
Ro　8:28 have been called according to his *p.*
　9:11 in order that God's *p*
　9:17 "I raised you up for this very *p,*
1Co　3: 8 the man who waters have one *p,*
2Co　5: 5 who has made us for this very *p*
Gal　4:18 be zealous, provided the *p* is good,
Eph　1:11 in conformity with the *p* of his will,
　3:11 according to his eternal *p* which he
Php　2: 2 love, being one in spirit and *p.*
　2:13 and to act according to his good *p.*
2Ti　1: 9 but because of his own *p* and grace.

PURPOSED (PURPOSE)

Isa　14:24 and as I have *p,* so it will stand.
　14:27 For the LORD Almighty has *p,*
Eph　1: 9 which he *p* in Christ, to be put

PURPOSES (PURPOSE)

Ps　33:10 he thwarts the *p* of the peoples.
Jer　23:20 the *p* of his heart.

Jer　32:19 great are your *p* and mighty are

PURSE (PURSES)

Hag　1: 6 to put them in a *p* with holes in it.''
Lk　10: 4 Do not take a *p* or bag or sandals;
　22:36 "But now if you have a *p,* take it,

PURSES (PURSE)

Lk　12:33 Provide *p* for yourselves that will

PURSUE (PURSUES)

Ps　34:14 seek peace and *p* it.
Pr　15: 9 he loves those who *p* righteousness
Ro　9:30 who did not *p* righteousness,
1Ti　6:11 and *p* righteousness, godliness,
2Ti　2:22 and *p* righteousness, faith,
1Pe　. 3: 1 he must seek peace and *p* it.

PURSUES (PURSUE)

Pr　21:21 He who *p* righteousness and love
　28: 1 wicked man flees though no one *p,*

QUAIL

Ex　16:13 That evening *q* came and covered
Nu　11:31 and drove *q* in from the sea.

QUALITIES* (QUALITY)

Da　6: 3 by his exceptional *q* that the king
Ro　1:20 of the world God's invisible *q*—
2Pe　1: 8 For if you possess these *q*

QUALITY (QUALITIES)

1Co　3:13 and the fire will test the *q*

QUARREL (QUARRELING QUARRELS QUARRELSOME)

Pr　15:18 but a patient man calms a *q.*
　17:14 Starting a *q* is like breaching a dam;
　17:19 He who loves a *q* loves sin;
　20: 3 but every fool is quick to *q.*
　26:17 in a *q* not his own.
　26:20 without gossip a *q* dies down.
2Ti　2:24 And the Lord's servant must not *q;*
Jas　4: 2 You *q* and fight.

QUARRELING (QUARREL)

1Co　3: 3 For since there is jealousy and *q*
2Ti　2:14 before God against *q* about words;

QUARRELS (QUARREL)

Pr　13:10 Pride only breeds *q,*
Isa　45: 9 Woe to him who *q* with his Maker,
2Ti　2:23 because you know they produce *q.*
Jas　4: 1 What causes fights and *q*

QUARRELSOME (QUARREL)

Pr　19:13 a *q* wife is like a constant dripping.
　21: 9 than share a house with a *q* wife.
　26:21 so is a *q* man for kindling strife.
1Ti　3: 3 not violent but gentle, not *q,*

QUEEN

1Ki 10: 1 When the *q* of Sheba heard about
2Ch　9: 1 When the *q* of Sheba heard
Mt　12:42 The *Q* of the South will rise

QUENCH (QUENCHED)

SS　8: 7 Many waters cannot *q* love;

QUENCHED (QUENCH)

Isa　66:24 nor will their fire be *q,*
Mk　9:48 and the fire is not *q.'*

QUICKEN see (make) ALIVE, (give) LIFE, RESTORE, REVIVE

QUICK-TEMPERED* (TEMPER)

Pr　14:17 A *q* man does foolish things,
　14:29 but a *q* man displays folly.
Tit　1: 7 not *q,* not given to drunkenness,

QUIET (QUIETNESS)

Ps　23: 2 he leads me beside *q* waters,
Pr　17: 1 Better a dry crust with peace and *q*
Ecc　9:17 The *q* words of the wise are more
Am　5:13 Therefore the prudent man keeps *q*
Zep　3:17 he will *q* you with his love,
Lk　19:40 he replied, "if they keep *q,*
1Th　4:11 it your ambition to lead a *q* life,

1Ti 2: 2 we may live peaceful and *q* lives
1Pe 3: 4 beauty of a gentle and *q* spirit,

QUIETNESS (QUIET)

Isa 30: 15 in *q* and trust is your strength,
    32: 17 the effect of righteousness will be *q*
1Ti 2: 11 A woman should learn in *q*

QUIVER

Ps 127: 5 whose *q* is full of them.

RACE

Ecc 9: 11 The *r* is not to the swift
Ac 20: 24 if only I may finish the *r*
1Co 9: 24 that in a *r* all the runners run,
Gal 2: 2 that I was running or had run my *r*
    5: 7 You were running a good *r*.
2Ti 4: 7 I have finished the *r*, I have kept
Heb 12: 1 perseverance the *r* marked out

RACHEL

Daughter of Laban (Ge 29:16); wife of Jacob (Ge 29:28); bore two sons (Ge 30:22-24; 35:16-24; 46:19). Stole Laban's gods (Ge 31:19, 32-35). Death (Ge 35:19-20).

RADIANCE (RADIANT)

Eze 1: 28 so was the *r* around him.
Heb 1: 3 The Son is the *r* of God's glory

RADIANT (RADIANCE)

Ex 34: 29 he was not aware that his face was *r*
Ps 34: 5 Those who look to him are *r*;
SS 5: 10 *Beloved* My lover is *r* and ruddy,
Isa 60: 5 Then you will look and be *r*,
Eph 5: 27 her to himself as a *r* church,

RAGE

Ac 4: 25 " 'Why do the nations *r*
Col 3: 8 *r*, malice, slander, and filthy

RAGS

Isa 64: 6 our righteous acts are like filthy *r*;

RAHAB

Prostitute of Jericho who hid Israelite spies (Jos 2; 6:22-25; Heb 11:31; Jas 2:25). Mother of Boaz (Mt 1:5).

RAIN (RAINBOW)

Ge 7: 4 from now I will send *r* on the earth
1Ki 17: 1 nor *r* in the next few years
    18: 1 and I will send *r* on the land."
Mt 5: 45 and sends *r* on the righteous
Jas 5: 17 it did not *r* on the land for three
Jude : 12 They are clouds without *r*,

RAINBOW (RAIN)

Ge 9: 13 I have set my *r* in the clouds,

RAISE (RISE)

Jn 6: 39 but *r* them up at the last day.
1Co 15: 15 he did not *r* him if in fact the dead

RAISED (RISE)

Isa 52: 13 he will be *r* and lifted up
Mt 17: 23 on the third day he will be *r* to life
Lk 7: 22 the deaf hear, the dead are *r*,
Ac 2: 24 But God *r* him from the dead,
Ro 4: 25 was *r* to life for our justification.
    6: 4 as Christ was *r* from the dead
    8: 11 And if the Spirit of him who *r* Jesus
    10: 9 in your heart that God *r* him
1Co 15: 4 that he was *r* on the third day
    15: 20 But Christ has indeed been *r*

RALLY*

Isa 11: 10 the nations will *r* to him,

RAM (RAMS)

Ge 22: 13 there in a thicket he saw a *r* caught
Da 8: 3 before me was a *r* with two horns,

RAMPART*

Ps 91: 4 will be your shield and *r*.

RAMS (RAM)

1Sa 15: 22 to heed is better than the fat of *r*.
Mic 6: 7 pleased with thousands of *r*,

RAN (RUN)

Jnh 1: 3 But Jonah *r* away from the LORD

RANSOM (RANSOMED)

Isa 50: 2 Was my arm too short to *r* you?
Hos 13: 14 "I will *r* them from the power
Mt 20: 28 and to give his life as a *r* for many."
Mk 10: 45 and to give his life as a *r* for many."
1Ti 2: 6 who gave himself as a *r* for all men
Heb 9: 15 as a *r* to set them free

RANSOMED (RANSOM)

Isa 35: 10 and the *r* of the LORD will return.

RARE

Pr 20: 15 that speak knowledge are a *r* jewel.

RAVEN (RAVENS)

Ge 8: 7 made in the ark and sent out a *r*,
Job 38: 41 Who provides food for the *r*

RAVENS (RAVEN)

1Ki 17: 6 The *r* brought him bread
Ps 147: 9 and for the young *r* when they call.
Lk 12: 24 Consider the *r*: They do not sow

READ (READING READS)

Dt 17: 19 he is to *r* it all the days of his life
Jos 8: 34 Joshua *r* all the words of the law—
2Ki 23: 2 He *r* in their hearing all the words
Ne 8: 8 They *r* from the Book of the Law
Jer 36: 6 and *r* to the people from the scroll
2Co 3: 2 known and *r* by everybody.

READING (READ)

1Ti 4: 13 to the public *r* of Scripture,

READS (READ)

Rev 1: 3 Blessed is the one who *r* the words

REAFFIRM

2Co 2: 8 therefore, to *r* your love for him.

REAL* (REALITIES REALITY)

Jn 6: 55 is *r* food and my blood is *r* drink.
1Jn 2: 27 all things and as that anointing is *r*,

REALITIES* (REAL)

Heb 10: 1 are coming—not the *r* themselves.

REALITY* (REAL)

Col 2: 17 the *r*, however, is found in Christ.

REALM (REALMS)

Hab 2: 9 "Woe to him who builds his *r*

REALMS (REALM)

Eph 1: 3 the heavenly *r* with every spiritual
    2: 6 in the heavenly *r* in Christ Jesus,

REAP (REAPER REAPS)

Job 4: 8 and those who sow trouble *r* it.
Ps 126: 5 will *r* with songs of joy.
Hos 8: 7 and *r* the whirlwind.
    10: 12 *r* the fruit of unfailing love,
Jn 4: 38 you to *r* what you have not worked
Ro 6: 22 the benefit you *r* leads to holiness,
2Co 9: 6 generously will also *r* generously.
Gal 6: 8 from that nature will *r* destruction;

REAPER (REAP)

Jn 4: 36 and the *r* may be glad together.

REAPS (REAP)

Pr 11: 18 who sows righteousness *r* a sure
    22: 8 He who sows wickedness *r* trouble,
Gal 6: 7 A man *r* what he sows.

REASON (REASONED)

Ge 2: 24 For this *r* a man will leave his
Isa 1: 18 "Come now, let us *r* together,"
Mt 19: 5 'For this *r* a man will leave his
Jn 12: 27 it was for this very *r* I came
    15: 25 'They hated me without *r*.'
1Pe 3: 15 to give the *r* for the hope that you
2Pe 1: 5 For this very *r*, make every effort

REASONED (REASON)

1Co 13: 11 thought like a child, I *r* like a child.

REBEKAH

Sister of Laban, secured as bride for Isaac (Ge 24). Mother of Esau and Jacob (Ge 25:19-26). Taken by Abimelech as sister of Isaac; returned (Ge 26:1-11). Encouraged Jacob to trick Isaac out of blessing (Ge 27:1-17).

REBEL (REBELLED REBELLION REBELS)

Nu 14: 9 Only do not *r* against the LORD.
1Sa 12: 14 and do not *r* against his commands,
Mt 10: 21 children will *r* against their parents

REBELLED (REBEL)

Ps 78: 56 and *r* against the Most High;
Isa 63: 10 Yet they *r*

REBELLION (REBEL)

Ex 34: 7 and forgiving wickedness, *r* and sin
Nu 14: 18 in love and forgiving sin and *r*.
1Sa 15: 23 For *r* is like the sin of divination,
2Th 2: 3 will not come until the *r* occurs

REBELS (REBEL)

Ro 13: 2 he who *r* against the authority is
1Ti 1: 9 but for lawbreakers and *r*,

REBIRTH* (BEAR)

Tit 3: 5 us through the washing of *r*

REBUILD (BUILD)

Ezr 5: 2 set to work to *r* the house of God
Ne 2: 17 let us *r* the wall of Jerusalem,
Ps 102: 16 For the LORD will *r* Zion
Da 9: 25 and *r* Jerusalem until the Anointed
Am 9: 14 they will *r* the ruined cities
Ac 15: 16 Its ruins I will *r*,

REBUILT (BUILD)

Zec 1: 16 and there my house will be *r*.

REBUKE (REBUKED REBUKES REBUKING)

Lev 19: 17 *R* your neighbor frankly
Ps 141: 5 let him *r* me—it is oil on my head.
Pr 3: 11 and do not resent his *r*,
    9: 8 *r* a wise man and he will love you.
    15: 31 He who listens to a life-giving *r*
    17: 10 A *r* impresses a man
    19: 25 a discerning man, and he will gain
    25: 12 is a wise man's *r* to a listening ear.
    27: 5 Better is open *r*
    30: 6 or he will *r* you and prove you a liar
Ecc 7: 5 It is better to heed a wise man's *r*
Isa 54: 9 never to *r* you again.
Jer 2: 19 your backsliding will *r* you.
Lk 17: 3 "If your brother sins, *r* him,
1Ti 5: 1 Do not *r* an older man harshly,
2Ti 4: 2 correct, *r* and encourage—
Tit 1: 13 Therefore, *r* them sharply,
    2: 15 Encourage and *r* with all authority.
Rev 3: 19 Those whom I love I *r*

REBUKED (REBUKE)

Mk 16: 14 he *r* them for their lack of faith
1Ti 5: 20 Those who sin are to be *r* publicly,

REBUKES (REBUKE)

Job 22: 4 "Is it for your piety that he *r* you
Pr 28: 23 He who *r* a man will
    29: 1 remains stiff-necked after many *r*
Heb 12: 5 do not lose heart when he *r* you,

REBUKING (REBUKE)

2Ti 3: 16 *r*, correcting and training

RECEIVE (RECEIVED RECEIVES)

Mt 10: 41 a righteous man will *r* a righteous
Mk 10: 15 anyone who will not *r* the kingdom
Jn 20: 22 and said, "*R* the Holy Spirit.
Ac 1: 8 you will *r* power when the Holy
    2: 38 you will *r* the gift of the Holy Spirit
    19: 2 "Did you *r* the Holy Spirit
    20: 35 'It is more blessed to give than to *r*
1Co 9: 14 the gospel should *r* their living
2Co 6: 17 and I will *r* you."
1Ti 1: 16 believe on him and *r* eternal life.
Jas 1: 7 should not think he will *r* anything
2Pe 1: 11 and you will *r* a rich welcome

1Jn 3: 22 and *r* from him anything we ask,
Rev 4: 11 to *r* glory and honor and power,
    5: 12 to *r* power and wealth and wisdom

RECEIVED (RECEIVE)

Mt 6: 2 they have *r* their reward in full.
    10: 8 Freely you have *r*, freely give.
Mk 11: 24 believe that you have *r* it,
Jn 1: 12 Yet to all who *r* him,
    1: 16 his grace we have all *r* one blessing
Ac 8: 17 and they *r* the Holy Spirit.
    10: 47 They have *r* the Holy Spirit just
Ro 8: 15 but you *r* the Spirit of sonship.
1Co 11: 23 For I *r* from the Lord what I
2Co 1: 4 the comfort we ourselves have *r*
Col 2: 6 just as you *r* Christ Jesus as Lord,
1Pe 4: 10 should use whatever gift he has *r*

RECEIVES (RECEIVE)

Pr 18: 22 and *r* favor from the LORD.
    27: 21 but man is tested by the praise he *r*.
Mt 7: 8 everyone who asks *r*; he who seeks
    10: 40 he who *r* me *r* the one who sent me.
    10: 40 "He who *r* you *r* me, and he who
Ac 10: 43 believes in him *r* forgiveness of sins

RECITE

Ps 45: 1 as I *r* my verses for the king;

RECKLESS

Pr 12: 18 *R* words pierce like a sword,
    14: 16 but a fool is hotheaded and *r*.

RECKONING

Isa 10: 3 What will you do on the day of *r*,
Hos 9: 7 the days of *r* are at hand.

RECLAIM* (CLAIM)

Isa 11: 11 time to *r* the remnant that is left

RECOGNITION (RECOGNIZE)

1Co 16: 18 Such men deserve *r*.
1Ti 5: 3 Give proper *r* to those widows who

RECOGNIZE (RECOGNITION RECOGNIZED)

Mt 7: 16 By their fruit you will *r* them.
1Jn 4: 2 This is how you can *r* the Spirit
    4: 6 This is how we *r* the Spirit of truth

RECOGNIZED (RECOGNIZE)

Mt 12: 33 for a tree is *r* by its fruit.
Ro 7: 13 in order that sin might be *r* as sin,

RECOMPENSE*

Isa 40: 10 and his *r* accompanies him.
    62: 11 and his *r* accompanies him.' ' '

RECONCILE* (RECONCILED RECONCILIATION RECONCILING)

Ac 7: 26 He tried to *r* them by saying, 'Men,
Eph 2: 16 in this one body to *r* both of them
Col 1: 20 him to *r* to himself all things,

RECONCILED* (RECONCILE)

Mt 5: 24 First go and be *r* to your brother;
Lk 12: 58 try hard to be *r* to him on the way,
Ro 5: 10 how much more, having been *r*,
    5: 10 we were *r* to him through the death
1Co 7: 11 or else be *r* to her husband.
2Co 5: 18 who *r* us to himself through Christ
    5: 20 you on Christ's behalf: Be *r* to God.
Col 1: 22 he has *r* you by Christ's physical

RECONCILIATION* (RECONCILE)

Ro 5: 11 whom we have now received *r*.
    11: 15 For if their rejection is the *r*
2Co 5: 18 and gave us the ministry of *r*:
    5: 19 committed to us the message of *r*.

RECONCILING* (RECONCILE)

2Co 5: 19 that God was *r* the world to himself

RECORD (RECORDED)

Ps 130: 3 If you, O LORD, kept a *r* of sins,
Hos 13: 12 his sins are kept on *r*.
1Co 13: 5 is not easily angered, it keeps no *r*

RECORDED (RECORD)

Job 19: 23 "Oh, that my words were *r*,
Jn 20: 30 which are not *r* in this book.

RECOUNT*

Ps 40: 5 no one can *r* to you;
    79: 13 we will *r* your praise.
    119: 13 With my lips I *r*

RED

Ex 15: 4 are drowned in the *R* Sea.
Ps 106: 9 He rebuked the *R* Sea,
Pr 23: 31 Do not gaze at wine when it is *r*,
Isa 1: 18 though they are *r* as crimson,

REDEEM (KINSMAN-REDEEMER REDEEMED REDEEMER REDEEMS REDEMPTION)

Ex 6: 6 will *r* you with an outstretched arm
2Sa 7: 23 on earth that God went out to *r*
Ps 44: 26 *r* us because of your unfailing love.
    49: 7 No man can *r* the life of another
    49: 15 God will *r* my life from the grave;
    130: 8 He himself will *r* Israel
Hos 13: 14 I will *r* them from death.
Gal 4: 5 under law, to *r* those under law,
Tit 2: 14 for us to *r* us from all wickedness

REDEEMED (REDEEM)

Job 33: 28 He *r* my soul from going
Ps 71: 23 I, whom you have *r*.
    107: 2 Let the *r* of the LORD say this—
Isa 35: 9 But only the *r* will walk there,
    63: 9 In his love and mercy he *r* them;
Gal 3: 13 Christ *r* us from the curse
1Pe 1: 18 or gold that you were *r*

REDEEMER (REDEEM)

Job 19: 25 I know that my *R* lives,
Ps 19: 14 O LORD, my Rock and my *R*.
Isa 44: 6 and *R*, the LORD Almighty:
    48: 17 your *R*, the Holy One of Israel:
    59: 20 "The *R* will come to Zion,

REDEEMS (REDEEM)

Ps 34: 22 The LORD *r* his servants;
    103: 4 he *r* my life from the pit

REDEMPTION (REDEEM)

Ps 130: 7 and with him is full *r*.
Lk 21: 28 because your *r* is drawing near."
Ro 3: 24 grace through the *r* that came
    8: 23 as sons, the *r* of our bodies.
1Co 1: 30 our righteousness, holiness and *r*.
Eph 1: 7 In him we have *r* through his blood
    1: 14 until the *r* of those who are God's
    4: 30 you were sealed for the day of *r*.
Col 1: 14 in whom we have *r*, the forgiveness
Heb 9: 12 having obtained eternal *r*.

REED

Isa 42: 3 A bruised *r* he will not break,
Mt 12: 20 A bruised *r* he will not break,

REFINE*

Jer 9: 7 "See, I will *r* and test them,
Zec 13: 9 I will *r* them like silver
Mal 3: 3 and *r* them like gold and silver.

REFLECT (REFLECTS)

2Co 3: 18 unveiled faces all *r* the Lord's

REFLECTS (REFLECT)

Pr 27: 19 As water *r* a face,

REFRESH (REFRESHED REFRESHING)

Phm : 20 in the Lord; *r* my heart in Christ.

REFRESHED (REFRESH)

Pr 11: 25 refreshes others will himself be *r*.

REFRESHING* (REFRESH)

Ac 3: 19 that times of *r* may come

REFUGE

Nu 35: 11 towns to be your cities of *r*,
Dt 33: 27 The eternal God is your *r*,
Jos 20: 2 to designate the cities of *r*,

Ru 2: 12 wings you have come to take *r*."
2Sa 22: 3 God is my rock, in whom I take *r*,
    22: 31 a shield for all who take *r* in him.
Ps 2: 12 Blessed are all who take *r* in him.
    5: 11 But let all who take *r* in you be glad
    9: 9 The LORD is a *r* for the oppressed,
    16: 1 for in you I take *r*.
    17: 7 those who take *r* in you
    18: 2 God is my rock, in whom I take *r*.
    31: 2 be my rock of *r*,
    34: 8 blessed is the man who takes *r*
    36: 7 find *r* in the shadow of your wings.
    46: 1 God is our *r* and strength,
    62: 8 for God is our *r*.
    71: 1 In you, O LORD, I have taken *r*;
    91: 2 "He is my *r* and my fortress,
    144: 2 my shield, in whom I take *r*,
Pr 14: 26 and for his children it will be a *r*.
    30: 5 a shield to those who take *r* in him.
Na 1: 7 a *r* in times of trouble.

REFUSE (REFUSED)

Jn 5: 40 yet you *r* to come to me to have life

REFUSED (REFUSE)

2Th 2: 10 because they *r* to love the truth
Rev 16: 9 but they *r* to repent and glorify him

REGARD (REGARDS)

1Th 5: 13 Hold them in the highest *r* in love

REGARDS (REGARD)

Ro 14: 14 But if anyone *r* something

REGRET

2Co 7: 10 leads to salvation and leaves no *r*,

REHOBOAM

Son of Solomon (1Ki 11:43; 1Ch 3:10). Harsh treatment of subjects caused divided kingdom (1Ki 12:1-24; 14:21-31; 2Ch 10-12).

REIGN (REIGNED REIGNS)

Ex 15: 18 The LORD will *r*
Ps 68: 16 mountain where God chooses to *r*,
Isa 9: 7 He will *r* on David's throne
    24: 23 for the LORD Almighty will *r*
    32: 1 See, a king will *r* in righteousness
Jer 23: 5 a King who will *r* wisely
Lk 1: 33 and he will *r* over the house
Ro 6: 12 Therefore do not let sin *r*
1Co 15: 25 For he must *r* until he has put all
2Ti 2: 12 we will also *r* with him.
Rev 11: 15 and he will *r* for ever and ever."
    20: 6 will *r* with him for a thousand years
    22: 5 And they will *r* for ever and ever.

REIGNED (REIGN)

Ro 5: 21 so that, just as sin *r* in death,
Rev 20: 4 and *r* with Christ a thousand years.

REIGNS (REIGN)

Ps 9: 7 The LORD *r* forever;
    47: 8 God *r* over the nations;
    93: 1 The LORD *r*, he is robed
    96: 10 among the nations, "The LORD *r*
    97: 1 The LORD *r*, let the earth be glad;
    99: 1 The LORD *r*, / let the nations tremble;
    146: 10 The LORD *r* forever,
Isa 52: 7 "Your God *r*!"
Rev 19: 6 For our Lord God Almighty *r*.

REIN

Jas 1: 26 and yet does not keep a tight *r*

REJECT (REJECTED REJECTION REJECTS)

Ps 94: 14 For the LORD will not *r* his people
Ro 11: 1 I ask then: Did God *r* his people?

REJECTED (REJECT)

1Sa 8: 7 it is not you they have *r*
1Ki 19: 10 The Israelites have *r* your covenant
2Ki 17: 15 They *r* his decrees
Ps 66: 20 who has not *r* my prayer
    118: 22 The stone the builders *r*
Isa 5: 24 for they have *r* the law
    41: 9 chosen you and have not *r* you.

Isa 53: 3 He was despised and *r* by men,
Jer 8: 9 Since they have *r* the word
Mt 21:42 '' 'The stone the builders *r*
1Ti 4: 4 nothing is to be *r* if it is received
1Pe 2: 4 *r* by men but chosen by God
    2: 7 ''The stone the builders *r*

REJECTION* (REJECT)

Ro 11:15 For if their *r* is the reconciliation

REJECTS (REJECT)

Lk 10:16 but he who *r* me *r* him who sent me
Jn 3:36 whoever *r* the Son will not see life,
1Th 4: 8 he who *r* this instruction does not

REJOICE (JOY)

Dt 12: 7 shall *r* in everything you have put
1Ch 16:10 of those who seek the LORD *r*.
    16:31 Let the heavens *r*, let the earth be
Ps 2:11 and *r* with trembling.
    5:11 those who love your name may *r*
    9:14 and there in your salvation.
    34: 2 let the afflicted hear and *r*.
    63:11 But the king will *r* in God;
    66: 6 come, let us *r* in him.
    68: 3 and *r* before God;
    105: 3 of those who seek the LORD *r*.
    118:24 let us *r* and be glad in it.
    119:14 I *r* in following your statutes
    119:162 I *r* in your promise
    149: 2 Let Israel *r* in their Maker;
Pr 5:18 may you *r* in the wife of your youth
    23:25 may she who gave you birth *r!*
    24:17 stumbles, do not let your heart *r*,
Isa 9: 3 as men *r*
    35: 1 the wilderness will *r* and blossom.
    61: 7 they will *r* in their inheritance;
    62: 5 so will your God *r* over you.
Jer 31:12 they will *r* in the bounty
Zep 3:17 he will *r* over you with singing.''
Zec 9: 9 *R* greatly, O Daughter of Zion!
Lk 6:23 ''*R* in that day and leap for joy,
    10:20 but *r* that your names are written
    15: 6 '*R* with me; I have found my lost
    15: 9 '*R* with me; I have found my lost
Ro 5: 2 And we *r* in the hope of the glory
    12:15 Rejoice with those who *r;* mourn
Php 2:17 I am glad and *r* with all of you.
    3: 1 Finally, my brothers, *r* in the Lord!
    4: 4 *R* in the Lord always.
1Pe 4:13 But *r* that you participate
Rev 19: 7 Let us *r* and be glad

REJOICES (JOY)

Ps 13: 5 my heart *r* in your salvation.
    16: 9 my heart is glad and my tongue *r;*
Isa 61:10 my soul *r* in my God.
    62: 5 as a bridegroom *r* over his bride,
Lk 1:47 and my spirit *r* in God my Savior,
Ac 2:26 my heart is glad and my tongue *r;*
1Co 12:26 if one part is honored, every part *r*
    13: 6 delight in evil but *r* with the truth.

REJOICING (JOY)

2Sa 6:12 to the City of David with *r*.
Ne 12:43 *r* because God had given them
Ps 30: 5 but *r* comes in the morning.
Lk 15: 7 in the same way there will be more *r*
Ac 5:41 *r* because they had been counted
2Co 6:10 sorrowful, yet always *r;* poor,

RELATIVES

Pr 19: 7 A poor man is shunned by all his *r*
Mk 6: 4 among his *r* and in his own house is
Lk 21:16 betrayed by parents, brothers, *r*
1Ti 5: 8 If anyone does not provide for his *r*

RELEASE (RELEASED)

Isa 61: 1 and *r* from darkness,
Lk 4:18 to *r* the oppressed,

RELEASED (RELEASE)

Ro 7: 6 we have been *r* from the law
Rev 20: 7 Satan will be *r* from his prison

RELENTED (RELENTS)

Ex 32:14 the LORD *r* and did not bring
Ps 106:45 and out of his great love he *r*.

RELENTS* (RELENTED)

Joel 2:13 and he *r* from sending calamity.
Jnh 4: 2 a God who *r* from sending calamity

RELIABLE (RELY)

Pr 22:21 teaching you true and *r* words,
Jn 8:26 But he who sent me is *r*,
2Ti 2: 2 witnesses entrust to *r* men who will

RELIANCE* (RELY)

Pr 25:19 is *r* on the unfaithful in times

RELIED (RELY)

2Ch 13:18 were victorious because they *r*
    16: 8 Yet when you *r* on the LORD,
Ps 71: 6 From birth I have *r* on you;

RELIEF

Job 35: 9 they plead for *r* from the arm
Ps 94:13 you grant him *r* from days
    143: 1 come to my *r*.
La 3:49 without *r*,
    3:56 to my cry for *r*.''
2Th 1: 7 and give *r* to you who are troubled,

RELIGION* (RELIGIOUS)

Ac 25:19 dispute with him about their own *r*
    26: 5 to the strictest sect of our *r*,
1Ti 5: 4 all to put their *r* into practice
Jas 1:26 himself and his *r* is worthless;
    1:27 *R* that God our Father accepts

RELIGIOUS (RELIGION)

Jas 1:26 If anyone considers himself *r*

RELY (RELIABLE RELIANCE RELIED)

Isa 50:10 and *r* on his God.
Eze 33:26 you then possess the land? You *r*
2Co 1: 9 this happened that we might not *r*
Gal 3:10 All who *r* on observing the law are
1Jn 4:16 and *r* on the love God has for us.

REMAIN (REMAINS)

Nu 33:55 allow to *r* will become barbs
Ps 102:27 But you *r* the same,
Jn 1:32 from heaven as a dove and *r* on him
    15: 4 *R* in me, and I will *r* in you.
    15: 7 If you *r* in me and my words
    15: 9 Now *r* in my love.
Ro 13: 8 Let no debt *r* outstanding,
1Co 13:13 And now these three *r:* faith,
2Ti 2:13 he will *r* faithful,
Heb 1:11 They will perish, but you *r;*
1Jn 2:27 just as it has taught you, *r* in him.

REMAINS (REMAIN)

Ps 146: 6 the LORD, who *r* faithful forever.
Heb 7: 3 Son of God he *r* a priest forever.

REMEDY

Isa 3: 7 ''I have no *r*.

REMEMBER (REMEMBERED REMEMBERS REMEMBRANCE)

Ge 9:15 I will *r* my covenant between me
Ex 20: 8 ''*R* the Sabbath day
    33:13 *R* that this nation is your people.''
Dt 5:15 *R* that you were slaves in Egypt
1Ch 16:12 *R* the wonders he has done,
Job 36:24 *R* to extol his work,
Ps 25: 6 *R*, O LORD, your great mercy
    63: 6 On my bed I *r* you;
    74: 2 *R* the people you purchased of old,
    77:11 I will *r* the deeds of the LORD;
Ecc 12: 1 *R* your Creator
Isa 46: 8 ''*R* this, fix it in mind,
Jer 31:34 and will *r* their sins no more.''
Hab 3: 2 in wrath *r* mercy.
Lk 1:72 and to *r* his holy covenant,
Gal 2:10 we should continue to *r* the poor,
Php 1: 3 I thank my God every time I *r* you.
2Ti 2: 8 *R* Jesus Christ, raised
Heb 8:12 and will *r* their sins no more.''

REMEMBERED (REMEMBER)

Ex 2:24 he *r* his covenant with Abraham,
    3:15 am to be *r* from generation
Ps 98: 3 He has *r* his love

Ps 106:45 for their sake he *r* his covenant
    111: 4 He has caused his wonders to be *r;*
    136:23 to the One who *r* us
Isa 65:17 The former things will not be *r*,
Eze 18:22 offenses he has committed will be *r*
    33:13 things he has done will be *r;*

REMEMBERS (REMEMBER)

Ps 103:14 he *r* that we are dust.
    111: 5 he *r* his covenant forever.
Isa 43:25 and *r* your sins no more.

REMEMBRANCE (REMEMBER)

Lk 22:19 given for you; do this in *r* of me.''
1Co 11:24 which is for you; do this in *r* of me.
    11:25 whenever you drink it, in *r* of me.''

REMIND

Jn 14:26 will *r* you of everything I have said
2Pe 1:12 I will always *r* you of these things,

REMNANT

Ezr 9: 8 has been gracious in leaving us a *r*
Isa 11:11 time to reclaim the *r* that is left
Jer 23: 3 ''I myself will gather the *r*
Zec 8:12 inheritance to the *r* of this people.
Ro 11: 5 the present time there is a *r* chosen

REMOVED

Ps 30:11 you *r* my sackcloth and clothed me
    103:12 so far has he *r* our transgressions
Jn 20: 1 and saw that the stone had been *r*

REND

Joel 2:13 *R* your heart

RENEW (RENEWAL RENEWED RENEWING RENEWS)

Ps 51:10 and *r* a steadfast spirit within me.
Isa 40:31 will *r* their strength.

RENEWAL (RENEW)

Isa 57:10 You found *r* of your strength,
Tit 3: 5 of rebirth and *r* by the Holy Spirit,

RENEWED (RENEW)

Ps 103: 5 that my youth is *r* like the eagle's.
2Co 4:16 yet inwardly we are being *r* day

RENEWING* (RENEW)

Ro 12: 2 transformed by the *r* of your mind.

RENEWS* (RENEW)

Ps 119:50 Your promise *r* my life.

RENOUNCE (RENOUNCED RENOUNCES)

Da 4:27 *R* your sins by doing what is right,

RENOUNCED (RENOUNCE)

2Co 4: 2 we have *r* secret and shameful

RENOUNCES (RENOUNCE)

Pr 28:13 confesses and *r* them finds

RENOWN*

Ge 6: 4 were the heroes of old, men of *r*.
Ps 102:12 *r* endures through all generations.
    135:13 *r*, O LORD, through all
Isa 26: 8 your name and *r*
    55:13 This will be for the LORD's *r*,
    63:12 to gain for himself everlasting *r*,
Jer 13:11 to be my people for my *r* and praise
    32:20 have gained the *r* that is still yours.
    33: 9 Then this city will bring me *r*, joy,
    49:25 the city of *r* not been abandoned,
Eze 26:17 How you are destroyed, O city of *r*,
Hos 12: 5 the LORD is his name of *r!*

REPAID (PAY)

Lk 6:34 to 'sinners,' expecting to be *r* in full
    14:14 you will be *r* at the resurrection
Col 3:25 Anyone who does wrong will be *r*

REPAY (PAY)

Dt 7:10 But those who hate him he will *r*
    32:35 It is mine to avenge; I will *r*.
Ru 2:12 May the LORD *r* you
Ps 103:10 or *r* us according to our iniquities.

Ps 116: 12 How can I r the LORD
Jer 25: 14 I will r them according
Ro 12: 17 Do not r anyone evil for evil.
12: 19 "It is mine to avenge; I will r,"
1Pe 3: 9 Do not r evil with evil

REPAYING (PAY)

2Ch 6: 23 r the guilty by bringing
1Ti 5: 4 so r their parents and grandparents

REPEATED

Heb 10: 1 the same sacrifices r endlessly year

REPENT (REPENTANCE REPENTED REPENTS)

1Ki 8: 47 r and plead with you in the land
Job 36: 10 commands them to r of their evil.
42: 6 and r in dust and ashes.''
Jer 15: 19 "If you r, I will restore you
Eze 18: 30 R! Turn away from all your
18: 32 R and live! ''Take up a lament
Mt 3: 2 ''R, for the kingdom of heaven is
4: 17 ''R, for the kingdom of heaven is
Mk 6: 12 and preached that people should r.
Lk 13: 3 unless you r, you too will all perish.
Ac 2: 38 Peter replied, ''R and be baptized,
3: 19 R, then, and turn to God,
17: 30 all people everywhere to r.
26: 20 also, I preached that they should r
Rev 2: 5 R and do the things you did at first.

REPENTANCE (REPENT)

Isa 30: 15 ''In r and rest is your salvation,
Mt 3: 8 Produce fruit in keeping with r.
Mk 1: 4 a baptism of r for the forgiveness
Lk 3: 8 Produce fruit in keeping with r.
5: 32 call the righteous, but sinners to r.''
24: 47 and r and forgiveness of sins will be
Ac 20: 21 that they must turn to God in r
26: 20 and prove their r by their deeds.
Ro 2: 4 kindness leads you toward r?
2Co 7: 10 Godly sorrow brings r that leads
2Pe 3: 9 but everyone to come to r.

REPENTED (REPENT)

Mt 11: 21 they would have r long ago

REPENTS (REPENT)

Lk 15: 7 in heaven over one sinner who r
15: 10 of God over one sinner who r.''
17: 3 rebuke him, and if he r, forgive him

REPORTS

Ex 23: 1 ''Do not spread false r.

REPOSES*

Pr 14: 33 Wisdom r in the heart

REPRESENTATION*

Heb 1: 3 and the exact r of his being,

REPROACH

Job 27: 6 my conscience will not r me
Isa 51: 7 Do not fear the r of men
1Ti 3: 2 Now the overseer must be above r,

REPUTATION

1Ti 3: 7 also have a good r with outsiders,

REQUESTS

Ps 20: 5 May the LORD grant all your r.
Php 4: 6 with thanksgiving, present your r

REQUIRE (REQUIRED REQUIRES)

Mic 6: 8 And what does the LORD r of you

REQUIRED (REQUIRE)

1Co 4: 2 it is r that those who have been

REQUIRES (REQUIRE)

1Ki 2: 3 what the LORD your God r:
Heb 9: 22 the law r that nearly everything be

RESCUE (RESCUED RESCUES)

Ps 22: 8 let the LORD r him.
31: 2 come quickly to my r;
69: 14 R me from the mire,
91: 14 says the LORD, ''I will r him;
143: 9 R me from my enemies, O LORD,

Da 6: 20 been able to r you from the lions?''
Ro 7: 24 Who will r me from this body
Gal 1: 4 himself for our sins to r us
2Pe 2: 9 how to r godly men from trials

RESCUED (RESCUE)

Ps 18: 17 He r me from my powerful enemy,
Pr 11: 8 The righteous man is r
Col 1: 13 For he has r us from the dominion

RESCUES (RESCUE)

Da 6: 27 He r and he saves;
1Th 1: 10 who r us from the coming wrath.

RESENT* (RESENTFUL RESENTS)

Pr 3: 11 and do not r his rebuke,

RESENTFUL* (RESENT)

2Ti 2: 24 to everyone, able to teach, not r.

RESENTS* (RESENT)

Pr 15: 12 A mocker r correction;

RESERVE (RESERVED)

1Ki 19: 18 Yet I r seven thousand in Israel—

RESERVED (RESERVE)

Ro 11: 4 ''I have r for myself seven

RESIST (RESISTED RESISTS)

Da 11: 32 know their God will firmly r him.
Mt 5: 39 I tell you, Do not r an evil person.
Lk 21: 15 of your adversaries will be able to r
Jas 4: 7 R the devil, and he will flee
1Pe 5: 9 R him, standing firm in the faith,

RESISTED (RESIST)

Job 9: 4 Who has r him and come out

RESISTS* (RESIST)

Ro 9: 19 For who r his will?'' But who are

RESOLVED

Ps 17: 3 I have r that my mouth will not sin.
Da 1: 8 But Daniel r not to defile himself
1Co 2: 2 For I r to know nothing while I was

RESOUNDING*

Ps 150: 5 praise him with r cymbals.
1Co 13: 1 I am only a r gong or a clanging

RESPECT (RESPECTABLE RESPECTED RESPECTS)

Lev 19: 3 '' 'Each of you must r his mother
19: 32 show r for the elderly and revere
Pr 11: 16 A kindhearted woman gains r,
Mal 1: 6 where is the r due me?'' says
Eph 5: 33 and the wife must r her husband.
6: 5 obey your earthly masters with r
1Th 4: 12 so that your daily life may win the r
5: 12 to r those who work hard
1Ti 3: 4 children obey him with proper r.
3: 8 are to be men worthy of r, sincere,
3: 11 are to be women worthy of r,
6: 1 their masters worthy of full r.
Tit 2: 2 worthy of r, self-controlled,
1Pe 2: 17 Show proper r to everyone:
3: 7 them with r as the weaker partner
3: 16 But do this with gentleness and r,

RESPECTABLE* (RESPECT)

1Ti 3: 2 self-controlled, r, hospitable,

RESPECTED (RESPECT)

Pr 31: 23 Her husband is r at the city gate,

RESPECTS (RESPECT)

Pr 13: 13 he who r a command is rewarded.

RESPLENDENT*

Ps 76: 4 You are r with light,
132: 18 but the crown on his head will be r

RESPOND

Ps 102: 17 He will r to the prayer
Hos 2: 21 ''I will r to the skies,

RESPONSIBILITY (RESPONSIBLE)

Ac 18: 6 your own heads! I am clear of my r.

RESPONSIBLE (RESPONSIBILITY)

Nu 1: 53 The Levites are to be r for the care
1Co 7: 24 Brothers, each man, as r to God,

REST (RESTED RESTS SABBATH-REST)

Ex 31: 15 the seventh day is a Sabbath of r,
33: 14 go with you, and I will give you r.''
Lev 25: 5 The land is to have a year of r.
Dt 31: 16 going to r with your fathers,
Jos 14: 15 Then the land had r from war.
21: 44 The LORD gave them r
1Ki 5: 4 The LORD my god has given me r
1Ch 22: 9 who will be a man of peace and r,
Job 3: 17 and there the weary are at r.
Ps 16: 9 my body also will r secure,
33: 22 May your unfailing love r upon us,
62: 1 My soul finds r in God alone;
62: 5 Find r, O my soul, in God alone;
90: 17 of the Lord our God r upon us;
91: 1 will r in the shadow
95: 11 ''They shall never enter my r.''
Pr 6: 10 a little folding of the hands to r—
Isa 11: 2 Spirit of the LORD will r on him—
11: 10 and his place of r will be glorious.
30: 15 ''In repentance and r is your
32: 18 in undisturbed places of r.
57: 20 which cannot r,
Jer 6: 16 and you will find r for your souls.
47: 6 'how long till you r?
Mt 11: 28 and burdened, and I will give you r.
2Co 12: 9 so that Christ's power may r on me
Heb 3: 11 'They shall never enter my r.' ''
4: 3 'They shall never enter my r.' ''
4: 10 for anyone who enters God's r
Rev 14: 13 ''they will r from their labor,

RESTED (REST)

Ge 2: 2 so on the seventh day he r
Heb 4: 4 ''And on the seventh day God r

RESTITUTION

Ex 22: 3 ''A thief must certainly make r,
Lev 6: 5 He must make r in full, add a fifth
Nu 5: 8 the r belongs to the LORD

RESTORE (RESTORES)

Ps 51: 12 R to me the joy of your salvation,
80: 3 R us, O God,
126: 4 R our fortunes, O LORD,
Jer 31: 18 R me, and I will return,
La 5: 21 R us to yourself, O LORD,
Da 9: 25 From the issuing of the decree to r
Na 2: 2 The LORD will r the splendor
Gal 6: 1 are spiritual should r him gently.
1Pe 5: 10 will himself r you and make you

RESTORES (RESTORE)

Ps 23: 3 he r my soul.

RESTRAINED (RESTRAINT)

Ps 78: 38 Time after time he r his anger

RESTRAINING (RESTRAINT)

Pr 27: 16 r her is like r the wind
Col 2: 23 value in r sensual indulgence.

RESTRAINT (RESTRAINED RESTRAINING)

Pr 17: 27 of knowledge uses words with r,
23: 4 have the wisdom to show r.
29: 18 no revelation, the people cast off r;

RESTS (REST)

Dt 33: 12 and the one the LORD loves r
Pr 19: 23 one r content, untouched
Lk 2: 14 to men on whom his favor r.''

RESULT

Lk 21: 13 This will r in your being witnesses
Ro 6: 22 to holiness, and the r is eternal life.
11: 31 as a r of God's mercy to you.
2Co 2: 3 from Christ, the r of our ministry,
2Th 1: 5 as a r you will be counted worthy
1Pe 1: 7 may be proved genuine and may r

RESURRECTION*

Mt 22: 23 who say there is no *r*, came to him
22: 28 at the *r*, whose wife will she be
22: 30 At the *r* people will neither marry
22: 31 But about the *r* of the dead—
27: 53 and after Jesus' *r* they went
Mk 12: 18 who say there is no *r*, came to him
12: 23 At the *r* whose wife will she be,
Lk 14: 14 repaid at the *r* of the righteous.''
20: 27 who say there is no *r*, came to Jesus
20: 33 at the *r* whose wife will she be,
20: 35 in the *r* from the dead will neither
20: 36 since they are children of the *r*.
Jn 11: 24 again in the *r* at the last day.''
11: 25 Jesus said to her, ''I am the *r*
Ac 1: 22 become a witness with us of his *r*.''
2: 31 he spoke of the *r* of the Christ,
4: 2 in Jesus the *r* of the dead.
4: 33 to testify to the *r* of the Lord Jesus,
17: 18 good news about Jesus and the *r*.
17: 32 When they heard about the *r*
23: 6 of my hope in the *r* of the dead.''
23: 8 Sadducees say that there is no *r*,
24: 15 that there will be a *r*
24: 21 'It is concerning the *r*
Ro 1: 4 Son of God by his *r* from the dead:
6: 5 also be united with him in his *r*.
1Co 15: 12 some of you say that there is no *r*
15: 13 If there is no *r* of the dead,
15: 21 the *r* of the dead comes
15: 29 if there is no *r*, what will those do
15: 42 So will it be with the *r* of the dead.
Php 3: 10 power of his *r* and the fellowship
3: 11 to attain to the *r* from the dead.
2Ti 2: 18 say that the *r* has already taken
Heb 6: 2 on of hands, the *r* of the dead,
11: 35 so that they might gain a better *r*.
1Pe 1: 3 hope through the *r* of Jesus Christ
3: 21 It saves you by the *r* of Jesus Christ
Rev 20: 5 This is the first *r*.
20: 6 those who have part in the first *r*.

RETALIATE*

1Pe 2: 23 he did not *r*; when he suffered,

RETRIBUTION

Ps 69: 22 may it become a *r* and a trap.
Jer 51: 56 For the LORD is a God of *r*;
Ro 11: 9 a stumbling block and a *r* for them.

RETURN (RETURNED RETURNS)

Ge 3: 19 and to dust you will *r*.''
2Sa 12: 23 go to him, but he will not *r* to me.''
2Ch 30: 9 If you *r* to the LORD, then your
Ne 1: 9 but if you *r* to me and obey my
Job 10: 21 joy before I go to the place of no *r*,
16: 22 before I go on the journey of no *r*,
22: 23 If you *r* to the Almighty, you will
Ps 80: 14 *R* to us, O God Almighty!
126: 6 with songs of joy,
Isa 10: 21 A remnant will *r*, a remnant
35: 10 the ransomed of the LORD will *r*.
55: 11 It will not *r* to me empty,
Jer 24: 7 for they will *r* to me
31: 8 a great throng will *r*.
La 3: 40 and let us *r* to the LORD.
Hos 6: 1 ''Come, let us *r* to the LORD.
12: 6 But you must *r* to your God;
14: 1 *R*, O Israel, to the LORD your
Joel 2: 12 ''*r* to me with all your heart,
Zec 1: 3 '*R* to me,' declares the LORD
10: 9 and they will *r*.

RETURNED (RETURN)

Ps 35: 13 When my prayers *r*
Am 4: 6 yet you have not *r* to me,''
1Pe 2: 25 now you have *r* to the Shepherd

RETURNS (RETURN)

Pr 3: 14 and yields better *r* than gold.
Isa 52: 8 When the LORD *r* to Zion,
Mt 24: 46 finds him doing so when he *r*.

REUBEN

Firstborn of Jacob by Leah (Ge 29:32; 46:8;
1Ch 2:1). Attempted to rescue Joseph (Ge 37:
21-30). Lost birthright for sleeping with Bilhah
(Ge 35:22; 49:4). Tribe of blessed (Ge 49:3-4; Dt

33:6), numbered (Nu 1:21; 26:7), allotted land
east of Jordan (Nu 32; 34:14; Jos 13:15), west (Eze
48:6), failed to help Deborah (Jdg 5:15-16), supported David (1Ch 12:37), 12,000 from (Rev 7:5).

REVEAL (REVEALED REVEALS REVELATION REVELATIONS)

Mt 11: 27 to whom the Son chooses to *r* him.
Gal 1: 16 was pleased to *r* his Son in me

REVEALED (REVEAL)

Dt 29: 29 but the things *r* belong to us
Isa 40: 5 the glory of the LORD will be *r*,
43: 12 I have *r* and saved and proclaimed
53: 1 the arm of the LORD been *r*?
65: 1 I *r* myself to those who did not ask
Mt 11: 25 and *r* them to little children.
Jn 12: 38 the arm of the Lord been *r*?''
17: 6 ''I have *r* you to those whom you
Ro 1: 17 a righteousness from God is *r*,
8: 18 with the glory that will be *r* in us.
10: 20 I *r* myself to those who did not
16: 26 but now *r* and made known
1Co 2: 10 but God has *r* it to us by his Spirit.
2Th 1: 7 happen when the Lord Jesus is *r*
2: 3 and the man of lawlessness is *r*,
1Pe 1: 7 and honor when Jesus Christ is *r*.
1: 20 but was *r* in these last times
4: 13 overjoyed when his glory is *r*.

REVEALS* (REVEAL)

Nu 23: 3 Whatever he *r* to me I will tell you
Job 12: 22 He *r* the deep things of darkness
Da 2: 22 He *r* deep and hidden things;
2: 28 a God in heaven who *r* mysteries.
Am 4: 13 and *r* his thoughts to man,

REVELATION* (REVEAL)

2Sa 7: 17 David all the words of this entire *r*.
1Ch 17: 15 David all the words of this entire *r*.
Pr 29: 18 Where there is no *r*, the people cast
Da 10: 1 a *r* was given to Daniel (who was
Hab 2: 2 ''Write down the *r*
2: 3 For the *r* awaits an appointed time;
Lk 2: 32 a light for *r* to the Gentiles
Ro 16: 25 according to the *r*
1Co 14: 6 I bring you some *r* or knowledge
14: 26 a *r*, a tongue or an interpretation.
14: 30 And if a *r* comes to someone who is
Gal 1: 12 I received it by *r* from Jesus Christ.
2: 2 I went in response to a *r*
Eph 1: 17 you the Spirit of wisdom and *r*,
3: 3 mystery made known to me by *r*,
Rev 1: 1 *r* of Jesus Christ, which God gave

REVELATIONS* (REVEAL)

2Co 12: 1 on to visions and *r* from the Lord.
12: 7 of these surpassingly great *r*,

REVELED* (REVELRY)

Ne 9: 25 they *r* in your great goodness.

REVELRY (REVELED)

Ex 32: 6 drink and got up to indulge in *r*.
1Co 10: 7 and got up to indulge in pagan *r*.''

REVENGE (VENGEANCE)

Lev 19: 18 ''Do not seek *r* or bear a grudge
Ro 12: 19 Do not take *r*, my friends,

REVERE* (REVERENCE REVERENT REVERING)

Lev 19: 32 for the elderly and *r* your God.
Dt 4: 10 so that they may learn to *r* me
13: 4 must follow, and him you must *r*.
14: 23 to *r* the LORD your God always.
17: 19 learn to *r* the LORD his God
28: 58 and do not *r* this glorious
Job 37: 24 Therefore, men *r* him,
Ps 22: 23 *R* him, all you descendants
33: 8 let all the people of the world *r* him
102: 15 of the earth will *r* your glory.
Ecc 3: 14 God does it so that men will *r* him.
Isa 25: 3 cities of ruthless nations will *r* you.
59: 19 of the sun, they will *r* his glory.
63: 17 hearts so we do not *r* you?
Jer 10: 7 Who should not *r* you,
Hos 10: 3 because we did not *r* the LORD.

Mal 4: 2 But for you who *r* my name,

REVERENCE (REVERE)

Lev 19: 30 and have *r* for my sanctuary.
Ne 5: 15 of *r* for God I did not act like that.
Ps 5: 7 in *r* will I bow down
Da 6: 26 people must fear and *r* the God
2Co 7: 1 perfecting holiness out of *r* for God
Eph 5: 21 to one another out of *r* for Christ.
Col 3: 22 of heart and *r* for the Lord.
1Pe 3: 2 when they see the purity and *r*
Rev 11: 18 and those who *r* your name,

REVERENT* (REVERE)

Ecc 8: 12 with God-fearing men, who are *r*
Tit 2: 3 women to be *r* in the way they live,
Heb 5: 7 because of his *r* submission.
1Pe 1: 17 as strangers here in *r* fear.

REVERING* (REVERE)

Dt 8: 6 walking in his ways and *r* him.
Ne 1: 11 who delight in *r* your name.

REVERSE*

Isa 43: 13 When I act, who can *r* it?''

REVIVE* (REVIVING)

Ps 80: 18 *r* us, and we will call on your name.
85: 6 Will you not *r* us again,
Isa 57: 15 and to *r* the heart of the contrite.
57: 15 to *r* the spirit of the lowly
Hos 6: 2 After two days he will *r* us;

REVIVING* (REVIVE)

Ps 19: 7 *r* the soul.

REVOKED

Isa 45: 23 a word that will not be *r*:

REWARD (REWARDED REWARDING REWARDS)

Ge 15: 1 your very great *r*.''
1Sa 24: 19 May the LORD *r* you well
Ps 19: 11 in keeping them there is great *r*.
62: 12 Surely you will *r* each person
127: 3 children a *r* from him.
Pr 9: 12 are wise, your wisdom will *r* you;
11: 18 sows righteousness reaps a sure *r*.
13: 21 prosperity is the *r* of the righteous.
19: 17 he will *r* him for what he has done.
25: 22 and the LORD will *r* you.
31: 31 Give her the *r* she has earned,
Isa 40: 10 See, his *r* is with him,
49: 4 and my *r* is with my God.''
61: 8 In my faithfulness I will *r* them
62: 11 See, his *r* is with him,
Jer 17: 10 to a man according to his conduct
32: 19 you *r* everyone according
Mt 5: 12 because great is your *r* in heaven,
6: 1 you will have no *r*
6: 5 they have received their *r* in full.
10: 41 a prophet will receive a prophet's *r*,
16: 27 and then he will *r* each person
Lk 6: 23 because great is your *r* in heaven.
6: 35 Then your *r* will be great,
1Co 3: 14 built survives, he will receive his *r*.
Eph 6: 8 know that the Lord will *r* everyone
Col 3: 24 an inheritance from the Lord as a *r*.
Heb 11: 26 he was looking ahead to his *r*.
Rev 22: 12 I am coming soon! My *r* is with me

REWARDED (REWARD)

Ru 2: 12 May you be richly *r* by the LORD,
2Sa 22: 21 of my hands he has *r* me.
2Ch 15: 7 for your work will be *r*.''
Ps 18: 24 The LORD has *r* me according
Pr 13: 13 he who respects a command is *r*.
14: 14 and the good man *r* for his.
Jer 31: 16 for your work will be *r*,''
1Co 3: 8 and each will be *r* according
Heb 10: 35 your confidence; it will be richly *r*.
2Jn : 8 but that you may be *r* fully.

REWARDING* (REWARD)

Rev 11: 18 for *r* your servants the prophets

REWARDS (REWARD)

1Sa 26: 23 The LORD *r* every man

Pr 12: 14 the work of his hands *r* him.
Heb 11: 6 that he *r* those who earnestly seek

RIBS

Ge 2: 21 he took one of the man's *r*

RICH (RICHES RICHEST)

Job 34: 19 does not favor the *r* over the poor,
Ps 49: 16 overawed when a man grows *r*,
145: 8 slow to anger and *r* in love.
Pr 21: 17 loves wine and oil will never be *r*.
22: 2 *R* and poor have this in common:
23: 4 Do not wear yourself out to get *r*;
28: 6 than a *r* man whose ways are
28: 20 to get *r* will not go unpunished.
28: 22 A stingy man is eager to get *r*
Ecc 5: 12 but the abundance of a *r* man
Isa 33: 6 a *r* store of salvation and wisdom
53: 9 and with the *r* in his death,
Jer 9: 23 or the *r* man boast of his riches,
Zec 3: 4 and I will put *r* garments on you.''
Mt 19: 23 it is hard for a *r* man
Lk 1: 53 but has sent the *r* away empty.
6: 24 ''But woe to you who are *r*,
12: 21 for himself but is not *r* toward God
16: 1 ''There was a *r* man whose
21: 1 Jesus saw the *r* putting their gifts
2Co 6: 10 yet making many *r*; having nothing
8: 2 poverty welled up in *r* generosity.
8: 9 he was *r*, yet for your sakes he
8: 11 You will be made *r* in every way
Eph 2: 4 love for us, God, who is *r* in mercy,
1Ti 6: 9 want to get *r* fall into temptation
6: 17 Command those who are *r*
6: 18 to do good, to be *r* in good deeds,
Jas 1: 10 the one who is *r* should take pride
2: 5 the eyes of the world to be *r* in faith
5: 1 you *r* people, weep and wail
Rev 2: 9 I know your poverty—yet you are *r*!
3: 18 you can become *r*; and white

RICHES (RICH)

Job 36: 18 that no one entices you by *r*;
Ps 49: 6 and boast of their great *r*?
49: 12 despite his *r*, does not endure;
62: 10 though your *r* increase,
119: 14 as one rejoices in great *r*.
Pr 3: 16 in her left hand are *r* and honor.
11: 28 Whoever trusts in his *r* will fall,
22: 1 is more desirable than great *r*;
27: 24 for *r* do not endure forever,
30: 8 give me neither poverty nor *r*,
Isa 10: 3 Where will you leave your *r*?
60: 5 to you the *r* of the nations will
Jer 9: 23 or the rich man boast of his *r*,
Lk 8: 14 *r* and pleasures, and they do not
Ro 9: 23 to make the *r* of his glory known
11: 33 the depth of the *r* of the wisdom
Eph 2: 7 he might show the incomparable *r*
3: 8 to the Gentiles the unsearchable *r*
Col 1: 27 among the Gentiles the glorious *r*
2: 2 so that they may have the full *r*

RICHEST (RICH)

Isa 55: 2 and your soul will delight in the *r*

RID

Ge 21: 10 ''Get *r* of that slave woman
1Co 5: 7 Get *r* of the old yeast that you may
Gal 4: 30 ''Get *r* of the slave woman

RIDE (RIDER RIDING)

Ps 45: 4 In your majesty *r* forth victoriously

RIDER (RIDE)

Rev 6: 2 was a white horse! Its *r* held a bow,
19: 11 whose *r* is called Faithful and True.

RIDING (RIDE)

Zec 9: 9 gentle and *r* on a donkey,
Mt 21: 5 gentle and *r* on a donkey,

RIGGING

Isa 33: 23 Your *r* hangs loose;

RIGHT (RIGHTS)

Ge 4: 7 But if you do not do what is *r*,
18: 19 of the LORD by doing what is *r*

Ge 18: 25 the Judge of all the earth do *r?''*
48: 13 on his left toward Israel's *r* hand,
Ex 15: 6 Your *r* hand, O LORD,
15: 26 and do what is *r* in his eyes,
Dt 5: 32 do not turn aside to the *r*
6: 18 Do what is *r* and good
13: 18 and doing what is *r* in his eyes.
Jos 1: 7 do not turn from it to the *r*
1Sa 12: 23 you the way that is good and *r*.
1Ki 3: 9 to distinguish between *r* and wrong
15: 5 For David had done what was *r*
2Ki 7: 9 to each other, ''We're not doing *r*.
Ne 9: 13 and laws that are just and *r*,
Ps 16: 8 Because he is at my *r* hand,
16: 11 eternal pleasures at your *r* hand.
17: 7 you who save by your *r* hand
18: 35 and your *r* hand sustains me;
19: 8 The precepts of the LORD are *r*,
25: 9 He guides the humble in what is *r*
33: 4 For the word of the LORD is *r*
44: 3 it was your *r* hand, your arm,
45: 4 let your *r* hand display awesome
51: 4 so that you are proved *r*
63: 8 your *r* hand upholds me.
73: 23 you hold me by my *r* hand.
91: 7 ten thousand at your *r* hand,
98: 1 his *r* hand and his holy arm
106: 3 who constantly do what is *r*.
110: 1 ''Sit at my *r* hand
118: 15 LORD's *r* hand has done mighty
119:144 Your statutes are forever *r*;
137: 5 may my *r* hand forget its skill,
139: 10 your *r* hand will hold me fast.
Pr 1: 3 doing what is *r* and just and fair;
4: 27 Do not swerve to the *r* or the left;
14: 12 There is a way that seems *r*
18: 17 The first to present his case seems *r*
Ecc 7: 20 who does what is *r* and never sins.
SS 1: 4 How *r* they are to adore you!
Isa 1: 17 learn to do *r*!
7: 15 reject the wrong and choose the *r*.
30: 10 us no more visions of what is *r*!
30: 21 Whether you turn to the *r*
41: 10 you with my righteous *r* hand.
41: 13 who takes hold of your *r* hand
48: 13 my *r* hand spread out the heavens;
64: 5 to the help of those who gladly do *r*
Jer 23: 5 and do what is just and *r* in the land
Eze 18: 5 who does what is just and *r*.
18: 21 and does what is just and *r*,
33: 14 and does what is just and *r*—
Hos 14: 9 The ways of the LORD are *r*;
Mt 5: 29 If your *r* eye causes you to sin,
6: 3 know what your *r* hand is doing,
22: 44 ''Sit at my *r* hand
25: 33 He will put the sheep on his *r*
Jn 1: 12 he gave the *r* to become children
Ac 2: 34 ''Sit at my *r* hand
7: 55 Jesus standing at the *r* hand of God
Ro 3: 4 ''So that you may be proved *r*
8: 34 is at the *r* hand of God and is
9: 21 Does not the potter have the *r*
12: 17 careful to do what is *r* in the eyes
1Co 9: 4 Don't we have the *r* to food
2Co 8: 21 we are taking pains to do what is *r*,
Eph 6: 1 parents in the Lord, for this is *r*.
Php 4: 8 whatever is *r*, whatever is pure,
2Th 3: 13 never tire of doing what is *r*.
Heb 1: 3 down at the *r* hand of the Majesty
Jas 2: 8 as yourself,'' you are doing *r*.
1Pe 3: 14 if you should suffer for what is *r*,
1Jn 2: 29 who does what is *r* has been born
Rev 2: 7 I will give the *r* to eat from the tree
3: 21 I will give the *r* to sit with me
22: 11 let him who does *r* continue to do *r*

RIGHTEOUS (RIGHTEOUSLY RIGHTEOUSNESS)

Ge 6: 9 Noah was a *r* man, blameless
18: 23 ''Will you sweep away the *r*
Nu 23: 10 Let me die the death of the *r*,
Ne 9: 8 your promise because you are *r*.
Job 36: 7 He does not take his eyes off the *r*;
Ps 1: 5 nor sinners in the assembly of the *r*.
5: 12 O LORD, you bless the *r*;
11: 7 For the LORD is *r*,
15: 2 and who does what is *r*,

Ps 34: 15 The eyes of the LORD are on the *r*
37: 16 Better the little that the *r* have
37: 21 but the *r* give generously;
37: 25 yet I have never seen the *r* forsaken
37: 30 of the *r* man utters wisdom,
55: 22 he will never let the *r* fall.
64: 10 Let the *r* rejoice in the LORD
68: 3 But may the *r* be glad
112: 4 compassionate and *r* man.
118: 20 through which the *r* may enter.
119: 7 as I learn your *r* laws.
119:137 *R* are you, O LORD,
140: 13 Surely the *r* will praise your name
143: 2 for no one living is *r* before you.
145: 17 The LORD is *r* in all his ways
Pr 3: 33 but he blesses the home of the *r*.
4: 18 of the *r* is like the first gleam
10: 7 of the *r* will be a blessing,
10: 11 The mouth of the *r* is a fountain
10: 16 The wages of the *r* bring them life,
10: 20 The tongue of the *r* is choice silver,
10: 24 what the *r* desire will be granted.
10: 28 The prospect of the *r* is joy,
10: 32 of the *r* know what is fitting,
11: 23 The desire of the *r* ends only
11: 30 The fruit of the *r* is a tree of life,
12: 10 A *r* man cares for the needs
12: 21 No harm befalls the *r*,
13: 9 The light of the *r* shines brightly,
15: 28 of the *r* weighs its answers,
15: 29 but he hears the prayer of the *r*.
16: 31 it is attained by a *r* life.
18: 10 the *r* run to it and are safe.
20: 7 The *r* man leads a blameless life;
21: 15 justice is done, it brings joy to the *r*
23: 24 The father of a *r* man has great joy;
28: 1 but the *r* are as bold as a lion.
29: 6 but a *r* one can sing and be glad.
29: 7 The *r* care about justice
29: 27 The *r* detest the dishonest;
Ecc 7: 20 There is not a *r* man on earth
Isa 26: 7 The path of the *r* is level;
41: 10 with my *r* right hand.
45: 21 a *r* God and a Savior;
53: 11 his knowledge my *r* servant will
64: 6 and all our *r* acts are like filthy rags
Jer 23: 5 up to David a *r* Branch,
Eze 3: 20 when a *r* man turns
18: 5 ''Suppose there is a *r* man
18: 20 of the *r* man will be credited
33: 12 The *r* man, if he sins, will not be
Da 9: 18 requests of you because we are *r*,
Hab 2: 4 but he will live by his faith—
Zec 9: 9 *r* and having salvation,
Mal 3: 18 see the distinction between the *r*
Mt 5: 45 rain on the *r* and the unrighteous.
9: 13 For I have not come to call the *r*,
10: 41 and anyone who receives a *r* man
13: 43 Then the *r* will shine like the sun
13: 49 and separate the wicked from the *r*
25: 37 ''Then the *r* will answer him, 'Lord,
25: 46 to eternal punishment, but the *r*
Ac 24: 15 will be a resurrection of both the *r*
Ro 1: 17 as it is written: ''The *r* will live
2: 5 when his *r* judgment will be
2: 13 the law who will be declared *r*.
3: 10 ''There is no one *r*, not even one;
3: 20 Therefore no one will be declared *r*
5: 19 one man through the *r* will be made *r*.
Gal 3: 11 because, ''The *r* will live by faith.''
1Ti 1: 9 that law is made not for the *r*
2Ti 4: 8 which the Lord, the *r* Judge,
Tit 3: 5 because of *r* things we had done,
Heb 10: 38 But my *r* one will live by faith.
Jas 5: 16 The prayer of a *r* man is powerful
1Pe 3: 12 the eyes of the Lord are on the *r*
3: 18 the *r* for the unrighteous,
4: 18 ''If it is hard for the *r* to be saved,
1Jn 2: 1 defense—Jesus Christ, the *R* One.
3: 7 does what is right is *r*, just as he is *r*.
Rev 19: 8 stands for the *r* acts of the saints.)

RIGHTEOUSLY* (RIGHTEOUS)

Ps 9: 4 on your throne, judging *r*.
Isa 33: 15 He who walks *r*
Jer 11: 20 LORD Almighty, you who judge *r*

RIGHTEOUSNESS (RIGHTEOUS)

Ge 15: 6 and he credited it to him as *r*.
Dt   9: 4 of this land because of my *r*.''
1Sa 26: 23 LORD rewards every man for his *r*
1Ki 10: 9 to maintain justice and *r*.''
Job 37: 23 great *r*, he does not oppress.
Ps   7: 17 to the LORD because of his *r*
     9: 8 He will judge the world in *r*;
    17: 15 And I—in *r* I will see your face;
    23: 3 He guides me in paths of *r*
    33: 5 The LORD loves *r* and justice;
    35: 28 My tongue will speak of your *r*
    36: 6 Your *r* is like the mighty
    37: 6 He will make your *r* shine like
    40: 9 I proclaim *r* in the great assembly;
    45: 4 in behalf of truth, humility and *r*;
    45: 7 You love *r* and hate wickedness;
    48: 10 your right hand is filled with *r*.
    65: 5 us with awesome deeds of *r*,
    71: 2 Rescue me and deliver me in your *r*
    71: 15 My mouth will tell of your *r*,
    71: 19 Your *r* reaches to the skies, O God,
    85: 10 *r* and peace kiss each other.
    89: 14 *R* and justice are the foundation
    96: 13 He will judge the world in *r*
    98: 9 He will judge the world in *r*
   103: 6 The LORD works *r*
   103: 17 his *r* with their children's children
   106: 31 This was credited to him as *r*
   111: 3 and his *r* endures forever.
   118: 19 Open for me the gates of *r*;
   132: 9 May your priests be clothed with *r*;
   145: 7 and joyfully sing of your *r*.
Pr 11: 5 *r* of the blameless makes a straight
    11: 18 he who sows *r* reaps a sure reward.
    13: 6 *R* guards the man of integrity,
    14: 34 *R* exalts a nation,
    16: 8 Better a little with *r*
    16: 12 a throne is established through *r*.
    21: 21 He who pursues *r* and love
Isa 5: 16 will show himself holy by his *r*.
     9: 7 it with justice and *r*
    11: 4 but with *r* he will judge the needy,
    16: 5 and speeds the cause of *r*.
    26: 9 the people of the world learn *r*.
    32: 17 The fruit of *r* will be peace;
    42: 6 ''I, the LORD, have called you in *r*;
    42: 21 the LORD for the sake of his *r*
    45: 8 ''You heavens above, rain down *r*;
    51: 1 ''Listen to me, you who pursue *r*
    51: 6 my *r* will never fail.
    51: 8 But my *r* will last forever,
    58: 8 then your *r* will go before you,
    59: 17 He put on *r* as his breastplate,
    61: 10 and arrayed me in a robe of *r*,
    63: 1 ''It is I, speaking in *r*,
Jer 9: 24 justice and *r* on earth,
    23: 6 The LORD Our *R*.
Eze 3: 20 a righteous man turns from his *r*
    14: 20 save only themselves by their *r*.
    18: 20 The *r* of the righteous man will be
    33: 12 *r* of the righteous man will not save
Da   9: 24 to bring in everlasting *r*,
    12: 3 and those who lead many to *r*,
Hos 10: 12 Sow for yourselves *r*,
Am   5: 24 *r* like a never-failing stream!
Mic 7: 9 I will see his *r*.
Zep 2: 3 Seek *r*, seek humility;
Mal 4: 2 the sun of *r* will rise with healing
Mt   5: 6 those who hunger and thirst for *r*,
     5: 10 who are persecuted because of *r*,
     5: 20 unless your *r* surpasses that
     6: 1 to do your 'acts of *r*' before men,
     6: 33 But seek first his kingdom and his *r*
Jn 16: 8 world of guilt in regard to sin and *r*
Ac 24: 25 Paul discoursed on *r*, self-control
Ro   1: 17 For in the gospel a *r* from God is
     3: 5 brings out God's *r* more clearly,
     3: 22 This *r* from God comes
     4: 3 and it was credited to him as *r*.''
     4: 5 wicked, his faith is credited as *r*.
     4: 6 man to whom God credits *r* apart
     4: 9 faith was credited to him as *r*.
     4: 13 through the *r* that comes by faith.
     4: 22 why ''it was credited to him as *r*.''
     5: 18 of *r* was justification that brings life
     6: 13 body to him as instruments of *r*.

Ro   6: 16 or to obedience, which leads to *r*?
     6: 18 and have become slaves to *r*.
     6: 19 in slavery to *r* leading to holiness.
     8: 10 yet your spirit is alive because of *r*.
     9: 30 did not pursue *r*, have obtained it,
    10: 3 they did not know the *r* that comes
    14: 17 but of *r*, peace and joy
1Co 1: 30 our *r*, holiness and redemption.
2Co 3: 9 is the ministry that brings *r*!
     5: 21 that in him we might become the *r*
     6: 7 with weapons of *r* in the right hand
     6: 14 For what do *r* and wickedness have
     9: 9 his *r* endures forever.''
Gal 2: 21 for if *r* could be gained
     3: 6 and it was credited to him as *r*.''
     3: 21 then *r* would certainly have come
Eph 4: 24 created to be like God in true *r*
     5: 9 *r* and truth) and find out what
     6: 14 with the breastplate of *r* in place,
Php 1: 11 filled with the fruit of *r* that comes
     3: 6 as for legalistic *r*, faultless.
     3: 9 not having a *r* of my own that
1Ti 6: 11 and pursue *r*, godliness, faith, love,
2Ti 2: 22 and pursue *r*, faith, love and peace,
     3: 16 correcting and training in *r*,
     4: 8 is in store for me the crown of *r*,
Heb 1: 8 and *r* will be the scepter
     5: 13 with the teaching about *r*.
     7: 2 his name means ''king of *r*'';
    11: 7 became heir of the *r* that comes
    12: 11 it produces a harvest of *r*
Jas 2: 23 and it was credited to him as *r*,''
     3: 18 sow in peace raise a harvest of *r*.
1Pe 2: 24 die to sins and live for *r*;
2Pe 2: 21 not to have known the way of *r*,
     3: 13 and a new earth, the home of *r*.

RIGHTS (RIGHT)

Ps 82: 3 maintain the *r* of the poor
Pr 31: 8 for the *r* of all who are destitute.
Isa 10: 2 to deprive the poor of their *r*
La   3: 35 to deny a man his *r*
Gal 4: 5 that we might receive the full *r*

RING

Pr 11: 22 Like a gold *r* in a pig's snout
Lk 15: 22 Put a *r* on his finger and sandals

RIOTS

2Co 6: 5 imprisonments and *r*; in hard work,

RIPE

Joel 3: 13 for the harvest is *r*.
Am   8: 1 showed me: a basket of *r* fruit.
Jn   4: 35 at the fields! They are *r* for harvest.
Rev 14: 15 for the harvest of the earth is *r*.''

RISE (RAISE RAISED RISEN ROSE)

Lev 19: 32 '' '*R* in the presence of the aged,
Nu 24: 17 a scepter will *r* out of Israel.
Isa 26: 19 their bodies will *r*
Mal 4: 2 of righteousness will *r* with healing
Mt 17: 9 ''After three days I will *r* again.'
Mt 27: 63 'After three days I will *r* again.'
Mk   8: 31 and after three days *r* again.
Lk 18: 33 On the third day he will *r* again.''
Jn   5: 29 those who have done good will *r*
    20: 9 had to *r* from the dead.)
Ac 17:_3 had to suffer and *r* from the dead.
1Th 4: 16 and the dead in Christ will *r* first.

RISEN (RISE)

Mt 28: 6 He is not here; he has *r*, just
Mk 16: 6 He has *r*! He is not here.
Lk 24: 34 The Lord has *r* and has appeared

RIVER (RIVERS)

Ps 46: 4 There is a *r* whose streams make
Isa 66: 12 ''I will extend peace to her like a *r*,
Eze 47: 12 grow on both banks of the *r*.
Rev 22: 1 Then the angel showed me the *r*

RIVERS (RIVER)

Ps 137: 1 By the *r* of Babylon we sat

ROAD (CROSSROADS ROADS)

Mt   7: 13 and broad is the *r* that leads

ROADS (ROAD)

Lk   3: 5 crooked *r* shall become straight,

ROARING

1Pe 5: 8 prowls around like a *r* lion looking

ROB (ROBBERS ROBBERY ROBS)

Mal 3: 8 ''Will a man *r* God? Yet you *r* me.

ROBBERS (ROB)

Jer 7: 11 become a den of *r* to you?
Mk 15: 27 They crucified two *r* with him,
Lk 19: 46 but you have made it 'a den of *r*.' ''
Jn 10: 8 came before me were thieves and *r*,

ROBBERY (ROB)

Isa 61: 8 I hate *r* and iniquity.

ROBE (ROBED ROBES)

Ge 37: 3 and he made a richly ornamented *r*
Isa 6: 1 the train of his *r* filled the temple.
    61: 10 arrayed me in a *r* of righteousness,
Rev 6: 11 each of them was given a white *r*,

ROBED (ROBE)

Ps 93: 1 the LORD is *r* in majesty
Isa 63: 1 Who is this, *r* in splendor,

ROBES (ROBE)

Ps 45: 8 All your *r* are fragrant with myrrh
Rev 7: 13 ''These in white *r*— who are they,

ROBS* (ROB)

Pr 19: 26 He who *r* his father and drives out
    28: 24 He who *r* his father or mother

ROCK

Ge 49: 24 of the Shepherd, the *R* of Israel,
Ex 17: 6 Strike the *r*, and water will come
Nu 20: 8 Speak to that *r* before their eyes
Dt 32: 4 He is the *R*, his works are perfect,
    32: 13 him with honey from the *r*,
2Sa 22: 2 ''The LORD is my *r*, my fortress
Ps 18: 2 The LORD is my *r*, my fortress
    19: 14 O LORD, my *R* and my Redeemer
    40: 2 he set my feet on a *r*
    61: 2 lead me to the *r* that is higher
    92: 15 he is my *R*, and there is no
Isa 26: 4 the LORD, is the *R* eternal.
    51: 1 to the *r* from which you were cut
Da   2: 34 you were watching, a *r* was cut out,
Mt   7: 24 man who built his house on the *r*.
    16: 18 and on this *r* I will build my church
Ro   9: 33 and a *r* that makes them fall,
1Co 10: 4 the spiritual *r* that accompanied
1Pe 2: 8 and a *r* that makes them fall.''

ROD (RODS)

2Sa 7: 14 I will punish him with the *r* of men,
Ps 23: 4 your *r* and your staff,
Pr 13: 24 He who spares the *r* hates his son,
    22: 15 the *r* of discipline will drive it far
    23: 13 if you punish him with the *r*,
    29: 15 *r* of correction imparts wisdom,
Isa 11: 4 the earth with the *r* of his mouth;

RODS (ROD)

2Co 11: 25 Three times I was beaten with *r*,

ROLL (ROLLED)

Mk 16: 3 ''Who will *r* the stone away

ROLLED (ROLL)

Lk 24: 2 They found the stone *r* away

ROMAN

Ac 16: 37 even though we are *R* citizens,
    22: 25 you to flog a *R* citizen who hasn't

ROOF (ROOFS)

Pr 21: 9 Better to live on a corner of the *r*

ROOFS

Mt 10: 27 in your ear, proclaim from the *r*.

ROOM (ROOMS)

Mt   6: 6 But when you pray, go into your *r*,
Mk 14: 15 He will show you a large upper *r*,
Lk   2: 7 there was no *r* for them in the inn.

Jn 8: 37 because you have no *r* for my word
21: 25 the whole world would not have *r*
2Co 7: 2 Make *r* for us in your hearts.

ROOMS (ROOM)
Jn 14: 2 In my Father's house are many *r;*

ROOSTER
Mt 26: 34 this very night, before the *r* crows,

ROOT (ROOTED ROOTS)
Isa 11: 10 In that day the *R* of Jesse will stand
53: 2 and like a *r* out of dry ground.
Mt 3: 10 already at the *r* of the trees,
13: 21 But since he has no *r*, he lasts only
Ro 11: 16 if the *r* is holy, so are the branches.
15: 12 "The *R* of Jesse will spring up,
1Ti 6: 10 of money is a *r* of all kinds of evil.
Rev 5: 5 the *R* of David, has triumphed.
22: 16 I am the *R* and the Offspring

ROOTED (ROOT)
Eph 3: 17 being *r* and established in love,

ROOTS (ROOT)
Isa 11: 1 from his *r* a Branch will bear fruit.

ROSE (RISE)
SS 2: 1 I am a *r* of Sharon,
1Th 4: 14 believe that Jesus died and *r* again

ROTS
Pr 14: 30 but envy *r* the bones.

ROUGH
Isa 42: 16 and make the *r* places smooth.
Lk 3: 5 the *r* ways smooth.

ROUND
Ecc 1: 6 *r* and *r* it goes,

ROYAL
Ps 45: 9 at your right hand is the *r* bride
Da 1: 8 not to defile himself with the *r* food
Jas 2: 8 If you really keep the *r* law found
1Pe 2: 9 a *r* priesthood, a holy nation,

RUBBISH*
Php 3: 8 I consider them *r*, that I may gain

RUBIES
Job 28: 18 the price of wisdom is beyond *r*.
Pr 3: 15 She is more precious than *r;*
8: 11 for wisdom is more precious than *r*,
31: 10 She is worth far more than *r*.

RUDDER*
Jas 3: 4 by a very small *r* wherever the pilot

RUDDY
1Sa 16: 12 He was *r*, with a fine appearance
SS 5: 10 *Beloved* My lover is radiant and *r*,

RUDE*
1Co 13: 5 It is not *r*, it is not self-seeking,

RUIN (RUINED RUINING RUINS)
Pr 10: 8 but a chattering fool comes to *r*.
10: 10 and a chattering fool comes to *r*.
10: 14 but the mouth of a fool invites *r*.
10: 29 but it is the *r* of those who do evil.
18: 24 many companions may come to *r*,
19: 13 A foolish son is his father's *r*,
26: 28 and a flattering mouth works *r*.
SS 2: 15 that *r* the vineyards,
Eze 21: 27 A *r!* A *r!* I will make it a *r!*
1Ti 6: 9 desires that plunge men into *r*

RUINED (RUIN)
Isa 6: 5 "I am *r!* For I am a man
Mt 9: 17 and the wineskins will be *r*.
12: 25 divided against itself will be *r*,

RUINING* (RUIN)
Tit 1: 11 they are *r* whole households

RUINS (RUIN)
Pr 19: 3 A man's own folly *r* his life,
Ecc 4: 5 and *r* himself.

2Ti 2: 14 and only *r* those who listen.

RULE (RULER RULERS RULES)
Ge 1: 26 let them *r* over the fish of the sea
3: 16 and he will *r* over you."
Jdg 8: 22 said to Gideon, "*R* over us—
1Sa 12: 12 'No, we want a king to *r* over us'—
Ps 2: 9 You will *r* them with an iron
67: 4 for you *r* the peoples justly
119:133 let no sin *r* over me.
Pr 17: 2 A wise servant will *r*
Isa 28: 10 *r* on *r*, *r* on *r;*
Eze 20: 33 I will *r* over you with a mighty
Zec 6: 13 and will sit and *r* on his throne.
9: 10 His *r* will extend from sea to sea
Ro 13: 9 are summed up in this one *r:*
15: 12 arise to *r* over the nations;
1Co 7: 17 This is the *r* I lay down in all
Gal 6: 16 and mercy to all who follow this *r*,
Eph 1: 21 far above all *r* and authority,
Col 3: 15 the peace of Christ *r* in your hearts,
2Th 3: 10 we gave you this *r:* "If a man will
Rev 2: 27 He will *r* them with an iron scepter;
12: 5 who will *r* all the nations
19: 15 He will *r* them with an iron scepter

RULER (RULE)
Ps 8: 6 You made him *r* over the works
Pr 19: 6 Many curry favor with a *r*,
23: 1 When you sit to dine with a *r*,
25: 15 Through patience a *r* can be
29: 26 Many seek an audience with a *r*,
Isa 60: 17 and righteousness your *r*.
Da 9: 25 the *r*, comes, there will be seven
Mic 5: 2 one who will be *r* over Israel,
Mt 2: 6 for out of you will come a *r*
Eph 2: 2 of the *r* of the kingdom of the air,
1Ti 6: 15 God, the blessed and only *R*,
Rev 1: 5 and the *r* of the kings of the earth.

RULERS (RULE)
Ps 2: 2 and the *r* gather together
119:161 *R* persecute me without cause,
Isa 40: 23 reduces the *r* of this world
Da 7: 27 and all *r* will worship and obey him
Mt 20: 25 "You know that the *r*
Ac 13: 27 and their *r* did not recognize Jesus,
Ro 13: 3 For *r* hold no terror
1Co 2: 6 of this age or of the *r* of this age,
Eph 3: 10 should be made known to the *r*
6: 12 the *r*, against the authorities,
Col 1: 16 or powers or *r* or authorities;

RULES (RULE)
Nu 15: 15 is to have the same *r* for you
2Sa 23: 3 when he *r* in the fear of God,
Ps 22: 28 and he *r* over the nations.
66: 7 He *r* forever by his power,
103: 19 and his kingdom *r* over all.
Isa 29: 13 is made up only of *r* taught by men.
40: 10 and his arm *r* for him.
Mt 15: 9 their teachings are but *r* taught
Lk 22: 26 one who *r* like the one who serves.
2Ti 2: 5 he competes according to the *r*.

RUMORS
Jer 51: 46 afraid when *r* are heard in the land;
Mt 24: 6 You will hear of wars and *r* of wars,

RUN (RAN RUNNERS RUNNING RUNS)
Ps 19: 5 champion rejoicing to *r* his course.
Pr 4: 12 when you *r*, you will not stumble.
18: 10 the righteous *r* to it and are safe.
Isa 10: 3 To whom will you *r* for help?
40: 31 they will *r* and not grow weary,
Joel 3: 18 ravines of Judah will *r* with water.
Hab 2: 2 so that a herald may *r* with it.
1Co 9: 24 *R* in such a way as to get the prize.
Gal 2: 2 that I was running or had *r* my race
Php 2: 16 on the day of Christ that I did not *r*
Heb 12: 1 let us *r* with perseverance the race

RUNNERS* (RUN)
1Co 9: 24 that in a race all the *r* run,

RUNNING (RUN)
Ps 133: 2 *r* down on Aaron's beard,
Lk 17: 23 Do not go *r* off after them.

1Co 9: 26 I do not run like a man *r* aimlessly;
Gal 5: 7 You were *r* a good race.

RUNS (RUN)
Jn 10: 12 he abandons the sheep and *r* away.

RUSH
Pr 1: 16 for their feet *r* into sin,
6: 18 feet that are quick to *r* into evil,
Isa 59: 7 Their feet *r* into sin;

RUST
Mt 6: 19 where moth and *r* destroy,

RUTH*
Moabitess; widow who went to Bethlehem with mother-in-law Naomi (Ru 1). Gleaned in field of Boaz; shown favor (Ru 2). Proposed marriage to Boaz (Ru 3). Married (Ru 4:1-12); bore Obed, ancestor of David (Ru 4:13-22), Jesus (Mt 1:5).

RUTHLESS
Pr 11: 16 but *r* men gain only wealth.
Ro 1: 31 are senseless, faithless, heartless, *r*.

SABBATH (SABBATHS)
Ex 20: 8 "Remember the *S* day
31: 14 " 'Observe the *S*, because it is holy
Lev 25: 2 the land itself must observe a *s*
Dt 5: 12 "Observe the *S* day
Isa 56: 2 keeps the *S* without desecrating it,
56: 6 all who keep the *S*
58: 13 if you call the *S* a delight
Jer 17: 21 not to carry a load on the *S* day
Mt 12: 1 through the grainfields on the *S*.
Lk 13: 10 On a *S* Jesus was teaching in one
Col 2: 16 a New Moon celebration or a *S* day

SABBATH-REST* (REST)
Heb 4: 9 then, a *S* for the people of God;

SABBATHS (SABBATH)
2Ch 2: 4 evening and on *S* and New Moons
Eze 20: 12 Also I gave them my *S*

SACKCLOTH
Ps 30: 11 you removed my *s* and clothed me
Da 9: 3 in fasting, and in *s* and ashes.
Mt 11: 21 would have repented long ago in *s*

SACRED
Lev 23: 2 are to proclaim as *s* assemblies.
Mt 7: 6 "Do not give dogs what is *s*;
Ro 14: 5 One man considers one day more *s*
1Co 3: 17 for God's temple is *s*, and you are
2Pe 1: 18 were with him on the *s* mountain.
2: 21 on the *s* commandment that was

SACRIFICE (SACRIFICED SACRIFICES)
Ge 22: 2 *S* him there as a burnt offering
Ex 12: 27 'It is the Passover *s* to the LORD,
1Sa 15: 22 To obey is better than *s*,
1Ki 18: 38 the LORD fell and burned up the *s*,
1Ch 21: 24 or a burnt offering that costs me
Ps 40: 6 *S* and offering you did not desire,
50: 14 *S* thank offerings to God,
51: 16 You do not delight in *s*,
54: 6 I will *s* a freewill offering to you;
107: 22 Let them *s* thank offerings
141: 2 of my hands be like the evening *s*.
Pr 15: 8 The LORD detests the *s*
21: 3 to the LORD than *s*.
Da 9: 27 that 'seven' he will put an end to *s*
12: 11 time that the daily *s* is abolished
Hos 6: 6 For I desire mercy, not *s*,
Mt 9: 13 this means: 'I desire mercy, not *s*.'
Ro 3: 25 God presented him as a *s*
Eph 5: 2 as a fragrant offering and *s* to God.
Php 4: 18 an acceptable *s*, pleasing to God.
Heb 9: 26 away with sin by the *s* of himself.
10: 5 "*S* and offering you did not desire,
10: 10 through the *s* of the body
10: 14 by one *s* he has made perfect
10: 18 there is no longer any *s* for sin.
11: 4 faith Abel offered a better *s*
13: 15 offer to God a *s* of praise—
1Jn 2: 2 He is the atoning *s* for our sins,
4: 10 as an atoning *s* for our sins.

SACRIFICED (SACRIFICE)

Ac 15: 29 are to abstain from food s to idols,
1Co 5: 7 our Passover lamb, has been s.
      8: 1 Now about food s to idols:
Heb 7: 27 He s for their sins once for all
      9: 28 so Christ was s once

SACRIFICES (SACRIFICE)

Ps 51: 17 The s of God are a broken spirit;
Mk 12: 33 than all burnt offerings and s.''
Ro 12: 1 to offer your bodies as living s,
Heb 9: 23 with better s than these.
     13: 16 for with such s God is pleased.
1Pe 2: 5 offering spiritual s acceptable

SAD

Lk 18: 23 he heard this, he became very s,

SADDUCEES

Mt 16: 6 the yeast of the Pharisees and S.''
Mk 12: 18 S, who say there is no resurrection,
Ac 23: 8 S say that there is no resurrection,

SAFE (SAVE)

Ps 27: 5 he will keep me s in his dwelling;
     37: 3 in the land and enjoy s pasture.
Pr 18: 10 the righteous run to it and are s.
     28: 26 he who walks in wisdom is kept s.
     29: 25 in the LORD is kept s.
Jer 12: 5 If you stumble in s country,
Jn 17: 12 kept them s by that name you gave
1Ti 2: 15 But women will be kept s
1Jn 5: 18 born of God keeps him s,

SAFETY (SAVE)

Ps   4: 8 make me dwell in s.
Hos 2: 18 so that all may lie down in s.
1Th 5: 3 people are saying, ''Peace and s,''

SAINTS

1Sa 2: 9 He will guard the feet of his s,
Ps 16: 3 As for the s who are in the land,
     30: 4 Sing to the LORD, you s of his;
     31: 23 Love the LORD, all his s!
     34: 9 Fear the LORD, you his s,
    116: 15 is the death of his s.
    149: 1 his praise in the assembly of the s.
    149: 5 Let the s rejoice in this honor
Da   7: 18 the s of the Most High will receive
Ro   8: 27 intercedes for the s in accordance
1Co 6: 2 not know that the s will judge
Eph 1: 15 Jesus and your love for all the s,
      1: 18 of his glorious inheritance in the s,
      6: 18 always keep on praying for all the s
Phm : 7 have refreshed the hearts of the s.
Rev 5: 8 which are the prayers of the s.
     19: 8 for the righteous acts of the s.)

SAKE (SAKES)

1Sa 12: 22 For the s of his great name
Ps 23: 3 righteousness for his name's s.
     44: 22 Yet for your s we face death all day
    106: 8 Yet he saved them for his name's s,
Isa 42: 21 for the s of his righteousness
     43: 25 your transgressions, for my own s,
     48: 9 For my own name's s I delay my
     48: 11 For my own s, for my own s,
Jer 14: 7 for the s of your name.
     14: 21 For the s of your name do not
Eze 20: 9 But for the s of my name I did what
     20: 14 But for the s of my name I did what
     20: 22 and for the s of my name I did what
     36: 22 But for the s of my holy name,
Da   9: 17 For your s, O Lord, look with favor
Mt 10: 39 life for my s will find it.
     19: 29 for my s will receive a hundred
1Co 9: 23 I do all this for the s of the gospel,
2Co 12: 10 for Christ's s, I delight
Php 3: 7 loss for the s of Christ.
Heb 11: 26 He regarded disgrace for the s
1Pe 2: 13 for the Lord's s to every authority
3Jn : 7 was for the s of the Name that they

SAKES* (SAKE)

2Co 8: 9 yet for your s he became poor,

SALEM

Ge 14: 18 king of S brought out bread

Heb 7: 2 ''king of S'' means ''king of peace.''

SALT

Ge 19: 26 and she became a pillar of s.
Nu 18: 19 covenant of s before the LORD
Mt   5: 13 ''You are the s of the earth.
Col 4: 6 with s, so that you may know how
Jas 3: 11 s water flow from the same spring?

SALVATION* (SAVE)

Ex 15: 2 he has become my s.
2Sa 22: 3 my shield and the horn of my s.
     23: 5 Will he not bring to, fruition my s
1Ch 16: 23 proclaim his s day after day.
2Ch 6: 41 O LORD God, be clothed with s,
Ps   9: 14 and there rejoice in your s.
     13: 5 my heart rejoices in your s.
     14: 7 that s for Israel would come out
     18: 2 is my shield and the horn of my s,
     27: 1 The LORD is my light and my s—
     28: 8 a fortress of s for his anointed one.
     35: 3 ''I am your s.''
     35: 9 and delight in his s.
     37: 39 The s of the righteous comes
     40: 10 I speak of your faithfulness and s.
     40: 16 those who love your s always say,
     50: 23 way so that I may show him the s
     51: 12 Restore to me the joy of your s
     53: 6 that s for Israel would come out
     62: 1 my s comes from him.
     62: 2 He alone is my rock and my s;
     62: 6 He alone is my rock and my s;
     62: 7 My s and my honor depend
     67: 2 your s among all nations.
     69: 13 answer me with your sure s.
     69: 27 do not let them share in your s.
     69: 29 may your s, O God, protect me.
     70: 4 those who love your s always say,
     71: 15 of your s all day long,
     74: 12 you bring s upon the earth.
     85: 7 and grant us your s.
     85: 9 Surely his s is near those who fear
     91: 16 and show him my s.''
     95: 1 to the Rock of our s.
     96: 2 proclaim his s day after day.
     98: 1 I have worked s for him.
     98: 2 The LORD has made his s known
     98: 3 the s of our God.
    116: 13 I will lift up the cup of s
    118: 14 he has become my s.
    118: 21 You have become my s.
    119: 41 your s according to your promise;
    119: 81 with longing for your s,
    119:123 My eyes fail, looking for your s,
    119:155 S is far from the wicked,
    119:166 I wait for your s, O LORD,
    119:174 I long for your s, O LORD,
    132: 16 I will clothe her priests with s,
    149: 4 he crowns the humble with s.
Isa 12: 2 Surely God is my s;
     12: 2 he has become my s.''
     12: 3 from the wells of s.
     25: 9 let us rejoice and be glad in his s.''
     26: 1 God makes s
     26: 18 We have not brought s to the earth;
     30: 15 ''In repentance and rest is your s,
     33: 2 our s in time of distress.
     33: 6 a rich store of s and wisdom
     45: 8 let s spring up,
     45: 17 the LORD with an everlasting s;
     46: 13 I will grant s to Zion,
     46: 13 and my s will not be delayed.
     49: 6 that you may bring my s
     49: 8 and in the day of s I will help you;
     51: 5 My s is on the way,
     51: 6 But my s will last forever,
     51: 8 my s through all generations.''
     52: 7 who proclaim s,
     52: 10 the s of our God.
     56: 1 for my s is close at hand
     59: 16 so his own arm worked s for him,
     59: 17 and the helmet of s on his head;
     60: 18 but you will call your walls S
     61: 10 me with garments of s
     62: 1 her s like a blazing torch.
     63: 5 so my own arm worked s for me,
Jer 3: 23 is the s of Israel.
La   3: 26 quietly for the s of the LORD.

Jnh 2: 9 S comes from the LORD.''
Zec 9: 9 righteous and having s,
Lk   1: 69 He has raised up a horn of s for us
      1: 71 of long ago), s from our enemies
      1: 77 give his people the knowledge of s
      2: 30 For my eyes have seen your s,
      3: 6 And all mankind will see God's s
     19: 9 ''Today s has come to this house,
Jn   4: 22 for s is from the Jews.
Ac   4: 12 S is found in no one else,
     13: 26 message of s has been sent.
     13: 47 that you may bring s to the ends
     28: 28 to know that God's s has been sent
Ro   1: 16 for the s of everyone who believes:
     11: 11 s has come to the Gentiles
     13: 11 because our s is nearer now
2Co 1: 6 it is for your comfort and s;
      6: 2 and in the day of s I helped you.''
      6: 2 of God's favor, now is the day of s.
      7: 10 brings repentance that leads to s
Eph 1: 13 word of truth, the gospel of your s.
      6: 17 Take the helmet of s and the sword
Php 2: 12 to work out your s with fear
1Th 5: 8 and the hope of s as a helmet.
      5: 9 to receive s through our Lord Jesus
2Ti 2: 10 they too may obtain the s that is
      3: 15 wise for s through faith
Tit 2: 11 of God that brings s has appeared
Heb 1: 14 to serve those who will inherit s?
      2: 3 This s, which was first announced
      2: 3 escape if we ignore such a great s?
      2: 10 of their s perfect through suffering,
      5: 9 of eternal s for all who obey him
      6: 9 case—things that accompany s.
      9: 28 to bring s to those who are waiting
1Pe 1: 5 the coming of the s that is ready
      1: 9 of your faith, the s of your souls.
      1: 10 Concerning this s, the prophets,
      2: 2 by it you may grow up in your s,
2Pe 3: 15 that our Lord's patience means s,
Jude : 3 to write to you about the s we share
Rev 7: 10 ''S belongs to our God,
     12: 10 have come the s and the power
     19: 1 S and glory and power belong

SAMARIA (SAMARITAN)

1Ki 16: 24 He bought the hill of S
2Ki 17: 6 the king of Assyria captured S
Jn   4: 4 Now he had to go through S.
      4: 5 came to a town in S called Sychar,

SAMARITAN (SAMARIA)

Lk 10: 33 But a S, as he traveled, came where
     17: 16 and thanked him—and he was a S.
Jn   4: 7 When a S woman came

SAMSON

Danite judge. Birth promised (Jdg 13). Married
to Philistine, but wife given away (Jdg 14). Vengeance on Philistines (Jdg 15). Betrayed by Delilah (Jdg 16:1-22). Death (Jdg 16:23-31). Feats of
strength: killed lion (Jdg 14:6), 30 Philistines (Jdg
14:19), 1,000 Philistines with jawbone (Jdg 15:
13-17), carried off gates of Gaza (Jdg 16:3),
pushed down temple of Dagon (Jdg 16:25-30).

SAMUEL

Ephraimite judge and prophet (Heb 11:32).
Birth prayed for (1Sa 1:10-18). Dedicated to temple by Hannah (1Sa 1:21-28). Raised by Eli (1Sa
2:11, 18-26). Called as prophet (1Sa 3). Led Israel
to victory over Philistines (1Sa 7). Asked by Israel
for a king (1Sa 8). Anointed Saul as king (1Sa
9-10). Farewell speech (1Sa 12). Rebuked Saul
for sacrifice (1Sa 13). Announced rejection of
Saul (2Sa 15). Anointed David as king (1Sa 16).
Protected David from Saul (1Sa 19:18-24). Death
(1Sa 25:1). Returned from dead to condemn Saul
(1Sa 28).

SANBALLAT

Led opposition to Nehemiah's rebuilding of
Jerusalem (Ne 2:10, 19; 4; 6).

SANCTIFIED* (SANCTIFY)

Jn 17: 19 that they too may be truly s.
Ac 20: 32 among all those who are s.
     26: 18 among those who are s by faith

Ro 15: 16 to God, *s* by the Holy Spirit.
1Co 1: 2 to those *s* in Christ Jesus
6: 11 But you were washed, you were *s*,
7: 14 and the unbelieving wife has been *s*
7: 14 the unbelieving husband has been *s*
1Th 4: 3 It is God's will that you should be *s*
Heb 10: 29 blood of the covenant that *s* him,

SANCTIFY* (SANCTIFIED SANCTIFYING)

Jn 17: 17 *S* them by the truth; your word is
17: 19 For them I *s* myself, that they too
1Th 5: 23 *s* you through and through.
Heb 9: 13 are ceremonially unclean *s* them

SANCTIFYING* (SANCTIFY)

2Th 2: 13 through the *s* work of the Spirit
1Pe 1: 2 through the *s* work of the Spirit,

SANCTUARY

Ex 25: 8 ''Then have them make a *s* for me,
Lev 19: 30 and have reverence for my *s*.
Ps 15: 1 Lord, who may dwell in your *s*?
63: 2 I have seen you in the *s*
68: 24 of my God and King into the *s*.
68: 35 are awesome, O God, in your *s*;
73: 17 me till I entered the *s* of God;
102: 19 looked down from his *s* on high,
134: 2 Lift up your hands in the *s*
150: 1 Praise God in his *s*;
Eze 37: 26 I will put my *s* among them forever
41: 1 the man brought me to the outer *s*
Da 9: 26 will destroy the city and the *s*.
Heb 6: 19 It enters the inner *s*
8: 2 in the *s*, the true tabernacle set up
8: 5 They serve at a *s* that is a copy
9: 24 enter a man-made *s* that was only

SAND

Ge 22: 17 and as the *s* on the seashore.
Mt 7: 26 man who built his house on *s*.

SANDAL (SANDALS)

Ru 4: 7 one party took off his *s*

SANDALS (SANDAL)

Ex 3: 5 off your *s*, for the place where you
Dt 25: 9 take off one of his *s*, spit in his face
Jos 5: 15 off your *s*, for the place where you
Mt 3: 11 whose *s* I am not fit to carry.

SANG (SING)

Ex 15: 1 and the Israelites *s* this song
15: 21 Miriam *s* to them:
Nu 21: 17 Then Israel *s* this song:
Jdg 5: 1 Barak son of Abinoam *s* this song:
1Sa 18: 7 As they danced, they *s*:
2Sa 22: 1 David *s* to the Lord the words
2Ch 5: 13 in praise to the Lord and *s*:
29: 30 So they *s* praises with gladness
Ezr 3: 11 thanksgiving they *s* to the Lord:
Job 38: 7 while the morning stars *s* together
Ps 106: 12 and *s* his praise.
Rev 5: 9 And they *s* a new song:
5: 12 In a loud voice they *s*:
14: 3 they *s* a new song before the throne
15: 3 and *s* the song of Moses the servant

SAP

Ro 11: 17 share in the nourishing *s*

SAPPHIRA*

Ac 5: 1 together with his wife *S*,

SARAH

Wife of Abraham, originally named Sarai; barren (Ge 11:29-31; 1Pe 3:6). Taken by Pharaoh as Abraham's sister; returned (Ge 12:10-20). Gave Hagar to Abraham; sent her away in pregnancy (Ge 16). Name changed; Isaac promised (Ge 17: 15-21; 18:10-15; Heb 11:11). Taken by Abimelech as Abraham's sister; returned (Ge 20). Isaac born; Hagar and Ishmael sent away (Ge 21:1-21; Gal 4:21-31). Death (Ge 23).

SARDIS

Rev 3: 1 the angel of the church in *S* write:

SASH (SASHES)

Rev 1: 13 with a golden *s* around his chest.

SASHES (SASH)

Rev 15: 6 wore golden *s* around their chests.

SAT (SIT)

Ps 137: 1 By the rivers of Babylon we *s*
Mk 16: 19 and he *s* at the right hand of God.
Lk 10: 39 who *s* at the Lord's feet listening
Heb 1: 3 he *s* down at the right hand
8: 1 who *s* down at the right hand
10: 12 he *s* down at the right hand of God.
12: 2 and *s* down at the right hand

SATAN

Job 1: 6 and *S* also came with them.
Zec 3: 2 said to *S*, ''The Lord rebuke you,
Mt 12: 26 If *S* drives out *S*, he is divided
16: 23 *S!* You are a stumbling block to me
Mk 4: 15 *S* comes and takes away the word
Lk 10: 18 ''I saw *S* fall like lightning
22: 3 *S* entered Judas, called Iscariot,
Ro 16: 20 The God of peace will soon crush *S*
1Co 5: 5 is present, hand this man over to *S*,
2Co 11: 14 for *S* himself masquerades
12: 7 a messenger of *S*, to torment me.
1Ti 1: 20 handed over to *S* to be taught not
Rev 12: 9 serpent called the devil or *S*,
20: 2 or *S*, and bound him for a thousand
20: 7 *S* will be released from his prison

SATISFIED (SATISFY)

Ps 17: 15 I will be *s* with seeing your likeness
22: 26 The poor will eat and be *s*;
63: 5 My soul will be *s* as with the richest
104: 28 they are *s* with good things.
105: 40 *s* them with the bread of heaven.
Pr 13: 4 the desires of the diligent are fully *s*
30: 15 are three things that are never *s*,
Ecc 5: 10 whoever loves wealth is never *s*
Isa 53: 11 he will see the light of life and be *s*
Mt 14: 20 They all ate and were *s*,
Lk 9: 17 and all ate and were *s*.

SATISFIES* (SATISFY)

Ps 103: 5 He *s* my desires with good things,
107: 9 for he *s* the thirsty
147: 14 and *s* you with the finest of wheat.

SATISFY (SATISFIED SATISFIES)

Ps 90: 14 *S* us in the morning
145: 16 *s* the desires of every living thing.
Pr 5: 19 may her breasts *s* you always,
Isa 55: 2 and your labor on what does not *s*?
58: 10 and *s* the needs of the oppressed,

SAUL

1. Benjamite; anointed by Samuel as first king of Israel (1Sa 9-10). Defeated Ammonites (1Sa 11). Rebuked for offering sacrifice (1Sa 13:1-15). Defeated Philistines (1Sa 14). Rejected as king for failing to annihilate Amalekites (1Sa 15). Soothed from evil spirit by David (1Sa 16:14-23). Sent David against Goliath (1Sa 17). Jealousy and attempted murder of David (1Sa 18:1-11). Gave David Michal as wife (1Sa 18:12-30). Second attempt to kill David (1Sa 19). Anger at Jonathan (1Sa 20:26-34). Pursued David: killed priests at Nob (1Sa 22), went to Keilah and Ziph (1Sa 23), life spared by David at En Gedi (1Sa 24) and in his tent (1Sa 26). Rebuked by Samuel's spirit for consulting witch at Endor (1Sa 28). Wounded by Philistines; took own life (1Sa 31; 1Ch 10). Lamented by David (2Sa 1:17-27). Children (1Sa 14:49-51; 1Ch 8).
2. See PAUL

SAVAGE

Ac 20: 29 *s* wolves will come in among you

SAVE (SAFE SAFETY SALVATION SAVED SAVES SAVIOR)

Ge 45: 5 to *s* lives that God sent me ahead
1Ch 16: 35 Cry out, ''*S* us; O God our Savior;
Job 40: 14 that your own right hand can *s* you.
Ps 17: 7 you who *s* by your right hand
18: 27 You *s* the humble

Ps 28: 9 *S* your people and bless your
31: 16 me in your unfailing love.
69: 35 for God will *s* Zion
71: 2 turn your ear to me and *s* me.
72: 13 and *s* the needy from death.
89: 48 or *s* himself from the power
91: 3 Surely he will *s* you
109: 31 to *s* his life from those who
146: 3 in mortal men, who cannot *s*.
Pr 2: 16 will *s* you also from the adulteress,
Isa 35: 4 he will come to *s* you.''
38: 20 The Lord will *s* me,
46: 7 it cannot *s* him from his troubles.
59: 1 of the Lord is not too short to *s*,
63: 1 mighty to *s*.''
Jer 17: 14 *s* me and I will be saved,
Eze 3: 18 ways in order to *s* his life,
7: 19 able to *s* them in the day
14: 14 they could *s* only themselves
33: 12 of the righteous man will not *s* him
34: 22 I will *s* my flock, and they will no
Da 3: 17 the God we serve is able to *s* us
Hos 1: 7 and I will *s* them—not by bow,
Zep 1: 18 will be able to *s* them
3: 17 he is mighty to *s*.
Zec 8: 7 ''I will *s* my people
Mt 1: 21 he will *s* his people from their sins
16: 25 wants to *s* his life will lose it,
Lk 19: 10 to seek and to *s* what was lost.''
Jn 3: 17 but to *s* the world through him.
12: 47 come to judge the world, but to *s* it.
Ro 11: 14 people to envy and *s* some of them.
1Co 7: 16 whether you will *s* your husband?
1Ti 1: 15 came into the world to *s* sinners—
Heb 7: 25 to *s* completely those who come
Jas 5: 20 of his way will *s* him from death
Jude : 23 others from the fire and *s* them;

SAVED (SAVE)

Ps 22: 5 They cried to you and were *s*;
33: 16 No king is *s* by the size of his army;
34: 6 he *s* him out of all his troubles.
106: 21 They forgot the God who *s* them,
116: 6 when I was in great need, he *s* me.
Isa 25: 9 we trusted in him, and he *s* us.
45: 22 ''Turn to me and be *s*,
64: 5 How then can we be *s*?
Jer 4: 14 from your heart and be *s*.
8: 20 and we are not *s*.''
Eze 3: 19 but you will have *s* yourself.
33: 5 warning, he would have *s* himself.
Joel 2: 32 on the name of the Lord will be *s*;
Mt 10: 22 firm to the end will be *s*.
24: 13 firm to the end will be *s*.
Mk 13: 13 firm to the end will be *s*.
16: 16 believes and is baptized will be *s*,
Jn 10: 9 enters through me will be *s*.
Ac 2: 21 on the name of the Lord will be *s*.'
2: 47 daily those who were being *s*.
4: 12 to men by which we must be *s*.''
15: 11 of our Lord Jesus that we are *s*,
16: 30 do to be *s*?'' They replied,
Ro 5: 9 how much more shall we be *s*
9: 27 only the remnant will be *s*.
10: 1 the Israelites is that they may be *s*.
10: 9 him from the dead, you will be *s*.
10: 13 on the name of the Lord will be *s*.''
11: 26 so all Israel will be *s*, as it is written:
1Co 1: 18 to us who are being *s* it is the power
3: 15 will suffer loss; he himself will be *s*,
5: 5 his spirit *s* on the day of the Lord.
10: 33 of many, so that they may be *s*.
15: 2 By this gospel you are *s*,
Eph 2: 5 it is by grace you have been *s*.
2: 8 For it is by grace you have been *s*,
2Th 2: 13 you to be *s* through the sanctifying
1Ti 2: 4 who wants all men to be *s*
2Ti 1: 9 who has *s* us and called us
Tit 3: 5 He *s* us through the washing
Heb 10: 39 but of those who believe and are *s*.

SAVES (SAVE)

Ps 7: 10 who *s* the upright in heart.
68: 20 Our God is a God who *s*;
145: 19 he hears their cry and *s* them.
1Pe 3: 21 It *s* you by the resurrection

SAVIOR* (SAVE)

Dt 32: 15 and rejected the Rock his S.
2Sa 22: 3 stronghold, my refuge and my s—
22: 47 Exalted be God, the Rock, my S!
1Ch 16: 35 Cry out, ''Save us, O God our S;
Ps 18: 46 Exalted be God my S!
24: 5 and vindication from God his S.
25: 5 for you are God my S,
27: 9 O God my S.
38: 22 O Lord my S.
42: 5 my S and
42: 11 my S and my God.
43: 5 my S and my God.
65: 5 O God our S,
68: 19 Praise be to the Lord, to God our S,
79: 9 Help us, O God our S,
85: 4 Restore us again, O God our S,
89: 26 my God, the Rock my S.'
Isa 17: 10 You have forgotten God your S;
19: 20 he will send them a s and defender,
43: 3 the Holy One of Israel, your S;
43: 11 and apart from me there is no s.
45: 15 O God and S of Israel.
45: 21 a righteous God and a S;
49: 26 that I, the LORD, am your S,
60: 16 know that I, the LORD, am your S,
62: 11 'See, your S comes!'
63: 8 and so he became their S.
Jer 14: 8 its S in times of distress,
Hos 13: 4 no S except me.
Mic 7: 7 I wait for God my S;
Hab 3: 18 I will be joyful in God my S.
Lk 1: 47 and my spirit rejoices in God my S,
2: 11 of David a S has been born to you;
Jn 4: 42 know that this man really is the S
Ac 5: 31 S that he might give repentance
13: 23 God has brought to Israel the S
Eph 5: 23 his body, of which he is the S.
Php 3: 20 we eagerly await a S from there,
1Ti 1: 1 by the command of God our S
2: 3 This is good, and pleases God our S
4: 10 who is the S of all men,
2Ti 1: 10 through the appearing of our S,
Tit 1: 3 me by the command of God our S,
1: 4 the Father and Christ Jesus our S.
2: 10 about God our S attractive.
2: 13 appearing of our great God and S,
3: 4 and love of God our S appeared,
3: 6 through Jesus Christ our S,
2Pe 1: 1 S Jesus Christ have received a faith
1: 11 eternal kingdom of our Lord and S
2: 20 and S Jesus Christ and are again
3: 2 and S through your apostles.
3: 18 and knowledge of our Lord and S
1Jn 4: 14 Son to be the S of the world.
Jude : 25 to the only God our S be glory,

SCALE (SCALES)

Ps 18: 29 with my God I can s a wall.

SCALES (SCALE)

Lev 11: 9 may eat any that have fins and s.
19: 36 Use honest s and honest weights,
Pr 11: 1 The LORD abhors dishonest s,
Da 5: 27 You have been weighed on the s
Rev 6: 5 Its rider was holding a pair of s

SCAPEGOAT (GOAT)

Lev 16: 10 by sending it into the desert as a s.

SCARECROW*

Jer 10: 5 Like a s in a melon patch,

SCARLET

Jos 2: 21 she tied the s cord in the window.
Isa 1: 18 ''Though your sins are like s,
Mt 27: 28 They stripped him and put a s robe

SCATTER (SCATTERED SCATTERS)

Dt 4: 27 The LORD will s you
Ne 1: 8 I will s you among the nations,
Jer 9: 16 I will s them among nations that
30: 11 the nations among which I s you,
Zec 10: 9 I s them among the peoples,

SCATTERED (SCATTER)

Isa 11: 12 he will assemble the s people
Jer 31: 10 'He who s Israel will gather them

Zec 2: 6 ''for I have s you to the four winds
13: 7 and the sheep will be s,
Mt 26: 31 and the sheep of the flock will be s.'
Jn 11: 52 but also for the s children of God,
Ac 8: 4 who had been s preached the word
Jas 1: 1 To the twelve tribes s
1Pe 1: 1 s throughout Pontus, Galatia,

SCATTERS (SCATTER)

Mt 12: 30 he who does not gather with me s.

SCEPTER

Ge 49: 10 The s will not depart from Judah,
Nu 24: 17 a s will rise out of Israel.
Ps 2: 9 You will rule them with an iron s;
45: 6 a s of justice will be the s
Heb 1: 8 and righteousness will be the s
Rev 2: 27 'He will rule them with an iron s;
12: 5 rule all the nations with an iron s.
19: 15 ''He will rule them with an iron s.''

SCHEMES

Pr 6: 18 a heart that devises wicked s,
24: 9 The s of folly are sin,
2Co 2: 11 For we are not unaware of his s.
Eph 6: 11 stand against the devil's s.

SCHOLAR*

1Co 1: 20 Where is the s? Where is

SCOFFERS

2Pe 3: 3 that in the last days s will come,

SCORN (SCORNED SCORNING SCORNS)

Ps 69: 7 For I endure s for your sake,
69: 20 S has broken my heart
89: 41 he has become the s
109: 25 I am an object of s to my accusers;
119: 22 Remove from me s and contempt,
Mic 6: 16 you will bear the s of the nations.''

SCORNED (SCORN)

Ps 22: 6 s by men and despised

SCORNING (SCORN)

Heb 12: 2 him endured the cross, s its shame,

SCORNS (SCORN)

Pr 13: 13 He who s instruction will pay for it,
30: 17 that s obedience to a mother,

SCORPION

Lk 11: 12 will give him a s? If you then,
Rev 9: 5 sting of a s when it strikes a man.

SCOUNDREL

Pr 6: 12 A s and villain,

SCRIPTURE (SCRIPTURES)

Jn 2: 22 Then they believed the S
7: 42 Does not the S say that the Christ
10: 35 and the S cannot be broken—
Ac 8: 32 was reading this passage of S:
1Ti 4: 13 yourself to the public reading of S,
2Ti 3: 16 All S is God-breathed
2Pe 1: 20 that no prophecy of S came about

SCRIPTURES (SCRIPTURE)

Mt 22: 29 because you do not know the S
Lk 24: 27 said in all the S concerning himself.
24: 45 so they could understand the S.
Jn 5: 39 These are the S that testify about
Ac 17: 11 examined the S every day to see
2Ti 3: 15 you have known the holy S,
2Pe 3: 16 as they do the other S,

SCROLL

Ps 40: 7 it is written about me in the s.
Isa 34: 4 and the sky rolled up like a s;
Eze 3: 1 eat what is before you, eat this s;
Heb 10: 7 it is written about me in the s
Rev 6: 14 The sky receded like a s, rolling up,
10: 8 take the s that lies open in the hand

SCUM

1Co 4: 13 this moment we have become the s

SEA (SEASHORE)

Ex 14: 16 go through the s on dry ground.
Dt 30: 13 ''Who will cross the s to get it
1Ki 7: 23 He made the S of cast metal,
Job 11: 9 and wider than the s.
Ps 93: 4 mightier than the breakers of the s
95: 5 The s is his, for he made it,
Ecc 1: 7 All streams flow into the s,
Isa 57: 20 the wicked are like the tossing s,
Jnh 1: 4 LORD sent a great wind on the s,
Mic 7: 19 iniquities into the depths of the s.
Hab 2: 14 as the waters cover the s.
Zec 9: 10 His rule will extend from s to s
Mt 18: 6 drowned in the depths of the s.
1Co 10: 1 that they all passed through the s.
Jas 1: 6 who doubts is like a wave of the s,
Jude : 13 They are wild waves of the s,
Rev 10: 2 He planted his right foot on the s
13: 1 I saw a beast coming out of the s.
20: 13 The s gave up the dead that were
21: 1 and there was no longer any s.

SEAL (SEALED SEALS)

Ps 40: 9 I do not s my lips,
SS 8: 6 Place me like a s over your heart,
Da 12: 4 and s the words of the scroll
Jn 6: 27 God the Father has placed his s
1Co 9: 2 For you are the s of my apostleship
2Co 1: 22 set his s of ownership on us,
Eph 1: 13 you were marked in him with a s,
Rev 6: 3 the Lamb opened the second s,
6: 5 When the Lamb opened the third s,
6: 7 the Lamb opened the fourth s,
6: 9 When he opened the fifth s,
6: 12 I watched as he opened the sixth s.
8: 1 When he opened the seventh s,
9: 4 people who did not have the s
22: 10 ''Do not s up the words

SEALED (SEAL)

Eph 4: 30 with whom you were s for the day
2Ti 2: 19 solid foundation stands firm, s
Rev 5: 1 on both sides and s with seven seals

SEALS (SEAL)

Rev 5: 2 ''Who is worthy to break the s
6: 1 I opened the first of the seven s.

SEAMLESS*

Jn 19: 23 This garment was s, woven

SEARCH (SEARCHED SEARCHES SEARCHING)

Ps 4: 4 s your hearts and be silent.
139: 23 S me, O God, and know my heart;
Pr 2: 4 and s for it as for hidden treasure,
25: 2 to s out a matter is the glory
SS 3: 2 I will s for the one my heart loves.
Jer 17: 10 ''I the LORD s the heart
Eze 34: 11 I myself will s for my sheep
34: 16 I will s for the lost and bring back
Lk 15: 8 and s carefully until she finds it?

SEARCHED (SEARCH)

Ps 139: 1 O LORD, you have s me
Ecc 12: 10 The Teacher s to find just the right
1Pe 1: 10 s intently and with the greatest

SEARCHES (SEARCH)

1Ch 28: 9 for the LORD s every heart
Ps 7: 9 who s minds and hearts,
Pr 11: 27 but evil comes to him who s for it.
20: 27 The lamp of the LORD s the spirit
Ro 8: 27 And he who s our hearts knows
1Co 2: 10 The Spirit s all things,
Rev 2: 23 will know that I am he who s hearts

SEARCHING (SEARCH)

Jdg 5: 15 there was much s of heart.
Am 8: 12 s for the word of the LORD,

SEARED

1Ti 4: 2 whose consciences have been s

SEASHORE (SEA)

Jos 11: 4 as numerous as the sand on the s.
1Ki 4: 29 as measureless as the sand on the s.

SEASON (SEASONED SEASONS)

Lev 26: 4 I will send you rain in its *s*,
Ps   1: 3 which yields its fruit in *s*
2Ti   4: 2 be prepared in *s* and out of *s;*

SEASONED* (SEASON)

Col   4: 6 full of grace, *s* with salt,

SEASONS (SEASON)

Ge   1:14 signs to mark *s* and days and years,
Gal   4:10 and months and *s* and years!

SEAT (SEATED SEATS)

Ps   1: 1 or sit in the *s* of mockers.
Pr   31:23 where he takes his *s*
Da   7: 9 and the Ancient of Days took his *s*.
Lk   14: 9 say to you, 'Give this man your *s*.'
2Co   5:10 before the judgment *s* of Christ,

SEATED (SEAT)

Ps   47: 8 God is *s* on his holy throne.
Isa   6: 1 I saw the Lord *s* on a throne,
Lk   22:69 of Man will be *s* at the right hand
Eph   1:20 and *s* him at his right hand
      2: 6 and *s* us with him in the heavenly
Col   3: 1 where Christ is *s* at the right hand
Rev 14:14 *s* on the cloud was one "like a son
     20:11 white throne and him who was *s*

SEATS (SEAT)

Lk   11:43 you love the most important *s*

SECLUSION*

Lk   1:24 and for five months remained in *s*.

SECRET (SECRETLY SECRETS)

Dt   29:29 The *s* things belong
Jdg 16: 6 Tell me the *s* of your great strength
Ps   90: 8 our *s* sins in the light
     139:15 when I was made in the *s* place.
Pr   11:13 but a trustworthy man keeps a *s*.
     21:14 A gift given in *s* soothes anger,
Jer 23:24 Can anyone hide in *s* places
Mt   6: 4 so that your giving may be in *s*.
      6:18 who sees what is done in *s*,
Mk   4:11 "The *s* of the kingdom
1Co   2: 7 No, we speak of God's *s* wisdom,
      4: 1 entrusted with the *s* things of God.
2Co   4: 2 we have renounced *s* and shameful
Eph   5:12 what the disobedient do in *s*.
Php   4:12 I have learned the *s*

SECRETLY (SECRET)

2Pe   2: 1 They will *s* introduce destructive
Jude : 4 about long ago have *s* slipped

SECRETS (SECRET)

Ps   44:21 since he knows the *s* of the heart?
Ro   2:16 day when God will judge men's *s*
1Co 14:25 the *s* of his heart will be laid bare.
Rev   2:24 Satan's so-called deep *s* (I will not

SECURE (SECURITY)

Dt   33:12 beloved of the LORD rest *s* in him.
Ps   16: 5 you have made my lot *s*.
     16: 9 my body also will rest *s*,
     112: 8 His heart is *s*, he will have no fear;
Pr   14:26 fears the LORD has a *s* fortress,
Heb   6:19 an anchor for the soul, firm and *s*.
2Pe   3:17 and fall from your *s* position.

SECURITY (SECURE)

Job 31:24 or said to pure gold, 'You are my *s*,'

SEED (SEEDS SEEDTIME)

Ge   1:11 on the land that bear fruit with *s*
Isa 55:10 so that it yields *s* for the sower
Mt   13: 3 "A farmer went out to sow his *s*.
     13:31 of heaven is like a mustard *s*,
     17:20 have faith as small as a mustard *s*,
Lk   8:11 of the parable: The *s* is the word
1Co   3: 6 I planted the *s*, Apollos watered it,
2Co   9:10 he who supplies *s* to the sower
Gal   3:29 then you are Abraham's *s*,
1Pe   1:23 not of perishable *s*,
1Jn   3: 9 because God's *s* remains in him;

SEEDS (SEED)

Jn   12:24 But if it dies, it produces many *s*.
Gal   3:16 Scripture does not say "and to *s*,"

SEEDTIME* (SEED)

Ge   8:22 *s* and harvest,

SEEK (SEEKING SEEKS SELF-SEEKING SOUGHT)

Lev 19:18 Do not *s* revenge or bear a grudge
Dt   4:29 if from there you *s* the LORD your
1Ki 22: 5 "First *s* the counsel of the LORD."
1Ch 28: 9 If you *s* him, he will be found
2Ch   7:14 themselves and pray and *s* my face
     15: 2 If you *s* him, he will be found
Ps   34:10 those who *s* the LORD lack no
     105: 3 of those who *s* the LORD rejoice.
     105: 4 *s* his face always.
     119: 2 and *s* him with all their heart.
     119:10 I *s* you with all my heart;
     119:176 *S* your servant,
Pr   8:17 and those who *s* me find me.
     18:15 the ears of the wise *s* it out.
     25:27 is it honorable to *s* one's own honor
     28: 5 those who *s* the LORD understand
Isa 55: 6 *S* the LORD while he may be
     65: 1 found by those who did not *s* me.
Jer 29:13 You will *s* me and find me
Hos 10:12 for it is time to *s* the LORD,
Am   5: 4 "*S* me and live;
Zep   2: 3 *S* the LORD, all you humble
Mt   6:33 But *s* first his kingdom
      7: 7 and it will be given to you; *s*
Lk   12:31 *s* his kingdom, and these things will
     19:10 For the Son of Man came to *s*
Jn   5:30 for I *s* not to please myself
Ro   10:20 found by those who did not *s* me;
1Co   7:27 you married? Do not *s* a divorce.
     10:24 Nobody should *s* his own good,
Heb 11: 6 rewards those who earnestly *s* him.
1Pe   3:11 he must *s* peace and pursue it.

SEEKING (SEEK)

2Ch 30:19 who sets his heart on *s* God—
Pr   20:18 Make plans by *s* advice;
Mal   3: 1 the Lord you are *s* will come
Jn   8:50 I am not *s* glory for myself;
1Co 10:33 For I am not *s* my own good

SEEKS (SEEK)

Pr   11:27 He who *s* good finds good will.
Mt   7: 8 he who *s* finds; and to him who
Jn   4:23 the kind of worshipers the Father *s*.
Ro   3:11 no one who *s* God.

SEER

1Sa   9: 9 of today used to be called a *s*.)

SELF-CONTROL* (CONTROL)

Pr   25:28 is a man who lacks *s*.
Ac   24:25 *s* and the judgment to come,
1Co   7: 5 you because of your lack of *s*.
Gal   5:23 faithfulness, gentleness and *s*.
2Ti   3: 3 slanderous, without *s*, brutal,
2Pe   1: 6 and to knowledge, *s*; and to *s*,

SELF-CONTROLLED* (CONTROL)

1Th   5: 6 are asleep, but let us be alert and *s*.
      5: 8 let us be *s*, putting on faith and love
1Ti   3: 2 *s*, respectable, hospitable,
Tit   1: 8 who is *s*, upright, holy
      2: 2 worthy of respect, *s*, and sound
      2: 5 to be *s* and pure, to be busy at home
      2: 6 encourage the young men to be *s*.
      2:12 to live *s*, upright and godly lives
1Pe   1:13 prepare your minds for action; be *s;*
      4: 7 and *s* so that you can pray.
      5: 8 Be *s* and alert.

SELF-DISCIPLINE* (DISCIPLINE)

2Ti   1: 7 a spirit of power, of love and of *s*.

SELF-INDULGENCE*

Mt   23:25 inside they are full of greed and *s*.
Jas   5: 5 lived on earth in luxury and *s*.

SELF-SEEKING* (SEEK)

Ro   2: 8 But for those who are *s*

SELFISH*

Ps 119:36 and not toward *s* gain.
Pr   18: 1 An unfriendly man pursues *s* ends;
Gal   5:20 fits of rage, *s* ambition, dissensions,
Php   1:17 preach Christ out of *s* ambition,
      2: 3 Do nothing out of *s* ambition
Jas   3:14 and *s* ambition in your hearts,
      3:16 you have envy and *s* ambition,

SELL (SELLING SELLS SOLD)

Ge   25:31 "First *s* me your birthright."
Mk   10:21 everything you have
Rev 13:17 or *s* unless he had the mark,

SELLING (SELL)

Lk   17:28 buying and *s*, planting and building

SELLS (SELL)

Pr   31:24 makes linen garments and *s* them,

SEND (SENDING SENDS SENT)

Ps   43: 3 *S* forth your light and your truth,
Isa   6: 8 He said, "Go and tell this
Mal   3: 1 "See, I will *s* my messenger,
Mt   9:38 to *s* out workers into his harvest
     24:31 And he will *s* his angels
Mk   1: 2 I will *s* my messenger ahead of you,
Lk   20:13 I will *s* my son, whom I love;
Jn   3:17 For God did not *s* his Son
      3:17 but if I go, I will *s* him to you.
1Co   1:17 For Christ did not *s* me to baptize;

SENDING (SEND)

Mt   10:16 I am *s* you out like sheep
Jn   20:21 Father has sent me, I am *s* you."
Ro   8: 3 God did by *s* his own Son

SENDS (SEND)

Ps   57: 3 God *s* his love and his faithfulness.

SENNACHERIB

Assyrian king whose siege of Jerusalem was
overthrown by the LORD following prayer of
Hezekiah and Isaiah (2Ki 18:13-19:37; 2Ch 32:
1-21; Isa 36-37).

SENSES*

Lk   15:17 "When he came to his *s*, he said,
1Co 15:34 Come back to your *s* as you ought,
2Ti   2:26 and that they will come to their *s*

SENSITIVITY*

Eph   4:19 Having lost all *s*, they have given

SENSUAL* (SENSUALITY)

Col   2:23 value in restraining *s* indulgence.
1Ti   5:11 For when their .. desires overcome

SENSUALITY* (SENSUAL)

Eph   4:19 have given themselves over to *s*

SENT (SEND)

Ex   3:14 to the Israelites: 'I AM has *s* me
Isa 55:11 achieve the purpose for which I *s* it.
     61: 1 He has *s* me to bind up
Jer 28: 9 as one truly *s* by the LORD only
Mt   10:40 me receives the one who *s* me.
Mk   6: 7 he *s* them out two by two
Lk   4:18 He has *s* me to proclaim freedom
      9: 2 and he *s* them out to preach
     10:16 rejects me rejects him who *s* me."
Jn   1: 6 There came a man who was *s*
      4:34 "is to do the will of him who *s* me
      5:24 believes him who *s* me has eternal
      8:16 I stand with the Father, who *s* me.
      9: 4 must do the work of him who *s* me.
     16: 5 "Now I am going to him who *s* me,
     17: 3 and Jesus Christ, whom you have *s*.
     17:18 As you *s* me into the world,
     20:21 As the Father has *s* me, I am
Ro   10:15 they preach unless they are *s*?
Gal   4: 4 God *s* his Son, born of a woman,
1Jn   4:10 but that he loved us and *s* his Son

SENTENCE

2Co   1: 9 in our hearts we felt the *s* of death.

SEPARATE (SEPARATED SEPARATES SEPARATION)

Mt 19: 6 has joined together, let man not s.''
Ro   8: 35 Who shall s us from the love
1Co 7: 10 wife must not s from her husband.
2Co 6: 17 and be s, says the Lord.
Eph 2: 12 at that time you were s from Christ,

SEPARATED (SEPARATE)

Isa 59: 2 But your iniquities have s
Eph 4: 18 in their understanding and s

SEPARATES (SEPARATE)

Pr 16: 28 and a gossip s close friends.
    17: 9 repeats the matter s close friends.
Mt 25: 32 as a shepherd s the sheep

SEPARATION (SEPARATE)

Nu   6: 2 a vow of s to the LORD

SERAPHS*

Isa 6: 2 Above him were s, each
     6: 6 Then one of the s flew to me

SERIOUSNESS*

Tit 2: 7 s and soundness of speech that

SERPENT (SERPENT'S)

Ge   3: 1 the s was more crafty than any
Isa 27: 1 Leviathan the coiling s;
Rev 12: 9 that ancient s called the devil
    20: 2 that ancient s, who is the devil,

SERPENT'S (SERPENT)

2Co 11: 3 Eve was deceived by the s cunning,

SERVANT (SERVANTS)

Ex 14: 31 trust in him and in Moses his s.
    21: 2 ''If you buy a Hebrew s, he is
1Sa 3: 10 ''Speak, for your s is listening.''
2Sa 7: 19 the future of the house of your s.
1Ki 20: 40 While your s was busy here
Job 1: 8 ''Have you considered my s Job?
Ps 19: 11 By them is your s warned;
    19: 13 Keep your s also from willful sins;
    31: 16 Let your face shine on your s;
    89: 3 I have sworn to David my s,
Pr 14: 35 A king delights in a wise s,
    17: 2 wise s will rule over a disgraceful
    22: 7 and the borrower is s to the lender.
    31: 15 and portions for her s girls.
Isa 41: 8 ''But you, O Israel, my s,
    49: 3 He said to me, ''You are my s,
    53: 11 my righteous s will justify
Zec 3: 8 going to bring my s, the Branch.
Mal 1: 6 his father, and a s his master.
Mt   8: 13 his s was healed at that very hour.
    20: 26 great among you must be your s,
    24: 45 Who then is the faithful and wise s,
    25: 21 'Well done, good and faithful s!'
Lk   1: 38 I am the Lord's s,'' Mary answered.
    16: 13 ''No s can serve two masters.
Jn 15: 15 and where I am, my s also will be.
Ro   1: 1 a s of Christ Jesus, called
    13: 4 For he is God's s to do you good.
Php 2: 7 taking the very nature of a s,
Col 1: 23 of which I, Paul, have become a s.
2Ti 2: 24 And the Lord's s must not quarrel;

SERVANTS (SERVANT)

Lev 25: 55 for the Israelites belong to me as s.
2Ki 17: 13 to you through my s the prophets.''
Ezr 5: 11 ''We are the s of the God of heaven
Ps 34: 22 The LORD redeems his s;
   103: 21 you his s who do his will.
   104: 4 flames of fire his s.
Isa 44: 26 who carries out the words of his s
    65: 8 so will I do in behalf of my s;
    65: 13 my s will drink,
Lk 17: 10 should say, 'We are unworthy s;
Jn 15: 15 longer call you s, because a servant
Ro 13: 6 for the authorities are God's s,
1Co 3: 5 And what is Paul? Only s,
Heb 1: 7 his s flames of fire.''

SERVE (SERVED SERVES SERVICE SERVING)

Dt 10: 12 to s the LORD your God
    11: 13 and to s him with all your heart
    13: 4 s him and hold fast to him.
    28: 47 you did not s the LORD your
Jos 22: 5 and to s him with all your heart
    24: 15 this day whom you will s,
    24: 18 We too will s the LORD,
1Sa 7: 3 to the LORD and s him only,
    12: 20 but s the LORD with all your heart
    12: 24 s him faithfully with all your heart;
2Ch 19: 9 ''You must s faithfully
Job 36: 11 If they obey and s him,
Ps   2: 11 S the LORD with fear
Da   3: 17 The God we s is able to save us
Mt   4: 10 Lord your God, and s him only.' ''
     6: 24 ''No one can s two masters.
    20: 28 but to s, and to give his life
Ro 12: 7 If it is serving, let him s;
Gal 5: 13 rather, s one another in love.
Eph 6: 7 S wholeheartedly,
1Ti 6: 2 they are to s them even better,
Heb 9: 14 so that we may s the living God!
1Pe 4: 10 gift he has received to s others,
     5: 2 greedy for money, but eager to s;
Rev 5: 10 kingdom and priests to s our God,

SERVED (SERVE)

Mt 20: 28 Son of Man did not come to be s,
Jn 12: 2 Martha, while Lazarus was
Ac 17: 25 And he is not s by human hands,
Ro   1: 25 and s created things rather
1Ti 3: 13 Those who have s well gain

SERVES (SERVE)

Lk 22: 26 one who rules like the one who s.
    22: 27 But I am among you as one who s.
Jn 12: 26 Whoever s me must follow me;
Ro 14: 18 because anyone who s Christ
1Pe 4: 11 If anyone s, he should do it

SERVICE (SERVE)

Lk   9: 62 fit for s in the kingdom
    12: 35 ''Be dressed ready for s
Ro 15: 17 in Christ Jesus in my s to God.
1Co 12: 5 There are different kinds of s,
    16: 15 themselves to the s of the saints.
2Co 9: 12 This s that you perform is not only
Eph 4: 12 God's people for works of s,
Rev 2: 19 and faith, your s and perseverance,

SERVING (SERVE)

Jos 24: 15 if s the LORD seems undesirable
2Ch 12: 8 learn the difference between s me
Ro 12: 7 If it is s, let him serve;
    12: 11 your spiritual fervor, s the Lord.
    16: 18 people are not s our Lord Christ,
Eph 6: 7 as if you were s the Lord, not men,
Col 3: 24 It is the Lord Christ you are s.
2Ti 2: 4 No one s as a soldier gets involved

SETH

Ge   4: 25 birth to a son and named him S,

SETTLE

Mt   5: 25 ''S matters quickly
2Th 3: 12 in the Lord Jesus Christ to s down

SEVEN (SEVENS SEVENTH)

Ge   7: 2 Take with you s of every kind
Jos 6: 4 march around the city s times.
1Ki 19: 18 Yet I reserve s thousand in Israel—
Pr   6: 16 s that are detestable to him:
    24: 16 a righteous man falls s times,
Isa 4: 1 In that day s women
Da   9: 25 comes, there will be s 'sevens,'
Mt 18: 21 Up to s times?'' Jesus answered,
Lk 11: 26 takes s other spirits more wicked
Ro 11: 4 for myself s thousand who have not
Rev 1: 4 To the s churches in the province
     6: 1 opened the first of the s seals.
     8: 2 and to them were given s trumpets.
    10: 4 And when the s thunders spoke,
    15: 7 to the s angels s golden bowls filled

SEVENS* (SEVEN)

Da   9: 24 ''Seventy 's' are decreed

Da   9: 25 will be seven 's,' and sixty-two 's.'
     9: 26 the sixty-two 's,' the Anointed

SEVENTH (SEVEN)

Ge   2: 2 By the s day God had finished
Ex 20: 10 but the s day is a Sabbath
    23: 11 but during the s year let the land lie
    23: 12 but on the s day do not work,
Heb 4: 4 ''And on the s day God rested

SEVERE

2Co 8: 2 Out of the most s trial, their
1Th 1: 6 of the Lord; in spite of s suffering.

SEWED (SEWS)

Ge   3: 7 so they s fig leaves together

SEWS (SEWED)

Mt   9: 16 No one s a patch of unshrunk cloth

SEXUAL (SEXUALLY)

Ex 22: 19 ''Anyone who has s relations
Lev 18: 6 relative to have s relations.
    18: 7 father by having s relations
    18: 20 Do not have s relations with
Mt 15: 19 murder, adultery, s immorality,
Ac 15: 20 by idols, from s immorality,
1Co 5: 1 reported that there is s immorality
     6: 13 body is not meant for s immorality,
     6: 18 Flee from s immorality.
    10: 8 should not commit s immorality,
2Co 12: 21 s sin and debauchery
Gal 5: 19 s immorality, impurity
Eph 5: 3 even a hint of s immorality,
Col 3: 5 s immorality, impurity, lust,
1Th 4: 3 that you should avoid s immorality

SEXUALLY (SEXUAL)

1Co 5: 9 to associate with s immoral people
     6: 9 Neither the s immoral nor idolaters
     6: 18 he who sins s sins against his own
Heb 12: 16 See that no one is s immoral,
    13: 4 the adulterer and all the s immoral.
Rev 21: 8 the murderers, the s immoral,

SHADE

Ps 121: 5 the LORD is your s
Isa 25: 4 and a s from the heat.

SHADOW

Ps 17: 8 hide me in the s of your wings
    23: 4 through the valley of the s of death,
    36: 7 find refuge in the s of your wings.
    91: 1 will rest in the s of the Almighty.
Isa 51: 16 covered you with the s of my hand
Col 2: 17 These are a s of the things that
Heb 8: 5 and s of what is in heaven.
    10: 1 The law is only a s

SHADRACH

Hebrew exiled to Babylon; name changed from Hananiah (Da 1:6-7). Refused defilement by food (Da 1:8-20). Refused to worship idol (Da 3:1-18); saved from furnace (Da 3:19-30).

SHAKE (SHAKEN SHAKING)

Ps 64: 8 all who see them will s their heads
    99: 1 let the earth s.
Hag 2: 6 I will once more s the heavens
Heb 12: 26 ''Once more I will s not only

SHAKEN (SHAKE)

Ps 16: 8 I will not be s.
    30: 6 ''I will never be s.''
    62: 2 he is my fortress, I will never be s.
   112: 6 Surely he will never be s;
Isa 54: 10 Though the mountains be s
Mt 24: 29 and the heavenly bodies will be s.'
Lk   6: 38 s together and running over.
Ac   2: 25 I will not be s.
Heb 12: 27 that what cannot be s may remain.

SHAKING* (SHAKE)

Ps   2: 7 they hurl insults, s their heads;
Mt 27: 39 insults at him, s their heads
Mk 15: 29 s their heads and saying, ''So!

SHALLUM

King of Israel (2Ki 15:10-16).

SHAME (ASHAMED SHAMED SHAMEFUL)

Ps 25: 3 will ever be put to s,
     34: 5 their faces are never covered with s
     69: 6 not be put to s because of me,
Pr 13: 18 discipline comes to poverty and s,
     18: 13 that is his folly and his s.
Jer 8: 9 The wise will be put to s;
      8: 12 No, they have no s at all;
Ro   9: 33 trusts in him will never be put to s.''
     10: 11 trusts in him will never be put to s.''
1Co 1: 27 things of the world to s the wise;
Heb 12: 2 endured the cross, scorning its s.

SHAMED (SHAME)

Jer 10: 14 every goldsmith is s by his idols.
Joel 2: 26 never again will my people be s.

SHAMEFUL (SHAME)

2Co 4: 2 have renounced secret and s ways;
2Pe 2: 2 Many will follow their s ways
Rev 21: 27 nor will anyone who does what is s

SHAMGAR

Judge; killed 600 Philistines (Jdg 3:31).

SHAPE (SHAPES SHAPING)

Job 38: 14 The earth takes s like clay

SHAPES (SHAPE)

Isa 44: 10 Who s a god and casts an idol,

SHAPING (SHAPE)

Jer 18: 4 the pot he was s from the clay was

SHARE (SHARED SHARERS SHARES SHARING)

Ge 21: 10 that slave woman's son will never s
Lev 19: 17 frankly so you will not s in his guilt.
Dt 10: 9 That is why the Levites have no s
1Sa 30: 24 All will s alike.''
Eze 18: 20 The son will not s the guilt
Mt 25: 21 and s your master's happiness!'
Lk   3: 11 ''The man with two tunics should s
Ro   8: 17 if indeed we s in his sufferings
     12: 13 S with God's people who are
2Co 1: 7 as you s in our sufferings,
Gal 4: 30 the slave woman's son will never s
      6: 6 in the word must s all good things
Eph 4: 28 something to s with those in need.
Col 1: 12 you to s in the inheritance
2Th 2: 14 that you might s in the glory
1Ti 5: 22 and do not s in the sins of others.
      6: 18 and to be generous and willing to s.
2Ti 2: 6 the first to receive a s of the crops.
Heb 12: 10 that we may s in his holiness.
     13: 16 to do good and to s with others,
Rev 22: 19 from him his s in the tree of life

SHARED (SHARE)

Ps 41: 9 he who s my bread,
Ac   4: 32 but they s everything they had.
Heb 2: 14 he too s in their humanity so that

SHARERS* (SHARE)

Eph 3: 6 and s together in the promise

SHARES (SHARE)

Pr 22: 9 for he s his food with the poor.
Jn 13: 18 'He who s my bread has lifted up

SHARING (SHARE)

1Co 9: 10 so in the hope of s in the harvest.
2Co 9: 13 for your generosity in s with them
Php 3: 10 the fellowship of s in his sufferings.
Phm : 6 you may be active in s your faith.

SHARON

SS   2: 1 I am a rose of S.

SHARP (SHARPENED SHARPENS SHARPER)

Pr   5: 4 s as a double-edged sword.
Isa 5: 28 Their arrows are s,
Rev 1: 16 came a s double-edged sword.
     19: 15 Out of his mouth comes a s sword

SHARPENED (SHARP)

Eze 21: 9 s and polished—

SHARPENS* (SHARP)

Pr 27: 17 As iron s iron,
     27: 17 so one man s another.

SHARPER* (SHARP)

Heb 4: 12 S than any double-edged sword.

SHATTER (SHATTERED SHATTERS)

Jer 51: 20 with you I s nations,

SHATTERED (SHATTER)

1Sa 2: 10 who oppose the LORD will be s.
Job 16: 12 All was well with me, but he s me;
     17: 11 days have passed, my plans are s,
Ecc 12: 6 before the pitcher is s at the spring,

SHATTERS (SHATTER)

Ps 46: 9 he breaks the bow and s the spear,

SHAVED

Jdg 16: 17 my head were s, my strength would
1Co 11: 5 it is just as though her head were s.

SHEAF (SHEAVES)

Lev 23: 11 is to wave the s before the LORD

SHEARER* (SHEARERS)

Ac   8: 32 and as a lamb before the s is silent,

SHEARERS (SHEARER)

Isa 53: 7 and as a sheep before her s is silent,

SHEAVES (SHEAF)

Ge 37: 7 while your s gathered around mine
Ps 126: 6 carrying s with him.

SHEBA

1. Benjamite who rebelled against David (2Sa 20).
2. See QUEEN.

SHECHEM

1. Raped Jacob's daughter Dinah; killed by Simeon and Levi (Ge 34).
2. City where Joshua renewed the covenant (Jos 24).

SHED (SHEDDING SHEDS)

Ge   9: 6 by man shall his blood be s;
Pr   6: 17 hands that s innocent blood,
Ro   3: 15 ''Their feet are swift to s blood;
Col 1: 20 through his blood, s on the cross.

SHEDDING (SHED)

Heb 9: 22 without the s of blood there is no

SHEDS (SHED)

Ge   9: 6 ''Whoever s the blood of man,

SHEEP (SHEEP'S SHEEPSKINS)

Nu 27: 17 LORD's people will not be like s
Dt 17: 1 a s that has any defect or flaw in it,
1Sa 15: 14 ''What then is this bleating of s
Ps 44: 22 we are considered as s
     78: 52 led them like s through the desert.
    100: 3 we are his people, the s
    119:176 I have strayed like a lost s.
SS   4: 2 teeth are like a flock of s just shorn,
Isa 53: 6 We all, like s, have gone astray,
     53: 7 as a s before her shearers is silent,
Jer 50: 6 ''My people have been lost s;
Eze 34: 11 I myself will search for my s
Zec 13: 7 and the s will be scattered,
Mt   9: 36 helpless, like s without a shepherd.
     10: 6 lost sheep to go
     12: 11 ''If any of you has a s and it falls
     18: 13 he is happier about that one s
     25: 32 as a shepherd separates the s
Jn 10: 1 man who does not enter the s pen
     10: 3 He calls his own s by name
     10: 7 the truth. I am the gate for the s.
     10: 15 and I lay down my life for the s.
     10: 27 My s listen to my voice; I know
     21: 17 Jesus said, ''Feed my s.
1Pe 2: 25 For you were like s going astray,

SHEEP'S* (SHEEP)

Mt   7: 15 They come to you in s clothing,

SHEEPSKINS* (SHEEP)

Heb 11: 37 They went about in s and goatskins

SHEKEL

Ex 30: 13 This half s is an offering

SHELTER

Ps 27: 5 me in the s of his tabernacle
     31: 20 In the s of your presence you hide
     55: 8 I would hurry to my place of s,
     61: 4 take refuge in the s of your wings,
     91: 1 in the s of the Most High
Ecc 7: 12 Wisdom is a s
Isa 4: 6 It will be a s and shade
     25: 4 a s from the storm
     32: 2 Each man will be like a s
     58: 7 the poor wanderer with s—

SHEM

Son of Noah (Ge 5:32; 6:10). Blessed (Ge 9: 26). Descendants (Ge 10:21-31; 11:10-32).

SHEPHERD (SHEPHERDS)

Ge 48: 15 the God who has been my s
     49: 24 because of the S, the Rock of Israel
Nu 27: 17 will not be like sheep without a s.''
2Sa 7: 7 commanded to s my people Israel,
1Ki 22: 17 on the hills like sheep without a s,
Ps 23: 1 LORD is my s, I shall not be in want.
     28: 9 be their s and carry them forever.
     80: 1 Hear us, O S of Israel,
Isa 40: 11 He tends his flock like a s:
Jer 31: 10 will watch over his flock like a s.'
Eze 34: 5 scattered because there was no s,
     34: 12 As a s looks after his scattered
Zec 11: 9 and said, ''I will not be your s.
     11: 17 ''Woe to the worthless s,
     13: 7 ''Strike the s,
Mt   2: 6 who will be the s of my people
      9: 36 and helpless, like sheep without a s.
     26: 31 '' 'I will strike the s,
Jn 10: 11 The good s lays down his life
     10: 14 ''I am the good s; I know my sheep
     10: 16 there shall be one flock and one s.
Heb 13: 20 that great S of the sheep, equip you
1Pe 5: 4 And when the Chief S appears,
Rev 7: 17 of the throne will be their s;

SHEPHERDS (SHEPHERD)

Jer 23: 1 ''Woe to the s who are destroying
     50: 6 their s have led them astray
Eze 34: 2 prophesy against the s of Israel;
Lk   2: 8 there were s living out in the fields
Ac 20: 28 Be s of the church of God,
1Pe 5: 2 of God's flock that is
Jude : 12 s who feed only themselves.

SHIBBOLETH*

Jdg 12: 6 No,'' they said, ''All right, say 'S.' ''

SHIELD (SHIELDED SHIELDS)

Ge 15: 1 I am your s,
2Sa 22: 3 my s and the horn of my salvation.
     22: 36 You give me your s of victory;
Ps   3: 3 But you are a s around me,
      5: 12 with your favor as with a s.
      7: 10 My s is God Most High,
     18: 2 He is my s and the horn
     28: 7 LORD is my strength and my s;
     33: 20 he is our help and our s.
     84: 11 For the LORD God is a sun and s;
     91: 4 his faithfulness will be your s
    115: 9 he is their help and s.
    119:114 You are my refuge and my s;
    144: 2 my s, in whom I take refuge.
Pr   2: 7 he is a s to those whose walk is
     30: 5 he is a s to those who take refuge
Eph 6: 16 to all this, take up the s of faith.

SHIELDED (SHIELD)

1Pe 1: 5 through faith are s by God's power

SHIELDS (SHIELD)

Dt 33: 12 for he s him all day long.

SHIFTLESS*

Pr 19: 15 and the *s* man goes hungry.

SHIMEI

Cursed David (2Sa 16:5-14); spared (2Sa 19: 16-23). Killed by Solomon (1Ki 2:8-9, 36-46).

SHINE (SHINES SHINING SHONE)

Nu 6: 25 the LORD make his face *s*
Job 33: 30 that the light of life may *s* on him.
Ps 4: 6 Let the light of your face *s* upon us,
37: 6 make your righteousness *s* like
67: 1 and make his face *s* upon us; *Selah*
80: 1 between the cherubim, *s* forth
118: 27 he has made his light *s* upon us.
Isa 60: 1 ''Arise, *s*, for your light has come,
Da 12: 3 are wise will *s* like the brightness
Mt 5: 16 let your light *s* before men,
13: 43 the righteous will *s* like the sun
2Co 4: 6 made his light *s* in our hearts
Eph 5: 14 and Christ will *s* on you.''
Php 2: 15 in which you *s* like stars

SHINES (SHINE)

Ps 50: 2 God *s* forth.
Pr 13: 9 The light of the righteous *s* brightly
Jn 1: 5 The light *s* in the darkness,

SHINING (SHINE)

Pr 4: 18 *s* ever brighter till the full light
2Pe 1: 19 as to a light *s* in a dark place,
Rev 1: 16 His face was like the sun *s*

SHIPS

Pr 31: 14 She is like the merchant *s*,

SHIPWRECKED*

2Co 11: 25 I was stoned, three times I was *s*,
1Ti 1: 19 and so have *s* their faith.

SHISHAK

1Ki 14: 25 *S* king of Egypt attacked Jerusalem
2Ch 12: 2 *S* king of Egypt attacked Jerusalem

SHOCKING*

Jer 5: 30 ''A horrible and *s* thing

SHONE (SHINE)

Mt 17: 2 His face *s* like the sun,
Lk 2: 9 glory of the Lord *s* around them,
Rev 21: 11 It *s* with the glory of God,

SHOOT

Isa 53: 2 up before him like a tender *s*,
Ro 11: 17 and you, though a wild olive *s*,

SHORE

Lk 5: 3 asked him to put out a little from *s*.

SHORT (SHORTENED)

Nu 11: 23 ''Is the LORD's arm too *s*?
Isa 50: 2 Was my arm too *s* to ransom you?
59: 1 of the LORD is not too *s* to save,
Mt 24: 22 If those days had not been cut *s*,
Ro 3: 23 and fall *s* of the glory of God,
1Co 7: 29 brothers, is that the time is *s*.
Heb 4: 1 of you be found to have fallen *s* of it
Rev 20: 3 he must be set free for a *s* time.

SHORTENED (SHORT)

Mt 24: 22 of the elect those days will be *s*.

SHOULDER (SHOULDERS)

Zep 3: 9 and serve him *s* to *s*.

SHOULDERS (SHOULDER)

Dt 33: 12 LORD loves rests between his *s*.''
Isa 9: 6 and the government will be on his *s*
Lk 15: 5 he joyfully puts it on his *s*

SHOUT (SHOUTED)

Ps 47: 1 *s* to God with cries of joy.
66: 1 *S* with joy to God, all the earth!
95: 1 let us *s* aloud to the Rock
98: 4 *S* for joy to the LORD, all the earth
100: 1 *S* for joy to the LORD, all the earth
Isa 12: 6 *S* aloud and sing for joy, people
26: 19 wake up and *s* for joy.

Isa 35: 6 the mute tongue *s* for joy.
40: 9 lift up your voice with a *s*,
42: 2 He will not *s* or cry out,
44: 23 *s* aloud, O earth beneath.
54: 1 burst into song, *s* for joy,
Zec 9: 9 *S*, Daughter of Jerusalem!

SHOUTED (SHOUT)

Job 38: 7 and all the angels *s* for joy?

SHOW (SHOWED)

Ex 18: 20 and *s* them the way to live
33: 18 Moses said, ''Now *s* me your glory
2Sa 22: 26 the faithful you *s* yourself faithful,
1Ki 2: 2 ''So be strong, *s* yourself a man,
Ps 17: 7 *S* the wonder of your great love,
25: 4 *S* me your ways, O LORD,
39: 4 ''*S* me, O LORD, my life's end
85: 7 *S* us your unfailing love, O LORD,
143: 8 *S* me the way I should go,
Pr 23: 4 have the wisdom to *s* restraint.
SS 2: 14 *s* me your face,
Isa 5: 16 the holy God will *s* himself holy
30: 18 he rises to *s* you compassion.
Eze 28: 25 I will *s* myself holy among them
Joel 2: 30 I will *s* wonders in the heavens
Zec 7: 9 *s* mercy and compassion
Ac 2: 19 I will *s* wonders in the heaven
10: 34 it is that God does not *s* favoritism
1Co 12: 31 now I will *s* you the most excellent
Eph 2: 7 ages he might *s* the incomparable
Tit 2: 7 In your teaching *s* integrity,
Jas 2: 18 I will *s* you my faith by what I do.
Jude : 23 to others *s* mercy, mixed with fear

SHOWED (SHOW)

1Ki 3: 3 Solomon *s* his love for the LORD
Lk 24: 40 he *s* them his hands and feet.
1Jn 4: 9 This is how God *s* his love

SHOWERS

Eze 34: 26 in season; there will be *s* of blessing
Hos 10: 12 and *s* righteousness on you.

SHREWD

2Sa 22: 27 to the crooked you show yourself *s*.
Mt 10: 16 Therefore be as *s* as snakes and

SHRINK (SHRINKS)

Heb 10: 39 But we are not of those who *s* back

SHRINKS* (SHRINK)

Heb 10: 38 And if he *s* back,

SHRIVEL

Isa 64: 6 we all *s* up like a leaf,

SHUDDER

Eze 32: 10 and their kings will *s* with horror

SHUHITE

Job 2: 11 Bildad the *S* and Zophar

SHUN* (SHUNS)

Job 28: 28 and to *s* evil is understanding.' ''
Pr 3: 7 fear the LORD and *s* evil.

SHUNS (SHUN)

Job 1: 8 a man who fears God and *s* evil.''
Pr 14: 16 man fears the LORD and *s* evil,

SHUT

Ge 7: 16 Then the LORD *s* him in.
Isa 22: 22 what he opens no one can *s*,
60: 11 they will never be *s*, day or night,
Da 6: 22 and he *s* the mouths of the lions.
Heb 11: 33 who *s* the mouths of lions,
Rev 3: 7 what he *s* no one can open,
21: 25 On no day will its gates ever be *s*,

SICK (SICKNESS)

Pr 13: 12 Hope deferred makes the heart *s*,
Eze 34: 4 or healed the *s* or bound up
Mt 9: 12 who need a doctor, but the *s*.
10: 8 Heal the *s*, raise the dead, cleanse
25: 36 I was *s* and you looked after me,
1Co 11: 30 many among you are weak and *s*,
Jas 5: 14 of you *s*? He should call the elders

SICKBED* (BED)

Ps 41: 3 LORD will sustain him on his *s*

SICKLE

Joel 3: 13 Swing the *s*,
Rev 14: 14 gold on his head and a sharp *s*

SICKNESS (SICK)

Mt 4: 23 and healing every disease and *s*

SIDE (SIDES)

Ps 91: 7 A thousand may fall at your *s*,
124: 1 If the LORD had not been on our *s*
Jn 18: 37 Everyone on the *s* of truth listens
20: 20 he showed them his hands and *s*.
2Ti 4: 17 But the Lord stood at my *s*
Heb 10: 33 at other times you stood *s* by *s*

SIDES (SIDE)

Nu 33: 55 in your eyes and thorns in your *s*.

SIFT

Lk 22: 31 Satan has asked to *s* you as wheat.

SIGHING

Isa 35: 10 and sorrow and *s* will flee away.

SIGHT

Ps 51: 4 and done what is evil in your *s*,
90: 4 For a thousand years in your *s*
116: 15 Precious in the *s* of the LORD
Pr 3: 4 in the *s* of God and man.
Mt 11: 5 The blind receive *s*, the lame walk,
Ac 4: 19 right in God's *s* to obey you rather
1Co 3: 19 this world is foolishness in God's *s*.
2Co 5: 7 We live by faith, not by *s*.
1Pe 3: 4 which is of great worth in God's *s*.

SIGN (SIGNS)

Ge 9: 12 ''This is the *s* of the covenant I am
17: 11 and it will be the *s* of the covenant
Isa 7: 14 the Lord himself will give you a *s*:
55: 13 for an everlasting *s*,
Eze 20: 12 I gave them my Sabbaths as a *s*
Mt 12: 38 to see a miraculous *s* from you.''
24: 3 what will be the *s* of your coming
24: 30 ''At that time the *s* of the Son
Lk 2: 12 This will be a *s* to you: You will
11: 29 looks for a miraculous *s*,
Ro 4: 11 he received the *s* of circumcision,
1Co 11: 10 to have a *s* of authority on her head
14: 22 are a *s*, not for believers

SIGNS (SIGN)

Ge 1: 14 let them serve as *s* to mark seasons
Ps 78: 43 day he displayed his miraculous *s*
105: 27 They performed his miraculous *s*
Da 6: 27 he performs *s* and wonders
Mt 24: 24 and perform great *s* and miracles
Mk 16: 17 these *s* will accompany those who
Jn 3: 2 perform the miraculous *s* you are
20: 30 Jesus did many other miraculous *s*
Ac 2: 19 and *s* on the earth below,
1Co 1: 22 Jews demand miraculous *s*
2Co 12: 12 *s*, wonders and miracles—
2Th 2: 9 *s* and wonders, and in every sort

SIHON

Nu 21: 21 to say to *S* king of the Amorites:
Ps 136: 19 *S* king of the Amorites

SILAS*

Prophet (Ac 15:22-32); co-worker with Paul on second missionary journey (Ac 16-18; 2Co 1:19). Co-writer with Paul (1Th 1:1; 2Th 1:1); Peter (1Pe 5:12).

SILENCE (SILENCED SILENT)

1Pe 2: 15 good you should *s* the ignorant talk
Rev 8: 1 there was *s* in heaven

SILENCED (SILENCE)

Ro 3: 19 so that every mouth may be *s*
Tit 1: 11 They must be *s*, because they are

SILENT (SILENCE)

Est 4: 14 For if you remain *s* at this time,
Ps 30: 12 to you and not be *s*.

Ps 32: 3 When I kept s,
39: 2 But when I was s and still,
Pr 17: 28 a fool is thought wise if he keeps s,
Ecc 3: 7 a time to be s and a time to speak,
Isa 53: 7 as a sheep before her shearers is s,
62: 1 For Zion's sake I will not keep s,
Hab 2: 20 let all the earth be s before him.''
Ac 8: 32 and as a lamb before the shearer is s,
1Co 14: 34 women should remain s
1Ti 2: 12 over a man; she must be s.

SILVER

Ps 12: 6 like s refined in a furnace of clay,
66: 10 you refined us like s.
Pr 2: 4 and if you look for it as for s
3: 14 for she is more profitable than s
8: 10 Choose my instruction instead of s,
22: 1 to be esteemed is better than s
25: 4 Remove the dross from the s,
25: 11 is like apples of gold in settings of s.
Isa 48: 10 I have refined you, though not as s;
Eze 22: 18 They are but the dross of s.
Da 2: 32 its chest and arms of s, its belly
Hag 2: 8 'The s is mine and the gold is mine,'
Zec 13: 9 I will refine them like s
Ac 3: 6 Peter said, ''S or gold I do not have,
1Co 3: 12 s, costly stones, wood, hay or straw
1Pe 1: 18 not with perishable things such as s

SILVERSMITH

Ac 19: 24 A s named Demetrius, who made

SIMEON

Son of Jacob by Leah (Ge 29:33; 35:23; 1Ch 2:
1). With Levi killed Shechem for rape of Dinah
(Ge 34:25-29). Held hostage by Joseph in Egypt
(Ge 42:24-43:23). Tribe of blessed (Ge 49:5-7),
numbered (Nu 1:23; 26:14), allotted land (Jos 19:
1-9; Eze 48:24), 12,000 from (Rev 7:7).

SIMON

1. See PETER.
2. Apostle, called the Zealot (Mt 10:4; Mk 3:
18; Lk 6:15; Ac 1:13).
3. Samaritan sorcerer (Ac 8:9-24).

SIMPLE

Ps 19: 7 making wise the s.
119:130 it gives understanding to the s.
Pr 8: 5 You who are s, gain prudence;
14: 15 A s man believes anything,

SIMPLEHEARTED* (HEART)

Ps 116: 6 The Lord protects the s;

SIN (SINFUL SINNED SINNER SINNERS SINNING SINS)

Ge 4: 7 s is crouching at your door;
Ex 32: 32 please forgive their s— but if not,
Nu 5: 7 and must confess the s he has
32: 23 be sure that your s will find you
Dt 24: 16 each is to die for his own s.
1Sa 12: 23 it from me that I should s
15: 23 For rebellion is like the s
1Ki 8: 46 for there is no one who does not s
2Ch 7: 14 and will forgive their s and will heal
Job 1: 22 Job did not s by charging God
Ps 4: 4 In your anger do not s,
17: 3 resolved that my mouth will not s.
32: 2 whose s the Lord does not count
32: 5 Then I acknowledged my s to you
36: 2 too much to detect or hate his s.
38: 18 I am troubled by my s.
39: 1 and keep my tongue from s;
51: 2 and cleanse me from my s.
66: 18 If I had cherished s in my heart,
119: 11 that I might not s against you.
119:133 let no s rule over me.
Pr 5: 22 the cords of his s hold him fast.
10: 19 words are many, s is not absent,
14: 9 Fools mock at making amends for s
16: 6 faithfulness s is atoned for;
17: 19 He who loves a quarrel loves s;
20: 9 I am clean and without s''?
Isa 3: 9 they parade their s like Sodom;
6: 7 is taken away and your s atoned
64: 5 But when we continued to s
Jer 31: 30 everyone will die for his own s;

Eze 3: 18 that wicked man will die for his s,
18: 26 his righteousness and commits s,
33: 8 that wicked man will die for his s,
Am 4: 4 ''Go to Bethel and s;
Mic 6: 7 of my body for the s of my soul?
7: 18 who pardons s and forgives
Zec 3: 4 ''See, I have taken away your s,
Mt 18: 6 little ones who believe in me to s,
Mk 3: 29 he is guilty of an eternal s.''
9: 43 If your hand causes you to s,
Lk 17: 1 people to s are bound to come,
Jn 1: 29 who takes away the s of the world!
8: 7 ''If any one of you is without s,
8: 34 everyone who sins is a slave to s.
8: 46 Can any of you prove me guilty of s
Ro 2: 12 All who s apart from the law will
5: 12 as s entered the world
5: 20 where s increased, grace increased
6: 2 By no means! We died to s;
6: 11 count yourselves dead to s
6: 14 For s shall not be your master,
6: 23 For the wages of s is death,
7: 7 I would not have known what s was
7: 25 sinful nature a slave to the law of s.
14: 23 that does not come from faith is s.
1Co 8: 12 When you s against your brothers
15: 56 The sting of death is s,
2Co 5: 21 God made him who had no s to be s
Gal 6: 1 if someone is caught in a s,
1Ti 5: 20 Those who s are to be rebuked
Heb 4: 15 just as we are—yet was without s.
9: 26 to do away with s by the sacrifice
11: 25 the pleasures of s for a short time.
12: 1 and the s that so easily entangles,
Jas 1: 15 it gives birth to s; and s,
1Pe 2: 22 ''He committed no s,
1Jn 1: 7 his Son, purifies us from all s.
1: 8 If we claim to be without s,
2: 1 But if anybody does s, we have one
3: 4 in fact, s is lawlessness.
3: 5 And in him is no s.
3: 6 No one who continues to s has
3: 9 born of God will continue to s,
5: 16 There is a s that leads to death.
5: 17 All wrongdoing is s, and there is s
5: 18 born of God does not continue to s;

SINAI

Ex 19: 20 descended to the top of Mount S
31: 18 speaking to Moses on Mount S,
Ps 68: 17 from S into his sanctuary.

SINCERE* (SINCERITY)

Da 11: 34 many who are not s will join them.
Ac 2: 46 ate together with glad and s hearts,
Ro 12: 9 Love must be s.
2Co 6: 6 in the Holy Spirit and in s love;
11: 3 somehow be led astray from your s
1Ti 1: 5 a good conscience and a s faith.
3: 8 s, not indulging in much wine,
2Ti 1: 5 have been reminded of your s faith,
Heb 10: 22 near to God with a s heart
Jas 3: 17 and good fruit, impartial and s.
1Pe 1: 22 the truth so that you have s love

SINCERITY* (SINCERE)

1Co 5: 8 bread without yeast, the bread of s
2Co 1: 12 in the holiness and s that are
2: 17 speak before God with s,
8: 8 but I want to test the s of your love
Eph 6: 5 and with s of heart, just
Col 3: 22 but with s of heart and reverence

SINFUL (SIN)

Ps 51: 5 Surely I was s from birth,
51: 5 s from the time my mother
Lk 5: 8 from me, Lord; I am a s man!''
Ro 7: 5 we were controlled by the s nature,
7: 18 lives in me, that is, in my s nature.
7: 25 but in the s nature a slave to the law
8: 3 Son in the likeness of s man
8: 4 not live according to the s nature
8: 7 the s mind is hostile to God.
8: 8 by the s nature cannot please God.
8: 9 are controlled not by the s nature
8: 13 if you live according to the s nature
13: 14 to gratify the desires of the s nature
1Co 5: 5 so that the s nature may be

Gal 5: 13 freedom to indulge the s nature;
5: 16 gratify the desires of the s nature.
5: 19 The acts of the s nature are obvious
5: 24 Jesus have crucified the s nature
6: 8 sows to please his s nature,
Col 2: 11 in the putting off of the s nature,
Heb 3: 12 brothers, that none of you has a s,
1Pe 2: 11 abstain from s desires, which war
1Jn 3: 8 He who does what is s is

SING (SANG SINGER SINGING SINGS SONG SONGS SUNG)

Ex 15: 1 ''I will s to the Lord,
Ps 5: 11 let them ever s for joy.
13: 6 I will s to the Lord,
30: 4 S to the Lord, you saints of his;
33: 1 S joyfully to the Lord, you
47: 6 S praises to God, s praises,
57: 7 I will s and make music.
59: 16 But I will s of your strength,
63: 7 I s in the shadow of your wings.
66: 2 S to the glory of his name;
89: 1 I will s of the Lord's great love
95: 1 Come, let us s for joy to the Lord
96: 1 S to the Lord a new song;
98: 1 S to the Lord a new song,
101: 1 I will s of your love and justice;
108: 1 I will s and make music
137: 3 ''S us one of the songs of Zion!''
147: 1 is to s praises to our God,
149: 1 S to the Lord a new song,
Isa 54: 1 ''S, O barren woman,
1Co 14: 15 also pray with my mind; I will s
Eph 5: 19 S and make music in your heart
Col 3: 16 and as you s psalms, hymns
Jas 5: 13 Is anyone happy? Let him s songs

SINGER* (SING)

2Sa 23: 1 Israel's s of songs:

SINGING (SING)

Ps 63: 5 with s lips my mouth will praise
68: 6 he leads forth the prisoners with s;
98: 5 with the harp and the sound of s,
Isa 35: 10 They will enter Zion with s;
Zep 3: 17 he will rejoice over you with s.''
Ac 16: 25 Silas were praying and s hymns
Rev 5: 13 on the sea, and all that is in them, s:

SINGLE

Ex 23: 29 I will not drive them out in a s year,
Mt 6: 27 you by worrying can add a s hour
Gal 5: 14 law is summed up in a s command:

SINGS (SING)

Eze 33: 32 more than one who s love songs

SINNED (SIN)

Lev 5: 5 confess in what way he has s
1Sa 24: 11 Then Saul said to Samuel, ''I have s
2Sa 12: 13 ''I have s against the Lord.''
24: 10 I have s greatly in what I have done
2Ch 6: 37 'We have s, we have done wrong
Job 1: 5 ''Perhaps my children have s
33: 27 'I s, and perverted what was right,
Ps 51: 4 Against you, you only, have I s
Jer 2: 35 because you say, 'I have not s.'
14: 20 we have indeed s against you.
Da 9: 5 we have s and done wrong.
Mic 7: 9 Because I have s against him,
Mt 27: 4 ''I have s,'' he said,
Lk 15: 18 I have s against heaven
Ro 3: 23 for all have s and fall short
5: 12 all s— for before the law was given,
2Pe 2: 4 did not spare angels when they s,
1Jn 1: 10 claim we have not s, we make him

SINNER (SIN)

Ecc 9: 18 but one s destroys much good.
Lk 15: 7 in heaven over one s who repents
18: 13 'God, have mercy on me, a s.'
1Co 14: 24 convinced by all that he is a s
Jas 5: 20 Whoever turns a s from the error
1Pe 4: 18 become of the ungodly and the s?''

SINNERS (SIN)

Ps 1: 1 or stand in the way of s
37: 38 But all s will be destroyed;

SINNING

Pr 1:10 My son, if *s* entice you,
23:17 Do not let your heart envy *s*,
Mt 9:13 come to call the righteous, but *s*.''
Ro 5: 8 While we were still *s*, Christ died
Gal 2:17 evident that we ourselves are *s*,
1Ti 1:15 came into the world to save *s*—
Heb 7:26 set apart from *s*, exalted

SINNING (SIN)

Ex 20:20 be with you to keep you from *s*.''
1Co 15:34 stop *s*; for there are some who are
Heb 10:26 If we deliberately keep on *s*
1Jn 3: 6 No one who lives in him keeps on *s*
3: 9 go on *s*, because he has been born

SINS (SIN)

Lev 5: 1 '' 'If a person *s* because he does not
16:30 you will be clean from all your *s*.
26:40 '' 'But if they will confess their *s*
Nu 15:30 '' But anyone who *s* defiantly,
1Sa 2:25 If a man *s* against another man,
2Ki 14: 6 each is to die for his own *s*.''
Ezr 9: 6 our *s* are higher than our heads
9:13 less than our *s* have deserved
Ps 19:13 your servant also from willful *s*;
32: 1 whose *s* are covered.
51: 9 Hide your face from my *s*
79: 9 deliver us and atone for our *s*
85: 2 and covered all their *s*.
103: 3 He forgives all my *s*
103:10 does not treat us as our *s* deserve
130: 3 O Lord, kept a record of *s*,
Pr 14:21 He who despises his neighbor *s*,
28:13 who conceals his *s* does not
29:22 one commits many *s*.
Ecc 7:20 who does what is right and never *s*.
Isa 1:18 ''Though your *s* are like scarlet,
38:17 you have put all my *s*
43:25 and remembers your *s* no more.
59: 2 your *s* have hidden his face
64: 6 like the wind our *s* sweep us away.
Jer 31:34 and will remember their *s* no more
La 3:39 complain when punished for his *s*?
Eze 18: 4 soul who *s* is the one who will die.
33:10 Our offenses and *s* weigh us down,
36:33 day I cleanse you from all your *s*,
Hos 14: 1 Your *s* have been your downfall!
Mt 1:21 he will save his people from their *s*
6:15 if you do not forgive men their *s*,
9: 6 authority on earth to forgive *s* . . . . .
18:15 ''If your brother *s* against you,
26:28 for many for the forgiveness of *s*.
Lk 5:24 authority on earth to forgive *s* . . . . .
11: 4 Forgive us our *s*,
17: 3 ''If your brother *s*, rebuke him,
Jn 8:24 you will indeed die in your *s*.''
20:23 If you forgive anyone his *s*,
Ac 2:38 for the forgiveness of your *s*.
3:19 so that your *s* may be wiped out,
10:43 forgiveness *s* through his name.''
22:16 be baptized and wash your *s* away,
26:18 they may receive forgiveness of *s*
Ro 4: 7 whose *s* are covered.
4:25 delivered over to death for our *s*
1Co 15: 3 died for our *s* according
2Co 5:19 not counting men's *s* against them.
Gal 1: 4 himself for our *s* to rescue us
Eph 2: 1 dead in your transgressions and *s*,
Col 2:13 us all our *s*, having canceled
1Ti 5:22 and do not share in the *s* of others.
Heb 1: 3 he had provided purification for *s*,
2:17 atonement for the *s* of the people.
7:27 He sacrificed for their *s* once for all
8:12 and will remember their *s* no more
9:28 to take away the *s* of many people;
10: 4 of bulls and goats to take away *s*
10:12 for all time one sacrifice for *s*,
10:26 of the truth, no sacrifice for *s* is left,
Jas 4:17 ought to do and doesn't do it, *s*.
5:16 Therefore confess your *s*
5:20 and cover over a multitude of *s*.
1Pe 2:24 He himself bore our *s* in his body
3:18 For Christ died for *s* once for all,
4: 8 love covers over a multitude of *s*.
1Jn 1: 9 If we confess our *s*, he is faithful
2: 2 He is the atoning sacrifice for our *s*,
3: 5 so that he might take away our *s*.
4:10 as an atoning sacrifice for our *s*.

Rev 1: 5 has freed us from our *s* by his blood

SISERA

Jdg 4: 2 The commander of his army was *S*,
5:26 She struck *S*, she crushed his head,

SISTER (SISTERS)

Lev 18: 9 have sexual relations with your *s*,
Mk 3:35 does God's will is my brother and *s*

SISTERS (SISTER)

Mt 19:29 or brothers or *s* or father or mother
1Ti 5: 2 as *s*, with absolute purity.

SIT (SAT SITS SITTING)

Dt 6: 7 them when you *s* at home
1Ki 8:25 fail to have a man to *s* before me
Ps 1: 1 or *s* in the seat of mockers.
26: 5 and refuse to *s* with the wicked.
80: 1 you who *s* enthroned
110: 1 ''*S* at my right hand
139: 2 You know when I *s* and when I rise
SS 2: 3 I delight to *s* in his shade,
Isa 16: 5 in faithfulness a man will *s* on it—
Mic 4: 4 Every man will *s* under his own
Mt 20:23 to *s* at my right or left is not for me
22:44 ''*S* at my right hand
Lk 22:30 in my kingdom and *s* on thrones,
Heb 1:13 ''*S* at my right hand
Rev 3:21 right to *s* with me on my throne,

SITS (SIT)

Ps 99: 1 *s* enthroned between the cherubim,
Isa 40:22 He *s* enthroned above the circle
Mt 19:28 of Man *s* on his glorious throne,
Rev 4: 9 thanks to him who *s* on the throne

SITTING (SIT)

Est 2:19 Mordecai was *s* at the king's gate.
Mt 26:64 the Son of Man *s* at the right hand
Rev 4: 2 in heaven with someone *s* on it.

SITUATION (SITUATIONS)

1Co 7:24 remain in the *s* God called him
Php 4:12 of being content in any and every *s*,

SITUATIONS* (SITUATION)

2Ti 4: 5 head in all *s*, endure hardship,

SKIES (SKY)

Ps 19: 1 the *s* proclaim the work
71:19 Your righteousness reaches to the *s*
108: 4 your faithfulness reaches to the *s*.

SKILL (SKILLED SKILLFUL)

Ps 137: 5 may my right hand forget its *s*.
Ecc 10:10 but *s* will bring success.

SKILLED (SKILL)

Pr 22:29 Do you see a man *s* in his work?

SKILLFUL (SKILL)

Ps 45: 1 my tongue is the pen of a *s* writer.
78:72 with *s* hands he led them.

SKIN (SKINS)

Job 19:20 with only the *s* of my teeth.
19:26 And after my *s* has been destroyed,
Jer 13:23 Can the Ethiopian change his *s*

SKINS (SKIN)

Ex 25: 5 ram *s* dyed red and hides
Lk 5:37 the new wine will burst the *s*,

SKULL

Mt 27:33 (which means The Place of the *S*).

SKY (SKIES)

Ge 1: 8 God called the expanse ''*s*.''
Pr 30:19 the way of an eagle in the *s*,
Isa 34: 4 and the *s* rolled up like a scroll;
Jer 33:22 stars of the *s* and as measureless
Mt 24:29 the stars will fall from the *s*,
24:30 coming on the clouds of the *s*,
Rev 20:11 Earth and *s* fled from his presence,

SLACK*

Pr 18: 9 One who is *s* in his work

SLAIN (SLAY)

1Sa 18: 7 ''Saul has *s* his thousands,
Eze 37: 9 into these *s*, that they may live.' ''
Rev 5: 6 as if it had been *s*, standing
5:12 ''Worthy is the Lamb, who was *s*,
6: 9 the souls of those who had been *s*

SLANDER (SLANDERED SLANDERER SLANDERERS SLANDEROUS)

Lev 19:16 '' 'Do not go about spreading *s*
Ps 15: 3 and has no *s* on his tongue,
Pr 10:18 and whoever spreads *s* is a fool.
2Co 12:20 outbursts of anger, factions, *s*,
Eph 4:31 rage and anger, brawling and *s*,
1Ti 5:14 the enemy no opportunity for *s*.
Tit 3: 2 to *s* no one, to be peaceable
1Pe 3:16 in Christ may be ashamed of their *s*
2Pe 2:10 afraid to *s* celestial beings;

SLANDERED (SLANDER)

1Co 4:13 when we are *s*, we answer kindly.

SLANDERER (SLANDER)

1Co 5:11 an idolater or a *s*, a drunkard

SLANDERERS (SLANDER)

Ro 1:30 They are gossips, *s*, God-haters,
1Co 6:10 nor the greedy nor drunkards nor *s*
Tit 2: 3 not to be *s* or addicted

SLANDEROUS (SLANDER)

2Ti 3: 3 unforgiving, *s*, without self-control
2Pe 2:11 do not bring *s* accusations

SLAUGHTER (SLAUGHTERED)

Isa 53: 7 he was led like a lamb to the *s*,
Jer 11:19 been like a gentle lamb led to the *s*;
Ac 8:32 ''He was led like a sheep to the *s*,

SLAUGHTERED (SLAUGHTER)

Ps 44:22 we are considered as sheep to be *s*.
Ro 8:36 we are considered as sheep to be *s*

SLAVE (ENSLAVED SLAVERY SLAVES)

Ge 21:10 ''Get rid of that *s* woman
Mt 20:27 wants to be first must be your *s*—
Jn 8:34 everyone who sins is a *s* to sin.
Ro 7:14 I am unspiritual, sold as a *s* to sin.
1Co 7:21 Were you a *s* when you were called
12:13 whether Jews or Greeks, *s* or free
Gal 3:28 nor free, male nor female,
4: 7 So you are no longer a *s*, but a son;
4:30 Get rid of the *s* woman and her son
Col 3:11 barbarian, Scythian, *s* or free,
1Ti 1:10 for *s* traders and liars and perjurers
Phm : 16 no longer as a *s*, but better than a *s*,
2Pe 2:19 a man is a *s* to whatever has

SLAVERY (SLAVE)

Ex 2:23 The Israelites groaned in their *s*
Ro 6:19 parts of your body in *s* to impurity
Gal 4: 3 under the basic principles
1Ti 6: 1 of *s* should consider their masters

SLAVES (SLAVE)

Ps 123: 2 As the eyes of *s* look to the hand
Ecc 10: 7 I have seen *s* on horseback,
Ro 6: 6 that we should no longer be *s* to sin
6:16 you are *s* to sin, which leads
6:22 and have become *s* to God,
Gal 2: 4 in Christ Jesus and to make us *s*.
4: 8 you were *s* to those who
Eph 6: 5 *S*, obey your earthly masters
Col 3:22 *S*, obey your earthly masters
4: 1 provide your *s* with what is right
Tit 2: 9 Teach *s* to be subject

SLAY (SLAIN)

Job 13:15 Though he *s* me, yet will I hope

SLEEP (ASLEEP SLEEPER SLEEPING SLEEPS)

Ge 2:21 the man to fall into a deep *s*;
15:12 Abram fell into a deep *s*,
28:11 it under his head and lay down to *s*.
Ps 4: 8 I will lie down and *s* in peace,
121: 4 will neither slumber nor *s*.
127: 2 for he grants *s* to those he loves.

Pr   6: 9 When will you get up from your *s?*
Ecc 5: 12 The *s* of a laborer is sweet,
1Co 15: 51 We will not all *s,* but we will all be
1Th 5: 7 For those who *s,* at night,

SLEEPER (SLEEP)

Eph 5: 14 "Wake up, O *s,*

SLEEPING (SLEEP)

Mk 13: 36 suddenly, do not find you *s.*

SLEEPLESS*

2Co 6: 5 in hard work, *s* nights and hunger;

SLEEPS (SLEEP)

Pr 10: 5 he who *s* during harvest is

SLIMY

Ps 40: 2 He lifted me out of the *s* pit,

SLING

1Sa 17: 50 over the Philistine with a *s*

SLIP (SLIPPING)

Dt   4: 9 let them *s* from your heart as long
Ps 121: 3 He will not let your foot *s*—

SLIPPING (SLIP)

Ps 66: 9 and kept our feet from *s.*

SLOW

Ex 34: 6 and gracious God, *s* to anger,
Jas 1: 19 *s* to speak and *s* to become angry,
2Pe 3: 9 The Lord is not *s* in keeping his

SLUGGARD

Pr   6: 6 Go to the ant, you *s;*
     13: 4 The *s* craves and gets nothing,
     20: 4 A *s* does not plow in season;
     26: 15 The *s* buries his hand in the dish;

SLUMBER

Ps 121: 3 he who watches over you will not *s;*
Pr   6: 10 A little sleep, a little *s,*
Ro 13: 11 for you to wake up from your *s,*

SLUR

Ps 15: 3 and casts no *s* on his fellow man,

SMELL

Ecc 10: 1 As dead flies give perfume a bad *s,*
2Co 2: 16 To the one we are the *s* of death;

SMITTEN

Isa 53: 4 *s* by him, and afflicted.

SMOKE

Ex 19: 18 Mount Sinai was covered with *s,*
Ps 104: 32 touches the mountains, and they *s.*
Isa   6: 4 and the temple was filled with *s.*
Joel 2: 30 blood and fire and billows of *s.*
Ac   2: 19 blood and fire and billows of *s.*
Rev 15: 8 filled with *s* from the glory

SMYRNA

Rev   2: 8 the angel of the church in *S* write:

SNAKE (SNAKES)

Nu 21: 8 "Make a *s* and put it up on a pole;
Pr 23: 32 In the end it bites like a *s*
Jn   3: 14 Moses lifted up the *s* in the desert,

SNAKES (SNAKE)

Mt 10: 16 as shrewd as *s* and as innocent
Mk 16: 18 they will pick up *s* with their hands;

SNARE (ENSNARE ENSNARED SNARED)

Dt   7: 16 for that will be a *s* to you.
Ps 69: 22 before them become a *s;*
     91: 3 from the fowler's *s.*
Pr 29: 25 Fear of man will prove to be a *s,*
Ro 11: 9 "May their table become a *s*

SNARED (SNARE)

Pr   3: 26 will keep your foot from being *s.*

SNATCH

Jn 10: 28 no one can *s* them out of my hand.

Jude   : 23 *s* others from the fire and save

SNOUT

Pr 11: 22 Like a gold ring in a pig's *s*

SNOW

Ps 51: 7 and I will be whiter than *s.*
Isa   1: 18 they shall be as white as *s;*

SNUFF (SNUFFED)

Isa 42: 3 a smoldering wick he will not *s* out.
Mt 12: 20 a smoldering wick he will not *s* out,

SNUFFED (SNUFF)

Pr 13: 9 but the lamp of the wicked is *s* out.

SOAP

Mal 3: 2 a refiner's fire or a launderer's *s.*

SOAR (SOARED)

Isa 40: 31 They will *s* on wings like eagles;

SOARED (SOAR)

2Sa 22: 11 he *s* on the wings of the wind.

SOBER

Ro 12: 3 think of yourself with *s* judgment,

SODOM

Ge 13: 12 and pitched his tents near *S.*
     19: 24 rained down burning sulfur on *S*
Isa   1: 9 we would have become like *S,*
Lk 10: 12 on that day for *S* than for that town
Ro   9: 29 we would have become like *S,*
Rev 11: 8 which is figuratively called *S*

SOIL

Ge   4: 2 kept flocks, and Cain worked the *s.*
Mt 13: 23 on good *s* is the man who hears

SOLD (SELL)

1Ki 21: 25 who *s* himself to do evil in the eyes
Mt 10: 29 Are not two sparrows *s* for a penny
     13: 44 then in his joy went and *s* all he had
Ro   7: 14 I am unspiritual, *s* as a slave to sin.

SOLDIER

1Co 9: 7 as a *s* at his own expense?
2Ti 2: 3 with us like a good *s* of Christ Jesus

SOLE

Dt 28: 65 place for the *s* of your foot.
Isa   1: 6 From the *s* of your foot to the top

SOLID

2Ti 2: 19 God's *s* foundation stands firm,
Heb 5: 12 You need milk, not *s* food!

SOLOMON

Son of David by Bathsheba; king of Judah (2Sa 12:24; 1Ch 3:5, 10). Appointed king by David (1Ki 1); adversaries Adonijah, Joab, Shimei killed by Benaiah (1Ki 2). Asked for wisdom (1Ki 3; 2Ch 1). Judged between two prostitutes (1Ki 3: 16-28). Built temple (1Ki 5-7; 2Ch 2-5); prayer of dedication (1Ki 8; 2Ch 6). Visited by Queen of Sheba (1Ki 9; 2Ch 9). Wives turned his heart from God (1Ki 11:1-13). Jeroboam rebelled against (1Ki 11:26-40). Death (1Ki 11:41-43; 2Ch 9:29-31).

Proverbs of (1Ki 4:32; Pr 1:1; 10:1; 25:1); psalms of (Ps 72; 127); song of (SS 1:1).

SON (SONS SONSHIP)

Ge 17: 19 your wife Sarah will bear you a *s,*
     21: 10 rid of that slave woman and her *s,*
     22: 2 "Take your *s,* your only *s,* Isaac.
Ex 11: 5 Every firstborn *s* in Egypt will die,
Dt   1: 31 father carries his *s,* all the way you
     6: 20 In the future, when your *s* asks you,
     8: 5 as a man disciplines his *s,*
    21: 18 rebellious *s* who does not obey his
2Sa 7: 14 be his father, and he will be my *s.*
1Ki 3: 20 and put her dead *s* by my breast.
Ps   2: 7 He said to me, "You are my *S;*
     2: 12 Kiss the *S,* lest he be angry
     8: 4 the *s* of man that you care for him?
Pr   3: 12 as a father the *s* he delights in.
     6: 20 My *s,* keep your father's

Pr 10: 1 A wise *s* brings joy to his father,
     13: 24 He who spares the rod hates his *s,*
     29: 17 Discipline your *s,* and he will give
Isa   7: 14 with child and will give birth to a *s,*
Eze 18: 20 The *s* will not share the guilt
Da   3: 25 the fourth looks like a *s* of the gods
     7: 13 before me was one like a *s* of man,
Hos 11: 1 and out of Egypt I called my *s.*
Am   7: 14 neither a prophet nor a prophet's *s,*
Mt   1: 1 of Jesus Christ the *s* of David,
     1: 21 She will give birth to a *s,*
     2: 15 "Out of Egypt I called my *s.*"
     3: 17 "This is my *S,* whom I love;
     4: 3 "If you are the *S* of God, tell these
     8: 20 but the *S* of Man has no place
    11: 27 one knows the *S* except the Father,
    12: 8 For the *S* of Man is Lord
    12: 32 a word against the *S* of Man will be
    12: 40 so the *S* of Man will be three days
    13: 41 *S* of Man will send out his angels,
    13: 55 "Isn't this the carpenter's *s?*
    14: 33 "Truly you are the *S* of God."
    16: 16 "You are the Christ, the *S*
    16: 27 For the *S* of Man is going to come
    17: 5 "This is my *S,* whom I love;
    19: 28 when the *S* of Man sits
    20: 18 and the *S* of Man will be betrayed
    20: 28 as the *S* of Man did not come
    21: 9 "Hosanna to the *S* of David!"
    22: 42 Whose *s* is he?" "The *s* of David,"
    24: 27 so will be the coming of the *S*
    24: 30 They will see the *S* of Man coming
    24: 44 the *S* of Man will come at an hour
    25: 31 "When the *S* of Man comes
    26: 63 if you are the Christ, the *S* of God."
    27: 54 "Surely he was the *S* of God!"
    28: 19 and of the *S* and of the Holy Spirit,
Mk   1: 11 "You are my *S,* whom I love;
    2: 28 So the *S* of Man is Lord
    8: 38 the *S* of Man will be ashamed
    9: 7 "This is my *S,* whom I love.
    10: 45 even the *S* of Man did not come
    13: 32 nor the *S,* but only the Father.
    14: 62 you will see the *S* of Man sitting
Lk   1: 32 and will be called the *S*
    2: 7 she gave birth to her firstborn, a *s.*
    3: 22 "You are my *S,* whom I love;
    9: 35 This is my *S,* whom I have chosen;
    9: 58 but the *S* of Man has no place
    12: 8 the *S* of Man will also acknowledge
    15: 20 he ran to his *s,* threw his arms
    18: 8 when the *S* of Man comes,
    18: 31 written by the prophets about the *S*
    19: 10 For the *S* of Man came to seek
Jn   1: 34 I testify that this is the *S* of God."
    3: 14 so the *S* of Man must be lifted up,
    3: 16 that he gave his one and only *S,*
    3: 36 believes in the *S* has eternal life,
    5: 19 the *S* can do nothing by himself;
    6: 40 is that everyone who looks to the *S*
    11: 4 so that God's *S* may be glorified
    17: 1 Glorify your *S,* that your *S* may
Ac   7: 56 and the *S* of Man standing
    13: 33 "'You are my *S;*
Ro   1: 4 with power to be the *S* of God
    5: 10 to him through the death of his *S,*
    8: 3 did by sending his own *S*
    8: 29 conformed to the likeness of his *S,*
    8: 32 He who did not spare his own *S,*
1Co 15: 28 then the *S* himself will be made
Gal   2: 20 I live by faith in the *S* of God,
    4: 4 God sent his *S,* born of a woman,
    4: 30 rid of the slave woman and her *s,*
1Th 1: 10 and to wait for his *S* from heaven,
Heb 1: 2 days he has spoken to us by his *S,*
    1: 5 "You are my *S;*
    2: 6 the *s* of man that you care for him?
    4: 14 Jesus the *S* of God, let us hold
    5: 5 "You are my *S;*
    7: 28 appointed the *S,* who has been
    10: 29 punished who has trampled the *S*
    12: 6 everyone he accepts as a *s.*"
2Pe 1: 17 saying, "This is my *S,* whom I love;
1Jn 1: 3 is with the Father and with his *S,*
    1: 7 his *S,* purifies us from all sin.
    2: 23 whoever acknowledges the *S* has
    3: 8 reason the *S* of God appeared was
    4: 9 only *S* into the world that we might

SONG

1Jn 4: 14 that the Father has sent his *S*
      5: 5 he who believes that Jesus is the *S*
      5: 11 eternal life, and this life is in his *S*.
Rev 1: 13 lampstands was someone ''like a *s*
     14: 14 on the cloud was one ''like a *s*

SONG (SING)

Ex 15: 2 LORD is my strength and my *s;*
Ps 40: 3 He put a new *s* in my mouth,
    69: 30 I will praise God's name in *s*
    96: 1 Sing to the LORD a new *s;*
    98: 4 burst into jubilant *s* with music;
   119: 54 Your decrees are the theme of my *s*
   149: 1 Sing to the LORD a new *s,*
Isa 49: 13 burst into *s,* O mountains!
    55: 12 will burst into *s* before you,
Rev 5: 9 And they sang a new *s:*
     15: 3 and sang the *s* of Moses the servant

SONGS (SING)

2Sa 23: 1 Israel's singer of *s;*
Job 35: 10 who gives *s* in the night,
Ps 100: 2 come before him with joyful *s.*
   126: 6 will return with *s* of joy,
   137: 3 ''Sing us one of the *s* of Zion!''
Eph 5: 19 with psalms, hymns and spiritual *s.*
Jas 5: 13 Is anyone happy? Let him sing *s*

SONS (SON)

Ge   6: 2 the *s* of God saw that the daughters
    10: 20 These are the *s* of Ham
Ru   4: 15 who is better to you than seven *s,*
Ps 127: 3 *s* are a heritage from the LORD,
   132: 12 if your *s* keep my covenant
Hos 1: 10 they will be called '*s*
Joel 2: 28 Your *s* and daughters will prophesy
Mt   5: 9 for they will be called *s* of God.
Lk   6: 35 and you will be *s* of the Most High,
Jn   1: 36 so that you may become *s* of light.''
Ro   8: 14 by the Spirit of God are *s* of God.
      9: 26 they will be called '*s*
2Co 6: 18 and you will be my *s* and daughters
Gal 3: 26 You are all *s* of God through faith
      4: 5 we might receive the full rights of *s.*
      4: 6 Because you are *s,* God sent
Heb 12: 7 discipline; God is treating you as *s.*

SONSHIP* (SON)

Ro   8: 15 but you received the Spirit of *s.*

SORCERY

Lev 19: 26 '' 'Do not practice divination or *s.*

SORROW (SORROWS)

Ps   6: 7 My eyes grow weak with *s;*
   116: 3 I was overcome by trouble and *s.*
Isa 60: 20 and your days of *s* will end.
Jer 31: 12 and they will *s* no more.
Ro   9: 2 I have great *s* and unceasing
2Co 7: 10 Godly *s* brings repentance that

SORROWS (SORROW)

Isa 53: 3 a man of *s,* and familiar

SOUGHT (SEEK)

2Ch 26: 5 As long as he *s* the LORD,
     31: 21 he *s* his God and worked
Ps 34: 4 I *s* the LORD, and he answered me
   119: 58 I have *s* your face with all my heart;

SOUL (SOULS)

Dt   6: 5 with all your *s* and with all your
    10: 12 all your heart and with all your *s,*
    30: 6 all your heart and with all your *s,*
Jos 22: 5 with all your heart and all your *s.''*
2Ki 3: 25 and with all his *s* and with all his
Ps 23: 3 he restores my *s.*
    34: 2 My *s* will boast in the LORD;
    42: 1 so my *s* pants for you, O God.
    42: 11 Why are you downcast, O my *s?*
    62: 5 Find rest, O my *s,* in God alone;
    63: 8 My *s* clings to you;
    94: 19 consolation brought joy to my *s.*
   103: 1 Praise the LORD, O my *s;*
Pr 13: 19 A longing fulfilled is sweet to the *s,*
    16: 24 sweet to the *s* and healing
    22: 5 he who guards his *s* stays far
Isa 55: 2 your *s* will delight in the richest

La   3: 20 and my *s* is downcast within me.
Eze 18: 4 For every living *s* belongs to me,
Mt 10: 28 kill the body but cannot kill the *s.*
    16: 26 yet forfeits his *s?* Or what can
    22: 37 with all your *s* and with all your
Heb 4: 12 even to dividing *s* and spirit,
3Jn   : 2 even as your *s* is getting along well.

SOULS (SOUL)

Pr 11: 30 and he who wins *s* is wise.
Jer 6: 16 and you will find rest for your *s.*
Mt 11: 29 and you will find rest for your *s.*

SOUND (FINE-SOUNDING)

Ge   3: 8 and his wife heard the *s*
Pr   3: 21 preserve *s* judgment
Eze 3: 12 I heard behind me a loud rushing *s*
Jn   3: 8 You hear its *s,* but you cannot tell
Ac   2: 2 Suddenly a *s* like the blowing
1Co 14: 8 if the trumpet does not *s* a clear call
    15: 52 the trumpet will *s,* the dead will
1Ti 1: 10 to the *s* doctrine that conforms
2Ti 4: 3 men will not put up with *s* doctrine.
Tit 1: 9 can encourage others by *s* doctrine
      2: 1 is in accord with *s* doctrine.

SOUR

Eze 18: 2 '' 'The fathers eat *s* grapes,

SOURCE

Heb 5: 9 became the *s* of eternal salvation

SOVEREIGN (SOVEREIGNTY)

Ge 15: 2 But Abram said, ''O *S* LORD,
2Sa 7: 18 O *S* LORD, and what is my family,
Ps 71: 16 your mighty acts, O *S* LORD;
Isa 25: 8 *S* LORD will wipe away the tears
    40: 10 the *S* LORD comes with power,
    50: 4 *S* LORD has given me
    61: 1 The Spirit of the *S* LORD is on me,
    61: 11 so the *S* LORD will make
Jer 32: 17 to the LORD: ''Ah, *S* LORD,
Eze 12: 28 fulfilled, declares the *S* LORD.' ''
Da   4: 25 that the Most High is *s*
2Pe 2: 1 denying the *s* Lord who bought
Jude   : 4 and deny Jesus Christ our only *S*

SOVEREIGNTY (SOVEREIGN)

Da   7: 27 Then the *s,* power and greatness

SOW (SOWER SOWN SOWS)

Job 4: 8 and those who *s* trouble reap it.
Ps 126: 5 Those who *s* in tears
Hos 8: 7 ''They *s* the wind
    10: 12 *S* for yourselves righteousness,
Mt   6: 26 they do not *s* or reap or store away
    13: 3 ''A farmer went out to *s* his seed.
1Co 15: 36 What you *s* does not come to life
Jas 3: 18 Peacemakers who *s*
2Pe 2: 22 and, ''A *s* that is washed goes back

SOWER (SOW)

Isa 55: 10 so that it yields seed for the *s*
Mt 13: 18 to what the parable of the *s* means:
Jn   4: 36 so that the *s* and the reaper may be
2Co 9: 10 Now he who supplies seed to the *s*

SOWN (SOW)

Mt 13: 8 sixty or thirty times what was *s.*
Mk   4: 15 along the path, where the word is *s.*
1Co 15: 42 The body that is *s* is perishable.

SOWS (SOW)

Pr 11: 18 he who *s* righteousness reaps a sure
    22: 8 He who *s* wickedness reaps trouble
2Co 9: 6 Whoever *s* sparingly will
Gal 6: 7 A man reaps what he *s.*

SPARE (SPARES SPARING)

Est 7: 3 *s* my people—this is my request.
Ro   8: 32 He who did not *s* his own Son,
    11: 21 natural branches, he will not *s* you
2Pe 2: 4 For if God did not *s* angels
      2: 5 if he did not *s* the ancient world

SPARES (SPARE)

Pr 13: 24 He who *s* the rod hates his son,

SPARING (SPARE)

Pr 21: 26 but the righteous give without *s.*

SPARKLE

Zec 9: 16 They will *s* in his land

SPARROW (SPARROWS)

Ps 84: 3 Even the *s* has found a home,

SPARROWS (SPARROW)

Mt 10: 29 Are not two *s* sold for a penny?

SPEAR (SPEARS)

1Sa 19: 10 as Saul drove the *s* into the wall.
Ps 46: 9 breaks the bow and shatters the *s,*

SPEARS (SPEAR)

Isa 2: 4 and their *s* into pruning hooks.
Joel 3: 10 and your pruning hooks into *s.*
Mic 4: 3 and their *s* into pruning hooks.

SPECIAL

Jas 2: 3 If you show *s* attention

SPECK

Mt   7: 3 look at the *s* of sawdust

SPECTACLE

1Co 4: 9 We have been made a *s*
Col 2: 15 he made a public *s* of them,

SPEECH

Ps 19: 3 There is no *s* or language
Pr 22: 11 pure heart and whose *s* is gracious
2Co 8: 7 in faith, in *s,* in knowledge,
1Ti 4: 12 set an example for the believers in *s*

SPEND (SPENT)

Pr 31: 3 do not *s* your strength on women,
Isa 55: 2 Why *s* money on what is not bread,
2Co 12: 15 So I will very gladly *s*

SPENT (SPEND)

Mk   5: 26 many doctors and had *s* all she had,
Lk   6: 12 and *s* the night praying to God.
    15: 14 After he had *s* everything,

SPIN

Mt   6: 28 They do not labor or *s.*

SPIRIT (SPIRIT'S SPIRITS SPIRITUAL SPIRITUALLY)

Ge   1: 2 and the *S* of God was hovering
      6: 3 ''My *S* will not contend
Ex 31: 3 I have filled him with the *S* of God,
Nu 11: 25 and put the *S* on the seventy elders.
Dt 34: 9 filled with the *s* of wisdom
Jdg 6: 34 Then the *S* of the LORD came
    11: 29 Then the *S* of the LORD came
    13: 25 and the *S* of the LORD began
1Sa 10: 10 the *S* of God came upon him
    16: 13 day on the *S* of the LORD came
    16: 14 the *S* of the LORD had departed
2Sa 23: 2 ''The *S* of the LORD spoke
2Ki 2: 9 inherit a double portion of your *s,''*
Ne   9: 20 You gave your good *S*
      9: 30 By your *S* you admonished them
Job 33: 4 The *S* of God has made me;
Ps 31: 5 Into your hands I commit my *s;*
    34: 18 saves those who are crushed in *s.*
    51: 10 and renew a steadfast *s* within me.
    51: 11 or take your Holy *S* from me.
    51: 17 sacrifices of God are a broken *s;*
   106: 33 rebelled against the *S* of God,
   139: 7 Where can I go from your *S?*
   143: 10 may your good *S*
Isa 11: 2 The *S* of the LORD will rest
    30: 1 an alliance, but not by my *S,*
    32: 15 till the *S* is poured upon us
    44: 3 I will pour out my *S*
    57: 15 him who is contrite and lowly in *s.*
    61: 1 The *S* of the Sovereign LORD is
    63: 10 and grieved his Holy *S.*
Eze 11: 19 an undivided heart and put a new *s*
    13: 3 prophets who follow their own *s*
    36: 26 you a new heart and put a new *s*
Da   4: 8 and the *s* of the holy gods is in him
Joel 2: 28 I will pour out my *S* on all people.

Zec 4: 6 but by my *S*,' says the LORD
Mt   1: 18 to be with child through the Holy *S*
     3: 11 will baptize you with the Holy *S*
     3: 16 he saw the *S* of God descending
     4: 1 led by the *S* into the desert
     5: 3 saying: "Blessed are the poor in *s*,
    10: 20 but the *S* of your Father speaking
    12: 31 against the *S* will not be forgiven.
    26: 41 *s* is willing, but the body is weak."
    28: 19 and of the Son and of the Holy *S*,
Mk   1: 8 he will baptize you with the Holy *S*
Lk   1: 35 "The Holy *S* will come upon you,
     1: 80 child grew and became strong in *s*;
     3: 16 will baptize you with the Holy *S*
     4: 18 "The *S* of the Lord is on me,
    11: 13 Father in heaven give the Holy *S*
    23: 46 into your hands I commit my *s*."
Jn   1: 33 who will baptize with the Holy *S*.'
     3: 5 a man is born of water and the *S*,
     4: 24 God is *s*, and his worshipers must
     6: 63 The *S* gives life; the flesh counts
     7: 39 Up to that time the *S* had not been
    14: 26 But the Counselor, the Holy *S*,
    16: 13 But when he, the *S* of truth, comes,
    20: 22 and said, "Receive the Holy *S*.
Ac   1: 5 will be baptized with the Holy *S*.'
     1: 8 when the Holy *S* comes on you;
     2: 4 of them were filled with the Holy *S*
     2: 17 I will pour out my *S* on all people.
     2: 38 will receive the gift of the Holy *S*.
     4: 31 they were all filled with the Holy *S*
     5: 3 that you have lied to the Holy *S*
     6: 3 who are known to be full of the *S*
     8: 15 that they might receive the Holy *S*,
     9: 17 and be filled with the Holy *S*.''
    11: 16 will be baptized with the Holy *S*.'
    13: 2 and fasting, the Holy *S* said,
    19: 2 ''Did you receive the Holy *S*
Ro   8: 4 nature but according to the *S*.
     8: 5 set on what the *S* desires.
     8: 9 And if anyone does not have the *S*
     8: 13 but if by the *S* you put
     8: 16 The *S* himself testifies
     8: 23 who have the firstfruits of the *S*,
     8: 26 the *S* helps us in our weakness.
1Co 2: 10 God has revealed it to us by his *S*.
     2: 14 man without the *S* does not accept
     5: 3 present, I am with you in *s*,
     6: 19 body is a temple of the Holy *S*,
    12: 13 baptized by one *S* into one body—
2Co 1: 22 and put his *S* in our hearts
     3: 3 but with the *S* of the living God,
     3: 6 the letter kills, but the *S* gives life.
     3: 17 Now the Lord is the *S*,
     5: 5 and has given us the *S* as a deposit,
     7: 1 that contaminates body and *s*,
Gal 3: 2 Did you receive the *S*
     5: 16 by the *S*, and you will not gratify
     5: 22 But the fruit of the *S* is love, joy,
     5: 25 let us keep in step with the *S*.
     6: 8 from the *S* will reap eternal life.
Eph 1: 13 with a seal, the promised Holy *S*,
     2: 22 in which God lives by his *S*.
     4: 4 There is one body and one *S*—
     4: 30 do not grieve the Holy *S* of God,
     5: 18 Instead, be filled with the *S*.
     6: 17 of salvation and the sword of the *S*,
Php 2: 2 being one in *s* and purpose.
1Th 5: 23 May your whole *s*, soul
2Th 2: 13 the sanctifying work of the *S*
1Ti 3: 16 was vindicated by the *S*,
2Ti 1: 7 For God did not give us a *s*
Heb 2: 4 of the Holy *S* distributed according
     4: 12 even to dividing soul and *s*,
    10: 29 and who has insulted the *S* of grace
1Pe 3: 4 beauty of a gentle and quiet *s*,
2Pe 1: 21 carried along by the Holy *S*.
1Jn 3: 24 We know it by the *S* he gave us.
     4: 1 Dear friends, do not believe every *s*
     4: 13 because he has given us of his *S*.
Jude   : 20 holy faith and pray in the Holy *S*.
Rev 2: 7 let him hear what the *S* says

SPIRIT'S* (SPIRIT)

1Co 2: 4 a demonstration of the *S* power,
1Th 5: 19 not put out the *S* fire; do not treat

SPIRITS (SPIRIT)

1Co 12: 10 the ability to distinguish between *s*,
    14: 32 The *s* of prophets are subject
1Jn 4: 1 test the *s* to see whether they are

SPIRITUAL (SPIRIT)

Ro 12: 1 to God—this is your *s* act of worship.
    12: 11 but keep your *s* fervor, serving
1Co 2: 13 expressing *s* truths in *s* words.
     3: 1 I could not address you as *s* but
    12: 1 Now about *s* gifts, brothers,
    14: 1 of love and eagerly desire *s* gifts,
    15: 44 a natural body, it is raised a *s* body.
Gal 6: 1 you who are *s* should restore him
Eph 1: 3 with every *s* blessing in Christ.
     5: 19 with psalms, hymns and *s* songs.
     6: 12 and against the *s* forces of evil
1Pe 2: 2 newborn babies, crave pure *s* milk,
     2: 5 are being built into a *s* house

SPIRITUALLY (SPIRIT)

1Co 2: 14 because they are *s* discerned.

SPIT

Mt 27: 30 They *s* on him, and took the staff
Rev 3: 16 I am about to *s* you out

SPLENDOR

1Ch 16: 29 the LORD in the *s* of his holiness.
    29: 11 the glory and the majesty and the *s*,
Job 37: 22 of the north he comes in golden *s*;
Ps 29: 2 in the *s* of his holiness.
    45: 3 clothe yourself with *s* and majesty.
    96: 6 *S* and majesty are before him;
    96: 9 in the *s* of his holiness;
   104: 1 you are clothed with *s* and majesty.
   145: 5 of the glorious *s* of your majesty,
   145: 12 and the glorious *s* of your kingdom.
   148: 13 his *s* is above the earth
Pr   4: 9 and present you with a crown of *s*.''
    16: 31 Gray hair is a crown of *s*;
    20: 29 gray hair the *s* of the old.
Isa 55: 5 for he has endowed you with *s*.''
    60: 21 for the display of my *s*.
    61: 3 the LORD for the display of his *s*.
    63: 1 Who is this, robed in *s*,
Hab 3: 4 His *s* was like the sunrise;
Mt   6: 29 in all his *s* was dressed like one
Lk   9: 31 appeared in glorious *s*, talking
2Th 2: 8 and destroy by the *s* of his coming.

SPOIL (SPOILS)

Ps 119:162 like one who finds great *s*.

SPOILS (SPOIL)

Isa 53: 12 he will divide the *s* with the strong,
Jn   6: 27 Do not work for food that *s*,

SPONTANEOUS*

Phm   : 14 so that any favor you do will be *s*

SPOTLESS

2Pe 3: 14 make every effort to be found *s*,

SPOTS (SPOTTED)

Jer 13: 23 or the leopard its *s*?

SPOTTED (SPOTS)

Ge 30: 32 and every *s* or speckled goat.

SPREAD (SPREADING SPREADS)

Ps 78: 19 "Can God *s* a table in the desert?
Ac   6: 7 So the word of God *s*.
    12: 24 of God continued to increase and *s*.
    13: 49 of the Lord *s* through the whole
    19: 20 the word of the Lord *s* widely
2Th 3: 1 message of the Lord may *s* rapidly

SPREADING (SPREAD)

Pr 29: 5 is a *s* net for his feet.
1Th 3: 2 God's fellow worker in *s* the gospel

SPREADS (SPREAD)

Pr 10: 18 and whoever *s* slander is a fool.

SPRING (SPRINGS WELLSPRING)

Jer 2: 13 the *s* of living water,
Jn   4: 14 in him a *s* of water welling up

Jas 3: 12 can a salt *s* produce fresh water.

SPRINGS (SPRING)

2Pe 2: 17 These men are *s* without water

SPRINKLE (SPRINKLED SPRINKLING)

Lev 16: 14 and with his finger *s* it on the front

SPRINKLED (SPRINKLE)

Heb 10: 22 having our hearts *s* to cleanse us

SPRINKLING (SPRINKLE)

1Pe 1: 2 to Jesus Christ and *s* by his blood:

SPROUT

Pr 23: 5 for they will surely *s* wings
Jer 33: 15 I will make a righteous Branch *s*

SPUR*

Heb 10: 24 how we may *s* one another

SPURNS*

Pr 15: 5 A fool *s* his father's discipline,

SPY

Gal 2: 4 ranks to *s* on the freedom we have

SQUANDERED (SQUANDERS)

Lk 15: 13 there *s* his wealth in wild living.

SQUANDERS* (SQUANDERED)

Pr 29: 3 of prostitutes *s* his wealth.

SQUARE

Rev 21: 16 The city was laid out like a *s*,

STABILITY*

Pr 29: 4 By justice a king gives a country *s*,

STAFF

Ge 49: 10 the ruler's *s* from between his feet,
Ex   7: 12 Aaron's *s* swallowed up their staffs.
Nu 17: 6 and Aaron's *s* was among them.
Ps 23: 4 your rod and your *s*,

STAIN (STAINED)

Eph 5: 27 without *s* or wrinkle or any other

STAINED (STAIN)

Isa 63: 1 with his garments *s* crimson?

STAKES

Isa 54: 2 strengthen your *s*.

STAND (STANDING STANDS STOOD)

Ex 14: 13 *S* firm and you will see
Jos 10: 12 ''O sun, *s* still over Gibeon,
2Ch 20: 17 *s* firm and see the deliverance
Job 19: 25 in the end he will *s* upon the earth.
Ps   1: 1 or *s* in the way of sinners
     1: 5 Therefore the wicked will not *s*
    24: 3 Who may *s* in his holy place?
    33: 11 of the LORD *s* firm forever,
    40: 2 and gave me a firm place to *s*.
    76: 7 Who can *s* before you
    93: 5 Your statutes *s* firm;
   119:120 I *s* in awe of your laws.
   130: 3 O Lord, who could *s*?
Ecc 5: 7 Therefore *s* in awe of God.
Isa 7: 9 If you do not *s* firm in your faith,
    29: 23 will *s* in awe of the God of Israel.
Eze 22: 30 *s* before me in the gap on behalf
Hab 3: 2 I *s* in awe of your deeds, O LORD.
Zec 14: 4 On that day his feet will *s*
Mal 3: 2 Who can *s* when he appears?
Mt 12: 25 divided against itself will not *s*.
Ro 14: 4 for the Lord is able to make him *s*.
    14: 10 we will all *s* before God's judgment
1Co 10: 3 out so that you can *s* up under it.
    15: 58 Therefore, my dear brothers, *s* firm
    16: 13 Be on your guard; *s* firm in the faith
Gal 5: 1 *S* firm, then, and do not let
Eph 6: 14 *S* firm then, with the belt
2Th 2: 15 *s* firm and hold to the teachings we
Jas 5: 8 You too, be patient and *s* firm,
Rev 3: 20 Here I am! I *s* at the door

STANDING (STAND)

Ex   3: 5 where you are *s* is holy ground.''

Jos   5: 15 the place where you are *s* is holy.''
Ru   1: 2 a man of *s*, whose name was Boaz.
      4: 11 May you have *s* in Ephrathah
Lk   21: 19 By *s* firm you will save yourselves.
1Ti   3: 13 have served well gain an excellent *s*
1Pe   5: 9 Resist him, *s* firm in the faith,

STANDS (STAND)

Ps   89: 2 that your love *s* firm forever,
     119: 89 it *s* firm in the heavens.
Pr   12: 7 the house of the righteous *s* firm.
Isa 40: 8 but the word of our God *s* forever.''
Mt   10: 22 but he who *s* firm to the end will be
2Ti   2: 19 God's solid foundation *s* firm,
1Pe   1: 25 but the word of the Lord *s* forever

STAR (STARS)

Nu   24: 17 A *s* will come out of Jacob;
Isa 14: 12 O morning *s*, son of the dawn!
Mt   2: 2 We saw his *s* in the east
2Pe   1: 19 the morning *s* rises in your hearts.
Rev   2: 28 I will also give him the morning *s*.
     22: 16 and the bright Morning *S*.''

STARS (STAR)

Ge   1: 16 He also made the *s*.
Job 38: 7 while the morning *s* sang together
Da   12: 3 like the *s* for ever and ever.
Php   2: 15 in which you shine like *s*

STATURE

1Sa   2: 26 boy Samuel continued to grow in *s*
Lk   2: 52 And Jesus grew in wisdom and *s*,

STATUTES

Ps   19: 7 *s* of the LORD are trustworthy,
     93: 5 Your *s* stand firm;
     119: 5 Blessed are they who keep his *s*
     119: 14 I rejoice in following your *s*
     119: 24 Your *s* are my delight;
     119: 36 Turn my heart toward your *s*
     119: 99 for I meditate on your *s*.
     119:111 Your *s* are my heritage forever;
     119:125 that I may understand your *s*.
     119:129 Your *s* are wonderful;
     119:138 The *s* you have laid
     119:152 Long ago I learned from your *s*
     119:167 I obey your *s*,

STEADFAST*

Ps   51: 10 and renew a *s* spirit within me.
     57: 7 My heart is *s*, O God,
     57: 7 my heart is *s*;
     108: 1 My heart is *s*, O God;
     111: 8 They are *s* for ever and ever,
     112: 7 his heart is *s*, trusting in the LORD
     119: 5 Oh, that my ways were *s*
Isa 26: 3 him whose mind is *s*,
1Pe   5: 10 and make you strong, firm and *s*.

STEADY

Isa 35: 3 *s* the knees that give way;

STEAL (STOLEN)

Ex   20: 15 ''You shall not *s*.
Lev 19: 11 '' 'Do not *s*.
Dt   5: 19 ''You shall not *s*.
Mt   19: 18 do not *s*, do not give false
Ro   13: 9 ''Do not *s*,'' ''Do not covet,''
Eph   4: 28 has been stealing must *s* no longer,

STEP (FOOTSTEPS STEPS)

Job 34: 21 he sees their every *s*.
Gal   5: 25 let us keep in *s* with the Spirit.

STEPHEN

Deacon (Ac 6:5). Arrested (Ac 6:8-15). Speech
to Sanhedrin (Ac 7). Stoned (Ac 7:54-60; 22:20).

STEPS (STEP)

Ps   37: 23 he makes his *s* firm;
Pr   14: 15 prudent man gives thought to his *s*.
     16: 9 but the LORD determines his *s*.
     20: 24 A man's *s* are directed
Jer 10: 23 it is not for man to direct his *s*.
1Pe   2: 21 that you should follow in his *s*.

STERN (STERNNESS)

Pr   15: 10 *S* discipline awaits him who leaves

STERNNESS* (STERN)

Ro   11: 22 and *s* of God: *s* to those who fell,

STICKS

Pr   18: 24 there is a friend who *s* closer

STIFF-NECKED (NECK)

Ex   34: 9 Although this is a *s* people,
Pr   29: 1 A man who remains *s*

STILL

Jos 10: 13 So the sun stood *s*, ·
Ps   37: 7 Be *s* before the LORD
     46: 10 ''Be *s*, and know that I am God;
     89: 9 its waves mount up, you *s* them.
Zec   2: 13 Be *s* before the LORD, all mankind
Mk   4: 39 said to the waves, ''Quiet! Be *s!*''

STIMULATE*

2Pe   3: 1 as reminders to *s* you

STING

1Co 15: 55 Where, O death, is your *s*?''

STINGY

Pr   28: 22 A *s* man is eager to get rich

STIRRED (STIRS)

Ps   45: 1 My heart is *s* by a noble theme

STIRS (STIRRED)

Pr   6: 19 and a man who *s* up dissension
     10: 12 Hatred *s* up dissension,
     15: 1 but a harsh word *s* up anger.
     15: 18 hot-tempered man *s* up dissension,
     16: 28 A perverse man *s* up dissension,
     28: 25 A greedy man *s* up dissension,
     29: 22 An angry man *s* up dissension,

STOLEN (STEAL)

Lev   6: 4 he must return what he has *s*
SS   4: 9 You have *s* my heart, my sister,

STOMACH

1Co   6: 13 Food for the *s* and the *s* for food''—
Php   3: 19 their god is their *s*, and their glory

STONE (CAPSTONE CORNERSTONE
MILLSTONE STONED STONES)

Ex   24: 4 set up twelve *s* pillars representing
     28: 10 on one *s* and the remaining six
     34: 1 ''Chisel out two *s* tablets like
Dt   4: 13 then wrote them on two *s* tablets.
     19: 14 your neighbor's boundary *s* set up
1Sa 17: 50 the Philistine with a sling and a *s;*
Ps   91: 12 will not strike your foot against a *s*.
     118: 22 The *s* the builders rejected
Pr   22: 28 not move an ancient boundary *s*
Isa   8: 14 a *s* that causes men to stumble
     28: 16 ''See, I lay a *s* in Zion,
Eze 11: 19 remove from them their heart of *s*
     36: 26 remove from you your heart of *s*
Mt   7: 9 will give him a *s*? Or if he asks
     21: 42 '' 'The *s* the builders rejected
     24: 2 not one *s* here will be left
Mk   16: 3 ''Who will roll the *s* away
Lk   4: 3 tell this *s* to become bread.''
Jn   8: 7 the first to throw a *s* at her.''
Ac   4: 11 '' 'the *s* you builders rejected,
Ro   9: 32 stumbled over the ''stumbling *s*.''
2Co   3: 3 not on tablets of *s* but on tablets
1Pe   2: 6 ''See, I lay a *s* in Zion,
Rev   2: 17 also give him a white *s*

STONED (STONE)

2Co 11: 25 once I was *s*, three times I was
Heb 11: 37 They were *s;* they were sawed

STONES (STONE)

Ex   28: 21 are to be twelve *s*, one for each
Jos   4: 3 to take up twelve *s* from the middle
1Sa 17: 40 chose five smooth *s*
Mt   3: 9 out of these *s* God can raise up
1Co   3: 12 silver, costly *s*, wood, hay or straw,
1Pe   2: 5 also, like living *s*, are being built

STOOD (STAND)

Jos 10: 13 So the sun *s* still,
Lk   22: 28 You are those who have *s* by me
2Ti   4: 17 But the Lord *s* at my side
Jas   1: 12 because when he has *s* the test,

STOOP (STOOPS)

2Sa 22: 36 you *s* down to make me great.

STOOPS (STOOP)

Ps 113: 6 who *s* down to look

STOP

Job 37: 14 *s* and consider God's wonders.
Isa   1: 13 *S* bringing meaningless offerings!
      1: 16 *S* doing wrong,
      2: 22 *S* trusting in man,
Jer 32: 40 I will never *s* doing good to them,
Mk   9: 39 ''Do not *s* him,'' Jesus said.
Jn   6: 43 ''*S* grumbling among yourselves,''
      7: 24 *S* judging by mere appearances,
     20: 27 *S* doubting and believe.''
Ro   14: 13 Therefore let us *s* passing judgment
1Co 14: 20 Brothers, *s* thinking like children.

STORE (STORED)

Pr   2: 1 and *s* up my commands within you,
      7: 1 and *s* up my commands within you.
     10: 14 Wise men *s* up knowledge,
Isa 33: 6 a rich *s* of salvation and wisdom
Mt   6: 19 not *s* up for yourselves treasures
      6: 26 or reap or *s* away in barns,
2Ti   4: 8 Now there is in *s* for me the crown

STORED (STORE)

Lk   6: 45 out of the good *s* up in his heart,
Col   1: 5 from the hope that is *s* up for you

STOREHOUSE (HOUSE)

Mal   3: 10 Bring the whole tithe into the *s*,

STORIES*

2Pe   1: 16 did not follow cleverly invented *s*
      2: 3 you with *s* they have made up.

STORM

Job 38: 1 LORD answered Job out of the *s*.
Ps 107: 29 He stilled the *s* to a whisper;
Lk   8: 24 the *s* subsided, and all was calm.

STOUTHEARTED* (HEART)

Ps 138: 3 you made me bold and *s*.

STRAIGHT

Ps   27: 11 lead me in a *s* path
     107: 7 He led them by a *s* way
Pr   2: 13 who leave the *s* paths
      3: 6 and he will make your paths *s*.
      4: 11 and lead you along *s* paths.
      4: 25 Let your eyes look *s* ahead,
     11: 5 of the blameless makes a *s* way
     15: 21 of understanding keeps a *s* course.
Isa 40: 3 make *s* in the wilderness
Mt   3: 3 make *s* paths for him.' ''
Jn   1: 23 'Make *s* the way for the Lord.' ''
2Pe   2: 15 They have left the *s* way

STRAIN (STRAINING)

Mt   23: 24 You *s* out a gnat but swallow

STRAINING (STRAIN)

Php   3: 13 and *s* toward what is ahead,

STRANGE (STRANGER STRANGERS)

Isa 28: 11 with foreign lips and *s* tongues
1Co 14: 21 ''Through men of *s* tongues
1Pe   4: 4 They think it *s* that you do not

STRANGER (STRANGE)

Ps 119: 19 I am a *s* on earth;
Mt   25: 35 I was a *s* and you invited me in,
Jn   10: 5 But they will never follow a *s;*

STRANGERS (STRANGE)

Heb 13: 2 Do not forget to entertain *s*,
1Pe   2: 11 as aliens and *s* in the world,

STRAW

Isa 11: 7 and the lion will eat s like the ox.
1Co 3: 12 silver, costly stones, wood, hay or s

STRAYED (STRAYS)

Ps 119:176 I have s like a lost sheep.
Jer 31: 19 After I s,

STRAYS (STRAYED)

Pr 21: 16 A man who s from the path
Eze 34: 16 for the lost and bring back the s.

STREAM (STREAMS)

Am 5: 24 righteousness like a never-failing s!

STREAMS (STREAM)

Ps 1: 3 He is like a tree planted by s
46: 4 is a river whose s make glad
Ecc 1: 7 All s flow into the sea,
Jn 7: 38 s of living water will flow

STREET

Mt 6: 5 on the s corners to be seen by men.
22: 9 Go to the s corners and invite
Rev 21: 21 The great s of the city was of pure gold,

STRENGTH (STRONG)

Ex 15: 2 The LORD is my s and my song;
Dt 4: 37 by his Presence and his great s,
6: 5 all your soul and with all your s.
Jdg 16: 15 told me the secret of your great s.''
2Sa 22: 33 It is God who arms me with s
2Ki 23: 25 with all his soul and with all his s,
1Ch 16: 11 Look to the LORD and his s;
16: 28 ascribe to the LORD glory and s,
29: 12 In your hands are s and power
Ne 8: 10 for the joy of the LORD is your s.''
Ps 18: 1 I love you, O LORD, my s.
21: 13 Be exalted, O LORD, in your s;
28: 7 The LORD is my s and my shield;
29: 11 The LORD gives s to his people;
33: 16 no warrior escapes by his great s.
46: 1 God is our refuge and s,
59: 17 O my S, I sing praise to you;
65: 6 having armed yourself with s,
73: 26 but God is the s of my heart
84: 5 Blessed are those whose s is in you,
96: 7 ascribe to the LORD glory and s.
105: 4 Look to the LORD and his s;
118: 14 The LORD is my s and my song;
147: 10 not in the s of the horse,
Pr 24: 5 a man of knowledge increases s;
30: 25 Ants are creatures of little s,
Isa 12: 2 the LORD, is my s and my song;
31: 1 and in the great s of their horsemen
40: 26 of his great power and mighty s,
40: 31 will renew their s.
63: 1 forward in the greatness of his s?
Jer 9: 23 or the strong man boast of his s
Mic 5: 4 flock in the s of the LORD,
Hab 3: 19 The Sovereign LORD is my s;
Mk 12: 30 of his glorious riches he may s you
1Co 1: 25 of God is stronger than man's s.
Eph 3: 16 of his glorious riches he may s you
Php 4: 13 through him who gives me s.
Heb 11: 34 whose weakness was turned to s;
1Pe 4: 11 it with the s God provides,

STRENGTHEN

2Ch 16: 9 to s those whose hearts are fully
Ps 119: 28 s me according to your word.
Isa 35: 3 S the feeble hands,
41: 10 I will s you and help you;
Lk 22: 32 have turned back, s your brothers.''
Eph 3: 16 of his glorious riches he may s you
1Th 3: 13 May he s your hearts
2Th 2: 17 and s you in every good deed
Heb 12: 12 s your feeble arms and weak knees.

STRENGTHENED (STRONG)

Col 1: 11 being s with all power according
Heb 13: 9 good for our hearts to be s by grace,

STRENGTHENING (STRONG)

1Co 14: 26 done for the s of the church.

STRETCHES

Ps 104: 2 he s out the heavens like a tent

STRICKEN (STRIKE)

Isa 53: 8 of my people he was s.

STRICT

1Co 9: 25 in the games goes into s training.

STRIFE (STRIVE)

Pr 17: 1 than a house full of feasting, with s.
20: 3 It is to a man's honor to avoid s,
22: 10 out the mocker, and out goes s;
30: 33 so stirring up anger produces s.''
1Ti 6: 4 s, malicious talk, evil suspicions

STRIKE (STRIKES STROKE)

Ge 3: 15 and you will s his heel.''
Zec 13: 7 ''S the shepherd,
Mt 4: 6 so that you will not s your foot
26: 31 '' 'I will s the shepherd,

STRIKES (STRIKE)

Mt 5: 39 If someone s you on the right

STRIPS

Lk 2: 12 You will find a baby wrapped in s
Jn 20: 5 in at the s of linen lying there

STRIVE* (STRIFE)

Ac 24: 16 I s always to keep my conscience
1Ti 4: 10 (and for this we labor and s),

STROKE (STRIKE)

Mt 5: 18 the smallest letter, not the least s

STRONG (STRENGTH STRENGTHEN STRENGTHENED STRENGTHENING STRONGER)

Dt 3: 24 your greatness and your s hand.
31: 6 Be s and courageous.
Jos 1: 6 ''Be s and courageous,
Jdg 5: 21 March on, my soul; be s!
2Sa 10: 12 Be s and let us fight bravely
1Ki 2: 2 ''So be s, show yourself a man,
1Ch 28: 20 ''Be s and courageous,
2Ch 32: 7 them with these words: ''Be s
Ps 24: 8 The LORD s and mighty,
31: 2 a s fortress to save me.
62: 11 that you, O God, are s,
Pr 18: 10 The name of the LORD is a s tower
31: 17 her arms are s for her tasks.
Ecc 9: 11 or the battle to the s,
SS 8: 6 for love is as s as death,
Isa 35: 4 ''Be s, do not fear;
53: 12 he will divide the spoils with the s,
Jer 9: 23 or the s man boast of his strength
50: 34 Yet their Redeemer is s;
Hag 2: 4 Be s, all you people of the land,'
Mt 12: 29 can anyone enter a s man's house
Lk 2: 40 And the child grew and became s;
Ro 15: 1 We who are s ought to bear
1Co 1: 8 He will keep you s to the end,
1: 27 things of the world to shame the s.
16: 13 in the faith; be men of courage; be s
2Co 12: 10 For when I am weak, then I am s.
Eph 6: 10 be s in the Lord and in his mighty
2Ti 2: 1 be s in the grace that is
1Pe 5: 10 restore you and make you s,

STRONGER (STRONG)

Dt 4: 38 before you nations greater and s
1Co 1: 25 of God is s than man's strength.

STRONGHOLD (STRONGHOLDS)

2Sa 22: 3 He is my s, my refuge and my
Ps 9: 9 a s in times of trouble.
18: 2 the horn of my salvation, my s.
27: 1 The LORD is the s of my life—
144: 2 my s and my deliverer,

STRONGHOLDS (STRONGHOLD)

Zep 3: 6 their s are demolished.
2Co 10: 4 have divine power to demolish s.

STRUGGLE (STRUGGLED STRUGGLING)

Ro 15: 30 me in my s by praying to God
Eph 6: 12 For our s is not against flesh
Heb 12: 4 In your s against sin, you have not

STRUGGLED (STRUGGLE)

Ge 32: 28 because you have s with God

STRUGGLING* (STRUGGLE)

Col 1: 29 To this end I labor, s
2: 1 to know how much I am s for you

STUDENT (STUDY)

Mt 10: 24 ''A s is not above his teacher,

STUDY (STUDENT)

Ezr 7: 10 Ezra had devoted himself to the s
Ecc 12: 12 and much s wearies the body.
Jn 5: 39 You diligently s the Scriptures

STUMBLE (STUMBLES STUMBLING)

Ps 37: 24 though he s, he will not fall,
119:165 and nothing can make them s.
Pr 3: 23 and your foot will not s;
Isa 8: 14 a stone that causes men to s
Jer 13: 16 before your feet s
31: 9 a level path where they will not s.
Eze 7: 19 for it has made them s into sin.
Hos 14: 9 but the rebellious s in them.
Mal 2: 8 teaching have caused many to s;
Jn 11: 9 A man who walks by day will not s,
Ro 9: 33 in Zion a stone that causes men to s
14: 20 that causes someone else to s.
1Co 10: 32 Do not cause anyone to s,
Jas 3: 2 We all s in many ways.
1Pe 2: 8 and, ''A stone that causes men to s
1Jn 2: 10 nothing in him to make him s.

STUMBLES (STUMBLE)

Pr 24: 17 when he s, do not let your heart
Jn 11: 10 is when he walks by night that he s,
Jas 2: 10 and yet s at just one point is guilty

STUMBLING (STUMBLE)

Lev 19: 14 put a s block in front of the blind,
Ps 56: 13 and my feet from s,
Mt 16: 23 Satan! You are a s block to me;
Ro 9: 32 They stumbled over the ''s stone.''
11: 9 a s block and a retribution for them
14: 13 up your mind not to put any s block
1Co 1: 23 a s block to Jews and foolishness
8: 9 freedom does not become a s block
2Co 6: 3 We put no s block in anyone's path,

STUMP

Isa 6: 13 so the holy seed will be the s
11: 1 up from the s of Jesse;

STUPID

Pr 12: 1 but he who hates correction is s.
2Ti 2: 23 to do with foolish and s arguments,

STUPOR

Ro 11: 8 ''God gave them a spirit of s,

SUBDUE (SUBDUED)

Ge 1: 28 in number; fill the earth and s it.

SUBDUED (SUBDUE)

Jos 10: 40 So Joshua s the whole region,
Ps 47: 3 He s nations under us,

SUBJECT (SUBJECTED)

Mt 5: 22 angry with his brother will be s
1Co 14: 32 of prophets are s to the control
15: 28 then the Son himself will be made s
Tit 2: 5 and to be s to their husbands,
2: 9 slaves to be s to their masters
3: 1 Remind the people to be s to rulers

SUBJECTED (SUBJECT)

Ro 8: 20 For the creation was s

SUBMISSION (SUBMIT)

1Co 14: 34 but must be in s, as the Law says.
1Ti 2: 11 learn in quietness and full s.

SUBMISSIVE (SUBMIT)

Jas 3: 17 then peace-loving, considerate, s,
1Pe 3: 1 in the same way be s
5: 5 in the same way be s

SUBMIT (SUBMISSION SUBMISSIVE SUBMITS)

Ro 13: 1 Everyone must s himself
     13: 5 necessary to s to the authorities,
1Co 16: 16 to s to such as these
Eph 5: 21 S to one another out of reverence
Col 3: 18 Wives, s to your husbands,
Heb 12: 9 How much more should we s
     13: 17 Obey your leaders and s
Jas 4: 7 S yourselves, then, to God.
1Pe 2: 18 s yourselves to your masters

SUBMITS* (SUBMIT)

Eph 5: 24 Now as the church s to Christ,

SUBTRACT*

Dt   4: 2 what I command you and do not s

SUCCEED (SUCCESS SUCCESSFUL)

Ps 20: 4 and make all your plans s.
Pr 15: 22 but with many advisers they s.
    16: 3 and your plans will s.
    21: 30 that can s against the LORD.

SUCCESS (SUCCEED)

Ge 39: 23 and gave him s in whatever he did.
1Sa 18: 14 In everything he did he had great s,
1Ch 12: 18 S, s to you, and s
    22: 13 you will have s if you are careful
2Ch 26: 5 the LORD, God gave him s.
Ecc 10: 1 but skill will bring s.

SUCCESSFUL (SUCCEED)

Jos 1: 7 that you may be s wherever you go.
2Ki 18: 7 he was s in whatever he undertook.
2Ch 20: 20 in his prophets and you will be s.''

SUFFER (SUFFERED SUFFERING SUFFERINGS SUFFERS)

Job 36: 15 those who s he delivers
Isa 53: 10 to crush him and cause him to s,
Mk   8: 31 the Son of Man must s many things
Lk 24: 26 the Christ have to s these things
    24: 46 The Christ will s and rise
2Co 1: 6 of the same sufferings we s.
Php 1: 29 to s for him, since you are going
Heb 9: 26 would have had to s many times
1Pe 3: 17 to s for doing good
     4: 16 However, if you s as a Christian,

SUFFERED (SUFFER)

Heb 2: 9 and honor because he s death,
     2: 18 Because he himself s
1Pe 2: 21 Christ s for you, leaving you
     4: 1 he who has s in his body is done

SUFFERING (SUFFER)

Job 36: 15 who suffer he delivers in their s;
Ps 22: 24 the s of the afflicted one;
Isa 53: 3 of sorrows, and familiar with s.
    53: 11 After the s of his soul,
La   1: 12 Is any s like my s
Ac   5: 41 worthy of s disgrace for the Name.
Ro   5: 3 know that s produces
2Ti 1: 8 But join with me in s for the gospel,
Heb 2: 10 of their salvation perfect through s.
    13: 3 as if you yourselves were s.
1Pe 4: 12 at the painful trial you are s,

SUFFERINGS (SUFFER)

Ro   5: 3 but we also rejoice in our s,
     8: 17 share in his s in order that we may
     8: 18 that our present s are not worth
2Co 1: 5 as the s of Christ flow
Php 3: 10 the fellowship of sharing in his s,
1Pe 4: 13 rejoice that you participate in the s
     5: 9 are undergoing the same kind of s.

SUFFERS (SUFFER)

Pr 13: 20 but a companion of fools s harm.
1Co 12: 26 If one part s, every part s with it;

SUFFICIENT

2Co 12: 9 said to me, ''My grace is s for you,

SUITABLE

Ge   2: 18 I will make a helper s for him.''

SUMMED* (SUMS)

Ro 13: 9 there may be, are s up
Gal 5: 14 The entire law is s up

SUMMONS

Ps 50: 1 speaks and s the earth
Isa 45: 3 God of Israel, who s you by name.

SUMS* (SUMMED)

Mt   7: 12 for this s up the Law

SUN (SUNRISE)

Jos 10: 13 So the s stood still,
Jdg 5: 31 may they who love you be like the s
Ps 84: 11 For the LORD God is a s
    121: 6 the s will not harm you by day,
    136: 8 the s to govern the day,
Ecc 1: 9 there is nothing new under the s.
Isa 60: 19 The s will no more be your light
Mal 4: 2 the s of righteousness will rise
Mt   5: 45 He causes his s to rise on the evil
    13: 43 the righteous will shine like the s
    17: 2 His face shone like the s,
Lk 23: 45 for the s stopped shining.
Eph 4: 26 Do not let the s go
Rev 1: 16 His face was like the s shining
    21: 23 The city does not need the s

SUNG (SING)

Mt 26: 30 When they had s a hymn, they

SUNRISE (SUN)

2Sa 23: 4 he is like the light of morning at s
Hab 3: 4 His splendor was like the s;

SUPERIOR

Heb 1: 4 he became as much s to the angels
     8: 6 ministry Jesus has received is as s

SUPERVISION

Gal 3: 25 longer under the s of the law.

SUPPER

Lk 22: 20 after the s he took the cup, saying,
1Co 11: 25 after s he took the cup,
Rev 19: 9 to the wedding s of the Lamb!' ''

SUPPLIED (SUPPLY)

Ac 20: 34 of mine have s my own needs
Php 4: 18 and even more; I am amply s,

SUPPLY (SUPPLIED SUPPLYING)

2Co 8: 14 your plenty will s what they need,
1Th 3: 10 and s what is lacking in your faith.

SUPPLYING* (SUPPLY)

2Co 9: 12 you perform is not only s the needs

SUPPORT (SUPPORTED SUPPORTING)

Ps 18: 18 but the LORD was my s.
Ro 11: 18 consider this: You do not s the root
1Co 9: 12 If others have this right of s

SUPPORTED (SUPPORT)

Ps 94: 18 your love, O LORD, s me.
Col 2: 19 s and held together by its ligaments

SUPPORTING (SUPPORT)

Eph 4: 16 held together by every s ligament,

SUPPRESS*

Ro   1: 18 wickedness of men who s the truth

SUPREMACY* (SUPREME)

Col 1: 18 in everything he might have the s.

SUPREME (SUPREMACY)

Pr   4: 7 Wisdom is s; therefore get wisdom.

SURE

Nu 28: 31 Be s the animals are without defect
    32: 23 you may be s that your sin will find
Dt   6: 17 Be s to keep the commands
    14: 22 Be s to set aside a tenth
    29: 18 make s there is no root
Jos 23: 13 then you may be s that the LORD
1Sa 12: 24 But be s to fear the LORD
Ps 19: 9 The ordinances of the LORD are s
    132: 11 a s oath that he will not revoke:

Pr 27: 23 Be s you know the condition
Isa 28: 16 cornerstone for a s foundation;
Eph 5: 5 of this you can be s: No immoral,
Heb 11: 1 faith is being s of what we hope for
2Pe 1: 10 to make your calling and election s.

SURFACE

2Co 10: 7 You are looking only on the s

SURPASS* (SURPASSED SURPASSES SURPASSING)

Pr 31: 29 but you s them all.''

SURPASSED* (SURPASS)

Jn   1: 15 'He who comes after me has s me
     1: 30 man who comes after me has s me

SURPASSES* (SURPASS)

Pr   8: 19 what I yield s choice silver.
Mt   5: 20 unless your righteousness s that
Eph 3: 19 to know this love that s knowledge

SURPASSING* (SURPASS)

Ps 150: 2 praise him for his s greatness.
2Co 3: 10 in comparison with the s glory.
     9: 14 of the s grace God has given you.
Php 3: 8 the s greatness of knowing Christ

SURPRISE (SURPRISED)

1Th 5: 4 that this day should s you like

SURPRISED (SURPRISE)

1Pe 4: 12 do not be s at the painful trial you
1Jn 3: 13 Do not be s, my brothers,

SURRENDER

1Co 13: 3 and s my body to the flames,

SURROUND (SURROUNDED SURROUNDS)

Ps   5: 12 you s them with your favor
    32: 7 and s me with songs of deliverance.
    89: 7 awesome than all who s him.
    125: 2 As the mountains s Jerusalem,
Jer 31: 22 a woman will s a man.''

SURROUNDED (SURROUND)

Heb 12: 1 since we are s by such a great cloud

SURROUNDS* (SURROUND)

Ps 32: 10 s the man who trusts in him.
    89: 8 and your faithfulness s you.
    125: 2 so the LORD s his people

SUSA

Ezr 4: 9 and Babylon, the Elamites of S,
Ne   1: 1 while I was in the citadel of S,

SUSPENDS*

Job 26: 7 he s the earth over nothing.

SUSPICIONS*

1Ti 6: 4 evil s and constant friction

SUSTAIN (SUSTAINING SUSTAINS)

Ps 55: 22 and he will s you;
Isa 46: 4 I am he, I am he who will s you.

SUSTAINING* (SUSTAIN)

Heb 1: 3 s all things by his powerful word.

SUSTAINS (SUSTAIN)

Ps 18: 35 and your right hand s me;
    146: 9 and s the fatherless and the widow,
    147: 6 The LORD s the humble
Isa 50: 4 to know the word that s the weary.

SWALLOW (SWALLOWED)

Isa 25: 8 he will s up death forever.
Jnh 1: 17 provided a great fish to s Jonah,
Mt 23: 24 You strain out a gnat but s a camel.

SWALLOWED (SWALLOW)

1Co 15: 54 ''Death has been s up in victory.''
2Co 5: 4 so that what is mortal may be s up

SWAYED

Mt 11: 7 A reed s by the wind? If not,
    22: 16 You aren't s by men, because you

2Ti   3: 6 are *s* by all kinds of evil desires,

SWEAR (SWORE SWORN)

Lev 19: 12 `` 'Do not *s* falsely by my name
Ps 24: 4 or *s* by what is false.
Isa 45: 23 by me every tongue will *s*.
Mt   5: 34 Do not *s* at all: either by heaven,
Jas   5: 12 Above all, my brothers, do not *s*—

SWEAT*

Ge   3: 19 By the *s* of your brow
Lk 22: 44 his *s* was like drops of blood falling

SWEET (SWEETER SWEETNESS)

Job 20: 12 ''Though evil is *s* in his mouth
Ps 119:103 How *s* are your words
Pr   9: 17 ''Stolen water is *s;*
      13: 19 A longing fulfilled is *s* to the soul,
      16: 24 *s* to the soul and healing
      20: 17 by fraud tastes *s* to a man,
      24: 14 also that wisdom is *s* to your soul;
Ecc   5: 12 The sleep of a laborer is *s,*
Isa   5: 20 and *s* for bitter.
Eze   3: 3 it tasted as *s* as honey in my mouth.
Rev 10: 10 It tasted as *s* as honey in my mouth

SWEETER (SWEET)

Ps 19: 10 they are *s* than honey,
     119:103 *s* than honey to my mouth!

SWEETNESS* (SWEET)

SS   4: 11 Your lips drop *s* as the honeycomb,
      5: 16 His mouth is *s* itself;

SWEPT

Mt 12: 44 finds the house unoccupied, *s* clean

SWERVE*

Pr   4: 5 do not forget my words or *s*
      4: 27 Do not *s* to the right or the left;

SWIFT

Pr   1: 16 they are *s* to shed blood.
Ecc   9: 11 The race is not to the *s*
Isa 59: 7 they are *s* to innocent blood.
Ro   3: 15 ''Their feet are *s* to shed blood;
2Pe   2: 1 bringing *s* destruction

SWINDLER* (SWINDLERS)

1Co   5: 11 or a slanderer, a drunkard or a *s.*

SWINDLERS* (SWINDLER)

1Co   5: 10 or the greedy and *s*, or idolaters.
      6: 10 *s* will inherit the kingdom of God.

SWORD (SWORDS)

Ge   3: 24 and a flaming *s* flashing back
Dt 32: 41 when I sharpen my flashing *s*
Jos   5: 13 of him with a drawn *s* in his hand.
1Sa 17: 45 ''You come against me with *s*
      17: 47 here will know that it is not by *s*
      31: 4 so Saul took his own *s* and fell on it.
2Sa 12: 10 the *s* will never depart
Ps 44: 6 my *s* does not bring me victory;
      45: 3 Gird your *s* upon your side,
Pr 12: 18 Reckless words pierce like a *s,*
Isa   2: 4 Nation will not take up *s*
Mic   4: 3 Nation will not take up *s*
Mt 10: 34 come to bring peace, but a *s.*
      26: 52 all who draw the *s* will die by the *s.*
Lk   2: 35 a *s* will pierce your own soul too.''
Ro 13: 4 for he does not bear the *s*
Eph   6: 17 of salvation and the *s* of the Spirit,
Heb   4: 12 Sharper than any double-edged *s,*
Rev   1: 16 came a sharp double-edged *s.*
      19: 15 Out of his mouth comes a sharp *s*

SWORDS (SWORD)

Ps 64: 3 who sharpen their tongues like *s*
Isa   2: 4 They will beat their *s*
Joel 3: 10 Beat your plowshares into *s*

SWORE (SWEAR)

Heb   6: 13 for him to swear by, he *s* by himself

SWORN (SWEAR)

Ps 110: 4 The LORD has *s*
Eze 20: 42 the land I had *s* with uplifted hand
Heb   7: 21 ''The Lord has *s*

SYCAMORE-FIG (FIG)

Am   7: 14 and I also took care of *s* trees.
Lk 19: 4 and climbed a *s* tree to see him,

SYMBOLIZES*

1Pe   3: 21 this water *s* baptism that now saves

SYMPATHETIC* (SYMPATHY)

1Pe   3: 8 in harmony with one another; be *s,*

SYMPATHIZED* (SYMPATHY)

Heb 10: 34 You *s* with those in prison

SYMPATHY (SYMPATHETIC SYMPATHIZED)

Ps 69: 20 I looked for *s*, but there was none,

SYNAGOGUE

Lk   4: 16 the Sabbath day he went into the *s,*
Ac 17: 2 custom was, Paul went into the *s,*

TABERNACLE (TABERNACLES)

Ex 40: 34 the glory of the LORD filled the *t.*
Heb   8: 2 the true *t* set up by the Lord,
      9: 11 and more perfect *t* that is not
      9: 21 sprinkled with the blood both the *t*
Rev 15: 5 that is, the *t* of Testimony,

TABERNACLES (TABERNACLE)

Lev 23: 34 the LORD's Feast of *T* begins,
Dt 16: 16 Feast of Weeks and the Feast of *T.*
Zec 14: 16 and to celebrate the Feast of *T.*

TABLE (TABLES)

Ex 25: 23 ''Make a *t* of acacia wood—
Ps 23: 5 You prepare a *t* before me

TABLES (TABLE)

Jn   2: 15 changers and overturned their *t.*
Ac   6: 2 word of God in order to wait on *t.*

TABLET (TABLETS)

Pr   3: 3 write them on the *t* of your heart.
      7: 3 write them on the *t* of your heart.

TABLETS (TABLET)

Ex 31: 18 he gave him the two *t*
Dt 10: 5 and put the *t* in the ark I had made,
2Co   3: 3 not on *t* of stone but on *t*

TAKE (TAKEN TAKES TAKING TOOK)

Ge 15: 7 land to *t* possession of it.''
      22: 17 Your descendants will *t* possession
Ex   3: 5 ''*T* off your sandals,
      21: 23 you are to *t* life for life, eye for eye,
      22: 22 ''Do not *t* advantage of a widow
Lev 10: 17 given to you to *t* away the guilt
      25: 14 do not *t* advantage of each other.
Nu 13: 30 and *t* possession of the land,
Dt   1: 8 and *t* possession of the land that
      12: 32 do not add to it or *t* away from it.
      31: 26 ''*T* this Book of the Law
1Sa   8: 11 He will *t* your sons and make them
1Ch 17: 13 I will never *t* my love away
Job 23: 10 But he knows the way that I *t;*
Ps   2: 12 Blessed are all who *t* refuge in him.
      25: 18 and *t* away all my sins.
      27: 14 be strong and *t* heart
      31: 24 Be strong and *t* heart,
      49: 17 for he will *t* nothing with him
      51: 11 or *t* your Holy Spirit from me.
      73: 24 afterward you will *t* me into glory.
      118: 8 It is better to *t* refuge in the LORD
Pr 22: 23 for the LORD will *t* up their case
Isa 62: 4 for the LORD will *t* delight in you,
Eze   3: 10 and *t* to heart all the words I speak
      33: 11 I *t* no pleasure in the death
Mt 10: 38 anyone who does not *t* his cross
      11: 29 *T* my yoke upon you and learn
      16: 24 deny himself and *t* up his cross
      26: 26 saying, ''*T* and eat; this is my body
Mk 14: 36 *T* this cup from me.
1Ti   6: 12 *T* hold of the eternal life

TAKEN (TAKE)

Ge   2: 23 for she was *t* out of man.''
Lev   6: 4 must return what he has stolen or *t*
Nu   8: 16 I have *t* them as my own in place

Nu 19: 3 it is to be *t* outside the camp
Ecc   3: 14 added to it and nothing *t* from it.
Isa   6: 7 your guilt is *t* away and your sin
Zec   3: 4 ''See, I have *t* away your sin,
Mt 13: 12 even what he has will be *t* from him
      24: 40 one will be *t* and the other left.
      26: 39 may this cup be *t* from me.
Mk 16: 19 he was *t* up into heaven
Ac   1: 9 he was *t* up before their very eyes,
Ro   5: 13 But sin is not *t* into account
1Ti   3: 16 was *t* up in glory.

TAKES (TAKE)

1Ki 20: 11 should not boast like one who *t* it
Ps   5: 4 You are not a God who *t* pleasure
      34: 8 blessed is the man who *t* refuge
Lk   6: 30 and if anyone *t* what belongs to you
Jn   1: 29 who *t* away the sin of the world!
      10: 18 No one *t* it from me, but I lay it
Rev 22: 19 And if anyone *t* words away

TAKING (TAKE)

Ac 15: 14 by *t* from the Gentiles a people
Php   2: 7 *t* the very nature of a servant,

TALENT

Mt 25: 15 to another one *t*, each according

TALES*

1Ti   4: 7 with godless myths and old wives' *t*

TALL

1Sa 17: 4 He was over nine feet *t.*
1Ch 11: 23 who was seven and a half feet *t.*

TAMAR

1. Wife of Judah's sons Er and Onan (Ge 38: 1-10). Tricked Judah into fathering children when he refused her his third son (Ge 38:11-30).
2. Daughter of David, raped by Amnon (2Sa 13).

TAMBOURINE

Ps 150: 4 praise him with *t* and dancing,

TAME* (TAMED)

Jas   3: 8 but no man can *t* the tongue.

TAMED* (TAME)

Jas   3: 7 the sea are being *t* and have been *t*

TARSHISH

Jnh   1: 3 from the LORD and headed for *T.*

TARSUS

Ac   9: 11 ask for a man from *T* named Saul,

TASK (TASKS)

1Ch 29: 1 The *t* is great, because this palatial
Mk 13: 34 each with his assigned *t,*
Ac 20: 24 complete the *t* the Lord Jesus has
1Co   3: 5 the Lord has assigned to each his *t.*
2Co   2: 16 And who is equal to such a *t?*
1Ti   3: 1 an overseer, he desires a noble *t.*

TASKS (TASK)

Pr 31: 17 her arms are strong for her *t.*

TASTE (TASTED TASTY)

Ps 34: 8 *T* and see that the LORD is good;
     119:103 sweet are your words to my *t,*
Pr 24: 13 from the comb is sweet to your *t.*
SS   2: 3 and his fruit is sweet to my *t.*
Col   2: 21 Do not *t!* Do not touch!''?
Heb   2: 9 the grace of God he might *t* death

TASTED (TASTE)

Eze   3: 3 it *t* as sweet as honey in my mouth.
1Pe   2: 3 now that you have *t* that the Lord
Rev 10: 10 It *t* as sweet as honey in my mouth,

TASTY (TASTE)

Ge 27: 4 Prepare me the kind of *t* food I like

TATTOO*

Lev 19: 28 or put *t* marks on yourselves.

TAUGHT (TEACH)

1Ki   4: 33 He also *t* about animals and birds,

2Ki 17: 28 *t* them how to worship the LORD.
2Ch 17: 9 They *t* throughout Judah,
Ps 119:102 for you yourself have *t* me.
Pr   4: 4 he *t* me and said,
    31: 1 an oracle his mother *t* him:
Isa 29: 13 is made up only of rules *t* by men.
    50: 4 ear to listen like one being *t.*
Mt   7: 29 he *t* as one who had authority,
    15: 9 their teachings are but rules *t*
Lk   4: 15 He *t* in their synagogues,
Ac 20: 20 have *t* you publicly and from house
1Co 2: 13 but in words *t* by the Spirit,
Gal 1: 12 nor was I *t* it; rather, I received it
1Ti 1: 20 to Satan to be *t* not to blaspheme.
1Jn 2: 27 just as it has *t* you, remain in him.

TAX (TAXES)

Mt 11: 19 a friend of *t* collectors and "sinners
    17: 24 of the two-drachma *t* came to Peter

TAXES (TAX)

Mt 22: 17 Is it right to pay *t* to Caesar or not
Ro 13: 7 If you owe *t,* pay *t;* if revenue,

TEACH (TAUGHT TEACHER TEACHERS TEACHES TEACHING TEACHINGS)

Ex   4: 12 and will *t* you what to say."
    18: 20 *T* them the decrees and laws,
    33: 13 *t* me your ways so I may know you
Lev 10: 11 and you must *t* the Israelites all
Dt   4: 9 *T* them to your children
    6: 1 me to *t* you to observe
    8: 3 to *t* you that man does not live
    11: 19 *T* them to your children, talking
1Sa 12: 23 I will *t* you the way that is good
1Ki 8: 36 *T* them the right way to live,
Job 12: 7 ask the animals, and they will *t* you
Ps 32: 8 *t* you in the way you should go;
    34: 11 I will *t* you the fear of the LORD.
    51: 13 I will *t* transgressors your ways,
    78: 5 forefathers to *t* their children,
    90: 12 *T* us to number our days aright,
    119: 33 *T* me, O LORD, to follow your
    143: 10 *T* me to do your will,
Pr   9: 9 *t* a righteous man and he will add
Jer 31: 34 No longer will a man *t* his neighbor
Mic 4: 2 He will *t* us his ways,
Lk 11: 1 said to him, "Lord, *t* us to pray,
    12: 12 for the Holy Spirit will *t* you
Jn 14: 26 will *t* you all things and will remind
Ro 2: 21 who *t* others, do you not *t* yourself?
    15: 4 in the past was written to *t* us,
1Ti 2: 12 I do not permit a woman to *t*
    3: 2 respectable, hospitable, able to *t,*
2Ti 2: 2 also be qualified to *t* others.
    2: 24 kind to everyone, able to *t,*
Tit 2: 1 You must *t* what is in accord
    2: 15 then, are the things you should *t.*
Heb 8: 11 No longer will a man *t* his neighbor
Jas 3: 1 know that we who *t* will be judged
1Jn 2: 27 you do not need anyone to *t* you.

TEACHER (TEACH)

Ecc 1: 1 The words of the *T,* son of David,
Mt 10: 24 "A student is not above his *t.*
    13: 52 "Therefore every *t*
    23: 10 Nor are you to be called '*t,'*
Lk 6: 40 A student is not above his *t,*
Jn 3: 2 we know you are a *t* who has come
    13: 14 and *T,* have washed your feet,

TEACHERS (TEACH)

Ps 119: 99 I have more insight than all my *t,*
Pr 5: 13 I would not obey my *t*
Lk 20: 46 "Beware of the *t* of the law.
1Co 12: 28 third *t,* then workers of miracles,
Eph 4: 11 and some to be pastors and *t,*
2Ti 4: 3 around them a great number of *t*
Heb 5: 12 by this time you ought to be *t,*
Jas 3: 1 of you should presume to be *t,*
2Pe 2: 1 as there will be false *t* among you.

TEACHES (TEACH)

Ps 25: 9 and *t* them his way.
    94: 10 Does he who *t* man lack
Pr 15: 33 of the LORD *t* a man wisdom,
Isa 48: 17 who *t* you what is best for you,
Mt 5: 19 *t* these commands will be called

1Ti 6: 3 If anyone *t* false doctrines
Tit 2: 12 It *t* us to say "No" to ungodliness
1Jn 2: 27 his anointing *t* you about all things

TEACHING (TEACH)

Ezr 7: 10 to *t* its decrees and laws in Israel.
Pr 1: 8 and do not forsake your mother's *t.*
    3: 1 My son, do not forget my *t,*
    6: 23 this *t* is a light,
Mt 28: 20 *t* them to obey everything I have
Jn 7: 17 whether my *t* comes from God or
    8: 31 to my *t,* you are really my disciples.
    14: 23 loves me, he will obey my *t.*
Ac 2: 42 themselves to the apostles' *t*
Ro 12: 7 let him serve; if it is *t,* let him teach;
Eph 4: 14 and there by every wind of *t*
2Th 3: 6 to the *t* you received from us.
1Ti 4: 13 of Scripture, to preaching and to *t.*
    5: 17 whose work is preaching and *t,*
    6: 3 Lord Jesus Christ and to godly *t,*
2Ti 3: 16 is God-breathed and is useful for *t,*
Tit 1: 11 by *t* things they ought not
    2: 7 In your *t* show integrity,
Heb 5: 13 with the *t* about righteousness.
2Jn 9 and does not continue in the *t*

TEACHINGS (TEACH)

Pr 7: 2 guard my *t* as the apple of your eye.
2Th 2: 15 hold to the *t* we passed on to you,
Heb 6: 1 leave the elementary *t* about Christ

TEAR (TEARS)

Rev 7: 17 God will wipe away every *t*
    21: 4 He will wipe every *t*

TEARS (TEAR)

Ps 126: 5 Those who sow in *t*
Isa 25: 8 LORD will wipe away the *t*
Jer 31: 16 and your eyes from *t,*
    50: 4 in *t* to seek the LORD their God.
Lk 7: 38 she began to wet his feet with her *t.*
2Co 2: 4 anguish of heart and with many *t,*
Php 3: 18 and now say again even with *t,*

TEETH (TOOTH)

Job 19: 20 with only the skin of my *t.*
Ps 35: 16 they gnashed their *t* at me.
Jer 31: 29 and the children's *t* are set on edge
Mt 8: 12 will be weeping and gnashing of *t.''*

TEMPER (EVEN-TEMPERED HOT-TEMPERED ILL-TEMPERED QUICK-TEMPERED)

Pr 16: 32 a man who controls his *t*

TEMPERANCE see SELF-CONTROL

TEMPERATE*

1Ti 3: 2 *t,* self-controlled, respectable,
    3: 11 not malicious talkers but *t*
Tit 2: 2 Teach the older men to be *t,*

TEMPEST

Ps 50: 3 and around him a *t* rages.
    55: 8 far from the *t* and storm."

TEMPLE (TEMPLES)

1Ki 6: 1 began to build the *t* of the LORD.
    6: 38 the *t* was finished in all its details
    8: 10 the cloud filled the *t* of the LORD,
    8: 27 How much less this *t* I have built!
2Ch 36: 19 They set fire to God's *t*
    36: 23 me to build a *t* for him at Jerusalem
Ezr 6: 14 finished building the *t* according
Ps 27: 4 and to seek him in his *t.*
Isa 6: 1 and the train of his robe filled the *t.*
Eze 10: 4 cloud filled the *t,* and the court was
    43: 5 glory of the LORD entered the *t*
Hab 2: 20 But the LORD is in his holy *t;*
Mt 12: 6 that one greater than the *t* is here.
    26: 61 'I am able to destroy the *t* of God
    27: 51 of the *t* was torn in two from top
Lk 21: 5 about how the *t* was adorned
Jn 2: 14 In the *t* courts he found men selling
1Co 3: 16 that you yourselves are God's *t*
    6: 19 you not know that your body is a *t*
2Co 6: 16 For we are the *t* of the living God.
Rev 21: 22 I did not see a *t* in the city,

TEMPLES (TEMPLE)

Ac 17: 24 does not live in *t* built by hands.

TEMPORARY

2Co 4: 18 what is seen is *t,* but what is unseen

TEMPT* (TEMPTATION TEMPTED TEMPTER TEMPTING)

1Co 7: 5 satan so that Satan will not *t* you
Jas 1: 13 does he *t* anyone; but each one is

TEMPTATION* (TEMPT)

Mt 6: 13 And lead us not into *t,*
    26: 41 pray so that you will not fall into *t.*
Mk 14: 38 pray so that you will not fall into *t.*
Lk 11: 4 And lead us not into *t.' ''*
    22: 40 "Pray that you will not fall into *t.''*
    22: 46 pray so that you will not fall into *t.''*
1Co 10: 13 No *t* has seized you except what is
1Ti 6: 9 want to get rich fall into *t*

TEMPTED* (TEMPT)

Mt 4: 1 into the desert to be *t* by the devil.
Mk 1: 13 was in the desert forty days, being *t*
Lk 4: 2 for forty days he was *t* by the devil.
1Co 10: 13 But when you are *t,* he will
    10: 13 he will not let you be *t*
Gal 6: 1 yourself, or you also may be *t.*
1Th 3: 5 way the tempter might have *t* you
Heb 2: 18 able to help those who are being *t.*
    2: 18 he himself suffered when he was *t,*
    4: 15 but we have one who has been *t*
Jas 1: 13 For God cannot be *t* by evil,
    1: 13 When *t,* no one should say,
    1: 14 each one is *t* when, by his own evil

TEMPTER* (TEMPT)

Mt 4: 3 *t* came to him and said,
1Th 3: 5 some way the *t* might have

TEMPTING* (TEMPT)

Lk 4: 13 the devil had finished all this *t,*
Jas 1: 13 no one should say, "God is *t* me.''

TEN (TENTH TITHE TITHES)

Ex 34: 28 covenant—the *T* Commandments.
Lev 26: 8 of you will chase *t* thousand,
Dt 4: 13 covenant, the *T* Commandments,
    10: 4 The *T* Commandments he had
Ps 91: 7 *t* thousand at your right hand,
Da 7: 24 *t* horns are *t* kings who will come
Mt 25: 1 will be like *t* virgins who took
    25: 28 it to the one who has the *t* talents.
Lk 15: 8 suppose a woman has *t* silver coins
Rev 12: 3 and *t* horns and seven crowns

TENANTS

Mt 21: 34 servants to the *t* to collect his fruit.

TEND

Jer 23: 2 to the shepherds who *t* my people:
Eze 34: 14 I will *t* them in a good pasture,

TENDERNESS*

Isa 63: 15 Your *t* and compassion are
Php 2: 1 fellowship with the Spirit, if any *t*

TENT (TENTMAKER TENTS)

Ex 27: 21 In the *T* of Meeting,
    40: 2 "Set up the tabernacle, the *T*
Isa 54: 2 "Enlarge the place of your *t,*
2Co 5: 1 that if the earthly *t* we live
2Pe 1: 13 as long as I live in the *t* of this body,

TENTH (TEN)

Ge 14: 20 Abram gave him a *t* of everything.
Nu 18: 26 you must present a *t* of that tithe
Dt 14: 22 Be sure to set aside a *t*
1Sa 8: 15 He will take a *t* of your grain
Lk 11: 42 you give God a *t* of your mint,
    18: 12 I fast twice a week and give a *t*
Heb 7: 4 patriarch Abraham gave him a *t*

TENTMAKER* (TENT)

Ac 18: 3 and because he was a *t* as they were

TENTS (TENT)

Ge 13: 12 and pitched his *t* near Sodom.

Ps 84: 10 than dwell in the *t* of the wicked.

TERAH

Ge 11: 31 *T* took his son Abram, his

TERRIBLE (TERROR)

2Ti 3: 1 There will be *t* times

TERRIFIED (TERROR)

Dt   7: 21 Do not be *t* by them,
     20: 3 do not be *t* or give way to panic
Ps 90: 7 and *t* by your indignation.
Mt 14: 26 walking on the lake, they were *t*.
     17: 6 they fell facedown to the ground, *t*.
     27: 54 they were *t*, and exclaimed,
Mk   4: 41 They were *t* and asked each other,

TERRIFYING (TERROR)

Heb 12: 21 The sight was so *t* that Moses said,

TERRITORY

2Co 10: 16 done in another man's *t*.

TERROR (TERRIBLE TERRIFIED TERRIFYING)

Dt   2: 25 very day I will begin to put the *t*
    28: 67 of the *t* that will fill your hearts
Job   9: 34 so that his *t* would frighten me no
Ps 91: 5 You will not fear the *t* of night,
Pr 21: 15 but *t* to evildoers.
Isa 13: 8 *T* will seize them,
    24: 17 *T* and pit and snare await you,
    51: 13 live in constant *t* every day
    54: 14 *T* will be far removed;
Lk 21: 26 Men will faint from *t*, apprehensive
Ro 13: 3 For rulers hold no *t*

TEST (TESTED TESTING TESTS)

Dt   6: 16 Do not *t* the LORD your God
Jdg   3: 1 to *t* all those Israelites who had not
1Ki 10: 1 came to *t* him with hard questions.
1Ch 29: 17 that you *t* the heart and are pleased
Ps 26: 2 *T* me, O LORD, and try me,
    78: 18 They willfully put God to the *t*
   106: 14 wasteland they put God to the *t*
   139: 23 *t* me and know my anxious
Jer 11: 20 and *t* the heart and mind,
Lk   4: 12 put the Lord your God to the *t*.' ''
Ac   5: 9 How could you agree to *t* the Spirit
Ro 12: 2 Then you will be able to *t*
1Co 3: 13 and the fire will *t* the quality
    10: 9 We should not *t* the Lord,
2Co 13: 5 unless, of course, you fail the *t*?
1Th 5: 21 *T* everything.
Jas   1: 12 because when he has stood the *t*,
1Jn   4: 1 *t* the spirits to see whether they are

TESTAMENT see COVENANT

TESTED (TEST)

Ge 22: 1 Some time later God *t* Abraham.
Job 23: 10 when he has *t* me, I will come forth
    34: 36 that Job might be *t* to the utmost
Ps 66: 10 For you, O God, *t* us;
Pr 27: 21 man is *t* by the praise he receives.
Isa 28: 16 a *t* stone,
    48: 10 I have *t* you in the furnace
1Ti   3: 10 They must first be *t*; and then
Heb 11: 17 By faith Abraham, when God *t* him

TESTIFIES (TESTIFY)

Jn   5: 32 There is another who *t* in my favor,
Ro   8: 16 The Spirit himself *t*

TESTIFY (TESTIFIES TESTIMONY)

Pr 24: 28 Do not *t* against your neighbor
Jn   1: 7 a witness to *t* concerning that light,
    1: 34 and I *t* that this is the Son of God.''
    5: 39 are the Scriptures that *t* about me,
    7: 7 because I *t* that what it does is evil.
   15: 26 he will *t* about me; but you
Ac   4: 33 continued to *t* to the resurrection
   10: 43 All the prophets *t* about him that
2Ti   1: 8 ashamed to *t* about our Lord,
1Jn   4: 14 *t* that the Father has sent his Son
    5: 7 For there are three that *t*: the Spirit

TESTIMONY (TESTIFY)

Ex 20: 16 ''You shall not give false *t*

Ex 31: 18 gave him the two tablets of the *T*,
Nu 35: 30 only on the *t* of witnesses.
Dt 19: 18 giving false *t* against his brother,
Pr 12: 17 A truthful witness gives honest *t*,
Isa 8: 20 and to the *t*! If they do not speak
Mt 15: 19 sexual immorality, theft, false *t*,
    24: 14 preached in the whole world as a *t*
Lk 18: 20 not give false *t*, honor your father
Jn   2: 25 He did not need man's *t* about man
    21: 24 We know that his *t* is true.
1Jn   5: 9 but God's *t* is greater because it is
Rev 12: 11 and by the word of their *t*;

TESTING (TEST)

Lk   8: 13 but in the time of *t* they fall away.
Heb 3: 8 during the time of *t* in the desert,
Jas   1: 3 because you know that the *t*

TESTS (TEST)

Pr 17: 3 but the LORD *t* the heart.
1Th 2: 4 but God, who *t* our hearts.

THADDAEUS

   Apostle (Mt 10:3; Mk 3:18); probably also known as Judas son of James (Lk 6:16; Ac 1:13).

THANK (THANKFUL THANKFULNESS THANKS THANKSGIVING)

Php 1: 3 I *t* my God every time I remember
1Th 3: 9 How can we *t* God enough for you

THANKFUL (THANK)

Col 3: 15 And be *t*.
Heb 12: 28 let us be *t*, and so worship God

THANKFULNESS (THANK)

1Co 10: 30 If I take part in the meal with *t*,
Col 2: 7 taught, and overflowing with *t*.

THANKS (THANK)

1Ch 16: 8 Give *t* to the LORD, call
Ne 12: 31 assigned two large choirs to give *t*.
Ps   7: 17 I will give *t* to the LORD
    28: 7 and I will give *t* to him in song.
    30: 12 my God, I will give you *t* forever.
    35: 18 I will give you *t* in the great
    75: 1 we give *t*, for your Name is near;
   100: 4 give *t* to him and praise his name.
   107: 1 Give *t* to the LORD, for he is good;
   118: 28 are my God, and I will give you *t*;
   136: 1 Give *t* to the LORD, for he is good.
Ro   1: 21 as God nor gave *t* to him,
1Co 11: 24 when he had given *t*, he broke it
    15: 57 *t* be to God! He gives us the victory
2Co 2: 14 *t* be to God, who always leads us
    9: 15 *T* be to God for his indescribable
1Th 5: 18 give *t* in all circumstances,
Rev 4: 9 and *t* to him who sits on the throne

THANKSGIVING (THANK)

Ps 95: 2 Let us come before him with *t*
   100: 4 Enter his gates with *t*
1Co 10: 16 cup of *t* for which we give thanks
Php 4: 6 by prayer and petition, with *t*,
1Ti   4: 3 created to be received with *t*

THEFT (THIEF)

Mt 15: 19 sexual immorality, *t*, false .

THEFTS* (THIEF)

Rev 9: 21 their sexual immorality or their *t*.

THEME*

Ps 45: 1 My heart is stirred by a noble *t*
   119: 54 Your decrees are the *t* of my song

THIEF (THEFT THEFTS THIEVES)

Ex 22: 3 A *t* must certainly make restitution
Pr   6: 30 Men do not despise a *t* if he steals
Lk 12: 39 at what hour the *t* was coming,
1Th 5: 2 day of the Lord will come like a *t*
1Pe 4: 15 or *t* or any other kind of criminal,
Rev 16: 15 I come like a *t*! Blessed is he who

THIEVES (THIEF)

Mt   6: 19 and where *t* break in and steal.
Jn 10: 8 who ever came before me were *t*
1Co 6: 10 nor homosexual offenders nor *t*

THINK (THINKING THOUGHT THOUGHTS)

Ps 63: 6 I *t* of you through the watches
Isa 44: 19 No one stops to *t*,
Mt 22: 42 ''What do you *t* about the Christ?
Ro 12: 3 Do not *t* of yourself more highly
Php 4: 8 praiseworthy—*t* about such things

THINKING (THINK)

Pr 23: 7 who is always *t* about the cost.
1Co 14: 20 Brothers, stop *t* like children.
2Pe 3: 1 to stimulate you to wholesome *t*.

THIRST (THIRSTS THIRSTY)

Ps 69: 21 and gave me vinegar for my *t*.
Mt   5: 6 Blessed are those who hunger and *t*
Jn   4: 14 the water I give him will never *t*.
2Co 11: 27 I have known hunger and *t*
Rev 7: 16 never again will they *t*.

THIRSTS (THIRST)

Ps 42: 2 My soul *t* for God,

THIRSTY (THIRST)

Ps 107: 9 for he satisfies the *t*
Pr 25: 21 if he is *t*, give him water to drink.
Isa 55: 1 ''Come, all you who are *t*,
Mt 25: 35 I was *t* and you gave me something
Jn   7: 37 ''If a man is *t*, let him come to me
Ro 12: 20 if he is *t*, give him something
Rev 21: 6 To him who is *t* I will give to drink
    22: 17 Whoever is *t*, let him come;

THOMAS

   Apostle (Mt 10:3; Mk 3:18; Lk 6:15; Jn 11:16; 14:5; 21:2; Ac 1:13). Doubted resurrection (Jn 20: 24-28).

THONGS

Mk   1: 7 *t* of whose sandals I am not worthy

THORN (THORNBUSHES THORNS)

2Co 12: 7 there was given me a *t* in my flesh,

THORNBUSHES (THORN)

Lk   6: 44 People do not pick figs from *t*,

THORNS (THORN)

Ge   3: 18 It will produce *t* and thistles
Nu 33: 55 in your eyes and *t* in your sides.
Mt 13: 7 fell among *t*, which grew up
    27: 29 and then twisted together a crown of *t*
Heb 6: 8 But land that produces *t*

THOUGHT (THINK)

Pr 14: 15 a prudent man gives *t* to his steps.
    21: 29 an upright man gives *t* to his ways.
1Co 13: 11 I talked like a child, I *t* like a child,

THOUGHTS (THINK)

1Ch 28: 9 every motive behind the *t*.
Ps 94: 11 The LORD knows the *t* of man;
   139: 23 test me and know my anxious *t*.
Isa 55: 8 ''For my *t* are not your *t*,
Mt 15: 19 For out of the heart come evil *t*,
1Co 2: 11 among men knows the *t* of a man
Heb 4: 12 it judges the *t* and attitudes

THREE

Ge   6: 10 Noah had *t* sons: Shem, Ham
Ex 23: 14 ''*T* times a year you are
Dt 19: 15 the testimony of two or *t* witnesses.
2Sa 23: 8 a Tahkemonite, was chief of the *T*;
Pr 30: 15 ''There are *t* things that are never
    30: 18 ''There are *t* things that are too
    30: 21 ''Under *t* things the earth trembles,
    30: 29 ''There are *t* things that are stately
Ecc 4: 12 of *t* strands is not quickly broken.
Da   3: 24 ''Weren't there *t* men that we tied up
Am   1: 3 ''For *t* sins of Damascus,
Jnh 1: 17 inside the fish *t* days and *t* nights.
Mt 12: 40 so the Son of Man will be *t* days
    12: 40 *t* nights in the belly of a huge fish,
    12: 40 *t* nights in the heart of the earth.
    17: 4 I will put up *t* shelters—one
    18: 20 or *t* come together in my name,
    26: 34 you will disown me *t* times.''
    26: 75 you will disown me *t* times.''

Mt 27: 63 'After *t* days I will rise again.'
Mk 8: 31 and after *t* days rise again.
     9: 5 Let us put up *t* shelters—one
    14: 30 yourself will disown me *t* times.''
Jn   2: 19 and I will raise it again in *t* days.''
1Co 13: 13 And now these *t* remain: faith,
    14: 27 or at the most *t*— should speak,
2Co 13: 1 testimony of two or *t* witnesses.''
1Jn 5: 7 For there are *t* that testify:

THRESHER* (THRESHING)

1Co 9: 10 plowman plows and the *t* threshes,

THRESHING (THRESHER)

Ru   3: 6 So she went down to the *t* floor
2Sa 24: 18 an altar to the LORD on the *t* floor
Lk   3: 17 is in his hand to clear his *t* floor

THREW (THROW)

Da   6: 16 and *t* him into the lions' den.
Jnh 1: 15 took Jonah and *t* him overboard,

THRIVE

Pr 29: 2 When the righteous *t*, the people

THROAT (THROATS)

Ps   5: 9 Their *t* is an open grave;
Pr 23: 2 and put a knife to your *t*

THROATS (THROAT)

Ro   3: 13 ''Their *t* are open graves;

THROB*

Isa 60: 5 your heart will *t* and swell with joy;

THRONE (ENTHRONED ENTHRONES THRONES)

2Sa 7: 16 your *t* will be established forever
1Ch 17: 12 and I will establish his *t* forever.
Ps 11: 4 the LORD is in his heavenly *t*.
    45: 6 Your *t*, O God, will last for ever
    47: 8 God is seated on his holy *t*.
    89: 14 justice are the foundation of your *t*;
Isa   6: 1 I saw the Lord seated on a *t*,
    66: 1 ''Heaven is my *t*,
Eze 28: 2 I sit on the *t* of a god
Da   7: 9 His *t* was flaming with fire,
Mt 19: 28 Son of Man sits on his glorious *t*,
Ac   7: 49 prophet says: '' 'Heaven is my *t*,
Heb 1: 8 ''Your *t*, O God, will last for ever
    4: 16 Let us then approach the *t* of grace
    12: 2 at the right hand of the *t* of God.
Rev 3: 21 sat down with my Father on his *t*.
    3: 21 the right to sit with me on my *t*.
    4: 2 there before me was a *t* in heaven
    4: 10 They lay their crowns before the *t*
  20: 11 Then I saw a great white *t*
  22: 3 *t* of God and of the Lamb will be

THRONES (THRONE)

Mt 19: 28 me will also sit on twelve *t*,
Rev 4: 4 throne were twenty-four other *t*,

THROW (THREW)

Jn   8: 7 the first to *t* a stone at her.''
Heb 10: 35 So do not *t* away your confidence;
    12: 1 let us *t* off everything that hinders

THUNDER (THUNDERS)

Ps 93: 4 Mightier than the *t*
Mk 3: 17 which means Sons of *T*); Andrew,

THUNDERS (THUNDER)

Job 37: 5 God's voice *t* in marvelous ways;
Ps 29: 3 the God of glory *t*,
Rev 10: 3 the voices of the seven *t* spoke.

THWART* (THWARTED)

Isa 14: 27 has purposed, and who can *t* him?

THWARTED (THWART)

Job 42: 2 no plan of yours can be *t*.

THYATIRA

Rev 2: 18 the angel of the church in *T* write:

TIBNI

    King of Israel (1Ki 16:21-22).

TIDINGS

Isa 40: 9 You who bring good *t* to Jerusalem
    52: 7 who bring good *t*,

TIES

Hos 11: 4 with *t* of love;
Mt 12: 29 unless he first *t* up the strong man?

TIGHT*

Jas   1: 26 and yet does not keep a *t* rein

TIGHTFISTED*

Dt 15: 7 or *t* toward your poor brother.

TIME (TIMES)

Est   4: 14 come to royal position for such a *t*
Ecc 3: 1 There is a *t* for everything,
    8: 5 wise heart will know the proper *t*
Da   7: 25 to him for a *t*, times and half a *t*.
    12: 7 ''It will be for a *t*, times and half a *t*.
Hos 10: 12 for it is *t* to seek the LORD,
Jn   2: 4 Jesus replied, ''My *t* has not yet
    17: 1 prayed: ''Father, the *t* has come.
Ro   9: 9 ''At the appointed *t* I will return,
    13: 11 understanding the present *t*.
1Co 7: 29 brothers, is that the *t* is short.
2Co 6: 2 now is the *t* of God's favor,
2Ti   1: 9 Jesus before the beginning of *t*,
Tit   1: 2 promised before the beginning of *t*,
Heb 9: 28 and he will appear a second *t*,
   10: 12 for all *t* one sacrifice for sins,
1Pe 4: 17 For it is *t* for judgment to begin

TIMES (TIME)

Ps   9: 9 a stronghold in *t* of trouble.
    31: 15 My *t* are in your hands;
    62: 8 Trust in him at all *t*, O people;
Pr 17: 17 A friend loves at all *t*,
Isa 46: 10 from ancient *t*, what is still to come
Am   5: 13 for the *t* are evil.
Mt 16: 3 cannot interpret the signs of the *t*.
    18: 21 how many *t* shall I forgive my
Ac   1: 7 ''It is not for you to know the *t*
Rev 12: 14 *t* and half a time, out

TIMID (TIMIDITY)

1Th 5: 14 encourage the *t*, help the weak,

TIMIDITY* (TIMID)

2Ti   1: 7 For God did not give us a spirit of *t*

TIMOTHY

    Believer from Lystra (Ac 16:1). Joined Paul on second missionary journey (Ac 16-20). Sent to settle problems at Corinth (1Co 4:17; 16:10). Led church at Ephesus (1Ti 1:3). Co-writer with Paul (1Th 1:1; 2Th 1:1; Phm 1).

TIP

Job 33: 2 my words are on the *t* of my tongue

TIRE (TIRED)

2Th 3: 13 never *t* of doing what is right.

TIRED (TIRE)

Ex 17: 12 When Moses' hands grew *t*,
Isa 40: 28 He will not grow *t* or weary,

TITHE (TEN)

Lev 27: 30 ''A *t* of everything from the land,
Dt 12: 17 eat in your own towns the *t*
Mal 3: 10 the whole *t* into the storehouse,

TITHES (TEN)

Nu 18: 21 give to the Levites all the *t* in Israel
Mal 3: 8 'How do we rob you?' ''In *t*

TITUS*

    Gentile co-worker of Paul (Gal 2:1-3; 2Ti 4: 10); sent to Corinth (2Co 2:13; 7-8; 12:18), Crete (Tit 1:4-5).

TODAY

Ps   2: 7 *t* I have become your Father.
    95: 7 *T*, if you hear his voice,
Mt   6: 11 Give us *t* our daily bread.
Lk   2: 11 *T* in the town of David a Savior has
   23: 43 *t* you will be with me in paradise.''

TONGUE (TONGUES)

Ex   4: 10 I am slow of speech and *t*.''
Job 33: 2 my words are on the tip of my *t*.
Ps   5: 9 with their *t* they speak deceit.
    34: 13 keep your *t* from evil
    37: 30 and his *t* speaks what is just.
    39: 1 and keep my *t* from sin;
    51: 14 my *t* will sing of your righteousness
    52: 4 O you deceitful *t*!
    71: 24 My *t* will tell of your righteous acts
 119:172 May my *t* sing of your word,
   137: 6 May my *t* cling to the roof
   139: 4 Before a word is on my *t*
Pr   6: 17 a lying *t*,
   10: 19 but he who holds his *t* is wise.
   12: 18 but the *t* of the wise brings healing.
   15: 4 The *t* that brings healing is a tree
   17: 20 he whose *t* is deceitful falls
   21: 23 He who guards his mouth and his *t*
   25: 15 and a gentle *t* can break a bone.
   26: 28 A lying *t* hates those it hurts,
   28: 23 than he who has a flattering *t*.
   31: 26 and faithful instruction is on her *t*.
SS   4: 11 milk and honey are under your *t*.
Isa 32: 4 the stammering *t* will be fluent
   45: 23 by me every *t* will swear.
   50: 4 has given me an instructed *t*,
   59: 3 and your *t* mutters wicked things.
Lk 16: 24 of his finger in water and cool my *t*,
Ro 14: 11 every *t* will confess to God.'
1Co 14: 2 speaks in a *t* does not speak to men
   14: 4 He who speaks in a *t* edifies himself
   14: 9 intelligible words with your *t*,
   14: 13 in a *t* should pray that he may
   14: 19 than ten thousand words in a *t*.
   14: 26 revelation, a *t* or an interpretation.
   14: 27 If anyone speaks in a *t*, two—
Php 2: 11 every *t* confess that Jesus Christ is
Jas   1: 26 does not keep a tight rein on his *t*,
    3: 5 Likewise the *t* is a small part
    3: 8 but no man can tame the *t*.
1Jn 3: 18 or *t* but with actions and in truth.

TONGUES (TONGUE)

Ps 12: 4 ''We will triumph with our *t*;
   126: 2 our *t* with songs of joy.
Isa 28: 11 with foreign lips and strange *t*
   66: 18 and gather all nations and *t*,
Jer 23: 31 the prophets who wag their own *t*
Mk 16: 17 in new *t*; they will pick up snakes
Ac   2: 3 to be *t* of fire that separated
    2: 4 and began to speak in other *t*
  10: 46 For they heard them speaking in *t*
  19: 6 and they spoke in *t* and prophesied

TONGUES

Ac 13: 33 *t* I have become your Father.'
Heb 1: 5 *t* I have become your Father''?
    3: 7 ''*T*, if you hear his voice,
    3: 13 daily, as long as it is called *T*,
    5: 5 *t* I have become your Father.''
   13: 8 Christ is the same yesterday and *t*

TOIL (TOILED TOILING)

Ge   3: 17 through painful *t* you will eat of it

TOILED (TOIL)

2Co 11: 27 and *t* and have often gone

TOILING (TOIL)

2Th 3: 8 *t* so that we would not be a burden

TOLERANCE* (TOLERATE)

Ro   2: 4 for the riches of his kindness, *t*

TOLERATE (TOLERANCE)

Hab 1: 13 you cannot *t* wrong.
Rev 2: 2 that you cannot *t* wicked men,

TOMB

Mt 27: 65 make the *t* as secure as you know
Lk 24: 2 the stone rolled away from the *t*,

TOMORROW

Pr 27: 1 Do not boast about *t*,
Isa 22: 13 ''for *t* we die!''
Mt   6: 34 Therefore do not worry about *t*,
1Co 15: 32 for *t* we die.''
Jas   4: 13 ''Today or *t* we will go to this

Ro 3: 13 their *t* practice deceit.''
1Co 12: 10 still another the interpretation of *t*.
12: 28 speaking in different kinds of *t*.
12: 30 Do all speak in *t*? Do all interpret?
13: 1 If I speak in the *t* of men
13: 8 where there are *t*, they will be
14: 5 greater than one who speaks in *t*,
14: 18 speak in *t* more than all of you.
14: 21 ''Through men of strange *t*
14: 39 and do not forbid speaking in *t*.

TOOK (TAKE)

Isa 53: 4 Surely he *t* up our infirmities
Mt 8: 17 ''He *t* up our infirmities
26: 26 they were eating, Jesus *t* bread,
26: 27 Then he *t* the cup, gave thanks
1Co 11: 23 the night he was betrayed, *t* bread,
11: 25 after supper he *t* the cup, saying,
Php 3: 12 for which Christ Jesus *t* hold of me.

TOOTH (TEETH)

Ex 21: 24 eye for eye, *t* for *t*, hand for hand,
Mt 5: 38 'Eye for eye, and *t* for *t*.'

TOP

Dt 28: 13 you will always be at the *t*,
Isa 1: 6 of your foot to the *t* of your head
Mt 27: 51 torn in two from *t* to bottom.

TORMENT (TORMENTED TORMENTORS)

Lk 16: 28 also come to this place of *t*.'
2Co 12: 7 a messenger of Satan, to *t* me.

TORMENTED (TORMENT)

Rev 20: 10 They will be *t* day and night

TORMENTORS (TORMENT)

Ps 137: 3 our *t* demanded songs of joy;

TORN

Gal 4: 15 you would have *t* out your eyes
Php 1: 23 I do not know! I am *t*

TORTURED*

Heb 11: 35 Others were *t* and refused

TOSSED (TOSSING)

Eph 4: 14 *t* back and forth by the waves,
Jas 1: 6 of the sea, blown and *t* by the wind.

TOSSING (TOSSED)

Isa 57: 20 But the wicked are like the *t* sea,

TOUCH (TOUCHED TOUCHES)

Ge 3: 3 you must not *t* it, or you will die.' ''
Ex 19: 12 go up the mountain or *t* the foot
Ps 105: 15 ''Do not *t* my anointed ones;
Mt 9: 21 If I only *t* his cloak, I will be healed
Lk 18: 15 babies to Jesus to have him *t* them.
24: 39 It is I myself! *T* me and see;
2Co 6: 17 *T* no unclean thing,
Col 2: 21 Do not taste! Do not *t*!'' ?

TOUCHED (TOUCH)

1Sa 10: 26 men whose hearts God had *t*.
Isa 6: 7 With it he *t* my mouth and said,
Mt 14: 36 and all who *t* him were healed.
Lk 8: 45 ''Who *t* me?'' Jesus asked.
1Jn 1: 1 looked at and our hands have *t*—

TOUCHES (TOUCH)

Ex 19: 12 Whoever *t* the mountain shall
Zec 2: 8 for whoever *t* you *t* the apple

TOWER

Ge 11: 4 with a *t* that reaches to the heavens
Pr 18: 10 of the LORD is a strong *t*;

TOWN (TOWNS)

Mt 2: 23 and lived in a *t* called Nazareth.

TOWNS (TOWN)

Nu 35: 2 to give the Levites *t* to live
35: 15 These six *t* will be a place of refuge
Jer 11: 13 as many gods as you have *t*,
Mt 9: 35 Jesus went through all the *t*

TRACING*

Ro 11: 33 and his paths beyond *t* out!

TRACK

Job 14: 16 but not keep *t* of my sin.

TRADERS (TRADING)

1Ti 1: 10 for slave *t* and liars and perjurers—

TRADING (TRADERS)

1Ki 10: 22 The king had a fleet of *t* ships at sea
Pr 31: 18 She sees that her *t* is profitable,

TRADITION (TRADITIONS)

Mt 15: 2 ''Why do your disciples break the *t*
15: 6 word of God for the sake of your *t*.
Mk 7: 13 by your *t* that you have handed
Col 2: 8 which depends on human *t*

TRADITIONS (TRADITION)

Mk 7: 8 are holding on to the *t* of men.''
Gal 1: 14 zealous for the *t* of my fathers.

TRAIL

1Ti 5: 24 the sins of others *t* behind them.

TRAIN* (TRAINED TRAINING)

Ps 68: 18 you led captives in your *t*;
Pr 22: 6 *T* a child in the way he should go,
Isa 2: 4 nor will they *t* for war anymore.
6: 1 the *t* of his robe filled the temple.
Mic 4: 3 nor will they *t* for war anymore.
Eph 4: 8 he led captives in his *t*
1Ti 4: 7 rather, *t* yourself to be godly.
Tit 2: 4 they can *t* the younger women

TRAINED (TRAIN)

Lk 6: 40 everyone who is fully *t* will be like
Ac 22: 3 Under Gamaliel I was thoroughly *t*
2Co 11: 6 I may not be a *t* speaker,
Heb 5: 14 by constant use have *t* themselves
12: 11 for those who have been *t* by it.

TRAINING* (TRAIN)

1Co 9: 25 in the games goes into strict *t*.
Eph 6: 4 up in the *t* and instruction
1Ti 4: 8 For physical *t* is of some value,
2Ti 3: 16 correcting and *t* in righteousness,

TRAITOR (TRAITORS)

Lk 6: 16 and Judas Iscariot, who became a *t*.
Jn 18: 5 Judas the *t* was standing there

TRAITORS (TRAITOR)

Ps 59: 5 show no mercy to wicked *t*.

TRAMPLE (TRAMPLED)

Joel 3: 13 Come, *t* the grapes,
Am 2: 7 They *t* on the heads of the poor
5: 11 You *t* on the poor
8: 4 Hear this, you who *t* the needy
Mt 7: 6 they may *t* them under their feet,
Lk 10: 19 I have given you authority to *t*

TRAMPLED (TRAMPLE)

Isa 63: 6 I *t* the nations in my anger;
Lk 21: 24 Jerusalem will be *t*
Heb 10: 29 to be punished who has *t* the Son
Rev 14: 20 They were *t* in the winepress

TRANCE*

Ac 10: 10 was being prepared, he fell into a *t*.
11: 5 and in a *t* I saw a vision.
22: 17 into a *t* and saw the Lord speaking.

TRANQUILLITY*

Ecc 4: 6 Better one handful with *t*

TRANSACTIONS*

Ru 4: 7 method of legalizing *t* in Israel.)

TRANSCENDS*

Php 4: 7 which *t* all understanding,

TRANSFIGURED*

Mt 17: 2 There he was *t* before them.
Mk 9: 2 There he was *t* before them.

TRANSFORM* (TRANSFORMED)

Php 3: 21 will *t* our lowly bodies

TRANSFORMED (TRANSFORM)

Ro 12: 2 be *t* by the renewing of your mind.
2Co 3: 18 are being *t* into his likeness

TRANSGRESSED* (TRANSGRESSION)

Da 9: 11 All Israel has *t* your law

TRANSGRESSION* (TRANSGRESSED TRANSGRESSIONS TRANSGRESSORS)

Ps 19: 13 innocent of great *t*.
Isa 53: 8 for the *t* of my people he was
Da 9: 24 and your holy city to finish *t*,
Mic 1: 5 All this is because of Jacob's *t*,
1: 5 What is Jacob's *t*?
3: 8 to declare to Jacob his *t*,
6: 7 Shall I offer my firstborn for my *t*,
7: 18 who pardons sin and forgives the *t*
Ro 4: 15 where there is no law there is no *t*.
11: 11 Rather, because of their *t*,
11: 12 if their *t* means riches for the world

TRANSGRESSIONS* (TRANSGRESSION)

Ps 32: 1 whose *t* are forgiven,
32: 5 my *t* to the LORD''—
39: 8 Save me from all my *t*;
51: 1 blot out my *t*.
51: 3 For I know my *t*,
65: 3 you atoned for our *t*.
103: 12 so far has he removed our *t* from us
Isa 43: 25 your *t*, for my own sake,
50: 1 of your *t* your mother was sent
53: 5 But he was pierced for our *t*,
Mic 1: 13 for the *t* of Israel
Ro 7 whose *t* are forgiven,
Gal 3: 19 because of *t* until the Seed to whom
Eph 2: 1 you were dead in your *t* and sins,
2: 5 even when we were dead in *t*—

TRANSGRESSORS* (TRANSGRESSION)

Ps 51: 13 Then I will teach *t* your ways,
Isa 53: 12 and made intercession for the *t*.
53: 12 and was numbered with the *t*.
Lk 22: 37 'And he was numbered with the *t*';

TRAP (TRAPPED TRAPS)

Ps 69: 22 may it become retribution and a *t*.
Pr 20: 25 a *t* for a man to dedicate something
28: 10 will fall into his own *t*,
Isa 8: 14 a *t* and a snare.
Mt 22: 15 and laid plans to *t* him in his words.
Lk 21: 34 close on you unexpectedly like a *t*.
Ro 11: 9 their table become a snare and a *t*,
1Ti 3: 7 into disgrace and into the devil's *t*.
6: 9 and a *t* and into many foolish
2Ti 2: 26 and escape from the *t* of the devil,

TRAPPED (TRAP)

Pr 6: 2 if you have been *t* by what you said
12: 13 An evil man is *t* by his sinful talk,

TRAPS (TRAP)

Jos 23: 13 they will become snares and *t*
La 4: 20 was caught in their *t*.

TRAVEL (TRAVELER)

Pr 4: 15 Avoid it, do not *t* on it;
Mt 23: 15 You *t* over land and sea

TRAVELER (TRAVEL)

Job 31: 32 door was always open to the *t*—
Jer 14: 8 like a *t* who stays only a night?

TREACHEROUS (TREACHERY)

Ps 25: 3 who are *t* without excuse.
2Ti 3: 4 not lovers of the good, *t*, rash,

TREACHERY (TREACHEROUS)

Isa 59: 13 rebellion and *t* against the LORD,

TREAD (TREADING TREADS)

Ps 91: 13 You will *t* upon the lion

TREADING (TREAD)

Dt 25: 4 an ox while it is *t* out the grain.

1Co 9: 9 an ox while it is *t* out the grain.''
1Ti 5: 18 the ox while it is *t* out the grain,''

TREADS (TREAD)

Rev 19: 15 He *t* the winepress of the fury

TREASURE (TREASURED TREASURES TREASURY)

Pr   2: 4 and search for it as for hidden *t,*
Isa 33: 6 of the LORD is the key to this *t.*
Mt   6: 21 For where your *t* is, there your
     13: 44 of heaven is like *t* hidden in a field.
Lk 12: 33 a *t* in heaven that will not be
2Co 4: 7 But we have this *t* in jars of clay
1Ti 6: 19 In this way they will lay up *t*

TREASURED (TREASURE)

Ex 19: 5 you will be my *t* possession.
Dt   7: 6 to be his people, his *t* possession.
     26: 18 his *t* possession as he promised,
Job 23: 12 I have *t* the words
Mal 3: 17 when I make up my *t* possession.
Lk   2: 19 But Mary *t* up all these things
      2: 51 But his mother *t* all these things

TREASURES (TREASURE)

1Ch 29: 3 my God I now give my personal *t*
Pr 10: 2 Ill-gotten *t* are of no value,
Mt   6: 19 up for yourselves *t* on earth,
     13: 52 out of his storeroom new *t*
Col 2: 3 in whom are hidden all the *t*
Heb 11: 26 of greater value than the *t* of Egypt,

TREASURY (TREASURE)

Mk 12: 43 more into the *t* than all the others.

TREAT (TREATED TREATING TREATMENT)

Lev 22: 2 sons to *t* with respect the sacred
Ps 103: 10 he does not *t* us as our sins deserve
Mt 18: 17 *t* him as you would a pagan
     18: 35 my heavenly Father will *t* each
Eph 6: 9 *t* your slaves in the same way.
1Th 5: 20 do not *t* prophecies with contempt.
1Ti 5: 1 *T* younger men as brothers,
1Pe 3: 7 and *t* them with respect

TREATED (TREAT)

Lev 19: 34 The alien living with you must be *t*
     25: 40 He is to be *t* as a hired worker
1Sa 24: 17 ''You have *t* me well, but I have
Heb 10: 29 who has *t* as an unholy thing

TREATING (TREAT)

Ge 18: 25 *t* the righteous and the wicked
Heb 12: 7 as discipline; God is *t* you as sons.

TREATMENT (TREAT)

Col 2: 23 and their harsh *t* of the body,

TREATY

Ex 34: 12 not to make a *t* with those who live
Dt   7: 2 Make no *t* with them, and show
     23: 6 Do not seek a *t* of friendship with them

TREE (TREES)

Ge   2: 9 and the *t* of the knowledge of good
      2: 9 of the garden were the *t* of life
Dt 21: 23 hung on a *t* is under God's curse.
2Sa 18: 9 Absalom's head got caught in the *t.*
1Ki 14: 23 and under every spreading *t.*
Ps   1: 3 He is like a *t* planted by streams
     52: 8 But I am like an olive *t*
     92: 12 righteous will flourish like a palm *t,*
Pr   3: 18 She is a *t* of life to those who
     11: 30 of the righteous is a *t* of life,
     27: 18 He who tends a fig *t* will eat its fruit
Isa 65: 22 For as the days of a *t,*
Jer 17: 8 He will be like a *t* planted
Eze 17: 24 I the LORD bring down the tall *t*
Da   4: 10 before me stood a *t* in the middle
Mic 4: 4 and under his own fig *t,*
Zec 3: 10 to sit under his vine and fig *t,*'
Mt   3: 10 every *t* that does not produce good
     12: 33 for a *t* is recognized by its fruit.
Lk 19: 4 climbed a sycamore-fig *t* to see him
Ac   5: 30 killed by hanging him on a *t.*
Ro 11: 24 be grafted into their own olive *t!*

Gal 3: 13 is everyone who is hung on a *t.*''
Jas 3: 12 My brothers, can a fig *t* bear olives,
1Pe 2: 24 sins in his body on the *t,*
Rev 2: 7 the right to eat from the *t* of life,
     22: 2 side of the river stood the *t* of life,
     22: 14 they may have the right to the *t*
     22: 19 from him his share in the *t* of life

TREES (TREE)

Jdg 9: 8 One day the *t* went out
Ps 96: 12 Then all the *t* of the forest will sing
Isa 55: 12 and all the *t* of the field
Mt   3: 10 The ax is already at the root of the *t*
Mk   8: 24 they look like *t* walking around.''
Jude   : 12 autumn *t,* without fruit

TREMBLE (TREMBLED TREMBLES TREMBLING)

Ex 15: 14 The nations will hear and *t;*
1Ch 16: 30 *T* before him, all the earth!
Ps 114: 7 *T,* O earth, at the presence
Jer 5: 22 ''Should you not *t* in my presence?
Eze 38: 20 of the earth will *t* at my presence.
Joel 2: 1 Let all who live in the land *t,*
Hab 3: 6 he looked, and made the nations *t.*

TREMBLED (TREMBLE)

Ex 19: 16 Everyone in the camp *t.*
     20: 18 in smoke, they *t* with fear.
2Sa 22: 8 ''The earth *t* and quaked,
Ac   7: 32 Moses *t* with fear and did not dare

TREMBLES (TREMBLE)

Ps 97: 4 the earth sees and *t.*
    104: 32 he who looks at the earth, and it *t,*
Isa 66: 2 and *t* at my word.
Jer 10: 10 When he is angry, the earth *t;*
Na   1: 5 The earth *t* at his presence,

TREMBLING (TREMBLE)

Ps   2: 11 and rejoice with *t.*
Da 10: 10 set me *t* on my hands and knees.
Php 2: 12 out your salvation with fear and *t,*
Heb 12: 21 terrifying that Moses said, ''I am *t*

TRESPASS* (TRESPASSES)

Ro   5: 15 But the gift is not like the *t.*
      5: 15 died by the *t* of the one man,
      5: 17 For if, by the *t* of the one man,
      5: 18 result of one *t* was condemnation
      5: 20 added so that the *t* might increase.

TRESPASSES* (TRESPASS)

Ro   5: 16 but the gift followed many *t*

TRIAL (TRIALS)

Ps 37: 33 condemned when brought to *t.*
Mk 13: 11 you are arrested and brought to *t,*
2Co 8: 2 most severe *t,* their overflowing
Jas 1: 12 is the man who perseveres under *t,*
1Pe 4: 12 at the painful *t* you are suffering,
Rev 3: 10 to keep you from the hour of *t* that is going

TRIALS* (TRIAL)

Dt   7: 19 saw with your own eyes the great *t,*
     29: 3 own eyes you saw those great *t,*
Lk 22: 28 who have stood by me in my *t.*
1Th 3: 3 one would be unsettled by these *t.*
2Th 1: 4 the persecutions and *t* you are
Jas 1: 2 whenever you face *t* of many kinds,
1Pe 1: 6 had to suffer grief in all kinds of *t.*
2Pe 2: 9 how to rescue godly men from *t*

TRIBE (HALF-TRIBE TRIBES)

Heb 7: 13 no one from that *t* has ever served
Rev 5: 5 See, the Lion of the *t* of Judah,
      5: 9 God from every *t* and language
     11: 9 men from every people, *t,*
     14: 6 to every nation, *t,* language

TRIBES (TRIBE)

Ge 49: 28 All these are the twelve *t* of Israel,
Mt 19: 28 judging the twelve *t* of Israel.

TRIBULATION*

Rev 7: 14 who have come out of the great *t;*

TRICKERY*

Ac 13: 10 full of all kinds of deceit and *t,*

2Co 12: 16 fellow that I am, I caught you by *t!*

TRIED (TRY)

Ps 73: 16 When I *t* to understand all this,
     95: 9 where your fathers tested and *t* me,
Heb 3: 9 where your fathers tested and *t* me

TRIES (TRY)

Lk 17: 33 Whoever *t* to keep his life will lose

TRIMMED

Mt 25: 7 virgins woke up and *t* their lamps.

TRIUMPH (TRIUMPHAL TRIUMPHED TRIUMPHING TRIUMPHS)

Ps 25: 2 nor let my enemies *t* over me.
     54: 7 my eyes have looked in *t*
    112: 8 in the end he will look in *t*
    118: 7 I will look in *t* on my enemies.
Pr 28: 12 When the righteous *t,* there is great
Isa 42: 13 and will *t* over his enemies.

TRIUMPHAL* (TRIUMPH)

Isa 60: 11 their kings led in *t* procession.
2Co 2: 14 us in *t* procession in Christ

TRIUMPHED (TRIUMPH)

Rev 5: 5 of Judah, the Root of David, has *t.*

TRIUMPHING* (TRIUMPH)

Col 2: 15 of them, *t* over them by the cross.

TRIUMPHS* (TRIUMPH)

Jas 2: 13 Mercy *t* over judgment! What

TROUBLE (TROUBLED TROUBLES)

Ge 41: 51 God has made me forget all my *t*
Jos 7: 25 Why have you brought this *t* on us?
Job 2: 10 good from God, and not *t?*''
      5: 7 Yet man is born to *t*
     14: 1 is of few days and full of *t.*
     42: 11 him over all the *t* the LORD had
Ps   7: 14 conceives *t* gives birth
      7: 16 The *t* he causes recoils on himself;
      9: 9 a stronghold in times of *t.*
     10: 14 But you, O God, do see *t* and grief;
     22: 11 for *t* is near
     27: 5 For in the day of *t*
     32: 7 you will protect me from *t*
     37: 39 he is their stronghold in time of *t.*
     41: 1 LORD delivers him in times of *t.*
     46: 1 an ever-present help in *t.*
     50: 15 and call upon me in the day of *t;*
     59: 16 my refuge in times of *t.*
     66: 14 spoke when I was in *t.*
     86: 7 In the day of my *t* I will call to you,
     91: 15 I will be with him in *t,*
    107: 6 to the LORD in their *t,*
    107: 13 they cried to the LORD in their *t,*
    116: 3 I was overcome by *t* and sorrow.
    119:143 *T* and distress have come upon me,
    138: 7 Though I walk in the midst of *t,*
    143: 11 righteousness, bring me out of *t.*
Pr 11: 8 righteous man is rescued from *t,*
     11: 17 a cruel man brings *t* on himself
     11: 29 He who brings *t* on his family will
     12: 13 but a righteous man escapes *t.*
     12: 21 but the wicked have their fill of *t.*
     15: 27 A greedy man brings *t* to his family
     19: 23 one rests content, untouched by *t.*
     22: 8 He who sows wickedness reaps *t,*
     24: 10 If you falter in times of *t,*
     25: 19 on the unfaithful in times of *t.*
     28: 14 he who hardens his heart falls into *t*
Jer 30: 7 It will be a time of *t* for Jacob,
Na   1: 7 a refuge in times of *t.*
Zep 1: 15 a day of *t* and ruin,
Mt   6: 34 Each day has enough *t* of its own.
     13: 21 When *t* or persecution comes
Jn 16: 33 In this world you will have *t.*
Ro   8: 35 Shall *t* or hardship or persecution
2Co 1: 4 those in any *t* with the comfort we
2Th 1: 7 to those who trouble you
Jas 5: 13 one of you in *t?* He should pray.

TROUBLED (TROUBLE)

Ps 38: 18 I am *t* by my sin.
Isa 38: 14 I am *t;* O Lord, come to my aid!''

Mk 14: 33 began to be deeply distressed and *t.*
Jn 14: 1 "Do not let your hearts be *t.*
　　14: 27 Do not let your hearts be *t*
2Th 1: 7 and give relief to you who are *t,*

TROUBLES (TROUBLE)

Ps 34: 6 he saved him out of all his *t.*
　　34: 17 he delivers them from all their *t.*
　　34: 19 A righteous man may have many *t,*
　　40: 12 For *t* without number surround me
　　54: 7 he has delivered me from all my *t,*
1Co 7: 28 those who marry will face many *t*
2Co 1: 4 who comforts us in all our *t,*
　　4: 17 and momentary *t* are achieving
　　6: 4 in *t,* hardships and distresses;
　　7: 4 in all our *t* my joy knows no bounds
Php 4: 14 good of you to share in my *t.*

TRUE (TRUTH)

Nu 11: 23 not what I say will come *t* for you.''
　　12: 7 this is not *t* of my servant Moses;
Dt 18: 22 does not take place or come *t,*
Jos 23: 15 of the LORD your God has come *t*
1Sa 9: 6 and everything he says comes *t.*
1Ki 10: 6 and your wisdom is *t.*
2Ch 6: 17 your servant David come *t.*
　　15: 3 was without the *t* God,
Ps 33: 4 of the LORD is right and *t;*
　　119:142 and your law is *t.*
　　119:151 and all your commands are *t.*
　　119:160 All your words are *t;*
Pr 8: 7 My mouth speaks what is *t,*
　　22: 21 teaching you *t* and reliable words,
Jer 10: 10 But the LORD is the *t* God;
　　28: 9 only if his prediction comes *t.*''
Eze 33: 33 ''When all this comes *t*—
Lk 16: 11 who will trust you with *t* riches?
Jn 1: 9 The *t* light that gives light
　　4: 23 when the *t* worshipers will worship
　　6: 32 Father who gives you the *t* bread
　　7: 28 on my own, but he who sent me is *t*
　　15: 1 ''I am the *t* vine, and my Father is
　　17: 3 the only *t* God, and Jesus Christ,
　　19: 35 testimony, and his testimony is *t.*
　　21: 24 We know that his testimony is *t.*
Ac 10: 34 ''I now realize how *t* it is that God
　　11: 23 all to remain *t* to the Lord
　　14: 22 them to remain *t* to the faith.
　　16: 23 See he said if even if Paul said was *t.*
Ro 3: 4 Let God be *t,* and every man a liar.
Php 4: 8 whatever is *t,* whatever is noble,
1Jn 2: 8 and the *t* light is already shining.
　　5: 20 He is the *t* God and eternal life.
Rev 19: 9 ''These are the *t* words of God.''
　　22: 6 These words are trustworthy and *t.*

TRUMPET (TRUMPETS)

Isa 27: 13 And in that day a great *t* will sound
Eze 33: 5 Since he heard the sound of the *t*
Zec 9: 14 Sovereign LORD will sound the *t;*
Mt 24: 31 send his angels with a loud *t* call,
1Co 14: 8 if the *t* does not sound a clear call,
　　15: 52 For the *t* will sound, the dead will
1Th 4: 16 and with the *t* call of God,
Rev 8: 7 The first angel sounded his *t,*

TRUMPETS (TRUMPET)

Jdg 7: 19 They blew their *t* and broke the jars
Rev 8: 2 and to them were given seven *t.*

TRUST* (ENTRUST ENTRUSTED TRUSTED TRUSTFULLY TRUSTING TRUSTS TRUSTWORTHY)

Ex 14: 31 put their *t* in him and in Moses his
　　19: 9 and will always put their *t* in you.''
Nu 20: 12 ''Because you did not *t*
Dt 1: 32 you did not *t* in the LORD your
　　9: 23 You did not *t* him or obey him.
　　28: 52 walls in which you *t* fall down.
Jdg 11: 20 did not *t* Israel to pass
2Ki 17: 14 who did not *t* in the LORD their
　　18: 30 to *t* in the LORD when he says,
1Ch 5: 22 to their positions of *t* by David
Job 4: 18 If God places no *t* in his servants,
　　15: 15 If God places no *t* in his holy ones,
　　31: 24 ''If I have put my *t* in gold
　　39: 12 Can you *t* him to bring
Ps 4: 5 and *t* in the LORD.

Ps 9: 10 Those who know your name will *t*
　　13: 5 But I *t* in your unfailing love;
　　20: 7 Some *t* in chariots and some
　　20: 7 we *t* in the name of the LORD our
　　22: 4 In you our fathers put their *t;*
　　22: 9 you made me *t* in you
　　25: 2 I lift up my soul; in you I *t,*
　　31: 6 I *t* in the LORD.
　　31: 14 But I *t* in you, O LORD;
　　33: 21 for we *t* in his holy name.
　　37: 3 *T* in the LORD and do good;
　　37: 5 *t* in him and he will do this:
　　40: 3 and put their *t* in the LORD.
　　40: 4 who makes the LORD his *t,*
　　44: 6 I do not *t* in my bow,
　　49: 6 those who *t* in their wealth
　　49: 13 of those who *t* in themselves,
　　52: 8 I *t* in God's unfailing love
　　55: 23 But as for me, I *t* in you.
　　56: 3 I will *t* in you.
　　56: 4 in God I *t;* I will not be afraid.
　　56: 11 in God I *t;* I will not be afraid.
　　62: 8 *T* in him at all times, O people;
　　62: 10 Do not *t* in extortion
　　78: 7 Then they would put their *t* in God
　　78: 22 or *t* in his deliverance.
　　91: 2 my God, in whom I *t.*''
　　115: 8 and so will all who *t* in them.
　　115: 9 O house of Israel, *t* in the LORD—
　　115: 10 O house of Aaron, *t* in the LORD
　　115: 11 You who fear him, *t* in the LORD
　　118: 8 than to *t* in man.
　　118: 9 than to *t* in princes.
　　119: 42 for I *t* in your word.
　　125: 1 Those who *t* in the LORD are like
　　135: 18 and so will all who *t* in them.
　　143: 8 for I have put my *t* in you.
　　146: 3 Do not put your *t* in princes,
Pr 3: 5 *T* in the LORD with all your heart
　　21: 22 the stronghold in which they *t.*
　　22: 19 So that your *t* may be in the LORD
Isa 8: 17 I will put my *t* in him.
　　12: 2 I will *t* and not be afraid.
　　26: 4 *T* in the LORD forever,
　　30: 15 in quietness and *t* is your strength,
　　31: 1 who *t* in the multitude
　　36: 15 to *t* in the LORD when he says,
　　42: 17 But those who *t* in idols,
　　50: 10 *t* in the name of the LORD
Jer 2: 37 LORD has rejected those you *t;*
　　5: 17 the fortified cities in which you *t.*
　　7: 4 Do not *t* in deceptive words
　　7: 14 the temple you *t* in, the place I gave
　　9: 4 do not *t* your brothers.
　　12: 6 Do not *t* them,
　　28: 15 you have persuaded this nation to *t*
　　39: 18 you *t* in me, declares the LORD.' ''
　　48: 7 Since you *t* in your deeds
　　49: 4 you *t* in your riches and say,
　　49: 11 Your widows too can *t* in me.''
Mic 7: 5 Do not *t* a neighbor;
Na 1: 7 He cares for those who *t* in him,
Zep 3: 2 She does not *t* in the LORD,
　　3: 12 who *t* in the name of the LORD.
Lk 16: 11 who will *t* you with true riches?
Jn 12: 36 Put your *t* in the light
　　14: 1 *T* in God; *t* also in me.
Ac 14: 23 Lord in whom they had put their *t.*
Ro 15: 13 you with all joy and peace as you *t*
1Co 4: 2 been given a *t* must prove faithful.
　　9: 17 discharging the *t* committed
2Co 1: 9 I *t* that you will discover that we
Heb 2: 13 ''I will put my *t* in him.''

TRUSTED* (TRUST)

1Sa 27: 12 Achish *t* David and said to himself,
2Ki 18: 5 Hezekiah *t* in the LORD, the God
1Ch 5: 20 their prayers, because they *t*
Job 12: 20 He silences the lips of *t* advisers
Ps 5: 9 from their mouth can be *t;*
　　22: 4 they *t* and you delivered them.
　　22: 5 in you they *t* and were not
　　26: 1 I have *t* in the LORD
　　41: 9 Even my close friend, whom I *t,*
　　52: 7 but *t* in his great wealth
Isa 20: 5 Those who *t* in Cush and boasted
　　25: 9 This is the LORD, we *t* in him;
　　25: 9 we *t* in him, and he saved us.

Isa 47: 10 You have *t* in your wickedness
Jer 13: 25 and *t* in false gods.
　　38: 22 those *t* friends of yours.
　　48: 13 ashamed when they *t* in Bethel.
Eze 16: 15 '' 'But you *t* in your beauty
Da 3: 28 They *t* in him and defied the king's
　　6: 23 because he had *t* in his God.
Lk 11: 22 the armor in which the man *t*
　　16: 10 *t* with very little can also be *t*
Ac 12: 20 a *t* personal servant of the king,
Tit 2: 10 but to show that they can be fully *t,*
　　3: 8 so that those who have *t*

TRUSTFULLY* (TRUST)

Pr 3: 29 who lives *t* near you.

TRUSTING* (TRUST)

Job 15: 31 by *t* what is worthless,
Ps 112: 7 his heart is steadfast, *t*
Isa 2: 22 Stop *t* in man,
Jer 7: 8 you are *t* in deceptive words that

TRUSTS* (TRUST)

Job 8: 14 What he *t* in is fragile;
Ps 21: 7 For the king *t* in the LORD;
　　22: 8 ''He *t* in the LORD;
　　28: 7 my heart *t* in him, and I am helped.
　　32: 10 surrounds the man who *t* in him.
　　84: 12 blessed is the man who *t* in you.
　　86: 2 who *t* in you.
Pr 11: 28 Whoever *t* in his riches will fall,
　　16: 20 blessed is he who *t* in the LORD.
　　28: 25 he who *t* in the LORD will prosper.
　　28: 26 He who *t* in himself is a fool,
　　29: 25 whoever *t* in the LORD is kept safe
Isa 26: 3 because he *t* in you.
　　28: 16 one who *t* will never be dismayed.
Jer 17: 5 ''Cursed is the one who *t* in man,
　　17: 7 blessed is the man who *t*
Eze 33: 13 but then he *t* in his righteousness
Hab 2: 18 For he who makes it *t*
Mt 27: 43 He *t* in God.
Ro 4: 5 but *t* God who justifies the wicked,
　　9: 33 one who *t* in him will never be put
　　10: 11 ''Anyone who *t* in him will never
1Co 13: 7 always protects, always *t,*
1Pe 2: 6 and the one who *t* in him

TRUSTWORTHY* (TRUST)

Ex 18: 21 *t* men who hate dishonest gain—
2Sa 7: 28 you are God! Your words are *t,*
Ne 13: 13 these men were considered *t.*
Ps 19: 7 The statutes of the LORD are *t,*
　　111: 7 all his precepts are *t.*
　　119: 86 All your commands are *t;*
　　119:138 they are fully *t.*
Pr 11: 13 but a *t* man keeps a secret.
　　13: 17 but a *t* envoy brings healing.
　　25: 13 is a *t* messenger to those who send
Da 2: 45 and the interpretation is *t.*''
　　6: 4 he was *t* and neither corrupt
Lk 16: 11 So if you have not been *t*
　　16: 12 And if you have not been *t*
　　19: 17 'Because you have been *t*
1Co 7: 25 one who by the Lord's mercy is *t.*
1Ti 1: 15 Here is a *t* saying that deserves full
　　3: 1 Here is a *t* saying: If anyone sets his
　　3: 11 but temperate and *t* in everything.
　　4: 9 This is a *t* saying that deserves full
2Ti 2: 11 Here is a *t* saying:
Tit 1: 9 must hold firmly to the *t* message
　　3: 8 This is a *t* saying.
Rev 21: 5 for these words are *t* and true.
　　22: 6 ''These words are *t* and true.

TRUTH* (TRUE TRUTHFUL TRUTHFULNESS TRUTHS)

Ge 42: 16 tested to see if you are telling the *t.*
1Ki 17: 24 LORD from your mouth is the *t.*''
　　22: 16 the *t* in the name of the LORD?''
2Ch 18: 15 the *t* in the name of the LORD?''
Ps 15: 2 who speaks the *t* from his heart
　　25: 5 guide me in your *t* and teach me,
　　26: 3 and I walk continually in your *t.*
　　31: 5 redeem me, O LORD, the God of *t*
　　40: 10 do not conceal your love and your *t*
　　40: 11 your *t* always protect me.
　　43: 3 Send forth your light and your *t,*

Ps 45: 4 victoriously in behalf of *t*, humility
    51: 6 Surely you desire *t*
    52: 3 than speaking the *t*
    86: 11 and I will walk in your *t;*
    96: 13 and the peoples in his *t*.
  119: 30 I have chosen the way of *t;*
  119: 43 of *t* from my mouth,
  145: 18 to all who call on him in *t*.
Pr 16: 13 they value a man who speaks the *t*.
    23: 23 Buy the *t* and do not sell it;
Isa 45: 19 I, the LORD, speak the *t;*
    48: 1 but not in *t* or righteousness—
    59: 14 *t* has stumbled in the streets,
    59: 15 *T* is nowhere to be found,
    65: 16 will do so by the God of *t;*
    65: 16 will swear by the God of *t*.
Jer   5: 1 who deals honestly and seeks the *t*,
     5: 3 do not your eyes look for *t?*
   7: 28 *T* has perished; it has vanished
     9: 3 it is not by *t*
     9: 5 and no one speaks the *t*.
  26: 15 for in *t* the LORD has sent me
Da   8: 12 and *t* was thrown to the ground.
     9: 13 and giving attention to your *t*.
   10: 21 what is written in the Book of *T*.
   11: 2 "Now then, I tell you the *t:*
Am 5: 10 and despise him who tells the *t*
Zec 8: 3 will be called The City of *T*,
     8: 16 are to do: Speak the *t* to each other,
     8: 19 Therefore love *t* and peace."
Mt 5: 18 I tell you the *t*, until heaven
    5: 26 I tell you the *t*, you will not get out
    6: 2 I tell you the *t*, they have received
    6: 5 I tell you the *t*, they have received
    6: 16 I tell you the *t*, they have received
    8: 10 "I tell you the *t*, I have not found
   10: 15 I tell you the *t*, it will be more
   10: 23 I tell you the *t*, you will not finish
   10: 42 I tell you the *t*, he will certainly not
   11: 11 I tell you the *t:* Among those born
   13: 17 For I tell you the *t*, many prophets
   16: 28 I tell you the *t*, some who are
   17: 20 I tell you the *t*, if you have faith
   18: 3 And he said: "I tell you the *t*,
   18: 13 And if he finds it, I tell you the *t*,
   18: 18 "I tell you the *t*, whatever you bind
   19: 23 to his disciples, "I tell you the *t*,
   19: 28 "I tell you the *t*, at the renewal
   21: 21 Jesus replied, "I tell you the *t*,
   21: 31 Jesus said to them, "I tell you the *t*,
   22: 16 of God in accordance with the *t*.
   23: 36 I tell you the *t*, all this will come
   24: 2 "I tell you the *t*, not one stone here
   24: 34 I tell you the *t*, this generation will
   24: 47 I tell you the *t*, he will put him
   25: 12 'I tell you the *t*, I don't know you.'
   25: 40 The King will reply, 'I tell you the *t*
   25: 45 "He will reply, 'I tell you the *t*,
   26: 13 tell you the *t*, wherever this gospel
   26: 21 "I tell you the *t*, one
   26: 34 "I tell you the *t*," Jesus answered,
Mk 3: 28 I tell you the *t*, all the sins
    5: 33 with fear, told him the whole *t*.
    8: 12 I tell you the *t*, no sign will be given
    9: 1 he said to them, "I tell you the *t*,
    9: 41 I tell you the *t*, anyone who gives
   10: 15 I tell you the *t*, anyone who will not
   10: 29 "I tell you the *t*," Jesus replied,
   11: 23 "I tell you the *t*, if anyone says
   12: 14 of God in accordance with the *t*.
   12: 43 Jesus said, "I tell you the *t*,
   13: 30 I tell you the *t*, this generation will
   14: 9 I tell you the *t*, wherever the gospel
   14: 18 "I tell you the *t*, one
   14: 25 "I tell you the *t*, I will not drink
   14: 30 "I tell you the *t*," Jesus answered,
L   4: 24 "I tell you the *t*," he continued,
    9: 27 I tell you the *t*, some who are
   12: 37 I tell you the *t*, he will dress himself
   12: 44 I tell you the *t*, he will put him
   18: 17 I tell you the *t*, anyone who will not
   18: 29 "I tell you the *t*," Jesus said to them,
   20: 21 of God in accordance with the *t*.
   21: 3 "I tell you the *t*," he said, "this
   21: 32 tell you the *t*, this generation will
   23: 43 answered him, "I tell you the *t*,
Jn   1: 14 from the Father, full of grace and *t*.
    1: 17 and *t* came through Jesus Christ.

Jn   1: 51 "I tell you the *t*, you shall see
    3: 3 "I tell you the *t*, no one can see
    3: 5 Jesus answered, "I tell you the *t*,
    3: 11 I tell you the *t*, we speak
    3: 21 But whoever lives by the *t* comes
    4: 23 worship the Father in spirit and *t*,
    4: 24 must worship in spirit and in *t*."
    5: 19 "I tell you the *t*, the Son can do
    5: 24 "I tell you the *t*, whoever hears my
    5: 25 I tell you the *t*, a time is coming
    5: 33 and he has testified to the *t*.
    6: 26 "I tell you the *t*, you are looking
    6: 32 Jesus said to them, "I tell you the *t*,
    6: 47 I tell you the *t*, he who believes has
    6: 53 Jesus said to them, "I tell you the *t*,
    7: 18 the one who sent him is a man of *t;*
    8: 32 Then you will know the *t*,
    8: 32 and the *t* will set you free."
    8: 34 Jesus replied, "I tell you the *t*,
    8: 40 who has told you the *t* that I heard
    8: 44 to the *t*, for there is no *t* in him.
    8: 45 I tell the *t*, you do not believe me!
    8: 46 I am telling the *t*, why don't you
    8: 51 I tell you the *t*, if a man keeps my
    8: 58 "I tell you the *t*," Jesus answered,
   10: 1 "I tell you the *t*, the man who does
   10: 7 "I tell you the *t*, I am the gate
   12: 24 I tell you the *t*, unless a kernel
   13: 16 I tell you the *t*, no servant is greater
   13: 20 tell you the *t*, whoever accepts
   13: 21 "I tell you the *t*, one of you is going
   13: 38 I tell you the *t*, before the rooster
   14: 6 I am the way and the *t* and the life.
   14: 12 I tell you the *t*, anyone who has
   14: 17 with you forever—the Spirit of *t*.
   15: 26 the Spirit of *t* who goes out
   16: 7 But I tell you the *t:* It is
   16: 13 But when he, the Spirit of *t*, comes,
   16: 13 comes, he will guide you into all *t*.
   16: 20 I tell you the *t*, you will weep
   16: 23 I tell you the *t*, my Father will give
   17: 7 them by the *t;* your word is *t*.
   17: 23 if I spoke the *t*, why did you strike
   18: 37 into the world, to testify to the *t*.
   18: 37 on the side of *t* listens to me."
   18: 38 "What is *t?*" Pilate asked.
   19: 35 He knows that he tells the *t*,
   21: 18 I tell you the *t*, when you were
Ac 20: 30 and distort the *t* in order
   21: 24 everybody will know there is no *t*
   21: 34 commander could not get at the *t*
   24: 8 able to learn the *t* about all these
   28: 25 "The Holy Spirit spoke the *t*
Ro 1: 18 of men who suppress the *t*
    1: 25 They exchanged the *t* of God
    2: 2 who do such things is based on *t*.
    2: 8 who reject the *t* and follow evil,
    2: 20 embodiment of knowledge and *t*—
    9: 1 I speak the *t* in Christ—I am not
   15: 8 of the Jews on behalf of God's *t*,
1Co 5: 8 the bread of sincerity and *t*.
   13: 6 in evil but rejoices with the *t*.
2Co 4: 2 setting forth the *t* plainly we
   11: 10 As surely as the *t* of Christ is in me,
   12: 6 because I would be speaking the *t*.
   13: 8 against the *t*, but only for the *t*.
Gal 2: 5 so that the *t* of the gospel might
    2: 14 in line with the *t* of the gospel,
    4: 16 enemy by telling you the *t?*
    5: 7 and kept you from obeying the *t?*
Eph 1: 13 when you heard the word of *t*,
    4: 15 Instead, speaking the *t* in love,
    4: 21 him in accordance with the *t* that is
    5: 9 and *t*) and find out what pleases
    6: 14 with the belt of *t* buckled
Col 1: 5 heard about in the word of *t*,
    1: 6 understood God's grace in all its *t*.
2Th 2: 10 because they refused to love the *t*
    2: 12 who have not believed the *t*
    2: 13 and through belief in the *t*.
1Ti 2: 4 to come to a knowledge of the *t*.
    2: 7 I am telling the *t*, I am not lying—
    3: 15 the pillar and foundation of the *t*.
    4: 3 who believe and who know the *t*.
    6: 5 who have been robbed of the *t*
2Ti 2: 15 correctly handles the word of *t*.
    2: 18 have wandered away from the *t*.
    2: 25 them to a knowledge of the *t*,

2Ti 3: 7 never able to acknowledge the *t*.
    3: 8 so also these men oppose the *t*—
    4: 4 will turn their ears away from the *t*
Tit 1: 1 the knowledge of the *t* that leads
    1: 14 of those who reject the *t*.
Heb 10: 26 received the knowledge of the *t*,
Jas 1: 18 birth through the word of *t*,
    3: 14 do not boast about it or deny the *t*.
    5: 19 of you should wander from the *t*
1Pe 1: 22 by obeying the *t* so that you have
2Pe 1: 12 established in the *t* you now have.
    2: 2 the way of *t* into disrepute.
1Jn 1: 6 we lie and do not live by the *t*.
    1: 8 deceive ourselves and the *t* is not
    2: 4 commands is a liar, and the *t* is not
    2: 8 its *t* is seen in him and you,
    2: 20 and all of you know the *t*.
    2: 21 because no lie comes from the *t*.
    2: 21 because you do not know the *t*,
    3: 18 or tongue but with actions and in *t*.
    3: 19 we know that we belong to the *t*,
    4: 6 is how we recognize the Spirit of *t*
    5: 6 testifies, because the Spirit is the *t*.
2Jn   : 1 whom I love in the *t*—
     : 2 who know the *t*—because of the *t*,
     : 3 will be with us in *t* and love.
     : 4 of your children walking in the *t*,
3Jn   : 1 friend Gaius, whom I love in the *t*.
     : 3 how you continue to walk in the *t*.
     : 3 tell about your faithfulness to the *t*
     : 4 my children are walking in the *t*.
     : 8 we may work together for the *t*.
     : 12 everyone—and even by the *t* itself.

TRUTHFUL* (TRUTH)

Pr 12: 17 A *t* witness gives honest testimony,
   12: 19 *T* lips endure forever,
   12: 22 but he delights in men who are *t*.
   14: 5 A *t* witness does not deceive,
   14: 25 A *t* witness saves lives,
Jer 4: 2 and if in a *t*, just and righteous way
Jn   3: 33 it has certified that God is *t*.
2Co 6: 7 in *t* speech and in the power

TRUTHFULNESS* (TRUTH)

Ro 3: 7 "If my falsehood enhances God's *t*

TRUTHS* (TRUTH)

1Co 2: 13 expressing spiritual *t*
1Ti 3: 9 hold of the deep *t* of the faith
    4: 6 brought up in the *t* of the faith
Heb 5: 12 to teach you the elementary *t*

TRY (TRIED TRIES TRYING)

Ps 26: 2 Test me, O LORD, and *t* me,
Isa 7: 13 enough to *t* the patience of men?
Lk 12: 58 *t* hard to be reconciled to him
   13: 24 will *t* to enter and will not be able
1Co 10: 33 even as I *t* to please everybody
   14: 12 *t* to excel in gifts that build up
2Co 5: 11 is to fear the Lord, we *t*
1Th 5: 15 always *t* to be kind to each other
Tit 2: 9 to *t* to please them, not to talk back

TRYING (TRY)

2Co 5: 12 We are not *t* to commend ourselves
Gal 1: 10 If I were still *t* to please men,
1Th 2: 4 We are not *t* to please men but God
1Pe 1: 11 *t* to find out the time
1Jn 2: 26 things to you about those who are *t*

TUMORS

1Sa 5: 6 them and afflicted them with *t*.

TUNE

1Co 14: 7 anyone know what *t* is being

TUNIC (TUNICS)

Lk 6: 29 do not stop him from taking your *t*.

TUNICS (TUNIC)

Lk 3: 11 "The man with two *t* should share

TURMOIL

Ps 65: 7 and the *t* of the nations.
Pr 15: 16 than great wealth with *t*.

TURN (TURNED TURNING TURNS)

Ex 32: 12 *T* from your fierce anger; relent
Nu 32: 15 If you *t* away from following him,
Dt   5: 32 do not *t* aside to the right
      28: 14 Do not *t* aside from any
      30: 10 and *t* to the LORD your God
Jos   1: 7 do not *t* from it to the right
1Ki   8: 58 May he *t* our hearts to him,
2Ch   7: 14 and *t* from their wicked ways,
      30: 9 He will not *t* his face from you
Job 33: 30 to *t* back his soul from the pit,
Ps   28: 1 do not *t* a deaf ear to me.
      34: 14 *T* from evil and do good;
      51: 13 and sinners will *t* back to you.
      78: 6 they in *t* would tell their children.
     119: 36 *T* my heart toward your statutes
     119:132 *T* to me and have mercy on me,
Pr   22: 6 when he is old he will not *t* from it.
Isa 17: 7 *t* their eyes to the Holy One
      28: 6 to those who *t* back the battle
      29: 16 You *t* things upside down,
      30: 21 Whether you *t* to the right
      45: 22 "*T* to me and be saved,
      55: 7 Let him *t* to the LORD,
Jer 31: 13 I will *t* their mourning
Eze 33: 9 if you do warn the wicked man to *t*
      33: 11 *T!* *T* from your evil ways!
Jnh   3: 9 Who knows but *t* with compassion *t*
Mal   4: 6 He will *t* the hearts of the fathers
Mt   5: 39 you on the right cheek, *t*
      10: 35 For I have come to *t*
Lk   1: 17 to *t* the hearts of the fathers
Jn   12: 40 nor *t* — and I would heal them."
      16: 20 but your grief will *t* to joy.
Ac   3: 19 Repent, then, and *t* to God,
      26: 18 and *t* them from darkness to light,
1Co 14: 31 For you can all prophesy in *t*
      15: 23 But each in his own *t*: Christ,
1Ti   6: 20 *T* away from godless chatter
1Pe   3: 11 He must *t* from evil and do good;

TURNED (TURN)

Dt   23: 5 *t* the curse into a blessing for you,
1Ki 11: 4 his wives *t* his heart
2Ch 15: 4 But in their distress they *t*
Est   9: 1 but now the tables were *t*
       9: 22 when their sorrow was *t* into joy
Ps   14: 3 All have *t* aside,
      30: 11 You *t* my wailing into dancing;
      40: 1 he *t* to me and heard my cry.
Isa   9: 12 for all this, his anger is not *t* away,
      53: 6 each of us has *t* to his own way;
Hos   7: 8 Ephraim is a flat cake not *t* over.
Joel 2: 31 The sun will be *t* to darkness
Lk   22: 32 And when you have *t* back,
Ro   3: 12 All have *t* away,

TURNING (TURN)

2Ki 21: 13 wiping it and *t* it upside down.
Pr   2: 2 *t* your ear to wisdom
      14: 27 *t* a man from the snares of death.

TURNS (TURN)

2Sa 22: 29 the LORD *t* my darkness into light
Pr   15: 1 A gentle answer *t* away wrath,
Isa 44: 25 and *t* it into nonsense.
Jas   5: 20 Whoever *t* a sinner from the error

TWELVE

Ge   35: 22 Jacob had *t* sons: The sons of Leah:
      49: 28 All these are the *t* tribes of Israel.
Mt   10: 1 He called his *t* disciples to him
Lk   9: 17 the disciples picked up *t* basketfuls
Rev 21: 12 the names of the *t* tribes of Israel.
      21: 14 of the *t* apostles of the Lamb.

TWIN (TWINS)

Ge   25: 24 there were *t* boys in her womb.

TWINKLING*

1Co 15: 52 in a flash, in the *t* of an eye,

TWINS (TWIN)

Ro   9: 11 before the *t* were born

TWISTING* (TWISTS)

Pr   30: 33 and as *t* the nose produces blood,

TWISTS (TWISTING)

Ex   23: 8 and *t* the words of the righteous.

TYRANNICAL*

Pr   28: 16 A *t* ruler lacks judgment,

TYRE

Eze 28: 12 a lament concerning the king of *T*
Mt   11: 22 it will be more bearable for *T*

UNAPPROACHABLE*

1Ti   6: 16 immortal and who lives in *u* light,

UNASHAMED*

1Jn   2: 28 and *u* before him at his coming.

UNBELIEF* (UNBELIEVER
UNBELIEVERS UNBELIEVING)

Mk   9: 24 help me overcome my *u!*"
Ro   4: 20 through *u* regarding the promise
      11: 20 they were broken off because of *u*,
      11: 23 And if they do not persist in *u*,
1Ti   1: 13 because I acted in ignorance and *u*.
Heb   3: 19 able to enter, because of their *u*.

UNBELIEVER* (UNBELIEF)

1Co   7: 15 But if the *u* leaves, let him do so.
      10: 27 If some *u* invites you to a meal
      14: 24 if an *u* or someone who does not
2Co   6: 15 have in common with an *u*?
1Ti   5: 8 the faith and is worse than an *u*.

UNBELIEVERS* (UNBELIEF)

Lk   12: 46 and assign him a place with the *u*.
Ro   15: 31 rescued from the *u* in Judea
1Co   6: 6 another — and this in front of *u!*
      14: 22 however, is for believers, not for *u*,
      14: 22 not for believers but for *u*;
      14: 23 do not understand or some *u* come
2Co   4: 4 this age has blinded the minds of *u*,
       6: 14 Do not be yoked together with *u*.

UNBELIEVING* (UNBELIEF)

Mt   17: 17 "O *u* and perverse generation,"
Mk   9: 19 "O *u* generation," Jesus replied,
Lk   9: 41 "O *u* and perverse generation,"
1Co   7: 14 For the *u* husband has been
       7: 14 and the *u* wife has been sanctified
Heb   3: 12 a heart that turns away
Rev 21: 8 But the cowardly, the *u*, the vile,

UNBLEMISHED*

Heb   9: 14 the eternal Spirit offered himself *u*

UNCEASING

Ro   9: 2 and *u* anguish in my heart.

UNCERTAIN*

1Ti   6: 17 which is so *u*, but to put their hope

UNCHANGEABLE* (UNCHANGING)

Heb   6: 18 by two *u* things in which it is

UNCHANGING* (UNCHANGEABLE)

Heb   6: 17 wanted to make the *u* nature

UNCIRCUMCISED

Lev 26: 41 when their *u* hearts are humbled
1Sa 17: 26 Who is this *u* Philistine that he
Jer   9: 26 house of Israel is *u* in heart."
Ac   7: 51 stiff-necked people, with *u* hearts
Ro   4: 11 had by faith while he was still *u*.
1Co   7: 18 Was a man *u* when he was called?
Col   3: 11 circumcised or *u*, barbarian,

UNCIRCUMCISION

1Co   7: 19 is nothing and *u* is nothing.
Gal   5: 6 neither circumcision nor *u* has any

UNCLEAN

Ge   7: 2 and two of every kind of *u* animal,
Lev 10: 10 between the *u* and the clean,
      11: 4 it is ceremonially *u* for you.
      17: 15 he will be ceremonially *u* till evening.
Isa   6: 5 ruined! For I am a man of *u* lips,
      52: 11 Touch no *u* thing!
Mt   15: 11 mouth does not make him '*u*,'
Ac   10: 14 never eaten anything impure or *u*.'"

Ro   14: 14 fully convinced that no food is *u*
2Co   6: 17 Touch no *u* thing,

UNCLOTHED*

2Co   5: 4 because we do not wish to be *u*

UNCONCERNED*

Eze 16: 49 were arrogant, overfed and *u*;

UNCOVERED

Ru   3: 7 Ruth approached quietly, *u* his feet
1Co 11: 5 with her head *u* dishonors her head
      11: 13 to pray to God with her head *u*?
Heb   4: 13 Everything is *u* and laid bare

UNDERGOES* (UNDERGOING)

Heb 12: 8 (and everyone *u* discipline),

UNDERGOING* (UNDERGOES)

1Pe   5: 9 the world are *u* the same kind

UNDERSTAND (UNDERSTANDING
UNDERSTANDS UNDERSTOOD)

Ne   8: 8 the people could *u* what was being
Job 38: 4 Tell me, if you *u*.
      42: 3 Surely I spoke of things I did not *u*,
Ps   14: 2 men to see if there are any who *u*,
      73: 16 When I tried to *u* all this,
     119: 27 Let me *u* the teaching
     119:125 that I may *u* your statutes.
Pr   2: 5 then you will *u* the fear
       2: 9 Then you will *u* what is right
      30: 18 four that I do not *u*:
Ecc   7: 25 to *u* the stupidity of wickedness
      11: 5 so you cannot *u* the work of God.
Isa   6: 10 *u* with their hearts,
      44: 18 know nothing, they *u* nothing;
      52: 15 they have not heard, they will *u*.
Jer 17: 9 Who can *u* it?
      31: 19 after I came to *u*,
Da   9: 25 and *u* this: From the issuing
Hos 14: 9 Who is discerning? He will *u* them.
Mt   13: 15 with their hearts
      24: 15 Daniel — let the reader *u* —
Lk   24: 45 so they could *u* the Scriptures.
Ac   8: 30 "Do you *u* what you are reading?"
Ro   7: 15 I do not *u* what I do.
      15: 21 those who have not heard will *u*."
1Co   2: 12 that we may *u* what God has freely
       2: 14 and he cannot *u* them,
      14: 16 those who do not *u* say "Amen"
Eph   5: 17 but *u* what the Lord's will is.
Heb 11: 3 By faith we *u* that the universe was
2Pe   1: 20 you must *u* that no prophecy
       3: 3 you must *u* that in the last days
       3: 16 some things that are hard to *u*,

UNDERSTANDING (UNDERSTAND)

1Ki   4: 29 and a breadth of *u* as measureless
Job 12: 12 Does not long life bring *u*?
      28: 12 Where does *u* dwell?
      28: 28 and to shun evil is *u*.' "
      32: 8 of the Almighty, that gives him *u*.
      36: 26 How great is God — beyond our *u*!
      37: 5 he does great things beyond our *u*.
Ps 111: 10 follow his precepts have good *u*.
     119: 34 Give me *u*, and I will keep your law
     119:100 I have more *u* than the elders,
     119:104 I gain *u* from your precepts;
     119:130 it gives *u* to the simple.
     136: 5 who by his *u* made the heavens,
     147: 5 his *u* has no limit.
Pr   2: 2 and applying your heart to *u*,
       2: 6 his mouth come knowledge and *u*.
       3: 5 and lean not on your own *u*;
       3: 13 the man who gains *u*,
       4: 5 Get wisdom, get *u*;
       4: 7 Though it cost all you have, get *u*.
       7: 4 and call *u* your kinsman;
       9: 10 knowledge of the Holy One is *u*.
      10: 23 but a man of *u* delights in wisdom.
      11: 12 but a man of *u* holds his tongue.
      14: 29 A patient man has great *u*,
      15: 21 a man of *u* keeps a straight course.
      15: 32 whoever heeds correction gains *u*.
      16: 16 to choose *u* rather than silver!
      16: 22 *U* is a fountain of life
      17: 27 and a man of *u* is even-tempered.

Pr 18: 2 A fool finds no pleasure in *u*
    19: 8 he who cherishes *u* prospers.
    20: 5 but a man of *u* draws them out.
    23: 23 get wisdom, discipline and *u*.
Isa 11: 2 the Spirit of wisdom and of *u*,
    40: 28 and his *u* no one can fathom.
    56: 11 They are shepherds who lack *u;*
Jer 3: 15 you with knowledge and *u*.
    10: 12 stretched out the heavens by his *u*.
Da 5: 12 a keen mind and knowledge and *u*,
    10: 12 that you set your mind to gain *u*
Hos 4: 11 which take away the *u*
Mk 4: 12 and ever hearing but never *u;*
    12: 33 with all your *u* and with all your
Lk 2: 47 who heard him was amazed at his *u*
2Co 6: 6 in purity, *u*, patience and kindness;
Eph 1: 8 on us with all wisdom and *u*.
Php 4: 7 of God, which transcends all *u*,
Col 1: 9 through all spiritual wisdom and *u*,
    2: 2 have the full riches of complete *u*,
1Jn 5: 20 God has come and has given us *u*,

UNDERSTANDS (UNDERSTAND)

1Ch 28: 9 and *u* every motive
Jer 9: 24 that he *u* and knows me,
Mt 13: 23 man who hears the word and *u* it.
Ro 3: 11 there is no one who *u*.
1Ti 6: 4 he is conceited and *u* nothing.

UNDERSTOOD (UNDERSTAND)

Ne 8: 12 they now *u* the words that had
Ps 73: 17 then I *u* their final destiny.
Isa 40: 13 Who has *u* the mind of the LORD,
    40: 21 Have you not *u* since the earth was
Jn 1: 5 but the darkness has not *u* it.
Ro 1: 20 being *u* from what has been made,

UNDESIRABLE*

Jos 24: 15 But if serving the LORD seems *u*

UNDIVIDED*

1Ch 12: 33 to help David with *u* loyalty—
Ps 86: 11 give me an *u* heart,
Eze 11: 19 I will give them an *u* heart
1Co 7: 35 way in *u* devotion to the Lord.

UNDOING

Pr 18: 7 A fool's mouth is his *u*,

UNDYING*

Eph 6: 24 Lord Jesus Christ with an *u* love.

UNEQUALED*

Mt 24: 21 *u* from the beginning of the world
Mk 13: 19 of distress *u* from the beginning,

UNFADING*

1Pe 3: 4 the *u* beauty of a gentle

UNFAILING*

Ex 15: 13 ''In your *u* love you will lead
1Sa 20: 14 But show me *u* kindness like that
2Sa 22: 51 he shows *u* kindness
Ps 6: 4 save me because of your *u* love.
    13: 5 But I trust in your *u* love;
    18: 50 he shows *u* kindness
    21: 7 through the *u* love
    31: 16 save me in your *u* love.
    32: 10 but the LORD's *u* love
    33: 5 the earth is full of his *u* love.
    33: 18 those whose hope is in his *u* love,
    33: 22 May your *u* love rest upon us,
    36: 7 How priceless is your *u* love!
    44: 26 redeem us because of your *u* love.
    48: 9 we meditate on your *u* love.
    51: 1 according to your *u* love;
    52: 8 I trust in God's *u* love
    77: 8 Has his *u* love vanished forever?
    85: 7 Show us your *u* love, O LORD,
    90: 14 in the morning with your *u* love,
    107: 8 thanks to the LORD for his *u* love
    107: 15 thanks to the LORD for his *u* love
    107: 21 to the LORD for his *u* love
    107: 31 to the LORD for his *u* love
    119: 41 May your *u* love come to me,
    119: 76 May your *u* love be my comfort,
    130: 7 for with the LORD is *u* love
    143: 8 bring me word of your *u* love,

Ps 143: 12 In your *u* love, silence my enemies;
    147: 11 who put their hope in his *u* love.
Pr 19: 22 What a man desires is *u* love;
    20: 6 Many a man claims to have *u* love.
Isa 54: 10 yet my *u* love for you will not be
La 3: 32 so great is his *u* love.
Hos 10: 12 reap the fruit of *u* love,

UNFAITHFUL (UNFAITHFULNESS)

Lev 6: 2 is *u* to the LORD by deceiving his
Nu 5: 6 and so is *u* to the LORD,
1Ch 10: 13 because he was *u* to the LORD;
Pr 11: 6 the *u* are trapped by evil desires.
    13: 2 the *u* have a craving for violence.
    13: 15 but the way of the *u* is hard.
    22: 12 but he frustrates the words of the *u*.
    23: 28 and multiplies the *u* among men.
    25: 19 is reliance on the *u* in times
Jer 3: 20 But like a woman *u* to her husband,

UNFAITHFULNESS (UNFAITHFUL)

1Ch 9: 1 to Babylon because of their *u*.
Mt 5: 32 except for marital *u*, causes her
    19: 9 for marital *u*, and marries another

UNFIT*

Tit 1: 16 and *u* for doing anything good.

UNFOLDING

Ps 119:130 the *u* of your words gives light;

UNFORGIVING*

2Ti 3: 3 unholy, without love, *u*, slanderous

UNFRIENDLY*

Pr 18: 1 An *u* man pursues selfish ends;

UNFRUITFUL

1Co 14: 14 my spirit prays, but my mind is *u*.

UNGODLINESS (UNGODLY)

Tit 2: 12 It teaches us to say ''No'' to *u*

UNGODLY (UNGODLINESS)

Ro 5: 6 powerless, Christ died for the *u*.
1Ti 1: 9 the *u* and sinful, the unholy
2Ti 2: 16 in it will become more and more *u*.
2Pe 2: 6 of what is going to happen to the *u;*
Jude 15 and to convict all the *u*

UNGRATEFUL*

Lk 6: 35 he is kind to the *u* and wicked.
2Ti 3: 2 disobedient to their parents, *u*,

UNHOLY*

1Ti 1: 9 and sinful, the *u* and irreligious;
2Ti 3: 2 ungrateful, *u*, without love,
Heb 10: 29 as an *u* thing the blood

UNINTENTIONALLY

Lev 4: 2 'When anyone sins *u* and does
Nu 15: 22 'Now if you *u* fail to keep any
Dt 4: 42 flee if he had *u* killed his neighbor

UNIT

1Co 12: 12 body is a *u*, though it is made up

UNITE (UNITED UNITY)

1Co 6: 15 and *u* them with a prostitute?

UNITED (UNITE)

Ge 2: 24 and mother and be *u* to his wife,
Mt 19: 5 and mother and be *u* to his wife,
Ro 6: 5 If we have been *u* like this with him
Eph 5: 31 and mother and be *u* to his wife,
Php 2: 1 from being *u* with Christ,
Col 2: 2 encouraged in heart and *u* in love,

UNITY* (UNITE)

2Ch 30: 12 the people to give them *u* of mind
Ps 133: 1 is when brothers live together in *u!*
Jn 17: 23 May they be brought to complete *u*
Ro 15: 5 a spirit of *u* among yourselves
Eph 4: 3 effort to keep the *u* of the Spirit
    4: 13 up until we all reach *u* in the faith
Col 3: 14 them all together in perfect *u*.

UNIVERSE*

1Co 4: 9 made a spectacle to the whole *u*,

Eph 4: 10 in order to fill the whole *u*.)
Php 2: 15 which you shine like stars in the *u*
Heb 1: 2 and through whom he made the *u*.
    11: 3 understand that the *u* was formed

UNJUST

Ro 3: 5 That God is *u* in bringing his wrath
    9: 14 What then shall we say? Is God *u?*
1Pe 2: 19 up under the pain of *u* suffering

UNKNOWN

Ac 17: 23 TO AN *U* GOD.

UNLEAVENED

Ex 12: 17 ''Celebrate the Feast of *U* Bread,
Dt 16: 16 at the Feast of *U* Bread, the Feast

UNLIMITED*

1Ti 1: 16 Jesus might display his *u* patience

UNLOVED

Pr 30: 23 an *u* woman who is married,

UNMARRIED

1Co 7: 8 It is good for them to stay *u*,
    7: 27 Are you *u?* Do not look for a wife.
    7: 32 An *u* man is concerned about

UNPLOWED

Ex 23: 11 the seventh year let the land lie *u*
Hos 10: 12 and break up your *u* ground;

UNPRODUCTIVE

Tit 3: 14 necessities and not live *u* lives.
2Pe 1: 8 and *u* in your knowledge

UNPROFITABLE

Tit 3: 9 because these are *u* and useless.

UNPUNISHED

Ex 34: 7 Yet he does not leave the guilty *u;*
Pr 6: 29 no one who touches her will go *u*.
    11: 21 of this: The wicked will not go *u*,
    19: 5 A false witness will not go *u*,

UNQUENCHABLE

Lk 3: 17 he will burn up the chaff with *u* fire

UNREPENTANT*

Ro 2: 5 stubbornness and your *u* heart,

UNRIGHTEOUS*

Zep 3: 5 yet the *u* know no shame.
Mt 5: 45 rain on the righteous and the *u*.
1Pe 3: 18 the righteous for the *u*, to bring you
2Pe 2: 9 and to hold the *u* for the day

UNSEARCHABLE

Ro 11: 33 How *u* his judgments,
Eph 3: 8 preach to the Gentiles the *u* riches

UNSEEN*

Mt 6: 6 and pray to your Father, who is *u*.
    6: 18 who is *u*; and your Father,
2Co 4: 18 on what is seen, but on what is *u*.
    4: 18 temporary, but what is *u* is eternal.

UNSETTLED*

1Th 3: 3 so that no one would be *u*
2Th 2: 2 not to become easily *u*

UNSHRUNK

Mt 9: 16 patch of *u* cloth on an old garment,

UNSPIRITUAL*

Ro 7: 14 but I am *u*, sold as a slave to sin.
Col 2: 18 and his *u* mind puffs him up
Jas 3: 15 down from heaven but is earthly, *u*,

UNSTABLE*

Jas 1: 8 he is a double-minded man, *u*
2Pe 2: 14 they seduce the *u;* they are experts
    3: 16 ignorant and *u* people distort,

UNTHINKABLE*

Job 34: 12 It is *u* that God would do wrong,

UNTIE

Mk 1: 7 worthy to stoop down and *u*.

Lk   13: 15 each of you on the Sabbath *u* his ox

UNVEILED*

2Co   3: 18 with *u* faces all reflect the Lord's

UNWHOLESOME*

Eph   4: 29 Do not let any *u* talk come out

UNWISE

Eph   5: 15 how you live—not as *u* but as wise,

UNWORTHY*

Ge   32: 10 I am *u* of all the kindness
Job 40:   4 "I am *u*— how can I reply to you?
Lk   17: 10 should say, 'We are *u* servants;
1Co 11: 27 Lord in an *u* manner will be guilty

UPHOLD (UPHOLDS)

Isa   41: 10 I will *u* you with my righteous right
Ro   3: 31 Not at all! Rather, we *u* the law.

UPHOLDS* (UPHOLD)

Ps   37: 17 but the LORD *u* the righteous.
   37: 24 for the LORD *u* him with his hand.
   63:   8 your right hand *u* me.
   140: 12 and *u* the cause of the needy.
   145: 14 The LORD *u* all those who fall
   146:   7 He *u* the cause of the oppressed

UPRIGHT

Dt   32:   4 *u* and just is he.
Job   1:   1 This man was blameless and *u*;
Ps   7: 10 who saves the *u* in heart.
   11:   7 *u* men will see his face.
   25:   8 Good and *u* is the LORD;
   33:   1 it is fitting for the *u* to praise him.
   64: 10 let all the *u* in heart praise him!
   92: 15 proclaiming, "The LORD is *u*;
   97: 11 and joy on the *u* in heart.
   119:   7 I will praise you with an *u* heart
Pr   2:   7 He holds victory in store for the *u*,
   3: 32 but takes the *u* into his confidence.
   14:   2 whose walk is *u* fears the LORD,
   15:   8 but the prayer of the *u* pleases him.
   21: 29 an *u* man gives thought to his ways.
Isa   26:   7 O *u* One, you make the way
Tit   1:   8 who is self-controlled, *u*, holy
   2: 12 *u* and godly lives in this present

UPROOTED

Dt   28: 63 You will be *u* from the land you are
Jer   31: 40 The city will never again be *u*
Jude   : 12 without fruit and *u*— twice dead.

UPSET

Lk   10: 41 are worried and *u* about many

URIAH

Hittite husband of Bathsheba, killed by David's order (2Sa 11).

USEFUL

Eph   4: 28 doing something *u*
2Ti   2: 21 *u* to the Master and prepared
   3: 16 Scripture is God-breathed and is *u*
Phm   : 11 now he has become *u* both to you

USELESS

1Co 15: 14 our preaching is *u*
Tit   3:   9 these are unprofitable and *u*.
Phm   : 11 Formerly he was *u* to you,
Heb   7: 18 *u* (for the law made nothing perfect
Jas   2: 20 faith without deeds is *u*?

USURY

Ne   5: 10 But let the exacting of *u* stop!
Ps   15:   5 who lends his money without *u*

UTMOST

Job 34: 36 that Job might be tested to the *u*

UTTER (UTTERS)

Ps   78:   2 I will *u* things hidden from of old—
Mt   13: 35 I will *u* things hidden

UTTERS (UTTER)

1Co 14:   2 he *u* mysteries with his spirit.

UZZIAH

Son of Amaziah; king of Judah also known as Azariah (2Ki 15:1-7; 1Ch 6:24; 2Ch 26). Struck with leprosy because of pride (2Ch 26:16-23).

VAIN

Ps   33: 17 A horse is a *v* hope for deliverance;
   73: 13 in *v* have I kept my heart pure;
   127:   1 its builders labor in *v*.
Isa   65: 23 They will not toil in *v*
1Co 15:   2 Otherwise, you have believed in *v*.
   15: 58 labor in the Lord is not in *v*.
2Co   6:   1 not to receive God's grace in *v*.
Gal   2:   2 running or had run my race in *v*.

VALIANT

1Sa 10: 26 by *v* men whose hearts God had

VALID

Jn   8: 14 my own behalf, my testimony is *v*,

VALLEY (VALLEYS)

Ps   23:   4 walk through the *v* of the shadow
Isa   40:   4 Every *v* shall be raised up,
Joel   3: 14 multitudes in the *v* of decision!

VALLEYS (VALLEY)

SS   2:   1 a lily of the *v*.

VALUABLE (VALUE)

Lk   12: 24 And how much more *v* you are

VALUE (VALUABLE VALUED)

Lev 27:   3 set the *v* of a male between the ages
Pr   16: 13 they *v* a man who speaks the truth.
   31: 11 and lacks nothing of *v*.
Mt   13: 46 When he found one of great *v*,
1Ti   4:   8 For physical training is of some *v*,
Heb 11: 26 as of greater *v* than the treasures

VALUED (VALUE)

Lk   16: 15 What is highly *v* among men is

VANISHES

Jas   4: 14 appears for a little while and then *v*.

VASHTI*

Queen of Persia replaced by Esther (Est 1-2).

VAST

Ge   2:   1 completed in all their *v* array.
Dt   1: 19 of the Amorites through all that *v*
   8: 15 He led you through the *v*
Ps 139: 17 How *v* is the sum of them!

VEGETABLES

Pr   15: 17 of *v* where there is love
Ro   14:   2 whose faith is weak, eats only *v*.

VEIL

Ex   34: 33 to them, he put a *v* over his face.
2Co   3: 14 for to this day the same *v* remains

VENGEANCE (AVENGE AVENGER AVENGES AVENGING REVENGE)

Nu   31:   3 to carry out the LORD's *v* on them
Isa   34:   8 For the LORD has a day of *v*,
Na   1:   2 The LORD takes *v* on his foes

VERDICT

Jn   3: 19 This is the *v*: Light has come

VICTOR'S* (VICTORY)

2Ti   2:   5 he does not receive the *v* crown

VICTORIES* (VICTORY)

2Sa 22: 51 He gives his king great *v*;
Ps   18: 50 He gives his king great *v*;
   21:   1 great is his joy in the *v* you give!
   21:   5 Through the *v* you gave, his glory is
   44:   4 who decrees *v* for Jacob.

VICTORIOUS (VICTORY)

Ps   20:   5 for joy when you are *v*

VICTORIOUSLY* (VICTORY)

Ps   45:   4 In your majesty ride forth *v*

VICTORY (VICTOR'S VICTORIES VICTORIOUS VICTORIOUSLY)

2Sa   8:   6 gave David *v* wherever he
Ps   44:   6 my sword does not bring me *v*;
   60: 12 With God we will gain the *v*,
   129:   2 they have not gained the *v* over me.
Pr   11: 14 but many advisers make *v* sure.
1Co 15: 54 "Death has been swallowed up in *v*
   15: 57 He gives us the *v* through our Lord
1Jn   5:   4 This is the *v* that has overcome

VIEW

Pr   5: 21 are in full *v* of the LORD,
2Ti   4:   1 and in *v* of his appearing

VILLAGE

Mk   6:   6 went around teaching from *v* to *v*.

VINDICATED (VINDICATION)

Job 13: 18 I know I will be *v*,
1Ti   3: 16 was *v* by the Spirit,

VINDICATION (VINDICATED)

Ps   24:   5 and *v* from God his Savior.

VINE (VINEYARD)

Ps 128:   3 Your wife will be like a fruitful *v*
Isa   36: 16 one of you will eat from his own *v*
Jnh   4:   6 Jonah was very happy about the *v*.
Jn   15:   1 "I am the true *v*, and my Father is

VINEGAR

Pr   10: 26 As *v* to the teeth and smoke
Mk 15: 36 filled a sponge with wine *v*,

VINEYARD (VINE)

1Ki 21:   1 an incident involving a *v* belonging
Pr   31: 16 out of her earnings she plants a *v*.
SS   1:   6 my own *v* I have neglected.
Isa   5:   1 My loved one had a *v*
1Co   9:   7 Who plants a *v* and does not eat

VIOLATION

Heb   2:   2 every *v* and disobedience received

VIOLENCE (VIOLENT)

Ge   6: 11 in God's sight and was full of *v*.
Isa 53:   9 though he had done no *v*,
   60: 18 No longer will *v* be heard
Eze 45:   9 Give up your *v* and oppression
Joel   3: 19 of *v* done to the people of Judah,
Jnh   3:   8 give up their evil ways and their *v*.

VIOLENT (VIOLENCE)

Eze 18: 10 "Suppose he has a *v* son, who sheds
1Ti   1: 13 and a persecutor and a *v* man,
   3:   3 not *v* but gentle, not quarrelsome,
Tit   1:   7 not *v*, not pursuing dishonest gain.

VIPERS

Ps 140:   3 the poison of *v* is on their lips.
Lk   3:   7 "You brood of *v*! Who warned you
Ro   3: 13 "The poison of *v* is on their lips."

VIRGIN (VIRGINS)

Dt   22: 15 shall bring proof that she was a *v*
Isa   7: 14 The *v* will be with child
Mt   1: 23 "The *v* will be with child
Lk   1: 34 I am a *v*?" The angel answered,
2Co 11:   2 that I might present you as a pure *v*

VIRGINS (VIRGIN)

Mt 25:   1 will be like ten *v* who took their
1Co   7: 25 Now about *v*: I have no command

VIRTUES*

Col   3: 14 And over all these *v* put on love,

VISIBLE

Eph   5: 13 exposed by the light becomes *v*,
Col   1: 16 and on earth, *v* and invisible,

VISION (VISIONS)

Da   9: 24 to seal up *v* and prophecy
Ac   26: 19 disobedient to the *v* from heaven.

VISIONS (VISION)

Nu   12:   6 I reveal myself to him in *v*,
Joel   2: 28 your young men will see *v*.

Ac   2: 17 your young men will see v,

VOICE

Dt   30: 20 listen to his v, and hold fast to him.
1Sa 15: 22 as in obeying the v of the LORD?
Job 40:   9 and can your v thunder like his?
Ps   19:   4 their v goes out into all the earth,
     29:   3 The v of the LORD is
     66: 19 and heard my v in prayer.
     95:   7 Today, if you hear his v,
Pr   8:   1 Does not understanding raise her v
Isa 30: 21 your ears will hear a v behind you,
     40:   3 A v of one calling:
Mk   1:   3 "a v of one calling in the desert,
Jn   5: 28 are in their graves will hear his v •
    10:   3 and the sheep listen to his v.
Ro   10: 18 "Their v has gone out
Heb   3:   7 "Today, if you hear his v,
Rev   3: 20 If anyone hears my v and opens

VOMIT

Lev 18: 28 it will v you out as it vomited out
Pr   26: 11 As a dog returns to its v,
2Pe   2: 22 "A dog returns to its v," and,

VOW (VOWS)

Nu   6:   2 a v of separation to the LORD
     30:   2 When a man makes a v
Jdg 11: 30 Jephthah made a v to the LORD:

VOWS (VOW)

Ps 116: 14 I will fulfill my v to the LORD
Pr   20: 25 and only later to consider his v.

VULTURES

Mt   24: 28 is a carcass, there the v will gather.

WAGE (WAGES WAGING)

2Co 10:   3 we do not w war as the world does.

WAGES (WAGE)

Mal   3:   5 who defraud laborers of their w,
Lk   10:   7 for the worker deserves his w.
Ro   4:   4 his w are not credited to him
     6: 23 For the w of sin is death,
1Ti   5: 18 and "The worker deserves his w."

WAGING (WAGE)

Ro   7: 23 w war against the law of my mind

WAILING

Ps   30: 11 You turned my w into dancing;

WAIST

2Ki   1:   8 and a leather belt around his w."
Mt   3:   4 he had a leather belt around his w.

WAIT (AWAITS WAITED WAITING WAITS)

Ps   27: 14 W for the LORD;
   130:   5 I w for the LORD, my soul waits,
Isa 30: 18 Blessed are all who w for him!
Ac   1:   4 w for the gift my Father promised,
Ro   8: 23 as we w eagerly for our adoption
1Th   1: 10 and to w for his Son from heaven,
Tit   2: 13 while we w for the blessed hope—

WAITED (WAIT)

Ps   40:   1 I w patiently for the LORD;

WAITING (WAIT)

Heb   9: 28 to those who are w for him.

WAITS (WAIT)

Ro   8: 19 creation w in eager expectation

WAKE (AWAKE WAKENS)

Eph   5: 14 "W up, O sleeper,

WAKENS* (WAKE)

Isa 50:   4 He w me morning by morning,
     50:   4 w my ear to listen like one being

WALK (WALKED WALKING WALKS)

Lev 26: 12 I will w among you and be your
Dt   5: 33 W in all the way that the LORD
     6:   7 and when you w along the road,
   10: 12 to w in all his ways, to love him,
   11: 19 and when you w along the road,

Dt   11: 22 to w in all his ways and to hold fast
     26: 17 and that you will w in his ways,
Jos 22:   5 to w in all his ways,
Ps   1:   1 who does not w in the counsel
     15:   2 He whose w is blameless
     23:   4 Even though I w
     84: 11 from those whose w is blameless.
     89: 15 who w in the light of your presence
  119: 45 I will w about in freedom,
Pr   4: 12 When you w, your steps will not be
     6: 22 When you w, they will guide you;
Isa   2:   3 so that we may w in his paths."
     2:   5 let us w in the light of the LORD.
   30: 21 saying, "This is the way; w in it."
   40: 31 they will w and not be faint.
   57:   2 Those who w uprightly
Jer   6: 16 ask where the good way is, and w
Da   4: 37 And those who w in pride he is able
Am   3:   3 Do two w together
Mic   4:   5 All the nations may w
     6:   8 and to w humbly with your God.
Mk   2:   9 'Get up, take your mat and w'?
Jn   8: 12 Whoever follows me will never w
1Jn   1:   6 with him yet w in the darkness,
     1:   7 But if we w in the light,
2Jn   6 his command is that you w in love.

WALKED (WALK)

Ge   5: 24 Enoch w with God; then he was no
Jos 14:   9 which your feet have w will be your
Mt   14: 29 and w on the water, and came toward Jesus.

WALKING (WALK)

1Ki   3:   3 love for the LORD by w according
Da   3: 25 I see four men w around in the fire,
2Jn   4 of your children w in the truth,

WALKS (WALK)

Pr   10:   9 The man of integrity w securely,
     13: 20 He who w with the wise grows wise
Isa 33: 15 He who w righteously
Jn   11:   9 A man who w by day will not

WALL (WALLS)

Jos   6: 20 w collapsed; so every man charged
Ne   2: 17 let us rebuild the w of Jerusalem,
Eph   2: 14 the dividing w of hostility,
Rev 21: 12 It had a great, high w

WALLOWING

2Pe   2: 22 back to her w in the mud."

WALLS (WALL)

Isa 58: 12 be called Repairer of Broken W,
     60: 18 but you will call your w Salvation
Heb 11: 30 By faith the w of Jericho fell,

WANDER (WANDERED)

Nu   32: 13 he made them w in the desert forty
Jas   5: 19 one of you should w from the truth

WANDERED (WANDER)

Eze 34:   6 My sheep w over all the mountains
Mt   18: 12 go to look for the one that w off?
1Ti   6: 10 have w from the faith and pierced
2Ti   2: 18 who have w away from the truth.

WANT (WANTED WANTING WANTS)

1Sa   8: 19 "We w a king over us.
Mt   19: 21 Jesus answered, "If you w
Lk   19: 14 'We don't w this man to be our king
Ro   7: 15 For what I w to do I do not do,
     13:   3 Do you w to be free from fear
2Co 12: 14 what I w is not your possessions
Php   3: 10 I w to know Christ and the power

WANTED (WANT)

1Co 12: 18 of them, just as he w them to be.
Heb   6: 17 Because God w to make

WANTING (WANT)

Da   5: 27 weighed on the scales and found w.
2Pe   3:   9 with you, not w anyone to perish,

WANTS (WANT)

Mt   5: 42 from the one who w to borrow
     20: 26 whoever w to become great

Mk   8: 35 For whoever w to save his life will
     10: 43 whoever w to become great
Ro   9: 18 he hardens whom he w to harden.
1Ti   2:   4 who w all men to be saved
1Pe   5:   2 you are willing, as God w you to be;

WAR (WARRIOR WARS)

Jos 11: 23 Then the land had rest from w.
1Sa 15: 18 make w on them until you have
Ps   68: 30 the nations who delight in w.
   120:   7 but when I speak, they are for w.
   144:   1 who trains my hands for w,
Isa   2:   4 nor will they train for w anymore.
Da   9: 26 W will continue until the end,
Ro   7: 23 waging w against the law
2Co 10:   3 we do not wage w as the world does
1Pe   2: 11 which w against your soul.
Rev 12:   7 And there was w in heaven.
     19: 11 With justice he judges and makes w

WARN* (WARNED WARNING WARNINGS)

Ex   19: 21 w the people so they do not force
Nu   24: 14 let me w you of what this people
1Sa   8:   9 but w them solemnly and let them
1Ki   2: 42 swear by the LORD and w you,
2Ch 19: 10 you are to w them not to sin
Ps   81:   8 O my people, and I will w you—
Jer   42: 19 I w you today that you made a fatal
Eze   3: 18 and you do not w him or speak out
     3: 19 But if you do w the wicked man
     3: 20 Since you did not w him, he will die
     3: 21 if you do w the righteous man not
     33:   3 blows the trumpet to w the people,
     33:   6 blow the trumpet to w the people
     33:   9 if you do w the wicked man to turn
Lk   16: 28 Let him w them, so that they will
Ac   4: 17 we must w these men
1Co   4: 14 not to w you, as my dear children.
Gal   5: 21 I w you, as I did before, that those
1Th   5: 14 brothers, w those who are idle,
2Th   3: 15 an enemy, but w him as a brother.
2Ti   2: 14 W them before God
Tit   3: 10 and then w him a second time.
     3: 10 W a divisive person once,
Rev 22: 18 I w everyone who hears the words

WARNED (WARN)

2Ki 17: 13 The LORD w Israel and Judah
Ps   19: 11 By them is your servant w;
Jer   22: 21 I w you when you felt secure,
Mt   3:   7 Who w you to flee
1Th   4:   6 have already told you and w you.
Heb 11:   7 when w about things not yet seen,
     12: 25 they refused him who w them

WARNING (WARN)

Jer   6:   8 Take w, O Jerusalem,
1Ti   5: 20 so that the others may take w.

WARNINGS (WARN)

1Co 10: 11 and were written down as w for us,

WARRIOR (WAR)

Ex   15:   3 The LORD is a w;
1Ch 28:   3 you are a w and have shed blood.'
Pr   16: 32 Better a patient man than a w,

WARS (WAR)

Ps   46:   9 He makes w cease to the ends
Mt   24:   6 You will hear of w and rumors of w,

WASH (WASHED WASHING)

Ps   51:   7 w me, and I will be whiter
Jer   4: 14 w the evil from your heart
Jn   13:   5 and began to w his disciples' feet,
Ac   22: 16 be baptized and w your sins away,
Jas   4:   8 W your hands, you sinners,
Rev 22: 14 Blessed are those who w their robes

WASHED (WASH)

Ps   73: 13 in vain have I w my hands
1Co   6: 11 you were w, you were sanctified,
Heb 10: 22 and having our bodies w
2Pe   2: 22 and, "A sow that is w goes back
Rev   7: 14 they have w their robes

WASHING (WASH)

Eph 5: 26 cleansing her by the *w* with water
1Ti 5: 10 showing hospitality, *w* the feet
Tit 3: 5 us through the *w* of rebirth

WASTED (WASTING)

Jn 6: 12 Let nothing be *w*.''

WASTING (WASTED)

2Co 4: 16 Though outwardly we are *w* away,

WATCH (WATCHER WATCHES WATCHING WATCHMAN)

Ge 31: 49 ''May the LORD keep *w*
Ps 90: 4 or like a *w* in the night.
141: 3 keep *w* over the door of my lips.
Pr 4: 6 love her, and she will *w* over you.
6: 22 when you sleep, they will *w*
Jer 31: 10 will *w* over his flock like a shepherd
Mic 7: 7 I *w* in hope for the LORD,
Mt 24: 42 ''Therefore keep *w*, because you do
26: 41 *W* and pray so that you will not fall
Mk 13: 35 ''Therefore keep *w* because you do
Lk 2: 8 keeping *w* over their flocks at night
1Ti 4: 16 *W* your life and doctrine closely.
Heb 13: 17 They keep *w* over you

WATCHER* (WATCH)

Job 7: 20 O *w* of men?

WATCHES* (WATCH)

Nu 19: 5 While he *w*, the heifer is
Job 24: 15 The eye of the adulterer *w* for dusk;
Ps 1: 6 For the LORD *w* over the way
33: 14 from his dwelling place he *w*
63: 6 of you through the *w* of the night.
119:148 through the *w* of the night,
121: 3 he who *w* over you will not slumber
121: 4 indeed, he who *w* over Israel
121: 5 The LORD *w* over you—
127: 1 Unless the LORD *w* over the city,
145: 20 LORD *w* over all who love him,
146: 9 The LORD *w* over the alien
Pr 31: 27 She *w* over the affairs
Ecc 11: 4 Whoever *w* the wind will not plant;
La 2: 19 as the *w* of the night begin;
4: 16 he no longer *w* over them.

WATCHING (WATCH)

Lk 12: 37 whose master finds them *w*

WATCHMAN (WATCH)

Eze 3: 17 I have made you a *w* for the house
33: 6 but I will hold the *w* accountable

WATER (WATERED WATERING WATERS WELL-WATERED)

Ex 7: 20 all the *w* was changed into blood.
17: 1 but there was no *w* for the people
Nu 20: 2 there was no *w* for the community,
Ps 1: 3 like a tree planted by streams of *w*,
22: 14 I am poured out like *w*,
42: 1 As the deer pants for streams of *w*,
Pr 25: 21 if he is thirsty, give him *w* to drink.
Isa 12: 3 With joy you will draw *w*
30: 20 of adversity and the *w* of affliction,
32: 2 like streams of *w* in the desert
49: 10 and lead them beside springs of *w*.
Jer 2: 13 broken cisterns that cannot hold *w*.
17: 8 will be like a tree planted by the *w*
31: 9 I will lead them beside streams of *w*
Eze 36: 25 I will sprinkle clean *w* on you.
Zec 14: 8 On that day living *w* will flow out
Mt 14: 29 and walked on the *w*, and came toward Jesus.
Mk 9: 41 anyone who gives you a cup of *w*
Lk 5: 4 to Simon, ''Put out into deep *w*,
Jn 3: 5 unless he is born of *w* and the Spirit.
4: 10 he would have given you living *w*.''
7: 38 streams of living *w* will flow
Eph 5: 26 washing with *w* through the word.
Heb 10: 22 our bodies washed with pure *w*.
1Pe 3: 21 this *w* symbolizes baptism that now
2Pe 2: 17 These men are springs without *w*
1Jn 5: 6 This is the one who came by *w*
5: 6 come by *w* only, but by *w*
5: 8 the Spirit, the *w* and the blood;
Rev 7: 17 to springs of living *w*.

Rev 21: 6 cost from the spring of the *w* of life.

WATERED (WATER)

1Co 3: 6 I planted the seed, Apollos *w* it,

WATERING (WATER)

Isa 55: 10 it without *w* the earth

WATERS (WATER)

Ps 23: 2 he leads me beside quiet *w*,
Ecc 11: 1 Cast your bread upon the *w*,
SS 8: 7 Many *w* cannot quench love;
Isa 11: 9 as the *w* cover the sea.
43: 2 When you pass through the *w*,
55: 1 come to the *w*;
58: 11 like a spring whose *w* never fail.
Hab 2: 14 as the *w* cover the sea.
1Co 3: 7 plants nor he who *w* is anything,

WAVE (WAVES)

Lev 23: 11 He is to *w* the sheaf
Jas 1: 6 he who doubts is like a *w* of the sea,

WAVER*

1Ki 18: 21 ''How long will you *w*
Ro 4: 20 Yet he did not *w* through unbelief

WAVES (WAVE)

Isa 57: 20 whose *w* cast up mire and mud,
Mt 8: 27 Even the winds and the *w* obey him
Eph 4: 14 tossed back and forth by the *w*,

WAY (WAYS)

Ex 13: 21 of cloud to guide them on their *w*
18: 20 and show them the *w* to live
Dt 1: 33 to show you the *w* you should go.
32: 6 Is this the *w* you repay the LORD,
1Sa 12: 23 I will teach you the *w* that is good
2Sa 22: 31 ''As for God, his *w* is perfect;
1Ki 8: 23 wholeheartedly in your *w*.
8: 36 Teach them the right *w* to live,
Job 23: 10 But he knows the *w* that I take;
Ps 1: 1 or stand in the *w* of sinners
32: 8 teach you in the *w* you should go;
37: 5 Commit your *w* to the LORD;
86: 11 Teach me your *w*, O LORD,
119: 9 can a young man keep his *w* pure?
139: 24 See if there is any offensive *w* in me
Pr 4: 11 I guide you in the *w* of wisdom
12: 15 The *w* of a fool seems right to him,
14: 12 There is a *w* that seems right
16: 17 he who guards his *w* guards his soul
19: 2 nor to be hasty and miss the *w*.
22: 6 Train a child in the *w* he should go,
30: 19 and the *w* of a man with a maiden.
Isa 30: 21 saying, ''This is the *w*; walk in it.''
35: 8 it will be called the *W* of Holiness.
40: 3 the *w* for the LORD;
48: 17 you in the *w* you should go.
53: 6 each of us has turned to his own *w*;
55: 7 Let the wicked forsake his *w*
Jer 5: 31 and my people love it this *w*.
Mal 3: 1 who will prepare the *w* before me.
Mt 3: 3 'Prepare the *w* for the Lord,
Lk 7: 27 who will prepare your *w* before you
Jn 14: 6 ''I am the *w* and the truth
Ac 1: 11 in the same *w* you have seen him go
9: 2 any there who belonged to the *W*,
24: 14 of the *W*, which they call a sect.
1Co 10: 13 also provide a *w* out so that you can
12: 31 will show you the most excellent *w*.
14: 1 Follow the *w* of love and eagerly
Col 1: 10 and may please him in every *w*;
Tit 2: 10 that in every *w* they will make
Heb 4: 15 who has been tempted in every *w*,
9: 8 was showing by this that the *w*
10: 20 and living *w* opened for us
13: 18 desire to live honorably in every *w*.

WAYS (WAY)

Ex 33: 13 teach me your *w* so I may know
Dt 10: 12 to walk in all his *w*, to love him,
26: 17 and that you will walk in his *w*,
30: 16 in his *w*, and to keep his commands
32: 4 and all his *w* are just.
Jos 22: 5 in all his *w*, to obey his commands,
2Ch 11: 17 walking in the *w* of David
Job 34: 21 ''His eyes are on the *w* of men;

Ps 25: 4 Show me your *w*, O LORD,
25: 10 All the *w* of the LORD are loving
37: 7 fret when men succeed in their *w*,
51: 13 I will teach transgressors your *w*,
77: 13 Your *w*, O God, are holy.
119: 59 I have considered my *w*
139: 3 you are familiar with all my *w*.
145: 17 The LORD is righteous in all his *w*
Pr 3: 6 in all your *w* acknowledge him,
4: 26 and take only *w* that are firm.
5: 21 For a man's *w* are in full view
16: 2 All a man's *w* seem innocent
16: 7 When a man's *w* are pleasing
Isa 2: 3 He will teach us his *w*,
55: 8 neither are your *w* my *w*,''
Eze 28: 15 You were blameless in your *w*
33: 8 out to dissuade him from his *w*,
Hos 14: 9 The *w* of the LORD are right;
Ro 1: 30 they invent *w* of doing evil;
Jas 3: 2 We all stumble in many *w*.

WEAK (WEAKER WEAKNESS WEAKNESSES)

Ps 41: 1 is he who has regard for the *w*;
72: 13 He will take pity on the *w*
82: 3 Defend the cause of the *w*
Eze 34: 4 You have not strengthened the *w*
Mt 26: 41 spirit is willing, but the body is *w*.''
Ac 20: 35 of hard work we must help the *w*,
Ro 14: 1 Accept him whose faith is *w*,
15: 1 to bear with the failings of the *w*
1Co 1: 27 God chose the *w* things
8: 9 become a stumbling block to the *w*.
9: 22 To the *w* I became *w*, to win the *w*.
11: 30 That is why many among you are *w*
2Co 12: 10 For when I am *w*, then I am strong.
1Th 5: 14 help the *w*, be patient
Heb 12: 12 your feeble arms and *w* knees.

WEAK-WILLED (WILL)

2Ti 3: 6 and gain control over *w* women,

WEAKER* (WEAK)

2Sa 3: 1 the house of Saul grew *w* and *w*.
1Co 12: 22 seem to be *w* are indispensable,
1Pe 3: 7 them with respect as the *w* partner

WEAKNESS* (WEAK)

La 1: 6 in *w* they have fled
Ro 8: 26 the Spirit helps us in our *w*.
1Co 1: 25 and the *w* of God is stronger
2: 3 I came to you in *w* and fear.
15: 43 it is sown in *w*, it is raised in power;
2Co 11: 30 boast of the things that show my *w*.
12: 9 for my power is made perfect in *w*
13: 4 he was crucified in *w*, yet he lives
Heb 5: 2 since he himself is subject to *w*.
11: 34 whose *w* was turned to strength;

WEAKNESSES* (WEAK)

2Co 12: 5 about myself, except about my *w*.
12: 9 all the more gladly about my *w*,
12: 10 I delight in *w*, in insults,
Heb 4: 15 unable to sympathize with our *w*,

WEALTH

Dt 8: 18 gives you the ability to produce *w*,
2Ch 1: 11 and you have not asked for *w*,
Ps 39: 6 he heaps up *w*, not knowing who
Pr 3: 9 Honor the LORD with your *w*,
10: 4 but diligent hands bring *w*.
11: 4 *W* is worthless in the day of wrath,
13: 7 to be poor, yet has great *w*.
15: 16 than great *w* with turmoil,
22: 4 bring *w* and honor and life.
Ecc 5: 10 whoever loves *w* is never satisfied
5: 13 *w* hoarded to the harm of its owner,
SS 8: 7 all the *w* of his house for love,
Mt 13: 22 and the deceitfulness of *w* choke it,
Mk 10: 22 away sad, because he had great *w*.
12: 44 They all gave out of their *w*; but she
Lk 15: 13 and there squandered his *w*
1Ti 6: 17 nor to put their hope in *w*,
Jas 5: 2 Your *w* has rotted, and moths have
5: 3 You have hoarded *w*

WEAPON (WEAPONS)

Ne 4: 17 work with one hand and held a *w*

WEAPONS (WEAPON)

Ecc 9: 18 Wisdom is better than w of war,
2Co 6: 7 with w of righteousness
      10: 4 The w we fight with are not

WEAR (WEARING)

Dt   8: 4 Your clothes did not w out
    22: 5 nor a man w women's clothing,
Ps 102: 26 they will all w out like a garment,
Pr 23: 4 Do not w yourself out to get rich;
Isa 51: 6 the earth will w out like a garment
Heb 1: 11 they will all w out like a garment.
Rev 3: 18 and white clothes to w,

WEARIES (WEARY)

Ecc 12: 12 and much study w the body.

WEARING (WEAR)

Jn 19: 5 When Jesus came out w the crown
Jas   2: 3 attention to the man w fine clothes
1Pe 3: 3 as braided hair and the w
Rev 7: 9 They were w white robes

WEARY (WEARIES)

Isa 40: 28 He will not grow tired or w,
    40: 31 they will run and not grow w,
    50: 4 know the word that sustains the w.
Mt 11: 28 all you who are w and burdened,
Gal   6: 9 Let us not become w in doing good,
Heb 12: 3 so that you will not grow w
Rev 2: 3 my name, and have not grown w.

WEDDING

Mt 22: 11 who was not wearing w clothes.
Rev 19: 7 For the w of the Lamb has come,

WEEDS

Mt 13: 25 and sowed w among the wheat,

WEEK

Mt 28: 1 at dawn on the first day of the w,
1Co 16: 2 On the first day of every w,

WEEP (WEEPING WEPT)

Ecc   3: 4 a time to w and a time to laugh,
Lk   6: 21 Blessed are you who w now,
    23: 28 w for yourselves and for your

WEEPING (WEEP)

Ps 30: 5 w may remain for a night,
   126: 6 He who goes out w,
Jer 31: 15 Rachel w for her children
Mt   2: 18 Rachel w for her children
     8: 12 where there will be w and gnashing

WEIGH (OUTWEIGHS WEIGHED WEIGHS WEIGHTIER WEIGHTS)

1Co 14: 29 others should w carefully what is

WEIGHED (WEIGH)

Job 28: 15 nor can its price be w in silver.
Da   5: 27 You have been w on the scales
Lk 21: 34 or your hearts will be w

WEIGHS (WEIGH)

Pr 12: 25 An anxious heart w a man down,
    15: 28 of the righteous w its answers,
    21: 2 but the LORD w the heart.
    24: 12 not he who w the heart perceive

WEIGHTIER* (WEIGH)

Jn   5: 36 "I have testimony w than that

WEIGHTS (WEIGH)

Lev 19: 36 Use honest scales and honest w,
Dt 25: 13 Do not have two differing w
Pr 11: 1 but accurate w are his delight.

WELCOME (WELCOMES)

Mk   9: 37 welcomes me does not w me
2Pe 1: 11 and you will receive a rich w

WELCOMES (WELCOME)

Mt 18: 5 whoever w a little child like this
2Jn   : 11 Anyone who w him shares

WELL (WELLED WELLING WELLS)

Mt 15: 31 crippled made w, the lame walking
Lk 14: 5 falls into a w on the Sabbath day.

Lk 17: 19 your faith has made you w."
Jas   5: 15 in faith will make the sick person w

WELL-WATERED (WATER)

Isa 58: 11 You will be like a w garden,

WELLED* (WELL)

2Co 8: 2 and their extreme poverty w up

WELLING* (WELL)

Jn   4: 14 of water w up to eternal life."

WELLS (WELL)

Isa 12: 3 from the w of salvation.

WELLSPRING* (SPRING)

Pr   4: 23 for it is the w of life.

WEPT (WEEP)

Ps 137: 1 of Babylon we sat and w
Lk 22: 62 And he went outside and w bitterly
Jn 11: 35 Jesus w.

WEST

Ps 103: 12 as far as the east is from the w,
   107: 3 from east and w, from north

WHEAT

Mt   3: 12 gathering his w into the barn
    13: 25 and sowed weeds among the w,
Lk 22: 31 Satan has asked to sift you as w.
Jn 12: 24 a kernel of w falls to the ground

WHEELS

Eze 1: 16 appearance and structure of the w:

WHIRLWIND (WIND)

2Ki 2: 1 to take Elijah up to heaven in a w,
Hos 8: 7 and reap the w.
Na   1: 3 His way is in the w and the storm,

WHISPER (WHISPERED)

1Ki 19: 12 And after the fire came a gentle w.
Job 26: 14 how faint the w we hear of him!
Ps 107: 29 He stilled the storm to a w;

WHISPERED (WHISPER)

Mt 10: 27 speak in the daylight; what is w

WHITE (WHITER)

Isa   1: 18 they shall be as w as snow;
Da   7: 9 His clothing was as w as snow;
     7: 9 the hair of his head was w like wool
Mt 28: 3 and his clothes were w as snow.
Rev 1: 14 hair were w like wool, as w as snow,
     3: 4 dressed in w, for they are worthy.
     6: 2 and there before me was a w horse!
     7: 13 "These in w robes—who are they,
    19: 11 and there before me was a w horse,
    20: 11 Then I saw a great w throne

WHITER (WHITE)

Ps 51: 7 and I will be w than snow.

WHOLE

Ge   1: 29 plant on the face of the w earth
     2: 6 and watered the w surface
   11: 1 Now the w world had one language
Ex 12: 47 The w community
    19: 5 Although the w earth is mine,
Lev 16: 17 and the w community of Israel.
Nu 14: 21 of the LORD fills the w earth,
    32: 13 until the w generation
Dt 13: 16 w burnt offering to the LORD your
    19: 8 gives you the w land he promised
Jos   2: 3 come to spy out the w land."
1Sa 1: 28 For his w life he will be given
    17: 46 the w world will know that there is
1Ki 10: 24 The w world sought audience
2Ki 21: 8 and will keep the w Law that my
Ps 72: 19 may the w earth be filled
Pr   4: 22 and health to a man's w body.
     8: 31 rejoicing in his w world
Ecc 12: 13 for this is the w duty of man.
Isa   1: 5 Your w head is injured,
     6: 3 the w earth is full of his glory."
    14: 26 plan determined for the w world;
Eze 34: 6 were scattered over the w earth,
    37: 11 these bones are the w house

Da   2: 35 mountain and filled the w earth.
Zep 1: 18 the w world will be consumed,
Zec 14: 9 will be king over the w earth.
Mal 3: 10 the w tithe into the storehouse,
Mt   5: 29 than for your w body to be thrown
     6: 22 your w body will be full of light.
    16: 26 for a man if he gains the w world,
    24: 14 will be preached in the w world
Lk 21: 35 live on the face of the w earth.
Jn 12: 19 Look how the w world has gone
    13: 10 to wash his feet; his w body is clean
    21: 25 the w world would not have room
Ac 17: 26 they should inhabit the w earth;
    20: 27 proclaim to you the w will of God.
Ro   1: 9 whom I serve with my w heart
     3: 19 and the w world held accountable
     8: 22 know that the w creation has been
1Co 4: 9 made a spectacle to the w universe,
    12: 17 If the w body were an ear,
Gal   3: 22 declares that the w world is
     5: 3 obligated to obey the w law.
Eph 4: 10 in order to fill the w universe.)
     4: 13 attaining to the w measure
1Th 5: 23 May your w spirit, soul
Jas   2: 10 For whoever keeps the w law
1Jn   2: 2 but also for the sins of the w world.
Rev 3: 10 going to come upon the w world

WHOLEHEARTED* (HEART)

2Ki 20: 3 you faithfully and with w devotion
1Ch 28: 9 and serve him with w devotion
    29: 19 my son Solomon the w devotion
Isa 38: 3 you faithfully and with w devotion

WHOLEHEARTEDLY* (HEART)

Nu 14: 24 a different spirit and follows me w,
    32: 11 they have not followed me w,
    32: 12 for they followed the LORD w."
Dt   1: 36 because he followed the LORD w
Jos 14: 8 followed the LORD my God w.'
    14: 9 followed the LORD my God w.'
    14: 14 the LORD, the God of Israel, w.
1Ki 8: 23 with your servants who continue w
1Ch 29: 9 for they had given freely and w
2Ch 6: 14 with your servants who continue w
    15: 15 oath because they had sworn it w.
    19: 9 and w in the fear of the LORD.
    25: 2 in the eyes of the LORD, but not w
    31: 21 he sought his God and worked w.
Ro   6: 17 you w obeyed the form of teaching
Eph 6: 7 Serve w, as if you were serving

WHOLESOME*

2Ki 2: 22 And the water has remained w
2Pe 3: 1 to stimulate you to w thinking.

WICK

Isa 42: 3 a smoldering w he will not snuff out
Mt 12: 20 a smoldering w he will not snuff out

WICKED (WICKEDNESS)

Ge 13: 13 Now the men of Sodom were w
    39: 9 How then could I do such a w thing
Ex 23: 1 Do not help a w man
Nu 14: 35 things to this whole w community,
Dt 15: 9 not to harbor this w thought:
Jdg 19: 22 some of the w men
1Sa 2: 12 Eli's sons were w men; they had no
    15: 18 completely destroy those w people,
    25: 17 He is such a w man that no one can
2Sa 13: 12 in Israel! Don't do this w thing.
2Ki 17: 11 They did w things that provoked
2Ch 7: 14 and turn from their w ways,
    19: 2 "Should you help the w
Ne 13: 17 "What is this w thing you are doing
Ps   1: 1 walk in the counsel of the w
     1: 5 Therefore the w will not stand
     7: 9 to an end the violence of the w
   10: 13 Why does the w man revile God?
   11: 5 the w and those who love violence
   12: 8 The w freely strut about
   26: 5 and refuse to sit with the w.
   32: 10 Many are the woes of the w,
   36: 1 concerning the sinfulness of the w:
   37: 13 but the Lord laughs at the w,
   49: 5 when w deceivers surround me—
   50: 16 But to the w, God says:
   58: 3 Even from birth the w go astray;

Ps 73: 3 when I saw the prosperity of the w.
82: 2 and show partiality to the w? Selah
112: 10 the longings of the w will come
119: 61 Though the w bind me with ropes,
119:155 Salvation is far from the w,
140: 8 do not grant the w their desires,
141: 10 Let the w fall into their own nets,
146: 9 but he frustrates the ways of the w.
Pr 2: 12 you from the ways of w men,
4: 14 Do not set foot on the path of the w
6: 18 a heart that devises w schemes,
9: 7 whoever rebukes a w man incurs
10: 20 the heart of the w is of little value.
10: 28 the hopes of the w come to nothing
11: 5 w are brought down by their own
11: 10 when the w perish, there are shouts
11: 21 The w will not go unpunished,
12: 5 but the advice of the w is deceitful.
12: 10 the kindest acts of the w are cruel.
14: 19 the w at the gates of the righteous.
15: 3 keeping watch on the w
15: 26 detests the thoughts of the w,
21: 10 The w man craves evil;
21: 29 A w man puts up a bold front,
28: 1 w man flees though no one pursues,
28: 4 who forsake the law praise the w,
29: 7 but the w have no such concern.
29: 16 When the w thrive, so does sin,
29: 27 the w detest the upright.
Isa 11: 4 breath of his lips he will slay the w.
13: 11 the w for their sins.
26: 10 Though grace is shown to the w,
48: 22 says the LORD, ''for the w.''
53: 9 He was assigned a grave with the w
55: 7 Let the w forsake his way
57: 20 But the w are like the tossing sea,
Jer 35: 15 of you must turn from your w ways
Eze 3: 18 that w man will die for his sin,
13: 22 you encouraged the w not to turn
14: 7 and puts a w stumbling block
18: 21 ''But if a w man turns away
18: 23 pleasure in the death of the w?
21: 25 '' 'O profane and w prince of Israel,
33: 8 When I say to the w, 'O w man,
33: 11 pleasure in the death of the w,
33: 14 to the w man, 'You will surely die,'
33: 19 And if a w man turns away
Da 12: 10 but the w will continue to be w.
Mt 12: 39 w and adulterous generation asks
12: 45 be with this w generation.''
12: 45 with it seven other spirits more w
Lk 6: 35 he is kind to the ungrateful and w.
Ac 2: 23 and you, with the help of w men,
Ro 4: 5 but trusts God who justifies the w,
1Co 5: 13 ''Expel the w man from among you
6: 9 not know that the w will not inherit
Rev 2: 2 that you cannot tolerate w men,

WICKEDNESS (WICKED)

Ge 6: 5 The LORD saw how great man's w
Ex 34: 7 and forgiving w, rebellion and sin.
Lev 16: 21 and confess over it all the w
19: 29 to prostitution and be filled with w.
Dt 9: 4 it is on account of the w
Ne 9: 2 confessed their sins and the w
Ps 45: 7 You love righteousness and hate w;
92: 15 he is my Rock, and there is no w
Pr 13: 6 but w overthrows the sinner.
Jer 3: 2 land with your prostitution and w.
8: 6 No one repents of his w,
14: 20 O LORD, we acknowledge our w
Eze 18: 20 the w of the wicked will be charged
28: 15 created till w was found in you.
33: 19 wicked man turns away from his w
Da 4: 27 and your w by being kind
9: 24 to atone for w, to bring
Jnh 1: 2 its w has come up before me.''
Mt 24: 12 Because of the increase of w,
Lk 11: 39 inside you are full of greed and w.
Ac 1: 18 (With the reward he got for his w,
Ro 1: 18 who suppress the truth by their w,
1Co 5: 8 the yeast of malice and w,
2Co 6: 14 what do righteousness and w have
2Ti 2: 19 of the Lord must turn away from w
Tit 2: 14 for us to redeem us from all w
Heb 1: 9 loved righteousness and hated w;
8: 12 For I will forgive their w
2Pe 2: 15 who loved the wages of w.

WIDE

Ps 81: 10 Open w your mouth and I will fill it
Isa 54: 2 stretch your tent curtains w,
Mt 7: 13 For w is the gate and broad is
2Co 6: 13 my children—open w your hearts
Eph 3: 18 to grasp how w and long and high

WIDOW (WIDOWS)

Ex 22: 22 ''Do not take advantage of a w
Dt 10: 18 cause of the fatherless and the w,
Ps 146: 9 sustains the fatherless and the w,
Isa 1: 17 plead the case of the w.
Lk 21: 2 saw a poor w put in two very small
1Ti 5: 4 But if a w has children

WIDOWS (WIDOW)

Ps 68: 5 to the fatherless, a defender of w,
Ac 6: 1 their w were being overlooked
1Co 7: 8 to the unmarried and the w I say:
1Ti 5: 3 to those w who are really
Jas 1: 27 look after orphans and w

WIFE (WIVES WIVES')

Ge 2: 24 and mother and be united to his w,
19: 26 But Lot's w looked back,
24: 67 she became his w, and he loved her;
Ex 20: 17 shall not covet your neighbor's w,
Lev 20: 10 adultery with another man's w—
Dt 5: 21 shall not covet your neighbor's w.
24: 5 happiness to the w he has married.
Ru 4: 13 took Ruth and she became his w.
Pr 5: 18 in the w of your youth.
12: 4 w of noble character is her
18: 22 He who finds a w finds what is
19: 13 quarrelsome w is like a constant
31: 10 w of noble character who can find?
Hos 1: 2 take to yourself an adulterous w
Mal 2: 14 the witness between you and the w
Mt 1: 20 to take Mary home as your w,
19: 3 for a man to divorce his w for any
Lk 17: 32 Remember Lot's w! Whoever tries
18: 29 or w or brothers or parents
1Co 7: 2 each man should have his own w,
7: 33 how he can please his w—
Eph 5: 23 the husband is the head of the w
5: 33 must love his w as he loves himself,
1Ti 3: 2 husband of but one w, temperate,
Rev 21: 9 I will show you the bride, the w

WILD

Ge 1: 25 God made the w animals according
8: 1 Noah and all the w animals
Lk 15: 13 squandered his wealth in w living.
Ro 11: 17 and you, though a w olive shoot,

WILL (WEAK-WILLED WILLFUL WILLING WILLINGNESS)

Ps 40: 8 I desire to do your w, O my God;
143: 10 Teach me to do your w,
Isa 53: 10 Yet it was the LORD's w
Mt 6: 10 your w be done
7: 21 who does the w of my Father
10: 29 apart from the w of your Father.
12: 50 does the w of my Father
26: 39 Yet not as I w, but as you w.''
26: 42 I drink it, may your w be done.''
Jn 6: 38 but to do the w of him who sent me.
7: 17 If any one chooses to do God's w,
Ac 20: 27 to you the whole w of God.
Ro 12: 2 and approve what God's w is—
1Co 7: 37 but has control over his own w,
Eph 5: 17 understand what the Lord's w is.
Php 2: 13 for it is God who works in you to w
1Th 4: 3 God's w that you should be sanctified;
5: 18 for this is God's w for you
2Ti 2: 26 has taken them captive to do his w.
Heb 2: 4 distributed according to his w.
9: 16 In the case of a w, it is necessary
10: 7 I have come to do your w, O God
13: 21 everything good for doing his w,
Jas 4: 15 ''If it is the Lord's w,
1Pe 3: 17 It is better, if it is God's w,
4: 2 but rather for the w of God.
2Pe 1: 21 never had its origin in the w
1Jn 5: 14 we ask anything according to his w,
Rev 4: 11 and by your w they were created

WILLFUL (WILL)

Ps 19: 13 Keep your servant also from w sins;

WILLING (WILL)

1Ch 28: 9 devotion and with a w mind,
29: 5 who is w to consecrate himself
Ps 51: 12 grant me a w spirit, to sustain me.
Da 3: 28 were w to give up their lives rather
Mt 18: 14 Father in heaven is not w that any
23: 37 her wings, but you were not w.
26: 41 The spirit is w, but the body is weak
1Ti 6: 18 and to be generous and w to share.
1Pe 5: 2 not because you are w,

WILLINGNESS* (WILL)

2Co 8: 11 so that your eager w
8: 12 For if the w is there, the gift is

WIN (WINS WON)

1Co 9: 19 myself a slave to everyone, to w
Php 3: 14 on toward the goal to w the prize
1Th 4: 12 your daily life may w the respect

WIND (WHIRLWIND WINDS)

Ps 1: 4 that the w blows away.
Ecc 2: 11 meaningless, a chasing after the w;
Hos 8: 7 ''They sow the w
Mk 4: 41 Even the w and the waves obey
Jn 3: 8 The w blows wherever it pleases.
Eph 4: 14 and there by every w of teaching
Jas 1: 6 blown and tossed by the w.

WINDOW

Jos 2: 21 she tied the scarlet cord in the w.
Ac 20: 9 in a w was a young man named
2Co 11: 33 in a basket from a w in the wall

WINDS (WIND)

Ps 104: 4 He makes w his messengers,
Mt 24: 31 gather his elect from the four w,
Heb 1: 7 ''He makes his angels w,

WINE

Ps 104: 15 w that gladdens the heart of man,
Pr 20: 1 W is a mocker and beer a brawler;
23: 20 join those who drink too much w
23: 31 Do not gaze at w when it is red,
31: 6 w to those who are in anguish;
SS 1: 2 your love is more delightful than w.
Isa 28: 7 And these also stagger from w
55: 1 Come, buy w and milk
Mt 9: 17 before that pour new w
Lk 23: 36 They offered him w vinegar
Jn 2: 3 When the w was gone, Jesus'
Ro 14: 21 not to eat meat or drink w
Eph 5: 18 on w, which leads to debauchery.
1Ti 5: 23 a little w because of your stomach
Rev 16: 19 with the w of the fury of his wrath.

WINEPRESS

Isa 63: 2 like those of one treading the w?
Rev 19: 15 He treads the w of the fury

WINESKINS

Mt 9: 17 do men pour new wine into old w.

WINGS

Ex 19: 4 and how I carried you on eagles' w
Ru 2: 12 under whose w you have come
Ps 17: 8 hide me in the shadow of your w
91: 4 under his w you will find refuge;
Isa 6: 2 him were seraphs, each with six w;
40: 31 They will soar on w like eagles;
Eze 1: 6 of them had four faces and four w.
Zec 5: 9 in their w! They had w like those
Mal 4: 2 rise with healing in its w.
Lk 13: 34 hen gathers her chicks under her w,
Rev 4: 8 the four living creatures had six w

WINS (WIN)

Pr 11: 30 and he who w souls is wise.

WINTER

Mk 13: 18 that this will not take place in w.

WIPE (WIPED)

Isa 25: 8 The Sovereign LORD will w away
Rev 7: 17 God will w away every tear

Rev 21: 4 He will *w* every tear

WIPED (WIPE)

Lk 7: 38 Then she *w* them with her hair,
Ac 3: 19 so that your sins may be *w* out,

WISDOM (WISE)

Ge 3: 6 and also desirable for gaining *w*.
1Ki 4: 29 God gave Solomon *w* and very
2Ch 1: 10 Give me *w* and knowledge,
Ps 51: 6 you teach me *w* in the inmost place
111: 10 of the *w* is the beginning of *w*;
Pr 2: 6 For the LORD gives *w*,
3: 13 Blessed is the man who finds *w*,
4: 7 *W* is supreme; therefore get
8: 11 for *w* is more precious than rubies,
11: 2 but with humility comes *w*,
13: 10 *w* is found in those who take advice
23: 23 get *w*, discipline and understanding
29: 3 A man who loves *w* brings joy
29: 15 The rod of correction imparts *w*,
31: 26 She speaks with *w*,
Isa 11: 2 Spirit of *w* and of understanding,
28: 29 in counsel and magnificent in *w*.
Jer 10: 12 he founded the world by his *w*
Mic 6: 9 and to fear your name is *w*—
Mt 11: 19 But *w* is proved right by her actions
Lk 2: 52 And Jesus grew in *w* and stature,
Ac 6: 3 known to be full of the Spirit and *w*.
Ro 11: 33 the depth of the riches of the *w*
1Co 1: 17 not with words of human *w*,
1: 30 who has become for us *w* from God
12: 8 through the Spirit the message of *w*
Eph 1: 17 may give you the Spirit of *w*
Col 2: 3 are hidden all the treasures of *w*
2: 23 indeed have an appearance of *w*,
Jas 1: 5 of you lacks *w*, he should ask God,
3: 13 in the humility that comes from *w*.
Rev 5: 12 and wealth and *w* and strength

WISE (WISDOM WISER)

1Ki 3: 12 give you a *w* and discerning heart,
Job 5: 13 He catches the *w* in their craftiness
Ps 19: 7 making the *w* simple.
Pr 3: 7 Do not be *w* in your own eyes;
9: 8 rebuke a *w* man and he will love
10: 1 A *w* son brings joy to his father,
11: 30 and he who wins souls is *w*.
13: 1 A *w* son heeds his father's
13: 20 He who walks with the *w* grows *w*,
16: 23 A *w* man's heart guides his mouth,
17: 28 Even a fool is thought *w*
Ecc 9: 17 The quiet words of the *w* are more
Jer 9: 23 "Let not the *w* man boast
Eze 28: 6 "'Because you think you are *w*,
Da 2: 21 He gives wisdom to the *w*
12: 3 Those who are *w* will shine like
Mt 11: 25 hidden these things from the *w*
25: 2 them were foolish and five were *w*.
1Co 1: 19 I will destroy the wisdom of the *w*;
1: 27 things of the world to shame the *w*;
3: 19 He catches the *w* in their craftiness
Eph 5: 15 but as *w*, making the most
2Ti 3: 15 able to make you *w* for salvation
Jas 3: 13 Who is *w* and understanding

WISER (WISE)

Pr 9: 9 a wise man and he will be *w* still;
1Co 1: 25 of God is *w* than man's wisdom.

WISH (WISHES)

Jn 15: 7 ask whatever you *w*, and it will be
Ro 9: 3 For I could *w* that I myself were
Rev 3: 15 I *w* you were either one

WISHES (WISH)

Rev 22: 17 let him come; and whoever *w*,

WITCHCRAFT

Dt 18: 10 engages in *w*, or casts spells,
Gal 5: 20 idolatry and *w*; hatred, discord,

WITHDREW

Lk 5: 16 But Jesus often *w* to lonely places

WITHER (WITHERS)

Ps 1: 3 and whose leaf does not *w*.
37: 19 In times of disaster they will not *w*;

WITHERS (WITHER)

Isa 40: 7 The grass *w* and the flowers fall,
1Pe 1: 24 the grass *w* and the flowers fall,

WITHHELD (WITHHOLD)

Ge 22: 12 you have not *w* from me your son,

WITHHOLD (WITHHELD WITHHOLDS)

Ps 84: 11 no good thing does he *w*
Pr 23: 13 Do not *w* discipline from a child;

WITHHOLDS (WITHHOLD)

Dt 27: 19 "Cursed is the man who *w* justice

WITNESS (EYEWITNESSES WITNESSES)

Pr 12: 17 truthful *w* gives honest testimony,
19: 9 A false *w* will not go unpunished,
Jn 1: 8 he came only as a *w* to the light.

WITNESSES (WITNESS)

Dt 19: 15 by the testimony of two or three *w*.
Mt 18: 16 by the testimony of two or three *w*.'
Ac 1: 8 and you will be my *w* in Jerusalem,

WIVES (WIFE)

Eph 5: 22 *W*, submit to your husbands
5: 25 love your *w*, just as Christ loved
1Pe 3: 1 talk by the behavior of their *w*,

WIVES' (WIFE)

1Ti 4: 7 with godless myths and old *w* tales

WOE

Isa 6: 5 "*W* to me!" I cried.
Eze 34: 2 *W* to the shepherds
Mt 18: 7 *W* to the world
23: 13 "*W* to you, teachers of the law
Jude : 11 *W* to them! They have taken

WOLF (WOLVES)

Isa 65: 25 *w* and the lamb will feed together.

WOLVES (WOLF)

Mt 10: 16 you out like sheep among *w*.

WOMAN (MAN)

Ge 2: 22 God made a *w* from
2: 23 she shall be called '*w*,'
3: 6 *w* saw that the fruit
3: 12 The *w* you put here with
3: 15 between you and the *w*,
3: 16 To the *w* he said,
12: 11 a beautiful *w* you are.
20: 3 because of the *w* you have
24: 5 if the *w* is unwilling
Ex 2: 1 married a Levite *w*
3: 22 Every *w* is to ask her
21: 10 If he marries another *w*
21: 22 hit a pregnant *w*
Lev 12: 2 *w* who becomes pregnant
15: 19 *w* has her regular flow
15: 25 a *w* has a discharge
18: 17 sexual relations with both a *w*
20: 13 as one lies with a *w*,
Nu 5: 29 when a *w* goes astray
30: 3 young *w* still living in
30: 9 by a widow or divorced *w*
30: 10 *w* living with her husband
Dt 20: 7 become pledged to a *w*
21: 11 the captives a beautiful *w*
22: 5 *w* must not wear men's
22: 13 married this *w* but when
Jdg 4: 9 hand Sisera over to a *w*.
13: 6 the *w* went to her husband
14: 2 have seen a Philistine *w*
16: 4 he fell in love with a *w*
20: 4 husband of the murdered *w*
Ru 3: 11 a *w* of noble character
1Sa 1: 15 a *w* who is deeply troubled
25: 3 intelligent and beautiful *w*,
28: 7 a *w* who is a medium.
2Sa 11: 2 he saw a *w* bathing
13: 17 "Get this *w* out of here
14: 2 had a wise *w* brought
20: 16 a wise *w* called from
1Ki 3: 18 this *w* also had a baby.
17: 24 the *w* said to Elijah.
2Ki 4: 8 a well-to-do *w* was there.

2Ki 8: 1 Elisha had said to the *w*
9: 34 "Take care of that cursed *w*,"
Job 14: 1 Man born of *w* is of few
Pr 11: 16 A kindhearted *w* gains respect,
11: 22 a beautiful *w* who shows no
14: 1 a wise *w* builds her house,
30: 23 unloved *w* who is married,
31: 30 a *w* who fears the LORD
Isa 54: 1 O barren *w*, you who never
Mt 5: 28 looks at a *w* lustfully
9: 20 a *w* who had been subject
15: 28 *W* you have great faith!
26: 7 a *w* came to him with
Mk 5: 25 a *w* was there who had
7: 25 a *w* whose little daughter
Lk 7: 39 what kind of a *w* she is
10: 38 a *w* named Martha opened
13: 12 "*W*, you are set free
15: 8 suppose a *w* has ten silver
Jn 2: 4 *w*, why do you involve
4: 7 a Samaritan *w* came
8: 3 a *w* caught in adultery.
19: 26 *w*, here is your son,"
20: 15 *W*, 'he said, "Why are you crying?
Ac 9: 40 Turning toward the dead *w*,
16: 14 was a *w* named Lydia,
Ro 7: 2 a married *w* is bound to
1Co 7: 2 each *w* her own husband
7: 15 a believing man or *w* is
7: 34 an unmarried *w* or virgin
7: 39 *w* is bound to her husband
11: 3 the head of the *w* is man,
11: 7 the *w* is the glory of man
11: 13 a *w* to pray to God with
Gal 4: 4 his Son, born of a *w*,
4: 31 not children of the slave *w*,
1Ti 2: 11 A *w* should learn in
5: 16 any *w* who is a believer
Rev 2: 20 You tolerate that *w* Jezebel,
12: 1 a *w* clothed with the sun
12: 13 he pursued the *w* who had
17: 3 a *w* sitting on a scarlet

WOMEN (MAN)

Mt 11: 11 among those born of *w*,
28: 5 The angel said to the *w*,
Mk 15: 41 Many other *w* who had come
Lk 1: 42 Blessed are you among *w*,
8: 2 also some *w* who had been
23: 27 *w* who mourned and wailed
24: 11 they did not believe the *w*,
Ac 1: 14 along with the *w* and Mary
16: 13 speak to the *w* who had
17: 4 not a few prominent *w*.
Ro 1: 26 *w* exchanged natural relations
1Co 14: 34 *w* should remain silent in
Php 4: 3 help these *w* who have
1Ti 2: 9 want *w* to dress modestly
5: 2 older *w* as mothers,
Tit 2: 3 teach the older *w* to be
2: 4 train the younger *w* to love
Heb 11: 35 *W* received back their dead
1Pe 3: 5 the holy *w* of the past

WOMB

Job 1: 21 Naked I came from my mother's *w*,
Ps 139: 13 in my mother's *w*,
Pr 31: 2 "O my son, O son of my *w*,
Jer 1: 5 you in the *w* I knew you,
Lk 1: 44 the baby in my *w* leaped for joy.
Jn 3: 4 into his mother's *w* to be born!"

WON (WIN)

1Pe 3: 1 they may be *w* over without words

WONDER (WONDERFUL WONDERS)

Ps 17: 7 Show the *w* of your great love.
SS 3: 3 No *w* the maidens love you!

WONDERFUL* (WONDER)

2Sa 1: 26 Your love for me was *w*,
1: 26 more *w* than that of women.
1Ch 16: 9 tell of all his *w* acts,
Job 42: 3 things too *w* for me to know.
Ps 26: 7 and telling of all your *w* deeds.
31: 21 for he showed his *w* love to me
75: 1 men tell of your *w* deeds.
105: 2 tell of all his *w* acts.

Ps 107: 8 and his *w* deeds for men,
107: 15 and his *w* deeds for men.
107: 21 and his *w* deeds for men.
107: 24 his *w* deeds in the deep.
107: 31 and his *w* deeds for men.
119: 18 *w* things in your law.
119:129 Your statutes are *w;*
131: 1 or things too *w* for me.
139: 6 Such knowledge is too *w* for me,
139: 14 your works are *w,*
145: 5 I will meditate on your *w* works.
Isa 9: 6 *W* Counselor, Mighty God,
28: 29 *w* in counsel and magnificent
Mt 21: 15 of the law saw the *w* things he did
Lk 13: 17 with all the *w* things he was doing.
1Pe 2: 9 out of darkness into his *w* light.

WONDERS (WONDER)

Ex 3: 20 with all the *w* that I will perform
Dt 10: 21 and awesome *w* you saw
2Sa 7: 23 awesome *w* by driving out nations
Job 37: 14 stop and consider God's *w.*
Ps 9: 1 I will tell of all your *w.*
89: 5 The heavens praise your *w,*
119: 27 then I will meditate on your *w.*
Joel 2: 30 I will show *w* in the heavens
Ac 2: 11 we hear them declaring the *w*
2: 19 I will show *w* in the heaven above
5: 12 many miraculous signs and *w*
2Co 12: 12 that mark an apostle—signs, *w*
2Th 2: 9 and *w,* and in every sort
Heb 2: 4 also testified to it by signs, *w*

WOOD

Isa 44: 19 Shall I bow down to a block of *w?''*
1Co 3: 12 costly stones, *w,* hay or straw,

WOOL

Pr 31: 13 She selects *w* and flax
Isa 1: 18 they shall be like *w.*
Da 7: 9 hair of his head was white like *w.*
Rev 1: 14 and hair were white like *w,*

WORD (BYWORD WORDS)

Nu 30: 2 he must not break his *w*
Dt 8: 3 but on every *w* that comes
2Sa 22: 31 the *w* of the LORD is flawless.
Ps 56: 4 In God, whose *w* I praise,
119: 9 By living according to your *w.*
119: 11 I have hidden your *w* in my heart
119:105 Your *w* is a lamp to my feet
Pr 12: 25 but a kind *w* cheers him up.
15: 1 but a harsh *w* stirs up anger.
25: 11 A *w* aptly spoken
30: 5 ''Every *w* of God is flawless;
Isa 55: 11 so is my *w* that goes out
Jer 23: 29 ''Is not my *w* like fire,'' declares
Mt 4: 4 but on every *w* that comes
12: 36 for every careless *w* they have
15: 6 Thus you nullify the *w* of God
Mk 4: 14 parable? The farmer sows the *w.*
Jn 1: 1 was the *W,* and the *W* was
1: 14 The *W* became flesh and lived for a
17: 17 them by the truth; your *w* is truth.
Ac 6: 4 and the ministry of the *w.''*
2Co 2: 17 we do not peddle the *w* of God
4: 2 nor do we distort the *w* of God
Eph 6: 17 of the Spirit, which is the *w* of God.
Php 2: 16 as you hold out the *w* of life—
Col 3: 16 Let the *w* of Christ dwell
2Ti 2: 15 and who correctly handles the *w*
Heb 4: 12 For the *w* of God is living
Jas 1: 22 Do not merely listen to the *w,*
2Pe 1: 19 And we have the *w* of the prophets

WORDS (WORD)

Dt 11: 18 Fix these *w* of mine in your hearts
Ps 12: 6 the *w* of the LORD are flawless,
119:103 How sweet are your *w* to my taste,
119:130 The unfolding of your *w* gives light;
119:160 All your *w* are true;
Pr 2: 1 My son, if you accept my *w*
10: 19 When *w* are many, sin is not absent
16: 24 Pleasant are the honeycomb,
30: 6 Do not add to his *w,*
Ecc 12: 11 The *w* of the wise are like goads,
Jer 15: 16 When your *w* came, I ate them;
Mt 24: 35 but my *w* will never pass away.

Lk 6: 47 and hears my *w* and puts them
Jn 6: 68 You have the *w* of eternal life.
15: 7 in me and my *w* remain in you,
1Co 2: 13 but in *w* taught by the Spirit,
14: 19 rather speak five intelligible *w*
Rev 22: 19 And if anyone takes *w* away

WORK (WORKED WORKER WORKERS WORKING WORKMAN WORKMANSHIP WORKS)

Ge 2: 2 day he rested from all his *w.*
Ex 23: 12 ''Six days do your *w,*
Nu 8: 11 ready to do the *w* of the LORD.
Dt 5: 14 On it you shall not do any *w,*
Ps 19: 1 the skies proclaim the *w*
Ecc 5: 19 his lot and be happy in his *w*—
Jer 48: 10 lax in doing the LORD's *w!*
Mt 20: 1 to hire men to *w* in his vineyard.
Jn 6: 27 Do not *w* for food that spoils,
6: 29 the *w* of him who sent
Ac 13: 2 for the *w* to which I have called
1Co 3: 13 test the quality of each man's *w.*
4: 12 We *w* hard with our own hands.
Eph 4: 16 up in love, as each part does its *w.*
Php 1: 6 that he who began a good *w*
2: 12 continue to *w* out your salvation
Col 3: 23 Whatever you do, *w* at it
1Th 4: 11 and to *w* with your hands,
5: 12 to respect those who *w* hard
2Th 3: 10 If a man will not *w,* he shall not eat
2Ti 3: 17 equipped for every good *w.*
Heb 6: 10 he will not forget your *w*
2Jn : 11 him shares in his wicked *w.*
3Jn : 8 men so that we may *w* together

WORKED (WORK)

1Co 15: 10 No, I *w* harder than all of them—
2Th 3: 8 On the contrary, we *w* night

WORKER (WORK)

Lk 10: 7 for the *w* deserves his wages.
1Ti 5: 18 and ''The *w* deserves his wages.''

WORKERS (WORK)

Mt 9: 37 is plentiful but the *w* are few.
1Co 3: 9 For we are God's fellow *w;*

WORKING (WORK)

Col 3: 23 as *w* for the Lord, not for men,

WORKMAN (WORK)

2Ti 2: 15 a *w* who does not need

WORKMANSHIP* (WORK)

Eph 2: 10 For we are God's *w,* created

WORKS (WORK)

Ps 66: 5 how awesome his *w* in man's behalf
145: 6 of the power of your awesome *w,*
Pr 8: 22 As the first of his *w,*
31: 31 let her *w* bring her praise
Ro 4: 2 in fact, Abraham was justified by *w*
8: 28 in all things God *w* for the good
Eph 2: 9 not by *w,* so that no one can boast.
4: 12 to prepare God's people for *w*

WORLD (WORLDLY)

Ps 9: 8 He will judge the *w*
50: 12 for the *w* is mine, and all that is in it
96: 13 He will judge the *w*
Pr 8: 23 before the *w* began.
Isa 13: 11 I will punish the *w* for its evil,
Zep 1: 18 the whole *w* will be consumed,
Mt 5: 14 ''You are the light of the *w.*
16: 26 for a man if he gains the whole *w,*
Mk 16: 15 into all the *w* and preach the good
Jn 1: 29 who takes away the sin of the *w!*
3: 16 so loved the *w* that he gave his one
8: 12 he said, ''I am the light of the *w,*
15: 19 As it is, you do not belong to the *w,*
16: 33 In this *w* you will have trouble.
17: 5 had with you before the *w* began.
17: 14 not of the *w* any more than I am
18: 36 ''My kingdom is not of this *w.*
Ac 17: 24 ''The God who made the *w*
Ro 3: 19 and the whole *w* held accountable
10: 18 their words to the ends of the *w.''*
1Co 1: 27 things of the *w* to shame the strong.

1Co 3: 19 the wisdom of this *w* is foolishness
6: 2 that the saints will judge the *w?*
2Co 5: 19 that God was reconciling the *w*
10: 3 For though we live in the *w,*
1Ti 6: 7 For we brought nothing into the *w,*
Heb 11: 38 the *w* was not worthy of them.
Jas 2: 5 poor in the eyes of the *w* to be rich
4: 4 with the *w* is hatred toward God?
1Pe 1: 20 before the creation of the *w,*
1Jn 2: 2 but also for the sins of the whole *w.*
2: 15 not love the *w* or anything in the *w.*
5: 4 born of God overcomes the *w.*
Rev 13: 8 slain from the creation of the *w.*

WORLDLY (WORLD)

1Co 3: 1 address you as spiritual but as *w*—
Tit 2: 12 to ungodliness and *w* passions,

WORM

Mk 9: 48 '' 'their *w* does not die,

WORRY (WORRYING)

Mt 6: 25 I tell you, do not *w* about your life,
10: 19 do not *w* about what to say

WORRYING (WORRY)

Mt 6: 27 of you by *w* can add a single hour

WORSHIP (WORSHIPED WORSHIPS)

Jos 22: 27 that we will *w* the LORD
2Ki 17: 36 arm, is the one you must *w.*
1Ch 16: 29 *w* the LORD in the splendor
Ps 95: 6 Come, let us bow down in *w,*
100: 2 *w* the LORD with gladness;
Zec 14: 17 up to Jerusalem to *w* the King,
Mt 2: 2 and have come to *w* him.
4: 9 ''if you will bow down and *w* me.''
Jn 4: 24 and his worshipers must *w* in spirit
Ro 12: 1 to God—this is your spiritual act of *w.*
Heb 10: 1 perfect those who draw near to *w.*

WORSHIPED (WORSHIP)

2Ch 29: 30 and bowed their heads and *w.*
Mt 28: 9 clasped his feet and *w* him.

WORSHIPS (WORSHIP)

Isa 44: 15 But he also fashions a god and *w* it;

WORTH (WORTHY)

Job 28: 13 Man does not comprehend its *w;*
Pr 31: 10 She is *w* far more than rubies.
Mt 10: 31 are *w* more than many sparrows.
Ro 8: 18 sufferings are not *w* comparing
1Pe 1: 7 of greater *w* than gold,
3: 4 which is of great *w* in God's sight.

WORTHLESS

Pr 11: 4 Wealth is *w* in the day of wrath,
Jas 1: 26 himself and his religion is *w.*

WORTHY (WORTH)

1Ch 16: 25 For great is the LORD and most *w*
Mt 10: 37 more than me is not *w* of me;
Lk 15: 19 I am no longer *w* to be called your
Eph 4: 1 to live a life *w* of the calling you
Php 1: 27 in a manner *w* of the gospel
Col 1: 10 in order that you may live a life *w*
1Ti 3: 8 are to be men of respect, sincere,
Heb 3: 3 Jesus has been found *w*
3Jn : 6 on their way in a manner *w* of God.
Rev 5: 2 ''Who is *w* to break the seals

WOUND (WOUNDS)

1Co 8: 12 and *w* their weak conscience,

WOUNDS (WOUND)

Pr 27: 6 *w* from a friend can be trusted
Isa 53: 5 and by his *w* we are healed.
Zec 13: 6 'What are these *w* on your body?'
1Pe 2: 24 by his *w* you have been healed.

WRAPS

Ps 104: 2 He *w* himself in light

WRATH

2Ch 36: 16 scoffed at his prophets until the *w*
Ps 2: 5 and terrifies them in his *w,* saying,
76: 10 Surely your *w* against men brings
Pr 15: 1 A gentle answer turns away *w,*

WRESTLED (continued)

Isa 13: 13 at the *w* of the LORD Almighty,
   51: 17 the cup of his *w*,
Jer 25: 15 filled with the wine of my *w*
Eze 5: 13 my *w* against them will subside,
   20: 8 So I said I would pour out my *w*
Am 1: 3 I will not turn back ,my *w*,
Na 1: 2 maintains his *w* against his enemies
Zep 1: 15 That day will be a day of *w*,
Jn 3: 36 for God's *w* remains on him.''
Ro 1: 18 The *w* of God is being revealed
   2: 5 you are storing up *w*
   5: 9 saved from God's *w* through him!
   9:22 choosing to show his *w*
1Th 5: 9 God did not appoint us to suffer *w*
Rev 6: 16 and from the *w* of the Lamb!
   19: 15 the fury of the *w* of God Almighty.

WRESTLED

Ge 32: 24 and a man *w* with him till daybreak

WRITE (WRITER WRITING WRITTEN WROTE)

Dt 6: 9 *W* them on the doorframes
   10: 2 I will *w* on the tablets the words
Pr 7: 3 *w* them on the tablet of your heart.
Jer 31: 33 and *w* it on their hearts.
Heb 8: 10 and *w* them on their hearts.
Rev 3: 12 I will also *w* on him my new name.

WRITER* (WRITE)

Ps 45: 1 my tongue is the pen of a skillful *w*.

WRITING (WRITE)

1Co 14: 37 him acknowledge that what I am *w*

WRITTEN (WRITE)

Dt 28: 58 which are *w* in this book,
Jos 1: 8 careful to do everything *w* in it.
   23: 6 to obey all that is *w* in the Book
Ps 40: 7 it is *w* about me in the scroll.
Da 12: 1 everyone whose name is found *w*
Mal 3: 16 A scroll of remembrance was *w*
Lk 10: 20 but rejoice that your names are *w*
   24:44 must be fulfilled that is *w* about me
Jn 20: 31 these are *w* that you may believe
   21: 25 for the books that would be *w*.
Ro 2: 15 of the law are *w* on their hearts,
1Co 4: 6 ''Do not go beyond what is *w*.''
   10: 11 as examples and were *w* down
2Co 3: 3 *w* not with ink but with the Spirit
Col 2: 14 having canceled the *w* code,
Heb 10: 7 it is *w* about me in the scroll—
   12: 23 whose names are *w* in heaven.
Rev 21: 27 but only those whose names are *w*

WRONG (WRONGDOING WRONGED WRONGS)

Ex 23: 2 Do not follow the crowd in doing *w*
Nu 5: 7 must make full restitution for his *w*,
Dt 32: 4 A faithful God who does no *w*,
Job 34: 12 unthinkable that God would do *w*,
Ps 5: 5 you hate all who do *w*.
Gal 2: 11 to his face, because he was clearly in the *w*.

1Th 5: 15 that nobody pays back *w* for *w*,

WRONGDOING (WRONG)

Job 1: 22 sin by charging God with *w*.
1Jn 5: 17 All *w* is sin, and there is sin that

WRONGED (WRONG)

1Co 6: 7 not rather be *w*? Why not rather

WRONGS (WRONG)

Pr 10: 12 but love covers over all *w*.
1Co 13: 5 angered, it keeps no record of *w*.

WROTE (WRITE)

Ex 34: 28 And he *w* on the tablets the words
Jn 5: 46 for he *w* about me.
   8: 8 down and *w* on the ground.

XERXES

King of Persia, husband of Esther. Deposed Vashti; replaced her with Esther (Est 1-2). Sealed Haman's edict to annihilate the Jews (Est 3). Received Esther without having called her (Est 5: 1-8). Honored Mordecai (Est 6). Hanged Haman (Est 7). Issued edict allowing Jews to defend themselves (Est 8). Exalted Mordecai (Est 8:1-2, 15; 9:4; 10).

YEAR (YEARS)

Ex 34: 23 Three times a *y* all your men are
Lev 16: 34 to be made once a *y* for all the sins
   25: 4 But in the seventh *y* the land is
   25: 11 The fiftieth *y* shall be a jubilee
Heb 10: 1 repeated endlessly *y* after *y*,

YEARS (YEAR)

Ge 1: 14 to mark seasons and days and *y*,
Ex 12: 40 lived in Egypt was 430 *y*.
   16: 35 The Israelites ate manna forty *y*,
Job 36: 26 of his *y* is past finding out.
Ps 90: 4 For a thousand *y* in your sight
   90: 10 The length of our days is seventy *y*
Pr 3: 2 they will prolong your life many *y*
Lk 3: 23 Jesus himself was about thirty *y* old
2Pe 3: 8 the Lord a day is like a thousand *y*,
Rev 20: 2 and bound him for a thousand *y*.

YEAST

Ex 12: 15 are to eat bread made without *y*.
Mt 16: 6 guard against the *y* of the Pharisees
1Co 5: 6 you know that a little *y* works

YESTERDAY

Heb 13: 8 Jesus Christ is the same *y*

YOKE (YOKED)

1Ki 12: 4 and the heavy *y* he put on us,
Mt 11: 29 Take my *y* upon you and learn
Gal 5: 1 be burdened again by a *y*

YOKED (YOKE)

2Co 6: 14 Do not be *y* together

YOUNG (YOUNGER YOUTH)

2Ch 10: 14 he followed the advice of the *y* men
Ps 37: 25 I was *y* and now I am old,
   119: 9 How can a *y* man keep his way
Pr 20: 29 The glory of *y* men is their strength
Isa 40: 11 he gently leads those that have *y*.
Joel 2: 28 your *y* men will see visions.
Ac 2: 17 your *y* men will see visions,
   7: 58 at the feet of a *y* man named Saul.
1Ti 4: 12 down on you because you are *y*,
Tit 2: 6 encourage the *y* men
1Pe 5: 5 *Y* men, in the same way be
1Jn 2: 13 I write to you, *y* men,

YOUNGER (YOUNG)

1Ti 5: 1 Treat *y* men as brothers, older
Tit 2: 4 Then they can train the *y* women

YOUTH (YOUNG)

Ps 103: 5 so that your *y* is renewed like
Ecc 12: 1 Creator in the days of your *y*,
2Ti 2: 22 Flee the evil desires of *y*,

ZACCHAEUS

Lk 19: 2 A man was there by the name of *Z*:

ZEAL (ZEALOUS)

Ps 69: 9 for *z* for your house consumes me,
Pr 19: 2 to have *z* without knowledge,
Isa 59: 17 and wrapped himself in *z*
Jn 2: 17 ''*Z* for your house will consume me
Ro 10: 2 their *z* is not based on knowledge.
   12: 11 Never be lacking in *z*,

ZEALOUS (ZEAL)

Nu 25: 13 he was *z* for the honor of his God
Pr 23: 17 always be *z* for the fear
Eze 39: 25 and I will be *z* for my holy name.
Gal 4: 18 fine to be *z*, provided the purpose is

ZEBULUN

Son of Jacob by Leah (Ge 30:20; 35:23; 1Ch 2: 1). Tribe of blessed (Ge 49:13; Dt 33:18-19), numbered (Nu 1:31; 26:27), allotted land (Jos 19: 10-16; Eze 48:26), failed to fully possess (Jdg 1: 30), supported Deborah (Jdg 4:6-10; 5:14, 18), David (1Ch 12:33), 12,000 from (Rev 7:8).

ZECHARIAH

1. Son of Jeroboam II; king of Israel (2Ki 15: 8-12).

2. Post-exilic prophet who encouraged rebuilding of temple (Ezr 5:1; 6:14; Zec 1:1).

ZEDEKIAH

1. False prophet (1Ki 22:11-24; 2Ch 18:10-23).

2. Mattaniah, son of Josiah (1Ch 3:15), made king of Judah by Nebuchadnezzar (2Ki 24:17-25: 7; 2Ch 36:10-14; Jer 37-39; 52:1-11).

ZEPHANIAH

Prophet; descendant of Hezekiah (Zep 1:1).

ZERUBBABEL

Descendant of David (1Ch 3:19; Mt 1:3). Led return from exile (Ezr 2:2; Ne 7:7). Governor of Israel; helped rebuild altar and temple (Ezr 3; Hag 1-2; Zec 4).

ZILPAH

Servant of Leah, mother of Jacob's sons Gad and Asher (Ge 30:9-12; 35:26, 46:16-18).

ZIMRI

King of Israel (1Ki 16:9-20).

ZION

2Sa 5: 7 David captured the fortress of *Z*,
Ps 2: 6 King on *Z*, my holy hill.''
   9: 11 to the LORD, enthroned in *Z*;
   74: 2 Mount *Z*, where you dwelt.
   87: 2 the LORD loves the gates of *Z*
   102: 13 and have compassion on *Z*,
   137: 3 ''Sing us one of the songs of *Z*!''
Isa 2: 3 The law will go out from *Z*,
   28: 16 ''See, I lay a stone in *Z*,
   51: 11 They will enter *Z* with singing;
   52: 8 When the LORD returns to *Z*,
Jer 50: 5 They will ask the way to *Z*
Joel 3: 21 The LORD dwells in *Z*!
Am 6: 1 to you who are complacent in *Z*,
Mic 4: 2 The law will go out from *Z*,
Zec 9: 9 Rejoice greatly, O Daughter of *Z*!
Ro 9: 33 I lay in *Z* a stone that causes men
   11: 26 ''The deliverer will come from *Z*:
Heb 12: 22 But you have come to Mount *Z*,
Rev 14: 1 standing on Mount *Z*,

ZIPPORAH*

Daughter of Reuel; wife of Moses (Ex 2:21-22; 4:20-26; 18:1-6).

ZOPHAR

One of Job's friends (Job 11; 20).

HELPS

FOR
BIBLE
STUDY

CHRONOLOGY OF BIBLICAL EVENTS

T he accompanying table includes both precise dates—some quite certain and others less provable which may be a year or two off—and round numbers, indicated by italic type, which indicate general periods or approximations. To this italic class must belong most of the dates included for the biblical and other books.

CHRONOLOGICAL TABLE

Dates in italics represent periods rather than exact years. Names of persons mentioned in the Bible are printed in boldface type at their first appearance.

BC *The Background of the Patriarchs*

8000 Stone Age inhabitants of Palestine leave evidences of village life and agriculture.

5500 Pottery invented.

4500 Use of metals begins with gold and copper.

3500 Sumerians settle in S Mesopotamia and develop complex civilization, including pictographic writing.

3300 Bronze is discovered as harder metal for tools and weapons.

3200 Sumerians adapt pictographs to cuneiform system of punching syllabic characters into clay tablets.

3000 Egyptians become united under first dynasty and develop advanced civilization. They adapt pictographs to hieroglyphic writing, invent papyrus.

2300 Sargon, a Semite, conquers Sumer and builds vast Akkadian empire. His people learn Sumerian arts and culture.

2000 Ur-Nammu, Sumerian king of Ur, gains control of all Sumer and Akkad, issues earliest known code of laws.

1900 Abraham migrates to S Palestine. Sodom and Gomorrah destroyed.

1750 Hyksos invaders seize control of Palestine and Egypt. Hammurabi, Semitic ruler of first Babylonian Empire, issues elaborate law code. Kings of Mari preserve archive of cuneiform tablets which reveal customs like some in Genesis stories and mention Habiru (Hebrews?) and Benjaminites.

1650 Alphabet invented, probably by Canaanites.

1570 Ahmose I of Egypt expels Hyksos, destroying many Palestinian cities.

1468 Thutmose III of Egypt reconquers Palestine, establishes empire soon reaching the Euphrates.

1400 At Nuzi, Hurrians (Horites) leave cuneiform tablets revealing customs like some in Genesis stories and mentioning Habiru. At Ugarit (Ras Shamra) in N Syria, Canaanites leave tablets, especially of Baal myths, in a language much like Hebrew.

1360 Palestinian vassals ask Pharaoh Akhenaton, in cuneiform letters preserved at his capital, Akhetaton (Tell el-Amarna), for protection against Habiru, apparently Hebrew tribes entering Palestine, possibly with **Jacob** as a leader. Perhaps it is under Akhenaton that **Joseph** holds office and some Hebrew tribes settle in Egypt.

The Exodus and Settlement in Palestine

1302 Seti I accedes in Egypt, revives empire in Palestine, and undertakes to drive Hittites from Syria.

1290 Ramses II succeeds Seti, continues his father's military campaigns in Syria-Palestine, begins extensive building projects in Delta region with enforced labor that includes Apiru, i.e., Habiru or Hebrews.

1250 **Moses** leads exodus of Hebrews from Egypt.

1225 Hebrew tribes under **Joshua** destroy a number of major Canaanite cities.

1220 Merneptah, Ramses' son and successor, erects victory stele naming Israel among peoples defeated in Palestine.

1200 Iron comes into use.

1188 Invasion of Egypt by Sea Peoples is turned back. Part of them, the Philistines, settle on the S Palestinian coast.

1120 N Israelite tribes join in defeating **Sisera**.

1100 **Abimelech** destroys Shechem.

1075 Gibeah destroyed in intertribal war against Benjamin.

1050 Philistines destroy temple at Shiloh, also other Israelite and Canaanite cities.

The United Kingdom

1020 **Saul** unites Israelite tribes as first king.

1009/8 Saul dies. **David** is chosen king of Judah in Hebron.

1002/1 David is anointed king of Israel, captures Jerusalem and makes it his capital.

990 David's interest in poetry stimulates written collections of old poems as well as new compositions.

970/69 **Solomon** anointed king. David dies.

965 Building of temple is begun in April/May.

959 Temple completed in October/November.

950 Solomon encourages collection and composition of wisdom sayings. Literature flourishes, e.g., stories of Saul and David.

The Divided Kingdoms

931/30 **Rehoboam** succeeds Solomon. N tribes secede, choose **Jeroboam** king of Israel.

926/25 Egyptian invader **Shishak** (Sheshonk I) despoils Jerusalem, destroys several cities of both Israel and Judah.

920 Gezer calendar, earliest example of written Hebrew yet found.

913 **Abijam** succeeds Rehoboam in Judah.

911/10 **Asa** succeeds Abijam in Judah.

910/9 **Nadab** succeeds Jeroboam in Israel.

909/8 Nadab killed; **Baasha** usurps in Israel.

886/85 **Elah** succeeds Baasha in Israel.

885/84 Elah killed by **Zimri**, who reigns seven days. **Omri** and **Tibni** lay rival claims to throne of Israel.

880 Omri overcomes Tibni, builds Samaria as his capital.

874/73 **Ahab** succeeds Omri in Israel.

873/72 **Jehoshaphat** coregent with Asa in Judah.

870/69 Asa dies; Jehoshaphat sole ruler in Judah.

865 Prophet **Elijah** sparks revival of Yahwism in Israel.

854/53 **Jehoram** (Joram) coregent with Jehoshaphat in Judah.

853 Assyrian record of Shalmaneser III mentions Ahab of Israel at Battle of Qarqar. **Ahaziah** succeeds Ahab.

852 **Jehoram** (Joram) succeeds Ahaziah in Israel.

850 **Elisha** succeeds Elijah as influential prophet of Yahwism in Israel. King **Mesha** of Moab erects stele to commemorate his winning independence from Israel.

848 Jehoshaphat dies; Jerhoram (Joram) sole ruler in Judah.

841 **Ahaziah** succeeds Jehoram in Judah. He and Jehoram of Israel are killed in revolt of **Jehu**. Assyrian obelisk shows Jehu as king of Israel paying tribute to Shalmaneser III. **Athaliah** seizes rule in Judah.

835 Athaliah killed; **Jehoash** (Joash) enthroned in Judah.

830 Yahwist revival in Israel stimulates collection and writing of traditions of judges and beginning of monarchy.

814/13 **Jehoahaz** (Joahaz) succeeds Jehu in Israel.

798 **Jehoash** (Joash) succeeds Jehoahaz in Israel.

796 Jehoash of Judah assassinated; **Amaziah** succeeds.

793/92 **Jeroboam II** coregent with Jehoash in Israel.

792/91 War between Israel and Judah results in capture of Amaziah of Judah. **Azariah** (Uzziah) is enthroned in his place.

782/81 Jehoash of Israel dies; Jeroboam II sole ruler. He frees Amaziah, who resumes rule in Judah.

767 Amaziah assassinated; Azariah sole ruler in Judah.

755 **Amos** is banished from Bethel. **Hosea** begins to prophesy.

753 **Zechariah** succeeds Jeroboam II in Israel.

752 Zechariah killed; **Shallum** usurps, reigns one month; **Menahem** usurps.

750 **Jotham** coregent in Judah when Azariah becomes leper.

742/41 Menahem of Israel pays tribute to **Tiglath-pileser III** of Assyria. **Pekahiah** succeeds Menahem.

740/39 Pekahiah killed in Israel; **Pekah** usurps, dates reign from 752. Azariah dies in Judah; Jotham sole ruler. **Isaiah** called to prophesy.

735 **Ahaz** coregent with Jotham in Judah.

734 Syro-Ephraimitic War sets Israel and Syria (Aram-Damascus) against Judah. Ahaz asks help from Tiglath-pileser.

733/32 Tiglath-pileser invades Israel, seizes Galilee and **Transjordan**, exiles many of inhabitants.

732/31 Pekah of Israel is killed; **Hoshea** usurps as Assyrian vassal. Jotham of Judah dies; Ahaz sole ruler.

725/24 Hoshea revolts. **Shalmaneser V** of Assyria besieges Samaria. **Micah** prophesies the city's destruction.

723/22 Fall of Samaria brings end to N kingdom, exile to many Israelites.

The S Kingdom Alone

716/15 **Hezekiah** succeeds Ahaz in Judah.

710 Hezekiah encourages immigration of N Yahwists who escaped exile. They bring traditions and documents, which stimulate literary activity, e.g., probably compiling of core of Deuteronomy.

701 Assyrian record of **Sennacherib** reports his siege of Jerusalem.

697/96 **Manasseh** coregent with Hezekiah.

687/86 Hezekiah dies; Manasseh sole ruler. As Assyrian vassal he promotes Assyrian cults, represses Yahwism.

663 Ashurbanipal (**Osnappar**) destroys Thebes and adds Egypt to the Assyrian Empire, bringing it to its widest extent.

643/42 **Amon** succeeds Manasseh.

641/40 **Josiah** succeeds Amon.

630 **Zephaniah** prophesies.

628/27 **Jeremiah** called to prophesy.

623/22 Law scroll found in temple is made basis for drastic Yahwist reform. Josiah extends rule to N as Assyrian power is weakened by revolts.

615 Editors under influence of Deuteronomy compile historical records of Israel.

612 **Nahum** prophesies destruction of Assyrian capital, Nineveh, which is accomplished by Cyaxares, king of Media.

609 Josiah killed in June/July as indicated by Babylonian record of expedition of **Pharaoh Neco** to support Assyrian forces holding out in W.

Jehoahaz succeeds, is deposed by Neco after three months. **Jehoiakim** is enthroned as Egyptian vassal.

607 **Habakkuk** begins to prophesy.

605 **Nebuchadrezzar** defeats Neco and Assyrian remnants at Carchemish in May/June, takes Palestine from Egypt. In September he accedes as Babylonian king.

604/3 Jeremiah dictates oracles to **Baruch** in December/January.

601 Nebuchadrezzar suffers heavy losses in attempt to invade Egypt. As a result Jehoiakim withholds tribute.

598/97 **Jehoiachin** succeeds Jehoiakim in December/January, *ca.* when Nebuchadrezzar besieges Jerusalem.

597 Babylonian Chronicle dates Nebuchadrezzar's capture of Jerusalem March 16. Jehoiachin and many leading citizens exiled; **Zedekiah** made regent as Babylonian puppet.

593 **Ezekiel** called to prophesy July 31.

589 Pro-Egyptian party forces Zedekiah to revolt.

588 Nebuchadrezzar besieges Jerusalem January 15. Later the siege is lifted for a time as the Babylonians drive back invasion of Palestine by **Pharaoh Hophra**.

586 Wall of Jerusalem breached July 18; Zedekiah flees and is captured. Destruction of city and temple begins August 14 or 17. Many more are exiled.

The Exile and Persian Rule

562 **Evil-merodach** succeeds Nebuchadrezzar in September.

561 Jehoiachin released from prison March 31 or April 2.

550 **Cyrus** the Persian gains control of Median Empire.

546 Cyrus conquers Lydia in Asia Minor.

540 Isaiah prophesies Cyrus will free exiles for return to Jerusalem.

539 Cyrus' army takes Babylon without a battle.

538 Cyrus authorizes return to ancestral lands of displaced peoples. **Sheshbazzar** leads a body of Jews to Jerusalem.

530 Cambyses succeeds Cyrus.

525 Cambyses adds Egypt to Persian Empire.

522 **Darius I** overcomes rival to secure Persian throne.

520 **Zerubbabel** begins rebuilding of temple in August/September at urging of **Haggai** and **Zechariah**.

515 Temple completed March 12.

486 Xerxes I (**Ahasuerus**) succeeds Darius.

480 Xerxes attempts conquest of Greece.

465 **Artaxerxes I** succeeds Xerxes.

450 Malachi composed.

445 **Nehemiah** appointed governor of Judea, plans rebuilding of walls of Jerusalem.

433 Nehemiah ends first term as governor.

404 Accession of **Artaxerxes II**.

397 **Ezra** brings the Law, probably the completed Pentateuch, to Jerusalem and gains its acceptance as the constitution of the Jewish state.

380 I, II Chronicles, Ezra, Nehemiah, Joel composed.

Hellenistic Rule and the Maccabean Revolt

334 **Alexander** the Great begins his conquest of the Persian Empire.

332 Alexander conquers Syria-Palestine, taking Tyre by a seven-month siege.

331 Alexander conquers Egypt, founds Alexandria.

323 Alexander dies, leaving his empire for his generals to squabble over. Ptolemy, founder of the Ptolemaic dynasty, gets control of Egypt, claims but is unable to hold Palestine.

312 Seleucus, founder of the Seleucid dynasty, gets control of Babylonia. He dates his reign, on which the Seleucid Era is based, from October.

301 Seleucus adds Syria to his realm. Ptolemy secures firm hold on Palestine.

300 Seleucus founds Antioch in Syria as his capital.

250 LXX, Greek translation of the Law (Pentateuch), is made in Alexandria, followed in time by translation of other books. Regular readings in the synagogues accord them wide familiarity and acceptance.

198 Seleucid **Antiochus III**, the Great, takes Palestine from Ptolemy V.

190 Romans defeat Antiochus the Great at Magnesia, remove Asia Minor from his control, impose heavy tribute and hostages.

187 **Seleucus IV** succeeds his father, Antiochus the Great.

180 **Jeshua ben Sira** writes Ecclesiasticus.

175 **Antiochus IV Epiphanes** succeeds his brother, Seleucus IV. He deposes the Jewish high priest, **Onias III**, appointing **Jason**.

172 **Menelaus** outbids Jason for the high priesthood.

169 Antiochus invades Egypt. Jason makes armed attack on Jerusalem. Antiochus brings army to quell revolt, enters temple, takes some of its treasures.

168 Roman ultimatum halts Antiochus in another invasion of Egypt.

167 Antiochus bans Jewish religious practices, desecrates temple on December 6.

166 **Judas Maccabeus** takes lead in Jewish revolt, organizes guerrilla force.

165 Antiochus sets out on campaign in E, leaves **Lysias** in charge of Syria and Palestine. Daniel is written.

164 Judas defeats Lysias, enters Jerusalem, rededicates the temple on December 14.

163 Antiochus IV dies in the E. His young son, **Antiochus V Eupator**, succeeds with Lysias as regent.

162 **Demetrius I**, son of Seleucus IV, seizes the throne.

160 Judas killed in battle. His brother **Jonathan** takes command of the revolt.

152 **Alexander Balas**, pretender to the Seleucid throne, appoints Jonathan high priest.

150 Qumran community formed. Judith, Testaments of the Twelve Patriarchs written.

143 Jonathan murdered. His brother **Simon** takes over.

Judean Independence and Conquest by Rome

142 Simon secures from **Demetrius II** recognition as high priest and ruler of an independent state of Judea.

134 Simon murdered; his son **John Hyrcanus I** succeeds.

130 Jeshua ben Sira's grandson translates Ecclesiasticus into Greek.

120 Jubilees written.

110 Hyrcanus conquers most of Palestine, forcibly proselytizes many. Pharisees gain wide following as opponents of aristocratic Sadducees. **Simon of Cyrene** writes five-volume history of Maccabean revolt.

104 Aristobulus I succeeds Hyrcanus, conquers Galilee.

103 Alexander Janneus succeeds his brother Aristobulus, issues coins with title "king," completes conquest of Palestine.

100 I Maccabees written.

90 Pharisees lead six-year revolt against Janneus, ended by his crucifying eight hundred rebels.

80 Epitomist condenses Simon of Cyrene's history to form II Maccabees. Main part of Enoch written.

76 Janneus dies; his widow, Alexandra, rules as queen, favors Pharisees.

67 Alexandra dies, bequeathing rule to her elder son, Hyrcanus II; but the younger, Aristobulus II, backed by the Sadducees, seizes it by force.

65 Hyrcanus is incited by Antipater, an Idumean, to besiege Jerusalem. Both parties seek Roman support.

63 Pompey captures Jerusalem, brings Palestine under Roman rule, appoints Hyrcanus II high priest.

50 Wisdom of Solomon written.

48 Julius Caesar defeats Pompey, becomes absolute Roman ruler. Antipater appointed governor of Palestine.

44 Caesar assassinated by Brutus, Cassius, and others. Palestine comes under control of Cassius.

42 Mark Antony and Octavius Caesar defeat Brutus and Cassius. Palestine under Antony.

40 Parthians invade Palestine, help Antigonus, son of Aristobulus II, to seize control. Roman Senate proclaims **Herod**, son of Antipater, king of the Jews.

37 Herod defeats Antigonus, establishes himself as king.

31 Octavius defeats Antony, becomes master of Roman world.

27 Octavius proclaimed **Augustus** Octavianus, Roman emperor.

20/19 Rebuilding of temple begun.

The Life of Jesus

7 Jesus is born.

4 Herod dies in April. His realm is divided among three sons: Judea, Samaria to **Archelaus**; Galilee, Perea to **Herod** Antipas; NE region to **Philip**.

AD

6 Augustus deposes Archelaus, puts Judea under Roman prefect.

14 **Tiberius Caesar** succeeds Augustus August 19.

25 Philo of Alexandria writes to harmonize Judaism and Greek philosophy.

26 **Pontius Pilate** becomes prefect of Judea.

28 **John** begins baptizing in fifteenth year of Tiberius.

30 Jesus crucified Friday, April 7.

The Career of Paul

33 **Paul** is converted, goes into Nabatean Arabia.

36 Paul visits Jerusalem, goes to Syria and Cilicia. Pilate replaced as prefect of Judea.

37 Caligula succeeds Tiberius March 16.

41 **Claudius** succeeds Caligula January 25. **Herod** Agrippa I appointed king of Judea, executes **James**, imprisons **Peter**.

44 Herod Agrippa dies. Judea put under procuratorship.

47 Paul and **Barnabas** begin "first missionary journey," to Cyprus, S Galatia.

49 Paul confers with apostles in Jerusalem, wins approval of Gentile mission. He and **Silas** begin "second missionary journey," going overland through Asia Minor and crossing to Macedonia. Claudius expels Jews from Rome.

50 Paul works in Macedonia, Athens. He arrives in Corinth, meets **Aquila** and **Prisca**, recent refugees from Rome, writes I Thessalonians.

51 Paul is hailed before proconsul **Gallio** after eighteen months in Corinth.

52 Paul leaves Corinth, sails for Ephesus, then Syria.

53 Paul arrives at Ephesus on "third missionary journey," beginning three-year residence there.

54 Nero succeeds Claudius.

55 Paul perhaps writes Philippians, Colossians, Philemon while imprisoned for a time in Ephesus.

56 Paul writes I Corinthians. He makes a brief "painful" visit to Corinth, returns to Ephesus, writes a "severe" letter to the Corinthians (II Corinthians 10–13 in the view of some scholars). Perhaps at this time he writes Galatians, Philippians 3. He goes to Macedonia, where he writes part or all of II Corinthians. He begins three-month stay in Corinth.

57 Paul writes Romans at Corinth, spends Passover at Philippi, arrives at Jerusalem for Pentecost. He is arrested and sent to the procurator **Felix** at Caesarea.

59 **Festus** replaces Felix as procurator. Paul appeals to Caesar, is sent to Rome.

60 Paul arrives in Rome, perhaps writes Philippians, Colossians, Philemon while imprisoned there. I Peter written ca. this time if by Peter.

64 Fire destroys much of Rome in July. Christians are blamed and persecuted. Perhaps Peter and Paul are among the martyrs.

The Period of the Later NT Books

66 Jews revolt against Rome.

68 Nero commits suicide; Galba succeeds. Roman troops destroy Qumran community.

69 Galba succeeded by Otho, Vitellius, and finally Vespasian, the general besieging Jerusalem.

70 Vespasian's son Titus takes Jerusalem in August, destroys temple, and razes city.

73 Last Jewish rebels commit suicide at Masada.

75 Mark written. Josephus writes an account of the war in Aramaic, later translates it into Greek.

79 Titus succeeds Vespasian.

81 Domitian succeeds Titus.

85 Matthew written.

90 Luke-Acts written. Rabbis at Jamnia close Hebrew canon.

92 Paul's letters collected and circulated together.

93 Josephus writes his Antiquities of the Jews.

95 Hebrews, Revelation written.

96 Nerva succeeds Domitian. I Clement written, perhaps also I Peter if pseudonymous.

98 Trajan succeeds Nerva.

100 John, James, and main part of II Esdras written.

110 Letters of John written.

115 Letters of Ignatius and Polycarp written.

117 Hadrian succeeds Trajan.

125 Jude written. Oldest extant NT manuscript copied—a papyrus fragment of John.

130 Pastorals, Letter of Barnabas written.

132 Hadrian's plan to rebuild Jerusalem as Roman colony incites second Jewish revolt, led by Simon ben Koseba.

135 Romans put down revolt, proceed to build Aelia Capitolina on site of Jerusalem.

138 Hadrian succeeded by Antoninus Pius.

140 Shepherd of Hermas written.

144 Marcion promotes his expurgated version of Luke and Paul's letters to replace the OT in Christian usage.

150 II Peter, Teaching of the Twelve Apostles (Didache) written.

MEASURES AND MONEY IN THE BIBLE

A Canadian motorist visiting the United States finds that more gallons are needed to fill his tank, and a pharmacist or jeweler soon learns that the ounces on his scales are heavier than those at the post office. Ancient people also had to take different standards for measures into account (cf., e.g., Genesis 23:16; Exodus 30:13; Deuteronomy 3:11; II Samuel 14:26; II Chronicles 3:3; Ezekiel 40:5). Archaeological discovery of inscribed weights and containers from biblical times shows further that there was considerable tolerance in the standards, for no two examples have been found in agreement. Evidently the repeated injunctions against false measures (e.g. Leviticus 19:35-36; Deuteronomy 25:13-15; Proverbs 20:10; Amos 8:5) were aimed at rather gross deviations. That the values varied at different periods would seem almost certain (cf. II Chronicles 3:3), and that some of the relations stated in the Bible (cf. esp. Ezekiel 45:11-15) and other ancient writings are later harmonizings of systems originally independent is to be suspected.

In spite of much scholarly study, therefore, calculations of biblical measures are at best approximate. For convenience the equivalents in the tables given here have been chosen as "round" numbers. Though obviously not exact, they lie within the limits indicated by the varying data and in view of the uncertainties may sometimes be as close as other computations to several decimal places.

Lengths and Areas

The measure of length most often mentioned in the Bible is the *cubit*, which originated as the distance from elbow to tip of middle finger. The *span*, originally the distance between the tips of thumb and little finger of the outstretched hand, came to be considered half a cubit. Various archaeological data—e.g., the inscription stating

the length of Hezekiah's conduit (cf. II Kings 20:20)—point to a usual cubit of seventeen-and-a-half to eighteen inches, so that the convenient equivalents of Table 1 are fairly close.

In the vision of the restored temple in Ezekiel 40–48 the dimensions are given in cubits described as a handbreadth longer than usual (40:5; 43:13). Probably this represents a return to a standard known or at least believed to have been in use when Solomon's Temple was built (cf. II Chronicles 3:3). Egyptian and Mesopotamian analogies suggest that the longer cubit contained seven handbreadths, equaling twenty to twenty-one inches, though it is not certain that handbreadths under the two standards were identical. Apparently the span of Ezekiel 43:13 is intended to be equal to the half cubit of verse 17 and thus in this system contained three-and-a-half handbreadths.

In the NT *fathom* translates a Greek measure based on the distance between fingertips of the outstretched arms, *ca.* six feet. It was used for land as well as water. *Mile* in Matthew 5:41 is probably the Roman mile of 1,000 paces (double steps), standardized at *ca.* fifty-eight inches each, or a total of *ca.* 1,618 yards. Elsewhere in the RSV miles are conversions into modern terms of Greek distances in stadia, the stadion being four hundred cubits, *ca.* two hundred yards. Similarly *hundred yards* (John 21:8) is a conversion of two hundred cubits.

A *sabbath day's journey* was the distance scribal interpretation permitted one to go from his home on the sabbath without violating the injunction of Exodus 16:29. Most evidence indicates it was 2,000 cubits, *ca.* 1,000 yards (cf. Joshua 3:4). *Day's journey* was apparently not a standardized distance.

Area, when not indicated by dimensions in cubits, was measured by the "yoke," translated *acre*—i.e., the land a yoke of oxen could plow in a day, perhaps *ca.* six-tenths of an acre like the corresponding Roman term—or else by the amount of grain needed to seed the plot (cf. Leviticus 27:16; I Kings 18:32).

Volumes

The units in Tables 2 and 3 are classified as dry or liquid measures on the basis of their use in the Bible. Possibly some were used for both kinds of materials, but all except the largest may represent containers—pots and perhaps baskets—of standardized shapes especially suited for one or the other. In the description of a vision of a woman in an *ephah* (Zechariah 5:6-11), the vessel is evidently so identified because of its form rather than its size. Here a lead cover is needed to keep the woman inside; contrast the excavated specimens of jars inscribed *bath*, which have small mouths. The demand that ephah and bath be "of the same measure" (Ezekiel 45:11) thus may be an effort to standardize the capacities of vessels of similar size but differing shapes.

The derivation of the name *homer* shows that originally it was an assload of grain, which would be carried in a large sack (cf. Genesis 42:27). No doubt the quantity early became standardized along the trade routes, and at various places local smaller measures came to be adjusted to convenient fractions of this major

unit. The series in Table 2 may represent a combination of two or more systems that developed in this way. The *cor*, originally a Sumerian measure, is used in reports of large quantities of grain (cf., e.g., I Kings 4:22; 5:11; Ezra 7:22). Whether it was equivalent to the homer is not entirely certain because of the corrupt text in Ezekiel 45:14, and because of the corruption here and in I Kings 5:11 (cf. II Chronicles 2:10), there is question whether it was ever used of liquids. The *lethech*, originally Canaanite, is mentioned only once, and the value given by the later rabbis may be merely a guess.

Measure is the regular RSV translation for seah (Genesis 18:6; Ruth 3:15, 17; I Samuel 25:18; I Kings 18:32; II Kings 7:1, 16, 18; Matthew 13:33; Luke 13:32) and is used in Isaiah 40:12c for the literal "third," which presumably means a seah pot as a third of an ephah. It is also occasionally the translation for ephah (Deuteronomy 25:14-15; Proverbs 20:10; Micah 6:10), bath (Luke 16:6), and cor (Luke 16:7). In Bel and the Dragon 3 *bushel* translates a Persian measure adopted in Egypt which was probably equivalent to *ca.* 1.8 U.S. bushels, but *fifty gallons* is a conversion into modern terms of the literal "six metretes." Probably this Greek measure was equivalent to *ca.* ten U.S. gallons, so that the total should be sixty gallons, corresponding to the conversion in John 2:6, where the literal "two or three metretes" becomes "twenty or thirty gallons." In Matthew 5:15; Mark 4:21; Luke 11:33 "bushel" probably refers to a Roman measure equivalent to *ca.* a U.S. peck. *Quart* (Revelation 6:6) denotes a Greek measure equivalent to *ca.* a U.S. dry quart.

Weights and Weighed Money

Most references to weights in the OT concern precious metals used as money. Until the introduction of coins into Palestine during the Persian period, pieces of gold, silver, and bronze used in exchange had to be valued by weighing in balances.

All the biblical data about relationships among weights are found in connection with the *shekel of the sanctuary* (Exodus 30:13-14; Leviticus 5:15; Numbers 3:47-48) as the standard for offerings, especially the contribution of a half shekel, or *beka* (Exodus 38:24-26), required yearly of each adult male. In several of the passages the sanctuary shekel is defined as containing twenty *gerahs*, evidently in distinction from a shekel containing another number. Calculation from the figures in Exodus 38:24-26 shows that there were 3,000 sanctuary shekels in a *talent*. Ezekiel 45:12 states the relation of the sanctuary shekel to the *mina*, but the text is in doubt. On the basis of the LXX the RSV says fifty shekels to the mina, but the Hebrew text seems to indicate sixty.

The repeated insistence in portions of the Pentateuch on the sanctuary standard might suggest that it was heavier than the commercial standard, and this has often been assumed. On the other hand the reference in Nehemiah 10:32 to the yearly temple contribution as a third of a shekel, presumably commercial, implies otherwise. If the same amount as half a sanctuary shekel is intended, the commercial shekel would be

heavier by a ratio of three to two. Other evidence, however, suggests a lesser difference. In Babylonia the shekel contained twenty-four gerahs, a relation that may well have been customary in Palestine also, even though the values were probably different. Evidence indicates that the Canaanites counted fifty shekels to the mina and fifty minas to the talent, in contrast to Babylonian ratios of sixty each; and thus it is likely that by the Palestinian commercial standard there were 2,500 shekels in a talent. If so, 2,500 twenty-four-gerah shekels by the commercial standard would make a talent of the same weight as the 3,000 twenty-gerah shekels by the sanctuary standard indicated in Exodus 38:24-26. Probably, therefore, the sanctuary standard differed from the commercial by having a shekel a sixth lighter. No doubt the name "beka"—derived from a root word meaning "split"—was used for a half of either shekel.

Archaeological support for this assumption is perhaps to be found in the inscribed weights from pre-exilic times which have been uncovered in Palestine. Among these the largest number are labeled *netseph*, a word not appearing in the OT. The ratio of the average of these weights to the probable weight of the commercial shekel is close enough to five to six to suggest that "shekel of the sanctuary" may be a postexilic designation for the netseph. In fact the inclusion of what may be an abbreviation for "shekel" on one of the netseph weights may indicate that this unit was sometimes called a shekel in pre-exilic times. If portions of the Pentateuch were based on an older custom of contributing half a netseph,

the renaming would be aimed at maintaining this equivalent of ten gerahs rather than a third of a commercial shekel, equivalent to only eight gerahs. If, on the other hand, the contribution was a postexilic innovation, the legislation might be an effort to raise the requirement. In either case the repeated emphasis on the lighter standard becomes understandable as the basis for a higher actual rate.

Tables 4 and 5 display the assumed relations and equivalents of the OT weights according to the sanctuary and commercial standards as explained above. The *pim* is included on the basis of excavated weights so inscribed. No example has been found, however, of the *qesitah* (Genesis 33:19; Joshua 24:32; Job 42:11; see RSV footnotes) and its value and relations are unknown.

In the NT weights are specified only in John 12:3; 19:39, where *pound* probably means the Roman pound of *ca.* eleven-and-a-half ounces, and Revelation 16:21, were *hundredweight* is a translation of "talent." Elsewhere in the NT both "pound" and "talent" refer to sums of money (see below).

Coined Money

Coins seem to have been invented in Asia Minor or Greece in the seventh century B.C., and some of them soon found their way into Palestine, as revealed by excavations. The first coins officially used there, however, were the Persian gold *darics* issued by Darius the Great (522–486). Sums in darics appear in Ezra-Nehemiah; a reference to them in the time of David (I Chronicles 29:7) is of course an anachronism. The Persians also

issued silver *shekels*, valued at twenty to the daric, which weighed only half a shekel by the Palestinian commercial standard. Whether a tax of forty shekels which Nehemiah mentions (5:15) refers to these coins or to weighed silver is uncertain.

Alexander the Great introduced Greek *drachmas* throughout the Near East. In the Greek monetary system, which had developed in Asia Minor under Babylonian influence, the terms *mina* and *talent* were used for larger sums, mina meaning one hundred drachmas and talent sixty minas, so that a talent was 6,000 drachmas. Since the drachmas issued by the Ptolemies in Egypt in the third century approached the weight of half a sanctuary shekel, the LXX translators in some of the passages translated "shekel of the sanctuary" as "didrachma," i.e., two-drachma coin. For "gerah" they used "obol," the smallest Greek silver coin, which was actually a sixth of a drachma rather than a tenth.

Later the drachma was devalued so that a talent became one hundred minas or 10,000 drachmas, while silver shekels minted in the Phoenician coastal cities of Tyre and Sidon followed a heavier standard than that of Table 5. Thus in NT times the shekel was equated with the tetradrachma, i.e., four-drachma coin. In the RSV of Matthew 17:24 *half-shekel tax* is an interpretation of the literal "didrachma," and *shekel* in verse 27 stands for "stater," here meaning a tetradrachma. The lost coin in Luke 15:8-9 is a drachma, and the *pounds* in the parable of Luke 19:11-27 represent minas. The payment to Judas, literally "thirty of silver" (Matthew 26:15), means thirty shekels as in the corresponding Hebrew phrase in Zechariah 11:12. Since the Jews first minted shekels during their revolt against Rome in A.D. 66–70, the coins given Judas would have to be Phoenician shekels or else tetradrachmas counted as shekels.

The money most often mentioned in the NT is the *denarius,* a Roman silver coin bearing the "likeness and inscription" of the emperor (Matthew 22:20; Mark 12:16; Luke 20:24). Though slightly lighter than a drachma, it was valued more highly because officially required for paying taxes (cf. Matthew 22:19). The implication that a denarius was a normal day's wage for a field laborer (Matthew 20:2; cf. Tobit 5:14, where a drachma is the daily wage for a guide and bodyguard on a long journey) provides a basis for judging the actual value of money in ancient times. Perhaps the suggestion that two hundred denarii would buy a minimum meal for 5,000 (Mark 6:37, 44) gives a clue to its purchasing power.

Penny as a price for sparrows (Matthew 10:29; Luke 12:6) refers to the assarion, a bronze coin issued by local rulers as an approximate equivalent for the official Roman bronze as, which was valued at a sixteenth of a denarius. Elsewhere (Matthew 5:26; Mark 12:42) "penny" stands for the quadrans, the smallest Roman bronze coin, worth a fourth of an as. The smallest Greek bronze coin, the lepton, is represented by the *two copper coins* contributed by a poor widow, which together are said to equal a quadrans (Mark 12:42).

Table 1. Lengths

UNIT	RELATION TO CUBIT	APPROXIMATE EQUIVALENT
finger	÷24	.75 inch
handbreadth	÷6	3 inches
span	÷2	9 inches
cubit		1.5 feet

Table 2. Dry Volumes

UNIT	RELATION TO EPHAH	APPROXIMATE EQUIVALENT
kab	÷18	.89 quart
omer	÷10	1.6 quart
seah	÷3	.67 peck
ephah		.5 bushel
lethech	×5	2.5 bushel
homer	×10	5 bushels
cor	×10	5 bushels

Table 3. Liquid Volumes

UNIT	RELATION TO BATH	APPROXIMATE EQUIVALENT
log	÷72	.56 pint
hin	÷6	3.33 quarts
bath		5 gallons
cor	×10	50 gallons

Table 4. Weights, Sanctuary Standard

UNIT	RELATION TO SHEKEL	APPROXIMATE EQUIVALENT
gerah	÷20	.017 ounce
beka	÷2	.17 ounce
shekel		.33 ounce
mina	×60	1.25 pounds
talent	×3,000	62.5 pounds

Table 5. Weights, Commercial Standard

UNIT	RELATION TO SHEKEL	APPROXIMATE EQUIVALENT
gerah	÷24	.017 ounce
beka	÷2	.2 ounce
pim	÷1.5	.267 ounce
shekel		.4 ounce
mina	×50	1.25 pounds
talent	×2,500	62.5 pounds

THE HEBREW CALENDAR

The beginning of the Hebrew year shown here falls at our March 21, the spring equinox. The Hebrews took this point of beginning from the Babylonians, probably after 605 B.C., when the Babylonians gained control of Judah and the West. After the conquest of Canaan (late thirteenth century B.C.) and through the periods of the united and divided monarchies (roughly eleventh through the seventh centuries B.C.), the Hebrews followed the Canaanite calendar, which began the year at the fall equinox (September 21).

The names of the Hebrew months shown here are of Babylonian origin. The earlier names given for some are Canaanite.

The Hebrew calendar was solar-lunar. The year ran from one equinox to another. Months were calculated from new moon to new moon. Thus months were of about 30 days' length (one lunation actually lasts about 29½ days, and twelve lunations about 354½ days). To make up the loss of 11 days per year (the solar year is 365½ days) an extra month was inserted every two or three years. Usually Adar, the twelfth month, was duplicated.

The Essenes of Qumran by the Dead Sea seem to have followed a purely solar calendar of 364 days, divided into four seasons of 13 weeks each (91 days), each season having two months of 30 days and one of 31. This scheme caused festivals to fall always on the same day of the week. We do not know when this calendar first arose.

The Hebrew day began at sundown.

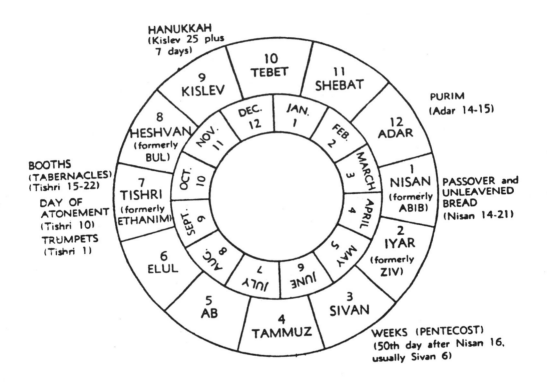

HANUKKAH
(Kislev 25 plus
7 days)

PURIM
(Adar 14-15)

BOOTHS
(TABERNACLES)
(Tishri 15-22)

DAY OF
ATONEMENT
(Tishri 10)

TRUMPETS
(Tishri 1)

PASSOVER and
UNLEAVENED
BREAD
(Nisan 14-21)

WEEKS (PENTECOST)
(50th day after Nisan 16,
usually Sivan 6)

| 10 TEBET | 11 SHEBAT | 12 ADAR | 1 NISAN (formerly ABIB) | 2 IYAR (formerly ZIV) | 3 SIVAN | 4 TAMMUZ | 5 AB | 6 ELUL | 7 TISHRI (formerly ETHANIM) | 8 HESHVAN (formerly BUL) | 9 KISLEV |

DEC. 12 · JAN. 1 · FEB. 2 · MARCH 3 · APRIL 4 · MAY 5 · JUNE 6 · JULY 7 · AUG. 8 · SEPT. 9 · OCT. 10 · NOV. 11

PROGRAMS FOR READING THE BIBLE

THE LONGER PROGRAM

The New Testament

1. Mark
2. Matthew
3. John
4-5. Luke-Acts
6. I Thessalonians
7. II Thessalonians
8. I Corinthians
9. II Corinthians (chief attention to chapters 1–9)
10. Galatians
11. Romans
12. Philemon
13. Colossians
14. Philippians
15. Ephesians
16. II Timothy
17. Titus
18. I Timothy
19. I Peter
20. Hebrews
21. James
22. I John
23. II John
24. III John
25. Jude
26. II Peter
27. Revelation (chapters 1–5 and 19:6–22:21; sample 6:1–19:5)

The Old Testament

28. Genesis
29. Exodus (chief attention to chapters 1–24)
30. Leviticus (scan and sample)
31. Numbers (chief attention to 10:11–21:35)
32. Deuteronomy (chief attention to chapters 1-11 and 27-34)
33. Joshua (chief attention to chapters 1–12 and 22-24)
34. Judges (chief attention to chapters 1–16)
35-36. I-II Samuel
37-38. I-II Kings (scan and sample)
39-40. I-II Chronicles (scan and sample)

The Old Testament—Longer Program, continued

41-42. Ezra-Nehemiah (chief attention to Nehemiah)
43. Amos
44. Hosea
45. Micah
46. Isaiah (chapters 1–39; chief attention to chapters 1–12)
47. Zephaniah
48. Jeremiah (chief attention to chapters 1–25 and 30–33)
49. Nahum
50. Habakkuk
51. Ezekiel (chief attention to chapters 1-24 and 33-39)
52. Obadiah
53. Lamentations
54. Isaiah (chapters 40–66)
55. Haggai
56. Zechariah (chief attention to chapters 1–8)
57. Malachi
58. Joel
59. Ruth
60. Jonah
61. Psalms
62. Job (less attention to chapters 32–37)
63. Proverbs (chief attention to chapters 1–9)
64. Song of Solomon
65. Ecclesiastes
66. Esther
67. Daniel

THE SHORTER PROGRAM

The New Testament

1. Mark
2. John
3. Luke–Acts
4. I Thessalonians
5. I Corinthians
6. Romans
7. Philemon
8. Philippians
9. Ephesians
10. II Timothy
11. I Peter
12. I John
13. Revelation (chapters 1–5 and 19:6–22:21; sample 6:1–19:5)

The Old Testament

14. Genesis
15. Exodus (chapters 1–24)
16. Numbers (10:11–21:35)
17. Deuteronomy (chapters 1–11)
18. Joshua (chapters 1–12 and 22–24)
19. Judges (sample)
20. I–II Samuel (sample)
21. I–II Kings (sample)
22. Nehemiah
23. Amos
24. Isaiah (chapters 1–12)
25. Jeremiah (chapters 1–25, 30–33)
26. Isaiah (chapters 40–55)
27. Ruth
28. Jonah
29. Psalms
30. Job (chapters 1–14 and 38–42)
31. Proverbs (chapters 1–9)
32. Daniel (chapters 1–6; sample chapters 7–12) 🔥

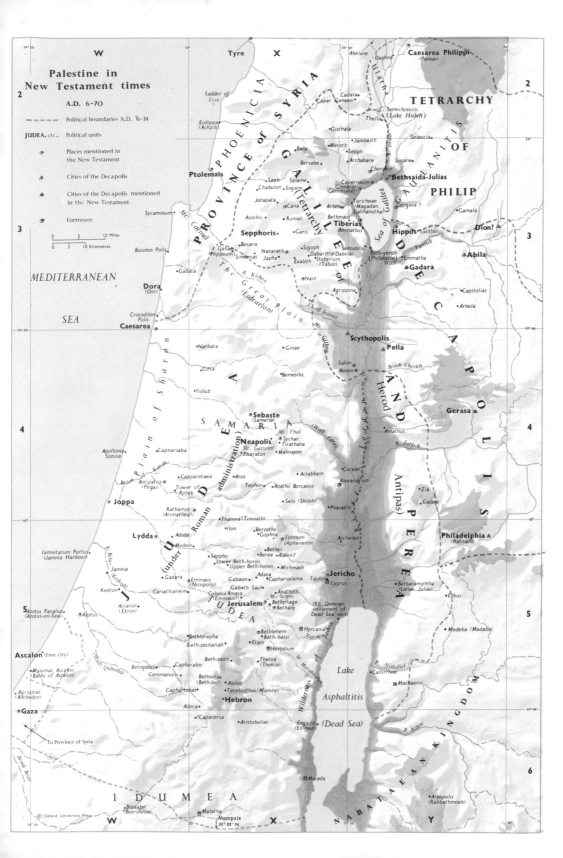

Palestine in New Testament times

A.D. 6-70

- – – – – Political boundaries A.D. '6-34

JUDEA, etc., Political units

○ Places mentioned in the New Testament

△ Cities of the Decapolis

▲ Cities of the Decapolis mentioned in the New Testament

▣ Fortresses

0   5   10 Miles
0   5   10 Kilometres

MEDITERRANEAN

SEA

PHOENICIA

PROVINCE OF SYRIA

TETRARCHY

Tyre

Ladder of Tyre
Ecdippa (Achzib)

Sycaminum

Mt. Carmel

Ptolemais

Saab
Chabulon
Sogane
Jotapata
Cana
Asochis
Rumah
Sepphoris
Besara
Gabae (Hippeum)
Simonias
Nazareth
Japha

Dora (Dor)

Crocodilon Polis

Caesarea

Bucolon Polis

The Great Plain (Esdraelon)

R. Kishon

Gischala
Baca
Bersabe
Saalem
Garis
Sigoph
Exaloth

Cadasa
Capar Canaeoi
Jamneith
Meroth
Sepph
Acchabare
Sogane
Chorazin
Capernaum (Gennesaret)
Arbela
Bethmaus
Tiberias
Ammathus
Sennabris
Dabaritta Dabira
Itaburium (Tabor)
Nain

Abelane
Daphne
Caesarea Philippi (Paneas)

Semechonitis (Lake Huleh)
Thella
Seleucia
Sogane

PHILIP

Bethsaida-Julias
Taricheae (Magadan Dalmanutha?)
Gergesa?
Gamala
Dion?
Hippos Susitha?
Beth-yerah (Philoteria) Wadi
Gadara
Emmatha
Capitolias
Arbela
Abila

GALILEE (Tetrarchy of

Sea of Galilee

Yarmuk

DECAPOLIS

Agrippina
V of Jezreel
Mt. Gilboa

Scythopolis
Pella

Salim
Aenon
Brook Cherith

HEROD

ANTIPAS

Gerasa

GAULANITIS OF

Ginae
Bemeslis

Narbata
Gitta
Yishub

Plain of Sharon

Sebaste (Samaria)
Neapolis
Mt. Gerizim
Pharaton

SAMARIA

Roman administration

Mt. Ebal
Sychar
Tirathana
Mahnayim
Arus
Tephon
Anathu Borcaeus
Selo (Shiloh)

Acrabbein
Coreae
Alexandrium

Zia
Gadara

Amathus
R. Jabbok

Philadelphia (Rabbah)

Apollonia Sozusa
Capnarsaba
Brook Aur Kanah
Capparetaea
Antipatris (Pegai)
Tower of Aphek

Joppa

PEREA (Tetrarchy of Antipas)

Lydda
Rathamin (Arimathea?)
Thamna (Timnath)
Ilon
Adida
Modein
Berzetho
Gophna

Phasaelis
Archelais

Esbus

Iamnitarum Portus (Jamnia Harbour)
Jamnia

Gazara
Cariathiareim
Emmaus (Nicopolis)
Colonia Amasa (Emmaus?)

Ephraim (Aphairema)
Bethel
Berea
Ailon?
Adasa
Gabath Saul
Michmash
Apathoth

Jericho
Cyprus

Betharamphtha (Livias Julias)

R. Belus
Kedron
Accaron (Ekron)
Sappho
Lower Beth-horon
Upper Beth-horon
Gabaon
Capharsalama
Mt. Scopus
Bethphage
Jerusalem
Bethany

Medeba (Madaba)

JUDEA (under

Azotus Paraliu (Azotus-on-Sea)
Azotus
Bethletepha
Bethlehem
Beth-bassi
Sidon Judaea
Hyrcania

Kh. Qumran: settlement of Dead Sea sect

Ascalon (Free city)
Maiumas Ascalon (Baths of Ascalon)
Betogabris
Capharabis
Gemmaruris
Beth-zechariah
Etam
Beth-zaith
Thecoa (Thekoa)
Bethsura (Beth-zur)
Alulos
Terebinthus (Mamre)
Caphartobas
Hebron
Adora

Agrippias (Anthedon)

Wadi Qubelba

Gaza

To Province of Syria

Brook Besor

Wilderness of Judaea

W. Murabba'at

Lake

Asphaltitis

(Dead Sea)

Nahaliel
Callirrhoe
Machaerus

R. Arnon

NABATAEAN KINGDOM

Caparorsa
Aristobulias
Engaddi (En-gedi)

Areopolis (Rabbathmoab)

Masada

IDUMEA

© Oxford University Press

Bersabe (Beersheba)
Malatha
Mampsis
31° 01' N